with MyBCommLab

- **Enhanced eText**—Keeps students engaged in learning on their own time, while helping them achieve greater conceptual understanding of course material. The worked examples bring learning to life, and algorithmic practice allows students to apply the very concepts they are reading about. Combining resources that illuminate content with accessible self-assessment, MyLab with Enhanced eText provides students with a complete digital learning experience—all in one place.

- **Reporting Dashboard**—View, analyze, and report learning outcomes clearly and easily, and get the information you need to keep your students on track throughout the course with the new Reporting Dashboard. Available via the MyLab Gradebook and fully mobile-ready, the Reporting Dashboard presents student performance data at the class, section, and program levels in an accessible, visual manner.

- **Quizzes and Tests**—Pre-built quizzes and tests allow you to quiz students without having to grade the assignments yourself.

- **Video Exercises**—These engaging videos explore a variety of business topics related to the theory students are learning in class. Quizzes assess students' comprehension of the concepts covered in each video.

- **Learning Catalytics™**—Is an interactive, student response tool that uses students' smartphones, tablets, or laptops to engage them in more sophisticated tasks and thinking. Now included with MyLab with eText, Learning Catalytics enables you to generate classroom discussion, guide your lecture, and promote peer-to-peer learning with real-time analytics. Instructors, you can:
  - Pose a variety of open-ended questions that help your students develop critical thinking skills
  - Monitor responses to find out where students are struggling
  - Use real-time data to adjust your instructional strategy and try other ways of engaging your students during class
  - Manage student interactions by automatically grouping students for discussion, teamwork, and peer-to-peer learning

Giving Students the Skills and Insights They Need to Thrive in Today's Digital Business Environment

The essential skills of writing, listening, collaborating, and public speaking are as important as ever, but they're not enough to succeed in today's business world. As business communication continues to get rocked by waves of innovation—first digital media, then social media, now mobile communication, and watch out for the upcoming invasion of chatbots—the nature of communication is changing. And the changes go far deeper than the tools themselves.

In this exciting but complex new world, no other textbook can match the depth and range of coverage offered *by Business Communication Today*.

Tools, Techniques, and Insights for Communicating Successfully in a Mobile, Digital, Social World

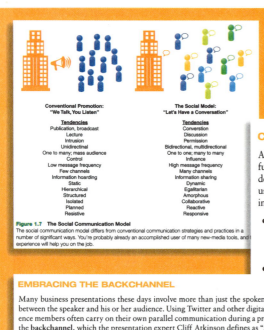

Conventional Promotion: "We Talk, You Listen"

Tendencies
Publication, broadcast
Lecture
Intrusion
Unidirectional
One to many; mass audience
Control
Low message frequency
Few channels
Information hoarding
Static
Hierarchical
Structured
Isolated
Planned
Resistive

The Social Model: "Let's Have a Conversation"

Tendencies
Conversion
Discussion
Permission
Bidirectional, multidirectional
One to one; many to many
Influence
High message frequency
Many channels
Information sharing
Dynamic
Egalitarian
Amorphous
Collaborative
Reactive
Responsive

Figure 1.7   The Social Communication Model
The social communication model differs from conventional communication strategies and practices in a number of significant ways. You're probably already an accomplished user of many new-media tools, and experience will help you on the job.

COMPOSITIONAL MODES FOR DIGITAL AND SOCIAL MEDIA

As you practice using various media and channels in this course, it's best to focus on the fundamentals of planning, writing, and completing messages, rather than on the specific details of any one medium or system.[2] Fortunately, the basic communication skills required usually transfer from one system to another. You can succeed with written communication in virtually all digital media by using one of nine *compositional modes*:

- **Conversations.** Messaging is a great example of a written medium that mimics spoken conversation. And just as you wouldn't read a report to someone sitting in your office, you wouldn't use conversational modes to exchange large volumes of information or to communicate with more than a few people at once.
- **Comments and critiques.** One of the most powerful aspects of social media is the ity for interested parties to express opinions and provide feedback, whether

EMBRACING THE BACKCHANNEL

Many business presentations these days involve more than just the spoken conv between the speaker and his or her audience. Using Twitter and other digital medi ence members often carry on their own parallel communication during a presenta the backchannel, which the presentation expert Cliff Atkinson defines as "a line munication created by people in an audience to connect with others inside or out room, with or without the knowledge of the speaker."[29] Chances are you've parti

Producing Business Videos

No matter what career path you pursue, chances are you'll have the need or opportunity to produce (or star in) a business video. For videos that require the highest production quality, companies usually hire specialists with the necessary skills and equipment. For most routine needs, however, any business communicator with modest equipment and a few basic skills can create effective videos.

The three-step process adapts easily to video; professionals refer to the three steps as *production*, and *postproduction* (see Figure 9.15). You can refer to one of ks available on basic video production techniques for more detail, but here ints to consider in all three steps. (A note on terminology: digital video-herited a number of terms from film that don't make strict technical sense mmon use anyway, including *footage* to indicate any amount of recorded *ing* to indicate video recording.)

6   LEARNING OBJECTIVE
Identify the most important considerations in the preproduction, production, and postproduction stages of producing basic business videos.

The process of creating videos is divided into preproduction, production, and postproduction.

The Internet of Everything Democratizes Energy

Like many large corporations, Xerox has a variety of blogs. This menu give quick access to all of them.

The search box lets visitors quickly find posts on topics of interest.

A large photo helps draw readers in.

Readers can subscribe to future posts via email or RSS newsfeed.

The post title is brief and clear, and it incorporates key terms likely to trigger hits in search engines (Internet of Everything and energy).

These links provide access to other posts by this author and other posts tagged with "innovation."

Social media share buttons make it easy for readers to share this post with their followers.

The sidebar lists recent posts and recent comments left by readers.

The post positions the company as an expert in an important technology field, without overtly selling Xerox products and services.

Figure 8.2   Business Applications of Blogging
This Xerox blog illustrates the content, writing style, and features that make an effective, reader-friendly company blog.
Source: Courtesy of Xerox Corporation.

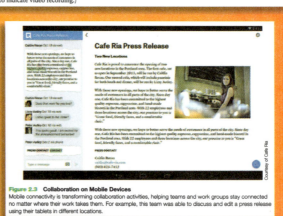

Cafe Ria Press Release

Two New Locations

Cafe Ria is proud to announce the opening of two new locations in the Portland area. The first cafe, set to open in September 2015, will be run by Caitlin Renae. Our second cafe, which will include premises for both lunch and dinner, will be run by Lizzy Astley.

With these new openings, we hope to better serve the needs of customers in all parts of the city. Since day one, Cafe Ria has been committed to the highest quality espresso, cappuccino, and hand-made biscotti in the Portland area. With 22 employees and three locations across the city, our promise to you is "Great food, friendly faces, and a comfortable chair."

PRESS CONTACT

Caitlin Renae
(503) 825-7412

Figure 2.3   Collaboration on Mobile Devices
Mobile connectivity is transforming collaboration activities, helping teams and work groups stay connected no matter where their work takes them. For example, this team was able to discuss and edit a press release using their tablets in different locations.

The Mobile Revolution

As much of a game changer as social media have been, some experts predict that mobile com... mon... tech... calls... to grow. ... not their ... access th...

THE RISE OF MOBILE AS A COMMUNICATION PLATFORM

Whether it's emailing, social networking, watching videos, or doing research, the percent-age of co...

HOW MOBILE TECHNOLOGIES ARE CHANGING BUSINESS COMMUNICATION

The rise of mobile communication has some obvious implications, such as the need for websites on a tiny sc... you know h... be mobile fr...

Writing Messages for Mobile Devices

One obvious adaptation to make for audiences using mobile devices is to modify the design and layo... features (see Cha... step. Reading is ... hend what they ...

DESIGNING MESSAGES FOR MOBILE DEVICES

In addition to making your content mobile-friendly using the writing tips in Chapter 4 (see pa...

The Unique Demands of Mobile Business Communication

Why Are Employees Leaving?

DIGITAL + SOCIAL + MOBILE: TODAY'S COMMUNICATION ENVIRONMENT

Job-Search Strategies: Maximize Your Mobile

The mobile business communication revolution is changing the way employers recruit new talent and the way job candidates look for opportunities. Many companies have optimized ... her career and the industry as a whole. Many of the tools you can use to build your personal brand are available as mobile apps, including blogging platforms, Twitter, Facebook, and LinkedIn.

Dozens of apps are available to help with various aspects ...

Optimizing for mobile includes writing short headlines that get right to the point.

This introduction conveys only the information readers need in order to grasp the scope of the article.

All the key points of the documents appear here on the first screen.

Readers who want more detail can swipe down for background infor-mation on the five points.

Writing for Mobile Devices

To write effectively for readers on mobile devices, use these five essential techniques:

- Use a linear flow
- Prioritize information for readers
- Create short, focused messages
- Use shorter subject lines and headings
- Use shorter paragraphs

Continue reading for background information on these guidelines.

Notes from strategy meeting March 14

Strategy mtg - 3/14
—Ask JF about wireless
—2018 forecast sounds off-Claire knows?
—Battery life too low!!

Figure 17.6 Using Mobile Devices in Presentations
A variety of mobile apps and cloud-based systems can free presenters and audiences from the c... a conventional conference room.

THE FUTURE OF COMMUNICATION

Communication Bots

The bots are back. Automated bots (short for *robots*) made a small wave... ing on w... with cus... widespr... from cus... niture pr...

THE FUTURE OF COMMUNICATION

The Internet of Things

The *Internet of Things (IoT)* refers to the billions of devices now connected to ... of having all these ... data into vast info... ple and the physi... simple sensors tha... parameters all the ...

THE FUTURE OF COMMUNICATION

Real-Time Translation

If you've ever tried to converse in a language other than you native tong... listener, y... words an... sentences... a written... instanta...

THE FUTURE OF COMMUNICATION

Emotion Recognition Software

Assessing an audience's emotional response is an important step in judging the success of many communication efforts. If you're presenting a new idea to upper management, for exam-ple, you can try to read facial clues and other nonverbal signals to determine whether the executives seem excited, annoyed, bored, or anywhere in between.

But what if you're not there in person and your message has to stand on its own? How can you judge the audience's reaction?

Intriguing Glimpses into the Future of Business Communication

Business Communication Today

Courtland L. Bovée

PROFESSOR OF BUSINESS COMMUNICATION
C. ALLEN PAUL DISTINGUISHED CHAIR
GROSSMONT COLLEGE

John V. Thill

CHAIRMAN AND CHIEF EXECUTIVE OFFICER
GLOBAL COMMUNICATION STRATEGIES

New York, NY

Vice President, Business Publishing: Donna Battista
Director of Portfolio Management: Stephanie Wall
Portfolio Manager: Dan Tylman
Editorial Assistant: Linda Siebert Albelli
Vice President, Product Marketing: Roxanne McCarley
Director of Strategic Marketing: Brad Parkins
Strategic Marketing Manager: Deborah Strickland
Product Marketer: Becky Brown
Field Marketing Manager: Lenny Ann Kucenski
Product Marketing Assistant: Jessica Quazza
Vice President, Production and Digital Studio, Arts and Business: Etain O'Dea
Director of Production, Business: Jeff Holcomb
Managing Producer, Business: Ashley Santora

Operations Specialist: Carol Melville
Creative Director: Blair Brown
Manager, Learning Tools: Brian Surette
Content Developer, Learning Tools: Lindsey Sloan
Managing Producer, Digital Studio, Arts and Business: Diane Lombardo
Digital Studio Producer: Monique Lawrence
Digital Studio Producer: Darren Cormier
Digital Studio Producer: Alana Coles
Full-Service Project Management and Composition: SPi Global
Interior Design: SPi Global
Cover Design: Laurie Entringer
Cover Art: Jesus Sanz/Shutterstock
Printer/Binder: LSC Communications
Cover Printer: LSC Communications

Library of Congress Cataloging-in-Publication Data on File
4 17

ISBN 10:   0-13-456218-6
ISBN 13: 978-0-13-456218-6

Dedication

This book is dedicated to the many thousands of instructors and students who use Bovée and Thill texts to develop career-enhancing skills in business communication. We appreciate the opportunity to play a role in your education, and we wish you the very best with your careers.

Courtland L. Bovée

John V. Thill

Brief Contents

Contents

6 Completing Business Messages **153**

PART 3
Digital, Social, and Visual Media **179**

7 Digital Media **181**

8 Social Media **205**

9 Visual Media **229**

PART 6
Developing and Delivering Business Presentations **457**

16 Developing Presentations in a Social Media Environment **459**

17 Enhancing Presentations with Slides and Other Visuals **485**

PART 7
Writing Employment Messages and Interviewing for Jobs **511**

18 Building Careers and Writing Résumés **513**

Real-Time Updates—Learn More

Real-Time Updates—Learn More is a unique feature you will see strategically located throughout the text, connecting you with dozens of carefully selected online media items. These elements—categorized by the icons shown below representing interactive websites, online videos, infographics, PowerPoint presentations, podcasts, PDF files, and articles—complement the text's coverage by providing contemporary examples and valuable insights from successful professionals.

REAL-TIME UPDATES
LEARN MORE BY READING THIS ARTICLE

REAL-TIME UPDATES
LEARN MORE BY LISTENING TO THESE PODCASTS

REAL-TIME UPDATES
LEARN MORE BY WATCHING THESE VIDEO

REAL-TIME UPDATES
LEARN MORE BY READING THIS PDF

REAL-TIME UPDATES
LEARN MORE BY VIEWING THIS PRESENTATION

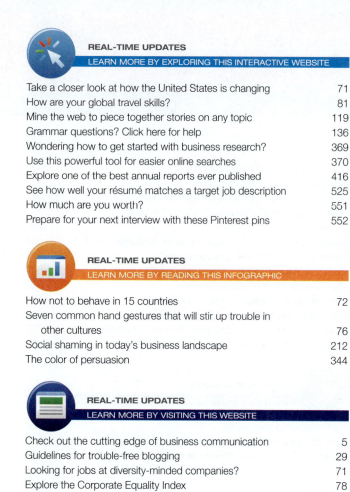

REAL-TIME UPDATES

LEARN MORE BY EXPLORING THIS INTERACTIVE WEBSITE

REAL-TIME UPDATES

LEARN MORE BY READING THIS INFOGRAPHIC

REAL-TIME UPDATES

LEARN MORE BY VISITING THIS WEBSITE

REAL-TIME UPDATES

LEARN MORE BY VISITING THIS WIKI

Major Changes and Improvements in This Edition

Here are the major changes in the 14th Edition of *Business Communication Today*:

- Twelve new chapter-opening vignettes with accompanying end-of-chapter individual and team challenges:
  - Kaiser Permanente's strategic approach to communicating with its diverse stakeholder groups (Chapter 3)
  - Wolff Orlis's use of storytelling in business communication, including using an award-winning novelist as its chief storytelling officer (Chapter 4)
  - Type Together's contemporary typeface designs, emphasizing readability in business documents and other messages (Chapter 6)
  - Slack's workplace messaging system, which is changing the way many organizations communicate (Chapter 7)
  - Jill Duffy's advice for handling the daily deluge of routine messages more productively (Chapter 10)
  - Strategyzer's revolutionary alternative to the traditional annual report, now embraced by thousands of entrepreneurs (Chapter 13)
  - Warby Parker's whimsical and audience-focused approach to annual reports (Chapter 14)
  - WPP's use of web interactivity to create one of the most readable annual reports ever published (Chapter 15)
  - Gina Barnett's "whole-body" public speaking advice, which can help all business professionals improve their onstage presence (Chapter 16)
  - Nancy Duarte's timeless advice for creating audience-friendly presentation slides (Chapter 17)
  - Burning Glass's application of artificial intelligence to the critical job-search challenge of matching employer needs and employee skill sets (Chapter 18)
  - VMWare's enthusiastic embrace of social media to transform its approach to employee recruiting (Chapter 19)

- A new highlight box theme, *The Future of Communication*, giving students a glimpse into some fascinating technologies that could reshape the practice of business communication in the coming years: the Internet of Things, real-time translation, haptic communication, telepathy, virtual and augmented reality, gestural computing, smart communication bots, emotion recognition, and holograms

- More than 70 new or redesigned business communication examples and figures. The 14th Edition includes
  - 78 annotated model documents
  - 26 examples of mobile communication in business communication
  - 25 examples of social media in business communication

- Revised annotations for all the before/after model document pairs, making it easier for students to see the specific changes made to transform ineffective messages into effective ones

- Updated coverage of the advantages and disadvantages of teams (Chapter 2), overcoming resistance (Chapter 2), gender differences (Chapter 3), digital messaging

(Chapter 7), the business communication uses of social networks (Chapter 8), content curation (Chapter 8), and effective and ethical apologies (Chapter 11)

- 24 New communication cases
- More than three dozen new end-of-chapter questions and exercises

Preparing the Next Generation of Professional Communicators with the Most Current and Most Comprehensive Text in the Field

Communication is the most valuable skill that graduates can bring into the workforce, and it is one of the six cornerstones of true professionalism emphasized in *Business Communication Today*. The business communication course is uniquely positioned to help students develop as professionals because it addresses such vital topics as respect, credibility, dependability, ethical decision making, and collaboration.

An essential part of being a professional is being conversant in the methods and practices of the contemporary workplace. To this end, *Business Communication Today* presents the full range of on-the-job skills that today's communicators need, from writing conventional printed reports to using the latest digital, social, mobile, and visual media (including a concise primer on producing digital business video). Each chapter adapts the fundamentals of effective writing to specific workplace challenges and media applications, so students will be better prepared to succeed from their first day on the job.

Although it stays on the leading edge of workplace practices and communication tools, *Business Communication Today* never loses sight of the fact that communication

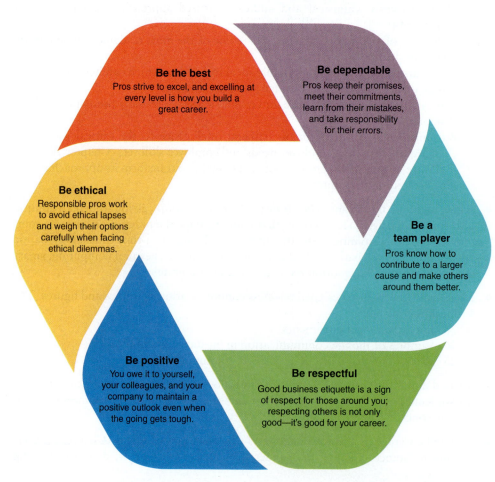

Be the best
Pros strive to excel, and excelling at every level is how you build a great career.

Be dependable
Pros keep their promises, meet their commitments, learn from their mistakes, and take responsibility for their errors.

Be ethical
Responsible pros work to avoid ethical lapses and weigh their options carefully when facing ethical dilemmas.

Be a team player
Pros know how to contribute to a larger cause and make others around them better.

Be positive
You owe it to yourself, your colleagues, and your company to maintain a positive outlook even when the going gets tough.

Be respectful
Good business etiquette is a sign of respect for those around you; respecting others is not only good—it's good for your career.

is a human activity in the deepest sense. It emphasizes the importance of developing a strong sense of etiquette, recognizing ethical dilemmas, advancing ethical communication, and respecting the rights and needs of audience members at every stage of the writing process.

By integrating all the key skills and insights that students need in order to succeed in today's dynamic workplace, *Business Communication Today* is an unmatched resource for preparing the next generation of business professionals.

Why Business Communication Instructors Continue to Choose Bovée and Thill

- **Market-leading innovation.** For more than three decades, Bovée and Thill texts have pioneered coverage of emerging trends and their implications for business communication. Bovée and Thill were the first authors in the field to give in-depth coverage to digital media, social media, and mobile communication.

- **Up-to-date coverage that reflects today's business communication practices and employer expectations.** Technology, globalization, and other forces have dramatically changed the practice of business communication in recent years, even to the point of altering how people read and how messages should be constructed. To prepare students for today's workplace, a business communication course needs to address contemporary skills, issues, and concepts.

- **Practical advice informed by deep experience.** Beyond the research and presentation of new ideas and tools, Bovée and Thill are among the most active and widely followed users of social media in the entire field of business communication. They don't just write about new concepts; they have years of hands-on experience with social media, blogging, content curation, search technologies, and other important tools. They are active participants in more than 45 social media sites.

 Scooped by Bovee & Thill's Online Magazines for Business Communication

Business Communication Instruction: How Students Can Learn More Through Online Media

Business Communication Instruction: How Student...

From www.youtube.com - June 15, 7:58 PM

Business Communication Instruction: How Students Can Learn More "Learn More" media items (more than 60 in all) integrate Bovee & Thill textbooks with online materials.

- **Engaging coverage of real companies and contemporary issues in business communication.** Bovée and Thill texts emphasize companies and issues students already know about or are likely to find intriguing. For example, cases in recent editions have addressed Comic-Con, location-based social networking, employer restrictions on social media, the use of Twitter in the job-search process, video gaming, alternative energy, and the challenges of reading and writing on smartphones.

- **Integrated learning.** In sharp contrast to texts that tack on coverage of social media and other new topics, Bovée and Thill continually revise their coverage to fully integrate the skills and issues that are important in today's workplace. This integration is carried through chapter-opening vignettes, chapter content, model documents, end-of-chapter questions, communication cases, and test banks to make sure students practice the skills they'll need, not just read about them in some anecdotal fashion.

- **Added value with unique, free resources for instructors and students.** From the groundbreaking Real-Time Updates to *Business Communication Headline News* to videos specially prepared for instructors, Bovée and Thill adopters can take advantage of an unmatched array of free resources to enhance the classroom experience and keep course content fresh. Please see pages xxix–xxx for a complete list.

In-Depth Coverage of Digital, Social, and Mobile Media Topics in the 14th Edition

Business Communication Today offers in-depth coverage of new and emerging media skills and concepts. These tables show where you can find major areas of coverage, figures, and communication cases that expose students to professional use of social media, mobile media, and other new technologies.

Major Coverage of Digital, Social, and Mobile Media

Topic	Page
Backchannel in presentations	477
Blogging and microblogging	214–220
Collaboration technologies	43–46
Community Q&A websites	214
Compositional modes for digital media	183–185
Content curation	213–214
Creating content for social media	212
Data visualization	242–244
Digital, social, and mobile media options	182–183
Email	186-189
Infographics	246
Instant messaging, text messaging, and workgroup messaging	190–192
Interview media	554–555
Meeting technologies	50–51
Mobile devices in presentations	498
Mobile etiquette	60
Mobile media	16–18, 108–109
Online and social media résumés	534–535

(continued)

Topic	Page
Online etiquette	59–60
Podcasting	196–197
Social communication model	15–16
Social networking	207–212
User-generated content	213
Web writing	195–197
Wikis	221
Writing and designing messages for mobile devices	22–25, 169
Writing persuasive messages for mobile media	346
Writing persuasive messages for social media	344–346

Figures and Model Documents Highlighting Digital, Social, and Mobile Media (not including email, IM, or PowerPoint slides)

Title	Figure	Page
The Social Communication Model	1.7	15
Mobile Communication Tools	1.8	16
Wearable Technology	1.9	17
Mobile Communication: Opportunities and Challenges	1.10	19
Unethical Communication	1.11	27
Ethical Communication	1.12	28
Powerful Tools for Communicating Effectively	Feature	22–25
Shared Online Workspaces	2.2	44
Collaboration on Mobile Devices	2.3	45
Capturing Key Decisions and Discoveries from a Meeting	2.5	49
Virtual Meetings	2.6	50
Telepresence	2.7	51
Mobile Language Tools	3.3	83
Writing for Multilingual Audiences	3.5	88
Using Audience Analysis to Plan a Message	4.2	101
Media and Channel Choices: Written + Digital	4.4	107
Mind Mapping	4.5	114
Business Communicators Innovating with Mobile	Feature	110–111
Fostering a Positive Relationship with an Audience	5.1	127
Building Credibility	5.2	131
Plain Language at Creative Commons	5.3	135
Making Effective Word and Phrase Choices	5.4	137
Writing for Mobile Devices	5.6	145
Designing for Readability	6.3	165
Designing for Mobile Devices	6.4	168
Compositional Modes: Status Updates and Announcements	7.1	185
Augmented Reality	7.2	186
Reader-Friendly Web Design	7.5	194
Writing for the Web	7.6	195
Mobile Podcasting	7.7	197
Community Building via Social Media	8.1	207
Business Applications of Blogging	8.2	217

(continued)

Figures and Model Documents Highlighting Digital, Social, and Mobile Media (not including email, IM, or PowerPoint slides) (*Continued*)

Title	Figure	Page
Business Applications of Microblogging	8.3	219
Business Communicators Innovating with Social Media	Feature	210–211
Data Visualization	9.10	244
Geographic Information Systems	9.12	245
Infographics	9.13	247
Visual Displays on Mobile Devices	9.14	250
Framing Your Shots: Finding the Right Range	9.16	253
Framing Your Shots: Finding the Right Balance	9.17	254
Announcing Good News	10.6	278
Goodwill Messages	10.7	279
Internal Message Providing Bad News About Company Operations	11.6	310
Appealing to Audience Needs	12.1	331
Promotional Messages in Social Media	12.6	345
Executive Dashboards	14.3	393
Executive Summary	15.2	425
Nonlinear Presentations	16.3	465
Using Mobile Devices in Presentations	17.6	499
Mobile Job-Search Tools	18.2	519
Job Task Simulations	19.4	555
Interview Simulators	19.5	560

Communication Cases Involving Digital, Social, Mobile, or Video Media (not including email, IM, or PowerPoint slides)

Case	Media	Page
7.27	Mobile media	202
7.29	Web writing	203
7.30	Web writing, mobile media	203
7.31	Web writing	203
7.32	Podcasting	203
7.33	Podcasting	203
8.24	Social networking	226
8.25	Social networking	226
8.26	Social networking	226
8.27	Blogging	226
8.28	Blogging	226
8.29	Blogging, mobile media	226
8.30	Blogging	227
8.31	Microblogging	227
8.32	Microblogging	227
8.33	Microblogging	227
8.34	Wiki writing	227
10.30	Blogging	286
10.42	Podcasting	288
10.43	Blogging	288

(*continued*)

Case	Media	Page
10.45	Microblogging	288
10.47	Social networking	289
10.48	Web writing	289
10.49	Blogging	289
10.50	Social networking	290
10.51	Social networking	290
11.35	Microblogging	322
11.40	Microblogging	323
11.41	Blogging	323
11.43	Podcasting	324
11.45	Social networking	324
11.48	Microblogging	325
11.49	Blogging	325
11.50	Blogging	325
11.51	Blogging	325
11.52	Social networking	326
11.53	Social networking	326
11.56	Mobile media	326
12.37	Microblogging	354
12.38	Blogging	354
12.51	Web writing	357
12.52	Web writing/mobile skills	357
12.53	Podcasting	357
12.55	Web writing	357
12.56	Web writing	358
12.57	Social networking	358
12.58	Microblogging	358
12.59	Social networking	358
12.60	Microblogging	358
18.24	Video	542
19.29	Video	574
19.31	Microblogging	574
19.33	Blogging	574

Extending the Value of Your Textbook with Free Multimedia Content

Business Communication Today's unique Real-Time Updates system automatically provides weekly content updates, including interactive websites, infographics, podcasts, PowerPoint presentations, online videos, and articles. You can subscribe to updates chapter by chapter, so you get only the material that applies to your current chapter. Visit **real-timeupdates.com/bct14** to subscribe.

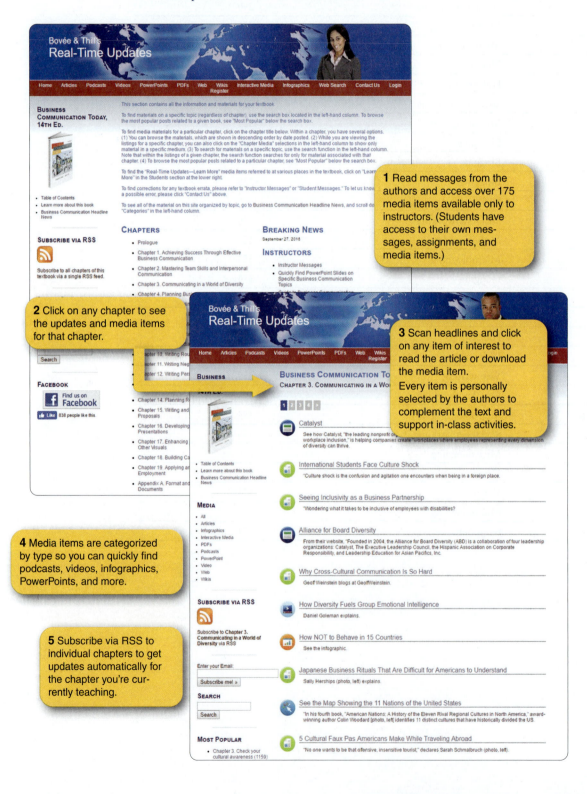

For Instructors: Features and Resources to Enhance the Course Experience

TARGET AUDIENCE

Everyone who teaches business communication is motivated to help students master the fundamentals of professional communication while also preparing them for the broader expectations they'll encounter in today's workplace. As the field of business communication continues to expand and get more complex, however, balancing those two objectives continues to get more difficult. Basing your course on a textbook that hasn't kept up with contemporary business media and professional practices puts both you and your students at a distinct disadvantage, and yet you obviously can't ignore basic writing skills.

With its treatment of business communication in the broadest sense (including digital video and managerial issues such as crisis communication), *Business Communication Today* is ideal for comprehensive business communication and managerial communication courses in any curriculum, in any format—in class, online, or hybrid.

For courses with a particular emphasis on written communication, you may find the authors' 16-chapter text *Excellence in Business Communication* to be an optimal fit. And for introductory courses that emphasize business English, the 14-chapter *Business Communication Essentials* offers balanced coverage of basic business English, communication strategies, and cutting-edge technologies. Its compact organization is particularly well suited to quarter calendars as well as to longer courses in which an instructor wants to have time available to supplement the text with service projects, business plan development, or other special activities.

Colleges and universities vary in the prerequisites established for the business communication course, but we advise at least one course in English composition. Some coursework in business studies will also give students a better perspective on communication challenges in the workplace. However, we have taken special care not to assume students have any in-depth business experience, so *Business Communication Today* works quite well for those with limited work experience or business coursework.

A TOTAL TEACHING AND LEARNING SOLUTION

Business Communication Today has helped more than 2 million students master essential skills for succeeding in the workplace. This 14th Edition continues that tradition by offering an unmatched set of tools that simplify teaching, promote active learning, and stimulate critical thinking. These components work together at four levels to provide seamless coverage of vital knowledge and skills: previewing, developing, enhancing, and reinforcing.

Previewing

Each chapter provides clear learning objectives that prepare students for the material to come and provide a framework for the chapter content. New in this edition, each learning objective aligns with a major heading in the chapter, and this structure is carried through to the end-of-chapter and online activities, making it easier for instructors and students to gauge learning progress.

After the learning objectives, a compelling Communication Close-Up vignette featuring a successful professional role model shows students how the material they will encounter in the chapter is put to use in actual business situations.

Developing

Chapter content develops, explains, and elaborates on concepts with a carefully organized presentation of textual and visual material. The three-step process of planning, writing, and completing is clearly explained and reinforced throughout the course. Some texts introduce a writing process model and then rarely, if ever, discuss it again, giving students few opportunities to practice it and leaving them to wonder just how important the process really is. *Business Communication Today* adapts the three-step process to every category of messages in every medium, from traditional letters and reports to email, blogs, IM, podcasts, wikis, and online videos.

Enhancing

Contemporary examples show students the specific elements that contribute to—or detract from—successful messages. *Business Communication Today* has an unmatched portfolio of realistic examples for students to emulate. In addition, Real-Time Updates—Learn More connects students with dozens of carefully selected online media elements that provide examples and insights from successful professionals.

Business Communication Today also extends students' awareness beyond the functional aspects of communication, with thorough and well-integrated coverage of business etiquette and ethics—vital issues that some texts raise briefly and then quickly forget. In light of employer concerns about the etiquette shortcomings of today's new hires and the continuing struggles with business ethics, we integrate ethics and etiquette throughout the book and give students numerous opportunities to ponder ethical dilemmas and practice communication etiquette.

Reinforcing

Hundreds of realistic exercises and activities help students practice vital skills and put newfound knowledge to immediate use. Unique features include downloadable Word documents, podcasts, PowerPoint presentations for students to analyze, and the innovative Bovée and Thill wiki simulator. Interactive Document Makeovers, pioneered by Bovée and Thill, let students experience firsthand the elements that make a document successful, giving them the insights they need in order to analyze and improve their own business messages. More than 140 communication cases, featuring dozens of real companies, encourage students to think about contemporary business issues as they put their skills to use in a variety of media, including blogging, social networking, and podcasting.

At every stage of the learning experience, *Business Communication Today* provides the tools instructors and students need to succeed.

Features that Help Students Build Essential Knowledge and Skills	Previewing	Developing	Enhancing	Reinforcing
Learning objectives (beginning of chapter)	•			
Communication Close-up (beginning of chapter)	•			
Concise presentations of fundamentals (within chapter)		•		
Managerial and strategic perspectives on key topics (within chapter)		•		
Three-step writing process discussion and diagrams (within chapter)		•		
Real-life examples (within chapter)			•	
Annotated model documents (within chapter)			•	
Highlight boxes (within chapter)			•	
Handbook of Grammar, Mechanics, and Usage (end of book)			•	
Learn More media resources (online)			•	
MyBCommLab (online)			•	•
Real-Time Updates (online)			•	•
Marginal notes for quick review (within chapter)				•
Checklists (within chapter)				•
Communication Challenges (end of chapter)				•
Quick Learning Guide (end of chapter)				•
Test Your Knowledge questions (end of chapter)				•
Apply Your Knowledge questions (end of chapter)				•

(continued)

Features that Help Students Build Essential Knowledge and Skills	Previewing	Developing	Enhancing	Reinforcing
Practice Your Skills activities and exercises (end of chapter)				•
Expand Your Skills web activities (end of chapter/online)				•
Bovée and Thill wiki simulator (online)				•
Cases (following Chapters 7, 8, 9, 10, 11, 12, 15, 17, 18, and 19)				•
Document Makeovers (online)				•

FULL SUPPORT FOR AACSB LEARNING STANDARDS

The American Association of Collegiate Schools of Business (AACSB) is a not-for-profit corporation of educational institutions, corporations, and other organizations devoted to the promotion and improvement of higher education in business administration and accounting. A collegiate institution offering degrees in business administration or accounting may volunteer for AACSB accreditation review. The AACSB makes initial accreditation decisions and conducts periodic reviews to promote continuous quality improvement in management education. Pearson Education is a proud member of the AACSB and is pleased to provide advice to help you apply AACSB Learning Standards.

Curriculum quality is one of the most important criteria for AACSB accreditation. Although no specific courses are required, the AACSB expects a curriculum to include learning experiences in the following areas:

- Written and oral communication
- Ethical understanding and reasoning
- Analytical thinking
- Information technology
- Interpersonal relations and teamwork
- Diverse and multicultural work environments
- Reflective thinking
- Application of knowledge

Throughout *Business Communication Today*, you'll find student exercises and activities that support the achievement of these important goals, and the questions in the accompanying test bank are tagged with the appropriate AACSB category.

UNMATCHED COVERAGE OF ESSENTIAL COMMUNICATION TECHNOLOGIES

The Bovée and Thill series continues to lead the field with unmatched coverage of communication technologies, reflecting the expectations and opportunities in today's workplace:

- Applicant tracking systems
- Assistive technologies
- Automated reputation analysis
- Backchannel
- Blogs
- Cloud computing
- Community Q&A websites
- Computer animation
- Content curation
- Crowdsourcing
- Crowdspeaking
- Data visualization
- Digital documents (PDFs)
- Digital whiteboards
- Email
- Emoticons
- Emotion recognition software
- Enterprise instant messaging
- E-portfolios
- Extranets
- Gamification
- Geographic information systems
- Gestural computing
- Graphics software
- Groupware and shared online workspaces
- Haptic communication
- Holograms
- Infographics
- Information architecture
- Instant messaging
- Intellectual property rights
- Interactivity
- Internet of Things
- Internet telephony (Skype)
- Interview simulators
- Intranets
- Knowledge management systems
- Linked and embedded documents
- Location-based social networking
- Microblogs
- Mobile business apps
- Multimedia documents
- Multimedia presentations
- Multimedia résumés

- Newsfeeds
- Online brainstorming systems
- Online research techniques
- Online survey tools
- Online video
- Podcasts
- PowerPoint animation
- Really Simple Syndication (RSS)
- Real-time translation
- Screencasts
- Search and metasearch engines
- Search engine optimization (SEO)
- Security and privacy concerns in digital media
- Sentiment analysis
- Smart communication bots
- Social bookmarking
- Social commerce
- Social media
- Social media résumés
- Social networking
- Tagging
- Teleconferencing and telepresence
- Telepathy
- Text messaging
- Translation software
- User-generated content
- Video interviews
- Video résumés
- Videoconferencing
- Virtual and augmented reality
- Virtual communities
- Virtual meetings
- Virtual whiteboards
- Web content management systems
- Webcasts
- Web directories
- Website accessibility
- Wikis
- Workforce analytics
- Workplace messaging systems

COURSE PLANNING GUIDE

Although *Business Communication Today* follows a conventional sequence of topics, it is structured so that you can address topics in whatever order best suits your needs. For instance, if you want to begin by reviewing grammar, sentence structure, and other writing fundamentals, you can ask students to read Chapter 5, Writing Business Messages, and then the Handbook of Grammar, Mechanics, and Usage. Conversely, if you want to begin with employment-related communication, you can start with the Prologue, Building a Career with Your Communication Skills, followed by Chapters 18 and 19.

The following table suggests a sequence and a schedule for covering the chapters in the textbook, with time allocations based on the total number of class hours available.

Chapter/Section Number and Title		Hours Devoted to Each Chapter/Section		
		30-Hour Course	**45-Hour Course**	**60-Hour Course**
Prologue	Building a Career with Your Communication Skills	1	1	1
1	Professional Communication in a Digital, Social, Mobile World	1	1	1
2	Collaboration, Interpersonal Communication, and Business Etiquette	1	1	2
3	Communication Challenges in a Diverse, Global Marketplace	1	2	3
4	Planning Business Messages	2	3	4
5	Writing Business Messages	2	3	4
6	Completing Business Messages	2	3	4
	Handbook of Grammar, Mechanics, and Usage	1	2	2
A	Format and Layout of Business Documents	1	1	1
7	Digital Media	1	2	3
8	Social Media	1	2	3
9	Visual Media	1	1	2
10	Writing Routine and Positive Messages	2	2	3
11	Writing Negative Messages	2	2	3
12	Writing Persuasive Messages	2	2	3
13	Finding, Evaluating, and Processing Information	1	2	3
14	Planning Reports and Proposals	1	2	3
15	Writing and Completing Reports and Proposals	1	2	3
B	Documentation of Report Sources	1	1	2
16	Developing Presentations in a Social Media Environment	1	3	3

(continued)

Chapter/Section Number and Title	Hours Devoted to Each Chapter/Section		
	30-Hour Course	45-Hour Course	60-Hour Course
17 Enhancing Presentations with Slides and Other Visuals	1	1	1
18 Building Careers and Writing Résumés	2	3	3
19 Applying and Interviewing for Employment	1	3	3

INSTRUCTOR RESOURCES AND SUPPORT OPTIONS

Business Communication Today is backed by an unmatched selection of resources for instructors and students, many of which were pioneered by the authors and remain unique in the field.

Online Communities and Media Resources

Instructors are welcome to take advantage of the many free online resources provided by Bovée and Thill:

- Sponsorship of Teaching Business Communication instructors' communities (open to all) and Bovée & Thill's Inner Circle for Business Communication (for adopters only) on LinkedIn and Facebook
- Instructor tips and techniques in Bovée and Thill's Business Communication Blog and Twitter feed
- The Bovée & Thill channel on YouTube, with videos that offer advice on teaching the new elements of business communication
- The unique Real-Time Updates content-updating service (see page xxiv)
- The popular Business Communication Headline News service (see page xxix–xxx)
- A variety of videos and PowerPoint presentations on SlideShare
- More than 500 infographics, videos, articles, podcasts, and PowerPoints on Business Communication Pictorial Gallery on Pinterest
- The Ultimate Guide to Resources for Teaching Business Communication

We also invite you to peruse Bovée & Thill's Online Magazines for Business Communication on Scoop.it:

- Business Communication 2.0: Social Media and Digital Communication
- Teaching a Modern Business Communication Course
- How the Mobile Revolution Is Changing Business Communication
- Teaching Business Communication and Workplace Issues
- Teaching Business Communication and Interpersonal Communication
- Teaching Business Presentations in a Business Communication Course
- Teaching Business Communication and Employment
- Teaching Visual Communication in a Business Communication Course
- Exclusive Teaching Resources for Business Communication Instructors

Links to all these services and resources can be found at **blog.businesscommunicationnetwork .com/resources**.

Business Communication Headline News

Stay on top of hot topics, important trends, and new technologies with Business Communication Headline News (**bchn.businesscommunicationnetwork.com**), the most comprehensive business communication site on the Internet. Every weekday during the school year, we offer fresh lecture content and provide a wide range of research and teaching tools on the website, including a custom web search function that we created expressly for business communication research.

Take advantage of the newsfeeds to get late-breaking news in headlines with concise summaries. You can scan incoming items in a matter of seconds and simply click through to read the full articles that interest you. All articles and accompanying multimedia resources are categorized by topic and chapter for easy retrieval at any time.

This free service for adopters offers numerous ways to enhance lectures and student activities:

- Keep current with the latest information and trends in the field
- Easily update your lecture notes with fresh material
- Create visuals for your classroom presentations
- Supplement your lectures with cutting-edge handouts
- Gather podcasts, online video, and other new media examples to use in the classroom
- Enhance your research projects with the newest data
- Compare best practices from other instructors
- Improve the quality and effectiveness of your teaching by reading about new teaching tips and techniques

At the website, you also get free access to these powerful instructional resources:

- **Business Communication Web Search**, featuring a revolutionary approach to searching developed by the authors that automatically formats more than 325 specific types of online search requests. The tool uses a simple and intuitive interface engineered to help business communication instructors find precisely what they want, whether it's Power-Point files, PDF files, Microsoft Word documents, Excel files, videos, podcasts, or more.
- **Real-Time Updates** are newsfeeds and content updates tied directly to specific points throughout the text. Each content update is classified by the type of media featured: interactive website, infographic, article, video, podcast, PowerPoint, or PDF. Additional sections on the site include Instructor Messages and Instructor Media (both password protected), Student Messages, and Student Assignments.

You can subscribe to Business Communication Headline News and get delivery by email, RSS newsreader, mobile phone, instant messenger, MP3, Twitter, Facebook, and a host of other options.

Bovée & Thill Business Communication Blog

The Bovée & Thill Business Communication Blog (**blog.businesscommunicationnetwork .com/**) offers original articles that help instructors focus their teaching to help students learn more efficiently and effectively. Articles discuss a wide variety of topics, including new topics instructors should be teaching their students, resources instructors can use in their classes, solutions to common teaching challenges, and great examples and activities instructors can use in class.

Authors' Email Hotline for Faculty

Integrity, excellence, and responsiveness are our hallmarks. That means providing you with textbooks that are academically sound, creative, timely, and sensitive to instructor and student needs. As an adopter of *Business Communication Today*, you are invited to use our Email Hotline (hotline@boveeandthillbusinesscommunicationblog.com) if you ever have a question or concern related to the text or its supplements.

Instructor's Resource Center

At the Instructor Resource Center, **www.pearsonhighered.com/irc**, instructors can access a variety of digital and presentation resources available with this text in downloadable format. As a registered faculty member, you can download resource files and receive immediate access and instructions for installing course management content on your campus server.

If you ever need assistance, our dedicated technical support team is ready to help with the media supplements that accompany this text. Visit **support.pearson.com/getsupport** for answers to frequently asked questions and toll-free user support phone numbers.

The following supplements are available to adopting instructors (for detailed descriptions, please visit **www.pearsonhighered.com/educator**):

- Instructor's Resource Manual
- Test Bank
- TestGen® Computerized Test Bank (and various conversions)
- PowerPoint Presentations

For Students: How This Course Will Help You

No matter what profession you want to pursue, the ability to communicate will be an essential skill—and a skill that employers expect you to have when you enter the workforce. This course introduces you to the fundamental principles of business communication and gives you the opportunity to develop your communication skills. You'll discover how business communication differs from personal and social communication, and you'll see how today's companies are using blogs, social networks, podcasts, virtual worlds, wikis, and other technologies. You'll learn a simple three-step writing process that works for all types of writing and speaking projects, both in college and on the job. Along the way, you'll gain valuable insights into ethics, etiquette, listening, teamwork, and nonverbal communication. Plus, you'll learn effective strategies for the many types of communication challenges you'll face on the job, from routine messages about transactions to complex reports and websites.

Few courses can offer the three-for-the-price-of-one value you get from a business communication class. Check out these benefits:

- **In your other classes.** The communication skills you learn in this class can help you in every other course you take in college. From simple homework assignments to complicated team projects to class presentations, you'll be able to communicate more effectively with less time and effort.
- **During your job search.** You can reduce the stress of searching for a job and stand out from the competition. Every activity in the job-search process relies on communication. The better you can communicate, the more successful you'll be at landing interesting and rewarding work.
- **On the job.** After you get that great job, the time and energy you have invested in this course will continue to yield benefits year after year. As you tackle each project and every new challenge, influential company leaders—the people who decide how quickly you'll get promoted and how much you'll earn—will be paying close attention to how well you communicate. They will observe your interactions with colleagues, customers, and business partners. They'll take note of how well you can collect data, find the essential ideas buried under mountains of information, and convey those points to other people. They'll observe your ability to adapt to different audiences and circumstances. They'll be watching when you encounter tough situations that require careful attention to ethics and etiquette. The good news: Every insight you gain and every skill you develop in this course will help you shine in your career.

HOW TO SUCCEED IN THIS COURSE

Although this course explores a wide range of message types and seems to cover quite a lot of territory, the underlying structure of the course is actually rather simple. You'll learn a few basic concepts, identify some key skills to use and procedures to follow—and then practice, practice, practice. Whether you're writing a blog posting in response to one of the real-company cases or drafting your own résumé, you'll be practicing the same skills again and again. With feedback and reinforcement from your instructor and your classmates, your confidence will grow and the work will become easier and more enjoyable.

The following sections offer advice on approaching each assignment, using your textbook, and taking advantage of some other helpful resources.

APPROACHING EACH ASSIGNMENT

In the spirit of practice and improvement, you will have a number of writing (and possibly speaking) assignments throughout this course. These suggestions will help you produce better results with less effort:

- **First, don't panic!** If the thought of writing a report or giving a speech sends a chill up your spine, you're not alone. Everybody feels that way when first learning business communication skills, and even experienced professionals can feel nervous about major projects. Keeping three points in mind will help. First, every project can be broken down into a series of small, manageable tasks. Don't let a big project overwhelm you; it's nothing more than a bunch of smaller tasks. Second, remind yourself that you have the skills you need in order to accomplish each task. As you move through the course, the assignments are carefully designed to match the skills you've developed up to that point. Third, if you feel panic creeping up on you, take a break and regain your perspective.

- **Focus on one task at a time.** A common mistake writers make is trying to organize and express their ideas while simultaneously worrying about audience reactions, grammar, spelling, formatting, page design, and a dozen other factors. Fight the temptation to do everything at once; otherwise, your frustration will soar and your productivity will plummet. In particular, don't worry about grammar, spelling, and word choices during your first draft. Concentrate on the organization of your ideas first, then the way you express those ideas, and then the presentation and production of your messages. Following the three-step writing process is an ideal way to focus on one task at a time in a logical sequence.

- **Give yourself plenty of time.** As with every other school project, putting things off to the last minute creates unnecessary stress. Writing and speaking projects in particular are much easier if you tackle them in small stages with breaks in between, rather than trying to get everything done in one frantic blast. Moreover, there will be instances when you simply get stuck on a project, and the best thing to do is walk away and give your mind a break. If you allow room for breaks in your schedule, you'll minimize the frustration and spend less time overall on your homework, too.

- **Step back and assess each project before you start.** The writing and speaking projects you'll have in this course cover a wide range of communication scenarios, and it's essential that you adapt your approach to each new challenge. Resist the urge to dive in and start writing without a plan. Ponder the assignment for a while, consider the various approaches you might take, and think carefully about your objectives before you start writing. Nothing is more frustrating than getting stuck halfway through because you're not sure what you're trying to say or you've wandered off track. Spend a little time planning, and you'll spend a lot less time writing.

- **Use the three-step writing process.** Those essential planning tasks are the first step in the three-step writing process, which you'll learn about in Chapter 4 and use throughout the course. This process has been developed and refined by professional writers with decades of experience and thousands of projects ranging from short blog posts to 500-page textbooks. It works, so take advantage of it.

- **Learn from the examples and model documents.** This textbook offers dozens of realistic examples of business messages, many with notes along the sides that explain strong and weak points. Study these and any other examples that your instructor provides. Learn what works and what doesn't, then apply these lessons to your own writing.

- **Learn from experience.** Finally, learn from the feedback you get from your instructor and from other students. Don't take the criticism personally; your instructor and your classmates are commenting about the work, not about you. View every bit of feedback as an opportunity to improve.

Using This Textbook Package

This book and its accompanying online resources introduce you to the key concepts in business communication while helping you develop essential skills. As you read each chapter, start by studying the learning objectives. They will help you identify the most important concepts in the chapter and give you a feel for what you'll be learning. Each learning objective corresponds to one major heading within the chapter, so you can easily find the information it relates to. After the learning objectives, a compelling Communication Close-Up vignette featuring a successful company or professional shows you how the material you will encounter in the chapter is put to use in actual business situations.

At the end of each chapter, the Summary of Learning Objectives gives you the chance to quickly verify your grasp of important concepts. Following that, you'll see two sets of questions that will help you test and apply your knowledge, and two sets of projects that will help you practice and expand your skills. Nine chapters also feature communication cases, which are more involved projects that require you to plan and complete a variety of messages and documents. All these activities are tagged by learning objective, so if you have any questions about the concepts you need to apply, just revisit that part of the chapter.

Several chapters have activities with downloadable media such as presentations and podcasts; if your instructor assigns these elements, follow the instructions in the text to locate the correct files.

In addition to the 19 chapters of the text itself, here are some special features that will help you succeed in the course and on the job:

- **Prologue: Building a Career with Your Communication Skills.** This section (immediately following this Preface) helps you understand today's dynamic workplace, the steps you can take to adapt to the job market, and the importance of creating an employment portfolio and building your personal brand.
- **Handbook.** The Handbook of Grammar, Mechanics, and Usage (see page 601) is a convenient reference of essential business English.
- **Real-Time Updates.** You can use this unique newsfeed service to make sure you're always kept up to date on important topics. Plus, at strategic points in every chapter, you will be directed to the Real-Time Updates website to get the latest information about specific subjects. To sign up, visit **real-timeupdates.com/bct14**.
- **Business Communication Web Search.** With our unique web search approach, you can quickly format more than 325 specific types of online searches. This tool uses a simple and intuitive interface engineered to help you find precisely what you want, whether it's PowerPoint files, PDF files, Microsoft Word documents, Excel files, videos, podcasts, videos, or social bookmarks. Check it out at **websearch .businesscommunicationnetwork.com**.

About the Authors

Courtland L. Bovée and John V. Thill have been leading textbook authors for more than two decades, introducing millions of students to the fields of business and business communication. Their award-winning texts are distinguished by proven pedagogical features, extensive selections of contemporary case studies, hundreds of real-life examples, engaging writing, thorough research, and the unique integration of print and electronic resources. Each new edition reflects the authors' commitment to continuous refinement and improvement, particularly in terms of modeling the latest practices in business and the use of technology.

Professor Bovée has 22 years of teaching experience at Grossmont College in San Diego, where he has received teaching honors and was accorded that institution's C. Allen Paul Distinguished Chair. Mr. Thill is a prominent communications consultant who has worked with organizations ranging from Fortune 500 multinationals to entrepreneurial start-ups. He formerly held positions with Pacific Bell and Texaco.

Courtland Bovée and John Thill were recently awarded proclamations from the governor of Massachusetts for their lifelong contributions to education and for their commitment to the summer youth baseball program that is sponsored by the Boston Red Sox.

Acknowledgments

The 14th Edition of *Business Communication Today* reflects the professional experience of a large team of contributors and advisors. We express our thanks to the many individuals whose valuable suggestions and constructive comments influenced the success of this book.

REVIEWERS OF MODEL DOCUMENTS

Thank you to these professors for their thoughtful reviews of model documents: Zenobein Adams, Cleveland State University and Cuyahoga Community College; Judy

Bello, Lander University; Scott Buechler, Elon University; Herb Brown, Appalachian State University; Terry Engebretsen, Idaho State University; Linda Gregory, Seminole State College of Florida; Kathleen Norris, Loyola Marymount University; Elisabeth Power, Saint Martin's University; Joanne M. Slutsky, University at Buffalo; Melvin Charles Washington, Howard University; and Gail Yosh, Montclair State University.

REVIEWERS OF PREVIOUS EDITIONS

Thank you to the following professors: Lydia E. Anderson, Fresno City College; Victoria Austin, Las Positas College; Faridah Awang, Eastern Kentucky University; Jeanette Baldridge, University of Maine at Augusta; Diana Baran, Henry Ford Community College; JoAnne Barbieri, Atlantic Cape Community College; Kristina Beckman, John Jay College; Judy Bello, Lander University; Carol Bibly, Triton College; Nancy Bizal, University of Southern Indiana; Yvonne Block, College of Lake County; Edna Boroski, Trident Technical College; Nelvia M. Brady, Trinity Christian College; Arlene Broeker, Lincoln University; David Brooks, Indiana University Southeast; Carol Brown, South Puget Sound Community College; Domenic Bruni, University of Wisconsin; Jeff Bruns, Bacone College; Gertrude L. Burge, University of Nebraska; Sharon Burton, Brookhaven College; Robert Cabral, Oxnard College; Dorothy Campbell, Brevard Community College; Linda Carr, University of West Alabama; Alvaro Carreras Jr., Florida International University; Sharon Carson, St. Philip's College; Rick Carter, Seattle University; Dacia Charlesworth, Indiana University–Purdue University Fort Wayne; Jean Chenu, Genesee Community College; Connie Clark, Lane Community College; Alvin Clarke, Iowa State University; Jerrie Cleaver, Central Texas College; Clare Coleman, Temple University; Michael P. Collins, Northern Arizona University; M. Cotton, North Central Missouri College; Pat Cowherd, Campbellsville University; Pat Cuchens, University of Houston–Clear Lake; Walt Dabek, Post University; Cathy Daly, California State University–Sacramento; Linda Davis, Copiah–Lincoln Community College; Christine R. Day, Eastern Michigan University; Harjit Dosanjh, North Seattle Community College; Amy Drees, Defiance College; Cynthia Drexel, Western State College of Colorado; Lou Dunham, Spokane Falls Community College; Donna Everett, Morehead State University; Donna Falconer, Anoka–Ramsey Community College; Kate Ferguson Marsters, Gannon University; Darlynn Fink, Clarion University of Pennsylvania; Bobbi Fisher, University of Nebraska–Omaha; Laura Fitzwater, Community College of Philadelphia; Lynda K. Fuller, Wilmington University; Matthew Gainous, Ogeechee Technical College; Yolande Gardner, Lawson State Community College; Gina Genova, University of California–Santa Barbara; Lonny Gilbert, Central State University; Camille Girardi-Levy, Siena College; Nancy Goehring, Monterey Peninsula College; Dawn Goellner, Bethel College; Robert Goldberg, Prince George's Community College; Jeffrey Goldberg, MassBay Community College; Helen Grattan, Des Moines Area Community College; Barbara Grayson, University of Arkansas at Pine Bluff; Deborah Griffin, University of Houston–Clear Lake; Alice Griswold, Clarke College; Bonnie Grossman, College of Charleston; Lisa Gueldenzoph, North Carolina A&T State University; Wally Guyot, Fort Hays State University; Valerie Harrison, Cuyamaca College; Tim Hartge, The University of Michigan–Dearborn; Richard Heiens, University of South Carolina–Aiken; Maureece Heinert, Sinte Gleska University; Leighanne Heisel, University of Missouri–St. Louis; Gary Helfand, University of Hawaii–West Oahu; Cynthia Herrera, Orlando Culinary Academy; Kathy Hill, Sam Houston State University; Pashia Hogan, Northeast State Tech Community College; Sarah Holmes, New England Institute of Technology; Ruth Hopkins Zajdel, Ohio University–Chillicothe; Sheila Hostetler, Orange Coast College; Michael Hricik, Westmoreland County Community College; Rebecca Hsiao, East Los Angeles College; Mary Ann Hurd, Sauk Valley Community College; Pat Hurley, Leeward Community College; Harold Hurry, Sam Houston State University; Marcia James, University of Wisconsin–Whitewater; Frank Jaster, Tulane University; Jonatan Jelen, Parsons The New School For Design; Irene Joanette Gallio, Western Nevada Community College; Edgar Dunson Johnson III,

Augusta State University; Mark Johnson, Rhodes State College; Joanne Kapp, Siena College; Jeanette A. Karjala, Winona State University; Christy L. Kinnion, Lenior Community College; Deborah Kitchin, City College of San Francisco; Lisa Kirby, North Carolina Wesleyan College; Claudia Kirkpatrick, Carnegie Mellon University; Betty Kleen, Nicholls State University; Fran Kranz, Oakland University; Jana Langemach, University of Nebraska–Lincoln; Joan Lantry, Jefferson Community College; Kim Laux, Saginaw Valley State University; Kathryn J. Lee, University of Cincinnati; Anita Leffel, The University of Texas, San Antonio; Ruth Levy, Westchester Community College; Nancy Linger, Moraine Park Technical College; Jere Littlejohn, University of Mississippi; Dana Loewy, California State University–Fullerton; Jennifer Loney, Portland State University; Susan Long, Portland Community College; Sue Loomis, Maine Maritime Academy; Thomas Lowderbaugh, University of Maryland–College Park; Jayne Lowery, Jackson State Community College; Lloyd Matzner, University of Houston–Downtown; Ron McNeel, New Mexico State University at Alamogordo; Dr. Bill McPherson, Indiana University of Pennsylvania; Phyllis Mercer, Texas Woman's University; Donna Meyerholz, Trinidad State Junior College; Annie Laurie I. Meyers, Northampton Community College; Catherine "Kay" Michael, St. Edward's University; Kathleen Miller, University of Delaware; Gay Mills, Amarillo College; Julie Mullis, Wilkes Community College; Pamela Mulvey, Olney Central College; Jimidene Murphey, Clarendon College; Cindy Murphy, Southeastern Community College; Dipali Murti-Hali, California State University–Stanislaus; Shelley Myatt, University of Central Oklahoma; Cora Newcomb, Technical College of the Lowcountry; Ron Newman, Crafton Hills College; Linda Nitsch, Chadron State College; Leah Noonan, Laramie County Community College; Mabry O'Donnell, Marietta College; Diana Oltman, Central Washington University; Ranu Paik, Santa Monica College; Lauren Paisley, Genesee Community College; Patricia Palermo, Drew University; John Parrish, Tarrant County College; Diane Paul, TVI Community College; John T. Pauli, University of Alaska–Anchorage; Michael Pennell, University of Rhode Island; Sylvia Beaver Perez, Nyack College; Melinda Phillabaum, Indiana University; Ralph Phillips, Geneva College; Laura Pohopien, Cal Poly Pomona; Diane Powell, Utah Valley State College; Christine Pye, California Lutheran University; Norma Pygon, Triton College; Dave Rambow, Wayland Baptist University; Richard David Ramsey, Southeastern Louisiana University; Charles Riley, Tarrant County College–Northwest Campus; Jim Rucker, Fort Hays State University; Dr. Suzan Russell, Lehman College; Danielle Scane, Orange Coast College; Calvin Scheidt, Tidewater Community College; Nancy Schneider, University of Maine at Augusta; Brian Sheridan, Mercyhurst College; Melinda Shirey, Fresno City College; Bob Shirilla, Colorado State University; Joyce Simmons, Florida State University; Gordon J. Simpson, SUNY Cobleskill; Peggy Simpson, Dominican University; Eunice Smith, Bismarck State College; Jeff Smith, University of Southern California; Lorraine M. Smith, Fresno City College; Harvey Solganick, LeTourneau University–Dallas campus; Stephen Soucy, Santa Monica College; Linda Spargo, University of Mississippi; W. Dees Stallings, Park University; Sally Stanton, University of Wisconsin–Milwaukee; Mark Steinbach, Austin Community College; Angelique Stevens, Monroe Community College; Steven Stovall, Wilmington College; Alden Talbot, Weber State University; Michele Taylor, Ogeechee Technical College; Wilma Thomason, Mid-South Community College; Ed Thompson, Jefferson Community College; Ann E. Tippett, Monroe Community College; Lori Townsend, Niagara County Community College; Lani Uyeno, Leeward Community College; Wendy Van Hatten, Western Iowa Tech Community College; Jay Wagers, Richmond Community College; John Waltman, Eastern Michigan University; Jie Wang, University of Illinois at Chicago; Chris Ward, The University of Findlay; Dorothy Warren, Middle Tennessee State University; Glenda Waterman, Concordia University; Kellie Welch, Jefferson Community College; Bradley S. Wesner, Nova Southeastern University; Mathew Williams, Clover Park Technical College; Beth Williams, Stark State College of Technology; Brian Wilson, College of Marin; and Sandra D. Young, Orangeburg–Calhoun Technical College.

REVIEWERS OF DOCUMENT MAKEOVERS

We sincerely thank the following reviewers for their assistance with the Document Makeover feature: Lisa Barley, Eastern Michigan University; Marcia Bordman, Gallaudet University; Jean Bush-Bacelis, Eastern Michigan University; Bobbye Davis, Southern Louisiana University; Cynthia Drexel, Western State College of Colorado; Kenneth Gibbs, Worcester State College; Ellen Leathers, Bradley University; Diana McKowen, Indiana University; Bobbie Nicholson, Mars Hill College; Andrew Smith, Holyoke Community College; Jay Stubblefield, North Carolina Wesleyan College; and Dawn Wallace, Southeastern Louisiana University.

MYLAB CONTRIBUTORS

George Bernard, Seminole State College of Florida; Gina L. Genova, University of California, Santa Barbara; Nancy Nygaard, University of Wisconsin Milwaukee; Storm Russo, Valencia College; and Susan C. Schanne, Eastern Michigan University.

PERSONAL ACKNOWLEDGMENTS

We extend a heartfelt thanks to our many friends, acquaintances, and business associates who provided materials or agreed to be interviewed so that we could bring the real world into the classroom.

A very special acknowledgment goes to George Dovel, whose superb writing skills, distinguished background, and wealth of business experience assured this project of clarity and completeness. Also, recognition and thanks to Jackie Estrada for her outstanding skills and excellent attention to details. Her creation of the "Peak Performance Grammar and Mechanics" material is especially noteworthy.

We also feel it is important to acknowledge and thank the Association for Business Communication, an organization whose meetings and publications provide a valuable forum for the exchange of ideas and for professional growth.

In addition, we thank Susan Schanne of Eastern Michigan University, Christine Laursen of Red Rocks Community College, and Laura A. LeDoux of Fullerton College for their assistance in preparing supplements for this new edition.

We extend our warmest appreciation to the devoted professionals at Pearson Higher Education for their commitment to producing high-value, student-focused texts, including Donna Battista, Vice President, Business Publishing; Stephanie Wall, Director of Portfolio Management; Daniel Tylman, Portfolio Manager; Ashley Santora, Managing Producer, Business; Linda Albelli, Editorial Assistant; Jeff Holcomb, Director of Production, Business; Becky Brown, Product Marketer; and Lenny Ann Kucenski, Field Marketing Manager. We are also grateful to Nicole Suddeth and Julie Kidd of SPi Global.

Courtland L. Bovée
John V. Thill

Prologue

BUILDING A CAREER WITH YOUR COMMUNICATION SKILLS

Using This Course to Help Launch Your Career

This course will help you develop vital communication skills that you'll use throughout your career—and those skills can help you launch an interesting and rewarding career, too. This brief prologue sets the stage by helping you understand today's dynamic workplace, the steps you can take to adapt to the job market, and the importance of creating an employment portfolio and building your personal brand. Take a few minutes to read it while you think about the career you hope to create for yourself.

UNDERSTANDING THE CHANGING WORLD OF WORK

Even as the U.S. economy recovers from the Great Recession and employment levels improve, you're likely to encounter some challenges as you start or continue with your business career. As companies around the world try to gain competitive advantages and cost efficiencies, employment patterns will vary from industry to industry and region to region.

The ups and downs of the economic cycle are not the only dynamic elements that will affect your career, however. The nature of employment itself is changing, with a growing number of independent workers and loosely structured *virtual organizations* that engage these workers for individual projects or short-term contracts, rather than hiring employees. In fact, one recent study predicted that independent workers will outnumber conventional employees in the United States by 2020.[1]

This new model of work offers some compelling advantages for workers and companies alike. Companies can lower their fixed costs, adapt more easily to economic fluctuations and competitive moves, and get access to specialized talent for specific project needs.[2] Workers can benefit from the freedom to choose the clients and projects that interest them the most, the flexibility to work as much or as little as they want, and (thanks to advances in communication technology) access to compelling work even if they live far from major employment centers such as New York City or California's Silicon Valley.[3]

On the other hand, this new approach also presents some significant challenges for all parties. These flexibilities and freedoms can create more complexity for workers and managers, diminished loyalties on both sides, uncertainty about the future, issues with skill development and training, and problems with accountability and liability.[4] Many of these challenges involve communication, making solid communication skills more important than ever.

These changes could affect you even if you pursue traditional employment throughout your career. Within organizations, you're likely to work with a combination of "inside" employees and "outside" contractors, which can affect the dynamics of the workplace. And the availability of more independent workers in the talent marketplace gives employers more options and more leverage, so full-time employees may find themselves competing against freelancers, at least indirectly.

As you navigate this uncertain future, keep two vital points in mind. First, don't wait for your career to just happen: Take charge of your career and stay in charge of it. Explore all your options and have a plan, but be prepared to change course as opportunities and

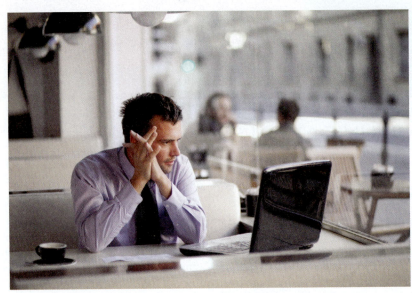

Are you comfortable working on your own? Independent workers have become an important part of the global workforce.

threats appear on the horizon. Second, don't count on employers to take care of you. The era of lifetime employment, in which an employee committed to one company for life with the understanding it would return the loyalty, is long gone. From finding opportunities to developing the skills you need in order to succeed, it's up to you to manage your career and look out for your own best interests.

How Employers View Today's Job Market

From an employer's perspective, the employment process is always a question of balance. Maintaining a stable workforce can improve practically every aspect of business performance, yet many employers want the flexibility to shrink and expand payrolls as business conditions change. Employers obviously want to attract the best talent, but the best talent is more expensive and more vulnerable to offers from competitors, so there are always financial trade-offs to consider.

Employers also struggle with the ups and downs of the economy. When unemployment is low, the balance of power shifts to employees, and employers have to compete in order to attract and keep top talent. When unemployment is high, the power shifts back to employers, who can afford to be more selective and less accommodating. In other words, pay attention to the economy; at times you can be more aggressive in your demands, but at other times you need to be more accommodating.

Companies view employment as a complex business decision with lots of variables to consider. To make the most of your potential, regardless of the career path you pursue, you need to view employment in the same way.

What Employers Look for in Job Applicants

Given the complex forces in the contemporary workplace and the unrelenting pressure of global competition, what are employers looking for in the candidates they hire? The short answer: a lot. Like all "buyers," companies want to get as much as they can for the money they spend. The closer you can present yourself as the ideal candidate, the better your chances of getting a crack at the most exciting opportunities.

Specific expectations vary by profession and position, of course, but virtually all employers look for the following general skills and attributes:[5]

- **Communication skills.** The reason this item is listed first isn't that you're reading a business communication textbook. Communication is listed first because it is far and away the most commonly mentioned skill set when employers are asked about

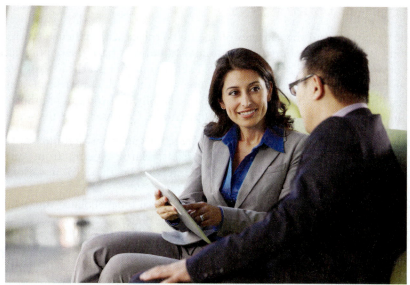

Communication skills will benefit your career, no matter what path or profession you pursue.

what they look for in employees. Improving your communication skills will help in every aspect of your professional life.

- **Interpersonal and team skills.** You will have many individual responsibilities on the job, but chances are you won't work alone very often. Learn to work with others and help them succeed as you succeed.
- **Intercultural and international awareness and sensitivity.** Successful employers tend to be responsive to diverse workforces, markets, and communities, and they look for employees with the same outlook.
- **Data collection, analysis, and decision-making skills.** Employers want people who know how to identify information needs, find the necessary data, convert the data into useful knowledge, and make sound decisions.
- **Digital, social, and mobile media skills.** Today's workers need to know how to use common office software and to communicate using a wide range of digital media and systems.
- **Time and resource management.** If you've had to juggle multiple priorities during college, consider that great training for the business world. Your ability to plan projects and manage the time and resources available to you will make a big difference on the job.
- **Flexibility and adaptability.** Stuff happens, as they say. Employees who can roll with the punches and adapt to changing business priorities and circumstances will go further (and be happier) than employees who resist change.
- **Professionalism.** Professionalism is the quality of performing at the highest possible level and conducting oneself with confidence, purpose, and pride. True professionals strive to excel, continue to hone their skills and build their knowledge, are dependable and accountable, demonstrate a sense of business etiquette, make ethical decisions, show loyalty and commitment, don't give up when things get tough, and maintain a positive outlook.

Adapting to Today's Job Market

Adapting to the workplace is a lifelong process of seeking the best fit between what you want to do and what employers (or clients, if you work independently) are willing to pay you to do. It's important to think about what you want to do during the many thousands of hours you will spend working, what you have to offer, and how to make yourself more attractive to employers.

WHAT DO YOU WANT TO DO?

Economic necessities and the vagaries of the marketplace will influence much of what happens in your career, of course, and you may not always have the opportunity to do the kind of work you would really like to do. Even if you can't get the job you want right now, though, start your job search by examining your values and interests. Doing so will give you a better idea of where you want to be eventually, and you can use those insights to learn and grow your way toward that ideal situation. Consider these questions:

- **What would you like to do every day?** Research occupations that interest you. Find out what people really do every day. Ask friends, relatives, alumni from your school, and contacts in your social networks. Read interviews with people in various professions to get a sense of what their careers are like.
- **How would you like to work?** Consider how much independence you want on the job, how much variety you like, and whether you prefer to work with products, machines, people, ideas, figures, or some combination thereof.
- **How do your financial goals fit with your other priorities?** For instance, many high-paying jobs involve a lot of stress, sacrifices of time with family and friends, and frequent travel or relocation. If location, lifestyle, intriguing work, or other factors are more important to you, you may well have to sacrifice some level of pay to achieve them.
- **Have you established some general career goals?** For example, do you want to pursue a career specialty such as finance or manufacturing, or do you want to gain experience in multiple areas with an eye toward upper management?
- **What sort of corporate culture are you most comfortable with?** Would you be happy in a formal hierarchy with clear reporting relationships? Or do you prefer less structure? Teamwork or individualism? Do you like a competitive environment?

You might need some time in the workforce to figure out what you really want to do or to work your way into the job you really want, but it's never too early to start thinking about where you want to be. Filling out the assessment in Table 1 might help you get a clearer picture of the nature of work you would like to pursue in your career.

TABLE 1   Career Self-Assessment

Activity or Situation	Strongly Agree	Agree	Disagree	No Preference
1. I want to work independently.	_____	_____	_____	_____
2. I want variety in my work.	_____	_____	_____	_____
3. I want to work with people.	_____	_____	_____	_____
4. I want to work with technology.	_____	_____	_____	_____
5. I want physical work.	_____	_____	_____	_____
6. I want mental work.	_____	_____	_____	_____
7. I want to work for a large organization.	_____	_____	_____	_____
8. I want to work for a nonprofit organization.	_____	_____	_____	_____
9. I want to work for a small business.	_____	_____	_____	_____
10. I want to work for a service business.	_____	_____	_____	_____
11. I want to start or buy a business someday.	_____	_____	_____	_____
12. I want regular, predictable work hours.	_____	_____	_____	_____
13. I want to work in a city location.	_____	_____	_____	_____
14. I want to work in a small town or suburb.	_____	_____	_____	_____
15. I want to work in another country.	_____	_____	_____	_____
16. I want to work outdoors.	_____	_____	_____	_____
17. I want to work in a structured environment.	_____	_____	_____	_____
18. I want to avoid risk as much as possible.	_____	_____	_____	_____
19. I want to enjoy my work, even if that means making less money.	_____	_____	_____	_____
20. I want to become a high-level corporate manager.	_____	_____	_____	_____

WHAT DO YOU HAVE TO OFFER?

Knowing what you want to do is one thing. Knowing what a company is willing to pay you to do is another thing entirely. You may already have a good idea of what you can offer employers. If not, some brainstorming can help you identify your skills, interests, and characteristics. Start by jotting down achievements you're proud of and experiences that were satisfying, and think carefully about what specific skills these achievements demanded of you. For example, leadership skills, speaking ability, and artistic talent may have helped you coordinate a successful class project. As you analyze your achievements, you may well begin to recognize a pattern of skills. Which of them might be valuable to potential employers?

Next, look at your educational preparation, work experience, and extracurricular activities. What do your knowledge and experience qualify you to do? What have you learned from volunteer work or class projects that could benefit you on the job? Have you held any offices, won any awards or scholarships, mastered a second language? What skills have you developed in nonbusiness situations that could transfer to a business position?

Take stock of your personal characteristics. Are you aggressive, a born leader? Or would you rather follow? Are you outgoing, articulate, great with people? Or do you prefer working alone? Make a list of what you believe are your four or five most important qualities. Ask a relative or friend to rate your traits as well.

If you're having difficulty figuring out your interests, characteristics, or capabilities, consult your college career center. Many campuses administer a variety of tests that can help you identify interests, aptitudes, and personality traits. These tests won't reveal your "perfect" job, but they'll help you focus on the types of work best suited to your personality.

HOW CAN YOU MAKE YOURSELF MORE VALUABLE?

While you're figuring out what you want from a job and what you can offer an employer, you can take positive steps toward building your career. First, look for volunteer projects, temporary jobs, freelance work, or internships that will help expand your experience base and skill set.[6] You can look for freelance projects on Craigslist and numerous other websites; some of these jobs have only nominal pay, but they do provide an opportunity for you to display your skills. Also consider applying your talents to *crowdsourcing* projects, in which companies and nonprofit organizations invite the public to contribute solutions to various challenges.

These opportunities help you gain valuable experience and relevant contacts, provide you with important references and work samples for your employment portfolio, and help you establish your personal brand (see the following sections).

Second, learn more about the industry or industries in which you want to work and stay on top of new developments. Join networks of professional colleagues and friends who can help you keep up with trends and events. Many professional societies have student chapters or offer students discounted memberships. Take courses and pursue other educational or life experiences that would be difficult while working full time.

BUILDING AN EMPLOYMENT PORTFOLIO

Employers want proof that you have the skills to succeed on the job, but even if you don't have much relevant work experience, you can use your college classes to assemble that proof. Simply create and maintain an *employment portfolio*, which is a collection of projects that demonstrate your skills and knowledge. You can create a *print portfolio* and an *e-portfolio*; both can help with your career effort. A print portfolio gives you something tangible to bring to interviews, and it lets you collect project results that might not be easy to show online, such as a handsomely bound report. An e-portfolio is a multimedia presentation of your skills and experiences.[7] Think of it as a website that contains your résumé, work samples, letters of recommendation, relevant videos or podcasts you have recorded, any blog posts or articles you have written, and other information about you and your skills. The portfolio can be burned on a CD or DVD for physical distribution or, more commonly, it can be posted online—whether on a personal website, your college's site (if student pages are available), or a specialized portfolio hosting site such as Behance. To see a selection of student e-portfolios from colleges around the United States, go to **real-timeupdates.com/bct14**, select Student Assignments, and locate the link to student e-portfolios.

Throughout this course, pay close attention to the assignments marked "Portfolio Builder" (they start in Chapter 7). These items will make particularly good samples of not only your communication skills but also your ability to understand and solve business-related challenges. By combining these projects with samples from your other courses, you can create a compelling portfolio when you're ready to start interviewing. Your portfolio is also a great resource for writing your résumé because it reminds you of all the great work you've done over the years. Moreover, you can continue to refine and expand your portfolio throughout your career; many professionals use e-portfolios to advertise their services.

As you assemble your portfolio, collect anything that shows your ability to perform, whether it's in school, on the job, or in other venues. However, you *must* check with employers before including any items that you created while you were an employee, and check with clients before including any *work products* (anything you wrote, designed, programmed, and so on) they purchased from you. Many business documents contain confidential information that companies don't want distributed to outside audiences.

For each item you add to your portfolio, write a brief description that helps other people understand the meaning and significance of the project. Include such items as these:

- **Background.** Why did you undertake this project? Was it a school project, a work assignment, or something you did on your own initiative?
- **Project objectives.** Explain the project's goals, if relevant.
- **Collaborators.** If you worked with others, be sure to mention that and discuss team dynamics if appropriate. For instance, if you led the team or worked with others long distance as a virtual team, point that out.
- **Constraints.** Sometimes the most impressive thing about a project is the time or budget constraints under which it was created. If such constraints apply to a project, consider mentioning them in a way that doesn't sound like an excuse for poor quality. If you had only one week to create a website, for example, you might say that "One of the intriguing challenges of this project was the deadline; I had only one week to design, compose, test, and publish this material."
- **Outcomes.** If the project's goals were measurable, what was the result? For example, if you wrote a letter soliciting donations for a charitable cause, how much money did you raise?
- **Learning experience.** If appropriate, describe what you learned during the course of the project.

Keep in mind that the portfolio itself is a communication project, so be sure to apply everything you'll learn in this course about effective communication and good design. Assume that potential employers will find your e-portfolio site (even if you don't tell them about it), so don't include anything that could come back to haunt you. Also, if you have anything embarrassing on Facebook, Twitter, or any other social networking site, remove it immediately.

To get started, first check with the career center at your college; many schools offer e-portfolio systems for their students. (Some schools now require e-portfolios, so you may already be building one.) You can also find plenty of advice online; search for "e-portfolio," "student portfolio," or "professional portfolio."

BUILDING YOUR PERSONAL BRAND

Products and companies have brands that represent collections of certain attributes, such as the safety emphasis of Volvo cars, the performance emphasis of BMW, or the luxury emphasis of Cadillac. Similarly, when people who know you think about you, they have a particular set of qualities in mind based on your professionalism, your priorities, and the various skills and attributes you have developed over the years. Perhaps without even being conscious of it, you have created a *personal brand* for yourself.

As you plan the next stage of your career, start managing your personal brand deliberately. The branding specialist Mohammed Al-Taee defines personal branding succinctly as "a way of clarifying and communicating what makes you different and special."[8]

You will have multiple opportunities to plan and refine your personal brand during this course. For example, Chapter 8 offers tips on business applications of social media, which are key to personal branding, and Chapters 18 and 19 guide you through the process of creating a résumé, building your network, and presenting yourself in interviews. To get you started, here are the basics of a successful personal branding strategy:[9]

- **Figure out the "story of you."** Simply put, where have you been in life, and where are you going? Every good story has dramatic tension that pulls readers in and makes them wonder what will happen next. Where is your story going next? Chapter 18 offers more on this personal brand-building approach.
- **Clarify your professional theme.** Volvos, BMWs, and Cadillacs can all get you from point A to point B in safety, comfort, and style, but each brand emphasizes some attributes more than others to create a specific image in the minds of potential buyers. Similarly, you want to be seen as something more than just an accountant, a supervisor, a salesperson. What will your theme be? Brilliant strategist? Hard-nosed, get-it-done tactician? Technical guru? Problem solver? Creative genius? Inspirational leader?
- **Reach out and connect.** Major corporations spread the word about their brands with multimillion-dollar advertising campaigns. You can promote your brand at little or no cost. The secret is networking, which you'll learn more about in Chapter 18. You build your brand by connecting with like-minded people, sharing information, demonstrating skills and knowledge, and helping others succeed.
- **Deliver on your brand's promise—every time, all the time.** When you promote a brand, you make a promise—a promise that whoever buys that brand will get the benefits you are promoting. All of this planning and communication is of no value if you fail to deliver on the promises your branding efforts make. Conversely, when you deliver quality results time after time, your talents and professionalism will speak for you.

USING ALL THE JOB-SEARCH TOOLS AT YOUR DISPOSAL

As a final note, be sure to use all the job-search tools and resources available to you. For example, many companies now offer mobile apps that give you a feel for what it's like to work there and let you search for job openings. A variety of apps and websites can help you find jobs, practice interviewing, and build your professional network.

We wish you great success in this course and in your career!

Endnotes

1. Ryan Kim, "By 2020, Independent Workers Will Be the Majority," *GigaOm*, 8 December 2011, gigaom.com.

2. Darren Dahl, "Want a Job? Let the Bidding Begin," *Inc.*, March 2011, 93–96; Thomas W. Malone, Robert J. Laubacher, and Tammy Johns, "The Age of Hyperspecialization," *Harvard Business Review*, July–August 2011, 56–65; Jennifer Wang, "The Solution to the Innovator's Dilemma," *Entrepreneur*, August 2011, 24–32.

3. "LiveOps and Vision Perry Create New Work Opportunities for Rural Tennessee," LiveOps press release, 18 July 2011, www.liveops.com; Malone et al., "The Age of Hyperspecialization."

4. Adapted from Dahl, "Want a Job? Let the Bidding Begin"; Malone et al., "The Age of Hyperspecialization"; Wang, "The Solution to the Innovator's Dilemma"; Marjorie Derven, "Managing the Matrix in the New Normal," *T+D*, July 2010, 42–47.

5. Courtland L. Bovèe and John V. Thill, *Business in Action*, 5th ed. (Upper Saddle River, N.J.: Pearson Prentice Hall, 2010), 18–21; Randall S. Hansen and Katharine Hansen, "What Do Employers Really Want? Top Skills and Values Employers Seek from Job-Seekers," QuintCareers.com, accessed 17 August 2010, www.quintcareers.com.

6. Nancy M. Somerick, "Managing a Communication Internship Program," *Bulletin of the Association for Business Communication* 56, no. 3 (1993): 10–20.

7. Jeffrey R. Young, "'E-Portfolios' Could Give Students a New Sense of Their Accomplishments," *The Chronicle of Higher Education*, 8 March 2002, A31.

8. Mohammed Al-Taee, "Personal Branding," Al-Taee blog, accessed 17 August 2010, altaeeblog.com.

9. Pete Kistler, "Seth Godin's 7-Point Guide to Bootstrap Your Personal Brand," Personal Branding blog, 28 July 2010, www.personalbrandingblog; Kyle Lacy, "10 Ways to Building Your Personal Brand Story," Personal Branding blog, 5 August 2010, www.personalbrandingblog; Al-Taee, "Personal Branding"; Scot Herrick, "30 Career Management Tips—Marketing AND Delivery Support Our Personal Brand," Cube Rules blog, 8 September 2007, cuberules.com; Alina Tugend, "Putting Yourself Out There on a Shelf to Buy," *New York Times*, 27 March 2009, www.nytimes.com.

PART 1

Understanding the Foundations of Business Communication

No other skill can help your career in as many ways as communication. Discover what business communication is all about, why communication skills are essential to your career, how social and mobile technologies are revolutionizing business communication, and how to adapt your communication experiences in life and college to the business world. Improve your skills in such vital areas as team interaction, etiquette, listening, and nonverbal communication. Explore the advantages and the challenges of a diverse workforce and develop the skills that every communicator needs to succeed in today's global, multicultural business environment.

El Nariz/Shutterstock

Professional Communication in a Digital, Social, Mobile World

LEARNING OBJECTIVES

After studying this chapter, you will be able to

1 Explain the importance of effective communication to your career and to the companies where you will work.

2 Explain what it means to communicate as a professional in a business context.

3 Describe the communication process model and the ways social media are changing the nature of business communication.

4 Outline the challenges and opportunities of mobile communication in business.

5 List four general guidelines for using communication technology effectively.

6 Define *ethics*, explain the difference between an ethical dilemma and an ethical lapse, and list six guidelines for making ethical communication choices.

COMMUNICATION CLOSE-UP AT

JetBlue

twitter.com/jetblue

If you have ever worked in retail, customer service, or a similar job, you know what a challenge it can be to make sure each customer has a great experience with your company. Imagine the challenge of keeping 35 million customers happy. That's how many passengers JetBlue carries every year—an average of roughly 95,000 customers per day.

As a relatively new airline, taking its first flight in 2000, JetBlue has always tried to differentiate itself from the older carriers in the business. A great example is its pioneering use of Twitter as a customer service platform. JetBlue joined Twitter in 2007, only a year after the microblogging service launched and well before most companies were aware of its potential for business communication. The company views its website as the central hub of its online presence, but social media (the company is quite active on Facebook as well, with over a million likes) provide a vital connection between customers and the website. In fact, digital communication of all forms is so important that the company considers itself a digital brand.

The airline was also one of the first companies to truly get the *social* part of social media—that Twitter and other systems were about more than just pushing information outward. Morgan Johnstone, the JetBlue communications staffer who got the company started on Twitter, recognized early on the power of listening via social media. He wanted to hear what people

JetBlue's use of social media for customer support coincides perfectly with air travelers' use of mobile devices.

were saying about the company, whether it was plea for help during travel, a compliment for a company employee, or even an unpleasant criticism. This interaction became so valuable to the company that it now has more than two dozen Twitter agents all ready to interact in real time with the 2 million travelers who follow the company. They answer questions, resolve problems and complaints, and even rebook flights on the spot if needed. (When a customer needs specific help, JetBlue's Twitter team usually takes the conversation private via direct messaging, and its Twitter homepage now encourages customer with service issues to phone or email for help.)

For a company that is all about moving people from point A to point B, it's no surprise that mobile communication has become an essential part of JetBlue's connection with its customers. Customers who ask for help or who post complaints on Twitter often do so via their mobile devices, whether they're on their way to catch a flight, stuck in an airport trying to rebook on a different flight, or even on board an aircraft waiting to take off. Mobile is now a core element in the company's communication strategy, with a mobile-friendly website and JetBlue smartphone apps. However the company innovates as it moves forward, its focus will be on using digital, social, and mobile communication to make sure customers have the best possible experience.[1]

Understanding Why Communication Matters

1 LEARNING OBJECTIVE
Explain the importance of effective communication to your career and to the companies where you will work.

Communication is the process of transferring information and meaning between senders and receivers.

Whether it's as simple as a smile or as ambitious as JetBlue's social media program (profiled in the chapter-opening Communication Close-Up), **communication** is the process of transferring information and meaning between *senders* and *receivers*, using one or more media and communication channels. The essence of communication is sharing—providing data, information, insights, and inspiration in an exchange that benefits both you and the people with whom you are communicating.[2] As Figure 1.1 indicates, this sharing can happen in a variety of ways, including simple and successful transfers of information, negotiations in which the sender and receiver arrive at an agreed-on meaning, and unsuccessful attempts in which the receiver creates a different message than the one the sender intended.

You will invest a lot of time and energy in this course developing your communication skills, so it's fair to ask whether the effort will be worthwhile. This section outlines the many ways in which good communication skills are critical for your career and for any company you join.

COMMUNICATION IS IMPORTANT TO YOUR CAREER

Ambition and great ideas aren't enough; you need to be able to communicate with people to succeed in business.

Improving your communication skills may be the single most important step you can take in your career. You can have the greatest ideas in the world, but they're no good to your company or your career if you can't express them clearly and persuasively. Some jobs, such as sales and customer support, are primarily about communicating. In fields such as engineering or finance, you often need to share complex ideas with executives, customers, and colleagues, and your ability to connect with people outside your field can be as important as your technical expertise. If you have the entrepreneurial urge, you will need to communicate with a wide range of audiences—from investors, bankers, and government regulators to employees, customers, and business partners.

The changing nature of employment is putting new pressure on communication skills, too. Many companies now supplement their permanent workforces with independent contractors who are brought on for a short period or even just a single project. Chances are you will spend some of your career as one of these freelancers, working without the support network that an established company environment provides. You will have to "sell yourself" into each new contract, communicate successfully in a wide range of work situations, and take full responsibility for your career growth and success.

If you launch a company or move into an executive role in an existing organization, you can expect communication to consume the majority of your time. Top executives spend most of their workdays communicating, and businesspeople who can't communicate well don't stand much chance of reaching the top.

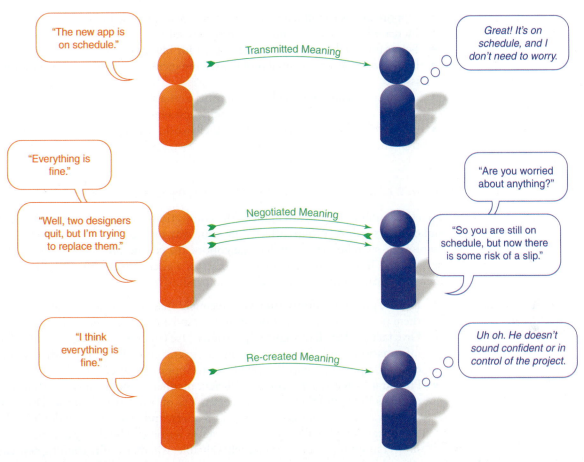

Figure 1.1 **Sharing Information**
These three exchanges between a software project manager (*left*) and his boss (*right*) illustrate the variety of ways in which information is shared between senders and receivers. In the top exchange, the sender's meaning is transmitted intact to the receiver, who accepts what the sender says at face value. In the middle exchange, the sender and receiver negotiate the meaning by discussing the situation. The negotiated meaning is that everything is fine *so far*, but the risk of a schedule slip is now higher than it was before. In the bottom exchange, the receiver has a negative emotional reaction to the word *think* and as a result creates her own meaning—that everything probably *is not* fine, despite what the sender says.

In fact, improving your communication skills may be the single most important step you can take in your career. The world is full of good marketing strategists, good accountants, good engineers, and good attorneys—but it is not full of good communicators. View this as an opportunity to stand out from your competition in the job market.

Employers sometimes express frustration at the poor communication skills of many employees—particularly recent college graduates who haven't yet learned how to adapt their communication styles to a professional business environment.[3] If you learn to write well, speak well, listen well, and recognize the appropriate way to communicate in any situation, you'll gain a major advantage that will serve you throughout your career.[4]

Strong communication skills give you an advantage in the job market.

> **REAL-TIME UPDATES**
> LEARN MORE BY VISITING THIS WEBSITE
> **Check out the cutting edge of business communication**
> This Pinterest board created by the authors highlights some of the most important changes taking place in the field of business communication. Go to **real-timeupdates.com/bct14** and select Learn More in the Students section.

COMMUNICATION IS IMPORTANT TO YOUR COMPANY

Aside from the personal benefits, communication should be important to you because it is important to your company. Effective communication helps businesses in numerous ways, by promoting[5]

- A stronger sense of trust between individuals and organizations
- Closer ties with important communities in the marketplace

Effective communication yields numerous business benefits.

- Opportunities to influence conversations, perceptions, and trends
- Increased productivity and faster problem solving
- Better financial results and higher return for investors
- Earlier warning of potential problems, from increasing business costs to critical safety issues
- Stronger decision making based on timely, reliable information
- Clearer and more persuasive marketing messages
- Greater employee engagement with their work, leading to higher employee satisfaction and lower employee turnover

WHAT MAKES BUSINESS COMMUNICATION EFFECTIVE?

Effective communication strengthens the connections between a company and all of its **stakeholders**—those groups affected in some way by the company's actions: customers, employees, shareholders, suppliers, neighbors, the community, the nation, and the world as a whole.[6] To make your communication efforts as effective as possible, focus on making them practical, factual, concise, clear, and persuasive:

> Effective messages are *practical*, *factual*, *concise*, *clear*, and *persuasive*.

- **Provide practical information.** Give recipients useful information, whether it's to help them perform a desired action or understand a new company policy.
- **Give facts rather than vague impressions.** Use concrete language, specific detail, and information that is clear, convincing, accurate, and ethical. Even when an opinion is called for, present compelling evidence to support your conclusion.
- **Present information in a concise, efficient manner.** Concise messages show respect for people's time, and they increase the chances of a positive response. Do your best to simplify complex subjects to help your readers, and make sure you don't inadvertently complicate simple subjects through careless writing.[7] The ability to explain a complex subject in simple terms is immensely valuable, whether you're training new employees or pitching a business plan to investors.
- **Clarify expectations and responsibilities.** Craft messages to generate a specific response from a specific audience. When appropriate, clearly state what you expect from audience members or what you can do for them.
- **Offer compelling, persuasive arguments and recommendations.** Show your readers precisely how they will benefit by responding to your message in the way you want them to.

Keep these five important characteristics in mind as you compare the ineffective and effective versions of the message in Figure 1.2.

Communicating as a Professional

2 LEARNING OBJECTIVE Explain what it means to communicate as a professional in a business context.

You've been communicating your entire life, of course, but if you don't have a lot of work experience yet, meeting the expectations of a professional environment might require some adjustment. A good place to start is to consider what it means to be a professional. **Professionalism** is the quality of performing at a high level and conducting oneself with purpose and pride. It means doing more than putting in the hours and collecting a paycheck: True professionals go beyond minimum expectations and commit to making meaningful contributions. Professionalism can be broken down into six distinct traits: striving to excel, being dependable and accountable, being a team player, demonstrating a sense of etiquette, making ethical decisions, and maintaining a positive outlook (see Figure 1.3 on page 8).

> Communication is an essential part of being a successful professional.

A key message to glean from Figure 1.3 is how much these elements of professionalism depend on effective communication. For example, to be a team player, you have to be able to collaborate, resolve conflicts, and interact with a wide variety of personalities. Without strong communication skills, you won't be able to perform to your potential, and others won't recognize you as the professional you'd like to be.

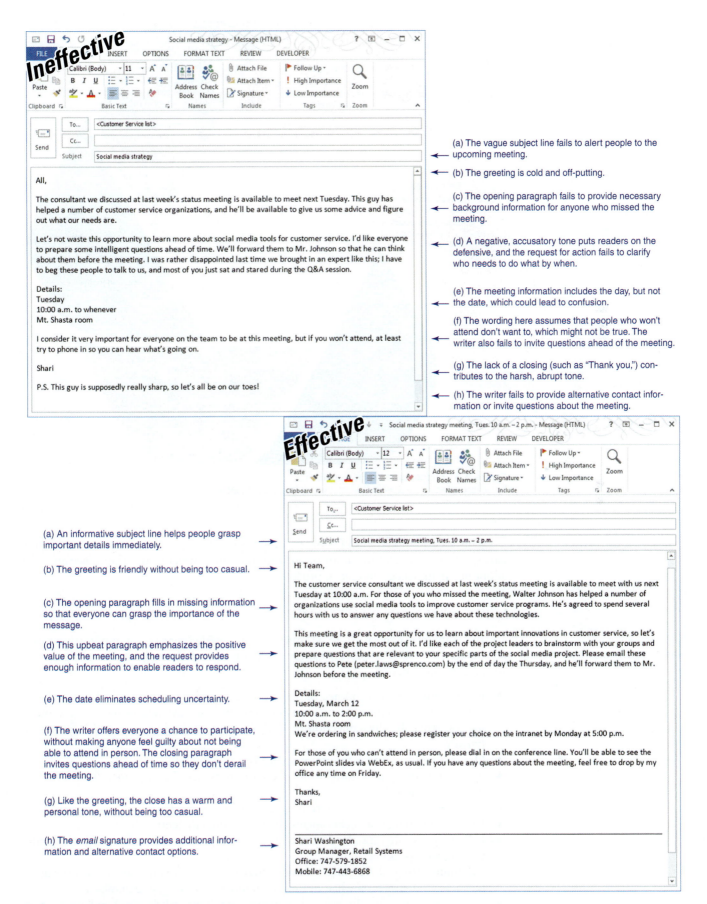

Ineffective

(a) The vague subject line fails to alert people to the upcoming meeting.

(b) The greeting is cold and off-putting.

(c) The opening paragraph fails to provide necessary background information for anyone who missed the meeting.

(d) A negative, accusatory tone puts readers on the defensive, and the request for action fails to clarify who needs to do what by when.

(e) The meeting information includes the day, but not the date, which could lead to confusion.

(f) The wording here assumes that people who won't attend don't want to, which might not be true. The writer also fails to invite questions ahead of the meeting.

(g) The lack of a closing (such as "Thank you,") contributes to the harsh, abrupt tone.

(h) The writer fails to provide alternative contact information or invite questions about the meeting.

Effective

(a) An informative subject line helps people grasp important details immediately.

(b) The greeting is friendly without being too casual.

(c) The opening paragraph fills in missing information so that everyone can grasp the importance of the message.

(d) This upbeat paragraph emphasizes the positive value of the meeting, and the request provides enough information to enable readers to respond.

(e) The date eliminates scheduling uncertainty.

(f) The writer offers everyone a chance to participate, without making anyone feel guilty about not being able to attend in person. The closing paragraph invites questions ahead of time so they don't derail the meeting.

(g) Like the greeting, the close has a warm and personal tone, without being too casual.

(h) The *email* signature provides additional information and alternative contact options.

Figure 1.2 Effective Professional Communication

At first glance, the top email message here looks like a reasonable attempt at communicating with the members of a project team. However, compare it with the bottom version by referencing the notes lettered (a) through (h) to see just how many problems the original message really has.

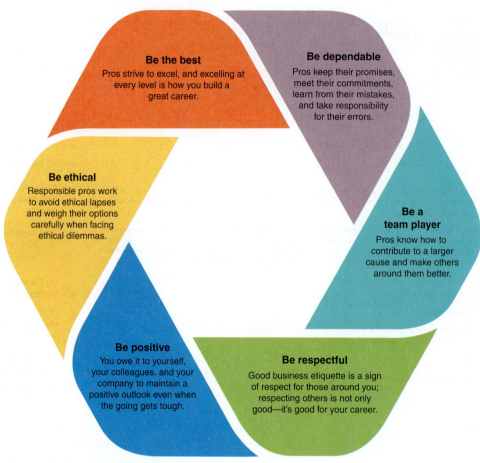

Figure 1.3 **Elements of Professionalism**
To be respected as a true professional, develop these six qualities.

This section offers a brief look at the skills employers will expect you to have, the nature of communication in an organizational environment, and the importance of adopting an audience-centered approach.

UNDERSTANDING WHAT EMPLOYERS EXPECT FROM YOU

Employers expect you to possess a wide range of communication skills.

Today's employers expect you to be competent at a wide range of communication tasks. Fortunately, the skills employers expect from you are the same skills that will help you advance in your career:[8]

- Recognizing information needs, using efficient search techniques to locate reliable sources of information (particularly from online sources), and using gathered information ethically; this collection of skills is often referred to as *digital information fluency*[9]
- Organizing ideas and information logically and completely
- Expressing ideas and information coherently, persuasively, and concisely
- Actively listening to others
- Communicating effectively with people from diverse backgrounds and experiences
- Using communication technologies effectively and efficiently
- Following accepted standards of grammar, spelling, and other aspects of high-quality writing and speaking
- Communicating in a civilized manner that reflects contemporary expectations of business etiquette, even when dealing with indifferent or hostile audiences
- Communicating ethically, even when choices aren't crystal clear or you have to share news that people don't want to hear

- Managing your time wisely and using resources efficiently
- Using **critical thinking**, which is the ability to evaluate evidence completely and objectively in order to form logical conclusions and make sound recommendations

You'll have the opportunity to practice these skills throughout this course, but don't stop there. Successful professionals continue to hone communication skills throughout their careers.

COMMUNICATING IN AN ORGANIZATIONAL CONTEXT

In addition to having the proper skills, you need to learn how to apply those skills in the business environment, which can be quite different from the social and scholastic environments you are accustomed to. Every organization has a **formal communication network**, in which ideas and information flow along the lines of command (the hierarchical levels) in the company's organization structure (see Figure 1.4). Throughout the formal network, information flows in three directions. *Downward communication* flows from executives to employees, conveying executive decisions and providing information that helps employees do their jobs. *Upward communication* flows from employees to executives, providing insight into problems, trends, opportunities, grievances, and performance, thus allowing executives to solve problems and make intelligent decisions. *Horizontal communication* flows between departments to help employees share information, coordinate tasks, and solve complex problems.[10]

> A company's formal communication network mirrors its organizational structure.

Every organization also has an **informal communication network**, often referred to as the *grapevine* or the *rumor mill*, which encompasses all communication that occurs outside the formal network. Some of this informal communication takes place naturally as a result of employee interaction on the job and in social settings, and some of it takes place when the formal network doesn't provide information that employees want. In fact, the inherent limitations of formal communication networks helped spur the growth of social media in the business environment.

ADOPTING AN AUDIENCE-CENTERED APPROACH

An **audience-centered approach** involves understanding and respecting the members of your audience and making every effort to get your message across in a way that is meaningful to them. This approach is also known as adopting the **"you" attitude**, in contrast

> An audience-centered approach involves understanding, respecting, and meeting the needs of your audience members.

Examples of downward communication
Examples of upward communication
Examples of horizontal communication

Figure 1.4 Formal Communication Network
The formal communication network is defined by the relationships between the various job positions in the organization. Messages can flow upward (from a lower-level employee to a higher-level employee), downward (from a higher-level employee to a lower-level employee), and horizontally (between employees at the same or similar levels across the organization).

REAL-TIME UPDATES

LEARN MORE BY WATCHING THIS VIDEO

The fundamentals of emotional intelligence

Understand the five elements that make up this essential quality for business success. Go to **real-timeupdates.com/bct14** and select Learn More in the Students section.

to messages that are about "me." Learn as much as possible about the biases, education, age, status, style, and personal and professional concerns of your receivers. If you're addressing people you don't know and you're unable to find out more about them, try to project yourself into their position by using common sense and imagination. This ability to relate to the needs of others is a key part of *emotional intelligence*, a combination of emotional and social skills that is widely considered to be a vital characteristic of successful managers and leaders.[11] The more you know about the people you're communicating with, the easier it is to concentrate on their needs—which, in turn, makes it easier for them to hear your message, understand it, and respond positively.

A vital element of audience-centered communication is **etiquette**, the expected norms of behavior in any particular situation. In today's hectic, competitive world, etiquette might seem a quaint and outdated notion. However, the way you conduct yourself and interact with others can have a profound influence on your company's success and your career. When executives hire and promote you, they expect your behavior to protect the company's reputation. The more you understand such expectations, the better chance you have of avoiding career-damaging mistakes. The principles of etiquette discussed in Chapter 2 will help you communicate with an audience-centered approach in a variety of business settings.

> Etiquette, the expected norms of behavior in a particular situation, can have a profound influence on your company's success and your career.

Exploring the Communication Process

3 LEARNING OBJECTIVE
Describe the communication process model and the ways social media are changing the nature of business communication.

Viewing communication as a process helps you identify steps you can take to improve your success as a communicator.

Even with the best intentions, communication efforts can fail. Messages can get lost or simply ignored. The receiver of a message can interpret it in ways the sender never imagined. In fact, two people receiving the same information can reach different conclusions about what it means.

Fortunately, by understanding communication as a process with distinct steps, you can improve the odds that your messages will reach their intended audiences and produce their intended effects. This section explores the communication process in two stages: first by following a message from one sender to one receiver in the basic communication model and then by expanding on that approach with multiple messages and participants in the social communication model.

THE BASIC COMMUNICATION MODEL

By viewing communication as a process (Figure 1.5), you can identify and improve the skills you need to be more successful. Many variations on this process model exist, but these eight steps provide a practical overview:

- **The sender has an idea.** Whether a communication effort will ultimately be effective starts right here and depends on the nature of the idea and the motivation for sending it.

Figure 1.5 The Basic Communication Process
This eight-step model is a simplified view of how communication works in real life; understanding this basic model is vital to improving your communication skills.

For example, if your motivation is to offer a solution to a problem, you have a better chance of crafting a meaningful message than if your motivation is merely to complain about a problem.

- **The sender encodes the idea as a message.** When someone puts an idea into a message—which you can think of as the "container" for an idea—he or she is **encoding** it, or expressing it in words or images. Much of the focus of this course is on developing the skills needed to successfully encode your ideas into effective messages.

- **The sender produces the message in a transmittable medium.** With the appropriate message to express an idea, the sender now needs a **communication medium** to present that message to the intended audience. To update your boss on the status of a project, for instance, you might have a dozen or more media choices, from a phone call to an instant message to a slideshow presentation.

- **The sender transmits the message through a channel.** Just as technology continues to increase the number of media options at your disposal, it continues to provide new **communication channels** you can use to transmit your messages. The distinction between medium and channel can get a bit murky, but think of the medium as the *form* a message takes (such as a Twitter update) and the channel as the system used to *deliver* the message (such as a mobile phone).

- **The audience receives the message.** If the channel functions properly, the message reaches its intended audience. However, mere arrival at the destination is no guarantee that the message will be noticed or understood correctly. As "How Audiences Receive Messages" (page 12) explains, many messages are either ignored or misinterpreted as noise.

- **The audience decodes the message.** After a message is received, the receiver needs to extract the idea from the message, a step known as **decoding**. "How Audiences Decode Messages" (page 13) takes a closer look at this complex and subtle step in the process.

- **The audience responds to the message.** By crafting messages in ways that show the benefits of responding, senders can increase the chances that recipients will respond in positive ways. However, as "How Audiences Respond to Messages" (page 14) points out, whether a receiver responds as the sender hopes depends on the receiver (1) *remembering* the message long enough to act on it, (2) being *able* to act on it, and (3) being *motivated* to respond.

- **The audience provides feedback to the sender.** In addition to responding (or not responding) to the message, audience members may give **feedback** that helps the sender evaluate the effectiveness of the communication effort. Feedback can be verbal (using written or spoken words), nonverbal (using gestures, facial expressions, or other signals), or both. Just like the original message, however, this feedback from the receiver also needs to be decoded carefully. A smile, for example, can have many meanings.

> The medium is the form a message takes, whereas the channel is the system used to deliver the message.

Considering the complexity of this process—and the barriers and distractions that often stand between sender and receiver—it should come as no surprise that communication efforts often fail to achieve the sender's objective. Fortunately, the better you understand the process, the more successful you'll be.

The following sections take a closer look at two important aspects of the process: environmental barriers that can block or distort messages and the steps audiences take to receive, decode, and respond to messages.

Barriers in the Communication Environment

Within any communication environment, messages can be disrupted by a variety of **communication barriers**. These barriers include noise and distractions, competing messages, filters, and channel breakdowns:

- **Noise and distractions.** External distractions range from uncomfortable meeting rooms to computer screens cluttered with instant messages and reminders popping up all over the place. Internal distractions are thoughts and emotions that prevent audiences from focusing on incoming messages. The common habit of *multitasking*—attempting more than one task at a time—is practically guaranteed to create communication distractions. Multitasking dramatically increases the workload on

> A number of barriers can block or distort messages before they reach the intended audience.

your brain because you're forcing it to constantly switch between sets of rules and contexts, which requires it to reorient each time.[12] Rather than getting more done, research shows that chronic multitasking often reduces productivity and increases errors.[13] As more communication takes place on mobile devices, the need to insulate yourself from noise and distractions will keep growing.

- **Competing messages.** Having your audience's undivided attention is a rare luxury. In most cases you must compete with other messages that are trying to reach your audience at the same time.
- **Filters.** Messages can be blocked or distorted by *filters*, any human or technological interventions between the sender and the receiver. Filtering can be both intentional (such as automatically filing incoming messages based on sender or content) or unintentional (such as an overly aggressive spam filter that deletes legitimate emails). As mentioned previously, the structure and culture of an organization can also inhibit the flow of vital messages. And in some cases the people or companies you rely on to deliver your message can distort it or filter it to meet their own needs.
- **Channel breakdowns.** Sometimes the channel simply breaks down and fails to deliver your message. A colleague you were counting on to deliver a message to your boss might have forgotten to do so, or a computer server might have crashed and prevented your blog from updating.

Minimizing barriers and distractions in the communication environment is everyone's responsibility.

Everyone in an organization can help minimize barriers and distractions. As a communicator, try to be aware of any barriers that could prevent your messages from reaching their intended audiences. As a manager, keep an eye out for any organizational barriers that could be inhibiting the flow of information. A small dose of common sense and courtesy goes a long way in any situation. Silence your phone before you step into a meeting. Don't talk across the tops of other people's cubicles. Be sensitive to volume when you're listening to music or podcasts or watching videos; even if you're wearing headphones, audio that leaks into your colleagues' spaces can disrupt their workflow and concentration.

Finally, take steps to insulate yourself from distractions. Don't let messages interrupt you every minute of the day. Instead, set aside time to attend to messages all at once so that you can focus the rest of the time. If the environment is noisy or busy, find ways to block out distractions, such as wearing noise-canceling headphones.

Inside the Mind of Your Audience

After a message works its way through the communication channel and reaches the intended audience, it encounters a whole new set of challenges. Understanding how audiences receive, decode, and respond to messages will help you create more effective messages.

To truly receive a message, audience members need to sense it, select it, then perceive it as a message.

How Audiences Receive Messages   For an audience member to receive a message, three events need to occur: The receiver has to *sense* the presence of a message, *select* it from all the other messages clamoring for attention, and *perceive* it as an actual message (as opposed to random, pointless noise).[14] You can appreciate the magnitude of this challenge by driving down any busy street in a commercial section of town. You'll encounter hundreds of messages—billboards, posters, store window displays, car stereos, pedestrians waving or talking on mobile phones, car horns, street signs, traffic lights, and so on. However, you'll sense, select, and perceive only a small fraction of these messages.

Today's business audiences are much like drivers on busy streets. They are inundated with so many messages and so much noise that they can miss or ignore many of the messages intended for them. Through this course, you will learn a variety of techniques to craft messages that get noticed. In general, follow these five principles to increase your chances of success:

To improve the odds that your messages will be successfully perceived by your audience, pay close attention to expectations, ease of use, familiarity, empathy, and technical compatibility.

- **Consider audience expectations.** Deliver messages using the media and channels that the audience expects. If colleagues expect meeting notices to be delivered by email, don't suddenly switch gears and start delivering the notices via blog postings without telling anyone. Of course, sometimes going *against* expectations can stimulate audience attention, which is why advertisers sometimes do wacky and creative things to get noticed. For most business communication efforts, however, following the expectations of your audience is the most efficient way to get your message across.

- **Ensure ease of use.** Even if audiences are actively looking for your messages, they probably won't see them if you make them hard to find, hard to navigate, or hard to read.
- **Emphasize familiarity.** Use words, images, and designs that are familiar to your audience. For example, most visitors to company websites expect to see information about the company on a page called "About" or "About Us."
- **Practice empathy.** Make sure your messages speak to the audience by clearly addressing *their* wants and needs—not yours. People are inclined to notice messages that relate to their individual concerns.[15]
- **Design for compatibility.** For the many messages delivered electronically these days, be sure to verify technological compatibility with your audience. For instance, if your website requires visitors to have a particular video capability in their browsers, you won't reach those audience members who don't have that software installed or updated.

How Audiences Decode Messages   A received message doesn't "mean" anything until the recipient decodes it and assigns meaning to it, and there is no guarantee the receiver will assign the same meaning the sender intended. Even well-crafted, well-intentioned communication efforts can fail at this stage because assigning meaning through decoding is a highly personal process that is influenced by culture, individual experience, learning and thinking styles, hopes, fears, and even temporary moods. Moreover, audiences tend to extract the meaning they expect to get from a message, even if it's the opposite of what the sender intended.[16] In fact, rather than "extract" your meaning, it's more accurate to say that your audience members re-create their own meaning—or meanings—from the message.

Cultural and personal beliefs and biases influence the meaning audiences get from messages. For instance, the human brain organizes incoming sensations into a mental "map" that represents the person's individual **perception** of reality. If an incoming detail doesn't fit into that perception, a message recipient may simply distort the information to make it fit rather than rearrange his or her mental map—a phenomenon known as **selective perception**.[17] For example, an executive who has staked her reputation on a particular business strategy might distort or ignore evidence that suggests the strategy is failing.

Differences in language and usage also influence received meaning. If you ask an employee to send you a report on sales figures "as soon as possible," does that mean within 10 seconds, 10 minutes, or 10 days? By clarifying expectations and resolving potential ambiguities in your messages, you can minimize such uncertainties. In general, the more experiences you share with another person, the more likely you are to share perception and thus share meaning (see Figure 1.6).

Individual thinking styles are another important factor in message decoding. For example, someone who places a high value on objective analysis and clear logic might interpret a message differently than someone who values emotion or intuition (reaching conclusions without using rational processes).

> Decoding is a complex process; receivers often extract different meanings from messages than senders attempt to encode in them.

> Selective perception occurs when people ignore or distort incoming information to fit their preconceived notions of reality.

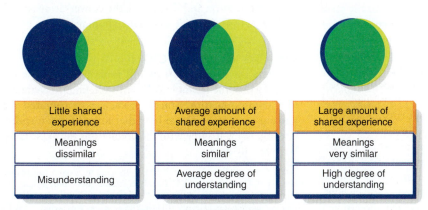

Figure 1.6   How Shared Experience Affects Understanding
The more two people or two groups of people share experiences—personal, professional, and cultural—the more likely it is that receivers will extract the intended meanings senders encode into the messages.

How Audiences Respond to Messages   Your message has been delivered, received, and correctly decoded. Now what? Will audience members respond in the way you'd like them to? Only if three events occur.

> Audiences will likely respond to a message if they remember it, if they're able to respond, and if they're properly motivated to do so.

First, the recipient has to *remember* the message long enough to act on it. Simplifying greatly, memory works in several stages: *Sensory memory* momentarily captures incoming data from the senses; then, whatever the recipient pays attention to is transferred to *short-term memory*. Information in short-term memory quickly disappears if it isn't transferred to *long-term memory*, which can be done either actively (such as when a person memorizes a list of items) or passively (such as when a new piece of information connects with something else the recipient already has stored in long-term memory). Finally, the information needs to be *retrieved* when the recipient wants to act on it.[18] In general, people find it easier to remember and retrieve information that is important to them personally or professionally. Consequently, by communicating in ways that are sensitive to your audience's wants and needs, you greatly increase the chance that your messages will be remembered and retrieved.

> By explaining how audiences will benefit by responding positively to your messages, you'll increase their motivation to respond.

Second, the recipient has to be *able* to respond as you wish. Obviously, if recipients simply cannot do what you want them to do, they will not respond according to your plan. By understanding your audience (you'll learn more about audience analysis in Chapter 4), you can work to minimize these unsuccessful outcomes.

Third, the recipient has to be *motivated* to respond. You'll encounter many situations in which your audience has the option of responding but isn't required to. For instance, a record company may or may not offer your band a contract, or your boss may or may not respond to your request for a raise. Throughout this course, you'll learn techniques for crafting messages that can help motivate readers to respond positively to your messages.

REAL-TIME UPDATES
LEARN MORE BY WATCHING THIS VIDEO
The Internet of Things
See how the IoT is reshaping numerous business processes, including business communication. Go to **real-timeupdates.com/bct14** and select Learn More in the Students section.

THE FUTURE OF COMMUNICATION

The Internet of Things

The *Internet of Things (IoT)* refers to the billions of devices now connected to the Internet and the networking potential of having all these gadgets communicate with each other, feed data into vast information warehouses, and interact with people and the physical environment. These "things" range from simple sensors that measure temperature, location, and other parameters all the way up to robots and other complex systems. People and animals with Internet-capable sensors (such as implanted chips) or devices also qualify as things in this model.

Imagine you walk into a department store and your mobile phone automatically gives you directions to the aisle where you could find the clothing styles you have recently been browsing online or discussing in social media. When you reach that aisle and start browsing, a coupon pops up on your phone, offering discounts on the specific items you're considering. When you pull a garment off the rack, the store's customer database checks other purchases you've made and suggests which items you already own that coordinate with this piece. If you could use an accessory to complete the outfit, the store's computers can tell your phone just where to take you. And if you need more advice, you can text or talk—and possibly not know whether you're conversing with a store employee or an automated chatbot on a computer somewhere.

Now imagine this simple concept expanded and applied in various ways to industrial facilities, agriculture, transportation, buildings, health care, and other systems. By relying on networked IoT devices for such communication functions as observing, measuring, and reporting, these enhanced systems can supplement or replace communication flows that were previously carried out by human participants.

IoT is poised to reshape many business processes on a scale that some experts compare to the Industrial Revolution of the 19th century. It also seems likely to influence business communication as it takes over some routine tasks and brings the power of smart networking and computing to others. Basic communication skills will remain as essential as ever, but don't be surprised if some of the conversations you have in the future aren't with your fellow humans.

WHAT'S YOUR PREDICTION?

Research the current state of IoT innovation to identify one way in which the technology has the potential to change business communication practices, such as automated report writing or conversational bots that mimic human speech or writing. Do you agree with the predictions the experts make? Why or why not?

Sources: Stacey Higginbotham, "IBM Is Bringing in Watson to Conquer the Internet of Things," *Fortune*, 15 December 2015, fortune.com; Jacques Bughin, Michael Chui, and James Manyika, "An Executive's Guide to the Internet of Things," *McKinsey Quarterly*, August 2015, www.mckinsey.com; Cora Cloud, "Internet of Things (IOT) Role in Business Communications," *Digium*, 9 April 2015, blogs.digium.com; Danial Burrus, "The Internet of Things Is Far Bigger Than Anyone Realizes," *Wired*, accessed 3 March 2016, www.wired.com.

THE SOCIAL COMMUNICATION MODEL

The basic model presented in Figure 1.5 illustrates how a single idea moves from one sender to one receiver. In a larger sense, it also helps represent the traditional nature of much business communication, which was primarily defined by a *publishing* or *broadcasting* mindset. For external communication, a company issued carefully scripted messages to a mass audience that didn't have many options for responding to those messages or initiating messages of their own. Customers and other interested parties had few ways to connect with one another to ask questions, share information, or offer support. Internal communication tended to follow the same "we talk, you listen" model, with upper managers issuing directives to lower-level supervisors and employees.

In recent years, however, a variety of technologies have enabled and inspired a new approach to business communication. In contrast to the publishing mindset, this **social communication model** is interactive, conversational, and usually open to all who wish to participate. Audience members are no longer passive recipients of messages but active participants in a conversation. Social media have given customers and other stakeholders a voice they did not have in the past. And businesses are listening to that voice. In fact, one of the most common uses of social media among U.S. businesses is monitoring online discussions about a company and its brands.[19]

Instead of transmitting a fixed message, a sender in a social media environment initiates a conversation by asking a question or sharing valuable information. Information shared this way is often revised and reshaped by the web of participants as they forward it and comment on it. People can add to it or take pieces from it, depending on their needs and interests. Figure 1.7 lists some of the significant differences between the traditional and social models of business communication.

The social communication model offers many advantages, but it has a number of disadvantages as well. Potential problems include information overload, a lower level

The conversational and interactive *social communication model* is revolutionizing business communication.

The social communication model can increase the speed of communication, reduce costs, improve access to expertise, and boost employee satisfaction.

For all their advantages, social media tools also present a number of communication challenges.

Conventional Promotion:
"We Talk, You Listen"

Tendencies
Publication, broadcast
Lecture
Intrusion
Unidirectinal
One to many; mass audience
Control
Low message frequency
Few channels
Information hoarding
Static
Hierarchical
Structured
Isolated
Planned
Resistive

The Social Model:
"Let's Have a Conversation"

Tendencies
Converstion
Discussion
Permission
Bidirectional, multidirectional
One to one; many to many
Influence
High message frequency
Many channels
Information sharing
Dynamic
Egalitarian
Amorphous
Collaborative
Reactive
Responsive

Figure 1.7   The Social Communication Model
The social communication model differs from conventional communication strategies and practices in a number of significant ways. You're probably already an accomplished user of many new-media tools, and this experience will help you on the job.

of engagement with tasks and other people, fragmented attention, information security risks, reduced productivity, and the difficulty of maintaining a healthy boundary between personal and professional lives.[20] All business professionals and managers need to choose and use digital tools wisely to control the flow of information they receive.

Of course, no company, no matter how enthusiastically it embraces the social communication model, is going to be run as a club in which everyone has a say in every business matter. Instead, a hybrid approach is emerging in which some communications (such as strategic plans and policy documents) follow the traditional approach, whereas others (such as project management updates and customer support messages) follow the social model.

You can learn more about business uses of social media in Chapter 8.

The Mobile Revolution

4 **LEARNING OBJECTIVE**
Outline the challenges and opportunities of mobile communication in business.

As much of a game changer as social media have been, some experts predict that mobile communication will change the nature of business and business communication even more. The venture capitalist Joe Schoendorf says that "mobile is the most disruptive technology that I have seen in 48 years in Silicon Valley."[21] The researcher Maribel Lopez calls mobile "the biggest technology shift since the Internet."[22]

Companies recognize the value of integrating mobile technology, from communication platforms to banking to retail. Mobile apps and communication systems can boost employee productivity, help companies form closer relationships with customers and business partners, and spur innovation in products and services (see Figure 1.8). Given the advantages and the rising expectations of employees and customers, firms on the leading edge of the mobile revolution are working to integrate mobile technology throughout their organizations.[23]

This section offers a high-level view of the mobile revolution, and you'll see coverage of specific topics integrated throughout the book—everything from collaborative writing and research to presentations and job search strategies.

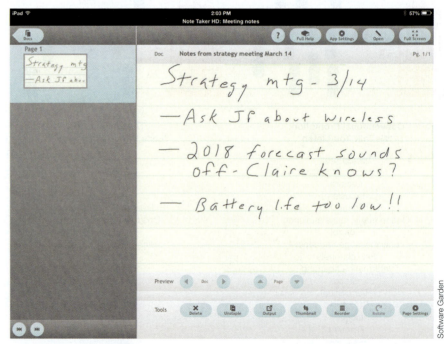

Figure 1.8 **Mobile Communication Tools**
Mobile technologies offer multiple ways to improve communication and other key business processes. For example, note-taking apps such as Note Taker HD offer an easy and unobtrusive way to take notes during meetings, site visits, and other business functions.

THE RISE OF MOBILE AS A COMMUNICATION PLATFORM

Whether it's emailing, social networking, watching videos, or doing research, the percentage of communication and media consumption performed on mobile devices continues to grow. For millions of people around the world, a mobile device is their primary way, if not their only way, to access the Internet. Globally, more than 80 percent of Internet users access the web with a mobile device at least some of the time.[24]

Mobile has become the primary communication tool for many business professionals, including a majority of executives under age 40.[25] Email and web browsing rank first and second in terms of the most common nonvoice uses of smartphones, and more email messages are now opened on mobile devices than on PCs.[26] Roughly half of U.S. consumers use a mobile device exclusively for their online search needs, and many online activities that eventually migrate to a PC screen start out on a mobile screen.[27] For many people, the fact that a smartphone can make phone calls is practically a secondary consideration; data traffic from mobile devices far outstrips voice traffic.[28]

Moreover, mobile phones—particularly smartphones—have become intensely personal devices in ways that PCs never did. For many users, the connection is so close they feel a sense of panic when they don't have frequent access to their phones.[29] When people are closely attached to their phones, day and night, they are more closely tied to all the information sources, conversations, and networks that those phones can connect to. As a result, mobile connectivity can start to resemble a continuous stream of conversations that never quite end, which influences the way businesses need to interact with their stakeholders. If *wearable technologies* become mainstream devices, they will contribute even more to this shift in behaviors (see Figure 1.9).

The parallels between social media and mobile communication are striking: Both sets of technologies change the nature of communication, alter the relationships between senders and receivers, create opportunities as well as challenges, and force business professionals to hone new skills. In fact, much of the rise in social communication can be attributed to the connectivity made possible by mobile devices. Companies that work to understand and embrace mobile, both internally and externally, stand the best chance of capitalizing on this monumental shift in the way people communicate.

> Mobile devices are rapidly taking over as the primary communication platform for many business professionals.

REAL-TIME UPDATES

LEARN MORE BY VIEWING THESE PRESENTATIONS

Exploring the potential of wearable technologies

Will wearable technologies influence business and business communication? These presentations explore the potential. Go to **real-timeupdates.com/bct14** and select Learn More in the Students section.

HOW MOBILE TECHNOLOGIES ARE CHANGING BUSINESS COMMUNICATION

The rise of mobile communication has some obvious implications, such as the need for websites to be mobile friendly. If you've ever tried to browse a conventional website on a tiny screen or fill in complicated online forms using the keypad on your phone, you know how frustrating the experience can be. Users increasingly expect websites to be mobile friendly, and they're likely to avoid sites that aren't optimized for mobile.[30]

Used by permission of Uno Inc.

Figure 1.9   Wearable Technology
Smartwatches and other wearable mobile devices offer intriguing possibilities for business communication. The Uno Noteband incorporates Spritz speed-reading technology that makes it easier to read message content quickly.

As mobile access overtakes computer-based access, some companies now take a *mobile-first* approach, in which websites are designed for optimum viewing on smartphones and tablets rather than conventional PC screens.[31] Another successful approach is creating mobile apps that offer a more interactive and mobile-friendly experience than a conventional website can provide.

However, device size and portability are only the most obvious changes. Just as with social media, the changes brought about by mobile go far deeper than the technology itself. Mobile changes the way people communicate, with profound implications for virtually every aspect of business communication.

People who grew up with mobile phones often expect to have the same level of connectivity in their roles as both customers and as employees.

The social media pioneer Nicco Mele coined the term *radical connectivity* to describe "the breathtaking ability to send vast amounts of data instantly, constantly, and globally."[32] Mobile plays a major and ever-expanding role in this phenomenon by keeping people connected 24/7, wherever they may be. People who've grown up with mobile communication technology expect to have immediate access to information and the ability to stay connected to their various social and business networks.[33]

Here are the most significant ways mobile technology is changing the practice of business communication:

Constant connectivity is a mixed blessing: You can work from anywhere at any time, but it's more difficult to disconnect from work and recharge yourself.

- Constant connectivity is a mixed blessing. As with social media, mobile connectivity can blur the boundaries between personal and professional time and space, preventing people from fully disengaging from work during personal and family time. On the other hand, it can give employees more flexibility to meet their personal and professional obligations.[34] In this regard, mobile plays an important role in efforts to reduce operating costs through telecommuting and other nontraditional work models.[35]
- Small mobile displays and sometimes-awkward input technologies present challenges for creating and consuming content, whether it's typing an email message or watching a video. As you'll read in Chapter 6, for example, email messages need to be written and formatted differently to make them easier to read on mobile devices.
- Mobile users are often multitasking—roughly half of mobile phone usage happens while people are walking, for instance—so they can't give full attention to the information on their screens.[36] Moreover, mobile use often occurs in environments with multiple distractions and barriers to successful communication.
- Mobile communication, particularly text messaging, has put pressure on traditional standards of grammar, punctuation, and writing in general. Chapter 4 has more on this topic.
- Mobile devices can serve as sensory and cognitive extensions.[37] For example, they can help people experience more of their environment (such as augmented reality apps that superimpose information on a live camera view) and have instant access to information without relying on faulty and limited human memory. The addition of *location-aware content*, such as facility maps and property information, enhances the mobile experience.
- Mobile devices create a host of security and privacy concerns for end users and corporate technology managers alike.[38] Companies are wrestling with the "bring your own device" or "BYOD" phenomenon, in which employees want to be able to access company networks and files with their personal smartphones and tablets, both in the office and away from it. These devices don't always have the rigorous security controls that corporate networks need, however, and users don't always use the devices in secure ways.
- Mobile tools can enhance productivity and collaboration by making it easier for employees to stay connected and giving them access to information and work tasks during forced gaps in the workday or while traveling.[39]
- Mobile apps can assist in a wide variety of business tasks, from research to presentations[40] (see Figure 1.10). Companies aren't restricted to commercially available apps, either. With digital publishing tools, companies can create custom apps with content and capabilities geared specifically toward their customers or employees.[41]

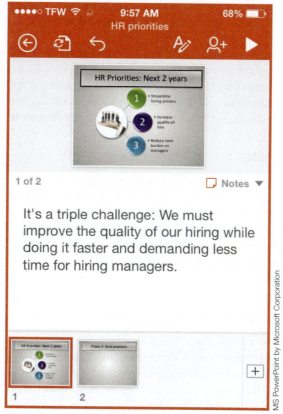

Figure 1.10 Mobile Communication: Opportunities and Challenges
From 24/7 connectivity to business-oriented apps that let professionals perform work tasks on the go (such as making notes for a presentation, as shown here on the mobile version of PowerPoint), mobile technology is revolutionizing business communication.

- Mobile connectivity can accelerate decision making and problem solving by putting the right information in the hands of the right people at the right time. For example, if the people in a decision-making meeting need more information, they can do the necessary research on the spot.[42] Mobile communication also makes it easier to quickly tap into pockets of expertise within a company.[43] Customer service can be improved by making sure technicians and other workers always have the information they need right at hand.[44] Companies can also respond and communicate faster during crises.[45]

- With interactivity designed to take advantage of the capabilities of mobile devices (including cameras, accelerometers, compasses, and GPS), companies can create more engaging experiences for customers and other users.[46]

The mobile revolution complicates business communication in some ways, but it can enhance communication in many other ways if done thoughtfully. You'll read more about mobile in the chapters ahead.

> Collaboration and problem solving are two key areas where mobile connectivity can boost productivity by enabling real-time interaction and access to vital information.

Using Technology to Improve Business Communication

Today's businesses rely heavily on technology to enhance communication. In fact, many of the technologies you might use in your personal life, from microblogs to video games, are also used in business. Technology is discussed extensively throughout this book, with specific advice on using both common and emerging tools. The four-page

5 LEARNING OBJECTIVE
List four general guidelines for using communication technology effectively.

photo essay "Powerful Tools for Communicating Effectively" (see pages 22–25) provides an overview of the technologies that connect people in offices, factories, and other business settings.

However, anyone who has used advanced technology knows the benefits are not automatic. Poorly designed or inappropriately used technology can hinder communication more than help. To communicate effectively, learn to keep technology in perspective, guard against information overload and information addiction, use technological tools productively, and frequently disengage from the computer to communicate in person.

KEEPING TECHNOLOGY IN PERSPECTIVE

Perhaps the single most important point to remember about technology is that it is simply a tool, a means by which you can accomplish certain tasks. Technology is an aid to interpersonal communication, not a replacement for it. Technology can't think for you or communicate for you, and if you lack some essential skills, technology can't fill in the gaps. Throughout the book, you'll see advice on keeping the focus on your messages and your audiences, and using technology to enhance the communication process.

GUARDING AGAINST INFORMATION OVERLOAD

The overuse or misuse of communication technology can lead to **information overload**, in which people receive more information than they can effectively process. Information overload makes it difficult to discriminate between useful and useless information, reduces productivity, and amplifies employee stress both on the job and at home, even to the point of causing health and relationship problems.[47]

You often have some level of control over the number and types of messages you choose to receive. Use the filtering features of your communication systems to isolate high-priority messages that deserve your attention. Also, be wary of subscribing to too many Twitter streams and other sources. Focus on the information you truly need in order to do your job.

As a sender, you can help reduce information overload by making sure you don't send unnecessary messages. In addition, when you send messages that aren't urgent or crucial, let people know so they can prioritize. Also, most communication systems let you mark messages as urgent; however, use this feature only when it is truly needed. Its overuse leads to annoyance and anxiety, not action.

USING TECHNOLOGICAL TOOLS PRODUCTIVELY

Facebook, Twitter, YouTube, and other technologies are key parts of what has been called the *information technology paradox*, in which information tools can waste as much time as they save. Social media are a particular source of concern: While they offer great opportunities for connecting with customers and other stakeholders, the potential for distraction can waste significant amounts of employee time.

Inappropriate web use not only distracts employees from work responsibilities, it can leave employers open to lawsuits for sexual harassment if inappropriate images are displayed in or transmitted around the company.[48] Social media have created another set of managerial challenges, given the risk that employee blogs or social networking pages can expose confidential information or damage a firm's reputation in the marketplace. With all these technologies, the best solution lies in developing clear policies that are enforced evenly for all employees.[49]

Managers need to guide their employees in the productive use of information tools because the speed and simplicity of these tools are also among their greatest weaknesses. The flood of messages from an expanding array of digital sources can significantly affect employees' ability to focus on their work. In one study, workers exposed to a constant barrage of emails, instant messages, and phone calls experienced an average 10-point drop in their functioning intelligence quotient.[50]

MOBILE APP
Pocket collects content you'd like to read or view later and syncs it across your mobile devices.

Don't rely too much on technology or let it overwhelm the communication process.

Information overload results when people receive more information than they can effectively process.

An important step in reducing information overload is to avoid sending unnecessary messages.

MOBILE APP
WhatsApp lets you send and receive messages, videos, and other content via your phone's Internet connection.

Communicating in today's business environment requires at least a basic level of technical competence.

DIGITAL + SOCIAL + MOBILE: TODAY'S COMMUNICATION ENVIRONMENT

It's All Fun and Games—and Effective Business Communication

The fact that millions of people spend billions of hours playing games on their mobile devices is not lost on companies looking for ways to enhance communication with employees and customers. Whether they feature skill, chance, or compelling story lines, successful games try to engage users intellectually and emotionally—just as successful business communicators try to do.

Gamification is the addition of game-playing aspects to an activity or a process with the goal of increasing user engagement, and it's a natural fit for social media and mobile devices. Foursquare's check-in competitions, in which the person who "checks in" using Foursquare the most times during a certain time window is crowned the "mayor" of that location, were an early use of gamification. Foursquare wasn't invented as a way for people to become imaginary mayors of places where they shop or eat, of course. It is an advertising platform that relies on user activity and user-generated content, and the game element encourages people to use the app more frequently.

Foursquare is a simple example of gamification, but other companies are pushing the concept in new ways to engage and motivate employees and other stakeholders. For example, Bunchball's Nitro software applies gamification concepts to a number of business communication platforms. On a customer-service system, the software rewards employees for increasing their productivity, meeting their service commitments to customers, and sharing knowledge with their colleagues. On several collaboration and brainstorming systems, gamification encourages people to make more connections, share ideas, and boost their influence within a community. Employee orientation systems can use game concepts to help new hires learn their way around the organization.

Gamification is also a key strategy for many companies trying to improve customer loyalty. Badgeville's Reputation Mechanics system, for example, boosts the profile of knowledgeable customers who share expertise on social media sites and other online forums. By rewarding their *product champions* (see page 345) this way, companies encourage them to keep contributing their expertise, thereby helping other customers be successful and satisfied.

Incidentally, if you are in the Millennial generation—those born between about 1981 and 1995—you're a special target of gamification in the workplace and the marketplace, given your generation's enthusiasm for video games. Don't be surprised to find more gamified apps and systems on the job and everywhere you turn as a consumer.

CAREER APPLICATIONS

1. Gamification is about influencing employee and customer behaviors in ways that benefit a company. Is this ethical? Explain your answer.
2. Assume a company provides a job-search game app that helps you navigate your way through applying for a job, explore various job openings, and understand what it would be like to work there. Would the app make you feel more positively about the company, or would you find that using a game for this purpose would trivialize something as important as your job search? Explain your answer.

Sources: Bunchball website, accessed 3 March 2016, www.bunchball.com; Badgeville website, accessed 3 March 2016, badgeville.com; Foursquare for Business website, accessed 3 March 2016, business.foursquare.com; Christopher Swan, "Gamification: A New Way to Shape Behavior," *Communication World*, May–June 2012, 13–14.

In addition to using your tools appropriately, knowing how to use them efficiently can make a big difference in your productivity. You don't have to become an expert in most cases, but you do need to be familiar with the basic features and functions of the tools you are expected to use on the job. As a manager, you also need to ensure that your employees have sufficient training to productively apply the tools you expect them to use.

> **REAL-TIME UPDATES**
> LEARN MORE BY VISITING THIS WIKI
>
> **Get the latest news on gamification**
>
> The Gamification Wiki offers information on gamification concepts and examples across a variety of industries. Go to **real-timeupdates.com/bct14** and select Learn More in the Students section.

RECONNECTING WITH PEOPLE

Even the best technologies can hinder communication if they are overused. For instance, a common complaint among employees is that managers rely too heavily on email and don't communicate face to face often enough.[51] Speaking with people over the phone or in person can take more time and effort and can sometimes force you to confront unpleasant situations directly, but it is often essential for solving tough problems and maintaining productive relationships.[52]

Moreover, even the best communication technologies can't show people who you really are. Remember to step out from behind the technology frequently to learn more about the people you work with and to let them learn more about you.

No matter how much technology is involved, communication is still about people connecting with people.

POWERFUL TOOLS FOR COMMUNICATING EFFECTIVELY

The tools of business communication evolve with every advance in digital technology. The 20 technologies highlighted on the next four pages help businesses redefine the office, collaborate and share information, connect with stakeholders, and build communities of people with shared interests and needs. For more examples of business uses of social media tools in particular, see pages 207–214 in Chapter 8.

REDEFINING THE OFFICE

Thanks to advances in mobile and distributed communication, the "office" is no longer what it used to be. Technology lets today's professionals work on the move while staying in close contact with colleagues, customers, and suppliers. These technologies are also redefining the very nature of some companies, as they replace traditional hierarchies with highly adaptable, virtual networks.

Web-Based Meetings

Andrey Popov/Shutterstock

Web-based meetings allow team members from all over the world to interact in real time. Meetings can also be recorded for later playback and review. Various systems support instant messaging, video, collaborative editing tools, and more.

Videoconferencing and Telepresence

dotshock/Shutterstock

Videoconferencing provides many of the benefits of in-person meetings at a fraction of the cost. Advanced systems feature *telepresence*, in which the video images of meeting participants are life-sized and extremely realistic.

Shared Online Workspaces

Microsoft Office 2013, copyright © 2013 Microsoft Corporation.

Online workspaces help teams work productively, even if they are on the move or spread out across the country. In addition to providing controlled access to shared files and other digital resources, some systems include such features as project management tools and real-time document sharing (letting two or more team members view and edit a document on screen at the same time).

Voice Technologies

Speech recognition (converting human speech to computer commands) and *speech synthesis* (converting computer commands to human speech) can enhance communication in many ways, including simplifying mobile computing, assisting workers who are unwilling or unable to use keyboards, and allowing "one-sided" conversations with information systems. *Speech analytics software* can evaluate conversations to improve customer service and other interactions. *Mobile VoIP* lets people make voice calls on WiFi networks to save connection and roaming charges.

Fancy Collection/Superstock

iTranslateapp.com

Courtesy of Hipmunk, http://www.hipmunk.com

Mobile Business Apps

As the range of business software applications on smartphones and tablet computers continues to expand, almost anything that can be accomplished on a regular computer can be done on a mobile device (although not always as efficiently or with the same feature sets).

22

Courtesy of bossjock studio, www.bossjockstudio.com

Instant Messaging

Instant messaging (IM) is one of the most widely used digital communication tools in the business world, replacing many conversations and exchanges that once took place via email or phone calls. *Enterprise IM systems* are similar to consumer IM systems in many respects but have additional security and collaboration features. *Group messaging systems* add file sharing and information-management tools to help teams work more efficiently.

Crowdsourcing and Collaboration Platforms

Crowdsourcing, inviting input from groups of people inside or outside the organization, can give companies access to a much wider range of ideas, solutions to problems, and insights into market trends.

COLLABORATING AND SHARING INFORMATION

The need to work with and share information quickly and easily is a constant in business. A wide variety of tools have been developed to facilitate collaboration and sharing, from general purpose systems such as instant messaging to more specialized capabilities such as data visualization.

Wikis promote collaboration by simplifying the process of creating and editing online content. Anyone with access (some wikis are private; some are public) can add and modify pages as new information becomes available.

Wikis

Data Visualization

Data visualization is a powerful tool for presenting and exploring sets of data that are very large, complex, or dynamic. As more companies rely on "big data" to identify and capitalize on market opportunities, the ability to extract insights from these large data sets can be an important competitive advantage.

Internet of Things

The *Internet of Things (IoT)* refers to the billions of smart, autonomous devices that are now connected via the Internet. These "things" are sensors, controllers, and other devices that send, receive, or process data. This machine-based communication can support or even replace conventional methods of business communication.

CONNECTING WITH STAKEHOLDERS

Electronic media and social media in particular have redefined the relationships businesses have with internal and external stakeholders. Any groups affected by a company's decisions now have tools to give voice to their opinions and needs, and companies have many more conversational threads that need to be monitored and managed.

Applicant Tracking Systems

Screenshot from Recruit by ZOHO Corporation. Copyright © by Mason Hering. Used by permission of Mason Hering.

Applicant tracking systems now play a huge role in employment-related communications. At virtually all large companies and many medium and small companies, your résumé and application information will be entered into one of these systems. Recruiters use various tools to identify promising candidates and manage the interview and selection process. After hiring, some firms use *talent management systems* to track employee development through workers' entire careers at the company.

Blogging

Courtesy of Xerox Corporation

Blogs let companies connect with customers and other audiences in a fast and informal way. Commenting features let readers participate in the conversation, too.

Content Curation

Bovee and Thill, LLC website

Content curation, selecting videos and other items of interest to followers of a website or blog, has become one of the most popular ways to connect with stakeholders. Pinterest and Scoop.it are among the leading technologies in this area.

Podcasting

RoBeDeRo/E+/Getty Images

With the portability and convenience of downloadable audio and video recordings, podcasts have become a popular means of delivering everything from college lectures to marketing messages. Podcasts are also used for internal communication, replacing conference calls, newsletters, and other media.

Online Video

Google and the Google logo are registered trademarks of Google Inc., used with permission.

The combination of low-cost digital video cameras and video-sharing websites such as YouTube has spurred a revolution in business video. Product demonstrations, company overviews, promotional presentations, and training seminars are among the most popular applications of business video. *Branded channels* allow companies to present theirvideos as an integrated collection in a customized user interface.

User-Generated Content Sites

User-generated content sites let businesses host photos, videos, software programs, technical solutions, and other valuable content for their customer communities.

BUILDING COMMUNITIES

One of the most significant benefits of new communication technologies is the ease with which companies can foster a sense of community among customers, enthusiasts, and other groups. In some instances, the company establishes and manages the online community, while in others the community is driven by *product champions* or other enthusiasts.

Gaming Technologies

Adding game-playing elements to business processes (such as competitions for sales or service teams) can increase engagement from employees and customers alike.

Community Q&A Sites

Many companies now rely heavily on communities of customers to help each other with product questions and other routine matters.

Businesses use a variety of social networks as specialized channels to engage customers, find new employees, attract investors, and share ideas and challenges with peers.

Microblogging

Microblogging services (of which Twitter is by far the best known) are a great way to share ideas, solicit feedback, monitor market trends, and announce special deals and events.

Social Networking

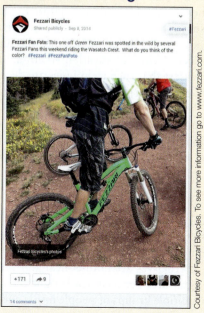

Committing to Ethical and Legal Communication

Ethics are the accepted principles of conduct that govern behavior within a society. Ethical behavior is a companywide concern, but because communication efforts are the public face of a company, they are subjected to particularly rigorous scrutiny from regulators, legislators, investors, consumer groups, environmental groups, labor organizations, and anyone else affected by business activities. **Ethical communication** includes all relevant information, is true in every sense, and is not deceptive in any way. In contrast, unethical communication can distort the truth or manipulate audiences in a variety of ways:[53]

Misleading audiences in any way is unethical.

- **Plagiarizing.** Plagiarism is presenting someone else's words or other creative product as your own. Note that plagiarism can be illegal if it violates a **copyright**, which is a form of legal protection for the expression of creative ideas.[54]
- **Omitting essential information.** Your audience must have all the information necessary to make an intelligent, objective decision.
- **Selective misquoting.** Distorting or hiding the true intent of someone else's words is unethical.
- **Misrepresenting numbers.** Statistics and other data can be unethically manipulated by increasing or decreasing numbers, exaggerating, altering statistics, or omitting numeric data.
- **Distorting visuals.** Images can be manipulated in unethical ways, such as altering photos to deceive audiences or changing the scale of graphs and charts to exaggerate or conceal differences.
- **Failing to respect privacy or information security needs.** Failing to respect the privacy of others or failing to adequately protect information entrusted to your care can also be considered unethical (and is sometimes illegal).

Transparency gives audience members access to all the information they need in order to process messages accurately.

The widespread adoption of social media has increased the attention given to the issue of **transparency**, which in this context refers to a sense of openness, of giving all participants in a conversation access to the information they need to accurately process the messages they are receiving. In addition to the information itself, audiences deserve to know when they are being marketed to and who is behind the messages they read or hear.

For example, with *stealth marketing*, companies recruit people to promote products to friends and other contacts in exchange for free samples or other rewards, without requiring them to disclose the true nature of the communication. This can range from paying consumers to give product samples as "gifts" to paying popular Vine contributors to work products and brand names into the segments they post on the popular video-sharing service.[55] Critics of stealth marketing, including the U.S. Federal Trade Commission (FTC), assert that such techniques are deceptive because they don't give targets the opportunity to raise their instinctive defenses against the persuasive powers of marketing messages.[56]

Aside from ethical concerns, trying to fool the public is simply bad for business. As the LaSalle University communication professor Michael Smith puts it, "The public backlash can be long, deep, and damaging to a company's reputation."[57]

DISTINGUISHING ETHICAL DILEMMAS FROM ETHICAL LAPSES

An ethical dilemma is a choice between alternatives that may not be clearly right or clearly wrong.

Some ethical questions are easy to recognize and resolve, but others are not. Deciding what is ethical can be a considerable challenge in complex business situations. An **ethical dilemma** involves choosing among alternatives that aren't clear-cut. Perhaps two conflicting alternatives are both ethical and valid, or perhaps the alternatives lie somewhere in the gray area between clearly right and clearly wrong. Every company has responsibilities to multiple groups of people inside and outside the firm, and those groups often have competing interests. For instance, employees naturally want higher wages and more

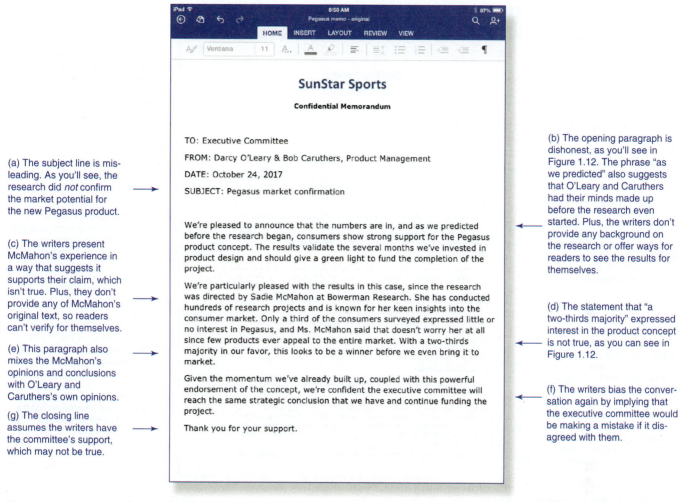

Figure 1.11   Unethical Communication
The writers of this memo clearly want the company to continue funding their pet project, even though the marketing research doesn't support such a decision. By comparing this memo with the version shown in Figure 1.12 (be sure to read the lettered annotations), you can see how the writers twisted the truth and omitted evidence in order to put a positive "spin" on the research.

benefits, but investors who have risked their money in the company want management to keep costs low so that profits are strong enough to drive up the stock price. Both sides have a valid ethical position.

In contrast, an **ethical lapse** is a clearly unethical choice. With both internal and external communication efforts, the pressure to produce results or justify decisions can make unethical communication a tempting choice. Telling a potential customer you can complete a project by a certain date when you know you can't is simply dishonest, even if you need the contract to save your career or your company. There is no ethical dilemma here.

> An ethical lapse is making a choice you know to be unethical.

Compare the messages in Figures 1.11 and 1.12 for examples of how business messages can be unethically manipulated.

ENSURING ETHICAL COMMUNICATION

Ensuring ethical business communication requires three elements: ethical individuals, ethical company leadership, and the appropriate policies and structures to support employees' efforts to make ethical choices.[58] Moreover, these three elements need to work in harmony. If employees see company executives making unethical decisions and flouting company guidelines, they might conclude that the guidelines are meaningless and emulate their bosses' unethical behavior.

MOBILE APP
The **PRSA Ethics** app is a mobile version of the Publish Relations Society of America's code of ethics.

(a) This neutral subject line doesn't try to sell the conclusion before readers have the opportunity to review the evidence for themselves.

(c) By providing the complete text of the researcher's summary, the memo allows readers to reach their own conclusions about what she wrote.

(e) The writers are careful to separate the researcher's observations and opinions from their own, even to the point of grouping them under separate subheadings.

(g) The close invites further discussion of the situation, without assuming agreement of the writers' conclusions.

(b) Rather than hardselling a conclusion that isn't even true, this opening offers a quick overview of the research and emphasizes the experience of the researcher. In the second paragraph, the writers continue by offering full disclosure of all background information related to the research project.

(d) The numbers here show how the original memo skewed the results. Just because one-third had no interest in the product does not mean two-thirds did. Moreover, the second paragraph from the researcher clearly indicates that she is concerned about the product's viability in the marketplace—a critical point completely missing in the original memo.

(f) The recommendation states clearly and objectively that the project probably will not live up to original hopes.

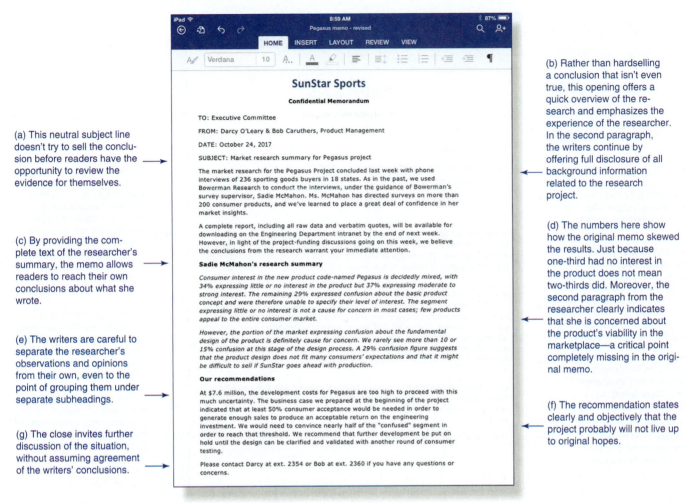

Figure 1.12   Ethical Communication
This version of the memo from Figure 1.11 presents the evidence in a more honest and ethical manner.

Responsible employers establish clear ethical guidelines for their employees to follow.

Employers have a responsibility to establish clear guidelines and set examples for ethical behavior, including ethical business communication. Many companies establish an explicit ethics policy by using a written **code of ethics** to help employees determine what is acceptable. A code is often part of a larger program of employee training and communication channels that allow employees to ask questions and report instances of questionable ethics. To ensure ongoing compliance with their codes of ethics, many companies also conduct **ethics audits** to monitor ethical progress and to point out any weaknesses that need to be addressed.

However, whether or not formal guidelines are in place, every employee has a responsibility to communicate in an ethical manner. In the absence of clear guidelines, ask yourself the following questions about your business communications:[59]

If you can't decide whether a choice is ethical, picture yourself explaining your decision to someone whose opinion you value.

- Have you defined the situation fairly and accurately?
- What is your intention in communicating this message?
- What impact will this message have on the people who receive it or who might be affected by it?
- Will the message achieve the greatest possible good while doing the least possible harm?
- Will the assumptions you've made change over time? That is, will a decision that seems ethical now seem unethical in the future?

- Are you comfortable with your decision? Would you be embarrassed if it were printed in tomorrow's newspaper or spread across the Internet? Think about a person whom you admire and ask yourself what he or she would think of your decision.

ENSURING LEGAL COMMUNICATION

In addition to ethical guidelines, business communication is also bound by a wide variety of laws and regulations, including the following areas:

- **Promotional communication.** Marketing specialists need to be aware of the many laws that govern truth and accuracy in advertising. These laws address such issues as product reviews written by bloggers who receive compensation from the companies involved, false and deceptive advertising, misleading or inaccurate labels on product packages, and bait-and-switch tactics in which a store advertises a lower-priced product to lure consumers into a store but then tries to sell them a more expensive item.[60] Chapter 12 explores this area in more detail.

- **Contracts.** A **contract** is a legally binding promise between two parties in which one party makes a specified offer and the other party accepts. Contracts are fundamental to virtually every aspect of business, from product sales to property rental to credit cards and loans to professional service agreements.[61]

- **Employment communication.** A variety of local, state, and federal laws govern communication between employers and both potential and current employees. For example, job descriptions must be written in a way that doesn't intentionally or unintentionally discriminate against women, minorities, or people with disabilities.[62]

- **Intellectual property.** In an age when instant global connectivity makes copying and retransmitting digital files effortless, the protection of intellectual property has become a widespread concern. **Intellectual property (IP)** includes patents, copyrighted materials, trade secrets, and even Internet domain names.[63] Bloggers and social media users in particular need to be careful about IP protection, given the carefree way that some post the work of others without offering proper credit.

> **REAL-TIME UPDATES**
> LEARN MORE BY VISITING THIS WEBSITE
> **Guidelines for trouble-free blogging**
> The Electronic Frontier Foundation offers a free *Legal Guide for Bloggers*. Go to **real-timeupdates.com/bct14** and select Learn More in the Students section.

- **Financial reporting.** Finance and accounting professionals who work for publicly traded companies (those that sell stock to the public) must adhere to stringent reporting laws. For instance, a number of corporations have recently been targets of both government investigations and shareholder lawsuits for offering misleading descriptions of financial results and revenue forecasts.

- **Defamation.** Negative comments about another party raise the possibility of **defamation**, the intentional communication of false statements that damage character or reputation.[64] (Written defamation is called *libel*; spoken defamation is called *slander*.) Someone suing for defamation must prove (1) that the statement is false, (2) that the language is injurious to the person's reputation, and (3) that the statement has been published.

- **Transparency requirements.** Governments around the world are taking steps to help ensure that consumers and other parties know who is behind the information they receive, particularly when it appears online. The European Union, for instance, outlaws a number of online marketing tactics, including "flogs," short for "fake blogs," in which an employee or a paid agent posing as an independent consumer posts positive stories about a company's products.[65] In the United States, FTC guidelines require bloggers and other social media users who review products to disclose if they receive compensation for writing reviews.[66]

If you have any doubts about the legality of a message you intend to distribute, ask for advice from your company's legal department. A small dose of caution can prevent huge legal headaches and protect your company's reputation in the marketplace.

For the latest information on ethical and legal issues in business communication, visit **real-timeupdates.com/bct14** and select Chapter 1.

> Business communication is governed by a wide variety of laws designed to ensure accurate, complete messages.

COMMUNICATION CHALLENGES AT JetBlue

Imagine that you've joined the Twitter team at JetBlue as one of the more than two dozen communication specialists tasked with monitoring conversations about the company in the Twittersphere and responding to questions, requests, and complaints from passengers. Use what you've learned in this chapter to address the following challenges.

INDIVIDUAL CHALLENGE: Find a recent Twitter conversation between a passenger and JetBlue. It can be a compliment, a complaint, or a question. How well do you think the JetBlue team handled the conversation? Does the conversation reflect well on JetBlue? If you had been the passenger, would you have been satisfied with the outcome? Why or why not?

TEAM CHALLENGE: With a team assigned by your instructor, analyze the writing style of several dozen JetBlue tweets. Next, choose another well-known company that is on Twitter and analyze a series of its tweets. How do the two companies compare in terms of the general tone of their social media writing? Is one more formal than the other? Does one emphasize self-promotion more than the other? Does one engage with customers more, answering queries and resolving complaints? Summarize your analysis, with examples from both companies.

Quick Learning Guide

KEY TERMS

audience-centered approach Understanding and respecting the members of your audience and making every effort to get your message across in a way that is meaningful to them

code of ethics A written set of ethical guidelines that companies expect their employees to follow

communication The process of transferring information and meaning using one or more media and communication channels

communication barriers Forces or events that can disrupt communication, including noise and distractions, competing messages, filters, and channel breakdowns

communication channels Systems used to deliver messages

communication medium The form in which a message is presented; the three primary categories of media are oral, written, and visual

contract A legally binding promise between two parties in which one party makes a specified offer and the other party accepts

copyright A form of legal protection for the expression of creative ideas

critical thinking The ability to evaluate evidence completely and objectively in order to form logical conclusions and make sound recommendations

decoding Extracting the idea from a message

defamation The intentional communication of false statements that damage someone's character or reputation

encoding Putting an idea into a message (using words, images, or a combination of both)

ethical communication Communication that includes all relevant information, is true in every sense, and is not deceptive in any way

ethical dilemma Situation that involves making a choice when the alternatives aren't completely wrong or completely right

ethical lapse A clearly unethical choice

ethics The accepted principles of conduct that govern behavior within a society

ethics audits Ongoing efforts to monitor ethical progress and to point out any weaknesses that need to be addressed

etiquette The expected norms of behavior in a particular situation

feedback Information from receivers regarding the quality and effectiveness of a message

SUMMARY OF LEARNING OBJECTIVES

1 **Explain the importance of effective communication to your career and to the companies where you will work.** Effective communication is important to your career because no matter what line of work you pursue, you need to be able to share information with other people. You can have the greatest business ideas in the world, but they're no good to anyone if you can't express them clearly and persuasively. In addition to benefiting you personally, your communication skills will help your company in multiple ways, offering (1) closer ties with important communities in the marketplace; (2) opportunities to influence conversations, perceptions, and trends; (3) increased productivity and faster problem solving; (4) better financial results; (5) earlier warning of potential problems; (6) stronger decision making; (7) clearer and more persuasive marketing messages; and (8) greater employee engagement with work.

2 **Explain what it means to communicate as a professional in a business context.** Communicating as a professional starts with being a professional, which embodies striving to excel, being dependable and accountable, being a team player, demonstrating a sense of etiquette, making ethical decisions, and maintaining a positive outlook.

As a professional, you will be expected to apply a wide range of communication skills, including organizing ideas and information; expressing yourself coherently and persuasively in a variety of media; building persuasive arguments; critically evaluating data and information; actively listening to others; communicating effectively with diverse audiences; using communication technologies; following accepted standards of grammar, spelling, and other aspects of high-quality writing and speaking; adapting your messages and communication styles as needed; demonstrating strong business etiquette; communicating ethically; respecting confidentiality; following applicable laws and regulations; and managing your time wisely and using resources efficiently.

Applying these skills effectively in an organizational context involves learning how to use both the *formal* and *informal* communication networks in your organization. The formal network mirrors the official hierarchy and structure of the organization; the informal network involves all the communication among members of the organization, regardless of their job positions. Adopting an *audience-centered approach* involves understanding and respecting the members of your audience and making every effort to get your message across in a way that is meaningful to them. This approach is also known as adopting the *"you" attitude* (where "you" is the recipient of the message you are sending).

3 **Describe the communication process model and the ways social media are changing the nature of business communication.** Communication is a complex and subtle process, and any attempt to model it involves some simplification, but it is helpful to view the process as eight steps: (1) the sender starts with an idea to share; (2) the sender encodes the meaning of that idea as a message; (3) the sender produces the message in a transmittable medium; (4) the sender transmits the message through a channel; (5) the audience receives the message; (6) the audience decodes the message to extract its meaning; (7) the audience responds to the message; and (8) the audience provides feedback to the sender.

Social media are transforming the practice of business communication and changing the nature of the relationships between companies and their stakeholders. Traditional business communication can be thought of as having a "publishing" mindset, in which a company produces carefully scripted messages and distributes them to an audience that has few options for responding to the company or interacting with one another. In contrast, the social model uses social media tools to create an interactive and participatory environment in which all parties have a chance to join the conversation. Many of the old rules and expectations, including tight control of the content and distribution of the message, no longer apply in this new environment.

4 **Outline the challenges and opportunities of mobile communication in business.** The challenges of mobile communications in business include the need for websites to be mobile friendly, the difficulty of creating and consuming content on small screens and keyboards, the potential for always-on connectivity to blur the lines between personal and professional time, the difficulty of getting and keeping the attention of multitasking audiences, and a variety of security and privacy concerns. The opportunities include giving employees more flexibility to meet their personal and professional obligations, using mobile devices as sensory and cognitive extensions, enhancing productivity and collaboration, assisting in a

formal communication network Communication channels that flow along the lines of command

informal communication network All communication that takes place outside the formal network; often referred to as the *grapevine* or the *rumor mill*

information overload Condition in which people receive more information than they can effectively process

intellectual property (IP) Assets including patents, copyrighted materials, trade secrets, and even Internet domain names

message The "container" in which an idea is transmitted from a sender to a receiver

perception A person's awareness or view of reality; also, the process of detecting incoming messages

professionalism The quality of performing at a high level and conducting oneself with purpose and pride

selective perception The inclination to distort or ignore incoming information rather than change one's beliefs

social communication model An interactive, conversational approach to communication in which formerly passive audience members are empowered to participate fully

stakeholders Groups affected by a company's actions: customers, employees, shareholders, suppliers, neighbors, the community, and the world at large

transparency Giving all participants in a conversation access to the information they need to accurately process the messages they are receiving

"you" attitude Communicating with an audience-centered approach; creating messages that are about "you," the receiver, rather than "me," the sender

wide variety of business tasks, accelerating decision making and problem solving, and creating more engaging experiences for customers and other users.

5 **List four general guidelines for using communication technology effectively.** First, keep technology in perspective. Make sure it supports the communication effort rather than overwhelming or disrupting it. Second, guard against information overload and information technology addiction. Third, learn how to use technological tools productively—and avoid using them in deliberately unproductive ways. Fourth, reconnect in person from time to time to ensure that communication is successful and that technology doesn't come between you and the people you need to reach.

6 **Define *ethics*, explain the difference between an ethical dilemma and an ethical lapse, and list six guidelines for making ethical communication choices.** Ethics are the accepted principles of conduct that govern behavior within a society. Ethical communication is particularly important in business because communication is the public face of a company, which is why communication efforts are intensely scrutinized by company stakeholders. The difference between an ethical dilemma and an ethical lapse is a question of clarity. An ethical dilemma occurs when the choice is unclear because two or more alternatives seem equally right or equally wrong. In contrast, an ethical lapse occurs when a person makes a conscious choice that is clearly unethical.

To make ethical choices in any situation, ask yourself these six questions: (1) Have I defined the situation fairly and accurately? (2) What is my intention in communicating this message? (3) What impact will this message have on the people who receive it or who might be affected by it? (4) Will the message achieve the greatest possible good while doing the least possible harm? (5) Will the assumptions I've made change over time? That is, will a decision that seems ethical now seem unethical in the future? (6) Am I truly comfortable with my decision?

MyBCommLab
Go to **mybcommlab.com** to complete the problems marked with this icon .

Test Your Knowledge

To review chapter content related to each question, refer to the indicated Learning Objective.

1-1. What benefits does effective communication give you and your organization? [LO-1]

1-2. What are the five attributes of effective business communication? [LO-1]

1-3. What are the six traits of professionalism? [LO-2]

1-4. Why should communicators take an audience-centered approach to communication? [LO-2]

1-5. What steps have to occur before an audience member perceives the presence of an incoming message? [LO-3]

1-6. What are the most common barriers to successful communication? [LO-3]

1-7. What does "BYOD" refer to, and what are the implications of this phenomenon? [LO-4]

1-8. How is communication affected by information overload? [LO-5]

1-9. What is an ethical dilemma? [LO-6]

1-10. What is an ethical lapse? [LO-6]

Apply Your Knowledge

To review chapter content related to each question, refer to the indicated Learning Objective.

1-11. Why do you think communication is vital to the success of every business organization? Explain briefly. [LO-1]

1-12. How does a company's use of social media reflect audience-centered communication? [LO-2]

1-13. How might overuse of social media on the job affect a person's ability to truly receive important business messages? [LO-3]

1-14. What changes would you make to your email messages if you know your recipients are typically walking or riding on mass transit when they read your messages? [LO-4]

1-15. You're the CEO of a company whose sales are declining, and there is a 50/50 chance you will need to lay off some of your employees sometime in the next two to three months. You have to decide whether to tell them now so they can look for new jobs as soon as possible, even though you're not yet sure layoffs will be necessary, or wait until you are sure layoffs will occur. Explain why this is an ethical dilemma. Be sure to consider the effect a sudden exodus of valuable employees could have on the company's prospects. [LO-6]

Practice Your Skills

1-16. **Message for Analysis: Analyzing Communication Effectiveness [LO-1]** Read the following blog posting, and then (1) analyze whether the message is effective or ineffective (be sure to explain why) and (2) revise the message so that it follows this chapter's guidelines.

It has come to my attention that many of you are lying on your time cards. If you come in late, you should not put 8:00 on your card. If you take a long lunch, you should not put 1:00 on your time card. I will not stand for this type of cheating. I simply have no choice but to institute an employee monitoring system. Beginning next Monday, video cameras will be installed at all entrances to the building, and your entry and exit times will be logged each time you use electronic key cards to enter or leave.

Anyone who is late for work or late coming back from lunch more than three times will have to answer to me. I don't care if you had to take a nap or if you girls had to shop. This is a place of business, and we do not want to be taken advantage of by slackers who are cheaters to boot.

It is too bad that a few bad apples always have to spoil things for everyone.

Exercises

Each activity is labeled according to the primary skill or skills you will need to use. To review relevant chapter content, you can refer to the indicated Learning Objective. In some instances, supporting information will be found in another chapter, as indicated.

1-17. **Writing: Compositional Modes: Summaries [LO-1], Chapter 4** Write a paragraph introducing yourself to your instructor and your class. Address such areas as your background, interests, achievements, and goals. Submit your paragraph using an email, blog, or social network, as indicated by your instructor.

1-18. **Media Skills: Microblogging [LO-1], Chapter 8** Write four effective messages (no more than 140 characters each) to persuade other college students to take the business communication course. Think of the first message as the "headline" of an advertisement that makes a bold promise regarding the value this course offers every aspiring business professional. The next three messages should be supporting points that provide evidence to back up the promise made in the first message.[67]

1-19. **Fundamentals: Analyzing Communication Effectiveness [LO-1]** Identify a video clip (on YouTube or another online source) that you believe represents an example of effective communication. It can be in any context, business or otherwise, but make sure it is something appropriate to discuss in class. Post a link to the video on your class blog, along with a brief written summary of why you think this example shows effective communication in action.

1-20. **Planning: Assessing Audience Needs [LO-2], Chapter 3** Choose a business career that sounds interesting to you and imagine that you are getting ready to apply for jobs in that field. Naturally, you want to create a compelling, audience-focused résumé that answers the key questions a hiring manager is most likely to ask. Identify three personal or professional qualities you have that would be important for someone in this career field. Write a brief statement (one or two sentences) regarding each quality, describing in audience-focused terms how you can contribute to a company in this respect. Submit your statements via email or the class blog.

1-21. **Communication Etiquette: Communicating with Sensitivity and Tact [LO-2]** Potential customers frequently visit your production facility before making purchase decisions. You and the people who report to you in the sales department have received extensive training in etiquette issues because you deal with high-profile clients so often. The rest of the workforce has not received such training, however, and you worry that someone might inadvertently say or do something that would offend one of these potential customers. In a two-paragraph email, explain to the general manager why you think anyone who might come in contact with customers should receive basic etiquette training.

1-22. **Collaboration: Team Projects; Planning: Assessing Audience Needs [LO-2], Chapter 2, Chapter 4** Your boss has asked your work group to research and report on corporate child-care facilities. Of course, you'll want to know who (besides your boss) will be reading your report. Working with two team members, list four or five other things you'll want to know about the situation and about your audience before starting your research. Briefly explain why each of the items on your list is important.

1-23. **Planning: Constructing a Persuasive Argument [LO-2], Chapter 12** Blogging is a popular way for employees to communicate with customers and other parties outside the company. In some cases employee blogs have been quite beneficial for both companies and their customers by providing helpful information and "putting a human face" on other formal and imposing corporations. In other cases, however, employees have been fired for posting information that their employers said was inappropriate. One particular area of concern is criticism of the company or individual managers. Should employees be allowed to criticize their employers in a public forum such as a blog? In a brief email message, argue for or against company policies that prohibit critical information in employee blogs.

1-24. **Fundamentals: Analyzing Communication Effectiveness [LO-3]** Use the eight phases of the communication process to analyze a miscommunication you've recently had with a coworker, supervisor, classmate, teacher, friend, or family member. What idea were you trying to share? How did you encode and transmit it? Did the receiver get the message? Did the receiver correctly decode the message? How do you know? Based on your analysis, identify and explain the barriers that prevented your successful communication in this instance.

1-25. **Fundamentals: Analyzing Communication Effectiveness [LO-4]** Using a mobile device, visit the websites of five companies that make products or provide services you buy or might buy in the future. Which of the websites is the most user friendly? How does it differ from the other sites? Do any of the companies offer a mobile shopping app for your device?

1-26. **Technology: Using Communication Tools [LO-5]** Find a free online communication service that you have no experience using as a content creator or contributor. Services to consider include blogging (such as Blogger), microblogging (such as Twitter), community Q&A sites (such as YahooAnswers), and user-generated content sites (such as Flickr). Perform a basic task such as opening an account or setting up a blog. Was the task easy to perform? Were the instructions clear? Could you find help online if you needed it? Is there anything about the experience that could be improved? Summarize your conclusions in a brief email message to your instructor.

1-27. **Communication Ethics: Distinguishing Ethical Dilemmas and Ethical Lapses [LO-6]** Knowing that you have numerous friends throughout the company, your boss relies on you for feedback concerning employee morale and other issues affecting the staff. She recently asked you to start reporting any behavior that might violate company policies, from taking office supplies home to making personal long-distance calls. List the issues you'd like to discuss with her before you respond to her request.

1.28. **Communication Ethics: Distinguishing Ethical Dilemmas and Ethical Lapses [LO-6]** Briefly explain why you think each of the following is or is not ethical.

a. Keeping quiet about a possible environmental hazard you've just discovered in your company's processing plant

b. Overselling the benefits of instant messaging to your company's managers; they never seem to understand the benefits of technology, so you believe it's the only way to convince them to make the right choice

c. Telling an associate and close friend that she needs to pay more attention to her work responsibilities, or management will fire her

d. Recommending the purchase of equipment your department doesn't really need in order to use up your allocated funds before the end of the fiscal year so that your budget won't be cut next year, when you might have a real need for the money

1-29. **Communication Ethics: Providing Ethical Leadership [LO-6]** Cisco, a leading manufacturer of equipment for the Internet and corporate networks, has developed a code of ethics that it expects employees to abide by. Visit the company's website at **www.cisco.com** and find its *Code of Conduct*. In a brief paragraph describe three specific examples of things you could do that would violate these provisions; then list at least three opportunities that Cisco provides its employees to report ethics violations or ask questions regarding ethical dilemmas.

Expand Your Skills

Critique the Professionals

Locate an example of professional communication from a reputable online source. It can reflect any aspect of business communication, from an advertisement or a press release to a company blog or website. Evaluate this communication effort in light of any aspect of this chapter that is relevant to the sample and interesting to you. For example, is the piece effective? Audience-centered? Ethical? Using whatever medium your instructor requests, write a brief analysis of the piece (no more than one page) citing specific elements from the piece and support from the chapter.

Sharpening Your Career Skills Online

Bovée and Thill's Business Communication Web Search, at **websearch.businesscommunicationnetwork.com**, is a unique research tool designed specifically for business communication research. Use the Web Search function to find a website, video, article, podcast, or presentation that describes an innovative use of mobile technology in business communication. Write a brief email message to your instructor or a post for your class blog describing the item and summarizing the information you found.

MyBCommLab

Go to **mybcommlab.com** for Auto-graded writing questions as well as the following Assisted-graded writing questions:

1-30. Why is critical thinking considered an essential communication skill? [LO-3]

1-31. How is mobile technology changing the practice of business communication? [LO-4]

Endnotes

1. JetBlue website, accessed 3 March 2016, www.jetblue.com; Jet-Blue Facebook page, accessed 3 March 2016, www.facebook.com/jetblue; Yuyu Chen, "What Twitter Marketers Can Learn from JetBlue, Emirates and Royal Dutch Airlines," *ClickZ*, 18 November 2015, www.clickz.com; "5 Social Media All-Stars," *CNNMoney*, 29 August 2013, money.cnn.com; JetBlue Twitter account, accessed 3 March 2016, https://twitter.com/JetBlue; Todd Wasserman, "How JetBlue's Social Media Strategy Took Flight," *Mashable*, 1 June 2011, mashable.com; "A Day In The Life: Social Media," BlueTales blog, 19 January 2012, blog.jetblue.com, Chantal Tode, "JetBlue Exec: Mobile Is Discovery Piece for Travelers," *Mobile Marketer*, 22 January 2013, www.mobilemarketer.com.
2. Richard L. Daft, *Management*, 6th ed. (Cincinnati: Thomson South-Western, 2003), 580.
3. "Employers: 13 Common Complaints About Recent Grads," Youturn, 2 October 2012, www.youturn.com.
4. Julie Connelly, "Youthful Attitudes, Sobering Realities," *New York Times*, 28 October 2003, E1, E6; Nigel Andrews and Laura D'Andrea Tyson, "The Upwardly Global MBA," *Strategy + Business* 36 (Fall 2004): 60–69; Jim McKay, "Communication Skills Found Lacking," *Pittsburgh Post-Gazette*, 28 February 2005, www.delawareonline.com.
5. Martin Zwilling, "How Effective Is Your Business Communication Skill?" *Forbes*, 20 January 2015, www.forbes.com; Brian Solis, *Engage!* (Hoboken, N.J.: John Wiley & Sons, 2010), 11–12; "Majority of Global Companies Face an Engagement Gap," Internal Comms Hub website, 23 October 2007, www.internalcommshub.com; Gary L. Neilson, Karla L. Martin, and Elizabeth Powers, "The Secrets to Successful Strategy Execution," *Harvard Business Review*, June 2008, 61–70; Nicholas Carr, "Lessons in Corporate Blogging," *BusinessWeek*, 18 July 2006, 9; Susan Meisinger, "To Keep Employees, Talk—and Listen—to Them!" *HR Magazine*, August 2006, 10.
6. Daft, *Management*, 147.
7. Zwilling, "How Effective Is Your Business Communication Skill?"
8. Susan Adams, "How to Communicate Effectively at Work," *Forbes*, 17 November 2015, www.forbes.com; "CEOs to Communicators: 'Stick to Common Sense,'" Internal Comms Hub website, 23 October 2007, www.internalcommshub.com; "A Writing Competency Model for Business," BizCom101.com, 14 December 2007, www.business-writing-courses.com; Sue Dewhurst and Liam Fitz-Patrick, "What Should Be the Competency of Your IC Team?" white paper, 2007, competentcommunicators.com.
9. "Digital Information Fluency Model," 21cif.com, accessed 11 February 2014, 21cif.com.
10. Philip C. Kolin, *Successful Writing at Work*, 6th ed. (Boston: Houghton Mifflin, 2001), 17–23.
11. "The Explainer: Emotional Intelligence," *Harvard Business Review* video, 18 August 2015, accessed 2 March 2016, hbr.org; Laura L. Myers and Mary L. Tucker, "Increasing Awareness of Emotional Intelligence in a Business Curriculum," *Business Communication Quarterly*, March 2005, 44–51.
12. Walter Frick, "The Curious Science of When Multitasking Works," *Harvard Business Review*, 6 January 2015, hbr.org.
13. Pete Cashmore, "10 Web Trends to Watch in 2010," CNN Tech, 3 December 2009, www.cnn.com.
14. Paul Martin Lester, *Visual Communication: Images with Messages* (Belmont, Calif.: Thomson South-Western, 2006), 6–8.
15. Michael R. Solomon, *Consumer Behavior: Buying, Having, and Being*, 6th ed. (Upper Saddle River, N.J.: Pearson Prentice Hall, 2004), 65.
16. Anne Field, "What You Say, What They Hear," *Harvard Management Communication Letter*, Winter 2005, 3–5.
17. Chuck Williams, *Management*, 2nd ed. (Cincinnati: Thomson South-Western, 2002), 690.
18. Charles G. Morris and Albert A. Maisto, *Psychology: An Introduction*, 12th ed. (Upper Saddle River, N.J.: Pearson Prentice Hall, 2005), 226–239; Saundra K. Ciccarelli and Glenn E. Meyer, *Psychology* (Upper Saddle River, N.J.: Prentice Hall, 2006), 210–229; Mark H. Ashcraft, *Cognition*, 4th ed. (Upper Saddle River, N.J.: Prentice Hall, 2006), 44–54.
19. Ben Hanna, *2009 Business Social Media Benchmarking Study*, Business.com, 2 November 2009, 11.
20. "Managing Yourself: Conquering Digital Distraction," *Harvard Business Review*, June 2015, 110–113, hbr.org; Michael Killian, "The Communication Revolution—'Deep Impact' About to Strike," Avaya Insights blog, 4 December 2009, www.avayablog.com.
21. "The Mobile Revolution Is Just Beginning," press release, World Economic Forum, 13 September 2013, www.weforum.org.
22. Maribel Lopez, "Three Trends That Change Business: Mobile, Social and Cloud," *Forbes*, 28 January 2012, www.forbes.com.

23. Kevin Custis, "Three Ways Business Can Be Successful on Mobile," *Forbes*, 15 November 2013, www.forbes.com; "IBM Survey: Speed and Analytics Key Drivers in Mobile Adoption for Organizations," press release, IBM, 19 November 2013, www.ibm.com.

24. "More Than Nine in 10 Internet Users Will Go Online via Phone," eMarketer, 6 January 2014, www.emarketer.com.

25. Christina "CK" Kerley, *The Mobile Revolution & B2B*, white paper, 2011, www.b2bmobilerevolution.com.

26. Jordie van Rijn, "The Ultimate Mobile Email Statistics Overview," Emailmonday.com, accessed 9 February 2014, www.emailmonday.com.

27. Jessica Lee, "46% of Searchers Now Use Mobile Exclusively to Research [Study]," Search Engine Watch, 1 May 2013, searchenginewatch.com.

28. Dennis McCafferty, "10 Awesome Facts About the Mobile Revolution," *CIO Insight*, 6 December 2013, www.cioinsight.com.

29. Yun-Sen Chan, "Smartphones Are Changing Person-to-Person Communication," Modern Media Mix, 23 April 2013, modernmediamix.com.

30. "Mobile Facts and Market Stats," Mocapay, accessed 10 February 2014, www.mocapay.com.

31. Richa Jain, "Making a Case for Mobile First Designs," Sitepoint, 21 November 2014, www.sitepoint.com; *Mobile Revolution* (Nashua, NH: Extron, 2011, PDF ebook).

32. Nicco Mele, *The End of Big: How the Internet Makes David the New Goliath* (New York: St. Martin's Press, 2013), 1–2.

33. "JWT's 13 Mobile Trends for 2013 and Beyond," J. Walter Thompson website, 2 April 2013, www.jwt.com.

34. *The Changing Role of Mobile Communications in the Workplace*, white paper, Frost & Sullivan, accessed 8 February 2014, www.frost.com.

35. *Top 10 Ways Successful Small Businesses Use Mobile Tech*, white paper, T-Mobile, 2012.

36. Armen Ghazarian, "How Do Users Interact with Mobile Devices," Medium.com, 29 November 2013, medium.com.

37. "JWT's 13 Mobile Trends for 2013 and Beyond."

38. "Bring Your Own Device: BYOD Is Here and You Can't Stop It," Garner, accessed 9 February 2014, www.garner.com.

39. Jessica Twentyman, "Deploying Smartphones, Tables, and Apps for a New Employee Communication Era," *SCM*, January/February 2013, 28–29; *The Changing Role of Mobile Communications in the Workplace*.

40. Aaref Hilaly, "The Biggest Opportunity in Mobile That No One Is Talking About," LinkedIn, 17 December 2013, www.linkedin.com.

41. Adobe Digital Publishing Solution, accessed 3 March 2016, www.adobe.com.

42. Michael Saylor, *The Mobile Wave: How Mobile Intelligence Will Change Everything* (New York: Vanguard Press, 2012), 10.

43. *The Changing Role of Mobile Communications in the Workplace*.

44. *Top 10 Ways Successful Small Businesses Use Mobile Tech*.

45. Milton Kazmeyer, "The Impact of Wireless Communication in the Workplace," *Houston Chronicle*, accessed 10 February 2014, smallbusiness.chron.com.

46. Gregg Hano, "The Power of Corporate Communications on Mobile Apps," Mag+, 1 August 2013, www.magplus.com.

47. Tara Craig, "How to Avoid Information Overload," *Personnel Today*, 10 June 2008, 31; Jeff Davidson, "Fighting Information Overload," *Canadian Manager*, Spring 2005, 16+.

48. Eric J. Sinrod, "Perspective: It's My Internet—I Can Do What I Want," News.com, 29 March 2006, www.news.com.

49. Eric J. Sinrod, "Time to Crack Down on Tech at Work?" News.com, 14 June 2006, www.news.com.

50. Jack Trout, "Beware of 'Infomania,'" *Forbes*, 11 August 2006, www.forbes.com.

51. "Many Senior Managers Communicate Badly, Survey Says," *Internal Comms Hub*, 6 August 2007, www.internalcommshub.com.

52. Mike Schaffner, "Step Away from the Computer," *Forbes*, 7 August 2009, www.forbes.com.

53. Philip C. Kolin, *Successful Writing at Work*, 6th ed. (Boston: Houghton Mifflin, 2001), 24–30.

54. Nancy K. Kubasek, Bartley A. Brennan, and M. Neil Browne, *The Legal Environment of Business*, 3rd ed. (Upper Saddle River, N.J.: Prentice Hall, 2003), 172.

55. Kurt Wagner, "Stealth Marketing: How Brands Infiltrate Vine With Product Placement," *Mashable*, 22 July 2014, mashable.com.

56. Word of Mouth Marketing Association, "WOM 101," accessed 2 June 2010, womma.org; Nate Anderson, "FTC Says Stealth Marketing Unethical," *Ars Technica*, 13 December 2006, arstechnica.com; "Undercover Marketing Uncovered," CBSnews.com, 25 July 2004, www.cbsnews.com; Stephanie Dunnewind, "Teen Recruits Create Word-of-Mouth 'Buzz' to Hook Peers on Products," *Seattle Times*, 20 November 2004, www.seattletimes.com.

57. Linda Pophal, "Tweet Ethics: Trust and Transparency in a Web 2.0 World," International Association of Business Communicators, 1 September 2009, www.iabc.com.

58. Daft, *Management*, 155.

59. Based in part on Robert Kreitner, *Management*, 9th ed. (Boston: Houghton Mifflin, 2004), 163.

60. Henry R. Cheeseman, *Contemporary Business and E-Commerce Law*, 4th ed. (Upper Saddle River, N.J.: Prentice Hall, 2003), 841–843.

61. Cheeseman, *Contemporary Business and E-Commerce Law*, 201.

62. John Jude Moran, *Employment Law: New Challenges in the Business Environment*, 2nd ed. (Upper Saddle River, N.J.: Prentice Hall, 2002), 186–187; Kubasek et al., *The Legal Environment of Business*, 562.

63. Cheeseman, *Contemporary Business and E-Commerce Law*, 325.

64. Kubasek et al., *The Legal Environment of Business*, 306.

65. Robert Plummer, "Will Fake Business Blogs Crash and Burn?" *BBC News*, 22 May 2008, news.bbc.co.uk.

66. Liza Darwin, "Why Those FTC Blogger Requirements Aren't Working," Refinery29, 7 April 2015, www.refinery29.com.

67. The concept of a four-tweet summary is based on Cliff Atkinson, *The Backchannel* (Berkeley, Calif.: New Riders, 2010), 120–121.

Collaboration, Interpersonal Communication, and Business Etiquette

LEARNING OBJECTIVES

After studying this chapter, you will be able to

1 List the advantages and disadvantages of working in teams, describe the characteristics of effective teams, and highlight four key issues of group dynamics.

2 Offer guidelines for collaborative communication, identify major collaboration technologies, and explain how to give constructive feedback.

3 List the key steps needed to ensure productive team meetings.

4 Identify the major technologies used to enhance or replace in-person meetings.

5 Identify three major modes of listening, describe the listening process, and explain the problem of selective listening.

6 Explain the importance of nonverbal communication, and identify six major categories of nonverbal expression.

7 Explain the importance of business etiquette, and identify four key areas in which good etiquette is essential.

MyBCommLab®

⭐ **Improve Your Grade!** More than 10 million students improved their results using the Pearson MyLabs. Visit **mybcommlab.com** for simulations, tutorials, and end-of-chapter problems.

COMMUNICATION CLOSE-UP AT
Cemex

www.cemex.com

You probably have been on a lab team or other project team that had trouble collaborating. Maybe you couldn't get everyone in the same room at the same time, or important messages got buried in long email threads, or good ideas were lost because the right information didn't get to the right people at the right time.

Imagine trying to collaborate when you have thousands of potential team members spread across dozens of countries. The Mexican company Cemex is one of the world's largest producers of concrete and its two primary components, cement and aggregates (crushed stone, sand, and gravel). Cemex faces teamwork challenges on a global scale, with 44,000 employees in more than 50 countries. After a period of worldwide expansion that began in the 1990s, the century-old company now operates quarries, cement plants, and other facilities on every continent except Antarctica.

Concrete and cement are two of the oldest products on earth and might not spring to mind when most people think of innovation. However, innovation is key to Cemex's long-term success, for several reasons. First, architects and builders continue to push the envelope by creating designs that require concrete with new performance and handling qualities. Second, Cemex's ability to operate profitably depends on running efficient operations, from raw material extraction to processing to transportation. Third, the production and distribution of concrete-related products have significant environmental

An innovative collaboration platform helps the global cement company Cemex operate with the agility and flexibility of a small company.

impacts, including the acquisition and consumption of heating fuels required by high-temperature cement kilns.

To stay competitive and profitable and to minimize the environmental effects of its operations, Cemex knew it needed to accelerate the pace of innovation. Company leaders figured the way to do that was to enable better collaboration, and the way to do *that* was to enable better communication.

The company's response to this multilayered challenge is a comprehensive online collaboration platform called *Shift*, which combines social networking, wikis, blogs, a Twitter-like microblogging system, social bookmarking, videoconferencing, a trend-spotting tool called *Shift Radar*, and more. A custom mobile app lets employees access the system wherever their work takes them.

By connecting people and information quickly and easily, Shift helps overcome the barriers of geography, time zones, and organizational boundaries. Employees and managers can tap into expertise anywhere in the company, workers with similar responsibilities can share ideas on improving operations, and problems and opportunities can be identified and brought to management's attention in much less time.

Technology is only part of the solution, however. Many companies that have implemented social platforms struggle to get employees to change ingrained behaviors and use the new tools. By getting top-level executives on board early, Cemex achieved nearly universal adoption, with 95 percent of employees using Shift and forming more than 500 online communities based on technical specialties and shared interests. That level of engagement is paying off in numerous ways, such as launching a new global brand of ready-mix concrete in one-third the expected time, nearly tripling the company's use of renewable energy, and reducing carbon dioxide emissions by almost 2 million metric tons.

Perhaps most impressive, Shift has lived up to its name by shifting the entrenched hierarchical culture of a large, old-school company to a more agile and responsive social business that is better prepared to face the future in its highly competitive markets. As Gilberto Garcia, Cemex's innovation director, puts it, social collaboration "can make a big company look like a small company" by connecting people and ensuring the free exchange of ideas.[1]

Communicating Effectively in Teams

1 **LEARNING OBJECTIVE**
List the advantages and disadvantages of working in teams, describe the characteristics of effective teams, and highlight four key issues of group dynamics.

Collaboration—working together to solve complex problems—is an essential skill for workers in nearly every profession.

Team members have a shared mission and are collectively responsible for their work.

The interactions among the employees at Cemex (profiled in the chapter-opening Communication Close-Up) represent one of the most essential elements of interpersonal communication. **Collaboration**—working together to meet complex challenges—is a prime skill expected in a wide range of professions. No matter what career path you pursue, it's a virtual guarantee that you will need to collaborate in at least some of your work activities. Your communication skills will pay off handsomely in these interactions because the productivity and quality of collaborative efforts depend heavily on the communication skills of the professionals involved.

A **team** is a unit of two or more people who share a mission and the responsibility for working to achieve a common goal.[2] **Problem-solving teams** and **task forces** assemble to resolve specific issues and then disband when their goals have been accomplished. Such teams are often *cross-functional*, pulling together people from a variety of departments who have different areas of expertise and responsibility. The diversity of opinions and experiences can lead to better decisions, but competing interests can cause tensions that highlight the need for effective communication. **Committees** are formal teams that usually have a long life span and can become a permanent part of the organizational structure. Committees typically deal with regularly recurring tasks, such as an executive committee that meets monthly to plan strategies and review results.

ADVANTAGES AND DISADVANTAGES OF TEAMS

When teams are successful, they can improve productivity, creativity, employee involvement, and even job security.[3] Teams are often at the core of **participative management**, the effort to involve employees in the company's decision making. A successful team can provide a number of advantages:[4]

Effective teams can pool knowledge, take advantage of diverse viewpoints, increase acceptance of solutions the team proposes, and achieve higher performance.

- **Increased information and knowledge.** By pooling the experience of several individuals, a team has access to more information.
- **Increased diversity of views.** Team members can bring a variety of perspectives to the decision-making process—as long as these diverse viewpoints are guided by a shared goal.[5]

Solving the Case of the Missing Team

When the company president assembled the team to find creative solutions to the company's cash flow problems, few people thought it would succeed. Through plenty of hard work, however, you and your colleagues have found new sources of investment capital. Now it's time to present your accomplishments to the board of directors, and your entire team has been looking forward to this meeting for weeks. Because appearing in front of the board can be a major career boost, the team planned to present the results together, giving each person a few minutes in the limelight.

However, Jackson Mueller, the chief financial officer and leader of your team, had a surprise for you this morning. He'd received word at the last minute that the board wanted a short, concise presentation, and he said the best way to comply was with a single presenter. No one was happy about the change, but Mueller is the highest-ranking employee on the team and the only one with experience presenting to the board.

Disappointment turned to dismay as you and your teammates watched from the back of the conference room. Mueller deftly compressed your 60-minute presentation down to 20 minutes, and the board showered him with praise. However, he never introduced any of the other team members, so your potential moment in the sun passed without recognition.

ANALYSIS

1. Did Mueller behave unethically by not introducing you and your colleagues to the board? Explain your answer.
2. Later, you complain to a colleague that by stressing "my team" so often, Mueller actually made the presentation all about him, not the team. But one of your colleagues argues that the team's assignment was to solve the problem, not to score career points with the board, so that goal shouldn't have been such a top priority. Explain why you agree or disagree.

- **Increased acceptance of a solution.** Those who participate in making a decision are more likely to support it and encourage others to accept it.
- **Higher performance levels.** Working in teams can unleash new levels of creativity and energy in workers who share a sense of purpose and mutual accountability. Effective teams can be better than top-performing individuals at solving complex problems.[6]

Although teamwork has many advantages, it also has a number of potential disadvantages. At the worst, working in teams can be a frustrating waste of time. Teams and business leaders need to be aware of and work to counter the following potential disadvantages:

- **Groupthink.** Like other social structures, business teams can generate tremendous pressure to conform with accepted norms of behavior. **Groupthink** occurs when peer pressure causes individual team members to withhold contrary or unpopular opinions. Teams afflicted with groupthink can be so focused on protecting group harmony that they oversimplify problems, ignore information that threatens consensus, and fail to consider risks and negative consequences.[7]
- **Hidden agendas.** Some team members may have a **hidden agenda**—a private, counterproductive motive, such as a desire to take control of the group, to undermine someone else on the team, or to pursue a business goal that runs counter to the team's mission.
- **Cost.** Aligning schedules, arranging meetings, and coordinating individual parts of a project can eat up a lot of time and money.
- **Overload.** Some companies have embraced collaborative work approaches to such an extent that they're overloading employees with team assignments. Moreover, as a company's best contributors gain a reputation for helping others and getting things done, they often find themselves assigned or invited to even more team efforts. As a result, team activities can take up so much of a person's day that individual responsibilities get pushed to nights and weekends, leading to exhaustion and lower productivity.[8]

> Teams need to avoid the negative impact of groupthink, hidden agendas, excessive costs, and employee overload.

CHARACTERISTICS OF EFFECTIVE TEAMS

The most effective teams have a clear objective and shared sense of purpose, have a strong sense of trust in each other, communicate openly and honestly, reach decisions by consensus, think creatively, know how to resolve conflict, and believe that their work matters.[9] Teams that have these attributes can focus their time and energy on their work, without being disrupted by destructive conflict (see page 41).

> Effective teams have a clear sense of purpose, open and honest communication, consensus-based decision making, creativity, and effective conflict resolution.

REAL-TIME UPDATES

LEARN MORE BY READING THIS ARTICLE

Google's research into effective teamwork

Google used its world-class data analysis capabilities to identify five factors that most effective teams consistently exhibit. Go to real-timeupdates.com/bct14 and select Learn More in the Students section.

In contrast, teams lacking one or more of these attributes can get bogged down in conflict or waste time and resources pursuing unclear goals. Common reasons for dysfunctional team efforts include management expectations that are either unclear or not accepted by all team members, a reluctance by team members to prioritize team goals over their personal goals, reward systems that don't recognize team contributions, and leadership that tolerates negative and counterproductive behaviors.[10]

GROUP DYNAMICS

Group dynamics are the interactions and processes that take place within a team.

The interactions and processes that take place among the members of a team are called **group dynamics.** Productive teams tend to develop clear **norms,** informal standards of conduct that members share and that guide member behavior. Group dynamics are influenced by several factors: the roles team members assume, the current phase of team development, the team's success in resolving conflict, and the team's success in overcoming resistance.

Assuming Team Roles

Each member of a group plays a role that affects the outcome of the group's activities.

Members of a team can play various roles, which fall into three categories (see Table 2.1). Members who assume **self-oriented roles** are motivated mainly to fulfill personal needs, so they tend to be less productive than other members. "Dream teams" comprising multiple superstars often don't perform as well as one might expect because high-performing individuals can have trouble putting the team's needs ahead of their own.[11] In addition, highly skilled and experienced people with difficult personalities might not contribute, for the simple reason that other team members may avoid interacting with them.[12] Far more likely to contribute to team goals are members who assume **team-maintenance roles** to help everyone work well together and those who assume **task-oriented roles** to help the team reach its goals.[13]

Allowing for Team Evolution

Teams typically evolve through a number of phases on their way to becoming productive. A variety of models have been proposed to describe the evolution toward becoming a productive team. Figure 2.1 shows how one commonly used model identifies the phases a problem-solving team goes through as it evolves:[14]

Teams typically evolve through a variety of phases, such as orientation, conflict, brainstorming, emergence, and reinforcement.

1. **Orientation.** Team members socialize, establish their roles, and begin to define their task or purpose. Team-building exercises and activities can help teams break down barriers and develop a sense of shared purpose.[15] For geographically dispersed virtual teams, creating a "team operating agreement" that sets expectations for online meetings, communication processes, and decision making can help overcome the disadvantages of distance.[16]

TABLE 2.1   Team Roles—Functional and Dysfunctional

Dysfunctional: Self-Oriented Roles	Functional: Team-Maintenance Roles	Functional: Task-Oriented Roles
Controlling: Dominating others by exhibiting superiority or authority	**Encouraging:** Drawing out other members by showing verbal and nonverbal support, praise, or agreement	**Initiating:** Getting the team started on a line of inquiry
Withdrawing: Retiring from the team either by becoming silent or by refusing to deal with a particular aspect of the team's work	**Harmonizing:** Reconciling differences among team members through mediation or by using humor to relieve tension	**Information giving or seeking:** Offering (or seeking) information relevant to questions facing the team
Attention seeking: Calling attention to oneself and demanding recognition from others	**Compromising:** Offering to yield on a point in the interest of reaching a mutually acceptable decision	**Coordinating:** Showing relationships among ideas, clarifying issues, and summarizing what the team has done
Diverting: Focusing the team's discussion of topics of interest to the individual rather than of those relevant to the task		**Procedure setting:** Suggesting decision-making procedures that will move the team toward a goal

Figure 2.1   Phases of Group Development
Groups generally progress through several stages on their way to becoming productive and reaching their objectives.
Sources: B. Aubrey Fisher, *Small Group Decision Making: Communication and the Group Process*, 2nd ed. (New York: McGraw-Hill, 1980), 145–149; Stephen P. Robbins and David A. DeCenzo, *Fundamentals of Management: Essential Concepts and Applications*, 4th ed. (Upper Saddle River, N.J.: Prentice Hall, 2004), 334–335; Richard L. Daft, *Management*, 6th ed. (Cincinnati: Thomson South-Western, 2003), 602–603.

2. **Conflict.** Team members begin to discuss their positions and become more assertive in establishing their roles. Disagreements and uncertainties are natural in this phase.
3. **Brainstorming.** Team members air all the options and fully discuss the pros and cons of each. At the end of this phase, members begin to settle on a single solution to the problem. Note that although group brainstorming remains a highly popular activity in today's companies, it may not always be the most productive way to generate new ideas. Some research indicates that having people brainstorm individually and then bring their ideas to a group meeting is more successful.[17]
4. **Emergence.** Consensus is reached when the team finds a solution that all members are willing to support (even if they have reservations).
5. **Reinforcement.** The team clarifies and summarizes the agreed-on solution. Members receive their assignments for carrying out the group's decision, and they make arrangements for following up on those assignments.

You may also hear the process defined as *forming, storming, norming, performing,* and *adjourning,* the phases identified by researcher Bruce Tuckman when he proposed one of the earliest models of group development.[18] Regardless of the model you consider, these stages are a general framework for team development. Some teams may move forward and backward through several stages before they become productive, and other teams may be productive right away, even though some or all members are in a state of conflict.[19]

REAL-TIME UPDATES
LEARN MORE BY READING THIS ARTICLE
Three factors that distinguish smart teams
Common sense might tell you that smarter individuals make for a smarter team, but these researchers discovered otherwise. Go to **real-timeupdates.com/bct14** and select Learn More in the Students section.

Resolving Conflict

Conflict in team activities can arise for a number of reasons: competition for resources, disagreement over goals or responsibilities, poor communication, power struggles, or fundamental differences in values, attitudes, and personalities.[20] Although the term *conflict* sounds negative, conflict isn't necessarily bad. It can be *constructive* if it forces important issues into the open, increases the involvement of team members, and generates creative ideas for solving a problem. Teamwork isn't necessarily about happiness and harmony; even teams that have some interpersonal friction can excel with effective leadership and team players who are committed to strong results. As the teamwork experts Andy Boynton and Bill Fischer put it, "Virtuoso teams are not about getting polite results."[21]

In contrast, conflict is *destructive* if it diverts energy from more important issues, destroys the morale of teams or individual team members, or polarizes or divides the team.[22] Destructive conflict can lead to *win-lose* or *lose-lose* outcomes, in which one or both sides lose, to the detriment of the entire team. If you approach conflict with the idea that both sides can satisfy their goals to at least some extent (a *win-win* strategy), you can minimize losses for everyone. For a win-win strategy to work, everybody must believe that (1) it's possible to find a solution that both parties can accept, (2) cooperation is better for the organization than competition, (3) the other party can be trusted, and (4) greater power or status doesn't entitle one party to impose a solution.

Conflict in teams can be either constructive or destructive.

Destructive conflict can lead to win-lose or lose-lose outcomes.

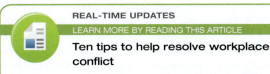

REAL-TIME UPDATES
LEARN MORE BY READING THIS ARTICLE
Ten tips to help resolve workplace conflict
Use these techniques to defuse conflict and help people focusing on solving problems. Go to **real-timeupdates.com/bct14** and select Learn More in the Students section.

The following seven measures can help team members successfully resolve conflict:

- **Proactive behavior.** Deal with minor conflict before it becomes major conflict. In team settings, conflict between two people can spread if it isn't addressed early.
- **Communication.** Get those directly involved in a conflict to participate in resolving it. These participants should choose their words and nonverbal gestures carefully in order to maintain focus on the problem at hand and to avoid further inflaming an already uncomfortable situation.[23]
- **Openness.** Get feelings out in the open before dealing with the main issues.
- **Research.** Seek factual reasons for a problem before seeking solutions.
- **Flexibility.** Don't let anyone lock into a position before considering other solutions.
- **Fair play.** Insist on fair outcomes; don't let anyone avoid a fair solution by hiding behind the rules.
- **Alliance.** Get opponents to fight together against an "outside force" instead of against each other.

Overcoming Resistance

One particular type of conflict that can impede progress is resistance to change. Sometimes this resistance is clearly irrational, such as when people resist any kind of change, whether the change makes sense or not. Sometimes, however, resistance is perfectly logical. A change may require someone to relinquish authority or give up comfortable ways of doing things.

When you encounter resistance or hostility, try to maintain your composure and address the other person's emotional needs.

Whenever you encounter resistance, your first instinct might be to argue even more force-fully for the proposed change. However, this approach is often counterproductive because it doesn't get at the roots of the resistance, and the other party is likely to dig in even deeper.

Rather than pushing harder, stop talking and start listening. Apply the *active listening* skills discussed on page 52, and let people express their reservations about the change. Make sure the other party knows you are listening, too, by choosing your nonverbal gestures carefully and by expressing interest in and sympathy for their concerns. Listening encourages others to open up about their worries, which can help you address them, and it can unveil legitimate issues that you have failed to consider.

With a line of communication open, recognize that your primary goal is not to win the argument but rather to build a relationship that can lead to solving the dilemma at hand.[24] Even if you have the authority to force the change, if you rely on force alone you'll create resentment and probably fail to get the level of emotional agreement needed for true success.

As you establish a comfortable working relationship, continue to be aware of elements of resistance that remain unspoken. For example, employees who bring up technical reasons for resisting a plan to improve efficiency may be worried deep down that the

---

THE ART OF PROFESSIONALISM

Being a Team Player

Professionals know that they are contributors to a larger cause, that it's not all about them. Just as in athletics and other team efforts, being a team player in business is something of a balancing act. On the one hand, you need to pay enough attention to your own efforts and skills to make sure you're pulling your own weight. On the other hand, you need to pay attention to the overall team effort to make sure the team succeeds. Remember that if the team fails, you fail, too.

Great team players know how to make those around them more effective, whether it's by lending a hand during crunch time, sharing resources, removing obstacles, making introductions, or offering expertise. In fact, the ability to help others improve their performance is one of the key attributes executives look for when they want to promote people into management.

Being a team player also means showing loyalty to your organization and protecting your employer's reputation—one of the most important assets any company has. Pros don't trash their employers in front of customers or in their personal blogs. When they have a problem, they solve it; they don't share it.

CAREER APPLICATIONS

1. If you prefer to work by yourself, should you take a job in a company that uses a team-based organization structure? Why or why not?
2. You can see plenty of examples of unprofessional business behavior in the news media and in your own consumer and employee experiences. Why should you bother being professional yourself?

company will get so efficient it will no longer need them. Through the various types of active listening described later in the chapter, you can get a better idea of what's really behind the reluctance to change. Ask questions to make sure you understand the resistance and to confirm your understanding of it, then acknowledge the other party's concerns.

With a better understanding of the resistance, the next step is to move toward a resolution through collaborative effort. Resisters will be more likely to listen to your reasoning after you've shown a willingness to listen to theirs, so calmly explain again why the change is in the organization's best interests. Even if you pursue the original plan without modification, those who initially resisted will now be more likely to cooperate and contribute.

Collaborating on Communication Efforts

When a team collaborates on reports, websites, presentations, and other communication projects, the collective energy and expertise of the various members can produce results that transcend what each individual could do alone.[25] However, collaborating on team messages requires special effort and planning.

GUIDELINES FOR COLLABORATIVE WRITING

In any collaborative effort, team members coming from different backgrounds may have different work habits or priorities: A technical expert may focus on accuracy and scientific standards, an editor may be more concerned about organization and coherence, and a manager may focus on schedules, costs, and corporate goals. In addition, team members differ in writing styles, work habits, and personality traits.

To collaborate effectively, everyone must be flexible and open to other opinions, focusing on team objectives rather than on individual priorities.[26] Successful writers know that most ideas can be expressed in many ways, so they avoid the "my way is best" attitude. The following guidelines will help you collaborate more successfully:[27]

- **Select collaborators carefully.** Whenever possible, choose a combination of people who together have the experience, information, and talent needed for each project.
- **Agree on project goals before you start.** Starting without a clear idea of what the team hopes to accomplish inevitably leads to frustration and wasted time.
- **Give your team time to bond before diving in.** If people haven't had the opportunity to work together before, make sure they can get to know each other before being asked to collaborate.
- **Clarify individual responsibilities.** Because members will be depending on each other, make sure individual responsibilities are clear.
- **Establish clear processes.** Make sure everyone knows how the work will be managed from start to finish.
- **Avoid composing as a group.** The actual composition is the only part of collaborative communication that does not usually benefit from group participation. Brainstorming the wording of short pieces of text such as headlines and slogans can be an effective way to stimulate creative word choices. For longer projects, however, it is usually more efficient to plan, research, and outline together but assign the task of writing to one person or divide larger projects among multiple writers. If you divide the writing, try to have one person do a final revision to ensure a consistent style.
- **Make sure tools and techniques are ready and compatible across the team.** Even minor details such as different versions of software can delay projects.
- **Check to see how things are going along the way.** Don't assume that everything is working just because you don't hear anything negative.

TECHNOLOGIES FOR COLLABORATIVE WRITING

A variety of tools and systems are available to help writers collaborate on everything from short documents to entire websites. The simplest tools are software features such as *commenting* (which lets colleagues write comments in a document without modifying the

2 LEARNING OBJECTIVE
Offer guidelines for collaborative communication, identify major collaboration technologies, and explain how to give constructive feedback.

MOBILE APP
The **Basecamp** app provides mobile access to this popular project management system.

Successful collaboration on writing projects requires a number of steps, from selecting the right partners and agreeing on project goals to establishing clear processes and avoiding writing as a group.

A wide variety of collaboration tools now exist to help professionals work on reports, presentations, and other communication efforts.

document text) and *tracking changes* (which lets one or more writers propose changes to the text while keeping everyone's edits separate and reversible). The widely used Adobe Acrobat digital document system (PDFs) also has group review and commenting features, including the option for live collaboration.

Collaboration Systems

Writing for websites often involves the use of a **content management system**, which organizes and controls website content and can include features that help team members work together on webpages and other documents. These tools range from simple blogging systems to more extensive *enterprise* systems that manage web content across an entire corporation. Many systems include *workflow* features that control how pages or documents can be created, edited, and published.

In contrast to the formal controls of a content management system, a **wiki**, from the Hawaiian word for *quick*, is a website that allows anyone with access to add new material and edit existing material. Public wikis (Wikipedia is the best known) allow any registered user to edit pages; private wikis are accessible only with permission. A key benefit of wikis is the freedom to post new or revised material without prior approval. Chapter 8 offers guidelines for effective wiki collaboration.

Teams and other work groups can also take advantage of a set of broader technologies often referred to as *groupware* or *collaboration platforms*. These technologies let people communicate, share files, review previous message threads, work on documents simultaneously, and connect using social networking tools. These systems help companies capture and share knowledge from multiple experts, bringing greater insights to bear on tough challenges.[28] Collaboration systems often take advantage of *cloud computing*, a somewhat vague term that refers to on-demand capabilities delivered over the Internet, rather than through conventional on-site software.[29]

Shared workspaces are online "virtual offices" that give everyone on a team access to the same set of resources and information (see Figure 2.2). You may see some of these workspaces referred to as *intranets* (restricted-access websites that are open to employees only) or *extranets* (restricted sites that are available to employees and to outside parties

> Wiki benefits include simple operation and the ability to post new or revised material instantly without a formal review process.

Figure 2.2   Shared Online Workspaces
Shared online workspaces give employees instant access to the all the files they need, from company reports to website content.

Courtesy of SAP

by invitation only). Many intranets have now evolved into social networking systems that include a variety of communication and collaboration tools, from microblogging to video clip libraries. For example, the performance troupe Blue Man Group uses a *social intranet* to help its 500 employees plan, stage, and promote shows all over the world.[30]

Social Networks and Virtual Communities

Social networking technologies are redefining teamwork and team communication by helping erase the constraints of geographic and organization boundaries. Some companies use social networks to form *virtual communities* or *communities of practice* that link employees with similar professional interests throughout the company and sometimes with customers and suppliers as well.

A *community of practice* links professionals with similar job interests; a key benefit is accumulating long-term organizational knowledge.

Social networks foster collaboration by identifying and connecting the best people to work on each problem or project, no matter where they are around the world or what their official roles are in the organization. Such communities are similar to teams in many respects, but one major difference is in the responsibility for accumulating organizational knowledge over the long term, beyond the duration of any specific project. For example, the pharmaceutical company Pfizer has a number of permanent product-safety communities that provide specialized advice on drug safety issues to researchers throughout the organization.[31]

Internal social networks help companies assemble the best resources for a given task, regardless of where the employees are located.

Social networking can also help a company maintain a sense of community even as it grows beyond the size that normally permits extensive daily interaction. At the online retailer Zappos, fostering a supportive work environment is the company's top priority. To encourage the sense of community among its expanding workforce, Zappos uses social networking tools to track employee connections and encourage workers to reach out and build relationships.[32]

Collaboration via Mobile Devices

Mobile devices add another layer of options for collaborative writing and other communication projects, particularly when used with cloud computing. Today's mobile systems can do virtually everything that fixed-web collaboration systems can do, from writing on virtual whiteboards to sharing photos, videos, and other multimedia files.[33] Mobility lets workers participate in online brainstorming sessions, seminars, and other formal or informal events from wherever they happen to be at the time (see Figure 2.3). This flexibility can

Collaboration apps for mobile devices support nearly all the features of computer-based platforms.

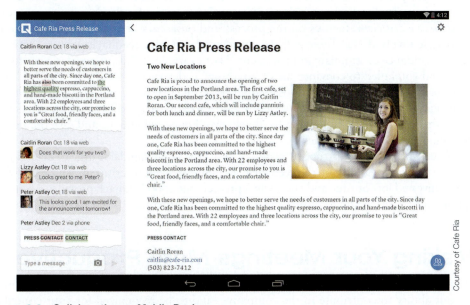

Figure 2.3 Collaboration on Mobile Devices
Mobile connectivity is transforming collaboration activities, helping teams and work groups stay connected no matter where their work takes them. For example, this team was able to discuss and edit a press release using their tablets in different locations.

TABLE 2.2   Giving Constructive Feedback

How to Be Constructive	Explanation
Think through your suggested changes carefully.	Many business documents must illustrate complex relationships between ideas and other information, so isolated and superficial edits can do more harm than good.
Discuss improvements rather than flaws.	Instead of saying "this is confusing," for instance, explain how the writing can be improved to make it clearer.
Focus on controllable behavior.	The writer may not have control over every variable that affected the quality of the message, so focus on those aspects the writer can control.
Be specific.	Comments such as "I don't get this" or "Make this clearer" don't give the writer much direction.
Keep feedback impersonal.	Focus comments on the message, not on the person who created it.
Verify understanding.	If in doubt, ask for confirmation from the recipient to make sure that the person understood your feedback.
Time your feedback carefully.	Respond in a timely fashion so that the writer has sufficient time to implement the changes you suggest.
Highlight any limitations your feedback may have.	If you didn't have time to give the document a thorough edit, or if you're not an expert in some aspect of the content, let the writer know so that he or she can handle your comments appropriately.

be particularly helpful during the review and production stages of major projects, when deadlines are looming and decisions and revisions need to be made quickly.

An important aspect of mobile collaboration and mobile communication in general is **unified communication**, which integrates such capabilities as voice and video calling, voice and video conferencing, instant messaging, and real-time collaboration software into a single system. By minimizing or eliminating the need to manage multiple communication systems and devices, unified communication promises to improve response times, productivity, and collaboration efforts.[34]

REAL-TIME UPDATES

LEARN MORE BY READING THIS ARTICLE

The benefits of mobile collaboration

Going mobile helps teams work faster and more effectively. Go to **real-timeupdates.com/bct14** and select Learn More in the Students section.

GIVING—AND RESPONDING TO—CONSTRUCTIVE FEEDBACK

When you give writing feedback, make it constructive by focusing on how the material can be improved.

Aside from processes and tools, collaborative communication often involves giving and receiving feedback about writing efforts. **Constructive feedback**, sometimes called *constructive criticism*, focuses on the process and outcomes of communication, not on the people involved (see Table 2.2). In contrast, **destructive feedback** delivers criticism with no guidance to stimulate improvement.[35] For example, "This proposal is a confusing mess, and you failed to convince me of anything" is destructive feedback. The goal is to be more constructive: "Your proposal could be more effective with a clearer description of the manufacturing process and a well-organized explanation of why the positives outweigh the negatives." When giving feedback, avoid personal attacks and give the person clear guidelines for improvement.

When you receive constructive feedback on your writing, keep your emotions in check and view it as an opportunity to improve.

When you receive constructive feedback, resist the understandable urge to defend your work or deny the validity of the feedback. Remaining open to criticism isn't easy when you've invested lots of time and energy in a project, but good feedback provides a valuable opportunity to learn and to improve the quality of your work.

Making Your Meetings More Productive

3 LEARNING OBJECTIVE
List the key steps needed to ensure productive team meetings.

Much of your workplace communication will occur during in-person or online meetings, so your ability to contribute to the company—and to be recognized for your contributions—will depend to a large degree on your meeting skills. Well-run meetings can help companies solve problems, develop ideas, and identify opportunities. Meetings can also be a great way to promote team building through the experience of social interaction.[36] As useful as meetings can be, though, they can be a waste of time if they aren't planned and managed well. You can help ensure productive meetings by preparing carefully, conducting meetings efficiently, and using meeting technologies wisely.

PREPARING FOR MEETINGS

The first step in preparing for a meeting is to make sure the meeting is really necessary. Meetings can consume hundreds or thousands of dollars of productive time while taking people away from other work, so don't hold a meeting if some other form of communication (such as a blog post) can serve the purpose as effectively.[37] If a meeting is truly necessary, proceed with these four planning tasks:

- **Define your purpose.** Meetings can focus on exchanging information, reaching decisions, or collaborating to solve problems or identify opportunities. Whatever your purpose, define the best possible result of the meeting (such as "we carefully evaluated all three product ideas and decided which one to invest in"). Use this hoped-for result to shape the direction and content of the meeting.[38]

- **Select participants for the meeting.** The rule here is simple: Invite everyone who really needs to be involved, and don't invite anyone who doesn't. For decision-making meetings, for example, invite only those people who are in a direct position to help the meeting reach its objective. The more people you have, the longer it will take to reach consensus. Meetings with more than 10 or 12 people can become unmanageable if everyone is expected to participate in the discussion and decision making.

- **Choose the venue and the time.** Online meetings (see page 50) are often the best way—and sometimes the only way—to connect people in multiple locations or to reach large audiences. For in-person meetings, review the facility and the seating arrangements. Is theater-style seating suitable, or do you need a conference table or some other layout? Pay attention to room temperature, lighting, ventilation, acoustics, and refreshments; these details can make or break a meeting. If you have control over the timing, morning meetings are often more productive because people are generally more alert and not yet engaged with the work of the day.

- **Set the agenda.** The success of a meeting depends on the preparation of the participants. Distribute a carefully written agenda to participants, giving them enough time to prepare as needed (see Figure 2.4 on the next page). A productive agenda answers three key questions: (1) What do we need to do in this meeting to accomplish our goals? (2) What issues are of greatest importance to all participants? (3) What information must be available in order to discuss these issues?[39]

> To ensure a successful meeting, decide on your purpose ahead of time, select the right participants, choose the venue and time, and set a clear agenda.

CONDUCTING AND CONTRIBUTING TO EFFICIENT MEETINGS

Everyone in a meeting shares the responsibility for making the meeting productive. If you're the leader, however, you have an extra degree of responsibility and accountability. The following guidelines will help leaders and participants contribute to more effective meetings:

> Everyone shares the responsibility for successful meetings.

- **Keep the discussion on track.** A good meeting draws out the best ideas and information the group has to offer. Good leaders occasionally need to guide, mediate, probe, stimulate, summarize, and redirect discussions that have gotten off track.

- **Follow agreed-on rules.** The larger the meeting, the more formal you need to be to maintain order. Formal meetings use **parliamentary procedure**, a time-tested method for planning and running effective meetings. The best-known guide to this procedure is *Robert's Rules of Order*.

- **Encourage participation.** You may discover that some participants are too quiet and others are too talkative. Draw out nonparticipants by asking for their input. For the overly talkative, you can say that time is limited and others need to be heard.

- **Participate actively.** Make a point to contribute to the progress of the meeting and the smooth interaction of participants. Use your listening skills and powers of observation to size up the interpersonal dynamics of the group, then adapt your behavior to

Figure 2.4   Typical Meeting Agenda
Agenda formats vary widely depending on the complexity of the meeting and the presentation technologies that will be used. One good approach is to first distribute a detailed planning agenda so that presenters know what they need in order to prepare, then create a simpler display agenda such as this PowerPoint slide to guide the progress of the meeting. Note how the agenda includes the time limit for each topic.

help the group achieve its goals. Speak up if you have something useful to say, but don't talk or ask questions just to demonstrate how much you know about the subject at hand.

- **Use mobile devices respectfully.** Tweeting key points from a convention speech or using your phone or tablet to jot down essential ideas and follow-up questions can be productive and respectful ways to use a device during a meeting. Checking Facebook or working on unrelated tasks is not. If you intend to use your device to take notes during a meeting, consider letting the meeting leader know that's what you're doing.[40]

- **Close effectively.** At the conclusion of the meeting, verify that the objectives have been met or arrange for follow-up work, if needed. Summarize the general conclusion of the discussion and any actions that need to be taken. Make sure all participants have a chance to clear up any misunderstandings.

PUTTING MEETING RESULTS TO PRODUCTIVE USE

In most cases, the value of a meeting doesn't end when the meeting ends. For example, problems or opportunities brought up during a meeting need to be addressed, any action items assigned during the meeting need to be acted on, and key decisions and announcements should be distributed to anyone who is affected but was unable to attend. Having a written, audio, or video record of a meeting also gives the participants a chance to verify their impressions and conclusions.

The conventional method of recording meetings is through written **minutes**, a summary of the important information presented and the decisions made. One person is usually assigned to keep notes as the meeting progresses and then to share them afterward. The specific format of the minutes is less important than making sure you record all the key information, particularly regarding responsibilities that were assigned during

Minutes are written summaries of important information presented and the decisions made in meetings.

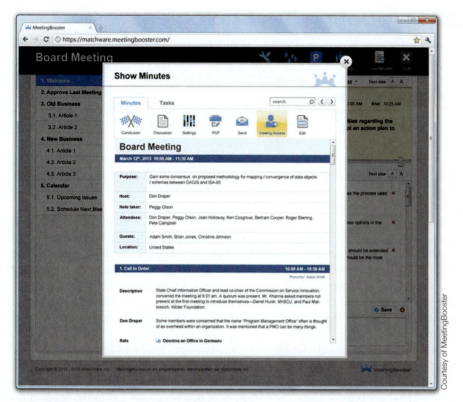

Figure 2.5 Capturing Key Decisions and Discoveries from a Meeting
Meeting technologies such as the MeetingBooster system help teams and other groups capture decisions and discoveries from meetings and put this information to productive use.

the meeting. Typical elements include a list of those present and a list of those who were invited but didn't attend, followed by the times the meeting started and ended, all major decisions reached at the meeting, all tasks assigned to meeting participants, and all subjects that were deferred to a later meeting. In addition, the minutes objectively summarize important discussions, noting the names of those who contributed major points. Any handouts, slides, or supporting documents can be attached to the minutes when they are distributed.

Depending on the meeting technologies at your disposal, you may have software specifically designed to record, distribute, and store meeting minutes (see Figure 2.5). Some systems automatically forward action items to each employee, record audio discussions for future playback, and make all the relevant documents and files available in one convenient place.[41]

To review the tasks that contribute to productive meetings, refer to "Checklist: Improving Meeting Productivity."

CHECKLIST ✔ Improving Meeting Productivity

A. Prepare carefully.
- Make sure the meeting is necessary
- Decide on your purpose
- Select participants carefully
- Choose the venue and the time
- Establish and distribute a clear agenda

B. Lead effectively and participate fully.
- Keep the meeting on track
- Follow agreed-on rules
- Encourage participation
- Participate actively
- Close effectively

C. Put the results to effective use.
- Distribute meeting minutes to participants and other interested parties
- Make sure task assignments are clearly communicated

Using Meeting Technologies

Virtual meeting technologies connect people spread around the country or around the world.

Conducting successful virtual meetings requires extra planning and more diligence during the meeting.

Today's companies use a number of technologies to enhance or even replace traditional in-person meetings. Holding **virtual meetings** can dramatically reduce costs and resource usage, reduce wear and tear on employees, and give teams access to a wider pool of expertise (see Figure 2.6).

Instant messaging (IM) and teleconferencing are the simplest forms of virtual meetings. Videoconferencing lets participants see and hear each other, demonstrate products, and transmit other visual information. *Telepresence* (see Figure 2.7) enables realistic conferences in which participants thousands of miles apart almost seem to be in the same room.[42] The ability to convey nonverbal subtleties such as facial expressions and hand gestures makes these systems particularly good for negotiations, collaborative problem solving, and other complex discussions.[43]

The most sophisticated web-based meeting systems combine the best of real-time communication, shared workspaces, and videoconferencing with other tools, such as *virtual whiteboards*, that let teams collaborate in real time. Such systems are used for everything from spontaneous discussions among small groups to carefully planned formal events such as press conferences, training sessions, sales presentations, and *webinars* (web-based seminars).[44] One of the newest virtual tools is online brainstorming, in which a company can conduct "idea campaigns" to generate new ideas from people across the organization.

Conducting successful virtual meetings requires extra planning beforehand and more diligence during the meeting. Recognizing the limitations of the virtual meeting format is a key to using it successfully.[45] Because virtual meetings offer less visual contact and nonverbal communication than in-person meetings, for example, leaders need to make sure everyone stays engaged and has the opportunity to contribute. Participants have a responsibility to pay attention and avoid the temptation to work on other tasks. To keep everyone focused, make sure the meeting time is dedicated to discussion and interaction, rather than getting everyone up to speed on the issues. Distribute background information before the meeting so that participants can join the meeting ready to collaborate.[46]

For the latest information on meeting technologies, visit **real-timeupdates.com/bct14** and select Chapter 2.

Figure 2.6 Virtual Meetings
With broadband wireless connections, virtual meetings are easy to conduct using smartphones or tablets.

Peter Wynn Thompson/The New York Times/Redux Pictures

Figure 2.7   Telepresence
How many people are actually in this conference room in Chicago? Only the two people in the foreground are in the room; the other participants are in Atlanta or London. Virtual meeting technologies such as this telepresence system connect people spread across the country or around the world.

Improving Your Listening Skills

Your long-term career prospects are closely tied to your ability to listen effectively. In fact, some 80 percent of top executives say listening is the most important skill needed to get things done in the workplace.[47] Plus, today's younger employees place a high premium on being heard, so listening is becoming even more vital for managers.[48]

Effective listening strengthens organizational relationships, alerts the organization to opportunities for innovation, and allows the organization to manage growing diversity both among the workforce and among the customers it serves.[49] Companies whose employees and managers listen effectively are able to stay informed, up to date, and out of trouble. Conversely, poor listening skills can cost companies millions of dollars per year as a result of lost opportunities, legal mistakes, and other errors. Effective listening is also vital to the process of building trust between organizations and between individuals.[50]

RECOGNIZING VARIOUS TYPES OF LISTENING

Effective listeners adapt their listening approaches to different situations. The primary goal of **content listening** is to understand and retain the information in the speaker's message. Because you're not evaluating the information at this point, it doesn't matter whether you agree or disagree, approve or disapprove—only that you understand. Try to overlook the speaker's style and any limitations in the presentation; just focus on the information.[51]

The goal of **critical listening** is to understand and evaluate the meaning of the speaker's message on several levels: the logic of the argument, the strength of the evidence, the validity of the conclusions, the implications of the message, the speaker's intentions and motives, and the omission of any important or relevant points. If you're skeptical, ask questions to explore the speaker's point of view and credibility. Be on the lookout for bias that could color the way the information is presented, and be careful to separate opinions from facts.[52]

The goal of **empathic listening** is to understand the speaker's feelings, needs, and wants so that you can appreciate his or her point of view, regardless of whether you share that perspective. By listening with empathy, you help the individual vent the emotions that

5   LEARNING OBJECTIVE
Identify three major modes of listening, describe the listening process, and explain the problem of selective listening.

Listening is one of the most important skills in the workplace.

To be a good listener, adapt the way you listen to suit the situation.

prevent a calm, clear-headed approach to the subject. Avoid the temptation to jump in with advice unless the person specifically asks for it. Also, don't judge the speaker's feelings, and don't try to tell people they shouldn't feel this or that emotion. Instead, let the speaker know that you appreciate his or her feelings and understand the situation. After you establish that connection, you can help the speaker move on to search for a solution.[53]

No matter what mode they are using at any given time, effective listeners try to engage in **active listening**, making a conscious effort to turn off their own filters and biases to truly hear and understand what the other party is saying. They ask questions to verify key points and encourage the speaker through positive body language.[54]

Listening actively means making the effort to turn off your internal "filters" and biases to truly hear and understand what the other person is saying.

UNDERSTANDING THE LISTENING PROCESS

Listening is a far more complex process than most people think—and most of us aren't very good at it. People typically listen at no better than a 25 percent efficiency rate, remember only about half of what's said during a 10-minute conversation, and forget half of that within 48 hours.[55] Furthermore, when questioned about material they've just heard, they are likely to get the facts mixed up.[56]

Why is such a seemingly simple activity so difficult? The reason is that listening is not a simple process, by any means. Listening follows the same sequence as the general communication process model described in Chapter 1 (page 10), with the added challenge that it happens in real time. To listen effectively, you need to successfully complete five steps:[57]

Listening involves five steps: receiving, decoding, remembering, evaluating, and responding.

1. **Receiving.** You start by physically hearing the message and acknowledging it. Physical reception can be blocked by noise, impaired hearing, or inattention. Some experts also include nonverbal messages as part of this stage because these factors influence the listening process as well.
2. **Decoding.** Your next step is to assign meaning to the words and phrases, which you do according to your own values, beliefs, ideas, expectations, roles, needs, and personal history. Decoding is also influenced by the circumstances, the speaker's tone, facial gestures, and other nonverbal signals. For example, if someone says, "Well, that's just lovely," a sarcastic tone signals that the intended meaning is the opposite of the literal meaning of the words.
3. **Remembering.** Before you can act on the information, you need to store it for future processing. As you learned in Chapter 1, incoming messages must first be captured in short-term memory before being transferred to long-term memory for more permanent storage.
4. **Evaluating.** The next step is to evaluate the message by applying critical thinking skills to separate fact from opinion and evaluate the quality of the evidence.
5. **Responding.** After you've evaluated the speaker's message, you react. If you're communicating one-on-one or in a small group, the initial response generally takes the form of verbal feedback. If you're one of many in an audience, your initial response may take the form of applause, laughter, or silence. Later, you may act on what you have heard.

If any one of these steps breaks down, the listening process becomes less effective or may even fail entirely. As both a sender and a receiver, you can reduce the failure rate by recognizing and overcoming a variety of physical and mental barriers to effective listening.

OVERCOMING BARRIERS TO EFFECTIVE LISTENING

Good listeners actively try to overcome barriers to successful listening.

Good listeners look for ways to overcome potential barriers throughout the listening process (see Table 2.3). You may not be able to control some factors, such as conference room acoustics or poor phone reception. You can control other factors, however, such as not interrupting speakers and not creating distractions that make it difficult for others to pay attention. And don't think you're not interrupting just because you're not talking.

TABLE 2.3   What Makes an Effective Listener?

Effective Listeners	Ineffective Listeners
Listen actively	Listen passively
Take careful and complete notes, when applicable	Take no notes or ineffective notes
Make frequent eye contact with the speaker (depends on culture to some extent)	Make little or no eye contact—or inappropriate eye contact
Stay focused on the speaker and the content	Allow their minds to wander, are easily distracted, work on unrelated tasks
Mentally paraphrase key points to maintain attention level and ensure comprehension	Fail to paraphrase
Adjust listening style to the situation	Listen with the same style, regardless of the situation
Give the speaker nonverbal cues (such as nodding to show agreement or raising eyebrows to show surprise or skepticism)	Fail to give the speaker nonverbal feedback
Save questions or points of disagreement until an appropriate time	Interrupt whenever they disagree or don't understand
Overlook stylistic differences and focus on the speaker's message	Are distracted by or unduly influenced by stylistic differences; are judgmental
Make distinctions between main points and supporting details	Are unable to distinguish main points from details
Look for opportunities to learn	Assume they already know everything that's important to know

Sources: Madelyn Burley-Allen, *Listening: The Forgotten Skill* (New York: Wiley, 1995), 70–71, 119–120; Judi Brownell, *Listening: Attitudes, Principles, and Skills* (Boston: Allyn & Bacon, 2002), 3, 9, 83, 89, 125; Larry Barker and Kittie Watson, *Listen Up* (New York: St. Martin's, 2000), 8, 9, 64.

Such actions as texting or checking your watch can interrupt a speaker and lead to communication breakdowns.

Selective listening is one of the most common barriers to effective listening. If your mind wanders, you may stay tuned out until you hear a word or phrase that gets your attention again. But by that time, you're unable to recall what the speaker *actually* said; instead, you remember what you think the speaker *probably* said.[58]

One reason listeners' minds tend to wander is that people think faster than they speak. Most people speak at about 120 to 150 words per minute, but listeners can process audio information at up to 500 words per minute or more.[59] Consequently, your brain has a lot of free time whenever you're listening, and if left unsupervised, it will find a thousand other things to think about. Make the effort to focus on the speaker and use the extra time to analyze and paraphrase what you hear or to take relevant notes.

Overcoming interpretation barriers can be difficult because you may not even be aware of them. As Chapter 1 notes, selective perception leads listeners to mold messages to fit their own conceptual frameworks. Listeners sometimes make up their minds before fully hearing the speaker's message, or they engage in *defensive listening*—protecting their egos by tuning out anything that doesn't confirm their beliefs or their view of themselves.

Even when your intentions are good, you can still misinterpret incoming messages if you and the speaker don't share enough language or experience. When listening to a speaker whose native language or life experience is different from yours, try to paraphrase that person's ideas. Give the speaker a chance to confirm what you think you heard or to correct any misinterpretation.

If the information you hear will be important to use later, write it down or otherwise record it. Don't rely on your memory. If you do need to memorize, you can hold information in short-term memory by repeating it silently or organizing a long list of items into several shorter lists. Four techniques can help to store information in long-term memory: (1) associate new information with something closely related (such as the restaurant in which you met a new client), (2) categorize the new information into logical groups (such as alphabetizing a list of names), (3) visualize words and ideas as pictures, and (4) create mnemonics such as acronyms or rhymes.

For a reminder of the steps you can take to overcome listening barriers, see "Checklist: Overcoming Barriers to Effective Listening."

Your mind can process information much faster than most speakers talk, so you need to focus to listen effectively.

CHECKLIST ✔ Overcoming Barriers to Effective Listening

- Lower barriers to message reception whenever you can (such as avoiding interrupting speakers by asking questions or by exhibiting disruptive nonverbal behaviors).
- Avoid selective listening by focusing on the speaker and carefully analyzing what you hear.
- Keep an open mind by avoiding any prejudgment and by not listening defensively.

- Don't count on your memory; write down or record important information.
- Improve your short-term memory by repeating information or breaking it into shorter lists.
- Improve your long-term memory by using association, categorization, visualization, and mnemonics.

Improving Your Nonverbal Communication Skills

6 LEARNING OBJECTIVE
Explain the importance of nonverbal communication, and identify six major categories of nonverbal expression.

Nonverbal communication can supplement or even replace verbal messages (those that use words).

Nonverbal communication is the interpersonal process of sending and receiving information, both intentionally and unintentionally, without using written or spoken language. Nonverbal signals play a vital role in communication because they can strengthen a verbal message (when the nonverbal signals match the spoken words), weaken a verbal message (when nonverbal signals don't match the words), or replace words entirely. For example, you might tell a client that a project is coming along nicely, but your forced smile and nervous glances will send an entirely different message.

RECOGNIZING NONVERBAL COMMUNICATION

You've been tuned in to nonverbal communication since your first contact with other human beings. Paying special attention to nonverbal signals in the workplace will enhance your ability to communicate successfully. Moreover, as you work with a diverse range of people in the global marketplace, you'll also need to grasp the different meanings of common gestures, expressions, and other signals in various cultures. Six types of signals are particularly important:

Nonverbal signals include facial expression, gesture and posture, vocal characteristics, personal appearance, touch, and time and space.

- **Facial expression.** Your face is the primary vehicle for expressing your emotions; it reveals both the type and the intensity of your feelings.[60] Your eyes are especially effective for indicating attention and interest, influencing others, regulating interaction, and establishing dominance.[61]
- **Gesture and posture.** The way you position and move your body expresses both specific and general messages, some voluntary and some involuntary. Many gestures—a wave of the hand, for example—have specific and intentional meanings. Other types of body movement are unintentional and express more general messages. Slouching, leaning forward, fidgeting, and walking briskly are all unconscious signals that can reveal whether you feel confident or nervous, friendly or hostile, assertive or passive, powerful or powerless.
- **Vocal characteristics.** Voice carries both intentional and unintentional messages. A speaker can intentionally control pitch, pace, and stress to convey a specific message. For instance, compare "*What* are you doing?" and "What are *you* doing?" Unintentional vocal characteristics can convey happiness, surprise, fear, and other emotions (for example, fear often increases the pitch and pace of your speaking voice).
- **Personal appearance.** People respond to others on the basis of their physical appearance, sometimes fairly and other times unfairly. Although an individual's body type and facial features impose some limitations on appearance, you can control grooming, clothing, accessories, piercings, tattoos, and hairstyle. To make a good impression, adopt the style of the people you want to impress. Many employers also have guidelines concerning attire, body art, and other issues, so make sure you understand and follow them.[62]
- **Touch.** Touch is an important way to convey warmth, comfort, and reassurance—as well as control. Touch is so powerful, in fact, that it is governed by cultural customs

that establish who can touch whom and how in various circumstances. Even within each culture's norms, however, individual attitudes toward touch vary widely. A manager might be comfortable using hugs to express support or congratulations, but his or her subordinates could interpret those hugs as a show of dominance or sexual interest.[63] Touch is a complex subject. The best advice: When in doubt, don't touch.

- **Time and space.** Like touch, time and space can be used to assert authority, imply intimacy, and send other nonverbal messages. For instance, some people try to demonstrate their own importance or disregard for others by making other people wait; others show respect by being on time. Similarly, taking care not to invade private space, such as standing too close when talking, is a way to show respect for others. Keep in mind that expectations regarding both time and space vary by culture.

USING NONVERBAL COMMUNICATION EFFECTIVELY

Paying attention to nonverbal cues makes you a better speaker and a better listener. When you're talking, be more conscious of the nonverbal cues you could be sending. Are they effective without being manipulative? Consider a situation in which an employee has come to you to talk about a raise. This situation is stressful for the employee, so don't say you're interested in what she has to tell you and then spend your time glancing at your computer or checking your watch. Conversely, if you already know you won't be able to give her the raise, be honest in your expression of emotions. Don't overcompensate for your own stress by smiling too broadly or shaking her hand too vigorously. Both nonverbal signals would raise her hopes without justification. In either case, match your nonverbal cues to the tone of the situation.

Also consider the nonverbal signals you send when you're not talking—the clothes you wear, the way you sit, the way you walk (see Figure 2.8). Are you talking like a serious business professional but dressing like you belong in a dance club or a frat house? Whether or not you think it is fair to be judged on superficial matters, the truth is that you *are* judged this way. Don't let careless choices or disrespectful habits undermine all the great work you're doing on the job.

When you listen, be sure to pay attention to the speaker's nonverbal cues. Do they amplify the spoken words or contradict them? Is the speaker intentionally using nonverbal

Work to make sure your non-verbal signals match the tone and content of your spoken communication.

What signals does your personal appearance send?

Radoslaw Korga/Shutterstock

Figure 2.8   Nonverbal Signals
The nonverbal signals you send in any business setting influence how others perceive you and your ideas.

CHECKLIST ✔ Improving Nonverbal Communication Skills

- Understand the roles that nonverbal signals play in communication, complementing verbal language by strengthening, weakening, or replacing words.
- Note that facial expressions (especially eye contact) reveal the type and intensity of a speaker's feelings.
- Watch for cues from gestures and posture.
- Listen for vocal characteristics that can signal the emotions underlying the speaker's words.

- Recognize that listeners are influenced by physical appearance.
- Be careful with physical contact; touch can convey positive attributes but can also be interpreted as dominance or sexual interest. If there is any doubt, don't touch.
- Pay attention to the use of time and space.

---

signals to send you a message that he or she can't put into words? Be observant, but don't assume that you can "read someone like a book." Nonverbal signals are powerful, but they aren't infallible, particularly if you don't know a person's normal behavioral patterns.[64] For example, contrary to popular belief, avoiding eye contact and covering one's face while talking are not reliable clues that someone is lying. Even when telling the truth, most people don't make uninterrupted eye contact with the listeners, and various gestures such as touching one's face might be normal behavior for particular people.[65] Moreover, these and other behaviors may be influenced by culture (in some cultures, sustained eye contact can be interpreted as a sign of disrespect) or might just be ways of coping with stressful situations.[66]

If something doesn't feel right, ask the speaker an honest and respectful question; doing so may clear everything up, or it may uncover issues you need to explore further. See "Checklist: Improving Nonverbal Communication Skills" for a summary of key ideas regarding nonverbal skills.

Developing Your Business Etiquette

7 LEARNING OBJECTIVE
Explain the importance of business etiquette, and identify four key areas in which good etiquette is essential.

Etiquette is an essential element of every aspect of business communication.

You may have noticed a common thread running through the topics of successful teamwork, productive meetings, effective listening, and nonverbal communication: All these activities depend on mutual respect and consideration among all participants. Nobody wants to work with someone who is rude to colleagues or an embarrassment to the company. Moreover, shabby treatment of others in the workplace can be a huge drain on morale and productivity.[67] Poor etiquette can drive away customers, investors, and other critical audiences—and it can limit your career potential.

This section addresses some key etiquette points to remember when you're in the workplace, out in public, online, and using mobile devices. Long lists of etiquette rules can be difficult to remember, but you can get by in almost every situation by remembering to be aware of your effect on others, treating everyone with respect, and keeping in mind that the impressions you leave behind can have a lasting effect on you and your company. As the etiquette expert Cindy Post Senning points out, "The principles of respect, consideration, and honesty are universal and timeless."[68]

BUSINESS ETIQUETTE IN THE WORKPLACE

Personal appearance can have considerable impact on your success in business.

Workplace etiquette includes a variety of behaviors, habits, and aspects of nonverbal communication. Although it isn't always thought of as an element of etiquette, your personal appearance in the workplace sends a strong signal to managers, colleagues, and customers (see Figure 2.9). Pay attention to the style of dress where you work and adjust your style to match. Expectations for specific jobs, companies, and industries can vary widely. The financial industries tend to be more formal than high-tech firms, for instance, and sales and executive positions usually involve more formal expectations than positions in engineering or manufacturing. Observe others, and don't be afraid to ask for advice. If you're not sure, dress modestly and simply—earn a reputation for what you can do,

Paul Bradbury/OJO Images Ltd/Alamy

Figure 2.9 **Showing Respect for Organizational Culture**
Being aware of expectations for personal appearance in a business setting is not only a sign of respect; it will help keep you from making career-limiting mistakes.

not for what you wear. Table 2.4 offers some general guidelines on assembling a business wardrobe that's cost-effective and flexible.

Grooming is as important as attire. Pay close attention to cleanliness, and avoid using products with powerful scents, such as perfumed soaps, colognes, shampoos, and after-shaves (many people are bothered by these products, and some are allergic to them).

IM and other text-based tools have taken over many exchanges that used to take place over the phone, but phone skills are still essential. Because phone calls lack the visual richness of face-to-face conversations, you have to rely on your attitude and

Your telephone skills will be vital to your business success.

TABLE 2.4 Assembling a Business Wardrobe

1 Smooth and Finished (Start with This)	2 Elegant and Refined (Add This to Column 1)	3 Crisp and Starched (Add This to Column 2)	4 Up-to-the-Minute Trendy (Add This to Column 3)
• Choose well-tailored clothing that fits well; it doesn't have to be expensive, but it does have to fit and be appropriate for business. • Keep buttons, zippers, and hemlines in good repair. • Select shoes that are comfortable enough for long days but neither too casual nor too dressy for the office; keep shoes clean and in good condition. • Make sure the fabrics you wear are clean, are carefully pressed, and do not wrinkle easily. • Choose colors that flatter your height, weight, skin tone, and style; sales advisors in good clothing stores can help you choose.	• Choose form-fitting (but not skin-tight) clothing—not swinging or flowing fabrics, frills, or fussy trimmings. • Choose muted tones and soft colors or classics, such as a dark blue suit or a basic black dress. • If possible, select a few classic pieces of jewelry (such as a string of pearls or diamond cuff links) for formal occasions. • Wear jackets that complement an outfit and lend an air of formality to your appearance. Avoid jackets with more than two tones; one color should dominate.	• Wear blouses or shirts that are or appear starched. • Choose closed top-button shirts or button-down shirt collars, higher-neckline blouses, or long sleeves with French cuffs and cuff links. • Wear creased trousers or skirts with a lower hemline.	• Supplement your foundation with pieces that reflect the latest styles. • Add a few pieces in bold colors but wear them sparingly to avoid a garish appearance. • Embellish your look with the latest jewelry and hairstyles but keep the overall effect looking professional.

COMMUNICATING ACROSS CULTURES

Whose Skin Is This, Anyway?

Generational differences abound in the workplace, but few are quite as visible as *body art*: tattoos, piercings (other than ear lobes), and hair dyes in unconventional colors. According to survey data from the Pew Research Center, people younger than 40 are much more inclined than those older than 40 to display some form of body art. For example, people 26 to 40 years old are four times more likely to have tattoos than people who are 41 to 64 years old.

With such profound differences, it's no surprise that in many workplaces body art has become a contentious issue between employees wanting to express themselves and employers wanting to maintain particular standards of professional appearance. As the employment law attorney Danielle S. Urban notes, the issue gets even more complicated when religious symbolism is involved.

Who is likely to win this battle? Will the body art aficionados who continue to join the workforce and who are now rising up the managerial ranks force a change in what is considered acceptable appearance in the workplace? Or will they be forced to cover up to meet traditional standards?

So far, most companies seem to be relying on the judgment of their employees and managers, rather than enforcing strict guidelines. Many seem to accept that tastes and norms are changing and that body art has become a widespread form of self-expression rather than a mode of rebellion. Starbucks, which used to require employees to hide tattoos under long sleeves, recently revised its policy to allow employees to display tattoos everywhere except on their faces. The semiconductor giant Intel even featured photos of employee tattoos in its online technology newsletter.

Job seekers and active employees are still advised to be discreet, however, particularly with facial piercings and large, visible tattoos. In one recent survey about a third of employers said they would be less likely to promote an employee with visible piercings or tattoos. The nonverbal signals you think you are sending might not be the signals a manager receives—or wants to receive.

CAREER APPLICATIONS

1. Should companies have stricter standards of appearance for "customer-facing" employees than for employees who do not interact with customers? Why or why not?
2. Should companies allow their employees the same freedom of expression and appearance as their customers exhibit? For example, if a firm's clientele tends to be heavily tattooed, should employees be allowed the same freedom? Why or why not?

Sources: "Employers Reveal the Top Factors Preventing Workers' Chance of Promotion in New CareerBuilder Survey," CareerBuilder, 2 July 2015, www .careerbuilder.com; Micah Solomon, "Starbucks to Allow Tattoos, Piercings: Wise or Risky Customer Service, HR Move?" *Forbes*, 17 October 2014, www.forbes .com; "Intel Tattoos Speak Volumes," 17 March 2011, *Intel Free Press*, www .intelfreepress.com; Rita Pyrillis, "Body of Work," *Workforce Management*, November 2010, www.workforce.com; Danielle S. Urban, "What to Do About 'Body Art' at Work," *Workforce Management*, March 2010, www.work force.com; "Tattooed Gen Nexters," Pew Research Center, 9 December 2008, pewresearch.org.

---

tone of voice to convey confidence and professionalism. Here are some important tips for using phones at work (for etiquette points specifically about mobile devices, see page 60):[69]

Basic courtesy on the phone makes communication more efficient and more pleasant for everyone involved.

- **Be conscious of how your voice sounds.** Don't speak in a monotone; vary your pitch and inflections so people know you're interested. Slow down when conversing with people whose native language isn't the same as yours.
- **Be courteous when you call someone.** Identify yourself and your organization, briefly describe why you're calling, and verify that you've called at a good time. Minimize the noise level in your environment as much as possible. For important or complicated conversations, plan what you want to say before calling.
- **Convey a positive, professional attitude when you answer the phone.** Answer promptly and with a smile so that you sound welcoming. Identify yourself and your company (some companies have specific instructions for what to say when you answer). Establish the needs of your caller by asking, "How may I help you?" If you know the caller's name, use it. If you can't answer the caller's questions, either forward the call to a colleague who can or advise the caller on how to get his or her questions resolved. If you do forward a call, put the caller on hold and call the next person yourself to verify that he or she is available.
- **End calls with courtesy and clarity.** Close in a friendly, positive manner and double-check all vital information such as meeting times and dates.

If you never or rarely check your voicemail, disable it or record an outgoing message advising callers to reach you another way.

- **Use your own voicemail features to help callers.** Record a brief, professional-sounding outgoing message for regular use. When you will be away or unable to answer the phone for an extended period, record a temporary greeting that tells callers when you will respond to their messages. If you don't check your messages regularly or at all, disable your voicemail. Letting messages pile up for days or weeks without answering them is extremely thoughtless.

- **Be considerate when leaving voicemail messages.** Retrieving voicemail messages can be a chore, so be thoughtful about leaving them. Unless voicemail is the best or only choice, consider leaving a message through other means, such as text messaging or email. If you do leave a voicemail message, make it as brief as possible. Leave your name, number (don't assume the recipient has caller ID), reason for calling, and times you can be reached. State your name and telephone number slowly so the other person can easily write them down; repeat both if the other person doesn't know you.

BUSINESS ETIQUETTE IN SOCIAL SETTINGS

From business lunches to industry conferences, you may be asked to represent your company in public. Make sure your appearance and actions are appropriate to the situation. Get to know the customs of other cultures when it comes to meeting new people. For example, in North America, a firm handshake is expected when two people meet, whereas a respectful bow of the head is more appropriate in Japan. If you are expected to shake hands, be aware that the passive "dead fish" handshake creates an extremely negative impression for many people. If you are physically able, always stand when shaking someone's hand.

When introducing yourself, include a brief description of your role in the company. When introducing two other people, speak their first and last names clearly and then offer some information (perhaps a shared professional interest) to help the two people ease into a conversation.[70] Generally speaking, the lower-ranking person is introduced to the senior-ranking person, without regard to gender.[71]

Business is often conducted over meals, and knowing the basics of dining etiquette will make you more effective in these situations.[72] Start by choosing foods that are easy to eat. Avoid alcoholic beverages in most instances, but if drinking one is appropriate, save it for the end of the meal. Leave business documents under your chair until entrée plates have been removed; the business aspect of the meal doesn't usually begin until then.

Remember that business meals are a forum for business. Don't discuss politics, religion, or any other topic likely to stir up emotions. Don't complain about work, don't ask deeply personal questions, avoid profanity, and be careful with humor—a joke that entertains some people could easily offend others.

Etiquette is particularly important when you represent your company in public.

MOBILE APP
The **Good Manners** iPhone app helps you make appropriate choices in a variety of social situations.

REAL-TIME UPDATES
LEARN MORE BY WATCHING THIS VIDEO
Dining etiquette simplified
The etiquette expert Barbara Pachter offers tips to help you get comfortable at business lunches and dinners. Go to **real-timeupdates.com/bct14** and select Learn More in the Students section.

BUSINESS ETIQUETTE ONLINE

Digital media seem to be a breeding ground for poor etiquette. Learn the basics of professional online behavior to avoid mistakes that could hurt your company or your career. Here are some guidelines to follow whenever you are representing your company while using digital media:[73]

- **Avoid personal attacks.** The anonymous and instantaneous nature of online communication can cause even level-headed people to strike out in blog postings, social networks, and other media.
- **Stay focused on the original topic.** If you want to change the subject of an email exchange, a forum discussion, or a blog comment thread, start a new message.
- **Don't present opinions as facts, and support facts with evidence.** This guideline applies to all communication, of course, but online venues in particular seem to tempt people into presenting their beliefs and opinions as unassailable truths.

When you represent your company online, you must adhere to a high standard of etiquette and show respect for others.

- **Follow basic expectations of spelling, punctuation, and capitalization.** Sending careless, acronym-filled messages that look like you're texting your high school buddies makes you look like an amateur.
- **Use virus protection and keep it up to date.** Sending or posting a file that contains a computer virus puts others at risk.
- **Use difficult-to-break passwords on email, Twitter, and other accounts.** If someone hacks your account, it can create spam headaches—or worse—for your contacts and followers.
- **Ask if this is a good time for an IM chat.** Don't assume that just because a person is showing as "available" on your IM system that he or she wants to chat at this moment.
- **Watch your language and keep your emotions under control.** A single indiscretion could haunt you forever.
- **Avoid multitasking while using IM and other tools.** You might think you're saving time by doing a dozen things at once, but you're probably making the other person wait while you bounce back and forth between IM and your other tasks.
- **Never assume privacy.** Assume that anything you type will be stored forever, could be forwarded to other people, and might be read by your boss or the company's security staff.
- **Don't use "Reply All" in email unless everyone can benefit from your reply.** If one or more recipients of an email message don't need the information in your reply, remove their addresses before you send.
- **Don't waste others' time with sloppy, confusing, or incomplete messages.** Doing so is disrespectful.

Respect personal and professional boundaries when using Facebook and other social networking tools.

- **Respect boundaries of time and virtual space.** For instance, don't start using an employee's personal Facebook page for business messages unless you've discussed it beforehand, and don't assume people are available to discuss work matters around the clock, even if you do find them online in the middle of the night.
- **Be careful of online commenting mechanisms.** For example, many blogs and websites now use your Facebook login to let you comment on articles. If your Facebook profile includes your job title and company name, those could show up along with your comment.

BUSINESS ETIQUETTE USING MOBILE DEVICES

Your mobile phone habits send a signal about the degree of respect you have for those around you.

Like every other aspect of communication, your mobile device habits say a lot about how much respect you have for the people around you. Selecting obnoxious ringtones, talking loudly in open offices or public places, using your phone right next to someone else, making excessive or unnecessary personal calls during work hours, invading someone's privacy by using your phone's camera without permission, taking or making calls in restrooms and other inappropriate places, texting during a meal or while someone is talking to you, allowing incoming calls to interrupt meetings or discussions—these are all disrespectful choices that reflect negatively on you.[74] In general, older employees, managers, and customers are less tolerant of mobile device use than younger people are, so don't assume that your habits will be universally acceptable.[75]

Virtual assistants and other mobile phone voice features can annoy and disrupt the workplace and social settings if not used with respect for others.

Virtual assistants, such as the Siri voice recognition system in Apple iPhones, raise another new etiquette dilemma. From doing simple web searches to dictating entire memos, these systems may be convenient for users, but they can create distractions and annoyances for other people.[76] As with other public behaviors, think about the effect you have on others before using these technologies.

Note that expectations and policies regarding mobile device use vary widely from company to company. At one extreme, the venture capitalist Ben Horowitz fines his employees if they even look at a mobile device while an entrepreneur is pitching a business plan because he considers it disrespectful to people making presentations.[77] Not all bosses are quite so strict, but make sure you understand the situation in your workplace.

COMMUNICATION CHALLENGES AT **Cemex**

You recently joined Cemex and quickly became an enthusiastic user of the company's Shift collaboration platform, particularly its wiki capability. In your brief time being involved with the wiki, you have observed some behavior that runs counter to the spirit of collaborative writing. Study these two scenarios and decide how to respond.

INDIVIDUAL CHALLENGE: An employee in Spain keeps editing your pages on the wiki, often making changes that seem to add no value as far as you can tell. She doesn't seem to be editing other employees' pages nearly so often, so you are beginning to wonder whether she has a personal grudge against you. You want to address this uncomfortable situation without dragging your boss into it. First, decide how to approach your contentious colleague. Should you call her on the phone, send her an email message, or perhaps insert a sarcastic comment about excessive editing on one of her wiki pages? Second, whichever mode of communication you've chosen, outline the message you think you should share with her.

TEAM CHALLENGE: A common dilemma in every form of collaborative writing is deciding how soon to share early drafts with your colleagues to get their feedback and contributions. Should you send out an unpolished rough draft for the team's input before investing a lot of time in polishing and formatting, or should you do a second or third draft to enhance readability—knowing the team might delete entire sections you've worked hard to polish? On one of the Cemex wikis where you collaborate with colleagues, some contributors seem to go into "grammar attack mode" whenever a rough draft appears. They seem to ignore the message and content altogether and instead focus on punctuation, grammar, and formatting concerns. With a small team of fellow students, draft some brief guidelines for wiki contributors, conveying these three points: (1) Punctuation, grammar, and formatting are definitely important, but worrying about them too early in the writing process can hamper the free exploration of ideas and information. (2) When reviewing early drafts, wiki users need to make a conscious effort to look past the presentation and focus on the information. (3) Contributors who post rough drafts seeking input should make the pages at least minimally readable so that reviewers can focus on the content and ideas. (To learn more about editing and working with wikis, you can peek ahead to page 221 in Chapter 8.)

Quick Learning Guide

KEY TERMS

active listening Making a conscious effort to turn off filters and biases to truly hear and understand what someone is saying

collaboration Working together to meet complex challenges

committees Formal teams that usually have a long life span and can become a permanent part of the organizational structure

constructive feedback Critique that focuses on the process and outcomes of communication, not on the people involved

content listening Listening to understand and retain the speaker's message

content management systems Computer systems that organize and control the content for websites

critical listening Listening to understand and evaluate the meaning of the speaker's message

destructive feedback Criticism delivered with no guidance to stimulate improvement

empathic listening Listening to understand the speaker's feelings, needs, and wants so that you can appreciate his or her point of view

group dynamics Interactions and processes that take place among the members of a team

groupthink Situation in which peer pressure causes individual team members to withhold contrary or unpopular opinions

hidden agenda Private, counterproductive motives, such as a desire to take control of a group

minutes Written summary of the important information presented and the decisions made during a meeting

nonverbal communication Information sent and received, both intentionally and unintentionally, without using written or spoken language

norms Informal standards of conduct that group members share and that guide member behavior

parliamentary procedure A time-tested method for planning and running effective meetings; the best-known guide to this procedure is *Robert's Rules of Order*

participative management An effort to involve employees in a company's decision making

problem-solving teams Teams that assemble to resolve specific issues and then disband when their goals have been accomplished

selective listening Listening to only part of what a speaker is saying; ignoring the parts one doesn't agree with or find interesting

SUMMARY OF LEARNING OBJECTIVES

1 List the advantages and disadvantages of working in teams, describe the characteristics of effective teams, and highlight four key issues of group dynamics. Teams can achieve a higher level of performance than individuals because of the combined intelligence and energy of the group. Motivation and creativity can flourish in team settings. Moreover, individuals tend to perform better because they achieve a sense of purpose by belonging to a group. Teams also bring more input and a greater diversity of views, which tends to result in better decisions. And because team members participate in the decision process, they are more committed to seeing the team succeed. Teams are not without disadvantages, however. Poorly managed teams can be a waste of everyone's time. For example, if members are pressured to conform, they may develop groupthink, which can lead to poor-quality decisions and ill-advised actions. Some members may let their private motives get in the way.

Four important aspects of group dynamics are assuming team roles, allowing for team evolution, resolving conflict, and overcoming resistance.

2 Offer guidelines for collaborative communication, identify major collaboration technologies, and explain how to give constructive feedback. Key guidelines for collaborative writing include (1) carefully selecting collaborators, (2) agreeing on project goals before starting, (3) giving the team time to bond before starting the work, (4) clarifying individual responsibilities, (5) establishing clear processes, (6) avoiding composing as a group, (7) making sure tools and techniques are ready and compatible, and (8) checking to see how things are going along the way.

Major collaboration technologies include web content management systems, wikis, groupware, and shared workspaces.

To give constructive feedback, focus on the work and how it can be improved, rather than on the person and the mistakes.

3 List the key steps needed to ensure productive team meetings. The most important step in planning a meeting is to make sure that a meeting is necessary and is the best way to accomplish the given objective. If it is, proceed by identifying the purpose of the meeting, selecting the right mix of participants to accomplish the goal, choosing the venue and time carefully, and setting a clear agenda.

Once the meeting is under way, work to keep the discussion on track, follow agreed-upon rules, encourage participation, participate actively yourself, and close the meeting effectively to make sure all decisions and action items are clearly understood.

4 Identify the major technologies used to enhance or replace in-person meetings. Meeting enhancement and replacement technologies range from simple audio teleconferencing and IM chat sessions to videoconferences, telepresence systems, web-based meetings, and virtual worlds such as realistic-looking online conference rooms.

5 Identify three major modes of listening, describe the listening process, and explain the problem of selective listening. *Content listening* is listening to understand and retain the information in the speaker's message. *Critical listening* is listening to understand and evaluate the meaning of the speaker's message on several levels, including the logic of the argument and the strength of the evidence. *Empathic listening* is listening to understand the speaker's feelings, needs, and wants. Regardless of the mode used, effective listeners try to engage in *active listening*, making a conscious effort to turn off their own filters and biases to truly hear and understand what the other party is saying.

The listening process involves five activities: (1) receiving (physically hearing the message), (2) decoding (assigning meaning to what you hear), (3) remembering (storing the message for future reference), (4) evaluating (thinking about the message), and (5) responding (reacting to the message, taking action, or giving feedback).

The listening process can be hampered by a variety of barriers, one of the most common of which is selective listening. When people listen selectively, they hear only parts of the speaker's message, because either they allow their minds to wander or they engage in defensive listening by tuning out information that threatens their beliefs or egos.

6 Explain the importance of nonverbal communication and identify six major categories of nonverbal expression. *Nonverbal communication* is important because nonverbal signals can strengthen, weaken, or even replace verbal messages. The major categories of

self-oriented roles Unproductive team roles in which people are motivated mainly to fulfill personal needs

shared workspaces Online "virtual offices" that give everyone on a team access to the same set of resources and information

task forces A form of problem-solving teams, often with members from more than one organization

task-oriented roles Productive team roles directed toward helping a team reach its goals

team A unit of two or more people who share a mission and the responsibility for working to achieve a common goal

team-maintenance roles Productive team roles directed toward helping everyone work well together

unified communication A single system of communication that integrating voice and video calling, voice and video conferencing, instant messaging, real-time collaboration software, and other capabilities

virtual meetings Meetings that take place online rather than in person

wiki Special type of website that allows anyone with access to add new material and edit existing material

nonverbal signals are facial expression, gestures and posture, vocal characteristics, personal appearance, touch, and the use of time and space.

7 **Explain the importance of business etiquette and identify four key areas in which good etiquette is essential.** Attention to etiquette is essential to success in every form of business communication—so much so that etiquette is considered an important business skill. Poor etiquette can hinder team efforts, drain morale and productivity, drive away customers and investors, and limit your career potential. Four key areas in which good etiquette is essential are the workplace, social settings in which you represent your employer, online interactions in which you represent your employer, and when using mobile devices.

MyBCommLab®

Go to **mybcommlab.com** to complete the problems marked with this icon .

Test Your Knowledge

To review chapter content related to each question, refer to the indicated Learning Objective.

2-1. How can organizations and employees benefit from successful teamwork? [LO-1]

2-2. What is groupthink, and how can it affect an organization? [LO-1]

2-3. How can employees and companies take advantage of social networking technologies to promote teamwork? [LO-2]

2-4. What is parliamentary procedure? [LO-3]

2-5. What are the advantages of virtual meetings? [LO-4]

2-6. What are the main activities that make up the listening process? [LO-5]

2-7. How does content listening differ from critical listening and empathic listening? [LO-5]

2-8. What are the six major categories of nonverbal communication? [LO-6]

2-9. Why do mobile devices present unique etiquette challenges? [LO-7]

Apply Your Knowledge

To review chapter content related to each question, refer to the indicated Learning Objective.

2-10. You head up the interdepartmental design review team for a manufacturer of high-performance motorcycles, and things are not going well. The design engineers and marketing strategists keep arguing about which should be a higher priority, performance or aesthetics, and the accountants say both groups are driving up the cost of the new model by adding too many new features. Everyone has valid points to make, but the team is bogging down in conflict. Explain how you could go about resolving the stalemate. [LO-1]

2-11. You and another manager in your company disagree about whether employees should be encouraged to create online profiles on LinkedIn and other business-oriented social networking websites. You say these connections can be valuable to employees by helping them meet their peers throughout the industry and valuable to the company by identifying potential sales leads and business partners. The other manager says that encouraging employees to become better known in the industry will only make it easier for competitors to lure them away with enticing job offers. Write a brief email message that outlines your argument. (Make up any information you need about the company and its industry.) [LO-2]

2-12. How can nonverbal communication help you run a meeting? How can it help you call a meeting to order, emphasize important topics, show approval, express reservations, regulate the flow of conversation, and invite a colleague to continue with a comment? [LO-3], [LO-6]

2-13. Why do you think people are more likely to engage in rude behaviors during online communication than during in-person communication? [LO-7]

2-14. You're giving your first major presentation at your new job and you notice at least half the people in the small conference room are looking at their mobile devices more than they are looking at you. How should you handle the situation? [LO-7]

Practice Your Skills

2-15. **Message for Analysis: Planning Meetings [LO-3]**
A project leader has made notes about covering the following items at the quarterly budget meeting. Prepare a formal agenda by putting these items into a logical order and rewriting, where necessary, to give phrases a more consistent sound.

- Budget Committee Meeting to be held on December 12, 2018, at 9:30 a.m., and we have allotted one hour for the meeting
- I will call the meeting to order.
- Real estate director's report: A closer look at cost overruns on Greentree site. (10 minutes)
- The group will review and approve the minutes from last quarter's meeting. (5 minutes)
- I will ask the finance director to report on actual versus projected quarterly revenues and expenses. (15 minutes)
- I will distribute copies of the overall divisional budget and announce the date of the next budget meeting.
- Discussion: How can we do a better job of anticipating and preventing cost overruns? (20 minutes)
- Meeting will take place in Conference Room 3, with WebEx active for remote employees.
- What additional budget issues must be considered during this quarter?

Exercises

Each activity is labeled according to the primary skill or skills you will need to use. To review relevant chapter content, you can refer to the indicated Learning Objective. In some instances, supporting information will be found in another chapter, as indicated.

2-16. **Collaboration: Working in Teams [LO-1], [LO-2]** In teams assigned by your instructor, prepare a 10-minute presentation on the potential disadvantages of using social media for business communication. When the presentation is ready, discuss how effective the team was using the criteria of (a) having a clear objective and a shared sense of purpose, (b) communicating openly and honestly, (c) reaching decisions by consensus, (d) thinking creatively, and (e) knowing how to resolve conflict. Be prepared to discuss your findings with the rest of the class.

2-17. **Negotiation and Conflict Resolution: Resolving Conflicts; Communication Ethics: Providing Ethical Leadership [LO-1], Chapter 1** During team meetings, one member constantly calls for votes or decisions before all the members have voiced their views. As the leader, you asked this member privately about his behavior. He replied that he is trying to move the team toward its goals, but you are concerned that he is really trying to take control. How can you deal with this situation without removing the member from the group?

2-18. **Collaboration: Collaborating on Writing Projects; Media Skills: Blogging [LO-2]** In this project you will conduct research on your own and then merge your results with those of the rest of your team. Search Twitter for messages on the subject of workplace safety. (You can use Twitter's advanced search function or use the "twitter.com" site qualifier on a regular search engine.) Compile at least five general safety tips that apply to any office setting, and then meet with your team to select the five best tips from all those the team has collected. Collaborate on a blog post that lists the team's top five tips.

2-19. **Communication Etiquette: Etiquette in the Workplace, Participating in Meetings [LO-3], [LO-7]** In group meetings, some of your colleagues have a habit of interrupting and arguing with the speaker, taking credit for ideas that aren't theirs, and shooting down ideas they don't agree with. As the newest person in the group, you're not sure if this is accepted behavior in this company, but it concerns you both personally and professionally. Should you go with the flow and adopt their behavior or stick with your own communication style, even though you might get lost in the noise? In a two-paragraph email message or post for your class blog, explain the pros and cons of both approaches.

2-20. **Collaboration: Participating in Meetings [LO-3]** With a classmate, attend a local community or campus meeting where you can observe a group discussion, vote, or take other group action. Take notes individually during the meeting and, afterward, work together to answer the following questions.

a. What is your evaluation of this meeting? In your answer, consider (1) the leader's ability to clearly articulate the meeting's goals, (2) the leader's ability to engage members in a meaningful discussion, (3) the group's dynamics, and (4) the group's listening skills.

b. How did group members make decisions? Did they vote? Did they reach decisions by consensus? Did those with dissenting opinions get an opportunity to voice their objections?

c. How well did the individual participants listen? How could you tell?

d. Did any participants change their expressed views or their votes during the meeting? Why might that have happened?

e. Did you observe any of the communication barriers discussed in Chapter 1? Identify them.

f. Compare the notes you took during the meeting with those of your classmate. What differences do you notice? How do you account for these differences?

2-21. **Collaboration: Leading Meetings [LO-3], Chapter 3** Every month, each employee in your department is expected to give a brief oral presentation on the status of his or her project. However, your department has recently hired an employee who has a severe speech impediment that prevents people from understanding most of what he says. As the department manager, how will you resolve this dilemma? Please explain.

2-22. **Collaboration: Using Collaboration Technologies [LO-4]** In a team assigned by your instructor, use Zoho (free for personal use) or a comparable system to collaborate on a set of directions that out-of-town visitors could use to reach a specific point on your campus, such as a stadium or dorm. The team should choose the location and the mode(s) of transportation involved. Be creative—brainstorm the best ways to guide first-time visitors to the selected location using all the media at your disposal.

2-23. **Interpersonal Communication: Listening Actively [LO-5]** For the next several days, take notes on your listening performance during at least a half-dozen situations in class, during social activities, and at work, if applicable. Referring to the traits of effective listeners in Table 2.3, rate yourself on these positive listening habits using *always*, *frequently*, *occasionally*, or *never*. In a report no longer than one page, summarize your analysis and identify specific areas in which you can improve your listening skills.

2-24. **Nonverbal Communication: Analyzing Nonverbal Signals [LO-6]** Select a business letter and envelope you have received at work or home. Analyze their appearance. What nonverbal messages do they send? Are these messages consistent with the content of the letter? If not, what could the sender have done to make the nonverbal communication consistent with the verbal communication? Summarize your findings in a post on your class blog or in an email message to your instructor.

2-25. **Communication Etiquette: Etiquette in the Workplace [LO-7]** As the regional manager of an international accounting firm, you place high priority on professional etiquette. Not only does it communicate respect to your clients, it also instills confidence in your firm by showing that you and your staff are aware of and able to meet the expectations of almost any audience. Earlier today you took four new employees to lunch with an important client. You've done this for years, and it's usually an upbeat experience for everyone, but today's lunch was a disaster. One of the employees made not one, not two, but three calls on his mobile phone during lunch. Another interrupted the client several times and even got into a mild argument. The third employee kept telling sarcastic jokes about politics, making everyone at the table uncomfortable. And the fourth showed up dressed like she was expecting to bale hay or work in a coal mine, not have a business lunch in a posh restaurant. You've already called the client to apologize, but now you need to coach these employees on proper business etiquette. Draft a brief memo to these employees, explaining why etiquette is so important to the company's success—and to their individual careers.

Expand Your Skills

Critique the Professionals

Celebrities can learn from successful businesses when it comes to managing their careers, but businesses can learn from successful celebrities, too—particularly when it comes to building communities online using social media. Locate three celebrities (musicians, actors, authors, or athletes) who have sizable fan bases on Facebook and analyze how they use the social network. Using whatever medium your instructor requests, write a brief analysis (no more than one page) of the lessons, positive or negative, that a business could learn from these celebrities. Be sure to cite specific elements from the Facebook pages you've chosen, and if you think any of the celebrities have made mistakes in their use of Facebook, describe those as well.

Sharpening Your Career Skills Online

Bovée and Thill's Business Communication Web Search, at **websearch.businesscommunicationnetwork.com,** is a unique research tool designed specifically for business communication research. Use the Web Search function to find a website, video, article, podcast, or presentation that offers advice on improving your active listening skills in business situations. Write a brief email message to your instructor, describing the item you found and summarizing the career skills information you learned from it.

MyBCommLab

Go to **mybcommlab.com** for Auto-graded writing questions as well as the following Assisted-graded writing questions:

2-26. Should teams try to resolve all conflicts that come up in the course of doing their work? Why or why not? [LO-1]

2-27. Considering what you've learned about nonverbal communication, what are some of the ways in which communication might break down during an online meeting in which the participants can see video images of only the person presenting at any given time—and then only his or her head? [LO-6]

Endnotes

1. "Company Profile," Cemex website, accessed 8 March 2016, www.cemex.com; "Transforming the Way We Work," Cemex website, accessed 8 February 2015, www.cemex.com; *Cemex: Building the Future*, accessed 11 May 2013, www.cemex.com; Cemex Shift Twitter account, accessed 11 May 2013, twitter.com/CX_Shift; Dion Hinchcliffe, "Social Business Success: CEMEX," *ZDNet*, 1 February 2012, www.zdnet.com; "Cemex and Becoming a Social Business with IBM Software," video embedded in Jesus Gilberto Garcia, Miguel Angel Lozano Martinez, and Arturo San Vicente, "Shift Changes the Way Cemex Works," *Management Exchange*, 15 July 2011, www.managementexchange.com; Debra Donston-Miller, "Social Business Leader Cemex Keeps Ideas Flowing," *InformationWeek*, 6 November 2012, www.informationweek.co.uk.

2. Courtland L. Bovée and John V. Thill, *Business in Action*, 5th ed. (Upper Saddle River, N.J.: Pearson Prentice Hall, 2011), 172.

3. "Five Case Studies on Successful Teams," *HR Focus*, April 2002, 18+.

4. Stephen R. Robbins, *Essentials of Organizational Behavior*, 6th ed. (Upper Saddle River, N.J.: Prentice Hall, 2000), 98.

5. Max Landsberg and Madeline Pfau, "Developing Diversity: Lessons from Top Teams," *Strategy + Business*, Winter 2005, 10–12.

6. "Groups Best at Complex Problems," *Industrial Engineer*, June 2006, 14.

7. Natalie D. Brecher, "Breaking Bad: Stop Deceptive Groupthink," *Journal of Property Management* 80, no. 6 (November–December 2015): 45.

8. Rob Cross, Reb Rebele, and Adam Grant, "Collaborative Overload," *Harvard Business Review*, January–February 2016, 74–79.

9. Martha Mendoza and Michael Liedtke, "Google Study of Teamwork Finds 'How' Is More Important Than 'Who,'" *Columbus Dispatch*, 23 November 2015, www.dispatch.com; Nicola A. Nelson, "Leading Teams," *Defense AT&L*, July–August 2006, 26–29; Larry Cole and Michael Cole, "Why Is the Teamwork Buzz Word Not Working?" *Communication World*, February–March 1999, 29; Patricia Buhler, "Managing in the 90s: Creating Flexibility in Today's Workplace," *Supervision*, January 1997, 241; Allison W. Amason, Allen C. Hochwarter, Wayne A. Thompson, and Kenneth R. Harrison, "Conflict: An Important Dimension in Successful Management Teams," *Organizational Dynamics* 24, no. 2 (August 1995): 201.

10. David Dye, "Broken Teamwork," *Leadership Excellence Essentials*, February 2016, 16.

11. Geoffrey Colvin, "Why Dream Teams Fail," *Fortune*, 8 June 2006, 87–92.

12. Tiziana Casciaro and Miguel Sousa Lobo, "Competent Jerks, Lovable Fools, and the Formation of Social Networks," *Harvard Business Review*, June 2005, 92–99.

13. Stephen P. Robbins and David A. DeCenzo, *Fundamentals of Management: Essential Concepts and Applications*, 4th ed. (Upper Saddle River, N.J.: Prentice Hall, 2004), 266–267; Jerald Greenberg and Robert A. Baron, *Behavior in Organizations*, 8th ed. (Upper Saddle River, N.J.: Prentice Hall, 2003), 279–280.

14. B. Aubrey Fisher, *Small Group Decision Making: Communication and the Group Process*, 2nd ed. (New York: McGraw-Hill, 1980), 145–149; Robbins and DeCenzo, *Fundamentals of Management*, 334–335; Richard L. Daft, *Management*, 6th ed. (Cincinnati: Thomson South-Western, 2003), 602–603.

15. Michael Laff, "Effective Team Building: More Than Just Fun at Work," *Training + Development* 6, no. 8 (August 2006): 24–35.

16. Claire Sookman, "Building Your Virtual Team," *Network World*, 21 June 2004, 91.

17. Jared Sandberg, "Brainstorming Works Best if People Scramble for Ideas on Their Own," *Wall Street Journal*, 13 June 2006, B1.

18. Mark K. Smith, "Bruce W. Tuckman—Forming, Storming, Norming, and Performing in Groups," Infed.org, accessed 5 July 2005, www.infed.org.

19. Robbins and DeCenzo, *Fundamentals of Management*, 258–259.

20. Daft, *Management*, 609–612.

21. Andy Boynton and Bill Fischer, *Virtuoso Teams: Lessons from Teams That Changed Their Worlds* (Harrow, UK: FT Press, 2005), 10.

22. Thomas K. Capozzoli, "Conflict Resolution—A Key Ingredient in Successful Teams," *Supervision* 56, no. 12 (November 1999), 14–16.

23. Amy Gallo, "Choose the Right Words in an Argument," *Harvard Business Review*, 16 June 2014, hbr.org.

24. Mark Goulston, "Practical Tips for Overcoming Resistance," *Harvard Business Review*, 1 July 2013, hbr.org.

25. Jon Hanke, "Presenting as a Team," *Presentations*, January 1998, 74–82.

26. William P. Galle Jr., Beverly H. Nelson, Donna W. Luse, and Maurice F. Villere, *Business Communication: A Technology-Based Approach* (Chicago: Irwin, 1996), 260.

27. Mary Beth Debs, "Recent Research on Collaborative Writing in Industry," *Technical Communication* 38, no. 4 (November 1991): 476–484.

28. Rob Koplowitz, "Building a Collaboration Strategy," *KM World*, November/December 2009, 14–15.

29. Eric Knorr and Galen Gruman, "What Cloud Computing Really Means," *InfoWorld*, 3 May 2012, www.infoworld.com; Lamont Wood, "Cloud Computing Poised to Transform Communication," *LiveScience*, 8 December 2009, www.livescience.com.

30. "How Blue Man Group Gets Creative with Its Social Intranet," Socialtext website, accessed 1 May 2012, www.socialtext.com.

31. Richard McDermott and Douglas Archibald, "Harnessing Your Staff's Informal Networks," *Harvard Business Review*, March 2010, 82–89.

32. Tony Hsieh, "Why I Sold Zappos," *Inc.*, 1 June 2010, www.inc.com.

33. "Adobe Connect Mobile," Adobe website, accessed 27 February 2014, www.adobe.com.

34. Parks Associates, "Mobile Collaborative Communications for Business," white paper, accessed 27 February 2014, www.parksassociates.com.

35. Chuck Williams, *Management*, 2nd ed. (Cincinnati: Thomson South-Western, 2002), 706–707.

36. Ron Ashkenas, "Why We Secretly Love Meetings," *Harvard Business Review* blogs, 5 October 2010, blogs.hbr.org.

37. Douglas Kimberly, "Ten Pitfalls of Pitiful Meetings," *Payroll Manager's Report*, January 2010, 1, 11; "Making the Most of Meetings," *Journal of Accountancy*, 28 February 2009, 22.

38. Cyrus Farivar, "How to Run an Effective Meeting," BNET website, accessed 12 August 2008, www.bnet.com.

39. "Better Meetings Benefit Everyone: How to Make Yours More Productive," *Working Communicator Bonus Report*, July 1998, 1.

40. Janine Popick, "Business Meeting Etiquette: 8 Pet Peeves," *Inc.*, 9 April 2012, www.inc.com.

41. "Features Overview," MeetingSense website, accessed 11 May 2013, www.meetingsense.com.

42. Roger O. Crockett, "The 21st Century Meeting," *BusinessWeek*, 26 February 2007, 72–79.

43. Steve Lohr, "As Travel Costs Rise, More Meetings Go Virtual," *New York Times*, 22 July 2008, www.nytimes.com.

44. GoToMeeting website, accessed 3 May 2012, www.gotomeeting .com; "Unlock the Full Power of the Web Conferencing," *CEO World*, 20 November 2007, www.ceoworld.biz.

45. Nick Morgan, "How to Conduct a Virtual Meeting," *Harvard Business Review* blogs, 1 March 2011, blogs.hbr.org.

46. Keith Ferrazzi, "How to Run a Great Virtual Meeting," *Harvard Business Review*, 27 March 2015, www.hbr.org.

47. Judi Brownell, *Listening*, 2nd ed. (Boston: Allyn & Bacon, 2002), 9, 10.

48. Carmine Gallo, "Why Leadership Means Listening," *Business-Week*, 31 January 2007, www.businessweek.com.

49. Augusta M. Simon, "Effective Listening: Barriers to Listening in a Diverse Business Environment," *Bulletin of the Association for Business Communication* 54, no. 3 (September 1991): 73–74.

50. Robyn D. Clarke, "Do You Hear What I Hear?" *Black Enterprise*, May 1998, 129.

51. Dennis M. Kratz and Abby Robinson Kratz, *Effective Listening Skills* (New York: McGraw-Hill, 1995), 45–53; J. Michael Sproule, *Communication Today* (Glenview, Ill.: Scott Foresman, 1981), 69.

52. Brownell, *Listening*, 230–231.

53. Kratz and Kratz, *Effective Listening Skills*, 78–79; Sproule, *Communication Today*, 69.

54. Bill Brooks, "The Power of Active Listening," *American Salesman*, June 2003, 12; "Active Listening," Study Guides and Strategies website, accessed 5 February 2005, www.studygs.net.

55. Bob Lamons, "Good Listeners Are Better Communicators," *Marketing News*, 11 September 1995, 13+; Phillip Morgan and H. Kent Baker, "Building a Professional Image: Improving Listening Behavior," *Supervisory Management* (November 1985): 35–36.

56. Clarke, "Do You Hear What I Hear?"; Dot Yandle, "Listening to Understand," *Pryor Report Management Newsletter Supplement* 15, no. 8 (August 1998): 13.

57. Brownell, *Listening*, 14; Kratz and Kratz, *Effective Listening Skills*, 8–9; Sherwyn P. Morreale and Courtland L. Bovée, *Excellence in Public Speaking* (Orlando, Fla.: Harcourt Brace, 1998), 72–76; Lyman K. Steil, Larry L. Barker, and Kittie W. Watson, *Effective Listening: Key to Your Success* (Reading, Mass.: Addison Wesley, 1983), 21–22.

58. Patrick J. Collins, *Say It with Power and Confidence* (Upper Saddle River, N.J.: Prentice Hall, 1997), 40–45.

59. Morreale and Bovée, *Excellence in Public Speaking*, 296.

60. Dale G. Leathers, *Successful Nonverbal Communication: Principles and Applications* (New York: Macmillan, 1986), 19.

61. Gerald H. Graham, Jeanne Unrue, and Paul Jennings, "The Impact of Nonverbal Communication in Organizations: A Survey of Perceptions," *Journal of Business Communication* 28, no. 1 (Winter 1991): 45–62.

62. Danielle S. Urban, "What to Do About 'Body Art' at Work," *Workforce Management*, 24 March 2010, www.workforce.com.

63. Virginia P. Richmond and James C. McCroskey, *Nonverbal Behavior in Interpersonal Relations*, 4th ed. (Boston: Allyn & Bacon, 2000), 153–157.

64. Mary Ellen Slayter, "Pamela Meyer on the Science Behind 'Liespotting,'" SmartBlog on Workforce, 14 September 2010, smartblogs .com.

65. Slayter, "Pamela Meyer on the Science Behind 'Liespotting.'"

66. Joe Navarro, "Body Language Myths," *Psychology Today*, 25 October 2009, www.psychologytoday.com; Richmond and McCroskey, *Nonverbal Behavior in Interpersonal Relations*, 2–3.

67. John Hollon, "No Tolerance for Jerks," *Workforce Management*, 12 February 2007, 34.

68. Linton Weeks, "Please Read This Story, Thank You," NPR, 14 March 2012, www.npr.org.

69. Alan Cole, "Telephone Etiquette at Work," Work Etiquette website, 14 March 2012, www.worketiquettc.co.uk; Alf Nucifora, "Voice Mail Demands Good Etiquette from Both Sides," *Puget Sound Business Journal*, 5–11 September 2003, 24; Ruth Davidhizar and Ruth Shearer, "The Effective Voice Mail Message," *Hospital Material Management Quarterly* 22, no. 2 (2000): 45–49; "How to Get the Most Out of Voice Mail," *CPA Journal* 70, no. 2 (February 2000): 11; Jo Ind, "Hanging on the Telephone," *Birmingham Post*, 28 July 1999, PS10; Larry Barker and Kittie Watson, *Listen Up* (New York: St. Martin's Press, 2000), 64–65; Lin Walker, *Telephone Techniques* (New York: AMACOM, 1998), 46–47; Dorothy Neal, *Telephone Techniques*, 2nd ed. (New York: Glencoe McGraw-Hill, 1998), 31; Jeannie Davis, *Beyond "Hello"* (Aurora, Colo.: Now Hear This Inc., 2000), 2–3; "Ten Steps to Caller-Friendly Voice Mail," *Managing Office Technology*, January 1995, 25; Rhonda Finniss, "Voice Mail: Tips for a Positive Impression," *Administrative Assistant's Update*, August 2001, 5.

70. Dana May Casperson, *Power Etiquette: What You Don't Know Can Kill Your Career* (New York: AMACOM, 1999), 10–14; Ellyn Spragins, "Introducing Politeness," *Fortune Small Business*, November 2001, 30.

71. Tanya Mohn, "The Social Graces as a Business Tool," *New York Times*, 10 November 2002, sec. 3, 12.

72. Casperson, *Power Etiquette*, 44–46.

73. "Are You Practicing Proper Social Networking Etiquette?" *Forbes*, 9 October 2009, www.forbes.com; Pete Babb, "The Ten Commandments of Blog and Wiki Etiquette," *InfoWorld*, 28 May 2007, www.infoworld.com; Judith Kallos, "Instant Messaging Etiquette," NetM@ blog, accessed 3 August 2008, www.netmanners .com; Michael S. Hyatt, "E-Mail Etiquette 101," From Where I Sit blog, 1 July 2007, www.michaelhyatt.com.

74. J. J. McCorvey, "How to Create a Cell Phone Policy," *Inc.*, 10 February 2010, www.inc.com.

75. Chad Brooks, "Poor Mobile Manners Not Lost on Bosses," Fox Business, 29 October 2013, smallbusiness.foxbusiness.com.

76. Nick Wingfield, "Oh, for the Good Old Days of Rude Cellphone Gabbers," *New York Times*, 2 December 2011, www.nytimes.com.

77. Cromwell Schubarth, "VC Ben Horowitz on What He Wants in a Startup and Why Rap Genius Is It," *Silicon Valley Business Journal*, 4 February 2014, www.bizjournals.com.

Communication Challenges in a Diverse, Global Marketplace

LEARNING OBJECTIVES

After studying this chapter, you will be able to

1 Discuss the opportunities and challenges of intercultural communication.

2 Define *culture*, explain how culture is learned, and define *ethnocentrism* and *stereotyping*.

3 Explain the importance of recognizing cultural variations, and list eight categories of cultural differences.

4 List four general guidelines for adapting to any business culture.

5 Identify seven steps you can take to improve your intercultural communication skills.

MyBCommLab®

⭐ **Improve Your Grade!** More than 10 million students improved their results using Pearson MyLabs. Visit **mybcommlab.com** for simulations, tutorials, and end-of-chapter problems.

Kaiser Permanente CEO Bernard J. Tyson believes a culturally competent workforce is essential to the health provider's aim of serving the diverse U.S. population.

COMMUNICATION CLOSE-UP AT
Kaiser Permanente

kp.org

Delivering quality health care is difficult enough, given the complexities of technology, government regulations, evolving scientific and medical understanding, and the variability of human performance. It gets even more daunting when you add the challenges of communication among medical staff and between patients and their caregivers, which often takes place under stressful circumstances. Those communication efforts are challenging enough in an environment where everyone speaks the same language and feels at home in a single cultural context—but they're infinitely more complex in the United States, whose residents identify with dozens of different cultures and speak several hundred languages.

The Oakland-based health-care system Kaiser Permanente has been embracing the challenges and opportunities of diversity since its founding in 1945. It made a strong statement with its very first hospital when it refused to follow the then-common practice of segregating patients by race. Now, as the largest not-for-profit health system in the United States, Kaiser's client base includes more than 10 million members from over 100 distinct cultures.

At the core of Kaiser's approach is *culturally competent care*, which it defines as "health care that acknowledges cultural diversity in the clinical setting, respects members' beliefs and practices, and ensures that cultural needs are considered and respected at every point of contact." These priorities are woven into Kaiser's organizational culture, structure, and business practices.

Delivering this standard of care requires a mix of skills and knowledge that range from an awareness of medical issues of concern to specific cultures to language fluency (and translation skills in more than 100 languages) to the awareness needed to handle cultural traditions and values in a sensitive manner. Kaiser's Centers of Excellence in Culturally Competent Care at facilities around the country are a good

REUTERS/Mario Anzuoni

example of the extent the company takes to serve its diverse clientele. Each center focuses on one or more cultures prominent in a given locale, with a particular emphasis on improving care outcomes for population segments that have historically been underserved.

Kaiser believes that effectively serving a diverse client base requires an equally diverse staff. As the chairman and CEO Bernard J. Tyson explains, "The rich diversity of our organization reflects the diversity of the people we serve each and every day." Nearly half the executive team are women, for example, and people of color make up nearly 60 percent of the company's workforce.

In addition to helping Kaiser communicate more effectively with its customers, the strategic emphasis on diversity and inclusion is good for businesses. Its target market segments also happen to be among the country's fastest-growing demographic groups, and Kaiser's ability to connect with these audiences gives it an important competitive advantage.[1]

Understanding the Opportunities and Challenges of Communication in a Diverse World

1 LEARNING OBJECTIVE Discuss the opportunities and challenges of intercultural communication.

Diversity includes all the characteristics that define people as individuals.

MOBILE APP

Culture Compass offers insights into more than 100 countries around the world.

Kaiser Permanente (profiled in the chapter-opening Communication Close-Up) illustrates the opportunities and the challenges for business professionals who know how to communicate with diverse audiences. Although the concept is often framed in terms of ethnic background, a broader and more useful definition of **diversity** includes "all the characteristics and experiences that define each of us as individuals."[2] As one example, the pharmaceutical company Merck identifies 19 separate dimensions of diversity, including race, age, military experience, parenting status, marital status, and thinking style.[3] As you'll learn in this chapter, these characteristics and experiences can have a profound effect on the way businesspeople communicate.

Intercultural communication is the process of sending and receiving messages between people whose cultural backgrounds could lead them to interpret verbal and nonverbal signs differently. Every attempt to send and receive messages is influenced by culture, so to communicate successfully, you need a basic understanding of the cultural differences you may encounter and how you should handle them. Your efforts to recognize and bridge cultural differences will open up business opportunities throughout the world and maximize the contributions of all the employees in a diverse workforce.

OPPORTUNITIES IN A GLOBAL MARKETPLACE

You will communicate with people from many other cultures throughout your career.

Chances are good that you'll be working across international borders sometime in your career. Thanks to communication and transportation technologies, natural boundaries and national borders are no longer the impassable barriers they once were. Local markets are opening to worldwide competition as businesses of all sizes look for new growth opportunities outside their own countries. Thousands of U.S. businesses depend on exports for significant portions of their revenues. Every year, these companies export hundreds of billions of dollars' worth of materials and merchandise, along with billions more in personal and professional services. If you work in one of these companies, you may well be called on to visit or at least communicate with a wide variety of people who speak languages other than English and who live in cultures quite different from what you're used to. Among the United States's top 10 global trading partners, only Canada and Great Britain have English as an official language; Canada also has French as an official language.[4]

Not surprisingly, effective communication is important to cross-cultural and global business. In a recent survey, nearly 90 percent of executives said their companies' profits, revenue, and market share would all improve with better international communication skills. In addition, half of these executives said communication or collaboration breakdowns had affected major international business efforts in their companies.[5] The good news here is that improving your cultural communication skills could make you a more valuable job candidate at every stage of your career.

ADVANTAGES OF A DIVERSE WORKFORCE

Even if you never visit another country or transact business on a global scale, you will interact with colleagues from a variety of cultures and with a wide range of characteristics and life experiences. Many innovative companies are changing the way they approach diversity, from seeing it as a legal requirement (providing equal opportunities for all) to seeing it as a strategic opportunity to connect with customers and take advantage of the broadest possible pool of talent.[6] Smart business leaders recognize the competitive advantages of a diverse workforce that offers a broader spectrum of viewpoints and ideas, helps businesses understand and identify with diverse markets, and enables companies to benefit from a wider range of employee talents. "It just makes good business sense," says Gord Nixon, the CEO of the Royal Bank of Canada.[7]

The diversity of today's workforce brings distinct advantages to businesses:

- A broader range of views and ideas
- A better understanding of diverse, fragmented markets
- A broader pool of talent from which to recruit

Diversity is simply a fact of life for all companies. The United States has been a nation of immigrants from the beginning, and that trend continues today. The western and northern Europeans who made up the bulk of immigrants during the nation's early years now share space with people from across Asia, Africa, Eastern Europe, and other parts of the world. Across the United States, the term *minority* as it is traditionally applied to nonwhite residents makes less and less sense every year. Non-Hispanic white Americans now account for about 60 percent of the overall U.S. population, but that figure will drop below 50 percent in two or three decades. Caucasian Americans already make up less than half the population in hundreds of cities and counties.[8]

REAL-TIME UPDATES

LEARN MORE BY VISITING THIS WEBSITE

Looking for jobs at diversity-minded companies?

DiversityWorking.com connects job searchers with companies that recognize the value of diverse workforces. Go to **real-timeupdates.com/bct14** and select Learn More in the Students section.

However, you and your colleagues don't need to be recent immigrants to constitute a diverse workforce. Differences in everything from age and gender identification to religion and ethnic heritage to geography and military experience enrich the workplace. Immigration and workforce diversity create advantages—and challenges—for business communicators throughout the world.

REAL-TIME UPDATES

LEARN MORE BY EXPLORING THIS INTERACTIVE WEBSITE

Take a closer look at how the United States is changing

The U.S. population is aging and becoming more diverse; dive into the details with this interactive presentation. Go to **real-timeupdates.com/bct14** and select Learn More in the Students section.

THE CHALLENGES OF INTERCULTURAL COMMUNICATION

Today's increasingly diverse workforce encompasses a wide range of skills, traditions, backgrounds, experiences, outlooks, and attitudes toward work—all of which can affect communication in the workplace. Supervisors face the challenge of connecting with these diverse employees, motivating them, and fostering cooperation and harmony among them. Teams face the challenge of working together closely, and companies are challenged to coexist peacefully with business partners and with the community as a whole.

The interaction of culture and communication is so pervasive that separating the two is virtually impossible. The way you communicate is deeply influenced by the culture in which you were raised. The meaning of words, the significance of gestures, the importance of time and space, the rules of human relationships—these and many other aspects of communication are defined by culture. To a large degree, your culture influences the way you think, which naturally affects the way you communicate as both a sender and a receiver.[9] Intercultural communication is much more complicated than simply matching language between sender and receiver; it goes beyond mere words to beliefs, values, and emotions.

A company's cultural diversity affects how its business messages are conceived, composed, delivered, received, and interpreted.

Culture influences everything about communication, including

- Language
- Nonverbal signals
- Word meaning
- Time and space issues
- Rules of human relationships

Elements of human diversity can affect every stage of the communication process, from the ideas a person deems important enough to share to the habits and expectations of giving feedback. In particular, your instinct is to encode your message using the assumptions of *your* culture. Members of your audience, however, decode your message according to the assumptions of *their* culture. The greater the difference between cultures, the greater the chance for misunderstanding.[10]

Throughout this chapter, you'll see examples of how communication styles and habits vary from one culture to another. These examples are intended to illustrate the major themes of intercultural communication, not to give an exhaustive list of the styles and habits of any particular culture. With an understanding of these major themes, you'll be prepared to explore the specifics of any culture.

Developing Cultural Competency

2 LEARNING OBJECTIVE
Define *culture*, explain how culture is learned, and define *ethnocentrism* and *stereotyping*.

Cultural competency requires a combination of attitude, knowledge, and skills.

Cultural competency includes an appreciation for cultural differences that affect communication and the ability to adjust one's communication style to ensure that efforts to send and receive messages across cultural boundaries are successful. In other words, it requires a combination of attitude, knowledge, and skills.[11] Kaiser Permanente, profiled at the beginning of the chapter, is a good example of a contemporary organization that values cultural competency so highly that it makes it a high-level strategic imperative.

Achieving cultural competency can take time and effort, but the good news is you're already an expert in culture—at least the culture in which you grew up. You understand how your society works, how people are expected to communicate, what common gestures and facial expressions mean, and so on. The bad news is that because you're such an expert in your own culture, your communication is largely automatic; that is, you rarely stop to think about the communication rules you're following. An important step toward successful intercultural communication is becoming more aware of these rules and the way they influence your communication.

REAL-TIME UPDATES
LEARN MORE BY READING THIS INFOGRAPHIC
How not to behave in 15 countries
These brief and occasionally humorous pointers will help keep you out of trouble. Go to **real-timeupdates.com/bct14** and select Learn More in the Students section.

UNDERSTANDING THE CONCEPT OF CULTURE

Culture is a shared system of symbols, beliefs, attitudes, values, expectations, and behavioral norms.

Culture is a shared system of symbols, beliefs, attitudes, values, expectations, and norms for behavior. Your cultural background influences the way you prioritize what is important in life, helps define your attitude toward what is appropriate in a given situation, and establishes rules of behavior.[12]

You belong to several cultures, each of which affects the way you communicate.

Actually, you belong to several cultures. In addition to the culture you share with all the people who live in your own country, you belong to other cultural groups, including an ethnic group, possibly a religious group, and perhaps a profession that has its own special language and customs. With its large population and long history of immigration, the United States is home to a vast array of cultures (see Figure 3.1).[13] In contrast, Japan is much more homogeneous, having only a few distinct cultural groups.[14]

Members of a given culture tend to have similar assumptions about how people should think, behave, and communicate, and they all tend to act on those assumptions in much the same way. Cultures can vary in their rate of change, degree of complexity, and tolerance toward outsiders. These differences affect the level of trust and openness you can achieve when communicating with people of other cultures.

You learn culture both directly (by being instructed) and indirectly (by observing others).

People learn culture directly and indirectly from other members of their group. As you grow up in a culture, you are taught by the group's members who you are and how best to function in that culture. Sometimes you are explicitly told which behaviors are acceptable. At other times you learn by observing which values work best in a particular group. In these ways, culture is passed on from person to person and from generation to generation.[15]

Cultures tend to offer views of life that are both coherent (internally logical) and complete (able to answer all of life's big questions).

In addition to being automatic, culture tends to be *coherent*; that is, a culture seems to be fairly logical and consistent when viewed from the inside. Certain norms within a culture may not make sense to someone outside the culture, but they probably make sense to those inside. Such coherence generally helps a culture function more smoothly internally, but it can create disharmony between cultures that don't view the world in the same way.

Finally, cultures tend to be *complete*; that is, they provide their members with most of the answers to life's big questions. This idea of completeness dulls or even suppresses curiosity about life in other cultures. Not surprisingly, such completeness can complicate communication with other cultures.[16]

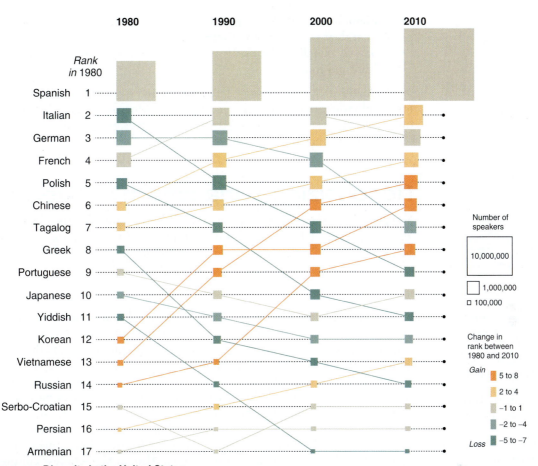

Figure 3.1   **Language Diversity in the United States**
Language is one of the distinguishing factors of population diversity. This chart shows the trend in the relative ranking of a number of languages other than English spoken in the United States since 1980.
Source: "Top Languages Other than English Spoken in 1980 and Changes in Relative Rank, 1990-2010," U.S. Census Bureau, 14 February 2013, www.census.gov.

OVERCOMING ETHNOCENTRISM AND STEREOTYPING

Ethnocentrism is the tendency to judge other groups according to the standards, behaviors, and customs of one's own group. Given the automatic influence of one's own culture, when people compare their culture with others, they often conclude that their own is superior.[17] An even more extreme reaction is **xenophobia**, a fear of strangers and foreigners. Clearly, businesspeople who take these views are not likely to communicate successfully across cultures.

Distorted views of other cultures or groups also result from **stereotyping**, assigning a wide range of generalized attributes to an individual on the basis of membership in a particular culture or social group. For instance, assuming that an older colleague will be out of touch with the youth market or that a younger colleague can't be an inspiring leader would be stereotyping age groups.

Those who want to show respect for others and to communicate effectively in business need to adopt a more positive viewpoint in the form of **cultural pluralism**—the practice of accepting multiple cultures on their own terms. When crossing cultural boundaries, you'll be more effective if you move beyond simple acceptance and adapt your communication style to that of the new cultures you encounter—even integrating aspects of those cultures into your own.[18] A few simple habits can help:

- **Avoid assumptions.** Don't assume that others will act the same way you do, use language and symbols the same way you do, or even operate from the same values and beliefs. For instance, in a comparison of the 10 most important values in three cultures, people from the United States had *no* values in common with people from Japanese or Arab cultures.[19]

Ethnocentrism is the tendency to judge all other groups according to the standards, behaviors, and customs of one's own group.

Stereotyping is assigning generalized attributes to an individual on the basis of membership in a particular group.

Cultural pluralism is the acceptance of multiple cultures on their own terms.

You can avoid ethnocentrism and stereotyping by avoiding assumptions, withholding judgment, and accepting differences.

- **Withhold judgment.** When people act differently, don't conclude that they are in error or that their way is invalid or inferior.
- **Acknowledge distinctions.** Don't ignore the differences between another person's culture and your own.

Unfortunately, overcoming ethnocentrism and stereotyping is not a simple task, even for people who are highly motivated to do so. Moreover, research suggests that people often have beliefs and biases that they're not even aware of—and that may even conflict with the beliefs they *think* they have.[20]

Recognizing Variations in a Diverse World

3 **LEARNING OBJECTIVE**
Explain the importance of recognizing cultural variations, and list eight categories of cultural differences.

Cultural context is the pattern of physical cues, environmental stimuli, and implicit understanding that conveys meaning between members of the same culture.

High-context cultures rely heavily on nonverbal actions and environmental setting to convey meaning; low-context cultures rely more on explicit verbal communication.

You can begin to learn how people in other cultures want to be treated by recognizing and accommodating eight main types of cultural differences: contextual, legal and ethical, social, nonverbal, age, gender, religious, and ability.

CONTEXTUAL DIFFERENCES

Every attempt at communication occurs within a **cultural context**, which is the pattern of physical cues, environmental stimuli, and implicit understanding that convey meaning between two members of the same culture. However, cultures around the world vary widely in the role that context plays in communication.

In a **high-context culture**, people rely less on verbal communication and more on the context of nonverbal signals and environmental setting to convey meaning. For instance, a Chinese speaker often expects the receiver to discover the essence of a message and uses indirectness and metaphor to provide a web of meaning.[21] The indirect style can be a source of confusion during discussions with people from low-context cultures, who are more accustomed to receiving direct answers. Also, in high-context cultures the rules of everyday life are rarely explicit; instead, as individuals grow up, they learn how to recognize situational cues (such as gestures and tone of voice) and how to respond as expected.[22] The primary role of communication in high-context cultures is building relationships, not exchanging information.[23]

In a **low-context culture** such as the United States, people rely more on verbal communication and less on circumstances and cues to convey meaning. In such cultures rules and expectations are usually spelled out through explicit statements such as "Please wait until I'm finished" or "You're welcome to browse."[24] The primary task of communication in low-context cultures is exchanging information.[25]

Contextual differences are apparent in the way businesspeople approach situations such as decision making, problem solving, negotiating, interacting among levels in the organizational hierarchy, and socializing outside the workplace.[26] For instance, businesspeople in low-context cultures tend to focus on the results of the decisions they face, a reflection of the cultural emphasis on logic and progress (for example, "Will this be good for our company? For my career?"). In comparison, higher-context cultures emphasize the means or the method by which a decision will be made. Building or protecting relationships can be as important as the facts and information used in making the decisions.[27] Consequently, negotiators working on business deals in such cultures may spend most of their time together building relationships rather than hammering out contractual details.

The distinctions between high and low context are generalizations, of course, but they are important to keep in mind as guidelines. Communication tactics that work well in a high-context culture may backfire in a low-context culture and vice versa.

LEGAL AND ETHICAL DIFFERENCES

Cultural context influences legal and ethical behavior, which in turn can affect communication. For example, the meaning of business contracts can vary from culture to culture. Whereas a manager from a U.S. company would tend to view a signed contract as the end of the negotiating process, with all the details resolved, his or her counterpart in many Asian cultures might view the signed contract as an agreement to do business—and only then begin to negotiate the details of the deal.[28]

As you conduct business around the world, you'll find that both legal systems and ethical standards differ from culture to culture. Making ethical choices across cultures can seem complicated, but you can keep your messages ethical by applying four basic principles:[29]

- **Actively seek mutual ground.** To allow the clearest possible exchange of information, both parties must be flexible and avoid insisting that an interaction take place strictly in terms of one culture or another.
- **Send and receive messages without judgment.** To allow information to flow freely, both parties must recognize that values vary from culture to culture, and they must trust each other.
- **Send messages that are honest.** To ensure that information is true, both parties must see things as they are—not as they would like them to be. Both parties must be fully aware of their personal and cultural biases.
- **Show respect for cultural differences.** To protect the basic human rights of both parties, each must understand and acknowledge the other's needs and preserve the other's dignity by communicating without deception.

Honesty and respect are cornerstones of ethical communication, regardless of culture.

SOCIAL DIFFERENCES

The nature of social behavior varies among cultures, sometimes dramatically. Some behavioral rules are formal and specifically articulated (table manners are a good example), whereas others are informal and learned over time (such as the comfortable distance to stand from a colleague during a discussion). The combination of formal and informal rules influences the overall behavior of most people in a society most of the time. In addition to the factors already discussed, *social norms* can vary from culture to culture in the following areas:

Formal rules of etiquette are explicit and well defined, but informal rules are learned through observation and imitation.

- **Attitudes toward work and success.** In the United States, for instance, a widespread view is that people who attain success through individual effort and initiative are to be admired.
- **Roles and status.** Culture influences the roles people play, including who communicates with whom, what they communicate, and in what way. Culture also dictates how people show respect and signify rank. For example, it would sound odd to address your boss in the United States as "Manager Jones," but including a professional title is common in China.[30]
- **Use of manners.** What is polite in one culture may be considered rude in another. For instance, asking a colleague "How was your weekend?" is a common way of making small talk in the United States, but the question sounds intrusive to people in cultures in which business and private lives are seen as separate spheres.
- **Concepts of time.** People in low-context cultures see time as a way to plan the business day efficiently, often focusing on only one task during each scheduled period and viewing time as a limited resource. However, executives from high-context cultures often see time as more flexible. Meeting a deadline is less important than building a business relationship.[31]
- **Future orientation.** Successful companies tend to have a strong *future orientation*, planning for and investing in the future, but national cultures around the world vary widely in this viewpoint. Some societies encourage a long-term outlook that emphasizes planning and investing—making sacrifices in the short term for the promise of better outcomes in the future. Others are oriented more toward the present, even to the point of viewing the future as hopelessly remote and not worth planning for.[32]
- **Openness and inclusiveness.** At the national level as well as within smaller groups, cultures vary on how open they are to accepting people from other cultures and people who don't necessarily fit the prevailing norms within the culture. An unwillingness to accommodate others can range from outright exclusion to subtle pressure to conform to majority expectations.

Respect and rank are reflected differently from culture to culture in the way people are addressed and in their working environment.

The rules of polite behavior vary from country to country.

Attitudes toward time, such as strict adherence to meeting schedules, can vary throughout the world.

Cultures around the world exhibit varying degrees of openness toward both outsiders and people whose personal identities don't align with prevailing social norms.

- **Use of communication technologies.** Don't assume that colleagues and customers around the world use the same communication tools you do. For example, although mobile phone usage is high in most countries around the world, the percentage of users with smartphones and the broadband service required for communication services such as video varies widely.[33]

NONVERBAL DIFFERENCES

As discussed in Chapter 2, nonverbal communication can be a helpful guide to determining the meaning of a message—but this situation holds true only if the sender and receiver assign the same meaning to nonverbal signals. For instance, the simplest hand gestures have different meanings in different cultures. A gesture that communicates good luck in Brazil is the equivalent of giving someone "the finger" in Colombia.[34] Don't assume that the gestures you grew up with will translate to another culture; doing so could lead to embarrassing mistakes.

> The meaning of nonverbal signals can vary widely from culture to culture, so you can't rely on assumptions.

When you have the opportunity to interact with people in another culture, the best advice is to study the culture in advance and then observe the way people behave in the following areas:

- **Greetings.** Do people shake hands, bow, or kiss lightly (on one side of the face or both)? Do people shake hands only when first introduced or every time they say hello or goodbye?
- **Personal space.** When people are conversing, do they stand closer together or farther apart than you are accustomed to?
- **Touching.** Do people touch each other on the arm to emphasize a point or slap each other on the back to show congratulations? Or do they refrain from touching altogether?
- **Facial expressions.** Do people shake their heads to indicate "no" and nod them to indicate "yes"? This is what people are accustomed to in the United States, but it is not universal.

- **Eye contact.** Do people make frequent eye contact or avoid it? Frequent eye contact is often taken as a sign of honesty and openness in the United States, but in other cultures it can be a sign of aggressiveness or disrespect.
- **Posture.** Do people slouch and relax in the office and in public, or do they sit up and stand up straight?
- **Formality.** In general, does the culture seem more or less formal than yours?

Following the lead of people who grew up in the culture is not only a great way to learn but a good way to show respect as well.

REAL-TIME UPDATES

LEARN MORE BY READING THIS INFOGRAPHIC

Seven common hand gestures that will stir up trouble in other cultures

Find out what gestures that have positive meanings in the United States can have intensively negative meanings in other cultures. Go to **real-timeupdates.com/bct14** and select Learn More in the Students section.

AGE DIFFERENCES

> A culture's views on youth and aging affect how people communicate with one another.

In U.S. culture youth is often associated with strength, energy, possibilities, and freedom, and age is sometimes associated with declining powers and the inability to keep pace. Older workers can, however, offer broader experience, the benefits of important business relationships nurtured over many years, and high degrees of "practical intelligence"—the ability to solve complex, poorly defined problems.[35]

In contrast, in cultures that value age and seniority, longevity earns respect and increasing power and freedom. For instance, in many Asian societies the oldest employees hold the most powerful jobs, the most impressive titles, and the greatest degrees of freedom and decision-making authority. If a younger employee disagrees with one of these senior executives, the discussion is never conducted in public. The notion of "saving face"—avoiding public embarrassment—is too strong. Instead, if a senior person seems to be in error about something, other employees will find a quiet, private way to communicate whatever information they feel is necessary.[36]

The multiple generations within a culture present another dimension of diversity. Today's workplaces can have three, four, or even five generations working side by side.[37]

Each has been shaped by dramatically different world events, social trends, and technological advances, so it is not surprising that they often have different values, expectations, and communication habits. For instance, Generation Y workers (see "Us Versus Them: Generational Conflict in the Workplace") have a strong preference for communicating via short digital messages, but Baby Boomers and Generation Xers sometimes find these brief messages to be abrupt and impersonal.[38]

GENDER DIFFERENCES

Gender influences workplace communication in several important ways. First, the perception of gender roles in business varies from culture to culture, and gender bias can range from overt discrimination to subtle and even unconscious beliefs.

Second, although the ratios of men and women in entry-level professional positions is roughly equal, the share of management roles held by men increases steadily the further

---

COMMUNICATING ACROSS CULTURES

Us Versus Them: Generational Conflict in the Workplace

The way adults view the world is profoundly shaped by the social and technological trends they experienced while growing up, so it's no surprise that each generation entering the workforce has a different perspective than the generations already at work. Throw in the human tendencies to resist change and to assume that whatever way one is doing something must be the best way to do it, and you have a recipe for conflict. Moreover, generations in a workplace sometimes feel they are competing for jobs, resources, influence, and control. The result can be tension, mistrust, and communication breakdowns.

Lumping people into generations is an imprecise science at best, but it helps to know the labels commonly applied to various age groups and to have some idea of their broad characteristics. These labels are not official, and there is no general agreement on when some generations start and end, but you will see and hear references to the following groups (approximate years of birth are shown in parentheses):

- **The Radio Generation (1925–1945).** People in this group are beyond what was once considered the traditional retirement age of 65, but some want or need to continue working.
- **Baby Boomers (1946–1964).** This large segment of the workforce, which now occupies many mid- and upper-level managerial positions, got its name from the population boom in the years following World War II. The older members of this generation have now reached retirement age, but many will continue to work beyond age 65—meaning that younger workers waiting for some of these management spots to open up might have to wait a while longer.
- **Generation X (1965–1980).** This relatively smaller "MTV generation" is responsible for many of the innovations that have shaped communication habits today but sometimes feels caught between the large mass of baby boomers ahead of them and the younger Generation Y employees entering the workforce. As Generation X begins to take over the management ranks, it is managing in a vastly different business landscape—one in which virtual organizations and networks of independent contractors replace much of the hierarchy inherited from the Baby Boomers.

- **Generation Y (1981–1995).** Also known as *millennials*, this youngest generation currently in the workforce is noted for its entrepreneurial instincts and technological savvy. This generation's comfort level with social media and other communication technologies is helping to change business communication practices but is also a source of concern for managers worried about information leaks and employee productivity.
- **Generation Z (after 1996).** If you're a member of Generation Y, those footsteps you hear behind you are coming from Generation Z, also known as *Generation I* (for Internet) or the *Net Generation*. Those in the first full generation to be born after the World Wide Web was invented are now entering the workforce.

These brief summaries can hardly do justice to entire generations of workers, but they give you some idea of the different generational perspectives and the potential for communication problems. As with all cultural conflicts, successful communication starts with recognizing and understanding both differences and similarities. Beneath the superficial differences in technology usage and other factors, various generations are a lot more alike than they are different.

CAREER APPLICATIONS

1. How would you resolve a conflict between a Baby Boomer manager who worries about the privacy and productivity aspects of social networking and a Generation Y employee who wants to use these tools on the job?
2. Consider the range of labels from the Radio Generation to the Net Generation. What does this tell you about the possible influence of technology on business communication habits?

Sources: Rebecca Knight, "Managing People from 5 Generations," *Harvard Business Review*, 25 September 2014, hbr.org; Anne Fisher, "When Gen X Runs the Show," *Time*, 14 May 2009, www.time.com; Deloitte, "Generation Y: Powerhouse of the Global Economy," research report, 2009, www.deloitte.com; "Generation Y," *Nightly Business Report* website, 30 June 2010, www.pbs.org; Sherry Posnick-Goodwin, "Meet Generation Z," *California Educator*, February 2010, www.cta.org; Ernie Stark, "Lost in a Time Warp," *People & Strategy* 32, no. 4 (2009): 58–64.

one looks up the corporate ladder. This imbalance can significantly affect communication in such areas as mentoring, which is a vital development opportunity for lower and middle managers who want to move into senior positions. In one survey, for example, some men in executive positions expressed reluctance to mentor women, partly because they find it easier to bond with other men and partly out of concerns over developing relationships that might seem inappropriate.[39]

Broadly speaking, men tend to emphasize content in their messages, whereas women tend to emphasize relationship maintenance.

Third, evidence suggests that men and women tend to have somewhat different communication styles. Broadly speaking, men emphasize content and outcomes in their communication efforts, whereas women place a higher premium on relationship maintenance.[40] As one example, men are more likely than women to try to negotiate a pay raise. Moreover, according to research by Linda Babcock of Carnegie Mellon University, both men and women tend to accept this disparity, viewing assertiveness as a positive quality in men but a negative one in women. Changing these perceptions could go a long way toward improving communication and equity in the workplace.[41]

Fourth, outdated concepts of gender and sexual orientation continue to be a source of confusion, controversy, and discrimination. Many people do not fit or wish to be fit into a simplistic heterosexual, male/female categorization scheme, but discriminatory company policies and the behaviors and attitudes of supervisors and coworkers can deprive these individuals of a fair and satisfying work experience. In response, many companies have taken steps to ensure equal opportunities and fair treatment for lesbian, gay, bisexual, and transgender (LGBT) job applicants and employees. Companies can also take steps to make sure their nondiscrimination policies protect employees' right to gender expression based on personal gender identity.[42] Communication plays a critical role in all these efforts, from listening to the needs of diverse employee groups to providing clear policies and educating employees on important issues.

REAL-TIME UPDATES

LEARN MORE BY VISITING THIS WEBSITE

Explore the Corporate Equality Index

The Human Rights Campaign assesses corporate policies and practices regarding equal rights and opportunities for LGBT employees. Go to **real-timeupdates.com/bct14** and select Learn More in the Students section.

RELIGIOUS DIFFERENCES

U.S. law requires employers to accommodate employees' religious beliefs to a reasonable degree.

As one of the most personal and influential aspects of life, religion brings potential for controversy and conflict in the workplace setting—as evidenced by a significant rise in the number of religious discrimination lawsuits in recent years.[43] Many employees believe they should be able to follow and express the tenets of their faith in the workplace. However, companies may need to accommodate employee behaviors that can conflict with each other and with the demands of operating the business. The situation is complicated, with no simple answers that apply to every situation. As more companies work to establish inclusive workplaces, you can expect to see this issue being discussed more often in the coming years.

REAL-TIME UPDATES

LEARN MORE BY READING THIS ARTICLE

Legal aspects of religion in the workplace

Get an overview of the laws that govern religious expression in the workplace. Go to **real-timeupdates.com/bct14** and select Learn More in the Students section.

ABILITY DIFFERENCES

Colleagues and customers with disabilities that affect communication represent an important aspect of the diversity picture. People whose hearing, vision, cognitive ability, or physical ability to operate electronic devices is impaired can be at a significant disadvantage in today's workplace. As with other elements of diversity, success starts with respect for individuals and sensitivity to differences.

Assistive technologies help employers create more inclusive workplaces and benefit from the contributions of people with physical or cognitive impairments.

Employers can also invest in a variety of *assistive technologies* that help people with disabilities perform activities that might otherwise be difficult or impossible. These technologies include devices and systems that help workers communicate orally and visually, interact with computers and other equipment, and enjoy greater mobility in the workplace. For example, designers can emphasize *web accessibility*, taking steps to make websites more accessible to people whose vision is limited. Assistive technologies create a vital link for thousands of employees with disabilities, giving them opportunities to pursue a greater range of career paths and giving employers access to a broader base of talent.[44]

Adapting to Other Business Cultures

Whether you're trying to work productively with members of another generation in your own office or with a business partner on the other side of the world, adapting your approach is essential to successful communication. This section offers general advice on adapting to any business culture and specific advice for professionals from other cultures on adapting to U.S. business culture.

4 LEARNING OBJECTIVE
List four general guidelines for adapting to any business culture.

GUIDELINES FOR ADAPTING TO ANY BUSINESS CULTURE

You'll find a variety of specific tips in "Improving Intercultural Communication Skills" on page 80, but here are four general guidelines that can help all business communicators improve their cultural competency:

- **Become aware of your own biases.** Successful intercultural communication requires more than just an understanding of the other party's culture; you need to understand your own culture and the way it shapes your communication habits.[45] For instance, knowing that you value independence and individual accomplishment will help you communicate more successfully in a culture that values consensus and group harmony.
- **Be careful about applying the "Golden Rule."** You probably heard this growing up: "Treat people the way you want to be treated." The problem with the Golden Rule is that other people don't always want to be treated the same way you want to be treated, particularly across cultural boundaries. The best approach: Treat people the way *they* want to be treated.
- **Exercise tolerance, flexibility, and respect.** As IBM's Ron Glover puts it, "To the greatest extent possible, we try to manage our people and our practices in ways that are respectful of the core principles of any given country or organization or culture."[46]
- **Practice patience and maintain a sense of humor.** Even the most committed and attuned business professionals can make mistakes in intercultural communication, so it is vital for all parties to be patient with one another. As business becomes ever more global, even people in the most tradition-bound cultures are learning to deal more patiently with outsiders and to overlook occasional cultural blunders.[47] A sense of humor is a helpful asset as well, allowing people to move past awkward and embarrassing moments. When you make a mistake, simply apologize and, if appropriate, ask the other person to explain the accepted way; then move on.

An important step in understanding and adapting to other cultures is to recognize the influences that your own culture has on your communication habits.

GUIDELINES FOR ADAPTING TO U.S. BUSINESS CULTURE

If you are a recent immigrant to the United States or grew up in a culture outside the U.S. mainstream, you can apply all the concepts and skills in this chapter to help adapt to U.S. business culture. Here are some key points to remember as you become accustomed to business communication in this country:[48]

- **Individualism.** In contrast to cultures that value group harmony and group success, U.S. culture generally expects individuals to succeed by their own efforts, and it rewards individual success. Even though teamwork is emphasized in many companies, competition between individuals is often expected and even encouraged.
- **Equality.** Although the country's historical record on equality has not always been positive and some inequalities still exist, equality is considered a core American value. This principle applies to race, gender, social background, and even age. To a greater degree than people in many other cultures, Americans believe that every person should be given the opportunity to pursue whatever dreams and goals he or she has in life.
- **Privacy and personal space.** Although this seems to be changing somewhat with the popularity of social networking and other personal media, people in the United States are accustomed to a fair amount of privacy. That also applies to their "personal space" at work. For example, they expect you to knock before entering a closed office and to avoid asking questions about personal beliefs or activities until they get to know you well.

The values espoused by American culture include individualism, equality, and privacy.

- **Time and schedules.** U.S. businesses value punctuality and the efficient use of time. For instance, meetings are expected to start and end at designated times.
- **Religion.** The United States does not have an official state religion. Many religions are practiced throughout the country, and people are expected to respect each other's beliefs.
- **Communication style.** Communication tends to be direct and focus more on content and transactions than on relationships or group harmony.

As with all observations about culture, these are generalizations, of course. Any nation of more than 300 million people will exhibit a wide variety of behaviors. However, following these guidelines will help you succeed in most business communication situations.

Improving Intercultural Communication Skills

5 LEARNING OBJECTIVE
Identify seven steps you can take to improve your intercultural communication skills.

Communicating successfully between cultures requires a variety of skills (see Figure 3.2). You can improve your intercultural skills throughout your career by studying other cultures and languages, respecting preferences for communication styles, learning to write and speak clearly, listening carefully, knowing when to use interpreters and translators, and helping others adapt to your culture.

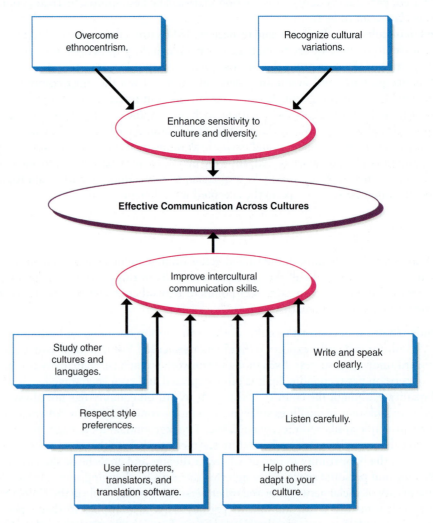

Figure 3.2   Components of Successful Intercultural Communication
Communicating in a diverse business environment is not always an easy task, but you can continue to improve your sensitivity and build your skills as you progress in your career.

STUDYING OTHER CULTURES

Effectively adapting your communication efforts to another culture requires not only knowledge about the culture but also the ability and motivation to change your personal habits as needed.[49] Fortunately, you don't need to learn about the whole world all at once. Many companies appoint specialists for countries or regions, giving employees a chance to focus on just one culture at a time. And if your employer conducts business internationally, it may offer training and support for employees who need to learn more about specific cultures.

REAL-TIME UPDATES

LEARN MORE BY EXPLORING THIS INTERACTIVE WEBSITE

How are your global travel skills?

Take this quiz to see if you have the knowledge to travel like a pro. Go to **real-timeupdates.com/bct14** and select Learn More in the Students section.

Even a small amount of research and practice will help you get through many business situations. In addition, most people respond positively to honest effort and good intentions, and many business associates will help you along if you show an interest in learning more about their cultures. Don't be afraid to ask questions. People will respect your concern and curiosity. You will gradually accumulate considerable knowledge, which will help you feel comfortable and be effective in a wide range of business situations.

Numerous websites and books offer advice on traveling to and working in specific cultures. Also try to sample newspapers, magazines, and even the music and movies of another country. For instance, a movie can demonstrate nonverbal customs even if you don't grasp the language. (However, be careful not to rely solely on entertainment products. If people in other countries based their opinions of U.S. culture only on the silly teen flicks and violent action movies that the United States exports around the globe, what sort of impression do you imagine they'd get?) For some of the key issues to research before doing business in another country, refer to Table 3.1 on the next page.

STUDYING OTHER LANGUAGES

As commerce continues to become more globalized and many countries become more linguistically diverse, the demand for multilingual communicators continues to grow as well. The ability to communicate in more than one language can make you a more competitive job candidate and open up a wider variety of career opportunities.

Even if your colleagues or customers in another country speak your language, it's worth the time and energy to learn common phrases in theirs. Doing so not only helps you get through everyday business and social situations but also demonstrates your commitment to the business relationship. After all, the other person probably spent years learning your language.

Mobile devices can be a huge help in learning another language and in communicating with someone in another language. A wide variety of apps and websites are available that help with essentials words and phrases, grammar, pronunciation, text translation, and even real-time audio translation (see Figure 3.3 on page 83).

Finally, don't assume that people from two countries who speak the same language speak it the same way. The French spoken in Québec and other parts of Canada is often noticeably different from the French spoken in France. Similarly, it's often said that the United States and the United Kingdom are two countries divided by a common language. For instance, *period* (punctuation), *elevator*, and *gasoline* in the United States are *full stop*, *lift*, and *petrol* in the United Kingdom.

Successful intercultural communication can require the modification of personal communication habits.

Making an effort to learn about another person's culture is a sign of respect.

MOBILE APP

iTranslate translates more than 80 languages and features voice input and output.

English is the most prevalent language in international business, but don't assume that everyone understands it or speaks it the same way.

RESPECTING PREFERENCES FOR COMMUNICATION STYLE

Communication style—including the level of directness, the degree of formality, media preferences, and other factors—varies widely from culture to culture (see Figures 3.4a–d on pages 84–87). Knowing what your communication partners expect can help you adapt to their particular style. Once again, watching and learning are the best ways to improve your skills. However, you can infer some generalities by learning more about the culture. For instance, U.S. workers typically prefer an open and direct communication style; they

TABLE 3.1 Doing Business in Other Cultures

Action	Details to Consider
Understand social customs	• How do people react to strangers? Are they friendly? Hostile? Reserved? • How do people greet each other? Should you bow? Nod? Shake hands? • How do you express appreciation for an invitation to lunch, dinner, or someone's home? Should you bring a gift? Send flowers? Write a thank-you note? • Are any phrases, facial expressions, or hand gestures considered rude? • How do you attract the attention of a waiter? Do you tip the waiter? • When is it rude to refuse an invitation? How do you refuse politely? • What topics may or may not be discussed in a social setting? In a business setting? • How do social customs dictate interaction between men and women? Between younger people and older people?
Learn about clothing and food preferences	• What occasions require special attire? • What colors are associated with mourning? Love? Joy? • Are some types of clothing considered taboo for one gender or the other? • How many times a day do people eat? • How are hands or utensils used when eating? • Where is the seat of honor at a table?
Assess political patterns	• How stable is the political situation? • Does the political situation affect businesses in and out of the country? • Is it appropriate to talk politics in social or business situations?
Understand religious and social beliefs	• To which religious groups do people belong? • Which places, objects, actions, and events are sacred? • Do religious beliefs affect communication between men and women or between any other groups? • Is there a tolerance for minority religions? • How do religious holidays affect business and government activities? • Does religion require or prohibit eating specific foods? At specific times?
Learn about economic and business institutions	• Is the society homogeneous or heterogeneous? • What languages are spoken? • What are the primary resources and principal products? • Are businesses generally large? Family controlled? Government controlled? • What are the generally accepted working hours? • How do people view scheduled appointments? • Are people expected to socialize before conducting business?
Appraise the nature of ethics, values, and laws	• Is money or a gift expected in exchange for arranging business transactions? • Do people value competitiveness or cooperation? • What are the attitudes toward work? Toward money? • Is politeness more important than factual honesty?

THE FUTURE OF COMMUNICATION

Real-Time Translation

If you've ever tried to converse in a language other than you native tongue, you know what a challenge this can be. As a listener, you have to convert the incoming sounds to discrete words and assemble these words into coherent phrases and sentences in order to extract the meaning. And unlike reading a written document, you have to do all this processing almost instantaneously, without the luxury of going back over something you didn't get. As a speaker, you have to find the right words, assemble them into phrases and sentences using the second language's grammar rules, and then pronounce them all correctly enough so they make sense to the other party. Reaching this level of proficiency can take years of study and practice.

Translating speech in real time is a challenging technical proposition, but a number of companies are making progress. Perhaps most notable so far is Skype Translator, which can translate voice and video calls and instant messages in multiple languages. A variety of smartphone and smartwatch apps offer translation, where speakers take turns talking to the device, then listen as it outputs the translated speech. The technology promises to keep evolving, becoming more versatile and more accurate, but it has already reached the point of being a useful business communication tool.

WHAT'S YOUR PREDICTION?

Research several apps and other solutions that offer real-time translation. Are they being used successfully in business communication? Do you think they will ever make it unnecessary to learn other languages in order to communicate effectively with diverse, global audiences?

Sources: "Skype Translator," Skype, accessed 14 March 2016, www.skype.com; Stu Robarts, "Google Translate App Now Translates Street Signs and Real-Time Conversations," Gizmag, 14 January 2015, www.gizmag.com; iTranslate Voice website, accessed 14 March 2016, itranslatevoice.com.

Figure 3.3   Mobile Language Tools
Translation apps are handy tools for working in multilingual business settings. Even if you don't speak a word of a particular language, you can get fast translations of essential phrases.

find other styles frustrating or suspect. Directness is also valued in Sweden as a sign of efficiency, but heated debates and confrontations are unusual. Italian, German, and French executives usually don't put colleagues at ease with praise before they criticize; doing so seems manipulative to them. Meanwhile, professionals from high-context cultures, such as Japan or China, tend to be less direct.[50] Finally, in general, business correspondence in other countries is often more formal than the style used by U.S. businesspeople.

WRITING CLEARLY

Writing clearly is always important, of course, but it is essential when you are writing to people whose first language is not English. Follow these recommendations to make sure your message can be understood (see Figure 3.5 on page 88):[51]

- **Choose words carefully.** Use precise words that don't have the potential to confuse with multiple meanings. For instance, the word *right* has several dozen different meanings and usages, so look for a synonym that conveys the specific meaning you intend, such as *correct, appropriate, desirable, moral, authentic,* or *privilege.*[52]
- **Be brief.** Use simple sentences and short paragraphs, breaking information into smaller chunks that are easier for readers to process.
- **Use plenty of transitions.** Help readers follow your train of thought by using transitional words and phrases. For example, tie related points together with expressions such as *in addition* and *first, second,* and *third.*
- **Address international correspondence properly.** Refer to Appendix A for more information.
- **Cite numbers and dates carefully.** In the United States, 12-05-18 means December 5, 2018, but in many other countries it means May 12, 2018. Dates in Japan and China are usually expressed with the year first, followed by the month and then the day; therefore, to write December 5, 2018, in Japan, write it as 2018-12-05. Similarly, in the United States and Great Britain, 1.000 means one with three decimal places, but it means one thousand in many European countries.
- **Avoid slang, idiomatic phrases, and business jargon.** Everyday speech and writing are full of slang and **idiomatic phrases**—phrases that mean more than the sum of their literal parts. Examples from U.S. English include "Knocked one out of the park" and "More bang for the buck." Your audience may have no idea what you're talking about when you use such phrases.
- **Avoid humor and references to popular culture.** Jokes and references to popular entertainment usually rely on culture-specific information that might be completely unknown to your audience.

Although some of these differences may seem trivial, meeting the expectations of an international audience illustrates both knowledge of and respect for the other cultures.

Clarity and simplicity are essential when writing to or speaking with people who don't share your native language.

Humor does not "travel well" because it usually relies on intimate knowledge of a particular culture.

4308 Preston Highway
Louisville, KY 40213
Toll Free: 1.800.FLY.RITE
Fax: (502) 555-1324
www.updraftrc.com

Zhejang Shan Tou Manufacturing Company, Ltd.
Guoliwei Industry Park
Libang Road, Longgang District
Shenzhen, Guangdong, China

Dear Mr. Li,

My company, Updraft RC, has designed a cool new line of radio-control toys that use smartphones as the controller. We are looking for a manufacturing partner, and your firm is one of the candidates we're having a look at.

Before we discuss technical details, I must say I have two sets of concerns about working with a foreign manufacturer. The first involves all the usual—transportation costs, delays, quality control, and risk of intellectual property theft. I'll need some assurances on how you address these issues to make sure they don't become problems in our relationship.

Second, companies here in the States that use foreign manufacturers often have to deal with heavy news coverage and activist publicity on such matters as workplace safety, worker rights, and environmentally sensitive manufacturing. Even though the U.S. company doesn't directly control what happens in the overseas contract manufacturer, the U.S. company takes the heat when the media uncovers abuse, neglect, pollution, etc. I know that Nike and other U.S. companies have spent millions and worked for years to promote positive conditions in overseas factories, but even these major corporations haven't been able to completely avoid problems and bad press. How can I be sure that a small company such as ours will? I do not want our product launch to get caught up in some scandal over "sweatshops."

I look forward to seeing your comprehensive response as soon as possible.

All the best,

Henry Gatlin

Henry Gatlin
Founder, CEO
Updraft RC

5 August 2017

Annotations (right margin):

Language such as "cool" and "having a look at" is too informal for external business communication, particularly for international correspondence.

The tone of this paragraph is too demanding.

"Here in the States" is too informal, and referring to the reader as "foreign" is potentially insulting.

Inflammatory language such as *bad press, scandal,* and *sweatshops* will put the reader on the defensive and discourage a positive response.

The request for a response sounds too demanding, and it lacks a specific deadline.

The closing is too informal.

Figures 3.4a   Intercultural Business Letter: Ineffective Original Draft
This letter (from a Kentucky company that designs radio-controlled airplanes) exhibits a number of problems that would create difficulties for its intended reader (the manager of a manufacturing company in China). Follow the changes in Figure 3.4b, c, and d to see how the letter was adapted and then translated for its target audience.

SPEAKING AND LISTENING CAREFULLY

Languages vary considerably in the significance of tone, pitch, speed, and volume, which can create challenges for people trying to interpret the explicit meaning of words themselves as well as the overall nuance of a message. The English word *progress* can be a noun or a verb, depending on which syllable you emphasize. In Chinese the meaning of the word *mà* changes depending on the speaker's tone; it can mean *mother, pileup, horse,* or *scold.* And routine Arabic speech can sound excited or angry to an English-speaking U.S. listener.[53]

To ensure successful conversations between parties who speak different native languages or even regional variations of the same language, speakers and listeners alike need to make accommodations.[54] Speakers should adjust the content of their messages and the style of their delivery to accommodate the needs of their listeners and the circumstances of the conversation. For example, if you are speaking in person or over an

Speaking clearly and getting plenty of feedback are two of the keys to successful intercultural conversations.

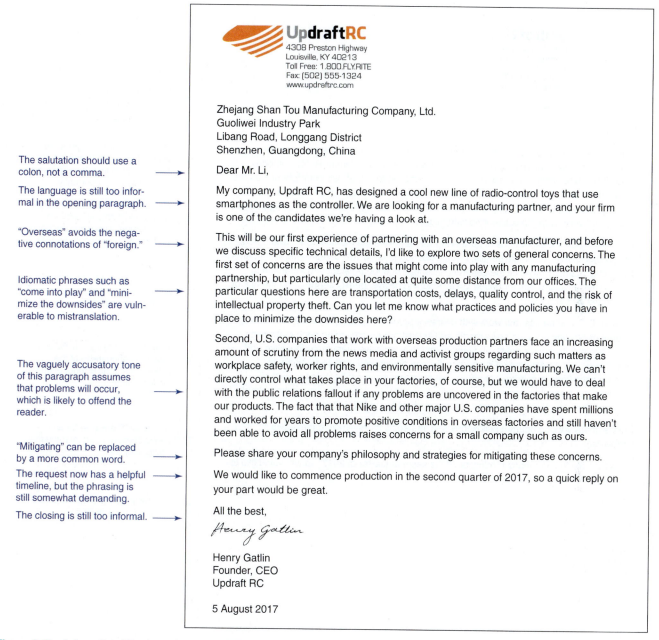

The salutation should use a colon, not a comma.

The language is still too informal in the opening paragraph.

"Overseas" avoids the negative connotations of "foreign."

Idiomatic phrases such as "come into play" and "minimize the downsides" are vulnerable to mistranslation.

The vaguely accusatory tone of this paragraph assumes that problems will occur, which is likely to offend the reader.

"Mitigating" can be replaced by a more common word.

The request now has a helpful timeline, but the phrasing is still somewhat demanding.

The closing is still too informal.

UpdraftRC
4308 Preston Highway
Louisville, KY 40213
Toll Free: 1.800.FLY.RITE
Fax: (502) 555-1324
www.updraftrc.com

Zhejiang Shan Tou Manufacturing Company, Ltd.
Guoliwei Industry Park
Libang Road, Longgang District
Shenzhen, Guangdong, China

Dear Mr. Li,

My company, Updraft RC, has designed a cool new line of radio-control toys that use smartphones as the controller. We are looking for a manufacturing partner, and your firm is one of the candidates we're having a look at.

This will be our first experience of partnering with an overseas manufacturer, and before we discuss specific technical details, I'd like to explore two sets of general concerns. The first set of concerns are the issues that might come into play with any manufacturing partnership, but particularly one located at quite some distance from our offices. The particular questions here are transportation costs, delays, quality control, and the risk of intellectual property theft. Can you let me know what practices and policies you have in place to minimize the downsides here?

Second, U.S. companies that work with overseas production partners face an increasing amount of scrutiny from the news media and activist groups regarding such matters as workplace safety, worker rights, and environmentally sensitive manufacturing. We can't directly control what takes place in your factories, of course, but we would have to deal with the public relations fallout if any problems are uncovered in the factories that make our products. The fact that that Nike and other major U.S. companies have spent millions and worked for years to promote positive conditions in overseas factories and still haven't been able to avoid all problems raises concerns for a small company such as ours.

Please share your company's philosophy and strategies for mitigating these concerns.

We would like to commence production in the second quarter of 2017, so a quick reply on your part would be great.

All the best,

Henry Gatlin

Henry Gatlin
Founder, CEO
Updraft RC

5 August 2017

Figure 3.4b   Intercultural Business Letter: First Revision
This version eliminates most of the problems with overly informal phrases and potentially offensive language. With these revisions, it would function well as a message between native speakers of English, but it still has some wording and formatting issues that could create difficulties for a Chinese reader. Compare with Figure 3.4c.

electronic connection that includes a video component, you can use hand gestures and other nonverbal signals to clarify your spoken message. When you don't have a visual connection, however, you must take extra care to convey your meaning through words and vocal characteristics alone. Conversely, listeners need to be tolerant of accents, vocabulary choices, gestures, and other factors that might distract them from hearing the meaning of a speaker's message.

When talking with people whose native language is different from yours, remember that the processing of even everyday conversations can be difficult. For instance, speakers from the United States sometimes string together multiple words into a single, mystifying pseudoword, such as turning "Did you eat yet?" into "Jeetyet?" In spoken French, many word pairs are joined as a matter of rule, and the pronunciation can change depending on which words are next to one another. In these instances, nonnative French speakers can have a hard time telling when one word ends and the next one begins.

UpdraftRC
4308 Preston Highway
Louisville, KY 40213
Toll Free: 1.800.FLY.RITE
Fax: (502) 555-1324
www.updraftrc.com

Dear Mr. Li:

With the widespread adoption of mobile phones, more and more accessories and associated products are being developed to meet new market demands. My company, Updraft RC, has designed a new line of radio-controlled toys that use smartphones as the controller. Our market tests show strong potential for demand among younger consumers, who are often eager to try new products. We are now looking for a manufacturing partner, and we are very willing to collaborate with you.

This will be our first experience of partnering with an overseas manufacturer, and before we discuss specific technical details, I would like you to know two of our general concerns. The first concern involves all the general challenges of a long-distance manufacturing partnership, including transportation costs, shipping delays, quality control, and the risk of intellectual property theft.

Second, U.S. companies that work with overseas production partners face an increasing amount of scrutiny from the news media and activist groups regarding such matters as workplace safety, worker rights, and environmentally sensitive manufacturing. Nike and other major U.S. companies have spent millions of dollars and worked for years to improve conditions in overseas factories, but even they have not be able to avoid all problems. As a small company with no ability to monitor factories, we are worried about any manufacturing-related problems that could affect our public image.

Please share your company's philosophy and strategies for minimizing these two concerns.

We would like to commence production in the second quarter of 2017, so we would like to hear your reply as soon as possible.

Thank you,

Henry Gatlin

Henry Gatlin
Founder, CEO
Updraft RC

5 August 2017

An inside address is typically not used in Chinese correspondence.

The salutation uses a colon rather than a comma.

The revised opening gives the reader some helpful context and the assurance that this is a meaningful business opportunity.

The phrase "we are very willing to collaborate with you" shows respect for the reader and suggests the interest in forming a partnership.

This paragraph has been shortened to eliminate the redundant request for information.

This revised paragraph still conveys the seriousness of the writer's concerns without offending the reader.

"Minimizing" is easier for a non-native speaker to understand than "mitigating."

"Thank you" is a simple and adequately formal closing.

Figure 3.4c   Intercultural Business Letter: Final Revision
Here is the final English version, revised to ensure more successful translation into Chinese and to conform to standard practices in Chinese business communication (including removing the inside address).

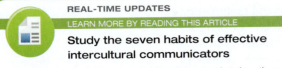

REAL-TIME UPDATES
LEARN MORE BY READING THIS ARTICLE
Study the seven habits of effective intercultural communicators

The willingness to take risks is a key habit; see what the other six are. Go to real-timeupdates.com/bct14 and select Learn More in the Students section.

To be more effective in intercultural conversations, speak slowly and clearly, but avoid talking down to the other person by overenunciating words or oversimplifying sentences. Don't rephrase until it's obviously necessary, because immediately rephrasing something you've just said doubles the translation workload for the listener. As the conversation progresses, look for and ask for feedback to make sure your message is getting through. At the end of the conversation, double-check to make sure you and the listener agree on what has been said and decided.

To listen more effectively in intercultural situations, accept what you hear without judgment and let people finish what they have to say.

As a listener, you'll need some practice to get a sense of vocal patterns. The key is simply to accept what you hear, without jumping to conclusions about meaning or motivation. Let other people finish what they have to say. If you interrupt, you may miss something important. You'll also show a lack of respect. If you do not understand a comment,

4308 Preston Highway
Louisville, KY 40213
Toll Free: 1.800.FLY.RITE
Fax: (502) 555-1324
www.updraftrc.com

李华先生：

　　随着智能手机的普及，越来越多的配件和周边产品正在被研发以满足市场的需求。我们的公司，Updraft RC,已经设计了一种新型的用智能手机控制的遥控玩具。我们的市场测试表明年轻客户，一个愿意尝试新产品的群体，（对我们的产品）有巨大的潜在需求。我们现在正在寻找制造伙伴，所以我们非常愿意与你们合作。

　　这是我们第一次与海外制造伙伴合作，在我们讨论具体细节之前，我非常愿意让你们知道我们的两个问题。第一个问题对远距制造商合作关系来说都是一个挑战，这个挑战包括运输费用，运输延迟，质量控制和知识产权盗窃。

　　第二，与大洋对岸合作的美国公司面临着越来越高的来自新媒体和活跃组织的审查。这些审查包括工作场所安全性，劳工权益和可能对环境产生损害的制造。耐克和其他主要的美国公司已经花费了数百万美元，工作了几十年用来提升海外工厂的情况，但是他们仍然不能避免所有的问题。对于没有能力监控（海外）工厂的小公司来说，我们比较当心与制造相关的一系列问题可能影响到我们公司的形象。

　　所以请让我们知道你们公司解决这两个问题的策略和方法。

　　我们计划在 2017 年的第二个季度投入产品的生产。所以我们希望尽快得到你们公司的回应。

　　　　　　　　　　　　　　亨利 加特林
　　　　　　　　　　　　　　创始人，首席执行官
　　　　　　　　　　　　　　2017年8月5日

Figure 3.4d Intercultural Business Letter: Translated Version
Here is the translated version, formatted in accordance with Chinese business communication practice.

ask the person to repeat it. Any momentary awkwardness you might feel in asking for extra help is less important than the risk of unsuccessful communication.

USING INTERPRETERS, TRANSLATORS, AND TRANSLATION SOFTWARE

You may encounter business situations that require using an *interpreter* (for spoken communication) or a *translator* (can be used for both spoken and written communication). Interpreters and translators can be expensive, but skilled professionals provide invaluable assistance for communicating in other cultural contexts.[55] Keeping up with current language usage in a given country or culture is also critical to avoid embarrassing blunders. In marketing and advertising, where being in tune with contemporary culture is critical, companies sometimes use *transcreation*, which essentially amounts to re-creating the material for a new cultural context, rather than simply translating the text.[56]

For important business communication, use a professional interpreter (for oral communication) or translator (for oral or written communication).

Figure 3.5   Writing for Multilingual Audiences
In today's global and diversified work environment, chances are that many of your messages will be read by people whose native language is not English. Notice how specific wording changes and modifications to sentence structure make the "Effective" version easier for nonnative speakers to read.

Some companies use *back-translation* to ensure accuracy. Once a translator encodes a message into another language, a different translator retranslates the same message into the original language. This back-translation is then compared with the original message to discover any errors or discrepancies.

The time and cost required for professional translation has encouraged the development of computerized translation tools. Dedicated software tools, mobile apps, and online services such as WorldLingo and Google Translate offer various forms of automated translation. Major search engines let you request translated versions of the websites you find. Although none of these tools can translate as well as human translators, they are getting better all the time.

HELPING OTHERS ADAPT TO YOUR CULTURE

Everyone can contribute to successful intercultural communication. Whether a younger person is unaccustomed to the formalities of a large corporation or a colleague from another country is working on a team with you, look for opportunities to help people fit in and adapt their communication style. For example, if a nonnative English speaker is making mistakes that could hurt his or her credibility, you can offer advice on the appropriate words and phrases to use. Most language learners truly appreciate this sort of assistance, as long as it is offered in a respectful manner. Moreover, chances are that while you're helping, you'll learn something about the other person's culture and language, too.

> Help others adapt to your culture; it will create a more productive workplace and teach you about their cultures as well.

You can also take steps to simplify the communication process. For instance, oral communication in a second language is usually more difficult than written forms of communication, so instead of asking a foreign colleague to provide information in a conference call, you could ask for a written response instead of or in addition to the live conversation.

For a brief summary of ideas to improve intercultural communication in the workplace, see "Checklist: Improving Intercultural Communication Skills." For additional information on communicating in a world of diversity, visit **real-timeupdates.com/bct14** and select Chapter 3.

CHECKLIST ✔ Improving Intercultural Communication Skills

- Understand your own culture so that you can recognize its influences on your communication habits.
- Study other cultures so that you can appreciate cultural variations.
- Study the languages of people with whom you communicate, even if you can learn only a few basic words and phrases.
- Help nonnative speakers learn your language.
- Respect cultural preferences for communication style.
- Write clearly, using brief messages, simple language, generous transitions, and appropriate international conventions.
- Avoid slang, humor, and references to popular culture.
- Speak clearly and slowly, giving listeners time to translate your words.
- Ask for feedback to verify that communication was successful.
- Listen carefully and ask speakers to repeat anything you don't understand.
- Use interpreters and translators for important messages.

COMMUNICATION CHALLENGES AT Kaiser Permanente

Kaiser Permanente puts a high priority on appreciating diversity and fostering a sense of inclusiveness among employees and patients. Imagine you're a department manager in a Kaiser medical center, where you're expected to maintain a climate of inclusion and support for employees of every cultural background. How would you address these challenges?

INDIVIDUAL CHALLENGE: Mihai Ciceu joined your department after relocating from Romania last year. He is a brilliant pricing and underwriting analyst, but he resists working with other employees, even in team settings where collaboration is expected. Given the importance that you place on teamwork, how should you handle the situation? List several alternatives for addressing this dilemma, identify which approach you would choose, and explain why you would do so.

TEAM CHALLENGE: Your employees are breaking into ethnically based cliques. Members of ethnic groups eat together, socialize together, and often chat in their native languages while they work. You appreciate how these groups give their members a sense of community, but you worry that these informal communication channels are alienating employees who are outside these groups and fragmenting the flow of information. How can you encourage a stronger sense of community and teamwork within your department? Brainstorm at least three steps you can take to encourage better cross-cultural communication in your department.

Quick Learning Guide

KEY TERMS

cultural competency An appreciation for cultural differences that affect communication and the ability to adjust one's communication style to ensure that efforts to send and receive messages across cultural boundaries are successful

cultural context The pattern of physical cues, environmental stimuli, and implicit understanding that convey meaning between two members of the same culture

cultural pluralism The practice of accepting multiple cultures on their own terms

culture A shared system of symbols, beliefs, attitudes, values, expectations, and norms for behavior

diversity All the characteristics and experiences that define each of us as individuals

ethnocentrism The tendency to judge other groups according to the standards, behaviors, and customs of one's own group

high-context culture Culture in which people rely less on verbal communication and more on the context of nonverbal actions and environmental setting to convey meaning

idiomatic phrases Phrases that mean more than the sum of their literal parts; such phrases can be difficult for nonnative speakers to understand

intercultural communication The process of sending and receiving messages between people whose cultural backgrounds could lead them to interpret verbal and nonverbal signs differently

low-context culture Culture in which people rely more on verbal communication and less on circumstances and nonverbal cues to convey meaning

stereotyping Assigning a wide range of generalized attributes to an individual on the basis of membership in a particular culture or social group

xenophobia Fear of strangers and foreigners

SUMMARY OF LEARNING OBJECTIVES

1 Discuss the opportunities and challenges of intercultural communication. The global marketplace spans natural boundaries and national borders, allowing worldwide competition between businesses of all sizes. Therefore, today's businesspeople are likely to communicate across international borders with people who live in different cultures. Moreover, even domestic workforces are becoming more diverse, with employees having different national, religious, and ethnic backgrounds. In this environment, companies can benefit from a broad range of viewpoints and ideas, get a good understanding of diverse markets, and recruit workers from the broadest possible pool of talent. However, intercultural communication presents challenges as well, including motivating diverse employees to cooperate and to work together in teams as well as understanding enough about how culture affects language to prevent miscommunication.

2 Define *culture*, explain how culture is learned, and define *ethnocentrism* and *stereotyping*. Culture is a shared system of symbols, beliefs, attitudes, values, expectations, and norms for behavior. Culture is learned by listening to advice from other members of a society and by observing their behaviors. This double-edged method uses direct and indirect learning to ensure that culture is passed from person to person and from generation to generation.

Ethnocentrism is the tendency to judge other groups according to the standards, behaviors, and customs of one's own group. Stereotyping is assigning a wide range of generalized attributes to individuals on the basis of their membership in a particular culture or social group, without considering an individual's unique characteristics. To overcome ethnocentrism and stereotyping, work to avoid assumptions, withhold judgment, and acknowledge distinctions.

3 Explain the importance of recognizing cultural variations and list eight categories of cultural differences. People from different cultures encode and decode messages differently, increasing the chances of misunderstanding. By recognizing and accommodating cultural differences, we avoid automatically assuming that everyone's thoughts and actions are just like ours. Begin by focusing on eight categories of differences: contextual differences (the degree to which a culture relies on verbal or nonverbal actions to convey meaning), legal and ethical differences (the degree to which laws and ethics are regarded and obeyed), social differences (how members value work and success, recognize status, define manners, and think about time), nonverbal differences (differing attitudes toward greetings, personal space, touching, facial expression, eye contact, posture, and formality), age differences (how members think about youth, seniority, and longevity), gender differences (how men and women communicate and the spectrum of gender identification), religious differences (how beliefs affect workplace relationships), and ability differences (inclusive strategies that enable people with disabilities to communicate more fully with the rest of the workforce).

4 List four general guidelines for adapting to any business culture. You can adapt to any business culture by (1) becoming aware of your own cultural biases so that you can understand how these forces shape your communication habits; (2) ignoring the Golden Rule (treating people the way you want them to treat you) and instead treating them the way *they* want to be treated; (3) exercising tolerance, flexibility, and respect; and (4) practicing patience and maintaining a sense of humor to get you through the bumpy spots.

5 Identify seven steps you can take to improve your intercultural communication skills. Communicating successfully between cultures requires a variety of skills, all of which you can continue to improve throughout your career. Make your intercultural communication effective by (1) studying other cultures; (2) studying other languages; (3) respecting your audience's preferences for communication style; (4) writing as clearly as possible; (5) speaking as clearly as you can; (6) listening carefully and using interpreters, translators, and translation software when necessary; and (7) helping others adapt to your own culture.

MyBCommLab®
Go to **mybcommlab.com** to complete the problems marked with this icon .

Test Your Knowledge

To review chapter content related to each question, refer to the indicated Learning Objective.

3-1. What are the potential advantages of a diverse workforce? [LO-1]

3-2. What is cultural competence? [LO-2]

3-3. What is ethnocentrism, and how can it be overcome in communication? [LO-2]

3-4. How do high-context cultures differ from low-context cultures? [LO-3]

3-5. In addition to contextual differences, what other categories of cultural differences exist? [LO-3]

3-6. How does a sense of humor come in handy during intercultural communication? [LO-4]

3-7. How can the Golden Rule cause problems in intercultural communication? [LO-4]

3-8. What steps can you take to help someone from another culture adapt to your culture? [LO-5]

Apply Your Knowledge

To review chapter content related to each question, refer to the indicated Learning Objective.

3-9. Make a list of the top five priorities in your life (for example, fame, wealth, family, spirituality, peace of mind, individuality, artistic expression). Compare your list with the priorities that seem to be valued in the culture in which you are currently living. (You can be as broad or as narrow as you like in defining *culture* for this exercise, such as overall U.S. culture or the culture in your college or university.) Do your personal priorities align with the culture's priorities? If not, how might this disparity affect your communication with other members of the culture? [LO-2]

3-10. How does making an effort to avoid assumptions contribute to the practice of cultural pluralism? [LO-2]

3-11. Why is it important to understand your own culture when attempting to communicate with people from other cultures? [LO-4]

3-12. Think about the last three movies or television shows set in the United States that you've watched. In what ways would these entertainment products be helpful or unhelpful for people from other countries trying to learn about U.S. culture? [LO-5]

3-13. How can helping someone adapt to your culture help you gain a better understand of it yourself? [LO-5]

Practice Your Skills

3-14. **Message for Analysis: Adapting to Cultural Differences** [LO-5] Your boss wants to send a brief email message welcoming employees recently transferred to your department from the company's Hong Kong branch. These employees, all of whom are Hong Kong natives, speak English, but your boss asks you to review his message for clarity. What would you suggest your boss change in the following email message? Why? Would you consider this message to be audience centered? Why or why not? (Hint: Do some quick research on Hong Kong to identify the style of English that people there are likely to speak.)

I wanted to welcome you ASAP to our little family here in the States. It's high time we shook hands in person and not just across the sea. I'm pleased as punch about getting to know you all, and I for one will do my level best to sell you on America.

Exercises

Each activity is labeled according to the primary skill or skills you will need to use. To review relevant chapter content, you can refer to the indicated Learning Objective. In some instances, supporting information will be found in another chapter, as indicated.

3-15. **Intercultural Communication: Recognizing Cultural Variations [LO-1], [LO-3], [LO-4]** Review the definitions of the generations on page 77. Based on your year of birth, to which generation do you belong? Do you feel a part of this generation? Why or why not? If you were born outside the United States, do the generational boundaries seem accurate to you? Now consider the biases that you might have regarding other generations. For example, if you are a member of Generation Y, what do you think about the Baby Boomers and their willingness to embrace new ideas? Identify several of your generational biases that could create friction in the workplace. Summarize your responses to these questions in a post on your class blog or an email message to your instructor.

3-16. **Intercultural Communication: Adapting to Cultural Variations [LO-4]** You are a new manager at K & J Brick, a masonry products company that is now run by the two sons of the man who founded it 50 years ago. For years, the co-owners have invited the management team to a wilderness lodge for a combination of outdoor sports and annual business planning meetings. You don't want to miss the event, but you know that the outdoor activities weren't designed for someone like you, whose physical impairments prevent participation in the sporting events. Draft a short email message to the rest of the management team, suggesting changes to the annual event that will allow all managers to participate.

3-17. **Intercultural Communication: Writing for Multiple-Language Audiences [LO-5]** Reading English-language content written by nonnative English speakers can be a good reminder of the challenges of communicating in another language. The writing can be confusing or even amusing at first glance, but the key to remember here is that your writing might sound just as confusing or amusing to someone else if your roles were reversed.

Identify a company that is based in a non-English-speaking country but that includes English-language text on its website. (The advanced search capabilities of your favorite search engine can help you locate websites from a particular country.) Study the language on this site. Does it sound as though it was written by someone adept at English? If the first site you've found does have writing that sounds natural to a native U.S. English speaker, find another company whose website doesn't. Select a section of text (at least several sentences long) and rewrite it to sound more "American." Submit the original text and your rewritten version to your instructor.

3-18. **Intercultural Communication: Writing for Multiple-Language Audiences; Collaboration: Team Projects [LO-5], Chapter 2** With a team assigned by your instructor, review the Facebook pages of five companies and look for words and phrases that might be confusing to a non-native speaker of English. If you (or someone on the team) are a nonnative speaker, explain to the team why those word choices could be confusing. Choose three sentences, headlines, company slogans, or other pieces of text that contain potentially confusing words and rewrite them to minimize the chances of misinterpretation. As much as possible, try to retain the tone of the original—although you may find that this is impossible in some instances. Use Google Docs to compile the original selections and your revised versions, then email the documents to your instructor.

3-19. **Intercultural Communication: Speaking with Multiple-Language Audiences; Collaboration: Team Projects [LO-5], Chapter 2** Working with two other students, prepare a list of 10 examples of slang (in your own language) that might be misinterpreted or misunderstood during a business conversation with someone from another culture. Next to each example, suggest other words you might use to convey the same message. Do the alternatives mean *exactly* the same as the original slang or idiom? Submit your list of original words and suggested replacements, with an explanation of why each replacement is better than the original.

3-20. **Intercultural Communication: Writing for Multiple-Language Audiences [LO-5]** Explore the powers and limitations of free online translation services such as Google Translate. Enter a sentence from this chapter, such as "It gets even more daunting when you add the challenges of communication among medical staff and between patients and their caregivers, which often takes place under stressful circumstances." First, translate the sentence from English to Spanish. Next, copy the Spanish version and paste it into the translation entry box and back-translate it from Spanish to English. Now repeat this test for another language. Did the sentence survive the round trip? Does it still sound like normal business writing when translated back into English?

(a) What are the implications for the use of automated translation services for international correspondence? (b) Would you feel comfortable using an online tool such as this to translate an important business message? (c) How might you use this website to sharpen your intercultural communication skills? Summarize your findings in a brief report.

3-21. **Intercultural Communication: Speaking with Multiple-Language Audiences; Media Skills: Podcasting [LO-5], Chapter 7** Your company was one of the first to use podcasting as a business communication tool. Executives frequently record messages (such as monthly sales summaries) and post them on the company's intranet; employees from the 14 offices in Europe, Asia, and North America then download the files to their music players or other devices and listen to the messages while riding the train to work, eating lunch at their desks, and so on. Your boss asks you to draft the opening statement for a podcast that will announce a revenue drop caused by intensive competitive pressure. She reviews your script and hands it back with a gentle explanation that it needs to be revised for international listeners. Improve the following statement in as many ways as you can:

Howdy, comrades. Shouldn't surprise anyone that we took a beating this year, given the insane pricing moves our knucklehead competitors have been making. I mean, how those clowns can keep turning a profit is beyond me, what with steel costs still going through the roof and labor costs heating up—even in countries where everybody goes to find cheap labor—and hazardous waste disposal regs adding to operating costs, too.

Expand Your Skills

Critique the Professionals

Find an online business document—such as a company webpage, blog post, Facebook Info tab, or LinkedIn profile—that you believe commits an intercultural communication blunder by failing to consider the needs of at least some of its target readers. For example, a website might use slang or idiomatic language that could confuse some readers, or it might use language that offends some readers. In a post on your class blog, share the text you found and explain why you think it does not succeed as effective intercultural communication. Be sure to include a link back to the original material.

Sharpening Your Career Skills Online

Bovée and Thill's Business Communication Web Search, at **websearch.businesscommunicationnetwork.com**, is a unique research tool designed specifically for business communication research. Use the Web Search function to find a website, video, article, podcast, or presentation that offers advice on communicating with business contacts in another country or culture. Write a brief email message to your instructor, describing the item you found and summarizing the career skills information you learned from it.

MyBCommLab

Go to **mybcommlab.com** for Auto-graded writing questions as well as the following Assisted-graded writing questions:

3-22. What three habits can help you develop a sense of cultural pluralism? [LO-2]
3-23. What four principles apply to ethical intercultural communication? [LO-3]

Endnotes

1. Bernard J. Tyson, "Diversity and Inclusion Are in Kaiser Permanente's DNA," Kaiser Permanente website, accessed 11 March 2016, kp.org; Marianne Aiello, "Diversity No Gimmick in Kaiser Permanente Ad Campaign," *HealthLeaders Media*, 25 November 2015, www.healthleadersmedia.com; "Top Reasons to Join Kaiser Permanente As a Woman in Tech," Kaiser Permanente website, accessed 11 March 2016, kp.org; "Kaiser Permanente—Achieving Our Mission and Growing the Business Through the National Diversity Agenda," Catalyst, 25 January 2011, www.catalyst.org; "DiversityInc Top 50" and "Diversity Leadership: Dr. Ronald Copeland, Kaiser Permanente," DiversityInc, accessed 11 March 2016, www.diversityinc.com; "Census Bureau Reports at Least 350 Languages Spoken in U.S. Homes," U.S. Census Bureau, 3 November 2015, www.census.gov. "Local and National Diversity Programs," Kaiser Permanente website, accessed 12 March 2016, kp.org.
2. Michael R. Carrell, Everett E. Mann, and Tracey Honeycutt-Sigler, "Defining Workforce Diversity Programs and Practices in Organizations: A Longitudinal Study," *Labor Law Journal* 57, no. 1 (Spring 2006): 5–12.
3. "Dimensions of Diversity—Workforce," Merck website, accessed 4 January 2011, www.merck.com.
4. "Top Trading Partners - January 2016," U.S. Census Bureau website, accessed 12 March 2016, www.census.gov.
5. Economist Intelligence Unit, "Competing Across Borders: How Cultural and Communication Barriers Affect Business," *Economist*, 2012, 4, www.economistinsights.com.
6. Nancy R. Lockwood, "Workplace Diversity: Leveraging the Power of Difference for Competitive Advantage," *HR Magazine*, June 2005, special section, 1–10.
7. Alan Kline, "The Business Case for Diversity," *USBanker*, May 2010, 10–11.
8. "Quick Facts: United States," U.S. Census Bureau website, accessed 12 March 2016, www.census.gov; Paul Taylor, "The Next America," Pew Research Center, 10 April 2014, www.pewresearch.org; "More Than 300 Counties Now 'Majority–Minority,'" press release, U.S. Census Bureau website, 9 August 2007, www.census.gov; Robert Kreitner, *Management*, 9th ed. (Boston: Houghton Mifflin, 2004), 84.
9. Tracy Novinger, *Intercultural Communication: A Practical Guide* (Austin: University of Texas Press, 2001), 15.
10. Larry A. Samovar and Richard E. Porter, "Basic Principles of Intercultural Communication," in *Intercultural Communication: A Reader*, 6th ed., edited by Larry A. Samovar and Richard E. Porter (Belmont, Calif.: Wadsworth, 1991), 12.
11. Arthur Chin, "Understanding Cultural Competency," *New Zealand Business*, December 2010/January 2011, 34–35; Sanjeeta R. Gupta, "Achieve Cultural Competency," *Training*, February 2009, 16–17; Diane Shannon, "Cultural Competency in Health Care

Organizations: Why and How," *Physician Executive*, September–October 2010, 15–22.
12. Linda Beamer and Iris Varner, *Intercultural Communication in the Workplace*, 2nd ed. (New York: McGraw-Hill Irwin, 2001), 3.
13. "Summary by Country," Ethnologue website, accessed 12 March 2016, www.ethnologue.com.
14. Philip R. Harris and Robert T. Moran, *Managing Cultural Differences*, 3rd ed. (Houston: Gulf, 1991), 394–397, 429–430.
15. Lillian H. Chaney and Jeanette S. Martin, *Intercultural Business Communication*, 2nd ed. (Upper Saddle River, N.J.: Prentice Hall, 2000), 6.
16. Beamer and Varner, *Intercultural Communication in the Workplace*, 4.
17. Chaney and Martin, *Intercultural Business Communication*, 2nd ed., 9.
18. Richard L. Daft, *Management*, 6th ed. (Cincinnati: Thomson South-Western, 2003), 455.
19. Lillian H. Chaney and Jeanette S. Martin, *Intercultural Business Communication*, 4th ed. (Upper Saddle River, N.J.: Pearson Prentice Hall, 2007), 53.
20. Project Implicit website, accessed 29 December 2010, implicit.harvard.edu/implicit.
21. Linda Beamer, "Teaching English Business Writing to Chinese-Speaking Business Students," *Bulletin of the Association for Business Communication* 57, no. 1 (1994): 12–18.
22. Edward T. Hall, "Context and Meaning," in *Intercultural Communication*, 6th ed., edited by Larry A. Samovar and Richard E. Porter (Belmont, Calif.: Wadsworth, 1991), 46–55.
23. Daft, *Management*, 459.
24. Charley H. Dodd, *Dynamics of Intercultural Communication*, 3rd ed. (Dubuque, Ia.: Brown, 1991), 69–70.
25. Daft, *Management*, 459.
26. Hannah Seligson, "For American Workers in China, a Culture Clash," *New York Times*, 23 December 2009, www.nytimes.com.
27. Beamer and Varner, *Intercultural Communication in the Workplace*, 230–233.
28. Ed Marcum, "More U.S. Businesses Abandon Outsourcing Overseas," *Seattle Times*, 28 August 2010, www.seattletimes.com.
29. Guo-Ming Chen and William J. Starosta, *Foundations of Intercultural Communication* (Boston: Allyn & Bacon, 1998), 288–289.
30. Joyce Millet, "Chinese Etiquette & Protocol," Protocol Professionals, accessed 12 March 2016, www.protocolprofessionals.com.
31. Chaney and Martin, *Intercultural Business Communication*, 2nd ed., 122–123.
32. Mansour Javidan, "Forward-Thinking Cultures," *Harvard Business Review*, July–August 2007, 20.
33. "The 100 Million Club 2013: The Top 14 Mobile Markets by Number of Mobile Subscriptions and 3G/4G Subscribers," *MobiThinking*, 26 November 2013, www.mobithinking.com.
34. Novinger, *Intercultural Communication*, 54.

35. Peter Coy, "Old. Smart. Productive." *BusinessWeek*, 27 June 2005, www.businessweek.com; Beamer and Varner, *Intercultural Communication in the Workplace*, 107–108.

36. Beamer and Varner, *Intercultural Communication in the Workplace*, 107–108.

37. Rebecca Knight, "Managing People from 5 Generations," *Harvard Business Review*, 25 September 2014, hbr.org.

38. Steff Gelston, "Gen Y, Gen X and the Baby Boomers: Workplace Generation Wars," *CIO*, 30 January 2008, www.cio.com.

39. Joanna Barsh and Lareina Yee, "Changing Companies' Minds About Women," *McKinsey Quarterly*, no. 4 (2011): 48–59.

40. John Gray, *Mars and Venus in the Workplace* (New York: HarperCollins, 2002), 10, 25–27, 61–63.

41. Jennifer Luden, "Ask for a Raise? Most Women Hesitate," *NPR*, 14 February 2011, www.npr.org.

42. "First Step: Gender Identity in the Workplace," Catalyst, June 2015, www.catalyst.org.

43. "Religious Bias a Growing Issue," *Business Insurance*, 13 February 2012, 8; Mark D. Downey, "Keeping the Faith," *HR Magazine*, January 2008, 85–88.

44. IBM Accessibility Center, accessed 24 August 2006, www-03 .ibm.com/able; AssistiveTech.net, accessed 24 August 2006, www .assistivetech.net; Business Leadership Network website, accessed 24 August 2006, www.usbln.org; National Institute on Disability and Rehabilitation Research website, accessed 24 August 2006, www .ed.gov/about/offices/list/osers/nidrr; Rehabilitation Engineering & Assistive Technology Society of North America website, accessed 24 August 2006, www.resna.org.

45. Daphne A. Jameson, "Reconceptualizing Cultural Identity and Its Role in Intercultural Business Communication," *International Journal of Business Communication* 44, no. 3 (July 2007): 199–235.

46. Leslie Knudson, "Diversity on a Global Scale," *HR Management*, accessed 17 August 2008, www.hrmreport.com.

47. Craig S. Smith, "Beware of Green Hats in China and Other Cross-Cultural Faux Pas," *New York Times*, 30 April 2002, C11.

48. Sana Reynolds and Deborah Valentine, *Guide for Internationals: Culture, Communication, and ESL* (Upper Saddle River, N.J.: Pearson Prentice Hall, 2006), 3–11, 14–19, 25.

49. P. Christopher Earley and Elaine Mosakowsi, "Cultural Intelligence," *Harvard Business Review*, October 2004, 139–146.

50. Bob Nelson, "Motivating Workers Worldwide," *Global Workforce*, November 1998, 25–27.

51. Mona Casady and Lynn Wasson, "Written Communication Skills of International Business Persons," *Bulletin of the Association for Business Communication* 57, no. 4 (1994): 36–40.

52. Lynn Gaertner-Johnston, "Found in Translation," Business Writing blog, 25 November 2005, www.businesswritingblog.com.

53. Myron W. Lustig and Jolene Koester, *Intercultural Competence*, 4th ed. (Boston: Allyn & Bacon, 2003), 196.

54. Pamela Rogerson-Revell, "'Can You Spell That for Us Nonnative Speakers?' Accommodation Strategies in International Business Meetings," *International Journal of Business Communication* 47, no. 4 (October 2010): 432–454.

55. James Wilfong and Toni Seger, *Taking Your Business Global* (Franklin Lakes, N.J.: Career Press, 1997), 232.

56. "Transcreation Services," Lionbridge, accessed 14 March 2016, www.lionbridge.com; Nataly Kelly, "Six Ways Transcreation Differs from Translation," Smartling, 21 July 2014, www.smartling.com.

Applying the Three-Step Writing Process

Every professional can learn to write more effectively while spending less time and energy in creating successful messages. Discover a proven writing process that divides the challenge of communicating into three simple steps: planning, writing, and completing messages. The process works for everything from blog posts to formal reports to your résumé. With a bit of practice, you'll be using the process to write more effectively without even thinking about it.

Photobee/Fotolia

PART

2 Applying the Three-Step Writing Process

Planning Business Messages

LEARNING OBJECTIVES

After studying this chapter, you will be able to

1 Describe the three-step writing process.

2 Explain why it's important to analyze a communication situation in order to define your purpose and profile your audience before writing a message.

3 Discuss information-gathering options for simple messages, and identify three attributes of quality information.

4 List the factors to consider when choosing the most appropriate medium for a message.

5 Explain why good organization is important to both you and your audience, and list the tasks involved in organizing a message.

MyBCommLab®

⭐ **Improve Your Grade!** More than 10 million students improved their results using the Pearson MyLabs. Visit **mybcommlab.com** for simulations, tutorials, and end-of-chapter problems.

COMMUNICATION CLOSE-UP AT

Wolff Olins

www.wolffolins.com

What do the following activities have in common: watching a movie, reading a novel, and listening to a friend tell you how she learned about herself during an amazing summer she spent volunteering? The common thread is *dramatic tension*—the need to know how the story is going to turn out. If you care about the person in the story, chances are you'll want to stick around to the end.

Storytelling might sound like an odd topic for a business communication course, but storytelling is at the heart of some of the most-effective communication efforts, from heart-tugging TV commercials to engaging training materials to rousing motivational speeches. With more and more professionals and companies recognizing the power of storytelling, storytelling techniques have become a hot topic in the business communication field.

As one of the most respected novelists and essayists of his generation, it's no surprise that the Pakistani writer Mohsin Hamid is an expert at storytelling. But it might come as a surprise to his many fans that he has a second career as the chief storytelling officer (CSO) for Wolff Olins, an international creativity consultancy based in London. In this role Hamid helps business professionals and executives use the art of storytelling as a means to engage with both internal and external audiences.

For example, the company heard from a number of top executives about the challenges of conveying to employees a clear sense of their companies' purpose and empowering them to apply their individual creative energies to achieving that purpose. Hamid explains that's it unrealistic to expect an executive to give everyone in the organization explicit task assignments. Instead, he or she can tell the company's story—where it came from, the reason it exists, and where it is heading—to help employees align their efforts in that shared mission.

Hamid advises executives to engage in this sort of strategic storytelling at three key stages of a company's evolution: when it is first

© D Legakis/Alamy Stock Photo

Novelist and essayist Mohsin Hamid has a second career as the chief storytelling officer at the London-based creative consultancy Wolff Olins.

launched, so that everyone knows where and how the company intends to grow; whenever major changes occur, so that everyone understands how the narrative has changed; and whenever the company's growth trajectory stalls, to reiterate what the company stands for and how it can overcome the odds. For instance, if a company is facing new competition, the CEO could relate a story from the company's past about how people came together to find better ways to satisfy customers and thereby protect the business.

By the way, business storytelling has an important personal angle as well. You can map out your career using storytelling (see page 117), and when you're interviewing for jobs you should be prepared in case an interviewer pops the classic question, "So, what's your story?" By visualizing a satisfying ending to your own career story, you'll have a better idea of what it takes to get there.[1]

Understanding the Three-Step Writing Process

1 LEARNING OBJECTIVE Describe the three-step writing process.

The emphasis that Wolff Olins (profiled in the chapter-opening Communication Close-Up) puts on connecting with audiences is a lesson that applies to business messages for all stakeholders. By following the process introduced in this chapter, you can create successful messages that meet audience needs and highlight your skills as a perceptive business professional.

The three-step writing process consists of *planning*, *writing*, and *completing* your messages.

The three-step writing process (see Figure 4.1) helps ensure that your messages are both *effective* (meeting your audience's needs and getting your points across) and *efficient* (making the best use of your time and your audience's time):

- **Step 1: Planning business messages.** To plan any message, first *analyze the situation* by defining your purpose and developing a profile of your audience. When you're sure what you need to accomplish with your message, *gather the information* that will meet your audience's needs. Next, *select the best combination of medium and*

1 Plan →	**2** Write →	**3** Complete
Analyze the Situation Define your purpose and develop an audience profile. **Gather Information** Determine audience needs and obtain the information necessary to satisfy those needs. **Choose Medium and Channel** Identify the best combination for the situation, message, and audience. **Organize the Information** Define your main idea, limit your scope, select a direct or an indirect approach, and outline your content.	**Adapt to Your Audience** Be sensitive to audience needs by using a "you" attitude, politeness, positive emphasis, and unbiased language. Build a strong relationship with your audience by establishing your credibility and projecting your company's preferred image. Control your style with a conversational tone, plain English, and appropriate voice. **Compose the Message** Choose strong words that will help you create effective sentences and coherent paragraphs.	**Revise the Message** Evaluate content and review readability, edit and rewrite for conciseness and clarity. **Produce the Message** Use effective design elements and suitable layout for a clean, professional appearance. **Proofread the Message** Review for errors in layout, spelling, and mechanics. **Distribute the Message** Deliver your message using the chosen medium; make sure all documents and all relevant file sare distributed successfully.

Figure 4.1   The Three-Step Writing Process
This three-step process will help you create more effective messages in any medium. As you get more practice with the process, it will become easier and more automatic.
Sources: Based in part on Kevin J. Harty and John Keenan, *Writing for Business and Industry: Process and Product* (New York: Macmillan Publishing Company, 1987), 3–4; Richard Hatch, *Business Writing* (Chicago: Science Research Associates, 1983), 88–89; Richard Hatch, *Business Communication Theory and Technique* (Chicago: Science Research Associates, 1983), 74–75; Center for Humanities, *Writing as a Process: A Step-by-Step Guide* (Mount Kisco, N.Y.: Center for Humanities, 1987); Michael L. Keene, *Effective Professional Writing* (New York: D. C. Heath, 1987), 28–34.

channel to deliver your message. Then *organize the information* by defining your main idea, limiting your scope, selecting the direct or indirect approach, and outlining your content. Planning messages is the focus of this chapter.

- **Step 2: Writing business messages.** After you've planned your message, *adapt to your audience* by using sensitivity, relationship skills, and an appropriate writing style. Then you're ready to *compose your message* by choosing strong words, creating effective sentences, and developing coherent paragraphs. Writing business messages is discussed in Chapter 5.
- **Step 3: Completing business messages.** After writing your first draft, *revise your message* by evaluating the content, reviewing readability, and editing and rewriting until your message comes across concisely and clearly, with correct grammar, proper punctuation, and effective format. Next, *produce your message*. Put it into the form that your audience will receive and review all design and layout decisions for an attractive, professional appearance. *Proofread* the final product to ensure high quality and then *distribute your message*. Completing business messages is discussed in Chapter 6.

Throughout this book, you'll learn how to apply these steps to a wide variety of business messages.

OPTIMIZING YOUR WRITING TIME

The more you use the three-step writing process, the more intuitive and automatic it will become. You'll also get better at allotting time for each task during a writing project. Start by figuring out how much time you have. Then, as a general rule, set aside roughly 50 percent of that time for planning, 25 percent for writing, and 25 percent for completing.

As a starting point, allot roughly half your available time for planning, one-quarter for writing, and one-quarter for completing a message.

Reserving half your time for planning might seem excessive, but as the next section explains, careful planning usually saves time overall by focusing your writing and reducing the need for reworking. Of course, the ideal time allocation varies from project to project. Simpler and shorter messages require less planning than long reports, websites, and other complex projects. Also, the time required to produce and distribute messages can vary widely, depending on the media, the size of the audience, and other factors. Start with the 50-25-25 split as a guideline, and use your best judgment for each project.

PLANNING EFFECTIVELY

As soon as the need to create a message appears, inexperienced communicators are often tempted to dive directly into writing. However, skipping or shortchanging the planning stage often creates extra work and stress later in the process. First, thoughtful planning is necessary to make sure you provide the right information in the right format to the right people. Taking the time to understand your audience members and their needs helps you find and assemble the facts they're looking for and deliver that information in a concise and compelling way. Second, with careful planning, the writing stage is faster, easier, and much less stressful. Third, planning can save you from embarrassing blunders that could hurt your company or your career.

For everything beyond brief and simple messages, resist the urge to skip the planning step.

Analyzing the Situation

Every communication effort takes place in a particular situation, meaning you have a specific message to send to a specific audience under a specific set of circumstances. For example, describing your professional qualifications in an email message to an executive in your own company differs significantly from describing your qualifications in your LinkedIn profile. The email message is likely to be focused on a single goal, such as explaining why you would be a good choice to head up a major project,

2 LEARNING OBJECTIVE
Explain why it's important to analyze a communication situation in order to define your purpose and profile your audience before writing a message.

and you have the luxury of focusing on the needs of a single, personally identifiable reader. In contrast, your social networking profile could have multiple goals, such as connecting with your peers at other companies and presenting your qualifications to potential employers, and it might be viewed by hundreds or thousands of readers, each with his or her own needs.

The underlying information for these two messages could be roughly the same, but the level of detail to include, the tone of the writing, the specific word choices—these and other decisions you need to make will differ from one situation to another. Making the right choices starts with clearly defining your purpose and understanding your audience's needs.

DEFINING YOUR PURPOSE

Business messages have both a general purpose and a specific purpose.

All business messages have a **general purpose**: to inform, to persuade, or to collaborate with the audience. This purpose helps define the overall approach you'll need to take, from gathering information to organizing your message. Within the scope of its general purpose, each message also has a **specific purpose**, which identifies what you hope to accomplish with your message and what your audience should do or think after receiving your message. For instance, is your goal simply to update your audience about some upcoming event, or do you want people to take immediate action? State your specific purpose as precisely as possible, even to the point of identifying which audience members should respond, how they should respond, and when.

After defining your purpose, verify that the message will be worth the time and effort required to create, send, and receive it.

After you have defined your specific purpose, take a moment for a reality check. Decide whether that purpose merits the time and effort required for you to prepare and send the message—and for your audience to spend the time required to read it, view it, or listen to it. Test your purpose by asking these four questions:

- **Will anything change as a result of your message?** Don't contribute to information overload by sending messages that won't change anything. For instance, if you don't like your company's latest advertising campaign but you're not in a position to influence it, sending a critical message to your colleagues won't change anything and won't benefit anyone.
- **Is your purpose realistic?** Recognizing whether a goal is realistic is an important part of having good business sense. For example, if you request a raise while the company is struggling, you might send the message that you're not tuned in to the situation around you.
- **Is the time right?** People who are busy or distracted when they receive your message are less likely to pay attention to it. Many professions and departments have recurring cycles in their workloads, for instance, and messages sent during peak times may be ignored.
- **Is your purpose acceptable to your organization?** Your company's business objectives and policies, and even laws that apply to your particular industry, may dictate whether a particular purpose is acceptable. For example, if you work for a discount stock brokerage, one that doesn't offer investing advice, it would be inappropriate to write a newsletter article on the pros and cons of investing in a particular company.

When you are satisfied that you have a clear and meaningful purpose and that this is a smart time to proceed, your next step is to understand the members of your audience and their needs.

DEVELOPING AN AUDIENCE PROFILE

Ask yourself some key questions about your audience:
- Who are they?
- How many people do you need to reach?
- How much do they already know about the subject?
- What is their probable reaction to your message?

Before audience members will take the time to read or listen to your messages, they have to be interested in what you're saying. They need to know the message is relevant to their needs—even if they don't necessarily want to read or see it. The more you know about

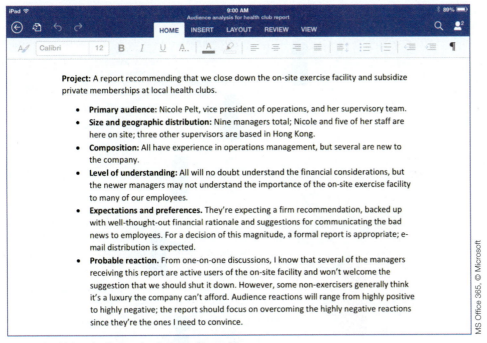

Figure 4.2 **Using Audience Analysis to Plan a Message**
For simple, routine messages, you usually don't need to analyze your audience in depth. However, for complex messages or messages for indifferent or hostile audiences, take the time to study their information needs and potential reactions to your message.

your audience members, their needs, and their expectations, the more effectively you'll be able to communicate with them. Follow these steps to conduct a thorough audience analysis (see Figure 4.2):

- **Identify your primary audience.** For some messages, certain audience members may be more important than others. Don't ignore the needs of less influential members, but make sure you address the concerns of the key decision makers.
- **Determine audience size and geographic distribution.** A message aimed at 10,000 people spread around the globe will probably require a different approach than one aimed at a dozen people down the hall.
- **Determine audience composition.** Look for similarities and differences in culture, language, age, education, organizational rank and status, attitudes, experience, motivations, biases, beliefs, and any other factors that might affect the success of your message (see Figure 4.3 on the next page).
- **Gauge audience members' level of understanding.** If audience members share your general background, they'll probably understand your material without difficulty. If not, your message will need an element of education to help people understand it.
- **Understand audience expectations and preferences.** For example, will members of your audience expect complete details or just a summary of the main points? In general, for internal communication, the higher up the organization your message goes, the fewer details people want to see.
- **Forecast probable audience reaction.** As you'll read later in the chapter, potential audience reaction affects message organization. If you expect a favorable response, you can state conclusions and recommendations up front and offer minimal supporting evidence. If you expect skepticism, you can introduce conclusions gradually and provide more proof.

> If audience members have different levels of understanding of the topic, aim your message at the most influential decision makers.

REAL-TIME UPDATES
LEARN MORE BY READING THIS PDF

Dig deep into audience needs with this planning tool

This in-depth tool can help you analyze audiences for even the most complex communication scenarios. Go to **real-timeupdates.com/bct14** and select Learn More in the Students section.

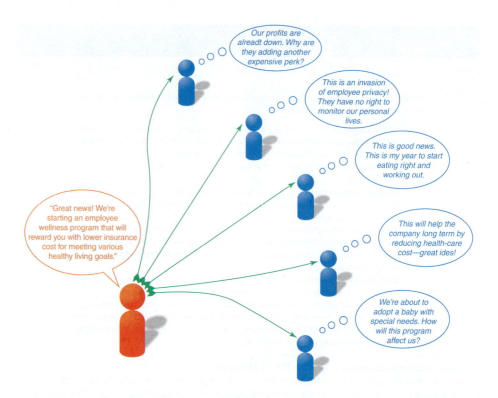

Figure 4.3 Predicting the Effects of Audience Composition

As just one example of why it's important to analyze the composition of your audience, the attitudes and beliefs of individual audience members can have a significant impact on the success of a message. In this scenario, for instance, a seemingly positive message about employee benefits can generate a wide range of responses from employees with different beliefs and concerns.

Gathering Information

3 **LEARNING OBJECTIVE**
Discuss information-gathering options for simple messages, and identify three attributes of quality information.

If a project doesn't require formal research techniques, or if you need answers in a hurry, you can use a variety of informal techniques to gather the information your audience needs.

MOBILE APP
The note-taking apps **Evernote** and **Notebook** help you collect, organize, and retrieve information for planning writing projects.

When you have a clear picture of your audience, your next step is to assemble the information to include in your message. For simple messages, you may already have all the information at hand, but for more complex messages, you may need to do considerable research and analysis before you're ready to begin writing. Chapter 13 explores formal techniques for finding, evaluating, and processing information, but you can often use a variety of informal techniques to gather insights and guide your research efforts.

- **Consider the audience's perspective.** Put yourself in the audience's position. What are these people thinking, feeling, or planning? What information do they need to move forward? If you are initiating a conversation in a social media context, what information will stimulate discussion among your target communities?
- **Listen to the community.** For almost any subject related to business these days, chances are there is a community of customers, product enthusiasts, or other people who engage in online discussions. Find them and listen to what they have to say.
- **Read reports and other company documents.** Annual reports, financial statements, news releases, blogs by industry experts, marketing reports, and customer surveys are just a few of the many potential information sources. Find out whether your company has a *knowledge management system*, a centralized database that collects the experiences and insights of employees throughout the organization.
- **Talk with supervisors, colleagues, or customers.** Fellow workers and customers may have information you need, or they may have good insights into the needs of your target audience.
- **Ask your audience for input.** If you're unsure what audience members need from your message, ask them, if possible. Admitting you don't know but want to meet their needs will impress an audience more than guessing and getting it wrong.

UNCOVERING AUDIENCE NEEDS

In many situations your audience's information needs will be obvious, or readers will be able to tell you what they need. In other situations, though, people may be unable to articulate exactly what they want. If someone makes a vague or broad request, ask questions to narrow the focus. If your boss says, "Find out everything you can about Interscope Records," narrow the investigation by asking which aspect of the organization and its business is most important. Asking a question or two often forces the person to think through the request and define more precisely what is required.

In addition, try to think of relevant information needs that your audience may not have expressed. Suppose you've been asked to compare two health insurance plans for your firm's employees, but your research has uncovered a third alternative that might be even better. You could then expand your report to include a brief explanation of why the third plan should be considered and compare it with the two original plans. Use judgment, however; in some situations you need to provide only what the audience expects and nothing more.

Audience members might not be able to describe all the information they need, or you might not have the opportunity to ask them, so you may have to engage in some detective work.

FINDING YOUR FOCUS

You may encounter situations in which the assignment or objective is so vague that you have no idea how to get started in determining what the audience needs to know. In such cases you can use some *discovery techniques* to help generate ideas and uncover possible avenues to research. One popular technique is **free writing**, in which you write whatever comes to mind, without stopping to make any corrections, for a set period of time. The big advantage of free writing is that you silence your "inner critic" and just express ideas as they come to you. You might end up with a rambling mess by any conventional measure, but that's not important. Within that tangle of expressions, you might also find some useful ideas and angles that hadn't occurred to you yet—perhaps the crucial idea that will jumpstart the entire project.

The best discovery option in some cases might not be writing at all, but rather *sketching*. If you're unable to come up with any words, grab a sketchpad and start drawing. While you're thinking visually, your brain might release some great ideas that were trapped behind words.

The techniques listed under "Defining Your Main Idea" on page 113 can also be helpful if you don't know where to start.

Use free writing and other discovery techniques if you need to the find the focus of a new writing project.

PROVIDING REQUIRED INFORMATION

After you have defined your audience's information needs, your next step is to satisfy those needs completely. One good way to test the thoroughness of your message is to use the **journalistic approach**: Check to see whether your message answers *who, what, when, where, why,* and *how*. Using this method, you can quickly tell whether a message fails to deliver. For example, consider this message requesting information from employees:

> We are exploring ways to reduce our office space leasing costs and would like your input on a proposed plan in which employees who telecommute on alternate days could share offices. Please let me know what you think of this proposal.

The message fails to tell employees everything they need to know to provide meaningful responses. The *what* could be improved by identifying the specific points of information the writer needs from employees (such as whether individual telecommuting patterns are predictable enough to allow scheduling of shared offices). The writer also doesn't specify *when* the responses are needed or *how* the employees should respond. By failing to address such points, the request is likely to generate a variety of responses, some possibly helpful but some probably not.

The journalistic approach asks who, what, when, where, why, and how.

Be Sure the Information Is Accurate

The *quality* of the information you provide is every bit as important as the *quantity*. Inaccurate information in business messages can cause a host of problems, from embarrassment and lost productivity to serious safety and legal issues. You might commit the organization

You have a responsibility to provide quality information to your readers.

to promises it can't keep—and the error could harm your reputation as a reliable businessperson. Thanks to the Internet, inaccurate information may persist for years after you distribute it.

You can minimize mistakes by double-checking every piece of information you collect. If you are consulting sources outside the organization, ask yourself whether the information is current and reliable. As Chapter 13 notes, you must be particularly careful when using sources you find online. Be sure to review any mathematical or financial calculations. Check all dates and schedules and examine your own assumptions and conclusions to be certain they are valid.

Be Sure the Information Is Ethical

By working hard to ensure the accuracy of the information you gather, you'll also avoid many ethical problems in your messages. If you do make an honest mistake, such as delivering information you initially thought to be true but later found to be false, contact the recipients of the message immediately and correct the error. No one can reasonably fault you in such circumstances, and people will respect your honesty.

Omitting important information can be an unethical decision.

Messages can also be unethical if important information is omitted (see "Ethics Detective: Solving the Case of the Missing Safety Warning"). Of course, as a business professional, you may have legal or other sound business reasons for not including every detail about every matter. Just how much detail should you include? Make sure you include enough to avoid misleading your audience. If you're unsure how much information your audience needs, offer as much as you believe best fits your definition of complete and then offer to provide more upon request.

Be Sure the Information Is Pertinent

Select the information to include based on how pertinent it is to your readers.

When gathering information for your message, remember that some points will be more important to your audience than others. Audience members will appreciate your efforts to prioritize the information they need and filter out the information they don't. Moreover, by focusing on the information that concerns your audience the most, you increase your chances of accomplishing your own communication goals.

ETHICS DETECTIVE

Solving the Case of the Missing Safety Warning

Your company, Furniture Formations, creates a variety of home furniture products, with extensive use of fine woods. To preserve the look and feel of the wood, your craftspeople use an linseed oil–based finish that you purchase from a local wholesaler. The workers apply the finish with rags, which are thrown away after each project. After a news report about spontaneous combustion of waste rags occurring in other furniture shops, you grow concerned enough to contact the wholesaler and ask for verification of the product's safety. The wholesaler knows you've been considering a nonflammable, water-based alternative from another source but tries to assure you with the following message:

> Seal the rags in an approved container and dispose of it according to local regulations. As you probably already know, county regulations require all commercial users of oil-based materials to dispose of leftover finishes at the county's hazardous waste facility.

You're still not satisfied. You visit the website of the oil's manufacturer and find the following cautionary statement about the product you're currently using:

> Finishes that contain linseed oil or tung oil require specific safety precautions to minimize the risk of fire. Oil-soaked rags and other materials such as steel wool must be sealed in water-filled metal containers and then disposed of in accordance with local waste management regulations. Failure to do so can lead to spontaneous combustion that results from the heat-producing chemical reaction that takes place as the finish dries. In particular, DO NOT leave wet, oil-soaked rags in a pile or discard them with other waste.

ANALYSIS

Was the wholesaler guilty of an ethical lapse in this case? If yes, explain what you think the lapse is and why you believe it is unethical. If no, explain why you think the statement qualifies as ethical.

If you don't know your audience or if you're communicating with a large group of people who have diverse interests, use common sense to identify points of interest. Audience factors such as age, job, location, income, and education can give you clues. If you're trying to sell memberships in a health club, you might adjust your message for athletes, busy professionals, families, and people in different locations or in different income brackets. The comprehensive facilities and professional trainers would appeal to athletes, whereas the low monthly rates would appeal to college students on tight budgets.

Some messages necessarily reach audiences with a diverse mix of educational levels, subject awareness, and other variables. If possible, provide each audience segment with its own targeted information, such as by using sections in a brochure or links on a webpage.

Selecting the Best Combination of Media and Channels

With the necessary information in hand, your next decision involves the best combination of media and channels to reach your target audience. As you recall from Chapter 1, the medium is the *form* a message takes and the channel is the *system* used to deliver the message. The distinction between the two isn't always crystal clear, and some people use the terms in different ways, but these definitions are a useful way to think about the possibilities for business communication.

Most media can be distributed through more than one channel, so whenever you have a choice, think through your options to select the optimum combination. For example, a brief written message could be distributed as a printed letter or memo, or it could be distributed through a variety of digital channels, from email to blogging to social networking.

4 LEARNING OBJECTIVE
List the factors to consider when choosing the most appropriate medium for a message.

THE MOST COMMON MEDIA AND CHANNEL OPTIONS

The simplest way to categorize media choices is to divide them into *oral* (spoken), *written*, and *visual*. Each of these media can be delivered through *digital* and *nondigital channels*, which creates six basic combinations, discussed in the following sections. Table 4.1 on the next page summarizes the general advantages and disadvantages of the six medium/channel combinations. Specific options within these categories have their own strengths and weaknesses to consider as well. (For simplicity's sake, subsequent chapters occasionally use "digital media" to indicate any of the three media types delivered through digital channels.)

Media can be divided into *oral*, *written*, and *visual* forms, and all three can be distributed through *digital* and *nondigital* channels.

Oral Medium, In-Person Channel

The oral medium, in-person combo involves talking with people who are in the same location, whether it's a one-on-one conversation over lunch or a more formal speech or presentation. Being in the same physical space is a key distinction because it enables the nuances of nonverbal communication more than any other media/channel combo. As Chapter 2 points out, these nonverbal signals can carry as much weight in the conversation as the words being spoken.

By giving people the ability to see, hear, and react to each other, in-person communication is useful for encouraging people to ask questions, make comments, and work together to reach a consensus or decision. Face-to-face interaction is particularly helpful in complex, emotionally charged situations in which establishing or fostering a business relationship is important.[2] Managers who engage in frequent "walk-arounds," chatting with employees face-to-face, can get input, answer questions, and interpret important business events and trends.[3]

The nonverbal and interactive aspects of in-person communication are difficult to replicate in most other media/channel combinations.

Oral Medium, Digital Channel

Oral media via digital channels include any transmission of voice via electronic means, both live and recorded, including telephone calls, podcasts, and voicemail messages. Live phone conversations offer the give-and-take of in-person conversations and can be the best

TABLE 4.1 Medium/Channel Combinations: Advantages and Disadvantages

Medium/Channel	Advantages	Disadvantages
Oral, in-person	• Provide opportunity for immediate feedback • Easily resolve misunderstandings and negotiate meanings • Involve rich nonverbal cues (both physical gesture and vocal inflection) • Allow expression of the emotion behind your message	• Restrict participation to those physically present • Unless recorded, provide no permanent, verifiable record of the communication • Reduce communicator's control over the message
Oral, digital	• Can provide opportunity for immediate feedback (live phone or online conversations) • Not restricted to participants in the same location • Allow time-shifted consumption (for example, podcasts)	• Lack nonverbal cues other than voice inflections • Can be tedious to listen to if not audience focused (recorded messages)
Written, printed	• Allow writers to plan and control their messages • Can reach geographically dispersed audiences • Offer a permanent, verifiable record • Minimize the distortion that can accompany oral messages • Can be used to avoid immediate interactions • Deemphasize any inappropriate emotional components • Give recipients time to process messages before responding (compared to oral communication)	• Offer limited opportunities for timely feedback • Lack the rich nonverbal cues provided by oral media • Often take more time and more resources to create and distribute • Can require special skills to prepare or produce if document is elaborate
Written, digital	Generally, all the advantages of written printed documents plus: • Fast delivery • Can reach geographically dispersed audiences • Flexibility of multiple formats and channels, from microblogs to wikis • Flexibility to structure messages in creative ways, such as writing a headline on Twitter and linking to the full message on a blog • Ability to link to related and more in-depth information • Can increase accessibility and openness in an organization through broader sharing • Enable audience interaction through social media features • Ease of integrating with other media types, such as embedded videos or photos	• Can be limited in terms of reach and capability (for example, on Twitter you can reach only those people who follow you or search for you) • Require Internet or mobile phone connectivity • Vulnerable to security and privacy problems • Are easy to overuse (sending too many messages to too many recipients) • Create privacy risks and concerns (exposing confidential data, employer monitoring, accidental forwarding) • Entail security risks (viruses, spyware; network breaches) • Create productivity concerns (frequent interruptions, nonbusiness usage)
Visual, printed	• Can quickly convey complex ideas and relationships • Often less intimidating than long blocks of text • Can reduce the burden on the audience to figure out how the pieces of a message or concept fit • Can be easy to create in spreadsheets and other software (simple charts and graphs), then integrate with reports	• Can require artistic skills to design • Require some technical skills to create • Can require more time to create than equivalent amount of text • Can be expensive to print
Visual, digital	Generally, all the advantages of visual printed documents and all the advantages of written digital formats plus: • Can personalize and enhance the experience for audience members • Offer the persuasive power of multimedia formats, particularly video	• Potential time, cost, and skills needed to create • Can require large amounts of bandwidth

alternative to talking in person. Without a video component, however, they can't provide the nuances of nonverbal communication. Podcasts can be a good way to share lectures, commentary, and other spoken content. You can read about podcasting in Chapter 7.

Written Medium, Print Channel

Written, printed documents are the classic format of business communication. **Memos** are brief printed documents traditionally used for the routine, day-to-day exchange of information within an organization. **Letters** are brief written messages sent to customers and other recipients outside the organization. Reports and proposals are usually longer than memos and letters, although both can be created in memo or letter format. These documents come in a variety of lengths, ranging from a few pages to several hundred, and usually have a fairly formal tone.

Although printed documents are still a useful format, they have been replaced by digital alternatives in many instances. However, here are several situations in which you should consider a printed message over electronic alternatives:

- When you want to make a formal impression
- When you are legally required to provide information in printed form
- When you want to stand out from the flood of electronic messages
- When you need a permanent, unchangeable, or secure record

Obviously, if you can't reach a particular audience electronically, you'll need to use a printed message. Appendix A offers guidelines on formatting printed memos and letters.

Digital media/channel formats have replaced printed documents in many instances, but print is still the best choice for some messages and situations.

Written Medium, Digital Channel

Most of your business communication efforts will involve written digital messages, with everything from super-short tweets to website content to book-length reports distributed as portable document format (PDF) files (see Figure 4.4). Business uses of written digital messages keep evolving as companies look for ways to communicate more effectively. For

Most of your business communication efforts will involve the combination of written medium and digital channel.

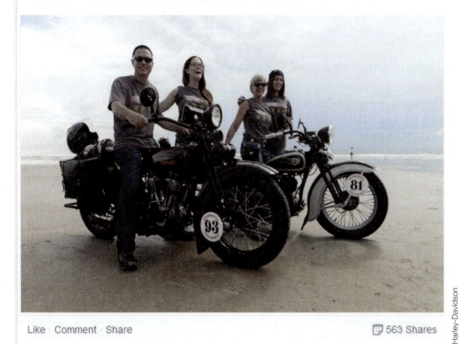

Figure 4.4 Media and Channel Choices: Written + Digital
Harley-Davidson could've chosen a variety of media/channel combinations to share this information about Harley fans taking a cross-country ride on vintage motorcycles. Facebook was an appealing choice because of the company's huge fan base (more than 7 million people) and the ease of sharing the message on the social network.

example, email has been a primary business medium for several decades, but it is being replaced in many cases by a variety of other digital formats.[4] Chapters 7 and 8 take a closer look at various written-digital combinations, from email to instant messaging (IM) to social networks.

Visual Medium, Print Channel

Photographs and diagrams can be effective communication tools for conveying emotional content, spatial relationships, technical processes, and other content that can be difficult to describe using words alone. You may occasionally create visual printed messages as stand-alone items, but most will be used as supporting material in printed documents.

Visual Medium, Digital Channel

Business messages can come alive when conveyed by visual media in digital channels. Info-graphics, interactive diagrams, animation, and digital video have the potential to engage audiences in ways that other formats can't, which is why the use of visual elements in business communication continues to grow.

Traditional business messages rely primarily on text, with occasional support from graphics such as charts, graphs, or diagrams to help illustrate points discussed in the text. However, many business communicators are discovering the power of messages in which the visual element is dominant and supported by small amounts of text. For the purposes of this discussion, think of visual media as formats in which one or more visual elements play a central role in conveying the message content.

Messages that combine powerful visuals with supporting text can be effective for a number of reasons. Today's audiences are pressed for time and bombarded with messages, so anything that communicates quickly is welcome. Visuals are also effective at describing complex ideas and processes because they can reduce the work required for an audience to identify the parts and relationships that make up the whole. Also, in a multilingual business world, diagrams, symbols, and other images can lower communication barriers by requiring less language processing. Finally, visual images can be easier to remember than purely textual descriptions or explanations.

The Unique Challenges of Communication on Mobile Devices

Mobile devices can be used to create and consume virtually every digital form of oral, written, and visual media. Thanks to the combination of portability and the flexibility enabled by a wide array of business-focused apps, mobile devices have become a primary tool in business communication. In addition to the factors discussed on pages 17–19 in Chapter 1, consider these issues whenever your messages are likely to be viewed on mobile devices:

- **Screen size and resolution.** The screen resolution of phones and tablets has improved considerably in recent years, but the limited size of these screens still presents a challenge simply because many messages are significantly larger than the screens they will be viewed on. The result is a dilemma that pits clarity against context. Readers can zoom in to make text readable and visuals understandable, but the inability to see an entire document page or visual at once—particularly on phone screens—can limit a reader's ability to grasp its full meaning. This can be particularly troublesome if you are collaborating on writing or presentation projects and team members need to review documents or slides.
- **Input technologies.** Even for accomplished texters, typing on mobile keyboards can be a challenge. Voice recognition is one way around the keyboard limitation, but anyone using it in public areas or in communaloffices runs the risk of sharing private message content and annoying anyone within earshot. Moreover, voice recognition software can make mistakes that require manual editing, particularly for users who don't enunciate clearly or when there is a lot of competing background noise. Using a stylus is an option for many devices, but this can be a slow and laborious process. If your website content or other messages and materials require a significant amount of input activity from recipients, make it as easy as possible for them. Even simple steps such as increasing the size of buttons and text-entry fields can help.

The combination of the visual medium and a digital channel can be the most compelling and engaging choice for many messages, although it is not always the easiest or cheapest format.

The mobile digital channel has become significant in business communication of all types, but it presents some challenges that must be considered.

Maintaining a Confident, Positive Outlook

Spend a few minutes around successful people in any field, and chances are you'll notice how optimistic they are. They believe in what they're doing, and they believe in themselves and their ability to solve problems and overcome obstacles.

Being positive doesn't mean displaying mindless optimism or spewing happy talk all the time. It means acknowledging that things may be difficult but then buckling down and getting the job done anyway. It means no whining and no slacking off, even when the going gets tough. We live in an imperfect world, no question; jobs can be boring or difficult, customers can be unpleasant, and bosses can be unreasonable. But when you're a pro, you find a way to power through.

Your energy, positive or negative, is contagious. Both in person and online, you'll spend as much time with your colleagues as you spend with family and friends. Personal demeanor is therefore a vital element of workplace harmony. No one expects (or wants) you to be artificially upbeat and bubbly every second of the day, but one negative personality can make an entire office miserable and unproductive. Every person in a company has a responsibility to contribute to a positive, energetic work environment.

CAREER APPLICATIONS

1. Do you have an ethical obligation to maintain a positive outlook on the job? Why or why not?
2. How can you lift your spirits when work is dragging you down?

- **Bandwidth, speed, and connectivity limitations.** The speed and quality of mobile connectivity varies widely by device, carrier, service plan, and geographic location. Even users with high-bandwidth service don't always enjoy the advertised transfer speeds they are paying for. Moreover, mobile users can lose connectivity while traveling, passing through network "dead spots," or during peak-demand hours or events (trade shows and conventions are notorious for this). Don't assume that your mobile recipients will be able to satisfactorily consume the content that you might be creating on a fast, reliable, in-office network.

- **Data usage and operational costs.** As the amount of video traffic in particular increases (video requires much higher bandwidth than text or audio), data consumption is becoming a key concern for mobile carriers and customers alike. Many mobile users do not have unlimited data-usage plans and have to manage their data consumption carefully to avoid excess fees. Some carriers offer unlimited data plans, but even those can come with restrictions such as bandwidth throttling that reduces the speed of a user's connection.[5] Given these factors, be careful about expecting or requiring mobile users to consume a lot of video or other data-intensive content.

FACTORS TO CONSIDER WHEN CHOOSING MEDIA AND CHANNELS

You don't always have the option of choosing which medium or channel to use for a particular message. For example, many companies have internal IM or social networking systems that you are expected to use for certain types of communication, such as project updates. However, when you do have a choice, consider these factors:

- **Richness.** *Richness* is a medium's ability to (1) convey a message through more than one informational cue (visual, verbal, vocal), (2) facilitate feedback, and (3) establish personal focus.[6] Face-to-face communication is a rich medium because it delivers information both verbally and nonverbally, it allows immediate feedback through both verbal and nonverbal responses, and it has the potential to be intimate and personal, at least in one-on-one and small-group settings. In contrast, lean media are limited in one or more of these three aspects. For example, texting and IM allow rapid feedback and can easily be personalized. However, they usually deliver information through only one informational cue (words), which can lead to misinterpretation. Emoticons (see page 188), which attempt to add emotional nuances that might otherwise be conveyed through visual means such as facial expressions, are a response to the one-dimensional leanness of text-only messages. In general, use richer media to

Media vary widely in terms of *richness*, which encompasses the number of information cues, feedback mechanisms, and opportunities for personalization.

(continued on page 112)

BUSINESS COMMUNICATORS INNOVATING WITH MOBILE

As the third major revolution in business communication in the past two decades (after the World Wide Web and social media), mobile communication has the potential to change nearly every aspect of business communication. Here is a small sample of the ways companies are putting mobile to work.

Training

In the face of changing markets, government regulations, and other forces in the business environment, developing and maintaining employee skill sets is an ongoing challenge for most companies. The challenge is made even more difficult when employees are constantly on the move or geographically dispersed. With training materials developed specifically for mobile devices, companies can deliver training content when and where it helps employees the most.

Distributed Decision Making

A complementary aspect to managing remote workers via mobile apps is giving employees the authority to make decisions in the field, rather than relying on managers back in the office. In the oil and gas industry, for instance, specialized mobile apps include tools for data visualization, collaboration, and data collection to help on-site employees and supervisors communicate and coordinate their efforts. This capability can be particularly vital after accidents or other crisis events, because it lets employees who are on the scene choose the best course of action without delay.

Mobile Glossary

In addition to terms defined elsewhere in the book, here are some helpful mobile terms.

3G, 4G, and 5G

Successive generations of mobile phone technology, although the generational boundaries are loosely defined and each generation includes a number of competing technologies; roughly speaking, we're in a transition from 3G to 4G now, and 5G (whatever it ends up being) won't arrive for at least several more years.

Android and iOS

The two major operating systems/platforms for mobile devices. Android devices are made by a wide variety of manufacturers, but iOS devices are made only by Apple.

Bandwidth

A measure of the data-carrying capacity of a mobile, Wi-Fi, or other network connection; streaming video and other demanding applications require a *broadband* connection, but there's no general agreement on exactly what constitutes broadband.

Cellular Versus Mobile

Two terms for the same concept; *cellular* (derived from the way phone networks are configured) is used mainly in the United States, whereas *mobile* is used more generally around the world and is also more descriptive, so that's the term used in this book

Context Awareness

A mobile device's ability to modify its operation based on knowledge of where it is; silencing the ringer when you arrive at your office is a simple example.

Geofencing

Using the location-sensing capabilities of mobile devices to remotely monitor and control the device and its user; delivery companies, for example, can monitor where their drivers are and make sure they stay within designated areas.

Over-the-Top (OTT) Application

A digital service that bypasses a traditional distribution network to provide similar capability, often by using cloud capabilities; an example is WhatsApp using Internet connections to create services traditionally provided by mobile phone carriers.

Phablet

A rather ungainly name for mobile devices that are larger than phones but smaller than tablets.

Quick Response (QR) Codes and Near-Field Communication (NFC)

Two ways for a mobile device to access additional information; QR codes are square, phone-scannable barcodes that connect the phone to a website; NFC is a short-distance radio technology that enables a data link between a phone and tags that can be attached to products or other locations.

Ndoeljindoel/Shutterstock

Remote Workforce Management

Dispersed workforces also present a variety of supervision and management difficulties. Mobile workforce management apps can address many of these problems, from basic functions such as ensuring that workers show up on time at remote job sites to rescheduling customer appointments on the fly to collecting information to share with technical support staff. Sales managers can give just-in-time coaching and encouragement to representatives who are about to call on potential customers. Some systems can even embed information on best practices from experienced workers and deliver virtual coaching to less-experienced workers in the field.

Shipfactory/Shutterstock and Photobank.ch/Shutterstock

Project Management

Work teams are often dispersed over wide geographic ranges and frequently on the move, so mobile communication is an essential element of contemporary project management. Instant access to task status and other vital information helps project managers stay on top of rapidly moving projects and helps team members communicate efficiently.

Miroslava Levina/Shutterstock

Recruiting

With a target population that is often on the move, companies are responding by integrating mobile into their recruiting processes. These efforts include mobile-friendly job postings, mobile application and recruiting apps, and interviewing systems that let candidates and recruiters connect using their mobile devices.

send nonroutine or complex messages, to humanize your presence throughout the organization, to communicate caring to employees, and to gain employee commitment to company goals. Use leaner media to send routine messages or to transfer information that doesn't require significant explanation.[7]

- **Formality.** Your media choice is a nonverbal signal that affects the style and tone of your message. For example, a printed memo or letter is likely to be perceived as a more formal gesture than an IM or email message.
- **Media and channel limitations.** Every medium and channel has limitations. For instance, IM is perfect for communicating simple, straightforward messages between two people, but it is less effective for complex messages or conversations that involve three or more people.
- **Urgency.** Some media establish a connection with the audience faster than others, so choose wisely if your message is urgent. However, be sure to respect audience members' time and workloads. If a message isn't urgent and doesn't require immediate feedback, choose a medium such as email or blogging that allows people to respond at their convenience.
- **Cost.** Cost is both a real financial factor and a perceived nonverbal signal. For example, depending on the context, extravagant (and expensive) video or multimedia presentations can send a nonverbal signal of sophistication and professionalism—or careless disregard for company budgets.
- **Audience preferences.** If you know that your audience prefers a particular media and channel combination, use that format if it works well for the message and the situation. Otherwise you risk annoying the audience or having your message missed or ignored.
- **Security and privacy.** Your company may have restrictions on the media and channels that can be used for certain types of messages, but even if it doesn't, think carefully whenever your messages include sensitive information. Never assume that your email, IM, and other digital communications are private. Many companies monitor these channels, and there is always the risk that networks could get hacked or that messages will be forwarded beyond their original recipients.

Many types of media/channel combinations offer instantaneous delivery, but take care not to interrupt people unnecessarily (for example, with IM or phone calls) if you don't need an immediate answer.

Remember that media and channel choices can also send a nonverbal signal regarding costs; make sure your choices are financially appropriate.

When choosing media and channels, don't forget to consider your audience's expectations and preferences.

Organizing Your Information

5 LEARNING OBJECTIVE
Explain why good organization is important to both you and your audience, and list the tasks involved in organizing a message.

Good organization benefits your audiences by helping them understand and accept your message in less time.

Good organization helps you by reducing the time and creative energy needed to create effective messages.

Organization can make the difference between success and failure. Good organization helps your readers or listeners in three key ways. First, it helps them understand your message by making the main point clear at the outset, presenting additional points to support that main idea, and satisfying all their information needs. But if your message is poorly organized, your meaning can be obscured, and your audiences may form inaccurate conclusions about what you've written or said.

Second, good organization helps receivers accept your message. If your writing appears confused and disorganized, people will likely conclude that the *thinking* behind the writing is also confused and disorganized. Moreover, effective messages often require a bit more than simple, clear logic. A diplomatic approach helps receivers accept your message, even if it's not exactly what they want to hear. In contrast, a poorly organized message on an emotionally charged topic can alienate the audience before you have the chance to get your point across.

Third, good organization saves your audience time. Well-organized messages are efficient: They contain only relevant ideas, and they are brief. Moreover, each piece of information is located in a logical place in the overall flow; each section builds on the one before to create a coherent whole, without forcing people to look for missing pieces.

In addition to saving time and energy for your readers, good organization saves *you* time and consumes less of your creative energy. Writing moves more quickly because you don't waste time putting ideas in the wrong places or composing material that you don't need. You spend far less time rewriting, trying to extract sensible meaning from disorganized rambling. Last but far from least, organizational skills are good for your career because they help you develop a reputation as a clear thinker who cares about your readers.

TABLE 4.2 Topics Versus Main Ideas

General Purpose	Example of Specific Purpose	Example of Topic	Example of Main Idea
To inform	Teach customer service representatives how to edit and expand the technical support wiki	Technical support wiki	Careful, thorough edits and additions to the wiki help the entire department provide better customer support.
To persuade	Convince top managers to increase spending on research and development	Funding for research and development	Competitors spend more than we do on research and development, enabling them to create more innovative products.
To collaborate	Solicit ideas for a companywide incentive system that ties wages to profits	Incentive pay	Tying wages to profits motivates employees and reduces compensation costs in tough years.

DEFINING YOUR MAIN IDEA

The **topic** of your message is the overall subject, and your **main idea** is a specific statement about that topic (see Table 4.2). For example, if you believe that the current system of using paper forms for filing employee insurance claims is expensive and slow, you might craft a message in which the topic is employee insurance claims and the main idea is that a new web-based system would reduce costs for the company and reduce reimbursement delays for employees.

In longer documents and presentations, you often need to unify a mass of material with a main idea that encompasses all the individual points you want to make. Finding a common thread through all these points can be a challenge. Sometimes you won't even be sure what your main idea is until you sort through the information. For tough assignments like these, consider a variety of techniques to generate creative ideas:

- **Brainstorming.** Working alone or with others, generate as many ideas and questions as you can, without stopping to criticize or organize. After you capture all these pieces, look for patterns and connections to help identify the main idea and the groups of supporting ideas. For example, if your main idea concerns whether to open a new restaurant in Denver, you'll probably find a group of ideas related to financial return, another related to competition, and so on. Identifying such groups helps you see the major issues that will lead you to a conclusion you can feel confident about.
- **Journalistic approach.** The journalistic approach (see page 103) asks *who, what, when, where, why,* and *how* questions to distill major ideas from unorganized information.
- **Question-and-answer chain.** Start with a key question, from the audience's perspective, and work back toward your message. You'll often find that each answer generates new questions until you identify the information that needs to be in your message.
- **Storyteller's tour.** Some writers find it best to talk through a communication challenge before they try to write. Record yourself as you describe what you intend to write. Then listen to the playback, identify ways to tighten and clarify the message, and repeat the process until you distill the main idea down to a single concise message.
- **Mind mapping.** You can generate and organize ideas using a graphic method called *mind mapping* (see Figure 4.5 on the next page). Start with a main idea and then branch out to connect every other related idea that comes to mind. You can find a number of free mind-mapping tools online.

> The topic is the broad subject; the main idea makes a statement about the topic.

REAL-TIME UPDATES
LEARN MORE BY VIEWING THIS PRESENTATION
Smart advice for brainstorming sessions
Generate better ideas in less time with these helpful tips. Go to **real-timeupdates.com/bct14** and selectLearn More in the Students section.

LIMITING YOUR SCOPE

The **scope** of your message is the range of information you present, the overall length, and the level of detail—all of which need to correspond to your main idea. The length of some business messages has a preset limit, whether from a boss's instructions, the technology

> Limit the scope of your message so that you can convey your main idea as briefly as possible.

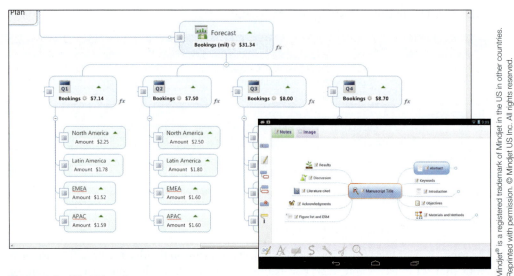

Figure 4.5 **Mind Mapping**
Mind-mapping tools such as Mindjet MindManager make it easy to explore the organization of your material, and mobile apps (see inset) bring this capability to tablets and other mobile devices.

you're using, or a time frame such as individual speaker slots during a seminar. Even if you don't have a preset length, it's vital to limit yourself to the scope needed to convey your main idea—and no more.

Whatever the length of your message, limit the number of major supporting points to half a dozen or so—and if you can get your idea across with fewer points, all the better. Offering a long list of supporting points might feel as though you're being thorough, but your audience is likely to view such detail as rambling and mind-numbing. Instead, group your supporting points under major headings, such as finance, customers, competitors, employees, or whatever is appropriate for your subject. Look for ways to combine your supporting points so that you have a smaller number with greater impact.

The ideal length of a message depends on your topic, your audience members' familiarity with the material, their receptivity to your conclusions, and your credibility. You'll need fewer words to present routine information to a knowledgeable audience that already knows and respects you. You'll need more words to build a consensus about a complex and controversial subject, especially if the members of your audience are skeptical or hostile strangers.

CHOOSING BETWEEN DIRECT AND INDIRECT APPROACHES

After you've defined your main idea and supporting points, you're ready to decide on the sequence you will use to present your information. You have two basic options:

- The **direct approach** starts with the main idea (such as a recommendation, a conclusion, or a request) and follows that with supporting evidence.
- The **indirect approach** starts with the evidence and builds up to the main idea.

To choose between these two alternatives, analyze your audience's likely reaction to your purpose and message (see Figure 4.6). Bear in mind, however, that Figure 4.6 presents only general guidelines; always consider the unique circumstances of each message and audience situation. The following sections offer more insight on choosing the best approach.

The type of message also influences the choice of the direct or indirect approach. In the coming chapters, you'll get specific advice on choosing the best approach for a variety of communication challenges.

With the direct approach, you open with the main idea of your message and support it with reasoning, evidence, and examples.

With the indirect approach, you withhold the main idea until you have built up to it logically and persuasively with reasoning, evidence, and examples.

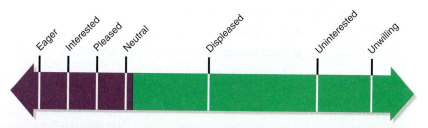

	Direct Approach	Indirect Approach	
Audience Reaction	Eager/interested/ pleased/neutral	Displeased	Uninterested/unwilling
Message Opening	Start with the main idea, the request, or the good news.	Start with a neutral statement that acts as a transition to the reasons for the bad news.	Start with a statement or question that captures attention.
Message Body	Provide necessary details.	Give reasons to build up to the negative answer or announcement. State or imply the bad news, and make a positive suggestion.	Arouse the audience's interest in the subject. Build the audience's desire to comply.
Message Close	Close with a cordial comment, a reference to the good news, or a statement about the specific action desired.	Close cordially.	Request action.

Figure 4.6 **Choosing Between the Direct and Indirect Approaches**
Think about the way your audience is likely to respond before choosing your approach.

OUTLINING YOUR CONTENT

After you have chosen the best approach, it's time to figure out the most logical and effective way to present your major points and supporting details. Get into the habit of creating outlines when you're preparing business messages. You'll save time, get better results, and do a better job of navigating through complicated business situations. Even if you're just jotting down three or four key points, making an outline will help you organize your thoughts for faster writing. When you're preparing a longer, more complex message, an outline is indispensable because it helps you visualize the relationships among the various parts.

Outlining saves time and helps you create more effective messages.

You're no doubt familiar with the basic outline formats that identify each point with a number or letter and that indent certain points to show which ones are of equal status. A good outline divides a topic into at least two parts, restricts each subdivision to one category, and ensures that each subdivision is separate and distinct (see Figure 4.7 on the next page).

Another way to visualize the outline of your message is to create an organization chart similar to the charts used to show a company's management structure. Put the main idea in the highest-level box to establish the big picture. The lower-level ideas, like lower-level employees, provide the details. All the ideas should be logically organized into divisions of thought, just as a company is organized into divisions and departments.[8] Using a visual chart instead of a traditional outline has many benefits. Charts help you (1) see the various levels of ideas and how the parts fit together, (2) develop new ideas, and (3) restructure your information flow. The mind-mapping technique used to generate ideas works in a similar way.

Whichever outlining or organizing scheme you use, start your message with the main idea, follow that with major supporting points, and then illustrate these points with evidence.

REAL-TIME UPDATES

LEARN MORE BY VIEWING THIS PRESENTATION

Get helpful tips on creating an outline for any project

Learn these proven steps for creating robust, practical outlines. Go to **real-timeupdates.com/bct14** and select Learn More in the Students section.

MOBILE APP

Outliner is one of several apps that make it easy to create and modify writing outlines.

Figure 4.7   Organizing Your Thoughts with a Clear Outline
No matter what outlining format you use, think through your major supporting points and the examples and evidence that can support each point.

Start with the Main Idea

The main idea establishes what you want your readers to do or think and why they should do so.

The main idea helps you establish the goals and general strategy of the message, and it summarizes two vital considerations: (1) *what* you want your audience members to do or think and (2) *why* they should do so. Everything in your message should either support the main idea or explain its implications. As discussed earlier, the direct approach states the main idea quickly and directly, whereas the indirect approach delays the main idea until after the evidence is presented.

State the Major Points

You need to support your main idea with major points that clarify and explain the main idea in concrete terms. If your purpose is to inform and the material is factual, your major points may be based on something physical or financial—something you can visualize or measure, such as activities to be performed, functional units, spatial or chronological relationships, or parts of a whole. When you're describing a process, the major points are almost inevitably steps in the process. When you're describing an object, the major points often correspond to the parts of the object. When you're giving a historical account, major points represent episodes in the chronological chain of events. If your purpose is to persuade or to collaborate, select major points that develop a line of reasoning or a logical argument that proves your central message and motivates your audience to act.

Provide Examples and Evidence

Choose supporting points, evidence, and examples carefully; a few strong points will make your case better than a large collection of weaker points.

After you've defined the main idea and identified major supporting points, think about examples and evidence that can confirm, illuminate, or expand your supporting points. Choose examples and evidence carefully so that these elements support your overall message without distracting or overwhelming your audience. One good example, particularly if it is conveyed through a compelling story (see the next section), is usually more powerful than several weaker examples. Similarly, a few strong points of evidence are usually more persuasive than a large collection of minor details. Keep in mind that you can back up your major supporting points in a variety of ways, depending on the subject material and the available examples and evidence (see Table 4.3).

If your schedule permits, put your outline aside for a day or two before you begin composing your first draft. Then review it with a fresh eye, looking for opportunities to improve the flow of ideas.

Figure 4.8 on page 118 illustrates several of the key themes about organizing a message: helping readers get the information they need quickly, defining and conveying the main idea, limiting the scope of the message, choosing the approach, and outlining your information.

TABLE 4.3   Six Types of Detail

Type of Detail	Comment	Example
Facts and figures	Enhances credibility more than any other type, but can become boring if used excessively	Sales are strong this month. We have two new contracts worth $5 million and a good chance of winning another worth $2.5 million.
Example or illustration	Adds life to a message, but one example does not prove a point. Idea must be supported by other evidence as well	We've spent four months trying to hire recent accounting graduates, but so far, only one person has joined our firm. One candidate told me that she would love to work for us, but she can get $10,000 more a year elsewhere.
Description	Helps audience visualize the subject by creating a sensory impression	Upscale hamburger restaurants target burger lovers who want more than the convenience and low prices of McDonald's. These places feature wine and beer, half-pound burgers, and generous side dishes (nachos, potato skins). Atmosphere is key.
Narration (storytelling)	Stimulates audience interest through the use of dramatic tension; in many instances, must be supplemented with facts and figures in order to convincingly prove a point convincingly	When Rita Longworth took over as CEO, she faced a tough choice: shut down the tablet PC division entirely or outsource manufacturing as a way to lower costs while keeping the division alive. As her first step, she convened a meeting with all the managers in the division to get their input on the two options. (Story continues from there.)
Reference to authority	Bolsters a case while adding variety and credibility; works only if authority is recognized and respected by audience	I discussed this idea with Jackie Loman in the Chicago plant, and she was very supportive. As you know, Jackie has been in charge of that plant for the past six years. She is confident that we can speed up the number 2 line by 150 units an hour if we add another worker.
Visual aids	Helps audience grasp the key points about sets of data or visualize connections between ideas	Graphs, charts, tables, infographics, data visualization, photos, video

BUILDING READER INTEREST WITH STORYTELLING TECHNIQUES

As the Wolff Olins vignette at the beginning of the chapter points out, narrative techniques can be an effective way to organize messages in a surprising number of business situations, from recruiting and training employees to enticing investors and customers. Storytelling is such a vital means of communicating that, in the words of the management consultant Steve Tobak, "It's hard to imagine your career going anywhere if you can't tell a story."[9] Fortunately, you've been telling stories all your life, so narrative techniques already come naturally to you; now it's just a matter of adapting those techniques to business situations.

You've already been on the receiving end of thousands of business stories: Storytelling is one of the most common structures used in television commercials and other advertisements. People love to share stories about themselves and others, too, which makes social media ideal for storytelling.[10]

Career-related stories, such as how someone sought and found the opportunity to work on projects he or she is passionate about, can entice skilled employees to consider joining a firm. Entrepreneurs use stories to help investors see how their new ideas have the potential to affect people's lives (and therefore generate lots of sales). Stories can be cautionary tales as well, dramatizing the consequences of career blunders, ethical mistakes, and strategic missteps.

A key reason storytelling can be so effective is that stories help readers and listeners imagine themselves living through the experience of the person in the story. Chip Heath of Stanford University and his brother, Dan Heath of Duke University, have spent years exploring the question of why some ideas "stick" and others disappear. One of their conclusions is that ideas conveyed through storytelling tend to thrive because stories "put knowledge into a framework that is more lifelike, more true to our day-to-day existence."[11]

In addition, stories can demonstrate cause-and-effect relationships in a compelling fashion.[12] Imagine attending a new-employee orientation and listening to the trainer read off a list of ethics rules and guidelines. Now imagine the trainer telling the story of

Storytelling is an effective way to organize many business messages because it helps readers personalize the message and understand causes and consequences.

Ineffective

Incorporation - Message (HTML)

File | Insert | Options | Format Text | Review | ♀ Tell me what you want to do

From ▾ | e.ankerson@smityardlaw.com
To... | b.courson@smityardlaw.com
Cc...
Subject | Incorporation

Hi Bethany,

I have to admit, my research had me longing for the simplicity of a sole proprietorship or the security of a corporate job. But we have decided to move forward with this grand adventure, so onward it is!

Regarding partnerships, I find it really annoying that people in some professions (but not ours) can form limited liability partnerships to protect themselves from unlimited financial liability. Hardly seems fair.

Anyway, incorporation is clearly the better choice for us. It protects us from unlimited liability, it makes it easier to add or remove executives (since they're not partners), and it lets us sell stock to raise capital.

Partnership does have two advantages. First, in terms of paperwork and legal hassles, a partnership is easier to establish and simpler to run. Second, partnerships are subject to only a single layer of taxation on income.

These advantages are compelling, but they are outweighed by unlimited liability, the difficulty of adding or replacing partners, and the lack of any means to sell shares to the public. Corporations are more complicated to set up and run, and income is taxed twice (first on company profits and then on any dividends we might pay out). However, these are relatively minor concerns when we consider the powerful advantages and protections that incorporation would give us.

Please let me know your thoughts,
Erik

(a) The vague subject line wastes an opportunity to begin building the message.

(b) The opening has an irrelevant discussion, doesn't explain what research this refers to, and fails to introduce the topic of the message.

(c) The beginning of this paragraph suggests it will discuss partnerships, but instead then digresses with another personal observation.

(d) The main idea, that the pair should incorporate, is delayed until the middle of the message.

(e) With the pros of partnerships in one paragraph and the cons of partnership, cons of incorporation, then pros of incorporation in the next paragraph.

Effective

Advantages of incorporation over partnership - Message (HTML)

Insert | Options | Format Text | Review | ♀ Tell me what you want to do

From ▾ | e.ankerson@smityardlaw.com
To... | b.courson@smityardlaw.com
Cc...
Subject | Advantages of incorporation over partnership

Hi Bethany,

After comparing the advantages and disadvantages of partnership and corporate structures in light of our long-range plans for the business, I believe the clear choice for us is incorporation.

Partnership does have two advantages. First, in terms of admin and legal requirements, a partnership is easier to establish and simpler to run. Second, partnerships are subject to only a single layer of taxation.

However, these advantages are outweighed by three disadvantages. First, the general partners in a partnership face unlimited legal liability, which puts our personal assets at risk. Second, growth and succession can be tricky if we decide to bring in another partner or one of us wants to leave the company. Third, the inability to sell shares of stock limits our opportunity to raise capital for expansion.

Incorporation addresses all three disadvantages of partnerships: Our personal assets are not vulnerable in the event of lawsuits or company bankruptcy, adding or replacing managers is simpler because we are all employees of the corporation, and—most significantly—we can sell shares of stock to raise capital.

Yes, corporations are more complicated to set up and run, and income is taxed twice (first on company profits and then on any dividends we might pay out to shareholders). However, these are relatively minor concerns when we consider the powerful advantages and protections that incorporation would give us.

Please let me know your thoughts,
Erik

(a) The subject line conveys the topic (incorporation vs. partnership) and the main idea (incorporation is the better choice).

(b) The opening provides some brief context by referencing their previous conversation, then immediately shares the main idea.

(c) Avoiding any digressions, the message moves right into key support points.

(d) With the main idea already expressed, the writer can devote the bulk of the message to supporting information.

(e) The support points are clearly organized: pros and cons of partnerships, then pros and cons of corporations.

This organization makes it easy for him to explain how incorporation overcomes all three key disadvantages of partnerships.

He completes the comparison by identifying two disadvantages of incorporation but states that these are outweighed by the advantages.

Figure 4.8 **Improving the Organization of a Message**
This writer is following up on a conversation from the previous day, in which he and the recipient discussed which of two forms of ownership, a partnership or a corporation, they should use for their new company. (*Partnership* has a specific legal meaning in this context.) That question is the topic of the message; the main idea is the recommendation that they incorporate, rather than form a partnership. Notice how the *Effective* version uses the direct approach to quickly get to the main idea and then supports that by comparing the advantages and disadvantages of both forms of ownership. In contrast, the *Ineffective* version contains irrelevant information, makes the comparison difficult to follow, and buries the main idea in the middle of the message.

someone who sounds a lot like you in the near future: fresh out of college and full of energy and ambition. Desperate to hit demanding sales targets, the person in the story began entering transactions before customers had actually agreed to purchase, hoping the sales would eventually come through and no one would be the wiser. The scheme was exposed during a routine audit, however, and the rising star was booted out of the company with an ethical stain that would haunt him for years. You may not remember all the rules and guidelines, but chances are you will remember what happened to that person who sounded a lot like you. This ability to share organizational values is one of the major benefits of using storytelling in business communication, particularly across diverse workforces.[13]

REAL-TIME UPDATES

LEARN MORE BY EXPLORING THIS INTERACTIVE WEBSITE

Mine the web to piece together stories on any topic

Storify is a content curation engine that lets you tell or follow a story by linking voices from multiple social media platforms. Go to **real-timeupdates.com/bct14** and select Learn More in the Students section.

A classic story has three basic parts. The beginning of the story presents someone the audience can identify with in some way, and this person has a dream to pursue or a problem to solve. (Think of how movies and novels often start by introducing a likable character who immediately gets into danger, for example.) The middle of the story shows this character taking action and making decisions as he or she pursues the goal or tries to solve the problem. The storyteller's objective here is to build the audience's interest by increasing the tension: Will the "hero" overcome the obstacles in his or her path and defeat whatever adversary is keeping him or her away from the goal?[14] The end of the story answers that question and usually offers a lesson to be learned about the outcome as well.

By the way, even though these are "stories," they must not be made-up tales. Telling stories that didn't happen to people who don't exist while presenting them as real-life events is a serious breach of ethics that damages a company's credibility.[15]

Consider adding an element of storytelling whenever your main idea involves the opportunity to inspire, to persuade, to teach, or to warn readers or listeners about the potential outcomes of a particular course of action.

In addition to its important communication function, storytelling can also serve as a means of strategic business analysis. For example, if you're having trouble articulating a story that you're trying to tell about a project you would like to pursue, it might be because you haven't fully thought through the purpose of the project. With a clearer definition in mind, you'll find it easier to tell your story.

For fresh ideas and media materials on planning messages, visit **real-timeupdates .com/bct14** and select Chapter 4. For a quick refresher on message-planning tasks, see "Checklist: Planning Business Messages."

> Organize stories in three parts: a beginning that introduces a sympathetic person with a dream or a challenge, a middle that shows the obstacles to be overcome, and an ending that resolves the situation and highlights the moral or message of the story.

CHECKLIST ✔ Planning Business Messages

A. Analyze the situation.
- Determine whether the purpose of your message is to inform, persuade, or collaborate.
- Identify what you want your audience to think or do after receiving the message.
- Make sure your purpose is worthwhile and realistic.
- Make sure the time is right for your message.
- Make sure your purpose is acceptable to your organization.
- Identify the primary audience.
- Determine the size and composition of your audience.
- Estimate your audience's level of understanding and probable reaction to your message.

B. Gather information.
- Decide whether to use formal or informal techniques for gathering information.
- Find out what your audience needs to know.
- Provide all required information and make sure it's accurate, ethical, and pertinent.

C. Select the best combination of medium and channel for your message.
- Understand the advantages and disadvantages of oral, written, and visual media distributed through both digital and nondigital channels.
- Consider media richness, formality, media limitations, urgency, cost, and audience preference.

D. Organize your information.
- Define your main idea.
- Limit your scope.
- Choose the direct or indirect approach.
- Outline content by starting with the main idea, adding major points, and illustrating with evidence.
- Look for opportunities to use storytelling to build audience interest.

COMMUNICATION CHALLENGES AT Wolff Olins

You've joined the Wolff Olins team at the company's New York office, where you work as a creative consultant helping entrepreneurs and company leaders write and tell stories. Use what you've learned in this chapter to address these two challenges.

INDIVIDUAL CHALLENGE: Look ahead to "Writing the Story of You" on page 488 in Chapter 18. You've been asked to write your career story as an example that Wolff Olins can use to teach clients about applying storytelling in a business context. If you are already established in your career, you can tell the story of how you got to where you are now, or you can imagine a fictitious career or a path you didn't take and write that story. If you have yet to start your business career, visualize where you'd like to be in 20 or 25 years and imagine the steps it would take to get there. Write your story in 150–200 words, making up whatever details you need. Be as creative as you want, and feel free to make your story a cautionary tale if you'd prefer—as in, "don't make the mistakes I made."

TEAM CHALLENGE: With a team assigned by your instructor, research a product or product category that used to be extremely popular but is now much rarer or perhaps even off the market. It could be something long gone, such as horse-drawn carriages or hoop skirts, or it might be something more recent, such as the Sony Walkman portable cassette player or floppy disks. Find out why it was initially popular, how big it was during its heyday, and why it fell into decline. Using whatever medium/channel combination your instructor asks, tell the story of this product or product category from introduction to decline, pointing out lessons that future businesspeople should take to heart.

Quick Learning Guide

KEY TERMS

direct approach Message organization that starts with the main idea (such as a recommendation, a conclusion, or a request) and follows that with supporting evidence

free writing An exploratory technique in which you write whatever comes to mind, without stopping to make any corrections, for a set period of time

general purpose The broad intent of a message—to inform, to persuade, or to collaborate with the audience

indirect approach Message organization that starts with the evidence and builds a case before presenting the main idea

journalistic approach Verifying the completeness of a message by making sure it answers the *who, what, when, where, why,* and *how* questions

letters Brief written messages sent to customers and other recipients outside an organization

main idea A specific statement about the topic of a message

memos Brief printed documents traditionally used for the routine, day-to-day exchange of information within an organization

scope The range of information presented in a message, its overall length, and the level of detail provided

specific purpose Identifies what you hope to accomplish with your message and what your audience should do or think after receiving your message

topic The overall subject of a message

SUMMARY OF LEARNING OBJECTIVES

1 Describe the three-step writing process. (1) Planning consists of four tasks: analyzing the situation (defining your purpose and profiling your audience), gathering the information to meet your audience's needs, selecting the best combination of medium and channel for the message and the situation, and organizing the information (defining your main idea, limiting your scope, selecting an approach, and outlining your content). (2) The writing step consists of two tasks: adapting to your audience and composing the message. Adapt your message to your audience by being sensitive to audience needs, building a strong relationship with your audience, and controlling your style. Compose your message by drafting your thoughts with strong words, effective sentences, and coherent paragraphs. (3) Completing your message consists of four tasks: revising your message by evaluating content and then rewriting and editing for clarity and conciseness, producing your message by using effective design elements and suitable delivery methods, proofreading your message for mistakes in spelling and mechanics, and distributing it in a way that meets both your needs and your audience's needs.

2 Explain why it's important to analyze a communication situation in order to define your purpose and profile your audience before writing a message. You must know enough about your purpose to shape your message in a way that will achieve your goal. Moreover, without a clear purpose to guide you, you are bound to waste time and energy. To decide whether you should proceed with your message, answer four questions: (1) Will anything change as a result of this message? (2) Is my purpose realistic? (3) Is this the right time for this message? (4) Is the purpose acceptable to my organization? Developing an audience profile is also essential because doing so helps you identify the information you need to include in your message and the most effective way to structure your message.

3 Discuss information-gathering options for simple messages, and identify three attributes of quality information. Gathering the information that will fulfill your audience's needs is a vital step before you attempt to organize your content. For more complex documents, you may need to plan a research project to acquire all the necessary information. For simple messages, however, if you don't already have all the information you need, you can often gather it by using informal methods such as considering the audience's perspective, reading existing reports and other company documents, talking with supervisors and others who have information and insight, and asking your audience members directly for their input. To determine whether the information you've gathered is good enough, verify that it is accurate, ethical, and pertinent to the audience's needs.

4 List the factors to consider when choosing the most appropriate medium for a message. The first factor to consider is media richness. Richness is determined by the medium's ability to (1) convey a message using more than one informational cue, such as sound, motion, nonverbal cues, and so on; (2) facilitate feedback; and (3) establish personal focus. Other factors to consider when selecting media include the level of formality, the specific limitations of each medium, the level of urgency, the cost of various media options, and your audience's preferences.

5 Explain why good organization is important to both you and your audience, and list the tasks involved in organizing a message. When you organize messages carefully, you save time and conserve creative energy because the writing process is quicker and you spend less time rewriting. Good organization also helps your audience members understand your message, helps them accept your message, and saves them time. The tasks involved in organizing your message include defining your main idea, limiting your scope to the information needed to convey and support that main idea, choosing the direct or indirect approach, and then outlining your content.

MyBCommLab

Go to **mybcommlab.com** to complete the problems marked with this icon .

Test Your Knowledge

To review chapter content related to each question, refer to the indicated Learning Objective.

4-1. What are the three major steps in the writing process? [LO-1]

⭐ 4-2. What are the benefits of planning your messages carefully, particularly longer and more complex messages? [LO-1]

4-3. What two types of purposes do all business messages have? [LO-2]

4-4. What do you need to know to develop an audience profile? [LO-2]

4-5. What is the value of free writing and other discovery techniques? [LO-3]

⭐ 4-6. Why are in-person conversations considered a rich medium? [LO-4]

4-7. What are four disadvantages of written, printed messages? [LO-4]

4-8. How does the topic of a message differ from its main idea? [LO-5]

4-9. Why is it important to limit the scope of a message? [LO-5]

4-10. What three elements do you need to consider when choosing between the direct and indirect approaches? [LO-5]

Apply Your Knowledge

To review chapter content related to each question, refer to the indicated Learning Objective.

4-11. Some writers argue that planning messages wastes time because they inevitably change their plans as they proceed. How would you respond to this argument? Briefly explain. [LO-1]

4-12. A day after sending an email to all 1,800 employees in your company regarding the income tax implications of the company's retirement plan, you discover that one of the sources you relied on for your information plagiarized from other sources. You quickly double-check all the information in your message and confirm that it is accurate. However, you are concerned about using plagiarized information, even though you did nothing wrong. Write a brief email message to your instructor, explaining how you would handle the situation. [LO-3]

4-13. You are organizing an exploratory in-person meeting with engineering representatives from a dozen manufacturers around the world to discuss updates to a technical standard that all the companies' products must adhere to. The representatives have a wide range of firmly held opinions on the subject, because the changes could help some companies and hurt others. They can't even agree on what should be addressed in the first meeting, so you need to develop a minimum level of consensus on what

should be on the agenda. Which combination of media and channels would you use to move the conversation forward and finalize the agenda? Each company has one representative, and any discussions need to be kept confidential. [LO-4]

4-14. How might the inability to view an entire document at once on a mobile screen hinder a reader's ability to grasp the full meaning of the message? [LO-4]

4-15. You have been invited to speak at an annual industry conference. After preparing the outline for your presentation, you see that you've identified 14 separate points to support your main idea. Should you move ahead with creating the slides for your presentation or go back and rethink your outline? Why? [LO-5]

Practice Your Skills

4-16. **Message for Analysis: Outlining Your Content** [LO-5]
A writer is working on an insurance information brochure and is having trouble grouping the ideas logically into an outline. Using the following information, prepare the outline, paying attention to the appropriate hierarchy of ideas. If necessary, rewrite phrases to make them all consistent.

Accident Protection Insurance Plan
- Coverage is only pennies a day
- Benefit is $100,000 for accidental death on common carrier
- Benefit is $100 a day for hospitalization as result of motor vehicle or common carrier accident
- Benefit is $20,000 for accidental death in motor vehicle accident
- Individual coverage is only $17.85 per quarter; family coverage is just $26.85 per quarter
- No physical exam or health questions
- Convenient payment—billed quarterly
- Guaranteed acceptance for all applicants
- No individual rate increases
- Free, no-obligation examination period
- Cash paid in addition to any other insurance carried
- Covers accidental death when riding as fare-paying passenger on public transportation, including buses, trains, jets, ships, trolleys, subways, or any other common carrier
- Covers accidental death in motor vehicle accidents occurring while driving or riding in or on automobile, truck, camper, motor home, or nonmotorized bicycle

Exercises

Each activity is labeled according to the primary skill or skills you will need to use. To review relevant chapter content, you can refer to the indicated Learning Objective. In some instances, supporting information will be found in another chapter, as indicated.

4.17. Planning: Identifying Your Purpose [LO-2] For each of the following communication tasks, state a specific purpose (if you have trouble, try beginning with "I want to . . . ").

a. A report to your boss, the store manager, about the outdated items in the warehouse

b. An email message to clients about your booth at the upcoming trade show

c. A letter to a customer who hasn't made a payment for three months

d. A memo to employees about the department's high phone bills

e. A phone call to a supplier, checking on an overdue parts shipment

f. A wiki entry for your office colleagues about the best ways to find information in the company's knowledge management system

4.18. Planning: Assessing Audience Needs [LO-2] For each communication task that follows, write brief answers to three questions: Who is the audience? What is the audience's general attitude toward my subject? What does the audience need to know?

a. A final-notice collection letter from an appliance manufacturer to an appliance dealer that is 3 months behind on payments, sent 10 days before initiating legal collection procedures

b. An advertisement for smartphones

c. A proposal to top management, suggesting that the four sales regions in the United States be combined into just two regions

d. Fliers announcing reduced rates for chimney cleaning or repairs, to be attached to doorknobs in the neighborhood

e. A cover letter sent along with your résumé to a potential employer

f. A website that describes the services offered by a consulting firm that helps accounting managers comply with government regulations

4-19. Planning: Assessing Audience Needs [LO-2] Choose a fairly simple electronic device (such as a digital music player) that you know how to operate well. Write two sets of instructions for operating the device: one set for a reader who has never used that type of device and one set for someone who is generally familiar with that type of machine but has never operated the specific model. Briefly explain how your two audiences affect your instructions.

4-20. Planning: Analyzing the Situation; Collaboration: Planning Meetings [LO-2], Chapter 2 How can the material discussed in this chapter also apply to meetings, as discussed in Chapter 2? Outline your ideas in a brief presentation or a post for your class blog.

4-21. Planning: Creating an Audience Profile; Collaboration: Team Projects [LO-2], [LO-3], Chapter 2 With a team assigned by your instructor, compare the Facebook pages of three companies in the same industry. Analyze the content on all the available tabs. What can you surmise about the intended audience for each company? Which of the three does the best job of presenting the information its target audience is likely to need? Prepare a brief presentation, including slides that show samples of the Facebook content from each company.

4-22. Planning: Analyzing the Situation, Selecting Media; Media Skills: Email [LO-2], [LO-4], Chapter 11 You are the head of public relations for a cruise line that operates out of Miami. You are shocked to read a letter in a local newspaper from a disgruntled passenger complaining about the service and entertainment on a recent cruise. You need to respond to these publicized criticisms in some way. What audiences will you need to consider in your response? What medium or media should you choose? If the letter had been published in a travel publication widely read by travel agents and cruise travelers, how might your course of action have differed? In an email message to your instructor, explain how you will respond.

4-23. Planning: Assessing Audience Needs; Media Skills: Blogging; Communication Ethics: Making Ethical Choices [LO-3], Chapter 1 Your supervisor has asked you to withhold important information that you think should be included in a report you are preparing. Disobeying him could be disastrous for your working relationship and your career. Obeying him could violate your personal code of ethics. What should you do? On the basis of the discussion in Chapter 1, would you consider this situation to be an ethical dilemma or an ethical lapse? Explain your analysis in a brief email message to your instructor.

4-24. Planning: Limiting Your Scope [LO-5] Suppose you are preparing to recommend that top management install a new heating system that uses the cogeneration process. The following information is in your files. Eliminate topics that aren't essential and then arrange the other topics so that your report will give top managers a clear understanding of the heating system and a balanced, concise justification for installing it.

- History of the development of the cogeneration heating process
- Scientific credentials of the developers of the process
- Risks assumed in using this process
- Your plan for installing the equipment in the headquarters building
- Stories about the successful use of cogeneration technology in comparable facilities
- Specifications of the equipment that would be installed
- Plans for disposing of the old heating equipment
- Costs of installing and running the new equipment
- Advantages and disadvantages of using the new process
- Detailed 10-year cost projections
- Estimates of the time needed to phase in the new system
- Alternative systems that management might want to consider

4-25. Planning: Choosing the Direct or Indirect Approach [LO-5] Indicate whether the direct or indirect approach would be best in each of the following situations and briefly explain why. Would any of these messages be inappropriate for email? Explain.

a. A message to the owner of an automobile dealership, complaining about poor service work

b. A message from a recent college graduate requesting a letter of recommendation from a former instructor

c. A message turning down a job applicant

d. A message announcing that because of high air-conditioning costs, the plant temperature will be held at 78°F during the summer

e. A message from an advertising agency to a troublesome long-term client, explaining that the agency will no longer be able to work on the client's account

4-26. **Planning: Using Storytelling Techniques; Communication Ethics: Providing Ethical Leadership; Media Skills: Podcasting [LO-5], Chapter 1** Research recent incidents of ethical lapses by business professionals or executives in any industry. Choose one example that has a clear story "arc" from beginning to end. Outline a cautionary tale that explains the context of the ethical lapse, the choice the person made, and the consequences of the ethical lapse. Script a podcast (aim for roughly three to five minutes) that tells the story. If your instructor directs, record your podcast and post to your class blog.

Expand Your Skills

Critique the Professionals

Locate an example of professional communication in any medium/channel that you think would work equally well—or perhaps better—in another medium. Using the information in this chapter and your understanding of the communication process, write a brief analysis (no more than one page) of the company's media/channel choice and explain why your choice would be at least as effective. Use whatever medium your instructor requests for your report and be sure to cite specific elements from the piece and support from the chapter.

Sharpening Your Career Skills Online

Bovée and Thill's Business Communication Web Search, at **websearch.businesscommunicationnetwork.com**, is a unique research tool designed specifically for business communication research. Use the Web Search function to find a website, video, article, podcast, or presentation that offers advice on planning a report, speech, or other business message. Write a brief email message to your instructor, describing the item you found and summarizing the career skills information you learned from it.

MyBCommLab

Go to **mybcommlab.com** for Auto-graded writing questions as well as the following Assisted-graded writing questions:

4-27. Email lacks both the visual element and the instantaneous connection of some other media. Could these supposed shortcomings actually help some employees communicate more comfortably and effectively? Explain your answer. [LO-4]

4-28. Would you use the direct or indirect approach to ask employees to work overtime to meet an important deadline? Please explain. [LO-5]

Endnotes

1. Michael Grothaus, "Why Companies Need Novelists," *Fast Company*, 1 May 2015, www.fastcompany.com; Wolff Olins website, accessed 17 March 2016, www.wolffolins.com; Haniya Rae, "Inside the Agency Wolff Olins," *Digiday*, 13 February 2014, digiday.com; "Is Corporate Storytelling Replacing the News Business?" *Fast Company*, 8 May 2014, www.fastcompany.com.

2. Carol Kinsey Gorman, "What's So Great About Face-to-Face?" *Communication World*, May–June 2011, 38–39.

3. Linda Duyle, "Get Out of Your Office," *HR Magazine*, July 2006, 99–101.

4. Caroline McCarthy, "The Future of Web Apps Will See the Death of Email," Webware blog, 29 February 2008, news.cnet.com; Kris Maher, "The Jungle," *Wall Street Journal*, 5 October 2004, B10; Kevin Maney, "Surge in Text Messaging Makes Cell Operators," *USA Today*, 28 July 2005, B1–B2.

5. Roger Cheng, "Verizon CEO: Unlimited Data Plans Just Aren't Sustainable," *CNET*, 24 September 2013, news.cnet.com; Brian Bennet, "Sprint Officially Outs New Unlimited Plans," *CNET*, 11 July 2013, reviews.cnet.com; footnotes on Sprint website, accessed 2 March 2014, shop.sprint.com.

6. Laurey Berk and Phillip G. Clampitt, "Finding the Right Path in the Communication Maze," *IABC Communication World*, October 1991, 28–32.

7. Samantha R. Murray and Joseph Peyrefitte, "Knowledge Type and Communication Media Choice in the Knowledge Transfer Process," *Journal of Managerial Issues* 19, no. 1 (Spring 2007): 111–133.

8. Holly Weeks, "The Best Memo You'll Ever Write," *Harvard Management Communication Letter*, Spring 2005, 3–5.

9. Steve Tobak, "How to Be a Great Storyteller and Win Over Any Audience," *BNET*, 12 January 2011, www.bnet.com.

10. Debra Askanase, "10 Trends in Sustainable Social Media," Community Organizer 2.0 blog, 13 May 2010, www.communityorganizer20.com.

11. Chip Heath and Dan Heath, *Made to Stick: Why Some Ideas Survive and Others Die* (New York: Random House, 2008), 214.

12. Heath and Heath, *Made to Stick*, 206, 214.

13. Randolph T. Barker and Kim Gower, "Strategic Application of Storytelling in Organizations," *Journal of Business Communication* 47, no. 3 (July 2010): 295–312.

14. David Meerman Scott, "Effective Storytelling for Business," WebInkNow blog, 18 February 2013, www.webinknow.com.

15. Jennifer Aaker and Andy Smith, "7 Deadly Sins of Business Storytelling," American Express Open Forum, accessed 21 March 2011, www.openforum.com.

LEARNING OBJECTIVES

After studying this chapter, you will be able to

1 Identify the four aspects of being sensitive to audience needs when writing business messages.

2 Explain how establishing your credibility and projecting your company's image are vital aspects of building strong relationships with your audience.

3 Explain how to achieve a tone that is conversational but businesslike, explain the value of using plain language, and define *active voice* and *passive voice*.

4 Describe how to select words that are both correct and effective.

5 Define the four types of sentences, and explain how sentence style affects emphasis within a message.

6 Define the three key elements of a paragraph, and list five ways to develop unified, coherent paragraphs.

7 List five techniques for writing effective messages for mobile readers.

COMMUNICATION CLOSE-UP AT
She Takes on the World

shetakesontheworld.com

Natalie MacNeil is not a dreamer of small dreams. Here's how she introduces herself on one of her online profiles: "My name is Natalie MacNeil, and I want to change the world." For MacNeil, that change means inspiring and helping women launch their own businesses and take more control over their careers. As she puts it, "I want to see more women leading companies, organizations, and countries."

MacNeil knows a thing or two about launching a business. She started her first when she was 18 and by her mid-20s had founded or cofounded a small portfolio of companies, including an Emmy-winning digital media production company, a collaborative workspace for entrepreneurs in the early startup phase, and She Takes on the World, which MacNeil describes as "a training platform and community for women entrepreneurs."

Communication is at the heart of MacNeil's world-changing quest. On the She Takes on the World website and in a book by the same name, MacNeil shares firsthand knowledge on everything from finding investors to expanding a company internationally. Her writing has appeared in a variety of other popular forums as well, including AllBusiness, American Express OPEN Forum, Mashable, *Forbes*, Entrepreneur.com, and *The Wall Street Journal*.

Plenty of entrepreneurs, executives, and other experts offer advice on launching businesses, so what sets MacNeil apart?

Image by Ashley Wessel

Women who run or aspire to run their own businesses are the target audience for Natalie MacNeil's She Takes on the World, a training and community platform that offers advice on all aspects of launching and managing a company.

One key element is a clear idea of who her audience is and the type of information these readers are likely to need. When promoting her book, for example, she emphasizes that no business book can appeal to every reader, and she lists the specific types of readers who can benefit from her book. She also does something that many business "how-to" writers don't: She addresses the personal side of being a successful entrepreneur.

Another key element is her positive writing style. The editor of *ForbesWoman* calls MacNeil's blog and book "smart, upbeat, inspirational, and full of practical advice for women who want to own their dream careers." As someone who came of age in the postdigital economy, MacNeil is also tuned in to the new world of work, where individuals must manage their personal brands and take control of their careers. In fact, one of her target audiences is college students who might want to create their own companies right out of college, without ever pursuing traditional employment.

The content and style of her messages is clearly connecting with readers. She Takes on the World has grown to include several dozen bloggers who cover every aspect of managing an entrepreneurial career in the new economy. The site was named one of *Forbes* magazine's top 10 entrepreneurial websites for women, among numerous other awards and recognitions it has received. MacNeil shows no signs of slowing down, either, with new investors behind her and ambitious expansion plans.[1]

Adapting to Your Audience: Being Sensitive to Audience Needs

1 **LEARNING OBJECTIVE**
Identify the four aspects of being sensitive to audience needs when writing business messages.

Natalie MacNeil (profiled in the chapter-opening Communication Close-Up) knows it takes more than just a great idea to change the way people think. Expressing ideas clearly and persuasively starts with adapting to one's audience.

Whether consciously or not, audiences greet most incoming messages with a selfish question: "What's in this for me?" If your readers or listeners don't think you understand or care about their needs, they won't pay attention, plain and simple. You can improve your audience sensitivity by adopting the "you" attitude, maintaining good standards of etiquette, emphasizing the positive, and using bias-free language.

Readers and listeners are more likely to respond positively when they believe messages are about them and their concerns.

USING THE "YOU" ATTITUDE

Adopting the "you" attitude means speaking and writing in terms of your audience's wishes, interests, hopes, and preferences.

Chapter 1 introduced the notion of audience-centered communication and the "you" attitude—speaking and writing in terms of your audience's wishes, interests, hopes, and preferences. On the simplest level, you can adopt the "you" attitude by replacing terms such as *I*, *me*, *mine*, *we*, *us*, and *ours* with *you* and *yours*:

Instead of This	Write This
Tuesday is the only day that we can promise quick response to purchase order requests; we are swamped the rest of the week.	If you need a quick response, please submit your purchase order requests on Tuesday.
We offer MP3 players with 50, 75, or 100 gigabytes of storage capacity.	You can choose an MP3 player with 50, 75, or 100 gigabytes of storage.

However, the "you" attitude is more than simply using particular pronouns. It's a matter of demonstrating genuine interest in your readers and concern for their needs (see Figure 5.1). You can use *you* 25 times in a single page and still offend your audience or ignore readers' true concerns. If you're writing to a retailer, try to think like a retailer; if you're dealing with a production supervisor, put yourself in that position; if you're writing to a dissatisfied customer, imagine how you would feel at the other end of the transaction.

Be aware that on some occasions it's better to avoid using *you*, particularly if doing so will sound overly authoritative or accusing:

Avoid using *you* and *your* if doing so
- Will make you sound dictatorial
- Will make someone else feel guilty
- Goes against your organization's style

Instead of This	Write This
You failed to deliver the customer's order on time.	The customer didn't receive the order on time.
You must correct all five copies by noon.	All five copies must be corrected by noon.

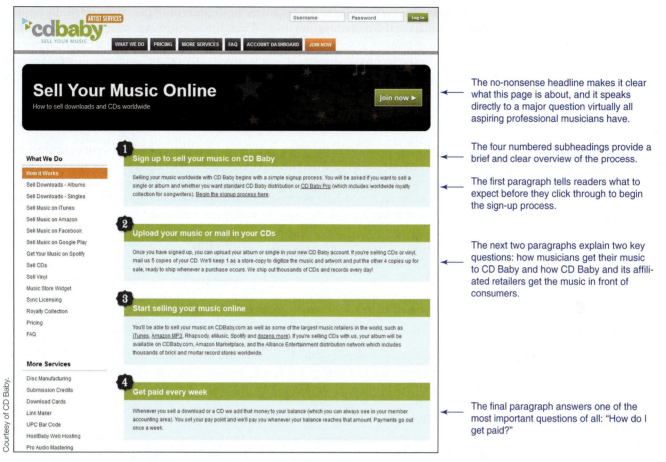

Figure 5.1 Fostering a Positive Relationship with an Audience
CD Baby, the world's largest retailer of independent music, uses clear, positive language to help musicians understand the process of selling their music through the company and its affiliates. By making the effort to communicate clearly and succinctly, the company encourages a positive response from its target readers.

As you practice using the "you" attitude, be sure to consider the attitudes of other cultures and the policies of your organization. In some cultures it is improper to single out one person's achievements because the whole team is responsible for the outcome; in that case, using the pronoun *we* or *our* (when you and your audience are part of the same team) would be more appropriate. Similarly, some companies have a tradition of avoiding references to *you* and *I* in most messages and reports.

MAINTAINING STANDARDS OF ETIQUETTE

Good etiquette not only indicates respect for your audience but also helps foster a more successful environment for communication by minimizing negative emotional reactions:

Even if a situation calls for you to be brutally honest, express the facts of the matter in a kind and thoughtful manner.

Instead of This	**Write This**
Once again, you've managed to bring down the entire website through your incompetent programming.	Let's review the last website update to explore ways to improve the process.
You've been sitting on our order for two weeks, and we need it now!	Our production schedules depend on timely delivery of parts and supplies, but we have not yet received the order you promised to deliver two weeks ago. Please respond today with a firm delivery commitment.

Of course, some situations require more diplomacy than others. If you know your audience well, a less formal approach may be more appropriate. However, when you are communicating with people who outrank you or with people outside your organization, an added measure of courtesy is usually needed.

Use extra tact when communicating with people higher up in the organization or outside the company.

Written communication and most forms of digital communication generally require more tact than oral communication does. When you're speaking, your words can be softened by your tone of voice and facial expression. Plus, you can adjust your approach according to the feedback you get. If you inadvertently offend someone in writing or in a podcast, for example, you don't usually get the immediate feedback you would need to resolve the situation. In fact, you may never know that you offended your audience.

EMPHASIZING THE POSITIVE

You can communicate negative news without being negative.

During your career, you will have many occasions in which you need to communicate bad news. However, there is a big difference between *delivering* negative news and *being* negative. When the tone of your message is negative, you put unnecessary strain on business relationships. Never try to hide negative news, but always be on the lookout for positive points that will foster a good relationship with your audience:[2]

Instead of This	Write This
It is impossible to repair your laptop today.	Your computer can be ready by Tuesday. Would you like a loaner until then?
We wasted $300,000 advertising in that magazine.	Our $300,000 advertising investment did not pay off. Let's analyze the experience and apply the insights to future campaigns.

If you find it necessary to criticize or correct, don't dwell on the other person's mistakes. Avoid referring to failures, problems, or shortcomings. Focus instead on what the audience members can do to improve the situation:

Instead of This	Write This
The problem with this department is a failure to control costs.	The performance of this department can be improved by tightening cost controls.
You failed to provide all the necessary information on the previous screen.	Please review the items marked in red on the previous screen so that we can process your order as quickly as possible.

Show audience members how they will benefit by responding to your message.

If you're trying to persuade audience members to buy a product, pay a bill, or perform a service, emphasize what's in it for them. When people recognize the benefits of doing so, they are more likely to respond positively to your appeal.

Instead of This	Write This
We will notify all three credit reporting agencies if you do not pay your overdue bill within 10 days.	Paying your overdue bill within 10 days will prevent a negative entry on your credit record.
I am tired of seeing so many errors in the customer service blog.	Proofreading your blog postings will help you avoid embarrassing mistakes that generate more customer service complaints.

Euphemisms are milder synonyms that can express an idea while triggering fewer negative connotations, but they should never be used to obscure the truth.

In general, try to state your message without using words that may hurt or offend your audience. Look for appropriate opportunities to use **euphemisms**—words or phrases that express a thought in milder terms—that convey your meaning without carrying negative or unpleasant connotations. For example, one common euphemism is referring to people beyond a certain age as "senior citizens" rather than "old people." *Senior* conveys respect in a way that *old* does not.

Euphemisms can bring a tone of civility to unpleasant communication, but they must be used with great care because they are so easy—and so tempting—to misuse. Euphemisms can be annoying if they force readers to "read between the lines" to get the message, and they can be unethical if they obscure the truth. For instance, one of the toughest messages a manager ever has to write is an internal memo or email announcing layoffs. This is a difficult situation for everyone involved, and managers can be tempted to resort to euphemisms such as *streamlining, restructuring, improving efficiency, reducing layers,* or *eliminating redundancies* to avoid using the word *layoff*.[3] Doing so might ease the emotional burden on the writer and promote the illusion that the message isn't as negative as it really is. However, these euphemisms can fail the "you" attitude test, as well as the standards of ethical information, by failing to answer the question every reader in these situations has, which is simply, *Am I going to lose my job?*

If you are considering using a euphemism, ask yourself this question: Are you trying to protect the reader's feelings or your own feelings? Even if it is unpleasant, people generally respond better to an honest message delivered with integrity than they do to a sugar-coated message that obscures the truth.

MOBILE APP
Dragon Dictation uses voice recognition to convert speech to text up to five times faster than typing.

USING BIAS-FREE LANGUAGE

Bias-free language avoids words and phrases that unfairly and even unethically categorize or stigmatize people in ways related to gender, race, ethnicity, age, disability, or other personal characteristics. Contrary to what some may think, biased language is not simply about "labels." To a significant degree, language reflects the way we think and what we believe, and biased language may well perpetuate the underlying stereotypes and prejudices it represents.[4] Moreover, because communication is all about perception, simply *being* fair and objective isn't enough. To establish a good relationship with your audience, you must also *appear* to be fair.[5] Good communicators make every effort to change biased language (see Table 5.1). Bias can come in a variety of forms:

Bias-free language avoids words and phrases that unfairly and even unethically categorize or stigmatize people.

- **Gender bias.** Avoid sexist language by using the same labels for everyone, regardless of gender. Don't refer to a woman as *chairperson* and then to a man as *chairman*. Use chair, chairperson, or chairman consistently. (Note that it is not uncommon to use chairman when referring to a woman who heads a board of directors. Archer

TABLE 5.1 Overcoming Bias in Language

Examples	Unacceptable	Preferable
Gender Bias		
Using words containing *man*	Man-made	Artificial, synthetic, manufactured, constructed, human-made
	Mankind	Humanity, human beings, human race, people
	Manpower	Workers, workforce
	Businessman	Executive, manager, businessperson, professional
	Salesman	Sales representative, salesperson
	Foreman	Supervisor
Using female-gender words	Actress, stewardess	Actor, flight attendant
Using special designations	Woman doctor, male nurse	Doctor, nurse
Using *he* to refer to "everyone"	The average worker . . . he	The average worker . . . he or she *OR* Average workers . . . they
Identifying roles with gender	The typical executive spends four hours of his day in meetings.	Most executives spend four hours a day in meetings.
	the consumer . . . she	consumers . . . they
	the nurse/teacher . . . she	nurses/teachers . . . they
Identifying women by marital status	Mrs. Norm Lindstrom	Maria Lindstrom *OR* Ms. Maria Lindstrom
	Norm Lindstrom and Ms. Drake	Norm Lindstrom and Maria Drake *OR* Mr. Lindstrom and Ms. Drake
Racial and Ethnic Bias		
Assigning stereotypes	Not surprisingly, Shing-Tung Yau excels in mathematics.	Shing-Tung Yau excels in mathematics.
Identifying people by race or ethnicity	Mario M. Cuomo, Italian American politician and ex-governor of New York	Mario M. Cuomo, politician and ex-governor of New York
Age Bias		
Including age when irrelevant	Mary Kirazy, 58, has just joined our trust department.	Mary Kirazy has just joined our trust department.
Disability Bias		
Putting the disability before the person	Disabled workers face many barriers on the job.	Workers with physical disabilities face many barriers on the job.
	An epileptic, Tracy has no trouble doing her job.	Tracy's epilepsy has no effect on her job performance.

Daniels Midland's Patricia Woertz and Xerox's Ursula Burns, for example, both refer to themselves as "chairman."[6]) Reword sentences to use *they* or to use no pronoun at all rather than refer to all individuals as *he*. Note that the preferred title for women in business is *Ms.* unless the individual asks to be addressed as *Miss* or *Mrs.* or has some other title, such as *Dr.*

- **Racial and ethnic bias.** Avoid identifying people by race or ethnic origin unless such a label is relevant to the matter at hand—and it rarely is.
- **Age bias.** Mention the age of a person only when it is relevant. Moreover, be careful of the context in which you use words that refer to age; such words carry a variety of positive and negative connotations. For example, *young* can imply energy, youthfulness, inexperience, or even immaturity, depending on how it's used.
- **Disability bias.** Physical, mental, sensory, or emotional impairments should never be mentioned in business messages unless those conditions are directly relevant to the subject. If you must refer to someone's disability, put the person first and the disability second.[7] For example, by saying "employees with physical handicaps," not "handicapped employees," you focus on the whole person, not the disability. Finally, never use outdated terminology such as *crippled* or *retarded*.

REAL-TIME UPDATES

LEARN MORE BY READING THIS PDF

Get detailed advice on using bias-free language

This in-depth guide offers practical tips for avoiding many types of cultural bias in your writing and speaking. Go to **real-timeupdates .com/bct14** and select Learn More in the Students section.

Adapting to Your Audience: Building Strong Relationships

2 LEARNING OBJECTIVE
Explain how establishing your credibility and projecting your company's image are vital aspects of building strong relationships with your audience.

Successful communication relies on a positive relationship between sender and receiver. Establishing your credibility and projecting your company's image are two vital steps in building and fostering positive business relationships.

ESTABLISHING YOUR CREDIBILITY

People are more likely to react positively to your message when they have confidence in you.

Audience responses to your messages depend heavily on your **credibility**, a measure of your believability based on how reliable you are and how much trust you evoke in others. With audiences who don't know you and trust you already, you need to establish credibility before they'll accept your messages (see Figure 5.2). On the other hand, when you do establish credibility, communication becomes much easier because you no longer have to spend time and energy convincing people that you are a trustworthy source of information and ideas. To build, maintain, or repair your credibility, emphasize the following characteristics:

To enhance your credibility, emphasize such factors as honesty, objectivity, and awareness of audience needs.

- **Honesty.** Demonstrating honesty and integrity will earn you the respect of your audiences, even if they don't always agree with or welcome your messages.
- **Objectivity.** Show that you can distance yourself from emotional situations and look at all sides of an issue.
- **Awareness of audience needs.** Let your audience members know, directly or indirectly, that you understand what's important to them.
- **Credentials, knowledge, and expertise.** Audiences need to know that you have whatever it takes to back up your message, whether it's education, professional certification, special training, past successes, or simply the fact that you've done your research.
- **Endorsements.** An *endorsement* is a statement on your behalf by someone who is accepted by your audience as an expert.
- **Performance.** Demonstrating impressive communication skills is not enough; people need to know they can count on you to get the job done.
- **Sincerity.** When you offer praise, don't use *hyperbole*, such as "you are the most fantastic employee I could ever imagine." Instead, point out specific qualities that warrant praise.

REAL-TIME UPDATES

LEARN MORE BY READING THIS ARTICLE

Building credibility online

Follow these steps to build your credibility as an online voice. Go to **real-timeupdates.com/bct14** and select Learn More in the Students section.

Photography plays an important role because clients are essentially "buying" Fraley when they buy his services. These images show him to be friendly, engaging, and confident.

The first paragraph summarizes his business background, which sends a strong message that he has the experience to back up the advice he gives.

Describing some of his career accomplishments provides persuasive support to his high-level message of being an innovator himself—not just somebody who knows how to talk about innovation.

Listing publications that have quoted him adds to his credibility as a respected expert in the field.

Courtesy of Gregg Fraley.

Figure 5.2 Building Credibility
Gregg Fraley is a highly regarded expert in the field of creativity and business innovation, but because his services are intangible, potential clients can't "test drive" those services before making a purchase decision. He therefore takes special care to build credibility as part of his communication efforts.

In addition, audiences need to know that you believe in yourself and your message. If you lack faith in yourself, you're likely to communicate an uncertain attitude that undermines your credibility. In contrast, if you are convinced that your message is sound, you can state your case with authority. Look out for phrases containing words such as *hope* and *trust*, which can drain the audience's confidence in your message.

Instead of This	Write This
We hope this recommendation will be helpful.	We're pleased to make this recommendation.
We trust that you'll want to extend your service contract.	By extending your service contract, you can continue to enjoy top-notch performance from your equipment.

Finally, keep in mind that credibility can take a long time to establish—and it can be wiped out in an instant. An occasional mistake or letdown is usually forgiven, but major lapses in honesty or integrity can destroy your reputation.

PROJECTING YOUR COMPANY'S IMAGE

When you communicate with anyone outside your organization, it is more than a conversation between two individuals. You represent your company and therefore play a vital role in helping the company build and maintain positive relationships with all its stakeholders. Most successful companies work hard to foster a specific public image, and your

---

THE ART OF PROFESSIONALISM

Being Dependable and Accountable

By any definition, a "pro" is somebody who gets the job done. Develop a reputation as somebody people can count on. This means meeting your commitments, including keeping on schedule and staying within budgets. These are skills that take some time to develop as you discover how much time and money are required to accomplish various tasks and projects. With experience, you'll learn to be conservative with your commitments. You don't want to be known as someone who overpromises and underdelivers.

If you can't confidently predict how long a project will take or how much it will cost, be sure to let your client, colleagues, or supervisor know. And if changing circumstances threaten your ability to meet a previous commitment, be sure to share that information with anyone who might be affected by your performance.

Being accountable also means owning up to your mistakes and learning from failure so that you can continue to improve. Pros don't make excuses or blame others. When they make mistakes—and everybody does—they face the situation head on, make amends, and move on.

CAREER APPLICATIONS

1. What steps could you take to make realistic commitments on tasks and projects in which you have little or no experience?
2. Does being accountable mean you never make mistakes? Explain your answer.

Your company's interests and reputation take precedence over your personal views and communication style.

external communication efforts need to project that image. As part of this responsibility, the interests and preferred communication style of your company must take precedence over your own views and personal communication style.

Many organizations have specific communication guidelines that show everything from the correct use of the company name to preferred abbreviations and other grammatical details. Specifying a desired style of communication is more difficult, however. Observe more experienced colleagues, and never hesitate to ask for editorial help to make sure you're conveying the appropriate tone. For instance, because clients entrust thousands or millions of dollars to an investment firm, it must communicate in a style quite different from that of a clothing retailer. And a clothing retailer specializing in high-quality business attire communicates in a different style than a store catering to the latest trends in casual wear.

Adapting to Your Audience: Controlling Your Style and Tone

3 **LEARNING OBJECTIVE**
Explain how to achieve a tone that is conversational but businesslike, explain the value of using plain language, and define *active voice* and *passive voice*.

Your communication **style** involves the choices you make to express yourself: the words you select, the manner in which you use those words in sentences, and the way you build paragraphs from individual sentences. Your style creates a certain **tone**, or overall impression, in your messages. The right tone depends on the nature of your message and your relationship with the reader.

CREATING A CONVERSATIONAL TONE

Most business messages aim for a conversational style that is warm but businesslike.

The tone of your business messages can range from informal to conversational to formal. When you're communicating with your superiors or with customers, your tone may tend to be more formal and respectful.[8] However, that formal tone might sound distant and cold if used with close colleagues.

Compare the three versions of the message in Table 5.2. The first is too formal for today's audiences, whereas the third is inappropriately casual for business. The second message demonstrates the **conversational tone** used in most business communication—plain language that sounds businesslike without being stuffy at one extreme or too laid-back and informal at the other extreme. You can achieve a tone that is conversational but still businesslike by following these guidelines:

- **Understand the difference between texting and writing.** Texting can be an efficient way to communicate quickly, particularly on mobile devices with cramped keyboards.

TABLE 5.2   Finding the Right Tone

Tone	Example
Stuffy: too formal for today's audiences	Dear Ms. Navarro:
	Enclosed please find the information that was requested during our telephone communication of May 14. As was mentioned at that time, Midville Hospital has significantly more doctors of exceptional quality than any other health facility in the state.
	As you were also informed, our organization has quite an impressive network of doctors and other health-care professionals with offices located throughout the state. Should you need a specialist, our professionals will be able to make an appropriate recommendation.
	In the event that you have questions or would like additional information, you may certainly contact me during regular business hours.
	Most sincerely yours,
	Samuel G. Berenz
Conversational: just right for most business communication	Dear Ms. Navarro:
	Here's the information you requested during our phone conversation on Friday. As I mentioned, Midville Hospital has the highest-rated doctors and more of them than any other hospital in the state.
	In addition, we have a vast network of doctors and other health professionals with offices throughout the state. If you need a specialist, they can refer you to the right one.
	If you would like more information, please call any time between 9:00 and 5:00, Monday through Friday.
	Sincerely,
	Samuel G. Berenz
Unprofessional: too casual for business communication	Here's the 411 you requested. IMHO, we have more and better doctors than any other hospital in the state.
	FYI, we also have a large group of doctors and other health professionals w/ offices close to U at work/home. If U need a specialist, they'll refer U to the right one.
	Any? just ring or msg.
	L8R,
	S

However, it's best to view texting as a mode of conversation, rather than as a mode of writing—and to keep the two modes clear in your mind when you are writing. Communication effectiveness and your personal credibility can suffer if you let texting habits (such as using sentence fragments, sloppy punctuation, and lots of acronyms) creep into your business writing.

- **Avoid stale and pompous language.** Most companies now shy away from such dated phrases as "attached please find" and "please be advised that." Similarly, avoid using obscure words, stale or clichéd expressions, and overly complicated sentences designed only to impress others (see Table 5.3 on the next page).
- **Avoid preaching and bragging.** Readers tend to get irritated by know-it-alls who like to preach or brag. However, if you need to remind your audience of something that should be obvious, try to work in the information casually, perhaps in the middle of a paragraph, where it will sound like a secondary comment rather than a major revelation.
- **Be careful with intimacy.** Business messages should generally avoid intimacy, such as sharing personal details or adopting a casual, unprofessional tone. However, when you have a close relationship with audience members, such as among the members of a close-knit team, a more intimate tone is sometimes appropriate and even expected.
- **Be careful with humor.** Humor can easily backfire and divert attention from your message. If you don't know your audience well or you're not skilled at using humor in a business setting, don't use it at all. Avoid humor in formal messages and when you're communicating across cultural boundaries.

REAL-TIME UPDATES
LEARN MORE BY READING THIS ARTICLE
Ten tips for conversational writing
These easy-to-use ideas will help you achieve a business-friendly conversational tone. Go to **real-timeupdates.com/bct14** and select Learn More in the Students section.

TABLE 5.3   Weeding Out Obsolete Phrases

Obsolete Phrase	Up-to-Date Replacement
we are in receipt of	we received
kindly advise	please let me/us know
attached please find	enclosed is or I/we have enclosed
it has come to my attention	I have just learned or [someone] has just informed me
the undersigned	I/we
in due course	(specify a time or date)
permit me to say that	(omit; just say whatever you need to say)
pursuant to	(omit; just say whatever you need to say)
in closing, I'd like to say	(omit; just say whatever you need to say)
we wish to inform you that	(omit; just say whatever you need to say)
please be advised that	(omit; just say whatever you need to say)

USING PLAIN LANGUAGE

Audiences can understand and act on plain language without reading it over and over.

An important aspect of creating a conversational tone is using *plain language* (or *plain English* specifically when English is involved). Plain language presents information in a simple, unadorned style that allows your audience to easily grasp your meaning—language that recipients "can read, understand and act upon the first time they read it."[9] You can see how this definition supports using the "you" attitude and shows respect for your audience. In addition, plain language can make companies more productive and more profitable because people spend less time trying to figure out messages that are confusing or aren't written to meet their needs.[10] Plain language is also easier for nonnative speakers to read, a major benefit when you're addressing diverse, global audiences.

Creative Commons, a not-for-profit organization that provides content creators with an alternative to traditional copyright law, offers a great example of adapting to readers with plain language. Its licensing terms are available in three versions: a complete "legal code" document that spells out contractual details in specific legal terms that meet the needs of legal professionals, a "human readable" version that explains the licensing terms in nontechnical language that anyone can understand, and a "machine readable" version fine-tuned for search engines and other systems (see Figure 5.3).[11]

SELECTING THE ACTIVE OR PASSIVE VOICE

Your choice of the active or passive voice affects the tone of your message. In **active voice**, the subject performs the action and the object receives the action: "Jodi sent the email message." In **passive voice**, the subject receives the action: "The email message was sent by Jodi." As you can see, the passive voice combines the helping verb *to be* with a form of the verb that is usually similar to the past tense.

Active sentences are usually stronger than passive ones.

Using the active voice helps make your writing more direct, livelier, and easier to read (see Table 5.4). In contrast, the passive voice is often cumbersome, can be unnecessarily vague, and can make sentences overly long. In most cases, the active voice is your best choice.[12] Nevertheless, using the passive voice can help you demonstrate the "you" attitude in some situations:

Use passive sentences to soften bad news, to put yourself in the background, or to create an impersonal tone when needed.

- When you want to be diplomatic about pointing out a problem or an error of some kind (the passive version seems less like an accusation)
- When you want to point out what's being done without taking or attributing either the credit or the blame (the passive version shifts the spotlight away from the person or persons involved)
- When you want to avoid personal pronouns in order to create an objective tone (the passive version may be used in a formal report, for example)

The second half of Table 5.4 illustrates several other situations in which the passive voice helps you focus your message on your audience.

The notion of three layers is carried through the text and reinforced with the diagram.

The introductory sentence expresses the main idea, that the licenses are built in three layers (note that "use" would be a simpler alternative to "incorporate").

The paragraph on the "human readable" version explains why it exists and whom it benefits.

The purpose and function of the "machine readable" version are less obvious than in the other two versions, so this paragraph offers a more extensive explanation.

Figure 5.3 **Plain Language at Creative Commons**
Creative Commons uses this diagram and text to explain the differences among its three versions of content licenses.

TABLE 5.4   Choosing Active or Passive Voice

In general, avoid passive voice to make your writing lively and direct.

Dull and Indirect in Passive Voice	Lively and Direct in Active Voice
The new procedure was developed by the operations team.	The operations team developed the new procedure.
Legal problems are created by this contract.	This contract creates legal problems.
Reception preparations have been undertaken by our PR people for the new CEO's arrival.	Our PR people have begun planning a reception for the new CEO.

However, passive voice is helpful when you need to be diplomatic or want to focus attention on problems or solutions rather than on people.

Accusatory or Self-Congratulatory in Active Voice	More Diplomatic in Passive Voice
You lost the shipment.	The shipment was lost.
I recruited seven engineers last month.	Seven engineers were recruited last month.
We are investigating the high rate of failures on the final assembly line.	The high rate of failures on the final assembly line is being investigated.

Composing Your Message: Choosing Powerful Words

After you have decided how to adapt to your audience, you're ready to begin composing your message. As you write your first draft, let your creativity flow. Don't try to write and edit at the same time or worry about getting everything perfect. Make up words if you can't think of the right word, draw pictures, talk out loud—do whatever it takes to get the ideas out of your head and onto screen or paper. If you've scheduled carefully, you should have time to revise and refine the material later. In fact, many writers find it helpful to establish a personal rule of never showing a first draft to anyone. By working in this "safe zone," away from the critical eyes of others, your mind will stay free to think clearly and creatively.

4   LEARNING OBJECTIVE
Describe how to select words that are both correct and effective.

If you get stuck and feel unable to write, try to overcome writer's block by jogging your brain in creative ways. The introduction is often the hardest part to write, so put it aside and work on whichever parts of the document you're most comfortable with at any given moment. In most cases you don't need to write the sections in any particular order.[13] Work on nontext elements such as graphics or your cover page. Revisit your purpose and confirm your intent in writing the message. Give yourself a mental break by switching to a different project. Sometimes all you need to do is start writing without worrying about the words you're using or how they will sound to the audience. Words will start flowing, your mind will engage, and the writing will come easier.

You may find it helpful to hone your craft by viewing your writing at three levels: strong words, effective sentences, and coherent paragraphs. Starting at the word level, successful writers pay close attention to the correct use of words.[14] If you make errors of grammar or usage, you lose credibility with your audience—even if your message is otherwise correct. Poor grammar suggests to readers that you're unprofessional, and they may choose not to trust you as a result. Moreover, poor grammar may imply that you don't respect your audience enough to get things right.

Correctness is the first consideration when choosing words.

The rules of grammar and usage can be a source of worry for writers because some of them are complex and some evolve over time. Even professional editors and grammarians occasionally have questions about correct usage, and they may disagree about the answers. For example, the word *data* is the plural form of *datum*, yet some experts now prefer to treat *data* as a singular noun when it's used in nonscientific material to refer to a body of facts or figures.

With practice, you'll become more skilled in making correct choices over time. If you have doubts about what is correct, you have many ways to find the answer. Check the Handbook of Grammar, Mechanics, and Usage at the end of this book, or consult the many special reference books and resources available in libraries, in bookstores, and on the Internet.

Effectiveness is the second consideration when choosing words.

In addition to using words correctly, successful writers and speakers take care to use the most effective words and phrases. Selecting and using words effectively is often more challenging than using words correctly because doing so is a matter of judgment and experience. Careful writers continue to work at their craft to find words that communicate with power (see Figure 5.4).

UNDERSTANDING DENOTATION AND CONNOTATION

A word may have both a denotative and a connotative meaning. The **denotative meaning** is the literal, or dictionary, meaning. The **connotative meaning** includes all the associations and feelings evoked by the word.

The denotative meaning of *desk* is "a piece of furniture with a flat work surface and various drawers for storage." The connotative meaning of *desk* may include thoughts associated with work or study, but the word *desk* has fairly neutral connotations—neither strong nor emotional. However, some words have much stronger connotations than others and should be used with care. For example, the connotations of the word *fail* are negative and can have a dramatic emotional impact. If you say the sales department *failed* to meet its annual quota, the connotative meaning suggests that the group is inferior, incompetent, or below some standard of performance. However, the reason for not achieving 100 percent might be an inferior product, incorrect pricing, or some other factor outside the control of the sales department. In contrast, by saying the sales department achieved 85 percent of its quota, you clearly communicate that the results were less than expected without triggering all the negative emotions associated with *failure*.

BALANCING ABSTRACT AND CONCRETE WORDS

The more abstract a word is, the more it is removed from the tangible, objective world of things that can be perceived with the senses.

Words vary dramatically in their degree of abstraction or concreteness. An **abstract word** expresses a concept, quality, or characteristic. Abstractions are usually broad, encompassing a category of ideas, and they are often intellectual, academic, or philosophical. *Love, honor,*

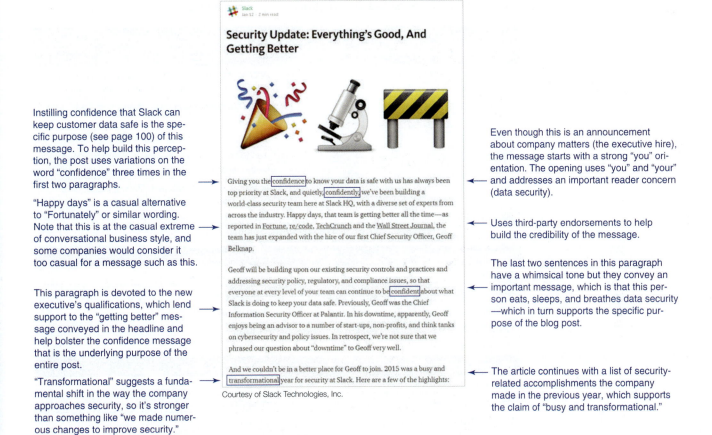

Instilling confidence that Slack can keep customer data safe is the specific purpose (see page 100) of this message. To help build this perception, the post uses variations on the word "confidence" three times in the first two paragraphs.

"Happy days" is a casual alternative to "Fortunately" or similar wording. Note that this is at the casual extreme of conversational business style, and some companies would consider it too casual for a message such as this.

This paragraph is devoted to the new executive's qualifications, which lend support to the "getting better" message conveyed in the headline and help bolster the confidence message that is the underlying purpose of the entire post.

"Transformational" suggests a fundamental shift in the way the company approaches security, so it's stronger than something like "we made numerous changes to improve security."

Even though this is an announcement about company matters (the executive hire), the message starts with a strong "you" orientation. The opening uses "you" and "your" and addresses an important reader concern (data security).

Uses third-party endorsements to help build the credibility of the message.

The last two sentences in this paragraph have a whimsical tone but they convey an important message, which is that this person eats, sleeps, and breathes data security —which in turn supports the specific purpose of the blog post.

The article continues with a list of security-related accomplishments the company made in the previous year, which supports the claim of "busy and transformational."

Security Update: Everything's Good, And Getting Better

Giving you the confidence to know your data is safe with us has always been top priority at Slack, and quietly, confidently, we've been building a world-class security team here at Slack HQ, with a diverse set of experts from across the industry. Happy days, that team is getting better all the time—as reported in Fortune, re/code, TechCrunch and the Wall Street Journal, the team has just expanded with the hire of our first Chief Security Officer, Geoff Belknap.

Geoff will be building upon our existing security controls and practices and addressing security policy, regulatory, and compliance issues, so that everyone at every level of your team can continue to be confident about what Slack is doing to keep your data safe. Previously, Geoff was the Chief Information Security Officer at Palantir. In his downtime, apparently, Geoff enjoys being an advisor to a number of start-ups, non-profits, and think tanks on cybersecurity and policy issues. In retrospect, we're not sure that we phrased our question about "downtime" to Geoff very well.

And we couldn't be in a better place for Geoff to join. 2015 was a busy and transformational year for security at Slack. Here are a few of the highlights:

Courtesy of Slack Technologies, Inc.

Figure 5.4   Making Effective Word and Phrase Choices
The opening paragraphs of this blog post from Slack, the maker of a popular group messaging service, illustrate a number of effective word and phrase choices. Slack's usual communication tone is upbeat and casual, even a little bit playful, but data and network security is a critically important issue that had already affected the young company by this point in time, so this post strikes a balance between conversational and serious.

progress, *tradition*, and *beauty* are abstractions, as are such important business concepts as *productivity*, *profits*, *quality*, and *motivation*. In contrast, a **concrete word** stands for something you can touch, see, or visualize. Most concrete terms are anchored in the tangible, material world. *Chair*, *table*, *horse*, *rose*, *kick*, *kiss*, *red*, *green*, and *two* are concrete words; they are direct, clear, and exact. Things don't need to have a physical presence to be considered concrete, by the way; *software*, *database*, and *website* are all concrete terms as well.

As you can imagine, abstractions tend to cause more trouble for writers and readers than concrete words. Abstractions tend to be "fuzzy" and can be interpreted differently, depending on the audience and the circumstances. The best way to minimize such problems is to blend abstract terms with concrete ones, the general with the specific. State the concept, and then pin it down with details expressed in more concrete terms. Save the abstractions for ideas that cannot be expressed any other way. In addition, abstract words such as *small*, *numerous*, *sizable*, *near*, *soon*, *good*, and *fine* are imprecise, so try to replace them with terms that are more accurate. Instead of referring to a sizable loss, give an exact number.

FINDING WORDS THAT COMMUNICATE WELL

By practicing your writing, learning from experienced writers and editors, and reading extensively, you'll find it easier to choose words that communicate exactly what you want to say. When you compose your business messages, think carefully to find the most powerful words for each situation and to avoid obscure words, clichés, and buzzwords that are turning into clichés (see Table 5.5 on the next page):

- **Choose strong, precise words.** Choose words that express your thoughts clearly, specifically, and dynamically. If you find yourself using a lot of adjectives and adverbs, you're probably trying to compensate for weak nouns and verbs. Saying that *sales*

Try to use words that are powerful and familiar.

TABLE 5.5 Examples of Finding Powerful Words

Potentially Weak Words and Phrases	Stronger Alternatives (Effective Usage Depends on the Situation)
Increase (as a verb)	Accelerate, amplify, augment, enlarge, escalate, expand, extend, magnify, multiply, soar, swell
Decrease (as a verb)	Curb, cut back, depreciate, dwindle, shrink, slacken
Large, small	(Use a specific number, such as $100 million)
Good	Admirable, beneficial, desirable, flawless, pleasant, sound, superior, worthy
Bad	Abysmal, corrupt, deficient, flawed, inadequate, inferior, poor, substandard, worthless
We are committed to providing . . .	We provide . . .
It is in our best interest to . . .	We should . . .
Unfamiliar Words	**Familiar Words**
Ascertain	Find out, learn
Consummate	Close, bring about
Peruse	Read, study
Circumvent	Avoid
Unequivocal	Certain
Clichés and Buzzwords	**Plain Language**
An uphill battle	A challenge
Writing on the wall	Prediction
Call the shots	Lead
Take by storm	Attack
Costs an arm and a leg	Expensive
A new ball game	Fresh start
Fall through the cracks	Be overlooked
Think outside the box	Be creative
Run it up the flagpole	Find out what people think about it
Eat our own dog food	Use our own products
Mission-critical	Vital
Disintermediate	Get rid of
Green light (as a verb)	Approve
Architect (as a verb)	Design
Space (as in, "we compete in the XYZ space")	Market or industry
Blocking and tackling	Basic skills
Trying to boil the ocean	Working frantically but without focus
Human capital	People, employees, workforce
Low-hanging fruit	Tasks that are easy to complete or sales that are easy to close
Pushback	Resistance

plummeted is stronger and more efficient than saying sales *dropped dramatically* or sales *experienced a dramatic drop*.

- **Choose familiar words.** You'll communicate best with words that are familiar to both you and your readers. Efforts to improve a situation certainly can be *ameliorative*, but saying they are *helpful* is a lot more effective. Moreover, trying to use an unfamiliar word for the first time in an important document can lead to embarrassing mistakes.
- **Avoid clichés and be careful with buzzwords.** Although familiar words are generally the best choice, avoid *clichés*—terms and phrases so common that they have

Avoid clichés, be extremely careful with trendy buzzwords, and use jargon only when your audience is completely familiar with it.

lost some of their power to communicate. *Buzzwords*, newly coined terms often associated with technology, business, or cultural changes, are slightly more difficult to handle than clichés, but they can be useful in small doses and in the right situation. The careful use of a buzzword can signal that you're an insider, someone in the know.[15] However, buzzwords quickly become clichés, and using them too late in their "life cycle" can mark you as an outsider desperately trying to look like an insider. When people use clichés and overuse buzzwords, they often sound as though they don't know how to express themselves otherwise and don't invest the energy required for original writing.[16]

- **Use jargon carefully.** *Jargon*, the specialized language of a particular profession or industry, has a bad reputation, but it's not always bad. Using jargon is usually an efficient way to communicate within the specific groups that understand these terms. After all, that's how jargon develops in the first place, as people with similar interests devise ways to communicate complex ideas quickly. For instance, when a recording engineer wants to communicate that a particular piece of music is devoid of reverberation and other sound effects, it's a lot easier to simply describe the track as "dry." Of course, to people who aren't familiar with such insider terms, jargon is meaningless and intimidating—one more reason it's important to understand your audience before you start writing.

MOBILE APP
The **Advanced English Dictionary and Thesaurus** helps you find the right word by organizing words according to their relationship with other words.

Composing Your Message: Creating Effective Sentences

Arranging your carefully chosen words in effective sentences is the next step in creating powerful messages. Start by selecting the best type of sentence to communicate each point you want to make.

5 LEARNING OBJECTIVE
Define the four types of sentences, and explain how sentence style affects emphasis within a message.

CHOOSING FROM THE FOUR TYPES OF SENTENCES

Sentences come in four basic varieties: simple, compound, complex, and compound-complex. A **simple sentence** has one main *clause* (a single subject and a single predicate), although it may be expanded by nouns and pronouns that serve as objects of the action and by modifying phrases. Here's an example with the subject noun underlined once and the predicate verb underlined twice:

A simple sentence has one main clause.

> Profits increased in the past year.

A **compound sentence** has two main clauses that express two or more independent but related thoughts of equal importance, usually joined by a conjunction (such as *and*, *but*, or *or*). In effect, a compound sentence is a merger of two or more simple sentences (independent clauses) that are related. For example:

A compound sentence has two main clauses.

> Wage rates have declined by 5 percent, and employee turnover has been high.

The independent clauses in a compound sentence are always separated by a comma or by a semicolon (in which case the conjunction—*and*, *but*, *or*—is dropped).

A **complex sentence** expresses one main thought (the independent clause) and one or more subordinate, related thoughts (dependent clauses that cannot stand alone as valid sentences). Independent and dependent clauses are usually separated by a comma:

A complex sentence has one main clause and one subordinate clause.

> Although you may question Gerald's conclusions, you must admit that his research is thorough.

In this example, "Although you may question Gerald's conclusions" is a subordinate thought expressed in a dependent clause.

A **compound-complex sentence** has two main clauses, at least one of which contains a subordinate clause:

A compound-complex sentence has two main clauses and at least one dependent clause.

> Profits increased 35 percent in the past year, so although the company faces long-term challenges, I agree that its short-term prospects look quite positive.

When constructing sentences, choose the form that matches the relationship of the ideas you want to express. If you have two ideas of equal importance, express them as two simple sentences or as one compound sentence. However, if one of the ideas is less important than the other, place it in a dependent clause to form a complex sentence. For example, although the following compound sentence uses a conjunction to join two ideas, they aren't truly equal:

> The chemical products division is the strongest in the company, and its management techniques should be adopted by the other divisions.

By making the first thought subordinate to the second, you establish a cause-and-effect relationship and emphasize the more important idea (that the other divisions should adopt the chemical division's management techniques):

> Because the chemical products division is the strongest in the company, its management techniques should be adopted by the other divisions.

Maintain some variety among the four sentence types to keep your writing from getting choppy (too many short, simple sentences) or exhausting (too many long sentences).

In addition to selecting the best type for each thought you want to express, using a variety of sentence types throughout a document can make your writing more interesting and effective. For example, if you use too many simple sentences in a row, you may struggle to properly express the relationships among your ideas, and your writing will sound choppy and abrupt. At the other extreme, a long series of compound, complex, or compound-complex sentences can be tiring to read.

USING SENTENCE STYLE TO EMPHASIZE KEY THOUGHTS

In every message of any length, some ideas are more important than others. You can emphasize these key ideas through your sentence style. One obvious technique is to give important points the most space. When you want to call attention to a thought, use extra words to describe it. Consider this sentence:

Emphasize specific parts of sentences by
• Devoting more words to them
• Putting them at the beginning or at the end of the sentence
• Making them the subject of the sentence

> The chairperson called for a vote of the shareholders.

To emphasize the importance of the chairperson, you might describe her more fully:

> Having considerable experience in corporate takeover battles, the chairperson called for a vote of the shareholders.

You can increase the emphasis even more by adding a separate, short sentence to augment the first:

> The chairperson called for a vote of the shareholders. She has considerable experience in corporate takeover battles.

You can also call attention to a thought by making it the subject of the sentence. In the following example, the emphasis is on the person:

> I can write letters much more quickly by using voice dictation.

By changing the subject, however, the voice dictation capability takes center stage:

> Using voice dictation enables me to write letters much more quickly.

Another way to emphasize an idea (in this instance, the idea of stimulating demand) is to place it either at the beginning or at the end of a sentence:

> **Less emphatic:** We are cutting the price to stimulate demand.

> **More emphatic:** To stimulate demand, we are cutting the price.

The best placement of a dependent clause depends on the relationship between the ideas in the sentence.

In complex sentences the placement of the dependent clause hinges on the relationship between the ideas expressed. If you want to emphasize the subordinate idea, put the dependent clause at the end of the sentence (the most emphatic position) or at the beginning (the second most emphatic position). If you want to downplay the idea, put the dependent clause within the sentence:

> **Most emphatic:** The electronic parts are manufactured in Mexico, <u>which has lower wage rates than the United States</u>.

Emphatic: <u>Because wage rates are lower in Mexico than in the United States</u>, the electronic parts are manufactured there.

Least emphatic: Mexico, <u>which has lower wage rates than the United States</u>, was selected as the production site for the electronic parts.

Techniques such as these give you a great deal of control over the way your audience interprets what you have to say.

Composing Your Message: Crafting Unified, Coherent Paragraphs

Paragraphs organize sentences related to the same general topic. Readers expect every paragraph to be *unified*—focusing on a single topic—and *coherent*—presenting ideas in a logically connected way. By carefully arranging the elements of each paragraph, you help your readers grasp the main idea of your document and understand how the specific pieces of support material back up that idea.

6 LEARNING OBJECTIVE
Define the three key elements of a paragraph, and list five ways to develop unified, coherent paragraphs.

CREATING THE ELEMENTS OF A PARAGRAPH

Paragraphs vary widely in length and form, but a typical paragraph contains three basic elements: a topic sentence, support sentences that develop the topic, and transitional words and phrases.

Most paragraphs consist of
- A topic sentence that reveals the subject of the paragraph
- Related sentences that support and expand the topic
- Transitions that help readers move between sentences and paragraphs

Topic Sentence

An effective paragraph deals with a single topic, and the sentence that introduces that topic is called the **topic sentence** (see Figure 5.5). In informal and creative writing the

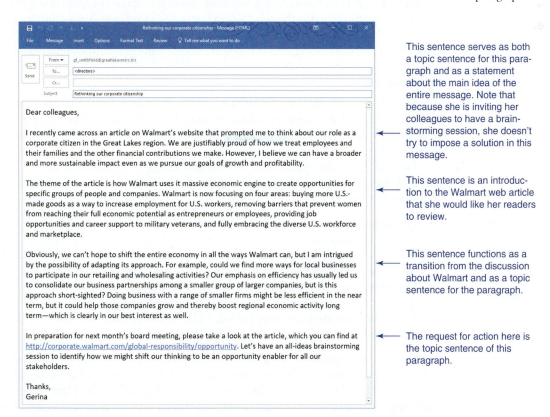

This sentence serves as both a topic sentence for this paragraph and as a statement about the main idea of the entire message. Note that because she is inviting her colleagues to have a brainstorming session, she doesn't try to impose a solution in this message.

This sentence is an introduction to the Walmart web article that she would like her readers to review.

This sentence functions as a transition from the discussion about Walmart and as a topic sentence for the paragraph.

The request for action here is the topic sentence of this paragraph.

Figure 5.5 Topic Sentences
This article from Walmart's website uses topic sentences effectively. Note how the first two sentences are actually multipurpose topic sentences.

topic sentence may be implied rather than stated. In business writing the topic sentence is generally explicit and is often the first sentence in the paragraph. The topic sentence gives readers a summary of the general idea that will be covered in the rest of the paragraph. The following examples show how a topic sentence can introduce the subject and suggest the way the subject will be developed:

> The medical products division has been troubled for many years by public relations problems. [In the rest of the paragraph, readers will learn the details of the problems.]

> To get a refund, please supply us with the following information. [The details of the necessary information will be described in the rest of the paragraph.]

In addition to helping your readers, topic sentences help you as a writer because they remind you of the purpose of each paragraph and thereby encourage you to stay focused. In fact, a good way to test the effectiveness of your writing is to prepare a summary version that consists of only the first sentences of all your paragraphs. If this summary communicates the essence of your message in a sensible, compelling way, you've probably done a good job of presenting your information.[17]

Support Sentences

In most paragraphs, the topic sentence needs to be explained, justified, or extended with one or more support sentences. These related sentences must all have a bearing on the general subject and must provide enough specific details to make the topic clear.

> The medical products division has been troubled for many years by public relations problems. Since 2014, the local newspaper has published 15 articles that portray the division in a negative light. We have been accused of everything from mistreating laboratory animals to polluting the local groundwater. Our facility has been described as a health hazard. Our scientists are referred to as "Frankensteins," and our profits are considered "obscene."

The support sentences are all more specific than the topic sentence. Each one provides another piece of evidence to demonstrate the general truth of the main thought. Also, each sentence is clearly related to the general idea being developed, which gives the paragraph unity. A paragraph is well developed if it contains enough information to make the topic sentence understood and convincing, and if it doesn't contain any extraneous, unrelated sentences.

Transitions

Transitions connect ideas by showing how one thought is related to another. They also help alert the reader to what lies ahead so that shifts and changes don't cause confusion. In addition to helping readers understand the connections you're trying to make, transitions give your writing a smooth, even flow.

Depending on the specific need within a document, transitional elements can range in length from a single word to an entire paragraph or more. You can establish transitions in a variety of ways:

Transitional elements include
• Connecting words (conjunctions)
• Repeated words or phrases
• Pronouns
• Words that are frequently paired

- **Use connecting words.** Use conjunctions such as *and, but, or, nevertheless, however, in addition,* and so on.
- **Echo a word or phrase from a previous paragraph or sentence.** "A system should be established for monitoring inventory levels. *This system* will provide . . . "
- **Use a pronoun that refers to a noun used previously.** "Ms. Arthur is the leading candidate for the president's position. *She* has excellent qualifications."
- **Use words that are frequently paired.** "The machine has a *minimum* output of . . . Its *maximum* output is . . . "

Some transitions serve as mood changers, alerting the reader to a change in mood from the previous material. Some announce a total contrast with what's come before, some announce a causal relationship, and some signal a change in time. Here is a list of transitions frequently used to move readers smoothly between clauses, sentences, and paragraphs:

Additional detail: moreover, furthermore, in addition, besides, first, second, third, finally

Cause-and-effect relationship: therefore, because, accordingly, thus, consequently, hence, as a result, so
Comparison: similarly, here again, likewise, in comparison, still
Contrast: yet, conversely, whereas, nevertheless, on the other hand, however, but, nonetheless
Condition: although, if
Illustration: for example, in particular, in this case, for instance
Time sequence: formerly, before, after, when, meanwhile, sometimes
Intensification: indeed, in fact, in any event
Summary: in brief, in short, to sum up
Repetition: that is, in other words, as mentioned previously

Consider using a transition whenever it could help the reader better understand your ideas and follow you from point to point. You can use transitions inside paragraphs to tie related points together and between paragraphs to ease the shift from one distinct thought to another. In longer reports, a transition that links major sections or chapters may be a complete paragraph that serves as a mini introduction to the next section or as a summary of the ideas presented in the section just ending. Here's an example:

> Given the nature of this product, our alternatives are limited. As the previous section indicates, we can stop making it altogether, improve it, or continue with the current model. Each of these alternatives has advantages and disadvantages, which are discussed in the following section.

This paragraph makes it clear to the reader that the analysis of the problem (offered in the previous section) is now over and that the document is making a transition to an analysis of the possible solutions (to be offered in the next section).

CHOOSING THE BEST WAY TO DEVELOP EACH PARAGRAPH

You have a variety of options for developing paragraphs, each of which can convey a specific type of idea. Five of the most common approaches are illustration, comparison or contrast, cause and effect, classification, and problem and solution (see Table 5.6).

Five ways to develop paragraphs:
- *Illustration*
- *Comparison or contrast*
- *Cause and effect*
- *Classification*
- *Problem and solution*

TABLE 5.6 Five Techniques for Developing Paragraphs

Technique	Description	Example
Illustration	Giving examples that demonstrate the general idea	Some of our most popular products are available through local distributors. For example, Everett & Lemmings carries our frozen soups and entrees. The J. B. Green Company carries our complete line of seasonings, as well as the frozen soups. Wilmont Foods, also a major distributor, now carries our new line of frozen desserts.
Comparison or contrast	Using similarities or differences to develop the topic	When the company was small, the recruiting function could be handled informally. The need for new employees was limited, and each manager could comfortably screen and hire her or his own staff. However, our successful bid on the Owens contract means that we will be doubling our labor force over the next six months. To hire that many people without disrupting our ongoing activities, we will create a separate recruiting group within the human resources department.
Cause and effect	Focusing on the reasons for something	The heavy-duty fabric of your Wanderer tent probably broke down for one of two reasons: (1) a sharp object punctured the fabric, and without reinforcement, the hole was enlarged by the stress of pitching the tent daily for a week, or (2) the fibers gradually rotted because the tent was folded and stored while still wet.
Classification	Showing how a general idea is broken into specific categories	Successful candidates for our supervisor trainee program generally come from one of several groups. The largest group by far consists of recent graduates of accredited business management programs. The next largest group comes from within our own company, as we try to promote promising staff workers to positions of greater responsibility. Finally, we occasionally accept candidates with outstanding supervisory experience in related industries.
Problem and solution	Presenting a problem and then discussing the solution	Selling handmade toys online is a challenge because consumers are accustomed to buying heavily advertised toys from major chain stores or well-known websites such as Amazon.com. However, if we develop an appealing website, we can compete on the basis of product novelty and quality. In addition, we can provide unusual crafts at a competitive price: a rocking horse of birch, with a hand-knit tail and mane; a music box with the child's name painted on the top; and a real teepee made by Native American artisans.

In some instances combining approaches in a single paragraph is an effective strategy. Notice how the example provided for "Problem and solution" in Table 5.6 also includes an element of illustration by listing some of the unique products that could be part of the proposed solution. When combining approaches, however, do so carefully so that you don't lose readers partway through the paragraph.

In addition, before settling for the first approach that comes to mind, consider alternatives. Think through various methods before committing yourself, or even write several test paragraphs to see which method works best. By avoiding the easy habit of repeating the same old paragraph pattern time after time, you can keep your writing fresh and interesting.

Writing Messages for Mobile Devices

7 LEARNING OBJECTIVE
List five techniques for writing effective messages for mobile readers.

One obvious adaptation to make for audiences using mobile devices is to modify the design and layout of your messages to fit smaller screen sizes and different user interface features(see Chapter 6). However, modifying your approach to writing is also an important step. Reading is more difficult on small screens, and consequently users' ability to comprehend what they read on mobile devices is lower than it is on larger screens.[18] In fact, research shows that comprehension can drop by 50 percent when users move from reading on a full-size screen to reading on a smartphone, and they can scroll right past vital information without noticing it.[19] Use these five techniques to make your mobile messages more effective:

To write effectively for mobile devices
- Use a linear organization
- Prioritize information
- Write short, focused messages
- Use short subject lines and headings
- Use short paragraphs

- **Use a linear organization.** In a printed document or on a larger screen, readers can easily take in multiple elements on a page, such as preview or summary boxes, tables and other supporting visuals, and sidebars with related information. All these elements are in view at the same time, so readers can jump around the page to read various parts without feeling lost. With small mobile device screens, however, a complicated organization requires readers to zoom in and out and pan around to see all these elements at readable text sizes. This makes reading slower and increases the odds that readers will get disoriented and lose the thread of the message because they can't see the big picture. In addition, using a touch screen momentarily obscures some of the information, so the more that users have to hunt and scroll, the more likely they will miss something.[20] To simplify reading, organize with a linear flow from the top to the bottom of the message or article.
- **Prioritize information.** Small screens make it difficult for readers to scan the page to find the information they want most. Prioritize the information based on what you know about their needs and put that information first.[21] Use the *inverted pyramid* style favored by journalists, in which you reveal the most important information briefly at first and then provide successive layers of detail that readers can consume if they want. Note that you may need to avoid using the indirect approach (see page 114) if your message is complicated because it will be more difficult for readers to follow your chain of reasoning.
- **Write shorter and more focused messages and documents.** Mobile users often lack the patience or opportunity to read lengthy messages or documents, so keep it short.[22] In some cases this could require you to write two documents, a shorter *executive summary* (see page 425) for mobile use and a longer supporting document that readers can access with their PCs if they want more details.
- **Use shorter subject lines and headings.** Mobile devices, particularly phones, can't display as many characters in a single line of text as the typical computer screen can. Depending on the app or website, email subject lines and page headings will be truncated or will wrap around to take up multiple lines. Both formats make reading more difficult. A good rule of thumb is to keep subject lines and headlines to around 25 characters.[23] This doesn't give you much text to work with, so make every word count and make sure you start with the key words so readers can instantly see what the subject line or heading is about.[24]
- **Use shorter paragraphs.** In addition to structuring a message according to discrete blocks of information, paragraphs have a visual role in written communication as

well. Shorter paragraphs are less intimidating and let readers take frequent "micro rests" as they move through a document. Because far less text is displayed at once on a mobile screen, keep paragraphs as short as possible so readers don't have to swipe through screen after screen before getting to paragraph breaks.

Compare the two messages in Figure 5.6 to get a sense of how to write reader-friendly mobile content.

For a reminder of the tasks involved in writing messages, see "Checklist: Writing Business Messages."

Figure 5.6a

The text from this conventional report page is too small to read on a phone screen.

However, zooming in to read forces the reader to lose context and repeatedly move around to find all the pieces of the page.

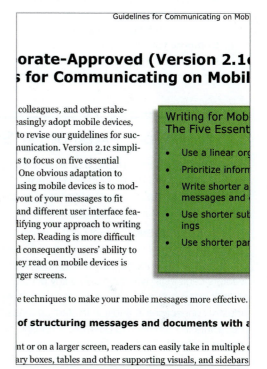

Figure 5.6b

Optimizing for mobile includes writing short headlines that get right to the point.

This introduction conveys only the information readers need in order to grasp the scope of the article.

All the key points of the documents appear here on the first screen.

Readers who want more detail can swipe down for background information on the five points.

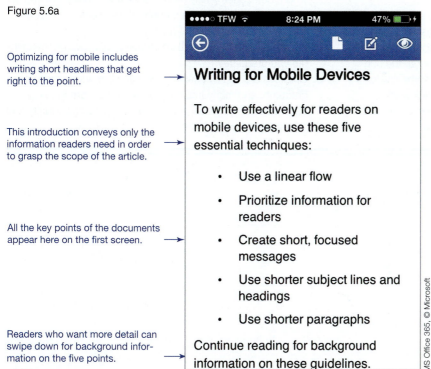

Figure 5.6c

Figure 5.6 **Writing for Mobile Devices**
Messages and documents created for printed pages and full-sized screens can be difficult and frustrating on mobile devices (Figure 5.6a and b). For mobile audiences, rewrite with short headlines and concise, linear content (Figure 5.6c).

CHECKLIST ✔ Writing Business Messages

A. Adapt to your audience.
- Use the "you" attitude.
- Maintain good etiquette through polite communication.
- Emphasize the positive whenever possible.
- Use bias-free language.
- Establish credibility in the eyes of your audience.
- Project your company's preferred image.
- Use a conversational but still professional and respectful tone.
- Use plain language for clarity.

B. Compose your message.
- Choose strong words that communicate efficiently.
- Pay attention to the connotative meaning of your words.
- Balance abstract and concrete terms to accurately convey your meaning.
- Avoid clichés and trendy buzzwords.
- Use jargon only when your audience understands it and prefers it.
- Vary your sentence structure for impact and interest.
- Develop coherent, unified paragraphs.
- Use transitions generously to help your audience follow your message.
- As needed, adapt your writing for the limitations of mobile devices.

COMMUNICATION CHALLENGES AT **She Takes on the World**

Natalie MacNeil recently hired you as an assistant editor at her website. One of your responsibilities is to review the work of guest article contributors and suggest improvements. Use what you've learned in this chapter to address these writing challenges.

INDIVIDUAL CHALLENGE: A prospective writer included the following sentence in a draft that aims to give entrepreneurs a realistic expectation about getting funding from venture capitalists: "Venture capitalists, who fund only a tiny percentage of all new companies, can provide valuable management expertise and industry connections in addition to start-up funds." How would you rewrite the sentence to put more emphasis on the fact that venture capitalists fund very few companies and most entrepreneurs can't count on getting funding from them?

TEAM CHALLENGE: You're reviewing a draft that encourages college students who are about to graduate to consider starting a business rather than applying for conventional jobs. The writer has two main reasons for making this suggestion. First, the current job market is tough in many professions, and some graduates will be forced to take jobs that are outside their intended fields and perhaps below the level of their qualifications. Second, the nature of employment is changing in many professions and

industries, and many companies now engage independent contractors (also known as freelancers) for short durations, rather than hiring employees for the long term. Which of these statements is the most sensitive to the audience's needs as they relate to this specific topic? What specific words and phrases make it the most sensitive?

a. The job market remains slow in many industries and professions, so you should seriously consider creating your own job by starting a small company and setting up shop as an independent contractor.

b. The job market remains slow in many industries and professions, and many of those jobs aren't coming back even when the economy fully recovers. Chances are you'll end up working as an independent contractor at some point anyway, so you might as well do it now.

c. What could be more fun than creating your own job the minute you graduate?

d. Chances are you'll be facing a tough job market when you graduate, and many traditional jobs are converting to contract work. Why not convert a challenge into opportunity and create your own job?

Quick Learning Guide

KEY TERMS

abstract word Word that expresses a concept, quality, or characteristic; abstractions are usually broad

active voice Sentence structure in which the subject performs the action and the object receives the action

bias-free language Language that avoids words and phrases that categorize or stigmatize people in ways related to gender, race, ethnicity, age, or disability

complex sentence Sentence that expresses one main thought (the independent clause) and one or more subordinate, related thoughts (dependent clauses that cannot stand alone as valid sentences)

compound sentence Sentence with two main clauses that express two or more independent but related thoughts of equal importance, usually joined by a conjunction such as *and*, *but*, or *or*

compound-complex sentence Sentence with two main clauses, at least one of which contains a subordinate clause

concrete word Word that represents something you can touch, see, or visualize; most concrete terms related to the tangible, material world

connotative meaning All the associations and feelings evoked by a word

conversational tone The tone used in most business communication; it uses plain language that sounds businesslike without being stuffy at one extreme or too laid-back and informal at the other extreme

credibility A measure of your believability based on how reliable you are and how much trust you evoke in others

denotative meaning The literal, or dictionary, meaning of a word

euphemisms Words or phrases that express a thought in milder terms

passive voice Sentence structure in which the subject receives the action

simple sentence Sentence with one main clause (a single subject and a single predicate)

style The choices you make to express yourself: the words you select, the manner in which you use those words in sentences, and the way you build paragraphs from individual sentences

tone The overall impression in your messages, created by the style you use

topic sentence Sentence that introduces the topic of a paragraph

transitions Words or phrases that tie ideas together by showing how one thought is related to another

SUMMARY OF LEARNING OBJECTIVES

1 Identify the four aspects of being sensitive to audience needs when writing business messages. First, the "you" attitude refers to speaking and writing in terms of your audience's wishes, interests, hopes, and preferences rather than your own. Writing with this attitude is essential to effective communication because it shows your audience that you have their needs in mind, not just your own. Second, good etiquette not only indicates respect for your audience but also helps foster a more successful environment for communication by minimizing negative emotional reaction. Third, sensitive communicators understand the difference between delivering negative news and being negative. Without hiding the negative news, they look for ways to emphasize positive aspects. Fourth, being sensitive includes taking care to avoid biased language that unfairly and even unethically categorizes or stigmatizes people in ways related to gender, race, ethnicity, age, or disability.

2 Explain how establishing your credibility and projecting your company's image are vital aspects of building strong relationships with your audience. Whether a one-time interaction or a series of exchanges over the course of many months or years, successful communication relies on a positive relationship existing between sender and receiver. Audience responses to your messages depend heavily on your credibility—a measure of your believability based on how reliable you are and how much trust you evoke in others. When you have established credibility with an audience, communication becomes much easier because you no longer have to spend time and energy convincing people that you are a trustworthy source of information and ideas. Project your company's desired image when communicating with external audiences. You represent your company and therefore play a vital role in helping the company build and maintain positive relationships with all of its stakeholders.

3 Explain how to achieve a tone that is conversational but businesslike, explain the value of using plain language, and define *active voice* and *passive voice*. To achieve a tone that is conversational but still businesslike, avoid obsolete and pompous language, avoid preaching and bragging, be careful with intimacy (sharing personal details or adopting an overly casual tone), and be careful with humor. Plain language is a way of presenting information in a simple, unadorned style so that your audience can easily grasp your meaning. By writing and speaking in plain terms, you demonstrate the "you" attitude and show respect for your audience. In the active voice, the subject performs the action and the object receives the action. In the passive voice, the subject receives the action. The passive voice combines the helping verb *to be* with a form of the verb that is usually in the past tense.

4 Describe how to select words that are both correct and effective. To select the best words, first make sure they are correct by checking grammar and usage guides. Then choose words that have few connotations (to reduce the chance of misinterpretation) and no unintended negative connotations (to reduce the chance of offending your audience). Select words that communicate clearly, specifically, and dynamically. Choose words that are strong and familiar, avoid clichés, be extremely careful with buzzwords, and use jargon only when your audience will understand it.

5 Define the four types of sentences, and explain how sentence style affects emphasis within a message. The four types of sentences are simple (one main clause), compound (two main clauses that express independent but related ideas of equal importance), complex (one main clause and one subordinate clause of lesser importance), and compound-complex (two main clauses, at least one of which contains a subordinate clause). Sentence style affects emphasis by playing up or playing down specific parts of a sentence. To emphasize a certain point, you can place it at the end of the sentence or make it the subject of the sentence. To deemphasize a point, put it in the middle of the sentence.

6 Define the three key elements of a paragraph, and list five ways to develop unified, coherent paragraphs. The three key elements of a paragraph are a topic sentence that identifies the subject of the paragraph, support sentences that develop the topic and provide examples and evidence, and transitional words and phrases that help readers connect one thought to the next. Effective paragraphs are both unified (focused on a single idea) and coherent (logically organized). You can develop paragraphs through illustration (giving examples), comparison or contrast (pointing out similarities or differences), cause and effect (giving reasons), classification (discussing categories), and problem and solution (stating a problem and showing how to solve it).

7 **List five techniques for writing effective messages for mobile readers.** Five techniques for writing effective messages for mobile readers are using a linear organization so readers don't have to jump around the screen to find important message elements; prioritizing information and delivering the most important information first; writing short, focused messages; using short subjects lines and headings; and using short paragraphs.

MyBCommLab

Test Your Knowledge

To review chapter content related to each question, refer to the indicated Learning Objective.

5-1. What is meant by the "you" attitude? [LO-1]
5-2. Why is it important to establish your credibility when communicating with an audience of strangers? [LO-2]
5-3. In what three situations is the passive voice appropriate? [LO-3]
5-4. How does an abstract word differ from a concrete word? [LO-4]
5-5. How does the denotative meaning of a word differ from its connotative meaning? [LO-4]
5-6. How can you use sentence style to emphasize key thoughts? [LO-5]
5-7. How can topic sentences help readers? [LO-6]
5-8. What functions do transitions serve? [LO-6]
5-9. How does reading comprehension on small, mobile devices compare with comprehension on full-size screens? [LO-7]

Apply Your Knowledge

To review chapter content related to each question, refer to the indicated Learning Objective.

5-10. Millions of people in the United States are allergic to one or more food ingredients, including 1 of every 13 children. Allergic reactions to food items or ingredients send more than 200,000 people to the emergency room every year. Many of these episodes are tied to poorly written food labels that either fail to identify dangerous allergens or use scientific terms that most consumers don't recognize.[25] Do food manufacturers have a responsibility to ensure that consumers read, understand, and follow warnings on food products? Explain your answer. [LO-1]
5-11. When composing business messages, how can you communicate with an authentic voice and project your company's image at the same time? [LO-2]
5-12. Does using plain language make you come across as less of an expert? Explain your answer. [LO-3]
5-13. Should you bother using transitions if the logical sequence of your message is obvious? Why or why not? [LO-6]
5-14. Why can it be difficult to use the indirect approach for a complex message that will be read on mobile devices? [LO-7]

Practice Your Skills

5-15. **Messages for Analysis: Creating a Businesslike Tone [LO-1], [LO-3]** Read the following email draft, then (a) analyze the strengths and weaknesses of each sentence and (b) revise the document so that it follows this chapter's guidelines. The message was written by the marketing manager of an online retailer of baby-related products in the hope of becoming a retail outlet for Inglesina strollers and high chairs. As a manufacturer of stylish, top-quality products, Inglesina (based in Italy) is extremely selective about the retail outlets through which it allows its products to be sold.

Our e-tailing site, **www.BestBabyGear.com**, specializes in only the very best products for parents of newborns, infants, and toddlers. We constantly scour the world looking for products that are good enough and well-built enough and classy enough—good enough to take their place alongside the hundreds of other carefully selected products that adorn the pages of our award-winning website, **www.bestbabygear.com**. We aim for the fences every time we select a product to join this portfolio; we don't want to waste our time with onesey-twosey products that might sell a half dozen units per annum—no, we want every product to be a top-drawer success, selling at least one hundred units per specific model per year in order to justify our expense and hassle factor in adding it to the above mentioned portfolio. After careful consideration, we thusly concluded that your Inglesina lines meet our needs and would therefore like to add it.

Exercises

Each activity is labeled according to the primary skill or skills you will need to use. To review relevant chapter content, you can refer to the indicated Learning Objective. In some instances, supporting information will be found in another chapter, as indicated.

Writing: Communicating with Sensitivity and Tact [LO-1] Substitute a better phrase for each of the following:

5-16. You claim that
5-17. It is not our policy to
5-18. You neglected to
5-19. In which you assert
5-20. We are sorry you are dissatisfied
5-21. You failed to enclose
5-22. We request that you send us
5-23. Apparently you overlooked our terms
5-24. We have been very patient
5-25. We are at a loss to understand

Writing: Demonstrating the "You" Attitude [LO-1] Rewrite these sentences to reflect your audience's viewpoint:

5-26. Your email order cannot be processed; we request that you use the order form on our website instead.
5-27. We insist that you always bring your credit card to the store.
5-28. We want to get rid of all our 15-inch LCD screens to make room in our warehouse for the new 19-, 23-, and 35-inch monitors. Thus, we are offering a 25 percent discount on all sales of 15-inch models this week.
5-29. I am applying for the position of accounting intern in your office. I feel my grades prove that I am bright and capable, and I think I can do a good job for you.
5-30. As requested, we are sending the refund for $25.

5-31. If you cared about doing a good job, you would've made the extra effort required to learn how to use the machinery properly.

5-32. Your strategy presentation this morning absolutely blew me away; there's no way we can fail with all the brilliant ideas you've pulled together—I'm so glad you're running the company now!

5-33. Regarding your email message from September 28 regarding the slow payment of your invoice, it's important for you to realize that we've just undergone a massive upgrade of our accounts payable system and payments have been delayed for everybody, not just you.

5-34. I know I'm late with the asset valuation report, but I haven't been feeling well and I just haven't had the energy needed to work through the numbers yet.

5-35. With all the online news sources available today, I can't believe you didn't know that MyTravel and Thomas Cook were in merger talks—I mean, you don't even have to get up from your computer to learn this!

Writing: Emphasizing the Positive [LO-1] Revise these sentences to be positive rather than negative:

5-36. To avoid damage to your credit rating, please remit payment within 10 days.

5-37. We don't offer refunds on returned merchandise that is soiled.

5-38. Because we are temporarily out of Baby Cry dolls, we won't be able to ship your order for 10 days.

5-39. You failed to specify the color of the blouse that you ordered.

5-40. You should have realized that waterbeds will freeze in unheated houses during winter. Therefore, our guarantee does not cover the valve damage, and you must pay the $9.50 valve-replacement fee (plus postage).

Writing: Using Unbiased Language [LO-1] Rewrite each of the following to eliminate bias:

5-41. For an Indian, Maggie certainly is outgoing.

5-42. He needs a wheelchair, but he doesn't let his handicap affect his job performance.

5-43. A pilot must have the ability to stay calm under pressure, and then he must be trained to cope with any problem that arises.

5-44. Renata Parsons, married and the mother of a teenager, is a top candidate for CEO.

5-45. Even at his age, Sam Nugent is still an active salesman.

5-46. **Writing: Establishing Your Credibility; Microblogging Skills [LO-2], Chapter 8** Search LinkedIn for the profile of an expert in any industry or profession. Now imagine that you are going to introduce this person as a speaker at a convention. You will make an in-person introduction at the time of the speech, but you decide to introduce him or her the day before on Twitter. Write four tweets: one that introduces the expert and three that cover three key supporting points that will enhance the speaker's credibility in the minds of potential listeners. Make up any information you need to complete this assignment, and then email the text of your proposed tweets to your instructor.

5-47. **Writing: Using Plain Language; Communication Ethics: Making Ethical Choices, [LO-3], Chapter 1** Your company has been a major employer in the local community for years, but shifts in the global marketplace have forced some changes in the company's long-term direction. In fact, the company plans to reduce local staffing by as much as 50 percent over the next 5 to 10 years, starting with a small layoff next month. The size and timing of future layoffs have not been decided, although there is little doubt that more layoffs will happen at some point. In the first draft of a letter aimed at community leaders, you write that "this first layoff is part of a continuing series of staff reductions anticipated over the next several years." However, your boss is concerned about the vagueness and negative tone of the language and asks you to rewrite that sentence to read "this layoff is part of the company's ongoing efforts to continually align its resources with global market conditions." Do you think this suggested wording is ethical, given the company's economic influence in the community? Explain your answer in an email message to your instructor.

5-48. **Writing: Creating Effective Sentences: Media Skills: Social Networking [LO-4], Chapter 8** If you are interested in business, chances are you've had an idea or two for starting a company. If you haven't yet, go ahead and dream up an idea now. Make it something you are passionate about, something you could really throw yourself into. Now write a four-sentence summary that could appear on the Info tab on a Facebook profile. Make sure the first sentence is a solid topic sentence, and make sure the next three sentences offer relevant evidence and examples. Feel free to make up any details you need. Email your summary to your instructor or post it on your class blog.

Writing: Choosing Powerful Words [LO-4] Write a concrete phrase for each of these vague phrases:

5-49. Sometime this spring

5-50. A substantial savings

5-51. A large number attended

5-52. Increased efficiency

5-53. Expanded the work area

5-54. Flatten the website structure

Writing: Choosing Powerful Words [LO-4] List terms that are stronger than the following:

5-55. Ran after

5-56. Seasonal ups and downs

5-57. Bright

5-58. Suddenly rises

5-59. Moves forward

Writing: Choosing Powerful Words [LO-4] As you rewrite these sentences, replace the clichés and buzzwords with plain language (for any terms you don't recognize, you can find definitions online):

5-60. Being a jack-of-all-trades, Dave worked well in his new general manager job.

5-61. Moving Leslie into the accounting department, where she was literally a fish out of water, was like putting a square peg into a round hole, if you get my drift.

5-62. My only takeaway from the offsite was that Laird threw his entire department under the bus for missing the deadline.

5-63. I'd love to help with that project, but I'm bandwidth-constrained.

5-64. The board green-lighted our initiative to repurpose our consumer products for the commercial space.

Writing: Choosing Powerful Words [LO-4] Suggest short, simple words to replace each of the following:

5-65. Inaugurate

5-66. Terminate

5-67. Utilize

5-68. Anticipate

5-69. Assistance

5-70. Endeavor

5-71. Ascertain

5-72. Procure

5-73. Consummate

5-74. Advise

5-75. Alteration

5-76. Forwarded

5-77. Fabricate

5-78. Nevertheless

5-79. Substantial

Writing: Choosing Powerful Words [LO-4] Write up-to-date, less-stuffy versions of these phrases; write "none" if you think there is no appropriate substitute or "delete" if the phrase should simply be deleted:

5-80. As per your instructions

5-81. Attached herewith

5-82. In lieu of

5-83. In reply I wish to state

5-84. Please be advised that

Writing: Creating Effective Sentences [LO-5] Rewrite each sentence so that it is active rather than passive:

5-85. The raw data are entered into the customer relationship management system by the sales representative each Friday.

5-86. High profits are publicized by management.

5-87. The policies announced in the directive were implemented by the staff.

5-88. Our computers are serviced by the Santee Company.

5-89. The employees were represented by Tamika Hogan.

5-90. **Writing: Crafting Unified, Coherent Paragraphs; Collaboration: Evaluating the Work of Others [LO-6], Chapter 6** Working with four other students, divide the following five topics among yourselves and each write one paragraph on your selected topic. Be sure each student uses a different technique when writing his or her paragraph: One student should use the illustration technique, one the comparison or contrast technique, one a discussion of cause and effect, one the classification technique, and one a discussion of problem and solution. Then exchange paragraphs within the team and pick out the main idea and general purpose of the paragraph one of your teammates wrote. Was everyone able to correctly identify the main idea and purpose? If not, suggest how the paragraph could be rewritten for clarity.
- Types of *phablets* available for sale
- Advantages and disadvantages of eating at fast-food restaurants
- Finding that first full-time job
- Good qualities of my car (or house, or apartment, or neighborhood)
- How to make a dessert (or barbecue a steak or make coffee)

Writing: Using Transitions [LO-6] Add transitional elements to the following sentences to improve the flow of ideas. (Note: You may need to eliminate or add some words to smooth out your sentences.)

5-91. Facing some of the toughest competitors in the world, Harley-Davidson had to make some changes. The company introduced new products. Harley's management team set out to rebuild the company's production process. New products were coming to market and the company was turning a profit. Harley's quality standards were not on par with those of its foreign competitors. Harley's costs were still among the highest in the industry. Harley made a U-turn and restructured the company's organizational structure. Harley's efforts have paid off.

5-92. Whether you're indulging in a doughnut in New York or California, Krispy Kreme wants you to enjoy the same delicious taste with every bite. The company maintains consistent product quality by carefully controlling every step of the production process. Krispy Kreme tests all raw ingredients against established quality standards. Every delivery of wheat flour is sampled and measured for its moisture content and protein levels. Krispy Kreme blends the ingredients. Krispy Kreme tests the doughnut mix for quality. Krispy Kreme delivers the mix to its stores. Financial critics are not as kind to the company as food critics have been. Allegations of improper financial reporting have left the company's future in doubt.

5-93. **Media Skills: Writing for Mobile Devices [LO-7]** Find an interesting website article on any business topic. Write a three-paragraph summary that would be easy to read on a phone screen.

Expand Your Skills

Critique the Professionals

Locate an example of professional communication from a reputable online source. Choose a paragraph that has at least three sentences. Evaluate the effectiveness of this paragraph at three levels, starting with the paragraph structure. Is the paragraph unified and cohesive? Does it have a clear topic sentence and sufficient support to clarify and expand on that topic? Second, evaluate each sentence. Are the sentences easy to read and easy to understand? Did the writer vary the types and lengths of sentences to produce a smooth flow and rhythm? Is the most important idea presented prominently in each sentence? Third, evaluate at least six word choices. Did the writer use these words correctly and effectively? Using whatever medium your instructor requests, write a brief analysis of the piece (no more than one page), citing specific elements from the piece and support from the chapter.

Sharpening Your Career Skills Online

Bovée and Thill's Business Communication Web Search, at **websearch.businesscommunicationnetwork.com**, is a unique research tool designed specifically for business communication research. Use the Web Search function to find a website, video, article, podcast, or presentation that offers advice on writing effective sentences. Write a brief email message to your instructor, describing the item that you found and summarizing the career skills information you learned from it.

MyBCommLab

Go to **mybcommlab.com** for Auto-graded writing questions as well as the following Assisted-graded writing questions:

5-94. Why are email, texting, and other forms of digital communication so prone to inadvertent etiquette breakdowns in which even well-intentioned writers insult or confuse readers? [LO-1]

5-95. What steps can you take to make abstract concepts such as *opportunity* feel more concrete in your messages? [LO-4]

Endnotes

1. Personal communication, Natalie MacNeil, 10 February 2015; *She Takes on the World*, accessed 20 March 2016, shetakesontheworld .com; Prashanth Gopalan, "Natalie MacNeil Vs. the World," *TechVibes*, 29 September 2010, www.techvibes.com; Natalie MacNeil website, accessed 9 June 2013, nataliemacneil.com; product page for *She Takes on the World: A Guide to Being Your Own Boss, Working Happy, and Living on Purpose*, accessed 9 June 2013, www.amazon .com; Natalie MacNeil bio, *Huffington Post*, accessed 9 June 2013, www.huffingtonpost.com/natalie-macneil.

2. Annette N. Shelby and N. Lamar Reinsch Jr., "Positive Emphasis and You Attitude: An Empirical Study," *Journal of Business Communication* 32, no. 4 (1995): 303–322.

3. Quinn Warnick, "A Close Textual Analysis of Corporate Layoff Memos," *Business Communication Quarterly* 73, no. 3 (September 2010): 322–326.

4. Sherryl Kleinman, "Why Sexist Language Matters," *Qualitative Sociology* 25, no. 2 (Summer 2002): 299–304.

5. Judy E. Pickens, "Terms of Equality: A Guide to Bias-Free Language," *Personnel Journal*, August 1985, 24.

6. Xerox website, accessed 20 March 2016, www.xerox.com; ADM website, accessed 20 March 2016, www.adm.com.

7. Lisa Taylor, "Communicating About People with Disabilities: Does the Language We Use Make a Difference?" *Bulletin of the Association for Business Communication* 53, no. 3 (September 1990): 65–67.

8. Susan Benjamin, *Words at Work* (Reading, Mass.: Addison Wesley, 1997), 136–137.

9. Plain English Campaign website, accessed 28 June 2010, www .plainenglish.co.uk.

10. Plain Language website, accessed 13 May 2016, www.plainlanguage .gov; Irene Etzkorn, "Amazingly Simple Stuff," presentation, 7 November 2008, www.slideshare.net.

11. Creative Commons website, accessed 20 March 2016, creativecommons.org.

12. Susan Jaderstrom and Joanne Miller, "Active Writing," *Office Pro*, November/December 2003, 29.

13. Mary Munter, *Guide to Managerial Communication*, 7th ed. (Upper Saddle River, N.J.: Pearson Prentice Hall, 2006), 41.

14. Portions of this section are adapted from Courtland L. Bovée, *Techniques of Writing Business Letters, Memos, and Reports* (Sherman Oaks, Calif.: Banner Books International, 1978), 13–90.

15. Catherine Quinn, "Lose the Office Jargon; It May Sunset Your Career," *The Age* (Australia), 1 September 2007, www.theage .com.au.

16. Robert Hartwell Fiske, *The Dimwit's Dictionary* (Oak Park, Ill.: Marion Street Press, 2002), 16–20.

17. Beverly Ballaro and Christina Bielaszka-DuVernay, "Building a Bridge over the River Boredom," *Harvard Management Communication Letter*, Winter 2005, 3–5.

18. Jakob Nielsen, "Mobile Content Is Twice as Difficult," Nielsen Norman Group, 28 February 2011, www.nngroup.com.

19. Jakob Nielsen and Raluca Budiu, *Mobile Usability* (Berkeley, Calif.: New Riders, 2013), 10, 102.

20. Nielsen and Budiu, *Mobile Usability*, 23.

21. "Mobile Web Best Practices," W3C website, accessed 12 March 2014, www.w3.org.

22. "Mobile Message Mayhem," Verne Ordman & Associates, accessed 12 March 2014, www.businesswriting.biz.

23. "Mobile Message Mayhem."

24. Marieke McCloskey, "Writing Hyperlinks: Salient, Descriptive, Start with Keyword," Nielsen Norman Group, 9 March 2014, www.nngroup.com.

25. Food Allergy Research & Education website, accessed 22 March 2016, www.foodallergy.org; Diana Keough, "Snacks That Can Kill; Schools Take Steps to Protect Kids Who Have Severe Allergies to Nuts," *Plain Dealer*, 15 July 2003, E1; "Dawdling over Food Labels," *New York Times*, 2 June 2003, A16; Sheila McNulty, "A Matter of Life and Death," *Financial Times*, 10 September 2003, 14.

Completing Business Messages

LEARNING OBJECTIVES

After studying this chapter, you will be able to

1 Discuss the value of careful revision, and describe the tasks involved in evaluating your first drafts and the work of other writers.

2 List four techniques you can use to improve the readability of your messages.

3 Describe eight steps you can take to improve the clarity of your writing, and give four tips on making your writing more concise.

4 List four principles of effective design, and explain the role of major design elements in document readability.

5 Explain the importance of proofreading and give eight tips for successful proofreading.

6 Discuss the most important issues to consider when distributing your messages.

Designers José Scaglione and Veronika Burian of Type Together focus on creating typefaces that are easy to read in lengthy stretches of text but that still display fresh and unique personalities.

Courtesy TypeTogether

COMMUNICATION CLOSE-UP AT

Type Together

www.type-together.com

Take a moment and look at the variety of textual messages all around you, from this book to whatever posters and signs might be in view to the displays on mobile devices. Wherever text is presented in print or digital form, someone had to make a decision about which typeface to use for each string of text. And behind the scenes, somebody designed every character of every typeface. (*Font* and *typeface* are often used interchangeably, although strictly speaking, a font is a set of characters that use a given typeface design.)

Typefaces aren't something most people think about very often, but they can have considerable influence on the success of a written message. Type design can contribute to or detract from a message in two major ways: readability and personality. Naturally, readability is essential. If people can't accurately read the words on the page or screen, they won't interpret a message as intended. If a typeface is legible but difficult to read for more than few a words, people will tend to give up and never finish reading the document.

Personality is more subtle but also important because the "look and feel" of a typeface sends a nonverbal message along with the verbal (written) message. Various typefaces can convey a wide range of these nonverbal messages, from serious and formal to casual and even playful. Just like showing up for a job interview in wildly inappropriate clothing, using a typeface with the wrong personality can detract from even a well-written message. (And as you can see from studying a variety of typefaces, personality needs to be balanced with readability; some typefaces with "strong" personalities can be difficult to read.) Personality is so important that some companies commission their own custom typefaces that become integral elements of their overall brand presence.

Type design has been an active art form for hundreds of years, and many contemporary designs are the result of efforts to adapt classic designs to contemporary uses. For some designs, this modernization is an effort to improve a typeface's readability or update its visual presence. For others, the modernization has a more technical aspect, creating typefaces that work more successfully with digital print or display technologies. For instance, the Georgia typeface was created in the 1990s primarily as a solution for that era's lower-resolution computer screens, although thanks to its attractive readability it is still a popular choice today.

Although thousands of typefaces are now available, type design remains a vibrant artistic profession, with new designs appearing all the time. Veronika Burian and José Scaglione are among the latest generation of designers lending their talents to the ageless challenge of balancing readability and personality. Their type foundry Type Together, based in the Czech Republic capital of Prague, specializes in editorial typefaces, those used for long blocks of text such as in newspapers and books. (As a nod to the days when all typefaces were made from metal, type design studios are still referred to as *foundries*.)

Burian and Scaglione focus on the challenge of making type that is highly readable while offering fresh new personalities and meeting the technical demands of contemporary digital publishing. As individual designers and together as the cofounders of Type Together, Burian and Scaglione have achieved international recognition for their designs and their contribution to the art of type design through workshops, teaching, and publications. Their commissioned work has ranged from customizing e-reader type for Apple's iBooks to creating a font that Levi's could use in multiple languages for a global ad campaign.

Your business audiences may not think about typefaces often, but their responses to your messages and documents depend more than they might imagine on the efforts of type designers such as Burian and Scaglione—and on your skill in using their designs.[1]

Revising Your Message: Evaluating the First Draft

1 LEARNING OBJECTIVE
Discuss the value of careful revision, and describe the tasks involved in evaluating your first drafts and the work of other writers.

Veronika Burian and José Scaglione (profiled in the chapter-opening Communication Close-Up) lend their creativity and talents to an essential stage of the writing process—producing professional-quality messages that convey the intended message both verbally and nonverbally. You'll read more about document design and production, including choosing and using typefaces, later in the chapter.

Before getting to the design stage, though, it's important to fine-tune the content you've diligently researched, organized, and composed. Successful communicators recognize that the first draft is rarely as tight, clear, and compelling as it needs to be. Careful revision can mean the difference between a rambling, unfocused message and a lively, direct message that gets results.

The revision task can vary somewhat, depending on the medium and the nature of your message. For informal messages to internal audiences, particularly when using instant messaging, text messaging, email, or blogging, the revision process is often as simple as quickly looking over your message to correct any mistakes before sending or posting it. However, don't fall into the common trap of thinking that you don't need to worry about grammar, spelling, clarity, and other fundamentals of good writing when you use such media. These qualities can be *especially* important in digital media, particularly if these messages are the only contact your audience has with you. Audiences are likely to equate the quality of your writing with the quality of your thinking. Poor-quality messages create an impression of poor-quality thinking and can cause confusion, frustration, and costly delays.

For important messages, schedule time to put your draft aside for a day or two before you begin the revision process.

With more complex messages, try to put your draft aside for a day or two before you begin the revision process so that you can approach the material with a fresh eye. Then start with the "big picture," making sure that the document accomplishes your overall goals before moving to finer points such as readability, clarity, and conciseness. Compare the letters in Figures 6.1 and 6.2 on the next two pages for an example of how careful revision improves a letter to a customer.

EVALUATING YOUR CONTENT, ORGANIZATION, STYLE, AND TONE

When you begin the revision process, focus your attention on content, organization, style, and tone. To evaluate the content of your message, answer these questions:

- Is the information accurate?
- Is the information relevant to the audience?
- Is there enough information to satisfy the readers' needs?

Figure 6.1 Improving a Letter Through Careful Revision

Careful revision makes this draft shorter, clearer, and more focused. The proofreading symbols you see here are still widely used whenever printed documents are edited and revised; you can find a complete list of symbols in Appendix C. Note that many business documents are now "marked up" using such software tools as revision marks in Microsoft Word and comments in Adobe Acrobat. No matter what the medium, however, careful revision is key to more effective messages.

Delauny Music
56 Commerce Circle • Davenport, IA 52806
(563) 555-4001• delaunymusic.net

June 21, 2018

Ms. Claudia Banks
122 River Heights Drive
Bettendorf, IA 52722

Dear Ms. Banks:

Thank you for your recent purchase. We wish you many years of satisfaction with your new Yamaha CG1 grand piano. The CG1 carries more than a century of Yamaha's heritage in design and production of world-class musical instruments and will give you many years of playing and listening pleasure.

The content is now organized in three coherent paragraphs, each with a distinct message.

Our commitment to your satisfaction doesn't stop with your purchase, however. As a vital first step, please remember to call us sometime within three to eight months after your piano is delivered to take advantage of the Yamaha Servicebond^{SM} Assurance Program. This free service program includes a thorough evaluation and adjustment of the instrument after you've had some time to play it and it has had time to adapt to its environment.

In addition to this important service appointment, a regular program of tuning is essential to ensure your piano's impeccable performance. Our piano specialists recommend four tunings during the first year and two tunings every year thereafter. As your local Yamaha dealer, we are ideally positioned to provide you with optimum service for both regular tuning and any maintenance or repair needs you may have.

The tone is friendly and engaging without being flowery.

Sincerely,

Madeline Delauny
Madeline Delauny
Owner

Figure 6.2 **Professional Business Letter**
Here is the revised and finished version of the edited letter from Figure 6.1. Note that the *block format* used here is just one of several layout options; Appendix A also describes the *modified block format* and the *simplified format*.

- Is there a good balance between general information (giving readers enough background information to appreciate the message) and specific information (giving readers the details they need to understand the message)?

When you are satisfied with the content of your message, you can review its organization. Answer another set of questions:

- Are all the points covered in the most logical order?
- Do the most important ideas receive the most space, and are they placed in the most prominent positions?
- Would the message be more convincing if it were arranged in a different sequence?
- Are any points repeated unnecessarily?
- Are details grouped together logically, or are some still scattered through the document?

Next, consider whether you have achieved the right tone for your audience. Is your writing formal enough to meet the audience's expectations without being too formal or academic? Is it too casual for a serious subject?

Spend a few extra moments on the beginning and end of your message; these sections usually have the greatest impact on the audience. Be sure that the opening is relevant, interesting, and geared to the reader's probable reaction. In longer messages, ensure that the first few paragraphs establish the subject, purpose, and organization of the material. Review the conclusion to be sure that it summarizes the main idea and leaves the audience with a positive impression.

EVALUATING, EDITING, AND REVISING THE WORK OF OTHERS

At many points in your career, you will be asked to evaluate, edit, or revise the work of others. Whether you're suggesting improvements or actually making the improvements yourself (as you might on a wiki site, for example), you can make a contribution by using all the skills you are learning in Chapter 4 through Chapter 6.

Before you dive into someone else's work, recognize the dual responsibility that doing so entails. First, unless you've been specifically asked to rewrite something in your own style or to change the emphasis of the message, remember that your job is to help the other writer succeed at his or her task, not to impose your writing style or pursue your own agenda. In other words, make sure your input focuses on making the piece more effective, not on making it more like something you would've written. Second, make sure you understand the writer's intent before you begin suggesting or making changes. If you try to edit or revise without knowing what the writer hoped to accomplish, you run the risk of making the piece less effective, not more. With those thoughts in mind, answer the following questions as you evaluate someone else's writing:

> When you evaluate, edit, or revise someone else's work, remember that your job is to help that person succeed, not to impose your own style.

- What is the purpose of this document or message?
- Who is the target audience?
- What information does the audience need?
- Does the document provide this information in a well-organized way?
- Does the writing demonstrate the "you" attitude toward the audience?
- Is the tone of the writing appropriate for the audience?
- Can the readability be improved?
- Is the writing clear? If not, how can it be improved?
- Is the writing as concise as it could be?
- Does the design support the intended message?

You can read more about using these skills in the context of wiki writing in Chapter 8.

Revising to Improve Readability

After confirming the content, organization, style, and tone of your message, make a second pass to improve *readability*. Most professionals are inundated with more reading material than they can ever hope to consume, and they'll appreciate your efforts to make your documents easier to read. You'll benefit from this effort, too: If you earn a reputation for creating well-crafted documents that respect the audience's time, people will pay more attention to your work.

2 LEARNING OBJECTIVE List four techniques you can use to improve the readability of your messages.

You may be familiar with one of the indexes that have been developed over the years in an attempt to measure readability. The Flesch-Kincaid Grade Level score computes reading difficulty relative to U.S. grade-level achievement. For instance, a score of 10 suggests that a document can be read and understood by the average 10th grader. The Flesch Reading Ease score, a similar scoring system, ranks documents on a 100-point scale. Higher scores suggest that the document should be easier to read, based on word size and sentence length. If these measurements aren't built into your word-processing software, you can find a number of calculators for various indexes online.

Readability indexes offer a useful reference point, but they are limited by what they are able to measure: word length, number of syllables, sentence length, and paragraph length. They can't measure any of the other factors that affect readability, such as document design, the "you" attitude, clear sentence structure, smooth transitions, and proper word usage. Compare these two paragraphs:

> Readability indexes offer a useful reference point, but they are all limited by what they are able to measure: word length, number of syllables, sentence length, and paragraph length. They can't measure any of the other factors that affect readability, from "you" orientation to writing clarity to document design.

> Readability indexes can help. But they don't measure everything. They don't measure whether your writing clarity is good. They don't measure whether your document design is good or not. Reading indexes are based on word length, syllables, sentences, and paragraphs.

The second paragraph scores much better on both grade level and reading ease, but it is choppy, unsophisticated, and poorly organized. As a general rule, then, don't assume that a piece of text is readable if it scores well on a readability index—or that it is difficult to read if it doesn't score well.

Beyond using shorter words and simpler sentences, you can improve the readability of a message by making the document interesting and easy to skim. Most business audiences—particularly influential senior managers—tend to skim documents, looking for key ideas, conclusions, and recommendations. If they think a document contains valuable information or requires a response, they will read it more carefully when time permits. Four techniques will make your message easier to read and easier to skim: varying sentence length, using shorter paragraphs, using lists and bullets instead of narrative, and adding effective headings and subheadings.

REAL-TIME UPDATES

LEARN MORE BY VISITING THIS WEBSITE

Editing and proofreading tips, with an error treasure hunt

This guide from the Writing Center at the University of North Carolina, Chapel Hill, offers advice on editing and proofreading, and a chance to find errors strategically embedded in the advice itself. Go to **real-timeupdates.com/bct14** and select Learn More in the Students section.

VARYING YOUR SENTENCE LENGTH

To keep readers' interest, look for ways to combine a variety of short, medium, and long sentences.

Varying the length of your sentences is a creative way to make your messages interesting and readable. By choosing words and sentence structure with care, you can create a rhythm that emphasizes important points, enlivens your writing style, and makes information more appealing to your reader. For example, a short sentence that highlights a conclusion at the end of a substantial paragraph of evidence makes your key message stand out. Try for a mixture of sentences that are short (up to 15 words or so), medium (15–25 words), and long (more than 25 words).

Each sentence length has its advantages. Short sentences can be processed quickly and are easier for nonnative speakers and translators to interpret. Medium-length sentences are useful for showing the relationships among ideas. Long sentences are often the best for conveying complex ideas, listing multiple related points, or summarizing or previewing information.

Of course, each sentence length also has disadvantages. Too many short sentences in a row can make your writing choppy. Medium sentences can lack the punch of short sentences and the informative power of longer sentences. Long sentences can be difficult to understand because they contain more information and usually have a more complicated structure. Because readers can absorb only a few words per glance, longer sentences are also more difficult to skim. By choosing the best sentence length for each communication need and remembering to mix sentence lengths for variety, you'll get your points across while keeping your messages lively and interesting.

KEEPING YOUR PARAGRAPHS SHORT

Short paragraphs have the major advantage of being easy to read.

Large blocks of text can be visually daunting, particularly on screen and even more so on small mobile devices, so the optimum paragraph length is short to medium in most cases. Unless you break up your thoughts somehow, you'll end up with lengthy paragraphs that are guaranteed to intimidate even the most dedicated reader. Short paragraphs, generally 100 words or fewer (this paragraph has 92 words), are easier to read than long ones, and they make your writing look inviting. You can also emphasize ideas by isolating them in short, forceful paragraphs.

However, don't go overboard with short paragraphs. In particular, be careful to use one-sentence paragraphs only occasionally and usually only for emphasis. Also, if you need to divide a subject into several pieces to keep paragraphs short, be sure to help your readers keep the ideas connected by guiding them with plenty of transitional elements.

USING LISTS TO CLARIFY AND EMPHASIZE

An effective alternative to using conventional sentences is to set off important ideas in a list—a series of words, names, or other items. Lists can show the sequence of your ideas, heighten their visual impact, and increase the likelihood that a reader will find key points. In addition, lists help simplify complex subjects, highlight main points, visually break up a page or screen, ease the skimming process for busy readers, and give readers a breather. Compare these two treatments of the same information:

Lists are effective tools for highlighting and simplifying material.

Narrative	List
Owning your own business has many potential advantages. One is the opportunity to pursue your own personal passion. Another advantage is the satisfaction of working for yourself. As a sole proprietor, you also have the advantage of privacy because you do not have to reveal your financial information or plans to anyone.	Owning your own business has three advantages: • Opportunity to pursue personal passion • Satisfaction of working for yourself • Financial privacy

You can separate list items with numbers, letters, or bullets (a general term for any kind of graphical element that precedes each item). Bullets are generally preferred over numbers, unless the list is in some logical sequence or ranking or you need to refer to specific list items elsewhere in the document.

Lists are easier to locate and read if the entire numbered or bulleted section is set off by a blank line before and after. Furthermore, make sure to introduce lists clearly so that people know what they're about to read. One way to introduce lists is to make them a part of the introductory sentence:

The board of directors met to discuss the revised annual budget. To keep expenses in line with declining sales, the directors voted to

● Cut everyone's salary by 10 percent
● Close the employee cafeteria
● Reduce travel expenses

Another way to introduce a list is to precede it with a complete introductory sentence, followed by a colon:

The decline in company profit is attributable to four factors:

● Slower holiday sales
● Increased transportation and fuel costs
● Higher employee wages
● Slower inventory turnover

Regardless of the format you choose, the items in a list should be parallel; that is, they should all use the same grammatical pattern. For example, if one list item begins with a verb, every item should begin with a verb. If one item is a noun phrase, all should be noun phrases.

Nonparallel List Items (a mix of verb and noun phrases)	Parallel List Items (all verb phrases)
• Improve our bottom line	• Improving our bottom line
• Identification of new foreign markets for our products	• Identifying new foreign markets for our products
• Global market strategies	• Developing our global market strategies
• Issues regarding pricing and packaging size	• Resolving pricing and packaging issues

TABLE 6.1   Achieving Parallelism

Method	Example
Parallel words	The plan was approved by Clausen, Whittaker, Merlin, and Carlucci.
Parallel phrases	We are gaining market share in supermarkets, in department stores, and in specialty stores.
Parallel clauses	I'd like to discuss the issue after Vicki gives her presentation but before Marvin shows his slides.
Parallel sentences	In 2015 we exported 30 percent of our production. In 2016 we exported 50 percent.

Parallel forms are easier to read and skim. You can create parallelism by repeating the pattern in words, phrases, clauses, or entire sentences (see Table 6.1).

ADDING HEADINGS AND SUBHEADINGS

Use headings to grab the reader's attention and organize material into short sections.

A **heading** is a brief title that tells readers about the content of the section that follows. **Subheadings** are subordinate to headings, indicating subsections within a major section. Headings and subheadings serve these important functions:

- **Organization.** Headings show your reader at a glance how the document is organized. They act as labels to group related paragraphs and organize lengthy material into shorter sections.
- **Attention.** Informative, inviting, and in some cases intriguing headings grab the reader's attention, make the text easier to read, and help the reader find the parts he or she needs to read—or skip.
- **Connection.** Using headings and subheadings together helps readers see the relationship between main ideas and subordinate ones so that they can understand your message more easily. Moreover, headings and subheadings visually indicate shifts from one idea to the next.

Informative headings are generally more helpful than descriptive ones.

Headings and subheadings fall into two categories. **Descriptive headings**, such as "Cost Considerations," identify a topic but do little more. **Informative headings**, such as "Redesigning Material Flow to Cut Production Costs," guide readers to think in a certain way about the topic. They are also helpful in guiding your work as a writer, especially if cast as questions you plan to address in your document. Well-written informative headings are self-contained, which means readers can read just the headings and subheadings and understand them without reading the rest of the document. For example, "Staffing Shortages Cost the Company $150,000 Last Year" provides a key piece of information and captures the reader's attention. Whatever types of headings you choose, keep them brief and use parallel construction throughout the document.

Editing for Clarity and Conciseness

3 LEARNING OBJECTIVE
Describe eight steps you can take to improve the clarity of your writing, and give four tips on making your writing more concise.

After you've reviewed and revised your message for readability, your next step is to make your message as clear and as concise as possible.

EDITING FOR CLARITY

Clarity is essential to getting your message across accurately and efficiently.

Verify that every sentence conveys the message you intend and that readers can extract that meaning without needing to read it more than once. To ensure clarity, look closely at your paragraph organization, sentence structure, and word choices (see Chapter 5). Can readers make sense of the related sentences in a paragraph? Is the meaning of each sentence easy to grasp? Is each word clear and unambiguous (meaning it doesn't have any risk of being interpreted in more than one way)?

See Table 6.2 for examples of the following tips:

- **Break up overly long sentences.** If you find yourself stuck in a long sentence, you're probably trying to make the sentence do more than it reasonably can, such as expressing two dissimilar thoughts or peppering the reader with too many pieces of supporting evidence at once. (Did you notice how difficult this long sentence was to read?)
- **Rewrite hedging sentences.** *Hedging* means pulling back from making a confident, definitive statement about a topic. Granted, sometimes you have to write *may* or *seems* to avoid stating a judgment or prediction as a fact. When you hedge too often or without good reason, however, you come across as being unsure of what you're saying.
- **Impose parallelism.** When you have two or more similar ideas to express, make them parallel by using the same grammatical construction. Parallelism shows that the ideas are related, of similar importance, and on the same level of generality.
- **Correct dangling modifiers.** Sometimes a modifier is not just an adjective or an adverb but an entire phrase modifying a noun or a verb. Be careful not to leave this type of modifier *dangling*, with no connection to the subject of the sentence.
- **Reword long noun sequences.** When multiple nouns are strung together as modifiers, the resulting sentence can be hard to read. See if a single well-chosen word will do the job. If the nouns are all necessary, consider moving one or more to a modifying phrase, as shown in Table 6.2.

> Hedging is appropriate when you can't be absolutely sure of a statement, but excessive hedging undermines your authority.

> When you use parallel grammatical patterns to express two or more ideas, you show that they are comparable thoughts.

TABLE 6.2 Revising for Clarity

Issues to Review	Ineffective	Effective
Overly Long Sentences (taking compound sentences too far)	The magazine will be published January 1, and I'd better meet the deadline if I want my article included because we want the article to appear before the trade show.	The magazine will be published January 1. I'd better meet the deadline because we want the article to appear before the trade show.
Hedging Sentences (overqualifying sentences)	I believe that Mr. Johnson's employment record seems to show that he may be capable of handling the position.	Mr. Johnson's employment record shows that he is capable of handling the position.
Unparallel Sentences (using dissimilar construction for similar ideas)	Mr. Simms had been drenched with rain, bombarded with telephone calls, and his boss shouted at him. To waste time and missing deadlines are bad habits.	Mr. Sims had been drenched with rain, bombarded with telephone calls, and shouted at by his boss. Wasting time and missing deadlines are bad habits.
Dangling Modifiers (placing modifiers close to the wrong nouns and verbs)	Walking to the office, a red sports car passed her. [suggests that the car was walking to the office] Reduced by 25 percent, Europe had its lowest semiconductor output in a decade. [suggests that Europe shrank by 25 percent]	A red sports car passed her while she was walking to the office. Europe reduced semiconductor output by 25 percent, its lowest output in a decade.
Long Noun Sequences (stringing too many nouns together)	The window sash installation company will give us an estimate on Friday.	The company that installs window sashes will give us an estimate on Friday.
Camouflaged Verbs (changing verbs into nouns)	The manager undertook implementation of the rules. Verification of the shipments occurs weekly. reach a conclusion about give consideration to	The manager implemented the rules. We verify shipments weekly. conclude consider
Subject-Predicate Separation (putting the predicate too far from the subject)	A 10% decline in market share, which resulted from quality problems and an aggressive sales campaign by Armitage, the market leader in the Northeast, was the major problem in 2016.	The major problem in 2016 was a 10% loss of market share, which resulted from quality problems and an aggressive sales campaign by Armitage, the market leader in the Northeast.
Modifier Separation (putting adjectives, adverbs, or prepositional phrases too far from the words they modify)	Our antique desk lends an air of strength and substance with thick legs and large drawers.	With its thick legs and large drawers, our antique desk lends an air of strength and substance.
Awkward References (linking ideas in ways that cause more work for the reader)	The Law Office and the Accounting Office distribute computer supplies for paralegals and accountants, respectively.	The Law Office distributes computer supplies for paralegals; the Accounting Office distributes them for accountants.

Subject and predicate should be placed as close together as possible, as should modifiers and the words they modify.

- **Replace camouflaged verbs.** Watch for words that end in -*ion*, -*tion*, -*ing*, -*ment*, -*ant*, -*ent*, -*ence*, -*ance*, and -*ency*. These endings often change verbs into nouns and adjectives, requiring you to add a verb to get your point across.
- **Clarify sentence structure.** Keep the subject and predicate of a sentence as close together as possible. When the subject and predicate are far apart, readers may need to read the sentence twice to figure out who did what. Similarly, adjectives, adverbs, and prepositional phrases usually make the most sense when they're placed as close as possible to the words they modify.
- **Clarify awkward references.** If you want readers to refer to a specific point in a document, avoid vague references such as *the above-mentioned*, *as mentioned above*, *the aforementioned*, *the former*, *the latter*, and *respectively*. Use a specific pointer such as "as described in the second paragraph on page 162."

EDITING FOR CONCISENESS

Make your documents tighter by removing unnecessary words, phrases, and sentences.

Many of the changes you make to improve clarity also shorten your message by removing unnecessary words. The next step is to examine the text with the specific goal of reducing the number of words. Readers appreciate conciseness and are more likely to read your documents if you have a reputation for efficient writing. See Table 6.3 for examples of the following tips:

- **Delete unnecessary words and phrases.** To test whether a word or phrase is essential, try the sentence without it. If the meaning doesn't change, leave it out.
- **Shorten long words and phrases.** Short words and phrases are generally more vivid and easier to read than long ones. Also, by using infinitives (the "to" form of a verb) in place of some phrases, you can often shorten sentences while making them clearer.
- **Eliminate redundancies.** In some word combinations, the words say the same thing. For instance, "visible to the eye" is redundant because *visible* is enough without further clarification; "to the eye" adds nothing.
- **Rewrite "It is/There are" starters.** If you start a sentence with an indefinite pronoun such as *it* or *there*, chances are the sentence could be shorter and more active. For instance, "We believe . . ." is a stronger opening than "It is believed that . . ." because it is shorter and because it identifies who is doing the believing.

As you rewrite, concentrate on how each word contributes to an effective sentence and on how each sentence helps build a coherent paragraph. For a reminder of the tasks involved in revision, see "Checklist: Revising Business Messages."

CHECKLIST ✔ Revising Business Messages

A. Evaluate content, organization, style, and tone.
- Make sure the information is accurate, relevant, and sufficient.
- Check that all necessary points appear in logical order.
- Verify that you present enough support to make the main idea convincing and compelling.
- Be sure the beginning and ending of the message are effective.
- Make sure you've achieved the right tone for the audience and the situation.

B. Review for readability.
- Consider using a readability index, but be sure to interpret the answer carefully.
- Use a mix of short, medium, and long sentences.
- Keep paragraphs short.
- Use bulleted and numbered lists to emphasize key points.
- Make the document easy to skim with headings and subheadings.

C. Edit for clarity.
- Break up overly long sentences and rewrite hedging sentences.
- Impose parallelism to simplify reading.
- Correct dangling modifiers.
- Reword long noun sequences and replace camouflaged verbs.
- Clarify sentence structure and awkward references.

D. Edit for conciseness.
- Delete unnecessary words and phrases.
- Shorten long words and phrases.
- Eliminate redundancies.
- Rewrite sentences that start with "It is" or "There are."

TABLE 6.3   Revising for Conciseness

Issues to Review	Less Effective	More Effective
Unnecessary Words and Phrases		
Using wordy phrases	for the sum of	for
	in the event that	if
	prior to the start of	before
	in the near future	soon
	at this point in time	now
	due to the fact that	because
	in view of the fact that	because
	until such time as	when
	with reference to	about
Using too many relative pronouns (such as *that* or *who*)	Cars that are sold after January will not have a six-month warranty.	Cars sold after January will not have a six-month warranty.
	Employees who are driving to work should park in the underground garage.	Employees driving to work should park in the underground garage.
		OR
		Employees should park in the underground garage.
Using too few relative pronouns	The project manager told the engineers last week the specifications were changed.	The project manager told the engineers last week that the specifications were changed.
		OR
		The project manager told the engineers that last week the specifications were changed
Long Words and Phrases		
Using overly long words	During the preceding year, the company accelerated productive operations.	Last year the company sped up operations.
	The action was predicated on the assumption that the company was operating at a financial deficit.	The action was based on the belief that the company was losing money.
Using wordy phrases rather than infinitives	If you want success as a writer, you must work hard.	To succeed as a writer, you must work hard.
	He went to the library for the purpose of studying.	He went to the library to study.
	The employer increased salaries so that she could improve morale.	The employer increased salaries to improve morale.
Redundancies		
Repeating meanings	absolutely complete	complete
	basic fundamentals	fundamentals
	follows after	follows
	free and clear	free
	refer back	refer
	repeat again	repeat
	collect together	collect
	future plans	plans
	return back	return
	important essentials	essentials
	end result	result
	actual truth	truth
	final outcome	outcome
	uniquely unusual	unique
	surrounded on all sides	surrounded
Using double modifiers	modern, up-to-date equipment	modern equipment
It Is **and** ***There Are*** **Starters**	It would be appreciated if you would sign the lease today.	Please sign the lease today.
Starting sentences with *It* or *There*	There are five employees in this division who were late to work today.	Five employees in this division were late to work today.

THE FUTURE OF COMMUNICATION

Haptic Technologies

As the most intimate form of communication, touch can convey shades of emotion and meaning in ways that other forms can't match. Think of the range of messages you can send by the way you greet someone, for example. A firm handshake, a light kiss on the cheek, an awkward embrace, and a fist bump all send different nonverbal signals. *Haptic communication* or *haptics* is the study of touch in a communication context.

Touch is a vital aspect of human-to-human and human-to-machine interaction, but it is missing from most forms of digital communication. You can't give someone a hearty handshake over email or feel the vibration patterns of a machine while viewing it over a video link.

However, the field of *haptic technology* is enabling touch and tactile sensations in a growing number of ways. Many arcade video games and video game controllers use *haptic feedback* to give players some sense of the feel of driving a racecar, for example. Moving beyond simple vibration feedback, some controllers can now simulate the sensation of holding and using specific weapons or other physical elements in a game.

Mobile devices and wearables such as smartwatches are incorporating haptic input and output in ways that simulate the nuances of human touch. For instance, you can use a smartwatch to send specific, personalized "touch messages" to other smartwatch wearers with complete privacy. The ability to remotely manipulate objects and machines through simulated touch (rather than abstracted devices such as joysticks) is another intriguing promise of haptics.

The technology has exciting potential in such diverse areas as training, online retailing, and making more devices usable by people with limited vision. Imagine being able to feel the texture of fabric from halfway around the world or letting an expert's hands remotely guide yours as you learn a new procedure. Now that display technologies have more or less reached the resolution capacity of human eyesight, the next wave of user interface advances is likely to come in the form of touch.

WHAT'S YOUR PREDICTION?

Research the current state of haptic technology to identify one way in which the technology has the potential to change business communication practices, such as replacing detailed verbal descriptions of products with touch-enabled virtual interaction. Do you agree with the predictions the experts make? Why or why not?

Sources: Maya Baratz, "The Communication of the Future Is So Real You Can Touch It," *Fast Company*, 12 January 2015, www.fastcodesign.com; JV Chamary, "The iPhone 7 Killer Feature Should Be Haptic Feedback," *Forbes*, 25 September 2015, www.forbes.com; Brian S. Hall, "Taptic, Haptics, and the Body Fantastic: The Real Apple Watch Revolution," *Macworld*, 3 October 2014, www.macworld.com.

Producing Your Message

4 LEARNING OBJECTIVE
List four principles of effective design, and explain the role of major design elements in document readability.

Now it's time to put your hard work on display. The *production quality* of your message—the total effect of page or screen design, graphical elements, typography, and so on—plays an important role in its effectiveness. A polished, inviting design not only makes your material easier to read but also conveys a sense of professionalism and importance.[2]

The quality of your document design, both on paper and on screen, affects readability and audience perceptions.

DESIGNING FOR READABILITY

Design affects readability in two important ways. First, carefully chosen design elements can improve the effectiveness of your message. In contrast, poor design decisions, such as using distracting background images behind text, pointless animations, or tiny typefaces, act as barriers to communication. Second, the visual design sends a nonverbal message to your readers, influencing their perceptions of the communication before they read a single word.

Good design enhances the readability of your material.

Effective design helps you establish the tone of your document and helps guide your readers through your message (see Figure 6.3). To achieve an effective design, pay careful attention to the following design elements:

For effective design, pay attention to
• Consistency
• Balance
• Restraint
• Detail

- **Consistency.** Throughout each message, be consistent in your use of margins, typeface, type size, and space. Also be consistent when using recurring design elements, such as vertical lines, columns, and borders. In many cases you'll want to be consistent from message to message as well; that way, audiences who receive multiple messages from you recognize your documents and know what to expect.

- **Balance.** Balance is an important but subjective issue. One document may have a formal, rigid design in which the various elements are placed in a grid pattern, whereas another may have a less formal design in which elements flow more freely across the

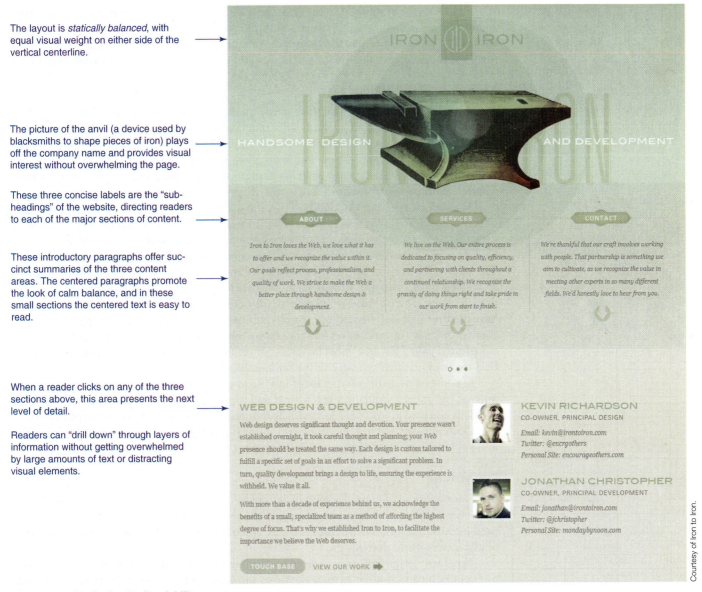

The layout is *statically balanced*, with equal visual weight on either side of the vertical centerline.

The picture of the anvil (a device used by blacksmiths to shape pieces of iron) plays off the company name and provides visual interest without overwhelming the page.

These three concise labels are the "sub-headings" of the website, directing readers to each of the major sections of content.

These introductory paragraphs offer succinct summaries of the three content areas. The centered paragraphs promote the look of calm balance, and in these small sections the centered text is easy to read.

When a reader clicks on any of the three sections above, this area presents the next level of detail.

Readers can "drill down" through layers of information without getting overwhelmed by large amounts of text or distracting visual elements.

Figure 6.3   Designing for Readability
The website of the web development firm Iron to Iron is a model of elegant design that promotes easy reading.

page—and both could be in balance. Like the tone of your language, visual balance can be too formal, just right, or too informal for a given message.

- **Restraint.** Strive for simplicity in design. Don't clutter your message with too many design elements, too many typeface treatments, too many colors, or too many decorative touches. Let "simpler" and "fewer" be your guiding concepts.
- **Detail.** Pay attention to details that affect your design and thus your message. For instance, extremely wide columns of text can be difficult to read; in many cases a better solution is to split the text into two narrower columns.

Even without special training in graphic design, you can make your print and digital messages more effective by understanding the use of white space, margins and line justification, typefaces, and type styles.

White Space

Any space that doesn't contain text or artwork, both in print and online, is considered **white space**. (Note that "white space" isn't necessarily white; it is simply blank.) These unused areas provide visual contrast and important resting points for your readers. White

MOBILE APP
Genius Scan lets you scan documents with your phone and create PDFs on the go.

White space separates elements in a document and helps guide the reader's eye.

space includes the margins, paragraph indents, space around images, open areas surrounding headings, vertical space between columns, and horizontal space between paragraphs or lines of text. To increase the chance that readers will read your messages, be generous with white space; it makes pages and screens feel less intimidating and easier to read.[3]

Margins and Justification

Most business documents use a flush left margin and a ragged right margin.

Margins define the space around text and between text columns. In addition to their width, the look and feel of margins are influenced by the way lines of text are arranged. They can be set (1) *justified* (which means they are *flush*, or aligned vertically, on both the left and the right), (2) flush left with a *ragged right* margin, (3) flush right with a *ragged left* margin, or (4) centered. This paragraph is justified, whereas the paragraphs in Figure 6.2 on page 156 are flush left with a ragged right margin.

Magazines, newspapers, and books often use justified type because it can accommodate more text in a given space. However, justified type needs to be used with care. First, it creates a denser look because the uniform line lengths decrease the amount of white space along the right margin. Second, it produces a more formal and less personalized look. Third, unless it is used with some skill and attention, justified type can be more difficult to read because it can produce large gaps between words and excessive hyphenation at the ends of lines. The publishing specialists who create magazines, newspapers, and books have the time and skill needed to carefully adjust character and word spacing to eliminate these problems. (In some cases sentences are even rewritten to improve the appearance of the printed page.) Because most business communicators don't have that time or skill, it's best to avoid justified type in routine business documents.

In contrast to justified type, flush-left, ragged-right type creates a more open appearance on the page, producing a less formal and more contemporary look. Spacing between words is consistent, and only long words that fall at the ends of lines are hyphenated.

Centered type is rarely used for text paragraphs but is commonly used for headings and subheadings. Flush-right, ragged-left type is rarely used in business documents.

Typefaces

Typeface refers to the visual design of letters, numbers, and other text characters. As the Type Together vignette at the beginning of the chapter noted, *typeface* and *font* are often used interchangeably, but typeface is the design of the type itself, and a font is a collection of characters using that design.

Typeface design influences the tone of your message, making it look authoritative or friendly, businesslike or casual, classic or modern, and so on (see Table 6.4). Veronika Burian, José Scaglione, and other type designers know how to make design choices that evoke specific emotional reactions and trigger particular visual associations, so be sure to choose fonts that are appropriate for your message. (Note that many of the fonts on your computer are not appropriate for normal business use.)

The classic style of document design uses a sans serif typeface for headings and a serif typeface for regular paragraph text; however, many contemporary documents and webpages now use all sans serif.

Serif typefaces have small crosslines (called serifs) at the ends of each letter stroke. **Sans serif typefaces**, in contrast, lack these serifs. For years, the conventional wisdom in typography was that serif faces were easier to read in long blocks of text because the serifs

TABLE 6.4   Typeface Personalities: Serious to Casual to Playful

Serif Typefaces	Sans Serif Typefaces	Specialty Typefaces (rarely used for routine business communication)
Bookman Old Style	Arial	Bauhaus
Century Schoolbook	News Gothic Com	**Broadway**
Courier	**Eras Bold**	*Civilite MJ*
Garamond	Franklin Gothic Book	*Commercial Script*
Georgia	Gill Sans	**Forte MT**
Times New Roman	Verdana	**STENCIL**

made it easier for the eye to pick out individual letters. Accordingly, the standard advice was to use serif faces for the body of a document and sans serif for headings and subheadings.

However, the research behind the conventional wisdom is not as conclusive as once thought.[4] In fact, many sans serif typefaces work as well or better for body text than some serif typefaces. This seems to be particularly true on screens, which often have lower resolution than printed text. Many contemporary documents and webpages now use sans serif faces for body text.

For most documents, you shouldn't need more than two typefaces, although if you want to make captions or other text elements stand out, you can use another font.[5] Using more typefaces can clutter a document and produce an amateurish look.

REAL-TIME UPDATES

LEARN MORE BY READING THIS ARTICLE

Improve your document designs by learning the fundamentals of typography

Knowing the basics of type usage will help you create more effective page and screen layouts. Go to **real-timeupdates.com/bct14** and select Learn More in the Students section.

Type Styles

Type style refers to any modification that lends contrast or emphasis to type, including boldface, italic, underlining, color, and other highlighting and decorative styles. Using boldface type for subheads breaks up long expanses of text. You can also set individual words or phrases as bold to draw more attention to them. For example, the key terms in each chapter in this book are set in boldface. Italic type also creates emphasis, although not as pronounced as boldface. Italic type has specific uses as well, such as highlighting quotations and indicating foreign words, irony, humor, book and movie titles, and unconventional usage.

As a general rule, avoid using any style in a way that slows your audience's progress through the message. For instance, underlining or using all uppercase letters can interfere with a reader's ability to recognize the shapes of words, and shadowed or outlined type can seriously hinder legibility. Also, avoid overusing any type style. For example, putting too many words in boldface dilutes the impact of the special treatment by creating too many focal points in the paragraph.

Type size is an important consideration as well. For most printed business messages, use a size of 10 to 12 points for regular text and 12 to 18 points for headings and subheadings (1 point is approximately 1/72 inch). Resist the temptation to reduce type size too much in order to squeeze in extra text or to enlarge type to fill up space. Type that is too small or too large can be difficult to read. Be particularly careful with small type online. Small type that looks fine on a medium-resolution screen can be hard to read on both low-resolution screens (because these displays can make letters look jagged or fuzzy) and high-resolution screens (because these monitors reduce the apparent size of the type even further).

Avoid using any type style that inhibits your audience's ability to read your messages.

REAL-TIME UPDATES

LEARN MORE BY VISITING THIS WEBSITE

See the newest designs from some of the brightest minds in typography

Type design is a fascinating and dynamic field; this portfolio shows dozens of innovative new typefaces. Go to **real-timeupdates.com/bct14** and select Learn More in the Students section.

FORMATTING FORMAL LETTERS AND MEMOS

Formal business letters usually follow certain design conventions, as the letter in Figure 6.2 illustrates. Most business letters are printed on *letterhead stationery*, which includes the company's name, address, and other contact information. The first element to appear after the letterhead is the date, followed by the inside address, which identifies the person receiving the letter. Next is the salutation, usually in the form of *Dear Mr.* or *Ms. Last Name*. The message comes next, followed by the complimentary close, usually *Sincerely* or *Cordially*. And last comes the signature block: space for the signature, followed by the sender's printed name and title. Your company will probably have a standard format to follow for letters, possibly along with a template in Microsoft Word or whatever word processor is standard in the organization. For in-depth information on letter formats, see Appendix A, "Format and Layout of Business Documents."

Like letters, business memos usually follow a preset design. Memos have largely been replaced by digital media in many companies, but if they are still in use at the firm you join, the company may have a standard format or template for you to use. Most memos begin with a title such as *Memo, Memorandum,* or *Interoffice Correspondence.* Following that are usually four headings: *Date, To, From,* and *Subject.* (*Re:,* short for

Regarding, is sometimes used instead of *Subject*.) Memos usually don't use a salutation, complimentary close, or signature, although signing your initials next to your name on the *From* line is standard practice in most companies. Bear in mind that memos are often distributed without sealed envelopes, so they are less private than most other message formats.

DESIGNING MESSAGES FOR MOBILE DEVICES

In addition to making your content mobile-friendly using the writing tips in Chapter 5 (see page 144), you can follow these steps in formatting that content for mobile devices:

- **Think in small chunks.** Remember that mobile users consume information one screen at a time, so try to divide your message into independent, easy-to-consume bites. If readers have to scroll through a dozen screens to piece together your message, they might miss your point or just give up entirely.
- **Make generous use of white space.** White space is always helpful, but it's critical on small screens because readers are trying to get the point of every message as quickly as possible. Keep your paragraphs short (four to six lines), and separate them with blank lines so the reader's eyes can easily jump from one point to the next.[6]
- **Format simply.** Avoid anything that is likely to get in the way of fast, easy reading, including busy typefaces, complex graphics, and complicated layouts.
- **Consider horizontal and vertical layouts.** Most phones and tablets can automatically rotate their screen content from horizontal to vertical as the user rotates the device. A layout that doesn't work well with the narrow vertical perspective might be acceptable at the wider horizontal perspective.

Compare the two messages in Figure 6.4; notice how much more difficult the screen in Figure 6.4a is to read.

Figure 6.4a

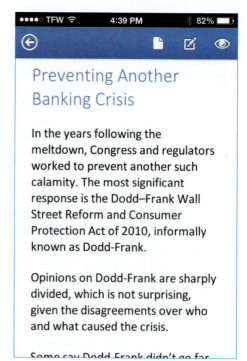

Figure 6.4b

Figure 6.4   Designing for Mobile Devices

Compare the readability of Figures 6.4a and 6.4b. Even simple changes such as revising with shorter paragraphs, choosing cleaner typefaces, and making generous use of white space in and around the text can dramatically improve readability on mobile screens.

Proofreading Your Message

Proofreading is the quality inspection stage for your documents, your last chance to make sure that your document is ready to carry your message—and your reputation—to the intended audience. Even a small mistake can doom your efforts, so take proofreading seriously.

Look for two types of problems: (1) undetected mistakes from the writing, design, and layout stages and (2) mistakes that crept in during production. For the first category, you can review format and layout guidelines in Appendix A on page 578 and brush up on writing basics with the Handbook of Grammar, Mechanics, and Usage on page 601. The second category can include anything from computer glitches such as missing fonts to broken web links to problems with the ink used in printing. Be particularly vigilant with complex documents and complex production processes that involve multiple colleagues and multiple computers. Strange things can happen as files move from computer to computer, especially when lots of fonts and multimedia elements are involved.

Resist the temptation to treat proofreading as a casual scan up and down the page or screen. Instead, approach it as a methodical procedure in which you look for specific problems that may occur. Use these techniques from professional proofreaders to help ensure high-quality output:

- **Make multiple passes.** Go through the document several times, focusing on a different aspect each time. For instance, look for content errors the first time and layout errors the second time.
- **Use perceptual tricks.** You've probably experienced the frustration of reading over something a dozen times and still missing an obvious error. This happens because your brain has developed a wonderful skill of subconsciously supplying missing pieces and correcting mistakes when it knows what is *supposed* to be on the page. To keep your brain from tricking you, you need to trick it by changing the way you process the visual information. Try (1) reading each page backward, from the bottom to the top, (2) placing your finger under each word and reading it silently, (3) making a slit in a sheet of paper that reveals only one line of type at a time, and (4) reading the document aloud and pronouncing each word carefully.
- **Double-check high-priority items.** Double-check the spelling of names and the accuracy of dates, addresses, and any number that could cause grief if incorrect (such as telling a potential employer that you'd be happy to work for $5,000 a year when you meant to say $50,000).
- **Give yourself some distance.** If possible, don't proofread immediately after finishing a document; let your mind wander off to new topics and then come back fresh later.
- **Be vigilant.** Avoid reading large amounts of material in one sitting and try not to proofread when you're tired.
- **Stay focused.** Concentrate on what you're doing. Try to block out distractions and focus as completely as possible on your proofreading task.
- **Review complex digital documents on paper.** Some people have trouble proofreading webpages, online reports, and other digital documents on screen. If you have trouble, print the materials so you can review them on paper.
- **Take your time.** Quick proofreading is not careful proofreading.

The amount of time you need to spend on proofing depends on the length and complexity of the document and the situation. A typo in an email message to your team may not be a big deal, but a typo in a financial report, a contract, or a medical file certainly could be serious. See "Checklist: Proofing Business Messages" for a handy list of items to review during proofing.

5 **LEARNING OBJECTIVE**
Explain the importance of proofreading and give eight tips for successful proofreading.

Your credibility is affected by your attention to the details of mechanics and form.

The types of details to look for when proofreading include language errors, missing material, design errors, and typographical errors.

MOBILE APP
The **NounPlus English Grammar Checker** can check your writing for a variety of basic grammatical issues.

REAL-TIME UPDATES
LEARN MORE BY LISTENING TO THIS PODCAST
Tips for proofing your papers
This advice for proofreading class assignments will help you on the job, too. Go to **real-timeupdates.com/bct14** and select Learn More in the Students section.

CHECKLIST ✔ Proofing Business Messages

A. Look for writing errors.
- Typographical mistakes
- Misspelled words
- Grammatical errors
- Punctuation mistakes

B. Look for missing elements.
- Missing text sections
- Missing exhibits (drawings, tables, photographs, charts, graphs, online images, and so on)
- Missing source notes, copyright notices, or other reference items

C. Look for design, formatting, and programming mistakes.
- Incorrect or inconsistent font selections
- Problems with column sizing, spacing, and alignment
- Incorrect margins
- Incorrect special characters
- Clumsy line and page breaks
- Problems with page numbers
- Problems with page headers and footers
- Lack of adherence to company standards
- Inactive or incorrect links
- Missing files

Distributing Your Message

6 LEARNING OBJECTIVE
Discuss the most important issues to consider when distributing your messages.

With the production finished, you're ready to distribute your message. As with every other aspect of business communication, your options for distribution multiply with every advance in technology. For many digital systems, distribution is a simple matter of selecting a Send or Publish option when you're ready to go. When you have a 100-page report with full-color graphics or a massive multimedia file, however, you need to plan the distribution carefully so that your message is received by everyone who needs it. When choosing a means to distribute messages, consider the following factors:

Consider cost, convenience, time, security, and privacy when choosing a distribution method.

- **Cost.** Cost isn't a concern for most messages, but for lengthy reports or multimedia productions, it may well be. Printing, binding, and delivering reports can be expensive, so weigh the cost versus the benefits. Be sure to consider the nonverbal message you send regarding cost as well. Overnight delivery of a printed report could seem responsive in one situation but wasteful in another, for example.
- **Convenience.** How much work is involved for you and your audience? For instance, if you use a file-compression utility to shrink the size of email attachments, make sure your recipients have the means to expand the files on arrival. For extremely large files, consider recordable media such as DVDs or one of the many free or low-cost file-hosting sites now available.
- **Time.** How soon does the message need to reach the audience? Don't waste money on overnight delivery if the recipient won't read the report for a week. And speaking of time, don't mark any messages, printed or digital, as "urgent" if they aren't truly urgent.
- **Security and privacy.** The convenience offered by digital communication needs to be weighed against security and privacy concerns. For the most sensitive messages, your company will probably restrict both the people who can receive the messages and the means you can use to distribute them. In addition, most computer users are wary of opening attachments these days. Instead of sending word processor files, you can use Adobe Acrobat or an equivalent product to convert your documents to PDF files (which are more immune to viruses).

MOBILE APP

SignEasy solves the problem of signing digital documents such as contracts; you can sign right on your phone screen.

For more advice on revision, proofreading, and other topics related to this chapter, visit **real-timeupdates.com/bct14** and select Chapter 6.

COMMUNICATION CHALLENGES AT **Type Together**

You've joined Type Together as a marketing communications specialist, and your responsibilities include writing new content as well as revising and editing content submissions from other people in the company. Use what you've learned in this chapter about revising and editing to address these two challenges.

INDIVIDUAL CHALLENGE: Type foundries such as Type Together can sell their wares through a variety of online stores, where graphic designers and other users can select from thousands of fonts. These sites typically include a short description of the foundry's history, design philosophy, product line, or other characteristics. Assume that a particular site has a 75-word limit for this description. Review the Info page on Type Together's website at **www.type-together.com**, including the About Us section and the biographies of José Scaglione and Veronika Burian. Identify three or four essential points that would be of interest to people shopping for fonts, then craft a compelling introductory paragraph of no more than 75 words.

TEAM CHALLENGE: As with many aspects of digital media, the tasks of selecting and using fonts were once the domain of trained specialists but are now within the reach of every computer user. In fact, users with no background in typography are often forced to make choices involving type, even if they would rather not do so. Not surprisingly, everyday computer users can make ill-informed choices that limit the effectiveness of their messages and documents. With a team assigned by your instructor, do the research needed to come up with a list of "dos and don'ts" for choosing and using the fonts available on a typical computer or tablet. Start with the information provided in this chapter, but review at least three other sources to expand your perspective. As your instructor directs, present your advice in class or in a post on your class blog. Assume your target audience is made up of business professionals with no training or experience in graphic design or typography.

Quick Learning Guide

KEY TERMS

descriptive headings Headings that simply identify a topic

heading A brief title that tells readers about the content of the section that follows

informative headings Headings that guide readers to think in a certain way about a topic

sans serif typefaces Typefaces whose letters lack serifs

serif typefaces Typefaces with small crosslines (called *serifs*) at the ends of letter strokes

subheadings Titles that are subordinate to headings, indicating subsections with a major section

type style Any modification that lends contrast or emphasis to type, including boldface, italic, underlining, color, and other highlighting and decorative styles

typeface The physical design of letters, numbers, and other text characters (*font* and *typeface* are often used interchangeably, although strictly speaking, a font is a set of characters in a given typeface)

white space Space (of any color) in a document or screen that doesn't contain any text or artwork

SUMMARY OF LEARNING OBJECTIVES

1 Discuss the value of careful revision and describe the tasks involved in evaluating your first drafts and the work of other writers. Revision is a vital step in producing effective business messages; even if the first draft conveys the necessary information, chances are it can be made tighter, clearer, and more compelling—making it more successful. Careful revision also helps you locate and correct errors that can reduce the effectiveness of messages and damage your reputation as a communicator.

When evaluating your first drafts, check the *content* (is the content accurate, relevant, complete, and well balanced between general and specific information?); the *organization* (are your points grouped and sequenced logically, with focus on the most important ideas?); and the *tone* (is the tone appropriate for the audience and the specific situation?).

2 List four techniques you can use to improve the readability of your messages. Four techniques that help improve readability are varying sentence length, keeping paragraphs short, using lists, and adding headings and subheadings. Varying sentence length helps keep your writing fresh and dynamic while giving you a chance to emphasize the most important points. Paragraphs, on the other hand, are usually best kept short to make it easier for readers to consume your information in manageable chunks. Lists are effective devices for delineating sets of items, steps in a procedure, or other collections of related information. Headings and subheadings organize your message, call attention to important information, and help readers make connections between related pieces of information.

3 Describe eight steps you can take to improve the clarity of your writing, and give four tips on making your writing more concise. To clarify your writing, (1) break up overly long sentences, (2) rewrite hedging sentences, (3) impose parallelism, (4) correct dangling modifiers, (5) reword long noun sequences, (6) replace camouflaged verbs, (7) improve sentence structure, and (8) clarify awkward references. To make messages more concise, (1) delete unnecessary words and phrases, (2) shorten overly long words and phrases, (3) eliminate redundancies, and (4) recast sentences that begin with "It is" and "There are."

4 List four principles of effective design and explain the role of major design elements in document readability. Four important principles of effective design are *consistency* (using design elements in a consistent and predictable way throughout a document); *balance* (creating a balanced effect on page or screen, whether that balance is dynamic and informal or symmetrical and formal); *restraint* (striving for visual simplicity to avoid drawing attention away from your ideas); and *detail* (making sure that details are handled correctly so that errors or design misjudgments don't detract from your message).

The major design elements for textual messages include white space, margins, typefaces, and type styles. White space provides contrast and gives readers a resting point. Margins define the space around the text and contribute to the amount of white space. Margins can affect both readability and the overall visual appeal of your messages. Typefaces influence the tone of the message and should be chosen carefully for each use to ensure maximum readability. Type styles such as boldface, italics, and underlining provide contrast or emphasis.

5 Explain the importance of proofreading and give eight tips for successful proofreading. Proofreading is essential because it is your final opportunity to verify the quality of your communication efforts and to make sure that no errors in writing, design, or production will undo all the hard work you've put in. Proofreading should be more than just a quick glance through the document. Use the techniques the pros use to make sure your documents are top quality: (1) Make multiple passes, looking for specific types of problems each time. (2) Use perceptual tricks such as reading aloud or reading backward to prevent your brain from fooling you by filling in pieces or correcting errors. (3) Double-check high-priority items such as names, dates, addresses, and financial data. (4) Give yourself some distance by putting the document aside for a few hours or even a few days if possible. (5) Stay vigilant by proofing only small sections at a time and not proofing when you are tired. (6) Stay focused on your work. (7) Review complex digital documents on paper if possible. (8) Take your time.

6 Discuss the most important issues to consider when distributing your messages. Consider cost, convenience, time, security, and privacy when choosing the method to distribute your messages. Cost isn't a major issue for most messages, although production, printing, and distribution of lengthy or complex reports can be a concern. In general, balance the cost with the importance and urgency of the message. Make sure the distribution method is convenient for your audience. For example, attaching a document to an email message might be easy for you, but that might not be the best approach for a given audience. As with cost, balance the time factor with your needs and the needs of your audience. Finally, consider security and privacy issues before distributing documents that contain sensitive or confidential information. Your company may have restrictions on the type of information that can be distributed through various media and channels.

Test Your Knowledge

To review chapter content related to each question, refer to the indicated Learning Objective.

6-1. What are the three main tasks involved in revising a business message? [LO-1]

6-2. What are your two primary responsibilities when editing or revising the work of another writer? [LO-1]

6-3. What are the relative advantages of short, medium, and long sentences? [LO-2]

6-4. What functions do headings serve? [LO-2]

6-5. What are some ways you can make a document more concise? [LO-3]

6-6. What are hedging sentences and why should they be avoided unless truly necessary? [LO-3]

6-7. What steps should you take to format content for mobile devices? [LO-4]

6-8. Why is proofreading an important part of the writing process? [LO-5]

6-9. What perceptual tricks can you use to improve your chances of spotting errors during proofreading? [LO-5]

6-10. What factors should you consider when choosing a distribution method for your messages (other than for systems where you don't have a choice)? [LO-6]

Apply Your Knowledge

To review chapter content related to each question, refer to the indicated Learning Objective.

6-11. How does careful revision reflect the "you" attitude? [LO-1]

6-12. Why should you limit the number of typefaces and type styles in most business documents? [LO-4]

6-13. Why is white space particularly critical when designing documents for mobile devices? [LO-4]

6-14. How can you demonstrate good business sense in the choices you make regarding message distribution? [LO-6]

Practice Your Skills

6-15. **Message for Analysis 6.A: Revising to Improve Readability [LO-2]**Analyze the strengths and weaknesses of this message, then revise it so that it follows the guidelines in Chapter 4 through Chapter 6:

As an organization, the North American Personal Motorsports Marketing Association has committed ourselves to helping our members—a diverse group comprising of dealers of motorcycles, all-terrain vehicles, Snowmobiles, and personal watercraft—achieve their business objectives. Consequently, our organization, which usually goes under the initials NAPMMA, has the following aims, goals, and objectives. Firstly, we endeavor to aid or assist our members in reaching their business objectives. Second, NAPMMA

communicates ("lobbying" in slang terms) with local, state, and national governmental agencies and leaders on issues of importance to our members. And lastly, we educate the motorsports public, that being current motorsports vehicle owners, and prospective owners of said vehicles, on the safe and enjoyable operation of they're vehicles.

6-16. **Message for Analysis 6.B: Designing for Readability [LO-4]** To access this message, visit **real-timeupdates.com/bct14**, select Student Assignments, then select Chapter 6, Message 6.B. Download and open the document. Using the various page, paragraph, and font formatting options available in your word processor, modify the formatting of the document so that its visual tone matches the tone of the message.

6-17. **Message for Analysis 6.C: Evaluating the Work of Another Writer [LO-1]**To access this message, visit **real-timeupdates.com/bct14**, select Student Assignments, then select Chapter 6, Message 6.C. Download and open the document. Using your knowledge of effective writing and the tips on page 157 for evaluating the work of other writers, evaluate this message. After you set Microsoft Word to track changes, make any necessary corrections. Insert comments, as needed, to explain your changes to the author.

Exercises

Each activity is labeled according to the primary skill or skills you will need to use. To review relevant chapter content, you can refer to the indicated Learning Objective. In some instances, supporting information will be found in another chapter, as indicated.

6-18. **Evaluating the Work of Other Writers [LO-1]** Find a blog post (at least three paragraphs long) on any business-related topic. Evaluate it using the 10 questions on page 157. Email your analysis to your instructor, along with a permalink (a permanent link to this specific post, rather than to the blog overall) to the blog post.

6-19. **Revising for Readability (Sentence and Paragraph Length) [LO-2]** Rewrite the following paragraph to vary the length of the sentences and to shorten the paragraph so it looks more inviting to readers:

Although major league baseball remains popular, more people are attending minor league baseball games because they can spend less on admission, snacks, and parking and still enjoy the excitement of America's pastime. Connecticut, for example, has three AA minor league teams, including the New Haven Ravens, who are affiliated with the St. Louis Cardinals; the Norwich Navigators, who are affiliated with the New York Yankees; and the New Britain Rock Cats, who are affiliated with the Minnesota Twins. These teams play in relatively small stadiums, so fans are close enough to see and hear everything, from the swing of the bat connecting with the ball to the thud of the ball landing in the outfielder's glove. Best of all, the cost of a family outing to see rising stars play in a local minor league game is just a fraction of what the family would spend to attend a major league game in a much larger, more crowded stadium.

6-20. Revising for Readability (Sentence Length) [LO-2] Break the following sentences into shorter ones by adding more periods, and revise as needed for smooth flow:

a. The next time you write something, check your average sentence length in a 100-word passage, and if your sentences average more than 16 to 20 words, see whether you can break up some of the sentences.

b. Don't do what the village blacksmith did when he instructed his apprentice as follows: "When I take the shoe out of the fire, I'll lay it on the anvil, and when I nod my head, you hit it with the hammer." The apprentice did just as he was told, and now he's the village blacksmith.

c. Unfortunately, no gadget will produce excellent writing, but using a yardstick like the Fog Index gives us some guideposts to follow for making writing easier to read because its two factors remind us to use short sentences and simple words.

d. Know the flexibility of the written word and its power to convey an idea, and know how to make your words behave so that your readers will understand.

e. Words mean different things to different people, and a word such as *block* may mean city block, butcher block, engine block, auction block, or several other things.

6-21. Editing for Conciseness (Unnecessary Words) [LO-3] Cross out unnecessary words in the following phrases:

a. Consensus of opinion
b. New innovations
c. Long period of time
d. At a price of $50
e. Still remains

6-22. Editing for Conciseness (Long Words) [LO-3] Revise the following sentences using shorter, simpler words:

a. My antiquated PC is ineffectual for solving sophisticated problems.

b. It is imperative that the pay increments be terminated before an inordinate deficit is accumulated.

c. There was unanimity among the executives that his behavior was cause for a mandatory meeting with the company's human resources director.

d. The impending liquidation of the company's assets was cause for jubilation among the company's competitors.

e. The expectations of the president for a stock dividend were accentuated by the preponderance of evidence that the company was in good financial condition.

6-23. Editing for Conciseness (Lengthy Phrases) [LO-3] Use infinitives as substitutes for the overly long phrases in these sentences:

a. For living, I require money.
b. They did not find sufficient evidence for believing in the future.
c. Bringing about the destruction of a dream is tragic.

6-24. Editing for Conciseness (Lengthy Phrases) [LO-3] Rephrase the following in fewer words:

a. In the near future
b. In the event that
c. In order that
d. For the purpose of
e. With regard to
f. It may be that
g. In very few cases
h. With reference to
i. At the present time
j. There is no doubt that

6-25. Editing for Conciseness (Lengthy Phrases) [LO-3] Revise to condense these sentences to as few words as possible:

a. We are of the conviction that writing is important.
b. In all probability, we're likely to have a price increase.
c. Our goals include making a determination about that in the near future.
d. When all is said and done at the conclusion of this experiment, I'd like to summarize the final windup.
e. After a trial period of three weeks, during which time she worked for a total of 15 full working days, we found her work was sufficiently satisfactory so that we offered her full-time work.

6-26. Editing for Conciseness (Unnecessary Modifiers) [LO-3] Remove all the unnecessary modifiers from these sentences:

a. Tremendously high pay increases were given to the extraordinarily skilled and extremely conscientious employees.
b. The union's proposals were highly inflationary, extremely demanding, and exceptionally bold.

6-27. Editing for Clarity (Hedging) [LO-3] Rewrite these sentences so that they no longer contain any hedging:

a. It would appear that someone apparently entered illegally.
b. It may be possible that sometime in the near future the situation is likely to improve.
c. Your report seems to suggest that we might be losing money.
d. I believe Yolanda apparently has somewhat greater influence over employees in the inbound marketing department.
e. It seems as if this letter of resignation means you might be leaving us.

6-28. Editing for Clarity (Indefinite Starters) [LO-3] Rewrite these sentences to eliminate the indefinite starters:

a. There are several examples here to show that Elaine can't hold a position very long.
b. It would be greatly appreciated if every employee would make a generous contribution to Draymond Cook's retirement party.
c. It has been learned in Washington today from generally reliable sources that an important announcement will be made shortly by the White House.

d. There is a rule that states that we cannot work overtime without permission.

e. It would be great if you could work late for the next three Saturdays.

6-29. Editing for Clarity (**Parallelism**) [LO-3] Revise these sentences to present the ideas in parallel form:

a. Mr. Hill is expected to lecture three days a week, to counsel two days a week, and must write for publication in his spare time.

b. She knows not only accounting, but she also reads Latin.

c. Both applicants had families, college degrees, and were in their thirties, with considerable accounting experience but few social connections.

d. This book was exciting, well written, and held my interest.

e. Don is both a hard worker and he knows the financial reporting standards.

6-30. Editing for Clarity (**Awkward References**) [LO-3] Revise the following sentences to delete the awkward references:

a. The vice president in charge of sales and the production manager are responsible for the keys to 34A and 35A, respectively.

b. The keys to 34A and 35A are in executive hands, with the former belonging to the vice president in charge of sales and the latter belonging to the production manager.

c. The keys to 34A and 35A have been given to the production manager, with the aforementioned keys being gold embossed.

d. A laser printer and an inkjet printer were delivered to John and Megan, respectively.

e. The walnut desk is more expensive than the oak desk, the former costing $300 more than the latter.

6-31. Editing for Clarity (**Dangling Modifiers**) [LO-3] Rewrite these sentences to clarify the dangling modifiers:

a. Full of trash and ripped-up newspapers, we left Dallas on a plane that apparently hadn't been cleaned in days.

b. Lying on the shelf, Ruby found the operations manual.

c. With leaking plumbing and outdated wiring, I don't think we should buy that property.

d. Being cluttered and filthy, Sandy took the whole afternoon to clean up her desk.

e. After proofreading every word, the letter was ready to be signed.

6-32. Editing for Clarity (**Noun Sequences**) [LO-3] Rewrite the following sentences to eliminate the long strings of nouns:

a. The focus of the meeting was a discussion of the bank interest rate deregulation issue.

b. Following the government task force report recommendations, we are revising our job applicant evaluation procedures.

c. The production department quality assurance program components include employee training, supplier cooperation, and computerized detection equipment.

d. The supermarket warehouse inventory reduction plan will be implemented next month.

e. The State University business school graduate placement program is one of the best in the country.

6-33. Editing for Clarity (**Sentence Structure**) [LO-3] Rearrange the following sentences to bring the subjects closer to their verbs:

a. Trudy, when she first saw the bull pawing the ground, ran.

b. It was Terri who, according to Ted, who is probably the worst gossip in the office (Tom excepted), mailed the wrong order.

c. William Oberstreet, in his book *Investment Capital Reconsidered*, writes of the mistakes that bankers through the decades have made.

d. Judy Schimmel, after passing up several sensible investment opportunities, despite the warnings of her friends and family, invested her inheritance in a jojoba plantation.

e. The president of U-Stor-It, which was on the brink of bankruptcy after the warehouse fire, the worst tragedy in the history of the company, prepared a press announcement.

6-34. Editing for Clarity (**Camouflaged Verbs**) [LO-3] Rewrite each sentence so that the verbs are no longer camouflaged:

a. Adaptation to the new rules was performed easily by the employees.

b. The assessor will make a determination of the tax due.

c. Verification of the identity of the employees must be made daily.

d. The board of directors made a recommendation that Mr. Ronson be assigned to a new division.

e. The auditing procedure on the books was performed by the vice president.

6-35. Completing: Designing for Readability; Media Skills: Blogging [LO-4], Chapter 8 Compare the home pages of Bloomberg (**www.bloomberg.com**) and MarketWatch (**www.marketwatch.com**), two websites that cover financial markets. What are your first impressions of these two sites? How do their overall designs compare in terms of information delivery and overall user experience? Choose three pieces of information that a visitor to these sites would be likely to look for, such as a current stock price, news from international markets, and commentary from market experts. Which site makes it easier to find this information? Why? Present your analysis in a post for your class blog.

6-36. Communication Ethics: Making Ethical Choices; Media Skills: Blogging [LO-3], Chapter 8 The time and energy required for careful revision can often benefit you or your company directly, such as by increasing the probability that website visitors will buy your products. But what about situations in which the quality of your writing and revision work really doesn't stand to benefit you directly? For instance, assume that you are putting a notice on your website, informing the local community about some upcoming construction to your manufacturing plant.

The work will disrupt traffic for nearly a year and generate a significant amount of noise and air pollution, but knowing the specific dates and times of various construction activities will allow people to adjust their commutes and other activities to minimize the negative impact on their daily lives. However, your company does not sell products in the local area, so the people affected by all this are not potential customers. Moreover, providing accurate information to the surrounding community and updating it as the project progresses will take time away from your other job responsibilities. Do you have an ethical obligation to keep the local community informed with accurate, up-to-date information? Why or why not?

6-37. **Proofreading [LO-5]** Proofread the following email message and revise it to correct any problems you find:

Our final company orrientation of the year will be held on Dec. 20. In preparation for this sesssion, please order 20 copies of the Policy handbook, the confidentiality agreenemt, the employee benefits Manual, please let me know if you anticipate any delays in obtaining these materials.

Expand Your Skills

Critique the Professionals

Identify a company website that in your opinion violates one or more of the principles of good design discussed on pages 164–167. Using whatever medium your instructor requests, write a brief analysis of the site (no more than one page), citing specific elements from the piece and support from the chapter.

Sharpening Your Career Skills Online

Bovée and Thill's Business Communication Web Search, at **websearch.businesscommunicationnetwork.com**, is a unique research tool designed specifically for business communication research. Use the Web Search function to find a website, video, article, podcast, or presentation that offers advice on effective proofreading. Write a brief email message to your instructor, describing the item you found and summarizing the career skills information you learned from it.

MyBCommLab

Go to **mybcommlab.com** for Auto-graded writing questions as well as the following Assisted-graded writing questions:

6-38. How does varying the length of one's sentences improve the flow and readability of business documents? [LO-2]

6-39. How do your typeface selections help determine the personality of your documents and messages? [LO-4]

Endnotes

1. Type Together website, accessed 27 March 2016, www.type-together .com; "Georgia," in "Microsoft Typography," accessed 27 March 2016, www.microsoft.com; "Women in Design: Veronika Burian," Fontshop, 9 March 2015, www.fontshop.com; Jan Middendorp, "Creative Characters: Veronika Burian," MyFonts, October 2008, www.myfonts.com.

2. Deborah Gunn, "Looking Good on Paper," *Office Pro*, March 2004, 10–11.

3. Jacci Howard Bear, "What are the Rules of Desktop Publishing?" About Tech, accessed 13 May 2016, desktoppub.about.com.

4. Kas Thomas, "The Serif Readability Myth," *blogorrhea*, 18 January 2013, asserttrue.blogspot.com; Ole Lund, "Knowledge Construction in Typography: The Case of Legibility Research and the Legibility of Sans Serif Typefaces" (PhD diss., University of Reading, October 1999).

5. Jacci Howard Bear, "Use Fewer Fonts: Desktop Publishing Rules for How Many Fonts to Use," About.com, accessed 22 August 2005, desktoppub.about.com.

6. "Mobile Message Mayhem," Verne Ordman & Associates, accessed 12 March 2014, www.businesswriting.biz.

Choosing the best medium for every business message and using it effectively are essential communication skills. Fortunately, you probably have a fair amount of experience with various digital, social, and visual media. The three chapters in this part will help you adapt that experience to the unique demands of business communication.

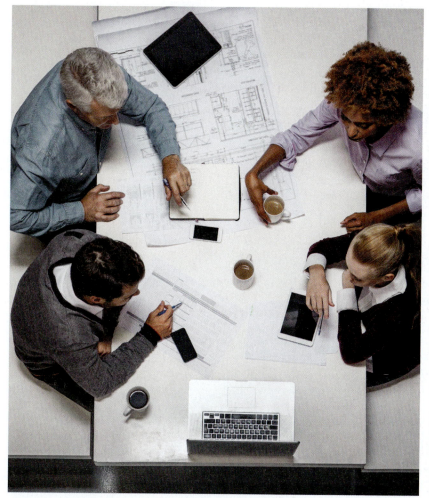

Porta Images/Getty Images

LEARNING OBJECTIVES

After studying this chapter, you will be able to

1 Identify the major digital media formats available for business messages, and list nine compositional modes used in digital media.

2 Describe the evolving role of email in business communication, and explain how to adapt the three-step writing process to email messages.

3 Identify the advantages and disadvantages of business messaging systems.

4 Explain why organizing website content is so challenging, and explain the concept of information architecture.

5 Explain how to adapt the three-step writing process to podcasting.

MyBCommLab®

⭐ **Improve Your Grade!** More than 10 million students improved their results using Pearson MyLabs. Visit **mybcommlab.com** for simulations, tutorials, and end-of-chapter problems.

COMMUNICATION CLOSE-UP AT

Slack

slack.com

If there's a business award for accidental success, Stewart Butterfield would surely be a leading contender for it. He has the unusual distinction of being the cofounder of two different video game companies that didn't succeed at their original missions but wound up spinning off secondary software features that became massive business successes on their own. The first turned into the photo-sharing web service Flickr, which was once just a feature inside an online role-playing game.

After selling Flickr to Yahoo! for a tidy sum, Butterfield cofounded another video game company. Again, the game business didn't work out, but he and his partners commercialized an instant messaging function the company had developed for internal use. That capability was expanded and became the Slack messaging system, and it is leading an upheaval in the world of business communication.

Slack offers several communication and information-management tools, but at its heart it is a workplace messaging system. Teams can set up a variety of channels to manage communication on specific topics, and individuals can configure alerts to make sure they get the messages they need without getting flooded by messages they don't (one of the banes of email). All communication is automatically archived, so it's easy for everyone on a team to find information. A key feature that Butterfield promotes with Slack is transparency, in that

Slack cofounder and CEO Stewart Butterfield guides the development of a workplace messaging system that thousands of companies are using to improve team communication.

communication threads are no longer lost or hidden in private email exchanges but out in the open for everyone on a team to see and share.

To understand the appeal of Slack, one needs to understand the love/hate relationship many business professionals have with email. Email is so ubiquitous that it's easy to forget what a revolutionary and disruptive medium it once was. In a world where internal memos could take hours to deliver and external letters could take days, nearly instantaneous email changed business communication forever, and it remains a vital communication tool.

However, email has long suffered from a serious case of too-much-of-a-good-thing. Many professionals complain of drowning in a flood of messages, with some getting dozens or hundreds of messages a day—even as they miss vital information when colleagues neglect to include them in message threads. Moreover, email is poorly suited to some of the tasks people use it for, such as project management, collaboration, information management, and other processes that require group communication and shared information access.

A variety of technologies that aim to overcome the disadvantages of email have recently entered the market, from basic instant messaging to full-featured collaboration systems. But few have caught on as quickly as Slack. Within a year of its 2013 launch, Slack had a half million daily users in 60,000 teams around the world and laid claim to being the fastest-growing business app in history. Within two years, the service had more than 2 million active users. Some describe it as more than a mere communication tool, calling it a radical way to transform how they work.

For many business communicators, Slack is clearly filling an unmet need. A majority of customers report greater productivity, more transparency, improved team culture, easier access to information, and a reduced need for meetings. On average, users say it has cut email use in their organizations almost in half, and many say it has nearly eliminated email entirely. By enabling communication and collaboration in ways that support how today's professionals want and need to work, Slack and other corporate messaging systems might finally be taming the dreaded email monster.[1]

Digital Media for Business Communication

1 **LEARNING OBJECTIVE**
Identify the major digital media formats available for business messages, and list nine compositional modes used in digital media.

The runaway success of Slack (profiled in the chapter-opening Communication Close-Up) highlights two important considerations in using digital media: choosing the best tools for the task at hand and using each tool wisely. This chapter offers advice on using tools you're likely to encounter in any profession: email, messaging, websites, and podcasting. (Digital media with a social component are covered in Chapter 8.)

DIGITAL AND SOCIAL MEDIA OPTIONS

The considerable range of digital media available for business messages continues to grow as communication technologies evolve:

Business communicators use the full range of digital media options, from conventional email and messaging to social networking tools.

- **Email.** Conventional email has long been a vital medium for business communication, although in many instances it is being replaced by other tools that provide better support for instant communication and real-time collaboration.
- **Messaging.** From basic text messaging on mobile devices to multifunction group systems such as those offered by Slack, messaging in various forms now rivals or exceeds email in many companies.
- **Web content.** Websites are one of the most important digital media types, from small-business sites with a few pages to large corporate sites with hundreds or thousands of pages.
- **Podcasting.** Businesses use podcasts to replace or supplement some conference calls, newsletters, training courses, and other communication activities.
- **Social networks.** Social networks have evolved into a major business communication technology, from well-known public networks to the private, internal networks that many companies now use.
- **Information- and content-sharing sites.** In addition to social networks, a variety of systems have been designed specifically for sharing content, including user-generated content sites, media curation sites, and community Q&A sites.
- **Wikis.** The collaborative nature of wikis—websites that can be expanded and edited by teams, user communities, or the public at large—make them a natural fit for

aggregating the knowledge of groups ranging from individual departments to the public at large.

- **Blogging and microblogging.** The ability to update content quickly and easily makes blogs and microblogs (such as Twitter) a natural medium when communicators want to get messages out in a hurry.

- **Online video.** Digital and online video have transformed what used to be a fairly specialized tool into a mainstream business communication medium.

The first four of these—email, messaging, web content, and podcasting—are covered in this chapter. Digital media with a strong social element, from social networks to microblogs, are addressed in Chapter 8. Online video, along with other visual media, is covered in Chapter 9.

Note that the lines between these media often get blurred as systems expand their capabilities or people use them in new ways. Moreover, the mobile variants of all these technologies add another layer of challenges and opportunities for business communicators. For example, the ability to scan coded labels such as barcodes or the similar *Quick Response (QR)* codes attached to printed materials, products, or store windows (or the ability to pick up radio signals from *near-field communication* tags) gives smartphone users a way to get more information—from companies themselves and from other consumers providing reviews on social websites.

Most of your business communication is likely to be via digital means, but don't overlook the benefits of printed messages. (For more on formatting printed letters and memos, see Chapter 6 and Appendix A.) Here are several situations in which you should consider using a printed message rather than digital alternatives:

- **When you want to make a formal impression.** For special messages, such as sending congratulations or condolences, the formality of printed documents usually makes them a much better choice than digital messages.

- **When you are legally required to provide information in printed form.** Business contracts and government regulations sometimes require that information be provided on paper.

- **When you want to stand out from the flood of digital messages.** If your audience's computers are overflowing with Twitter updates, email messages, and messaging notifications, sometimes a printed message can stand out enough to get noticed.

- **When you need a permanent, unchangeable, or secure record.** Letters and memos are reliable. Once printed, they can't be erased with a single keystroke or surreptitiously modified the way some digital messages can be. Printed documents also require more effort to copy and forward.

Even with the widespread use of digital media, printed memos and letters still play an important role in business communication.

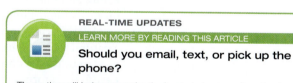

REAL-TIME UPDATES

LEARN MORE BY READING THIS ARTICLE

Should you email, text, or pick up the phone?

These tips will help you make the best choice in various business situations. Go to **real-timeupdates.com/bct14** and select Learn More in the Students section.

COMPOSITIONAL MODES FOR DIGITAL AND SOCIAL MEDIA

As you practice using various media and channels in this course, it's best to focus on the fundamentals of planning, writing, and completing messages, rather than on the specific details of any one medium or system.[2] Fortunately, the basic communication skills required usually transfer from one system to another. You can succeed with written communication in virtually all digital media by using one of nine *compositional modes*:

- **Conversations.** Messaging is a great example of a written medium that mimics spoken conversation. And just as you wouldn't read a report to someone sitting in your office, you wouldn't use conversational modes to exchange large volumes of information or to communicate with more than a few people at once.

- **Comments and critiques.** One of the most powerful aspects of social media is the opportunity for interested parties to express opinions and provide feedback, whether by leaving comments on a blog post or reviewing products on an e-commerce site. Sharing helpful tips and insightful commentary is also a great way to build your

Communicating successfully with digital media requires a wide range of writing approaches.

personal brand. To be an effective commenter, focus on short chunks of information that a broad spectrum of other site visitors will find helpful. Rants, insults, jokes, and blatant self-promotion are of little benefit to others.

- **Orientations.** The ability to help people find their way through an unfamiliar system or subject is a valuable writing skill and a talent that readers greatly appreciate. Unlike summaries (see the next item), orientations don't give away the key points in the collection of information but rather tell readers where to find those points. Writing effective orientations can be a delicate balancing act because you need to know the material well enough to guide others through it while being able to step back and view it from the inexperienced perspective of a "newbie."

- **Summaries.** At the beginning of an article or webpage, a summary functions as a miniature version of the document, giving readers all the key points while skipping over details. At the end of an article or webpage, a summary functions as a review, reminding readers of the key points they've just read. A series of key points extracted from an article or webpage can also serve as a summary.

- **Reference material.** One of the greatest benefits of the Internet is the access it can provide to vast quantities of reference materials—numerical or textual information that people typically don't read in a linear way but rather search through to find particular data points, trends, or other details. One of the challenges of writing reference material is that you can't always know how readers will want to access it. Making the information accessible via search engines is an important step. However, readers don't always know which search terms will yield the best results, so consider an orientation and organize the material in logical ways with clear headings that promote skimming.

- **Narratives.** The storytelling techniques covered in Chapter 4 can be effective in a wide variety of situations. Narratives work best when they have an intriguing beginning that ignites readers' curiosity, a middle section that moves quickly through the challenges that an individual or company faced, and an inspiring or instructive ending that gives readers information they can apply in their own lives and jobs.

- **Teasers.** Teasers intentionally withhold key pieces of information as a way to pull readers or listeners into a story or other document. Teasers are widely used in marketing and sales messages, such as a bit of copy on the outside of an envelope that promises important information on the inside. In digital media, the space limitations and URL linking capabilities of Twitter and other microblogging systems make them a natural tool for the teaser approach. Although they can certainly be effective, teasers need to be used with respect for readers' time and information needs. Be sure that the *payoff*, the information a teaser links to, is valuable and legitimate. You'll quickly lose credibility if readers think they are being tricked into clicking through to information they don't really want. (*Tweetables* are Twitter-ready bites of information extracted from a blog post or other messages. They often serve as teasers, although a series of them can make an effective summary as well.)

- **Status updates and announcements.** If you use social media frequently, much of your writing will involve status updates and announcements (see Figure 7.1). However, don't post trivial information that only you are likely to find interesting. Post only those updates that readers will find useful, and include only the information they need.

- **Tutorials.** Given the community nature of social media, the purpose of many messages is to share how-to advice. Becoming known as a reliable expert is a great way to build customer loyalty for your company while enhancing your own personal value.

As you approach a new communication task using digital media, ask yourself what kind of information audience members are likely to need, then choose the appropriate compositional mode. Of course, many of these modes are also used in written media, but over time, you may find yourself using all of them in various digital and social media contexts.

Figure 7.1   Compositional Modes: Status Updates and Announcements
Contests, such as this one featuring Fender musical equipment, are a popular message form on Facebook and other social media.

OPTIMIZING CONTENT FOR MOBILE DEVICES

Chapters 5 and 6 offer tips on writing and formatting messages for mobile devices. While keeping the limitations of the small screens of mobile devices and alternative input methods in mind, look for opportunities to take advantage of mobile-specific capabilities via apps and mobile-friendly websites. Mobile expands your options as a content creator, and it gives your audience members a wider range of engaging ways to consume your content:

- **Location-based services.** *Location-based social networking* links the virtual world of online social networking with the physical world of retail stores and other locations. As mobile web use in general continues to grow, location-based networking promises to become an important business communication medium because mobile consumers are a significant economic force—through the purchases they make directly and through their ability to influence other consumers.[3]
- **Gamification.** The addition of game-playing aspects to apps and web services, known as *gamification*, can increase audience engagement and encourage repeat use. The highlight box on page 27 has more on this intriguing business tool.
- **Augmented reality.** Superimposing data on live camera images can enrich experiences for consumers and supply useful information to business users (see Figure 7.2 on the next page). The Future of Communication box on page 213 has more on augmented reality and virtual reality.
- **Wearable technology.** From virtual-reality goggles to smartwatches to body-movement sensors, wearable technology pushes the radical connectivity of mobile to the next level. Some of these items work as auxiliary screens and controls for other mobile devices, but others are meant for independent use. One of the key promises of wearable technology is simplifying and enhancing everyday tasks for consumers and employees alike.[4]
- **Mobile blogging.** Smartphones and tablets are ideal for mobile blogs, sometimes known as *moblogs*. The mobile capability is great for workers whose jobs keep them

Mobile offers a range of exciting ways to enhance the audience experience.

Panasonic Corporation of North America

Figure 7.2 **Augmented Reality**
The *Maintenance Augmented Reality* feature in Panasonic's computer-integrated manufacturing software is a great example of using augmented reality for business communication. By simply pointing a mobile device at a machine, technicians can get detailed information needed for maintenance and repair.

on the move and for special-event coverage such as live-blogging trade shows and industry conventions.

- **Mobile podcasting.** Similarly, smartphone-based podcasting tools make it easy to record audio on the go and post finished podcasts to your blog or website.
- **Cloud-based services.** Mobile communication is ideal for cloud-based services—digital services that rely on resources stored in the cloud.

Email

2 LEARNING OBJECTIVE
Describe the evolving role of email in business communication, and explain how to adapt the three-step writing process to email messages.

Overuse is one of the major complaints about email.

Email has been a primary medium for many companies for several decades, and in the beginning it offered a huge advantage in speed and efficiency over the media it frequently replaced (printed and faxed messages). Over the years, email began to be used for many communication tasks simply because it was the only widely available digital medium for written messages and millions of users were comfortable with it. However, as Slack's growth illustrates, other tools are taking over specific tasks for which they are better suited.

In addition to the widespread availability of better alternatives for many communication purposes, the indiscriminate use of email has lowered its appeal in the eyes of many professionals. In a sense, email is too easy to use—it's too easy to send low-value messages to multiple recipients and to trigger long message chains that become impossible to follow as people chime in along the way. And because it is such a general-purpose tool, email gets used for everything from critically important messages to automated updates and confirmations with little or no value.

Email also suffers from an enormous problem with *spam* (unsolicited bulk email) and security risks such as *computer viruses* and *phishing* (fraudulent messages that prompt unwary users to divulge sensitivity information or grant access to protected networks). Spam accounts for roughly half of all email and requires great effort to keep it from flooding users' inboxes.[5] Most systems use spam and threat filters, but these filters are never 100 percent accurate and can also reject messages that are legitimate.

In spite of its shortcomings, email remains a major business communication medium.

Even with these drawbacks, email still has compelling advantages that will keep it in steady use in many companies. First, email is universal. Anybody with an email address can reach anybody else with an email address, no matter which systems the senders and receivers are on. Second, email is still the best medium for many private, short- to medium-length messages, particularly when the exchange is limited to two people. Unlike with microblogs or messaging, for instance, midsize messages are easy to compose and easy to read on email. Third, email's noninstantaneous nature is an advantage when used properly. Email lets senders compose substantial messages in private and on their own schedule, and it lets recipients read those messages at their leisure.

PLANNING EMAIL MESSAGES

The solution to email overload starts in the planning step, by making sure every message has a valid, business-related purpose. Also, be aware that many companies now have formal email policies that specify how employees can use email, including restrictions against using the company email service for personal messages, sending confidential information, or sending material that might be deemed objectionable. In addition, many employers now monitor email, either automatically with software programmed to look for sensitive content or manually via security staff actually reading selected email messages. Regardless of formal policies, every email user has a responsibility to avoid actions that could cause trouble, from downloading virus-infected software to sending inappropriate photographs.

Even with fairly short messages, spend a moment or two on the message planning tasks described in Chapter 4: analyzing the situation, gathering necessary information for your readers, and organizing your message. You'll save time in the long run because you will craft a more effective message on the first attempt. Your readers will get the information they need and won't have to generate follow-up messages asking for clarification or additional information.

> Cut down on message overload by making sure every email message you send has a valid business purpose.

WRITING EMAIL MESSAGES

Business email is a more formal medium than you are probably accustomed to with email for personal communication (see Figure 7.3). The expectations of writing quality for business email are higher than for personal email, and the consequences of bad writing or poor

> Business email messages are more formal than the email messages you send to family and friends.

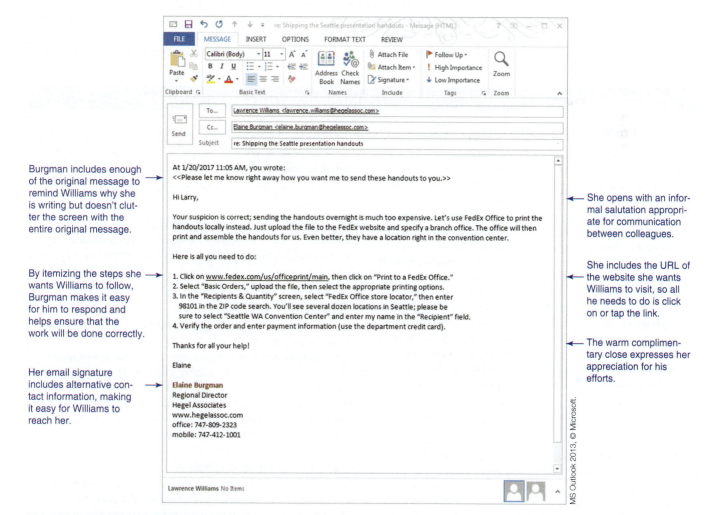

Burgman includes enough of the original message to remind Williams why she is writing but doesn't clutter the screen with the entire original message.

By itemizing the steps she wants Williams to follow, Burgman makes it easy for him to respond and helps ensure that the work will be done correctly.

Her email signature includes alternative contact information, making it easy for Williams to reach her.

She opens with an informal salutation appropriate for communication between colleagues.

She includes the URL of the website she wants Williams to visit, so all he needs to do is click on or tap the link.

The warm complimentary close expresses her appreciation for his efforts.

MS Outlook 2013, © Microsoft.

Figure 7.3   Email for Business Communication
In this response to an email query from a colleague, Elaine Burgman takes advantage of her email system's features to create an efficient and effective message.

judgment can be much more serious. For example, email messages and other digital documents have the same legal weight as printed documents, and they are often used as evidence in lawsuits and criminal investigations.[6]

The subject line is often the most important part of an email message because it can determine whether the message gets read.

The email subject line might seem like a small detail, but it is actually one of the most important parts of an email message because it helps recipients decide which messages to read and when to read them. To capture your audience's attention, make your subject lines informative and compelling. Go beyond simply describing or classifying your message; use the opportunity to build interest with keywords, quotations, directions, or questions.[7] For example, "July sales results" accurately describes the content of the message, but "July sales results: good news and bad news" is more intriguing. Readers will want to know why some news is good and some is bad.

In addition, many email programs display the first few words or lines of incoming messages, even before the recipient opens them. As noted by the social media public relations expert Steve Rubel, you can "tweetify" the opening lines of your email messages to make them stand out. In other words, choose the first few words carefully to grab your reader's attention.[8] Think of the first sentence as an extension of your subject line.

Attitudes about emoticons in business communication are changing; you'll have to use your best judgment in every case.

As a lean medium, email can present challenges when you need to express emotional nuances, whether positive or negative. For years, users of email (as well as messaging and text messaging) have used a variety of *emoticons* to express emotions in casual communication. For example, to express sympathy as a way to take some of the sting out of negative news, one might use a "frowny face," either the :(character string or a graphical emoticon such as ☺ or one of the colorful and sometimes animated characters available in some systems.

In past years, the use of emoticons was widely regarded as unprofessional and therefore advised against in business communication. Recently, though, an increasing number of professionals seem to be using them, particularly for communication with close colleagues, even as other professionals continue to view them as evidence of lazy or immature

---

DIGITAL + SOCIAL + MOBILE: TODAY'S COMMUNICATION ENVIRONMENT

Will Emoticons Give Your Career a Frowny Face?

Your project team has just been reprimanded by the boss for missing a deadline. Your colleagues left the meeting grumbling about being criticized in public after working nights and weekends, and you fear that morale will slip.

You could craft an inspirational message to soothe the bruised egos and get the team's energy turned around in a positive direction. However, writing such a message could be risky because world-weary teammates might just brush it off as "happytalk" and resent you for trying to be a cheerleader.

Alternatively, you could suggest that your colleagues lighten up and stay focused on the ultimate goal of the project. However, you already know that telling grumpy people to cheer up is a surefire way to make most of them even grumpier.

Instead, you opt for a quick bit of gentle sarcasm, designed to help release the negative emotions in a collegial way. When you get back to your desk, you write the following instant message:

Well, let's pick up the pieces of our shattered lives and move on ;-)

The over-the-top phrasing is a subtle way to remind everyone that the criticism wasn't all *that* traumatic, and that that winking emoticon tells everyone to lighten up without actually saying so. The apparent sarcasm connects with people who are marinating in their negative emotions, but it's really a pep talk disguised as sarcasm.

Then you worry that the emoticon will seem unprofessional, so you replace it with a simple period:

Well, let's pick up the pieces of our shattered lives and move on.

Oops. That one minor change to make the message more professional turned it into a statement of resigned sadness. You search your keyboard for any acceptable symbol that might help:

Well, let's pick up the pieces of our shattered lives and move on!

Great, now you've managed to sound bitter and demanding at the same time.

Given the difficulty of communicating emotional nuance in lean media such as messaging and email, are emoticons really all that bad? The answer depends on the situation, your relationship with your audience, and the company culture. Until emoticons become more widely accepted in business communication, it's wise to err on the side of caution.

CAREER APPLICATIONS

1. As a manager, what reaction would you have to job applicants who use emoticons in their email messages?
2. Are emoticons just a generational difference in perspective, or is there more to the issue? Explain your answer.

writing.[9] In the face of these conflicting perspectives, the best advice is to use caution. Avoid emoticons for all types of external communication and for formal internal communication, and avoid those bright yellow graphical emoticons (and particularly animated emoticons) in all business communication.

COMPLETING EMAIL MESSAGES

Particularly for important messages, taking a few moments to revise and proofread might save you hours of headaches and damage control. The more important the message, the more carefully you need to proofread. Also, favor simplicity when it comes to producing your email messages. A clean, easily readable font, in black on a white background, is sufficient for nearly all email messages. Take advantage of your email system's ability to include an **email signature**, a small file that automatically includes such items as your full name, title, company, and contact information at the end of your messages.

When you're ready to distribute your message, pause to verify what you're doing before you click "Send." Make sure you've included everyone necessary—and no one else. Don't click "Reply All" when you mean to select "Reply." The difference could be embarrassing or even career threatening. Don't include people in the cc (courtesy copy or "carbon copy," historically) or bcc (blind courtesy copy) fields unless you know how these features work. (Everyone who receives the message can see who is on the cc line but not who is on the bcc line.) Also, don't set the message priority to "high" or "urgent" unless your message is truly urgent. And if you intend to include an attachment, be sure that it is indeed attached.

To review the tips and techniques for successful email, see Table 7.1 and "Checklist: Creating Effective Email Messages," or select Chapter 7 at **real-timeupdates.com/bct14**.

> Think twice before hitting "Send." A simple mistake in your content or distribution can cause major headaches.

TABLE 7.1 Tips for Effective Email Messages

Tip	Why It's Important
When you request information or action, make it clear what you're asking for, why it's important, and how soon you need it; don't make your reader write back for details.	People will be tempted to ignore your messages if they're not clear about what you want or how soon you want it.
When responding to a request, either paraphrase the request or include enough of the original message to remind the reader what you're replying to.	Some businesspeople get hundreds of email messages a day and may need to be reminded what your specific response is about.
If possible, avoid sending long, complex messages via email.	Long messages are easier to read as attached reports or web content.
Adjust the level of formality to the message and the audience.	Overly formal messages to colleagues can be perceived as stuffy and distant; overly informal messages to customers or top executives can be perceived as disrespectful.
Activate a signature file, which automatically pastes your contact information into every message you create.	A signature saves you the trouble of retyping vital information and ensures that recipients know how to reach you through other means.
Don't let unread messages pile up in your inbox.	You'll miss important information and create the impression that you're ignoring other people.
Never type in all caps.	ALL CAPS ARE INTERPRETED AS SCREAMING.
Don't overformat your messages with background colors, multicolored type, unusual fonts, and so on.	Such messages can be difficult and annoying to read on screen.
Remember that messages can be forwarded anywhere and saved forever.	Don't let a moment of anger or poor judgment haunt you for the rest of your career.
Use the "return receipt requested" feature only for the most critical messages.	This feature triggers a message back to you whenever someone receives or opens your message; many consider this an invasion of privacy.
Make sure your computer has up-to-date virus protection.	One of the worst breaches of "netiquette" is infecting other computers because you haven't bothered to protect your own system.
Pay attention to grammar, spelling, and capitalization.	Some people don't think email needs formal rules, but careless messages make you look unprofessional and can annoy readers.
Use acronyms sparingly.	Shorthand such as IMHO (in my humble opinion) and LOL (laughing out loud) can be useful in informal correspondence with colleagues, but avoid using them in more formal messages.

CHECKLIST ✔ Creating Effective Email Messages

A. Planning email messages
- Make sure every email message you send is necessary.
- Don't cc or bcc anyone who doesn't really need to see the message.
- Follow company email policy; understand the restrictions your company places on email usage.
- Practice good email hygiene by not opening suspicious messages, keeping virus protection up to date, and following other company guidelines.
- Follow the chain of command.

B. Writing email messages
- Remember that business email is more formal than personal email.
- Recognize that email messages carry the same legal weight as other business documents.
- Pay attention to the quality of your writing and use correct grammar, spelling, and punctuation.
- Make your subject lines informative by clearly identifying the purpose of your message.
- Make your subject lines compelling by wording them in a way that intrigues your audiences.
- Use the first few words of the email body to catch the reader's attention.

C. Completing email messages
- Revise and proofread carefully to avoid embarrassing mistakes.
- Keep the layout of your messages simple and clean, particularly for mobile recipients.
- Use an email signature file to give recipients your contact information.
- Double-check your recipient list before sending.
- Don't mark messages as "urgent" unless they truly are urgent.

Messaging

3 LEARNING OBJECTIVE
Identify the advantages and disadvantages of business messaging systems.

The Slack profile at the beginning of the chapter highlights the rapid growth of **messaging**, a category of communication tools whose core focus is conversational exchanges. In contrast to email, which is a digital alternative to printed memos and letters, messaging is best thought of as a digital alternative to live voice conversation. Messaging technologies include text messaging on mobile phones, conventional instant messaging (IM) systems, online chat systems (such as those used by many companies for customer support), and workplace messaging systems such as Slack and its competitors.

A variety of digital messaging solutions are now available, from text messaging on mobile devices to private group messaging systems.

Messaging is a diverse category, and various systems offer a range of capabilities. They range from semipublic systems such as standard text messaging on mobile phones, in which anyone with your phone number can send you a message, to private systems that are closed to anyone other than invited members. Slack and other enterprise messaging systems are catching on with many businesses because they do a better job of enabling and capturing the communication flows that teams, departments, and other groups need in order to work together successfully. Messaging is also a function available on many collaboration platforms and social networks. And messaging isn't strictly limited to human-to-human exchanges. As the Future of Communication box on page 278 in Chapter 10 points out, automated messaging bots can participate in simple conversational exchanges and assist users with various business tasks.

MOBILE APP
Telegram is a free messaging app that offers one-on-one and group chat capabilities.

ADVANTAGES AND DISADVANTAGES OF MESSAGING

Messaging offers several key benefits over email:
- The ability to mimic live conversation
- Improved security
- Instantaneous delivery

Messaging offers several key benefits over email for specific communication purposes, so it's not surprising that it has been steadily replacing email in many applications in recent years. First, because it mimics voice conversation to a high degree, it is better suited to back-and-forth exchanges than email and other digital formats. If you've ever tried to carry on a conversation via email or Facebook comments, you know how agonizingly slow it can be to wait for the other person to respond. Second, with closed systems such as Slack, administrators can choose who is allowed to participate, which means they can block out all outside distractions and threats.[10] Unlike email, which has no centralized control mechanism on the Internet, these private messaging systems spare users from many of the overload problems and security threats that plague mail. Third, the instantaneous nature of messaging makes it the best choice when senders want messages to be seen and acted on immediately. (Email systems can be set up with alerts to tell receivers about incoming messages, but the email messages still need to be opened before they can be read.)

Messaging does have several potential drawbacks. First, for real-time conversational exchange, users of all systems are at the mercy of other users' typing speed and accuracy, which can make messaging annoyingly slow in some cases. Second, messaging systems vary widely in their levels of security and privacy, and public IM systems aren't as secure as private, enterprise-level systems. But even closed messaging systems such as Slack are at risk from security attacks. Third, like email, messaging is a lean medium with little opportunity to convey nonverbal signals, which increases the chances of misinterpretation.[11]

> **REAL-TIME UPDATES**
> **LEARN MORE BY READING THIS ARTICLE**
>
> **The security worries behind the surge in business messaging**
>
> Find out why mobile messaging apps can be security risks. Go to **real-timeupdates.com/bct14** and select Learn More in the Students section.

GUIDELINES FOR SUCCESSFUL MESSAGING

Although messages are often conceived, written, and sent within a matter of seconds, you can still apply key principles of the three-step process:

- **Planning instant messages.** View every exchange as a conversation; while you may not deliberately plan every individual statement you make or question you pose, take a moment to plan the overall exchange. If you're requesting something, think through exactly what you need and the most effective way to ask for it. If someone is asking you for something, consider his or her needs and your ability to meet them before you respond. And although you rarely need to organize instant messages in the sense of creating an outline, try to deliver information in a coherent, complete way that minimizes the number of individual messages required.

- **Writing instant messages.** As with email, the appropriate writing style for business messaging is more formal than the style you may be accustomed to with personal IM or text messaging. You should generally avoid acronyms (such as *FWIW* for "for what it's worth" or *HTH* for "hope that helps") except when communicating with close colleagues. In the exchange in Figure 7.4, notice how the participants communicate quickly and rather informally but still maintain good etiquette and a professional tone. This style is even more important if you or your staff use messaging to communicate with customers and other outside audiences.

- **Completing instant messages.** One of the biggest attractions of messaging is that the completing step is so easy. You don't have to produce the message in the usual sense, and distribution is as simple as hitting "Enter" or clicking a "Send" button. However, don't skip over the revising and proofreading tasks. Quickly scan each message before

Messaging is vulnerable to other people's typing skills, systems are vulnerable to security attacks (although generally less vulnerable than email), and it is a lean medium with potential for miscommunication.

Although you don't plan individual instant messages in the usual way, view important messaging exchanges as conversations with specific goals.

Figure 7.4   **Instant Messaging for Business Communication**
Instant messaging is widely used in business, but in most cases you should not use the same informal style of communication you probably use for messaging with your friends and family.

you send it, to make sure you don't have any missing or misspelled words and that your message is clear and complete. Keep in mind that many corporate messaging systems store every message, and systems such as Slack make them easily searchable, too, so even brief messages that you send in a hurry become part of a permanent record.

Regardless of the system you're using, you can make messaging more efficient and effective by following these tips:[12]

Successful messaging starts with being thoughtful and courteous.

- **Be thoughtful and courteous.** People can be overloaded by messages just as easily as they can by emails and social media updates, so don't waste time with chatter. When you want to start an exchange, ask the other person if he or she is free to chat, just as you would knock on someone's office door and ask if this is a good time to talk. Introduce yourself if you're messaging someone in your company for the first time.
- **Make yourself unavailable when you need to focus on other work.** You can reset your availability when a messaging conversation or meeting is scheduled.
- **If you're not on a secure system, don't send confidential information.** Your company's security policies may prohibit certain types of communication on its messaging system.
- **Be extremely careful about sending personal messages.** They clutter communication channels meant for business, and they can embarrass recipients if they pop up at awkward moments.
- **Don't use messaging for impromptu meetings if you can't verify that everyone concerned is available.** You risk leaving important contributors out of the loop otherwise.
- **Don't use messaging for lengthy, complex messages.** Email and other formats are better for those.
- **Try to avoid carrying on multiple conversations at once.** This minimizes the chance of sending messages to the wrong people or making one person wait while you tend to another conversation.
- **Follow all security guidelines.** These are designed to keep your company's information and systems safe from attack.

To review the advice for effective messaging in the workplace, see "Checklist: Using Messaging Productively" or select Chapter 7 at **real-timeupdates.com/bct14**.

CHECKLIST ✔ Using Messaging Productively

- Pay attention to security and privacy issues and be sure to follow all company guidelines.
- Treat messaging as a professional communication medium, not an informal, personal tool; avoid using messaging slang with all but close colleagues.
- Maintain good etiquette, even during simple exchanges.
- Protect your own productivity by making yourself unavailable when you need to focus.
- In most instances, don't use messaging for complex or personal messages.

Website Content

4 LEARNING OBJECTIVE Explain why organizing website content is so challenging, and explain the concept of information architecture.

You probably won't develop web content as often as you use email, social networks, and other media, but most companies have at least a basic website, and you might be involved in planning or expanding on it. Most of what you're learning about using other digital media is relevant to website content as well, although the unique nature of websites presents some special challenges. (The information here applies to conventional web content. Blogs and wikis are covered in Chapter 8.)

ORGANIZING WEBSITE CONTENT

The versatility of websites can be both a blessing and a curse. It's a blessing because a single web presence can serve multiple purposes for multiple audiences. For example, a company website can have sections for potential employees, investors, future customers,

THE FUTURE OF COMMUNICATION

Telepathic Communication

Mental telepathy—sending and receiving messages purely through the power of the mind—has long been a staple of science fiction and the province of psychics. However, some rudimentary experiments in technology-enabled telepathy show at least a hint of promise that telepathy could add an intriguing element to business communication in the future.

Using existing medical technologies for sensing and stimulating brain activity, scientists at the University of Washington demonstrated a simple video game in which one user's thoughts controlled a second user's physical motions. When the first user saw something on his screen and made a decision about how to react (without actually moving his hand), that brain activity was detected and transmitted to a second user. Using essentially the reverse technology, the decision the first user made would stimulate the brain of the second user and cause him to move his hand to implement the decision via his game controller. In a separate test, an international team of researchers showed it was possible to send simple verbal messages using a similar concept of encoding and decoding.

If the technology has practical applications, it is years away from being ready for the market. The potential is mindboggling to consider, though. Imagine just thinking up a message and having it appear on a colleague's mobile screen or, better yet, directly in his or her mind. Facebook CEO Mark Zuckerberg has speculated on this very possibility.

Even if it never achieves mainstream use, technological telepathy could be a boon for people with sensory or motor issues that prevent them from using existing modes of sending and receiving messages. They could put the full power of their creative and analytical minds directly to work without being stymied by layers of input/output technology.

WHAT'S YOUR PREDICTION?

Look into the current research on technology-enabled telepathy. Is it getting close to practical application? Aside from the technological hurdles, what other hurdlers will need to be overcome to make this a practical tool for communication?

Sources: Caitlin Dewey, "Mark Zuckerberg Says the Future of Communication Is Telepathy. Here's How That Would Actually Work," *Washington Post*, 1 July 2015, www.washingtonpost.com; University of Washington Neural Systems Laboratory, "Direct Brain-to-Brain Communication in Humans: A Pilot Study," 12 August 2013, neural.cs.washington.edu; Corinne Iozzio, "Scientists Prove That Telepathic Communication Is Within Reach," *Smithsonian*, 2 October 2014, smithsonianmag.com.

---

current customers, business partners, the media, and members of the local community. Anyone who wants to learn more about the company can visit the website and find what he or she needs.

That versatility can also be curse, however, because it makes websites more difficult to plan and organize than virtually any other type of communication. Each of the target audiences has unique information needs and possibly little interest in the other material that might be on the site. Visitors also enter the site at different points. Some will type in the top-level URL, some will link through to lower-level pages from other websites (a product review in a blog, for example), and many will land on specific pages after using a search engine.

Because the web is a multidimensional medium, readers move around in any order they please; there often is no beginning, middle, or end. When organizing a website, you need to anticipate the various paths your readers will want to follow and make sure you provide the right hyperlinks in the right places to help readers explore successfully. Professional website designers use the term **information architecture** to describe the content structure, labeling, and navigational flow of all the parts of a website.

In a sense, the information architecture is a three-dimensional outline of the site, showing (1) the vertical hierarchy of pages from the homepage down to the lower level, (2) the horizontal division of pages across the various sections of the site, and (3) the links that tie all these pages together, both internally (between various pages on the site) and externally (between the site and other websites).

On simpler sites with few content categories, the information architecture is fairly straightforward. A recent trend toward *one-page websites*, in which all the content is presented on a single, scrolling page, represents the ultimate in website simplicity. These sites can be particularly good

The versatility of websites can make them a challenge to organize because different visitors want different types of information.

Thinking through the information architecture of a website is essential to creating a rewarding experience for all visitors.

REAL-TIME UPDATES

LEARN MORE BY VISITING THIS WEBSITE

Examples of effective one-page web design

One Page Love has a large gallery of single-page web designs. Go to **real-timeupdates.com/bct14** and select Learn More in the Students section.

for mobile devices because navigating them requires nothing more than simple scrolling action by the user. Companies also use one-page designs for individual sections of a larger website.

However, on large corporate or organizational websites (such as your college or university's website), the architecture can be extremely complex, and it is the information architect's job to make each visitor's experience as simple as possible.

To organize a site effectively, follow these tips:[13]

Start developing the information architecture by brainstorming how all your potential visitors will want to use the site.

- Brainstorm all the likely usage scenarios—who will visit the site, where will they be coming from, what will they be looking for, and what terms will they use to identify the information they need?
- Identify all the likely entry points to the site and the target information for each visitor segment.
- Create a map or other visual tool (web designers refer to these as *wireframes*) that shows all the pathways between entry points and target information, then organize the content and links in the simplest, most direct way possible.
- Make sure visitors can always find their way back to the top level of the site, even if a search engine link plunked them onto a page deep within the site.
- Give visitors options for finding what they want (see Figure 7.5). Some will want to search by key terms, for example, whereas others will prefer to follow clearly defined paths that drill down into more specific information (such as Products ▶ Consumer Products ▶ Tools ▶ Handheld Power Tools, for example).

Figure 7.5   Reader-Friendly Web Design
This page from Zappos's website shows how to organize content in ways that help readers find desired information quickly. The numbered list on the left side serves as both a high-level overview and a clickable table of contents, and selecting any item displays a one-sentence summary and a more detailed description. Readers can quickly explore all 10 values without bouncing around from page to page.

- Be consistent with labels and link behaviors, and use commonly accepted terminology. For example, web visitors now expect information about a company to be on a page titled "About Us."

Think of your website as an information-delivery machine that visitors must learn how to operate in order to use efficiently. By making your machine as easy to use as possible, you'll help visitors find what they want quickly and encourage them to come back for more.

DRAFTING WEBSITE CONTENT

Everything you know about effective writing applies to web content, but keep these extra points in mind as well (see Figure 7.6):

- Take special care to build trust with your intended audiences, as careful readers can be skeptical of online content. Make sure your content is accurate, current, complete, and authoritative.
- Wherever you can, use the *inverted pyramid* style, in which you briefly cover the most important information first and then gradually reveal successive layers of detail—letting readers choose to see those additional layers if they want to.
- Help readers absorb information by breaking it into small, self-contained, easily readable chunks that are linked together logically. Many readers don't have the patience to read lengthy pages online.
- Present your information in a concise, skimmable format. Effective websites use a variety of means to help readers skim pages quickly, including lists, careful use of

With the inverted pyramid style, summarize the key points at the beginning of a webpage, then move on to provide details.

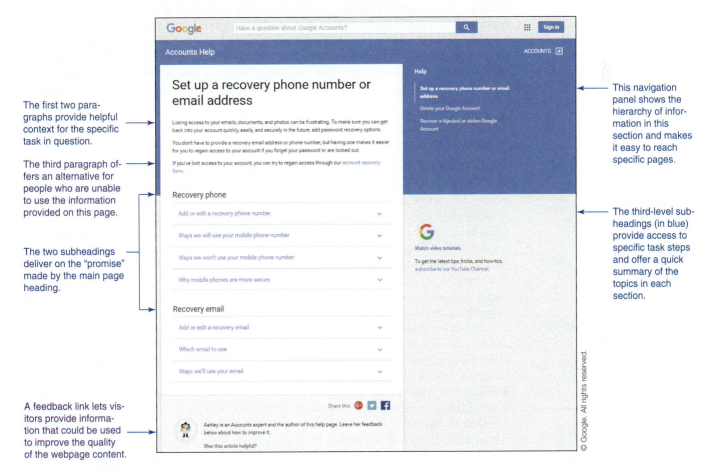

The first two paragraphs provide helpful context for the specific task in question.

The third paragraph offers an alternative for people who are unable to use the information provided on this page.

The two subheadings deliver on the "promise" made by the main page heading.

A feedback link lets visitors provide information that could be used to improve the quality of the webpage content.

This navigation panel shows the hierarchy of information in this section and makes it easy to reach specific pages.

The third-level subheadings (in blue) provide access to specific task steps and offer a quick summary of the topics in each section.

Figure 7.6 Writing for the Web
This page from the Google Help feature for Gmail demonstrates several important points about effective web writing.

color and boldface, informative headings, and helpful summaries that give readers a choice of learning more if they want to.

- Use direct and concise link names that serve for both site navigation and content skimming. Above all else, clearly identify where a link will take readers. Don't use cute wordplay that obscures the content, and don't force readers to click through in order to figure out where they're going.
- As much as possible, adapt your content for a global audience. Translating content is expensive, however, so some companies compromise by *localizing* the homepage while keeping the deeper, more detailed content in its original language.

Podcasting

Podcasting is the process of recording audio or video files and distributing them online. Podcasting combines the media richness of voice or visual communication with the convenience of portability. Audiences can listen to or watch podcasts on a blog or website, or they can download them to phones or portable music players to consume on the go. Particularly with audio podcasts, the hands-off, eyes-off aspect makes them great for listening while driving or exercising.

UNDERSTANDING THE BUSINESS APPLICATIONS OF PODCASTING

Podcasting can be used to deliver a wide range of audio and video messages.

Podcasting is a good choice to replace existing audio and video messages, such as one-way teleconferences in which a speaker provides information without expecting to engage in conversation with the listeners. Training is another good use of podcasting; you may have already taken a college course via podcasts. Marketing departments can replace expensive printed brochures with video podcasts that demonstrate new products in action. Sales representatives who travel to meet with potential customers can listen to audio podcasts or view video podcasts to get the latest information on their companies' products. Human resources departments can offer video tours of their companies to entice new recruits. Podcasts are also a useful feature on blogs to let audiences listen to or watch recordings of their favorite bloggers.

ADAPTING THE THREE-STEP PROCESS FOR SUCCESSFUL PODCASTING

The three-step process adapts quite well to podcasting.

Steering devices such as transitions, previews, and reviews are vital in podcasts.

Plan your podcast content carefully; editing is more difficult with podcasts than with textual messages.

Although it might not seem obvious at first, the three-step writing process adapts quite nicely to podcasting. First, focus the planning step on analyzing the situation, gathering the information you'll need, and organizing your material. One vital planning step depends on whether you intend to create podcasts for limited use and distribution (such as a weekly audio update to your virtual team) or a **podcasting channel** with regular recordings on a consistent theme, designed for a wider public audience. If you intend to create a podcasting channel, be sure to think through the range of topics you want to address over time to verify that you have a sustainable purpose.[14] If you bounce from one theme to another, you risk losing your audience.[15] Maintaining a consistent schedule is also important; listeners will stop paying attention if they can't count on regular updates.[16]

As you organize the content for a podcast, pay close attention to previews, transitions, and reviews. These steering devices are especially vital in audio recordings because audio lacks the headings and other elements that audiences rely on in print media. Moreover, scanning back and forth to find specific parts of an audio or video message is much more difficult than with textual messages, so you need to do everything possible to make sure your audience successfully receives and interprets your message on the first try.

One of the attractions of podcasting is the conversational, person-to-person feel of the recordings, so unless you need to capture exact wording, speaking from an outline and notes rather than a prepared script is often the best choice. However, no one wants to listen to rambling podcasts that take several minutes to get to the topic or struggle to make a point, so don't try to make up your content on the fly. Effective podcasts, like effective stories, have a clear beginning, middle, and end.

For basic podcasts, your computer and perhaps even your smartphone might have the hardware you already need, and you can download free recording software.

The completing step is where podcasting differs most dramatically from written communication, for the obvious reason that you are recording and distributing audio or video files. Particularly for more formal podcasts, start by revising your script or thinking through your speaking notes before you begin to record. The closer you can get to recording your podcasts in one take, the more productive you'll be.

Most personal computers, smartphones (see Figure 7.7), and other devices now have basic audio recording capability, including built-in microphones, and free editing software such as Audacity is available online. If you require higher production quality or greater flexibility, you'll need additional pieces of hardware and software, such as an audio processor (to filter out extraneous noise and otherwise improve the audio signal), a mixer (to combine multiple audio or video signals), a better microphone, more sophisticated recording and editing software, and perhaps some physical changes in your recording location to improve the acoustics.

Podcasts can be distributed in several ways, including through media stores such as iTunes, by dedicated podcast hosting services, or on a blog with content that supports the podcast channel.

For a quick review of the key points of business podcasting, see "Checklist: Planning and Producing Business Podcasts." For more news on podcasting, visit **real-timeupdates .com/bct14** and select Chapter 7.

Courtesy of bossjock studio, www.bossjockstudio.com.

Figure 7.7   Mobile Podcasting
Mobile podcasting apps make it easy to record podcasts on location.

CHECKLIST ✔ **Planning and Producing Business Podcasts**

- Consider podcasting whenever you have the opportunity to replace existing audio or video messages.
- If you plan a podcast channel with a regular stream of new content, make sure you've identified a theme or purpose that is rich enough to sustain your effort.
- Pay close attention to previews, transitions, and reviews to help prevent your audience from getting lost.

- Decide whether you want to improvise or speak from a written script.
- If you improvise, do enough planning and organization to avoid floundering and rambling in search of a point.
- Remember that editing is much more difficult to do with audio or video than with textual media, so plan your content and recording carefully.

COMMUNICATION CHALLENGES AT Slack

You work as a product manager in Slack's San Francisco offices. In this role you lead a cross-functional team responsible for defining new features for the Slack platform and working with professionals in engineering, marketing, sales, and finance to bring these new capabilities to market. These people are geographically dispersed, so much of your communication takes place via written team messaging, not in-person or online meetings. Apply what you've learned about messaging to address these two challenges.

INDIVIDUAL CHALLENGE: Software companies usually keep wish lists of new features, combining requests from customers, ideas submitted by insiders, and capabilities that are part of a long-term product plan. Choosing which of these ideas to implement for a given software update is no simple task and often requires trade-offs among time, cost, market demand, competitive moves, staffing, and other variables. Earlier this week, someone from the sales department said customers are clamoring for a particular feature, but the engineers responded that it will take too long to implement for the next scheduled software update, so they proposed an interim capability that they acknowledge is a good but not truly great solution. The marketing people then chimed in with the concern that promoting a less-than-ideal feature set could dampen the product's momentum in the marketplace. After this spirited discussion had been going on

for several days, someone on the team from accounting wrote, quite bluntly, that it was time to stop all this chatter and make a decision already. He said he was under pressure to update the engineering and marketing budgets, and he couldn't do his work if everyone else on the team was "wandering around in circles" without making a decision.

In your role as the leader of this team, write a brief response (no more than one paragraph). Be sure to consider the need to convey whatever information you intend to share and the need to smooth out the inevitable tension the accountant's message has produced. Make up whatever information you need while imagining yourself in the role of a product manager.

TEAM CHALLENGE: With a team assigned by your instructor, discuss the scenario described in the individual challenge above and identify several other business scenarios in which important questions need to be batted around by various members of a team before they can reach a decision. As with many decision-making challenges, there is tension between needing to make a decision and making sure you've collected and analyzed all the information you need in order to make the best possible decision. Brainstorm a set of guidelines that teams in any company could use to handle these decision-making challenges. Produce a brief document that could be posted on a collaboration platform such as Slack.

Quick Learning Guide

KEY TERMS

email signature A small file that automatically includes such items as your full name, title, company, and contact information at the end of your messages

information architecture Plan or map of the content structure, labeling, and navigational flow of all the parts of a website

messaging Category of communication system in which users' messages appear on each other's screens instantly, without the need to be opened individually, as with email; includes phone-based text messaging, conventional instant messaging, and workplace messaging

podcasting Process of recording audio or video files and distributing them online

podcasting channel Series of regular recordings on a consistent theme

SUMMARY OF LEARNING OBJECTIVES

1 Identify the major digital media formats available for business messages, and list nine compositional modes used in digital media. Major digital media for business messages include email, messaging, web content, podcasting, social networks, information- and media-sharing sites, wikis, blogging and microblogging, and online video. The nine compositional modes used in digital communication are conversations, comments and critiques, orientations, summaries, reference materials, narratives, teasers, status updates and announcements, and tutorials.

2 Describe the evolving role of email in business communication, and explain how to adapt the three-step writing process to email messages. As the earliest widely available digital written medium, email was applied to a broad range of communication tasks—some it was well suited for and some it wasn't. Over time, newer media such as instant messaging, blogs, and social networks have been taking over some of these tasks, but email remains a vital medium that is optimum for many private, short to medium-length messages.

The three-step process adapts easily to email communication. One of the most important planning decisions in crafting email is making sure every message has a valuable purpose. Any key planning decision should, in most instances, follow the chain of command in your organization; emailing over your boss's head is a good way to stir up resentment. When writing email messages, bear in mind that the expectations of writing quality and formality are higher in business email. Also, pay close attention to the wording of an email message's subject line; it often determines whether and when recipients open and read the message. Effective subject lines are both informative (concisely identifying what the message is about) and compelling (giving recipients a reason to read the message). Completing email messages is straightforward. Proof and revise messages (particularly important ones), stick with a clean design, make use of the email signature feature, and make sure you distribute the message to the right people.

3 Identify the advantages and disadvantages of business messaging systems. The benefits of messaging include its ability to mimic conversational exchanges, the ability to avoid many of the distractions and security threats that affect email, and its instantaneous nature. Messaging's disadvantages include its dependency on individual users' typing skills during real-time exchanges, some vulnerability to security threats, and the general disadvantages of lean media.

4 Explain why organizing website content is so challenging, and explain the concept of information architecture. The primary challenge in organizing website content is the medium's extreme versatility. This versatility can be a blessing because a single web presence can serve multiple purposes for multiple audiences, but it also creates the challenge of providing an efficient and successful experience for all these unique visitors. The key to organizing a website is careful consideration of its information architecture, which is a map of the content structure, labeling, and navigational links and pathways in a website.

5 Explain how to adapt the three-step writing process to podcasting. Although you'll be recording audio or video when creating podcasts, rather than writing messages, using the three-step process is an effective way to develop podcasts. Focus the planning step on analyzing the situation, gathering the information you'll need, and organizing your material. If you plan to create a series of podcasts on a given theme (the equivalent of starting a radio or TV show), make sure you've identified a range of topics extensive enough to keep your podcasts going over time. As you organize and begin to think about the words or images you'll use as content, pay close attention to previews, transitions, and reviews so that audiences don't get lost while listening or watching. Before you record, think through what you plan to say or shoot so that you don't ramble while trying to make your key points. Finally, consider the necessary level of production quality; good-quality podcasts usually require some specialized hardware and software.

MyBCommLab
Go to **mybcommlab.com** to complete the problems marked with this icon .

Test Your Knowledge

To review chapter content related to each question, refer to the indicated Learning Objective.

7-1. What are the situations in which a printed memo or letter might be preferable to a digital message? [LO-1]

7-2. How do the compositional modes of orientations, summaries, and teasers differ? [LO-1]

7-3. Why are subject lines important in email messages? [LO-2]

7-4. What are the benefits of using messaging in business communication? [LO-3]

7-5. Should you ever plan a messaging exchange? Explain your answer. [LO-3]

7-6. What is information architecture? [LO-3]

7-7. Why is it important to have a long-term, sustainable purpose in mind before you launch a podcast channel? [LO-5]

7-8. Is it wise to speak "off the cuff," with no notes or outline, when recording business podcasts? Why or why not? [LO-5]

Apply Your Knowledge

To review chapter content related to each question, refer to the indicated Learning Objective.

7-9. What are three innovative ways you could optimize your college's website for mobile devices? [LO-1]

7-10. If you wanted to get your employees' attention about the need to reduce costs without starting up the rumor mill about the possibility of layoffs, would it be wise to send out an email with the subject line "To save everyone's job, we must reduce costs now"? Explain your answer. [LO-2]

7-11. Should you ever use emoticons in business email messages? Explain your answer. [LO-2]

7-12. Communication on a major project is suffering because several team members are in the habit of writing cryptic or careless instant messages that often force recipients to engage in several rounds of follow-up messaging to figure out what the sender had in mind. As project leader, you've spoken with these team members about the need to write clearer messages, but they respond that careful planning and writing defeats the whole purpose of *instant* messaging. How should you handle the situation? [LO-3]

7-13. Your company's webmaster has become a big fan of tagging, the practice of identifying web content with category labels to make it easy to later retrieve all the content on a particular topic. She thinks tags are so powerful, in fact, that there is no longer any need to organize a website in any conventional, structured way. By using tag filtering, she claims, people can find whatever they need. In an email message, explain to her why information architecture is still necessary. [LO-2], [LO-4]

7-14. Imagine that you've been on the job for two or three decades, and you've amassed a deep store of leadership wisdom during the years. You'd like to share your wisdom with your 800 employees in a biweekly podcast. How should you go about planning this podcast series to make sure your employees will listen regularly? [LO-5]

Practice Your Skills

7-15. **Message 7.A: Media Skills: Messaging, Creating a Businesslike Tone [LO-3]** Review this messaging exchange and explain how the customer service agent could have handled the situation more effectively.

Agent:	Thanks for contacting Home Exercise Equipment. What's up?
Customer:	I'm having trouble assembling my home gym.
Agent:	I hear that a lot! LOL
Customer:	So is it me or the gym?
Agent:	Well, let's see ?g?. Where are you stuck?
Customer:	The crossbar that connects the vertical pillars doesn't fit.
Agent:	What do you mean doesn't fit?
Customer:	It doesn't fit. It's not long enough to reach across the pillars.
Agent:	Maybe you assembled the pillars in the wrong place. Or maybe we sent the wrong crossbar.
Customer:	How do I tell?
Agent:	The parts aren't labeled so could be tough. Do you have a measuring tape? Tell me how long your crossbar is.

7-16. **Message 7.B: Media Skills: Podcasting, Planning: Outlining Your Content [LO-5]** To access this message, visit real-timeupdates.com/bct14, select Student Assignments then Chapter 7, Message 7.B to listen to this podcast. Identify at least three ways in which the podcast could be improved, and draft a brief email message that you could send to the podcaster, giving your suggestions for improvement.

Exercises

Each activity is labeled according to the primary skill or skills you will need to use. To review relevant chapter content, you can refer to the indicated Learning Objective. In some instances, supporting information will be found in another chapter, as indicated.

7-17. **Collaboration: Working in Teams; Planning: Selecting Media [LO-1] Chapter 2** For each of these message needs, choose a medium that you think would work effectively and explain your choice. (More than one medium could work in some cases; just be able to support your particular choice.)

a. A technical support service for people trying to use their digital music players

b. A message of condolence to the family of an employee who passed away recently

c. A message from the CEO of a small company to the employees of the firm, explaining that she is leaving the company to join a competitor

d. A series of observations on the state of the industry, intended mostly for professionals within the industry

e. A series of messages, questions, and answers surrounding the work of a team on a confidential company project

7-18. Media Skills: Writing Email Subject Lines [LO-2] Using your imagination to make up whatever details you need, revise the following email subject lines to make them more informative:

a. New budget figures

b. Marketing brochure—your opinion?

c. Production schedule

7-19. Media Skills: Email [LO-2] The following email message contains numerous errors related to what you've learned about planning and writing business messages. Using the information it contains, write a more effective version.

TO: Felicia August <fb_august@evertrust.com>
SUBJECT: Those are the breaks, folks

Some of you may not like the rules about break times; however, we determined that keeping track of employees while they took breaks at times they determined rather than regular breaks at prescribed times was not working as well as we would have liked it to work. The new rules are not going to be an option. If you do not follow the new rules, you could be docked from your pay for hours when you turned up missing, since your direct supervisor will not be able to tell whether you were on a "break" or not and will assume that you have walked away from your job. We cannot be responsible for any errors that result from your inattentiveness to the new rules. I have already heard complaints from some of you and I hope this memo will end this issue once and for all. The decision has already been made.

Starting Monday, January 1, you will all be required to take a regular 15-minute break in the morning and again in the afternoon, and a regular thirty-minute lunch at the times specified by your supervisor, NOT when you think you need a break or when you "get around to it."

There will be no exceptions to this new rule!

Felicia August

Manager, Billing and Accounting

7-20. Media Skills: Messaging, Creating a Businesslike Tone [LO-3] Your firm, which makes professional-grade paint sprayers, uses messaging extensively for internal communication and frequently for external communication with customers and suppliers. Several customers have recently forwarded copies of messages they've received from your staff, asking if you know how casually some employees are treating this important medium. You decide to revise parts of several messages to show your staff a more appropriate writing style. Rewrite these sentences, making up any information you need, to convey a more businesslike style and tone. (Look up the acronyms online if you need to.)

a. IMHO, our quad turbo sprayer is best model 4U.

b. No prob; happy2help!

c. FWIW, I use the L400 myself & it rocks.

d. Most cust see 20–30% reduct in fumes w/this sprayer—of course, YMMV.

7-21. Media Skills: Web Writing, Planning: Outlining Your Content [LO-4] Find the website of a small company or nonprofit organization; make sure it is a fairly small and simple website. Identify all the individual pages on the site, then as best you can, "reverse engineer" the site's information architecture, identifying all the linkages between the individual pages. Draw a map of the architecture, showing how the various pages are linked together. (Hint: If the website has a "Site map" link, select that to see a hierarchical list of all the pages contained within the site.)

7-22. Media Skills: Podcasting, Planning: Outlining Your Content [LO-5] You began recording a weekly podcast to share information with your large and far-flung staff. After a month, you ask for feedback from several of your subordinates, and you're disappointed to learn that some people stopped listening to the podcast after the first couple of weeks. Someone eventually admits that many staffers feel the recordings are too long and rambling, and the information they contain isn't valuable enough to justify the time it takes to listen. You aren't pleased, but you want to improve. An assistant transcribes the introduction to last week's podcast so you can review it. You immediately see two problems. Revise the introduction based on what you've learned in this chapter.

So there I am, having lunch with Selma Gill, who just joined and took over the Northeast sales region from Jackson Stroud. In walks our beloved CEO with Selma's old boss at Uni-Plex; turns out they were finalizing a deal to co-brand our products and theirs and to set up a joint distribution program in all four domestic regions. Pretty funny, huh? Selma left Uni-Plex because she wanted to sell our products instead, and now she's back selling her old stuff, too. Anyway, try to chat with her when you can; she knows the biz inside and out and probably can offer insight into just about any sales challenge you might be running up against. We'll post more info on the co-brand deal next week; should be a boost for all of us. Other than those two news items, the other big news this week is the change in commission reporting. I'll go into the details in a minute, but when you log onto the intranet, you'll now see your sales results split out by product line and industry sector. Hope this helps you see where you're doing well and where you might beef things up a bit. Oh yeah, I almost forgot the most important bit. Speaking of our beloved CEO, Thomas is going to be our guest of honor, so to speak, at the quarterly sales meeting next week and wants an update on how petroleum prices are affecting customer behavior. Each district manager should be ready with a brief report. After I go through the commission reporting scheme, I'll outline what you need to prepare.

Expand Your Skills

Critique the Professionals

Check out the Twitter accounts of several companies that sell products or services you use or might use in the future. Find three teaser messages that attempt to persuade you to click through to another website. In a brief summary on your class blog or in an email message to your instructor, compare the effectiveness of the three teasers. Which was most effective, and which was least effective? Why? Were the payoffs for all three teasers satisfactory and in line with what you expected to see?

Sharpening Your Career Skills Online

Bovée and Thill's Business Communication Web Search, at websearch.businesscommunicationnetwork.com, is a unique research tool designed specifically for business communication research. Use the Web Search function to find a website, video, article, podcast, or presentation that offers advice on writing effective email and messages for mobile devices. Write a brief email message to your instructor, describing the item that you found and summarizing the career skills information you learned from it.

Cases

For all cases, feel free to use your creativity to make up any details you need in order to craft effective messages.

EMAIL SKILLS

7-23. Media Skills: Email; Message Strategies: Routine Messages [LO-2], Chapter 10 Team messaging apps are improving communication in all kinds of organizations, from small teams to entire companies to school groups and other non-business entities.

Your task: Imagine that you are responsible for choosing an organization's new messaging software. You can use an organization you are already a member of, such as a current or past employer, a nonprofit where you volunteer, or a project team in one of your classes. Alternatively, choose any real or imaginary organization in which at least a few people would need to coordinate their efforts using text-centric messaging.

Research the capabilities of Slack and two of its competitors, identifying the three or four most important features of each system. Write an email message (no more than four paragraphs) comparing these key features and recommending one of the systems for your chosen organization.

EMAIL SKILLS

7-24. Media Skills: Email; Message Strategies: Negative Messages [LO-2], Chapter 11 Many companies operate on the principle that the customer is always right, even when the customer *isn't* right. They take any steps necessary to ensure happy customers, lots of repeat sales, and a positive reputation among potential buyers. Overall, this is a smart and successful approach to business. However, most companies eventually encounter a nightmare customer who drains so much time, energy, and profits that the only sensible option is to refuse the customer's business. For example, the nightmare customer might be someone who constantly berates you and your employees, repeatedly makes outlandish demands for refunds and discounts, or simply requires so much help that you not only lose money on this person but also no longer have enough time to help your other customers. "Firing" a customer is an unpleasant step that should be taken only in the most extreme cases and only after other remedies have been attempted (such as talking with the customer about the problem), but it is sometimes necessary for the well-being of your employees and your company.

Your task: If you are currently working or have held a job in the recent past, imagine that you've encountered just such a customer. If you don't have job experience to call on, imagine that you work in a retail location somewhere around campus or in your neighborhood. Identify the type of behavior this imaginary customer exhibits and the reasons the behavior can no longer be accepted. Write a brief email message to the customer to explain that you will no longer be able to accommodate him or her as a customer. Calmly explain why you have had to reach this difficult decision. Maintain a professional tone and keep your emotions in check.

EMAIL SKILLS/TEAM SKILLS

7-25. Media Skills: Email; Collaboration: Team Projects [LO-2], Chapter 2 Colleges and universities are complex organizations that try to optimize results for students while wrestling with budgetary constraints, staffing issues, infrastructure concerns, limitations on available space, and a host of other issues. Even in the best-managed and most generously funded institutions, there are aspects of campus life that could be improved.

Your task: With a team assigned by your instructor, choose an issue of campus life that you think could and should be improved. It can be anything from transportation to housing to personal safety. Draft an email message that could be sent to your school's administration. In your message concisely describe the problem, speculate on why the problem or situation exists, offer suggestions on how it could be solved or improved, and explain how addressing it would improve campus life. (Don't send the message unless your instructor directs you to do so.)

EMAIL SKILLS/TEAM SKILLS

7-26. Media Skills: Email [LO-2] Studying real-life examples is a great way to get a feel for how various companies communicate with customers and other stakeholders.

Your task: With teammates assigned by your instructor, select five email messages from the Just Good Copy website at **www.goodemailcopy.com**. Evaluate them based on the criteria for effective email discussed in the chapter. Rank them from most effective to least effective and summarize your analysis in a presentation to your class or a post on your class blog.

EMAIL SKILLS/MOBILE SKILLS

7-27. Media Skills: Email [LO-2] The size limitations of smartphone screens call for a different approach to writing (see page 144) and formatting (see page 168) documents.

Your task: On the website of any company that interests you, find a news release (some companies refer to them as *press releases*) that announces the launch of a new product. Using Pages or any other writing app at your disposal, revise and format the material in a way that would be effective on smartphone screens.

MESSAGING SKILLS

7-28. Media Skills: Messaging; Compositional Modes: Tutorials [LO-1], [LO-3] High-definition television can be a joy to watch—but, oh, what a pain to buy. The field is cluttered with competing technologies and arcane terminology that is meaningless to most consumers. Moreover, it's nearly impossible to define one technical term without invoking two or three others, leaving consumers swimming in an alphanumeric soup of confusion. As a sales support manager for Crutchfield, a leading online retailer of audio and video systems, you understand the frustration buyers feel; your staff is deluged daily by their questions.

Your task: To help your staff respond quickly to consumers who ask questions via Crutchfield's online IM chat service, you are developing a set of "canned" responses to common questions. When a consumer asks one of these questions, a sales adviser can simply select the ready-made answer. Visit **www.crutchfield .com/Learn/** and conduct the research you need to write concise, consumer-friendly definitions of the following terms: *1080p, HDMI, 4K,* and *3D TV.*

WEB WRITING SKILLS/TEAM SKILLS

7-29. Message Strategies: Online Content; Collaboration: Team Projects [LO-4], Chapter 2 If you're like many other college students, your first year was more than you expected: more difficult, more fun, more frustrating, more expensive, more exhausting, more rewarding—more of everything, positive and negative. Oh, the things you know now that you didn't know then!

Your task: With several other students, identify five or six things you wish you would've realized or understood better before you started your first year of college. These can relate to your school life (such as "I didn't realize how much work I would have for my classes" or "I should've asked for help as sooner") and your personal and social life ("I wish I would've been more open to meeting people"). Use these items as the foundation of a brief informational report that you could post on a blog that is read by high school students and their families. Your goal with this report is to help the next generation of students make a successful and rewarding transition to college.

WEB WRITING SKILLS/MOBILE SKILLS/ PORTFOLIO BUILDER

7-30. Message Strategies: Online Content [LO-4] Adapting conventional web content to make it mobile friendly can require rethinking the site's information architecture to simplify navigation and content.

Your task: Choose the website of a company that makes products you find interesting. (Make it a conventional website, not one already optimized for mobile.) Analyze the section of the website that contains information about the company's products and determine the best way to present that material on mobile device screens. Mock up at least two screens showing how you would reformat the content to make it mobile friendly. Create a brief presentation with "before" and "after" views to show how your redesign would benefit mobile site visitors.

WEB WRITING SKILLS

7-31. Message Strategies: Online Content [LO-4] As you probably experienced, trying to keep all the different schools straight in one's mind while researching and applying for colleges can be rather difficult. Applicants and their families would no doubt appreciate a handy summary of your college or university's key points as they relate to the selection and application process.

Your task: Adapt content from your college or university's website to create a one-page "Quick Facts" sheet about your school. Choose the information you think prospective students and their families would find most useful. (Note that adapting existing content would be acceptable in a real-life scenario like this because you would be reusing content on behalf of the content owner. Doing so would definitely not be acceptable if you were using the content for yourself or for someone other than the original owner.)

PODCASTING SKILLS

7-32. Media Skills: Podcasting; Career Management: Personal Branding [LO-5], Prologue While writing the many letters and email messages that are part of the job search process, you find yourself wishing that you could just talk to some of these companies so your personality could shine through. Well, you've just gotten that opportunity. One of the companies that you've applied to has emailed you back, asking you to submit a two-minute podcast introducing yourself and explaining why you would be a good person to hire.

Your task: Identify a company that you'd like to work for after graduation and select a job that would be a good match for your skills and interests. Write a script for a two-minute podcast (roughly 250 words). Introduce yourself and the position you're applying for, describe your background, and explain why you think you're a good candidate for the job. Make up any details you need. If your instructor asks you to do so, record the podcast and submit the file.

PODCASTING SKILLS/PORTFOLIO BUILDER

7-33. Media Skills: Podcasting; Message Strategies: Marketing and Sales Messages [LO-5], Chapter 12 With any purchase decision, from a restaurant meal to a college education, recommendations from satisfied customers are often the strongest promotional messages.

Your task: Write a script for a one- to two-minute podcast (roughly 150–250 words), explaining why your college or university is a good place to get an education. Your audience is high school juniors and seniors. You can choose to craft a general message—something that would be useful to all prospective students—or you can focus on a specific academic discipline, the athletic program, or some other important aspect of your college experience. Either way, make sure your introductory comments make it clear whether you are offering a general recommendation or a specific recommendation. If your instructor asks you to do so, record the podcast and submit the file.

MyBCommLab

Go to **mybcommlab.com** for Auto-graded writing questions as well as the following Assisted-graded writing questions:

7-34. Why has email become overused and inappropriately used in many situations? [LO-2]

7-35. How can you use the inverted pyramid style of writing to craft effective website content? [LO-4]

Endnotes

1. Slack website, accessed 1 April 2016, slack.com; Adrienne Lafrance, "The Triumph of Email," *The Atlantic*, 6 January 2016, www.theatlantic.com; Harry McCracken, "With 500,000 Users, Slack Says It's The Fastest-Growing Business App Ever," *Fast Company*, 2 December 2015, www.fastcompany.com; Farhad Manjoo, "Slack, the Office Messaging App That May Finally Sink Email," *New York Times*, 11 March 2015, www.nytimes.com; Alyson Shontell and Eugene Kim, "Slack, a 2-Year-Old Messaging Platform, Is Raising $200 Million at Nearly a $4 Billion Valuation Led by Thrive Capital," *Business Insider*, 11 March 2016, www.businessinder.com; Ellis Hamburger, "Slack Is Killing Email," *The Verge*, 12 August 2014, www.theverge.com.

2. Richard Edelman, "Teaching Social Media: What Skills Do Communicators Need?," in *Engaging the New Influencers; Third Annual Social Media Academic Summit* (white paper), accessed 7 June 2010, www.newmediaacademicsummit.com.

3. Samantha Murphy, "Why Mobile Commerce Is on the Rise," *Mashable*, 7 March 2012, mashable.com.

4. Christina "CK" Kerley, "Wearables," AllThingsCK, accessed 6 April 2014, allthingsck.com.

5. Maria Vergelis, Tatyana Shcherbakova, Nadezhda Demidova, and Darya Gudkova, "Kaspersky Security Bulletin. Spam and Phishing in 2015," *Securelist*, 5 February 2016, securelist.com.

6. Hilary Potkewitz and Rachel Brown, "Spread of Email Has Altered Communication Habits at Work," *Los Angeles Business Journal*, 18 April 2005, labusinessjournal.com; Nancy Flynn, *Instant Messaging Rules* (New York: AMACOM, 2004), 47–54.

7. Mary Munter, Priscilla S. Rogers, and Jone Rymer, "Business Email: Guidelines for Users," *Business Communication Quarterly*, March 2003, 26; Renee B. Horowitz and Marian G. Barchilon, "Stylistic Guidelines for Email," *IEEE Transactions on Professional Communication* 37, no. 4 (December 1994): 207–212.

8. Steve Rubel, "Tip: Tweetify the Lead of Your Emails," The Steve Rubel Stream blog, 20 July 2010, www.steverubel.com.

9. Judith Newman, "If You're Happy and You Know It, Must I Know, Too?" *New York Times*, 21 October 2011, www.nytimes.com.

10. Eugene Kim, "The CEO of $2.8 Billion Slack Says It Has One Big Advantage over Facebook or LinkedIn," *Business Insider*, 11 February 2016, www.businessinsider.com.

11. Martin Zwilling, "Texting is Killing Real Business Communication," *Business Insider*, 13 January 2012, www.businessinsider.com.

12. Syndi Seid, "12 Tips for Instant Messaging in the Workplace," Advanced Etiquette, 1 June 2014, www.advancedetiquette.com; Leo Babauta, "17 Tips to Be Productive with Instant Messaging," *Web Worker Daily*, 14 November 2007, webworkerdaily.com; John Pallato, "Instant Messaging Unites Work Groups and Inspires Collaboration," *Internet World*, December 2002, 14.

13. Based in part on Shel Holtz, *Writing for the Wired World* (San Francisco: International Association of Business Communicators, 1999), 28–29.

14. "Set Up Your Podcast for Success," Feed For All website, accessed 4 October 2006, www.feedforall.com.

15. "Set Up Your Podcast for Success."

16. Nathan Hangen, "4 Steps to Podcasting Success," *Social Media Examiner*, 14 February 2011, www.socialmediaexaminer.com.

Social Media

LEARNING OBJECTIVES

After studying this chapter, you will be able to

1 Identify seven key points for using social media in business communication.

2 Describe the business communication applications of social networks.

3 Explain how information- and content-sharing sites are used in business communication.

4 Describe the role of blogging in business communication today, and explain how to adapt the three-step writing process to blogging.

5 Describe the business uses of Twitter and other microblogging systems.

6 Offer guidelines for becoming a valuable wiki contributor.

MyBCommLab®

⭐ **Improve Your Grade!** Over 10 million students improved their results using Pearson MyLabs. Visit **mybcommlab.com** for simulations, tutorials, and end-of-chapter problems.

Coffee shops are community gathering places, and a team of Starbucks employees use social media to extend that community feel into the virtual realm by connecting with fans and customers on a variety of social platforms.

© Iain Masterton/Alamy Stock Photo

Starbucks

www.starbucks.com

With its portfolio of worldwide locations pushing toward the 20,000 mark, Starbucks has a reputation for being nearby wherever and whenever anybody might be craving a cup of coffee. Not surprisingly, its online communications follows the same strategy of being everywhere its customers might be. Its broadest presence is on Facebook, with more than 50 company-sponsored pages, including local pages in more than 40 countries. Typical posts include contests and other special promotions, enticing photos of various coffee drinks, instructional videos on making a great cup of coffee at home, and updates on community involvement projects. Two of the company's most popular drinks, the Frappuccino and Pumpkin Spice Latte, even have their own social media accounts.

Starbucks also maintains several dozen Twitter accounts, many of which are country specific and tuned into local interests. In the Netherlands, for instance, fresh pastries are an essential part of the coffee experience, so employees alert customers on Twitter whenever a fresh batch is ready.

The company is active on a wide variety of other platforms as well, including Pinterest, YouTube, Foursquare, and Instagram. Although it is everywhere online, Starbucks takes care not to wear out its welcome. It posts new information relatively infrequently compared with many other major consumer brands. "They're not cluttering up your newsfeed," notes one industry observer.

Many companies use social media to offer digital coupons and sponsor online contests, but Starbucks takes things to an entirely new level. Its attention-getting efforts have included an online puzzle/scavenger hunt featuring Lady Gaga and an augmented-reality smartphone app that triggered animated movies when a phone was pointed at specially coded coffee cups.

Alexandra Wheeler, the company's vice president in charge of global digital marketing, emphasizes that these social media efforts are about more than gaining fans and building awareness. "They can have a material impact on the business," she says, citing one social media campaign that brought a million customers into Starbucks stores.

Like many companies still experimenting with social media as new tools and techniques emerge, Starbucks has had a stumble or two along the way. A notable example was a holiday Twitter hashtag campaign in the United Kingdom in which the company used a big-screen monitor at a national museum to display any tweet that included #spreadthecheer. Starbucks was embroiled in a public controversy over corporate taxes at the time, and some people used the opportunity of the unmonitored Twitter channel to post angry and occasionally obscene messages about the company.

This episode highlights one of the core dilemmas in social media: How much control should companies exercise over the social media channels they sponsor? If they try to exert too much control, they can stifle the very aspect of social engagement they're aiming for. If they exert too little, even well-intentioned efforts can spin out of control and lead to embarrassing public spectacles. As social media continue to reshape business communication, finding the right balance of conversation and control promises to be a never-ending challenge.[1]

Writing Strategies for Social Media

1 **LEARNING OBJECTIVE**
Identify seven key points for using social media in business communication.

Readers of social media expect to have a more engaged relationship with writers, so creating content for social media requires a new approach to writing.

Starbucks's use of social media (profiled in the chapter-opening Communication Close-Up) may seem like an obvious move, but these media represent a fundamental shift in the way companies handle business communication. The shift is still taking place, as more consumers adopt social media and more businesses experiment with the best ways to integrate these media and to adapt their internal and external communication practices.

No matter what media or compositional mode you are using for a particular message, writing for social media requires a different approach than for traditional media. Social media have changed the relationship between sender and receiver, so the nature of the messages needs to change as well. Whether you're writing a blog or posting a product demonstration video to YouTube, consider these tips for creating successful content for social media:[2]

- **Remember that it's a conversation, not a lecture or a sales pitch.** One of the great appeals of social media is the feeling of conversation, of people talking *with* one another instead of one person talking *at* everyone else (see Figure 8.1). For all their technological sophistication, in an important sense social media provide a new spin on the age-old practice of *word-of-mouth* communication. As more and more people gain a voice in the marketplace, companies that try to maintain the old "we talk, you listen" mindset are likely to be ignored in the social media landscape. People generally join social networks for the chance to interact, and you can help stimulate conversations by asking followers for their ideas, options, and feedback.[3]

- **Write informally but not carelessly.** Write as a human being, not as a cog in a faceless corporate machine. At the same time, don't get sloppy; no one wants to slog through misspelled words and half-baked sentences to find the message.

Readers—and search engines—don't like spending time trying to figure out clever puns and other wordplay; make your headlines clear and direct.

- **Create concise, specific, and informative headlines.** Avoid the temptation to engage in clever wordplay with headlines. This advice applies to all forms of business communication, of course, but it is essential for social media. Readers don't want to spend time and energy figuring out what your witty headlines mean. Search engines won't know what they mean, either, so fewer people will find your content.

- **Get involved and stay involved.** Social media understandably make some businesspeople nervous because they don't permit a high level of control over messages. However, don't hide from criticism—it can be valuable feedback. Take the opportunity to correct misinformation or explain how mistakes will be fixed.

- **If you need to promote something, do so indirectly.** Just as you shouldn't impose on people with a sales pitch during an informal social gathering, refrain from blatant promotional efforts in social media.

- **Be transparent and honest.** Honesty is always essential, of course, but a particular issue that has recently tripped up a few companies is hiding behind an online persona—either a fictitious character whose writing is actually done by a corporate marketing specialist or a real person who fails to disclose an affiliation with a corporate sponsor.

- **Think before you post!** Individuals and companies have been sued because of careless Twitter updates, employees have been fired for inappropriate Facebook posts, vital

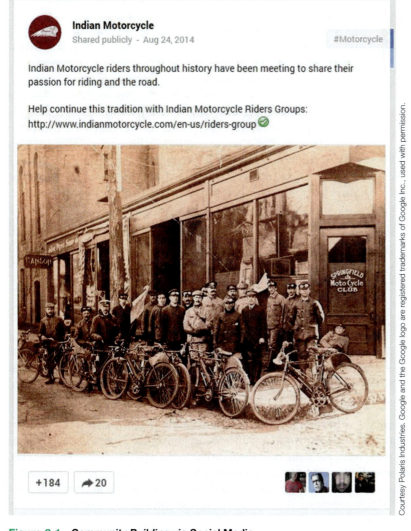

Courtesy Polaris Industries. Google and the Google logo are registered trademarks of Google Inc., used with permission.

Figure 8.1   Community Building via Social Media
Customer-affiliation groups can be an effective way to build stakeholder support for a company and its products. Indian Motorcycles used this Google+ post to spur interest in its rider groups.

company secrets have been leaked, and business and personal relationships have been strained. To be safe, assume that every message you post will be read by people far beyond your original audience.

A momentary lapse in judgment while writing messages for social media can cause tremendous damage to your career or your company.

Social Networks

Social networks, online services that help people and organizations form connections and share information, have recently become a major force in both internal and external business communication. In addition to Facebook, a variety of public and private social networks are used by businesses and professionals. These can be grouped into three categories:

2 LEARNING OBJECTIVE
Describe the business communication applications of social networks.

- **Public, general-purpose networks.** Facebook and Google+ are the largest and best-known of these networks. Additionally, regionally focused networks have significant user bases in some countries, such as China's Renren and Kaixin001.[4]
- **Public, specialized networks.** Whereas Facebook and Google+ serve a wide variety of personal and professional needs, other networks focus on a particular function or a particular audience. The most widely known is LinkedIn, with its emphasis on career- and sales-related networking. Other networks address the needs of entrepreneurs,

Business communicators make use of a wide range of specialized and private social networks, in addition to public networks such as Facebook and Google+.

small-business owners, specific professions, product enthusiasts, and other narrower audiences.

- **Private networks.** Some companies have built private social networks for internal use, either as standalone systems or as part of broader collaboration and communication systems (such as Cemex's Shift, profiled in Chapter 2). The Red Robin restaurant chain, for example, uses the Yammer social network to share information across the organization nationwide and up and down the corporate ladder. While many companies have found success with internal social networks, a recurring problem is getting enough people in an organization to use them. When top executives are visible participants and use the networks to share vital information, employees are more likely to stay active on them as well.[5]

Regardless of the purpose and audience, social networks are most beneficial when all participants give and receive information, advice, support, and introductions—just as in offline interactions. The following two sections describe how social networks are used in business communication and offer advice on using these platforms successfully.

BUSINESS COMMUNICATION USES OF SOCIAL NETWORKS

With their ability to reach virtually unlimited numbers of people through a variety of digital formats, social networks are a great fit for many business communication needs. Here are some of the key applications of social networks for internal and external business communication:

MOBILE APP

The social media management app **SocialOomph** lets you monitor multiple social media sites, schedule updates, and perform other time-saving tasks.

- **Integrating company workforces.** Just as public networks can bring friends and families together, internal social networks can help companies grow closer, including helping new employees navigate their way through the organization by finding experts, mentors, and other important contacts; encouraging workforces to jell after reorganizations or mergers; and overcoming structural barriers in communication channels, bypassing the formal communication system to deliver information where it is needed in a timely fashion.
- **Fostering collaboration.** Networks can play a major role in collaboration by identifying the best people, both inside the company and at other companies, to collaborate on projects; finding pockets of knowledge and expertise within the organization; giving meeting or seminar participants a way to meet before an event takes place and to maintain relationships after events; accelerating the development of teams by helping team members get to know one another and identify individual areas of expertise; and sharing information throughout the organization.
- **Building communities.** Social networks are a natural tool for bringing together *communities of practice*, people who engage in similar work, and *communities of interest*, people who share enthusiasm for a particular product or activity. Large and geographically dispersed companies can benefit greatly from communities of practice that connect experts who may work in different divisions or different countries. Communities of interest that form around a specific product are sometimes called

Community building, both within companies and with customers and other external parties, is an important function of social networking.

brand communities, and nurturing these communities can be a vital business communication task. Some communities spring up spontaneously when product enthusiasts connect online, whereas others are more formal organizations established by companies to help customers use their products more successfully and engage with like-minded individuals. The SAP Community Network, for instance, set up by the enterprise software company SAP, has more than 2.5 million members.[6]

- **Socializing brands and companies.** According to one survey of company executives, *socialization* now accounts for more than half of a company's or brand's global reputation.[7] **Brand socialization** is a measure of how effectively a company engages with its various online stakeholders in a mutually beneficial exchange of information. The game and doll maker Mattel engages its Twitter followers by answering product questions, reposting fan videos, and acknowledging enthusiastic praise from customers.[8]

  Socializing a brand is becoming an increasingly important element of marketing and public relations strategies.

- **Understanding target markets.** With hundreds of millions of people expressing themselves via social media, you can be sure that smart companies are listening. When asked about the value of having millions of Facebook fans, Coca-Cola's CEO Muhtar Kent replied, "The value is you can talk with them. They tell you things that are important for your business and brands."[9] In addition, a number of tools now exist to gather market intelligence from social media more or less automatically. For example, *sentiment analysis* and *reputation analysis* tools use advanced language-analysis algorithms to assess the reputations of companies and individuals, measure the emotional quality of online conversations, identify outrage "hot spots" on social media, and uncover trending topics of interest.[10]

  Social networks are vital tools for distributing information as well as for gathering information about the business environment.

- **Recruiting employees and business partners.** Companies use social networks to find potential employees, short-term contractors, subject-matter experts, product and service suppliers, and business partners. A key advantage here is that these introductions are made via trusted connections in a professional network. On LinkedIn, for example, members can recommend each other based on current or past business relationships, which helps remove the uncertainty of initiating business relationships with strangers.

- **Connecting with sales prospects.** Salespeople on networks such as LinkedIn can use their network connections to identify potential buyers and then ask for introductions through those shared connections. Sales networking can reduce *cold calling*, telephoning potential customers out of the blue—a practice that few people on either end of the conversation find pleasant.

- **Supporting customers.** Customer service is another one of the fundamental areas of business communication that have been revolutionized by social media. *Social customer service* involves using social networks and other social media tools to give customers a more convenient way to get help from the company and to help each other.

- **Extending the organization.** Social networking is also fueling the growth of *networked organizations*, sometimes known as *virtual organizations*, where companies supplement the talents of their employees with services from one or more external partners, such as a design lab, a manufacturing firm, or a sales and distribution company.

- **Crowdspeaking.** Companies, nonprofits, musicians, authors, and others can use *crowdspeaking* to "boost a signal." Crowdspeaking services such as Thunderclap and HeadTalker work in much the same manner as Kickstarter and other crowdfunding sites. Someone with a message to spread sets a campaign goal, such as recruiting 100 supporters to help share the message. If that goal is reached, the message is "triggered" and automatically sent to all the followers in all those supporters' social networks. By taking advantage of the *social reach* of their supporters, communicators can reach hundreds or thousands of times as many people as they could on their own.[11]

(continued on page 212)

BUSINESS COMMUNICATORS INNOVATING WITH SOCIAL MEDIA

Companies in virtually every industry use social media and continue to experiment with new ways to connect with customers and other stakeholders. From offering helpful tips on using products to helping customers meet each other, these companies show the enormous range of possibilities that new media continue to bring to business communication.

Recruiting and Business-Focused Social Networks

Marketo, a developer of digital marketing software, maintains a profile in LinkedIn, as do hundreds of its employees.

Tweetups

A powerful capability of online social media is bringing people with similar interests together offline. *Tweetups*, for example, are in-person meetings planned and organized over Twitter.

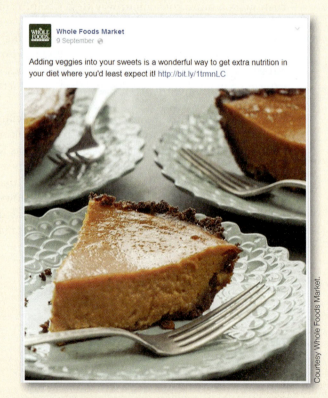

Value-Added Content via Social Networks

Thousands of companies are on social networking platforms, but blatantly promotional posts are not always welcome by fans and followers. Instead, companies such as Whole Foods use social networks to share information of interest, such as recipes and nutritional advice.

Value-Added Content via Blogging

One of the best ways to become a valued member of a network is to provide content that is useful to others in the network. The Quizzle personal finance blog offers a steady stream of articles and advice that help people manage their finances.

© Quizzle.

© 2013 by Lie-Nielsen Toolworks, Inc. Used by permission.

Value-Added Content via Online Video

Lie-Nielsen Toolworks of Warren, Maine, uses its YouTube channel to offer valuable information on choosing and using premium woodworking tools. By providing sought-after information for both current and potential customers free of charge, these videos help Lie-Nielsen foster relationships with the worldwide woodworking community and solidify its position as one of the leaders in this market. Animal Planet, Best Western, and Taco Bell are among the many other companies that make effective use of branded channels on YouTube.

Courtesy of Zappos.

Employee Recruiting

Zappos is one of the many companies now using Twitter as a recruiting tool. The company's @InsideZappos account gives potential employees an insider's look at the company's offbeat and upbeat culture.

REAL-TIME UPDATES

LEARN MORE BY READING THIS INFOGRAPHIC

Social shaming in today's business landscape

See how today's consumers use the power of social media to get satisfaction from companies. Go to **real-timeupdates.com/bct14** and select Learn More in the Students section.

STRATEGIES FOR BUSINESS COMMUNICATION ON SOCIAL NETWORKS

Social networks offer attractive opportunities for business communication, but they must be used with the same care as other professional media. Follow these guidelines to make the most of social networks for both personal branding and company communication:[12]

Choose the best composition mode (see Chapter 7) for every message type you post on social networks.

- **Choose the best compositional mode for each message, purpose, and network.** As you visit various social networks, take some time to observe the variety of message types you see in different parts of each website. For example, the informal status update mode works well for Facebook posts but would be less effective for company overviews and mission statements.
- **Offer valuable content to members of your online communities.** People don't join social networks to be sales targets. They join looking for connections and information. *Content marketing* is the practice of providing free information that is valuable to community members but that also helps a company build closer ties with current and potential customers.[13]
- **Join existing conversations.** Search for online conversations that are already taking place. Answer questions, solve problems, and respond to rumors and misinformation.
- **Anchor your online presence in your hub.** Although it's important to join those conversations and be visible where your stakeholders are active, it's equally important to anchor your presence at your own central *hub*—a web presence you own and control. (Control is important because trying to use Facebook, Twitter, or another service as a hub leaves you at the mercy of changes in design, terms of service, and other variables.) The hub can be a conventional website or a combination of a website, a blog, and a company-sponsored online community, for example.[14] Use the hub to connect the various pieces of your online "self" (as an individual or a company) to make it easier for people to find and follow you. For example, you can link to your blog from your LinkedIn profile or automatically announce new blog posts on Twitter.
- **Facilitate community building.** Make it easy for customers and other audiences to connect with the company and with each other. For instance, you can use the group feature on Facebook, LinkedIn, and other social networks to create and foster special-interest communities within your networks. Groups are a great way to connect people who are interested in specific topics, such as owners of a particular product.

Products can be promoted on social networks, but it needs to be done in a low-key, indirect way.

- **Restrict conventional promotional efforts to the right time and right place.** Persuasive communication efforts are still valid for specific communication tasks, such as regular advertising and the product information pages on a website, but efforts to inject blatant "salespeak" into social networking conversations are usually not welcome.
- **Maintain a consistent personality.** Each social network is a unique environment with particular norms of communication.[15] As a strictly business-oriented network, for example, LinkedIn has a more formal "vibe" than Facebook and Google+, which cater to both consumers and businesses. While adapting to the expectations of each network, however, be sure to maintain a consistent personality across all the networks in which you are active.[16]

See "Writing Promotional Messages for Social Media" in Chapter 12 (pages 344–346) for more tips on writing messages for social networks and other social media.

Information- and Content-Sharing Sites

3 **LEARNING OBJECTIVE**
Explain how information- and content-sharing sites are used in business communication.

Social networks allow members to share information and media as part of the networking experience, but a variety of systems have been designed specifically for sharing content. Though the field is diverse and still evolving, the possibilities can be divided into user-generated content sites, content curation sites, and community Q&A sites.

THE FUTURE OF COMMUNICATION

Augmented Reality and Virtual Reality

Augmented reality and virtual reality (VR) are two intriguing technologies that are starting to change the way employees perform a variety of job tasks, from training to research and development to customer service. Augmented reality provides a layer of digital information that enhances the immediate physical reality a person sees. This information can be as simple as text that displays on a mobile or wearable device pointed at a particular location or item, or as elaborate as 3D graphics that overlay whatever live scene the user is looking at through a device. For example, using an augmented reality app, technicians can point a smartphone or tablet at a machine and get information about its operation and repair. Travelers can use mobile devices to get additional information about environments they're moving through—everything from reviews of a restaurant they're walking past to details about the various businesses in an office building.

In contrast, VR creates a simulation in which the person experiences the sensation of being in an environment, even though that environment is entirely computer-generated. (Holograms, in which 3D representations of real people are projected into a physical space, are explored on page 487.) For training applications, for example, if it is difficult, expensive, or dangerous to put trainees in a real-life situation, a VR simulation can let employees experience the sensation of being there and doing whatever tasks are required. VR can also help people experience a product or structure before it is built. Ford uses VR to get feedback from drivers by letting them sit in and experience prototype designs before the cars are manufactured, and Audi lets buyers experience a virtual car with the options they'd like to order. The home improvement chain Lowes uses VR to let customers walk through rooms they want to build or redecorate in their homes. These simulated experiences can communicate much more powerfully than video, photos, or other conventional media.

WHAT'S YOUR PREDICTION?

Research an augmented or VR system that is currently used for business purposes (not games or other entertainment systems, in other words). Write a one-paragraph summary of how this technology is more effective than conventional business media and offer your prediction on whether it will enter the mainstream of business usage.

Sources: Peter Ray Allison, "Augmented Reality Business Applications Start to Get Real," *ComputerWeekly*, May 2015, www.computerweekly.com; Nicole Laskowski, "Augmented and Virtual Reality Make a Play for the Enterprise," *TechTarget*, February 2016, www.techtarget.com; Leo King, "Ford, Where Virtual Reality Is Already Manufacturing Reality," *Forbes*, 3 May 2014, www.forbes.com; Jack E. Gold, "Augmented-Reality Technology May Transform Work As We Know It," *TechTarget*, June 2015, www.techtarget.com; Lowe's Innovation Labs, accessed 23 February 2016, www.lowesinnovationlabs.com/holoroom.

USER-GENERATED CONTENT SITES

YouTube, Flickr, Yelp, and other **user-generated content (UGC) sites,** in which users, rather than website owners, contribute most or all of the content, have become serious business tools. On YouTube, for example, companies post everything from product demonstrations and TV commercials to company profiles and technical support explanations.

> YouTube and other user-generated content sites are now important business communication channels.

Moreover, the business communication value of sites such as YouTube goes beyond the mere ability to deliver content. The social aspects of these sites, including the ability to vote for, comment on, and share material, encourage enthusiasts to spread the word about the companies and products they endorse.[17]

Companies can also encourage UGC submissions on their own websites or through other social media platforms, such as Twitter and Facebook. Burberry, Starbucks, and Belkin are among the companies that generated thousands of responses when they invited customers to submit photos and other media.[18]

As one example of the way these sites are changing business communication, Yelp has become a major and sometimes controversial influence on consumer behavior at a local level by aggregating millions of reviews of stores, restaurants, and other businesses across the United States.[19] With the voice of the crowd affecting consumer behavior, businesses need to (1) focus on performing at a high level so that customers reward them with positive reviews and (2) get involved on Yelp (the site encourages business owners to tell potential customers about themselves as well). These efforts could pay off much more handsomely than advertising and other conventional communication efforts.

> The "voice of the crowd," which is enabled through social media sites, can dramatically influence the way businesses are managed.

CONTENT CURATION SITES

In many fields of business, so much original content is already available that sometimes the biggest value a communicator can offer audiences is guiding them to the best of what's out there, rather than creating new content. Similar to what museum curators do when they

Content curation is the process of collecting and presenting articles, videos, and other material on a particular topic in a way that makes it convenient for target readers.

decide which pieces in their collection to display, business communicators can find and share valuable material with the audiences through **content curation**.

At its simplest, content curation can involve sharing links to useful articles or video via blogs or social media accounts. Companies can also set up dedicated websites that publish links to original content in a variety of topic categories. The authors' Business Communication Headline News (bchn.businesscommunicationnetwork.com), for instance, is one of the earliest examples of content curation in the field of business communication. As an alternative, a number of websites offer ready-made content curation solutions. Pinterest and Scoop.it, for example, make it easy to assemble attractive online magazines or portfolios on specific topics.

Curating content for a target audience can be a great way to add value and stand out as an expert in your field. Not only can you save readers the time it would take to find material on their own, but you can use your knowledge to locate and present the most useful articles, videos, and other media on a given topic.

All content curators need to be aware of two key ethical concerns. First, you must not plagiarize, which is presenting someone else's content as your own. Second, you are promoting yourself as an expert when you curate content, and people will expect you to do a competent job of finding and filtering materials. As with any communication task, make sure you understand the needs of your target audience so that you can provide the best material possible to meet their needs.[20]

COMMUNITY Q&A SITES

Community Q&A sites offer great opportunities for building your personal brand.

Community Q&A sites, on which visitors answer questions posted by other visitors, are a contemporary twist on the early ethos of computer networking, which was people helping each other. (Groups of like-minded people connected online long before the World Wide Web was even created.) Community Q&A sites include dedicated customer support communities such as those hosted on Get Satisfaction and public sites such as Quora and Yahoo! Answers.

Responding to questions on Q&A sites can be a great way to build your personal brand, to demonstrate your company's commitment to customer service, and to counter misinformation about your company and its products. Keep in mind that when you respond to an individual query on a community Q&A site, you are also "responding in advance" to every person who comes to the site with the same question in the future. In other words, you are writing a type of reference material in addition to corresponding with the original questioner, so keep the long time frame and wider audience in mind.

Blogging

4 **LEARNING OBJECTIVE**
Describe the role of blogging in business communication today, and explain how to adapt the three-step writing process to blogging.

Blogs, online journals that are easier to personalize and update than conventional websites, are a major force in business communication. To maintain a positive connection with target audiences, business bloggers should follow several important guidelines:

Writing in a personal, authentic voice is key to attracting and keeping blog readers.

- **Communicate with personal style and an authentic voice.** Traditional business messages designed for large audiences tend to be carefully scripted and written in a "corporate voice" that is impersonal and objective. In contrast, successful business blogs tend to exhibit the personal style of their authors. Audiences relate to this fresh approach and often build closer emotional bonds with the blogger's organization as a result.

- **Deliver new information quickly.** Blogging tools let you post new material as soon as you create or find it. This feature not only allows you to respond quickly when needed—such as during a corporate crisis—but also lets your audiences know that active communication is taking place. Blogs that don't offer a continuous stream of new and interesting content are quickly ignored in today's online environment.

- **Choose topics of peak interest to audiences.** Successful blogs cover topics that readers care about, and they emphasize useful information while downplaying product

Community Manager: Keeping a Company Connected to Its Stakeholders

In the narrowest sense, a community manager is the social media interface between a company and its external stakeholders. More broadly, some community managers also plan and manage corporate events and oversee customer support operations. In smaller firms the community manager might be the sole voice in a company's social media presence (running its Twitter account and Facebook pages, for example). In larger firms the job often entails supervising a team of people who carry out a broad range of audience-engagement activities.

Not surprisingly, communication skills are essential for community managers, from handling the nuts and bolts of effectively using social media to fostering a sense of community and inspiring people to be passionate about a company and its brands. In addition, community management is a data-intensive job in many companies; managers are expected to make full use of analytical tools to measure the effects of social interaction and to use those results to plan new initiatives. Community managers also have to be well versed in their company's product and service offerings.

On a personal level, the job requires high energy, resilience, a thick skin for handling negative comments, and a willingness to be connected far beyond the limits of a 40-hour week. You are "the face of the brand," as Adobe's community manager Rachael King describes it, and when major events hit, social managers are expected to respond in real time.

If the attractions and challenges of this job sound appealing to you, be sure to add community manager to the list of career paths to explore as you get closer to graduation.

CAREER APPLICATIONS

1. Would someone with limited work experience but a long personal history of using social media be a good candidate for a community manager position? Why or why not?
2. What are the risks of having a single person be the voice of a company? How should companies address these risks?

Sources: Lindsay Kolowich, "What the Best Social Media Community Managers Actually Do in Their Jobs," HubSpot blog, 8 July 2015, blog.hubspot.com; Don Power, "In Their Own Words: What Community Managers Do Every Day," *SproutSocial*, 7 March 2013, sproutsocial.com; Ryan Lytle, "10 Qualities of an Effective Community Manager," *Mashable*, 27 January 2013, mashable.com; Jennifer Grayeb, "The 4 Pillars of Community Management," *Forbes*, 25 December 2013, www.forbes.com; Tim McDonald, "Community Manager: Key to the Future of Business," *Huffington Post*, 27 January 2014, www.huffingtonpost.

---

promotion.[21] These topics don't need to be earthshaking or cutting edge—they just need to be things that matter to target readers.

- **Encourage audiences to join the conversation.** Not all blogs invite comments, but many bloggers consider comments to be an essential feature. These comments can be a valuable source of news, information, and insights. In addition, the relatively informal nature of blogging seems to make it easier for company representatives to let their guards down and converse with their audiences. Of course, not all comments are helpful or appropriate, which is why many bloggers *moderate* comments, previewing them before allowing them to be displayed.

Most business blogs invite readers to leave comments as a way to encourage participation among stakeholders.

UNDERSTANDING THE BUSINESS APPLICATIONS OF BLOGGING

Blogs are a potential solution whenever you have a continuing stream of information to share with an online audience—and particularly when you want the audience to have the opportunity to respond. Here are some of the many ways businesses are using blogs:[22]

The business applications of blogs include a wide range of internal and external communication tasks.

- **Anchoring the social media presence.** As noted earlier, the multiple threads of any social media program should be anchored in a central hub that the company or an individual owns and controls. Blogs make an ideal social media hub.
- **Project management and team communication.** Using blogs is a good way to keep project teams up to date, particularly when team members are geographically dispersed.
- **Internal company news.** Companies can use blogs to keep employees informed about general business matters,

REAL-TIME UPDATES

LEARN MORE BY VISITING THIS WEBSITE

Big companies that blog well

Explore 10 blogs from such major brands as Coca-Cola and Disney. Go to **real-timeupdates.com/bct14** and select Learn More in the Students section.

from facility news to benefit updates. By reducing the need for grapevines to spring up, blogs can enhance communication across all levels of a company.

- **Customer support.** Customer support blogs answer questions, offer tips and advice, and inform customers about new products. Also, many companies monitor the *blogosphere* (and *Twittersphere*), looking for complaints and responding with offers to help dissatisfied customers.[23]

- **Public relations and media relations.** Many company employees and executives now share company news with both the general public and journalists via their blogs.

- **Recruiting.** Using a blog is a great way to let potential employees know more about your company, the people who work there, and the nature of the company culture. In the other direction, employers often find and evaluate the blogs and microblogs of prospective employees, making blogging a great way to build a name for yourself within your industry or profession.

- **Policy and issue discussions.** Executive blogs in particular provide a public forum for discussing legislation, regulations, and other broad issues of interest to an organization.

- **Crisis communication.** Using blogs is an efficient way to provide up-to-the-minute information during emergencies, to correct misinformation, or to respond to rumors.

- **Market research.** Blogs are a clever mechanism for soliciting feedback from customers and experts in the marketplace. In addition to using their own blogs for research, today's companies need to monitor blogs that are likely to discuss them, their executives, and their products. Negative product reviews, rumors, and other information can spread across the globe in a matter of hours, and managers need to know what the online community is saying—whether it's positive or negative.

- **Brainstorming.** Online brainstorming via blogs offers a way for people to toss around ideas and build on each others' contributions.

- **Employee engagement.** Blogs can enhance communication across all levels of a company, giving senior managers a channel they can use to communicate with employees and giving employees the chance to offer comments and ask questions.

- **Customer education.** Blogs are a great way to help current and potential customers understand and use your products and services. Doing so can also improve sales and support productivity by reducing the need for one-on-one communication.

- **Word-of-mouth marketing.** Bloggers and microbloggers often make a point of providing links to other blogs and websites that interest them, giving marketers a great opportunity to have their messages spread by enthusiasts. Word-of-mouth marketing is often called *viral marketing* in reference to the transmission of messages in much the same way that biological viruses are transmitted from person to person. However, viral marketing is not really an accurate metaphor. As author Brian Solis puts it, "There is no such thing as viral marketing."[24] Real viruses spread from host to host on their own, whereas word-of-mouth marketing requires "hosts" to spread messages *voluntarily*. The distinction is critical because you need to give people a good reason—good content, in other words—to pass along your message.

- **Influencing traditional media news coverage.** According to the social media consultant Tamar Weinberg, "The more prolific bloggers who provide valuable and consistent content are often considered experts in their subject matter" and are often called upon when journalists need insights into various topics.[25]

- **Community building.** Blogging is a great way to connect people with similar interests, and popular bloggers often attract a community of readers who connect with one another through the commenting function.

The possibilities of blogs are almost unlimited, so be on the lookout for new ways to use them to foster positive relationships with colleagues, customers, and other important audiences (see Figure 8.2).

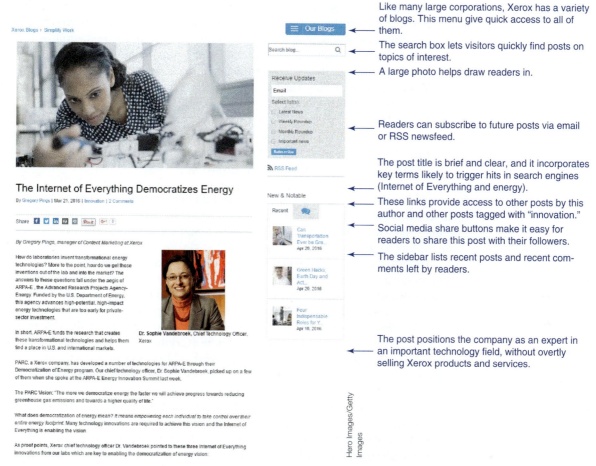

Like many large corporations, Xerox has a variety of blogs. This menu give quick access to all of them.

The search box lets visitors quickly find posts on topics of interest.

A large photo helps draw readers in.

Readers can subscribe to future posts via email or RSS newsfeed.

The post title is brief and clear, and it incorporates key terms likely to trigger hits in search engines (Internet of Everything and energy).

These links provide access to other posts by this author and other posts tagged with "innovation."

Social media share buttons make it easy for readers to share this post with their followers.

The sidebar lists recent posts and recent comments left by readers.

The post positions the company as an expert in an important technology field, without overtly selling Xerox products and services.

Hero Images/Getty Images

Figure 8.2 **Business Applications of Blogging**
This Xerox blog illustrates the content, writing style, and features that make an effective, reader-friendly company blog.
Source: Courtesy of Xerox Corporation.

ADAPTING THE THREE-STEP PROCESS FOR SUCCESSFUL BLOGGING

The three-step writing process is easy to adapt to blogging. The planning step is particularly important if you're considering starting a blog because you're planning an entire communication channel, not just a single message. Pay close attention to your audience, your purpose, and your scope.

- **Audience.** Except with team blogs and other efforts that have an obvious and well-defined audience, defining the target audience for a blog can be challenging. You want an audience that is large enough to justify the time you'll be investing but narrow enough that you can provide a clear focus. For instance, if you work for a firm that develops computer games, would you focus your blog on "hardcore" players, the types who spend thousands of dollars on super-fast PCs optimized for video games, or would you broaden the reach to include all video gamers? The decision often comes down to business strategy.
- **Purpose.** A business blog needs to have a business-related purpose that is important to your company and to your chosen audience. Moreover, the purpose has to "have legs"—that is, it needs to be something that can drive the blog's content for months or years—rather than focus on a single event or an issue of only temporary interest. For instance, if you're a technical expert, you might create a blog to give the audience tips and techniques for using your company's products more effectively—a never-ending subject that's important to both you and your audience.

Before you launch a blog, make sure you have a clear understanding of your target audience, the purpose of your blog, and the scope of subjects you plan to cover.

This would be the general purpose of your blog; each post would have a specific purpose within the context of that general purpose. Finally, if you are not writing an official company blog but rather blogging as an individual employee, make sure you understand your employer's blogging guidelines. IBM, for example, gives its employees 12 specific social computing guidelines, such as identifying their role as IBM employees if they are discussing matters related to the company and respecting intellectual property laws.[26]

- **Scope.** Defining the scope of your blog can be a bit tricky. You want to cover a subject area that is broad enough to offer ongoing discussion possibilities but narrow enough to have an identifiable focus. With a clear purpose in mind, you'll have a better idea of how wide or narrow your subject can be.

After you begin writing your blog, careful planning needs to continue with each message. Unless you're posting to a restricted-access blog, such as an internal blog on a company's intranet, you can never be sure who might see your posts or when other bloggers might link to them.

The ideal writing style for blog posts is personal and comfortable—but not careless.

Use a comfortable, personal writing style. Blog audiences don't want to hear from your company; they want to hear from *you*. Bear in mind, though, that comfortable does not mean careless. Sloppy writing annoys readers and damages your credibility.

Successful blog content also needs to be interesting, valuable to readers, and as brief as possible.[27] In addition, although audiences expect you to be knowledgeable in the subject area your blog covers, you don't need to know everything about a topic. If you don't have all the information yourself, provide links to other blogs and websites that supply relevant content. In fact, content curation (see page 213) is one of the most valuable aspects of blogging.

As with email subject lines, compelling headlines for blog posts are an essential tool to draw in readers. A headline needs to grab the reader's attention in a split second by promising something useful, surprising, challenging, or otherwise different from what he or she already knows. Headlines should be as short as possible and suggest that the information in the post will be easy to read and use. "List" headlines that cut right to the heart of something readers care about, such as "10 Reasons You Didn't Get That Promotion" or "Seven Ways to Save Money with Your Smartphone," are particularly popular among bloggers.

Completing messages for your blog is usually easy. Evaluate the content and readability of your message, proofread to correct any errors, and post it. Most blogging systems have built-in *newsfeed options* (often called RSS newsfeeds) so that your audience can automatically receive new posts from you.

Finally, make your material easier to find by **tagging** it with descriptive words. Your readers can then select these "content labels" to find additional posts about those topics. Tags are usually displayed with each post, and they can also be grouped in a *tag cloud* display, which shows all the tags in use on your blog.

"Checklist: Blogging for Business" summarizes some of the key points to remember when creating and writing a business blog.

CHECKLIST ✔ Blogging for Business

- Consider creating a blog or microblog account whenever you have a continuing stream of information to share with an online audience.
- Identify an audience that is broad enough to justify the effort but narrow enough to have common interests.
- Identify a purpose that is comprehensive enough to provide ideas for a continuing stream of posts.
- Consider the scope of your blog carefully; make it broad enough to attract an audience but narrow enough to keep you focused.

- Communicate with a personal style and an authentic voice, but don't write carelessly.
- Deliver new information quickly.
- Choose topics of peak interest to your audience.
- Encourage audiences to join the conversation.
- Consider using Twitter or other microblog updates to alert readers to new posts on your regular blog.

Microblogging

A **microblog** is a variation on blogging in which messages are sharply restricted to specific character counts. Twitter is the best known of these systems, but many others exist. Some companies have private microblogging systems for internal use only, either as standalone services or as part of broader collaboration systems.

Many of the concepts of regular blogging apply to microblogging as well, although the severe length limitations call for a different approach to composition. Microblog messages often involve short summaries or teasers that provide links to more information. In addition, microblogs tend to have a stronger social aspect that makes it easier for writers and readers to forward messages and for communities to form around individual writers.[28]

Like regular blogging, microblogging quickly caught on with business users and is now a mainstream business medium. Microblogs are used for virtually all of the blog applications mentioned on pages 215–216. In addition, microblogs are frequently used for providing company updates, offering coupons and notices of sales, presenting tips on product usage, sharing relevant and interesting information from experts, announcing the headlines of new blog posts, engaging with customers (see Figure 8.3), and serving as the *backchannel* in meetings and presentations (see page 477). By following top names in your field, you can also customize Twitter as your own real-time news source.[29]

Customer service is also becoming a popular use for Twitter, thanks to its ease and speed and the option of switching between public tweets and private direct messages as the situation warrants.[30] Even if a company doesn't want to use Twitter as a customer service channel, it should monitor the system to look for complaints or questions from customers, many of whom use Twitter these days to ask for help or publicize their disappointment.

The social networking aspect of Twitter and other microblogs also makes them good for *crowdsourcing* research questions: asking one's followers for input or advice.[31] Finally, the

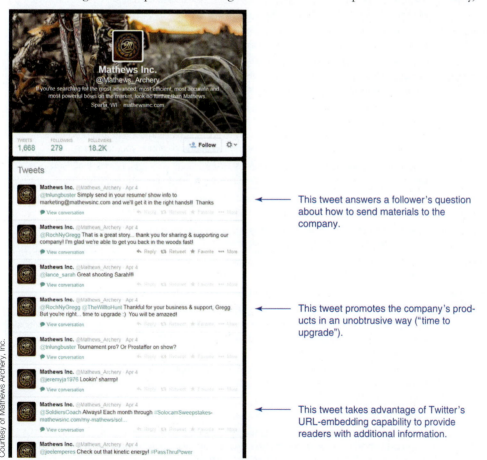

This tweet answers a follower's question about how to send materials to the company.

This tweet promotes the company's products in an unobtrusive way ("time to upgrade").

This tweet takes advantage of Twitter's URL-embedding capability to provide readers with additional information.

Courtesy of Mathews Archery, Inc.

Figure 8.3 **Business Applications of Microblogging**
Mathews, a small manufacturer of archery products, uses Twitter to foster relationships with customers and other interested parties. Notice how every tweet in this time line is part of a conversation.

REAL-TIME UPDATES

LEARN MORE BY READING THIS ARTICLE

Tips for ensuring a positive Twitter experience

Twitter offers advice for getting the most from the service while avoiding common blunders. Go to **real-timeupdates.com/bct14** and select Learn More in the Students section.

Don't let the speed and simplicity of microblogging lull you into making careless mistakes; every message should support your business communication objectives.

ease of *retweeting*, the practice of forwarding messages from other Twitter users, is the microblogging equivalent of sharing other content from other bloggers via content curation.

In addition to its usefulness as a standalone system, Twitter is integrated with other social media systems and a variety of publishing and reading tools and services. Many of these make use of the informal Twitter feature known as the *hashtag* (the # symbol followed by a word or phrase), which makes it easy for people to label and search for topics of interest and to monitor ongoing Twitter conversations about particular topics. As Starbucks discovered, however, hashtags can turn into "bashtags" when members of the public use a hashtag campaign to ridicule or criticize a company[32] (see page 205).

Although microblogs are designed to encourage spontaneous communication, when you're using the medium for business communication, don't just tweet whatever pops into your head. Make sure messages are part of your overall communication strategy. Twitter followers consider tweets that are entertaining, surprising, informative, or engaging (such as asking followers for advice) as the most valuable. In contrast, the least-valuable tweets tend to be complaints, conversations between the Twitter account owner and a specific follower, and relatively pointless messages such as saying "good morning."[33]

Table 8.1 summarizes the advice for successful blogging and microblogging in business.

TABLE 8.1   Tips for Effective Business Blogging and Microblogging

Tip	Why It's Important
Don't blog without a clear plan.	Without a clear plan, your blog or Twitter feed is likely to wander from topic to topic and fail to build a sense of community with your audience.
Post frequently, but don't overwhelm your readers.	If you won't have a constant supply of new information or new links, create a traditional website instead. On the other hand, blogging or tweeting too often can overwhelm your followers.
Make it about your audience and the issues important to them.	Readers want to know how your blog will help them, entertain them, or give them a chance to communicate with others who have similar interests.
Write in an authentic voice; never create an artificial character who supposedly writes a blog.	*Flogs*, or fake blogs, violate the spirit of blogging, show disrespect for your audience, and will turn audiences against you as soon as they uncover the truth. Fake blogs that are used to promote products are now illegal in some countries.
Link and retweet generously—but carefully.	Providing interesting links to other blogs and websites is a fundamental aspect of blogging, but make sure the links will be of value to your readers, and don't point to inappropriate material. Similarly, retweeting is a good way to share interesting content and build relationships with other Twitter users, but retweeting too often can annoy your followers.
Keep blog posts brief.	Most online readers don't have the patience to read lengthy reports. Rather than writing long, report-style posts, you can write brief posts that link to in-depth reports.
Don't post or tweet anything you wouldn't want the entire world to see.	Future employers, government regulators, competitors, journalists, and community critics are just a few of the people who might eventually see what you've written.
Minimize marketing and sales messages.	Even product enthusiasts and motivated shoppers don't want to be "sold to" on company blogs. They want information about how products and services will meet their needs.
Take time to write compelling, specific headlines for your posts.	Readers usually decide within a couple of seconds whether to read a post; boring or vague headlines will turn them away instantly.
Pay attention to spelling, grammar, and mechanics.	No matter how smart or experienced you are, poor-quality writing undermines your credibility with intelligent audiences.
Respond to criticism openly and honestly.	Hiding sends the message that you don't have a valid response to the criticism. If your critics are wrong, patiently explain why you think they're wrong. If they are right, explain how you'll fix the situation.
Listen and learn.	If you don't take the time to analyze the comments people leave on your blog or the comments other bloggers make about you, you're missing out on one of the most valuable aspects of blogging.
Respect intellectual property.	Improperly using material you don't own is not only unethical but can be illegal as well.
Be scrupulously honest and careful with facts.	Honesty is an absolute requirement for every ethical business communicator, of course, but you need to be extra careful online because inaccuracies (both intentional and unintentional) are likely to be discovered quickly and shared widely.
If you review products on your blog, disclose any beneficial relationships you have with the companies that make those products.	Bloggers who receive free products or other compensation from companies whose products they write about are now required to disclose the nature of these relationships.

Wikis

As Chapter 2 points out, using wikis is a great way for teams and other groups to collaborate on writing projects, from brief articles to long reports and reference works. The benefits of wikis are compelling, but they do require a unique approach to writing.

UNDERSTANDING THE WIKI PHILOSOPHY

To be a valuable wiki contributor, keep these points in mind:[34]

- Let go of traditional expectations of authorship, including individual recognition and control.
- Encourage all team members to improve each other's work.
- Use page templates and other formatting options to make sure your content matches the rest of the wiki.
- Many wikis provide both editing and commenting capabilities, and participants should use the appropriate tool for each. In other words, don't insert comments or questions into the main content; use the "talk page" or other commenting feature if you want to discuss the content.
- Take advantage of the *sandbox*, if available; this is a "safe," nonpublished section of the wiki where team members can practice editing and writing.

Wikis often have guideline pages to help new contributors integrate their work into the group's ongoing effort. Be sure to read and understand these guidelines, and don't be afraid to ask for help.

Being an effective wiki collaborator requires a different mindset when writing.

ADAPTING THE THREE-STEP PROCESS FOR SUCCESSFUL WIKI WRITING

You can easily adapt the three-step writing process for wikis, depending on whether you are creating a new wiki, adding new material to an existing wiki, or revising existing material on a wiki.

If you are creating a new wiki, think through your long-term purpose carefully, just as you would with a new blog or podcast channel. Doing so will help you craft appropriate guidelines, editorial oversight, and security policies.

If you are adding a page or an article to an existing wiki, figure out how this new material fits in with the existing organization. Determine whether any similar material already exists; it might be better to expand an existing article or add a subpage than to create a new item. Also, learn the wiki's preferred style for handling incomplete articles. For example, on the wiki that contains the user documentation for the popular WordPress blogging software, contributors are discouraged from adding new pages until the content is "fairly complete and accurate."[35]

Make sure you understand how a new wiki page will fit in with the existing content.

If you are revising or updating an existing wiki article, use the checklist on page 157 in Chapter 6 to evaluate the content before you make changes. If you don't agree with published content and plan to revise it, you can use the wiki's discussion facility to share your concerns with other contributors. The wiki environment should encourage discussions and even robust disagreements, as long as everyone remains civil and respectful.

For the latest advice on using social media in business, visit **real-timeupdates.com/bct14** and select Chapter 8.

COMMUNICATION CHALLENGES AT **Starbucks**

You've joined Alexandra Wheeler's social media team. Use what you've learned in the course so far to solve these communication dilemmas.

INDIVIDUAL CHALLENGE: You've written a blog entry describing an upcoming competition in which the small town that submits the most creative "community spirit" video will win a $50,000 makeover of a park or community center. Write a tweet of no more than 140 characters that could serve as a teaser to persuade your Twitter followers to click through to the blog post.

TEAM CHALLENGE: One member of the social media team is retiring, and you've been asked to recruit her replacement, whose primary responsibility will be blogging. Your plan is to send an email message to everyone in the company, providing a brief reminder of the blog's purpose, describing the writing style you're looking for, and inviting interested writers to submit sample blog entries for evaluation. (This message is for employees only; it won't be seen by the public.) With a team assigned by your instructor, brainstorm the ideal qualities of writer for the Starbucks blog, then draft the email invitation.

Quick Learning Guide

KEY TERMS

blog An easily updatable online journal; short for *weblog*

brand communities Groups of people united by their interest in and ownership or use of particular products

brand socialization A measure of how effectively a company engages with its various online stakeholders in a mutually beneficial exchange of information

community Q&A sites Websites on which visitors answer questions posted by other visitors or by company representatives

content curation The practice of collecting, filtering, and republishing material on a particular topic

microblog A variation on a blog in which messages are restricted to specific character counts; Twitter is the best-known example

social networks Online services that enable individual and organizational members to form connections and share information

tagging Attaching descriptive terms to blog posts and other articles to facilitate searching

user-generated content (UGC) sites Websites on which users, rather than website owners, contribute most or all of the content

SUMMARY OF LEARNING OBJECTIVES

1 **Identify seven key points for using social media in business communication.** Seven key points for using social media are (1) remember that it's a conversation, not a lecture or a sales pitch; (2) write informally but not carelessly; (3) create concise, specific, and informative headlines that don't force readers to solve clever wordplay puzzles; (4) get involved and stay involved with conversations that concern your company; (5) promote your company and products indirectly; (6) be transparent and honest; and (7) think before you post to avoid problems caused by careless messages.

2 **Describe the business communication applications of social networks.** Businesses now use a variety of social networks, including well-known public networks such as Facebook and business-oriented networks such as LinkedIn, as well as a variety of specialized networks, single-company networks for customers, and internal employee-only networks. The business communication applications of social networks are important and diverse; major uses include collaborating, gathering market intelligence, recruiting employees, connecting with business partners, marketing, and fostering brand communities.

3 **Explain how information- and content-sharing sites are used in business communication.** User-generated content sites such as YouTube allow companies to host media (such as videos) that customers and other stakeholders can view, comment on, and share. Content curation sites allow professionals and consumers with expertise or interest in a particular field to collect and republish material on a particular topic. Community Q&A sites give individuals the opportunity to build their personal brands by providing expertise, and they give companies the chance to address customer complaints and correct misinformation.

4 **Describe the role of blogging in business communication today, and explain how to adapt the three-step writing process to blogging.** Blogs are used in numerous ways in business today, such as for project management and team communication, company news, customer support, public relations and media relations, employee recruiting, policy and issue discussions, crisis communication, market research, brainstorming, employee engagement, viral marketing, influencing traditional media news coverage, and community building.

The three-step writing process adapts readily to blogging. When planning, be particularly careful in defining your audience, identifying the overall purpose of your blog and the specific purposes of each post, and establishing a scope that is narrow enough to be focused but broad enough to afford a steady supply of topics. Be sure to write in a personal, authentic style, without slipping into overly familiar or careless writing. Completing messages involves the usual tasks of proofing and revising before posting, along with the particular tasks needed to distribute your posts via newsfeeds.

5 **Describe the business uses of Twitter and other microblogging systems.** Microblogs such as Twitter are used for many of the same purposes as conventional blogging, along with digital coupons, sale announcements, one-on-one customer service queries, and customized news channels created by following experts of interest. Microblogs can also serve as the backchannel during meetings and presentations.

6 **Offer guidelines for becoming a valuable wiki contributor.** To become a valuable wiki contributor, let go of traditional expectations of authorship, including individual recognition and control; don't be afraid to edit and improve existing content; use page templates and other formatting options to make sure your content is formatted in the same style as the rest of the wiki; keep edits and comments separate by using the "talk page" to discuss content, rather than inserting comments directly into the text; take advantage of the sandbox to learn how use the wiki's writing and editing tools; and understand and follow the wiki's contributor guidelines.

MyBCommLab

Go to **mybcommlab.com** to complete the problems marked with this icon .

Test Your Knowledge

To review chapter content related to each question, refer to the indicated Learning Objective.

8-1. Why are straightforward, informative headlines better for social media than headlines with witty wordplay? [LO-1]

8-2. How have social media tools spurred the growth of communities of practice? [LO-2]

8-3. What does it mean to anchor your social media presence in a hub? [LO-2]

8-4. What is content curation? [LO-3]

8-5. How can blogs help with so-called viral marketing efforts? [LO-4]

8-6. Why is it important to have a long-term, sustainable purpose in mind before you launch a blog? [LO-4]

8-7. How can Twitter be used to crowdsource research? [LO-5]

8-8. How does the use of hashtags on Twitter help people find information of interest? [LO-5]

8-9. Why is it important to abandon traditional notions of ownership when writing on a wiki? [LO-6]

Apply Your Knowledge

To review chapter content related to each question, refer to the indicated Learning Objective.

8-10. Can your company stay in control of its messages if it stays off social media? Why or why not? [LO-1]

8-11. Is leveraging your connections on social networks for business purposes ethical? Why or why not? [LO-2]

8-12. If one of the benefits of blogging and microblogging is the personal, intimate style of writing, is it a good idea to limit your creativity by adhering to conventional rules of grammar, spelling, and mechanics? Why or why not? [LO-4]

8-13. What are some of the ways the president of a hiking equipment company can use Twitter to engage potential customers without being overtly promotional? [LO-5]

8-14. If you know that most readers of your management advice blog access it on mobile devices, should you switch to Twitter instead so the shorter messages would be easier to read on small screens? Why or why not? [LO-5]

Practice Your Skills

8-15. **Message for Analysis 8.A: Media Skills: Blogging, Creating a Businesslike Tone [LO-4]** Revise this blog post based on what you've learned in this chapter.

[headline]

We're DOOMED!!!!!

[post]

I was at the Sikorsky plant in Stratford yesterday, just checking to see how things were going with the assembly line retrofit we did for them last year. I think I saw the future, and it ain't pretty. They were demo'ing a prototype robot from Motoman that absolutely blows our stuff out of the water. They wouldn't let me really see it, but based on the 10-second glimpse I got, it's smaller, faster, and more maneuverable than any of our units. And when I asked about the price, the guy just grinned. And it wasn't the sort of grin designed to make me feel good.

I've been saying for years that we need to pay more attention to size, speed, and maneuverability instead of just relying on our historical strengths of accuracy and payload capacity, and you'd have to be blind not to agree that this experience proves me right. If we can't at least show a design for a better unit within two or three months, Motoman is going to lock up the market and leave us utterly in the dust.

Believe me, being able to say "I told you so" right now is not nearly as satisfying as you might think!!

8-16. **Message 8.B: Revising Web Content with a "You" Attitude [LO-6]** To access this wiki exercise, visit **real-timeupdates.com/bct14**, select Student Assignments, then select Chapter 8, Message 8.B. Follow the instructions for evaluating the existing content and revising it to make it more reader oriented.

8-17. **Message 8.C: Improving the Effectiveness of a Wiki Article [LO-6]** To access this wiki exercise, go to **real-timeupdates.com/bct14**, select Student Assignments, then select Chapter 8, Message 8.C. Follow the instructions for evaluating the existing content and revising it to make it clear and concise.

Exercises

Each activity is labeled according to the primary skill or skills you will need to use. To review relevant chapter content, you can refer to the indicated Learning Objective. In some instances, supporting information will be found in another chapter, as indicated.

8-18. **Media Skills: Social Networking [LO-2]** Pick a company in any industry that interests you. Imagine you are doing strategic planning for this firm, and identify one of your company's key competitors. (Hint: You can use the free listings on **www.hoovers.com** to find several top competitors for most medium-size and large companies in the United States.) Now search through social media sources to find three strategically relevant pieces of information about this competitor, such as the hiring of a new executive, the launch of a major new product, or a significant problem of some kind. In a post on your class blog, identify the information you found and the sources you used. (If you can't find useful information, pick another firm or try another industry.)

8-19. **Media Skills: Social Networking [LO-2]** Joining an ongoing social media conversation, such as a comment thread on Facebook, requires a delicate touch if you work for a company that has a commercial interest in the subject at hand. Imagine you work for a company that makes audiophile-quality headphones, acoustic guitars, or electronic drum kits (choose whichever product interests you most). While monitoring a Facebook group for enthusiasts of this product category, you see an active thread in which people are complaining about the quality of one of your competitor's products. You know that for years this company had a reputation for making high-quality equipment, but after a poorly executed plan to outsource manufacturing in order to cut costs, quality has suffered. A similar product that your company offers is slightly more expensive but has significantly higher quality, according to a recent survey conducted by a respected and impartial industry website.

Draft a brief comment that you could use to join the conversation. Decide what information you'll include and whether you will disclose your company affiliation. Assume that representatives from various companies do occasionally make posts and leave comments in this group, but overt selling is explicitly forbidden by the group's moderator.

8-20. **Media Skills: Blogging, Creating a Businesslike Tone; Mobile Skills [LO-4]** The members of the project team you lead have enthusiastically embraced blogging as a communication medium. Unfortunately, as emotions heat up during the project, some of the blog posts are becoming too casual, too personal, and even sloppy. Because your boss and other managers within the company also read this project blog, you don't want the team to seem unprofessional. Revise the following blog post so that it communicates in a more businesslike manner while retaining the informal, conversational tone of a blog. In addition, break it into smaller paragraphs that are more compatible with mobile devices. (Be sure to correct any spelling and punctuation mistakes you find as well.)

[post]

Well, to the profound surprise of absolutely nobody, we are not going to be able meet the June 1 commitment to ship 100 operating tables to Southeast Surgical Supply. (For those of you who have been living in a cave the past six month, we have been fighting to get our hands on enough high-grade chromium steel to meet our production schedule.) Sure enough, we got news, this morning that we will only get enough for 30 tables. Yes, we look like fools for not being able to follow through on promises we made to the customer, but no, this didn't have to happpen. Six month's ago, purchasing warned us about shrinking supplies and suggested we advance-buy as much as we would need for the next 12 months, or so. We naturally tried to followed their advice, but just as naturally were shot down by the bean counters at corporate who trotted out the policy about never buying more than three months worth of materials in

advance. Of course, it'll be us—not the bean counters who'll take the flak when everybody starts asking why revenues are down next quarter and why Southeast is talking to our friends at Crighton!!! Maybe, some day this company will get its head out of the sand and realize that we need to have some financial flexibility in order to compete.

8-21. **Media Skills: Blogging [LO-4]** Find a current political issue that could have a direct effect on business, such as immigration law, Internet sales tax, product safety, or international trade policy. Identify a company that is affected by this issue, and assume you are the president or CEO and want to speak out about it. Write a three-paragraph blog post that summarizes the issue, explains how it could affect your company, and urges a particular action from political leaders.

8-22. **Media Skills: Microblogging [LO-5]** Busy knitters can go through a lot of yarn in a hurry, so most keep a sharp eye out for sales. You're on the marketing staff of Knitting-Warehouse, and you like to keep your loyal shoppers up to date with the latest deals. Visit the Knitting-Warehouse website at **www.knitting-warehouse.com**, choose any on-sale product that catches your eye, and compose a tweet that describes the product and the sale. (Unless you are working on a private Twitter account that is accessible only by your instructor and your classmates, don't actually tweet this message. Email it to your instructor instead.)

8-23. **Media Skills: Microblogging [LO-5]** Choose a product you purchased recently or something you're considering purchasing. Compose a three-tweet sequence that (1) introduces the product, (2) lists two or three important advantages, and (3) identifies which groups of consumers can benefit from it. Email your tweets to your instructor rather than posting them on Twitter.

Expand Your Skills

Critique the Professionals

On Twitter, find two companies in the same industry and review a dozen recent tweets from each. Considering the tweets from the perspective of a potential customer, which company does a better job of engaging your attention and building your interest in its products? Using whatever medium your instructor requests, write a brief analysis of the two companies' Twitter activity, and explain why one is using the social network more effectively than the other.

Sharpening Your Career Skills Online

Bovée and Thill's Business Communication Web Search, at **websearch.businesscommunicationnetwork.com**, is a unique research tool designed specifically for business communication research. Use the Web Search function to find a website, video, article, podcast, or presentation that offers advice on using social media in business. In a brief email message to your instructor, describe the item that you found and summarize the career skills information you learned from it.

Cases

For all cases, feel free to use your creativity to make up any details you need in order to craft effective messages.

SOCIAL NETWORKING SKILLS

8-24. Media Skills: Social Networking; Media Skills: Micro-blogging [LO-2] [LO-5] Foursquare is one of the leading providers of location-based social networking services. Millions of people use Foursquare for social engagement and friendly competition, and many business owners are starting to recognize the marketing potential of having people who are on the move in local areas broadcast their locations and share information about stores, restaurants, clubs, and other merchants.

Your task: Review the information on Foursquare's Merchant Platform at business.foursquare.com. Now write four brief messages, no more than 140 characters long. The first should summarize the benefits to stores, restaurants, and other "brick-and-mortar" businesses of participating in Foursquare; the next three messages should convey three compelling points that support that overall benefit statement. If your class is set up with private Twitter accounts, use your private account to send your messages. Otherwise, email your four messages to your instructor or post them on your class blog, as your instructor directs.

SOCIAL NETWORKING SKILLS

8-25. Media Skills: Social Networking; Online Etiquette [LO-2], Chapter 2 Employees who take pride in their work are a priceless resource for any business. However, pride can sometimes manifest itself in negative ways when employees receive criticism—and public criticism is a fact of life in social media. Imagine that your company has recently experienced a rash of product quality problems, and these problems have generated some unpleasant and occasionally unfair criticism on a variety of social media sites. Someone even set up a Facebook page specifically to give customers a place to vent their frustrations.

You and your public relations team jumped into action, responding to complaints with offers to provide replacement products and help customers who have been affected by the quality problems. Everything seemed to be going as well as could be expected, until you were checking a few industry blogs one evening and discovered that a couple of engineers in your company's product design lab have been responding to complaints on their own. They identified themselves as company employees and defended their product design, blaming the company's production department and even criticizing several customers for lacking the skills needed to use such a sophisticated product. Within a matter of minutes, you see their harsh comments being retweeted and reposted on multiple sites, only fueling the fire of negative feedback against your firm. Needless to say, you are horrified.

Your task: You manage to reach the engineers by private message and tell them to stop posting messages, but you realize you have a serious training issue on your hands. Write a post for the internal company blog that advises employees on how to respond appropriately when they are representing the company online. Use your imagination to make up any details you need.

SOCIAL NETWORKING SKILLS/TEAM SKILLS

8-26. Media Skills: Social Networking [LO-2] Social media can be a great way to, well, socialize during your college years, but employers are increasingly checking the online activities of potential hires to avoid bringing in employees who may reflect poorly on the company.

Your task: Team up with another student and review each other's public presence on Facebook, Twitter, blogs, and any other website that an employer might check during the interview and recruiting process. Identify any photos, videos, messages, or other material that could raise a red flag when an employee is evaluating a job candidate. Write your teammate an email message that lists any risky material.

BLOGGING SKILLS

8-27. Media Skills: Blogging; Compositional Modes: Tutorials [LO-4] Studying abroad for a semester or a year can be a rewarding experience in many ways—improving your language skills, experiencing another culture, making contacts in the international business arena, and building your self-confidence.

Your task: Write a post for your class blog that describes your college's study abroad program and summarizes the steps involved in applying for international study. If your school doesn't offer study abroad opportunities, base your post on the program offered at another institution in your state.

BLOGGING SKILLS

8-28. Media Skills: Blogging [LO-4] Comic-Con International is an annual convention that highlights a wide variety of pop culture and entertainment media, from comic books and collectibles to video games and movies. From its early start as a comic book convention that attracted several hundred fans and publishing industry insiders, Comic-Con has become a major international event with more than 130,000 attendees.

Your task: Several readers of your pop culture blog have been asking for your recommendation about visiting Comic-Con in San Diego next summer. Write a two- or three-paragraph post for your blog that explains what Comic-Con is and what attendees can expect to experience at the convention. Be sure to address your post to fans, not industry insiders.[36]

BLOGGING SKILLS/MOBILE SKILLS

8-29. Media Skills: Blogging; Compositional Modes: Tutorials; Mobile Skills [LO-4] Tumblr has become a popular "short-form" blogging platform by combining the simplicity of Twitter with the ability to share photos and other media easily.

Your task: Write a 300- to 400-word mobile-friendly post for your class blog that explains how to set up an account on Tumblr and get involved in the Tumblr community. The help pages on Tumblr are a good place to get more information about the service.

BLOGGING SKILLS

8-30. Media Skills: Blogging [LO-4] Credit card debt can be a crippling financial burden with myriad side effects, from higher insurance rates to more expensive loans to difficulty getting a job or a promotion. Unfortunately, credit debt is also frighteningly easy to fall into, particularly for young people trying to get started in life with limited cash flow.

Your task: Write a three- to five-paragraph blog post that warns college students about the dangers of credit card debt. Be sure to cite the sources you find in your research.

MICROBLOGGING SKILLS

8-31. Media Skills: Microblogging; Compositional Modes: Summaries [LO-1] [LO-5] A carefully constructed series of tweets can serve as a summary of a blog post, video, or other message or document.

Your task: Find any article, podcast, video, or webpage on a business topic that interests you. Write four to six tweetables that summarize the content of the piece. Restrict the first tweetable to 120 characters to allow for a URL. Email the series to your instructor or publish them on Twitter if your instructor directs. If you quote phrases from the original directly, be sure to put them in quotation marks.

MICROBLOGGING SKILLS

8-32. Media Skills: Microblogging; Compositional Modes: Teasers [LO-5] Twitter updates are a great way to alert people to helpful articles, videos, and other online resources.

Your task: Find an online resource (it can be a website quiz, a YouTube video, a PowerPoint presentation, a newspaper article, or anything else appropriate) that offers some great tips to help college students prepare for job interviews. Write a teaser of no more than 120 characters that hints at the benefits other students can get from this resource. If your class is set up with private Twitter accounts, use your private account to send your message. Otherwise, email it to your instructor.

MICROBLOGGING SKILLS

8-33. Media Skills: Microblogging; Compositional Modes: Updates and Announcements [LO-5] JetBlue is known for its innovations in customer service and customer communication, including its pioneering use of the Twitter microblogging system. Nearly 2 million JetBlue fans and customers follow the company on Twitter to get updates on flight status during weather disruptions, facility upgrades, and other news.[37]

Your task: Write a message of no more than 140 characters that announces the limited-time availability of flights and travel packages—flights plus hotel rooms, for example—at JetBlue's store on eBay. The key selling point is that travelers may be able to purchase flights they want at steep discounts. If your class is set up with private Twitter accounts, use your private account to send your message. Otherwise, email it to your instructor.

WIKI SKILLS

8-34. Media Skills: Wiki Writing; Evaluating the Work of Other Writers [LO-6] Evaluating existing content is a vital step in making improvements to a wiki.

Your task: Find an article on Wikipedia that needs to be updated, corrected, or otherwise improved. You can use an article that has been flagged by Wikipedia editors or find an article on a subject you are familiar with, such as the profile of a favorite musical artist. To keep the project at a manageable size, feel free to select a portion of a longer article (roughly 500 to 1,000 words). Using the guidelines on page 157 for evaluating the work of other writers, evaluate the quality of the article and identify the steps you would take to improve it. Revise the piece and post your version on your class blog or email it to your instructor. Include a brief summary of the changes you made and your reasons for making them. (Do not edit the Wikipedia entry as part of this assignment.)

MyBCommLab

Go to **mybcommlab.com** for Auto-graded writing questions as well as the following Assisted-graded writing questions:

8-35. Why is "viral marketing" a misleading description? [LO-4]

8-36. Why does a personal style of writing help blogs build stronger relationships with audiences? [LO-4]

Endnotes

1. Starbucks website, accessed 11 February 2016, www.starbucks.com; "How Starbucks Social Media Team Captures the Personality of a Beverage," Starbucks news release, 6 May 2015, news.starbucks.com; David Moth, "How Starbucks Uses Pinterest, Facebook, Twitter and Google+" Econsultancy, 6 March 2013; Melissa Allison, "Starbucks Presses Social Media Onward," *Seattle Times*, 27 April 2013; Bethany Simpson, "3 Insane Starbucks Campaigns," iMedia Connection, 29 March 2012, www.imediaconnection.com; Starbucks U.S. and U.K. pages on Facebook, accessed 14 June 2013; Margaret Rhodes, "Most Creative People 2013: 12. Luz Muller," *Fast Company*, 13 May 2013.

2. Catherine Toole, "My 7 Deadly Sins of Writing for Social Media—Am I Right?" Econsultancy blog, 19 June 2007, www.econsultancy .com; Muhammad Saleem, "How to Write a Social Media Press Release," Copyblogger, accessed 16 September 2008, www.copyblogger .com; Melanie McBride, "5 Tips for (Better) Social Media Writing," Melanie McBride Online, 11 June 2008, accessed 16 September 2008, melaniemcbride.net.

3. "Tips for Effective Social Media Writing," MBO Partners, accessed 12 February 2016, www.mbopartners.com.

4. Renren website, accessed 11 February 2016, renren-inc.com; Jon Russell, "Why 'Going Global' Makes No Sense for China's Social Networks, for Now," The Next Web, 14 May 2012, thenextweb.com.

5. Charlene Li, "Why No One Uses the Corporate Social Network," *Harvard Business Review*, 7 April 2015, hbr.com.

6. Patrick Hong, "10 Exceptional Examples of Brand Communities," Momentology, 15 January 2015, www.momentology.com.

7. Todd Wasserman, "What Drives Brand Socialability?" *Mashable*, 12 October 2011, mashable.com.

8. Michelle Manafy, "Stop Acting Like a Robot and Start Socializing Your Brand," *Inc.*, 29 June 2015, www.inc.com; Mattel Twitter account, accessed 12 February 2016, twitter.com/mattel.

9. Muhtar Kent, "Shaking Things Up at Coca-Cola," *Harvard Business Review*, October 2011, 94–99.

10. Evolve24 website, accessed 10 February 2016, www.evolve24.com.

11. "The Top 20 Social Media Trends in 2016, According to the Experts," Bitly, 16 December 2015, blog.bitly.com; HeadTalker website, accessed 12 February 2016, headtalker.com.

12. Christian Pieter Hoffmann, "Holding Sway," *Communication World*, November–December 2011, 26–29; Josh Bernoff, "Social Strategy for Exciting (and Not So Exciting) Brands," *Marketing News*, 15 May 2009, 18; Larry Weber, *Marketing to the Social Web* (Hoboken, N.J.: Wiley, 2007), 12–14; David Meerman Scott, *The New Rules of Marketing and PR* (Hoboken, N.J.: Wiley, 2007), 62; Paul Gillin, *The New Influencers* (Sanger, Calif.: Quill Driver Books, 2007), 34–35; Jeremy Wright, *Blog Marketing: The Revolutionary Way to Increase Sales, Build Your Brand, and Get Exceptional Results* (New York: McGraw-Hill, 2006), 263–365.

13. Sonia Simone, "What's the Difference Between Content Marketing and Copywriting?" Copyblogger, accessed 4 June 2012, www.copyblogger.com.

14. Matt Rhodes, "Build Your Own Community or Go Where People Are? Do Both," FreshNetworks blog, 12 May 2009, www.freshnetworks.com.

15. Brian Solis, *Engage!* (Hoboken, N.J.: Wiley, 2010), 13.

16. Zachary Sniderman, "5 Ways to Clean Up Your Social Media Identity," *Mashable*, 7 July 2010, mashable.com.

17. Vanessa Pappas, "5 Ways to Build a Loyal Audience on YouTube," *Mashable*, 15 June 2010, www.mashable.com.

18. Eric Siu, "10 User Generated Content Campaigns That Actually Worked," HubSpot blog, 12 March 2015, blog.hubspot.com.

19. "About Us," Yelp, accessed 10 February 2016, www.yelp.com; Lisa Barone, "Keynote Conversation with Yelp Chief Operating Officer Geoff Donaker," Outspoken Media, 5 October 2010, outspokenmedia.com.

20. Ben Betts and Allison Anderson, "Diamond in the Rough," *TD: Talent Development*, January 2016, 30–34.

21. Amy Porterfield, "10 Top Business Blogs and Why They Are Successful," *Social Media Examiner*, 25 January 2011, www.socialmediaexaminer.com.

22. Debbie Weil, "Why Your Blog Is the Hub of Social Media Marketing," Social Media Insights blog, 12 January 2010, debbieweil .com; Ross Dawson, "A List of Business Applications for Blogging in the Enterprise," Trends in the Living Network blog, 7 July 2009, rossdawsonblog.com; Fredrik Wackå, "Six Types of Blogs—A Classification," CorporateBlogging.Info website, 10 August 2004, www.corporateblogging.info; Stephen Baker, "The Inside Story on Company Blogs," *BusinessWeek*, 14 February 2006, www.businessweek.com; Jeremy Wright, *Blog Marketing* (New York: McGraw-Hill, 2006), 45–56; Paul Chaney, "Blogs: Beyond the Hype!" Radiant Marketing Group blog, 26 May 2005, radiantmarketinggroup.com.

23. Solis, *Engage!*, 314.

24. Solis, *Engage!*, 86.

25. Tamara Weinberg, *The New Community Rules: Marketing on the Social Web* (Sebastopol, Calif.: O'Reilly Media, 2009), 89.

26. "IBM Social Computing Guidelines," IBM website, accessed 10 February 2016, www.ibm.com.

27. Joel Falconer, "Six Rules for Writing Great Web Content," Blog News Watch, 9 November 2007, accessed 14 February 2008, www.blognewswatch.com.

28. Dion Hinchcliffe, "Twitter on Your Intranet: 17 Microblogging Tools for Business," ZDNet, 1 June 2009, www.zdnet.com.

29. B. L. Ochman, "Why Twitter Is a Better Brand Platform Than Facebook," *Ad Age*, 1 June 2012, adage.com.

30. Leon Widrich, "4 Ways to Use Twitter for Customer Service and Support," *Social Media Examiner*, 12 April 2012, www.socialmediaexaminer.com.

31. Paul André, Michael Bernstein, and Kurt Luther, "What Makes a Great Tweet," *Harvard Business Review*, May 2012, 36–37.

32. Tom Hays and Jake Pearson, "Bashtag: NYPD Twitter Campaign Backfires," *Seattle Times*, 23 April 2014, www.seattletimes .com.

33. André et al., "What Makes a Great Tweet."

34. "Codex: Guidelines," WordPress website, accessed 10 February 2016, wordpress.org; Michael Shanks, "Wiki Guidelines," Traumwerk website, accessed 18 August 2006, metamedia.stanford .edu/projects/traumwerk/home; Joe Moxley, M. C. Morgan, Matt Barton, and Donna Hanak, "For Teachers New to Wikis," Writing Wiki, accessed 18 August 2006, writingwiki.org; "Wiki Guidelines," Psi, accessed 18 August 2006, psi-im.org.

35. "Codex: Guidelines."

36. Comic-Con website, accessed 27 February 2016, www.comic con.org; Tom Spurgeon, "Welcome to Nerd Vegas: A Guide to Visiting and Enjoying Comic-Con International 2014," The Comics Reporter, 25 May 2014, www.comicsreporter.com; Rebecca Winters Keegan, "Boys Who Like Toys," *Time*, 19 April 2007, www.time .com.

37. JetBlue Twitter page, accessed 3 February 2011, twitter.com/ JetBlue.

9 Visual Media

LEARNING OBJECTIVES

After studying this chapter, you will be able to

1 Explain the power of business images, discuss six principles of graphic design that help ensure effective visuals, and explain how to avoid ethical lapses when using visuals.

2 Explain how to choose which points in your message to illustrate.

3 Describe the most common options for presenting data in a visual format.

4 Describe the most common options for presenting information, concepts, and ideas.

5 Explain how to integrate visuals with text, and list three criteria to review in order to verify the quality of your visuals.

6 Identify the most important considerations in the preproduction, production, and postproduction stages of producing basic business videos.

COMMUNICATION CLOSE-UP AT

GoPro

gopro.com

If you've watched a daredevil video on YouTube in the past few years, chances are the video was shot with a GoPro camera. GoPro's digital cameras have captured everything from extreme snowboarders to Felix Baumgartner's epic 24-mile freefall leap from the edge of space. The "adrenaline market" is at the core of the GoPro brand, but the growing population of GoPro users also includes filmmakers, sports and wildlife photographers, oceanographers, atmospheric researchers, and others who need high-quality video footage from a small, rugged, and relatively inexpensive digital camera.

Not surprisingly, for its own business communication needs GoPro makes extensive use of video. Like many companies,

© epa european pressphoto agency b.v./Alamy Stock Photo

Viewer interest in extreme sports and other eye-catching events and phenomena created a huge market for GoPro's video cameras. Under the leadership of founder and CEO Nick Woodman, the company has capitalized on this visceral appeal with an extensive social media presence centered on online video.

it uses video to showcase new products and provide how-to advice for customers. However, GoPro has gone far beyond what many companies do with video by harnessing the amplifying power of social media. The company has taken user-generated content to the extreme, using a variety of recognition and reward mechanisms to encourage GoPro customers to submit video clips. For example, GoPro runs a nonstop contest that recognizes customers for the best footage shot on GoPro cameras. These photos and clips are then highlighted on the company's website and all across the major social media platforms, including YouTube, Facebook, Twitter, Google+, and Instagram.

The company's strategy of building a global video community has been a huge success. When Google (which owns YouTube) announced its first-ever monthly ranking of the highest-performing branded channels on YouTube, it determined that GoPro had the most engaged fan base. To measure engagement, Google factors in such variables as the amount of time visitors spending watching videos, the number of repeat visitors, and the number of times people "like" a video or leave a comment. When you consider that virtually every video on GoPro's YouTube channel functions as an advertisement for the company's cameras, you get an idea of the immense promotional power that this high level of engagement represents.

After several years of rocketing growth while amateurs and professionals scooped up its ever-improving cameras, GoPro captured 70 percent of the market for action cameras. However, the market became more or less saturated at that point, as most people who wanted a camera had one. With its primary market satisfied, the company faces the classic "now what?" question that many growing companies face. GoPro has decided to move into the drone market, where its cameras have been used on other companies' drones for some time. Whether it can gain a foothold as a drone manufacturer remains to be seen, but the company will surely continue to leverage the power of video and social outreach as it tries to repeat its early success.

Video is an obvious choice of medium for a company that makes video cameras, but video has become a primary business communication medium for companies in virtually every industry. From product tutorials and demonstrations to employee training to seminars and speeches, many companies now use video to supplement or replace other media choices. And video is part of the larger shift toward visual communication that has altered the business landscape in recent years. Even if your job doesn't involve snowboarding off cliffs or parachuting from space, you'll probably use video and other visual communication tools to connect with colleagues and customers.[1]

Understanding Visual Communication

As a company in the business of digital video, GoPro (profiled in the chapter-opening Communication Close-Up) emphasizes the visual element in every aspect of its communications. However, visual communication in all its forms has become important for companies in virtually every industry. This chapter is designed to help you appreciate the power of images and the visual evolution of business communication. It explains how to identify which points in your messages to illustrate; how to select the best visual for each of those points; how to create effective visuals in any medium, from memos to reports to webpages to presentations; and how to produce basic business videos.

THE POWER OF IMAGES

Well-designed visual elements can enhance the communication power of textual messages and, in some instances, even replace them. Visuals can often convey some message points (such as spatial relationships, correlations, procedures, and emotions) more effectively and more efficiently than words. In general, in a given amount of time, effective images can convey much more information than text.[2] In the numbers-oriented world of work, people rely heavily on trend lines, distribution curves, and other visual presentations of numeric quantities. Visuals attract and hold people's attention, helping your audience understand and remember your message. Busy readers often jump to visuals to try to get the gist of a message, and attractive visuals can draw readers more deeply into your reports and presentations. Using pictures is also an effective way to communicate with the diverse audiences that are common in today's business environment.

Like words, visuals often carry connotative or symbolic meanings.

In addition to their direct information value, visuals often convey connotative meaning as well. As you read in Chapter 5, many words and phrases carry connotative meanings, which are all the mental images, emotions, and other impressions that the word or phrase evokes in audience members. A significant part of the power—and risk—of visual elements derives from their connotative meanings. Even something as simple as a watermark symbol embedded in letterhead stationery can boost reader confidence in

Figure 9.1   **Visual Symbolism**
A red cross (with equal-length arms) on a white background is the well-known symbol of the Red Cross relief organization. It is also used to indicate the medical branches of many nations' military services. The red cross symbol is based on the flag of Switzerland (where the first Red Cross organization was formed), which over the course of hundreds of years developed from battle flags that originally used the Christian cross symbol. Although the Red Cross emblem is not based directly on the Christian symbol, the organization uses a red crescent in countries where Islam is the dominant religion and is known as the Red Crescent. To avoid any association with religious symbols, the International Federation of Red Cross and Red Crescent Societies (the global umbrella organization for all national Red Cross and Red Crescent organizations) recently adopted the Red Crystal as its new symbol.

the message printed on the paper.[3] Many colors, shapes, and other design elements carry **visual symbolism**, and their symbolic, connotative meaning can evolve over time and mean different things in different cultures (see Figure 9.1). Being aware of these symbolic meanings and using them to your advantage are important aspects of being an effective business communicator.

Because they have so much power to communicate, visuals must be carefully planned, competently created, and seamlessly integrated with text. An awkward sentence or grammatical error deep within a report might not be noticed by the majority of readers, but a poorly chosen or clumsily implemented visual will be noticed by most—and can confuse or alienate audiences and damage your credibility. You don't need to be a professional designer to use visuals effectively, but you do need to be aware of some basic design principles if you want to avoid making highly visible mistakes. This chapter gives you enough background to begin creating your own business visuals, and with some practice you'll be able to craft effective visuals for nearly any communication project you might encounter.

THE VISUAL EVOLUTION IN BUSINESS COMMUNICATION

Several technological and social factors are contributing to the increasing use and importance of visuals in business communication. The process of creating and working with visual elements used to be the domain of experts with complex and expensive tools. However, digital technology has changed this situation dramatically. Inexpensive digital cameras and smartphones can be used to produce high-quality images and video, and the software needed to create diagrams, process photos, edit video, and prepare other visual elements continues to get both easier and more powerful all the time. Design and production tasks that used to take days can now be completed in hours or even minutes. Business communicators have the tools to reach wider audiences in less time, using equipment that costs less and requires fewer skills.[4]

Thanks to advances in technology and changing audience expectations, business communication is becoming more visual.

While technology has been putting visual design and production into the hands of everyday business communicators in recent years, audience skills and expectations have been evolving as well. Two changes in particular could affect your communication efforts in the coming years. First, U.S. government research indicates that only half of the adult population in the United States has the literacy skills considered necessary for success in today's workplace.[5] In other words, depending on the nature of your work, you could find yourself communicating with audiences whose skills could prevent them from successfully reading your documents. Visuals could play a vital role in communicating your messages to audiences with lower reading skills. Second, because technology has multiplied the ways in which communicators can create visuals, and as people grow up and live in a more visual, media-saturated environment, audiences are likely to expect messages to be more visual.

As a result of these changes in both the tools and the communication environment, **visual literacy**—the ability to create effective images and to correctly interpret such images— has become a key business skill.[6] Whether you are using visuals to reach an audience with limited reading skills or to magnify the impact of your written messages, knowing how to help your audience see what you see will enable you to become a more effective communicator.

Visual literacy is the ability to create and interpret visuals successfully.

THE FUTURE OF COMMUNICATION

Gestural Computing

If you've ever wished that you could just wave your hands at your computer and have it do your bidding, that wish might come true in a few years. The aim of *gestural computing* is letting users control computers and other digital devices through modes of motion, such as waving your hands or moving your eyes.

Gestural computing can be accomplished through various means. One approach, which is already used widely in video games, involves handheld devices that convert motion to digital commands. The Nintendo Wii controller is a well-known example of this technology. Another approach involves sensors that detect and translate motion without requiring users to hold anything. Good examples are BMW's Gesture Control interface, which lets drivers wave their hands and move their fingers to select entertainment and navigation functions, and wireless control mechanisms for smartwatches and other wearables that let users interact with their devices simply by moving their fingers in the air (rather than reaching with one hand to use a touch interface).

Entertainment and other consumer applications of gestural control are intriguing, but the technology can also aid business communication. By simplifying interaction with mobile devices, it could make creating and consuming content on media devices more efficient. Imagine "typing" a report through your smartwatch by wiggling your fingers while you commute to work on your bicycle. In addition, like haptic computing (see page 164), gestural computing can open up possibilities for digital interaction for people with motor impairments that limit the use of conventional input devices such as keyboards.

WHAT'S YOUR PREDICTION?

Research the current state of gestural computing to identify one way in which the technology has the potential to change business communication practices. Do you agree with the predictions the experts make? Why or why not?

Sources: "Gesture Recognition," *TechTarget*, accessed 6 April 2016, whatis.techtarget.com; Deidre Richardson, "Aria Silicon Module Adds Gesture Control to Android Wear, Pebble Time," *ExtremeTech*, 3 June 2015, www.extremetech.com; Bill Howard, "AirTouch: BMW's Air Kiss for Touchscreen Gesture Controls," *ExtremeTech*, 4 January 2016, www.extremetech.com.

VISUAL DESIGN PRINCIPLES

Creating effective visuals requires basic knowledge of the principles of good design.

Just as creating effective sentences and paragraphs requires working knowledge of the principles of good writing, creating effective visuals requires some knowledge of the principles of good design. Even though few businesspeople have the opportunity to formally study the "language" of line, mass, space, size, color, pattern, and texture, anyone can learn enough of the basic concepts to craft effective basic visuals.

When you encounter visuals that you find appealing or unappealing, effective or ineffective, stop and ask yourself what caused your response. Did a particular design grab you and practically force you to pay attention, or did you pass right by with hardly a notice? Did one chart reveal its information quickly and easily, while another made you spend time decoding its confusing message? Did one photo appeal to you at an emotional level and therefore draw you into a document, whereas another was off-putting and caused you to lose interest? By thinking about your own reactions to visual designs, you can become a more effective designer yourself.

As you consider your reactions to various designs and create designs of your own, you'll begin to see how six fundamental principles help distinguish ineffective and effective designs:

- **Consistency.** Audiences view a series of visuals as a whole and assume that design elements will be consistent from one page to the next. Think of consistency as *visual parallelism*, in the same way that textual parallelism helps audiences understand and compare a series of ideas.[7] You can achieve visual parallelism in a variety of ways, including through consistent use of color, shape, size, texture, position, scale, or typeface.

- **Contrast.** To emphasize differences, depict items in contrasting colors, shapes, or sizes. For example, to highlight the difference between two quantities in a chart, don't use two shades of blue; instead, use blue for one and yellow or some other dramatically contrasting color for the other.

- **Balance.** Balance can be either *formal*, in which the elements in the images are arranged symmetrically around a central point or axis, or *informal*, in which elements are not distributed evenly, but rather stronger and weaker elements are arranged in a way that achieves an overall effect of balance. A common approach to informal balance is weighing one visually dominant element against several smaller or weaker elements.[8] In general, formal balance is more calming and serious, whereas informal balance tends to seem more dynamic and engaging.

- **Emphasis.** Audiences usually assume that the dominant element in a design is the most important, so make sure that the visually dominant element really does represent the most important information. You can do so through color, position, size, or placement, for example. Conversely, be sure to visually downplay less important items. For instance, avoid using strong colors for minor support points, and deemphasize background features such as the grid lines on a chart.

- **Convention.** Visual communication is guided by a variety of generally accepted rules or conventions, just as written communication is guided by an array of spelling, grammar, punctuation, and usage conventions. These conventions dictate virtually every aspect of design.[9] Moreover, many conventions are so ingrained that people don't even realize they are following these rules. For example, if English is your native language, you assume that ideas progress across the page from left to right because that's the direction in which English text is written. If you are a native Arabic or Hebrew speaker, however, you might automatically assume that flow on a page or screen is from right to left because that is the direction in which those languages are written. Flouting conventions often causes breakdowns in communication, but in some cases, it can be done to great effect.[10] For instance, flipping an organizational chart upside down to put the customers at the top, with frontline employees directly beneath them and on down to the chief executive at the bottom, can be an effective way to emphasize that customers come first and that the managers are responsible for supporting employees in their efforts to satisfy customers.

- **Simplicity.** As a general rule, simple is better when it comes to visuals for business communication. Remember that you're conveying information, not expressing your creative flair. Limit the number of colors and design elements you use, and take care to avoid *chartjunk*, a term coined by the visual communication specialist Edward R. Tufte for decorative elements that clutter documents and potentially confuse readers without adding any relevant information.[11] Computers make it far too easy to add chartjunk, from clip art illustrations to three-dimensional charts that really display only two dimensions of data.

Nearly every aspect of visual design is governed by conventions that set audience expectations.

THE ETHICS OF VISUAL COMMUNICATION

Power always comes with responsibility—and the potential power of visuals places an ethical burden on every business communicator. Ethical problems, both intentional and unintentional, can range from photos that play on racial or gender stereotypes, to images that imply cause-and-effect relationships that may not exist, to graphs that distort data (see Figure 9.2 on the next page).

Altering the scale of items in a visual is just one of many ways to emphasize or deemphasize certain aspects of information. For example, to increase the perceived size of a product, an advertiser might show a close-up of it being held by someone with smaller-than-average hands. Conversely, a large hand would make the product seem smaller.

You can work to avoid ethical lapses in your visuals by following these guidelines:[12]

- **Consider all possible interpretations—and misinterpretations.** Try to view your visuals from your audience members' perspective. Will their biases, beliefs, or backgrounds lead them to different conclusions than you've intended? For instance, assume that you want to show how easy your product is to use, and the photograph you've chosen just happens to show an older person operating the product. Will anyone conclude that what you really mean to say is that your product is so simple that "even an old person can use it"?

- **Provide context.** Even when they are completely accurate, visuals can show only a partial view of reality. Part of your responsibility as a communicator is to provide not only accurate visuals but enough background information to help audiences interpret the visual correctly.

Remember that the power to communicate with visuals comes with the responsibility to communicate ethically.

You can take many steps to emphasize or deemphasize specific elements in your visuals, but make sure you don't inadvertently commit an ethical lapse while doing so.

Visuals can't always speak for themselves; make sure your audience has enough context to interpret your visuals correctly.

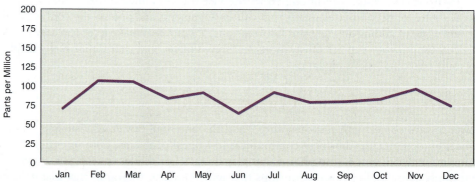

Figure 9.2 **Influencing Perception Through Visual Design**
Figure 9.2a shows impurities measured over the course of a 12-month period; the vertical scale is set from 0 to 120, sufficient to cover the range of variations in the data. However, what if you wanted to make the variations from month to month look more severe? Less severe? Figure 9.2b, with the scale "zoomed in" to a narrow range of 60 to 110, makes the variations look much more dramatic. The result could be a stronger emotional impact on the reader, creating the impression that these impurities are out of control. In contrast, Figure 9.2c expands the scale from 0 to 200, which minimizes the appearance of the variations in the data. This graph is visually "calmer," creating the opposite impression—that there's really nothing to worry about. The data shown in all three graphs are identical, but the graphs send three different messages to the reader. Are any of the graphs unethical? That depends on the communicator's intent and whether it inhibits the audience's ability to make informed decisions.

- **Don't hide or minimize negative information that runs counter to your argument.** Obscuring information prevents your audiences from making fully informed decisions regarding your content.
- **Don't exaggerate information that supports your argument.** Similarly, you have a responsibility not to oversell information in support of your argument. You should also resist the temptation to alter or enhance photographs and other images in order to support your arguments.

- **Don't oversimplify complex situations.** By their very nature, visuals tend to present simplified views of reality. This is usually a benefit and one of the key reasons for using visuals. However, take care not to mislead an audience by hiding complications that are important to the audience's understanding of the situation.

- **Don't imply cause-and-effect relationships without providing proof that they exist.** For example, if you create a line chart that shows how increasing sales seem to track with increasing advertising expenditures, you can claim a correlation but not necessarily a cause-and-effect relationship between the two. You can claim a causal relationship (meaning that the increase in advertising spending caused the increase in sales) only if you can isolate advertising spending as the *only* factor that can account for the increase in sales.

- **Avoid emotional manipulation or other forms of coercion.** For instance, a photograph of an unhappy child being treated as a social outcast because he or she doesn't own the trendiest new toys could be considered an unethical way to persuade parents to buy those products for their children.

- **Be careful with the way you aggregate data.** Preparing charts, graphs, and tables that present data often involves decisions about *aggregating*, or grouping, data. Such decisions can have a profound effect on the message your audience receives (see "Ethics Detective: Solving the Case of the Hidden Numbers"). For example, if you aggregate daily production levels to show only a single data point for each week, you might be obscuring important variations that happen from day to day.

> The ways in which you aggregate data for display can affect the messages and meanings that your audience extracts from your visuals.

Solving the Case of the Hidden Numbers

You've been assigned to present the results of an industrywide study of the effects of insecticides. Your audience consists of the department heads in your company, whose experience and educational backgrounds vary widely, from chemical engineering to insurance to law. You're convinced you need to keep your report as simple and as jargon-free as possible.

You're not a scientific expert on insecticides, but your supervisor has introduced you to a scientist who works for a trade association that represents chemical producers, including your firm. The scientist is familiar with the study you'll be reporting on, and she has experience in communicating technical subjects to diverse audiences. You jumped at the chance to have such a knowledgeable person review your presentation for technical accuracy, but you're uncomfortable with some of her feedback. In particular, you question her advice to replace the line chart shown here, which displays the number of insecticide poisonings and deaths by age.

The scientist suggests that this chart is too busy and too difficult for nonspecialists to understand. As an alternative, she provides this bar chart that selects four specific ages from the entire range. She says this chart communicates the same basic idea as the line chart but is much easier to read.

ANALYSIS

You agree with the scientist that the line chart is visually busy and takes more effort to process, but something bothers you about the bar chart. Does it present the insecticide situation accurately and honestly? Why or why not?

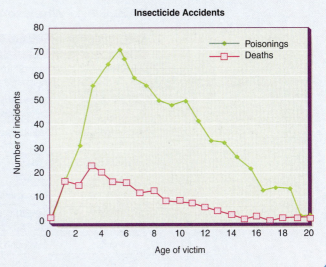

Identifying Points to Illustrate

2 **LEARNING OBJECTIVE**
Explain how to choose which points in your message to illustrate.

To help identify which parts of your message can benefit from visuals, step back and consider the flow of your message from the audience's point of view. Which parts of the message are likely to seem complex, open to misinterpretation, or even just a bit dull? Are there any connections between ideas that might not be obvious if they are addressed only in the text? Are there a lot of numeric data or is there other discrete factual content that would be difficult to read if presented in paragraph form? Is there a chance that the main idea won't "jump off the page" if it's covered only in the text?

If you answer yes to any of these questions, you probably need one or more visuals. When you're deciding which points to present visually, think of the five Cs:

Effective visuals are clear, complete, concise, connected, and compelling.

- **Clear.** The human mind is extremely adept at processing visual information, whether it's something as simple as the shape of a stop sign or as complicated as the floor plan for a new factory. If you're having difficultly conveying an idea in words, consider whether a visual element will do the job instead.
- **Complete.** Visuals, particularly tables, often serve to provide the supporting details for a main idea or recommendation. A table or another visual can provide these details without getting in the way of your main message.
- **Concise.** You've probably heard the expression "A picture is worth a thousand words." If a particular section of your message seems to require extensive description or explanation, see whether there's a way to convey this information visually. With a picture working in conjunction with text, you may be able to reduce your word count considerably.
- **Connected.** A key purpose of many business messages is showing connections of some sort—similarities or differences, correlations, cause-and-effect relationships, and so on. Whenever you want readers to see such a connection, determine whether a chart, a diagram, or another illustration might help.
- **Compelling.** Will one or more illustrations make your message more persuasive, more interesting, more likely to get read? You rarely want to insert visuals simply for decorative purposes, of course, but even if a particular point can be expressed equally well via text or visuals, consider adding the visual to make your report or presentation more compelling.

REAL-TIME UPDATES
LEARN MORE BY READING THIS ARTICLE

Four communication challenges where visuals can be more effective than text

Training, product reviews, complex data presentations, and social media can all benefit from visual content. Go to **real-timeupdates .com/bct14** and select Learn More in the Students section.

As you identify which points in your document would benefit from a visual, make sure that each visual you decide on has a clear purpose (see Table 9.1).

TABLE 9.1   When to Use Visuals

Purpose	Application
To clarify	Support text descriptions of "graphic" topics: quantitative or numeric information, explanations of trends, descriptions.
To simplify	Divide complicated descriptions into components that can be depicted with conceptual models, flowcharts, organization charts, or diagrams.
To emphasize	Call attention to particularly important points by illustrating them with line, bar, and pie charts.
To summarize	Review major points in the narrative by providing a chart or table that sums up the data.
To reinforce	Present information in visual form to supplement descriptions in text.
To attract	Make material seem more interesting by decorating the cover or title page and by breaking up the text with visual aids.
To impress	Build confidence by using visual forms to convey authenticity and precision.
To unify	Depict the relationships among various elements of a whole.

TABLE 9.2   Selecting the Best Visual

Communication Challenge	Effective Visual Choice
Presenting Data	
To present individual, exact values	Table
To show trends in one or more variables, or the relationship between those variables, over time	Line chart, bar chart
To compare two or more sets of data	Bar chart, line chart
To show frequency or distribution of parts in a whole	Pie chart
To show massive data sets, complex quantities, or dynamic data	Data visualization
Presenting Information, Concepts, and Ideas	
To show geographic relationships or comparisons	Map, geographic information system
To illustrate processes or procedures	Flowchart, diagram
To show conceptual or spatial relationships (simplified)	Illustration
To tell a data-driven story visually	Infographic
To show (realistic) spatial relationships	Photograph
To show processes, transformations, and other activities	Animation, video

Selecting Visuals for Presenting Data

After you have identified which points would benefit most from visual presentation, your next decision is choosing which type of visual to use for each message point. As you can see in Table 9.2, you have many choices for business graphics, which can be roughly divided into those for presenting data and those for presenting information, concepts, and ideas.

For some content, the decision is usually obvious. For example, to present a large set of numeric values or detailed textual information, a table is often the obvious choice. However, if you're presenting data broken down geographically, a color-coded map might be more effective, showing overall patterns rather than individual data points. Also, certain visuals are used more commonly for certain applications, as you'll see in the following sections.

Business professionals have a tremendous number of choices for presenting data, from general-purpose line, bar, and pie charts to specialized charts for product portfolios, financial analysis, and other professional functions. The visuals most commonly used to present data include tables; line and surface charts; bar charts, pictograms, and Gantt charts; scatter and bubble diagrams; and pie charts. (Note that most people use the terms *chart* and *graph* interchangeably.)

TABLES

When you need to present a large number of specific data points or pieces of information, choose a **table**, a systematic arrangement of data in columns and rows. Tables are ideal when your audience needs information that would be either difficult or tedious to handle in the main text.

Most tables contain the standard parts illustrated in Figure 9.3 on the next page. Every table includes vertical columns and horizontal rows, with useful headings along the top and side. For printed documents, you can adjust font size and column and row spacing to fit a considerable amount of information on the page and still maintain readability. For online documents, you may need to reduce the number of columns and rows to make sure your tables are easily readable, particularly on mobile devices. If you can't simplify a table enough to make it easily readable in a web or mobile browser, provide the full table as a downloadable PDF. If you want to give the audience the opportunity to manipulate the table's content, you can provide it as a downloadable or online spreadsheet. Tables for presentation slides usually need to be the simplest of all because you can't expect audiences to read detailed information from the screen.

Although complex information may require formal tables that are set apart from the text, you can present some data more simply within the text. You make the table, in essence,

3 LEARNING OBJECTIVE
Describe the most common options for presenting data in a visual format.

Printed tables can display extensive amounts of data, but tables for online display and presentation slides need to be simpler.

	Multicolumn Heading			Single-Column Heading
	Column Subheading	Column Subheading	Column Subheading	
Row Heading	xxx	xxx	xxx	xxx
Row Heading	xxx	xxx	xxx	xxx
Row Subheading	xxx	xxx	xxx	xxx
Row Subheading	xxx	xxx	xxx	xxx
Row Heading	xxx	xxx	xxx	xxx
Row Heading	xxx	xxx	xxx	xxx
TOTALS	xxx	xxx	xxx	xxx

Figure 9.3 **Parts of a Table**
Here are the standard parts of a table. No matter which design you choose, make sure the layout is clear and that individual rows and columns are easy to follow.

a part of the paragraph, typed in tabular format. Such text tables are usually introduced with a sentence that leads directly into the tabulated information. Here's an example:[13]

Here is how five leading full-service restaurant operators compare in terms of number of locations and annual revenue:

	OSI Restaurant Partners	**Dine Equity**	**Carlson**	**Brinker**	**Darden**
Major Chain(s)	Outback Steakhouse, Carrabba's	Applebee's, IHOP	Friday's, Pick Up Stix	Chili's, Maggiano's	Red Lobster, Olive Garden
Locations (n)	1,470	3,300	990	1,550	1,800
Revenue ($, Millions)	$3,600	$1,414	N/A	$2,859	7,113

Source: Hoover's website, accessed 25 February 2016, www.hoovers.com; "America's Largest Private Companies," *Forbes*, accessed 25 February 2016, www.forbes.com; company financial reports available on Google Finance, accessed 25 February 2016, www.google.com/finance.

When you prepare tables, follow these guidelines to make they are easy to read:

- Use common, understandable units and clearly identify which you're using, whether dollars, percentages, price per ton, or some other unit.
- Express all items in a column in the same unit and round off for simplicity whenever doing so won't eliminate essential details.
- Label column headings clearly and use a subheading if necessary.
- Separate columns or rows with lines or extra space to make the table easy to follow; in complex tables, consider highlighting every other row or column in a pale, contrasting color.
- Provide totals or averages of columns or rows when relevant.
- Document the source of the data, using the same format as a text footnote (see Appendix B).

Tables can contain numerals, text, symbols, or other facts and figures. Text tables are particularly appropriate for presenting survey findings or for comparing various items against a specific standard.

LINE AND SURFACE CHARTS

Line charts are commonly used to show trends over time or the relationship between two or more variables.

A **line chart** illustrates trends over time or plots the relationship of two or more variables. In line charts showing trends, the vertical axis—or y axis—shows the amount, and the horizontal axis, or x axis, shows the time or other quantity against which the amount is being

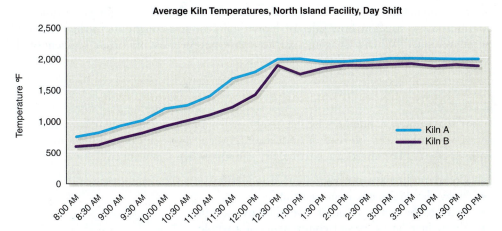

Figure 9.4   Line Chart
This line chart compares the temperatures measured inside two cement kilns at half-hour intervals from 8:00 A.M. to 5:00 P.M.

measured. Both axes often start at zero in the lower left corner, but you can exercise a fair amount of flexibility with both axes in order to present your data as clearly as possible. For instance, to show both positive and negative values (such as profit and loss), you can have the *y* axis span from a negative value up to a positive value, with zero somewhere in between. Of course, you should always avoid distorting the data in ways that could mislead your audience, as noted in the section "The Ethics of Visual Communication" on pages 233–235.

If you need to compare two or more sets of data, you can plot them on the same chart for instant visual comparison (see Figure 9.4). Two or three lines on a single chart are usually easy to read, but beyond that, things can get confusing, particularly if the lines cross.

Because they usually show the behavior of one or more variables in the past, line charts often raise the question, "What will happen in the future?" For instance, if you present sales data for the past 12 months, your audience may well ask what you think will happen in the next 12 months. Predicting the future is always risky, but you can use a spreadsheet's forecasting tool to extend a line into the future, using a statistical technique known as *regression analysis*. Check the program's Help function for more information on using its *linear regression*, *trend line*, or *forecasting* functions. However, when using these tools, be aware that all they can do is extract patterns from past data and extend them into the future. They don't have any awareness of the "real-life" factors that shaped the past data and that will shape the future data.

A **surface chart**, also called an **area chart**, is a form of line chart with a cumulative effect; all the lines add up to the top line, which represents the total (see Figure 9.5). This

Spreadsheet forecasting functions can help predict future values based on past values shown in a line chart.

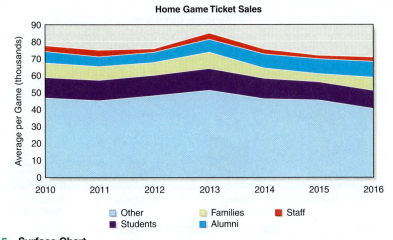

Figure 9.5   Surface Chart
Surface, or area, charts can show a combination of trends over time and the individual contributions of the components of a whole.

presentation helps you illustrate changes in the composition of something over time. One common use is to show how sales of individual products contribute to the company's overall revenue.[14] When preparing a surface chart, put the most important segment on the bottom and build up from there.

BAR CHARTS, PICTOGRAMS, AND GANTT CHARTS

A **bar chart** portrays numbers by the height or length of its rectangular bars, making a series of numbers easy to read or understand. (Vertical bar charts are sometimes called *column charts*.) Bar charts are particularly valuable when you want to

- Compare the sizes of several items at one time
- Show changes in one item over time
- Indicate the composition of several items over time
- Show the relative sizes of components of a whole

You can create bar charts in a wide variety of formats; choose the form that best illustrates the data and relationships in your message.

As the charts in Figure 9.6 show, the bar chart is a versatile tool that can serve many purposes. *Grouped* bar charts compare more than one set of data, using a different color or pattern for each set. *Deviation* bar charts identify positive and negative values, or winners and losers. *Segmented* bar charts, also known as *stacked* bar charts, show how individual components contribute to a total number, using a different color or pattern for each component. *Combination* bar and line charts compare quantities that require different intervals. *Paired* bar charts show the correlations between two items.

Figure 9.6 also suggests how creative you can be with bar charts. You might align the bars either vertically or horizontally, or you might use bar charts to show both positive and negative quantities. No matter what you do, however, be sure to space the bars evenly and place them in a logical order, such as chronological or alphabetical.

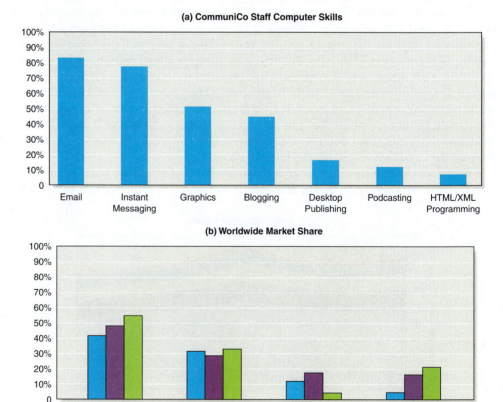

Figure 9.6 **Bar Charts**
Here are six of the many variations possible with bar charts: *singular* (9.6a), *grouped* (9.6b), *deviation* (9.6c), *segmented* (9.6d), *combination* (9.6e), and *paired* (9.6f).

(c) CommuniCo Stock Price

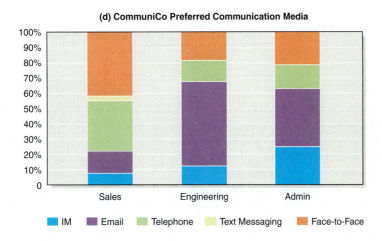

(d) CommuniCo Preferred Communication Media

(e) CommuniCo Employee Training Costs

(f) Conference Attendance by Gender

Figure 9.6   Bar Charts (*continued*)

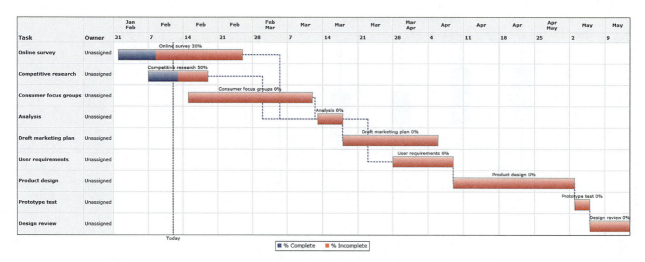

Figure 9.7 Gantt Chart
A Gantt chart is a specialized bar chart that uses bars to show durations of tasks and lines to show dependencies between tasks, such as when one task cannot be started before another one is completed.

You can also convert the bars of a bar chart into lines of symbols, so that the number or length of the symbols indicates the relative value of each item. A chart that portrays data as symbols instead of words or numbers is known as a **pictogram**. The chief value of pictograms is their novelty and ability to convey a more literal, visual message, but they can be more difficult to read if not designed with care, and they can present a less professional tone than a straightforward bar chart.

Closely related to the bar chart is the **time line chart**, which shows how much time is needed to complete each task in a given project. When you want to track progress toward completing a project, you can use a type of time line chart known as a **Gantt chart** (see Figure 9.7).

SCATTER AND BUBBLE DIAGRAMS

Scatter diagrams compare entities against two variables; bubble diagrams compare them against three.

If you need to compare several entities (companies, markets, employees, and so on) on two variables, such as revenue and profit margin, use a **scatter diagram**, also known as an **XY diagram**. This diagram is similar to a line chart in the sense that one variable is plotted along the x (horizontal) axis and another along the y (vertical) axis. In a scatter diagram, however, individual points are plotted, not continuous lines. A **bubble diagram** expands to three variables, with the size of the bubble representing the third variable (see Figure 9.8).

PIE CHARTS

Pie charts are used frequently in business reports, but they are often not as helpful to readers as bar charts and other types of visuals would be.

A **pie chart** is a commonly used tool for showing how the parts of a whole are distributed. Although pie charts are popular and can quickly highlight the dominant parts of a whole, they are often not as effective as bar charts or tables. For example, comparing percentages accurately is often difficult with a pie chart but can be fairly easy with a bar chart (see Figure 9.9). Making pie charts easier to read can require labeling each slice with data values, in which case a table might serve the purpose more effectively.[15]

DATA VISUALIZATION

Data visualization tools can overcome the limitations of conventional charts and other display types.

Data visualization is an important feature for companies using *big data*.

Conventional charts and graphs are limited in several ways: Most types can show only a limited number of data points before becoming too cluttered to interpret, they often can't show complex relationships among data points, and they can represent only numeric data. As computer technologies continue to generate large amounts of data that can be combined and connected in endless ways, a diverse class of display capabilities known as

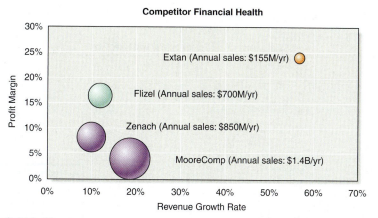

Figure 9.8   Bubble Diagram
A bubble diagram shows three variables: distance along the *x* and *y* axes, plus the diameter of each bubble. In this case the rate of revenue growth is plotted on the *x* axis, profit margin is plotted on the *y* axis, and the size of the bubbles represents annual revenues. For instance, MooreComp has the greatest revenues but the lowest profit margin, although it is growing faster than two of its three competitors.

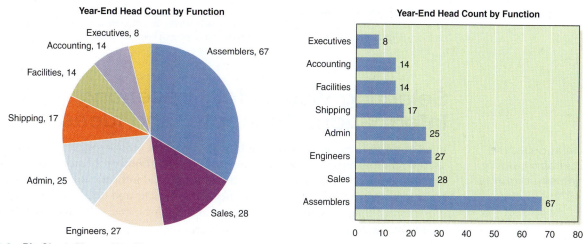

Figure 9.9   Pie Charts Versus Bar Charts
Pie charts are used frequently, but they aren't necessarily the best choice for many data presentations. This pie chart does make it easy to see that assemblers are the largest employee category, but other slice sizes (such as Sales, Engineers, and Admin) are not as easy to compare and require a numerical rather than a visual comparison. In contrast, the bar chart gives a quick visual comparison of every data point.

data visualization work to overcome all these drawbacks. In some instances data visualization is less about clarifying individual data points and more about extracting broad meaning from giant masses of data or putting the data into context.[16]

Data visualization has become an important tool for companies working with *big data*, a term used to describe massive collections of data from a variety of sources piling up at high speeds.[17] Interactive apps let users "drill down" into data sets to find details or look at data collections from a variety of perspectives (see Figure 9.10 on the next page).

In addition to displaying large data sets and linkages within data sets, other kinds of visualization tools combine data with textual information to communicate complex or dynamic data much faster than conventional presentations can. For example, a *tag cloud* shows the relative frequency of terms, or tags (content labels), in an article, a blog, a website, survey data, or another collection of text.[18]

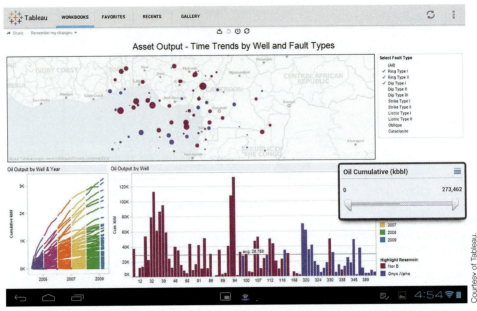

Figure 9.10 **Data Visualization**
Data visualization displays and software tools take a wide variety of forms. Here is a mobile app that lets users explore a large data set from different perspectives and at varying levels of detail.

Selecting Visuals for Presenting Information, Concepts, and Ideas

4 **LEARNING OBJECTIVE**
Describe the most common options for presenting information, concepts, and ideas.

In addition to facts and figures, you'll need to present other types of information, from spatial relationships to abstract ideas. In these situations professionals often look for visual solutions to complement or even replace textual information. The most common types of visuals for these applications include flowcharts and organization charts; maps; illustrations, diagrams, and photographs; infographics; and video (covered in the final section of the chapter).

FLOWCHARTS AND ORGANIZATION CHARTS

Use flowcharts to show a series of steps in a process or other sequential relationships.

If you need to show physical or conceptual relationships rather than numeric ones, you might want to use a flowchart or an organization chart. A **flowchart** (see Figure 9.11) illustrates a sequence of events from start to finish. It is particularly helpful when illustrating processes and procedures in which there are decision points, loops, and other complexities. For general business purposes, you don't need to be too concerned about the specific shapes, although do keep them consistent. However, be aware that there is a formal flowchart "language" in which each shape has a specific meaning (diamonds are decision points, rectangles are process steps, and so on). If you're communicating with computer programmers and others who are accustomed to formal flowcharting, make sure you use the correct symbols to avoid confusion. Graphics programs that have flowchart symbols usually label their functions, making it easy to use the right ones.

Use organization charts to depict the interrelationships among the parts of a whole.

As the name implies, an **organization chart** illustrates the positions, units, or functions of an organization and the ways they interrelate (refer to Figure 1.3 on page 8 for an example).

MAPS

Use maps for such tasks as representing statistics by geographic area or showing spatial relationships.

Maps can show location, distance, points of interest (such as competitive retail outlets), and geographic distribution of data, such as sales by region or population by state. In addition to presenting facts and figures, maps are useful for showing market territories, distribution routes, and facilities locations.

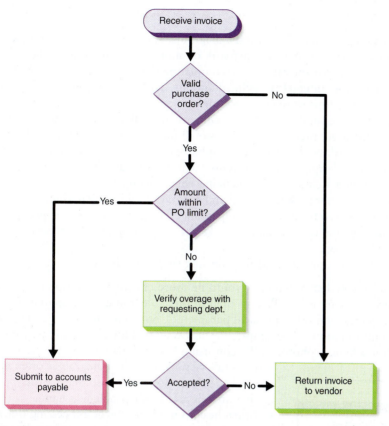

Figure 9.11   **Flowchart**

Flowcharts show sequences of events and are most valuable when the process or procedure has a number of decision points and variable paths.

Figure 9.12   **Geographic Information Systems**

Businesses use geographic information systems (GISs) in a variety of ways. By overlaying maps and aerial or satellite imagery with descriptive data (such as this map of gas prices in the Chicago area), companies can use these displays for such purposes as planning sales campaigns, optimizing transportation routing, and selecting retail or production sites.

When combined with databases and aerial or satellite photography in *geographic information systems (GISs)*, maps become extremely powerful visual reporting tools (see Figure 9.12). As one example, retailing specialists can explore the demographic and psychographic makeup of neighborhoods within various driving distances from a particular store location. Using such information, managers can plan everything from new building sites to delivery routes to marketing campaigns.

ILLUSTRATIONS, DIAGRAMS, AND PHOTOGRAPHS

Use illustrations and diagrams to show how something works or how it is made or used; illustrations are sometimes better than photographs because they let you focus on the most important details.

The opportunities to use illustrations, diagrams, and photographs are virtually endless. Simple illustrations can show the network of suppliers in an industry, the flow of funds through a company, or the process for completing the payroll each week. More-complex diagrams, including interactive online diagrams, can convey technical topics such as the operation of a machine or repair procedures.

Word processors and presentation software now offer fairly advanced drawing capabilities, but for more precise and professional illustrations, you may need a specialized package such as Adobe Illustrator or Trimble SketchUp. For more-technical illustrations, *computer-aided design (CAD)* systems such as Autodesk's AutoCAD can produce extremely detailed architectural and engineering drawings.

Use photographs for visual appeal and to show exact appearances.

Photographs offer both functional and decorative value, and nothing can top a photograph when you need to show exact appearances. Because audiences expect photographs to show literal visual truths, you must take care when using image-processing tools such as Adobe Photoshop.

To use photographs successfully, consider these guidelines:

- **Consider whether a diagram would be more effective than a photograph.** Photographs are often unmatched in their ability to communicate spatial relationships, sizes, shapes, and other physical parameters, but sometimes they communicate too much information. For example, to show how to adjust a specific part of a complicated machine, a photo can be confusing because it shows all the parts within the camera's view. A simplified diagram is often more effective because it allows you to emphasize the specific parts that are relevant to the problem at hand.

- **Learn how to use basic image-processing functions.** For most business reports, websites, and presentations, you won't need to worry about advanced image-processing functions and special effects. However, you need to know such basic operations such as the difference between resizing (changing the size of an image without removing any parts of it) and cropping (cutting away parts of an image).

- **Make sure the photographs have communication value.** Except for covers, title slides, and other special uses, it's usually best to avoid including photographs simply for decorative value.

Make sure you have the right to use photographs you find online.

- **Be aware of copyrights and model permissions.** As with textual information you find online, you can't simply insert online photographs into your documents. Unless they are specifically offered free, you have to assume that someone owns the photos and is entitled to payment or at least a photo credit. In addition, professional photographers are careful to have any person who poses in photos sign a model release form, which gives the photographer permission to use the person's image.

INFOGRAPHICS

Infographics can offer stylized versions of basic charts and graphs or more engaging narratives that tell a story or illustrate a process.

Infographics are a special class of diagrams that can convey both data and concepts or ideas. In addition, they contain enough visual and textual information to function as independent, standalone documents. Broadly speaking, there are two types of infographics: those that are stylized collections of charts or graphs and those that have a structured narrative. The first type don't necessarily convey any more information than basic charts and graphs in a conventional report would, but their communication value lies in their ability to catch the audience's attention and the ease with which they can be distributed online. The second type, represented by Figure 9.13, take full advantage of the visual medium to tell stories or show interconnected processes. Such infographics can be powerful communication tools, even to the point of replacing conventional reports.

Producing and Integrating Visuals

Now that you understand the communication power of visuals and have chosen the best visuals to illustrate key points in your report, website, or presentation, it's time to get creative. This section offers advice on creating visuals, integrating them with your text, and verifying the quality of your visual elements.

5 LEARNING OBJECTIVE
Explain how to integrate visuals with text, and list three criteria to review in order to verify the quality of your visuals.

CREATING VISUALS

Computers make it easy to create visuals, but they also make it easy to create ineffective, distracting, and even downright ugly visuals. However, by following the basic design principles discussed on pages 232–233, you can create all the basic visuals you need—ones that are both attractive and effective.

Whether you're using the charting functions offered in a spreadsheet or the design features of a specialized graphics program, take a few minutes to familiarize yourself with the software's quirks and capabilities. For important visuals, try to have a professional designer set up a template for the various types of visuals you and your colleagues need to create. In addition to helping ensure an effective design, using templates saves you the time of making numerous design decisions every time you create a chart or graphic.

No matter which tools you're using, take care to match the style and quality of your visuals with the subject matter and the situation at hand. The style of your visuals communicates a subtle message about your relationship with the audience. A simple sketch might be fine for a working meeting but inappropriate for a formal presentation or report. On the other hand, elaborate, full-color visuals may be viewed as extravagant for an informal report but may be entirely appropriate for a message to top management or influential outsiders.

Programs and apps offer a variety of graphical tools but don't automatically give you the design sensibility that is needed for effective visuals.

Learning how to use your computer tools will help you save enormous amounts of time and produce better results.

A visual's level of sophistication should match the communication situation.

MOBILE APP
Graph (Android) and **Numbers** (iOS) are two of the many apps available for creating charts and graphs on mobile devices.

INTEGRATING VISUALS WITH TEXT

For maximum effectiveness and minimum disruption for the reader, visual elements need to be carefully integrated with the text of your message. In some instances visual elements are somewhat independent from the text, as in the *sidebars* that occasionally accompany magazine articles or *photo essays* such as you see in Chapters 1, 4, and 8 in this textbook. Such images are related to the content of the main story, but they aren't referred to by a specific title or figure number.

For reports and most other business documents, however, visuals are tightly integrated with the text so that readers can move back and forth between text and visuals with as little disruption as possible. Successful integration involves four decisions: maintaining a balance between visuals and text, referring to visuals in the text, placing the visuals in a document, and writing titles and other descriptions.

Courtesy of Sustainable America.

Figure 9.13 Infographics
In general, infographics can be divided into simple presentations of data and visual narratives such as this one, which use the full power of the medium to tell stories or illustrate processes.

Maintaining a Balance Between Illustrations and Words

As far as the content allows, maintain a comfortable balance between text and visuals.

Strong visuals enhance the descriptive and persuasive power of your writing, but putting too many visuals into a report can distract your readers. If you're constantly referring to tables, illustrations, and other visual elements, the effort to switch back and forth from words to visuals can make it difficult for readers to maintain focus on the thread of your message. The space occupied by visuals can also disrupt the flow of text on the page or screen.

Make sure your visuals match the needs, expectations, and interpretation skills of your audience.

As always, take into account your readers' specific needs. If you're addressing an audience with multiple language backgrounds or widely varying reading skills, you can shift the balance toward more visual elements to help get around any language barriers. The professional experience, education, and training of your audience should influence your approach as well. For instance, detailed statistical plots and mathematical formulas are everyday reading material for quality-control engineers but not for most salespeople or top executives.

Referencing Visuals

To tie visuals to text, introduce them in the text and place them near the points they illustrate.

Unless a visual element clearly stands on its own, it should be referred to by number in the text of your report. Some report writers refer to all visuals as "exhibits" and number them consecutively throughout the report; many others number tables and figures separately (everything that isn't a table is regarded as a figure). In a long report with numbered sections, illustrations may have a double number (separated by a period or a hyphen) representing the section number and the individual illustration number within that section. Whatever scheme you use, make sure it's clear, consistent, and easy to follow.

Help your readers understand the significance of visuals by referring to them before readers encounter them in the document or on the screen. The following examples show how you can make this connection in the text:

Figure 1 summarizes the financial history of the motorcycle division over the past five years, with sales broken into four categories.

Total sales were steady over this period, but the mix of sales by category changed dramatically (see Figure 2).

The underlying reason for the remarkable growth in our sales of youth golf apparel is suggested by Table 4, which shows the growing interest in junior golf around the world.

Help your readers understand why each visual is important.

When describing the data shown in your visuals, be sure to emphasize the main point you are trying to make. Don't make the mistake of simply repeating the data to be shown. Paragraphs that do are guaranteed to put the reader to sleep. The visual will (or at least should) provide all these details; there is no need to repeat them in the text. Instead, use round numbers that sum up the message. For example, you might say, "As Table 4.2 shows, more than two-thirds of the respondents earn less than $20 per hour."

Placing Visuals

Place each visual as close as possible to its in-text reference to help readers understand the illustration's relevance and to minimize the effort of reading.

Try to position your visuals so that your audience won't have to flip back and forth (in printed documents) or scroll (on screen) between the visuals and the text. Ideally, it's best to place each visual within, beside, or immediately after the paragraph it illustrates so that readers can consult the explanation and the visual at the same time. This scheme works well both in print and online. If at all possible, avoid bunching visuals at the end of a section or the end of a document; doing so asks a lot of the reader. (Bunching is unavoidable in some cases, such as when multiple visuals accompany a single section of text—as in this chapter, for instance.) Word-processing, desktop-publishing, and web-design programs or apps let you place graphical elements virtually anywhere you wish, so take advantage of this flexibility.

Writing Titles, Captions, and Legends

A descriptive title simply identifies the topic of an illustration; an informative title helps the reader understand the conclusion to be drawn from the illustration.

Titles, captions, and legends help connect your visual and textual messages and ensure a seamless reading experience. A **title** identifies the content and purpose of the visual, along with whatever label and number you're using to refer to the visual. A **descriptive title** simply identifies the topic of the illustration, whereas an **informative title** calls attention to the conclusion that ought to be drawn from the data. Here's an example of the difference:

Descriptive Title	Informative Title
Relationship Between Petroleum Demand and Refinery Capacity in the United States	Refinery Capacity Declines as Petroleum Demand Continues to Grow

An informative title saves readers the work of interpreting the visual to extract the main idea from it. Regardless of whether your titles and legends are informative or descriptive, phrase them consistently throughout a document.

A **caption** usually offers additional discussion of a visual's content and can be up to several sentences long, if appropriate. Captions can also alert readers that additional discussion is available in the accompanying text. A **legend** helps readers "decode" the visual by explaining what various colors, symbols, or other design choices mean (several of the figures in this chapter use legends, for example). Legends aren't necessary for simple graphs, such as a line chart or bar chart with only one series of data, but they are invaluable with more complex graphics.

VERIFYING THE QUALITY OF YOUR VISUALS

Visuals have a particularly strong impact on your readers and on their perceptions of you and your work, so verifying the quality of your visuals is an essential step. Ask yourself three questions about every visual element:

- **Is the visual accurate?** Be sure to check for mistakes such as typographical errors, inconsistent color treatment, confusing or undocumented symbols, and misaligned elements. Also verify that the information in visuals and text matches. For data presentations, particularly if you're producing charts using a spreadsheet, verify any formulas used to generate the numbers and make sure you've selected the right numbers for each chart. For flowcharts, organization charts, diagrams, photos, and other visuals, make sure that each visual delivers your message accurately and that you have inserted the correct image files.

- **Is the visual properly documented?** As with the textual elements in your reports and presentations, visuals based on other people's research, information, and ideas require full citation. (Even if the graphical design is entirely yours, any underlying information taken from other sources needs to be documented.) Also, try to anticipate any questions or concerns your audience may have and address them with additional information, as needed. For instance, if you're presenting the results of survey research, many readers will want to know who participated in the survey, how many people responded, and when the questions were asked. You could answer these questions with a note in the caption along the lines of "652 accountants, surveyed the week of January 17." Similarly, if you found a visual in a secondary source, list that source on or near the graphic to help readers assess the information. Alternatively, you can list sources in an appendix.

- **Is the visual honest?** As a final precaution, step back and verify that your visuals communicate truthful messages. Make sure they don't hide information the audience needs, imply conclusions that your information doesn't support, or play on audience emotions in manipulative or coercive ways.

Review each visual to make sure it doesn't intentionally or unintentionally distort the meaning of the underlying information.

For a review of the important points to remember when creating visuals, see "Checklist: Creating Effective Visuals." For more information on visual communication, including design principles, ethical matters, and the latest tools for creating and displaying visuals, visit real-timeupdates.com/bct14 and select Chapter 9.

VISUAL MEDIA ON MOBILE DEVICES

Whether it's a training video, an interactive big-data tool, or a GIS system used for on-site analysis, more and more employees need to consume visual media on smartphones and tablets. The constraints of small screens are even more acute with visuals than they are with text, so preparing visual content for mobile users takes careful planning and the

CHECKLIST ✔ Creating Effective Visuals

- Emphasize visual consistency to connect parts of a whole and minimize audience confusion.
- Avoid arbitrary changes of color, texture, typeface, position, or scale.
- Highlight contrasting points through color, position, and other design choices.
- Decide whether you want to achieve formal or informal balance.
- Emphasize dominant elements and deemphasize less important pieces in a design.
- Understand and follow (at least most of the time) the visual conventions your audience expects.
- Strive for simplicity and clarity; don't clutter your visuals with meaningless decoration.
- Follow the guidelines for avoiding ethical lapses.

- Carefully consider your message, the nature of your information, and your audience to choose which points to illustrate.
- Select the proper types of graphics for the information at hand and for the objective of the message.
- Be sure the visual contributes to an overall understanding of the subject.
- Understand how to use your software tools to maximize effectiveness and efficiency.
- Integrate visuals and text by maintaining a balance between illustrations and words, clearly referring to visuals within the text, and placing visuals carefully.
- Use titles, captions, and legends to help readers understand the meaning and importance of your visuals.
- Verify the quality of your visuals by checking for accuracy, proper documentation, and honesty.

use of display tools designed for mobile devices. With screen space at a premium, think carefully about audience members' needs, including the circumstances in which they'll be using their devices, so you can prioritize and sequence the delivery of information (see Figure 9.14).[19]

Figure 9.14 **Visual Displays on Mobile Devices**
Think through your audience's needs carefully when designing mobile visuals. As with this mobile app from the Hipmunk airfare-search service, present only the most essential information on each screen, with no extraneous information, and let users tap through for more details.

Producing Business Videos

No matter what career path you pursue, chances are you'll have the need or opportunity to produce (or star in) a business video. For videos that require the highest production quality, companies usually hire specialists with the necessary skills and equipment. For most routine needs, however, any business communicator with modest equipment and a few basic skills can create effective videos.

The three-step process adapts easily to video; professionals refer to the three steps as *preproduction*, *production*, and *postproduction* (see Figure 9.15). You can refer to one of the many books available on basic video production techniques for more detail, but here are the key points to consider in all three steps. (A note on terminology: digital videography has inherited a number of terms from film that don't make strict technical sense but are in common use anyway, including *footage* to indicate any amount of recorded video and *filming* to indicate video recording.)

6 LEARNING OBJECTIVE
Identify the most important considerations in the preproduction, production, and postproduction stages of producing basic business videos.

The process of creating videos is divided into preproduction, production, and postproduction.

STEP 1: PREPRODUCTION

When you're recording speeches, seminars, and other events, planning is crucial because you have only one opportunity to get the footage you need. And even when you have the flexibility to retake footage, thoughtful planning will save time and money and lead to better-looking results. For any video, be sure to think through the following seven elements:

- **Purpose and scope.** With every communication effort, of course, it's essential to identify the purpose of your message and define the scope of what you will address before

1 Preproduction →	**2** Production →	**3** Postproduction
1. Verify your purpose and scope.	1. Frame each shot carefully.	1. Transfer your video footage to your computer and load it into the editing software.
2. Think about the composition of the scenes you want to film.	2. Keep the camera still while filming unless the situation demands that you move it.	2. Evaluate your material, identifying the shots you want to keep and those you can delete.
3. Decide where you'll place your camera or cameras.	3. Take B-roll footage.	3. Move sections of video around as needed to tell a coherent and compelling story.
4. Plan lighting.	4. Remember not to use the special effects in your camera so that you can export clean footage.	4. Weave in B-roll images and clips.
5. Make arrangements for sound recording.		5. Add transitions between video segments.
6. Writing a short list or full script as appropriate.		6. Synchronize the main audio track with the video and record narration.
7. Identify B-roll material that will enhance the final video.		7. Add an *intro* and an *outro*.
		8. Add text titles and other features as needed.
		9. Create a distributable file.

Figure 9.15 **Creating Effective Business Videos**
By following a methodical process in the preproduction, production, and postproduction stages, any business communicator with even basic equipment can create effective videos.

REAL-TIME UPDATES

LEARN MORE BY READING THIS ARTICLE

Using Snapchat for business communication

With its massive and still-growing audience, it's no surprise that the photo- and video-sharing network has caught the attention of business communicators. Go to **real-timeupdates.com/bct14** and select Learn More in the Students section.

you start. This is doubly important with video, however, because it is a linear medium that forces people to watch it in a predefined sequence. Most viewers won't sit through rambling or repetitive videos, so figure out what your point is and determine the briefest possible way to make it.

- **Scene composition.** Visualize what the camera is going to see. If you're demonstrating a new product, for example, do you want people to see it in a realistic setting, or would it be better to use a "clean stage" so that nothing else will compete for the viewer's attention? For "talking head" videos, in which someone talks directly into the camera at close range, an uncluttered background is preferred unless the setting is relevant. However, you don't need to resort to a bare white wall behind the subject; this can make the video feel more like an interrogation. A tastefully decorated office can look uncluttered without feeling stark or cold. Think carefully about the overall environment as well. Trying to conduct an interview outside or at a busy tradeshow, for example, can bring all kinds of noise and visual distractions into the equation.

Just as painters compose a scene, with a video camera you compose a scene by making decisions about what to show and where to place your camera.

- **Camera placement.** As you visualize the scene or scenes you plan to shoot, think about where to place your camera. Wide, medium, and close-up positions each have their own strengths and weaknesses, depending on what you're trying to convey. For example, showing a wide shot of a crowd's reaction can emphasize the emotional impact of a speech, but a wide shot looking at the speaker from a distance will have less impact because viewers won't able to see the emotions on the speaker's face. As a technical point, position the camera as close as you can for the shot you're trying to achieve, rather than using the camera's zoom capability. Using zoom makes the recording more vulnerable to shaking and makes it more difficult for you (or the camera's autofocus function) to keep the picture in focus.[20] If you need to zoom because you can't get the camera close enough, be sure to use *optical zoom* only, not *digital zoom*, which reduces the picture quality.

Invest the time and, if necessary, the money to get good lighting; it is essential to quality video production.

- **Lighting.** Good lighting is essential for a quality production, which is why professionals sometimes spend hours lighting a single shot. Lighting can be a complicated subject, but for most business videos, the simplest solution is to get a strong but soft light directed from behind the camera toward the subject (person, place, or thing) being filmed. This ensures that the subject is well lit and that the camera's exposure settings aren't overwhelmed by extraneous light coming from the background. Professionals use large "softboxes," reflectors, and other special equipment to direct light onto their subjects, but you can often take advantage of windows and natural daylight.[21] If you have artificial lighting that is too harsh, you can soften the light by filtering it through parchment paper.[22] When filming people, be particularly careful about strong overhead lights, which can create unflattering shadows. And when shooting outside, look for locations in full shade if possible to avoid the deep shadows created by direct sunlight.[23]

- **Sound.** Your camera or smartphone probably has a microphone to record sound along with video, but in most cases you should use an external microphone instead. The reason is that the camera's microphone will pick up too much noise because it is too far away from the person or persons who are speaking, and these *omnidirectional* microphones pick up sound from every angle.[24] In most cases the best solution is to pin a small *lavaliere* microphone on each speaker's lapel. Note that you can also record one or more audio sources separately (if you have speakers in different locations, for instance) and mix them together in postproduction.

A shot list serves as your outline and checklist while you're filming.

- **Shot list.** The director and professional videographer Steve Stockman advises to always think of a video in terms of discrete shots, rather than as one endless recording.[25] You can imagine shots as the equivalent of subsections or even the paragraphs in a report, each one leading smoothly to the next. Preparing a *shot list* ahead of time helps you identify all the footage you need to capture, and it serves as a checklist when you're shooting. And going beyond a shot list, whenever you're creating a video specifically (as opposed to recording a training session or some other event), consider writing a script that describes every scene and visual and contains speaking notes or even fully written dialogue. Some people are adept at improvising, and this is often fine for informal tutorials and other purposes. However, for important videos, a script is advised. The script is also an important planning and communication tool, helping you make sure all the pieces and people are ready when it's time to shoot.[26]

- **B-roll material.** The "B-roll" is another legacy term from film. It refers to a collection of secondary shots that can later be edited in to add visual interest, smooth over transitions, or otherwise improve the flow of the finished product.[27] For example, an interview with your company's CEO will look fairly static after a few minutes, but you can later cut in footage or images of your company's products, website, customers, manufacturing facilities, or other related scenes or images. The videographer Jefferson Graham makes it a point to show an image or clip of anything mentioned by a narrator or interview subject.[28] During postproduction, you can weave together your primary footage with B-roll video clips and still images, using the audio to maintain continuity from start to finish. Audiences will still get the full spoken message, only with a more interesting visual presentation.

B-roll is film terminology for extra scenes and images that can enhance your final production.

In addition to these planning considerations, be sure to identify and prepare all the equipment the shoot will require, from camera(s) to lights to props. If you plan to use a smartphone as your video camera, check out some of the apps that give you more control than the phone's built-in software provides.

REAL-TIME UPDATES

LEARN MORE BY VISITING THIS WEBSITE

Great advice for getting started in digital video

Indie Film Making offers a wealth of advice on producing quality videos. Go to **real-timeupdates.com/bct14** and select Learn More in the Students section.

STEP 2: PRODUCTION

With all your preproduction done, you're ready to shoot your video. These four tips will help you collect great footage:

- **Frame each shot carefully.** *Framing* refers to the decisions you make regarding what the camera sees and doesn't see when you aim it (see Figure 9.16). For example, if you're filming someone demonstrating a product, you'll have to decide where the camera should be aimed for each of your planned shots. If the presenter is talking at one point without using the product, you might frame the shot to emphasize the speaker's face. Then when the presenter interacts with the product, you might frame the shot to

Wide angle	Medium range	Close up
A wide-angle shot shows the full field of view; it can be great for capturing the size and composition of a crowd, suggesting a sense of scale, and establishing a scene. One drawback is the lack of visual and emotional intimacy. In this case, the speaker appears insignificant and distant.	A medium shot may or may not be useful, depending on what you are trying to convey. For example, if someone in the crowd was arguing with the speaker, using a medium range shot to zoom in as close as possible while still getting both people in frame would help you capture the emotion of the moment.	A close-up shot conveys intimacy and emotion, and it can remove distracting elements. On the downside, you lose the crowd reactions, and staying tight on the speaker for long periods can get tedious. Mixing it up with some crowd reaction shots is a good solution.

Digital Vision/Getty Images

Figure 9.16   Framing Your Shots: Finding the Right Range
Decisions about how you frame your shots can have a dramatic effect on information delivery and emotional impact. Compare the effect of these long, medium, and close shots, for example. Remember that your viewers can see everything the camera sees, but only what the camera sees.

Highlights from AGM
- 8K participants in Code for a Cause
- K-12 outreach now in 47 metro areas
- Budget projections still gloomy but improving

© IndiaPicture/Alamy Stock Photo

Figure 9.17   Framing Your Shots: Finding the Right Balance
Visual balance is another key decision when framing your shots. For a close-up of a person speaking directly to camera, for example, positioning the subject slightly off center makes the scene feel more dynamic. This also gives you room to display text on screen, if desired.

emphasize his or her hands. Just remember the obvious but sometimes overlooked point that the viewer sees everything the camera sees—but only what the camera sees. Framing decisions are particularly important if your videos will be watched on small-screen mobile devices, because small screens can limit the amount of detail viewers can see clearly. The question of balance (see page 232) is important as well. Keeping a speaker's face in the center of the screen can look dull and rigid after a while, so experiment with positioning him or her just off-center to create a more dynamically balanced scene (see Figure 9.17). Also, search for interesting angles for the shots you have planned.[29] In addition to filming the subject head on, for example, you might get some footage of him or her from the side or from high or low perspectives.

- **Keep the camera still.** If the camera moves around—intentionally or unintentionally—during a shot, the resulting footage puts a greater demand on your viewers. Shaky video from a handheld camera is uncomfortable to watch, so whenever possible, use a tripod or other stabilizing arrangement. And intentionally moving the camera forces viewers to process additional visual information that may or may not be relevant.[30] Moving during a shot also changes the background and lighting because the camera is looking at the scene differently. Sometimes you don't have a choice and have to follow a moving subject, but don't move the camera while filming unless you really need to.

- **Take B-roll footage.** In addition to the B-roll shots you planned in preproduction, keep an eye out for other interesting scenes and images that might enhance the finished video. It's better to shoot lots of footage you don't use than to regret not capturing something when you had the chance.

- **Don't use the special effects in your camera.** Many video cameras can add special effects such as pixilation or "old-timey" sepia tones, but using these features in the camera usually permanently alters the video. Instead, export "clean" footage to your editing software and add any effects in postproduction, where you can easily undo anything you try.[31]

> Resist the temptation to move around with your camera while filming unless it is absolutely necessary.

STEP 3: POSTPRODUCTION

Postproduction (often referred to simply as "post") is where interesting, high-quality videos come to life, as you use editing software to weave your main footage and B-roll footage into a seamless show and enhance it with music, titles, and other elements. Postproduction also lets you cut out clumsy bits of footage, record narration, potentially replace sections of dialogue, and make other fixes. With even low-cost video editing software, you can produce surprisingly sophisticated videos.

Here is a general overview of the postproduction process:[32]

1. Transfer your video footage to your computer and load it into the editing software.
2. Evaluate your material, identifying the shots you want to keep and those you can delete.
3. Use cut and paste to move sections of video around as needed to put the story in the desired order.
4. Weave in B-roll images and clips. Your company might also have a standard library of media elements to use in videos, including logos or introductory sequences.
5. Add transitions (such as a blend or quick fade to black) between video segments, if desired.
6. Synchronize the main audio track with the video and record narration as needed.
7. Add an *intro* (a brief sequence at the beginning) and an *outro* (a brief sequence at the end). Business videos often include company logos, website URLs, and other branding elements in intros and outros. Intros and outros often contain brief musical segments as well as a way to transition into and out of the spoken portion of the video.
8. Add text titles and other features as needed.
9. Create a distributable file. Video editors give you a variety of output options at different file sizes and screen resolutions, and some let you upload directly to YouTube.

As more and more companies rely on video for internal and external communication, learning some basic video skills will make you a more effective and more valuable communicator. For more on planning and producing business video, visit **real-timeupdates .com/bct14** and select Chapter 9.

> Postproduction involves the use of video editing software to place all your video and audio elements in the desired sequence.

COMMUNICATION CHALLENGES AT **GoPro**

You've joined the customer engagement team at GoPro, where your responsibilities include creating training materials to help customers use their GoPro cameras more effectively. Apply what you've learned in this chapter and throughout the course to the following challenges.

INDIVIDUAL CHALLENGE: A shot list is an important planning tool, particularly for complicated projects and situations in which you have limited time and opportunities to capture the footage you need. Your task is to create a sample shot list that customers can use to plan their own lists. Identify a part of your college campus or a section of your local area that has six distinct points of interest or special features. Imagine that you will be producing an orientation video, and prepare a shot list that identifies six locations where you would like to film. For each location, describe the specific shots you would like to get. For example, if you've chosen a monument in your town, you might want a wide-screen shot to establish the setting and a close-up shot that pans up the monument to show it in detail.

TEAM CHALLENGE: With a team assigned by your instructor, your task is to plan and produce a simple three- to four-minute video that shows viewers how to use some of the more important features of a smartphone. (Choose any phone that someone on your team has.) The purpose of the video is to serve as a sample for GoPro users who want to film production demonstration videos. Three or four minutes isn't a lot of time, so limit your scope to only a handful of major features. Follow the preproduction, production, and postproduction steps described on pages 251–253, then present your video the class. The emphasis with this process is on clear and effective communication, not professional-grade production quality, so don't worry too much about fancy effects or an elaborate set. Instead, focus your efforts on creating a video that communicates your key points well.

Quick Learning Guide

KEY TERMS

area chart Another name for a surface chart

bar chart Chart that portrays quantities by the height or length of its rectangular bars

bubble diagram Chart that expands the scatter diagram idea to three variables, with the size of the bubble representing the third variable

caption Brief commentary or explanation that accompanies a visual

data visualization A diverse class of displays that can show enormous sets of data in a single visual or show text and other complex information visually

descriptive title Title that simply identifies the topic of an illustration

flowchart Process diagram that illustrates a sequence of events from start to finish

Gantt chart The best-known type of time line chart

infographics Diagrams that contain enough visual and textual information to function as independent, standalone documents

informative title Title that highlights the conclusion to be drawn from the data

legend A "key" that helps readers decode a visual by explaining what various colors, symbols, or other design choices mean

line chart Chart that illustrates trends over time or plots the relationship of two or more variables

organization chart Diagram that illustrates the positions, units, or functions of an organization and their relationships

pictogram Chart that portrays data as symbols instead of words or numbers

pie chart Circular chart that shows how the parts of a whole are distributed

scatter diagram Chart that plots discrete data points, with one variable along the x (horizontal) axis and another along the y (vertical) axis

surface chart Form of line chart with a cumulative effect; all the lines add up to the top line, which represents the total

table A systematic arrangement of data in columns and rows

time line chart Chart that shows how much time is needed to complete each task in a project

title Text that identifies the content and purpose of a visual

visual literacy The ability to create effective images and to correctly interpret such images

visual symbolism The connotative (as opposed to the denotative, or literal) meaning of visuals

XY diagram Another name for a scatter diagram

SUMMARY OF LEARNING OBJECTIVES

1 Explain the power of business images, discuss six principles of graphic design that help ensure effective visuals, and explain how to avoid ethical lapses when using visuals. Well-designed visual elements can enhance the communication power of textual messages and, in some instances, even replace textual messages. Visuals can often convey some message points (such as spatial relationships, correlations, procedures, and emotions) more effectively and more efficiently than words. In the numbers-oriented world of work, readers rely heavily on trend lines, distribution curves, and other visual presentations of numeric quantities. Visuals attract and hold people's attention, helping your audience understand and remember your message. Visuals are also an effective way to communicate with diverse audiences.

When preparing visuals, (1) use elements of design consistently so you don't confuse your audience; (2) use color and other elements to show contrast effectively; (3) strive for a visual balance, either formal or informal, that creates a feel that is appropriate for your overall message; (4) use design choices to draw attention to key elements and to visually downplay less important items; (5) understand and follow design conventions that your audience expects (even if the expectation is subconscious), although you can consider unconventional design choices if they promise to convey your message more effectively; and (6) strive for simplicity in all your visuals, making design decisions that enhance the reception and understanding of information rather than obscure or confuse it.

Communicators are responsible for avoiding both intentional and unintentional ethical lapses when using visual elements. They can work to avoid these lapses by (1) considering all possible interpretations—and misinterpretations—of their messages and avoiding design choices that could lead to unwanted interpretations; (2) providing sufficient context, whether visual or verbal, for audiences to understand the meaning and significance of visuals; (3) not hiding or minimizing negative information that runs counter to their arguments; (4) not exaggerating information that supports their arguments; (5) not oversimplifying complex situations by hiding complications that are relevant to the audience's understanding; (6) not implying cause-and-effect relationships without providing proof that they exist; (7) avoiding emotional manipulation or other forms of coercion; and (8) being careful with the way they aggregate data.

2 Explain how to choose which points in your message to illustrate. To decide which points to illustrate, first step back and consider the overall flow of your message from the audience's point of view. Identify elements of the message that might be complex, vulnerable to misinterpretation, or even dull. Look for connections between ideas that should be highlighted or extensive collections of data and other discrete factual content that might be difficult to read in textual format.

3 Describe the most common options for presenting data in a visual format. The visuals most commonly used to present data include tables, line and surface charts, bar charts, pictograms, Gantt charts, scatter and bubble diagrams, and pie charts. You will probably use line, bar, and pie charts most often in your business communication efforts. Moving beyond basic display formats, designers continue to invent new data visualization tools to present large or complex sets of data.

4 Describe the most common options for presenting information, concepts, and ideas. Among the most commonly used visual formats in business communication are flowcharts (which depict a sequence of events in a process), organization charts (which show the relationships among people or elements in an organization), various types of maps (including data-driven map displays made possible by geographic information systems), illustrations (which are often used instead of photographs because they can focus attention on specific parts of an object), diagrams (used to convey designs, interrelated ideas, and other complex entities), photographs (used when realism or emotional impact is important), and infographics (hybrid elements that contain enough textual and visual information to function as standalone documents).

5 Explain how to integrate visuals with text and list three criteria to review in order to verify the quality of your visuals. To integrate visuals with text, strive for a balance between text and visuals; refer to visuals clearly; place visuals to maximize the smooth flow of reading; and write helpful titles, captions, and legends. To verify the quality of your visuals, make sure every visual is accurate (there are no mistakes or missing information), properly documented (the creator of any underlying data used in the visual has been given complete credit), and honest (the visual honestly reveals the real meaning of the underlying data or information).

6 Identify the most important considerations in the preproduction, production, and post-production stages of producing basic business videos. The key tasks in the preproduction stage are verifying your purpose and scope, thinking about the composition of the scenes you want to film, deciding where you'll place your camera(s), planning lighting, making arrangements for sound recording, writing a shot list or full script as appropriate, and identifying B-roll material that will enhance the final video.

During the production stage, be sure to frame each shot carefully, keep the camera still while filming unless the situation demands that you move it, take B-roll footage, and remember not to use the special effects in your camera so that you can export clean footage.

The postproduction stage generally consists of nine steps: (1) transfer your video footage to your computer and load it into the editing software; (2) evaluate your material, identifying the shots you want to keep and those you can delete; (3) move sections of video around as needed; (4) weave in B-roll images and clips; (5) add transitions between video segments, if desired; (6) synchronize the main audio track with the video and record narration as needed; (7) add an *intro* and an *outro*; (8) add text titles and other features as needed; and (9) create a distributable file.

MyBCommLab

Test Your Knowledge

To review chapter content related to each question, refer to the indicated Learning Objective.

⭐ 9-1. Why is simplicity important in business visuals? [LO-1]

9-2. What are the "five Cs" to consider when deciding which points to illustrate? [LO-2]

9-3. What type of data visual would you use to illustrate trends over time? [LO-3]

9-4. When would you use a bubble diagram instead of a scatter diagram? [LO-3]

9-5. For what purposes are Gantt charts used? [LO-3]

9-6. What is the purpose of adding titles, captions, and legends to visuals in reports? [LO-5]

⭐ 9-7. How do you check a visual for quality? [LO-5]

9-8. Why do experts recommend against using the built-in microphones in video cameras? [LO-6]

9-9. How does B-roll footage help enhance the appeal of business videos? [LO-6]

Apply Your Knowledge

To review chapter content related to each question, refer to the indicated Learning Objective.

⭐ 9-10. What similarities do you see between visuals and nonverbal communication? Explain your answer. [LO-1]

9-11. After studying the designs of corporate websites, Penn State University professor S. Shyam Sundar discovered quite an interesting phenomenon: The more interactive and engaging a website is, the more likely visitors are to "buy into whatever is being advocated" on the site. In other words, if two websites have identical content, the site with greater interactivity and more "bells and whistles" would be more persuasive.[33] Is it ethical to increase the persuasive power of a website simply by making it more interactive? Why or why not? [LO-1]

9-12. You're writing a report for the director of human resources on implementing team-based management throughout your company. You want to emphasize that since the new approaches were implemented six months ago, absenteeism and turnover have been sharply reduced in all but two departments. How do you visually present your data in the most favorable light while maintaining honest communication? Explain. [LO-1]

9-13. In addition to telling readers why an illustration is important, why else should you refer to it in the text of your document? [LO-5]

⭐ 9-14. Imagine that you are going to film your instructor's next lecture and you have the luxury of using three cameras. Where would you position them and why? (If you are taking an online course with no classroom, describe a generic classroom setting.) [LO-6]

Practice Your Skills

Messages for Analysis

9-15. **Message 9.A: Presenting Data (Bar Charts)** [LO-1], [LO-3] Examine the bar chart in Figure 9.18 and point out any problems or errors you notice.

9-16. **Message 9.B: Presenting Data (Line Charts)** [LO-1], [LO-3] Examine the line chart in Figure 9.19 and point out any problems or errors you notice.

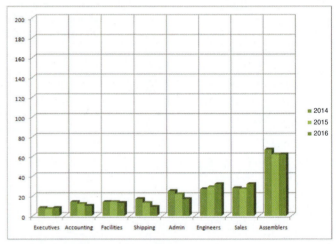

Figure 9.18 **Bar Chart for Analysis**

Figure 9.19 **Line Chart for Analysis**

Exercises

Each activity is labeled according to the primary skill or skills you will need to use. To review relevant chapter content, you can refer to the indicated Learning Objective.

9-17. Applying Visual Design Principles [LO-1] Find three visual presentations of data, information, or concepts on any business subject. Which of the three most clearly presents its data or information? What design choices promote this level of clarity? What improvements would you make to the other visuals to make them clearer?

9-18. Communication Ethics [LO-1] Using a spreadsheet, create a bar chart or line chart from data you find online or in a business publication. Alter the horizontal and vertical scales in several ways to produce different displays of the original data. How do the alterations distort the information? How might a reader detect whether a chart's scale has been altered?

9-19. Presenting Data (Bar and Pie Charts) [LO-3] As a market researcher for a statewide chain of car dealerships, you're examining car and truck ownership and lease patterns among single drivers in various age groups. By discovering which age groups have the highest percentages of owners, you will be better able to target advertising that promotes the leasing option. Using the information that follows, prepare a bar chart comparing the number of owners with the number of people who lease in each age category. Be sure to label your chart and include combined totals for owners and lessees ("total drivers"). Then prepare a pie chart showing the proportion of owners and lessees in the one age group you think holds the most promise for leasing a new vehicle. Write a sentence that prepares your company's management for the information shown in the pie chart.

Age Group	Number of Owners (in Thousands)	Number of Lessees (in Thousands)
18–24	1,830	795
25–29	1,812	1,483
30–34	1,683	1,413
35–44	1,303	1,932
45–54	1,211	1,894
55–64	1,784	1,435
65–74	3,200	1,142
75+	3,431	854

9-20. Presenting Data (Bar Charts) [LO-3] Team up with a classmate to design charts based on a comparison of the total tax burden of the U.S. taxpayer with that of people in other nations (see the data following this paragraph). One teammate should sketch a horizontal or vertical bar chart, and the other should sketch a pictogram from the estimates that follow. Then exchange charts and analyze how well each conveys the situation of the U.S. taxpayer. Would the bar chart look best with vertical or horizontal

bars? Why? What scale is best? How does the symbol used in the pictogram enhance or obscure the meaning or impact of the data? What suggestions can each student make for improving the other's visual aid?

Estimates show that Swedish taxpayers spend 51 percent of their incomes on taxes, British taxpayers spend 48 percent, French taxpayers spend 37 percent, Japanese taxpayers spend 28 percent, and U.S. taxpayers spend 27 percent.

9-21. Presenting Data (Line Charts) [LO-3] Here are last year's sales figures for the appliance and electronics megastore where you work. Construct a line chart that will help you explain to the store's general manager seasonal variations in each department.

STORE SALES (IN $ THOUSANDS)

Month	Home Electronics	Computers	Appliances
January	68	39	36
February	72	34	34
March	75	41	30
April	54	41	28
May	56	42	44
June	49	33	48
July	54	31	43
August	66	58	39
September	62	58	36
October	66	44	33
November	83	48	29
December	91	62	24

9-22. Presenting Data (Line Charts) [LO-3] Using rough approximations of the data, re-create the line chart in Figure 9.4 on page 239 as a bar chart (estimate the numerical values). Which of these two formats does the better job of conveying the information?

9-23. Presenting Data (Data Visualization) [LO-3] Explore several of the data visualization tools available through the Bovée & Thill Data Visualization and Infographics Gateway. (Go to real-timeupdates.com/bct14 and select Learn More in the Students section.) Choose one that has the potential to help business managers make decisions. Write a post for your class blog, explaining how this tool could assist with decision making. Be sure to include a link to the site where you found it.

9-24. Presenting Information, Concepts, and Ideas (Photographs) [LO-4] With a team assigned by your instructor, find a busy location on campus or in the surrounding neighborhood, someplace with lots of signs, storefronts, pedestrians, and traffic. Scout out two different photo opportunities: one that maximizes the visual impression of crowding and clutter, and one that minimizes this impression. For the first, assume that you are someone who advocates reducing the crowding and clutter, so you want to show how bad it is. For the second, assume you are a real estate agent or someone else who is motivated to show people that even though the location offers lots of shopping, entertainment, and other attractions, it's actually a rather calm and quiet neighborhood. Insert the two images in a document or blog post and write a caption for each that emphasizes the two opposite messages just described. Finally, write a brief paragraph discussing the ethical implications of what you've just done. Have you distorted reality or just presented it in ways that work to your advantage? Have you prevented audiences from gaining the information they would need to make informed decisions?

9-25. Presenting Information, Concepts, and Ideas (Maps) [LO-4] You work for C & S Holdings, a company that operates coin-activated, self-service car washes. Research shows that the farther customers live from a car wash, the less likely they are to visit. You know that 50 percent of customers at each of your car washes live within a 4-mile radius of the location, 65 percent live within 6 miles, 80 percent live within 8 miles, and 90 percent live within 10 miles. C & S's owner wants to open two new car washes in your city and has asked you to prepare a report recommending locations. Using a map of your city, choose two possible locations for car washes and create a visual depicting the customer base surrounding each location.

9-26. Presenting Information, Concepts, and Ideas (Organization Charts) [LO-4] Create an organization chart for your college or university. Start with the school's website to learn the various offices and departments.

9-27. Selecting the Right Type of Visual [LO-3], [LO-4] With a team of two or three other students, brainstorm and then sketch at least three types of charts you can use to compare the populations of all 50 states in the United States. You can use any of the graphic ideas presented in this chapter, as well as any ideas or examples you find from other sources.

9-28. Planning Business Videos; Mobile Skills [LO-6] Assume you are producing a video interview of your college or university's president. The purpose of the video is to encourage high school students to consider applying to your school. The interview will take place in the president's office, but you want to add some B-roll footage to make the video more visually appealing. Identify six scenes around campus that you could film for this purpose. Next, using a digital camera or the video capability in a phone, film these six scenes and share the B-roll footage with your class. Be sure to frame them in a way that they will be adequately viewable on mobile screens. As an option, add voiceover narration, titles, and other enhancements.

Expand Your Skills

Critique the Professionals

Find a business video on YouTube or another online source. This can be a product demonstration, a tutorial, a company profile, or most any other type of video other than an overt promotional video such as a TV commercial. Analyze its effectiveness in terms of lighting, sound, narration, camera placement, and the use of B-roll elements. How would you assess its overall effectiveness as a business message? Summarize your conclusions in a post on your class blog or an email message to your instructor. Be sure to include a link to the video.

Sharpening Your Career Skills Online

Bovée and Thill's Business Communication Web Search, at websearch.businesscommunicationnetwork.com, is a unique research tool designed specifically for business communication research. Use the Web Search function to find a website, video, article, podcast, or presentation that offers advice on creating effective visuals for documents and presentations. Write a brief email message to your instructor, describing the item that you found and summarizing the career skills information you learned from it.

MyBCommLab

Go to **mybcommlab.com** for Auto-graded writing questions as well as the following Assisted-graded writing questions:

9-29. Why might you use a simplified line illustration instead of a full-color digital photograph in a particular application? [LO-4]

9-30. You've been assigned the project of videotaping a new-employee welcome message by your company's vice president of human resources. You have top-notch equipment, attractive locations, and a solid script. There's just one problem: This executive is uncomfortable speaking on camera, and your first few shots are full of awkward gestures and nervous vocal tics. Assuming there isn't time for the executive to see a public speaking coach, how might you rethink your approach to the project in order to produce the most compelling video? [LO-6]

Endnotes

1. GoPro website, accessed 5 April 2016, www.gopro.com; Hilary Kramer, "GoPro Inc: Will Karma Be the Catalyst GPRO Stock Needs?" *InvestorPlace*, 4 April 2016, investorplace.com; Akin Oyedele, "Wall Street Analysts Say GoPro Isn't Going Mainstream and Now the Stock Is Falling," *Business Insider*, 20 June 2015, www.businessinsider.com; Nathan Ingraham, "GoPro Will Release a Quadcopter in the First Half of Next Year, *The Verge*, 27 May 2015, www.theverge.com; Ben Popper, "Here's Why GoPro Wants to Make Its Own Drones," *The Verge*, 26 November 2014, www.theverge.com; Garett Sloan, "The 10 Best Brand Channels on YouTube," *Adweek*, 2 April 2014, www.adweek.com; Christopher Ratcliff, "A Look Inside GoPro's Dazzling YouTube Strategy," Econsultancy website, 20 February 2014, econsultancy.com; GoPro channel on YouTube, accessed 5 April 2016, www.youtube.com/user/GoProCamera; "YouTube Brand Channel Leaderboard January–March 2014," *Google Think Insights*, 31 March 2014, www.thinkwithgoogle.com; Saya Weissman, "GoPro Might Have the Best Brand Content Around," *Digiday*, 6 February 2014, digiday.com; Shorty Industry Awards website, accessed 26 April 2014, industry.shortyawards.com; Anderson Cooper, "GoPro's Video Revolution," *60 Minutes*, 10 November 2013, www.cbsnews.com.

2. Alexis Gerard and Bob Goldstein, *Going Visual* (Hoboken, N.J.: Wiley, 2005), 18.

3. Charles Kostelnick and Michael Hassett, *Shaping Information: The Rhetoric of Visual Conventions* (Carbondale, Ill.: Southern Illinois University Press, 2003), 177.

4. Gerard and Goldstein, *Going Visual*, 25–27.

5. "PIAAC 2012/2014 Results," U.S. National Center for Education Statistics, accessed 5 April 2016, nces.ed.gov; "Fact Sheet Overview," *2003 National Assessment of Adult Literacy*, National Institute for Literacy, accessed 22 November 2006, www.nifl.gov.

6. Gerard and Goldstein, *Going Visual*, 103–106.

7. Edward R. Tufte, *Visual Explanations: Images and Quantities, Evidence and Narrative* (Cheshire, Conn.: Graphics Press, 1997), 82.

8. Joshua David McClurg-Genevese, "The Principles of Design," *Digital Web Magazine*, 13 June 2005, www.digital-web.com.

9. Kostelnick and Hassett, *Shaping Information*, 17.

10. Kostelnick and Hassett, *Shaping Information*, 216.

11. Edward R. Tufte, *The Visual Display of Quantitative Information* (Cheshire, Conn.: Graphic Press, 1983), 113.

12. Based in part on Tufte, *Visual Explanations*, 29–37, 53; Paul Martin Lester, *Visual Communication: Images with Messages*, 4th ed. (Belmont, Calif.: Thomson Wadsworth, 2006), 95–105, 194–196.

13. Data from Hoover's Online, accessed 3 December 2008, www.hoovers.com.

14. Robert L. Harris, *Information Graphics: A Comprehensive Illustrated Reference* (New York: Oxford University Press, 1999), 14.

15. Stephen Few, "Save the Pies for Dessert," *Visual Business Intelligence Newsletter*, August 2007, www.perceptualedge.com.

16. Maria Popova, "Data Visualization: Stories for the Information Age," *BusinessWeek*, 12 August 2009, www.businessweek.com.

17. "Big Data: What It Is and Why It Matters," SAS website, accessed 25 April 2014, www.sas.com.

18. "Data Visualization: Modern Approaches," *Smashing Magazine* website, 2 August 2007, www.smashingmagazine.com; "7 Things You Should Know About Data Visualization," Educause Learning Initiative, accessed 15 March 2008, www.educause.edu; TagCrowd website, accessed 15 March 2008, www.tagcrowd.com.

19. "Making Data Visualization Work: 4 Tips to Read Before You Start," Roambi blog, 13 August 2013, ww.roambi.com.

20. Steve Stockman, *How to Shoot Video That Doesn't Suck* (New York: Workman Publishing, 2011), Kindle edition.

21. Jefferson Graham, *Video Nation: A DIY Guide to Planning, Shooting, and Sharing Great Video from USA Today's Talking Tech Host* (Berkeley, Calif.: Peachpit Press, 2013), Kindle edition.

22. Graham, *Video Nation*.

23. Graham, *Video Nation*.

24. Graham, *Video Nation*.

25. Stockman, *How to Shoot Video That Doesn't Suck*.

26. Stockman, *How to Shoot Video That Doesn't Suck*.

27. Graham, *Video Nation*.

28. Graham, *Video Nation*.

29. Graham, *Video Nation*.

30. Stockman, *How to Shoot Video That Doesn't Suck*.

31. Stockman, *How to Shoot Video That Doesn't Suck*.

32. Based in part on Stockman, *How to Shoot Video That Doesn't Suck*; Graham, *Video Nation*.

33. "Interactive Web Sites Draw Minds, Shape Public Perception," *ScienceDaily*, 27 May 2008, www.sciencedaily.com.

Brief Messages

Most of your communication on the job will be through brief messages, from Twitter updates and blog posts to formal letters that might run to several pages. Learning how to write these messages quickly and effectively is key to maintaining productive working relationships with colleagues and customers. In these chapters you'll find specific techniques for crafting routine, positive, negative, and persuasive messages—techniques that will help you in everything from getting a raise to calming an angry customer to promoting your next great idea.

wong yu liang/Fotolia

10

Writing Routine and Positive Messages

LEARNING OBJECTIVES

After studying this chapter, you will be able to

1 Outline an effective strategy for writing routine business requests.

2 Describe three common types of routine requests.

3 Outline an effective strategy for writing routine replies and positive messages.

4 Describe six common types of routine replies and positive messages.

COMMUNICATION CLOSE-UP AT

Productivity Report

productivityreport.org

Every so often, you'll get the chance to craft a message or document that has the potential to reshape your career or your company, such as a major project proposal or a business plan. However, much of your business communication will take place through routine, everyday messages—asking someone for help or information, responding to such requests from others, sharing information with colleagues or customers, and congratulating or consoling other people.

Just because these messages are routine, though, doesn't make them unimportant. In fact, the cumulative effect of all these brief messages could have more influence on your career than the occasional major report or proposal. The way you handle communication, day in and day out, is a key factor in establishing your credibility as a professional.

Developing your skills at handling routine messages is only part of the challenge, however. Depending on your field and your position, you're likely to be inundated with routine messages. It's not uncommon for professionals to receive a hundred or more messages a day—and be expected to respond to many of them while generating many more messages themselves. So, not only do you need to be skilled at handling routine communication, you have to be hyperefficient at it, too, or else you'll get hopelessly swamped.

Jill Duffy offers research-based advice on handling the barrage of routine messages that most business communicators deal with on the job.

Image courtesy of Jill Duffy

Fortunately, you have a wise ally in Jill Duffy. Her career as a writer spans multiple industries, from academic journals to major newspapers to the trade journals *Game Developer* and *PCMag.com*. One of her areas of expertise is personal and organizational productivity, and she shares her ideas in the weekly Get Organized column for *PCMag.com*, in her book *Get Organized: How to Clean Up Your Messy Digital Life*, and via her newest venture, the website *Productivity Report*, which blends advice from research studies and personal experience. Her deep and diverse experience has given her useful insights into the challenges of digital productivity, and much of that involves how to handle a high volume of routine messages without losing focus on your audience or on your priorities.

For email, for instance, Duffy advises compartmentalizing message flows so that high-priority messages never get lost in the deluge of low-priority messages. Most email programs and apps offer the ability to filter messages based on sender, subject line, and other factors, so you can make sure important messages are always visible. Then develop a comprehensive system of software capabilities and daily habits to keep email in check. For example, if one of your goals is to respond to your boss's emails before you go home every day, set up an email filter to send those messages to a special folder and set an alarm to deal with them at 4:00 p.m. every day. Another skill she promotes is acting quickly and decisively on incoming email, whether that is deleting a message, filing it, responding immediately (for simple or critical messages), or scheduling time to respond. The key is to avoid looking at a message multiple times before deciding what to do with it.

Duffy doesn't subscribe to the approach taken by email users who never bother filtering and filing messages but who instead let them pile up in their inbox and use search functions to find specific messages whenever they need them. She points out several problems with this approach. First, if you can't remember who sent a message or the exact keywords that are in it, you'll never find it with search methods alone. Second, folders organized by subject serve as a "second memory" that she can browse whenever she wants. Third, that giant, unsorted pile of messages in your inbox will be a constant source of anxiety and distraction as you repeatedly scan though it trying to find a specific item or to make sure you haven't missed anything important.

Whether it's email, workgroup messaging, or any other communication platform, setting up and fine-tuning a system and set of habits that work best for you does take some time and effort. However, it will be time well spent because you'll be more efficient every day, and you'll be able to focus your attention and energy on the messages that matter the most.[1]

Strategy for Routine Requests

Jill Duffy (profiled in the chapter-opening Communication Close-Up) helps business professionals deal with a vital aspect of communication in today's digital workplace—how to productively handle the many routine messages that need to be sent or responded to day in and day out. Routine messages fall into two groups: routine requests, in which you ask for information from or action by another party, and a variety of routine and positive messages. Chapter 11 covers messages in which you need to convey negative information, and Chapter 12 addresses persuasive messages.

Making requests is a routine part of business, and in most cases your audience will be prepared to comply. By applying a clear strategy and tailoring your approach to each situation, you'll be able to generate effective requests quickly.

For routine requests and positive messages
• State the request or main idea
• Give necessary details
• Close with a cordial request for specific action

Like all other business messages, a routine request has three parts: an opening, a body, and a close. Using the direct approach, open with your main idea, which is a clear statement of your request. Use the body to give details and justify your request. Finally, close by requesting specific action.

Take care that your direct approach doesn't come across as abrupt or tactless.

STATING YOUR REQUEST UP FRONT

With routine requests, you can make your request at the beginning of the message. Of course, getting right to the point should not be interpreted as license to be abrupt or tactless:

• **Pay attention to tone.** Instead of demanding action ("Send me the latest version of the budget spreadsheet"), show respect by using words such as *please* and *I would appreciate*.

• **Assume that your audience will comply.** You can generally assume that your readers will comply with routine requests, so you don't need to devote a lot of time or energy toward trying to convince them to do so.

• **Be specific.** State precisely what you want. For example, if you request the latest market data from your research department, be sure to say whether you want a 1-page summary or 100 pages of raw data.

EXPLAINING AND JUSTIFYING YOUR REQUEST

Use the body of your message to explain your request, as needed. Make the explanation a smooth and logical outgrowth of your opening remarks. If complying with the request could benefit the reader, be sure to mention that. If you have multiple requests or questions, ask the most important questions first and deal with only one topic per question. If you have an unusual or complex request, break it down into specific, individual questions so that the reader can address each one separately. This consideration not only shows respect for your audience's time but also gets you a more accurate answer in less time.

REAL-TIME UPDATES
LEARN MORE BY VISITING THIS WEBSITE
Insight into mobile strategies for routine communication

ClickSoftware's MobileFever blog discusses a range of topics on mobile business communication. Go to **real-timeupdates.com/bct14** and select Learn More in the Students section.

REQUESTING SPECIFIC ACTION IN A COURTEOUS CLOSE

Close your message with three important elements: (1) a specific request that includes any relevant deadlines, (2) information about how you can be reached (if it isn't obvious), and (3) an expression of appreciation or goodwill. When you ask readers to perform a specific action, ask for a response by a specific date or time, if appropriate (for example, "Please send the figures by May 5 so that I can return first-quarter results to you before the May 20 conference."). Conclude your message with a sincere thanks. To review, see "Checklist: Writing Routine Requests."

Close request messages with
- A request for some specific action
- Information about how you can be reached
- An expression of appreciation

Common Examples of Routine Requests

The most common types of routine messages are asking for information or action, asking for recommendations, and making claims and requesting adjustments.

2 LEARNING OBJECTIVE
Describe three common types of routine requests.

ASKING FOR INFORMATION AND ACTION

Most simple requests can be handled with three message points:

- What you want to know or what you want your readers to do
- Why you're making the request (not required in all cases)
- Why it may be in your readers' interests to help you (not applicable in all cases)

For simple requests, using the direct approach gets the job done with a minimum of fuss. In more complex situations you may need to provide more extensive reasons and justification for your request. If applicable, point out any benefits to the reader of complying with your request. Naturally, be sure to adapt your request to your audience and the situation (see Figure 10.1 on the next page).

Routine requests can be handled with simple, straightforward messages, but more complicated requests may require additional justification and explanation.

CHECKLIST ✔ Writing Routine Requests

A. State your request up front.
- Write in a polite, undemanding, personal tone.
- Use the direct approach because your audience will probably respond favorably to your request.
- Be specific and precise in your request.

B. Explain and justify your request.
- Justify the request or explain its importance.
- Explain any potential benefits of responding.
- Ask the most important questions first.

- Break complex requests into individual questions that are limited to only one topic each.

C. Request specific action in a courteous close.
- Make it easy to comply by including appropriate contact information.
- Express your gratitude.
- Clearly state any important deadlines for the request.

1 Plan →	2 Write →	3 Complete
Analyze the Situation Verify that the purpose is to request information from company managers.	**Adapt to Your Audience** Show sensitivity to audience needs with a "you" attitude, politeness, positive emphasis, and bias-free language. The writer already has credibility, as manager of the department.	**Revise the Message** Evaluate content and review readability; avoid unnecessary details
Gather Information Gather accurate, complete information about local competitive threats.	**Compose the Message** Maintain a style that is conversational but still business like, using plain English and appropriate voice.	**Produce the Message** Simple email format is all the design this message needs.
Choose Medium and Channel Email is effective for this internal message, and it allows the attachment of a Word document to collect the information.		**Proofread the Message** Review for errors in layout, spelling, and mechanics.
Organize the Information Clarify that the main idea is collecting information that will lead to a better competitive strategy, which will in turn help the various district managers.		**Distribute the Message** Deliver the message via the company's email system.

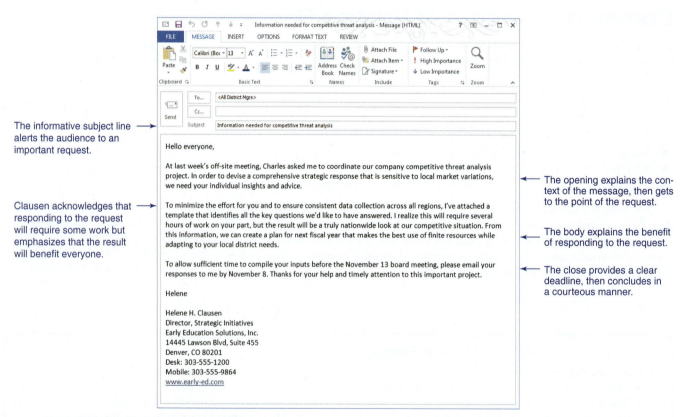

The informative subject line alerts the audience to an important request.

Clausen acknowledges that responding to the request will require some work but emphasizes that the result will benefit everyone.

The opening explains the context of the message, then gets to the point of the request.

The body explains the benefit of responding to the request.

The close provides a clear deadline, then concludes in a courteous manner.

Figure 10.1 Routine Message Requesting Action

In this email request to district managers across the country, Helene Clausen asks them to fill out an attached information collection form. Although the request is not unusual and responding to it is part of the managers' responsibilities, Clausen asks for their help in a courteous manner and points out the benefits of responding.

ASKING FOR RECOMMENDATIONS

The need to inquire about people arises often in business. For example, before awarding contracts, jobs, promotions, or scholarships, companies often ask applicants to supply references. Companies ask applicants to list people who can vouch for their ability, skills, integrity, character, and fitness for the job. Before you volunteer someone's name as a reference, ask permission. Some people don't want you to use their names, perhaps because they don't know enough about you to feel comfortable writing a letter or because they or their employers have a policy of not providing recommendations.

Always ask for permission before using someone as a reference.

Requests for recommendations and references are routine, so you can organize your inquiry using the direct approach. Open your message by clearly stating why the recommendation is required (if it's not for a job, be sure to explain its purpose) and that you would like your reader to write the letter. If you haven't had contact with the person for some time, use the opening to trigger the reader's memory of the relationship you had, the dates of association, and any special events or accomplishments that might bring a clear and favorable picture of you to mind.

Refresh the memory of any potential reference you haven't been in touch with for a while.

Close your message with an expression of appreciation and the full name and address (email or physical address) of the person to whom the message should be sent. When asking for an immediate recommendation, you should also mention the deadline. For printed letters, always be sure to enclose a stamped, preaddressed envelope as a convenience to the other party. Figure 10.2 on the next page provides an example of a request that follows these guidelines.

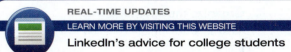

REAL-TIME UPDATES

LEARN MORE BY VISITING THIS WEBSITE

LinkedIn's advice for college students

Follow these tips to get the most from LinkedIn, including the most appropriate and effective ways to ask for recommendations. Go to **real-timeupdates.com/bct14** and select Learn More in the Students section.

MAKING CLAIMS AND REQUESTING ADJUSTMENTS

If you're dissatisfied with a company's product or service, you can opt to make a **claim** (a formal complaint) or request an **adjustment** (a settlement of a claim). In either case, it's important to maintain a professional tone in all your communication, no matter how angry or frustrated you are. Keeping your cool will help you get the situation resolved sooner.

When writing a claim or requesting an adjustment
- Explain the problem and give details
- Provide backup information
- Request specific action

Open with a clear and calm statement of the problem along with your request. In the body, give a complete, specific explanation of the details. Provide any information the recipient needs to verify your complaint. In your close, politely request specific action or convey a sincere desire to find a solution. And, if appropriate, suggest that the business relationship will continue if the problem is solved satisfactorily. Be prepared to back up your claim with invoices, sales receipts, canceled checks, dated correspondence, and any other relevant documents. Send copies and keep the originals for your files.

Be prepared to document any claims you make with a company. Send copies and keep the original documents.

If the remedy is obvious, tell your reader exactly what you expect to be done, such as exchanging incorrectly shipped merchandise for the right item or issuing a refund if the item is out of stock. However, if you're uncertain about the precise nature of the trouble, you could ask the company to assess the situation and then advise you on how the situation could be fixed. Supply your full contact information so that the company can discuss the situation with you, if necessary. Compare the ineffective and effective versions in Figure 10.3 on page 271 for an example of making a claim. To review the tasks involved in making claims and requesting adjustments, see "Checklist: Making Claims and Requesting Adjustments."

CHECKLIST ✓ Making Claims and Requesting Adjustments

- Maintain a professional tone, even if you're extremely frustrated.
- Open with a straightforward statement of the problem.
- Provide specific details in the body.
- Present facts honestly and clearly.

- Politely summarize the desired action in the closing.
- Clearly state what you expect as a fair settlement or ask the reader to propose a fair adjustment.
- Explain the benefits of complying with the request, such as your continued patronage.

Analyze the Situation
Verify that the purpose is to request a recommendation letter from a college professor.

Gather Information
Gather information on classes and dates to help the reader recall you and to clarify the position you seek.

Choose Medium and Channel
The letter format gives this message an appropriate level of formality, although many professors prefer to be contacted by email.

Organize the Information
Messages like this are common and expected, so a direct approach is fine.

Adapt to Your Audience
Show sensitivity to audience needs with a "you" attitude, politeness, positive emphasis, and bias-free language.

Compose the Message
Style is respectful and businesslike, while still using plain English and appropriate voice.

Revise the Message
Evaluate content and review readability; avoid unnecessary details.

Produce the Message
Simple letter format is all the design this message needs.

Proofread the Message
Review for errors in layout, spelling, and mechanics.

Distribute the Message
Deliver the message via postal mail or email if you have the professor's email address.

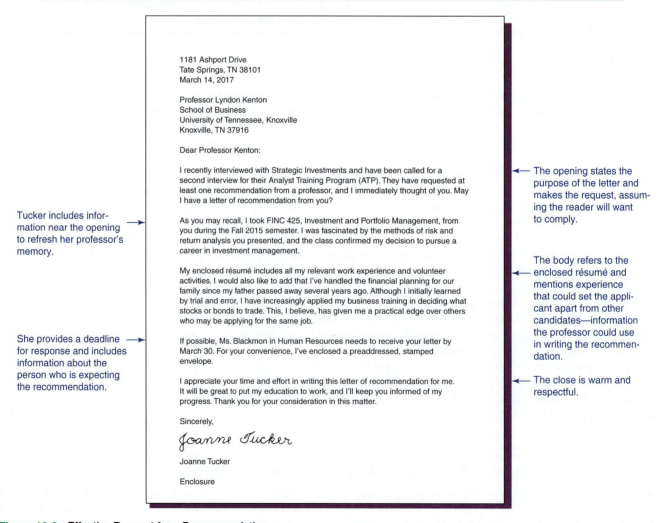

1181 Ashport Drive
Tate Springs, TN 38101
March 14, 2017

Professor Lyndon Kenton
School of Business
University of Tennessee, Knoxville
Knoxville, TN 37916

Dear Professor Kenton:

I recently interviewed with Strategic Investments and have been called for a second interview for their Analyst Training Program (ATP). They have requested at least one recommendation from a professor, and I immediately thought of you. May I have a letter of recommendation from you?

As you may recall, I took FINC 425, Investment and Portfolio Management, from you during the Fall 2015 semester. I was fascinated by the methods of risk and return analysis you presented, and the class confirmed my decision to pursue a career in investment management.

My enclosed résumé includes all my relevant work experience and volunteer activities. I would also like to add that I've handled the financial planning for our family since my father passed away several years ago. Although I initially learned by trial and error, I have increasingly applied my business training in deciding what stocks or bonds to trade. This, I believe, has given me a practical edge over others who may be applying for the same job.

If possible, Ms. Blackmon in Human Resources needs to receive your letter by March 30. For your convenience, I've enclosed a preaddressed, stamped envelope.

I appreciate your time and effort in writing this letter of recommendation for me. It will be great to put my education to work, and I'll keep you informed of my progress. Thank you for your consideration in this matter.

Sincerely,

Joanne Tucker

Joanne Tucker

Enclosure

Tucker includes information near the opening to refresh her professor's memory.

She provides a deadline for response and includes information about the person who is expecting the recommendation.

The opening states the purpose of the letter and makes the request, assuming the reader will want to comply.

The body refers to the enclosed résumé and mentions experience that could set the applicant apart from other candidates—information the professor could use in writing the recommendation.

The close is warm and respectful.

Figure 10.2 Effective Request for a Recommendation
This writer uses a direct approach when asking for a recommendation from a former professor. Note how she takes care to refresh the professor's memory because she took the class a year and a half ago. She also indicates the date by which the letter is needed and points to the enclosure of a stamped, preaddressed envelope.

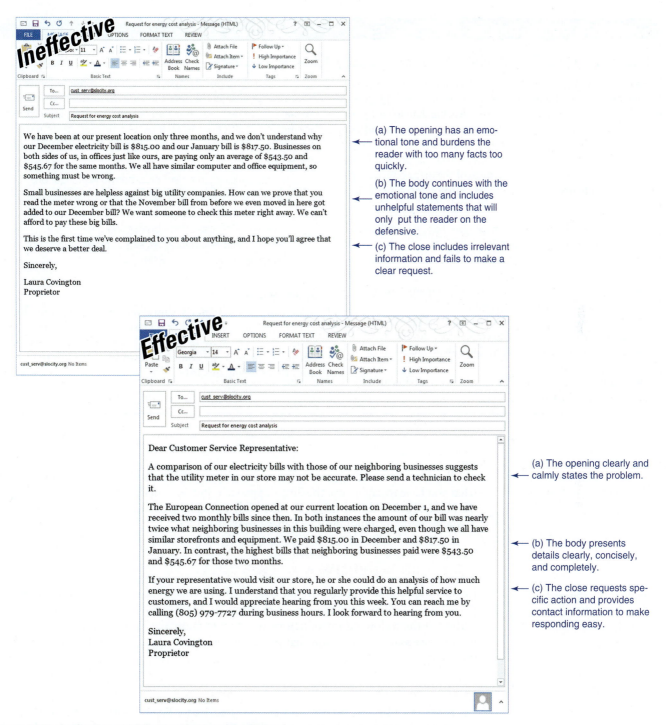

Figure 10.3   Ineffective and Effective Versions of a Claim
Note the difference in both tone and information content in these two versions. The ineffective version is emotional and unprofessional, whereas the effective version communicates calmly and clearly.

Strategy for Routine and Positive Messages

Just as you'll make numerous requests for information and action throughout your career, you'll also respond to similar requests from other people. When you are responding positively to a request, sending routine announcements, or sending a positive or goodwill message, you have several goals: to communicate the information or the good news, answer all questions, provide all required details, and leave your reader with a good impression of you and your firm.

3 LEARNING OBJECTIVE
Outline an effective strategy for writing routine replies and positive messages.

Solving the Case of the Imaginary Good News

To deal with a growing problem of employee turnover, your company recently hired a research firm to survey employees to find out why more of them have been leaving than in past years. You and a colleague were assigned to work with the consultants and present their findings to upper management. Neither one of you welcomed the assignment because you suspect you'll have to present information that is critical of the management team.

As you feared, the researchers deliver a mixture of news that is mostly negative:

- Seventy-eight percent of employees believe management cares more about profits than people.
- Fifty-five percent aren't sure what's expected of them anymore.
- Forty percent believe wages at the company have not kept up with the industry average.
- Thirty-eight percent think management has done a good job of responding to competitive advances.
- Fifty-two percent expect to finish their careers at the company.
- Eighty percent believe the economy is too slow to support a productive job search.

While you're poring over the report, trying to figure out how you'll present the information tomorrow, an instant message from the CEO pops up on your partner's computer, asking for a quick summary of the results. Your partner types the following and then asks you to review it before she sends it:

> As you'd expect in a no-holds-barred investigation like this, the researchers did uncover some areas for improvements. The good news: Only 20 percent of the workforce is even considering other options, and we could reasonably expect that only a fraction of that group will leave anytime soon.

ANALYSIS

You read your partner's summary twice, but something doesn't feel quite right. Does it present an accurate summary of the research? Why or why not? What's likely to happen when you present the complete research results to the CEO after first sending this IM?

Use a direct approach for routine replies and positive messages.

Readers receiving routine replies and positive messages will generally be interested in what you have to say, so use the direct approach. Put your main idea (the positive reply or the good news) in the opening. Use the body to explain all the relevant details, and close cordially, perhaps highlighting a benefit to your reader.

STARTING WITH THE MAIN IDEA

With the direct approach, open with a clear and concise expression of the main idea or good news.

By opening routine and positive messages with the main idea or good news, you're preparing your audience for the details that follow. Make your opening clear and concise. Although the following introductory statements make the same point, one is cluttered with unnecessary information that buries the purpose, whereas the other is brief and to the point:

Instead of This

I am pleased to inform you that after careful consideration of a diverse and talented pool of applicants, each of whom did a thorough job of analyzing Trask Horton Pharmaceuticals's training needs, we have selected your bid.

Write This

Trask Horton Pharmaceuticals has accepted your bid to provide public speaking and presentation training to the sales staff.

The best way to write a clear opening is to have a clear idea of what you want to say. Ask yourself, "What is the single most important message I have for the audience?"

MOBILE APP

If your email service doesn't allow huge file attachments, **Hightail** lets you post the file on its servers and send your recipients a link instead.

PROVIDING NECESSARY DETAILS AND EXPLANATION

Use the body to explain your point completely so that your audience won't be confused about or doubt your meaning. As you provide the details, maintain the supportive tone established in the opening. This tone is easy to continue when your message is entirely positive, as in this example:

> Your educational background and internship have impressed us, and we believe you would be a valuable addition to Green Valley Properties. As discussed during your interview, your salary will be $4,300 per month, plus benefits. Please plan to meet with our benefits manager, Paula Sanchez, at 8 A.M. on Monday, March 21. She will assist you with all the paperwork necessary to tailor our benefit package to your family situation. She will also arrange various orientation activities to help you get on board with the Green Valley team.

However, if your routine message is mixed and must convey mildly disappointing information, put the negative portion of your message into as favorable a context as possible:

Try to embed any negative information in a positive context.

Instead of This	**Write This**
No, we no longer carry the HealthTrakk Model V fitness watch.	The new HealthTrakk Optima has replaced the HealthTrakk Model V. The Optima model features a wider range of band colors and new tracking features, including GPS for outdoor fitness activities.

In this example, the more complete description is less negative and emphasizes how the recipient can benefit from the change. Be careful, though: Use negative information in this type of message only if you're reasonably sure the audience will respond positively. Otherwise, use the indirect approach (discussed in Chapter 11).

If you are communicating with a customer, you might also want to use the body of your message to assure the person of the wisdom of his or her purchase (without being condescending or self-congratulatory). Using such favorable comments, often known as *resale*, is a good way to build customer relationships. These comments are commonly included in acknowledgments of orders and other routine announcements to customers, and they are most effective when they are short and specific:

REAL-TIME UPDATES

LEARN MORE BY READING THIS ARTICLE

Using Twitter for routine customer communication

These 10 tips can help any company respond to the growing number of routine requests delivered on Twitter. Go to **real-timeupdates .com/bct14** and select Learn More in the Students section.

> The KitchenAid mixer you ordered is our best-selling model. It should meet your cooking needs for many years.

ENDING WITH A COURTEOUS CLOSE

The close of routine replies and positive messages is usually short and simple because you're leaving things on a neutral or positive note and not usually asking for the reader to do anything. Often, a simple thank you is all you need. However, if follow-up action is required or expected, use the close to identify who will do what and when that action will take place. For a quick reminder of the steps involved in writing routine replies and positive messages, see "Checklist: Writing Routine Replies and Positive Messages."

In the close, make sure audience members understand what to do next and how that action will benefit them (if applicable).

CHECKLIST ✔ Writing Routine Replies and Positive Messages

A. Start with the main idea.
- Be clear and concise.
- Identify the single most important message before you start writing.

B. Provide necessary details and explanation.
- Explain your point completely to eliminate any confusion or lingering doubts.
- Maintain a supportive tone throughout.

- Embed negative statements in positive contexts or balance them with positive alternatives.
- Talk favorably about the choices the customer has made.

C. End with a courteous close.
- Let your readers know you have their personal well-being in mind.
- If further action is required, tell readers how to proceed and encourage them to act promptly.

Common Examples of Routine and Positive Messages

Most routine and positive messages fall into six main categories: answers to requests for information and action, grants of claims and requests for adjustment, recommendations, routine information, good-news announcements, and goodwill messages.

ANSWERING REQUESTS FOR INFORMATION AND ACTION

Every professional answers requests for information and action from time to time. If the response is a simple yes or some other straightforward information, the direct approach is appropriate. A prompt, gracious, and thorough response will positively influence how people think about you and the organization you represent.

When you're answering requests and a potential sale is involved, you have three main goals: (1) to respond to the inquiry and answer all questions, (2) to leave your reader with a good impression of you and your firm, and (3) to encourage the future sale.

GRANTING CLAIMS AND REQUESTS FOR ADJUSTMENT

Responding to mistakes in a courteous, reader-focused way helps repair important business relationships.

No company wants to make mistakes, but these events represent turning points in relationships with customers. If you handle the situation well, your customer is likely to be even more loyal than before because you've proven that you're serious about customer satisfaction. However, if a customer believes that you mishandled a complaint, you'll make the situation even worse. Dissatisfied customers often take their business elsewhere without notice and tell numerous friends, colleagues, and social media followers about the negative experience. A transaction that might be worth only a small amount by itself could cost you many times that in lost business. In other words, every mistake is an opportunity to improve a relationship.

Your specific response to a customer complaint depends on your company's policies for resolving such issues and your assessment of whether the company, the customer, or some third party is at fault. In general, take the following steps:

- Acknowledge receipt of the customer's claim or complaint.
- Sympathize with the customer's inconvenience or frustration.
- Take (or assign) personal responsibility for setting matters straight.
- Explain precisely how you have resolved, or plan to resolve, the situation.
- Take steps to repair the relationship.
- Follow up to verify that your response was correct.

In addition to taking these positive steps, maintain a professional demeanor. Don't blame colleagues by name; don't make exaggerated, insincere apologies; don't imply that the customer is at fault; and don't promise more than you can deliver.

To grant a claim when the customer is at fault, try to discourage future mistakes without insulting the customer.

Communication about a claim is a delicate matter when the customer is clearly at fault. If you choose to grant the claim, open with that good news. However, the body needs special attention because you want to discourage similar claims in the future. Close in a courteous manner that expresses your appreciation for the customer's business (see Figure 10.4).

See "Checklist: Granting Claims and Adjustment Requests" to review the tasks involved in these kinds of business messages.

PROVIDING RECOMMENDATIONS AND REFERENCES

Recommendation letters are vulnerable to legal complications, so consult your company's legal department before writing one.

People who need endorsements from employers or colleagues (when applying for a job, for example) often request letters of recommendation. These messages used to be a fairly routine matter, but employment recommendations and references have raised some complex legal issues in recent years. Employees have sued employers and individual managers for providing negative information or refusing to provide letters of recommendation, and

Figure 10.4 Responding to a Claim When the Buyer Is at Fault

Responding to a claim when the buyer is at fault is a positive gesture, so the content and tone of the message need to reflect that. After all, there's no point in fostering a positive relationship through actions but then undermining that through negative communication. Notice how the ineffective version sounds like a crabby parent who gives in to a child's demand but sends a mixed message by being highly critical anyway. The effective version is much more subtle, letting the customer know how to take care of his skates, without blaming or insulting him.

CHECKLIST ✔ Granting Claims and Adjustment Requests

A. Responding when your company is at fault
- Be aware of your company's policies in such cases before you respond.
- For serious situations, refer to the company's crisis management plan.
- Start by acknowledging receipt of the claim or complaint.
- Take or assign personal responsibility for resolving the situation.
- Sympathize with the customer's frustration.
- Explain how you have resolved the situation (or plan to).
- Take steps to repair the customer relationship.
- Verify your response with the customer, and keep the lines of communication open.

B. Responding when the customer is at fault
- Weigh the cost of complying with or refusing the request.
- If you choose to comply, open with the good news.
- Use the body of the message to respectfully educate the customer about steps needed to avoid a similar outcome in the future.
- Close with an appreciation for the customer's business.

C. Responding when a third party is at fault
- Evaluate the situation and review your company's policies before responding.
- Avoid placing blame; focus on the solution.
- Regardless of who is responsible for resolving the situation, let the customer know what will happen to resolve the problem.

---

employers have sued other employers for failing to disclose negative information about job candidates. Before you write a letter of recommendation for a former employee or provide information in response to another employer's background check, make sure you understand your company's policies. The company may refuse to provide anything more than dates of employment and other basic details, for example.[2]

If you decide to write a letter of recommendation or respond to a request for information about a job candidate, your goal is to convince readers that the person being recommended has the characteristics necessary for the job, assignment, or other objective the person is seeking. A successful recommendation letter contains a number of relevant details (see Figure 10.5):

- The candidate's full name
- The position or other objective the candidate is seeking
- The nature of your relationship with the candidate
- Facts and evidence relevant to the candidate and the opportunity
- A comparison of this candidate's potential with that of peers, if available (for example, "Ms. Jonasson consistently ranked in the top 10 percent of our national salesforce.")
- Your overall evaluation of the candidate's suitability for the opportunity

REAL-TIME UPDATES

LEARN MORE BY VISITING THIS WEBSITE

Get expert tips on writing (or requesting) a letter of recommendation

Find helpful advice on employment recommendations, academic recommendations, and character references. Go to **real-timeupdates .com/bct14** and select Learn More in the Students section.

Keep in mind that every time you write a recommendation, you're putting your own reputation on the line. If the person's shortcomings are so pronounced that you don't think he or she is a good fit for the job, the only choice is to not write the letter at all. Unless your relationship with the person warrants an explanation, simply suggest that someone else might be in a better position to provide a recommendation.

SHARING ROUTINE INFORMATION

When sharing routine information
- *State the purpose at the beginning and briefly mention the nature of the information you are providing*
- *Provide the necessary details*
- *End with a courteous close*

Many messages involve sharing routine information, such as project updates and order status notifications. Use the opening of these routine messages to state the purpose and briefly mention the nature of the information you are providing. Give the necessary details in the body, and end your message with a courteous close.

Most routine communications are neutral, so you don't have to take special steps in anticipation of emotional reactions from readers. However, some routine informative messages may require additional care. For instance, policy statements or procedural changes may be good news for a company, perhaps by saving money. But it may not be obvious to

LeClerc specifies the duration and nature of the relationship in the body to give credibility to her evaluation. →

Point1 Promotions

105 E. Madison
Ann Arbor, MI 48103
tel: 800-747-9786
email: info@point1promo.net
www.point1promo.net

November 14, 2018

Ms. Clarice Gailey
Director of Operations
McNally and Associates, Inc.
8688 Southgate Ave.
Augusta, GA 30906

Dear Ms. Gailey:

I am pleased to recommend Talvin Biswas for the marketing position at McNally and Associates. Mr. Biswas has worked with Point1 Promotions as an intern for the past two summers while working toward his degree in marketing and advertising. His duties included customer correspondence, web content updates, and direct-mail campaign planning.

As his supervisor, in addition to knowing his work here, I also know that Mr. Biswas has served as secretary for the International Business Association at the University of Michigan. He tutored other international students in the university's writing center. His fluency in three languages (English, French, and Hindi) and thorough knowledge of other cultures will make him an immediate contributor to your international operations.

Mr. Biswas is a thoughtful and careful professional who will not hesitate to contribute ideas when invited to do so. In addition, because Mr. Biswas learns quickly, he will learn your company's routine with ease.

Mr. Biswas will make an excellent addition to your staff at McNally and Associates. If I can provide any additional information, please call me at the number above. If you prefer to communicate by email, my address is angela_leclerc@point1promo.net.

Sincerely,

Angela LeClerc

Angela LeClerc
Vice President, Marketing

← The opening clearly states the candidate's full name and the specific purpose of the letter.

← The body continues with specific examples to support the writer's positive evaluation.

← The close summarizes the writer's recommendation and invites further communication.

Figure 10.5   Effective Recommendation Letter
This letter clearly states the nature of the writer's relationship to the candidate and provides specific examples to support the writer's endorsements.

employees that such savings may make additional employee resources available or even lead to pay raises. In instances in which the reader may not initially view the information positively, use the body of the message to highlight the potential benefits from the reader's perspective. (For situations in which negative news will have a profound effect on the recipients, consider the indirect techniques discussed in Chapter 11.)

ANNOUNCING GOOD NEWS

To develop and maintain good relationships, smart companies recognize that it's good business to spread the word about positive developments. Such developments can include opening new facilities, hiring a new executive, introducing new products or services, or sponsoring community events. Because good news is always welcome, use the direct approach (see Figure 10.6 on the next page).

External good-news announcements are often communicated in a **news release**, also known as a *press release*, a specialized document used to share relevant information with the news media. (News releases are also used to announce negative news, such as plant closings.) In most companies, news releases are usually prepared or at least supervised by specially trained writers in the public relations department. The content follows the customary pattern for a positive message: good news followed by details and a positive close. However, traditional news releases have a critical difference: You're not writing directly

A news release, or press release, is a message (usually routine, but not always) designed to share information with the news media, although many are now written with customers and other stakeholders in mind as well.

THE FUTURE OF COMMUNICATION

Communication Bots

The bots are back. Automated bots (short for *robots*) made a small wave a decade or so ago when "chatbots" began appearing on websites to help companies handle online conversations with customers. Ikea's Anna, perhaps the first chatbot to get widespread attention, was built to answer routine questions from customers looking for advice regarding the chain's furniture products. Other chatbots followed, smartphones gained virtual "voicebot" assistants, and non-chatty bots continued to do automated work of various kinds on the Internet, but bots didn't really take off as a mainstream technology.

With advances in artificial intelligence and the growing use of messaging systems for both consumer and business communication, however, a new wave of bots as personal digital assistants has taken off. Microsoft CEO Satya Nadella goes so far as to say, "Bots are the new apps," suggesting they'll transform technology usage the same way mobile apps have. As bot capability is added to more messaging systems—through which a growing number of employees now conduct increasing amounts of their routine business communication—bots are finally entering the mainstream.

Bots are wildly popular on the Slack messaging system (see page 181), for example, where they can do everything from ordering lunch to monitoring the mood of team conversations. The Howdy bot, for example, can perform such tasks as simultaneously interviewing all the members of a project team to give the team leader a real-time status update. On Slack, bots are treated just like human team members in many ways—they can send and receive messages, be assigned tasks, and be invited to join specific groups and communication channels. As bots get better at understanding language, they'll be able to contribute to conversations, such as finding background information that could help solve a problem colleagues are discussing, without anyone asking for their help.

How far this bot revolution will go is anybody's guess, but the appeal of this new generation of digital genies is undeniable. They are more connected to the systems that people use every day on the job, and they can reduce the need to navigate yet another website or learn yet another app in order to get something done. Instead, you just message your bot and let it figure out how to make things happen.

To see a chatbot in action, check out BusCommBot, created by Courtland L. Bovée, one of the authors of this book. Log onto Facebook and search for Bovee & Thill's Business Communication Blog, then on that page, select "Message" under the photo at the top of the page.

WHAT'S YOUR PREDICTION?

Research the current state of bot communication to identify one way in which the technology is changing or has the potential to change business communication practices. Do you agree with the predictions the experts make? Why or why not?

Sources: Kelly Evans," "Chatbots Rise, and the Future May be 'Re-written,'" CNBC, 10 April 2016, www.cnbc.com; Casey Newton, "The Search for the Killer Bot," *The Verge*, 6 January 2016, www.theverge.com; Clint Boulton, "How Messaging Bots Will Change Workplace Productivity," *CIO*, 1 February 2016, www.cio.com; Ben Brown, "Your New Digital Coworker," Howdy blog, 20 October 2015, blog.howdy.ai; "Bot Users," Slack, accessed 10 April 2016, www.slack.com; Molly McHugh, "Slack Is Overrun with Bots. Friendly, Wonderful Bots." *Wired*, 21 August 2015, www.wired.com.

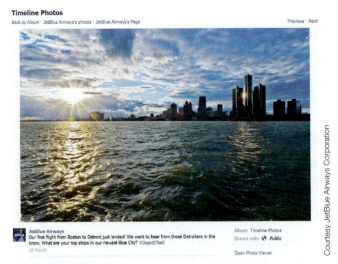

Figure 10.6 **Announcing Good News**
Encouraging online conversations is an important element of brand socialization. In this Facebook post celebrating its inaugural flight from Boston to Detroit, JetBlue asked residents of Detroit to recommend their favorite places around the city.

to the ultimate audience (such as the readers of a blog or newspaper); you're trying to spark the interest of an editor, reporter, blogger, or other intermediary in the hope that person will write a piece that carries your message to a larger audience.

Until recently, news releases were crafted in a way to provide information to reporters, who would then write their own articles if the subject matter was interesting to their readers. Thanks to the Internet and social media, however, the nature of the news release is changing. Many companies now view it as a general-purpose tool for communicating directly with customers and other audiences, creating *direct-to-consumer news releases*.[3] Many of these are considered *social media releases* because they include social networking links, "tweetables" (Twitter-ready statements that can be shared on Twitter at the click of a button), and other sharable content.

> The social media release includes ready-to-share content that is easy to reuse in blog posts, tweets, and other social media formats.

FOSTERING GOODWILL

All business messages should be written with an eye toward fostering positive relationships with audiences, but some messages are written specifically to build goodwill. You can use these messages to enhance your relationships with customers, colleagues, and other businesspeople by sending friendly, even unexpected, notes with no direct business purpose (see Figure 10.7). Whether you're thanking an employee for a job well done or congratulating a colleague for a personal or professional achievement, the small effort to send a goodwill message can have a positive and lasting effect on the people around you.

> Goodwill is the positive feeling that encourages people to maintain a business relationship.

In addition to creating messages for a specific goodwill reason, you can craft almost any routine message in a way to build goodwill. Two ways to do so are by providing information that your readers might find helpful and by maintaining a positive tone throughout your message.

> Many routine messages can be adapted to foster goodwill, either by sharing helpful information or providing an element of entertainment.

Sending Congratulations

One prime opportunity for sending goodwill messages is to congratulate individuals or companies for significant business achievements. Other reasons for sending congratulations include highlights in people's personal lives, such as weddings, births, graduations, and success in nonbusiness competitions. You may congratulate business acquaintances on their own achievements or on the accomplishments of a family member. You may also take note of personal events, even if you don't know the reader well. If you're already friendly with the reader, a more personal tone is appropriate.

> Taking note of significant events in someone's personal life helps foster your business relationship.

> **MOBILE APP**
> Looking for the special touch of a printed letter but have only your phone? **Lettrs** converts your digital message to print and puts it in the mail for you.

Figure 10.7   Goodwill Messages
Goodwill messages serve a variety of business functions. Fans who follow Steinway on Facebook love great pianos and great piano music. In this post the company offers its fan community something of value—a playlist of relaxing piano music as a Monday mood booster. The post doesn't attempt to sell anything (the "Buy" link shown in the video capture is for the album itself and isn't part of Steinway's message). It's just a way of fostering goodwill among fellow music lovers.

Sending Messages of Appreciation

An effective message of appreciation documents a person's contributions.

An important leadership quality is the ability to recognize the contributions of employees, colleagues, suppliers, and other associates. Your praise does more than just make the person feel good; it encourages further excellence. Moreover, a message of appreciation may become an important part of someone's personnel file. So when you write a message of appreciation, try to specifically mention the person or people you want to praise. The brief message that follows expresses gratitude and reveals the happy result:

> Thank you and everyone on your team for the heroic efforts you took to bring our servers back up after last Friday's flood. We were able to restore business right on schedule first thing Monday morning. You went far beyond the level of contractual service in restoring our data center within 16 hours. I would especially like to highlight the contribution of networking specialist Julienne Marks, who worked for 12 straight hours to reconnect our Internet service. If I can serve as a reference in your future sales activities, please do not hesitate to ask.

Hearing a sincere thank you can do wonders for morale.[4] Moreover, in today's digital media environment, a handwritten thank-you note can be a particularly welcome acknowledgment.[5]

Offering Condolences

The primary purpose of condolence messages is to let the audience know that you and the organization you represent care about the person's loss.

Condolence letters are brief personal messages written to comfort someone after the death of a loved one. You may have occasion to offer condolences to employees or other business associates (when the person has lost a family member) or to the family of an employee or business associate (when that person has died).

These messages can feel intimidating to write, but they don't need to be. Follow these three principles: short, simple, and sincere. You don't need to produce a work of literary art; the fact that you are writing sends a message that is as meaningful as anything you can say.

Timing and media choice are important considerations with condolence letters. The sooner your message is received, the more comforting it will be, so don't delay. And unless circumstances absolutely leave you no choice, avoid using email or another digital medium. A brief, handwritten note on quality stationery is the way to go.

Open a condolence message with a simple expression of sympathy, such as "I am deeply sorry to hear of your loss" or "I am sorry for your loss." How you continue from there depends on the circumstances and your relationships with the deceased and the person to whom you are writing. For example, if you are writing to the husband of a colleague who recently died and you have never met him, you might continue with "Having worked with Janice for more than a decade, I know what a kind and caring person she was." Such a statement accomplishes two goals: explaining why you in particular are writing and letting the recipient know that his loved one was appreciated in the workplace.

Conversely, if you are writing to a colleague who recently lost a loved one, you might continue with "After meeting Warren at last year's company picnic and hearing your stories about his involvement with your son's soccer league and the many other ways he contributed to his community, I know what a special person he was." Sharing brief and positive memories like this adds meaning and depth to your expression of sympathy.

You can conclude with a simple statement such as "My thoughts are with you during this difficult time." If appropriate for the situation and your relationship, you might also include an offer of assistance. "Please call if there is anything I do for you."

Keep your condolence message focused on the recipient, not your own emotions, and don't offer "life advice" or trite sayings.

As you decide what to include in the message, keep two points in mind. First, make it a personal expression of sympathy, but don't make the whole message about you and your sense of loss. You might be grieving as well, but unless you, the deceased, and the reader were all personally close, don't say things like "I was so devastated to hear the news about Kalinda."

Second, don't offer "life advice," and don't include trite sayings that you may have heard or read. At this point, soon after the loss, the recipient doesn't want your advice, only your sympathy. Also, don't bring religion into the discussion unless you have a close personal relationship with the recipient and religion is already a part of it. Otherwise, you risk offending with unwelcome or inappropriate sentiments.

Condolence letters are the most personal business messages you may ever have to write, so they require the utmost in care and respect for your reader. By keeping the messages simple, short, and sincere, you will be able to achieve the right tone.

To review the tasks involved in writing goodwill messages, see "Checklist: Sending Goodwill Messages." For the latest information on writing routine and positive messages, visit **real-timeupdates.com/bct14**.

CHECKLIST ✔ Sending Goodwill Messages

- Be sincere and honest.
- Don't exaggerate or use vague, grandiose language; support positive statements with specific evidence.
- Use congratulatory messages to build goodwill with clients and colleagues.

- Send messages of appreciation to emphasize how much you value the work of others.
- When sending condolence messages, open with a brief statement of sympathy, then adapt your message based on the circumstances and your relationship with the recipient.

COMMUNICATION CHALLENGES AT **Productivity Report**

You've joined *Productivity Report* as a freelance researcher and writer, helping Jill Duffy educate technology users on productivity and effective workplace communication. Use what you've learned in this and previous chapters to address these challenges.

INDIVIDUAL CHALLENGE: You've probably seen the acronym *tl;dr* in online discussions, which means "too long; didn't read." Web surfers, particularly those who are accessing content on mobile devices, crave concise articles they can absorb in a minute or two (maybe three). Find one of the articles in the Productivity category on *Productivity Report* and summarize it in 250 to 300 words—roughly what the average adult can read in one minute.

TEAM CHALLENGE: Duffy wrote a series of articles for *Productivity Report* titled "What's Wrong with Email" from which she would like to extract a series of "tweetable" teasers. Find these articles on the website and divide them among the members of your team. Evaluate each article and find three to five key points that you can convey as 140-character tweets. Assemble your collection of tweetables in a brief report, including one introductory tweet for the whole series.

Quick Learning Guide

KEY TERMS

adjustment Settlement of a claim

claim A formal complaint made in response to dissatisfaction over a product or service

condolence letters Brief personal messages written to comfort someone after the death of a loved one

news release A specialized document, also known as a *press release*, traditionally used to share relevant information with the local or national news media; today, many companies issue news releases directly to the public as well

SUMMARY OF LEARNING OBJECTIVES

1 **Outline an effective strategy for writing routine business requests.** When writing a routine request, open by stating your specific request. Use the body to justify your request and explain its importance. Close routine requests by asking for specific action (including a deadline, if appropriate) and expressing goodwill. A courteous close contains three important elements: (1) a specific request, (2) information about how you can be reached (if it isn't obvious), and (3) an expression of appreciation or goodwill.

2 **Describe three common types of routine requests.** The most common types of routine messages are asking for information or action, asking for recommendations, and making claims and requesting adjustments. Requests for information or action should explain what you want to know or what you want readers to do, why you're making the request, and why it may be in your reader's interest to help you (if applicable). Requests for recommendations should open by stating what it is you are requesting and asking the recipient to write the message in question. The body should list all the information the recipient would need to write the recommendation (refer to an attached résumé, if applicable). The close should contain an expression of appreciation and a deadline, if applicable. To make a claim (a formal complaint about a product or service) or request an adjustment (a settlement of a claim), open with a straightforward statement of the problem, use the body to give a complete explanation of the situation, and close with a polite request to resolve the situation.

3 **Outline an effective strategy for writing routine replies and positive messages.** The direct approach works well for routine replies and positive messages because recipients will generally be interested in what you have to say. Place your main idea (the positive reply or the good news) in the opening. Use the body to explain all the relevant details, and close cordially, perhaps highlighting a benefit to your reader.

4 **Describe six common types of routine replies and positive messages.** Most routine and positive messages fall into six categories: answers to requests for information and action, grants of claims and requests for adjustment, recommendations, informative messages, good-news announcements, and goodwill messages. Providing answers to requests for information or action is a simple task, often assisted with form responses that can be customized as needed. Granting claims and requests for adjustments is more complicated, and the right response depends on whether the company, the customer, or a third party was at fault. Recommendations also require a careful approach to avoid legal complications; some companies prohibit managers from writing recommendation letters or providing anything beyond basic employment history. Informative messages are often simple and straightforward, but some require extra care if the information affects recipients in a significant way. Good-news announcements are often handled by news releases, which used to be sent exclusively to members of the news media but are now usually made available to the public as well. Finally, goodwill messages, meant to foster positive business relationships, include congratulations, thank-you messages, and messages of condolence. To make goodwill messages effective, make them honest, sincere, and factual.

MyBCommLab

Go to **mybcommlab.com** to complete the problems marked with this icon .

Test Your Knowledge

To review chapter content related to each question, refer to the indicated Learning Objective.

10-1. What information should be included in a routine request? [LO-1]

10-2. Where in a routine message should you state your actual request? [LO-1]

10-3. What information should you include in a request for a recommendation? [LO-2]

10-4. How does a claim differ from an adjustment? [LO-2]

10-5. What is resale information? [LO-3]

⭐**10-6.** What is the appropriate strategy for responding to a request for a recommendation about a job candidate whose performance was poor? [LO-4]

⭐**10-7.** How can you avoid sounding insincere when writing a goodwill message? [LO-4]

10-8. What are three principles to follow for writing condolence messages? [LO-4]

Apply Your Knowledge

To review chapter content related to each question, refer to the indicated Learning Objective.

10-9. You have a complaint against one of your suppliers, but you have no documentation to back it up. Should you request an adjustment anyway? Why or why not? [LO-2]

⭐**10-10.** The latest issue of a local business newspaper names 10 area executives who have exhibited excellent leadership skills in the past year. You are currently searching for a job, and a friend suggests that you write each executive a congratulatory letter and mention in passing that you are looking for new career opportunities and would appreciate the opportunity for an interview. Is this a smart strategy? Why or why not? [LO-4]

⭐**10-11.** You've been asked to write a letter of recommendation for an employee who worked for you some years ago. You recall that the employee did an admirable job, but you can't remember any specific information at this point. Should you write the letter anyway? Explain. [LO-4]

10-12. Your company's error cost an important business customer a new client; you know it, and your customer knows it. Do you apologize, or do you refer to the incident in a positive light without admitting any responsibility? Briefly explain. [LO-4]

Practice Your Skills

Messages for Analysis

Read the following messages, then (1) analyze the strengths and weaknesses of each sentence and (2) revise each document so that it follows this chapter's guidelines.

10-13. Message 10.A: Message Strategies: Routine Requests [LO-2]

I'm fed up with the mistakes that our current accounting firm makes. I run a small construction company, and I don't have time to double-check every bookkeeping entry and call the accountants a dozen times when they won't return my messages. Please explain how your firm would do a better job than my current accountants. You have a good reputation among homebuilders, but before I consider hiring you to take over my accounting, I need to know that you care about quality work and good customer service.

10-14. Message 10.B: Message Strategies: Responding to Claims and Requests for Adjustments [LO-4]

We read your letter, requesting your deposit refund. We couldn't figure out why you hadn't received it, so we talked to our maintenance engineer, as you suggested. He said you had left one of the doors off the hinges in your apartment in order to get a large sofa through the door. He also confirmed that you had paid him $5.00 to replace the door since you had to turn in the U-Haul trailer and were in a big hurry.

This entire situation really was caused by a lack of communication between our housekeeping inspector and the maintenance engineer. All we knew was that the door was off the hinges when it was inspected by Sally Tarnley. You know that our policy states that if anything is wrong with the apartment, we keep the deposit. We had no way of knowing that George just hadn't gotten around to replacing the door.

But we have good news. We approved the deposit refund, which will be mailed to you from our home office in Teaneck, New Jersey. I'm not sure how long that will take, however. If you don't receive the check by the end of next month, give me a call.

Next time, it's really a good idea to stay with your apartment until it's inspected, as stipulated in your lease agreement. That way, you'll be sure to receive your refund when you expect it. Hope you have a good summer.

10-15. Message 10.C: Message Strategies: Providing Recommendations [LO-4] (Note: Assume that your company allows you to write recommendations.)

Your letter to Kunitake Ando, president of Sony, was forwarded to me because I am the human resources director. In my job as head of HR, I have access to performance reviews for all of the Sony employees in the United States. This means, of course, that I would be the person best qualified to answer your request for information on Nick Oshinski.

In your letter of the 15th, you asked about Nick Oshinski's employment record with us because he has applied to work for your company. Mr. Oshinski was employed with us from January 5, 2008, until March 1, 2016. During that time, Mr. Oshinski received ratings ranging from 2.5 up to 9.6, with 10 being the top score. As you can see, he must have done better reporting to some managers than to others. In addition, he took all vacation days, which is a bit unusual. Although I did not know Mr. Oshinski personally, I know that our best workers seldom use all the vacation time they earn. I do not know if that applies in this case.

In summary, Nick Oshinski performed his tasks well depending on who managed him.

Exercises

Each activity is labeled according to the primary skill or skills you will need to use. To review relevant chapter content, you can refer to the indicated Learning Objective. In some instances, supporting information will be found in another chapter, as indicated.

Message Strategies: Routine Requests; Revising for Conciseness [LO-1], Chapter 6 Critique the following closing paragraphs. How would you rewrite each to be concise, courteous, and specific?

10-16. I need your response sometime soon so I can order the parts in time for your service appointment. Otherwise, your air-conditioning system may not be in tip-top condition for the start of the summer season.

10-17. Thank you in advance for sending me as much information as you can about your products. I look forward to receiving your package in the very near future.

10-18. To schedule an appointment with one of our knowledgeable mortgage specialists in your area, you can always call our hotline at 1-800-555-8765. This is also the number to call if you have more questions about mortgage rates, closing procedures, or any other aspect of the mortgage process. Remember, we're here to make the home-buying experience as painless as possible.

Message Strategies: Routine Responses; Media Skills: Email [LO-3], Chapter 7 Revise the following short email messages so they are more direct and concise; develop a subject line for each revised message.

10-19. I'm contacting you about your recent email request for technical support on your cable Internet service. Part of the problem we have in tech support is trying to figure out exactly what each customer's specific problem is so that we can troubleshoot quickly and get you back in business as quickly as possible. You may have noticed that in the online support request form, there are a number of fields to enter your type of computer, operating system, memory, and so on. While you did tell us you were experiencing slow download speeds during certain times of the day, you didn't tell us which times specifically, nor did you complete all the fields telling us about your computer. Please return to our support website and resubmit your request, being sure to provide all the necessary information; then we'll be able to help you.

10-20. Thank you for contacting us about the difficulty you had collecting your luggage at Denver International Airport. We are very sorry for the inconvenience this has caused you. As you know, traveling can create problems of this sort regardless of how careful the airline personnel might be. To receive compensation, please send us a detailed list of the items that you lost and complete the following questionnaire. You can email it back to us.

10-21. Sorry it took us so long to get back to you. We were flooded with résumés. Anyway, your résumé made the final 10, and after meeting three hours yesterday, we've decided we'd like to meet with you. What is your schedule like for next week? Can you come in for an interview on June 15 at 3:00 p.m.? Please get back to us by the end of this workweek and let us know if you will be able to attend. As you can imagine, this is our busy season.

10-22. We're letting you know that because we use over a ton of paper a year and because so much of that paper goes into the wastebasket to become so much more environmental waste, starting Monday, we're placing white plastic bins outside the elevators on every floor to recycle that paper and in the process, minimize pollution.

Message Strategies: Routine and Positive Messages; Revising for Conciseness [LO-3], Chapter 6 Rewrite the following sentences so that they are direct and concise. If necessary, break your answer into two sentences.

10-23. We wanted to invite you to our special 40% off by-invitation-only sale; the sale is taking place on November 9.

10-24. We wanted to let you know that we are giving a tote bag and a voucher for five iTunes downloads with every $50 donation you make to our radio station.

10-25. The director planned to go to the meeting that will be held on Monday at a little before 11 am.

10-26. In today's meeting, we were happy to have the opportunity to welcome Paul Eccelson, who reviewed the shopping cart function on our website and offered some great advice; if you have any questions about these new forms, feel free to call him at his office.

10-27. **Message Strategies: Responding to Claims and Requests for Adjustments [LO-4]** Your company markets a line of automotive accessories for people who like to "tune" their cars for maximum performance. A customer has just written a furious email, claiming that a supercharger he purchased from your website didn't deliver the extra engine power he had expected. Your company has a standard refund process to handle situations such as this, and you have the information you need in order to inform the customer about that. You also have information that could help the customer find a more compatible supercharger from one of your competitors, but the customer's email message is so abusive that you don't feel obligated to help. Is this an appropriate response? Why or why not?

10-28. **Message Strategies: Writing Positive Messages; Media Skills: Microblogging [LO-4], Chapter 8** Locate an online announcement for a new product you find interesting or useful. Read enough about the product to be able to describe it to someone else in your own words, then writer four Twitter tweets: one to introduce the product to your followers and three follow-up tweets that describe three particularly compelling features or benefits of the product.

10-29. **Message Strategies: Writing Goodwill Messages [LO-4]** Identify someone in your life who has recently accomplished a significant achievement, such as graduating from high school or college, completing a major project, or winning an important professional award. Write a brief congratulatory message using the guidelines presented in the chapter.

Expand Your Skills

Critique the Professionals

Locate an online example of a news release in which a company announces good news, such as a new product, a notable executive hire, an expansion, strong financial results, or an industry award. Analyze the release using the guidance provided in the chapter. In what ways did the writer excel? What aspects of the release could be improved? Does the release provide social media–friendly content and features? Using whatever medium your instructor requests, write a brief analysis of the piece (no more than one page), citing specific elements from the piece and support from the chapter.

Sharpening Your Career Skills Online

Bovée and Thill's Business Communication Web Search, at websearch.businesscommunicationnetwork.com, is a unique research tool designed specifically for business communication research. Use the Web Search function to find a website, video, article, podcast, or presentation that offers advice on writing goodwill messages such as thank-you notes or congratulatory letters. Write a brief email message to your instructor, describing the item that you found and summarizing the career skills information you learned from it.

Cases

For all cases, feel free to use your creativity to make up any details you need in order to craft effective messages.

Routine Requests

BLOGGING SKILLS

10-30. Message Strategies: Requesting Information [LO-2]
You are writing a book about the advantages and potential pit-falls of using online collaboration systems for virtual team projects. You would like to include several dozen real-life examples from people in a variety of industries. Fortunately, you publish a highly respected blog on the subject, with several thousand regular readers.

Your task: Write a post for your blog that asks readers to submit brief descriptions of their experiences using collaboration tools for team projects. Ask them to email stories of how well a specific system or approach worked for them. Explain that they will receive an autographed copy of the book as thanks and that they will need to sign a release form if their stories are used. In addition, emphasize that you would like to use real names—of people, companies, and software—but you can keep the anecdotes anonymous if readers require. To stay on schedule, you need to have these stories by May 20.

MESSAGING SKILLS

10-31. Message Strategies: Routine Requests [LO-2]
One of the reasons you accepted the job offer from your current employer was the happy, relaxed vibe of the open-plan office. When you interviewed, it seemed as far away from a boring, conventional "cubicle farm" as you could get, which appealed to your nonconformist instincts. After a year in the job, however, you've experienced some of the disadvantages of the company's relaxed attitudes to just about every aspect of workplace behavior. People routinely bring pets to work, even though several people have explained they have allergies to dogs or cats. Some of the pets are less than ideally behaved, too, and a couple of dogs who are frequent visitors get into snarling matches when they see each other. One person even brings a pet bird, which has been known to fly loose around the office. Employees bring children of all ages to work, too, from infants still in diapers to teenagers who play video games on mobile devices—sometimes using headphones but sometimes not. Music lovers get into volume wars at least once a week, trying to drown each other out on their portable speaker systems.

You wonder how anybody can get any work done, until you privately interview several colleagues and realize that, like you, they aren't getting any work done. The office has become such a festival of distractions that people routinely bring work home on nights and weekends because home is the only place they can concentrate.

Your task: Write a brief request that could be sent out via the company's internal messaging system, asking people to consider the needs of their colleagues before bringing pets, children, and other potential distractions into the workplace.

EMAIL SKILLS

10-32. Message Strategies: Routine Requests [LO-2]
In the weeks after your company rolled out a new online collaboration system, you thought your eyesight was beginning to fail. You have to squint to read posted messages, and the file archive is almost impossible to navigate because you couldn't read the file names. Then you noticed people in the department you manage having the same problem, particularly people who work on laptops and tablets.

You began to wonder how the programmers in the information technology (IT) department who configured the system didn't notice the problem, until you walked through their department and realized they all had multiple, giant computer monitors. Everything you could see on their screens was displayed in large, easily readable type.

Your task: Write a brief email message to the head of IT, asking her group to meet with users in your department to discuss the question of on-screen readability with the new system.

EMAIL SKILLS

10-33. Message Strategies: Requesting a Recommendation [LO-2]
One of your colleagues, Katina Vander, was recently promoted to department manager and now serves on the company's strategic planning committee. At its monthly meeting next week, the committee will choose an employee to lead an important market research project that will help define the company's product portfolio for the next five years.

You worked side by side with Vander for five years, so she knows your abilities well and has complimented your business insights on many occasions. You know that because she has only recently been promoted to manager, she needs to build credibility among her peers and will therefore be cautious about making such an important recommendation. On the other hand, making a stellar recommendation for such an important project would show that she has a good eye for talent—an essential leadership trait.

Your task: Write an email message to Vander, telling her that you are definitely interested in leading the project and asking her to put in a good word for you with the committee. Mention four attributes that you believe would serve you well in the role: a dozen years of experience in the industry, an engineering degree that helps you understand the technologies involved in product design, a consistent record of excellent or exceptional ratings in annual employee evaluations, and the three years you spent working in the company's customer support group, which gave you a firsthand look at customer satisfaction and quality issues.

EMAIL SKILLS

10-34. Message Strategies: Requesting a Recommendation [LO-2]
After five years of work in the human resources department at Cell Genesys (a company that is developing cancer treatment drugs), you were laid off in a round of cost-cutting

moves that rippled through the biotech industry in recent years. The good news is that you found stable employment in the grocery distribution industry. The bad news is that in the three years since you left Cell Genesys, you have truly missed working in the exciting biotechnology field and having the opportunity to be a part of something as important as helping people recover from life-threatening diseases. You know careers in biotech are uncertain, but you have a few dollars in the bank now, and you're willing to ride that rollercoaster again.

Your task: Draft an email to Calvin Morris, your old boss at Cell Genesys, reminding him of the time you worked together and asking him to write a letter of recommendation for you.[6]

MESSAGING SKILLS

10-35. Message Strategies: Requesting Information [LO-2] Many companies now provide presales and postsales customer support through some form of instant messaging or online chat function. As a consumer looking for information, you'll get better service if you can frame your requests clearly and succinctly.

Your task: Imagine that you need to replace your old laptop computer, but you're not sure whether to go with another laptop or switch to a tablet or perhaps one of the new tablet/laptop hybrids. Think through the various ways you will use this new device, from researching and note-taking during class to watching movies and interacting with friends on social media. Now imagine you're in a chat session with a sales representative from a computer company, and this person has asked how he or she can help you. Draft a message (no more than 100 words) that summarizes your computing and media requirements and asks the representative to recommend the right type of device for you.

TEXT MESSAGING SKILLS

10-36. Message Strategies: Requesting Information [LO-2] The vast Consumer Electronics Show (CES) is the premier promotional event in the industry. More than 150,000 industry insiders from all over the world come to see the exciting new products on display from nearly 1,500 companies—everything from video game gadgets to Internet-enabled refrigerators with built-in computer screens.[7] You've just stumbled on a video game controller that has a built-in webcam to allow networked gamers to see and hear each other while they play. Your company also makes game controllers, and you're worried that your customers will flock to this new controller-cam. You need to know how much buzz around this new product is circulating through the show: Have people seen it? What are they saying about it? Are they excited about it?

Your task: Compose a text message to your colleagues at the show, alerting them to the new controller-cam and asking them to listen for any buzz it might be generating among the attendees at the Las Vegas Convention Center and the several surrounding hotels where the show takes place. Here's the catch: Your text-messaging service limits messages to 160 characters, including spaces and punctuation, so your message can't be any longer than this.

EMAIL SKILLS

10-37. Message Strategies: Requesting an Adjustment [LO-2] Love at first listen is the only way to describe the way you felt when you discovered the music-streaming service Song-Throng. You enjoy dozens of styles of music, from Afrobeat and Tropicalia to mainstream pop and the occasional blast of industrial metal, and SongThrong has them all for only $9.99 a month. You can explore every genre imaginable, listening to as many tracks as you like for a fixed monthly fee. The service sounded too good to be true—and sadly, it was. The service was so unreliable that you began keeping note of when it was unavailable. Last month, it was down for all or part of 12 days—well over a third of the month. As much as you like it, you've had enough.

Your task: Write an email to support@songthrong.com, requesting a full refund. To get the $9.99 monthly rate, you prepaid for an entire year ($119.88), and you've been a subscriber for two months now. You know the service has been out for at least part of the time on 12 separate days last month, and while you didn't track outages during the first month, you believe it was about the same number of days.

LETTER-WRITING SKILLS

10-38. Message Strategies: Requesting an Adjustment [LO-2] As a consumer, you've probably bought something that didn't work right or paid for a service that did not turn out the way you expected. Maybe it was a pair of jeans with a rip in a seam that you didn't find until you got home or a watch that broke a week after you bought it. Or maybe your family hired a lawn service to do some yard work and no one from the company showed up on the day promised, and when the gardeners finally appeared, they did not do what they'd been hired for but instead did other things that wound up damaging valuable plants.

Your task: Choose an incident from your own experience and write a claim letter, asking for a refund, repair, replacement, or other adjustment. You'll need to include all the details of the transaction, plus your contact address and phone number. If you can't think of such an experience, make up details for an imaginary situation. If your experience is real, you might want to mail the letter. The reply you receive will provide a good test of your claim-writing skills.

EMAIL SKILLS

10-39. Message Strategies: Requesting Action [LO-2] You head up the corporate marketing department for a nationwide chain of clothing stores. The company has decided to launch a new store-within-a-store concept, in which a small section of each store will showcase "business casual" clothing. To ensure a successful launch of this new strategy, you want to get input from the best retailing minds in the company. You also know it's important to get regional insights from around the country, because a merchandising strategy that works in one area might not succeed in another.

Your task: Write an email message to all 87 store managers, asking them to each nominate one person to serve on an advisory team (managers can nominate themselves if they are local market experts). Explain that you want to find people with at least five years of retailing experience, a good understanding of the local business climate, and thorough knowledge of the local retail competition. In addition, the best candidates will be good team players who are comfortable collaborating long distance using virtual meeting technologies. Also, explain that while you are asking each of the 87 stores to nominate someone, the team will be limited to no more than eight people. You've met many of the store managers, but not all of them, so be sure to introduce yourself at the beginning of the message.

Routine Messages

EMAIL SKILLS

10-40. Message Strategies: Granting Claims [LO-4] Your company sells flower arrangements and gift baskets. Holidays are always a rush, and the overworked staff makes the occasional mistake. Last week, somebody made a big one. As a furious email message from a customer named Anders Ellison explains, he ordered a Valentine's Day bouquet for his wife, but the company sent a bereavement arrangement instead.

Your task: Respond to Ellison's email message, apologizing for the error, promising to refund all costs that Ellison incurred, informing him that the correct arrangement will arrive tomorrow (and he won't be charged anything for it), and offering Ellison his choice of any floral arrangement or gift basket free on his wife's birthday.

EMAIL SKILLS

10-41. Message Strategies: Granting Claims [LO-4] Like many of the staff at Razer, you are an avid game player. You can therefore sympathize with Louis Hapsberg, a customer who got so excited during a hotly contested game that he slammed his Razer Anansi keyboard against his chair in celebration. Razer products are built for serious action, but no keyboard can withstand a blow like that. However, in the interest of building goodwill among the online gaming community, your manager has approved a free replacement. This sort of damage is rare enough that the company isn't worried about unleashing a flood of similar requests.

Your task: Respond to Hapsberg's email request for a replacement, in which he admitted to inflicting some abuse on this keyboard. Explain, tongue in cheek, that the company is "rewarding" him with a free keyboard in honor of his massive gaming win, but gently remind him that even the most robust electronic equipment needs to be used with care.

PODCASTING SKILLS/PORTFOLIO BUILDER

10-42. Message Strategies: Providing Routine Information; Media Skills: Podcasting [LO-4] As a training specialist in Winnebago Industry's human resources department, you're always on the lookout for new ways to help employees learn vital job skills. While watching a production worker page through a training manual while learning how to assemble a new recreational vehicle, you get what seems to be a great idea: Record the assembly instructions as audio files that workers can listen to while performing the

necessary steps. With audio instructions, they wouldn't need to keep shifting their eyes between the product and the manual—and constantly losing their place. They could focus on the product and listen for each instruction. Plus, the new system wouldn't cost much at all; any computer can record the audio files, and you'd simply make them available on an intranet site for download into smartphones, tablets, and digital music players.

Your task: You immediately run your new idea past your boss, who has heard about podcasting but doesn't think it has any place in business. He asks you to prove the viability of the idea by recording a demonstration. Choose a process you engage in yourself—anything from replacing the strings on a guitar to sewing a quilt to changing the oil in a car—and write a brief (one page or less) description of the process that could be recorded as an audio file. Think carefully about the limitations of the audio format as a replacement for printed text. (For instance, do you need to tell people to pause the audio while they perform a time-consuming task?) If directed by your instructor, record your instructions as a podcast.

BLOGGING SKILLS/PORTFOLIO BUILDER

10-43. Message Strategies: Providing Routine Information [LO-4] You are normally an easygoing manager who gives your employees a lot of leeway in using their own personal communication styles. However, the weekly staff meeting this morning pushed you over the edge. People were interrupting one another, asking questions that had already been answered, sending text messages during presentations, and exhibiting just about every other poor listening habit imaginable.

Your task: Review the advice in Chapter 2 on good listening skills, then write a post for the internal company blog. Emphasize the importance of effective listening, and list at least five steps your employees can take to become better listeners.

Routine Replies

EMAIL SKILLS

10-44. Message Strategies: Routine Responses [LO-4] As the administrative assistant to Walmart's director of marketing, you have just received a request from the company's webmaster to analyze Walmart's website from a consumer's point of view.

Your task: Visit www.walmart.com and browse through the site, considering the language, layout, graphics, and overall ease of use. In particular, look for aspects of the site that might be confusing or frustrating—annoyances that could prompt shoppers to abandon their quests and head to a competitor such as Target or Amazon. Summarize your findings and recommendations in an email message that could be sent to the webmaster.

MICROBLOGGING SKILLS

10-45. Message Strategies: Routine Announcements [LO-4] As a way to give back to the communities in which it does business, your company supports the efforts of the United Way, a global organization that works to improve lives through education, income stability, and healthy living choices.[8] Each year, your company runs a fundraising campaign in which employees are encouraged to donate money to their local United Way agencies, and it also grants employees up to three paid days off to volunteer their time for the United Way. This year, you are in charge of the company's campaign.

Your task: Compose a four-message sequence to be posted on the company's internal microblogging system (essentially a private version of Twitter). The messages are limited to 200 characters, including spaces and punctuation. The first message will announce the company's annual United Way volunteering and fundraising campaign (make up any details you need), and the other three messages will explain the United Way's efforts in the areas of education, income stability, and healthy living. Visit the United Way website to learn more about these three areas.

LETTER-WRITING SKILLS/TEAM SKILLS

10-46. Message Strategies: Providing Recommendations [LO-4] As a project manager at Expedia, one of the largest online travel services in the world, you've seen plenty of college interns in action. However, few have impressed you as much as Maxine "Max" Chenault. For one thing, she learned how to navigate the company's content management system virtually overnight and always used it properly, whereas other interns sometimes left things in a hopeless mess. She asked lots of intelligent questions about the business. You've been teaching her blogging and website design principles, and she's picked them up rapidly. Moreover, she is always on time, professional, and eager to assist. Also, she didn't mind doing mundane tasks.

On the downside, Chenault is a popular student. Early on, you often found her busy on the phone planning her many social activities when you needed her help. However, after you had a brief talk with her, this problem vanished.

You'll be sorry to see Chenault leave when she returns to school in the fall, but you're pleased to respond when she asks you for a letter of recommendation. She's not sure where she'll apply for work after graduation or what career path she'll choose, so she asks you to keep the letter fairly general.

Your task: Working with a team of your classmates, discuss what should and should not be in the letter. Prepare an outline based on your discussion and then draft the letter.

SOCIAL NETWORKING SKILLS

10-47. Message Strategies: Writing Routine Informative Messages; Composition Modes: Summarizing [LO-4] As energy costs trend ever upward and more people become attuned to the environmental and geopolitical complexities of petroleum-based energy, interest in solar, wind, and other alternative energy sources continues to grow. In locations with high *insolation* (a measure of cumulative sunlight), solar panels can be cost-effective solutions over the long term. However, the upfront costs of buying panels outright are still daunting for most homeowners. To help lower the entry barrier, the Foster City, California–based firm SolarCity now offers two options that require no entry costs: leasing solar panels or signing up for a Power Purchase Agreement, in which customers simply pay

for the power generated by panels that SolarCity installs and maintains on their homes.[9]

Your task: Visit the Solar City website at **www.solarcity.com**, select Residential, and then select the "What It Costs" tab. Read about the solar options the company currently offers. Next, study SolarCity's presence on Facebook at **www.facebook.com/solarcity** to get a feel for how the company presents itself in a social networking environment. Now assume that you have been assigned the task of writing a brief Facebook post that provides an overview of the solar options the company offers homeowners. In your own language and in 200 words or less, write the post and email it to your instructor.

Positive Messages

WEB-WRITING SKILLS

10-48. Message Strategies: Good-News Messages [LO-4] Amateur and professional golfers in search of lower scores want to find clubs that are optimized for their individual swings. This process of *club fitting* has gone decidedly high tech in recent years, with fitters using Doppler radar, motion-capture video, and other tools to evaluate golfers' swing and ball flight characteristics. Hot Stix Golf is a leader in this industry, having fitted more than 200 professionals and thousands of amateurs.[10]

Your task: Imagine that you are the communications director at the Indian Wells Golf Resort in Indian Wells, California. Your operation has just signed a deal with Hot Stix to open a fitting center on site. Write a three-paragraph article that could be posted on the resort website. The first paragraph should announce the news that the Hot Stix center will open in six months, the second should summarize the benefits of club fitting, and the third should offer a brief overview of the services that will be available at the Indian Wells Hot Stix Center. Information on club fitting can be found on the Hot Stix website at **www.hotstixgolf.com**.

BLOGGING SKILLS/PORTFOLIO BUILDER

10-49. Message Strategies: Good-News Messages [LO-4] Most people have heard of the Emmy, Grammy, Oscar, and Tony Awards for television, music, movies, and theater performances, but fewer know what the Webby Award is all about. Sponsored by the International Academy of Digital Arts and Sciences, the Webbys shine a spotlight on the best in website design, interactive media, and online film and video.[11]

Your task: Visit the Webby Awards website at **www.webbyawards.com**, select Winners, and choose one of the companies listed as a winner in the Websites or Advertising & Media categories. Now imagine you are the chief online strategist for this company, and you've just been informed your company has won a Webby. Winning this award is a nice validation of the work your team has put in during the past year, and you want to share their success with the entire company. Write a brief post for the internal company blog, describing what the Webby Awards are, explaining why they are a significant measure of accomplishment in the online industry, and congratulating the employees in your department who contributed to the successful web effort.

SOCIAL NETWORKING SKILLS

10-50. Message Strategies: Goodwill Messages [LO-4] As the largest employer in Loganville, your construction company provides jobs, purchasing activity, and tax receipts that make up a vital part of the city's economy. In your role as CEO, however, you realize that the relationship between your company and the community is mutually beneficial, and the company could not survive without the efforts of its employees, the business opportunities offered by a growing marketplace, and the physical and legal infrastructure that the government provides.

The company's dependence on the community was demonstrated in a moving and immediate way last weekend, when a powerful storm pushed the Logan River past flood stage and threatened to inundate your company's office and warehouse facilities. More than 200 volunteers worked alongside your employees through the night to fill and stack sandbags to protect your buildings, and the city council authorized the deployment of heavy equipment and additional staff to help in the emergency effort. As you watched the water rise nearly 10 feet behind the makeshift dike, you realized that the community came together to save your company.

Your task: Write a 100- to 200-word post for your company's Facebook page, thanking the citizens and government officials of Loganville for their help in protecting the company's facilities during the storm.

SOCIAL NETWORKING SKILLS

10-51. Message Strategies: Goodwill Messages [LO-4] Every April, your company stages a competition for the sales department called Spring Surge, which awards sales representatives who bring in the most new revenue during the month. The awards are significant, including a first prize of a trip to Hawai'i for the winning sales rep's entire family, and most people in the department take the competition seriously.

Here are the results of this years' competition:

1st place (trip for family to Hawai'i): Juanita Hermosa

2nd place (luxury box seats at an NFL playoff game): Jackson Peabody

3rd place ($500 prepaid credit card): Duane Redd

Total new revenue booked during April: $4.7 million

Your task: Write a brief post (150 to 200 words) for your company's internal social networking platform, incorporating these results and thanking everyone in the sales department for their efforts during the Spring Surge.

LETTER-WRITING SKILLS

10-52. Message Strategies: Goodwill Messages [LO-4] Shari Willison worked as a geologist in your civil engineering firm for 20 years before succumbing to leukemia last week. With only a few dozen employees, the company has always been a tight-knit group, and you feel like you've lost a good friend in addition to a valued employee.

Your task: Write a letter of condolence to Willison's husband, Arthur, and the couple's teenaged children, Jordan and Amy. You have known all three socially through a variety of company holiday parties and events over the years.

LETTER-WRITING SKILLS

10-53. Message Strategies: Goodwill Messages [LO-4] The office was somber this morning when you arrived to work, as employees learned that the partner of the chief operating officer, Leo West, had been killed in a car accident over the weekend. You never met Michael, and West is two levels above you in the corporate hierarchy (you're a first-level supervisor), so you don't have a close working relationship. However, you have been on comfortable terms with West during the ten years you've been at this company, and although you've never socialized with him outside of work, you've both occasionally shared personal and social news during casual conversations in the cafeteria.

Your task: Write a letter of condolence to West.

MyBCommLab

Go to **mybcommlab.com** for Auto-graded writing questions as well as the following Assisted-graded writing questions:

10-54. Should you use the direct or indirect approach for most routine messages? Why? [LO-1]

10-55. How can you prevent good-news announcements from being all about you and your company? [LO-4]

Endnotes

1. Jill Duffy author bio, *PC*, accessed 11 April 2016, www.pcmag
.com; Jill Duffy, "What's Wrong With Email Part 3: We Check, But
We Don't Process," *Productivity Report*, 1 February 2016,
productivityreport.org; "About," jilleduffy blog, accessed 11 April
2016, www.jilleduffy.com; Jill E. Duffy, *Get Organized: How to
Clean Up Your Messy Digital Life* (New York: PC Magazine, 2013).

2. "How to Write Reference Letters," National Association of Colleges and Employers website, accessed 5 July 2010, www.naceweb
.org; "Five (or More) Ways You Can Be Sued for Writing (or Not
Writing) Reference Letters," *Fair Employment Practices Guidelines*,
July 2006, 1, 3.

3. David Meerman Scott, *The New Rules of Marketing and PR*
(Hoboken, N.J.: Wiley, 2007), 62.

4. Pat Cataldo, "Op-Ed: Saying 'Thank You' Can Open More Doors
Than You Think," Penn State University Smeal College of Business
website, accessed 19 February 2008, www.smeal.psu.edu.

5. Jackie Huba, "Five Must-Haves for Thank-You Notes," Church of
the Customer blog, 16 November 2007, www.churchofthecustomer.
com.

6. Tom Abate, "Need to Preserve Cash Generates Wave of Layoffs in
Biotech Industry," *San Francisco Chronicle*, 10 February 2003,
www.sfgate.com.

7. CES website, accessed 11 April 2016, www.cesweb.org; Darren
Murph, "CES 2012 Sets All-Time Records for Attendance, Exhibi-
tors and Claimed Floor Space," *Engadget*, 13 January 2012,
www.engadget.com.

8. United Way website, accessed 11 April 2016, www.unitedway.org.

9. SolarCity website, accessed 11 April 2016, www.solarcity.com.

10. Hot Stix Golf website, accessed 11 April 2016, www.hotstixgolf
.com.

11. The Webby Awards website, accessed 11 April 2016, www
.webbyawards.com

LEARNING OBJECTIVES

After studying this chapter, you will be able to

1 Apply the three-step writing process to negative messages.

2 Explain how to effectively use the direct approach when conveying negative news.

3 Explain how to effectively use the indirect approach when conveying negative news.

4 Explain the importance of maintaining high standards of ethics and etiquette when delivering negative messages.

5 Describe successful strategies for sending negative messages on routine business matters.

6 List the important points to consider when conveying negative organizational news.

7 Describe successful strategies for sending negative employment-related messages.

MyBCommLab®

⭐ **Improve Your Grade!** More than 10 million students improved their results using Pearson MyLabs. Visit **mybcommlab.com** for simulations, tutorials, and end-of-chapter problems.

www.hailoapp.com

No one likes to hear about price increases, whether it's college tuition, your favorite Thai food, or a ride in a taxi. Unfortunately, price increases are a fact of life in business as costs increase or business conditions change.

At the same time, consumers don't like to be kept waiting when they want something. And when that something is a taxi ride to an important meeting or a favorite restaurant, consumers really don't like to wait.

This was the dilemma facing Hailo, a cab-hailing service based in London and now operating in many cities around the world. Hailo's business model is based on simplifying the process of getting a taxi. The company connects taxi drivers and passengers through a GPS-enabled smartphone app that lets passengers hail a cab simply by tapping their screens, similar to the apps used by Uber and other ride-sharing services. A driver in the vicinity can choose to make the pickup, and the passenger can then follow the taxi's progress on screen as it approaches.

For the thousands of taxi drivers who have registered with the service, Hailo offers the opportunity to gain more business without waiting by the curb at busy locations or cruising streets waiting for a people to flag them down. For passengers, Hailo simplifies the process of finding a cab, because drivers come directly to them; no more standing in the street

Paul Thompson Images/Alamy Stock Photo

In an attempt to balance the needs of passengers and taxi drivers during peak periods, the cab-hailing service Hailo announced a higher minimum fare via an email message to registered users.

hoping an available taxi will pass by or waiting in line at long taxi ranks.

Hailo's growth suggests that drivers and passengers alike find value in the service. In fact, Hailo was recently tagged as the fastest-growing technology startup in the United Kingdom. As popular as it is, though, there are times when the service doesn't operate to everyone's complete satisfaction. For example, a driver can respond to a Hailo request and on the way to the pickup pass by several people in the street trying to flag him or her down, only to discover that the Hailo customer just wants to be hauled a few hundred yards down the street to the next club or shop. The result is a double loss for the driver—unpaid time driving to the pickup location and the missed opportunity of potentially higher fares from those would-be customers passed along the way.

If drivers suspect that a potential passenger will want only a short ride, they are more likely not to respond to the request, because the short ride won't compensate for the time they have to invest. This phenomenon can be troublesome for the system as a whole during peak hours, when more passengers are trying to use it. To keep its app users happy, Hailo wants as many drivers as possible to participate during peak times. To encourage

drivers to pick up more Hailo customers, it guarantees drivers a minimum amount of revenue for every Hailo rider they pick up.

To boost driver participation, Hailo recently decided to increase the minimum fare passengers must pay during certain hours. Such news would be welcomed by drivers, of course, but not by those passengers accustomed to using the service for short hops around town.

Hailo announced the change in an email message to its customers, but it didn't just blurt out the news. Instead, it took the indirect approach, which you'll learn to use in this chapter. The email message started with a reader benefit, explaining that to increase the availability of cabs, the company was modifying its minimum fares. The message then provided a reminder of how Hailo works—and how it works best if it works well for both drivers and passengers. With that reasoning in place, the message moved on to deliver the unwelcome news about increases in the minimum fare during peak hours. The message ended on a positive note, pointing out that the increase wouldn't affect the majority of customers because most London cab rides already cost more than that amount. The message was a classic example of how to prepare readers, logically and emotionally, before delivering bad news.[1]

Using the Three-Step Writing Process for Negative Messages

1 LEARNING OBJECTIVE Apply the three-step writing process to negative messages.

You may never have to share unwelcome pricing news with customers, as Hailo (profiled in the chapter-opening Communication Close-Up) did, but you will have to share unwelcome news at many points in your career. Communicating negative information is a fact of life for all business professionals, whether it's saying no to a request, sharing unpleasant or unwelcome information, or issuing a public apology. With the techniques you'll learn in this chapter, however, you can successfully communicate unwelcome news while minimizing unnecessary stress for everyone involved.

Depending on the situation, you can have as many as five distinct goals when communicating negative information: (1) to convey the bad news, (2) to gain acceptance of the bad news, (3) to maintain as much of your audience's goodwill as possible, (4) to maintain a good image for your organization, and, if appropriate, (5) to reduce or eliminate the need for future correspondence on the matter. Five goals are clearly a lot to accomplish in one message, so careful planning and execution are particularly critical with negative messages.

Negative messages can have as many as five goals:
• Give the bad news
• Ensure acceptance of the bad news
• Maintain the reader's goodwill
• Maintain the organization's good image
• Minimize or eliminate future correspondence on the matter, as appropriate

STEP 1: PLANNING A NEGATIVE MESSAGE

When you need to convey negative news, you can't avoid the fact that your audience does not want to hear what you have to say. To minimize the damage to business relationships and to encourage the acceptance of your message, analyze the situation carefully so you can better understand the context in which the recipient will process your message.

Understanding your readers' concerns helps you be sensitive their needs while delivering an effective message.

Be sure to consider your purpose thoroughly—whether it's straightforward (such as rejecting a job applicant) or more complicated (such as drafting a negative performance review, in which you not only give the employee feedback on past performance but also help the person develop a plan to improve future performance). With a clear purpose and your audience's needs in mind, identify and gather the information your audience requires in order to understand and accept your message. Negative messages can be intensely personal to the recipient, and recipients often have a right to expect a thorough explanation of your answer.

Selecting the right medium and channel is also important. For instance, bad news for employees should be delivered in person whenever possible. This helps guard their privacy, demonstrates respect, and gives them an opportunity to ask questions. Doing so isn't always possible or feasible, though, so there will be times when you need to share important negative information through written or digital media.

> When preparing negative messages, choose the medium and channel with care.

Defining your main idea in a negative message is often more complicated than simply saying no. For instance, if you need to respond to a hardworking employee who requested a raise, your message might go beyond saying no to explaining how she can improve her performance by working smarter, not just harder.

Finally, the organization of a negative message requires particular care. One of the most critical planning decisions is choosing whether to use the direct or indirect approach (see Figure 11.1). A negative message using the *direct approach* opens with the bad news, proceeds to the reasons for the situation or the decision, and ends with a positive statement aimed at maintaining a good relationship with the audience. In contrast, the *indirect approach* opens with the reasons behind the bad news before presenting the bad news itself.

> Appropriate organization helps readers accept your negative news.

To help decide which approach to take in a particular situation, ask yourself the following questions:

- **Do you need to get the reader's attention immediately?** If the situation is an emergency, or if someone has ignored repeated messages, the direct approach can help you get attention quickly.
- **Does the recipient prefer a direct style of communication?** Some recipients prefer the direct approach no matter what, so if you know this, go with direct.

> You need to consider a variety of factors when choosing between direct and indirect approaches for negative messages.

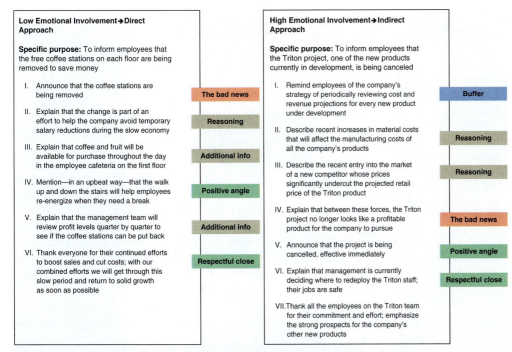

Low Emotional Involvement→Direct Approach

Specific purpose: To inform employees that the free coffee stations on each floor are being removed to save money

I. Announce that the coffee stations are being removed — *The bad news*

II. Explain that the change is part of an effort to help the company avoid temporary salary reductions during the slow economy — *Reasoning*

III. Explain that coffee and fruit will be available for purchase throughout the day in the employee cafeteria on the first floor — *Additional info*

IV. Mention—in an upbeat way—that the walk up and down the stairs will help employees re-energize when they need a break — *Positive angle*

V. Explain that the management team will review profit levels quarter by quarter to see if the coffee stations can be put back — *Additional info*

VI. Thank everyone for their continued efforts to boost sales and cut costs; with our combined efforts we will get through this slow period and return to solid growth as soon as possible — *Respectful close*

High Emotional Involvement→Indirect Approach

Specific purpose: To inform employees that the Triton project, one of the new products currently in development, is being canceled

I. Remind employees of the company's strategy of periodically reviewing cost and revenue projections for every new product under development — *Buffer*

II. Describe recent increases in material costs that will affect the manufacturing costs of all the company's products — *Reasoning*

III. Describe the recent entry into the market of a new competitor whose prices significantly undercut the projected retail price of the Triton product — *Reasoning*

IV. Explain that between these forces, the Triton project no longer looks like a profitable product for the company to pursue — *The bad news*

V. Announce that the project is being cancelled, effective immediately — *Positive angle*

VI. Explain that management is currently deciding where to redeploy the Triton staff; their jobs are safe — *Respectful close*

VII. Thank all the employees on the Triton team for their commitment and effort; emphasize the strong prospects for the company's other new products

Figure 11.1 Comparing the Direct and Indirect Approaches for Negative Messages
The direct and indirect approaches differ in two important ways: the position of the bad news within the sequence of message points and the use of a *buffer* in the indirect approach. ("Using the Indirect Approach for Negative Messages" on page 299 explains the use of a buffer.) Both these messages deal with changes made in response to negative financial developments, but the second example represents a much higher emotional impact for readers, so the indirect approach is called for in that case. Figure 11.2 on the next page explains how to choose the right approach for each situation.

- **How important is this news to the reader?** For minor or routine scenarios, the direct approach is nearly always best. However, if the reader has an emotional investment in the situation or the consequences to the reader are considerable, the indirect approach is often better, particularly if the bad news is unexpected.
- **Will the bad news come as a shock?** The direct approach is fine for many business situations in which people understand the possibility of receiving bad news. However, if the bad news might come as a shock to readers, use the indirect approach to help them prepare for it.

Figure 11.2 offers a convenient decision tree to help you decide which approach to use.

STEP 2: WRITING A NEGATIVE MESSAGE

Writing clearly and sensitively helps take some of the sting out of bad news.

By writing clearly and sensitively, you can take some of the sting out of bad news and help your reader accept the decision and move on. If your credibility hasn't already been established with an audience, clarify your qualifications so recipients won't question your authority or ability.

Protect your audience's pride by using language that conveys respect.

When you use language that conveys respect and avoids an accusing tone, you protect your audience's pride. This kind of communication etiquette is always important, but it demands special care with negative messages. Moreover, you can ease the sense of disappointment by using positive words rather than negative, counterproductive ones (see Table 11.1).

STEP 3: COMPLETING A NEGATIVE MESSAGE

The need for careful attention to detail continues as you complete your message. Revise your content to make sure everything is clear, complete, and concise. Even small flaws are likely to be magnified in readers' minds as they react to the negative news, because they can create

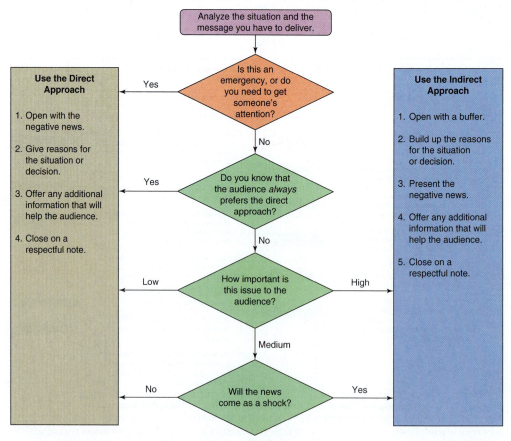

Figure 11.2 Choosing the Direct or Indirect Approach
Following this decision tree will help you decide whether the direct or indirect approach is better in a given situation. Of course, use your best judgment as well. Your relationship with the audience, for example, could affect your choice of approaches.

TABLE 11.1   Choosing Positive Words

Examples of Negative Phrasings	Positive Alternatives
Your request *doesn't make any sense*.	Please clarify your request.
The *damage won't be fixed* for a week.	The item will be repaired next week.
Although it *wasn't our fault*, there will be an *unavoidable delay* in your order.	We will process your order as soon as we receive an aluminum shipment from our supplier, which we expect within 10 days.
You are clearly *dissatisfied*.	I recognize that the product did not live up to your expectations.
I was *shocked* to learn that you're *unhappy*.	Thank you for sharing your concerns about your shopping experience.
The enclosed statement is *wrong*.	Please verify the enclosed statement and provide a correct copy.

the impression that you are careless or incompetent. Produce clean, professional documents and proofread carefully to eliminate mistakes. Finally, be sure to deliver messages promptly; withholding or delaying bad news can be unethical, even illegal. See Figure 11.3 on the next page for a message that conveys negative information clearly and concisely.

Using the Direct Approach for Negative Messages

A negative message using the direct approach opens with the bad news, proceeds to the reasons for the situation or the decision, and ends with a positive statement aimed at maintaining a good relationship with the audience. Depending on the circumstances, the message may also offer alternatives or a plan of action to fix the situation under discussion. Stating the bad news at the beginning can have two advantages: It makes a shorter message possible, and it allows the audience to reach the main idea of the message in less time.

2 LEARNING OBJECTIVE
Explain how to effectively use the direct approach when conveying negative news.

Use the direct approach when your negative answer or information will have minimal personal impact.

OPENING WITH A CLEAR STATEMENT OF THE BAD NEWS

No matter what the news is, come right out and say it, but maintain a calm, professional tone that keeps the focus on the news and not on individual failures or other personal factors. Also, if necessary, explain or remind the reader why you're writing.

PROVIDING REASONS AND ADDITIONAL INFORMATION

In most cases, follow the direct opening with an explanation of why the news is negative. The extent of your explanation depends on the nature of the news and your relationship with the reader. For example, if you want to preserve a long-standing relationship with an important customer, a detailed explanation could well be worth the extra effort such a message would require.

However, you will encounter some situations in which explaining negative news is neither appropriate nor helpful, such as when the reasons are confidential, excessively complicated, or irrelevant to the reader. To maintain a cordial working relationship with the reader, you might want to explain why you can't provide the information.

Should you apologize when delivering bad news or responding to negative situations? The answer isn't quite as simple as one might think, partly because the notion of *apology* is hard to pin down. To some people, it simply means an expression of sympathy that something negative has happened to another person. At the other extreme, it means admitting fault and taking responsibility for specific compensations or corrections to atone for the mistake.

Some experts have advised that a company should never apologize, even when it knows it has made a mistake, because the apology might be taken as a confession of guilt that could be used against the company in a lawsuit. However, several states have laws that specifically prevent expressions of sympathy from being used as evidence of legal liability. In fact, judges, juries, and plaintiffs tend to be more forgiving of companies that express

The amount of detail you should provide depends on your relationship with the audience.

Apologies can have legal ramifications, but refusing to apologize out of fear of admitting guilt can damage a company's relationships with its stakeholders.

1 Plan → 2 Write → 3 Complete

Analyze the Situation
Verify that the purpose is to decline a request and offer alternatives; audience is likely to be surprised by the refusal.

Gather Information
Determine audience needs and obtain the necessary information.

Choose Medium and Channel
For formal messages, printed letters on company letterhead are best.

Organize the Information
The main idea is to refuse the request so limit your scope to that; select the indirect approach based on the audience and the situation.

Adapt to Your Audience
Adjust the level of formality based on your degree of familiarity with the audience; maintain a positive relationship by using the "you" attitude, politeness, positive emphasis, and bias-free language.

Compose the Message
Use a conversational but professional style and keep the message brief, clear, and as helpful as possible.

Revise the Message
Evaluate content and review readability to make sure the negative information won't be misinterpreted; make sure your tone stays positive without being artificial.

Produce the Message
Maintain a clean, professional appearance on company letterhead

Proofread the Message
Review for errors in layout, spelling, and mechanics.

Distribute the Message
Deliver your message using the chosen medium.

927 Dawson Valley Road, Tulsa, Oklahoma 74151
Voice: (918) 669-4428   Fax: (918) 669-4429
www.infotech.com

March 6, 2018

Dr. Sandra Wofford, President
Whittier Community College
333 Whittier Avenue
Tulsa, OK 74150

Dear Dr. Wofford:

Infotech has been happy to support Whittier Community College in many ways over the years, and we appreciate the opportunities you and your organization provide to so many deserving students. Thank you for considering our grounds for your graduation ceremony on June 3.

We would certainly like to accommodate Whittier as we have in years past, but our companywide sales meetings will be held this year during the weeks of May 29 and June 5. With more than 200 sales representatives and their families from around the world joining us, activities will be taking place throughout our facility.

My assistant, Robert Seagers, suggests you contact the Municipal Botanical Gardens as a possible graduation site. He recommends calling Jerry Kane, director of public relations.

We remain firm in our commitment to you, President Wofford, and to the fine students you represent. Through our internship program, academic research grants, and other initiatives, we will continue to be a strong corporate partner to Whittier College and will support your efforts as you move forward.

Sincerely,

May Yee Kwan

May Yee Kwan
Public Relations Director

The buffer eases the recipient into the message by demonstrating respect and recapping the request.

Kwan suggests an alternative, showing that she cares about the college and has given the matter some thought.

She provides a meaningful reason for the negative response, without apologizing (because the company is not at fault).

Her close emphasizes the importance of the relationship and the company's continuing commitment.

Figure 11.3 **Effective Letter Declining a Routine Request**
In declining a college's request to use her company's facilities, May Yee Kwan took note of the fact that her company has a long-standing relationship with the college and wants to maintain that positive relationship. Because the news is unexpected based on past experience, she chose an indirect approach to build up to her announcement.

sympathy for wronged parties. Moreover, a sincere, effective apology can help repair—and even improve—a company's reputation.[2]

Creating an effective apology involves four key decisions.[3] First, the apology should be delivered by someone whose position in the organization corresponds with the gravity of the situation. The CEO doesn't need to apologize for a late package delivery, but he or she does need to be the public face of the company when a major problem occurs. Second, the apology needs to be real. Don't say "I'm sorry if anyone was offended." The conditional *if* implies that you're not sorry at all and that it's the other party's fault for being offended.[4] Third, apologies need to be delivered quickly, particularly in the social media age. A fast response makes the message more meaningful to the affected parties, and it helps the company maintain some control over the story, rather than reacting to social media outrage. Fourth, media and channel choices are crucial. The right choice can range from a private conversation to a written message posted or distributed online to a public press conference, depending on the situation.

Note that you can also express sympathy with someone's plight without suggesting that you are to blame. For example, if a customer damaged a product through misuse and suffered a financial loss as a result of not being able to use the product, you can say something along the lines of "I'm sorry to hear of your difficulties." This approach demonstrates sensitivity without accepting blame.

> **REAL-TIME UPDATES**
> LEARN MORE BY READING THIS ARTICLE
> ### In-depth advice on issuing an apology
> Balance the needs of all affected stakeholders with these timely tips. Go to **real-timeupdates.com/bct14** and select Learn More in the Students section.

CLOSING ON A RESPECTFUL NOTE

After you've explained the negative news, close the message in a manner that respects the impact the news is likely to have on the recipient. If appropriate, consider offering your readers an alternative solution if you can and if doing so is a good use of your time. Look for opportunities to include positive statements, but avoid creating false hopes or writing in a way that seems to suggest to the recipient that something negative didn't happen. Ending on a false positive can leave readers feeling "disrespected, disregarded, or deceived."[5]

In situations where you're responding after a mistake was made, an important aspect of a respectful close is describing the actions being taken to avoid similar mistakes in the future. Offering such explanations can underline the sincerity of an apology because doing so signals that the person or organization is serious about not repeating the error.

Using the Indirect Approach for Negative Messages

The indirect approach helps prepare readers for the bad news by presenting the reasons for it first. However, the indirect approach is *not* meant to obscure bad news, delay it, or limit your responsibility. Rather, the purpose of this approach is to ease the blow and help readers accept the situation. When done poorly, the indirect approach can be disrespectful and even unethical. But when done well, it is a good example of audience-oriented communication crafted with attention to ethics and etiquette. Showing consideration for the feelings of others is never dishonest.

3 LEARNING OBJECTIVE
Explain how to effectively use the indirect approach when conveying negative news.

Use the indirect approach when some preparation will help your audience accept your bad news.

OPENING WITH A BUFFER

Messages using the indirect approach open with a **buffer**: a neutral statement that establishes common ground with the reader without revealing the main idea (refer to Figure 11.1). A good buffer can express your appreciation for being considered (if you're responding to a request), assure the reader of your attention to the request, or indicate your understanding of the reader's needs. A good buffer also needs to be relevant and sincere.

A well-written buffer establishes common ground with the reader.

Poorly written buffers mislead or insult the reader.

In contrast, a poorly written buffer might trivialize the reader's concerns, divert attention from the problem with insincere flattery or irrelevant material, or mislead the reader into thinking your message actually contains good news.

Consider these possible responses to a manager of the order-fulfillment department who requested some temporary staffing help from your department (a request you won't be able to fulfill):

Our department shares your goal of processing orders quickly and efficiently.	← Establishes common ground with the reader and validates the concerns that prompted the original request—without promising a positive answer
As a result of the last downsizing, every department in the company is running shorthanded.	← Establishes common ground, but in a negative way that downplays the recipient's concerns
You folks are doing a great job over there, and I'd love to be able to help out.	← Potentially misleads the reader into concluding that you will comply with the request
Those new state labor regulations are driving me mad over here; how about in your department?	← Trivializes the reader's concerns by opening with an irrelevant issue

Only the first of these buffers can be considered effective; the other three are likely to damage your relationship with the other manager—and lower his or her opinion of you. Table 11.2 shows several types of effective buffers you could use to tactfully open a negative message.

PROVIDING REASONS AND ADDITIONAL INFORMATION

Phrase your reasons to signal the negative news ahead.

An effective buffer serves as a transition to the next part of your message, in which you build up the explanations and information that will culminate in your negative news. An ideal explanation section leads readers to your conclusion before you come right out and say it. In other words, the reader has followed your line of reasoning and is ready for the answer. By giving your reasons effectively, as Hailo did in its email message (see page 294), you help maintain focus on the issues at hand and defuse the emotions that always accompany significantly bad news.

Don't hide behind "company policy" when you deliver bad news; present logical answers instead.

As much as possible, avoid hiding behind company policy to cushion your bad news. If you say, "Company policy forbids our hiring anyone who does not have two years'

TABLE 11.2 Types of Buffers

Buffer	Strategy	Example
Agreement	Find a point on which you and the reader share similar views.	We both know how hard it is to make a profit in this industry.
Appreciation	Express sincere thanks for receiving something.	Your check for $127.17 arrived yesterday. Thank you.
Cooperation	Convey your willingness to help in any way you realistically can.	Employee Services is here to assist all associates with their health insurance, retirement planning, and continuing education needs.
Fairness	Assure the reader that you've closely examined and carefully considered the problem, or mention an appropriate action that has already been taken.	For the past week, we have had our bandwidth monitoring tools running around the clock to track your upload and download speeds.
Good news	Start with the part of your message that is favorable.	We have credited your account in the amount of $14.95 to cover the cost of return shipping.
Praise	Find an attribute or an achievement to compliment.	The Stratford Group has an impressive record of accomplishment in helping clients resolve financial reporting problems.
Resale	Favorably discuss the product or company related to the subject of the letter.	With their heavy-duty, full-suspension hardware and fine veneers, the desks and file cabinets in our Montclair line have long been popular with value-conscious professionals.
Understanding	Demonstrate that you understand the reader's goals and needs.	So that you can more easily find the printer with the features you need, I have attached a brochure that describes the full line of Epson printers.

supervisory experience," you imply that you won't consider anyone on his or her individual merits. By sharing the reasons behind the policy (if appropriate in the circumstances), you can give readers a more satisfying answer. Consider this response to an applicant:

> Because these management positions are quite challenging, the human resources department has researched the qualifications needed to succeed in them. The findings show that the two most important qualifications are a bachelor's degree in business administration and two years' supervisory experience.

← Shows the reader that the decision is based on a methodical analysis of the company's needs and not on some arbitrary guideline

← Establishes the criteria behind the decision and lets the reader know what to expect

This paragraph does a good job of stating reasons for the refusal:

- It provides enough detail to logically support the refusal.
- It implies that the applicant is better off avoiding a program in which he or she might fail.
- It shows that the company's policy is based on experience and careful analysis.
- It doesn't offer an apology for the decision because no one is at fault.
- It avoids negative personal expressions (such as "You do not meet our requirements").

Even valid, well-thought-out reasons won't convince every reader in every situation. However, if you've done a good job of laying out your reasoning, you've done everything you can to prepare the reader for the main idea, which is the negative news itself.

Well-written reasons are
- Detailed
- Tactful
- Individualized
- Unapologetic if no one is at fault
- Positive

CONTINUING WITH A CLEAR STATEMENT OF THE BAD NEWS

After you've thoughtfully and logically established your reasons and readers are prepared to receive the bad news, you can use three techniques to convey the negative information as clearly and as kindly as possible. First, deemphasize the bad news:

- Minimize the space or time devoted to the bad news—without trivializing it or withholding any important information.
- Subordinate bad news in a complex or compound sentence ("My department is already shorthanded, so I'll need all my staff for at least the next two months"). This construction presents the bad news in the middle of the sentence, the point of least emphasis.
- Place bad news in the middle of a paragraph or use parenthetical expressions ("Our profits, which are down, are only part of the picture").

Keep in mind, however, that it's possible to abuse deemphasis. For instance, if the primary point of your message is that profits are down, it would be inappropriate to marginalize that news by burying it in the middle of a sentence. State the negative news clearly, and then make a smooth transition to any positive news that might balance the story.

Second, if appropriate, use a conditional (*if* or *when*) statement to imply that the audience could have received, or might someday receive, a favorable answer ("When you have more managerial experience, you are welcome to reapply"). Such a statement could motivate applicants to improve their qualifications. However, avoid any suggestion that you might reverse the decision you've just made, and refrain from any phrasing that could give readers false hope.

Third, emphasize what you can do or have done rather than what you cannot do. Say "We sell exclusively through retailers, and the one nearest you that carries our merchandise is . . ." rather than "We are unable to serve you, so please call your nearest dealer." Also, by implying the bad news, you may not need to actually state it, thereby making the bad news less personal ("Our development budget for next year is fully committed to our existing slate of projects"). By focusing on the facts and implying the bad news, you make the impact less personal.

When implying bad news, however, be sure your audience will be able to grasp the entire message—including the bad news. Withholding negative information or overemphasizing positive information is unethical and unfair to your reader. If an implied message

To handle bad news carefully
- Deemphasize the bad news visually and grammatically
- Use a conditional statement, if appropriate
- Tell what you did do, not what you didn't do

Don't disguise bad news when you emphasize the positive.

MOBILE APP
Pocket Letter Pro for iOS includes templates for a variety of letter types to simplify writing business letters on your mobile device.

might lead to uncertainty, state your decision in direct terms. Just be sure to avoid overly blunt statements that are likely to cause pain and anger:

Instead of This	Write This
I *must refuse* your request.	I will be out of town on the day you need me.
We *must deny* your application.	The position has been filled.
I *am unable* to grant your request.	Contact us again when you have established . . .
We *cannot afford to* continue the program.	The program will conclude on May 1.
Much as I would like to attend . . .	Our budget meeting ends too late for me to attend.
We *must turn down* your extension request.	Please send in your payment by June 14.

CLOSING ON A RESPECTFUL NOTE

A positive close
- Builds goodwill
- Offers a suggestion for action
- Provides a look toward the future

As with the direct approach, the close in the indirect approach offers an opportunity to emphasize your respect for your audience, even though you've just delivered unpleasant news. Express best wishes without ending on a falsely upbeat note. If you can find a positive angle that's meaningful to your audience, by all means consider adding it to your conclusion. However, don't try to pretend that the negative news didn't happen or that it won't affect the reader. Suggest alternative solutions if such information is available and doing so is a good use of your time. If you've asked readers to decide between alternatives or to take some action, make sure that they know what to do, when to do it, and how to do it. Whatever type of conclusion you use, follow these guidelines:

- **Avoid an uncertain conclusion.** If the situation or decision is final, avoid statements such as "I trust our decision is satisfactory," which imply that the matter is open to discussion or negotiation.
- **Manage future correspondence.** Encourage additional communication *only* if you're willing to discuss the situation further. (If you're not, avoid statements such as "If you have further questions, please write.")
- **Express optimism, if appropriate.** If the situation might improve in the future, share that with your readers if it's relevant. However, don't suggest the possibility of a positive change if you don't have insight that it might happen.
- **Be sincere.** Steer clear of clichés that are insincere in view of the bad news. (If you can't help, don't say, "If we can be of any help, please contact us.")

Keep in mind that the close is the last thing audience members have to remember you by. Even though they're disappointed, leave them with the impression that they were treated with respect.

Maintaining High Standards of Ethics and Etiquette

4 LEARNING OBJECTIVE
Explain the importance of maintaining high standards of ethics and etiquette when delivering negative messages.

All business messages demand attention to ethics and etiquette, of course, but these considerations take on special importance when you are delivering bad news—for several reasons. First, a variety of laws and regulations dictate the content and delivery of many business messages with potentially negative content, such as the release of financial information by a public company. Second, negative messages can have a significant negative impact on the lives of those receiving them. Even if the news is conveyed legally and conscientiously, good ethical practice demands that these situations be approached with care and sensitivity. Third, emotions often run high when negative messages are involved, for both the sender and the receiver. Senders need to manage their own emotions and consider the emotional state of their audiences.

For example, in a message announcing or discussing workforce cutbacks, you have the emotional needs of several stakeholder groups to consider. The employees who are losing their jobs are likely to experience fear about their futures and possibly a sense of betrayal. The employees who are keeping their jobs are likely to feel anxiety about the long-term security of their jobs, the ability of company management to turn things around, and the level of care and respect the company has for its employees. These "survivors" may also feel guilty about keeping their jobs while some colleagues lost theirs. Outside the company, investors, suppliers, and segments of the community affected by the layoffs (such as retailers and homebuilders) will have varying degrees of financial interest in the outcome of the decision. Writing such messages requires careful attention to all these needs, while balancing respect for the departing employees with a positive outlook on the future.

The challenge of sending—and receiving—negative messages can tempt one to delay, downplay, or distort the bad news (see "Ethics Detective: Solving the Case of the Deceptive Soft Sell").[6] However, doing so may be unethical and even illegal. In recent years, numerous companies have been sued by shareholders, consumers, employees, and government regulators for allegedly withholding or delaying negative information in such areas as company finances, environmental hazards, and product safety. In many of these cases the problem was slow, incomplete, or inaccurate communication between the company and external stakeholders. In others, problems stemmed from a reluctance to send or receive negative news within the organization.

Effectively sharing bad news within an organization requires commitment from everyone involved. Employees must commit to sending negative messages when necessary and doing so in a timely fashion, even when that is unpleasant or difficult. Conversely, managers must commit to maintaining open communication channels, truly listening when employees have negative information to share and not punishing employees who deliver bad news.

Employees who observe unethical or illegal behavior within their companies and are unable to resolve the problems through normal channels may have no choice but to resort to **whistle-blowing**, expressing their concerns internally through company ethics hotlines—or externally through social media or the news media if they perceive no other options. The decision to "blow the whistle" on one's own employer is rarely easy or without consequences; more than 80 percent of whistle-blowers in one survey said they were punished in some way for coming forward with their concerns.[7]

Although whistle-blowing is sometimes characterized as "ratting on" colleagues or managers, it has an essential function. According to the international business expert Alex MacBeath, "Whistle-blowing can be an invaluable way to alert management to poor business practice within the workplace. Often whistle-blowing can be the only way that information about issues such as rule breaking, criminal activity, cover-ups, and fraud can be brought to management's attention before serious damage is suffered."[8]

Sharing bad news effectively requires commitment from everyone in the organization.

Whistle-blowing is a difficult decision for most employees to make, but it provides a vital element of feedback for managers.

ETHICS DETECTIVE

Solving the Case of the Deceptive Soft Sell

You and your colleagues are nervous. Sales have been declining for months, and you see evidence of budget tightening all over the place—the fruit and pastries have disappeared from the coffee stations, accountants are going over expense reports with magnifying glasses, and managers are slow to replace people who leave the company. Instant messages fly around the office; everyone wants to know whether anyone has heard anything about layoffs.

The job market in your area is weak, and you know you might have to sell your house—in one of the weakest housing markets in memory—and move your family out of state to find another position in your field. If your job is eliminated, you're ready to cope with the loss, but you need as much time as possible. You breathe a sigh of relief when the following item from the CEO appears on the company's internal blog:

> With news of workforce adjustments elsewhere in our industry, we realize many of you are concerned

about the possibility here. I'd like to reassure all of you that we remain confident in the company's fundamental business strategy, and the executive team is examining all facets of company operations to ensure our continued financial strength.

The message calms your fears. Should it?

A month later, the CEO announces a layoff of 20 percent of the company's workforce—nearly 700 people.

ANALYSIS

You're shocked by the news because you felt reassured by the blog posting from last month. In light of what happened, you retrieve a copy of the newsletter and reread the CEO's message. Does it seem ethical now? Why or why not? If you had been in charge of writing this newsletter item and your hands were tied because you couldn't come out and announce the layoffs yet, how would you have rewritten the message?

CHECKLIST ✔ Creating Negative Messages

A. Choose the better approach.
- Consider using the direct approach when the audience is aware of the possibility of negative news, when the reader is not emotionally involved in the message, when you know that the reader would prefer the bad news first, when you know that firmness is necessary, and when you want to discourage a response.
- Consider using the indirect approach when the news is likely to come as a shock or surprise, when your audience has a high emotional investment in the outcome, and when you want to maintain a good relationship with the audience.

B. For the indirect approach, open with an effective buffer.
- Establish common ground with the audience.
- Validate the request, if you are responding to one.
- Don't trivialize the reader's concerns.
- Don't mislead the reader into thinking the coming news might be positive.

C. Provide reasons and additional information.
- Explain why the news is negative.
- Adjust the amount of detail to fit the situation and the audience.

- Avoid explanations when the reasons are confidential, excessively complicated, or irrelevant to the reader.
- If appropriate, state how you plan to correct or respond to the negative news.
- Seek the advice of company lawyers if you're unsure what to say.

D. Clearly state the bad news.
- State the bad news as positively as possible, using tactful wording.
- To help protect readers' feelings, deemphasize the bad news by minimizing the space devoted to it, subordinating it, or embedding it.
- If your response might change in the future if circumstances change, explain the conditions to the reader.
- Emphasize what you can do or have done rather than what you can't or won't do.

E. Close on a respectful note.
- Express best wishes without being falsely positive.
- Suggest actions readers might take, if appropriate, and provide them with necessary information.
- Encourage further communication only if you're willing to discuss the situation further.

Recognizing the value of this feedback, many companies have formal reporting mechanisms that give employees a way to voice ethical and legal concerns to management. Various government bodies have also instituted protections for whistle-blowers, partly in recognition of the role that workers play in food safety and other vital areas.[9]

For a summary of the points to consider when crafting negative messages, see "Checklist: Creating Negative Messages."

Sending Negative Messages on Routine Business Matters

5 LEARNING OBJECTIVE
Describe successful strategies for sending negative messages on routine business matters.

Professionals and companies receive a wide variety of requests and cannot respond positively to every single one. In addition, mistakes and unforeseen circumstances can lead to delays and other minor problems that occur in the course of business. Occasionally, companies must send negative messages to suppliers and other parties. Whatever the purpose, crafting routine negative responses and messages quickly and graciously is an important skill for every businessperson.

MAKING NEGATIVE ANNOUNCEMENTS ON ROUTINE BUSINESS MATTERS

On occasion managers need to make unexpected negative announcements. For example, a company might decide to consolidate its materials purchasing with fewer suppliers and thereby need to tell several firms it will no longer be buying from them. Internally, management may need to announce the elimination of an employee benefit or other changes that employees will view negatively.

Negative announcements on routine business matters usually should be handled with the indirect approach because the news is unexpected.

Except in the case of minor changes, the indirect approach is usually the better choice. Follow the steps outlined for indirect messages: Open with a buffer that establishes some mutual ground between you and the reader, advance your reasoning, announce the change, and close with as much positive information and sentiment as appropriate under the circumstances.

REJECTING SUGGESTIONS AND PROPOSALS

Managers receive a variety of suggestions and proposals, both solicited and unsolicited, from internal and external sources. For an unsolicited proposal from an external source, you may not even need to respond if you don't already have a working relationship with the sender. However, if you need to reject a proposal you solicited, you owe the sender an explanation, and because the news may be unexpected, the indirect approach is better. In general, the closer your working relationship, the more thoughtful and complete you need to be in your response. For example, if you are rejecting a proposal from an employee, explain your reasons fully and carefully so that the employee can understand why the proposal was not accepted and so that you don't damage an important working relationship.

REFUSING ROUTINE REQUESTS

When you are unable to meet a request, your primary communication challenge is to give a clear negative response without generating negative feelings or damaging anyone's credibility. As simple as such messages may seem to be, they can test your skills as a communicator because you often need to deliver negative information while maintaining a positive relationship with the other party.

The direct approach works best for most routine negative responses. It helps your audience get your answer quickly and move on to other possibilities, and it saves time for you because messages with the direct approach are often easier to write than those with the indirect approach.

The indirect approach is a better choice when the stakes are high for you or for the receiver, when you or your company has an established relationship with the person making the request, or when you're forced to decline a request that you might have accepted in the past (as was the case in Figure 11.3).

Consider the following points as you develop your routine negative messages:

- Manage your time carefully; focus on the most important relationships and requests.
- If the matter is closed, don't imply that it's still open by using phrases such as "Let me think about it and get back to you" as a way to delay saying no.
- Offer alternative ideas if you can, particularly if the relationship is important.
- Don't imply that other assistance or information might be available if it isn't.

When turning down an invitation or a request for a favor, consider your relationship with the reader.

If you aren't in a position to offer additional information or assistance, don't imply that you are.

HANDLING BAD NEWS ABOUT TRANSACTIONS

Bad news about transactions is always unwelcome. When you send such messages, you have three goals: (1) to modify the customer's expectations, (2) to explain how you plan to resolve the situation, and (3) to repair whatever damage might have been done to the business relationship.

The specific content and tone of each message can vary widely, depending on the nature of the transaction and your relationship with the customer. Telling an individual consumer that his new sweater will be arriving a week later than you promised is much simpler than telling Toyota that 30,000 transmission parts will be a week late when you know the company will be forced to idle a multimillion-dollar production facility as a result.

If you haven't done anything specific to set the customer's expectations—such as promising delivery within 24 hours—the message simply needs to inform the customer of the situation, with little or no emphasis on apologies (see Figure 11.4 on the next page).

If you did set the customer's expectations and now find that you can't meet them, your task is more complicated. In addition to resetting those expectations and explaining how you'll resolve the problem, you should include an apology as part of your message. The scope of the apology depends on the magnitude of the mistake. For the customer who ordered the sweater, a simple apology followed by a clear statement of when the sweater will arrive would probably be sufficient. For larger business-to-business transactions, the customer may want an explanation of what went wrong to determine whether you'll be able to perform as you promise in the future.

To help repair the damage to the relationship and encourage repeat business, many companies offer discounts on future purchases, free merchandise, or other considerations.

Some negative messages regarding transactions carry significant financial and legal ramifications.

Your approach to bad news about business transactions depends on what you've done previously to set the customer's expectations.

If you've failed to meet expectations that you set for the customer, you should include an element of apology.

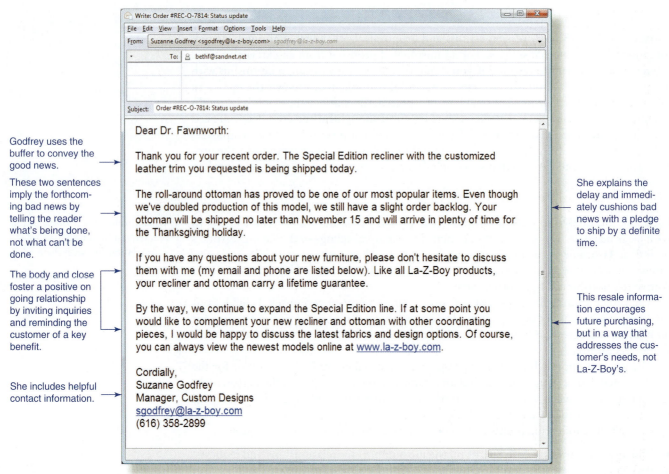

Godfrey uses the buffer to convey the good news.

These two sentences imply the forthcoming bad news by telling the reader what's being done, not what can't be done.

The body and close foster a positive on going relationship by inviting inquiries and reminding the customer of a key benefit.

She includes helpful contact information.

She explains the delay and immediately cushions bad news with a pledge to ship by a definite time.

This resale information encourages future purchasing, but in a way that addresses the customer's needs, not La-Z-Boy's.

Figure 11.4   Effective Negative Message Regarding a Transaction
This message, which is a combination of good and bad news, uses the indirect approach—with the good news serving as a buffer for the bad news. In this case the customer wasn't promised delivery by a certain date, so the writer simply informs the customer when to expect the rest of the order. The writer also takes steps to repair the relationship and encourage future business with her firm.

However, you don't always have a choice. Business-to-business purchasing contracts sometimes include performance clauses that legally entitle the customer to discounts or other restitution. To review the concepts covered in this section, see "Checklist: Handling Bad News About Transactions."

REFUSING CLAIMS AND REQUESTS FOR ADJUSTMENT

Customers who make a claim or request an adjustment tend to be emotionally involved, so the indirect approach is usually the better choice when you are denying such a request. Your delicate task is to avoid accepting responsibility for the unfortunate situation and yet avoid blaming or accusing the customer. To steer clear of these pitfalls, pay special attention to the tone of your letter. Demonstrate that you understand and have considered the complaint carefully, and then calmly explain why you are refusing the request.

Use the indirect approach in most cases of refusing a claim.

CHECKLIST ✔ Handling Bad News About Transactions

- Reset the customer's expectations regarding the transaction.
- Explain what happened and why, if appropriate.
- Explain how you will resolve the situation.
- Repair any damage done to the business relationship, perhaps offering future discounts, free merchandise, or other considerations.
- Offer a professional, businesslike expression of apology if your organization made a mistake.

Close on a respectful and action-oriented note (see Figure 11.5). And be sure to respond quickly. With so many instantaneous media choices at their disposal, some angry consumers will take their complaints public if they don't hear back from you within a few days or even a few hours.[10]

If you deal with enough customers over a long enough period, chances are you'll get a request that is outrageous, insulting, and perhaps even clearly dishonest. In such a scenario it's particularly important to control your emotions to avoid saying or writing anything that the recipient might interpret as defamation (see page 29 in Chapter 1). To avoid being accused of defamation, follow these guidelines:

- Avoid any kind of abusive language or terms that could be considered defamatory.
- Provide accurate information and stick to the facts.

When refusing a claim
- Demonstrate your understanding of the complaint
- Explain your refusal
- Suggest alternative action

You can help avoid committing defamation by not responding emotionally or abusively.

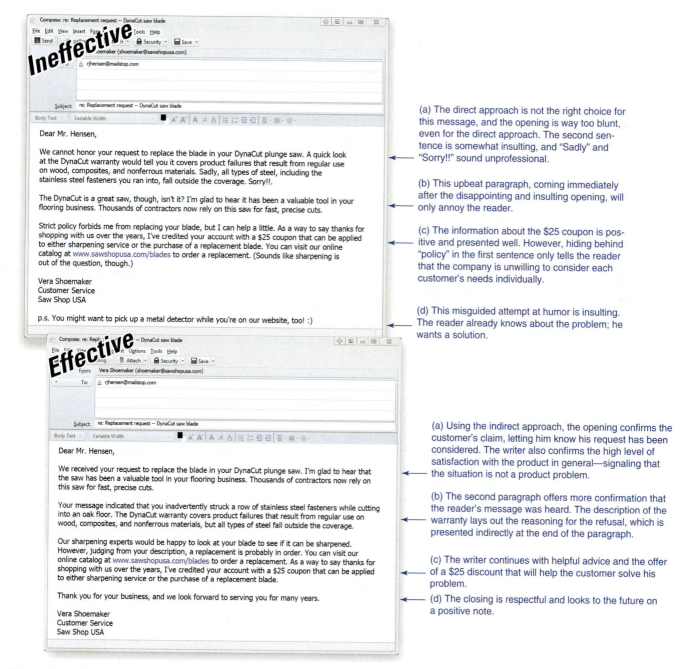

Figure 11.5 Message to Refuse a Claim
Vera Shoemaker diplomatically refuses this customer's request for a new saw blade; he inadvertently damaged his current blade after cutting into some steel fasteners. Without blaming the customer (even though the customer clearly made a mistake), she points out that the saw blade is not intended to cut steel, so the warranty doesn't cover a replacement in this instance.

- Use the indirect approach because the reader is expecting or hoping for a positive response.
- Indicate your full understanding of the nature of the complaint.
- Explain why you are refusing the request, without hiding behind company policy.
- Provide an accurate, factual account of the transaction.
- Emphasize ways things should have been handled rather than dwell on the reader's negligence.
- Avoid any appearance of defamation.
- Avoid expressing personal opinions.
- End with a positive, friendly, helpful close.
- Make any suggested action easy for readers to comply with.

- Never let anger or malice motivate your messages.
- Consult your company's legal advisers whenever you think a message might have legal consequences.
- Communicate honestly and make sure you believe what you're saying is true.
- Emphasize a desire for a good relationship in the future.

Keep in mind that nothing positive can come out of antagonizing a customer, even one who has verbally abused you or your colleagues. Reject the claim or request for adjustment in a professional manner and move on to the next challenge. For a brief review of the tasks involved when refusing claims, see "Checklist: Refusing Claims."

Sending Negative Organizational News

6 LEARNING OBJECTIVE List the important points to consider when conveying negative organizational news.

The messages described in the previous section deal with internal matters or individual interactions with external parties. From time to time, managers must also share negative information with the public at large, and sometimes respond to negative information as well. Most of these scenarios have unique challenges that must be addressed on a case-by-case basis, but the general advice offered here applies to all of them. One key difference among all these messages is whether you have time to plan the announcement. The following section addresses negative messages you do have time to plan for, and "Communicating in a Crisis" later in the chapter offers advice on communication during emergencies.

COMMUNICATING UNDER NORMAL CIRCUMSTANCES

Negative organizational messages to external audiences can require extensive planning.

Businesses may need to send a range of negative messages regarding their ongoing operations. As you plan such messages, take extra care to consider all your audiences and their unique needs. Keep in mind that a significant negative event such as a plant closing can affect hundreds or thousands of people in multiple stakeholder groups: Employees need to find new jobs, get training in new skills, or perhaps get emergency financial help. If many of your employees plan to move in search of new jobs, school districts may have to adjust budgets and staffing levels. Your customers need to find new suppliers. Your suppliers may need to find other customers of their own. Government agencies may need to react to everything from a decrease in tax revenues to an influx of people seeking unemployment benefits.

When making negative announcements, follow these guidelines:

- **Match your approach to the situation.** A modest price increase won't shock most customers, so the direct approach is fine. However, canceling a product that lots of people count on is another matter, so building up to the news via the indirect approach might be better.
- **Consider the unique needs of each group.** As the plant closing example illustrates, various people have different information needs.
- **Give each audience enough time to react as needed.** Negative news often requires readers to make decisions or take action in response, so don't increase their stress by not providing any warning.

Give people as much time as possible to react to negative organizational news.

- **Give yourself enough time to plan and manage a response.** Chances are you're going to be hit with complaints, questions, or product returns after you make your announcement, so make sure you're ready with answers and additional follow-up information.
- **Look for positive angles, but don't exude false optimism.** If eliminating a seldom-used employee benefit means the company can invest more in advertising, by all means promote that positive angle. On the other hand, laying off 10,000 people does not give them "an opportunity to explore new horizons." It's a traumatic event that can affect employees, their families, and their communities for years. The best you may be able to do is to thank people for their past support and wish them well in the future.
- **Seek expert advice if you're not sure.** Many significant negative announcements have important technical, financial, or legal elements that require the expertise of lawyers, accountants, or other specialists.

> Ask for legal help and other assistance if you're not sure how to handle a significant negative announcement.

Negative situations will challenge you as a communicator and leader. Inspirational leaders try to seize such opportunities as a chance to reshape or reinvigorate the organization, and they offer encouragement to those around them (see Figure 11.6 on the next page).

RESPONDING TO NEGATIVE INFORMATION IN A SOCIAL MEDIA ENVIRONMENT

For all the benefits they bring to business, social media and other communication technologies have created a major new challenge: responding to online rumors, false information, and attacks on a company's reputation. Customers who believe they have been treated unfairly can turn to Twitter, Facebook, and other tools to use public exposure as leverage.

However, false rumors and both fair and unfair criticisms can spread around the world in a matter of minutes. Responding to rumors and countering negative information requires an ongoing effort and case-by-case decisions about which messages require a response. Follow these four steps:[11]

> **MOBILE APP**
> The **Yelp** mobile app is an easy way to keep the consumer review site at your fingertips—and to monitor what's being said about your business.

- **Engage early, engage often.** The most important step in responding to negative information has to be done *before* the negative information appears, and that is to engage with communities of stakeholders as a long-term strategy. Companies that have active, mutually beneficial relationships with customers and other interested parties are less likely to be attacked unfairly online and more likely to survive such attacks if they do occur. In contrast, companies that ignore constituents or jump into "spin doctor" mode when a negative situation occurs don't have the same credibility as companies that have done the long, hard work of fostering relationships within their physical and online communities.
- **Monitor the conversation.** If people are interested in what your company does, chances are they are blogging, tweeting, podcasting, posting videos, writing on Facebook, and otherwise sharing their opinions. Use the available technologies to listen to what people are saying.
- **Evaluate negative messages.** When you encounter negative messages, resist the urge to fire back immediately. Instead, evaluate the source, the tone, and the content of the message—and then choose a response that fits the situation. For example, the Public Affairs Agency of the U.S. Air Force groups senders of negative messages into four categories: "trolls" (those whose only intent is to stir up conflict), "ragers" (those who are just ranting or telling jokes), "the misguided" (those who are spreading incorrect information), and "unhappy customers" (those who have had a negative experience with the Air Force).
- **Respond appropriately.** After you have assessed a negative message, make the appropriate response based on an overall public relations plan. The Air Force, for instance, doesn't respond to trolls or ragers, responds to misguided messages with correct information, and responds to unhappy customers with efforts to rectify the situation and reach a reasonable solution. In addition to replying

> Responding effectively to rumors and negative information in social media requires continual engagement with stakeholders and careful decisions about which messages should get a response.

REAL-TIME UPDATES
LEARN MORE BY VISITING THIS WEBSITE
Is there any truth to that rumor?
The Emergent website at Columbia University tracks and evaluates rumors spreading online. Go to **real-timeupdates** **.com/bct14** and select Learn More in the Students section.

promptly, make sure your response won't make the situation worse. For example, taking legal action against critics, even if technically justified, can rally people to their defense and create a public relations nightmare. In some instances the best response is to contact a critic privately (through direct messaging on Twitter, for example) to attempt a resolution away from the public forum.

Ineffective

Pulling the plug on Triton

JUNE 6 BY OSCAR HUERTA   LEAVE A COMMENT

Most of you probably don't follow the costs of materials on the world market, but let me tell you, it's been brutal for those of us who do. We're seeing some major increases in the cost of high-grade steel, ceramics, and semiconductor-grade silicon. We can accommodate moderate increases in these costs by raising our list prices, but there's only so far we can raise prices before sales start to drop.

Of course, we periodically revisit our sales forecasts for products in development, to make sure our revenue projections are valid. Sad to say, Triton looks like it will get hammered when it hits the market. AMG Magnetics recently introduced a product that will compete directly with Triton, and it has both higher performance and a lower price.

This won't come as a surprise to anyone who has been looking at the numbers: We have to pull the plug on Triton. It just won't fly under these new circumstances.

Now, I don't want to hear any gossip about the Triton team failing or not being up to the task or whatever. Sue Wentworth and her crew have been putting in long hours for months, and it was tough for me at the other top managers to deliver this news.

Disruptions like this always start the rumor mill going about job security, so I'm happy to report that there is no need to worry. We have plenty of other projects that could use some extra help, and other project managers are already lobbying to get their hands on the Triton staffers.

By the way, these reviews are something the management team does every quarter to make sure we focus our time and investment on new products with the greatest potential for strong sales and profit levels, the management team reviews the costing analysis and sales projections for every R&D project once a quarter. Sometimes circumstances change after we launch a project, and the financial assumptions we made at that point might no longer be valid.

(a) The writer attempts the indirect approach in the body of the message but gives away the bad news in the headline of the blog post.

(b) This opening makes it more about the writer than the readers or the company in general.

(c) Saying that Triton "will get hammered when it hits the market" is too blunt for such a sensitive message.

(d) He started the post by saying most people don't look at the numbers, so this news will come as a surprise. Also, "pull the plug" and "It just won't fly" feel too flippant for such an important message.

(e) This remark about gossip introduces an additional layer of negativity that serve no purpose.

(f) This paragraph has positive information about job security, but it starts with an unnecessary negative remark about the rumor mill.

(g) This information would make a good buffer (see the Effective example), but it makes a poor close because it doesn't leave the reader with anything to feel good about.

Effective

Triton project: important update

JUNE 6 BY OSCAR HUERTA   LEAVE A COMMENT

As part of the ongoing effort to make sure we focus our time and investment on new products with the greatest potential for strong sales and profit levels, the management team reviews the costing analysis and sales projections for every R&D project once a quarter. Conducting these reviews every quarter gives us time to respond in the event that current circumstances no longer align with the financial assumptions we made when a particular project was launched.

On the cost side of the equation, we're seeing some major increases in the cost of high-grade steel, ceramics, and semiconductor-grade silicon. We can accommodate moderate increases in these costs by raising our list prices, but there's only so far we can raise prices before sales start to drop.

Regarding sales projections, our forecasts still look solid for every new product, except for the Triton project. AMG Magnetics recently introduced a product that will compete directly with Triton, and it has both higher performance and a lower price. Accordingly, we have had to reduce Triton's sales forecasts by 35 percent.

Unfortunately, the increase in material costs and the decrease in projected sales volume put Triton in an impossible position. We believe the company has better opportunities for investing our development capital and the time and energy of our talented engineering staff. Accordingly, we have decided to cancel Triton, effectively immediately.

Please rest assured that this will not affect staffing levels. We have plenty of other projects that can use some extra help, and other project managers are already lobbying to get the Triton staffers on their teams.

Please join me in thanking Sue Wentworth and everyone on the Triton team for the months of dedication and creativity they devoted to this project. I know they are disappointed in this outcome but recognize the necessity of focusing on our brightest prospects.

(a) The post title preserves the indirect approach by not giving away the bad news.

(b) The opening serves as an effective buffer because it explains the process that was used to reach the decision. This will put the audience in a rational frame of mind, rather than an emotional one.

(c) This paragraph conveys the first of the two reasons that led to the decision, and it does so in a calm but authoritative way.

(d) This paragraph shares the second reason and narrows the focus from all products to just the Triton project. At this point, readers should be prepared for the bad news that is coming.

(e) He delivers the bad news while keeping the focus on the project and its financial parameters. He also immediately shifts into a positive stance, talking about the talented staff and other opportunities.

(f) This paragraph puts to rest any worries other readers will have about their jobs.

(g) The close is respectful and demonstrates sensitivity toward the people most affected by the decision.

Figure 11.6 **Internal Message Providing Bad News About Company Operations**
The cancelation of a major development project before completion can be a traumatic event for a company's employees. People who worked on the project are likely to feel that all their time and energy were wasted and worry that their jobs are in jeopardy. Employees who didn't work on the project might worry about the company's financial health and the stability of their own jobs. Such messages are therefore prime candidates for the indirect approach. Note how much more effectively the revised (effective) version manages the reader's emotions from beginning to end.

TABLE 11.3 How to Communicate in a Crisis

When a Crisis Hits:	
Do	**Don't**
Prepare for trouble ahead of time by identifying potential problems, appointing and training a response team, and preparing and testing a crisis management plan	Blame anyone for anything
Get top management involved immediately	Speculate in public
Set up a news center for company representatives and the media that is equipped with phones, computers, and other digital tools for preparing news releases and online updates. At the news center, take the following steps:	Refuse to answer questions
• Issue frequent news updates and have trained personnel available to respond to questions around the clock	Release information that will violate anyone's right to privacy
• Provide complete information packets to the media as soon as possible	Use the crisis to pitch products or services
• Prevent conflicting statements and provide continuity by appointing a single person trained in advance to speak for the company	Play favorites with media representatives
• Tell receptionists and other employees to direct all phone calls to the designated spokesperson in the news center	
• Provide updates when new information is available via blog postings, Twitter updates, text messaging, Facebook, and other appropriate media	
Tell the whole story—openly, completely, and honestly; if you are at fault, apologize	
Demonstrate the company's concern by your statements and your actions	

Whatever you do, keep in mind that positive reputations are an important asset and need to be diligently guarded and defended. Everybody has a voice now, and some of those voices don't care to play by the rules of ethical communication.

COMMUNICATING IN A CRISIS

Some of the most critical instances of business communication occur during crises, which can include industrial accidents, crimes or scandals involving company employees, on-site hostage situations, terrorist attacks, information theft, product tampering incidents, and financial calamities. During a crisis, customers, employees, local communities, and others will demand information. In addition, rumors can spread unpredictably and uncontrollably. You can also expect the news media to descend quickly, asking questions of anyone they can find.

The key to successful communication efforts during a crisis is having a **crisis management plan**. In addition to defining operational procedures to deal with a crisis, this plan outlines communication tasks and responsibilities, which can include everything from media contacts to news release templates (see Table 11.3). The plan should clearly specify which people are authorized to speak for the company, provide contact information for all key executives, and include a list of the news outlets and social media tools that will be used to disseminate information.

Although you can't predict catastrophes, you can prepare for them. Analysis of corporate crises over the past several decades reveals that companies that respond quickly with the information people need tend to fare much better in the long run than those that go into hiding or release inconsistent or incorrect information.[12]

Anticipation and planning are key to successful communication in a crisis.

Sending Negative Employment Messages

As a manager, you will find yourself in a variety of situations in which you have to convey bad news to individual employees or potential employees. Recipients often have an emotional stake in your message, so taking the indirect approach is usually advised. In addition, use great care in choosing media for these messages. For instance, email and other written forms let you control the message and avoid personal confrontation, but one-on-one conversations are often viewed as more sensitive and give both sides the opportunity to ask and answer questions.

7 LEARNING OBJECTIVE Describe successful strategies for sending negative employment-related messages.

REFUSING REQUESTS FOR EMPLOYEE REFERENCES AND RECOMMENDATION LETTERS

Managers may get requests for recommendation letters from other employers and from past employees. When sending refusals to prospective employers who have requested information about past employees, your message can be brief and direct:

> Our human resources department has authorized me to confirm that Yolanda Johnson worked for Tolson Logistics for three years, from June 2014 to July 2016. Best of luck as you interview applicants.

Implies that company policy prohibits the release of any more information but does provide what information is available

Ends on a positive note

This message doesn't need to say, "We cannot comply with your request." It simply gives the reader all the information that is allowable.

Refusing an applicant's direct request for a recommendation letter is another matter. Any refusal to cooperate may seem to be a personal slight and a threat to the applicant's future. Diplomacy and preparation help readers accept your refusal:

> Thank you for letting me know about your job opportunity with Coca-Cola. Your internship there and the MBA you've worked so hard to earn should place you in an excellent position to land the marketing job.
>
> Although we do not send out formal recommendations here at PepsiCo, I can certainly send Coca-Cola a confirmation of your employment dates. And if you haven't considered this already, be sure to ask several of your professors to write evaluations of your marketing skills.
> Best of luck to you in your career.

Uses the indirect approach because the other party is probably expecting a positive response

Announces that the writer cannot comply with the request, without explicitly blaming it on "policy"

Offers to fulfill as much of the request as possible and suggests an alternative

Ends on a positive note

This message tactfully avoids hurting the reader's feelings because it makes positive comments about the reader's recent activities, implies the refusal, suggests an alternative, and uses a polite close.

REFUSING SOCIAL NETWORKING RECOMMENDATION REQUESTS

Making recommendations in a social networking environment is more complicated than with a traditional recommendation letter because the endorsements you give become part of your online profile. On a network such as LinkedIn, others can see whom you've recommended and what you've written about these people. Much more so than with traditional letters, then, the recommendations you make in a social network become part of your personal brand.[13] Moreover, networks make it easy to find people and request recommendations, so you are likely to get more requests than you would have otherwise—and sometimes from people you don't know well.

Social networks have created new challenges in recommendation requests, but they also offer more flexibility in responding to these requests.

Fortunately, social networks give you a bit more flexibility when responding to these requests. You can simply ignore or delete the request—some people make it personal policy to ignore requests from networkers they don't know. Of course, if you do know someone, ignoring a request could create an uncomfortable situation, so you need to decide each case based on your relationship with the person. Another option is to refrain from making recommendations at all and just let people know this policy when they ask. Whatever you decide, remember that it is your choice.[14]

If you choose to make recommendations and want to respond to a request, you can write as much or as little information about the person as you are comfortable sharing. Unlike the situation with an offline recommendation, you

REAL-TIME UPDATES

LEARN MORE BY READING THIS ARTICLE

These templates make it easier to turn down recommendation requests

The career expert Alison Doyle offers advice and message templates to help you handle these uncomfortable messages. Go to **real-timeupdates.com/bct14** and select Learn More in the Students section.

don't need to write a complete letter. You can write a briefer statement, even just a single sentence that focuses on one positive aspect.[15] This flexibility allows you to respond positively in those situations in which you have mixed feelings about a person's overall abilities.

REJECTING JOB APPLICATIONS

Application rejections are routine communications, but saying no is never easy, and recipients are emotionally invested in the decision. Moreover, companies must be aware of the possibility of employment discrimination lawsuits.[16] Of course, having fair and nondiscriminatory hiring practices is essential, but rejections must also be written in a way that doesn't inadvertently suggest any hint of discrimination. Expert opinions differ on the level of information to include in a rejection message, but the safest strategy is to avoid sharing any explanations for the company's decision and to avoid making or implying any promises of future consideration (see Figure 11.7):[17]

Poorly written rejection letters can tarnish your company's reputation and can even invite legal troubles.

- **Personalize the email message or letter by using the recipient's name.** For example, mail merge makes it easy to insert each recipient's name into a form letter.
- **Open with a courteous expression of appreciation for having applied.** In a sense, this is like the buffer in an indirect message because it gives you an opportunity to begin the conversation without immediately and bluntly telling the reader that his or her application has been rejected.
- **Convey the negative news politely and concisely.** The passive voice is helpful in this situation because it shifts focus away from the people involved and thereby depersonalizes the response. For example, "Your application was not among those selected for an interview" is less blunt than the active phrase "We have rejected your application."
- **Avoid explaining why an applicant was rejected or why other applicants were chosen instead.** Although it was once more common to offer such explanations, and some

Fitcher opens with a simple expression of appreciation for being considered, which acts as a mini-buffer for the bad news to come.

He closes on a positive note without apologizing or implying that the matter is open for discussion.

Dear Ms. DeCicco:

Thank you for considering Bradley & Jackson as a place to launch your career in accounting. After a careful review of all applications we received for this position, your application was not among those selected for an interview.

We appreciate your interest, and I encourage you to apply again if a compatible job opening is posted on our website in the future.

Best wishes for success in your career.

Sincerely,
Marvin R. Fitcher
HR Director
Bradley & Jackson

The opening conveys the bad news quickly, using the passive voice to depersonalize the decision.

He invites her to reapply for any positions that may appear in the future, while avoiding any promise of reviewing her current application again.

Figure 11.7 Effective Message Rejecting a Job Applicant
This message rejecting a job applicant takes care to avoid making or implying any promises about future opportunities, beyond inviting the person to apply for positions that may appear in the future. Note that this would not be appropriate if the company did not believe the applicant was a good fit for the company in general.

experts still advocate this approach, the simplest strategy from a legal standpoint is to avoid offering reasons for the decision. Avoiding explanations lowers the possibility that an applicant will perceive discrimination in the hiring decision or be tempted to challenge the reasons given.

- **Don't state or imply that the application will be reviewed at a later date.** Saying that "we will keep your résumé on file for future consideration" can create false hopes for the recipient and leave the company vulnerable to legal complaints if a future hiring decision is made without actually reviewing this candidate's application again. If the candidate might be a good fit for another position in the company in the future, you can suggest he or she reapply if a new job opening is posted.
- **Close with positive wishes for the applicant's career success.** A brief statement such as "We wish you success in your career" is sufficient.

Naturally, you should adjust your tactics to the circumstances. A simple and direct message is fine when someone has only submitted a job application, but rejecting a candidate who has made it at least partway through the interview process requires greater care. Personal contact has already been established through the interview process, so a phone call may be more appropriate.

GIVING NEGATIVE PERFORMANCE REVIEWS

Performance reviews are designed to clarify job requirements, give employees feedback on their performance relative to those requirements, and establish a personal plan of action to ensure continued performance in the future. Performance reviews also help companies set organizational standards and communicate organizational values.[18] In addition, they document evidence of performance in the event that disciplinary action is needed or an employee later disputes management decisions regarding pay or promotions.[19]

The worst possible outcome in an annual review is a negative surprise, such as when an employee has been working toward different goals than the manager expects or has been unknowingly underperforming throughout the year but didn't receive any feedback or improvement coaching along the way.[20]

To avoid negative surprises, managers should provide regular feedback and coaching as needed throughout the year if employee performance falls below expectations. In fact, some companies have gone so far as to abandon the traditional performance review altogether. The online retailer Zappos, for example, has replaced annual performance reviews with frequent status reports that give employees feedback on routine job tasks and an annual assessment of how well each employee embodies the company's core values.[21]

Regardless of the specific approach a company takes, writing an effective performance review requires careful, objective assessment and a clear statement of how well an employee has done relative to agreed-on goals. If you need to write a review that includes negative information, keep the following points in mind:[22]

- **Document performance problems.** You will need this information in order to write an effective appraisal and to support any decisions that need to be made about pay, promotions, or termination.
- **Evaluate all employees consistently.** Consistency is not only fair but also helps protect the company from claims of discriminatory practices.
- **Write in a calm, objective voice.** The employee is not likely to welcome your negative assessment, but you can manage the emotions of the situation by maintaining professional reserve in your writing.
- **Focus on opportunities for improvement.** This information can serve as the foundation for an improvement plan for the coming year.
- **Keep job descriptions up to date.** If a job evolves over time in response to changes in the business, the employees' current activities may no longer match an outdated job description.

An important goal of any performance evaluation is to give the employee a plan of action for improving his or her performance.

By giving employees clear goals and regular feedback, you can help avoid unpleasant surprises in a performance review.

Negative evaluations should provide careful documentation of performance concerns.

REAL-TIME UPDATES

LEARN MORE BY READING THIS ARTICLE

IBM crowdsources a replacement for its annual performance reviews

CEO Ginni Rometty explains why the company turned to its employees to create a better alternative to the traditional approach. Go to **real-timeupdates.com/bct14** and select Learn More in the Students section.

TERMINATING EMPLOYMENT

If an employee's performance cannot be brought up to company standards or if factors such as declining sales warrant a reduction in the workforce, a company often has no choice but to terminate employment. As with other negative employment messages, termination is fraught with emotions and legal ramifications, so careful planning, complete documentation, and sensitive writing are essential.

Termination messages should always be written with input from the company's legal staff, but here are general writing guidelines to bear in mind:[23]

- Clearly present the reasons for this difficult action, whether it is the employee's performance or a business decision unrelated to performance.
- Make sure the reasons are presented in a way that cannot be construed as unfair or discriminatory.
- Follow company policy, contractual requirements, and applicable laws to the letter.
- Avoid personal attacks or insults of any kind.
- Ask another manager to review the letter before issuing it. An objective reviewer who isn't directly involved might spot troublesome wording or faulty reasoning.
- Deliver the termination letter in person if at all possible. Arrange a meeting that will ensure privacy and freedom from interruptions.

Carefully word a termination message to avoid creating undue ill will and grounds for legal action.

Any unplanned termination is clearly a negative outcome for both employer and employee, but careful attention to content and tone in the termination message can help the employee move on gracefully and minimize the misunderstandings and anger that can lead to expensive lawsuits. To review the tasks involved in this type of message, see "Checklist: Writing Negative Employment Messages."

For the latest information on writing negative messages, visit **real-timeupdates.com/ bct14** and select Chapter 11.

CHECKLIST ✔ **Writing Negative Employment Messages**

A. Refusing requests for employee references and recommendations
- Don't feel obligated to write a recommendation letter if you don't feel comfortable doing so.
- Take a diplomatic approach to minimize hurt feelings.
- Compliment the reader's accomplishments.
- Suggest alternatives, if available.
- Use the options available to you on social networks, such as ignoring a request from someone you don't know or writing a recommendation on a single positive attribute.

B. Rejecting job applicants
- If possible, respond to all applications, even if you use only a form message to acknowledge receipt.
- If you use the direct approach, take care to avoid being blunt or cold.
- If you use the indirect approach, don't mislead the reader in your buffer or delay the bad news for more than a sentence or two.
- Avoid explaining why the applicant was rejected.
- Suggest alternatives, if possible.

C. Giving negative performance reviews
- Document performance problems throughout the year.
- Evaluate all employees consistently.
- Keep job descriptions up to date as employee responsibilities change.
- Maintain an objective and unbiased tone.
- Use nonjudgmental language.
- Focus on problem resolution.
- Make sure negative feedback is documented and shared with the employee.
- Don't avoid confrontations by withholding negative feedback.
- Ask the employee for a commitment to improve.

D. Terminating employment
- State your reasons accurately and make sure they are objectively verifiable.
- Avoid statements that might expose your company to a wrongful termination lawsuit.
- Consult company lawyers to clarify all terms of the separation.
- Deliver the letter in person if at all possible.
- End the relationship on terms as positive as possible.

COMMUNICATION CHALLENGES AT **Hailo**

As Hailo expands around the world, it faces the challenges every growing business faces. You recently joined the company as an app development manager in the New York office. Use what you've learned in this chapter to address the following challenges.

INDIVIDUAL CHALLENGE: Another manager stopped by this morning with a request to borrow two of your best programmers for a three-week emergency. Under normal conditions, you wouldn't hesitate to help, but your team has its own scheduling challenges to deal with. Plus, this isn't the first time this manager has run into trouble, and you suspect that poor project management is the reason. In one or two sentences, diplomatically state your refusal to help while suggesting that your colleague's management skills need to be improved.

TEAM CHALLENGE: You've found it easy to say yes to recommendation letter requests from former employees who were top performers, and you've learned to say no to those people who didn't perform so well. The requests you struggle with are from employees in the middle—people who didn't really excel but didn't really cause any trouble either. You've just received a request from a computer systems specialist who falls smack in the middle of the middle. Unfortunately, he's applying for a job at a firm that you know places high demands on its employees and generally hires the best of the best. He's a great person, and you'd love to help, but in your heart you know that if by some chance he does get the job, he probably won't last. Plus, you don't want to get a reputation in the industry for recommending weak candidates. With your team, brainstorm a sensitive but effective buffer that will help you set the stage for the negative news.

Quick Learning Guide

KEY TERMS

buffer A neutral opening statement in an indirect negative message that establishes common ground with the reader without revealing the main idea

crisis management plan Plan that defines operational procedures to deal with a crisis, including communication tasks and responsibilities

performance review Employee evaluation procedure giving feedback on performance and guidance for future efforts

whistle-blowing Efforts by employees to report concerns about unethical or illegal behavior

SUMMARY OF LEARNING OBJECTIVES

1 Apply the three-step writing process to negative messages. Because the way you convey negative information can be as damaging as the fact that you're conveying it, planning negative messages carefully is crucial. Make sure your purpose is specific, necessary, and appropriate for the medium you've chosen. Find out how your audience prefers to receive bad news. Collect all the facts necessary to support your negative decision, and adapt your tone to the situation as well as to your audience. Negative messages may be organized according to the direct or the indirect approach, and your choice depends on audience preference as well as on the situation. In addition, carefully choose positive words to construct diplomatic sentences. Finally, revision, design, and proofreading are necessary to ensure that you are saying exactly what you want to say in the best possible way and that careless errors don't aggravate an already emotional situation.

2 Explain how to effectively use the direct approach effectively when conveying negative news. The direct approach to negative messages puts the bad news up front, follows with the reasons (and perhaps offers an alternative), and closes with a respectful statement that is as positive as possible under the circumstances. Use the direct approach when you know your audience prefers receiving bad news up front or if the bad news will cause readers relatively little pain or disappointment. Otherwise, use the indirect approach. Even though it is direct, however, don't use the direct approach as a license to be rude or overly blunt.

3 Explain how to effectively use the indirect approach effectively when conveying negative news. The indirect approach for negative messages begins with a buffer (a neutral or positive statement to establish common ground with the reader), explains the reasons leading up to the decision or news, clearly states the negative news without unduly emphasizing it, and closes with a respectful statement. When using the indirect approach, you need to be careful to avoid obscuring the bad news or misleading your audience into thinking you're actually delivering good news. The key to avoiding both problems is remembering that the purpose of the indirect approach is to cushion the blow, not to avoid delivering it. When using a buffer, you must be sure it is neither deceptive nor insincere. To write an effective buffer, look for opportunities to express your appreciation for being considered, to assure your reader of your attention to the request, or to indicate your understanding of the reader's needs.

4 Explain the importance of maintaining high standards of ethics and etiquette when delivering negative messages. Ethics and etiquette are important in every message, of course, but they take on particular significance with negative messages for three reasons. First, the communicator often needs to adhere to a variety of laws and regulations when delivering negative messages. Second, good ethical practice demands care and sensitivity in the content and delivery of negative messages, as these messages can have a profoundly negative effect on the people who receive them. Third, communicators need to manage their own emotions when crafting and distributing negative messages while at the same time considering the emotional needs of their audiences.

5 Describe successful strategies for sending negative messages on routine business matters. When making negative announcements on routine business matters, the indirect approach is usually preferred, although the direct approach can work for minor issues. When rejecting suggestions and proposals, tailor the approach to the situation. An unsolicited proposal from an external source doesn't need as much of your attention as a solicited proposal from an internal source, for example. For refusing routine requests, the direct approach is usually sufficient, except when the matter at hand is significant, you or your company have an established relationship with the person making the request, or you're forced to decline a request that you might have said yes to in the past.

When conveying bad news about transactions, you need to modify the customer's expectations, explain how you plan to resolve the situation, and repair whatever damage might have been done to the business relationship. Whether you should apologize depends in part on the magnitude of the situation and whether you previously established specific expectations about the transaction.

When refusing a claim or a request for adjustment, the indirect approach is usually preferred because the other party is emotionally involved and expects you to respond positively. Demonstrate that you understand and have carefully considered the complaint, then rationally and calmly explain why you are refusing the request.

6 **List the important points to consider when conveying negative organizational news.** Public communications about various organization matters fall into two categories: those you can plan for (and therefore have more time to prepare messages) and crises that hit without warning. The first category includes a variety of announcements, from relatively minor matters such as price increases to major matters such as layoffs and bankruptcy proceedings. For these messages, be sure to match your approach to the situation, consider the unique needs of each audience group, give each audience enough time to react as needed, give yourself enough time to plan and manage a response, look for positive angles but don't exude false optimism, and seek expert advice on legal, financial, or technical matters if you're not sure how to proceed.

To respond successfully to rumors and negative information in a social media environment, first be sure you are engaged with important stakeholders before negative situations occur. Second, monitor the conversations taking place about your company and its products. Third, when you see negative messages, evaluate them before responding. Fourth, after evaluating negative messages, take the appropriate response based on an overall public relations plan. Some messages are better ignored, whereas others should be addressed immediately with corrective information.

The second category of negative organizational news involves communication during times of crisis. Preparation is key for successful crisis management. Although you can't anticipate the nature and circumstances of every possible crisis, you can prepare by deciding such issues as who is in charge of communications, where the press and the public can get information, and what will be said in likely emergency scenarios. A good crisis communication plan includes such items as email and phone lists for important media contacts, website templates for various emergency scenarios, and after-hours contact information for key personnel in the company.

7 **Describe successful strategies for sending negative employment-related messages.** The indirect approach is usually the better choice for negative employment messages because the recipient is always emotionally involved and the decisions are usually significant. When refusing requests from other employers for performance-related information about past employees, your message can be brief and direct. Simply provide whatever information your company allows to be shared in these situations. Refusing a recommendation request directly from a former employee feels much more personal for the recipient, however, so the indirect approach is better. Responding to requests on social networks is somewhat easier because you have the option of recommending just one particular aspect of a person's overall skill set, even if you can't make an unqualified, overall endorsement.

Messages rejecting job applicants raise a number of emotional and legal issues and therefore must be approached with great care. Experts vary in their advice about how much information to include in these messages. However, the safest strategy is a brief message that opens with an expression of appreciation for being considered (which functions like a buffer in an indirect message), continues with a statement to the effect that the applicant was not chosen for the position applied for, and closes courteously without providing reasons for the rejection or making promises about future consideration.

Negative performance reviews should take care to document the performance problems, be sure that all employees are being evaluated consistently, be written in a calm and objective voice, and focus on opportunities for improvement. Moreover, they must be written with reference to accurate, current job descriptions that provide the basis for measuring employee performance.

Termination messages are the most challenging employment messages of all. They should clearly present the reasons for the decision, present the reasons in a way that cannot be construed as unfair or discriminatory, follow company policy and any relevant legal guidelines, and avoid personal attacks or insults of any kind. Asking a manager not directly involved in the situation to review your message can help you avoid troublesome wording or faulty reasoning. Finally, try to deliver the written message in person if possible.

MyBCommLab®

Go to **mybcommlab.com** to complete the problems marked with this icon .

Test Your Knowledge

To review chapter content related to each question, refer to the indicated Learning Objective.

11-1. Why is it particularly important to select your medium and channel carefully and adapt your tone to your audience's needs and preferences when writing a negative message? [LO-1]

11-2. Under what circumstances should you avoid offering explanations in negative indirect messages? [LO-3]

11-3. What is the sequence of presentation in a negative message that is organized using the indirect approach? [LO-3]

11-4. What is a buffer, and what steps must you take to ensure that buffers you write are ethical? [LO-3]

11-5. What is whistle-blowing? [LO-4]

11-6. What steps can you take to minimize chances of being accused of defamation when refusing a claim or request for adjustment? [LO-5]

11-7. Why is it important to be engaged with stakeholders before trying to use social media during a crisis or other negative scenario? [LO-6]

11-8. What is a crisis management plan? [LO-6]

11-9. What are the five guidelines for giving negative performance reviews? [LO-7]

Apply Your Knowledge

To review chapter content related to each question, refer to the indicated Learning Objective.

11-10. Would you choose the direct or indirect approach to announce that a popular employee benefit is being eliminated for cost reasons? Why? [LO-1]

11-11. Can you express sympathy with someone's negative situation without apologizing for the circumstances? Explain your answer. [LO-2]

11-12. Is intentionally deemphasizing bad news the same as distorting graphs and charts to deemphasize unfavorable data? Why or why not? [LO-3]

11-13. Why is it important to be engaged with stakeholders before trying to use social media during a crisis or other negative scenario? [LO-6]

11-14. If your social media monitoring efforts pick up a tweet that accuses your customer service staff of lying and claims to have evidence to back it up, how would you respond? [LO-6]

11-15. How would you respond to a LinkedIn network connection who asks for a recommendation when you barely remember working with this person and don't remember whether she was good at her job? [LO-7]

Practice Your Skills

Messages for Analysis

Read the following messages, then (1) analyze the strengths and weaknesses of each sentence and (2) revise each message so that it follows this chapter's guidelines.

11-16. Message 11.A: Sending Negative Organizational News [LO-6]

From: M. Juhasz, Travel & Meeting Services
To: [mailing list]
Subject: Travel

Dear Traveling Executives:
We need you to start using some of the budget suggestions we are going to issue as a separate memorandum. These include using videoconference equipment and web conferencing instead of traveling to meetings, staying in cheaper hotels, arranging flights for cheaper times, and flying from less-convenient but also less-expensive suburban airports.

The company needs to cut travel expenses by fifty percent, just as we've cut costs in all departments of Black & Decker. This means you'll no longer be able to stay in fancy hotels and make last-minute, costly changes to your travel plans.

You'll also be expected to avoid hotel surcharges for phone calls and Internet access. If the hotel you want to stay in doesn't offer free wireless, go somewhere else. And never, NEVER return a rental car with an empty tank! That causes the rental agency to charge us a premium price for the gas they sell when they fill it up upon your return.

You'll be expected to make these changes in your travel habits immediately.

Sincerely,
M. Juhasz
Travel & Meeting Services

11-17. Message 11.B: Refusing Requests for Claims and Adjustments [LO-5]

I am responding to your letter of about six weeks ago asking for an adjustment on your wireless hub, model WM39Z. We test all our products before they leave the factory; therefore, it could not have been our fault that your hub didn't work.

If you or someone in your office dropped the unit, it might have caused the damage. Or the damage could have been caused by the shipper if he dropped it. If so, you should file a claim with the shipper. At any rate, it wasn't our fault. The parts are already covered by warranty. However, we will provide labor for the repairs for $50, which is less than our cost, since you are a valued customer.

We will have a booth at the upcoming trade show there and hope to see you or someone from your office. We have many new models of hubs, routers, and other computer gear that we're sure you'll want to see. I've enclosed our latest catalog. Hope to see you there.

11-18. Message 11.C: Rejecting Job Applications [LO-7]

I regret to inform you that you were not selected for our summer intern program at Equifax. We had over a thousand résumés and cover letters to go through and simply could not get to them all. We have been asked to notify everyone that we have already selected students for the 25 positions based on those who applied early and were qualified.

We're sure you will be able to find a suitable position for summer work in your field and wish you the best of luck. We deeply regret any inconvenience associated with our reply.

Exercises

Each activity is labeled according to the primary skill or skills you will need to use. To review relevant chapter content, you can refer to the indicated Learning Objective.

Planning: Choosing the Direct or Indirect Approach [LO-1] Select which approach you would use (direct or indirect) for the following negative messages.

11-19. An email message to your boss, informing her that one of your key clients is taking its business to a different accounting firm

11-20. An email message to a customer, informing her that one of the books she ordered over the Internet is temporarily out of stock

11-21. An instant message to a customer, explaining that the DVD recorder he ordered for his new computer is on backorder and that, as a consequence, the shipping of the entire order will be delayed

11-22. A blog post to all employees, notifying them that the company parking lot will be repaved during the first week of June and that the company will provide a shuttle service from a remote parking lot during that period

11-23. A letter from a travel agent to a customer, stating that the airline will not refund her money for the flight she missed but that her tickets are valid for one year

11-24. A form letter from a U.S. airline to a customer, explaining that the company cannot extend the expiration date of the customer's frequent flyer miles even though the customer was living overseas for the past three years and unable to use the miles during that time

11-25. A letter from an insurance company to a policyholder, denying a claim for reimbursement for a special medical procedure that is not covered under the terms of the customer's policy

11-26. A letter from an electronics store, stating that the customer will not be reimbursed for a malfunctioning mobile phone that is still under warranty (because the terms of the warranty do not cover damages to phones that were accidentally dropped from a moving car)

11-27. An announcement to the repairs department, listing parts that are on backorder and will be three weeks late

11-28. **Message Strategies: Refusing Routine Requests [LO-4]** As a customer service supervisor for a mobile phone company, you're in charge of responding to customers' requests for refunds. You've just received an email from a customer who unwittingly ran up a $550 bill for data charges after forgetting to disable his smartphone's Wi-Fi hotspot feature. The customer says it wasn't his fault because he didn't know his roommates were using his phone to get free Internet access. However, you've dealt with this situation before and provided a notice to all customers to be careful about excess data charges resulting from the use of the hotspot capability. Draft a short buffer (one or two sentences) for your email reply, sympathizing with the customer's plight but preparing him for the bad news (that company policy specifically prohibits refunds in such cases).

Etiquette: Communicating with Sensitivity and Tact; Collaboration: Team Projects [LO-4] Working alone, revise the following statements to deemphasize the bad news. Then team up with a classmate and read each other's revisions. Did you both use the same approach in every case? Which approach seems to be most effective for each of the revised statements?

11-29. The airline can't refund your money. The "Conditions" section on the back of your ticket states that there are no refunds for missed flights. Sometimes the airline makes exceptions, but only when life and death are involved. Of course, your ticket is still valid and can be used on a flight to the same destination.

11-30. I'm sorry to tell you, we can't supply the custom decorations you requested. We called every supplier, and none of them can do what you want on such short notice. You can, however, get a standard decorative package on the same theme in time. I found a supplier that stocks these. Of course, it won't have quite the flair you originally requested.

11-31. We can't refund your money for the malfunctioning MP3 player. You shouldn't have immersed the unit in water while swimming; the users' manual clearly states that the unit is not designed to be used in adverse environments.

11-32. **Communication Ethics [LO-4]** The insurance company where you work is planning to raise all premiums for health-care coverage. Your boss has asked you to read a draft of her letter to customers announcing the new, higher rates. The first two paragraphs discuss some exciting medical advances and the expanded coverage offered by your company. Only in the final paragraph do customers learn that they will have to pay more for coverage starting next year. What are the ethical implications of this draft? What changes would you suggest?

11-33. **Sending Negative Organizational News [LO-6]** Public companies occasionally need to issue news releases to announce or explain downturns in sales, profits, demand, or other business factors. Search the web to locate a company that has issued a press release that recently reported lower earnings or other bad news and access the news release on the firm's website. You can also search for press releases at **www.prnewswire.com** or **www.businesswire .com**. How does the headline relate to the main message of the release? Is the release organized according to the direct or the indirect approach? What does the company do to present the bad news in a favorable light—and does this effort seem sincere and ethical to you?

Expand Your Skills

Critique the Professionals

Locate an example online of a negative-news message from any company. Possible examples include announcements of product recalls, poor financial results, layoffs, and fines or other legal troubles. Analyze the approach the company took; was it the most effective strategy possible? Did the company apologize, if doing so would have been appropriate under the circumstances, and does the apology seem sincere? Does the tone of the message match the seriousness of the situation? Does the message end on a positive note, if appropriate? Using whatever medium your instructor requests, write a brief analysis of the message (no more than one page), citing specific elements from the piece and support from the chapter.

Sharpening Your Career Skills Online

Bovée and Thill's Business Communication Web Search, at websearch.businesscommunicationnetwork.com, is a unique research tool designed specifically for business communication research. Use the Web Search function to find a website, video, article, podcast, or presentation that offers advice on writing messages that convey negative information. Write a brief email message to your instructor, describing the item you found and summarizing the career skills information you learned from it.

Cases

For all cases, feel free to use your creativity to make up any details you need in order to craft effective messages.

Negative Messages on Routine Business Matters

EMAIL SKILLS

11-34. Message Strategies: Rejecting Suggestions and Proposals; Communication Ethics: Making Ethical Choices [LO-5] Knowing how much online product reviews can shape consumer behavior, the other cofounder of your company has just circulated an internal email message with the not-so-subtle hint that everyone in your small start-up should pose as happy customers and post glowing reviews of your new product on Amazon and other shopping sites. You're horrified at the idea—not only is this highly unethical, but if (or more likely when) the scheme is exposed, the company's reputation will be severely damaged.

Your task: You would prefer to address this in a private conversation, but because your partner has already pitched the idea to everyone via email, you have no choice but to respond via email as well. You need to act quickly before anyone acts on the suggestion. Write a response explaining why this is a bad idea and telling employees not to do it. Keep in mind that you are chastising your business partner in front of all your employees. Make up any names or other details you need.

MICROBLOGGING SKILLS

11-35. Message Strategies: Making Routine Negative Announcements [LO-5] Professional musicians do everything they can to keep the show going, particularly for tours that are scheduled months in advance. However, illness and other unforeseeable circumstances can force an act to cancel shows, even after all the tickets have been sold.

Your task: Choose one of your favorite musical acts and assume that you are the tour manager who needs to tell 25,000 fans that an upcoming concert must be canceled because of illness. Ticket holders can apply for a refund at the artist's website or keep their tickets for a future concert date, which will be identified and announced as soon as possible. Write two tweets, one announcing the cancelation and one outlining the options for ticket holders. Make up any information you need, and send your tweets to your instructor via email (don't actually tweet them!).

EMAIL SKILLS

11-36. Message Strategies: Rejecting Suggestions and Proposals [LO-5] Imagine that you are the president of a student club or some other campus group that is unaffiliated with any larger national or international organization. (It can be any type of organization—recreational, charitable, academic, cultural, professional, or social—but try to use a real organization, even if you aren't a member.) You've just received a message from someone who is the president of a similar club in another college or university, proposing to form a national organizational structure. Her proposal has some appealing aspects, including unified branding and recruiting, the opportunity to share best practices, and the chance to socialize with and learn from like-minded students across the country. However, after talking it over with some of your members, you decide it's not right for you. You believe that the time, trouble, and costs of being part of a national organization would outweigh the benefits it could offer.

Your task: Draft an email response politely declining the offer.

EMAIL SKILLS

11-37. Message Strategies: Rejecting Suggestions and Proposals [LO-5] Walter Joss is one of the best employees in your department, a smart and hard worker with a keen mind for business. His upbeat attitude has helped the entire department get through some recent rough times, and on a personal level, his wise counsel helped you grow into a leadership role when you were promoted to marketing manager several years ago.

You generally welcome Joss's input on the department's operations, and you have implemented several of his ideas to improve the company's marketing efforts. However, the proposal he emailed you yesterday was not his best work, to put it mildly. He proposed that the company dump the advertising agency it has used for a decade and replace it with some new agency you've never heard of. The only reasons he offered were that the agency "had become unresponsive" and that a "smaller agency could meet our needs better." He failed to address any of the other criteria that are used to select advertising agencies, such as costs, creative skills, technical abilities, geographic reach, research capabilities, and media experience.

This is the first you've heard any criticism of the agency, and in fact, their work has helped your company increase sales every year.

Your task: Draft an email message to Joss, rejecting his proposal. (Note that in a real-life setting, you would want to discuss this with Joss in person, rather than through email, but use email for the purposes of this exercise.)

EMAIL SKILLS

11-38. Message Strategies: Making Routine Negative Announcements [LO-5] You've been proud of many things your gardening tool company has accomplished as it grew from just you working in your basement shop to a nationally known company that employs more than 200 people. However, nothing made you prouder than the company's Helping Our Hometown Grow program, in which employees volunteer on company time to help residents in your city start their own vegetable gardens, using tools donated by the company. Nearly 50 employees participated directly, helping some 500 families supplement their grocery budgets with home-grown produce. Virtually everyone in the company contributed, though, because employees who didn't volunteer to help in the gardens pitched in to cover the work responsibilities of the volunteers.

Sadly, 10 years after you launched the program, you have reached the inescapable conclusion that the company can no longer afford to keep the program going. With consumers around the country still struggling with the aftereffects of a deep recession, sales have been dropping for the past three years—even as lower-cost competitors step up their presence in the market. To save the program, you would have to lay off several employees, but your employees come first.

Your task: Write an email to the entire company, announcing the cancellation of the program.

TELEPHONE SKILLS

11-39. Message Strategies: Making Routine Negative Announcements [LO-5] Vail Products of Toledo, Ohio, manufactured a line of beds for use in hospitals and other institutions that have a need to protect patients who might otherwise fall out of bed and injure themselves (including patients with cognitive impairments or patterns of spasms or seizures). These "enclosed bed systems" use a netted canopy to keep patients in bed rather than the traditional method of using physical restraints such as straps or tranquilizing drugs. The intent is humane, but the design is flawed: At least 30 patients have become trapped in the various parts of the mattress and canopy structure, and 8 of them have suffocated.

Working with the U.S. Food and Drug Administration, Vail issued a recall on the beds, as manufacturers often do in the case of unsafe products. However, the recall is not really a recall. Vail will not be replacing or modifying the beds, nor will it accept returns. Instead, the company is urging institutions to move patients to other beds, if possible. Vail has also sent out revised manuals and warning labels to be placed on the beds. The company also announced that it is ceasing production of enclosed beds.

Your task: A flurry of phone calls from concerned patients, family members, and institutional staff is overwhelming the support staff. As a writer in Vail's corporate communications office, you've been asked to draft a short script to be recorded on the company's phone system. When people call the main number, they'll hear "Press 1 for information regarding the recall of Model 500, Model 1000, and Model 2000 enclosed beds." After they press 1, they'll hear the message you're about to write, explaining that although the action is classified as a recall, Vail will not be accepting returned beds, nor will it replace any of the affected beds. The message should also assure customers that Vail has already sent revised operating manuals and warning labels to every registered owner of the beds in question. The phone system has limited memory, and you've been directed to keep the message to 75 words or less.[24]

MICROBLOGGING SKILLS

11-40. Message Strategies: Making Routine Negative Announcements [LO-5] JetBlue was one of the first companies to incorporate the Twitter microblogging service into its customer communications, and thousands of fliers and fans now follow the airline's tweeting staff members. Messages include announcements about fare sales, celebrations of company milestones, schedule updates, and even personalized responses to people who tweet with questions or complaints about the company.[25]

Your task: Write a tweet alerting JetBlue customers to the possibility that Hurricane Isaac might disrupt flight schedules from August 13 through August 15. Tell them that decisions about delays and cancellations will be made on a city-by-city basis and will be announced on Twitter and the company's website.

BLOGGING SKILLS

11-41. Message Strategies: Making Routine Negative Announcements [LO-5] Marketing specialists usually celebrate when target audiences forward their messages to friends and family—essentially acting as unpaid advertising and sales representatives. In fact, the practice of viral marketing is based on this hope. For one Starbucks regional office, however, viral marketing started to make the company just a bit sick. The office sent employees in the Southeast an email coupon for a free iced drink and invited them to share the coupon with family and friends. To the surprise of virtually no one who understands the nature of online life, the email coupon multiplied rapidly, to the point that Starbucks stores all around the country were quickly overwhelmed with requests for free drinks. The company decided to immediately terminate the free offer, a month ahead of the expiration date on the coupon.[26]

Your task: Write a one-paragraph message that can be posted on the Starbucks website and at individual stores, apologizing for the mix-up and explaining that the offer is no longer valid.

EMAIL SKILLS

11-42. Message Strategies: Refusing Claims and Requests for Adjustment [LO-5] Your company markets a line of rugged smartphone cases designed to protect the sensitive devices from drops, spills, and other common accidents. Your guarantee states that you will reimburse customers for the cost of a new phone if the case fails to protect it from any of the following: (a) a drop of no more than 6 feet onto any surface; (b) spills of any beverage or common household chemical; (c) being crushed by any object weighing up to 100 pounds; or (d) being chewed on by dogs, cats, or other common household pets.

Jack Simmons, a rancher from Wyoming, emailed your customer support staff, requesting a reimbursement after he dropped his iPhone in his hog barn and a 900-pound boar crushed it in a single bite.

Your task: Write an email response to the customer, denying his request for a new phone.

PODCASTING SKILLS

11-43. Message Strategies: Negative Announcements on Routine Matters [LO-5] An employee concierge seemed like a great idea when you added it as an employee benefit last year. The concierge handles a wide variety of personal chores for employees, everything from dropping off dry cleaning to ordering event tickets to sending flowers. Employees love the service, and you know that the time they save can be devoted to work or family activities. Unfortunately, profits are way down and concierge usage is up—up so far that you'll need to add a second concierge to keep up with the demand. As painful as it will be for everyone, you decide that the company needs to stop offering the service.

Your task: Script a brief podcast announcing the decision and explaining why it is necessary. Make up any details you need. If your instructor asks you to do so, record your podcast and submit the file.

EMAIL SKILLS/PORTFOLIO BUILDER

11-44. Message Strategies: Negative Announcements on Routine Matters [LO-5] You can certainly sympathize with employees when they complain about having their email and instant messages monitored, but you're implementing a company policy that all employees agree to abide by when they join the company. Your firm, Webcor Builders of San Francisco, California, is one of the estimated 60 percent of U.S. companies with such monitoring systems in place. More and more companies use these systems (which typically operate by scanning messages for keywords that suggest confidential, illegal, or otherwise inappropriate content) in an attempt to avoid instances of sexual harassment and other problems.

As the chief information officer, the manager in charge of computer systems in the company, you're often the target when employees complain about being monitored. Consequently, you know you're really going to hear it when employees learn that the monitoring program will be expanded to personal blogs as well.

Your task: Write an email message to be distributed to the entire workforce, explaining that the automated monitoring program is about to be expanded to include employees' personal blogs. Explain that, while you sympathize with employee concerns regarding privacy and freedom of speech, it is the management team's responsibility to protect the company's intellectual property and the value of the company name. Therefore employees' personal blogs will be added to the monitoring system to ensure that employees don't intentionally or accidentally expose company secrets or criticize management in a way that could harm the company.[27]

SOCIAL NETWORKING SKILLS

11-45. Message Strategies: Rejecting Suggestions and Proposals [LO-5] All companies love *product enthusiasts*, those customers who are such fans that their activities help the company market its products and support its customers. Enthusiasts of a particular company or product often join *owners groups* or *user groups* to network, share ideas, and support one another.

These groups can be sponsored by the company or entirely independent. Social media are a natural forum for product enthusiasts as they meet online to share tips, tricks, rumors about upcoming products, and the pros and cons of various products, as well as provide feedback to the companies that make the products they use and enjoy.

Imagine you're on the social media team for Android, the operating system made by Google that is used in more than a billion mobile devices. With nearly 2 billion likes, the Android Facebook page is a popular online destination for Android smartphone and tablet users. After posting an item about some new software features, you get a comment from Shauna Roberts, who has commented on hundreds of posts over the past few years. She is definitely an Android enthusiast and has helped many other users with technical support issues—and helped the Android team with a number of great product suggestions.

Today she has a proposal for you: She wants Google to start paying the top commenters on the Android Facebook page, in return for the work they do to help both customers and the company. Her argument is that Google benefits from the enthusiasts' time and expertise, so it would be fair to offer some modest compensation in return.

Your task: Draft a response that you could post on the company's Facebook page in response to this proposal. The idea has come up before, and the company's response has always been that paying enthusiasts for social media activity, even if it helps the company through word-of-mouth marketing and lower support costs, would be too difficult to manage. First, judging the relative value of thousands of comments would be next to impossible. Second, quantity doesn't necessarily mean quality when it comes to sharing technical information. And third, the administrative and contractual overhead needed to make these work-for-hire relationships legal and legitimate would be overwhelming.[28]

LETTER-WRITING SKILLS

11-46. Message Strategies: Negative Announcements on Routine Matters [LO-5] Your company, PolicyPlan Insurance Services, is a 120-employee insurance claims processor based in Milwaukee. PolicyPlan has engaged Midwest Sparkleen for interior and exterior cleaning for the past five years. Midwest Sparkleen did exemplary work for the first four years, but after a change of ownership last year, the level of service has plummeted. Offices are no longer cleaned thoroughly, you've had to call the company at least six times to remind them to take care of spills and other messes they're supposed to address routinely, and they've left toxic cleaning chemicals in a public hallway on several occasions. You have spoken with the owner about your concerns twice in the past three months, but his assurances that service would improve have not resulted in any noticeable improvements. When the evening cleaning crew forgot to lock the lobby door last Thursday—leaving your entire facility vulnerable to theft from midnight until 8:00 Friday morning—you decided it was time for a change.

Your task: Write a letter to Jason Allred, owner of Midwest Sparkleen, 4000 South Howell Avenue, Milwaukee, WI, 53207, telling him that PolicyPlan will not be renewing its annual cleaning contract with Midwest Sparkleen when the current contract expires at the end of this month. Cite the examples identified above, and keep the tone of your letter professional.

LETTER-WRITING SKILLS

11-47. Message Strategies: Negative Announcements on Routine Matters [LO-5]   You enjoy helping other people learn, and your part-time work as a tutor for high school students has brought in some much-needed income during the past two years. You pride yourself on giving everything you can to help every one of your clients, but you've reached the end of the line with Drew Whitechapel. You know he has the ability, but he refuses to take tutoring seriously and continues to get failing grades in his American History class. You know he isn't getting much value from your tutoring, and you would rather devote your time and energy to a more serious student.

Your task: Write a letter to Drew's parents, explaining that you will no longer be able to tutor him after this month. (They've already paid you for this month's sessions.)

Negative Organizational News

MICROBLOGGING SKILLS

11-48. Message Strategies: Responding to Rumors [LO-6] Sheila Elliot, a well-known actress, appeared on a national talk show last night and claimed that your company's Smoothstone cookware was responsible for her toddler's learning disability. Elliot claimed that the nonstick surfaces of Smoothstone pots and pans contain a dangerous chemical that affected her child's cognitive development. There's just one problem with her story—well, three problems, actually: (a) your company's cookware line is called Moonstone, not Smoothstone; (b) Moonstone does not contain and never has contained the chemical Elliot mentioned; and (c) the product she is really thinking of was called Smoothfire, which was made by another company and was pulled off the market five years ago.

Thousands of worried parents aren't waiting for the fact checkers, however. They took to the blogosphere and Twitter-sphere with a vengeance overnight, warning people to throw away anything made by your company (Tatum Housewares). Several television stations have already picked up the Twitter chatter and repeated the rumor. Retailers are already calling your sales staff to cancel orders.

Your task: Write a three-message sequence to be posted on your company's Twitter account, correcting the rumor and conveying the three points outlined above.

BLOGGING SKILLS

11-49. Message Strategies: Negative Organizational Announcements [LO-6]   XtremityPlus is known for its outlandish extreme-sports products, and the Looney Launch is no exception. Fulfilling the dream of every childhood daredevil, the Looney Launch is an aluminum and fiberglass contraption that quickly unfolds to create the ultimate bicycle jump. The product has been

selling as fast as you can make it, even though it comes plastered with warning labels proclaiming that its use is inherently dangerous.

As XtremityPlus's CEO, you were nervous about introducing this product, and your fears were just confirmed: You've been notified of the first lawsuit by a parent whose child broke several bones after crash-landing off a Looney Launch.

Your task: Write a post for your internal blog, explaining that the Looney Launch is being removed from the market immediately. Tell your employees to expect some negative reactions from enthusiastic customers and retailers, but explain that (a) the company can't afford the risk of additional lawsuits, and (b) even for XtremityPlus, the Looney Launch pushes the envelope a bit too far. The product is simply too dangerous to sell in good conscience.

BLOGGING SKILLS/PORTFOLIO BUILDER

11-50. Message Strategies: Communicating in a Crisis [LO-6]   One of your company's worst nightmares has just come true. EQ Industrial Services (EQIS), based in Wayne, Michigan, operates a number of facilities around the country that dispose of, recycle, and transport hazardous chemical wastes. Last night, explosions and fires broke out at the company's Apex, North Carolina, facility, forcing the evacuation of 17,000 local residents.

Your task: It's now Friday, the day after the fire. Write a brief post for the company's blog, covering the following points:

- A fire broke out at the Apex facility at approximately 10 P.M. Thursday.
- No one was in the facility at the time.
- Because of the diverse nature of the materials stored at the plant, the cause of the fire is not yet known.
- Rumors that the facility stores extremely dangerous chlorine gas and that the fire was spreading to other nearby businesses are not true.
- Special industrial firefighters hired by EQIS have already brought the fire under control.
- Residents in the immediate area were evacuated as a precaution, and they should be able to return to their homes tomorrow, pending permission from local authorities.
- Several dozen residents were admitted to local hospitals with complaints of breathing problems, but most have been released already; about a dozen emergency responders were treated as well.
- At this point (Friday afternoon), tests conducted by the North Carolina State Department of Environment and Natural Resources "had not detected anything out of the ordinary in the air."

Conclude by thanking the local police and fire departments for their assistance and directing readers to EQIS's toll-free hot line for more information.[29]

BLOGGING SKILLS

11-51. Message Strategies: Responding to Rumors and Public Criticism [LO-6]   Spreading *FUD*—fear, uncertainty, and doubt—about other companies is one of the less-honorable ways of dealing with competition in the business world. For example, someone can start a "whisper campaign" in the marketplace, raising fears that a particular company is struggling financially. Customers who don't want to risk future instability in their supply chains might then shift their purchasing away from the company, based on nothing more than the false rumor.

Your task: Find the website of any company that seems interesting. Imagine you are the CEO and the company is the subject of an online rumor about impending bankruptcy. Explore the website to get a basic feel for what the company does. Making up any information you need, write a post for the company's blog, explaining that the bankruptcy rumors are false and that the company is on solid financial ground and plans to keep serving the industry for many years to come. (Be sure to review page 309 for tips.)

SOCIAL NETWORKING SKILLS

11-52. Message Strategies: Responding to Rumors and Public Criticism [LO-6] The consumer reviews on Yelp can be a promotional boon to any local business—provided the reviews are positive, of course. Negative reviews, fair or not, can affect a company's reputation and drive away potential customers. Fortunately for business owners, sites like Yelp give them the means to respond to reviews, whether they want to apologize for poor service, offer some form of compensation, or correct misinformation in a review.

Your task: Search Yelp for a negative review (one or two stars) on any business in any city. Find a review that has some substance to it, not just a simple, angry rant. Now imagine you are the owner of that business, and write a reply that could be posted via the "Add Owner Comment" feature. Use information you find on Yelp about the company and fill in any details by using your imagination. Remember that your comment will be visible to everyone who visits Yelp. (Be sure to review page 309 for tips.)

Negative Employment Messages

SOCIAL NETWORKING SKILLS/EMAIL SKILLS

11-53. Message Strategies: Refusing Requests for Recommendations [LO-7] You're delighted to get a message from an old friend and colleague, Heather Lang. You're delighted right up to the moment you read her request that you write a recommendation about her web design and programming skills for your LinkedIn profile. You would do just about anything for Lang—anything except recommend her web design skills. She is a master programmer whose technical wizardry saved more client projects than you can count, but when it comes to artistic design, Lang simply doesn't have "it." From gaudy color schemes to unreadable type treatment to confusing layouts, her design sense is as weak as her technical acumen is strong.

Your task: First, write a brief email to Lang, explaining that you would be most comfortable highlighting her technical skills

because that is where you believe her true strengths lie. Second, write a two-sentence recommendation that you could include in your LinkedIn profile, recommending Lang's technical skills. Make up or research any details you need.

TELEPHONE SKILLS

11-54. Message Strategies: Terminating Employment [LO-7] As the human resources manager at Alion Science and Technology, a military research firm in McLean, Virginia, you were thrilled when one of the nation's top computer visualization specialists accepted your job offer. Claus Gunnstein's skills would have made a major contribution to Alion's work in designing flight simulators and other systems. Unfortunately, the day after he accepted the offer, Alion received news that a major Pentagon contract had been canceled. In addition to letting several dozen current employees know that the company will be forced to lay them off, you need to tell Gunnstein that Alion has no choice but to rescind the job offer.

Your task: Outline the points you'll need to make in a telephone call to Gunnstein. Pay special attention to your opening and closing statements. (You'll review your plans for the phone call with Alion's legal staff to make sure everything you say follows employment law guidelines; for now, just focus on the way you'll present the negative news to Gunnstein. Feel free to make up any details you need.)[30]

EMAIL SKILLS

11-55. Message Strategies: Refusing Requests for Recommendations [LO-5] Well, this is awkward. Daniel Sturgis, who quit last year just as you were planning to fire him for consistently failing to meet agreed-on performance targets, has just emailed you from his new job, asking for a recommendation. He says his new job is awful and he regrets leaving your company. He knows you don't have any openings, but he would be grateful for a recommendation.

Your task: Write an email message to Sturgis, explaining that you will not be able to write him a recommendation. Make up any details you need.

MESSAGING SKILLS/MOBILE SKILLS

11-56. Message Strategies: Refusing Requests for Recommendations [LO-7] Your classmates could end up being important business contacts as you all progress through your careers. Of course, this also means you might be asked for favors that you're not comfortable giving, such as providing recommendations for someone whose skills or other attributes you don't admire. Choose a person who was in a course you recently took and imagine that a few years after graduation he or she texts you with a request for a job recommendation letter. You've kept in touch socially, at least online, and would like to continue to do so, but your memory of this person's professional potential is more negative than positive. (Make up any combination of negative traits, such as failing to contribute to team projects, giving up quickly in the face of adversity, struggling to understand basic concepts, or other limitations.)

Your task: You've decided to decline the request, so now you must figure out how to phrase your response. Draft a response that you could send in this scenario, making up any information you need. Don't use the person's real name and don't include any information that your instructor or anyone else could use to identify the person, but imagine that you are in fact writing to this individual. You're on a compatible mobile service that doesn't limit the length of text messages, but remember that your message will be read on a small mobile screen. Email your response to your instructor.

MEMO-WRITING SKILLS/PORTFOLIO BUILDER

11-57. Message Strategies: Negative Performance Reviews [LO-7] Elaine Bridgewater, the former professional golfer you hired to oversee your golf equipment company's relationship with retailers, knows the business inside and out. As a former touring pro, she has unmatched credibility. She also has seemingly boundless energy, solid technical knowledge, and an engaging personal style. Unfortunately, she hasn't been quite as attentive as she needs to be when it comes to communicating with retailers. You've been getting complaints about voicemail messages gone unanswered for days, confusing emails that require two or three rounds of clarification, and reports that are haphazardly thrown together. As valuable as Bridgewater's other skills are, she's going to cost the company sales if this goes on much longer. The retail channel is vital to your company's survival, and she's the employee most involved in this channel.

Your task: Draft a brief (one page maximum) informal performance appraisal and improvement plan for Bridgewater. Be sure to compliment her on the areas in which she excels but don't shy away from highlighting the areas in which she needs to improve, too: punctual response to customer messages; clear writing; and careful revision, production, and proofreading. Use what you've learned in this course so far to supply any additional advice about the importance of these skills.

MyBCommLab

Go to **mybcommlab.com** for Auto-graded writing questions as well as the following Assisted-graded writing questions:

11-58. What are three techniques for deemphasizing negative news? [LO-3]

11-59. Why should a company view employee whistle-blowing as a positive information resource, even if it subjects the company to potential legal trouble? [LO-4]

Endnotes

1. Hailo website, accessed 13 April 2016, www.hailoapp.com; email from Hailo dated 29 October 2013; Natasha Lomas, "Hailo Ups Its Minimum Fare in London to £10, Triggers Licensing Complaints," 31 October 2013, TechCrunch, techcrunch.com.
2. Maurice E. Schweitzer, Alison Wood Brooks, and Adam D. Galinsky, "The Organizational Apology," *Harvard Business Review*, September 2015, hbr.org; Adrienne Carter and Amy Borrus, "What if Companies Fessed Up?" *BusinessWeek*, 24 January 2005, 59–60; Patrick J. Kiger, "The Art of the Apology," *Workforce Management*, October 2004, 57–62.
3. Schweitzer, Brooks, and Galinsky, "The Organizational Apology."
4. John Guiniven, "Sorry! An Apology as a Strategic PR Tool," *Public Relations Tactics*, December 2007, 6.
5. Quinn Warnick, "A Close Textual Analysis of Corporate Layoff Memos," *Business Communication Quarterly*, September 2010, 322–326.
6. "Advice from the Pros on the Best Way to Deliver Bad News," report on *Customer Relationship Management*, 1 February 2003, www.elibrary.com.
7. Ben Levisohn, "Getting More Workers to Whistle," *Business-Week*, 28 January 2008, 18.
8. "Less Than Half of Privately Held Businesses Support Whistle-blowing," Grant Thornton website, accessed 13 October 2008, www.internationalbusinessreport.com.
9. Steve Karnowski, "New Food Safety Law Protects Whistleblowers," *Bloomberg Businessweek*, 11 February 2011, www.businessweek.com.
10. Christopher Elliott, "7 Ways Smart Companies Tell Customers 'No,'" *CBS Money Watch*, 7 June 2011, www.cbsnews.com.
11. Micah Solomon, "Mean Tweets: Managing Customer Complaints," CNBC, 22 February 2012, www.cnbc.com; "When Fans Attack: How to Defend a Brand's Reputation Online," Crenshaw Communications blog, 20 May 2010, crenshawcomm.com; Leslie Gaines-Ross, "Reputation Warfare," *Harvard Business Review*, December 2010, 70–76; David Meerman Scott, "The US Air Force: Armed with Social Media," WebInkNow blog, 15 December 2008, www.webinknow.com; Matt Rhodes, "How to React If Somebody Writes About Your Brand Online," FreshNetworks blog, 9 January 2009, www.freshnetworks.com; Matt Rhodes, "Social Media as a Crisis Management Tool," Social Media Today blog, 21 December 2009, www.socialmediatoday.com.
12. Courtland L. Bovée, John V. Thill, George P. Dovel, and Marian Burk Wood, *Advertising Excellence* (New York: McGraw-Hill, 1995), 508–509; John Holusha, "Exxon's Public-Relations Problem," *New York Times*, 12 April 1989, D1.
13. Omowale Casselle, "Really, You Want ME to Write YOU a LinkedIn Recommendation," RecruitingBlogs, 22 April 2010, www.recruitingblogs.com.
14. "LinkedIn Profiles to Career Introductions: When You Can't Recommend Your Friend," *Seattle Post-Intelligencer* Personal Finance blog, 16 November 2010, blog.seattlepi.com.
15. Neal Schaffer, "How Should I Deal with a LinkedIn Recommendation Request I Don't Want to Give?" Social Web School, 20 January 2010, humancapitalleague.com.

16. Dawn Wolf, "Job Applicant Rejection Letter Dos and Donts—Writing an Appropriate 'Dear John' Letter to an Unsuccessful Applicant," 31 May 2009, Employment Blawg.com, www.employmentblawg.com.

17. Wolf, "Job Applicant Rejection Letter Dos and Donts"; "Prohibited Employment Policies/Practices," U.S. Equal Employment Opportunity Commission, accessed 14 July 2010, www.eeoc.gov; Susan M. Heathfield, "Candidate Rejection Letter," About.com, accessed 14 July 2010, humanresources.about.com; "Rejection Letters Under Scrutiny: 7 Do's & Don'ts," *Business Management Daily*, 1 April 2009, www.businessmanagementdaily.com.

18. Judi Brownell, "The Performance Appraisal Interviews: A Multipurpose Communication Assignment," *Bulletin of the Association for Business Communication* 57, no. 2 (1994): 11–21.

19. Susan Friedfel, "Protecting Yourself in the Performance Review Process," *Workforce Management*, April 2009, www.workforce.com.

20. Kelly Spors, "Why Performance Reviews Don't Work—And What You Can Do About It," Independent Street blog, *Wall Street Journal*, 21 October 2008, blogs.wsj.com.

21. Rita Pyrillis, "Is Your Performance Review Underperforming?" *Workforce Management*, May 2011, 20–22, 24–25.

22. Friedfel, "Protecting Yourself in the Performance Review Process."

23. E. Michelle Bohreer and Todd J. Zucker, "Five Mistakes Managers Make When Terminating Employees," *Texas Lawyer*, 2 May 2006, www.law.com; Deborah Muller, "The Right Things to Do to Avoid Wrongful Termination Claims," *Workforce Management*, October 2008, www.workforce.com; Maria Greco Danaher, "Termination: Telling an Employee," *Workforce Management*, accessed 14 July 2010, www.workforce.com.

24. "FDA Notifies Public That Vail Products, Inc., Issues Nationwide Recall of Enclosed Bed Systems," U.S. Food and Drug Administration press release, 30 June 2005, www.fda.gov.

25. Twitter/JetBlue website, accessed 29 October 2008, twitter.com/JetBlue.

26. "Viral Effect of Email Promotion," Alka Dwivedi blog, accessed 19 October 2006, www.alkadwivedi.net; Teresa Valdez Klein, "Starbucks Makes a Viral Marketing Misstep," Blog Business Summit website, accessed 19 October 2006, www.blogbusinesssummit.com.

27. Pui-Wing Tam, Erin White, Nick Wingfield, and Kris Maher, "Snooping Email by Software Is Now a Workplace Norm," *Wall Street Journal*, 9 March 2005, B1+.

28. This scenario, and all the information presented in this case, is fictitious.

29. Environmental Quality Company press releases, accessed 27 October 2006, www.eqonline.com; "N.C. Residents to Return After Fire," *Science Daily*, 6 October 2006, www.sciencedaily.com; "Hazardous Waste Plant Fire in N.C. Forces 17,000 to Evacuate," *FOX News*, 6 October 2006, www.foxnews.com.

30. Alion website, accessed 19 August 2005, www.alionscience.com.

LEARNING OBJECTIVES

After studying this chapter, you will be able to

1 Apply the three-step writing process to persuasive messages.

2 Describe an effective strategy for developing persuasive business messages, and identify the three most common categories of persuasive business messages.

3 Describe an effective strategy for developing marketing and sales messages, and explain how to modify your approach when writing promotional messages for social media.

4 Identify steps you can take to avoid ethical lapses in marketing and sales messages.

MyBCommLab®

⭐ **Improve Your Grade!** More than 10 million students improved their results using Pearson MyLabs. Visit **mybcommlab.com** for simulations, tutorials, and end-of-chapter problems.

COMMUNICATION CLOSE-UP AT
Red Ants Pants

redantspants.com

Sarah Calhoun was fed up. The rugged work she was doing in her adopted home state of Montana, including clearing trails and peeling logs, was destroying her not-so-rugged clothes. She switched to men's work pants, which were tough enough for the job but didn't fit.

Tired of constantly putting down her tools so she could pull up her misfit britches, Calhoun decided to solve the problem herself. She launched Red Ants Pants with the focus on providing hardwearing pants for hardworking women, meeting the needs of customers whose work makes clothing a matter of practical utility and even on-the-job safety. Red Ants Pants are made from tough, heavy cloth and in both "straight" and "curvy" styles to

Sarah Calhoun connects with customers by communicating in a fun, authentic, respectful way.

Sarah Calhoun from www.redantspants.com by ErikPeterson. Copyright (c) Sarah Calhoun. Used by permission of Sarah Calhoun.

provide a better fit for more women. In addition, they come in two or three times as many waist/inseam combinations as typical pants, greatly increasing the chance that every woman will find exactly the size she needs.

Why "Red Ants Pants," by the way? In a conversation with a biologist about the social behaviors of ants, she learned that in red ant colonies, females do most of the work. In keeping with the cheeky style she adopted for all her company's communication, she uses the name as a salute to hardworking women everywhere.

Calhoun knew there was a market for her product, but launching a company in the fiercely competitive global clothing industry—and doing so from the tiny town of White Sulphur Springs, Montana, no less—was a huge challenge. However, from the start she has used size and independence to her advantage, making choices that fit her personal values and the needs of her customers. For example, unlike with most clothing brands, she chose to keep production in the United States, rather than offshoring in pursuit of the lowest possible costs.

That spirit of independence extends to her customer communication efforts, demonstrating both the greater flexibility that small companies often have compared with their larger, "more corporate" competitors—and the need to exercise creative brain power over brute-force budget power. Her communication style is more fun and more daring than a typical corporation would

attempt, for example, and it seems to resonate with buyers. How many clothing companies would use photographs (discreetly staged, to be sure) to suggest that hardworking women would rather wear no pants than wear pants that don't fit?

Without a significant marketing budget, Calhoun looks for low-cost, high-visibility ways to reach customers. Her most unusual is hitting the highway with her sales manager in an ant-decorated Airstream travel trailer on trips they call the "Tour de Pants." They invite women to stage in-home gatherings, much like old-school Tupperware parties. Through visiting customers in their homes and hearing stories about women working in what are often male-dominated professions, Calhoun also gains invaluable marketing research insights.

Calhoun's most ambitious communication effort so far has been sponsoring the Red Ants Pants Music Festival, which has attracted such major American artists as Lyle Lovett and Guy Clark. All profits go to the Red Ants Pants Foundation, which she started to "support family farms and ranches, women in business, and rural initiatives."

The combination of meeting customer needs with quality products and a creative marketing effort is paying off. Red Ants Pants now has customers all across the country and around the world, from Europe to Australia, and even women working the research stations in Antarctica.[1]

Using the Three-Step Writing Process for Persuasive Messages

1 LEARNING OBJECTIVE
Apply the three-step writing process to persuasive messages.

Persuasion is the attempt to change someone's attitudes, beliefs, or actions.

Sarah Calhoun (profiled in the chapter-opening Communication Close-Up) understands that successful businesses rely on persuasive messages in both internal and external communication. Whether you're trying to convince your boss to open a new office in Europe or encourage potential customers to try your products, you need to call on your abilities of **persuasion**—an attempt to change an audience's attitudes, beliefs, or actions.[2] Because persuasive messages ask audiences to give something of value (money in exchange for a product, for example) or take substantial action (such as changing a corporate policy), they are more challenging to write than routine messages. Successful professionals understand that persuasion is not about trickery or getting people to act against their own best interests; it's about letting audiences know they have choices and presenting your offering in the best possible light.[3]

STEP 1: PLANNING PERSUASIVE MESSAGES

Having a great idea or a great product is not enough; you need to be able to convince others of its merits.

In today's information-saturated business environment, having a great idea or a great product is no longer enough. Every day, untold numbers of good ideas go unnoticed and good products go unsold simply because the messages meant to promote them aren't compelling enough to be heard above the competitive noise. Creating successful persuasive messages in these challenging situations demands careful attention to all four tasks in the planning step, starting with an insightful analysis of your purpose and your audience.

Analyzing the Situation

Clarifying your purpose is an essential step with persuasive messages.

In defining your purpose, make sure you're clear about what you really hope to achieve. Suppose you want to persuade company executives to support a particular research project. But what does "support" mean? Do you want them to pat you on the back and wish

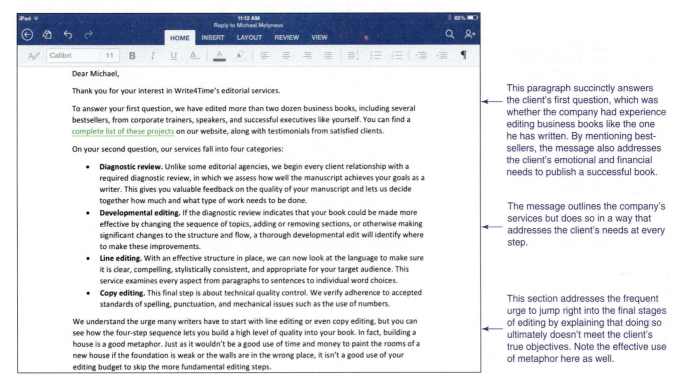

Figure 12.1 Appealing to Audience Needs
This draft of a response to an inquiry about an editorial company's services addresses the writer's concerns about the time, cost, and effectiveness of the company's services.

you well? Or do you want them to give you a staff of five researchers and a $1 million annual budget?

The best persuasive messages are closely connected to your audience's desires and interests (see Figure 12.1).[4] Consider these important questions: Who is my audience? What are my audience members' needs? What do I want them to do? How might they resist? Are there alternative positions I need to examine? What does the decision maker consider to be the most important issue? How might the organization's culture influence my strategy?

To understand and categorize audience needs, you can refer to specific information, such as **demographics** (the age, gender, occupation, income, education, and other quantifiable characteristics of the people you're trying to persuade) and **psychographics** (personality, attitudes, lifestyle, and other psychological characteristics). When analyzing your audiences, take into account their cultural expectations and practices so that you don't undermine your persuasive message by using an inappropriate appeal or by organizing your message in a way that seems unfamiliar or uncomfortable to your readers.

If you aim to change someone's attitudes, beliefs, or actions, it is vital to understand his or her **motivation**—the combination of forces that drive people to satisfy their needs. Table 12.1 on the next page lists some of the needs that psychologists have identified or suggested as being important in influencing human motivation. Obviously, the more closely a persuasive message aligns with a recipient's existing motivation, the more effective the message is likely to be. For example, if you try to persuade consumers to purchase a product on the basis of its fashion appeal, that message will connect with consumers who are motivated by a desire to be in fashion, but it probably won't connect with consumers driven more by functional or financial concerns.

Gathering Information

Once your situation analysis is complete, you need to gather the information necessary to create a compelling persuasive message. You'll learn more about the types of information to include in persuasive business messages and marketing and sales messages later in this chapter. Chapter 13 presents advice on how to find the information you need.

Demographics include characteristics such as age, gender, occupation, income, and education.

Psychographics include characteristics such as personality, attitudes, and lifestyle.

Motivation is the combination of forces that drive people to satisfy their needs.

TABLE 12.1 Human Needs That Influence Motivation

Need	Implications for Communication
Basic physiological requirements: The needs for food, water, sleep, oxygen, and other essentials	Everyone has these needs, but the degree of attention an individual gives to them often depends on whether the needs are being met; for instance, an advertisement for sleeping pills will have greater appeal to someone suffering from insomnia than to someone who has no problem sleeping.
Safety and security: The needs for protection from bodily harm, for the safety of loved ones, and for financial security, protection of personal identity, career security, and other assurances	These needs influence both consumer and business decisions in many ways; for instance, advertisements for life insurance often encourage parents to think about the financial security of their children and other loved ones.
Affiliation and belonging: The needs for companionship, acceptance, love, popularity, and approval	The need to feel loved, accepted, or popular drives a great deal of human behavior, from the desire to be attractive to potential mates to wearing the clothing style that a particular social group is likely to approve.
Power and control: The need to feel in control of situations or to exert authority over others	You can see many examples appealing to this need in advertisements: *Take control of your life*, *your finances*, *your future*, *your career*, and so on. Many people who lack power want to know how to get it, and people who have power often want others to know they have it.
Achievement: The need to feel a sense of accomplishment—or to be admired by others for accomplishments	This need can involve both *knowing* (when people experience a feeling of accomplishment) and *showing* (when people are able to show others that they've achieved success); advertising for luxury consumer products frequently appeals to this need.
Adventure and distraction: The need for excitement or relief from daily routine	People vary widely in their need for adventure; some crave excitement—even danger—whereas others value calmness and predictability. Some needs for adventure and distraction are met *virtually*, such as through horror movies, thriller novels, etc.
Knowledge, exploration, and understanding: The need to keep learning	For some people, learning is usually a means to an end, a way to fulfill some other need; for others, acquiring new knowledge is the goal.
Aesthetic appreciation: The desire to experience beauty, order, symmetry, etc.	Although this need may seem "noncommercial" at first glance, advertisers appeal to it frequently, from the pleasing shape of a package to the quality of the gemstones in a piece of jewelry.
Self-actualization: The need to "be all that one can be," to reach one's full potential as a human being	The psychologists Kurt Goldstein and Abraham Maslow popularized self-actualization as the desire to make the most of one's potential, and Maslow identified it as one of the higher-level needs in his classic hierarchy; even if people met most or all of their other needs, they would still feel the need to self-actualize. An often-quoted example of appealing to this need is the U.S. Army's one-time advertising slogan "Be all that you can be."
Helping others: The need to believe that one is making a difference in the lives of other people	This need is the central motivation in fundraising messages and other appeals to charity.

Sources: Courtland L. Bovée and John V. Thill, *Business in Action*, 8th ed. (Upper Saddle River, N.J.: Prentice Hall, 2017), 225–239; Saundra K. Ciccarelli and Glenn E. Meyer, *Psychology* (Upper Saddle River, N.J.: Prentice Hall, 2006), 336–346; Abraham H. Maslow, "A Theory of Human Motivation," *Psychological Review* 50 (1943): 370–396.

Selecting the Right Media and Channels

Persuasive messages can be found in virtually every communication format, from instant messages and podcasts to radio advertisements and skywriting. In fact, advertising agencies employ media specialists whose job is to analyze the options available and select the most cost-effective combination for each client and each advertising campaign.

In some situations, various members of your audience might prefer different media for the same message. Some consumers like to do all their car shopping in person, whereas others do most of their car-shopping research online. Some people don't mind promotional emails for products they're interested in; others resent every piece of commercial email they receive. If you can't be sure you can reach most or all of your audience through a single medium, you need to use two or more, such as following up an email campaign with printed letters.

Persuasive messages are often unexpected and sometimes even unwelcome, so choose your medium carefully to maximize the chance of getting through to your audience.

Social media provide some exciting options for persuasive messages, particularly marketing and sales messages. However, as "Writing Promotional Messages for Social Media" on page 344 explains, messages in these media require a unique approach.

Organizing Your Information

The most effective main ideas for persuasive messages have one thing in common: They are about the receiver, not the sender. For instance, if you're trying to convince others to join you in a business venture, explain how it will help them, not how it will help you.

Limiting your scope is vital. If you seem to be wrestling with more than one main idea, you haven't zeroed in on the heart of the matter. If you try to craft a persuasive message without focusing on the one central problem or opportunity your audience truly cares about, you're unlikely to persuade successfully.[5]

Because the nature of persuasion is to convince people to change their attitudes, beliefs, or actions, most persuasive messages use the indirect approach. That means you'll want to explain your reasons and build interest before asking for a decision or for action—or perhaps even before revealing your purpose. In contrast, when you have a close relationship with your audience and the message is welcome or at least neutral, the direct approach can be effective.

Most persuasive messages use the indirect approach.

For persuasive business messages, the choice between the direct and indirect approaches is also influenced by the extent of your authority, expertise, or power in an organization. For instance, if you are a highly regarded technical expert with years of experience, you might use the direct approach in a message to top executives. In contrast, if you aren't well known and therefore need to rely more on the strength of your message than the power of your reputation, the indirect approach will probably be more successful.

The choice of approach is influenced by your position (or authority within the organization) relative to your audience's.

STEP 2: WRITING PERSUASIVE MESSAGES

Encourage a positive response to your persuasive messages by (1) using positive and polite language, (2) understanding and respecting cultural differences, (3) being sensitive to organizational cultures, and (4) taking steps to establish your credibility.

Positive language is an essential feature of persuasive messages.

Positive language usually happens naturally with persuasive messages because you're promoting an idea or product you believe in. However, take care not to inadvertently insult your readers by implying that they've made poor choices in the past and that you're here to save them from their misguided ways.

Be sure to understand cultural expectations as well. For example, a message that seems forthright and direct in a low-context culture might seem brash and intrusive in a high-context culture.

Just as social culture affects the success of a persuasive message, so too does the culture within an organization. For instance, some organizations handle disagreement and conflict indirectly, behind the scenes, whereas others accept and even encourage open discussion and sharing differing viewpoints.

Organizational culture can influence persuasion as much as social culture.

Finally, when you are trying to persuade a skeptical or hostile audience, credibility is essential. You must convince people that you know what you're talking about and that you're not trying to mislead them (see "Ethics Detective: Solving the Case of the Incredible Credibility"). Use these techniques:

- Use simple language to avoid suspicions of fantastic claims and emotional manipulation.
- Provide objective evidence for the claims and promises you make.
- Identify your information sources.
- Establish common ground by emphasizing beliefs, attitudes, and experiences you have in common with the audience.
- Be objective and present fair and logical arguments.
- Display your willingness to keep your audience's best interests at heart.
- Persuade with logic, evidence, and compelling narratives, rather than trying to coerce with high-pressure, "hard sell" tactics.
- Whenever possible, try to build your credibility before you present a major proposal or ask for a major decision. That way, audiences don't have to evaluate both you and your message at the same time.[6]

Audiences often respond unfavorably to over-the-top language, so keep your writing simple and straightforward.

STEP 3: COMPLETING PERSUASIVE MESSAGES

The pros know from experience that details can make or break a persuasive message, so they're careful not to skimp on this part of the writing process. When you evaluate your content, try to judge your argument objectively and to not overestimate your credibility.

Careless production undermines your credibility, so revise and proofread with care.

Solving the Case of the Incredible Credibility

As the director of human resources in your company, you're desperate for some help. You want to keep the costs of employee benefits under control while making sure you provide employees with a fair benefits package. However, you don't have time to research all the options for health insurance, wellness programs, retirement plans, family counseling, educational benefits, and everything else, so you decide to hire a consultant. You receive the following message from a consultant interested in working with you:

> I am considered the country's foremost authority on employee health insurance programs. My clients offer universally positive feedback on the programs I've designed for them. They also love how much time I save them—hundreds and hundreds of hours.

> I am absolutely confident that I can thoroughly analyze your needs and create a portfolio that realizes every degree of savings possible. I invite you to experience the same level of service that has generated such comments as "Best advice ever!" and "Saved us an unbelievable amount of money."

You'd love to get results like that, but the message almost sounds too good to be true. Is it?

ANALYSIS

The consultant's message contains at least a dozen instances in which this writer's credibility might be questioned. Identify as many as you can, and explain how you would bolster reader confidence by providing additional or different information.

If possible, ask an experienced colleague who knows your audience well to review your draft. Make sure your design elements complement, rather than detract from, your persuasive argument. In addition, meticulous proofreading will help you identify any mechanical or spelling errors that would weaken your persuasive potential. Finally, make sure your distribution methods fit your audience's expectations and preferences.

Persuasive messages can be divided into *persuasive business messages* (those that try to convince audiences to approve new projects, enter into business partnerships, and so on) and *marketing and sales messages* (those that try to convince audiences to consider and then purchase products and services). The basic techniques of persuasion work for both types, but each has some unique considerations.

Developing Persuasive Business Messages

2 LEARNING OBJECTIVE Describe an effective strategy for developing persuasive business messages, and identify the three most common categories of persuasive business messages.

Your success as a businessperson is closely tied to your ability to encourage others to accept new ideas, change old habits, or act on your proposals and recommendations. Even if you have the power to compel others to do what you want them to do, persuading them is more effective than forcing them. People who are forced into accepting a decision or plan are less motivated to support it and more likely to react negatively than if they're persuaded.[7]

STRATEGIES FOR PERSUASIVE BUSINESS MESSAGES

Within the context of the three-step process, effective persuasion involves four essential strategies: framing your arguments, balancing emotional and logical appeals, reinforcing your position, and anticipating objections. (Note that all the concepts in this section apply as well to marketing and sales messages, covered later in the chapter.)

Framing Your Arguments

As noted previously, most persuasive messages use the indirect approach. Experts in persuasive communication have developed a number of indirect models for such messages. One of the best known is the **AIDA model**, which organizes messages into four phases (see Figure 12.2):

- **Attention.** Your first objective is to encourage your audience to want to hear about your problem, idea, or new product—whatever your main idea is. Be sure to find some common ground on which to build your case.

MOBILE APP

Want to persuade your local government to address a problem? The **CitySourced** app aims to facilitate civic engagement through mobile communication.

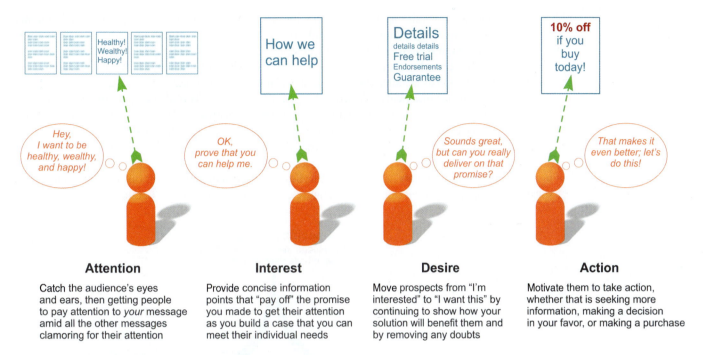

Attention

Catch the audience's eyes and ears, then getting people to pay attention to *your* message amid all the other messages clamoring for their attention

Interest

Provide concise information points that "pay off" the promise you made to get their attention as you build a case that you can meet their individual needs

Desire

Move prospects from "I'm interested" to "I want this" by continuing to show how your solution will benefit them and by removing any doubts

Action

Motivate them to take action, whether that is seeking more information, making a decision in your favor, or making a purchase

Figure 12.2   The AIDA Model for Persuasive Messages
With the AIDA model, you craft one or more messages to move recipients through the four stages of attention, interest, desire, and action. The model works well for both persuasive business messages (such as persuading your manager to fund a new project) and marketing and sales messages.

- **Interest.** Provide additional details that prompt audience members to imagine how the solution might benefit them.
- **Desire.** Help audience members embrace your idea by explaining how the change will benefit them and answering potential objections.
- **Action.** Suggest the specific action you want your audience to take. Include a deadline, when applicable.

The AIDA model is tailor-made for using the indirect approach, allowing you to save your main idea for the action phase. However, you can also use AIDA for the direct approach, in which case you use your main idea as an attention-getter, build interest with your argument, create desire with your evidence, and reemphasize your main idea in the action phase with the specific action you want your audience to take.

When your AIDA message uses the indirect approach and is delivered by memo or email, keep in mind that your subject line usually catches your reader's eye first. Your challenge is to make it interesting and relevant enough to capture the reader's attention without revealing your main idea. If you put your request in the subject line, you might get a quick no before you've had a chance to present your arguments:

Instead of This	Write This
Request for development budget to add automated IM response system	Reducing the cost of customer support inquiries

With either the direct or indirect approach, AIDA and similar models do have limitations. First, AIDA is a unidirectional method that essentially talks *at* audiences, not *with* them. Second, AIDA is built around a single event, such as asking an audience for a decision, rather than on building a mutually beneficial, long-term relationship.[8] AIDA is still a valuable tool for the right purposes, but as you'll read later in the chapter, a conversational approach is more compatible with today's social media environment.

Balancing Emotional and Logical Appeals

Imagine you're sitting at a control panel with one knob labeled "logic" and another labeled "emotion." As you prepare persuasive messages, carefully adjust each knob, tuning the

Margin notes:

The AIDA model is a useful approach for many persuasive messages:
- Attention
- Interest
- Desire
- Action

The AIDA model is ideal for the indirect approach.

The AIDA approach does have limitations:
- It essentially talks *at* audiences, not *with* them
- It focuses on one-time events, not long-term relationships

message for maximum impact (see Figure 12.3). Too little emotion, and your audience might not care enough to respond. Too much emotion, and your audience might think you are ignoring tough business questions or even being irrational.

In general, persuasive business messages rely more heavily on logical than on emotional appeals because the main idea is usually to save money, increase quality, or improve some other practical, measurable aspect of business. To find the optimum balance, consider four factors: (1) the actions you hope to motivate, (2) your readers' expectations, (3) the degree of resistance you need to overcome, and (4) your position in the formal and informal power structure of the organization.[9]

Emotional appeals attempt to connect with the reader's feelings or sympathies.

Emotional Appeals   As its name implies, an **emotional appeal** calls on audience feelings and sympathies rather than on facts, figures, and rational arguments. For instance, you can make

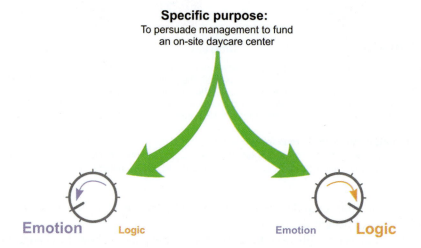

Specific purpose:
To persuade management to fund
an on-site daycare center

Emotion   Logic

Emotion   Logic

Proposal to improve employee satisfaction and work/life balance

Being separated during the day is stressful for both parents and children.

Many parents are now working more hours and second jobs to make ends meet, so the situation is getting worse.

The extra travel time every morning and evening to put children in day care adds to the stress and cost of coming to work.

When parents need to leave work to pick up sick children from day care or stay home with them, this often creates an unfair burden on other employees to pick up the slack.

Knowing that the company cares about them and their children would boost employee morale.

Therefore, the company should provide an on-site daycare facility with a separate infirmary where sick children could stay during the day.

Proposal to boost productivity and reduce absenteeism

Analysis of employee time records shows that employees with children under the age of 10 take unscheduled days off three times more often than employees without young children.

Daycare issues are cited as the number one reason for these unscheduled days off.

In the 98 exit interviews conducted last year, 24 departing employees mentioned the need to balance family and work commitments as the primary reason for leaving.

In the last six months, HR has logged 14 complaints from employees who say they have to take on extra work when colleagues leave the office to pick up sick children from day care.

Research shows that on-site day care can improve productivity by as much as 20 percent—among parents and nonparents alike.

Therefore, the company should provide an on-site daycare facility with a separate infirmary where sick children could stay during the day.

Figure 12.3   Balancing Logical and Emotional Appeals
Whenever you plan a persuasive message, imagine you have a knob that turns from *emotion* at one extreme to *logic* at the other, letting you adjust the relative proportions of each type of appeal. Compare these two outlines for a proposal that asks management to fund an on-site daycare center. The version on the left relies heavily on emotional appeals, whereas the version on the right uses logical appeals (inductive reasoning, specifically). Through your choice of words, images, and supporting details, you can adjust the emotion-to-logic ratio in every message.

use of the emotion surrounding certain words. The word *freedom* evokes strong feelings, as do words such as *success*, *prestige*, *compassion*, *security*, and *comfort*. Such words can help put your audience members in a positive frame of mind and help them accept your message. However, emotional appeals in business messages aren't usually effective by themselves because the audience wants proof that you can solve a business problem. Even if your audience members reach a conclusion based primarily on emotions, they'll look to you to provide logical support as well.

Logical Appeals   A logical appeal calls on reasoning and evidence. The basic approach with a logical appeal is to make a claim based on a rational argument, supported by solid evidence. When appealing to your audience's logic, you might use three types of reasoning:

- **Analogy.** With analogy, you reason from specific evidence to specific evidence, in effect "borrowing" from something familiar to explain something unfamiliar. For instance, to convince the executive committee to hire leadership coaches for newly promoted managers, you might say it's like hiring a nutritionist or a personal trainer to help one develop positive habits and healthy routines.
- **Induction.** With inductive reasoning, you work from specific evidence to a general conclusion. To convince your team to change to a new manufacturing process, for example, you could point out that every company that has adopted it has increased profits, so it must be a smart idea.
- **Deduction.** With deductive reasoning, you work from a generalization to a specific conclusion. To persuade your boss to hire additional customer support staff, you might point to industry surveys that show how crucial customer satisfaction is to corporate profits.

> Logical appeals are based on the reader's notions of reason; these appeals can use analogy, induction, or deduction.

Every method of reasoning is vulnerable to misuse, both intentional and unintentional, so verify your rational arguments carefully. For example, in the case of the manufacturing process, are there any other factors that affect the integrity of your reasoning? What if that process works well only for small companies with few products, but your firm is a multinational behemoth with 10,000 products? To guard against faulty logic, follow these guidelines:[10]

> Using logical appeals carries with it the ethical responsibility to avoid faulty logic.

- **Avoid hasty generalizations.** Make sure you have plenty of evidence before drawing conclusions.
- **Avoid circular reasoning.** *Circular reasoning* is a logical fallacy in which you try to support your claim by restating it in different words. The statement "We know temporary workers cannot handle this task because temps are unqualified for it" doesn't prove anything because the claim and the supporting evidence are essentially identical. It doesn't prove *why* the temps are unqualified.
- **Avoid attacking an opponent.** If your persuasive appeal involves countering a competitive appeal made by someone else, make sure you attack the argument your opponent is making, not his or her character or qualifications.
- **Avoid oversimplifying a complex issue.** Make sure you present all the factors and don't reduce a wide range of choices to a simple "either/or" scenario if that isn't the case.
- **Avoid mistaken assumptions of cause and effect.** If you can't isolate the impact of a specific factor, you can't assume that it's the cause of whatever effect you're discussing. You lowered prices, and sales went up. Were lower prices the cause? Maybe, but the sales increase might have been caused by a better advertising campaign, changes in the weather, or some other factor.
- **Avoid faulty analogies.** Be sure that the two objects or situations being compared are similar enough for the analogy to hold. For instance, explaining that an Internet firewall is like a prison wall is a poor analogy because a firewall keeps things out, whereas a prison wall keeps things in.
- **Avoid illogical support.** Make sure the connection between your claim and your support is truly logical and not based on a leap of faith, a missing premise, or irrelevant evidence.

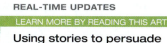

REAL-TIME UPDATES
LEARN MORE BY READING THIS ARTICLE
Using stories to persuade

Learn why stories are usually more effective than plain data when it comes to changing minds. Go to **real-timeupdates** **.com/bct14** and select Learn More in the Students section.

Reinforcing Your Position

Choose your words carefully to trigger the desired responses.

After you've worked out the basic elements of your argument, step back and look for ways to strengthen your position. Are all your claims supported by believable evidence? Would a quotation from a recognized expert help make your case?

Next, examine your language. Can you find more powerful words to convey your message? For example, if your company is in serious financial trouble, talking about *fighting for survival* is a more powerful emotional appeal than talking about *ensuring continued operations*. As with any other powerful tool, though, use vivid language and abstractions carefully and honestly.

In addition to examining individual word choices, consider using metaphors and other figures of speech. If you want to describe a quality-control system as being designed to detect every possible product flaw, you might call it a "spider web" to imply that it catches everything that comes its way. Similarly, anecdotes (brief stories) can help your audience grasp the meaning and importance of your arguments. Instead of just listing the number of times the old laptop computers in your department have failed, you could describe how you lost a sale when your computer broke down during a critical sales presentation.

Beyond specific words and phrases, look for other factors that can reinforce your position. When you're asking for something, your audience members will find it easier to grant your request if they stand to benefit from it as well.

Anticipating Objections

Even powerful persuasive messages can encounter audience resistance.

Even the most compelling ideas and proposals can be expected to encounter some initial resistance. The best way to deal with audience resistance is to anticipate as many objections as you can and address them in your message before your audience can even bring them up. For instance, if you know that your proposal to switch to lower-cost materials will raise concerns about product quality, address this issue head-on in your message. If you wait until people raise the concern after reading your message, they may gravitate toward another firm before you have a chance to address their concerns. By bringing up such potential problems right away, you also demonstrate a broad appreciation of the issue and imply confidence in your message.[11] This anticipation is particularly important when you're not delivering a message in person and won't have the opportunity to detect and respond to objections on the spot.

If you expect to encounter strong resistance, present all sides of an issue.

To uncover potential audience objections, try to poke holes in your own theories and ideas before your audience does. Then find solutions to the problems you've uncovered. If possible, ask your audience members for their thoughts on the subject before you put together your argument; people are more likely to support solutions they help create.

Keep two things in mind when anticipating objections. First, you don't always have to explicitly discuss a potential objection. You could simply mention that the lower-cost materials have been tested and approved by the quality-control department. Second, if you expect a hostile audience—one biased against your plan from the beginning—present all sides of the story. As you cover each option, explain the pros and cons. You'll gain additional credibility if you present these options before presenting your recommendation or decision.[12]

AVOIDING COMMON MISTAKES IN PERSUASIVE COMMUNICATION

Don't let confidence or enthusiasm lead you to some common mistakes in persuasive communication.

When you believe in a concept or project you are promoting, it's easy to get caught up in your own confidence and enthusiasm and thereby fail to see things from the audience's perspective. When putting together persuasive arguments, avoid these common mistakes (see Figure 12.4):[13]

- **Using a hard sell.** Don't push. No one likes being pressured into making a decision, and communicators who take this approach can come across as being more concerned with meeting their own goals than with satisfying the needs of their audiences. In

Ineffective

It's time to call the Fast Track program what it truly is—a disaster. Everyone was excited last year when we announced the plan to speed up our development efforts and introduce at least one new product every month. We envisioned rapidly expanding market share and strong revenue growth. What we got instead is a nightmare that is getting worse every month.

As a company, we clearly underestimated the resources it would take to market, sell, and support so many new products. We can't hire and train fast enough, and every department are overwhelmed. Forced to jump from one new product to the next, the sales and technical specialists can't develop the expertise needed to help buyers before the sale or support them after the sale. As a result, too many customers either buy the wrong product or buy the right product but then can't get knowledgeable help when they need it. We're losing credibility in the market, we're starting to lose sales, and it won't be long before we start losing employees who are fed up with the insanity.

To make matters even worse, some of the recent products were clearly rushed to market before they were ready. With numerous quality issues, returns and warranty costs are skyrocketing.

New products are the lifeblood of the company, to be sure, but there is no point in introducing products that only create enormous support headaches and cost more to support than they generate in profits. We need to put the Fast Track initiative on hold immediately so the entire company can regroup. The R&D lab can devote its time to fixing problems in the recent products, and the rest of us can catch our breath and try to figure out how to meet our sales and customer support goals.

(a) The company has clearly staked a lot on this program, so opening by calling it a disaster will only put the reader on the defensive.

(b) Word choices such as *nightmare* here and *insanity* in the next paragraph give the message an emotional, almost hysterical, tone that detracts from the serious message.

(c) The writer mingles together an observation that may be subjective (declining credibility), a hard data point (declining sales), and a prediction (possibility of employee defections).

(d) The claim that recent products were "clearly rushed to market" is unnecessarily inflammatory (because it blames another department) and distracts the reader from the more immediate problems of poor quality.

(e) The first sentence of the last paragraph is insulting to anyone with basic business sense—particularly the president of a company.

Effective

(a) This neutral summary of events serves as an effective buffer for the indirect approach and provides a subtle reminder of the original goals of the program.

(b) This paragraph contains the same information as the ineffective version, but does so in a calmer way that won't trigger the reader's defense mechanisms and will thereby keep the focus on the facts.

(c) The writer separates a personal hunch (about the possibility of losing employees) from an observation about the market and a measured data point (declining sales).

(d) The writer introduces the information about quality problems without directing blame.

(e) With the evidence assembled, the writer introduces the main idea of putting the program on hold. The recommendation is a judgment call and a suggestion to a superior, so the hedging phrase I *believe* is appropriate.

Everyone was excited last year when we launched the Fast Track program to speed up our development efforts and introduce at least one new product every month. We envisioned rapidly expanding market share and strong revenue growth in all our product lines.

While the R&D lab has met its goal of monthly releases, as a company, we clearly underestimated the resources it would take to market, sell, and support so many new products. We can't hire and train fast enough, and our teams in every department are overwhelmed. The sales and technical specialists haven't had time to develop the expertise needed to help buyers before the sale or support them after the sale. As a result, too many customers either buy the wrong product or buy the right product but then can't get knowledgeable help when they need it. We're losing credibility in the market, and we're starting to lose sales. If the situation continues, I fear we will being losing employees, too.

In addition, some of the recent products are generating multiple reports of hardware quality problems and buggy software. Returns and warranty costs are climbing at an unprecedented rate.

With costs rising faster than revenues and our people getting overwhelmed, I believe it is time to put the Fast Track initiative on hold until the company can regroup. The hiatus would give R&D time to address the quality problems and give the marketing, sales, and tech support team the chance to reassess our goals with the current product portfolio and our current staffing levels.

Figure 12.4 Persuasive Argumentation

Imagine you're the marketing manager in a company that decided to speed up its new product launches but did too much too fast and wound up creating chaos. You decide enough is enough and write a memo to the company president advocating that the new program be shut down until the company can regroup—a suggestion you know will meet with resistance. Notice how the ineffective version doesn't quite use the direct approach but comes out swinging, so to speak, and is overly emotional throughout. The effective version builds to its recommendation indirectly, using the same information but in a calm, logical way. Because it sticks to the facts, it is also shorter.

CHECKLIST ✔ Developing Persuasive Messages

A. Get your reader's attention.
- Open with an audience benefit, a stimulating question, a problem, or an unexpected statement.
- Establish common ground by mentioning a point on which you and your audience agree.
- Show that you understand the audience's concerns.

B. Build your reader's interest.
- Expand and support your opening claim or promise.
- Emphasize the relevance of your message to your audience.

C. Increase your reader's desire.
- Make audience members want to change by explaining how the change will benefit them.
- Back up your claims with relevant evidence.

D. Motivate your reader to take action.
- Suggest the action you want readers to take.
- Stress the positive results of the action.
- Make the desired action clear and easy.

E. Balance emotional and logical appeals.
- Use emotional appeals to help the audience accept your message.
- Use logical appeals when presenting facts and evidence for complex ideas or recommendations.
- Avoid faulty logic.

F. Reinforce your position.
- Provide additional evidence of the benefits of your proposal and your own credibility in offering it.
- Use abstractions, metaphors, and other figures of speech to bring facts and figures to life.

G. Anticipate objections.
- Anticipate and answer potential objections.
- Present the pros and cons of all options if you anticipate a hostile reaction.

---

contrast, a "soft sell" is more like a comfortable conversation that uses calm, rational persuasion.

- **Resisting compromise.** Successful persuasion is often a process of give-and-take, particularly in the case of persuasive business messages, where you don't always get everything you asked for in terms of budgets, investments, and other commitments.
- **Relying solely on great arguments.** Great arguments are important, but connecting with your audience on the right emotional level and communicating through vivid language are just as vital. Sometimes a well-crafted story can be even more compelling than dry logic.
- **Assuming that persuasion is a one-shot effort.** Persuasion is often a process, not a one-time event. In many cases you need to move your audience members along one small step at a time rather than try to convince them to say "yes" in one huge step.

To review the steps involved in developing persuasive messages, refer to "Checklist: Developing Persuasive Messages."

COMMON EXAMPLES OF PERSUASIVE BUSINESS MESSAGES

Throughout your career, you'll have numerous opportunities to write persuasive messages within your organization, such as reports suggesting more efficient operating procedures or memos requesting money for new equipment. Similarly, you may produce a variety of persuasive messages for people outside the organization, such as websites shaping public opinion or letters requesting adjustments that go beyond a supplier's contractual obligations. In addition, some of the routine requests you studied in Chapter 10 can become persuasive messages if you want a nonroutine result or believe that you haven't received fair treatment. Most of these messages can be divided into persuasive requests for action, persuasive presentations of ideas, and persuasive claims and requests for adjustment.

Persuasive Requests for Action

Most persuasive business messages involve a request for action.

The bulk of your persuasive business messages will involve requests for action. In some cases your request will be anticipated, so the direct approach is fine. In others you'll need to introduce your intention indirectly, and the AIDA model or a similar approach is ideal for this purpose (see Figure 12.5).

1 Plan → 2 Write → 3 Complete

Analyze the Situation
Verify that the purpose is to solve an ongoing problem, so the audience will be receptive.

Gather Information
Determine audience needs and obtain the necessary information on recycling problem areas.

Choose Medium and Channel
Verify that an email message is appropriate for this communication.

Organize the Information
Limit the scope to the main idea, which is to propose a recycling solution; use the indirect approach to lay out the extent of the problem.

Adapt to Your Audience
Adjust the level of formality based on the degree of familiarity with the audience; maintain a positive relationship by using the "you" attitude, politeness, positive emphasis, and bias-free language.

Compose the Message
Use a conversational but professional style and keep the message brief, clear, and as helpful as possible.

Revise the Message
Evaluate content and review readability to make sure the information is clear and complete without being overwhelming.

Produce the Message
Emphasize a clean, professional appearance.

Proofread the Message
Review for errors in layout, spelling, and mechanics.

Distribute the Message
Verify that the right file is attached and then deliver the message.

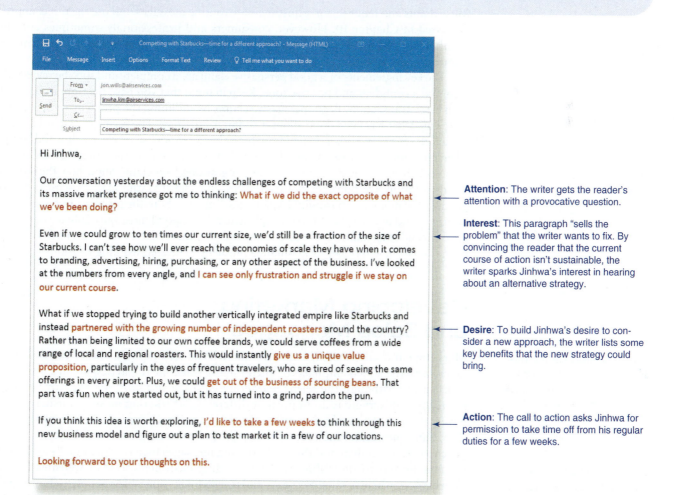

File Message Insert Options Format Text Review Q Tell me what you want to do

From ▾ jon.wills@airservices.com
To... jinwha.kim@airservices.com
Cc...
Subject Competing with Starbucks—time for a different approach?

Hi Jinhwa,

Our conversation yesterday about the endless challenges of competing with Starbucks and its massive market presence got me to thinking: What if we did the exact opposite of what we've been doing?

Attention: The writer gets the reader's attention with a provocative question.

Even if we could grow to ten times our current size, we'd still be a fraction of the size of Starbucks. I can't see how we'll ever reach the economies of scale they have when it comes to branding, advertising, hiring, purchasing, or any other aspect of the business. I've looked at the numbers from every angle, and I can see only frustration and struggle if we stay on our current course.

Interest: This paragraph "sells the problem" that the writer wants to fix. By convincing the reader that the current course of action isn't sustainable, the writer sparks Jinhwa's interest in hearing about an alternative strategy.

What if we stopped trying to build another vertically integrated empire like Starbucks and instead partnered with the growing number of independent roasters around the country? Rather than being limited to our own coffee brands, we could serve coffees from a wide range of local and regional roasters. This would instantly give us a unique value proposition, particularly in the eyes of frequent travelers, who are tired of seeing the same offerings in every airport. Plus, we could get out of the business of sourcing beans. That part was fun when we started out, but it has turned into a grind, pardon the pun.

Desire: To build Jinhwa's desire to consider a new approach, the writer lists some key benefits that the new strategy could bring.

If you think this idea is worth exploring, I'd like to take a few weeks to think through this new business model and figure out a plan to test market it in a few of our locations.

Looking forward to your thoughts on this.

Action: The call to action asks Jinhwa for permission to take time off from his regular duties for a few weeks.

Figure 12.5   Persuasive Message Using the AIDA Model
This writer uses the AIDA model to persuade his boss to give him a few weeks away from his regular duties to explore a new business strategy. The passages in red are key points in each step of the AIDA approach. (These passages would not appear in red in the actual email message.)

Open with an attention-getting device and show readers you understand their concerns. Use the interest and desire sections of your message to demonstrate that you have good reason for making such a request and to cover what you know about the situation: the facts and figures, the benefits of helping, and any history or experience that will enhance your appeal. Your goals are (1) to gain credibility (for yourself and your request) and (2) to make your readers believe that helping you will indeed help solve a significant problem. Close with a request for some specific action, and make that course of action as easy to follow as possible to maximize the chances of a positive response.

Persuasive Presentations of Ideas

Sometimes the objective of persuasive messages is simply to encourage people to consider a new idea.

You may encounter situations in which you simply want to change attitudes or beliefs about a particular topic, without asking the audience to decide or do anything—at least not yet. The goal of your first message might be nothing more than convincing your audience to reexamine long-held opinions or admit the possibility of new ways of thinking.

For instance, the World Wide Web Consortium (a global association that defines many of the guidelines and technologies behind the World Wide Web) launched a campaign called the Web Accessibility Initiative. Although the consortium's ultimate goal is making websites more accessible to people with disabilities or age-related limitations, a key interim goal is simply making website developers more aware of the need. As part of this effort, the consortium has developed a variety of presentations and documents that highlight the problems many web visitors face.[14]

Persuasive Claims and Requests for Adjustments

Most claims and requests for adjustment are routine messages and use the direct approach discussed in Chapter 10. However, consumers and professionals sometimes encounter situations in which they believe they haven't received a fair deal by following normal procedures. These situations require a more persuasive message.

The key ingredients of a good persuasive claim are a complete and specific review of the facts and a confident and positive tone. Keep in mind that you have the right to be satisfied with every transaction. Begin persuasive claims by outlining the problem and continue by reviewing what has been done about it so far, if anything. The recipient might be juggling numerous claims and other demands on his or her attention, so be clear, calm, and complete when presenting your case. Be specific about how you would like the situation to be resolved.

Next, give your reader a good reason for granting your claim. Show how the individual or organization is responsible for the problem, and appeal to your reader's sense of fair play, goodwill, or moral responsibility. Explain how you feel about the problem, but don't get carried away and don't make threats. People generally respond most favorably to requests that are calm and reasonable. Close on a respectful note that reflects how a successful resolution of the situation will repair or maintain a mutually beneficial working relationship.

Developing Marketing and Sales Messages

3 LEARNING OBJECTIVE
Describe an effective strategy for developing marketing and sales messages, and explain how to modify your approach when writing promotional messages for social media.

Marketing and sales messages use many of the same techniques as persuasive business messages.

Marketing and sales messages use the same basic techniques as other persuasive messages, with the added emphasis of encouraging someone to participate in a commercial transaction. Although the terms *marketing message* and *sales message* are often used interchangeably, there is an important difference: **Marketing messages** usher potential buyers through the purchasing process without asking them to make an immediate decision. **Sales messages** take over at that point, encouraging potential buyers to make a purchase decision then and there. Marketing messages focus on such tasks as introducing new brands to the public and encouraging customers to visit websites for more information, whereas sales messages make an explicit request for people to buy a specific product or service.

Most marketing and sales messages, particularly in larger companies, are created and delivered by professionals with specific training in marketing, advertising, sales, or public relations. However, you may be called on to review the work of these specialists or even to write such messages in smaller companies, and having a good understanding of how these messages work will help you be a more effective manager.

PLANNING MARKETING AND SALES MESSAGES

Everything you've learned about planning messages applies in general to marketing and sales messages, but the planning steps for these messages have some particular aspects to consider as well:

- **Assessing audience needs.** As with every other business message, successful marketing and sales messages start with an understanding of audience needs. Depending on the product and the market, these needs can range from a few functional considerations (such as the size, weight, and finish of office paper) to a complicated mix of emotional and logical issues (all the factors that play into buying a house, for example).

  Understanding the purchase decision from the buyer's perspective is a vital step in framing an effective marketing or sales message.

- **Analyzing your competition.** Marketing and sales messages nearly always compete with messages from other companies trying to reach the same audience. When Nike plans a marketing campaign to introduce a new shoe model to current customers, the company knows its audience has also been exposed to messages from Adidas, New Balance, Reebok, and other shoe companies. Finding a unique message in crowded markets can be quite a challenge.

  Marketing and sales messages have to compete for the audience's attention.

- **Determining key selling points and benefits.** With some insight into audience needs and the alternatives offered by your competitors, your next step is to decide which features and benefits to highlight. **Selling points** are the most attractive features of a product, whereas **benefits** are the particular advantages purchasers can realize from those features. In other words, selling points focus on what the product does. Benefits focus on what the user experiences or gains. Benefits can be practical, emotional, or a combination of the two. For example, the feature of a thin, flexible sole in a running shoe offers the practical benefit of a more natural feel while running. In contrast, the visual design features of the shoe offer no practical benefits but can offer the emotional benefit of wearing something stylish or unusual.

  Selling points focus on the product; benefits focus on the user.

- **Anticipating purchase objections.** Marketing and sales messages usually encounter objections, and as with persuasive business messages, the best way to handle them is to identify

  Anticipating objections is crucial to effective marketing and sales messages.

THE FUTURE OF COMMUNICATION

Emotion Recognition Software

Assessing an audience's emotional response is an important step in judging the success of many communication efforts. If you're presenting a new idea to upper management, for example, you can try to read facial clues and other nonverbal signals to determine whether the executives seem excited, annoyed, bored, or anywhere in between.

But what if you're not there in person and your message has to stand on its own? How can you judge the audience's reaction? This challenge has been taken up by a range of artificial intelligence software tools that attempt to measure people's emotional states based on their facial gestures or voice tones. This capability is being incorporated into mobile apps and other systems to measure such things as emotional reactions to TV commercials and other video material, stress levels, and emotional states as people interact with new products. The technology also holds some promise for people on the autism spectrum who have difficulty deciphering emotions from facial gestures.

Like many emerging technologies, emotion recognition has to navigate some complex issues surrounding ethics,

privacy, accuracy, and what might be called the "creepiness factor" of knowing that a device is trying to read your feelings. On the plus side, having apps that respond to user moods could make device usage more satisfying and give businesses a powerful tool for improving communication.

WHAT'S YOUR PREDICTION?

Research the current state of emotion recognition to identify one way in which the technology has the potential to change business communication practices. Do you agree with the predictions the experts make? Why or why not?

Sources: Hannah Jane Parkinson, "Happy? Sad? Forget Age, Microsoft Can Now Guess Your Emotions," *Guardian*, 11 November 2015, www.theguardian.com; Microsoft Cognitive Services, accessed 19 April 2016, www.microsoft.com; Eyeris website, accessed 19 April 2016, emovu.com; Bill Doerrfeld, "20+ Emotion Recognition APIs That Will Leave You Impressed, and Concerned," Nordic APIs blog, 31 December 2015, nordicapis.com; Nederlandse Omroep Stichting, "Computer Leert Autisten Emoties Herkennen," 14 November 2015, nos.nl.

these objections up front and address as many as you can. They can range from high price or low quality to a lack of compatibility with existing products or a perceived risk involved with the product. By identifying potential objections up front, you can craft your promotional messages in ways that address those concerns. If price is a likely objection, for instance, you can look for ways to increase the perceived value of the purchase and decrease the perception of high cost. When promoting a home gym, you might say that it costs less than a year's worth of health club dues. Of course, any attempts to minimize perceptions of price or other potential negatives must be done ethically.

WRITING CONVENTIONAL MARKETING AND SALES MESSAGES

Conventional marketing and sales messages are often prepared using the AIDA model or some variation of it. (See the next section on crafting messages for social media.) Here are the key points of using the AIDA model for these messages:

- **Getting the reader's attention.** By looking and listening during any given day, you'll notice the many ways advertisers try to get your attention. For example, a headline might offer an exciting product benefit, a piece of interesting news, an appeal to people's emotions or sense of financial value, or a unique solution to a common problem. Of course, words aren't the only attention-getting devices. Depending on the medium, marketers can use evocative images, music, animation, or video. "Cutting through the clutter" to get the audience's attention is one of the biggest challenges with marketing and sales messages.

- **Building interest.** After catching the reader's or viewer's attention, your next step is to build interest in the product, company, or idea you are promoting. A common technique is to "pay off" the promise made in the headline by explaining how you can deliver those benefits. For example, if the headline offers a way to "Get Fit for $2 a Day," the first paragraph could explain that the home gyms your company sells start at under $700, which works out to less than $2 a day over the course of a year.

> To build interest, expand on and support the promises in your attention-getting opening.

- **Increasing desire.** Now that you've given the audience some initial information to start building their interest, the next step is to boost their desire for the product by expanding on your explanation of how it will benefit them. Think carefully about the sequence of support points and use plenty of subheadings, hyperlinks, video demonstrations, and other devices to help people quickly find the information they need. By keeping the focus on potential customers and their practical and emotional needs, you can layer on information that helps convince people that your product really is the best solution for them. You can also use a variety of techniques to address potential objections and minimize doubts, including testimonials from satisfied users, articles written by industry experts, competitive comparisons, offers of product samples or free demonstrations, independent test results, and money-back guarantees.

> Add details and audience benefits to increase desire for the product or service.

- **Motivating action.** The final step in the AIDA model is persuading the audience to take action, such as encouraging people to pick up the phone to place an order or visit an online app store to download your software. The keys to a successful *call to action* are making it as easy and risk-free as possible. If the process is confusing or time-consuming, you'll lose potential customers.

> After you've generated sufficient interest and desire, you're ready to persuade readers to take the preferred action.

If you analyze the advertisements you encounter in any medium, you'll see variations of these techniques used again and again.

REAL-TIME UPDATES

LEARN MORE BY READING THIS INFOGRAPHIC

The color of persuasion

See the powerful influence of color in marketing and sales messages. Go to **real-timeupdates.com/bct14** and select Learn More in the Students section.

WRITING PROMOTIONAL MESSAGES FOR SOCIAL MEDIA

The AIDA model and similar approaches have been successful with marketing and sales messages for decades, but in the social media landscape consumers are more apt to look for product information from other consumers, not from the companies marketing those

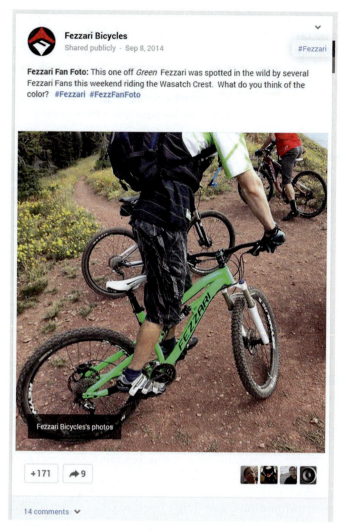

Figure 12.6   Promotional Messages in Social Media
Persuasive communication on social media often avoids overt promotion and instead tries to engage the target audience, as Fezzari Bicycles did with this post on Google+.

products. Consequently, your emphasis should shift to encouraging and participating in online conversations. Follow these guidelines (see Figure 12.6):[15]

- **Facilitate community building.** Give customers and other audiences an opportunity to connect with you and one another, such as on your Facebook page or through members-only online forums.
- **Listen at least as much as you talk.** Listening is just as essential for online conversations as it is for in-person conversations.
- **Initiate and respond to conversations within the community.** Through your website, blog postings, social network profiles and messages, newsletters, and other tools, make sure you provide the information customers need in order to evaluate your products and services. Use **conversation marketing**, rather than traditional promotion, to initiate and facilitate conversations in your networked community of customers, journalists, bloggers, and other interested parties.
- **Provide information people want.** Whether it's industry-insider news, in-depth technical guides to using your products, or brief answers to questions posted on community Q&A sites, fill the information gaps about your company and its products.
- **Identify and support your champions.** In marketing, *champions* are the most enthusiastic fans of your company and its products. Champions are so enthusiastic they

In a social media environment, persuasive efforts require a more conversational, interactive approach.

MOBILE APP
Talkwalker helps companies monitor social media conversations in real time.

help spread your message (through their social media accounts, for instance), defend you against detractors, and help other customers use your products.

- **Be real.** Social media audiences respond positively to companies that are open and conversational about themselves, their products, and subjects of shared interest. In contrast, if a company is serving its stakeholders poorly with shoddy products, bad customer service, or unethical behavior, an attempt to improve its reputation by adopting social media without fixing the underlying problems is likely to fail as soon as audiences see through the superficial attempt to "be social."

- **Integrate conventional marketing and sales strategies at the right time and in the right places.** AIDA and similar approaches are still valid for specific communication tasks, such as conventional advertising and the product promotion pages on your website.

CREATING PROMOTIONAL MESSAGES FOR MOBILE DEVICES

Mobile advertising and mobile commerce (sometimes referred to as *m-commerce*) are two of the hottest developments in marketing communications. Mobile advertising is already a multibillion-dollar business.[16] The types of marketing and sales messages created for mobile audiences range from short, simple text ads that appear next to search engine results to mobile-optimized video—the most common form of content marketing in the mobile arena.[17]

Companies are putting so much emphasis on mobile marketing because mobile devices now play such a big role in consumer buying behavior. Smartphone owners tend to use their devices for many shopping-related tasks, from searching for product reviews to finding stores and service businesses, looking for coupons and other promotions, and doing in-store price comparisons. In fact, some 80 percent of smartphone-equipped consumers use their devices to get shopping-related information.[18]

If you are involved with creating mobile marketing or sales messages, keep two essential points in mind. First, like all mobile messages, promotional messages need to be kept short and simple. Second, the mobile experience needs to be fast and straightforward. Mobile users are often time-constrained, and they will quickly abandon websites that don't load quickly or are confusing to navigate.

Promotional messages aimed at mobile audiences need to be short, simple, and easy to respond to.

Maintaining High Standards of Ethics, Legal Compliance, and Etiquette

4 LEARNING OBJECTIVE Identify steps you can take to avoid ethical lapses in marketing and sales messages.

The word *persuasion* has negative connotations for some people, especially in a marketing or sales context. However, ethical businesspeople view persuasion as a positive force, aligning their own interests with what is best for their audiences. They influence audience members by providing information and aiding understanding, which allows audiences the freedom to choose.[19] To maintain the highest standards of business ethics, always demonstrate the "you" attitude by showing honest concern for your audience's needs and interests.

Marketing and sales messages are covered by a wide range of laws and regulations.

As marketing and selling grow increasingly complex, so do the legal ramifications of marketing and sales messages. In the United States, the Federal Trade Commission (FTC; **www.ftc.gov**) has the authority to impose penalties (ranging from cease-and-desist orders to multimillion-dollar fines) on advertisers who violate federal standards for truthful advertising. Other federal agencies have authority over advertising in specific industries, such as transportation and financial services. Individual states have additional laws that may apply. The legal aspects of promotional communication can be quite complex, varying from state to state and from country to country, and most companies require marketing and salespeople to get clearance from company lawyers before sending messages.

Moreover, communicators must stay on top of changing regulations, such as the latest laws governing unsolicited bulk email ("spam"), disclosure requirements for bloggers who review products, privacy, and data security. For example, two ethical concerns that could produce new legislation are *behavioral targeting*, which tracks the online behavior of website visitors and serves up ads based on what they seem to be interested in, and *remarketing*, in which behaviorally targeted ads follow users even as they move on to other websites. Many users consider the practice invasive.[20]

For all marketing and sales efforts, pay close attention to the following legal considerations:[21]

- **Marketing and sales messages must be truthful and nondeceptive.** The FTC considers messages to be deceptive if they include statements that are likely to mislead reasonable customers and those statements are an important part of the purchasing decision. Failing to include important information is also considered deceptive. The FTC also looks at *implied claims*—claims you don't explicitly make but that can be inferred from what you do or don't say.
- **You must back up your claims with evidence.** According to the FTC, offering a money-back guarantee or providing letters from satisfied customers is not enough; you must still be able to support claims for your product with objective evidence such as a survey or scientific study. If you claim that your food product lowers cholesterol, you must have scientific evidence to support that claim.
- **"Bait-and-switch" advertising is illegal.** Trying to attract buyers by advertising a product that you don't intend to sell—and then trying to sell them another (and usually more expensive) product—is illegal.
- **Marketing messages and websites aimed at children are subject to special rules.** For example, online marketers must obtain consent from parents before collecting personal information about children under age 13.
- **Marketing and sales messages are considered binding contracts in many states.** If you imply or make an offer and then can't fulfill your end of the bargain, you can be sued for breach of contract.
- **In most cases you can't use a person's name, photograph, or other identity without permission.** Doing so is considered an invasion of privacy. You can use images of people considered to be public figures as long as you don't unfairly imply that they endorse your message.

Marketers have a responsibility to stay up to date on laws and regulations that restrict promotional messages.

Meeting your ethical and legal obligations will go a long way toward maintaining good communication etiquette. However, you may still face etiquette decisions within ethical and legal boundaries. For instance, you can produce a marketing campaign that complies with all applicable laws and yet is offensive or insulting to your audience. Taking an audience-centered approach, in which you show respect for your readers and their values, should help you avoid any such etiquette missteps.

Technology also gives communicators new ways to demonstrate sensitivity to user needs and gives audiences more control over which messages they receive. By liking a company's Facebook page, for instance, people choose to see posts from that company in their timelines. *Opt-in* email newsletters are another technology that shows the "you" attitude at work. Unlike the unwelcome spam messages that litter email inboxes these days, opt-in messages are sent only to those people who have specifically requested information.

For the latest information on writing persuasive messages, visit **real-timeupdates .com/bct14** and select Chapter 12.

COMMUNICATION CHALLENGES AT **Red Ants Pants**

Sarah Calhoun likes your style—your writing style, that is. She hired you to take care of all the company's customer communication efforts, from managing the website to writing an email newsletter. Use what you've learned in this chapter to address these challenges.

INDIVIDUAL CHALLENGE: Red Ants Pants are much tougher than regular jeans, so their higher price is in line with the lasting value they offer customers. However, paying $139 for a pair of pants is a tough decision for many working women. Visit the Red Ants Pants website and study the description of the original work pants. Write a short statement (50 to 100 words) that addresses the cost concerns some customers are likely to have and explains why the pants are a good value. Mimic the tone of company's website content.

TEAM CHALLENGE: Not many companies have the irreverent self-confidence to present their company history in the form of poetry—and fairly goofy poetry at that. The rhyming couplets in the "Our History" section of the Red Ants Pants website (under "Our Story") do the job quite nicely, but you need a shorter version to use on the company's Facebook page. Using that information (and any other information on the website), write a paragraph of approximately 100 words that describes the company's founding.

Quick Learning Guide

KEY TERMS

AIDA model Message sequence that involves attention, interest, desire, and action

benefits Particular advantages that readers will realize from a product's selling points

conversation marketing Approach in which companies initiate and facilitate conversations in a networked community of customers, journalists, bloggers, and other interested parties

demographics Quantifiable characteristics of a population, including age, gender, occupation, income, and education

emotional appeal Persuasive approach that calls on audience feelings and sympathies rather than facts, figures, and rational arguments

logical appeal Persuasive approach that calls on reasoning and evidence rather than audience feelings and sympathies

marketing messages Promotional messages that usher potential buyers through the purchasing process without asking them to make an immediate decision

motivation The combination of forces that drive people to satisfy their needs

persuasion The attempt to change an audience's attitudes, beliefs, or actions

psychographics Psychological characteristics of an audience, including personality, attitudes, and lifestyle

sales messages Promotional messages that encourage potential buyers to make a purchase decision then and there

selling points The most attractive features of a product or service

SUMMARY OF LEARNING OBJECTIVES

1 Apply the three-step writing process to persuasive messages. To plan persuasive messages, carefully clarify your purpose to make sure you focus on a single goal. Understand audience needs, which can involve research to identify relevant demographic and psychographic variables and to assess audience motivations. Persuasive messages usually ask people to give up time, money, or other resources, so gathering the right information to convince readers of the benefits of responding is essential. Media choices need to be considered carefully, particularly with marketing and sales messages in a social media landscape. For organizing persuasive messages, you will usually want to choose the indirect approach to establish awareness and interest before asking the audience to take action.

When writing persuasive messages, use positive and polite language, understand and respect cultural differences, be sensitive to organizational cultures when writing persuasive business messages, and take steps to establish your credibility. Seven common ways to establish credibility in persuasive messages are using simple language, supporting your claims, identifying your sources, establishing common ground, being objective, displaying good intentions, and avoiding the hard sell.

The steps for completing persuasive messages are the same as for other types of messages, but accuracy and completeness are especially important because they send signals about your credibility—a crucial element in persuasive messages.

2 Describe an effective strategy for developing persuasive business messages, and identify the three most common categories of persuasive business messages. Within the context of the three-step process, effective persuasion involves four essential strategies: framing your arguments, balancing emotional and logical appeals, reinforcing your position, and anticipating objections. One of the most commonly used methods for framing a persuasive argument is the AIDA model, in which you open your message by getting the audience's attention; build interest with facts, details, and additional benefits; increase desire by providing more evidence and answering possible objections; and motivate a specific action.

Persuasive business messages combine emotional appeals (which call on feelings and sympathies) and logical appeals (which call on reason using analogy, induction, or deduction). To reinforce your position, look for ways to add convincing evidence, quotations from experts, or other support material.

By identifying potential objections and addressing them as you craft your message, you can help prevent audience members from gravitating toward negative answers before you have the opportunity to ask them for a positive response. You can often resolve these issues before the audience has a chance to go on the defensive.

The most common types of these messages are (1) persuasive requests for action, in which you ask the recipient to make a decision or engage in some activity; (2) persuasive presentations of ideas, in which you aren't necessarily looking for a decision or action but rather would like the audience to consider a different way of looking at a particular topic; and (3) persuasive claims and requests for adjustments, in which you believe that you have not received fair treatment under an organization's standard policies and would like the recipient to give your case fresh consideration.

3 Describe an effective strategy for developing marketing and sales messages, and explain how to modify your approach when writing promotional messages for social media. Marketing and sales messages use the same basic techniques as other persuasive messages, with the added emphasis of encouraging someone to participate in a commercial transaction. Marketing messages do this indirectly, whereas sales messages do it directly. The basic strategy for creating these messages includes assessing audience needs, analyzing your competition, determining key selling points and benefits, anticipating purchase objections, applying AIDA or a similar model, adapting your writing to social media (if appropriate), and maintaining high standards of ethical and legal compliance.

To use social media for promotional communication, start by engaging audiences with efforts to build networked communities of potential buyers and other interested parties. Listen to conversations taking place about your company and its products. Initiate and respond to conversations within these communities, being sure to use an objective, conversational style. Provide the information interested parties want. Identify and support the enthusiastic product champions who want to help spread your message. Be authentic and transparent in all your communication. Speak directly to customers so you don't have to rely on the news media. Finally, continue to use the AIDA model or similar approaches, but only at specific times and places, as part of a broader, conversational approach.

4 Identify steps you can take to avoid ethical lapses in marketing and sales messages. Effective and ethical persuasive communicators focus on aligning their interests with the interests of their audiences. They help audiences understand how their proposals will provide benefits to the audience, using language that is persuasive without being manipulative. They choose words that are less likely to be misinterpreted and take care not to distort the truth. Throughout, they maintain a "you" attitude with honest concern for the audience's needs and interests. By following applicable laws and regulations, marketers can avoid many ethical problems.

Test Your Knowledge

To review chapter content related to each question, refer to the indicated Learning Objective.

12-1. What are four of the many ways you can build credibility with an audience when planning a persuasive message? [LO-1]

12-2. What is the AIDA model and what are its limitations? [LO-2]

12-3. How do emotional appeals differ from logical appeals? [LO-2]

12-4. What three types of reasoning can you use in logical appeals? [LO-2]

12-5. What is conversation marketing? [LO-3]

12-6. How do marketing and sales messages differ? [LO-3]

12-7. What is likely to happen if you don't anticipate audience objections when crafting your messages? [LO-2], [LO-3]

12-8. How do benefits differ from features? [LO-3]

12-9. Why do promotional messages need to be short and simple on mobile devices? [LO-4]

12-10. How does ethical behavior contribute to positive etiquette in persuasive messages? [LO-4]

Apply Your Knowledge

To review chapter content related to each question, refer to the indicated Learning Objective.

12-11. Why is it essential to understand your readers' likely motivations before writing a persuasive message? [LO-1]

12-12. Why is it important to present all sides of an argument when writing a persuasive message to a potentially hostile audience? [LO-2]

12-13. Are emotional appeals ethical? Why or why not? [LO-2]

12-14. What is likely to happen if a promotional message starts immediately with a call to action? Why? [LO-3]

12-15. Are promotional slogans such as "Best sushi in town" or "Atlanta's most popular restaurant" ethical? Why or why not? [LO-4]

Practice Your Skills

Messages for Analysis

For Message 12.A and Message 12.B, read the following documents, then (1) analyze the strengths and weaknesses of each sentence, and (2) revise each document so that it follows this chapter's guidelines.

12-16. **Message 12.A: Message Strategies: Persuasive Claims and Requests for Adjustment [LO-2]**

Dear TechStar Computing:

I'm writing to you because of my disappointment with my new multimedia PC display. The display part works all right, but the audio volume is set too high and the volume knob doesn't turn it down. It's driving us crazy. The volume knob doesn't seem to be connected to anything but simply spins around. I can't believe you would put out a product like this without testing it first.

I depend on my computer to run my small business and want to know what you are going to do about it. This reminds me of every time I buy electronic equipment from what seems like any company. Something is always wrong. I thought quality was supposed to be important, but I guess not. Anyway, I need this fixed right away. Please tell me what you want me to do.

12-17. **Message 12.B: Message Strategies: Sales Messages [LO-3]**

We know how awful dining hall food can be, and that's why we've developed the "Mealaweek Club." Once a week, we'll deliver food to your dormitory or apartment. Our meals taste great. We have pizza, buffalo wings, hamburgers and curly fries, veggie roll-ups, and more!

When you sign up for just six months, we will ask what day you want your delivery. We'll ask you to fill out your selection of meals. And the rest is up to us. At "Mealaweek," we deliver! And payment is easy. We accept MasterCard and Visa or a personal check. It will save money especially when compared with eating out.

Just fill out the enclosed card and indicate your method of payment. As soon as we approve your credit or check, we'll begin delivery. Tell all your friends about Mealaweek. We're the best idea since sliced bread!

12-18. **Message 12.C: Media Skills: Podcasting [LO-2]** To access this message, visit **real-timeupdates.com/bct14**, select Student Assignments, and select Chapter 12, Message 12.C. Listen to the podcast. Identify at least three ways in which the podcast could be more persuasive, and draft a brief email message you could send to the podcaster with your suggestions for improvement.

Exercises

Each activity is labeled according to the primary skill or skills you will need to use. To review relevant chapter content, you can refer to the indicated Learning Objective. In some instances, supporting information will be found in another chapter, as indicated.

Choosing a Message Strategy: [LO-1], Chapters 10 and 11 Now that you've explored routine, positive, negative, and persuasive messages, review the following message scenarios and identify which of the four message strategies would be most appropriate for the situation. Offer a brief justification for your choices. (Depending on the particular circumstances, a scenario might lend itself to more than one type of message; just be sure to offer compelling reasons for your choices.)

12-19. An unsolicited message to your department manager, explaining why you believe the company's experiment with self-managed work teams has not been successful

12-20. An unsolicited message to your department manager, explaining why you believe the company's experiment with self-managed work teams has not been successful and suggesting that one of the more experienced employees (such as yourself) should be promoted to supervisor

12-21. A message to a long-time industrial customer, explaining that a glitch in your accounting system resulted in the customer being overcharged on its last five orders, apologizing for the problem, and assuring the customer that you will refund the overcharged amount immediately

12-22. A news release announcing that your company plans to invite back 50 employees who were laid off earlier in the year

Message Strategies: Persuasive Business Messages; Collaboration: Team Projects [LO-2] With another student, analyze the persuasive email message in Figure 12.5 by answering the following questions:

12-23. What techniques are used to capture the reader's attention?

12-24. Does the writer use the direct or indirect organizational approach? Why?

12-25. Is the subject line effective? Why or why not?

12-26. How does the writer balance emotional and logical appeals?

12-27. What reader benefits are included?

12-28. How does the writer establish credibility?

Message Strategies: Persuasive Business Messages, Marketing and Sales Messages: Media Skills: Email [LO-2], [LO-3] Compose effective subject lines for the following persuasive email messages:

12-29. A recommendation to your branch manager to install wireless networking throughout the facility. Your primary reason is that management has encouraged more teamwork, but teams often congregate in meeting rooms, the cafeteria, and other places that lack network access—without which they can't do much of the work they are expected to do.

12-30. A message to area residents, soliciting customers for your new business, "Meals à la Car," a carryout dining service that delivers from most of the local restaurants.

12-31. A message to the company president, asking that employees be allowed to carry over their unused vacation days to the following year. Apparently, many employees canceled their fourth-quarter vacation plans to work on the installation of a new computer system. Under current policy, vacation days not used by December 31 can't be carried over to the following year.

12-32. **Communication Ethics: Making Ethical Choices [LO-2], [LO-4]** Your boss has asked you to post a message on the company's internal blog, urging everyone in your department to donate money to the company's favorite charity, an organization that operates a summer camp for children with physical disabilities. You wind up writing a lengthy posting, packed with facts and heartwarming anecdotes about the camp and the children's experiences. When you must work that hard to persuade your audience to take an action such as donating money to a charity, are you being manipulative and unethical? Explain.

Message Strategies: Marketing and Sales Messages (Customer Benefits) [LO-3] Determine whether the following sentences focus on features or benefits; rewrite as necessary to focus all the sentences on benefits.

12-33. All-Cook skillets are coated with a durable, patented nonstick surface.

12-34. You can call anyone and talk as long as you like on Saturdays and Sundays with our new FamilyTalk wireless plan.

12-35. With an eight-millisecond response time, the Samsung LN-S4095D 40-inch LCD TV delivers fast video action that is smooth and crisp.[22]

12-36. **Message Strategies: Marketing and Sales Messages [LO-3]** Have you ever wondered why certain websites and blogs appear at the top of the list when you use an online search engine? Or why a site you might expect to find doesn't show up at all? Such questions are at the heart of one of the most important activities in online communication: *search engine optimization* (SEO). (SEO applies to the *natural* or *organic* search results, not the sponsored, paid results you see above, beside, or below the main search results listing.)

SEO is a complex topic that factors in dozens of variables, but even without becoming an expert in SEO, every website owner can work toward improving rankings by focusing on three important areas. First, offer fresh, high-quality, audience-oriented content. Content that doesn't appeal to people won't appeal to search engines, either. Second, use relevant keywords judiciously, particularly in important areas such as the page title that displays at the top of the browser screen. Third, encourage links to your site from other high-quality sites with relevant content. These links from other sites are crucial because they tell the search engines that other people find your content interesting and useful. Not surprisingly, given the importance of links from other sites, the content sharing encouraged by social media has had a huge impact on SEO in recent years.[23]

Locate a website for any company that sells products to consumers and write a new title for the site's homepage (the title that appears at the top of a web browser). Make the title short enough to read quickly while still summarizing what the company offers. Be sure to use one or more keywords that online shoppers would likely use when searching for the types of products the company sells. Next, identify three high-quality websites that would be good ones to link to the site you chose. For instance, if you chose a website that sells automotive parts and supplies, one of the three linking sites could be a popular blog that deals with automotive repair. Or if the site you chose sells golf equipment, you might find a sports website that covers the professional golf tours or one that provides information about golf courses around the world.

Expand Your Skills

Critique the Professionals

Visit the Facebook pages of six companies in several industries. How do the companies make use of their timeline? Do any of the companies use timeline posts to promote their products? Compare the material on the About tabs. Which company has the most compelling information here? How about the use of custom tabs: which company does the best job of using this Facebook feature? Using whatever medium your instructor requests, write a brief analysis of the message (no more than one page), citing specific elements from the piece and support from the chapter.

Sharpening Your Career Skills Online

Bovée and Thill's Business Communication Web Search, at websearch.businesscommunicationnetwork.com, is a unique research tool designed specifically for business communication research. Use the Web Search function to find a website, video, article, podcast, or presentation that offers advice on writing persuasive messages (either persuasive business messages or marketing and sales messages). Write a brief email message to your instructor, describing the item you found and summarizing the career skills information you learned from it.

Cases

For all cases, feel free to use your creativity to make up any details you need in order to craft effective messages.

Persuasive Business Messages

MICROBLOGGING SKILLS

12-37. Message Strategies: Persuasive Business Messages [LO-2] You've been trying for months to convince your boss, company CEO Will Florence, to start using Twitter. You've told him that top executives in numerous industries now use Twitter as a way to connect with customers and other stakeholders without going through the filters and barriers of formal corporate communications, but he doesn't see the value.

Your task: You come up with the brilliant plan to demonstrate Twitter's usefulness using Twitter itself. First, find three executives from three companies who are on Twitter (choose any companies and executives you find interesting). Second, study their tweets to get a feel for the type of information they share. Third, if you don't already have a Twitter account set up for this class, set one up for the purposes of this exercise (you can deactivate later). Fourth, write four tweets to demonstrate the value of executive microblogging: one that summarizes the value of having a company CEO use Twitter and three support tweets, each one summarizing how your three real-life executive role models use Twitter.

BLOGGING SKILLS/TEAM SKILLS

12-38. Message Strategies: Persuasive Business Messages [LO-2] As a strong advocate for the use of social media in business, you are pleased by how quickly people in your company have taken up blogging, wiki writing, and other new-media activities. You are considerably less excited by the style and quality of your colleagues' writing. Many seem to have interpreted "authentic and conversational" to mean "anything goes." Several of the Twitter users in the company seem to have abandoned any pretense of grammar and spelling. A few managers have dragged internal disagreements about company strategy out into public view, arguing with each other through comments on various industry-related forums. Product demonstration videos have been posted to the company's YouTube channel virtually unedited, making the whole firm look unpolished and unprofessional. The company CEO has written some blog posts that bash competitors with coarse and even crude language.

You pushed long and hard for greater use of these tools, so you feel a sense of responsibility for this situation. In addition, you are viewed by many in the company as the resident expert on social media, so you have some "expert authority" on this issue. On the other hand, you are only a first-level manager, with three levels of managers above you, so while you have some "position authority" as well, you can hardly dictate best practices to the managers above you.

Your task: Working with two other students, write a post for the company's internal blog (which is not viewable outside the company), outlining your concerns about these communication practices. Use the examples mentioned previously and make up any additional details you need. Emphasize that while social media communication is often less formal and more flexible than traditional business communication, it shouldn't be unprofessional. You are thinking of proposing a social media training program for everyone in the company, but for this message you just want to bring attention to the problem.

EMAIL SKILLS/TEAM SKILLS

12-39. Message Strategies: Persuasive Business Messages [LO-2] At lunch with a colleague from your department last week, you discovered that as much as you both love your jobs, family obligations are making it difficult to keep working full time. Unfortunately, your company doesn't offer any conventional part-time jobs because it needs to keep positions such as yours staffed five days a week. However, you have heard about the concept of job sharing, in which two people divide a single job.

Your task: With a partner, research job sharing. Identify the pros and cons from the perspectives of the employer and the employees involved. Using the AIDA approach, draft a persuasive email message to your supervisor, outlining the benefits and addressing the potential problem areas. Your call to action should be to ask your supervisor to propose job sharing to company management.

EMAIL SKILLS

12-40. Message Strategies: Persuasive Business Messages [LO-2] While sitting at your desk during lunch break, slumped over as usual, staring at your computer screen, you see an online article about the dangers of sitting at your desk all day. Yikes. The article suggests trying a standing desk—or even better, a treadmill desk, which has an exercise treadmill built into a standing desk. You'd love to lose a few pounds while being healthier and feeling more alert during the day. Plus, you know the company is encouraging employees to live healthier lifestyles to improve their overall well-being and to reduce its health-care costs.

Your task: Research treadmill desks and write a persuasive email message to your boss, requesting that the company buy or rent a treadmill desk for you to try out. Offer to serve as a research subject for the whole office, tracking your weight loss, alertness levels, and any other relevant variables you can think of.

LETTER-WRITING SKILLS

12-41. Message Strategies: Persuasive Business Messages [LO-2] The coffee shop across the street from your tiny apartment is your haven away from home—great beverages, healthy snacks, free wireless, and an atmosphere that is convivial but not so lively that you can't focus on your homework. It lacks only one thing: some way to print out your homework and other files when you need hard copies. Your college's libraries and computer labs provide printers, but you live three miles from campus, and it's a long walk or an inconvenient bus ride.

Your task: Write a letter to the owner of the coffee shop, encouraging her to set up a printing service to complement the free wireless access. Propose that the service run at break-even prices, just enough to pay for paper, ink cartridges, and the cost of the printer itself. The benefit to the shop would be enticing patrons to spend more time—and, therefore, more of their coffee and tea money—in the shop. You might also mention that you had to take the bus to campus to print this letter, so you bought your afternoon latté somewhere else.

EMAIL SKILLS/PORTFOLIO BUILDER

12-42. Message Strategies: Persuasive Business Messages [LO-2] As someone who came of age in the "post-email" world of blogs, wikis, social networks, and other Web 2.0 technologies, you were rather disappointed to find your new employer solidly stuck in the age of email. You use email, of course, but it is only one of the tools in your communication toolbox. From your college years, you have hands-on experience with a wide range of social media tools, having used them to collaborate on school projects, to become involved in your local community, to learn more about various industries and professions, and to research potential employers during your job search. (In fact, without social media, you might never have heard about your current employer in the first place.) Moreover, your use of social media on the job has already paid several important dividends, including finding potential sales contacts at several large companies, connecting with peers in other companies to share ideas for working more efficiently, and learning about some upcoming legislative matters in your state that could profoundly hamper your company's current way of doing business.

You hoped that by setting an example through your own use of social media at work, your new colleagues and company management would quickly adopt these tools as well. However, just the opposite has happened. Waiting in your email in-box this morning was a message from the CEO, announcing that the company is now cutting off access to social networking websites and banning the use of any social media at work. The message says using company time and company computers for socializing is highly inappropriate and might be considered grounds for dismissal in the future if the problem gets out of hand.

Your task: You are stunned by the message. You fight the urge to fire off a hotly worded reply to straighten out the CEO's misperceptions. Instead, you wisely decide to send a message to your immediate superior first, explaining why you believe the new policy should be reversed. Using your boss's favorite medium (email, of course!), write a persuasive message explaining why Facebook, Twitter, and other social networking technologies are valid—and valuable—business tools. Bolster your argument with examples from other companies and advice from communication experts.

MESSAGING SKILLS

12-43. Message Strategies: Requests for Action [LO-2] At IBM, you're one of the coordinators for the annual Employee

Charitable Contributions Campaign. Since 1978, the company has helped employees contribute to more than 2,000 health and human service agencies. These groups may offer child care; treat substance abuse; provide health services; or fight illiteracy, homelessness, and hunger. Some offer disaster relief or care for the elderly. All deserve support. They're carefully screened by IBM, one of the largest corporate contributors of cash, equipment, and people to nonprofit organizations and educational institutions in the United States and around the world. As your literature states, the program "has engaged our employees more fully in the important mission of corporate citizenship."

During the winter holidays, you target agencies that cater to the needs of displaced families, women, and children. It's not difficult to raise enthusiasm. The prospect of helping children enjoy the holidays—children who otherwise might have nothing—usually awakens the spirit of your most distracted workers. But some of them wait until the last minute and then forget.

Workers have until December 16 to make cash contributions. To make it in time for holiday deliveries, they can also bring in toys, food, and blankets through Tuesday, December 20. They shouldn't have any trouble finding the collection bins; they're everywhere, marked with bright red banners. But some will want to call you with questions or (you hope) to make credit card contributions: 800-658-3899, ext. 3342.

Your task: It's December 14. Write a 75- to 100-word message for your department's workplace messaging systems, encouraging last-minute holiday gifts.[24]

EMAIL SKILLS

12-44. Message Strategies: Requests for Action [LO-2] Managing a new-product launch can be an aggravating experience as you try to coordinate a wide variety of activities and processes while barreling toward a deadline that is often defined more by external factors than a realistic assessment of whether you can actually meet it. You depend on lots of other people to meet their deadlines, and if they fail, you fail. The pressure is enough to push anybody over the edge. Unfortunately, that happened to you last week. After a barrage of bad news from suppliers and the members of the team you lead, you lost your cool in a checkpoint meeting. Shouting at people and accusing them of slacking off was embarrassing enough, but the situation got a hundred times worse this morning when your boss suggested you needed some low-pressure work for a while and removed you as the leader of the launch team.

Your task: Write an email message to your boss, Sunil, requesting to be reinstated as the project team leader. Make up any information you need.

EMAIL SKILLS

12-45. Message Strategies: Requests for Action [LO-2] You appreciate how important phones are to your company's operations, but the amount of conversational chatter in your work area has gotten so bad that it's hard to concentrate on your work. You desperately need at least a few quiet hours every day to engage in the analytical thinking your job requires.

Your task: Write an email message to the division vice president, Jeri Ross, asking her to designate one of the conference rooms as a quiet-zone work room. It would have Wi-Fi so that employees can stay connected to the corporate network, but it would not have any phone service, either landline or mobile. (Mobile reception is already weak in the conference rooms, but you will propose to equip the room with a mobile signal jammer to ensure that no calls can be made or received.) In addition, conversation of any kind would be strictly forbidden. Make up any details you need.

EMAIL SKILLS/MOBILE SKILLS

12-46. Message Strategies: Requests for Action [LO-2]

Your new company, WorldConnect Language Services, started well and is going strong. However, to expand beyond your Memphis, Tennessee, home market, you need a one-time infusion of cash to open branch offices in other cities around the Southeast. At the Entrepreneur's Lunch Forum you attended yesterday, you learned about several *angels*, as they are called in the investment community—private individuals who invest money in small companies in exchange for a share of ownership. One such angel, Melinda Sparks, told the audience she is looking for investment opportunities outside of high technology, where angels often invest their money. She also indicated that she looks for entrepreneurs who know their industries and markets well, who are passionate about the value they bring to the marketplace, who are committed to growing their businesses, and who have a solid plan for how they will spend an investor's money. Fortunately, you meet all of her criteria.

Your task: Draft an email message to Sparks, introducing yourself and your business and asking for a meeting at which you can present your business plan in more detail. Explain that your Memphis office was booked to capacity within two months of opening, thanks to the growing number of international business professionals looking for translators and interpreters. You've researched the entire Southeast region and identified at least 10 other cities that could support a language services office such as yours. Making up whatever other information you need, draft a four-paragraph message following the AIDA model, ending with a request for a meeting within the next four weeks. You know Sparks tends to read email on her phone, so craft your message to be mobile friendly.

EMAIL SKILLS

12-47. Message Strategies: Persuasive Claims and Requests for Adjustment [LO-2]

You thought it was strange that no one called you on your new mobile phone, even though you had given your family members, friends, and boss your new number. Two weeks after getting the new phone and agreeing to a $49 monthly fee, you called the service provider, InstantCall, just to see if everything was working. Sure enough, the technician discovered that your incoming calls were being routed to an inactive number. You're glad she found the problem, but then it took the company nearly two more weeks to fix it. When you called to complain about paying for service you didn't receive, the customer service agent suggests you send an email to Judy

Hinkley at the company's regional business office to request an adjustment.

Your task: Decide how much of an adjustment you think you deserve under the circumstances and then send an email message to Hinkley to request the adjustment to your account. Write a summary of events in chronological order, supplying exact dates for maximum effectiveness. Make up any information you need, such as problems that the malfunctioning service caused at home or at work.

EMAIL SKILLS

12-48. Message Strategies: Requests for Information [LO-2]

As a motivated, ambitious employee, you naturally care about your performance on the job—and about making sure your performance is being fairly judged and rewarded. Unfortunately, the company has recently gone through a period of turmoil, and you have reported to seven managers during the past five years. One year, your annual performance review was done by someone who had been your boss for only three weeks and knew almost nothing about you or your work. Last year, your boss was fired the day after he wrote your review, and you can't help but wonder whether you got a fair review from someone in that situation. Overall, you are worried that your career progression and wage increases have been hampered by inconsistent and ill-informed performance reviews.

The company allows employees to keep copies of their reviews, but you haven't been diligent about doing so. You would like to get copies of your last five reviews, but you heard from a colleague that the human resources department will not release copies of past reviews without approval from the managers who wrote them. In your case, however, three of the managers who reviewed you are no longer with the company, and you do not want your current boss to know you are concerned about your reviews.

Your task: Write an email message to the director of human resources, Leon Sandes, requesting copies of your performance reviews over the past five years. Use the information included above and make up any additional details you need.

Marketing and Sales Messages: Conventional Media

LETTER-WRITING SKILLS/PORTFOLIO BUILDER

12-49. Message Strategies: Marketing and Sales Messages [LO-3]

Like all other states, Kentucky works hard to attract businesses that are considering expanding into the state or relocating entirely from another state. The Kentucky Cabinet for Economic Development is responsible for reaching out to these companies and overseeing the many incentive programs the state offers to new and established businesses.

Your task: As the communication director of the Kentucky Cabinet for Economic Development, you play the lead role in reaching out to companies that want to expand or relocate to Kentucky. Visit **www.thinkkentucky.com** and read "Top 10

Reasons for Locating or Expanding Your Business in Kentucky" (look under "Why Kentucky" in the "Locating/Expanding in KY" dropdown menu). Identify the major benefits the state uses to promote Kentucky as a great place to locate a business. Summarize these reasons in a one-page form letter that will be sent to business executives throughout the country. Be sure to introduce yourself and your purpose in the letter, and close with a compelling call to action (have them reach you by telephone at 800-626-2930 or by email at econdev@ky.gov). As you plan your letter, try to imagine yourself as the CEO of a company and consider what a complex choice it would be to move to another state.[25]

LETTER-WRITING SKILLS/PORTFOLIO BUILDER

12-50. Message Strategies: Marketing and Sales Messages
[LO-3] Water polo is an active sport that provides great opportunities for exercise and for learning the collaborative skills involved in teamwork. You can learn more at **www.usawaterpolo.org**.

Your task: Write a one-page letter to parents of 10- to 14-year-old boys and girls, promoting the health and socialization benefits of water polo and encouraging them to introduce their children to the sport through a local club. Tell them they can learn more about the sport and find a club in their area by visiting the USA Water Polo website.

WEB-WRITING SKILLS

12-51. Message Strategies: Marketing and Sales Messages
[LO-3] Convincing people to give their music a try is one of the toughest challenges new bands and performers face.

Your task: Imagine you've taken on the job of promoting an amazing new band or performer you just discovered. Choose someone you've heard live or online and write 100 to 200 words of webpage copy describing the music in a way that will convince people to listen to a few online samples.

WEB-WRITING SKILLS/MOBILE SKILLS/TEAM SKILLS

12-52. Message Strategies: Marketing and Sales Messages
[LO-3] You never intended to become an inventor, but you saw a way to make something work more easily, so you set to work. You developed a model, found a way to mass-produce it, and set up a small manufacturing studio in your home. You know that other people are going to benefit from your invention. Now all you need to do is reach that market.

Your task: Team up with other students assigned by your instructor and imagine a useful product that you might have invented—perhaps something related to a hobby or sporting activity. List the features and benefits of your imaginary product and describe how it helps customers. Then write the copy for the first screen of a mobile-friendly website that would introduce and promote this product, using what you've learned in this chapter and making up details as you need them. With word processing software or another tool if your instructor indicates, format the screen to show how the information would appear on a typical smartphone screen.

PODCASTING SKILLS

12-53. Message Strategies: Marketing and Sales Messages
[LO-3] Your new podcast channel, School2Biz, offers advice to business students making the transition from college to career. You provide information on everything from preparing résumés to interviewing to finding a place in the business world and building a successful career. As you expand your audience, you'd eventually like to turn School2Biz into a profitable operation (perhaps by selling advertising time during your podcasts). For now, you're simply offering free advice.

Your task: As your instructor directs, either write a 50-word description of your new podcast or record a 30-second podcast describing the new service. Make up any information you need to describe School2Biz. Be sure to mention who you are and why the information you present is worth listening to.[26]

LETTER-WRITING SKILLS/PORTFOLIO BUILDER

12-54. Message Strategies: Marketing and Sales Messages
[LO-3] Kelly Services is a large staffing company based in Troy, Michigan. Client firms turn to Kelly to strategically balance their workloads and workforces during peaks and valleys of demand, to handle special projects, and to evaluate employees before making a full-time hiring decision. Facing the economic pressures of global competition, many companies now rely on a dynamic combination of permanent employees and temporary contractors hired through service providers such as Kelly. In addition to these staffing services, Kelly offers project services (managing both short- and long-term projects) and outsourcing and consulting services (taking over entire business functions).[27]

Your task: Write a one-page sales letter that would be sent to human resources executives at large U.S.-based corporations describing Kelly's three groups of business services. For current information, visit the Kelly website.

WEB-WRITING SKILLS/PORTFOLIO BUILDER

12-55. Message Strategies: Marketing and Sales Messages
[LO-3] After a shaky start as the technology matured and advertisers tried to figure out this new medium, online advertising has finally become a significant force in both consumer and business marketing. Companies in a wide variety of industries are shifting some of the ad budgets from traditional media such as TV and magazines to the increasing selection of advertising possibilities online—and more than a few companies now advertise almost exclusively online. That's fine for companies that sell advertising time and space online, but your job involves selling advertising in print magazines that are worried about losing market share to online publishers.

Online advertising has two major advantages that you can't really compete with: interactivity and the ability to precisely target individual audience members. On the other hand, you have several advantages going for you, including the ability to produce high-quality color photography, the physical presence of print (such as when a magazine sits on a table in a doctor's waiting room), portability, guaranteed circulation numbers, and close reader relationships that go back years or decades.

Your task: You work as an advertising sales specialist for the Time Inc. division of Time Warner, which publishes dozens of magazines around the world. Write a brief persuasive message about the benefits of magazine advertising; the statement will be posted on the individual websites of Time Inc.'s numerous magazines, so you can't narrow in on any single publication. Also, Time Inc. coordinates its print publications with an extensive online presence (including thousands of paid online ads), so you can't bash online advertising, either.[28]

Marketing and Sales Messages: Social Media

WEB-WRITING SKILLS

12-56. Message Strategies: Marketing and Sales Messages; Media Skills: Social Networking [LO-3], Chapter 8 Curves is a fitness center franchise that caters to women who may not feel at home in traditional gyms. With its customer-focused and research-based approach, Curves has become a significant force in the fitness industry and one of the most successful franchise operations in history.[29]

Your task: Read about the company on its website and imagine that you are adapting this material for the company's Facebook page. Write a "Company Overview" (95–100 words) and "Mission" statement (45–50 words).

SOCIAL NETWORKING SKILLS/TEAM SKILLS

12-57. Message Strategies: Marketing and Sales Messages; Media Skills: Social Networking [LO-3], Chapter 8 You chose your college or university based on certain expectations, and you've been enrolled long enough now to have some idea about whether those expectations have been met. In other words, you are something of an expert about the "consumer benefits" your school can offer prospective students.

Your task: In a team of four students, interview six other students who are not taking this business communication course. Try to get a broad sample of demographics and psychographics, including students in a variety of majors and programs. Ask these students (1) why they chose this college or university and (2) whether the experience has met their expectations so far. To ensure the privacy of your respondents, do not record their names with their answers. Each member of the team should then answer these same two questions, so that you have responses from a total of 10 students.

After compiling the responses (you might use Google Docs or a similar collaboration tool so that everyone on the team has easy access to the information), analyze them as a team to look for any recurring "benefit themes." Is it the quality of the education? Research opportunities? Location? The camaraderie of school sporting events? The chance to meet and study with fascinating students from a variety of backgrounds? Identify two or three strong benefits that your college or university can promise—and deliver—to prospective students.

Now nominate one member of the team to draft a short marketing message that could be posted on your school's Facebook page. The message should include a catchy title that makes it clear the message is a student's perspective on why this is a great place to get a college education. When the draft is ready, the other members of the team should review it individually. Finally, meet as a team to complete the message.

MICROBLOGGING SKILLS

12-58. Message Strategies: Marketing and Sales Messages; Media Skills: Microblogging [LO-3], Chapter 8 Effective microblogging messages emphasize clarity and conciseness—and so do effective sales messages.

Your task: Find the website of any product that can be ordered online (any product you find interesting and that is appropriate to use for a class assignment). Adapt the information on the website, using your own words, and write four tweets to promote the product. The first should get your audience's attention (with an intriguing benefit claim, for example), the second should build audience interest by providing some support for the claim you made in the first message, the third should increase readers' desire to have the product by layering on one or two more buyer benefits, and the fourth should motivate readers to take action to place an order.

If your class is set up with private Twitter accounts, use your private account to send your messages. Otherwise, email your four messages to your instructor or post them on your class blog, as your instructor directs.

SOCIAL NETWORKING SKILLS/TEAM SKILLS

12-59. Message Strategies: Marketing and Sales Messages; Media Skills: Social Networking [LO-3], Chapter 8 At this point in your collegiate career, you've developed areas of academic expertise that could benefit other students. After kicking around moneymaking ideas with friends, you decide that the tutoring business would be a more enjoyable way to share your expertise than a regular part-time job.

Your task: In a team assigned by your instructor, compile a list of all the subject areas in which your team would be qualified to tutor high school students or other college students. Now brainstorm the best way to present your offerings on Facebook and other social media sites. Come up with a name for your tutoring company and write a 100- to 200-word "About Us" statement.

MICROBLOGGING SKILLS/TEAM SKILLS

12-60. Message Strategies: Marketing and Sales Messages; Media Skills: Social Networking [LO-3], Chapter 8 You and your tutoring team (from the previous case) know you should take advantage of every social media platform to get the word out on your new company.

Your task: With the same team as in the previous case, compose four tweets to introduce your tutoring service on Twitter.

MyBCommLab

Go to **mybcommlab.com** for Auto-graded writing questions as well as the following Assisted-graded writing questions:

12-61. Why do persuasive business messages usually emphasize logical appeals over emotional appeals? [LO-2]

12-62. Why do the AIDA model and similar approaches need to be modified when writing persuasive messages in social media? [LO-3]

Endnotes

1. Red Ants Pants website, accessed 17 April 2016, redantspants .com; Becky Warren, "Ants on the Pants," *Country Woman*, February–March 2011, www.countrywomanmagazine.com; Dan Testa, "Red Ants Pants: By Working Women, for Working Women," *Flathead Beacon*, 4 March 2010, www.flatheadbeacon.com; Sammi Johnson, "Outdoor Woman: Red Ants Pants," *406 Woman*, April/May 2010, 52–53; Beth Judy, "Fit for Her," *Montana Magazine*, March–April 2010, 14–16; *Montana Quarterly*, Summer 2010, www .redantspants.com; Devan Grote, "Red Ants Pants," *Gettysburg*, Spring 2009, www.redantspants.com.

2. Jay A. Conger, "The Necessary Art of Persuasion," *Harvard Business Review*, May–June 1998, 84–95; Jeanette W. Gilsdorf, "Write Me Your Best Case for . . . ," *Bulletin of the Association for Business Communication* 54, no. 1 (March 1991): 7–12.

3. "Vital Skill for Today's Managers: Persuading, Not Ordering, Others," *Soundview Executive Book Summaries*, September 1998, 1.

4. Mary Cross, "Aristotle and Business Writing: Why We Need to Teach Persuasion," *Bulletin of the Association for Business Communication* 54, no. 1 (March 1991): 3–6.

5. Stephen Bayley and Roger Mavity, "How to Pitch," *Management Today*, March 2007, 48–53.

6. Robert B. Cialdini, "Harnessing the Science of Persuasion," *BusinessWeek*, 4 December 2007, www.businessweek.com.

7. Wesley Clark, "The Potency of Persuasion," *Fortune*, 12 November 2007, 48; W. H. Weiss, "Using Persuasion Successfully," *Supervision*, October 2006, 13–16.

8. Tom Chandler, "The Copywriter's Best Friend," Copywriter Underground blog, 20 December 2006, copywriterunderground .com.

9. Raymond M. Olderman, *10-Minute Guide to Business Communication* (New York: Macmillan Spectrum/Alpha Books, 1997), 57–61.

10. John D. Ramage and John C. Bean, *Writing Arguments: A Rhetoric with Readings*, 3rd ed. (Boston: Allyn & Bacon, 1995), 430–442.

11. Philip Vassallo, "Persuading Powerfully: Tips for Writing Persuasive Documents," *Et Cetera*, Spring 2002, 65–71.

12. Dianna Booher, *Communicate with Confidence* (New York: McGraw-Hill, 1994), 102.

13. Conger, "The Necessary Art of Persuasion."

14. "Social Factors in Developing a Web Accessibility Business Case for Your Organization," W3C website, accessed 17 April 2016, www.w3.org.

15. Tamar Weinberg, *The New Community Rules: Marketing on the Social Web* (Sebastapol, Calif.: O'Reilly Media, 2009), 22; 23–24; 187–191; Larry Weber, *Marketing to the Social Web* (Hoboken, N.J.: Wiley, 2007), 12–14; David Meerman Scott, *The New Rules of Marketing and PR* (Hoboken, N.J.: Wiley, 2007), 62; Paul Gillin, *The New Influencers* (Sanger, Calif.: Quill Driver Books, 2007), 34–35; Jeremy Wright, *Blog Marketing: The Revolutionary Way to Increase Sales, Build Your Brand, and Get Exceptional Results* (New York: McGraw-Hill, 2006), 263–365.

16. Ingrid Lunden, "Global Mobile Ad Spend Jumped 105% in 2013, on Track for $31.5B In 2014 Led by Google, Says eMarketer," *TechCrunch*, 19 March 2014, techcrunch.com.

17. Inessa Davydova, "The Rise in Mobile Video," *DigitalSurgeons*, 1 October 2013, www.digitalsurgeons.com.

18. Chris Kelley, "Why You Need a Mobile Website," *V2 Marketing Communications*, 18 June 2013, blog.marketingv2.com.

19. Gilsdorf, "Write Me Your Best Case for . . . ."

20. Robert Brady, "The Dark Side of Remarketing," *Clix*, 21 January 2014, www.clixmarketing.com; Miguel Helft and Tanzina Vega, "Retargeting Ads Follow Surfers to Other Sites," *New York Times*, 29 August 2010, www.nytimes.com.

21. "How to Comply with the Children's Online Privacy Protection Rule," U.S. Federal Trade Commission website, accessed 17 July 2010, www.ftc.gov; "Frequently Asked Advertising Questions: A Guide for Small Business," U.S. Federal Trade Commission website, accessed 17 July 2010, www.ftc.gov.

22. Samsung website, accessed 22 October 2006, www.samsung.com.

23. "Webmaster Guidelines," Google, accessed 5 February 2013, www.google.com; Brian Clark, "How to Create Compelling Content That Ranks Well in Search Engines," *Copyblogger*, May 2010, www.copyblogger.com; P. J. Fusco, "How Web 2.0 Affects SEO Strategy," *ClickZ*, 23 May 2007, www.clickz.com.

24. IBM website, accessed 15 January 2004, www.ibm.com; "DAS Faces an Assured Future with IBM," IBM website, accessed 16 January 2004, www.ibm.com; "Sametime," IBM website, accessed 16 January 2004, www.ibm.com.

25. Kentucky Cabinet for Economic Development website, accessed 8 May 2014, www.thinkkentucky.com.

26. Podcast Bunker website, accessed 19 July 2010, www.podcastbunker.com.

27. Kelly Services website, accessed 19 July 2010, www.kellyservices .com.

28. Time Inc. website, accessed 8 May 2014, www.timewarner.com.

29. Curves website, accessed 19 July 2010, www.curves.com

Reports and proposals are the "major leagues" of business communication. These are the tools you use to analyze complex problems, educate audiences, address opportunities in the marketplace, win contracts, and even launch new companies through compelling business plans. Adapt what you've learned so far to the particular challenges of these long-format messages, including some special touches that can make formal reports stand out from the crowd.

BraunS/Getty Images

13

Finding, Evaluating, and Processing Information

LEARNING OBJECTIVES

After studying this chapter, you will be able to

1 Describe an effective process for conducting business research.

2 Define *secondary research*, and explain how to evaluate, locate, and document information sources.

3 Define *primary research*, and outline the steps involved in conducting surveys and interviews.

4 Describe the major tasks involved in processing research results.

5 Explain how to summarize research results and present conclusions and recommendations.

COMMUNICATION CLOSE-UP AT

Strategyzer

strategyzer.com

Whenever you're gathering information for a major business writing project, you're likely to encounter the question of how much is enough? Collecting and processing information takes time and often costs money, and it's not always clear how much information you need in order to craft an effective report or proposal, or how much time and money you should invest to get it. Invest too little and you risk writing a flawed report. Invest too much and you'll waste time and money that would be better put to other uses.

Business plans are a great example of this dilemma, and they have a special twist that makes information collection even more challenging. As you'll read on page 396 in Chapter 14, a conventional business plan covers a lot of territory, from a high-level look at strategy to details on financing, operations, marketing, and other functional areas. These reports can run to 20, 30, 40 pages or more, and you can spend weeks gathering the necessary information and distilling it down to useful formats.

Spending that much time on research before writing the business plan and launching the company can seem like a good idea to entrepreneurs who want to reduce start-up risks as much as possible or who want to produce high-quality reports to impress lenders or investors. In many start-up situations, however, this is precious time that entrepreneurs should be

Author and entrepreneur Alex Osterwalder's approach to evaluating new business ideas offers a simpler, faster alternative than the traditional business plan.

Courtesy of Alex Osterwalder

spending getting a product in front of customers to test the viability of the business concept, rather than crafting an impressive-looking plan about an idea that is still unproven. Moreover, in fast-moving markets, it is possible to spend so much time researching and writing the business plan that the target market changes by the time the plan is ready.

The special twist with business plans involves the uncertainty surrounding some of the most important information they typically contain. For example, estimating demand for a new product or service is one of the most vital aspects of planning a business—and one of the most difficult. You might spend weeks or months gathering data on comparable products and refining spreadsheets with elegant forecasting models to predict how many products you can sell and how much profit you'll make. This projection will then be the basis of almost everything else in the business plan, from the amount of money you can attract from investors to the number of employees you should hire.

Here's the catch: You could spend all this time writing a plan and launching a business based on this number only to find out it's wildly off the mark. In the worst case scenario, you might've wasted months launching a weak business idea or a product with little or no market appeal. Even the most sophisticated estimates of market demand are still only predictions, and the only way to really know if a product is going to sell is to get it in front of customers and ask them to buy it.

In response to these uncertainties with conventional business plans, some experts now recommend a simplified, accelerated approach that gets a new business to the "point of proof" faster. One of the key thinkers behind this new approach is the Swiss author and entrepreneur Alex Osterwalder. Rather than launching businesses with elaborate planning and a conventional business plan, he proposes that companies use the Business Model Canvas. This single-sheet visual brainstorming tool helps entrepreneurs answer a handful of key questions to determine whether they have a financially viable business concept—and what to adjust if they don't. The canvas approach helps flag some of the common stumbling points of new businesses, including financial plans that are based on shaky assumptions (or outright fantasy) and untested hypotheses about market behavior.

The Business Model Canvas and its variants don't necessarily replace conventional business reports in all cases, and they don't cover all the details needed to operate a business after launch, but they help entrepreneurs decide whether it makes sense to move forward. By developing and testing business concepts quickly, entrepreneurs can find out whether they have a realistic idea before investing weeks of time in detailed planning and report-writing efforts. The canvas idea has definitely captured the imagination of entrepreneurs: More than a million people bought the book that first outlined the canvas idea, and more than 5 million have downloaded the Business Model Canvas.[1]

Planning Your Research

1 **LEARNING OBJECTIVE**
Describe an effective process for conducting business research.

Audiences expect you to support your business messages with solid research.

Whether you're brainstorming a new business idea using something like Strategyzer's Business Model Canvas (profiled in the chapter-opening Communication Close-Up) or planning a conventional business report or proposal, you need to make sure your reporting, analysis, and recommendations are supported with solid research. Figure 13.1 outlines a five-step research process that will help you gather and use information efficiently; you'll learn more about these steps in the following sections.

With so much information now online, it's tempting just to punch some keywords into a search engine and grab the first few results that show up. However, effective and efficient research requires a more thoughtful approach. Your favorite search engine might not be able to reach the webpages that have the information you need, the information might not be online at all, it might be online but not under the search terms you've used, or it might not even exist in any form.

Figure 13.1 The Research Process
By following a methodical research process, you can save time and money while uncovering better information.

To maximize your chances of finding useful information and to minimize the time you spend looking for it, follow these planning steps: Familiarize yourself with the subject so that you can frame insightful questions, identify the most critical gaps in your information, and then prioritize your research needs. However, before launching any research project, be sure to take a moment or two to consider the ethics and etiquette of your approach.

Researching without a plan can waste time and produce flawed results.

MAINTAINING ETHICS AND ETIQUETTE IN YOUR RESEARCH

Your research tactics affect the people you gather data and information from and the people who read and apply your results. To avoid ethical lapses, keep the following points in mind:

- **Don't force a specific outcome by skewing your research.** Approach your research with an open mind and a willingness to accept whatever you find, even if it's not what you expect or want to see.
- **Respect the privacy of your research participants.** Privacy is a contentious issue today. Businesses believe they have a right to protect their confidential information from competitors, and consumers believe they have a right to protect their personal information from businesses.
- **Document sources and give appropriate credit.** Whether you are using published documents, personal interviews, or company records, citing your sources not only is fair to the people who created and provided the information but also helps your audience members confirm your information or explore it in more detail, if they so choose.
- **Respect the intellectual property and digital rights of your sources.** For example, your research might turn up a great new way to sell services online, but that doesn't mean you're free to implement that process. It might be protected by one of the many patents that have been granted in recent years for business process models.
- **Don't extract more from your sources than they actually provide.** In other words, don't succumb to the temptation to put words in a source's mouth. For instance, if an industry expert says that a sales increase is possible, don't quote him or her as saying that a sales increase is probable.
- **Don't misrepresent who you are or what you intend to do with the research results.** One classic example of ethical lapses in this area is known as *sugging*, short for *selling under the guise of research*. For example, a firm might seem to be conducting a survey when it is, in fact, using the questions to identify hot sales leads. Another unethical variation on sugging is following up a real survey with sales calls, using information that respondents shared in the belief that they were only participating in a survey.[2]

Take precautions to avoid ethical lapses in your research.

Privacy is a contentious issue in the research field today.

Don't automatically assume that you can use all the ideas and information you find online.

Research etiquette deserves careful attention, too. For example, respect the time of anyone who agrees to be interviewed or to be a research participant, and maintain courtesy throughout the interview or research process. For more information on research ethics and etiquette, review the *Code of Standards and Ethics for Survey Research* published by the Council of America Survey Research Organizations (**www.casro.org**).

REAL-TIME UPDATES
LEARN MORE BY VISITING THIS WEBSITE
Get clear answers to murky copyright questions

Find out what is covered by copyright, what isn't, and how to secure a copyright for your own work. Go to **real-timeupdates.com/bct14** and select Learn More in the Students section.

FAMILIARIZING YOURSELF WITH THE SUBJECT

Give yourself some unstructured time at the beginning of the project to explore the general subject area, perhaps by reading industry publications and blogs, searching for trending topics on Twitter, visiting competitors' websites, and interviewing experts within your organization. Scanning the tables of contents and indexes of books on the subject can give you a sense of how a broad subject area is divided into component topics.

When you have a basic grasp of the subject area, develop a **problem statement** that defines the problem or purpose of your research—the decision you need to make or the

Avoid false starts and blind alleys by familiarizing yourself with new subject areas before you start your research.

The problem statement defines the purpose of your research and guides your investigation.

conclusion you need to reach at the end of the process. You may find it easier to phrase the problem as a question, such as "How can we improve customer satisfaction?" or "Does Apple's new TV system pose a competitive threat to us?"

IDENTIFYING INFORMATION GAPS

Focus your research by identifying the most important gaps in your information.

Your problem statement frames the purpose of your research, but it doesn't usually tell you what specific information you need to find. Your next task is to dig deeper to discover the *information gaps* that need to be filled through research. You or someone in your company may already have some of the information you need, and you don't want to waste time or money gathering information you already have.

For instance, the question "How can we improve customer satisfaction?" is too vague because many separate factors contribute to customer satisfaction. To get useful information, you would break this topic down into specific issues, such as product reliability and customer service skills. Digging further, you may discover that you don't need to research product reliability because the company already tracks data on product repairs. However, if no one has ever measured the employees' customer service skills, you would identify that as a definite information gap.

PRIORITIZING RESEARCH NEEDS

You usually won't have enough time or money to answer every question that comes to mind, so setting priorities is a must.

Prioritizing your research needs is important because you won't have the time or money to answer every question you might have. Moreover, if you'll be using interviews or surveys, you'll need to limit the number of questions you ask so that you don't consume more time than people are willing to give. One simple way to prioritize is to divide your questions into "need to know" and "nice to know" and then toss out all the "nice to know" questions. If you start with a technique such as information gap analysis, you will get a clear idea of the information you truly need to collect.

Conducting Secondary Research

2 LEARNING OBJECTIVE
Define *secondary research*, and explain how to evaluate, locate, and document information sources.

Secondary research efforts gather and analyze information that has been previously collected for other purposes.

Start your research by conducting secondary research first.

With a clear plan and careful prioritization, you're ready to conduct research, and the first step is to see whether anyone else has already done some or all of the research you need. Consulting research that was done previously for another purpose is considered **secondary research**. The sources for such information include print and online periodicals, online databases, books, and other research reports. (Some companies specialize in reports on particular industries, companies, technologies, market regions, and other subjects.)

Don't let the name *secondary* mislead you, though. You want to start with secondary research because it can save you considerable time and money, although you may have to pay to see someone else's results. In contrast, *primary research* (see page 372) is new research done specifically for the current project.

EVALUATING SOURCES

Evaluate your sources carefully to avoid embarrassing and potentially damaging mistakes.

No matter where you're searching, it is your responsibility to separate quality information from unreliable or misleading junk to avoid corrupting your results. Social media have complicated this challenge by making many new sources of information available. On the positive side, independent sources communicating through blogs, wikis, Twitter, user-generated content sites, and podcasting channels can provide valuable and unique insights, often from experts whose voices might never be heard otherwise. On the negative side, these nontraditional information sources often lack the editorial boards and fact-checkers commonly used in traditional publishing. You cannot assume that the information you find is accurate, objective, and current. Answer the following questions about each piece of material:

- **Does the source have a reputation for honesty and reliability?** Naturally, you'll feel more comfortable using information from an established source that has a reputation for accuracy. But don't let your guard down completely; even the finest reporters and editors can make mistakes. For sources that are new or relatively unknown, your safest bet is to corroborate anything you learn with information from several other sources.

- **Is the source potentially biased?** The individual or organization providing the information might have a particular bias or point of view regarding the information and its context. Such bias is neither inherently bad nor unethical (unless it is being intentionally hidden), but you need to be aware of it to interpret the information you find.
- **What is the purpose of the material?** Was the material designed to inform others of new research, advance a position, or stimulate discussion? Was it designed to promote or sell a product? Be sure to distinguish among advertising, advocating, and informing.
- **Is the author credible?** Find out whether the person or the publisher is known and respected in the field. Is the author someone with hands-on experience in the subject area or merely an observer with an opinion?
- **Where did the source get *its* information?** Many sources of secondary information get their material from other secondary sources, removing you even further from the original data.
- **Can you verify the material independently?** Verification can uncover biases or mistakes—which is particularly important when the information goes beyond simple facts to include projections, interpretations, and estimates. If you can't verify critical information, let your audience know that.
- **Is the material current?** Make sure you are using the most current information available by checking the publication or posting date.
- **Is the material complete?** Have you accessed the entire document or only a selection from it? If it's a selection, which parts were excluded? Do you need more detail?
- **Are all claims supported with evidence?** Are opinions presented as facts? Does the writer make broad claims, such as "most people believe . . .," without citing any surveys to prove his or her point?
- **Do the source's claims stand up to logical scrutiny?** Finally, step back and ask whether the information makes sense. If that little voice in your head says that something sounds suspicious, listen!

You probably won't have time to conduct a thorough background check on all your sources, so focus your efforts on the most important or most suspicious pieces of information.

LOCATING SOURCES

Even if you intend to eventually conduct primary research, start with a review of any available secondary research. Inside your company, you might be able to find a variety of documents prepared for other projects that offer helpful information. Be sure to ask whether your company has a *knowledge management system* or some other repository for research results. (See "Managing Information" on page 379 for more on this topic.) Outside the company, you can choose from a wide range of print and online resources, some of which are included in Table 13.1 on the next page.[3] (The list in this table represents a tiny fraction of the secondary resources available; ask a reference librarian for advice on researching specific business topics.) For instance, if you want to know more about a specific company, one of the first things you'll need to find out is whether the company is public (sells shares of stock to the general public) or private. Public corporations, which are required to submit extensive financial reports to government agencies, usually have more information available than private companies.

Finding Information at the Library

Public, corporate, and university libraries offer an enormous array of business books, databases, newspapers, periodicals, directories, almanacs, and government publications. Some of these printed sources provide information that is not available online, and some of the online sources provide information that is available by subscription. Don't assume that you can find everything you need through your own online research.

MOBILE APP
The **Instapaper** mobile app lets you instantly save webpages and articles to read later, a convenient capability when you're exploring a topic and want to collect potential sources for review.

Let your readers know if you were unable to verify critical pieces of information obtained in your research.

TABLE 13.1 Important Resources for Business Research*

COMPANY, INDUSTRY, AND PRODUCT RESOURCES

AnnualReports.com. Free access to annual reports from thousands of public companies.

Brands and Their Companies/Companies and Their Brands. Contains data on several hundred thousand consumer products, manufacturers, importers, marketers, and distributors. Available as an online database; ask at your library.

D&B Directories. Dun & Bradstreet publishes a variety of business databases and directories covering thousands of companies worldwide.

Hoover's Online. Database of millions of companies, including in-depth coverage of thousands of leading companies around the world. Basic information is available free; in-depth information requires a subscription.

Manufacturing & Distribution USA. Data on thousands of companies in the manufacturing, wholesaling, and retailing sectors.

NAICS Codes. North American Industry Classification System.

Reference USA. Concise information on millions of U.S. companies; subscription database.

SEC filings. U.S. Securities and Exchange Commission filings, including 10Ks, 10Qs, annual reports, and prospectuses, for U.S. public firms.

Standard & Poor's Net Advantage. Comprehensive range of directories and databases focusing on publicly traded companies and their industries and markets.

ThomasNet. Information on thousands of U.S. manufacturers, indexed by company name and product.

RESEARCH DIRECTORIES AND INDEXES

Books in Print. Database indexes millions of books, audiobooks, and video titles from around the world. Available in print and professional online versions.

Directories in Print. Information on thousands of business and industrial directories.

Encyclopedia of Associations. Index of thousands of associations, listed by broad subject category, specific subject, association, and location. Available as an online database as well.

Reader's Guide to Periodical Literature. Database of articles in general-interest magazines.

TRADEMARKS AND PATENTS

Official Gazette of the United States Patent and Trademark Office. Weekly publications (one for trademarks and one for patents) providing official record of newly assigned trademarks and patents, product descriptions, and product names.

United States Patent and Trademark Office. Trademark and patent information records.

STATISTICS AND OTHER BUSINESS DATA

U.S. Bureau of Economic Analysis. Large collection of economic and government data.

Europa—The European Union Online. A portal that provides up-to-date coverage of current affairs, legislation, policies, and EU statistics.

FedStats. Access to a full range of statistics and information from more than 70 U.S. government agencies.

Key Business Ratios (Dun & Bradstreet). Industry, financial, and performance ratios.

Information Please Almanac. Compilation of broad-range statistical data, with a strong focus on the labor force.

Annual Statement Studies. Industry, financial, and performance ratios published by the Risk Management Association.

Statistical Abstract of the United States. Annual compendium of U.S. economic, social, political, and industrial statistics.

The World Almanac and Book of Facts. Facts on economic, social, educational, and political events for major countries.

U.S. Bureau of Labor Statistics. Extensive national and regional information on labor and business, including employment, industry growth, productivity, the Consumer Price Index, and the overall U.S. economy.

U.S. Census Bureau. Demographic data and analysis on consumers and businesses based on census results.

COMMERCIAL DATABASES

A wide variety of commercial databases provide access to articles from trade and academic journals; ask your reference librarian to help you select the best databases for specific research projects.

*Note: Some of these resources are free, and some are available via subscription only; check with your librarian.

Libraries offer information and resources you can't find anywhere else—including reference librarians who can show you how to plan and conduct effective searches.

Libraries are also where you'll find one of your most important resources: librarians. Reference librarians are skilled in research strategies and can often help you locate obscure information you can't find on your own. They can also direct you to many sources of business information. Also, many library websites now have a business portal, with links to helpful resources and advice on finding information.

Whether you're looking for information in printed materials or in databases, each type of resource serves a special function:

- **Newspapers and periodicals.** Libraries offer access to a wide variety of popular magazines, general business magazines, *trade journals* (which provide information about specific professions and industries), and *academic journals* (which provide research-oriented articles from researchers and educators). Check the library's website or ask a librarian to find out which periodicals are available in print or digital formats.
- **Business books.** Although generally less timely than newspapers, periodicals, and online sources, business books provide in-depth coverage of a variety of business topics. Many libraries now offer online access to their card catalogs so you can see whether they have specific titles in their collections.
- **Directories.** Thousands of directories are published in print and digital formats in the United States, and many include membership information for all kinds of professions, industries, and special-interest groups.
- **Almanacs and statistical resources.** Almanacs are handy guides to factual and statistical information about countries, politics, the labor force, and so on. One of the most extensive, the *Statistical Abstract of the United States*, published annually by the U.S. Department of Commerce, contains statistics about occupations, government, population, health, business, crime, and the environment (also available online at **www.census.gov**).
- **Government publications.** Information on laws, court decisions, tax questions, regulatory issues, and other governmental concerns is often available in collections of government documents. A librarian can direct you to the information you want.
- **Databases.** Databases offer vast collections of searchable information, often in specific areas, such as business, law, science, technology, and education. Some of these are available only by institutional subscription, so the library may be your only way to gain access to them. Some libraries offer remote online access to some or all databases; for others, you need to visit in person.

Local, state, and federal government agencies publish a huge variety of information that is helpful to business researchers.

Finding Information Online

The Internet can be a tremendous source of business information, provided that you know how to approach a search, where to look, and how to use the tools available. Roughly speaking, the tools fall into two categories: those you can use to actively *search* for existing information and those you can use to *monitor* selected sources for new information. (Some tools can perform both functions.)

Online research tools can be used to search for existing information and to monitor for new information.

Online Search Tools The most familiar search tools are general-purpose **search engines**, such as Google and Bing, which scan millions of websites to identify individual webpages that contain a specific word or phrase and then attempt to rank the results from most useful to least useful. Search engines have the advantage of scanning millions or billions of individual webpages, and the best engines use powerful ranking algorithms to present the pages that are probably the most relevant to your search request.

To be a successful online researcher, you need to expand your toolkit beyond the popular search engines.

For all their ease and power, conventional search engines have three primary shortcomings: (1) no human editors are involved to evaluate the quality or ranking of the search results; (2) various engines use different search techniques, so they often find different material or present similar results in different order; and (3) search engines can't reach all the content on some websites (this part of the Internet is sometimes called the *hidden Internet* or the *deep web*).

Today's search engines are powerful tools, but they still have important limitations.

A variety of tools are available to overcome the three main weaknesses of general-purpose search engines, and you should consider using one or more of them in your business research. First, **web directories** such as DMOZ (**dmoz.org**) use human editors to categorize and evaluate websites. Some directories focus on specific media types, such as blogs or podcasts.

Web directories benefit from having human editors evaluate and select websites.

REAL-TIME UPDATES
LEARN MORE BY EXPLORING THIS INTERACTIVE WEBSITE
Wondering how to get started with business research?
Baruch College's Beginner's Guide to Business Research will point you in the right direction. Go to **real-timeupdates.com/bct14** and select Learn More in the Students section.

Second, **metasearch engines** help overcome the differences among search engines by formatting your search request for multiple search engines, making it easy to find a broader range of results. With a few clicks, you can compare results from multiple search engines to make sure you are getting a broad view of the material.

Third, **online databases** help address the challenge of the hidden Internet by offering access to newspapers, magazines, journals, digital copies of books, and other resources often not available with standard search engines. Some of these

Metasearch engines can save you time by using multiple search engines at once.

databases offer free access to the public, but others require a subscription (check with your library). Also, a variety of specialized search engines now exist to reach various parts of the hidden Internet.

Online databases can give you access to important resources that search engines often can't reach.

Online Monitoring Tools One of the most powerful aspects of online research is the ability to automatically monitor selected sources for new information so that you can get new information without repeating manual searches. The possibilities include subscribing to newsfeeds from blogs and websites; following people on Twitter and other microblogs; setting up alerts on search engines and online databases; and using specialized monitors such as TweetDeck and HootSuite to track tweets that mention specific companies or other terms.

To stay up to date on a research topic, subscribe to RSS feeds, search engine alerts, or Twitter updates from knowledgeable individuals.

Exercise care when setting up monitoring tools, however, because it's easy to get overwhelmed by the flood of information. Remember that you can always go back and search your sources if you need to gather additional information.

Search Tips

Search engines, metasearch engines, and databases offer a variety of ways to find information. Unfortunately, no two of them work in exactly the same way, and you have to learn how to use each one most effectively. This learning may take a few extra minutes at the beginning of your research, but it could save you hours of lost time later—and save you from embarrassing oversights. You can usually find a Help or Support page that explains both basic and advanced functions, with advice on how to use a particular tool most effectively.

Make sure you know how each search tool works; you can get unpredictable results if you don't know how a particular tool operates.

To make the best use of any search engine or database, keep the following points in mind:

Search engine results can create the illusion that the Internet is a complete, well-organized warehouse of reliable information. However, it is neither complete nor organized, and not all the information is reliable.

- **Think before you search.** The neatly organized results you get from a search engine can create the illusion that the Internet is an orderly warehouse of all the information in the universe, but the reality is far different. The Internet is an incomplete, unorganized hodgepodge of millions of independent websites with information that ranges in value from priceless to worse-than-worthless. After you have identified what you need to know, spend a few moments thinking about where that information might be found, how it might be structured, and what terms various websites might use to describe it.
- **Pay attention to the details.** Details can make all the difference in a search. On Google, for example, you can filter results according to when items were published online. This setting could drastically change your results, so make sure you haven't inadvertently limited your search by selecting a narrower time frame than you really want.
  - **Don't limit yourself to a regular web search engine.** Google, Bing, and other search engines are remarkably powerful, but they can't access all online content. Moreover, the content you need might not even be online.
  - **Review the search and display options carefully.** When using advanced search or while searching in databases, pay close attention to whether you are searching in the title, author, subject, or document field and whether the search is limited to particular types of documents (such as full-text documents only). Each choice will return

different results. And when the results are displayed, verify the presentation order; results might be sorted by date or by relevance.

- **Try variations of terms.** If you can't find what you're looking for, try abbreviations (*CEO, CPA*), synonyms (*man, male*), related terms (*child, adolescent, youth*), different spellings (*dialog, dialogue*), singular and plural forms (*woman, women*), nouns and adjectives (*manager, management, managerial*), and open and compound forms (*online, on line, on-line*). Some search engines automatically search for such synonyms.
- **Adjust the scope of your search, if needed.** If a search yields little or no information, broaden your search by specifying fewer terms. Conversely, if you're inundated with too many hits, use more terms to narrow your search.
- **Look beyond the first few pages of results.** Don't assume that the highest-ranking results are the best sources for you. For example, materials that haven't been optimized for search engines won't rank as highly (meaning they won't show up in the first few pages of results), but they may be far better for your purposes.

Other powerful search tools include *enterprise search engines* that search all the computers on a company's network and *research and content managers* such as LiveBinders and the Zotero browser extension. And don't overlook the search functions in workplace messaging systems, groupware, and other closed systems.

For research innovations from a mobile perspective, see "Research on the Go with Mobile Devices."

> Be sure to look beyond the first few pages of search results; there is no guarantee that the best information for your project will appear early in the listings.

MOBILE APP

Access and add to your Zotero research files with a variety of **Zotero**-compatible mobile apps.

DIGITAL + SOCIAL + MOBILE: TODAY'S COMMUNICATION ENVIRONMENT

Research on the Go with Mobile Devices

Smartphones and tablets have opened up new possibilities for collecting information for business reports and other communication purposes. Using built-in capabilities such as audio and video recording, as well as apps made specifically for research, business researchers can collect qualitative and quantitative information in a variety of ways:

- **Mobile surveys.** Tablets with interactive software can replace the clipboards long used by researchers for "mall intercept" surveys and other efforts to collect data from shoppers.
- **Collecting and sharing.** Collaborative apps such as Pearltrees make it easy to collect online information and organize it across multiple devices, then connect with relevant information collected by other users.
- **Note taking.** Evernote, OneNote, and other note-taking apps simplify the process of compiling notes, webpages, photos, and other pieces of research.
- **Sketching.** Sometimes a simple picture is more powerful than words or photos. With touchscreen apps on phones and tablets, researchers can quickly sketch maps, process diagrams, and other visuals on the spot.
- **Audio, photo, and video recording.** Whether it's snapping images of street scenes for a report on potential store locations or recording test subjects using a new product prototype, the audiovisual capabilities of today's mobile devices give researchers a host of new tools.
- **Document scanning.** Scanning apps let researchers record and organize images of documents that can't be removed from their storage locations.

- **Real-time thoughts and impressions.** Asking survey subjects to record information on their mobile devices while they are observing store displays or making purchase decisions, for example, promises to enhance some classic research methods. With the old methods, shoppers would answer survey questions about the choices they made well after the fact, leaving the accuracy of their answers up to the quality of their memories. With their mobile phones in hand, shoppers who've agreed to participate in research can describe their impressions and decisions on the spot and even take photos of displays that caught their eye.

As more consumers adopt mobile devices and software developers continue to create new research apps, mobile research promises to revolutionize research the same way it has changed business communication in general.

CAREER APPLICATIONS

1. Assume you're about to visit another college where you're applying for the master's program, and you want to learn as much as you can about the school in the limited time you have available. How could you use your mobile phone to improve your information collection?
2. Mobile research raises some important ethical and legal questions involving privacy. Identify three possible privacy violations that researchers need to guard against.

Sources: Shelly Terrell, "Research on the Go! Effective Research with Mobile Devices," presentation, 7 November 2013, www.slideshare.net; Derek Matisz, "Mobile-Enabled Ethnography: 4 Tips for Using Mobile Devices in Your Research," Vision Critical blog, 24 July 2013, www.visioncritical.com; "Let's Go Shopping: Using Mobile Qualitative Research for Shop-Alongs," 2020Research, accessed 9 May 2014, www.2020research.com.

DOCUMENTING YOUR SOURCES

Proper documentation of the sources you use is an ethical responsibility—and an important resource for your readers.

Documenting the sources you use in your writing serves three important functions: It properly and ethically credits the person who created the original material, it shows your audience that you have sufficient support for your message, and it helps your readers explore your topic in more detail, if desired. Your results might be used by people long after you conduct the research, and these people won't always have the opportunity to query you in person for more information.

Be sure to take advantage of source documentation tools whenever you can to help ensure that you accurately track all your sources. Most word-processing programs can automatically track and number endnotes for you, and you can use the "table of authorities" feature to create a bibliography of all the sources you've used. A wide variety of *citation management* or *reference management* tools are available with popular web browsers.

You may document your sources through footnotes, endnotes, or some similar system (see Appendix B, "Documentation of Report Sources"). Whatever method you choose, documentation is necessary for books, articles, tables, charts, diagrams, song lyrics, scripted dialogue, letters, speeches, and anything else you take from someone else, including ideas and information that you've re-expressed through paraphrasing or summarizing.

However, you do not have to cite a source for general knowledge or for specialized knowledge that's generally known among your readers. For example, almost everyone knows that Nike is a large sporting goods company and that computers are pervasive in business today. You can say so on your own authority, even if you've read an article in which the author says the same thing.

Copyright protections may prevent you from using some materials without obtaining permission from the copyright holder.

Chapter 1 notes that copyright law covers the expression of creative ideas, and copyrights can apply to a wide range of materials, including reports and other documents, web content, movies, musical compositions, lectures, computer programs, and even choreographed dance routines. Copyright protection is initiated the moment the expression is put into fixed form. Copyright law does not protect such elements as titles, names, short phrases, slogans, familiar symbols, or lists of ingredients or contents. It also doesn't protect ideas, procedures, methods, systems, processes, concepts, principles, discoveries, or devices, although it does cover their description, explanation, or illustration.[4] (Note that many of the entities that aren't covered under copyright law are covered under other legal protections, such as trademarks for slogans and patents for devices and processes.)

Merely crediting the source is not always enough. According to the *fair use doctrine*, you can use other people's work only as long as you don't unfairly prevent them from benefiting as a result. For example, if you reproduce someone else's copyrighted material in a report you're writing, even if you properly identify the source, you may be preventing the author from selling that material to your readers.

If you want to use copyrighted information in a report, contact the copyright holder (usually the author or publisher) for permission to reprint it. You'll often be asked to pay a fee. For more information on copyrights, visit **www.copyright.gov** or **www.creativecommons.org**.

Conducting Primary Research

3 **LEARNING OBJECTIVE**
Define *primary research*, and outline the steps involved in conducting surveys and interviews.

Primary research efforts collect data and information for the first time, rather than analyzing and reusing what other researchers have found.

If secondary research can't provide the information and insights you need, your next choice is to gather the information yourself. This is the task of **primary research**, which is collecting data and information for the first time, rather than analyzing and reusing what other researchers have found. The two most common primary research methods for business writing are surveys and interviews, the focus of this section. Other primary techniques include *observation* and *experiments*, such as test-marketing a new product.

GATHERING INFORMATION WITH SURVEYS

Surveys can provide invaluable insights on a wide variety of business topics, but they are useful only when they're reliable and valid. A survey is *reliable* if it produces identical results when repeated. A survey is *valid* if it measures what it's intended to measure. To conduct a survey that generates reliable and valid results, you need to choose research participants carefully and develop an effective set of questions. (A good research handbook can guide you through the process of selecting a sufficient number of representative participants. For important surveys on strategically important topics with much at stake, you're usually better off hiring a research specialist who knows how to avoid errors during planning, execution, and analysis.)

When selecting people to participate in a survey, the most critical task is getting a *representative sample* of the population in question. For instance, if you want to know how U.S. consumers feel about something, you can't just survey a few hundred people in a shopping mall. Different types of consumers shop at different times of the day and on different days of the week, and many consumers rarely, if ever, shop at malls. A survey that doesn't represent the overall population will suffer from *sampling bias*.

> For a survey to produce valid results, it must be based on a representative sample of the population of interest.

Online surveys offer a number of advantages, including speed, cost, and the ability to adapt the question set along the way based on a respondent's answers. However, they are also vulnerable to sampling bias because they capture only the opinions of people who visit particular websites and who want to participate, and these people might not be a representative sample of the population of interest.

> Online surveys are relatively quick and inexpensive, but they require the same care in planning and analysis as offline surveys.

To develop an effective survey questionnaire, start with the information gaps you identified earlier and then break these points into specific questions, choosing an appropriate type of question for each point. (Figure 13.2 on the next page shows various types of survey questions.) The following guidelines will help you produce results that are both valid and reliable:[5]

- Provide clear instructions to make sure people can answer every question correctly.
- Don't ask for information that people can't be expected to remember, such as how many times they went grocery shopping in the past year.
- Keep the questionnaire short and easy to answer; don't expect people to give you more than 10 or 15 minutes of their time.
- Whenever possible, formulate questions that provide answers that are easy to analyze. Numbers and facts are easier to summarize than opinions, for instance.
- Avoid *leading questions* that could bias your survey. If you ask, "Do you prefer that we stay open in the evenings for customer convenience?" you'll no doubt get a "yes." Instead, ask, "What time of day do you normally do your shopping?"
- Avoid ambiguous descriptors such as *often* or *frequently*. Such terms mean different things to different people.
- Avoid compound questions such as "Do you read books and magazines?" People who read one but not the other won't know whether to answer yes or no.
- Make the survey *adaptive*. With an online survey, you can program the survey to branch automatically based on audience inputs. Not only does this sort of real-time adaptation deliver better answers, it reduces frustration for survey respondents as well.[6]

> Provide clear instructions in questionnaires to prevent incorrect or ambiguous answers.

Before you conduct a survey, test it on a sample group first to identify questions that might be confusing or ambiguous.

> Be sure to test your survey before using it.

GATHERING INFORMATION WITH INTERVIEWS

Getting in-depth information straight from an expert or an individual concerned about an issue can be a great method for collecting primary information. Interviews can dig deeper than the "hands-off" approach of surveys, and skilled interviewers can also watch for nonverbal signals that provide additional insights. Interviews can take a variety of formats, from email exchanges to group discussions.

> Interviews are easy to conduct but require careful planning to produce useful results.

Be aware that the answers you receive in an interview are influenced by the types of questions you ask, by the way you ask them, and by each subject's cultural and language background. Potentially significant factors include the person's race, gender, age, educational level, and social status.[7]

Ask **open-ended questions** (such as "Why do you believe that South America represents a better opportunity than Europe for this product line?") to solicit opinions, insights, and information. Ask **closed questions** to elicit a specific answer, such as yes or

> Choose question types that will generate the specific kinds of information you need.

QUESTION TYPE	EXAMPLE
Open-ended	How would you describe the flavor of this ice cream?
Either-or	Do you think this ice cream is too rich? _____ Yes _____ No
Multiple choice	Which description best fits the taste of this ice cream? (Choose only one.) a. Delicious b. Too fruity c. Too sweet d. Too intense e. Bland f. Stale
Scale	Please mark an X on the scale to indicate how you perceive the texture of this ice cream. ⟵————————————————⟶ Too light Light Creamy Too creamy
Checklist	Which of the following ice cream brands do you recognize? (Check all that apply.) _____ Ben & Jerry's _____ Breyers _____ Carvel _____ Dreyer's _____ Häagen-Dazs
Ranking	Rank these flavors in order of your preference, from 1 (most preferred) to 5 (least preferred): _____ Vanilla _____ Cherry _____ Strawberry _____ Chocolate _____ Coconut
Short-answer	In the past 2 weeks, how many times did you buy ice cream in a grocery store? _____ In the past 2 weeks, how many times did you buy ice cream in an ice cream shop? _____

Figure 13.2 Types of Survey Questions
For each item in your survey, choose the type of question that will elicit the most useful answers.

no. However, don't use too many closed questions in an interview, or the experience will feel more like a simple survey and won't take full advantage of the interactive interview setting.

Think carefully about the sequence of your questions and the subject's potential answers so you can arrange questions in an order that helps uncover layers of information. Also, consider providing the person with a list of questions at least a day or two before the interview, especially if you'd like to quote your subject in writing or if your questions might require your subject to conduct research or think extensively about the answers. If you want to record the interview, ask the person ahead of time and respect his or her wishes. During the interview, be alert to new topics you might not have considered while planning the interview, and pursue them if they will shed light on your research questions.

CHECKLIST ✔ Conducting Effective Information Interviews

- Learn about the person you will be interviewing.
- Formulate your main idea to ensure effective focus.
- Choose the duration, style, and organization of the interview.
- Select question types to elicit the specific information you want.

- Design each question carefully to collect useful answers.
- Limit the number of questions you ask.
- During the interview, be alert to new topics that you might want to probe.
- Consider recording the interview if the subject permits.
- Review your notes as soon as the interview ends.

As soon as possible after the interview, take a few moments to write down your thoughts, go over your notes, and organize your material. Look for important themes, helpful facts or statistics, and direct quotes. If you recorded the interview, *transcribe* it (take down word for word what the person said) or take notes from the recording just as you would while listening to someone in person.

Face-to-face interviews give you the opportunity to gauge reactions to your questions and observe the nonverbal signals that accompany the answers, but interviews don't necessarily have to take place in person. For example, email interviews give subjects a chance to think through their responses thoroughly rather than rush to fit the time constraints of a face-to-face interview.[8] Also, email interviews might be the only way you will be able to access some experts.

In addition to individual interviews, business researchers can also use a form of group interview known as the **focus group**. In this format a moderator guides a group through a series of discussion questions while the rest of the research team members observe through a one-way mirror. The key advantage of focus groups is the opportunity to learn from group dynamics as the various participants bounce ideas and questions off each other. Allowing a group to discuss topics and problems in this manner can uncover much richer information than can a series of individual interviews.[9]

As a reminder of the tasks involved in interviews, see "Checklist: Conducting Effective Information Interviews."

> Face-to-face interviews give you the opportunity to gauge non-verbal responses.

Processing Data and Information

After you've collected all the necessary secondary and primary information, the next step is to transform it into the specific content you need. For simple projects, you may be able to insert your material directly into your report, presentation, or other application. However, when you have gathered a significant amount of information or raw data, you need to process the material before you can use it. This step can involve quoting, paraphrasing, or summarizing textual material; analyzing numeric data; drawing conclusions; and making recommendations.

4 LEARNING OBJECTIVE
Describe the major tasks involved in processing research results.

> After you have collected your research results, the next step is to convert them into usable information.

QUOTING, PARAPHRASING, AND SUMMARIZING

You can use textual information from secondary sources in three ways. *Quoting* a source means you reproduce the material exactly as you found it (giving full credit to the source, of course). Use direct quotations when the original language will enhance your argument or when rewording the passage would reduce its impact. However, be careful with direct quotes: Using too many creates a choppy patchwork of varying styles and gives the impression that all you've done is piece together the work of other people. When quoting sources, set off shorter passages with quotation marks and set off longer passages (generally, five lines or more) as separate, indented paragraphs.

You can often maximize the impact of secondary material in your own writing by *paraphrasing* it—restating it in your own words and with your own sentence structures.[10]

> Quoting a source means reproducing the content exactly and indicating who originally created the information.

REAL-TIME UPDATES
LEARN MORE BY READING THIS ARTICLE
Launch that new business idea with solid research

Get a helpful overview of research techniques for entrepreneurs. Go to **real-timeupdates.com/bct14** and select Learn More in the Students section.

Paraphrasing is expressing someone else's ideas in your own words.

Paraphrasing helps you maintain consistent tone, present information using vocabulary more familiar to your audience, and avoid the choppy feel of too many quotations. Of course, you still need to credit the originator of the information through a footnote, endnote, or in-text citation.

To paraphrase effectively, follow these tips:[11]

- Read and reread the original passage until you fully understand its meaning.
- Restate the central ideas of the original passage using your own words.
- Check your version against the source to verify that you have not altered the meaning.
- Use quotation marks to identify any unique terms or phrases you have borrowed exactly from the source.
- Record the source accurately so that you can give proper credit if you use this material in your report.

Summarizing is similar to paraphrasing but distills the content into fewer words.

Summarizing is similar to paraphrasing but presents the gist of the material in fewer words than the original. An effective summary identifies the main ideas and major support points from your source material but leaves out minor details, examples, and other information that is less critical to your audience. Like quotations and paraphrases, summaries also require complete documentation of sources.

Of course, all three approaches require careful attention to ethics. When quoting directly, take care not to distort the original intent of the material by quoting selectively or out of context. If an interview subject said, "This market could grow dramatically next year if we invest heavily in new products," using only "this market could grow dramatically next year" in a report would be unethical.

When paraphrasing and summarizing, preserve the intended message of the original while expressing the ideas in your own words and sentences. Remember that the goal is to help your audience relate to material that supports your message. Double-check your writing to make sure you didn't subconsciously skew the other writer's message to fit your own needs.

ANALYZING NUMERIC DATA

Research often produces numeric data—everything from sales figures to population statistics to survey answers. By themselves, these numbers might not provide the insights you or your audience require, so you'll need to process the data to extract useful insights.

Gaining Insights

Mean, median, and mode provide insight into sets of data.

Even without advanced statistical techniques, you can use simple arithmetic to extract powerful insights from sets of research data. Three common and useful measures are shown in Table 13.2. The **mean** (which is what most people refer to when they use the term *average*) is the sum of all the items in a group divided by the number of items in that group. The **median** is the "middle of the road," or the midpoint of a series (with an equal number of items above and below). The **mode** is the number that occurs more often than

TABLE 13.2 Three Types of Data Measures: Mean, Median, and Mode

Wilson	$3,000	
Green	5,000	
Carrick	6,000	
Cho	7,000	Mean
Keeble	7,500	Median
Lopes	8,500	
O'Toole	8,500	Mode
Mannix	8,500	
Caruso	9,000	
Total	$63,000	

any other in a sample. It's the best answer to a question such as "What is the usual amount?" Each of these three measures can give you different insights into a set of data.

Next, look at the data to spot **trends**—definite patterns taking place over time, including growth, decline, and cyclical trends that vary between growth and decline. By examining data over a period of time, you can detect patterns and relationships that help you answer important questions.

Statistical measures and trends identify *what* is happening. To help you understand *why* those things are happening, look at **causation** (the cause-and-effect linkage between two factors, in which one causes the other to happen) and **correlation** (the simultaneous change in two variables you're measuring, such as customer satisfaction dropping when product reliability drops).

Bear in mind that causation can be easy to assume but difficult to prove. The drop in customer satisfaction might have been caused by a new accounting system that fouled up customer invoices. To prove causation, you need to be able to isolate the suspected cause as the *only* potential source of the change in the measured effect. However, eliminating all but one possible cause isn't always feasible, so you often have to apply careful judgment to correlations. Researchers frequently explore the relationships between subsets of data using a technique called *cross-tabulation*. For instance, if you're trying to figure out why total sales rose or fell, you might look separately at sales data by customer age and gender, by purchase location, and by product type.

Guarding Against Mistakes and Misinterpretations

Numbers are easy to manipulate with spreadsheets and other computer tools, so be sure to guard against computational errors and misinterpretation of results. Double-check all calculations and document the operation of any spreadsheets you plan to share with colleagues. Common spreadsheet mistakes to watch for include errors in math formulas, references to unintended cells in the spreadsheet (resulting in the inclusion of data you don't want or the exclusion of data you do want), and failures to verify the specific operation of the spreadsheet's built-in math functions.

In addition to watching for computational errors, step back and look at your entire set of data before proceeding with any analysis. Do the numbers make sense, based on what you know about the subject? Are any data points suspicious? If the production numbers you've been measuring have never varied more than 10 percent month to month and then suddenly jumped 50 percent last month, is that new number real or an erroneous measurement?

Even when your data points are accurate and your analysis is technically correct, it's still possible to misinterpret or misrepresent the results. Many analysis errors require statistical expertise to identify and fix, but even without advanced skills, you can take these precautions:

- **Avoid faulty comparisons.** Make sure you compare "apples to apples" and not "apples to oranges," as the saying goes.
- **Don't push research results beyond their limits.** The temptation to extract insights and assurances that aren't really there can be quite strong, particularly in situations of great uncertainty. For instance, if you're about to recommend that your company invest millions of dollars in developing a new product based on your consumer research, you're likely to "see" every possible justification in the data. Have a trusted colleague review your data to see whether he or she extracts the same conclusions.
- **Steer clear of misleading presentations.** Even valid data can be presented in invalid ways (such as with distorted graphs), and it's your responsibility to make sure the visual presentation of your data is accurate.

Trends identify patterns that tend to repeat over time.

Causation shows cause-and-effect relationships; *correlation* indicates simultaneous changes in two variables that may not necessarily be causally related.

Watch out for errors that might have crept in during the collection and processing of data.

Applying Your Findings

After all your planning, research, and processing, you're finally ready to apply your findings. This step can involve summarizing your results, drawing conclusions based on those results, and making recommendations.

5 LEARNING OBJECTIVE
Explain how to summarize research results and present conclusions and recommendations.

SUMMARIZING YOUR RESEARCH

A summary is an unbiased presentation of information regarding a particular topic, without attempts to draw conclusions or make recommendations.

A research summary is an unbiased condensation of the information uncovered in your research. (*Summary* in this context means a summary of your entire research project, not just a summary of secondary source material.) Summaries should not include opinions, conclusions, or recommendations. Summarizing is not always a simple task, and your readers will judge your ability to separate significant issues from less significant details. Identify the main idea and the key support points; separate them from details, examples, and other supporting evidence (see Figure 13.3). Focus your efforts on your audience, highlighting the information that is most important to the person who assigned the project or to those who will be reading the report.

However, focusing on the audience doesn't mean conveying only the information your audience wants to hear. A good summary might contain nothing but bad news, if that's what your research uncovered. Even if the summary isn't pleasant, effective managers always appreciate and respect honest, complete, and perceptive information from their employees.

DRAWING CONCLUSIONS

A conclusion is a logical interpretation of research results.

A **conclusion** is a logical interpretation of the facts and other information in a report. Reaching valid conclusions based on the evidence at hand is one of the most important skills you can develop in your business career. For a conclusion to be sound, it must meet two criteria. First, it must be based strictly on the information in your report. You shouldn't introduce any new information in your conclusion. (If something is that important, it belongs in the body of the report.) Also, you can't ignore any of the information you've presented, even if it doesn't support your conclusion. Second, the conclusion must be logical, meaning it must follow accepted patterns of inductive or deductive reasoning. Conclusions that are based on unproven premises, appeal to emotion, make hasty generalizations, or contain any other logical fallacies are not valid.

Remember that your personal values or the organization's values may also influence your conclusions; just be sure that you're aware of how these biases can affect your judgment. If a bias affects your conclusion, you should explain it to your audience. Also, don't expect all team members to examine the evidence and arrive at the same conclusion. One

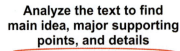

Original: 116 words

Our facilities costs spiraled out of control last year. The 23 percent jump was far ahead of every other cost category in the company and many times higher than the 4 percent average rise for commercial real estate in the Portland metropolitan area. The rise can be attributed to many factors, but the major factors include repairs (mostly electrical and structural problems at the downtown office), energy (most of our offices are heated by electricity, the price of which has been increasing much faster than for oil or gas), and last but not least, the loss of two sublease tenants whose rent payments made a substantial dent in our cost profile for the past five years.

Analyze the text to find main idea, major supporting points, and details

Main idea → Our facilities costs spiraled out of control last year. The 23 percent jump was far ahead of every other cost category in the company and many times higher than the 4 percent average rise for commercial real estate in the Portland metropolitan area. *Major support points* → The rise can be attributed to many factors, but the major factors include repairs (mostly electrical and structural problems at the downtown office), energy (most of our offices are heated by electricity, the price of which has been increasing much faster than for oil or gas), and last but not least, *Details* → the loss of two sublease tenants whose rent payments made a substantial dent in our cost profile for the past five years.

45-word summary

Our facilities costs jumped 23 percent last year, far ahead of every other cost category in the company and many times higher than the 4 percent local average. The major factors contributing to the increase are repairs, energy, and the loss of two sublease tenants.

22-word summary

Our facilities costs jumped 23 percent last year, due mainly to rising repair and energy costs and the loss of sublease income.

Figure 13.3 **Summarizing Effectively**
To summarize a section of text, first analyze it to find the main idea, the major support points, and the less important details. Then assemble the appropriate pieces with additional words and phrases as needed to ensure a smooth flow.

of the reasons for bringing additional people into a decision is to gain their unique perspectives and experiences.

Even though conclusions need to be logical, they may not automatically or obviously flow from the evidence. Many business decisions require assumptions, judgment calls, and creative thinking—in fact, the ability to see patterns and possibilities that others can't see is one of the hallmarks of innovative business leaders.

MAKING RECOMMENDATIONS

Whereas a conclusion interprets information, a **recommendation** suggests what to do about the information. The following example illustrates the difference between a conclusion and a recommendation:

A recommendation is a suggested course of action.

Conclusion	**Recommendation**
On the basis of its track record and current price, I believe that this company is an attractive buy.	I recommend that we offer to buy the company at a 10 percent premium over the current market value of its stock.

To be credible, recommendations must be based on logical analysis and sound conclusions. They must also be practical and acceptable to your readers—the people who have to make your recommendations work. Finally, when making a recommendation, be certain you have adequately described the steps that come next. Don't leave your readers wondering what they need to do to act on your recommendation.

MANAGING INFORMATION

Conducting your research well does more than provide strong support for your own writing projects. Your individual research projects are also an important contribution to your organization's collective knowledge base. To organize information and make it readily available to everyone in the company, many firms use some form of **knowledge management (KM)**, a set of technologies, policies, and procedures that let colleagues capture and share information throughout an organization. Social media tools have recently been enhancing the flexibility and capability of KM systems, making it easier for more people to contribute to and benefit from shared knowledge and transforming knowledge into more of a living entity that is part of an ongoing conversation.[12]

Knowledge management systems, often supplemented now by social media tools, help organizations share research results and other valuable information and insights.

COMMUNICATION CHALLENGES AT **Strategyzer**

You're a business development manager at Strategyzer with responsibility for expanding sales of the company's Business Model Canvas training courses and apps. Use what you've learned in this chapter to address these information gathering and processing challenges. You may find it helpful to familiarize yourself with the Business Model Canvas by watching the two-minute video at **businessmodelgeneration.com/canvas/bmc**.

INDIVIDUAL CHALLENGE: You've heard from a number of product managers and other mid-level business planners in big companies that they would like to use the Business Model Canvas but they can't convince company executives (their superiors, in other words) to give up the familiar approach of detailed business plans. You hit on the idea of a mini-course for corporate executives to help them understand the value of the canvas approach for early stage business planning. Before you can convince Strategyzer's content development team to create the course, you need to provide some evidence that *Fortune 500* executives would be interested in devoting half a day to such a course. You decide to conduct some research to gauge executive interest in the mini-course and to identify the most important topics it should cover. What would be an effective problem statement for guiding your research?

TEAM CHALLENGE: Collect the problem statements you and your teammates generated for the individual challenge and choose the statement that the team finds most effective. Using that statement as a guide, discuss the following four approaches and

decide which would be the best research approach to gathering the information you need to address the problem statement. Summarize your reasoning in an email message to your instructor.

a. Conduct a telephone survey of *Fortune 500* executives responsible for overseeing product development. Ask a series of questions designed to uncover the executives' awareness of the canvas approach and their attitudes toward it.

b. Conduct an email or in-app survey of current users of the Business Model Canvas app, asking them to report on the resistance they are receiving from executives in their companies.

c. Post a brief survey on Strategyzer's website, asking top-level corporate executives to explain their reasons for sticking with the traditional approach of detailed business plans, rather than trying a new method such as the Business Model Canvas.

d. Post an interactive survey on Strategyzer's website, asking site visitors to report on the attitudes toward Business Model Canvas and similar approaches in their organizations. Set up branching in the survey so that people who are interested in the canvas method but who have encountered resistance from upper management are asked a series of questions about the nature of the resistance they are encountering and what forms of proof could help convince these executives to give the new method a try.

Quick Learning Guide

KEY TERMS

causation Cause-and-effect linkage between two factors, where one of them causes the other to occur or change

closed questions Questions with a fixed range of possible answers

conclusion A logical interpretation of the facts and other information in a report

correlation The simultaneous change in two variables; changes in one variable may or may not cause changes in the other

focus group A form of group research interview in which a moderator guides a group through a series of discussion questions while the rest of the research team members observes

knowledge management (**KM**) Set of technologies, policies, and procedures that let colleagues capture and share information throughout an organization

mean Value equal to the sum of all the items in the group divided by the number of items in that group; what people refer to when they use the term *average*

median Midpoint of a series, with an equal number of items above and below

metasearch engines Search tools that format search requests for multiple search engines simultaneously

mode The number that occurs more often than any other in a sample

online databases Online compilations of newspapers, magazines, journals, and other information sources

open-ended questions Questions without simple, predetermined answers; used to solicit opinions, insights, and information

primary research New research done specifically for the current project

problem statement Statement that defines the problem or purpose of your research

recommendation A suggested course of action

search engines Online search tools that identify individual webpages that contain specific words or phrases you've asked for

secondary research Research done previously for another purpose

trends Repeatable patterns taking place over time

web directories Online lists of websites selected by human editors

SUMMARY OF LEARNING OBJECTIVES

1 Describe an effective process for conducting business research. Begin the research process with careful planning to make sure you familiarize yourself with the subject area, identify the most important information gaps you face, and prioritize the questions you need to ask to fill those gaps. Then locate the required data and information, using primary and secondary research as needed. Process the results of your research, analyzing both textual and numeric information to extract averages, trends, and other insights. Apply your findings by summarizing information for someone else's benefit, drawing conclusions based on what you've learned or developing recommendations. Finally, manage information effectively so that you and others can retrieve it later and reuse it in other projects.

2 Define *secondary research* and explain how to evaluate, locate, and document information sources. Secondary research involves collecting information that was originally gathered for another research project or another effort. Secondary research is generally done before primary research, to save time and money in the event someone else has already gathered the information needed.

Information should come from a credible source that has a reputation for being honest and reliable; the source should also be unbiased. The purpose of the material should be known, and the author should be credible. The information should include references to sources (if obtained elsewhere), and it should be independently verifiable. The material should be current, complete, and supported with evidence. Finally, the information should seem logical.

The tasks involved in locating secondary sources of data and information can vary widely depending on the project, but much of your efforts will involve finding information in a corporate, public, or university library or finding information online. Libraries offer an array of business books, databases, newspapers, periodicals, directories, almanacs, and government publications. Some of these printed sources provide information that is not available online, and some of the online sources provide information that is available by subscription. Librarians can be a huge help when you need advice on structuring an investigation or finding specific sources.

Finding information online is often more complicated than simply plugging a few terms into a search engine. General-purpose search engines are sophisticated tools, but even when they are used wisely, they are not able to find everything on the Internet. Moreover, with no human reviewers to evaluate the quality or ranking of the search results, you can't always be sure of the quality of what you find. Web directories, metasearch engines, and online databases all complement the capabilities of general-purpose search engines. Use online monitoring tools to be alerted to new materials on topics of interest.

To make the best use of any search engine or database, think about your information needs carefully before you start searching, read and understand the instructions for using each online research tool, pay attention to the details because even minor aspects of searching can dramatically influence results, review search and display options carefully to optimize results, try variations on your search terms if you can't find what you're looking for, and try narrower or broader searches to adjust the scope of what you're looking for.

3 Define *primary research* and outline the steps involved in conducting surveys and interviews. Primary research is research that is being conducted for the first time, and the two most common methods are surveys and interviews. Conducting a survey involves selecting a representative set of respondents from the population you are studying, developing a questionnaire using carefully written and sequenced questions, and administering the actual survey to collect information. Conducting an interview starts with learning about the person(s) you plan to interview and then formulating your main idea to make sure your interview will stay focused. Choose the length, style, and organization of the interview, and then select question types to elicit the sort of information you want, with each question designed to collect useful answers. Limit your questions to the most important queries. Record the interview if the person allows, and review your notes as soon as the interview ends.

4 Describe the major tasks involved in processing research results. In most cases you need to process your research results in some fashion before applying them in reports and presentations. The three basic ways to process verbal information are quoting (using someone else's words directly, with appropriate attribution), paraphrasing (restating someone else's words in your own language), and summarizing (creating a shorter version of an original piece of writing). Processing numeric data can involve a variety of statistical analysis techniques. Three basic computations are the mean (what people are referring to when they say "average"), the median (the midpoint in a series, indicating an equal number of lesser and greater values), and the mode (the most frequently occurring value in a series). Processing results can also involve looking for trends and distinguishing causal relationships from correlations and mere coincidences.

5 Explain how to summarize research results and present conclusions and recommendations. Research results can be applied in several ways, depending on the purpose of the report or presentation. A summary is an unbiased condensation of the information uncovered in your research. It filters out details and presents only the most important ideas. A conclusion is your analysis of what the findings mean (an interpretation of the facts). A recommendation is your opinion (based on reason and logic) about the course of action that should be taken.

MyBCommLab

Go to **mybcommlab.com** to complete the problems marked with this icon .

TEST YOUR KNOWLEDGE

To review chapter content related to each question, refer to the indicated Learning Objective.

13-1. What are the five steps in the research process? [LO-1]

13-2. What is the purpose of identifying information gaps before starting research? [LO-1]

13-3. Should you conduct secondary research first or primary research? Why? [LO-2]

13-4. What is the *hidden Internet*? [LO-2]

13-5. What does it mean to make a survey adaptive? [LO-3]

13-6. What is paraphrasing and what is its purpose? [LO-4]

13-7. What are the differences between the mean, median, and mode? [LO-4]

13-8. What are the characteristics of a sound conclusion? [LO-5]

13-9. How does a conclusion differ from a recommendation? [LO-5]

APPLY YOUR KNOWLEDGE

To review chapter content related to each question, refer to the indicated Learning Objective.

13-10. Companies occasionally make mistakes that expose confidential information, such as when employees lose laptop computers containing sensitive data files or webmasters forget to protect confidential webpages from search engine indexes. If you conducted a search that turned up competitive information on webpages that were clearly intended to be private, what would you do? Explain your answer. [LO-1]

13-11. Why must you be careful when citing information from online sources? [LO-2]

13-12. One of your employees submitted a report comparing the market opportunities for two product ideas your company might develop. The report concludes that because the first idea yielded 340,000 hits in a Google search, whereas the second idea yielded only 128,000 hits, the first idea clearly has more sales potential. Is this a valid conclusion? Why or why not? [LO-4]

13-13. While analyzing last year's sales data, you notice that sales were 10 to 15 percent higher than average during August, September, and November. The marketing department invested heavily in a search engine advertising campaign from August through December. Can you conclude that the advertising campaign caused the increase in sales? Why or why not? [LO-5]

PRACTICE YOUR SKILLS

13-14. Message for Analysis: Primary Research: Conducting Interviews [LO-4] Imagine you are going to interview a mid-level manager in a large corporation about the company's meeting practices. Read the questions and then

(1) critique them, as a whole, indicating what is effective or ineffective about this series of questions, and (2) select five questions and revise them to make them more effective.

a. What is your position in the company?

b. To whom do you report?

c. Do you attend or run many meetings?

d. Do your meetings start on time? Run late?

e. Do you distribute or receive a meeting agenda several days in advance of the meeting?

f. Do you like your job?

g. Do you travel a lot for your job?

h. Has your company cut back on travel expenditures? If so, how and why?

i. Does your company use videoconferencing or online meetings as an alternative to travel?

j. Does your company own its own videoconferencing equipment?

k. Are virtual meetings more or less effective than face-to-face meetings?

l. How long have you worked at this company?

m. Who are your most important customers?

n. How often does your management team meet with the managers of other companies?

o. Does your company produce a wide range of products or only a few specialty items?

p. How do you keep your meetings on track?

q. Does someone prepare written minutes of meetings? Are the minutes distributed to meeting members?

Exercises

Each activity is labeled according to the primary skill or skills you will need to use. To review relevant chapter content, you can refer to the indicated Learning Objective. In some instances, supporting information will be found in another chapter, as indicated.

Planning Your Research; Collaboration: Team Projects [LO-1] In a team assigned by your instructor, decide how you would structure a research project to answer the following questions. Identify any shortcomings in the approaches you have chosen.

13-15. Has the litter problem on campus been reduced since the cafeteria began offering fewer take-out choices this year than in past years?

13-16. Has the school attracted more transfer students since it waived the formal application process and allowed students at other colleges simply to send their transcripts and a one-page letter of application?

13-17. Have the number of traffic accidents at the school's main entrance been reduced since a traffic light was installed?

13-18. Did student satisfaction with campus libraries decline after budget cuts forced the libraries to reduce opening hours?

13-19. Planning a Research Project [LO-1] You and your business partners are considering buying several franchises in the fast-food business. You are all experienced managers or entrepreneurs, but none of you has experience in franchising. Visit www.amazon.com and search for books on this subject. Explore some of the books that you find by reading reviews and using the "search inside" feature.

   a. Use the information you find to develop a list of subquestions to help you narrow your focus.
   b. Write down the names of three books you might purchase to further aid your research.
   c. Summarize how a search like this can assist you with your research efforts and identify any risks of using this technique.

13-20. Planning a Research Project [LO-1] Analyze any recent school or work assignment that required you to conduct research. How did you approach your investigation? Did you rely mostly on sources of primary information or mostly on sources of secondary information? Now that you have studied this chapter, can you identify two ways to improve the research techniques you used during that assignment? Briefly explain.

Conducting Secondary Research (Company and Industry Data) [LO-2] Using online or printed sources, find the following information. Be sure to properly cite your sources, using the formats discussed in Appendix B.

13-21. Contact information for the American Management Association

13-22. Median weekly earnings of men and women by occupation

13-23. Current market share for Perrier water

13-24. Performance ratios for office supply retailers

13-25. Annual stock performance for Nike

13-26. Number of franchise outlets in the United States

13-27. Composition of the U.S. workforce by profession

Conducting Secondary Research (Finding Sources) [LO-2] Businesspeople have to know where to look for secondary information when they conduct research. Identify five periodicals or online resources in each the following professions:

13-28. Marketing and advertising

13-29. Insurance

13-30. Telecommunications

13-31. Accounting

13-32. Conducting Secondary Research (Documenting Sources) [LO-2] Select five business articles from sources such as journals, books, newspapers, or websites. Develop a resource list, using Appendix B as a guideline.

13-33. Conducting Secondary Research (Evaluating Sources) [LO-2] Find three websites that provide business information such as company or industry news, trends, analysis, facts, or performance data. Using the criteria discussed under "Evaluating Sources" on page 366, evaluate the credibility of the information presented at these websites.

13-34. Conducting Secondary Research (Online Monitoring); Media Skills: Microblogging [LO-2], Chapter 8 Select a business topic that interests you and configure a Twitter monitoring tool such as TweetDeck (www.tweetdeck.com) to track tweets on this topic. After you've found at least a dozen tweets, identify three that provide potentially useful information and describe them in a brief email message to your instructor.

13-35. Conducting Secondary Research (Company Data) [LO-2] Select any publicly traded company and find the following information:

   • Names of the company's current officers
   • List of the company's products or services (summarized by product lines or divisions, if the company offers many products and services)
   • Current issues in the company's industry
   • Outlook for the company's industry as a whole

13-36. Conducting Secondary Research (Industry Issues) [LO-2] You'd like to know if it's a good idea to buy banner ads on other websites to drive more traffic to your company's website. You're worried about the expense and difficulty of running an experiment to test banner effectiveness, so you decide to look for some secondary data. Identify three secondary sources that might offer helpful data on this question.

13-37. Conducting Primary Research (Surveys) [LO-3] You work for a movie studio that is producing a young director's first motion picture, the story of a group of unknown musicians finding work and making a reputation in a competitive industry. Unfortunately, some of your friends leave the first complete screening, saying that the 182-minute movie is simply too long. Others said they couldn't imagine any sequences to cut out. Your boss wants to test the movie on a regular audience and ask viewers to complete a questionnaire that will help the director decide whether edits are needed and, if so, where. Design a questionnaire you can use to solicit valid answers for a report to the director about how to handle the audience members' reactions to the movie.

13-38. Conducting Primary Research (Interviews) [LO-3] Plan an information interview with a professional working in your chosen field of study. Plan the structure of the interview and create a set of interview questions. Conduct the interview. Using the information you gathered, write a memo to another student, describing the tasks, advantages, and disadvantages of jobs in this field of study. (Assume that your reader is a person who also plans to pursue a career in this field of study.)

13-39. Conducting Primary Research (Interviews) [LO-3] You're conducting an information interview with a manager in another division of your company. Partway through the interview, the manager shows clear signs of impatience. How should you respond? What might you do differently to prevent this from happening in the future? Explain your answers.

13-40. Processing Data and Information [LO-4] Select an article from a business periodical such as *Bloomberg Businessweek*, *Fortune*, or *Forbes*. Read the article and highlight its key points. Summarize the article in fewer than 100 words, paraphrasing the key points.

13-41. **Processing Data and Information [LO-4]** Your boss has asked you to analyze and report on your division's sales for the first nine months of this year. Using the following data from company invoices, calculate the mean for each quarter and all averages for the year to date. Then identify and discuss the quarterly sales trends.

January	$24,600
February	$25,900
March	$23,000
April	$21,200
May	$24,600
June	$26,800
July	$29,900
August	$30,500
September	$26,600

EXPAND YOUR SKILLS

Critique the Professionals

Find a recent example of a significant business blunder, such as a new product that failed in the marketplace. Based on what you can learn about the episode, how might better research have helped the company in question avoid the blunder? Using whatever medium your instructor requests, write a brief conclusion of your analysis.

Sharpening Your Career Skills Online

Bovée and Thill's Business Communication Web Search, at **websearch.businesscommunicationnetwork.com**, is a unique research tool designed specifically for business communication research. Use the Web Search function to find a website, video, article, podcast, or presentation that offers advice on using online search tools in business research. Write a brief email message to your instructor, describing the item you found and summarizing the career skills information you learned from it.

MyBCommLab

Go to **mybcommlab.com** for Auto-graded writing questions as well as the following Assisted-graded writing questions:

13-42. How can online monitoring tools help you with research? [LO-2]

13-43. What search terms could you use to find estimates of the lifetime financial value of a college education? [LO-2]

Endnotes

1. Kavi Guppta, "How to Convince Leaders to Avoid Business Plans When Validating New Ideas," Strategyzer blog, 18 April 2016, blog .strategyzer.com; Strategyzer website, accessed 23 April 2016, strategyzer.com; Alexander Ostenwalder and Yves Pigneur, *Business Model Generation: A Handbook for Visionaries, Game Changers, and Challengers* (Hoboken, N.J.: Wiley, 2009), ebook; Alex Cowan, "The 20 Minute Business Plan: Business Model Canvas Made Easy," Cowan+, 6 February 2013, www.alexandercowan.com.
2. Annie Pettit, "Mugging, Sugging and Now Rugging: I Take a Hard Stance on Privacy," LoveStats blog, 29 January 2010, lovestats .wordpress.com.
3. Information for this section originally based in part from "Finding Industry Information," accessed 3 November 1998, www.pitt .edu/~buslibry/industries.htm; Thomas P. Bergman, Stephen M. Garrison, and Gregory M. Scott, *The Business Student Writer's Manual and Guide to the Internet* (Upper Saddle River, N.J.: Prentice Hall, 1998), 67–80; Ernest L. Maier, Anthony J. Faria, Peter Kaatrude, and Elizabeth Wood, *The Business Library and How to Use It* (Detroit: Omnigraphics, 1996), 53–76; Sherwyn P. Morreale and Courtland L. Bovée, *Excellence in Public Speaking* (Fort Worth, Tex.: Harcourt Brace College Publishers, 1998), 166–171.

4. "Copyright Office Basics," U.S. Copyright Office website, accessed 2 November 2006, www.copyright.gov.
5. Naresh K. Malhotra, *Basic Marketing Research* (Upper Saddle River, N.J.: Prentice Hall, 2002), 314–317; "How to Design and Conduct a Study," *Credit Union Magazine,* October 1983, 36–46.
6. "Using Skip Logic in a Survey," SurveyMonkey.com, accessed 19 August 2016, www.surveymonkey.com.
7. Morreale and Bovée, *Excellence in Public Speaking,* 177.
8. Morreale and Bovée, *Excellence in Public Speaking,* 182.
9. A. B. Blankenship and George Edward Breen, *State of the Art Marketing Research* (Lincolnwood, Ill.: NTC Business Books, 1992), 225.
10. Lynn Quitman Troyka, *Simon & Schuster Handbook for Writers,* 6th ed. (Upper Saddle River, N.J.: Prentice Hall, 2002), 481.
11. "How to Paraphrase Effectively: 6 Steps to Follow," Research paper.com, accessed 26 October 1998, www.researchpaper.com.
12. Jonathan Reichental, "Knowledge Management in the Age of Social Media," O'Reilly Radar, 16 March 2011, radar.oreilly.com; Venkatesh Rao, "Social Media vs. Knowledge Management: A Generational War," *Social Computing,* 17 November 2008, www.social computingmagazine.com; Jeff Kelly, "KM vs. Social Media: Beware the Warmongers," *Social Computing,* 17 November 2008, www.socialcomputingmagazine.com.

14

Planning Reports and Proposals

LEARNING OBJECTIVES

After studying this chapter, you will be able to

1 Adapt the three-step writing process to reports and proposals.

2 List the options for organizing informational reports, and identify the key parts of a business plan.

3 Discuss three major ways to organize analytical reports.

4 Explain how to choose an organizational strategy when writing a proposal.

MyBCommLab®

⭐ **Improve Your Grade!** More than 10 million students improved their results using Pearson MyLabs. Visit **mybcommlab.com** for simulations, tutorials, and end-of-chapter problems.

COMMUNICATION CLOSE-UP AT
Warby Parker

www.warbyparker.com

When a company sets out to disrupt an entire industry, it's not surprising that its communication efforts don't follow all the old rules, either.

Much of the worldwide market for eyeglasses is controlled by the Italian company Luxottica Group, which owns such well-known brands as Ray-Ban and Oakley and manufactures glasses for a host of high-fashion labels, from Dolce & Gabbana to Versace. Luxottica also operates more than 7,000 retail stores, including LensCrafters and Sunglass Hut. If you've ever purchased a pair of prescription glasses or sunglasses, chances are you've done business with Luxottica in one form or another. And business has been very good for Luxottica, earning it some 80 percent of the global market for glasses.

Much of the remaining 20 percent of the market is in the hands of Costco and Walmart, two companies that compete on cost more than fashion. Between high fashion on one hand and low prices on the other, these three giants seem to have wrapped up the market.

Neil Blumenthal and David Gilboa looked at the data and drew a different conclusion, however. They believed an

Neil Blumenthal and David Gilboa's unconventional ideas behind the eyewear startup Warby Parker are reflected in the company's cheeky communication style.

opportunity existed for a company to compete on fashion *and* price. Together with their University of Pennsylvania classmates Andrew Hunt and Jeffrey Raider, they crafted a business model that combines fashion-forward designs and a brand image that appeals to younger consumers with the operational efficiency of online commerce. Echoing their unconventional aspirations, they named the company Warby Parker after two characters from the works of the Beat Generation writer Jack Kerouac.

The quest to connect with buyers in a market dominated by a handful of major corporations gives Warby Parker's communication efforts a different look and feel. You won't find supermodels posing on yachts in the company's promotional campaigns. You're more likely to find a blog post about what company employees are reading or a wistful goodbye note to a summer intern heading back to high school.

The company's "annual reports" are a great example of how unconventional thinking can lead to communications that connect with audiences in fresh ways. All U.S. companies that sell stock to the public are required to issue annual reports that disclose a variety of financial details. Most companies expand on these minimum requirements with glossy, persuasive messages about their operations, products, and prospects. As a privately held company, Warby Parker isn't required to publish an annual report, but it does so anyway— sort of. Its annual reports are anything but normal. One year, the report was an online calendar of major, minor, and just plain goofy things that happened around the company, from product launches to a survey about how many pairs of pants employees wear in a typical month. The following year, it was an interactive message generator that created personalized reports for website visitors based on how good or bad *their* year had been.

This tradition-defying approach to communication fits the transparent, social, and conversational style of today's younger consumers. And it helps position Warby Parker as a different kind of company—one more in touch with those customers and their needs and aspirations. The company won't dethrone Luxottica anytime soon, but it has already carved out a nice chunk of the eyewear market and continues to grow as it heads toward a possible initial public offering in the stock market. At that point it will have to bend to convention just a little, at least enough to meet government reporting requirements, but it will surely maintain an offbeat approach in the rest of its communication efforts.[1]

Applying the Three-Step Writing Process to Reports and Proposals

1 LEARNING OBJECTIVE
Adapt the three-step writing process to reports and proposals.

Whether they are routine documents or the unconventional messages that Warby Parker (profiled in the chapter-opening Communication Close-Up) tends to create, **reports** are written accounts that objectively communicate information about some aspect of a business (see Figure 14.1). **Informational reports** offer data, facts, feedback, and other types of information, without analysis or recommendations. **Analytical reports** offer both information and analysis and can also include recommendations. **Proposals** are a special category of reports that combine information delivery and persuasive communication.

The purpose and content of business reports varies widely; in some cases you'll follow strict guidelines, but in others the organization and format will be up to you.

The nature of these reports can vary widely, depending on the circumstances. Some of the reports you write will be voluntary, launched on your own initiative and following whatever structure you find most effective. Other reports will be in response to a manager's or customer's request, and you may or may not receive guidance regarding the organization and content. You may also write certain reports that follow strict, specific guidelines for content and layout.

Many of your reports will be written for internal audiences, but you may also write reports for a wide range of outside readers.

Your audience will sometimes be internal, which gives you more freedom to discuss sensitive information. Other times your audience might include customers, investors, community members, or news media, any of which can create additional demands as you present company information to such external groups.

No matter what the circumstances, preparing reports requires all the skills and knowledge that you've gained throughout this course and will continue to gain on the job. View every business report as an opportunity to demonstrate your understanding of business challenges and your ability to contribute to your organization's success.

By adapting the three-step writing process, you can reduce the time required to write effective reports and still produce documents that make lasting and positive impressions on your audiences. The concepts are the same as those you explored in Chapters 4 through 6 and applied to shorter messages in Chapters 10 through 12. However, the emphasis on specific tasks can vary considerably. For instance, planning can take days or weeks for a complex report or proposal.

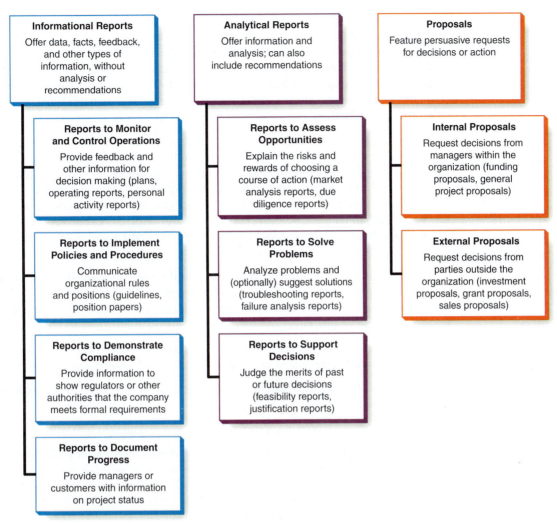

Figure 14.1   Common Types of Business Reports and Proposals
You will have the opportunity to read and write many types of reports in your career; here are some of the most common.

ANALYZING THE SITUATION

The complexity of most reports and the magnitude of the work involved heighten the need to analyze the situation carefully. With an email or another short message, you can change direction halfway through the first draft and perhaps lose only a few minutes of work. In contrast, if you change direction halfway through a major report, you could lose days of work. To minimize that chance, pay special attention to your statement of purpose. In addition, for anything beyond the simplest reports, take the time to prepare a work plan before you start writing.

Given the length and complexity of many reports, it's crucial to clearly define your purpose so you don't waste time with avoidable rework.

Defining Your Purpose

Informational reports often address a predetermined need and must meet specific audience expectations. For example, you may be asked to write reports that verify your company's compliance with government regulations, that summarize sales, or that monitor a process—all of which have audiences who expect certain information in a certain format. With other informational reports, you will need to uncover audience needs before you can define the optimum purpose.

In some cases you'll be told the purpose of the report; in others, it's up to you to identify the purpose.

Analytical reports and proposals are almost always written in response to a perceived problem or a perceived opportunity. A clear statement of this problem or opportunity helps frame the communication challenge by identifying *what* you're going to write about, but it's insufficient to guide your writing efforts. To plan effectively, address the problem or opportunity with a clear **statement of purpose** that defines *why* you are preparing the report (see Table 14.1).

The most useful way to phrase your purpose statement is to begin with an infinitive (*to* plus a verb). Using an infinitive encourages you to take control and decide where you're going before you begin. When you choose an infinitive (such as *to inform, to confirm, to analyze, to persuade,* or *to recommend*), you pin down your general goal in preparing the report. Consider these examples for informational reports:

- To update clients on the progress of the research project (progress report)
- To develop goals and objectives for the coming year (strategic plan)
- To identify customers and explain how the company will serve them (marketing plan)
- To submit monthly sales statistics to management (operating report)
- To summarize what occurred at the annual sales conference (personal activity report)
- To explain building access procedures (policy implementation report)
- To submit required information to the Securities and Exchange Commission (compliance report)

The statement of purpose for an analytical report often needs to be more comprehensive than a statement for an informational report. For example, a report suggesting ways to reduce employee travel and entertainment (T&E) costs might have the following as a statement of purpose:

> . . . to analyze the T&E budget, evaluate the impact of recent changes in airfares and hotel costs, and suggest ways to tighten management's control over T&E expenses.

If the writer had been assigned an informational report instead, she might have stated her purpose differently:

> To summarize the company's spending on travel and entertainment

You can see from these two examples how much influence the purpose statement has on the scope of your report. Because she was assigned an analytical report rather than an informational report, the writer had to go beyond merely collecting data; she had to draw conclusions and make recommendations. (You can see the full report based on this statement of purpose in Chapter 15.)

Proposals must also be guided by a clear and specific statement of purpose to help you focus on crafting a persuasive message. Here are several examples:

> To secure $400k of funding in next year's capital budget for a new conveyor system in the warehouse (funding proposal)

> To get management approval to reorganize the North American salesforce (general project proposal)

> To secure $2 million in venture capital funding to complete design and production of the new line of titanium mountain bikes (investment proposal as part of a business plan)

> To convince Boeing to purchase a trial subscription to our latest database offering (sales proposal)

TABLE 14.1 Problem Statements Versus Purpose Statements

Problem Statement	Statement of Purpose
Our company's market share is steadily declining.	To explore new ways of promoting and selling our products and to recommend the approaches most likely to stabilize our market share
Our computer network lacks sufficient bandwidth and cannot be upgraded to meet our future needs.	To analyze various networking options and to recommend the system that will best meet our current and future needs
We need $2 million to launch our new product.	To convince investors that our new business would be a sound investment so that we can obtain desired financing
Our current operations are too decentralized and expensive.	To justify closing the Newark plant and transferring East Coast operations to a single Midwest location in order to save the company money

Preparing Your Work Plan

You're already accustomed to some schedule pressure with school reports. This is good practice for your business career, in which you'll be expected to produce quality reports quickly and efficiently. Carefully thinking out a work plan is the best way to make sure you produce good work on schedule. By identifying all the tasks that must be performed, you ensure that nothing is overlooked (see Figure 14.2).

If you are preparing a work plan for yourself, it can be relatively informal: a simple list of the steps you plan to take and an estimate of their sequence and timing. For more complicated projects, however, particularly those that involve multiple team members, you'll want to prepare a formal, detailed work plan that can guide the performance of many tasks over a span of time. For consultants and others whose work output is a formal

A detailed work plan saves time and often produces more effective reports.

The problem statement clearly and succinctly defines the problem the writers intend to address.

This section explains how the researchers will find the data and information they need.

This paragraph identifies exactly what will be covered by the research and addressed in the final report.

The preliminary outline has enough detail to guide the research and set reader expectations.

The assignments and schedule section clearly lists responsibilities and due dates.

STATEMENT OF THE PROBLEM
The rapid growth of our company over the past five years has reduced the sense of community among our staff. People no longer feel like part of an intimate organization that values teamwork.

PURPOSE AND SCOPE OF WORK
The purpose of this study is to determine whether social networking technology such as Facebook and Socialtext would help rebuild a sense of community within the workforce and whether encouraging the use of such tools in the workplace will have any negative consequences. The study will attempt to assess the impact of social networks in other companies in terms of community-building, morale, project communication, and overall productivity.

SOURCES AND METHODS OF DATA COLLECTION
Data collection will start with secondary research, including a review of recently published articles and studies on the use of social networking in business and a review of product information published by technology vendors. Primary research will focus on an employee and management survey to uncover attitudes about social networking tools. We will also collect anecdotal evidence from bloggers and others with experience using networks in the workplace.

PRELIMINARY OUTLINE
The preliminary outline for this study is as follows:
I. What experiences have other companies had with social networks in the workplace?
  A. Do social networks have a demonstrable business benefit?
  B. How do employees benefit from using these tools?
  C. Has network security and information confidentiality been an issue?
II. Is social networking an appropriate solution for our community-building needs?
  A. Is social networking better than other tools and methods for community building?
  B. Are employees already using social networking tools on the job?
  C. Will a company-endorsed system distract employees from essential duties?
  D. Will a company system add to managerial workloads in any way?
III. If we move ahead, should we use a "business-class" network such as Socialtext or a consumer tool such as Facebook?
  A. How do the initial and ongoing costs compare?
  B. Do the additional capabilities of a business-class network justify the higher costs?
IV. How should we implement a social network?
  A. Should we let it grow "organically," with employees choosing their own tools and groups?
  B. Should we make a variety of tools available and let employees improvise on their own?
  C. Should we designate one system as the official company social network and make it a permanent, supported element of the information technology infrastructure?
V. How can we evaluate the success of a new social network?
  A. What are the criteria of success or failure?
  B. What is the best way to measure these criteria?

TASK ASSIGNMENTS AND SCHEDULE
Each phase of this study will be completed by the following dates:
Secondary research: Hank Waters — September 15, 2017
Employee and management survey: Julienne Cho — September 22, 2017
Analysis and synthesis of research: Hank Waters/Julienne Cho — October 6, 2017
Comparison of business and consumer solutions: Julienne Cho — October 13, 2017
Comparison of implementation strategies: Hank Waters — October 13, 2017
Final report: Hank Waters — October 20, 2017

Figure 14.2 Work Plan for a Report
A formal work plan such as this is a vital tool for planning and managing complex writing projects. The preliminary outline here helps guide the research; the report writers may well modify the outline when they begin writing the report.

report, the work plan can also become the basis for a contract if the proposal is accepted. A formal work plan might include the following elements (especially the first two):

- **Statement of the problem or opportunity.** This statement clarifies the challenge or opportunity at hand, helps you (and anyone working with you) stay focused on the core issues, and helps everyone avoid the distractions that are likely to arise along the way.
- **Statement of the purpose and scope of your investigation.** The purpose statement describes what you plan to accomplish and therefore also defines the boundaries of your work. Delineating which subjects you will cover and which you won't is especially important for complex investigations.
- **Discussion of tasks to be accomplished.** For simple reports, the list of tasks to be accomplished will be short and probably obvious. However, longer reports and complex investigations require an exhaustive list so that you can reserve time with customers, with executives, or for outside services, such as market researchers or print shops.
- **Description of any additional products or activities that will result from your investigation.** Often the only outcome of your efforts will be the report itself. In other cases you'll need to produce something or perform some task in addition to completing the report. Make such expectations clear at the outset.
- **Review of project assignments, schedules, and resource requirements.** Indicate who will be responsible for what, when tasks will be completed, and how much the investigation will cost. If more than one person will be involved, you may also want to include a brief section on coordinating report writing and production, such as whether you'll use a wiki to develop the report content. If constraints on time, money, personnel, or data are likely to affect the quality of the report, identify these limitations up front.
- **Plans for following up after delivering the report.** Follow-up can be as simple as making sure people received the information they need or as complex as conducting additional research to evaluate the results of proposals included in your report. Even informal follow-up can help you improve your future reports and communicate that you care about your work's effectiveness and its impact on the organization.
- **Working outline.** Some work plans include a tentative outline of the report, as does the plan in Figure 14.2.

GATHERING INFORMATION

Some reports require formal research projects in order to gather all the necessary information.

The amount of information needed in many reports and proposals requires careful planning—and perhaps even a separate research project just to get the data and information you need. As Chapter 13 emphasizes, you should prioritize your information needs before you start and focus on the most important questions. Whenever possible, try to reuse or adapt existing information to save time.

SELECTING THE BEST MEDIA AND CHANNELS

In some situations you may be required to use a specific medium for your reports.

In addition to the general media selection criteria discussed in Chapter 4, consider several points for reports and proposals. First, audiences may have specific media requirements, and you might not have a choice. For instance, executives in many corporations now expect to review many reports via their in-house intranets, sometimes in conjunction with an *executive dashboard*, a customized online presentation of highly summarized business information. Executive dashboards are particularly helpful for accessing report content on mobile devices (see Figure 14.3).

Second, consider how your audience members want to provide feedback on your report or proposal. Do they prefer to write comments on a printed document or edit a wiki article? Third, will people need to search through your document or update it in the future? Fourth, bear in mind that your choice of medium sends a message. For instance, a routine sales report dressed up in expensive multimedia could look like a waste of valuable company resources.

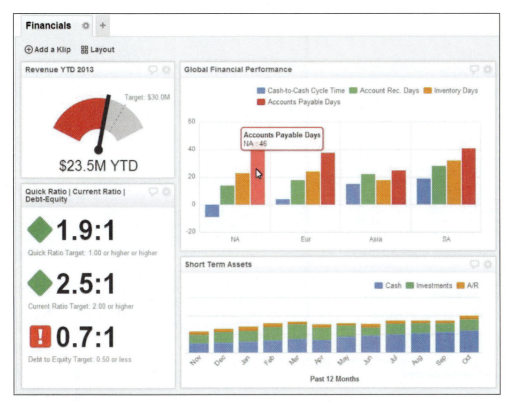

Figure 14.3 Executive Dashboards
To help managers avoid information overload, many companies now use executive dashboards to present carefully filtered highlights of key performance parameters. Dashboards are essentially super-summarized reports. The latest generation of software and mobile apps make it easy to customize screens to show each manager the specific summaries he or she needs to see.

ORGANIZING YOUR INFORMATION

The length and complexity of most reports and proposals require extra emphasis on clear, reader-oriented organization. Your readers might have the patience to struggle through a short, disorganized email message but not through a poorly organized 200-page report. As Chapter 4 discusses, when an audience is likely to be receptive or at least open-minded, use the direct approach: Lead with a summary of your key findings, conclusions, recommendations, or proposal—whichever is relevant. This "up-front" arrangement is by far the most popular and convenient for business reports. It saves time and makes the rest of the report easier to follow. For those who have questions or want more information, later parts of the report provide complete findings and supporting details. The direct approach also produces a more forceful report. You sound sure of yourself when you state your conclusions confidently at the outset.

Most business reports use the direct approach.

At times, however, confidence may be misconstrued as arrogance. If your position is relatively low in the organizational hierarchy, or if your audience is skeptical or hostile, consider the indirect approach: Introduce your findings and provide supporting evidence and reasoning before presenting your conclusions and recommendations. The indirect approach gives you a chance to prove your points and gradually overcome your audience's reservations.

Use the indirect approach when you need to build support for your main idea or you want to avoid coming across as arrogant.

Although the indirect approach has advantages, some readers will always be in a hurry to get to the answer and will immediately flip to the recommendations anyway, thus defeating your purpose. Therefore, consider length before choosing the direct or indirect approach. In general, the longer the message, the less effective an indirect approach is likely to be.

Because both direct and indirect approaches have merit, businesspeople often combine them. They reveal their conclusions and recommendations as they go along rather than put them either first or last. Figure 14.4 on the next page presents the introductions from

Long reports sometimes combine direct and indirect approaches, building support for interim conclusions or recommendations along the way.

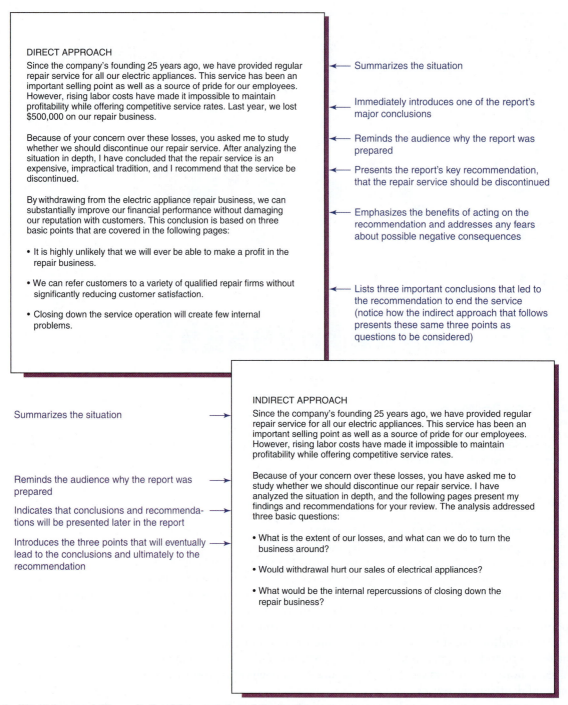

DIRECT APPROACH

Since the company's founding 25 years ago, we have provided regular repair service for all our electric appliances. This service has been an important selling point as well as a source of pride for our employees. However, rising labor costs have made it impossible to maintain profitability while offering competitive service rates. Last year, we lost $500,000 on our repair business.

Because of your concern over these losses, you asked me to study whether we should discontinue our repair service. After analyzing the situation in depth, I have concluded that the repair service is an expensive, impractical tradition, and I recommend that the service be discontinued.

By withdrawing from the electric appliance repair business, we can substantially improve our financial performance without damaging our reputation with customers. This conclusion is based on three basic points that are covered in the following pages:

- It is highly unlikely that we will ever be able to make a profit in the repair business.

- We can refer customers to a variety of qualified repair firms without significantly reducing customer satisfaction.

- Closing down the service operation will create few internal problems.

← Summarizes the situation

← Immediately introduces one of the report's major conclusions

← Reminds the audience why the report was prepared

← Presents the report's key recommendation, that the repair service should be discontinued

← Emphasizes the benefits of acting on the recommendation and addresses any fears about possible negative consequences

← Lists three important conclusions that led to the recommendation to end the service (notice how the indirect approach that follows presents these same three points as questions to be considered)

Summarizes the situation →

Reminds the audience why the report was prepared →

Indicates that conclusions and recommendations will be presented later in the report →

Introduces the three points that will eventually lead to the conclusions and ultimately to the recommendation →

INDIRECT APPROACH

Since the company's founding 25 years ago, we have provided regular repair service for all our electric appliances. This service has been an important selling point as well as a source of pride for our employees. However, rising labor costs have made it impossible to maintain profitability while offering competitive service rates.

Because of your concern over these losses, you have asked me to study whether we should discontinue our repair service. I have analyzed the situation in depth, and the following pages present my findings and recommendations for your review. The analysis addressed three basic questions:

- What is the extent of our losses, and what can we do to turn the business around?

- Would withdrawal hurt our sales of electrical appliances?

- What would be the internal repercussions of closing down the repair business?

Figure 14.4 **Direct Approach Versus Indirect Approach in an Introduction**
In the direct version of this introduction, the writer quickly presents the report's recommendation, followed by the conclusions that led to that recommendation. In the indirect version, the same topics are introduced in the same order, but no conclusions are drawn about them (the conclusions and the ultimate recommendation appear later, in the body of the report).

two reports that follow the same general outline. In the direct version, a series of statements summarizes the conclusion reached in relation to each main topic in the outline. In the indirect version, the same topics are introduced in the same order but without drawing any conclusions about them. Instead, the conclusions appear within the body of the report.

Regardless of the format, length, or order of your report, think carefully about how your ideas will be subdivided and developed. Take care to choose the most logical argument structure—one that suits your topic and goals and that makes sense to your audience.

Audience expectations are one of the most important considerations when deciding on the organization of your report.

As you outline your content, use informative ("talking") headings rather than simple descriptive ("topical") headings (see Table 14.2). Informative headings in a question or

TABLE 14.2   Types of Outline Headings

Descriptive (Topical) Outline	Informative (Talking) Outline	
	Question Form	Summary Form

1. Industry Characteristics
  a. Annual sales
  b. Profitability
  c. Growth rate
    i. Sales
    ii. Profit
	1. What is the nature of the industry?
	  a. What are the annual sales?
	  b. Is the industry profitable?
	  c. What is the pattern of growth?
	    i. Sales growth?
	    ii. Profit growth?
		1. Flour milling is a mature industry.
		  a. Market is large.
		  b. Profit margins are narrow.
		  c. Growth is modest.
		    i. Sales growth averages less than
		      3 percent a year.
		    ii. Profits are flat.

CHECKLIST ✔ Adapting the Three-Step Process to Reports and Proposals

A. Analyze the situation.
- Clearly define your purpose before you start writing.
- If you need to accomplish several goals in the report, identify them all in advance.
- Prepare a work plan to guide your efforts.

B. Gather information.
- Determine whether you need to launch a separate research project to collect the necessary information.
- Reuse or adapt existing material whenever possible.

C. Select the best medium.
- Base your decision on audience expectations or requirements.

- Consider the need for commenting, revising, distributing, and storing.
- Remember that the medium you choose also sends a message.

D. Organize your information.
- Use the direct approach if your audience is receptive.
- Use the indirect approach if your audience is skeptical.
- Use the indirect approach when you don't want to risk coming across as arrogant.
- Combine approaches if doing so will help build support for your primary message.

summary form force you to think through the content rather than simply identifying the general topic area. Using informative headings also facilitates collaborative writing by reducing ambiguity about what each person needs to write.

For a quick review of adapting the three-step process to longer documents, refer to "Checklist: Adapting the Three-Step Process to Reports and Proposals." The following sections provide specific advice on how to plan informational reports, analytical reports, and proposals.

Planning Informational Reports

Informational reports provide the information that employees, managers, and others need in order to make decisions and take action. Although dozens of particular formats exist, they can be grouped into four general categories:

- **Reports to monitor and control operations.** Just as doctors rely on medical reports to see how well the various systems in a patient's body are functioning, business managers rely on a wide range of reports to see how well the various systems in their companies are functioning. *Plans* establish expectations and guidelines to direct future action (see "Creating Successful Business Plans" on page 396). *Operating reports* provide feedback on a wide variety of an organization's functions, including sales, inventories, expenses, shipments, and other aspects of company operations. *Personal activity reports* provide information regarding an individual's experiences during sales calls, industry conferences, market research trips, and other activities.
- **Reports to implement policies and procedures.** *Policy reports* range from brief descriptions of business procedures to manuals that run dozens or hundreds of pages. *Position papers*, sometimes called *white papers* or *backgrounders*, outline an organization's official position on issues that affect the company's success.

2 LEARNING OBJECTIVE
List the options for organizing informational reports, and identify the key parts of a business plan.

Informational reports are used to monitor and control operations, to implement policies and procedures, to demonstrate compliance, and to document progress.

- **Reports to demonstrate compliance.** Even the smallest businesses are required to show that they are in compliance with government regulations of one sort or another. Some compliance reports, such as quarterly and annual tax reports, affect all businesses. Others concern particular industries, companies using hazardous materials, specific professional functions, or other special factors. Compliance reports are usually created in specific formats that must be followed exactly.

Progress reports range from simple, informal updates to comprehensive status reports.

- **Reports to document progress.** Progress reports range from simple updates to comprehensive reports that include such elements as measured progress toward goals, comparisons of budgeted versus actual expenses, and lists of ongoing concerns and risks.

ORGANIZATIONAL STRATEGIES FOR INFORMATIONAL REPORTS

Most informational reports use a **topical organization**, arranging the material by topic in one of the following ways:

A topical organization is built around the content itself, using such arrangements as comparison, importance, sequence, spatial orientation, chronology, geography, or category.

- **Comparison.** Showing similarities and differences (or advantages and disadvantages) between two or more entities
- **Importance.** Building up from the least important item to the most important (or from most important to the least, if you don't think your audience will read the entire report)
- **Sequence.** Organizing the steps or stages in a process or procedure
- **Spatial orientation.** Organizing parts of a physical space by their relative locations
- **Chronology.** Organizing a chain of events in order from oldest to newest or vice versa
- **Geography.** Organizing by region, city, state, country, or other geographic unit
- **Category.** Grouping by topical category, such as sales, profit, cost, or investment

Whichever pattern you choose, use it consistently so that readers can easily follow your discussion from start to finish. Of course, certain reports (such as compliance or monitor-and-control reports) must follow a prescribed flow.

CREATING SUCCESSFUL BUSINESS PLANS

A **business plan** is a comprehensive document that describes a company's mission, structure, objectives, and operations. In general, business plans can be written during three separate phases of a company's life: (1) before the company is launched, when the founders are defining their vision of what the company will be; (2) when the company is seeking funding, in which case the business plan takes on a persuasive tone to convince outsiders that investing in the firm would be a profitable decision; and (3) after the company is up and running and the business plan serves as a monitor-and-control mechanism to make sure operations are staying on track.

REAL-TIME UPDATES

LEARN MORE BY VISITING THIS WEBSITE

Step-by-step advice for developing a successful business plan

Take advantage of the Small Business Administration's comprehensive guide to preparing a business plan. Go to **real-timeupdates .com/bct14** and select Learn More in the Students section.

At any stage, a comprehensive business plan forces you to think about personnel, marketing, facilities, suppliers, distribution, and a host of other issues vital to a company's success. The specific elements to include in a business plan can vary based on the situation; here are the sections typically included in a plan written to attract outside investors:[2]

Formal business plans, particularly those used to solicit outside investment, must meet a specific set of reader expectations.

- **Summary.** In one or two paragraphs, summarize your business concept, particularly the *business model*, which defines how the company will generate revenue and produce a profit. The summary must be compelling, catching the investor's attention and giving him or her reasons to keep reading. Describe your product or service and its market potential. Highlight some things about your company and its leaders that will distinguish your firm from the competition. Summarize your financial projections and indicate how much money you will need from investors or lenders and where it will be spent.

- **Mission and objectives.** Explain the purpose of your business and what you hope to accomplish.
- **Company and industry.** Give full background information on the origins and structure of your venture and the characteristics of the industry in which you plan to compete.
- **Products or services.** Concisely describe your products or services, focusing on their unique attributes and their appeal to customers.
- **Market and competition.** Provide data that will persuade investors that you understand your target market and can achieve your sales goals. Be sure to identify the strengths and weaknesses of your competitors.
- **Management.** Summarize the background and qualifications of the key management personnel in your company. Include résumés in an appendix.
- **Marketing strategy.** Provide projections of sales volume and market share; outline a strategy for identifying and reaching potential customers, setting prices, providing customer support, and physically delivering your products or services. Whenever possible, include evidence of customer acceptance, such as advance product orders.
- **Design and development plans.** If your product requires design or development, describe the nature and extent of what needs to be done, including costs and possible problems. For new or unusual products, you may want to explain how the product will be manufactured.
- **Operations plan.** Provide information on facilities, equipment, and personnel requirements.
- **Overall schedule.** Forecast important milestones in the company's growth and development, including when you need to be fully staffed and when your products will be ready for the market.
- **Critical risks and problems.** Identify significant negative factors and discuss them honestly.
- **Financial projections and requirements.** Include a detailed budget of start-up and operating costs, as well as projections for income, expenses, and cash flow for the first few years of business. Identify the company's financing needs and potential sources, if appropriate.
- **Exit strategy.** Explain how investors will be able to profit from their investment, such as through a public stock offering, sale of the company, or a buyback of the investors' interest.

As Chapter 13's Communication Close-Up on page 363 notes, not everyone believes a conventional business plan is the right approach for every start-up company. If a company still needs to prove the viability of its business model or key product, the time it would take to write a full business plan might be better spent on getting the product or service operational and in front of customers in order to prove its viability. A regular business plan would make more sense after that, when the company needs to transition from start-up to ongoing operations.

REAL-TIME UPDATES

LEARN MORE BY READING THIS PDF

Crafting your "wow" statement

Bill Reichert of Garage Technology Ventures offers advice on capturing an investor's attention in just a matter of seconds. Go to **real-timeupdates.com/bct14** and select Learn More in the Students section.

Planning Analytical Reports

The purpose of analytical reports is to analyze, to understand, or to explain a problem or an opportunity and figure out how it affects the company and how the company should respond. In many cases you'll also be expected to make a recommendation based on your analysis. As you saw in Figure 14.1, analytical reports fall into three basic categories:

- **Reports to assess opportunities.** Every business opportunity carries some degree of risk and requires a variety of decisions and actions in order to capitalize on the opportunity. For instance, *market analysis reports* are used to judge the likelihood of success

3 LEARNING OBJECTIVE
Discuss three major ways to organize analytical reports.

Analytical reports are used to assess opportunities, to solve problems, and to support decisions.

for new products or sales initiatives by identifying potential opportunities as well as competitive threats and other risks. *Due diligence reports* examine the financial aspects of a proposed decision, such as acquiring another company.

- **Reports to solve problems.** Managers often assign *troubleshooting reports* when they need to understand why something isn't working properly and what can be done to fix the situation. A variation, the *failure analysis report*, studies events that happened in the past, with the hope of learning how to avoid similar failures in the future.

- **Reports to support decisions.** *Feasibility reports* are called for when managers need to explore the ramifications of a decision they're about to make (such as replacing an advertising agency or switching materials used in a manufacturing process). *Justification reports* justify a decision that has already been made.

Writing analytical reports presents a greater challenge than writing informational reports, for three reasons. First, you're doing more than simply delivering information; you're also analyzing a problem or an opportunity and presenting your conclusions. The best writing in the world can't compensate for flawed analysis. Second, when your analysis is complete, you need to present your thinking in a credible manner. Third, analytical reports often convince other people to make significant financial and personnel decisions, so your reports carry the added responsibility of the consequences of these decisions.

In some situations the problem or opportunity you address may be defined by the person who authorizes the report. In other cases you will have to define it yourself. Be careful not to confuse a simple topic (quarterly profits) with a problem (the decline in profits over the past six quarters). Moreover, if you're the only person who thinks a particular issue is a problem, your readers won't be interested in your solution unless your report first convinces them that a problem exists. As with marketing and sales messages, sometimes you need to "sell the problem" before you can sell the solution.

To help define the problem that your analytical report will address, answer these questions:

- What needs to be determined?
- Why is this issue important?
- Who is involved in the situation?
- Where is the trouble located?
- How did the situation originate?
- When did it start?

Not all these questions apply in every situation, but asking them helps you define the problem being addressed and limit the scope of your discussion.

Another effective way to tackle a complex problem is to divide it into a series of logical, connected questions, a process sometimes called **problem factoring**. You probably subconsciously approach most problems this way. When your car won't start, what do you do? You use the available evidence to organize your investigation and to start a search for cause-and-effect relationships. For example, if the engine doesn't turn over, you might suspect a dead battery. If the engine does turn over but won't fire, you can conclude that the battery is okay, but perhaps you're out of gas. When you speculate on the cause of a problem, you're forming a **hypothesis**, a potential explanation that needs to be tested. By subdividing a problem and forming hypotheses based on available evidence, you can tackle even the most complex situations. With a clear picture of the problem or opportunity in mind, you're ready to consider the best structure for your report.

Whenever you are preparing an analytical report, make sure you are clear in your own mind about whether you are advocating one particular line of thought or objectively exploring all the available options.[3] Even if advocating one position is appropriate in the circumstances, your readers will expect you to have considered the other options so that you can help them understand why your answer is preferred.

Clarify the problem in an analytical report by determining what you need to analyze, why the issue is important, who is involved, where the trouble is located, and how and when it started.

Use problem factoring to divide a complex problem into more manageable pieces.

ORGANIZATIONAL STRATEGIES FOR ANALYTICAL REPORTS

When you expect your audience to agree with you, use the direct approach to focus attention on conclusions and recommendations. When you expect your audience to disagree with you or to be hostile, use the indirect approach to focus attention on the rationale behind your conclusions and recommendations.

The three most common structural approaches for analytical reports are focusing on conclusions (a direct format), focusing on recommendations (another direct format), and focusing on logical arguments (an indirect format) (see Table 14.3).

Before you choose an approach, determine whether your audience is receptive or skeptical.

Focusing on Conclusions

When writing for audiences that are likely to accept your conclusions—either because they've asked you to perform an analysis or they trust your judgment—consider using a direct approach that focuses immediately on your conclusions. This structure communicates the main idea quickly, but it presents some risks. Even if audiences trust your judgment, they may have questions about your data or the methods you used. Moreover, starting with a conclusion may create the impression that you have oversimplified the situation. You're generally better off taking this direct approach in a report only when your credibility is high—when your readers trust you and are willing to accept your conclusions (see Figure 14.5 on the next page).

Focusing on conclusions is often the best approach when you're addressing a receptive audience.

Focusing on Recommendations

A slightly different approach is useful when your readers want to know what they ought to do in a given situation (as opposed to what they ought to conclude). You'll often be asked to solve a problem or assess an opportunity rather than just study it. The actions you want your readers to take become the main subdivisions of your report.

When structuring a report around recommendations, use the direct approach as you would for a report that focuses on conclusions. Then unfold your recommendations using a series of five steps:

When readers want to know what you think they should do, organize your report to focus on recommendations.

1. Establish or verify the need for action in the introduction by briefly describing the problem or opportunity
2. Introduce the benefit that can be achieved, without providing any details
3. List the steps (recommendations) required to achieve the benefit, using action verbs for emphasis
4. Explain each step more fully, giving details on procedures, costs, and benefits
5. Summarize your recommendations

If your recommendation carries any risks, be sure to clearly address them. Doing so not only makes your report more ethical but also offers you some protection in the event

Whenever a recommendation carries some element of risk, you owe it to your audience to make this clear.

TABLE 14.3   Common Ways to Structure Analytical Reports

Element	Focus on Conclusions or Recommendations	Focus on Logical Argument	
		Use 2 + 2 = 4 Model	Use Yardstick Model
Reader mindset	Are likely to accept	Hostile or skeptical	Hostile or skeptical
Approach	Direct	Indirect	Indirect
Writer credibility	High	Low	Low
Advantages	Readers quickly grasp conclusions or recommendations	Works well when you need to show readers how you built toward an answer by following clear, logical steps	Works well when you have a list of criteria (standards) that must be considered in a decision; alternatives are all measured against the same criteria
Drawbacks	Structure can make topic seem too simple	Can make report longer	Readers must agree on criteria; can be lengthy because of the need to address all criteria for every alternative

MEASURING QUALITY IMPROVEMENTS

In keeping with the direct approach, the report will open with the conclusion that the program is a success.

These two sections will support the conclusion with evidence from two key areas.

I. Introduction

II. Conclusion: Outsourcing employee training has reduced costs and improved quality

III. Cost reductions

    A. Exceeded 15 percent cost-reduction goal with 22 percent savings in first year

    B. Achieved actual reduction of 22 percent

    C. Reassigned three staffers who used to work on training full-time

    D. Reduced management time needed to oversee training

    E. Sold the computers that used to be reserved for training

IV. Quality improvements

    A. Employees say they are more confident in 7 out of 10 key skill areas

    B. Measurable mistakes have dropped by 12 percent

This section will complete the story by highlighting areas that still need improvement.

V. Areas needing improvement

    A. Three skill areas still need improvement

    B. Two trainers received approval ratings below 80 percent

    C. Outside trainers aren't always aware of internal company issues

    D. We have lost some flexibility for scheduling courses

VI. Summary

Figure 14.5 **Preliminary Outline of a Research Report Focusing on Conclusions**
A year after a bank decided to have an outside firm handle its employee training, an analyst was asked to prepare a report evaluating the results. The analysis shows that the outsourcing experiment was a success, so the report opens with that conclusion but supports it with clear evidence. Readers who accept the conclusion can stop reading, and those who desire more information can continue.

that your recommendation is implemented but doesn't work out as you had hoped. In short, make sure your readers know the potential disadvantages as well as the potential benefits.

Focusing on Logical Arguments

Two common logical patterns arguments are the 2 + 2 = 4 approach (adding everything up) and the yardstick approach (comparing solutions against criteria).

When readers are likely to be skeptical or hostile to the conclusion or recommendation you plan to make, use an indirect approach. If you guide people along a logical path toward the answer, they are more likely to accept it when they encounter it. The two most common logical approaches are known as the *2 + 2 = 4 approach* and the *yardstick approach*.

The 2 + 2 = 4 Approach   The **2 + 2 = 4 approach** is so named because it convinces readers of your point of view by demonstrating that everything adds up. The main points in your outline are the main reasons behind your conclusions and recommendations. You support each reason with the evidence you collected during your analysis.

Start by considering using the 2 + 2 = 4 approach; it's familiar and easy to develop.

Because of its natural feel and versatility, the 2 + 2 = 4 approach is generally the most persuasive and efficient way to develop an analytical report for skeptical readers. When organizing your own reports, try this structure first. You'll find that many business situations lend themselves nicely to this pattern of logical argumentation.

The yardstick approach compares a solution or several solutions to a set of predetermined standards.

The Yardstick Approach   The **yardstick approach** is useful when you need to use a number of criteria to evaluate one or more possible solutions. These criteria become the "yardstick" by which you measure the various alternatives. With this approach, you begin by discussing the problem or opportunity and then list the criteria that will guide the decision. The body of the report then evaluates the alternatives against those criteria.

The main points of the outline are either the criteria themselves or the alternatives (see Figure 14.6).

The yardstick approach is particularly useful for proposals when the audience has provided a list of criteria the solution must meet. Imagine that your company has been asked to bid on a contract to design and install a factory-floor distribution system for a large corporation. The client has listed the requirements (criteria) for the system, and you've developed a preliminary design to meet them. In the body of your proposal, you could use the client's list of requirements as the main headings and under each one explain how your preliminary design meets the requirement.

The yardstick approach has two potential drawbacks. First, your audience members need to agree with the criteria you're using in your analysis. If they don't, they won't agree with the results of the evaluation. If you have any doubt about their agreement, build consensus before you start your report, if possible, or take extra care to explain why the criteria you're using are the best ones in this particular case.

Second, the yardstick approach can get tedious when you have many options to consider or many criteria to compare them against. One way to minimize repetition is to compare the options in tables and then highlight the most unusual or important aspects of each alternative in the text so that you get the best of both worlds. This approach allows you to compare all the alternatives against the same yardstick while calling attention to the most significant differences among them.

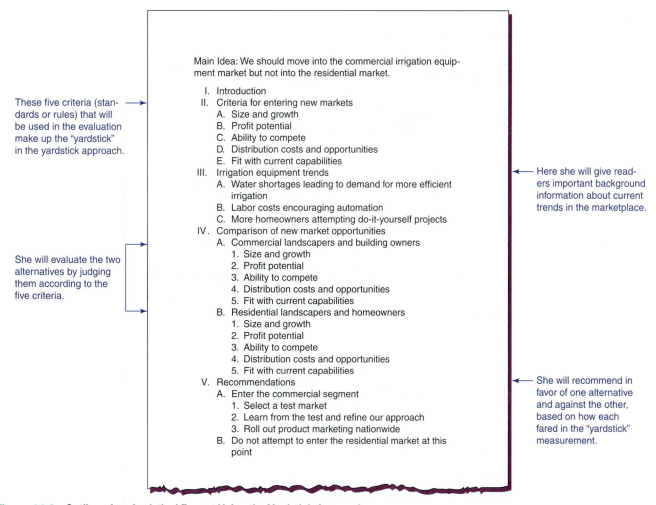

Figure 14.6   Outline of an Analytical Report Using the Yardstick Approach
This report was drafted by a market analyst for a company that makes irrigation equipment for farms and ranches. The company has been so successful in the agricultural market that it is starting to run out of potential customers. To keep growing, it needs to find another market. Two obvious choices to consider were commercial buildings and residences, but management needed to evaluate both carefully before making a decision.

EFFECTIVE ANALYTICAL REPORTS: AN EXAMPLE

As national sales manager of a New Hampshire sporting goods company, Binh Phan was concerned about his company's ability to sell to its major accounts, the giant national chains that now dominate retailing. Even though these customers are getting bigger, the company's sales to them are dropping, and it's critical to figure out why and propose a solution. Phan's boss, the vice president of marketing, asked Phan to analyze the situation and make a recommendation.

Phan's troubleshooting report appears in Figure 14.7. The main idea is that the company should establish a separate sales team for each these major national accounts rather than continuing to service them through the company's four regional divisions. However, Phan knew his plan would be controversial because it requires a big change in the company's organization and in the way sales reps are paid. His thinking had to be clear and easy to follow, so he used the 2 + 2 = 4 approach to focus on his reasons.

The first paragraph verifies who requested the report, when it was requested, and who wrote it.

MEMO

TO: Robert Mendoza, Vice President of Marketing
FROM: Binh Phan, National Sales Manager   *BP*
DATE: September 14, 2017
SUBJECT: Major accounts sales problems

As you requested on August 20, this report outlines the results of my investigation into the recent slowdown in sales to major accounts and the accompanying rise in sales- and service-related complaints from some of our largest customers.

Over the last four quarters, major account sales dropped 12%, whereas overall sales were up 7%. During the same time, we've all noticed an increase in both formal and informal complaints from larger customers, regarding how confusing and complicated it has become to do business with us.

The second paragraph highlights the serious nature of the problem.

This section explains how the information used in the analysis was collected.

My investigation started with in-depth discussions with the four regional sales managers, first as a group and then individually. The tension I felt in the initial meeting eventually bubbled to the surface during my meetings with each manager. Staff members in each region are convinced that other regions are booking orders they don't deserve, with one region doing all the legwork only to see another region get the sale, the commission, and the quota credit.

I followed up these formal discussions by talking informally and exchanging email with several sales representatives from each region. Virtually everyone who is involved with our major national accounts has a story to share. No one is happy with the situation, and I sense that some reps are walking away from major customers because the process is so frustrating.

The decline in sales to our major national customers and the increase in their complaints stem from two problems: (1) sales force organization and (2) commission policy.

ORGANIZATIONAL PROBLEMS

Organizational problems are the first "2" in Phan's 2 + 2 = 4 approach.

Phan describes the first problem and explains how it occurred, without blaming anyone personally.

When we divided the national sales force into four geographical regions last year, the idea was to focus our sales efforts and clarify responsibilities for each prospective and current customer. The regional managers have gotten to know their market territories very well, and sales have increased beyond even our most optimistic projections.

However, while solving one problem, we have created another. In the past 12 to 18 months, several regional customers have grown to national status, and a few retailers have taken on (or expressed interest in) our products. As a result, a significant portion of both current sales and future opportunities lies with these large national accounts.

I uncovered more than a dozen cases in which sales representatives from two or more regions found themselves competing with each other by pursuing the same customers from different locations. Moreover, the complaints from our major accounts about

(continued)

Figure 14.7 **Analytical Report Using the 2 + 2 = 4 Approach**
The 2 + 2 = 4 approach lets this writer present a logical argument that is both clear and compelling.

2

overlapping or nonexistent account coverage are a direct result of the regional organization. In some cases, customers aren't sure which of our representatives they're supposed to call with problems and orders. In other cases, no one has been in contact with them for several months.

For example, having retail outlets across the lower tier of the country, AmeriSport received pitches from reps out of our West, South, and East regions. Because our regional offices have a lot of negotiating freedom, the three were offering different prices. But all AmeriSport buying decisions were made at the Tampa headquarters, so all we did was confuse the customer. The irony of the current organization is that we're often giving our weakest selling and support efforts to the largest customers in the country.

COMMISSION PROBLEMS

The regional organization problems are compounded by the way we assign commissions and quota credit. Salespeople in one region can invest a lot of time in pursuing a sale, only to have the customer place the order in another region. So some sales rep in the second region ends up with the commission on a sale that was partly or even entirely earned by someone in the first region. Therefore, sales reps sometimes don't pursue leads in their regions, thinking that a rep in another region will get the commission.

For example, Athletic Express, with outlets in 35 states spread across all four regions, finally got so frustrated with us that the company president called our headquarters. Athletic Express has been trying to place a large order for tennis and golf accessories, but none of our local reps seem interested in paying attention. I spoke with the rep responsible for Nashville, where the company is headquartered, and asked her why she wasn't working the account more actively. Her explanation was that last time she got involved with Athletic Express, the order was actually placed from their L.A. regional office, and she didn't get any commission after more than two weeks of selling time.

RECOMMENDATIONS

Our sales organization should reflect the nature of our customer base. To accomplish that goal, we need a group of reps who are free to pursue accounts across regional borders—and who are compensated fairly for their work. The most sensible answer is to establish a national account group. Any customers whose operations place them in more than one region would automatically be assigned to the national group.

In addition to solving the problem of competing sales efforts, the new structure will also largely eliminate the commission-splitting problem because regional reps will no longer invest time in prospects assigned to the national accounts team. However, we will need to find a fair way to compensate regional reps who are losing long-term customers to the national team. Some of these reps have invested years in developing customer relationships that will continue to yield sales well into the future, and everyone I talked to agrees that reps in these cases should receive some sort of compensation. Such a "transition commission" would also motivate the regional reps to help ensure a smooth transition from one sales group to the other. The exact nature of this compensation would need to be worked out with the various sales managers.

3

SUMMARY

The regional sales organization is effective at the regional and local levels but not at the national level. We should establish a national accounts group to handle sales that cross regional boundaries. Then we'll have one set of reps who are focused on the local and regional levels and another set who are pursuing national accounts.

To compensate regional reps who lose accounts to the national team, we will need to devise some sort of payment to reward them for the years of work invested in such accounts. This can be discussed with the sales managers once the new structure is in place.

Figure 14.7 Analytical Report Using the 2 + 2 = 4 Approach (*continued*)

Planning Proposals

Proposals are written for both internal and external audiences. Internal proposals request decisions from managers within the organization, such as proposals to buy new equipment or launch new research projects. Examples of external proposals include *grant proposals*, which request funds from government agencies and other sponsoring organizations, and *sales proposals*, which suggest individualized solutions for potential customers and request purchase decisions.

4 LEARNING OBJECTIVE Explain how to choose an organizational strategy when writing a proposal.

Annotations:
- Phan brings the first problem to life by complementing the general description with a specific example.
- In discussing the second problem, he simplifies the reader's task by maintaining a parallel structure: a general description followed by a specific example.
- He explains how his recommendation (a new organizational structure) will solve both problems.
- He acknowledges that the recommended solution does create a temporary compensation problem but expresses confidence that a solution to that can be worked out.
- Commission problems are the second "2" in Phan's 2 + 2 = 4 approach.
- Phan concludes the 2 + 2 = 4 approach: organizational problems + commission problems = the need for a new sales structure.
- The summary concisely restates both the problem and the recommended solution.

Buyers often solicit proposals by publishing a request for proposals (RFP).

The most significant factor in planning any proposal is whether the intended recipient has asked you to submit a proposal. *Solicited proposals* are generally prepared at the request of external parties that require a product or a service, but they may also be requested by such internal sources as management or the board of directors. When organizations require complex products, services, or systems, they often prepare a formal invitation to bid on the contract, called a **request for proposals** (**RFP**), which includes instructions that specify exactly the type of work to be performed or products to be delivered, along with budgets, deadlines, and other requirements. To attract a large pool of qualified bidders, organizations send RFPs to firms with good records of performance in the field, print them in trade publications, and post them on the web.

REAL-TIME UPDATES

LEARN MORE BY READING THIS ARTICLE

Seven steps to successful proposals

A sales expert describes the process for crafting winning business proposals. Go to **real-timeupdates.com/bct14** and select Learn More in the Students section.

To write a proposal in response to an RFP, begin by reviewing the requirements. Next, define the scope of the deliverables, determine the methods and procedures to be used, and estimate time requirements, personnel requirements, and costs. Then put it all in writing—exactly as specified in the RFP, following the precise format it requires and responding meticulously to every point it raises.[4] RFPs can seem surprisingly picky, even to the point of specifying the paper size for the proposal and the number of copies to send, but you must follow every detail.

Unsolicited proposals are created by organizations attempting to obtain business or funding without a specific invitation from a potential client. Such proposals may also be initiated by employees or managers who want to convince company insiders to adopt a program, a policy, or an idea. In other words, with an unsolicited proposal, the writer makes the first move. Even so, an unsolicited proposal should not come as a surprise to the recipient, but rather should be the summation of an ongoing conversation between the sender and the recipient.[5] This approach helps ensure acceptance, and it gives you an opportunity to explore the recipient's needs and craft your proposal around them.

Unsolicited proposals require additional persuasive elements because the audience isn't expecting the proposal and might not even be conscious of the problem you propose to solve.

Unsolicited proposals differ from solicited proposals in another important respect: Your audience may not be aware of the problem you are addressing, so your proposal must first convince readers that a problem or an opportunity exists before convincing them that you can address it. Thus unsolicited proposals generally spend considerable time explaining why readers should take action and convincing them of the benefits of doing so.

Every proposal competes for something: money, time, attention, and so on.

With virtually any proposal, keep in mind that you are always competing for something—money, time, management attention, and so on. Even if yours is the only proposal on the table, you are still competing with all the other choices your audience members could make with their time, money, and attention.

Proposals can be significant writing projects, particularly when you are responding to a complex RFP. Fortunately, a variety of software products are available to considerably lighten the load. Basic features include the ability to automatically personalize the proposal, ensure proper structure, and organize storage of all your boilerplate material (identical sections of text used in every proposal, such as a description of your company). At a more advanced level, semiautomated proposal-writing systems can scan RFPs to identify questions and requirements and fill in potential answers from a centralized knowledge base that contains input from all the relevant experts in your company.[6]

ORGANIZATIONAL STRATEGIES FOR PROPOSALS

Your choice of structure for proposals depends on whether the proposal is solicited and, if so, whether you expect readers to be receptive to your specific recommendation. In general, your audience is likely to be more receptive to solicited proposals because the problem and the solution have already been identified. Submit your proposal for the solution specified in the RFP, and structure the proposal using the direct approach to focus on your recommendation. As soon as possible within the constraints of the RFP requirements, identify why your solution is unique and deserves close consideration.[7]

Depending on the circumstances and your relationship with the recipient, the indirect approach is often better for unsolicited proposals. When writing unsolicited proposals, you must first convince the audience that a problem exists and establish your credibility if you are unknown to the reader. At the same time, you need to give the reader a compelling reason to keep reading a document that he or she didn't request. Follow the AIDA model or a similar approach to grab the reader's attention quickly. For an external proposal, for instance, you might start off with an attention-getter such as "In working with other companies in your industry, our productivity specialists were able to reduce their operating costs by as much as 15 percent." Then, to convince the reader that you can back up that claim, present your solution in a logical fashion, with solid evidence, leading up to a request for a decision (see "Ethics Detective: Solving the Case of the Overblown Proposal").

> The indirect approach following AIDA or a similar model is often the best way to build your case in an unsolicited proposal.

EFFECTIVE PROPOSALS: AN EXAMPLE

A good proposal explains why a project or course of action is needed, what it will involve, and how the recipient will benefit. In Figure 14.8 on pages 406–409, a human resources manager responded to a request from his boss to explore ways to address three troublesome workforce issues. During his investigation, he discovered a better approach than the company had been considering, and that became the subject of his proposal.

ETHICS DETECTIVE

Solving the Case of the Overblown Proposal

As the manager in charge of your company's New Ventures Group, you've read your share of proposals—hundreds, maybe thousands, of them. You've developed a sixth sense about these documents, an ability to separate cautious optimism from self-doubt and distinguish justified enthusiasm from insupportable hype.

Your company invests in promising smaller firms that could grow into beneficial business partners or even future acquisitions. In a typical scenario, a small company invents a new product but needs additional funding to manufacture and market it, so the owners approach you with funding proposals. Because you make the first major decision in this investment process, your choices and recommendations to the board of directors are crucial.

Moreover, the risks are considerable: If one of your recommendations doesn't pan out, the company could lose all the money it invested (often millions), and that's only the start. Failures consume your team's precious time and energy and can even put the company at risk for shareholder lawsuits and other serious headaches. In other words, mistakes in your line of work are costly.

The proposal in front of you today is intriguing. A small company in Oklahoma has designed a product called the

Wireless Shopping List, and you think the idea might appeal to upscale homeowners. Small touchscreens are placed around the house, wherever occupants are likely to think of things they need to buy on the next shopping trip: on the refrigerator door, in the media room, in the nursery, in the garage, in the gardening shed. The system collects all these inputs and, on command, prints out a shopping list or downloads it to a smartphone. It's a clever idea, but one paragraph in the proposal bothers you:

> Everybody in our test market audience was absolutely stunned when we demonstrated the simulated system. They couldn't believe something like this was even possible. It was so handy and so convenient—everyone said it would change their lives forever. We haven't even specified the price yet, but every single person in the room wanted to place an order, on the spot.

ANALYSIS

This proposal potentially oversells the idea in at least three ways. Identify them and explain how they could lead you to decline the investment opportunity.

memo
CORPORATE HR

TO: Lailah Banks
FROM: Roger Hemmings
DATE: September 28, 2018
SUBJECT: Addressing Our High-Priority Personnel Issues

As you requested after last month's State of the Workforce meeting, I've been exploring potential responses to the top three personnel issues the team identified: job satisfaction, position readiness, and succession planning. We were all concerned about the cost and time commitment required to tackle these big issues, so the consensus reached at the meeting was to prioritize the issues and address them one at a time.

However, I believe there is a manageable way to address all three issues at once.

Areas of Concern: Finding Common Threads

The "big three" issues definitely feel overwhelming when we consider the changes needed in order to make meaningful improvements in all of them. There is hope in the details, however. Common threads run through all three areas, and we can address many of the problems with a single solution.

To review the three issues:

- **Job satisfaction:** Results from the last four internal surveys show a disturbing pattern of dissatisfaction, with many employees expressing uncertainty about where their careers are heading, confusion about how they fit into the big picture, and anger about not being given fair consideration for promotions.

- **Position readiness:** Managers frequently complain to us that our emphasis on promoting from within is difficult for them to adhere to because they can't find enough employees who are ready to move into positions of greater responsibility. Employees usually have the technical skills, but managers say that many lack the vision to see how their individual efforts contribute to the larger effort or lack the professionalism needed to function at a high level around customers, executives, and business partners.

- **Succession planning:** This has been a priority for several years, but we never seem to make much headway toward putting a real program in place. We've solved one side of the equation—identifying all the critical managerial and professional roles where we're vulnerable to employees leaving or being promoted—but we haven't figured out how to identify and prepare promising candidates to move into these positions.

As I dug through these issues, two themes kept popping up: a lack of shared purpose and inadequate relationship building.

The subject line establishes a connection to a topic previously discussed without divulging the main idea of the proposal (which uses the indirect approach).

The opening paragraph serves as a reminder of their previous discussion, the task he was given, and the expectations about how he would approach it.

This single-sentence paragraph is the attention-getter in the AIDA model; it promises a solution that is better than expected.

This section summarizes the previous discussion while laying the groundwork for introducing a key reason for the proposal he is going to make, which is that he has found a couple of common themes in the three areas of concern.

He introduces those two themes, which shape the proposal he is about to make. This works as the interest stage of the AIDA model, since it presents an intriguing and unexplored angle on issues previously discussed.

(continued)

Figure 14.8   Internal Proposal
The manager in charge of his company's employee development efforts has a solution to three worrisome workforce issues that he has previously discussed with his boss, the director of human resources. He uses this memo-format proposal to outline a new employee mentoring program and suggest how the company can get started on it.[9]

Page 2

The Lack of Shared Purpose

The company has always prided itself on attracting the best people in every functional specialty, but I believe this has resulted in an overemphasis on hard skills and individual output, to the detriment of soft skills and an overall sense of teamwork and shared contribution. It's no surprise that so many employees feel adrift and disconnected, when we don't foster a communal sense of how the company functions as an integrated enterprise. We have some of the brightest employees in the industry, but many are too focused on the tactics of their own jobs.

Inadequate Relationship Building

After reviewing the employee survey data, I wanted to get a more personal take on these issues, so I interviewed more than two dozen professional staffers and managers across all divisions. These interviews uncovered another troubling dynamic: We're not very good at building professional relationships throughout the organization.

Employees and their managers tend to stay isolated within their functional silos and don't seem to understand or even care about the challenges faced by their colleagues in other departments. One market analyst described cross-functional meetings as "strangers forced to cooperate with strangers." Managers trying to fill promotional opportunities sometimes don't know where to look because they rarely get to know employees outside their own chain of command. And every professional staffer I talked to expressed some variation of feeling lost, with no one to turn to for confidential career advice.

Proposed Solution: Employee Mentoring

Clearly, we have some challenges on our hands. The good news is that we have the potential to solve many of them with an employee mentoring program. Here is a brief overview of mentoring programs, their benefits, potential stumbling blocks, and a recommended strategy for launching our own program.

Common Features of Mentoring Programs

Here are the key features common to most mentoring programs:

- It's a formal program matchesinterested employees with managers and senior professional staff in one-on-one coaching relationships. The coaching can involve job-specific challenges, work-life balance, workplace conflicts, or anything else the participants decide is useful.

- Employees and their mentors meet or at least talk on a regular schedule. Continuity is essential.

Here he offers more information about the two themes he discovered as he continues to lay out the reasons for his proposed solution.

At this point, he is ready to shift from "selling the problem" and laying the groundwork to presenting his solution.

This brief overview of employee mentoring programs establishes common ground with his reader, so he can be sure they are thinking about the same thing.

(continued)

Figure 14.8 **Internal Proposal (*continued*)**

Page 3

- HR provides the "matchmaking service" to help find the optimum pairings and manage demand, but isn't involved in the actual mentoring.

- Mentoring relationships are confidential, giving both sides the freedom to talk openly.

Potential Benefits of Mentoring Programs

Mentoring can go a long way toward solving these problems of shared purpose and relationship building, but companies report an even wider range of benefits from their mentoring programs:

- Employees can learn how to professionally navigate the corporate environment, from subtle issues such as business etiquette to broader questions such as how they contribute to company growth.

- Employees can discuss problems and worries with a trusted advisor, without fear of retribution.

- Managers gain insights into the challenges employees are facing, beyond the tactical demands of their jobs, which will help them manage and lead more effectively.

- Managers and employees learn about the challenges and contributions of other functional areas, which will foster better cooperation between departments.

- Through their mentors, employees can meet other managers, executives, and influential senior staff, expanding their networks within the company and opening more career doors.

- Managers can monitor the progress of promising employees and guide them into new opportunities.

- As an employee benefit, mentoring can help us attract a wider and more diverse pool of outside job candidates.

- Mentoring can boost productivity by helping employees find the best ways to invest their time and creative energy.

- Proactive mentoring can help the company get the full potential from employees who don't feel like they are part of the "in crowd" within the company.

- Through "reverse mentoring," senior staff and managers may have opportunities to learn about digital media use and other valuable skills they haven't had to embrace in their careers.

The bottom-line impact of mentoring programs isn't always easy to measure, but my research found some compelling figures. For example, companies have seen

Here he presents the general benefits of mentoring programs in a way that connects them to the two themes he identified earlier.

(continued)

Figure 14.8 Internal Proposal *(continued)*

Page 4

turnover drop by as much as 20 percent in the year after mentoring was launched, and the majority of employees and mentors alike report improved job satisfaction as a result of being involved in mentoring.

Costs and Potential Challenges

The benefits of mentoring do need to be weighed against costs and some potential challenges:

- Many companies find themselves with more interested employees than their programs can support, so we need to manage the demand in a fair and transparent way.

- There will be some direct and indirect costs, including training for mentors, an automated system for matching mentors with employees as the program scales up, and clerical and supervisory workload for HR.

- Mentoring requires time and energy, so mentors' workloads will need to be adjusted accordingly.

- Mentoring can create conflicts with employees' direct supervisors, so HR will need to offer mediation.

We can predict some of these costs and complexities, but the most accurate way to assess them will be to run a pilot program, as I propose in the next section.

Next Steps: Develop a Business Case and Launch a Pilot Program

The research makes a clear case for mentoring, provided it is planned carefully and managed well. I propose that we develop a formal business case for a mentoring program and present it to the Executive Council. We need top-down support and the participation of executives themselves as mentors, so C-level buy-in is essential.

Rather than launching companywide, I think we should start with a limited pilot program, with perhaps two or three dozen participants. This will let us fine-tune the program and get a clearer estimate of costs in order to refine budgets before scaling up.

My rough estimate is that the pilot program will require one full-time staff member in HR to facilitate matchmaking, mediate conflicts, analyze results, and plan the companywide rollout. This new position will have a loaded cost of approximately $90k. I shouldn't have any problem clearing out this much in my operating budget, probably by canceling the lowest-rated training courses (as we've been discussing doing anyway).

Can I get on your calendar sometime next week to go over the potential structure of the program and answer any questions or concerns you may have?

Sharing the positive outcomes that other companies have experienced should heighten his boss's desire to explore the possibility of starting a program.

He is open about the downsides of mentoring programs, which addresses some potential objections and helps maintain his credibility on the subject.

"Next steps" signals his shift to the action phase of the AIDA model. He outlines a brief plan to move forward and concludes by asking for a meeting to get things rolling.

Figure 14.8 **Internal Proposal** (*continued*)

COMMUNICATION CHALLENGES AT Warby Parker

You work as a communication specialist at Warby Parker, reporting to co-CEO David Gilboa. Using the skills you've been practicing in this course, respond to these challenges.

INDIVIDUAL CHALLENGE: You're helping Gilboa prepare a report about the company. Gilboa characterizes the report as a "public business plan," in that it will discuss the company and its objectives, strategies, and operations without disclosing the sort of confidential information that a typical business plan includes. The target audience includes potential investors, employees, and business partners.

To help overcome shoppers' reluctance to buy eyewear online, Warby Parker offers Home Try-On, in which people can order five pairs of frames, keep them for five days at no cost, then decide which pair they would like to order. This gives shoppers lots of time to try on the frames they are considering and get the opinions of family and friends. Which of the following headings would you choose for a section in the report that explains this program? Explain your reasoning in a brief email message to your instructor.

a. Home Try-On: Making online shopping even better than in-store shopping
b. Home Try-On: Our tried-and-true way to eliminate the risk of buying eyewear online
c. Home Try-On: Now you can try on five frames in the comfort of your own home
d. Home Try-On: How we reduce a major perceived risk in the Warby Parker business model

TEAM CHALLENGE: Many companies offer a brief "fact sheet" (often a downloadable, one-page PDF) that summarizes the concept of the business, its product lines, unique technologies, target markets, biographies of key executives, and other information of potential interest to various stakeholders. In a team with two or three other students, review the fact sheets (sometimes called a "company overview" or something similar) offered on the websites of three companies in any industry, then collaborate on a one-page fact sheet for Warby Parker. (For the purposes of this activity, you can adapt and reuse content from the Warby Parker website.)

Quick Learning Guide

KEY TERMS

analytical reports Reports that offer both information and analysis; they can also include recommendations

business plan A comprehensive document that describes a company's mission, structure, objectives, and operations

hypothesis A potential explanation that needs to be tested

informational reports Reports that offer data, facts, feedback, and other types of information, without analysis or recommendations

problem factoring Dividing a problem into a series of logical, connected questions

proposals Reports that combine information delivery and persuasive communication

reports Written accounts that objectively communicate information about some aspect of a business

request for proposals (RFP) A formal invitation to bid on a contract

statement of purpose Planning statement that defines why you are preparing a report

topical organization Arrangement of material according to comparisons, importance, sequence, chronology, spatial orientation, geography, or category

yardstick approach Logical argumentation approach that uses a number of criteria to evaluate one or more possible solutions

2 + 2 = 4 approach Logical argumentation approach that convinces readers of your point of view by demonstrating how everything "adds up"

SUMMARY OF LEARNING OBJECTIVES

1 Adapt the three-step writing process to reports and proposals. The comprehensive nature of the three-step process is ideal for the work involved in most reports and proposals. Use all the advice you learned in Chapters 4 through 6, with added emphasis on a few specific points for longer documents: (1) Identify your purpose clearly to avoid rework, (2) prepare a work plan to guide the research and writing tasks, (3) determine whether a separate research project might be needed to gather the necessary information, (4) choose the appropriate medium (or media, in some cases) for your audience, and (5) organize your information by selecting the best approach for an informational or analytical report.

2 List the options for organizing informational reports and identify the parts of a business plan. Informational reports focus on the delivery of facts, figures, and other types of information. Most informational reports use a topical organization, arranging material by comparison, importance, sequence, chronology, geography, or category.

Formal business plans—those that are shown to outside audiences such as investors and bankers—typically contain the following elements: a summary of the business concept, the company's mission and objectives, background on the company and the industry in which it competes, descriptions of its products and services, an analysis of target markets and key competitors, a discussion of the management team, a summary of the marketing strategy, design and development plans, an operations plan, a schedule with major milestones, an analysis of critical risks and problems, financial projections and requirements, and a description of the proposed exit strategy.

3 Discuss three major ways to organize analytical reports. The three most common ways to organize analytical reports are by focusing on conclusions, focusing on recommendations, and focusing on logical arguments. The first two are direct approaches; the third is an indirect approach.

4 Explain how to choose an organizational strategy when writing a proposal. The most significant factor in planning a proposal is whether the proposal is solicited or unsolicited. Solicited proposals are obviously expected and welcomed by the recipient, but they often must follow a specific organization, particularly when they are submitted in response to a request for proposals (RFP). For unsolicited proposals, the writer has flexibility in choosing the most effective organization, format, and content. However, because unsolicited proposals are unexpected, the writer often needs to explain why the solution offered in the proposal is even necessary for the reader to consider. Because of this, the indirect approach is usually preferred for unsolicited proposals.

Test Your Knowledge

To review chapter content related to each question, refer to the indicated Learning Objective.

14-1. What is the major difference between informational and analytical reports? [LO-1]

14-2. What does a statement of purpose convey? [LO-1]

14-3. What should you include in the work plan for a complex report or proposal? [LO-1]

14-4. How are reports for monitoring and controlling operations used? [LO-2]

14-5. What are the three major ways to organize an analytical report? [LO-3]

14-6. How does a feasibility report differ from a justification report? [LO-3]

14-7. What is problem factoring? [LO-3]

14-8. What is an RFP and how does it relate to proposal writing? [LO-4]

Apply Your Knowledge

To review chapter content related to each question, refer to the indicated Learning Objective.

14-9. Would "Look into employee morale problems" be an effective problem statement for a report? Why or why not? [LO-1]

14-10. Which of the topical organization plans listed on page 396 would you use to organize an analytical report on a recent power outage in your manufacturing facility? Why? [LO-2]

14-11. If you want to make a particular recommendation in your report, should you include information that might support a different recommendation? Explain your answer. [LO-3]

14-12. Assume you are assigned the task of evaluating two firms to provide security for your company's office and factory facilities, but your analysis tells you that neither firm is capable of providing quality service at an acceptable cost. How should you structure your report? [LO-3]

14-13. In what ways are unsolicited proposals more challenging to write than solicited proposals? [LO-4]

Practice Your Skills

14-14. Message for Analysis: Comparing Two Report Formats [LO-1] The Securities and Exchange Commission (SEC) requires all public companies to digitally file a comprehensive annual report (form 10-K). Many companies post links to these reports on their websites, along with links to other company reports. Visit the website of any public corporation and find the company's most recent 10-K and Fiscal Year in Review reports. Compare the style and format of the two reports. For which audience(s) is the Year in Review targeted? Who besides the SEC might be interested in the 10-K? Which report do you find easier to read? More interesting? More detailed?

Exercises

Each activity is labeled according to the primary skill or skills you will need to use. To review relevant chapter content, you can refer to the indicated Learning Objective. In some instances, supporting information will be found in another chapter, as indicated.

14-15. Planning: Analyzing the Situation [LO-1] Sales at The Style Shop, a clothing store for men, have declined for the third month in a row. Your boss is not sure whether this decline is due to the weak economy or some other unknown reason. She has asked you to investigate the situation and to submit a report to her, highlighting some possible reasons for the decline. Develop a statement of purpose for your report.

14-16. Planning: Preparing the Work Plan [LO-1] South by Southwest (SXSW) is a family of conferences and festivals in Austin, Texas, that showcase some of the world's most creative talents in music, interactive media, and film. In addition to being a major entertainment venue for a week every March, SXSW is also an increasingly important *trade show*, an opportunity for companies to present products and services to potential customers and business partners. You work for a company that makes music training equipment such as an electronic keyboard with an integrated computer screen that guides learners through every step of learning to play a keyboard. Your manager has asked you to look into whether the company should rent an exhibition booth at SXSW next year. Prepare a work plan for an analytical report that will assess the promotional opportunities at SXSW and make a recommendation on exhibiting. Include the statement of purpose, a problem statement for any research you will conduct, a description of what will result from your investigation, the sources and methods of data collection, and a preliminary outline. Visit the SXSW website at www.sxsw.com for more information.[8]

Planning: Organizing Reports [LO-1] For each of the following scenarios, determine whether the direct or indirect approach would be advisable, and explain why.

14-17. A monthly financial report prepared by the accounting department for upper management

14-18. An accountant fresh out of college who wants to propose a new way to present those monthly financial results to upper management

14-19. An unsolicited proposal to provide payroll processing services

14-20. An analytical report, requested by the CEO, explaining why the company has been losing money in the eastern sales region for the past two years

14-21. An unsolicited proposal to the board of directors, outlining why it makes strategic sense for your company to expand into international markets; the board rejected a similar—but poorly presented—idea last year

14-22. Planning: Organizing Reports [LO-1] Look through recent issues (print or online) of *Bloomberg Businessweek*, *Fortune*, or other business publications for an article that describes how an executive's conclusions about his or her company's current situation or future opportunities led to changes in policy, plans, or products. Construct an outline of the material, first using a direct approach and then using an indirect approach. Which approach do you think the executive would use when reporting these conclusions to stockholders? When reporting to other senior managers? Explain your answers.

14-23. Planning: Organizing Reports (Informational Reports) [LO-2] Assume that your college president has received many student complaints about campus parking problems. You are appointed the chair of a student committee organized to investigate the problems and recommend solutions. The president gives you a file labeled "Parking: Complaints from Students," and you jot down the essence of the complaints as you inspect the contents. Your notes look like this:

- Inadequate student spaces at critical hours
- Poor night lighting near the computer center
- Inadequate attempts to keep resident neighbors from occupying spaces
- Dim marking lines
- Motorcycles taking up full spaces
- Discourteous security officers
- Spaces (often empty) reserved for college officials
- Relatively high parking fees
- Full fees charged to night students even though they use the lots only during low-demand periods
- Vandalism to cars and a sense of personal danger
- Inadequate total space
- Resident harassment of students parking on the street in front of neighboring houses

Prepare an outline for an informational report to be submitted to committee members. Use a topical organization that categorizes this information.

Planning: Organizing Reports (Analytical Reports) [LO-2] Three years ago, your company (a carpet manufacturer) modernized its Georgia plant in anticipation of increasing demand for carpets. Because of the depressed housing market, the increase in demand for new carpets has been slow to materialize. As a result, the company has excess capacity at both its Georgia and California plants. On the basis of your research, you have recommended that the company close the California plant. J. P. Lawrence, the company president, has asked you to prepare a justification report to support your recommendation. Here are the facts you gathered by interviewing the respective plant managers:

Operational Statistics

- Georgia plant: This plant has newer equipment, has higher productivity, employs 100 nonunion production workers, and ships $12 million in carpets a year; hourly base wage is $16
- California plant: California plant employs 80 union production workers and ships $8 million in carpets a year; hourly base wage is $20

Financial Implications

- Savings by closing California plant: (1) increase productivity by 17 percent; (2) reduce labor costs by 20 percent (total labor savings would be $1 million per year; see assumptions); (3) annual local tax savings of $120,000 (Georgia has a more favorable tax climate)
- Sale of Pomona, California, land: Purchased in 1952 for $200,000. Current market value $2.5 million. Net profit (after capital gains tax) over $1 million
- Sale of plant and equipment: Fully depreciated; any proceeds a windfall
- Costs of closing California plant: One-time deductible charge of $250,000 (relocation costs of $100,000 and severance payments totaling $150,000)

Assumptions

- Transfer five workers from California to Georgia
- Hire 45 new workers in Georgia
- Lay off 75 workers in California
- Georgia plant would require a total of 150 workers to produce the combined volume of both plants

14-24. Which approach (focus on conclusions, recommendations, or logical arguments) will you use to structure your report to the president? Why?

14-25. Suppose this report were to be circulated to plant managers and supervisors instead. What changes, if any, might you make in your approach?

14-26. List some conclusions you might draw from the preceding information to use in your report.

14-27. Using the structure you selected for your report to the president, draft a final report outline with first- and second-level informative headings.

Planning Reports and Proposals [LO-2], [LO-3], [LO-4] Using the information presented in this chapter, identify the report type represented by each of the following examples. In addition, write a brief paragraph about each, explaining who the audience is likely to be, what type of data would be used, and whether conclusions and recommendations would be appropriate.

14-28. A statistical study of the pattern of violent crime in a large city during the past five years

14-29. A report prepared by a seed company, demonstrating the benefits of its seed corn for farmers

14-30. A report prepared by an independent testing agency, evaluating various types of nonprescription cold remedies

14-31. A trip report submitted at the end of a week by a traveling salesperson

14-32. A report indicating how 45 acres of undeveloped land could be converted into an industrial park

14-33. An annual report to be sent to the shareholders of a large corporation

14-34. A report from a U.S. National Park wildlife officer to Washington, D.C., headquarters showing the status of an endangered animal species

14-35. A report outlining the risks of closing a chain of retail stores and moving the entire business online

14-36. Planning Informational Reports [LO-2] You're the vice president of operations for a Florida fast-food chain. In the aftermath of a major hurricane, you're drafting a report on the emergency procedures to be followed by personnel in each restaurant when storm warnings are in effect. Answer who, what, when, where, why, and how, then prepare a one-page outline of your report. Make up any details you need.

14-37. Planning Proposals [LO-4] You're getting ready to launch a new lawn-care business that offers mowing, fertilizing, weeding, and other services. The lawn surrounding a nearby shopping center looks as if it could use better care, so you target that business for your first unsolicited proposal. To help prepare this proposal, write your answers to these questions:

- What questions will you need to answer before you can write a proposal to solve the reader's problem? Be as specific as possible.
- What customer benefits will you include in your proposal?
- Will you use a letter or memo format for your proposal? Explain your answer.

14-38. Planning Proposals; Collaboration: Team Projects [LO-4], Chapter 2 Break into small groups and identify an operational problem occurring at your campus and involving one of the following: registration, university housing, food services, parking, or library services. Develop a workable solution to that problem. Finally, develop a list of pertinent facts that your team will need to gather to convince the reader that the problem exists and that your solution will work.

Expand Your Skills

Critique the Professionals

Download any of the free reports offered on the American Coatings Association website at **www.paint.org**. Identify the target audience(s) and purpose of the report you've chosen. Using whatever medium your instructor requests, write a brief analysis of the report, describing what works well and what doesn't work well.

Sharpening Your Career Skills Online

Bovée and Thill's Business Communication Web Search, at **websearch.businesscommunicationnetwork.com**, is a unique research tool designed specifically for business communication research. Use the Web Search function to find a website, video, article, podcast, or presentation that offers advice on writing effective business proposals. Write a brief email message to your instructor, describing the item you found and summarizing the career skills information you learned from it.

MyBCommLab

Go to **mybcommlab.com** for Auto-graded writing questions as well as the following Assisted-graded writing questions:

14-39. What elements should be included in a formal business plan? [LO-2]

14-40. When responding to an RFP, should you try to stand out from the crowd by organizing and formatting your proposal in a fresh, unexpected way? Explain your answer. [LO-4]

Endnotes

1. Warby Parker website, accessed 26 April 2016, www.warbyparker.com; Max Chafkin, "Warby Parker See the Future of Retail," *Fast Company*, 17 February 2015, www.fastcompany.com; Jessica Pressler, "20/30 Vision," *New York Magazine*, 11 August 2013, nymag.com; Andrew Mascio, "Luxottica: An Unstoppable Machine," *Seeking Alpha*, 29 December 2014, seekingalpha.com; Luxottica website, accessed 2 March 2015, www.luxottica.com; Manuela Mesco, "Italian Eyewear Marker Luxottica Profit, Sales Up," *MarketWatch*, 2 March 2015, www.marketwatch.com; Ross Crooks, "12 Lessons from Warby Parker's Annual Report," *Forbes*, 30 January 2014, www.forbes.com; Warby Parker profile, B Corporation website, accessed 3 March 2015, www.bcorporation.net.
2. Heidi Brown, "How to Write a Winning Business Plan," *Forbes*, 18 June 2010, www.forbes.com; Michael Gerber, "The Business Plan That Always Works," *Her Business*, May/June 2004, 23–25; J. Tol Broome Jr., "How to Write a Business Plan," *Nation's Business*, February 1993, 29–30; Albert Richards, "The Ernst & Young Business Plan Guide," *R & D Management*, April 1995, 253; David Lanchner, "How Chitchat Became a Valuable Business Plan," *Global Finance*, February 1995, 54–56; Marguerita Ashby-Berger, "My Business Plan—And What Really Happened," *Small Business Forum*, Winter 1994–1995, 24–35; Stanley R. Rich and David E. Gumpert, *Business Plans That Win $$$* (New York: Harper & Row, 1985).

3. David A. Garvin and Michael A. Roberto, "What You Don't Know About Making Decisions," Harvard Business School website, 15 October 2001, hbswk.hbs.edu.
4. Iris Varner, *Contemporary Business Report Writing*, 2nd ed. (Chicago: Dryden Press, 1991), 170.
5. Curt Kampmeier, "How to Write a Proposal That's Accepted Every Time," *Consulting to Management*, September 2000, 62.
6. Qvidian website, accessed 28 February 2011, www.qvidian.com; Dan MacDougall, "Orchestrating Your Proposal," *Canadian Consulting Engineer*, March–April 2003, 51–56.
7. "Why What You Learned in School About Writing Was Wrong," CapturePlanning.com, accessed 9 December 2008, www.captureplanning.com.
8. SXSW website, accessed 26 April 2016, sxsw.com; Catherine Holahan and Spencer E. Ante, "SXSW: Where Tech Mingles with Music," *BusinessWeek*, 7 March 2008, www.businessweek.com.
9. Report content based in part on Lorri Freifeld, "How-To: Start a Corporate Mentoring Program," *Training*, accessed 27 April 2016, trainingmag.com; Beth N. Carvin, "How to Start a Corporate Mentoring Program," Mentor Scout, accessed 27 April 2016, www.mentorscout.com; "Benefits of Mentoring Programs," Insala, accessed 27 April 2016, mentoringtalent.com; Heather R. Huhman, "Create a Corporate Mentoring Program and You May Reap the Benefits," *Entrepreneur*, 10 February 2015, www.entrepreneur.com.

LEARNING OBJECTIVES

After studying this chapter, you will be able to

1 Explain how to adapt to your audiences when writing reports and proposals.

2 Name five characteristics of effective report content, and list the topics commonly covered in the introduction, body, and close of formal reports.

3 List six strategies to strengthen a proposal argument, and identify the topics commonly covered in the introduction, body, and close of proposals.

4 Summarize the four tasks involved in completing business reports and proposals.

5 Identify the elements to include in a request for proposals (RFP).

COMMUNICATION CLOSE-UP AT
WPP

wpp.com

Corporate annual reports are among the most important reports a company produces—and among the most difficult, too. These reports must adhere to detailed financial reporting regulations while functioning as broader, multitopic informational reports for a diverse audience of investors, potential employees, business partners, activists, journalists, and others. Most have a strong promotional emphasis as well: They try to convince investors to buy the company's stock and encourage job seekers to consider the company.

Addressing the information needs of so many reader segments is a daunting task for any firm, but it's particularly challenging for WPP. The London-based holding company is the

Sir Martin Sorrell is CEO of the global advertising conglomerate WPP, whose annual reports take full advantage of the online environment to help readers find content of greatest interest.

ZUMA Press, Inc./Alamy Stock Photo

world's largest marketing communication services firm, with more than 150 component companies involved in every conceivable aspect of advertising and related business activities. Together, WPP companies have nearly 200,000 employees in more than 100 countries.

A lengthy formal report on an organization with so many moving parts could turn into an unreadable morass. However, by taking advantage of the flexibility of the web and making intelligent, reader-friendly choices, WPP crafts annual reports that are remarkably easy to navigate and consume.

One of WPP's recent reports offers multiple examples of creating reports with audience needs in mind. The homepage of the report is a single, scrollable screen (making it easy to navigate on the growing number of mobile and touch-screen devices) that offers clear and simple choices for every potential reader.

The top of the page offers links to read the full report, to read four major sections that are highlighted as standalone reports, or to watch a video message, for those who don't want to read at all. (This brief video of CEO Sir Martin Sorrell even has "subheadings" embedded in the timeline, making it much easier to skim than the typical online video.) The top section also offers links to two other annually issued reports that many site visitors will be curious about, one on the company's efforts toward sustainability and another that highlights its *pro bono* work (services offered for free, typically to nonprofit organizations).

Swiping or scrolling down to the middle of the page reveals a menu of "Fast Read" topics, each offering a highly compressed summary of major subject areas from the full report. A traditional annual report can take hours to read cover to cover, but these summaries can be read in just a few minutes. In each Fast Read section, readers can click through to additional layers of detail on that specific topic if they're interested.

Continuing down to the bottom of the page, readers are presented with a variety of links—to the full report, just the financial statements, or specific report sections. No matter where readers venture up and down this landing page, navigation choices are always clearly in view, making it just about impossible to get lost.

Within three short screens of information, WPP offers easy-to-read summaries and well-marked pathways to subtopics and deeper detail. The full annual report (available as a PDF) is 252 pages long, but the thoughtful, reader-friendly organization of the online report makes this mammoth document feel simple, clear, and unintimidating. Norman Pearlstine, an editor at Time Inc. with more than fifty years of experience reading company annual reports, said the WPP report "may be the best annual report I have ever read."

Of course, WPP is in the business of communication and has some of the best information architects, writers, and web designers in the industry, so one would expect top-notch online reports. However, every business communicator, even those with humble resources, can learn from the company's emphasis on starting with readers and structuring reports to meet their needs.[1]

Writing Reports and Proposals: Adapting to Your Audience

1 **LEARNING OBJECTIVE** Explain how to adapt to your audiences when writing reports and proposals.

The communicators at WPP (profiled in the chapter-opening Communication Close-Up) know that reports and proposals are most effective when they are adapted to the needs and interests of their intended audiences. To ensure your own success with reports, be sensitive to audience needs, build strong relationships with your audience, and control your style and tone.

BEING SENSITIVE TO YOUR AUDIENCE'S NEEDS

The "you" attitude is especially important with long or complex reports because they demand a lot from readers.

Chapter 5 discusses four aspects of audience sensitivity, and all four apply to reports and proposals: adopting the "you" attitude, maintaining a strong sense of etiquette, emphasizing the positive, and using bias-free language. Reports and proposals that are highly technical, complex, or lengthy can put heavy demands on readers, so the "you" attitude takes on special importance with these messages.

In addition, various audience members can have widely different information needs. For instance, if you're reporting on the results of a customer satisfaction survey, the service manager might want every detail, whereas the president might want only a top-level summary. With previews, summaries, appendixes, and other elements, you can meet the needs of a diverse audience—provided that you plan for these elements in advance.

Today's readers often lack the time or the inclination to plow through long reports page by page or screen by screen. They typically want to browse quickly, find a section of interest, dive in for details, browse for another section, and so on. If you want readers to understand and accept your message,

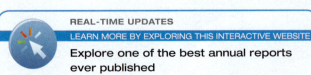

REAL-TIME UPDATES
LEARN MORE BY EXPLORING THIS INTERACTIVE WEBSITE

Explore one of the best annual reports ever published

Have a look at the WPP annual report discussed in the chapter-opening Communication Close-Up. Go to **real-timeupdates.com/bct14** and select Learn More in the Students section.

help them navigate your document by using headings and links, smooth transitions, and previews and reviews.

Help your audiences navigate through your reports by providing clear directions to key pieces of content.

Headings

Headings improve a document's readability and are especially useful for identifying the framework of a report. They also visually indicate shifts from one idea to the next and, when used in a combination of levels, help readers see the relationship between subordinate and main ideas. In addition, busy readers can quickly understand the gist of a document simply by scanning the headings. In online reports, headings serve all these functions, plus they can be used to provide links to other sections and other websites.

Many companies specify a format for headings, either through style guides or document templates. If yours does, use that recommended format. If you are creating your own scheme, make sure the hierarchy of headings and subheadings is clear. If you have three levels of headings in a report, for example, you might use 20-point bold type for the first-level headings, 16 points for the second level, and 12 points for the third level:

First level

SECOND LEVEL

Third level

Another option is to put the first-level headings in all capital letters or to emphasize them using color. The sample report on pages 431–445 does both of these, for instance.

Transitions

Transitions help readers move from one section of a report to the next and from key point to key point within sections. Transitions can be words, sentences, or complete paragraphs. Here's an example:

Transitions connect ideas by helping readers move from one thought to the next.

> . . . As you can see, our profits have decreased by 12 percent over the past eight months.
>
> To counteract this decline in profits, we can explore alternatives. First, we can raise our selling prices. Second, we can work to reduce our manufacturing costs. Third, we can introduce new products that will support higher profit margins. However, each of these alternatives has both advantages and disadvantages.

The phrase *As you can see* alerts readers to the fact that they are reading a summary of the information just presented. The phrase *this decline in profits* refers to the previous paragraph, letting readers know that the text will be saying something else about that topic. The words *first*, *second*, and *third* help readers stay on track as the three alternatives are introduced, and the word *however* alerts readers to the fact that evaluating the three alternatives requires some additional discussion. Effective transitions such as these can help readers summarize and remember what they've learned so far while giving them a mental framework to process new information.

Previews and Reviews

Preview sections introduce important topics by helping readers get ready for new information; they are particularly helpful when the information is complex, unexpected, or unfamiliar. Think of a preview as an opportunity for readers to arrange their mental file folders before you start giving them information to put in those folders.

Previews help readers prepare for upcoming information, whereas reviews help them verify and clarify what they've just read.

Review sections come after a body of material and summarize the information just covered. They help readers absorb details while keeping track of the big picture. Long reports and those dealing with complex subjects can often benefit from multiple review sections, one at the end of every major subject block, as well as a more comprehensive review at the very end of a document.

Previews and reviews can be written in sentence format, in bulleted lists, or using a combination of the two. Both are effective, but bullets can increase your document's readability by adding white space to the document design. Consider the following preview, shown using both formats:

Sentence Format

The next section discusses the advantages of online advertising. Among them are currency, global reach, affordability, and interactivity.

Bulleted List

As the next section shows, online advertising has four advantages:

- Currency
- Global reach
- Affordability
- Interactivity

For more on writing effective lists, see "Using Lists to Clarify and Emphasize" on page 159 in Chapter 6.

BUILDING STRONG RELATIONSHIPS WITH YOUR AUDIENCE

Your reports may continue to be read for months or years after you write them—and reach audiences you never envisioned.

Building relationships with your readers starts with planning how to adapt your style and language to meet their needs and expectations. Bear in mind that some reports— particularly those that can be transmitted online—can take on lives of their own, reaching a wider audience than you ever imagined and being read years after you write them. Consequently, choose your content and language with care. Also, because many companies have specific guidelines for communicating with public audiences, make sure you're aware of these preferences before you start writing.

As discussed in Chapter 5, establishing your credibility is vital to successful communication. To gain your audience's trust, research all sides of your topic and document your findings with credible sources. Also, be aware that setting audience expectations too high can lead to problems with your credibility if you can't deliver everything people expect you to, so take particular care with the introductory sections of important reports.

CONTROLLING YOUR STYLE AND TONE

Adjust the level of formality to match the situation and your audience's expectations.

If you know your readers reasonably well and your report is likely to meet with their approval, you can adopt a fairly informal tone—provided that doing so is acceptable in the situation and in your company's culture. To make your tone less formal, refer to readers as *you* and refer to yourself as *I* (or *we*, if there are multiple report authors).

A more formal tone is usually appropriate for longer reports, especially those that deal with controversial or complex information. You'll also want to use a more formal tone when your report will be sent to other parts of the organization or to outsiders, such as customers, suppliers, or members of the community (see Figure 15.1).

If the situation calls for a more formal tone, use the impersonal journalism style, eliminating all references to *you* and *I* (including *we*, *us*, and *our*). When you use an impersonal style, you impose a controlled distance between you and your readers. Your tone is not only objective but also businesslike and unemotional. Be careful to avoid jokes, and minimize the use of similes, metaphors, and overly colorful language.

However, when crafting a more formal tone, take care not to go overboard, or you'll end up sounding stiff or dull. In addition, don't inadvertently slip into the passive voice. You can avoid this potential weakness by making the report content itself the actor in a sentence. For example, to convert "I think we should buy TramCo" to a more formal tone, you could write "The financial analysis clearly shows that buying TramCo is the best alternative."

Drafting Report Content

2 **LEARNING OBJECTIVE**
Name five characteristics of effective report content, and list the topics commonly covered in the introduction, body, and close of formal reports.

With a clear picture of how you need to adapt to your audience, you're ready to begin composing your first draft. Before you put those first words down on paper, though, review your outline one last time. Verify that the organization you've chosen makes sense, given everything you've learned about your topic so far. Also, review the wording of the headings and subheadings to make sure they establish the right tone. For a hard-hitting,

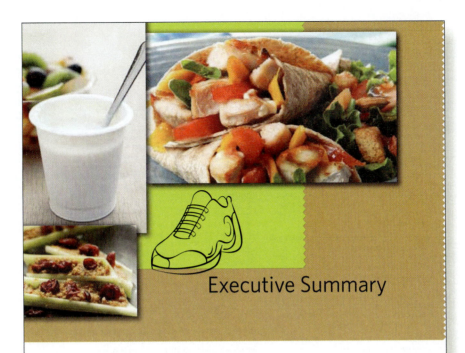

Long and somewhat rigorous sentences help give the report its formal tone. For a more consumer-oriented publication, this writing could certainly be simplified.

Executive Summary

Eating and physical activity patterns that are focused on consuming fewer calories, making informed food choices, and being physically active can help people attain and maintain a healthy weight, reduce their risk of chronic disease, and promote overall health. The *Dietary Guidelines for Americans, 2010* exemplifies these strategies through recommendations that accommodate the food preferences, cultural traditions, and customs of the many and diverse groups who live in the United States.

By law (Public Law 101-445, Title III, 7 U.S.C. 5301 et seq.), *Dietary Guidelines for Americans* is reviewed, updated if necessary, and published every 5 years. The U.S. Department of Agriculture (USDA) and the U.S. Department of Health and Human Services (HHS) jointly create each edition. *Dietary Guidelines for Americans, 2010* is based on the *Report of the Dietary Guidelines Advisory Committee on the Dietary Guidelines for Americans, 2010* and consideration of Federal agency and public comments.

Dietary Guidelines recommendations traditionally have been intended for healthy Americans ages 2 years and older. However, *Dietary Guidelines for Americans, 2010* is being released at a time of rising concern about the health of the American population. Poor diet and physical inactivity are the most important factors contributing to an epidemic of overweight and obesity affecting men, women, and children in all segments of our society. Even in the absence of overweight, poor diet and physical inactivity are associated with major causes of morbidity and mortality in the United States. Therefore, the *Dietary Guidelines for Americans, 2010* is intended for Americans ages 2 years and older, including those at increased risk of chronic disease.

Dietary Guidelines for Americans, 2010 also recognizes that in recent years nearly 15 percent of American households have been unable to acquire adequate food to meet their needs.[1] This dietary guidance can help them maximize the nutritional content of

A less-formal report might've said something along the lines of "Poor diet and physical inactivity are killing U.S. citizens" instead of the more formal (and more precise) "are associated with major causes of morbidity and mortality."

This paragraph mentions the troubling statistic that 15 percent of U.S. households can't afford to meet basic nutritional requirements, but because the report is presenting dietary recommendations and not public policy statements about economics or other issues, the tone is objective and dispassionate.

1. Nord M, Coleman-Jensen A, Andrews M, Carlson S. Household food security in the United States, 2009. Washington (DC): U.S. Department of Agriculture, Economic Research Service. 2010 Nov. Economic Research Report No. ERR-108. Available from http://www.ers.usda.gov/publications/err108.

viii   DIETARY GUIDELINES FOR AMERICANS, 2010

(continued)

Figure 15.1   Achieving the Appropriate Tone for a Report
This report excerpt (part of the executive summary of the *Dietary Guidelines for Americans* published by the U.S. Department of Agriculture and the U.S. Department of Health and Human Services) uses a number of techniques to create a formal tone. This is a formal policy document whose intended readers are educators, government regulators, and others charged with using the information to help inform consumers. If the document had been written with consumers in mind, you can imagine how the tone might have been lighter and less formal.

direct tone, use informative phrasing ("Quality Problems Result in Nearly 500 Customer Defections Every Year"). For an objective, indirect tone, use descriptive phrasing ("Effects of Product Quality on Customer Retention").

Writing lengthy reports and proposals can be a huge task, so be sure to take advantage of technological tools to help throughout the process. In addition to features such as automatic table of contents and index generators, look for opportunities to use *linked and embedded documents* to incorporate graphics, spreadsheets, databases, and other elements produced in other software programs. For instance, in Microsoft Office you can choose to either *link* to another file (which ensures that changes in that file are reflected in your file) or *embed* another file (which doesn't include the automatic updating feature).

Before you start writing, review your outline one more time and verify the wording of your headings and subheadings.

MOBILE APP

Redbooth's file and content management features help teams manage collaborative report writing.

This is an example of a sentence that is precise and uses language appropriate for the purpose of this report. In contrast, a document aimed primarily at consumers might have said "We've converted the latest nutritional insights into recommendations for healthy eating."

their meals. Many other Americans consume less than optimal intake of certain nutrients even though they have adequate resources for a healthy diet. This dietary guidance and nutrition information can help them choose a healthy, nutritionally adequate diet.

The intent of the Dietary Guidelines is to summarize and synthesize knowledge about individual nutrients and food components into an interrelated set of recommendations for healthy eating that can be adopted by the public. Taken together, the Dietary Guidelines recommendations encompass two overarching concepts:

- **Maintain calorie balance over time to achieve and sustain a healthy weight.** People who are most successful at achieving and maintaining a healthy weight do so through continued attention to consuming only enough calories from foods and beverages to meet their needs and by being physically active. To curb the obesity epidemic and improve their health, many Americans must decrease the calories they consume and increase the calories they expend through physical activity.

- **Focus on consuming nutrient-dense foods and beverages.** Americans currently consume too much sodium and too many calories from solid fats, added sugars, and refined grains.[2] These replace nutrient-dense foods and beverages and make it difficult for people to achieve recommended nutrient intake while controlling calorie and sodium intake. A healthy eating pattern limits intake of sodium, solid fats, added sugars, and refined grains and emphasizes nutrient-dense foods and beverages—vegetables, fruits, whole grains, fat-free or low-fat milk and milk products,[3] seafood, lean meats and poultry, eggs, beans and peas, and nuts and seeds.

A basic premise of the Dietary Guidelines is that nutrient needs should be met primarily through consuming foods. In certain cases, fortified foods and dietary supplements may be useful in providing one or more nutrients that otherwise might be consumed in less than recommended amounts. Two eating patterns that embody the Dietary Guidelines are the USDA Food Patterns and their vegetarian adaptations and the DASH (Dietary Approaches to Stop Hypertension) Eating Plan.

A healthy eating pattern needs not only to promote health and help to decrease the risk of chronic diseases, but it also should prevent foodborne illness. Four basic food safety principles (Clean, Separate, Cook, and Chill) work together to reduce the risk of foodborne illnesses. In addition, some foods (such as milks, cheeses, and juices that have not been pasteurized, and undercooked animal foods) pose high risk for foodborne illness and should be avoided.

The information in the *Dietary Guidelines for Americans* is used in developing educational materials and aiding policymakers in designing and carrying out nutrition-related programs, including Federal food, nutrition education, and information programs. In addition, the *Dietary Guidelines for Americans* has the potential to offer authoritative statements as provided for in the Food and Drug Administration Modernization Act (FDAMA).

The following are the *Dietary Guidelines for Americans, 2010* Key Recommendations, listed by the chapter in which they are discussed in detail. These Key Recommendations are the most important in terms of their implications for improving public health.[4] To get the full benefit, individuals should carry out the Dietary Guidelines recommendations in their entirety as part of an overall healthy eating pattern.

In a less-formal report, the authors might have written "One of our basic premises is that nutrient needs should be met primarily through consuming foods" or even "You should meet your nutrient needs by eating food, not by taking supplements." However, to maintain a formal tone, they avoid both first- and second-person usage.

2. Added sugars: Caloric sweeteners that are added to foods during processing, preparation, or consumed separately. Solid fats: Fats with a high content of saturated and/or *trans* fatty acids, which are usually solid at room temperature. Refined grains: Grains and grain products missing the bran, germ, and/or endosperm; any grain product that is not a whole grain.
3. Milk and milk products also can be referred to as dairy products.
4. Information on the type and strength of evidence supporting the Dietary Guidelines recommendations can be found at http://www.nutritionevidencelibrary.gov.

DIETARY GUIDELINES FOR AMERICANS, 2010   ix

Figure 15.1   Achieving the Appropriate Tone for a Report (*continued*)

Like other written business communications, reports and proposals have three main sections: an introduction (or *opening*), a body, and a close. The content and length of each section vary with the type and purpose of the document, the document's organizational structure, the length and depth of the material, the document's degree of formality, and your relationship with your audience.

At a minimum, an effective *introduction* accomplishes these four tasks:

The introduction needs to put the report in context for the reader, introduce the subject, preview main ideas, and establish the tone of the document.

- It helps the reader understand the context of the report by tying it to a problem or an assignment
- It introduces the subject matter and indicates why it is important
- It previews the main idea (if you're using the direct approach)
- It establishes the tone and the writer's relationship with the audience

The *body* presents, analyzes, and interprets the information gathered during your investigation and supports your recommendations or conclusions. The length and content of the body can vary widely based on the subject matter.

The *close* has three important functions:

- It summarizes your key points
- It emphasizes the benefits to the reader if the document suggests a change or some other course of action
- It brings all the action items together in one place

The final section of a report or proposal can leave a lasting impression, so use the close to make sure your report says what you intended.[2] In fact, readers who are in a hurry might skip the body of the report and read only the summary, so make sure it carries a strong, clear message.

Your credibility and prospects for the future are on the line with every business report you write, so make sure your content is

- **Accurate.** Information presented in a report must be factually correct. When writing reports, be sure to double-check your facts and references in addition to checking for typos. If an audience ever gets the inkling that your information is shaky, they'll start to view all your work with a skeptical eye.
- **Complete.** To help audiences make informed decisions, include all the information necessary for readers to understand the situation, problem, or proposal. Support all key assertions using an appropriate combination of illustrations, explanations, and facts.[3] Tell your readers what they need to know—no more, no less—and present the information in a way that is geared toward their needs. Mobile reporting apps can help you integrate text with "live" data that let readers explore if they need additional insights.
- **Balanced.** It's important to present all sides of the issue fairly and equitably and to include all the essential information, even if some of it doesn't support your line of reasoning. Omitting relevant information or facts can bias your report.
- **Clear and logical.** Save your readers time by making sure your sentences are uncluttered, contain well-chosen words, and proceed logically. To help your readers move from one point to the next, make your transitions clear and logical. For a successful report, identify the ideas that belong together and organize them in a way that's easy to understand.[4]
- **Documented properly.** If you use primary and secondary sources for your report or proposal, be sure to properly document and give credit to your sources, as Chapter 13 explains.

> The body of your report presents, analyzes, and interprets the information you gathered during your investigation and supports your recommendations or conclusions.

> Your close is often the last opportunity to get your message across, so make it clear and compelling.

> The close might be the only part of your report some readers have time for, so it should convey the full weight of your message.

> Effective report content is accurate, complete, balanced, clear, logical, and properly documented.

REAL-TIME UPDATES

LEARN MORE BY VISITING THIS WEBSITE

Get practical advice on developing research reports

Purdue's Online Writing Lab offers advice on developing all the sections of a typical research report. Go to **real-timeupdates.com/bct14** and select Learn More in the Students section.

Drafting Proposal Content

If you're writing an unsolicited proposal, you have some latitude in the scope and organization of content. However, the scope and organization of a solicited proposal are usually governed by the request for proposals. Most RFPs spell out precisely what you should cover and in what order. This uniformity lets the recipient evaluate competing proposals in a systematic way.

The general purpose of any proposal is to persuade readers to do something, such as purchase goods or services, fund a project, or implement a program. Thus your writing approach for a proposal is similar to that used for persuasive sales messages (see Chapter 12). Your proposal must sell your audience on your ideas, product, service, methods, and company. As with any other persuasive message, you can use the AIDA model to gain attention, build interest, create desire, and motivate action (of course, you may need to adapt it if you're responding to an RFP or working within some other

3 **LEARNING OBJECTIVE**
List six strategies to strengthen a proposal argument, and identify the topics commonly covered in the introduction, body, and close of proposals.

> The AIDA model works well for proposals, although you may need to adapt it if you're responding to an RFP.

constraints). Here are some additional strategies to strengthen your persuasive argument:[5]

- **Demonstrate your knowledge.** Everything you write should show the reader that you have the knowledge and experience to solve the problem or address the opportunity outlined in your proposal.
- **Provide concrete information and examples.** Avoid vague, unsupported generalizations such as "We are losing money on this program." Instead, provide quantifiable details such as the amount of money being lost, how, why, and so on. Explain how much money your proposed solution will save. Spell out your plan and give details on how the job will be done.
- **Research the competition.** Find out what alternatives your audience might choose over your proposal so that you can emphasize why your solution is the optimum choice. Potential customers sometimes face a "buy or build" decision, in which they must choose between buying a solution from an external party and building it themselves. In these cases you are effectively competing against your target customers.
- **Prove that your proposal is workable.** Your proposal must be appropriate and feasible for your audience. It should be consistent with your audience's capabilities. For instance, your proposal would be pointless if it recommended a plan of action that requires three times the number of available employees or twice the available budget.
- **Adopt the "you" attitude.** Relate your product, service, or personnel to the reader's exact needs, either as stated in the RFP for a solicited proposal or as discovered through your own investigation for an unsolicited proposal.
- **Package your proposal attractively.** Make sure your proposal is letter perfect, inviting, and readable. Readers will prejudge the quality of your products or services by the proposal you submit. Errors, omissions, and inconsistencies will work against you—and may even cost you important career and business opportunities.

> Business proposals need to provide more than just attractive ideas—readers look for evidence of practical, achievable solutions.

Proposals in various industries often have their own special challenges as well. For instance, management consultants have to convince every potential client that they have the skills and knowledge to solve the client's problem—without giving away the answer for free in the proposal. In other industries, such as transportation services, bidders may be asked to compute hundreds or thousands of individual pricing scenarios. Hands-on experience goes a long way when you're deciding what to include or exclude; whenever possible, get advice from a senior colleague who's been through it before.

Consider using proposal-writing software if you and your company need to submit proposals as a routine part of doing business. These programs can automatically personalize proposals, ensure proper structure (making sure you don't forget any sections, for instance), organize storage of all your boilerplate text, integrate contact information from sales databases, scan RFPs to identify questions (and even assign them to content experts), and fill in preliminary answers to common questions from a centralized knowledge base.[6]

As with reports, approach proposals by identifying the pieces to include in the introduction, body, and close. For solicited proposals, always follow the instructions in the RFP, but here are some guidelines for unsolicited proposals. The introduction presents and summarizes the problem you want to solve or the opportunity you want to pursue, along with your proposed solution. It orients readers to the remainder of the report. If your proposal is solicited, its introduction should refer to the RFP so that readers know which RFP you're responding to. If your proposal is unsolicited, the introduction should mention any factors that led you to submit your proposal, such as prior conversations with members of the recipient organization's staff.

The proposal's body gives complete details on the proposed solution and specifies the anticipated results. Because a proposal is by definition a persuasive message, your audience expects you to promote your offering in a confident, professional manner. Even when you're expressing an idea you believe in passionately, be sure to maintain an objective tone so that you don't risk overselling your message.

> Readers understand that a proposal is a persuasive message, so they're willing to accommodate a promotional style—as long as it is professional and focused on their needs.

The close of a proposal generally summarizes the key points, emphasizes the benefits readers will realize from your solution, summarizes the merits of your approach, restates why you and your firm are the ones to perform the service or provide the products in question, and asks for a decision from readers. The close is your last opportunity to persuade readers to accept your proposal. In both formal and informal proposals, make this section relatively brief, assertive (but not brash or abrupt), and confident.

See Table 15.1 for a summary of the content to include in reports and proposals. You can use this table as a handy reference whenever you need to write a report in school or on the job.

TABLE 15.1 Content Elements to Consider for Reports and Proposals

Reports	Proposals
Introduction: Establish the context, identify the subject, preview main ideas (if using the direct approach), and establish tone and reader relationship.	**Introduction:** Identify the problem you intend to solve or the opportunity you want to pursue.
• **Authorization.** Reiterate who authorized the report, if applicable. • **Problem/purpose.** Explain the reason for the report's existence and what the report will achieve. • **Scope.** Describe what will and won't be covered in the report. • **Background.** Review historical conditions or factors that led up to the report. • **Sources and methods.** Discuss the primary and secondary sources consulted and methods used. • **Definitions.** List terms and their definitions, including any terms that might be misinterpreted. Terms may also be defined in the body, explanatory notes, or glossary. • **Limitations.** Discuss factors beyond your control that affect report quality (but do not use this as an excuse for poor research or a poorly written report). • **Report organization.** Identify the topics to be covered and in what order.	• **Background or statement of the problem.** Briefly review the situation at hand, establish a need for action, and explain how things could be better. In unsolicited proposals, convince readers that a problem or an opportunity exists. • **Solution.** Briefly describe the change you propose, highlighting your key selling points and their benefits to show how your proposal will solve the reader's problem. • **Scope.** State the boundaries of the proposal—what you will and will not do. • **Report organization.** Orient the reader to the remainder of the proposal and call attention to the major divisions of thought.
Body: Present relevant information and support your recommendations or conclusions.	**Body:** Give complete details on the proposed solution and describe anticipated results.
• **Explanations.** Give complete details of the problem, project, or idea. • **Facts, statistical evidence, and trends.** Lay out the results of studies or investigations. • **Analysis of action.** Discuss potential courses of action. • **Pros and cons.** Explain the advantages, disadvantages, costs, and benefits of a particular course of action. • **Procedures.** Outline steps for a process. • **Methods and approaches.** Discuss how you've studied a problem (or gathered evidence) and arrived at your solution (or collected your data). • **Criteria.** Describe the benchmarks for evaluating options and alternatives. • **Conclusions and recommendations.** Discuss what you believe the evidence reveals and what you propose should be done about it. • **Support.** Give the reasons behind your conclusions or recommendations.	• **Facts and evidence to support your conclusions.** Give complete details of the proposed solution and anticipated results. • **Proposed approach.** Describe your concept, product, or service. Stress reader benefits and emphasize any advantages you have over your competitors. • **Work plan.** Describe how you'll accomplish what must be done (unless you're providing a standard, off-the-shelf item). Explain the steps you'll take, their timing, the methods or resources you'll use, and the person(s) responsible. State when work will begin, how it will be divided into stages, when you'll finish, and whether follow-up will be needed. • **Statement of qualifications.** Describe your organization's experience, personnel, and facilities—relating it all to readers' needs. Include a list of client references. • **Costs.** Prove that your costs are realistic—break them down so that readers can see the costs of labor, materials, transportation, travel, training, and other categories.
Close: Summarize key points, emphasize the benefits of any recommendations, list action items; label as "Summary" or "Conclusions and Recommendations."	**Close:** Summarize key points, emphasize the benefits and advantages of your proposed solution, ask for a decision from the reader.
• **For direct approach.** Summarize key points (except in short reports), listing them in the order in which they appear in the body. Briefly restate your conclusions or recommendations, if appropriate. • **For indirect approach.** If you haven't done so at the end of the body, present your conclusions or recommendations. • **For motivating action.** Spell out exactly what should happen next and provide a schedule with specific task assignments.	• **Review of argument.** Briefly summarize the key points. • **Review of reader benefits.** Briefly summarize how your proposal will help the reader. • **Review of the merits of your approach.** Briefly summarize why your approach will be more effective than alternatives. • **Restatement of qualifications.** For external proposals, briefly reemphasize why you and your firm should do the work. • **Request.** Ask for a decision from the reader.

Completing Reports and Proposals

4 **LEARNING OBJECTIVE**
Summarize the four tasks involved in completing business reports and proposals.

The revision process for long reports can take considerable time, so be sure to plan ahead.

Tight, efficient writing is especially important with online content.

As with shorter messages, when you have finished your first draft, you need to perform four tasks to complete your document: revise, produce, proofread, and distribute. The revision process is essentially the same for reports as for other business messages, although it may take considerably longer, depending on the length and complexity of your documents. Evaluate your organization, style, and tone, making sure your content is clear, logical, and reader oriented. Then work to improve the report's readability by varying sentence length, keeping paragraphs short, using lists and bullets, and adding headings and subheadings. Remember that even minor mistakes can affect your credibility.

Tight, efficient writing that is easy to skim is always a plus, but it's especially important for impatient online audiences.[7] Review online content carefully; strip out all information that doesn't meet audience needs and condense everything else as much as possible. Audiences will gladly return to sites that deliver quality information quickly—and they'll avoid sites that don't.

After assembling your report or proposal in its final form, review it thoroughly one last time, looking for inconsistencies, errors, and missing components. Don't forget to proof your visuals thoroughly and make sure they are positioned correctly. For online reports, make sure all links work as expected and all necessary files are active and available. If you need specific tips on proofreading documents, look back at Chapter 6.

The number and variety of parts you include in a report depend on the type of report, audience requirements, organizational expectations, and report length.

PRODUCING FORMAL REPORTS AND PROPOSALS

Formal reports and proposals can include a variety of features beyond the text and visuals (see Table 15.2). Most of these elements provide additional information; a few are more decorative and add a degree of formality.

TABLE 15.2 Production Elements to Consider for Formal Reports and Proposals

Reports	Proposals
Prefatory elements (before the introduction)	**Prefatory elements** (before the introduction)
• **Cover.** Include a concise title that gives readers the information they need to grasp the purpose and scope of the report. For a formal printed report, choose heavy, high-quality *cover stock*.	• **Cover, title fly, title page.** Same uses as with reports; be sure to follow any instructions in the RFP, if relevant.
• **Title fly.** Some formal reports open with a plain sheet of paper that has only the title of the report on it, although this is certainly not necessary.	• **Copy of or reference to the RFP.** Instead of having a letter of authorization, a solicited proposal should follow the instructions in the RFP. Some will instruct you to include the entire RFP in your proposal; others may want you to simply identify it by a name and tracking number.
• **Title page.** Typically includes the report title, name(s) and title(s) of the writer(s), and date of submission; this information can be put on the cover instead.	• **Synopsis or executive summary.** These components are less common in formal proposals than in reports. In an unsolicited proposal, your letter of transmittal will catch the reader's interest. In a solicited proposal, the introduction will provide an adequate preview of the contents.
• **Letter of authorization.** If you received written authorization to prepare the report, you may want to include that letter or memo in your report.	• **Letter of transmittal.** If the proposal is solicited, treat the transmittal letter as a positive message, highlighting those aspects of your proposal that may give you a competitive advantage. If the proposal is unsolicited, the transmittal letter should follow the advice for persuasive messages (see Chapter 12)—the letter must persuade the reader that you have something worthwhile to offer that justifies reading the proposal.
• **Letter of transmittal.** "Cover letter" that introduces the report and can include scope, methods, limitations, and highlights of the report; offers to provide follow-on information or assistance; and acknowledges help received while preparing the report.	
• **Table of contents.** List all section headings and major subheadings to show the location and hierarchy of the information in the report.	
• **List of illustrations.** Consider including if the illustrations are particularly important and you want to call attention to them.	
• **Synopsis or executive summary.** See discussion on page 425.	
Supplementary elements (after the close)	**Supplementary elements** (after the close)
• **Appendixes.** Additional information related to the report but not included in the main text because it is too lengthy or lacks direct relevance. List appendixes in your table of contents and refer to them as appropriate in the text.	• **Appendixes.** Same uses as with reports; be sure to follow any instructions in the RFP, if relevant.
• **Bibliography.** List the secondary sources you consulted; see Appendix B.	• **Résumés of key players.** For external proposals, résumés can convince readers that you have the talent to achieve the proposal's objectives.
• **Index.** List names, places, and subjects mentioned in the report, along with the pages on which they occur.	

One of the most important elements to consider is an introductory feature that helps time-pressed readers get a sense of what's in the document or even get all the key points without reading the document. A **synopsis**—sometimes called an **abstract**—is a brief overview (one page or less) of a report's most important points. The phrasing of a synopsis can be *informative* (presenting the main points in the order in which they appear in the text) if you're using the direct approach or *descriptive* (simply describing what the report is about, without "giving away the ending") if you're using the indirect approach. As an alternative to a synopsis or an abstract, a longer report may include an **executive summary**—a fully developed "mini" version of the report, for readers who lack the time or motivation to read the entire document (see Figure 15.2).

Following the body of the report, possible supplemental parts (those coming after the main text of the report or proposal) include one or more appendixes, a bibliography, and an index. In general, place here supporting materials that could be of interest to some or all of your readers but that aren't crucial to the main thrust of your message.

For an illustration of how the various parts fit together in a report, see "Report Writer's Notebook: Analyzing a Formal Report," starting on page 431.

In contrast to formal reports, synopses and executive summaries are less common in proposals. In an unsolicited proposal, the letter of transmittal should catch the reader's interest. In a solicited proposal, the introduction provides an adequate preview of the contents. Moreover, proposals often take the indirect approach, which means they build up

A synopsis is a brief overview of a report's key points; an executive summary is a fully developed "mini" version of the report.

MOBILE APP

For report writing on the go, **LogMeIn** lets you access your computer's programs and files from your mobile device.

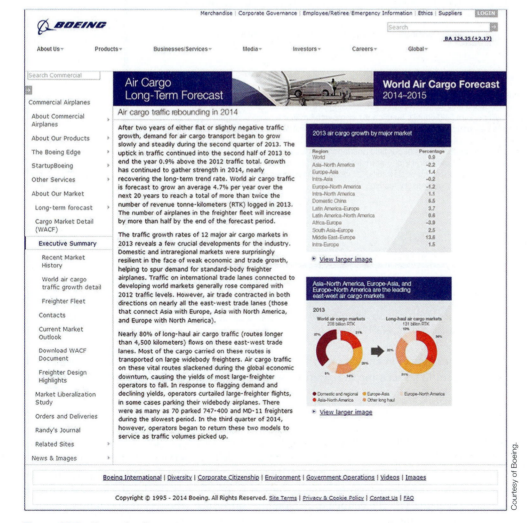

Figure 15.2 **Executive Summary**
This executive summary from a Boeing report on worldwide air cargo markets highlights key facts, figures, and trends using both text and visuals.

O'Donnell & Associates, Inc.

1793 East Westerfield Road, Arlington Heights, Illinois 60005
(847) 398-1148 Fax: (847) 398-1149 Email: dod@ix.netcom.com

July 31, 2017

Ms. Joyce Colton, P.E.
AGI Builders, Inc.
1280 Spring Lake Drive
Belvidere, Illinois, 61008

Subject: Proposal No. F-0087 for AGI Builders, Elgin Manufacturing Campus

Dear Ms. Colton:

The opening paragraph serves as an introduction. →

O'Donnell & Associates is pleased to submit the following proposal to provide construction testing services for the mass grading operations and utility work at the Elgin Manufacturing Campus, 126th St., Elgin, Illinois. Our company has been providing construction-testing services in the Chicago area since 1972 and has performed numerous large-scale geotechnical investigations across Illinois, including more than 100 at O'Hare International Airport, Midway Airport, Meig's Field, and other airports.

← *The introduction grabs the reader's attention by highlighting company qualifications.*

Headings divide the proposal into logical segments for easy reading. →

Background

It is our understanding that the work consists of two projects: (1) the mass grading perations will require approximately six months, and (2) the utility work will require approximately three months. The two operations are scheduled as follows:

← *The project background section acknowledges the two projects and their required timeline.*

Mass Grading Operation	September 2017–February 2018
Utility Work	March 2018–May 2018

Proposed Approach and Work Plan

The work plan describes the scope of the project and outlines specific tests the company will perform. →

O'Donnell & Associates will perform observation and testing services during both the mass grading operations and the excavation and backfilling of the underground utilities. Specifically, we will perform field density tests on the compacted material using a nuclear moisture/density gauge, as required by the job specifications. We will also conduct appropriate laboratory tests such as ASTM D-1557 Modified Proctors. We will prepare detailed reports summarizing the results of our field and laboratory testing. Fill materials to be placed at the site may consist of natural granular materials (sand), processed materials (crushed stone, crushed concrete, slag), or clay soils. O'Donnell & Associates will provide qualified personnel to perform the necessary testing.

(continued)

Figure 15.3 External Solicited Proposal
This proposal was submitted by a geotechnical engineering firm that conducts a variety of environmental testing services. The company is bidding on the mass grading and utility work specified by the prospective client, AGI Builders.

to the call to action at the end of the report, and summarizing this information at the beginning could undermine the carefully structured persuasive build-up (see Figure 15.3).

MOBILE APP
Dropbox lets you store files in the cloud and access or share them from PCs and mobile devices.

DISTRIBUTING REPORTS AND PROPOSALS

For physical distribution of important printed reports or proposals, consider spending the extra money for a professional courier or package delivery service. Doing so can help you stand out in a crowd, and it lets you verify receipt. Alternatively, if you've prepared the document for a single person or small group in your office or the local area, delivering it in person will give you the chance to personally "introduce" the report and remind readers why they're receiving it.

The work plan also explains who will be responsible for the various tasks.

Ms. Joyce Colton, AGI Builders   Page 2   July 31, 2017

Kevin Patel will be the lead field technician responsible for the project. A copy of his résumé is included with this proposal for your review. Kevin will coordinate field activities with your job site superintendent and make sure that appropriate personnel are assigned to the job site. Overall project management will be the responsibility of Joseph Proesel. Project engineering services will be performed under the direction of Dixon O'Donnell, P.E. All field personnel assigned to the site will be familiar with and abide by the Project Site Health and Safety Plan prepared by Carlson Environmental, Inc., dated April 2017.

The project leader's résumé is attached to the proposal, providing additional detail without cluttering up the body of the proposal.

Qualifications

O'Donnell & Associates has been providing quality professional services since 1972 in the areas of

The qualifications section grabs attention by mentioning compelling qualifications.

- Geotechnical engineering
- Materials testing and inspection
- Pavement evaluation
- Environmental services
- Engineering and technical support (CADD) services

The company provides Phase I and Phase II environmental site assessments, preparation of LUST site closure reports, installation of groundwater monitoring wells, and testing of soil/groundwater samples for environmental contaminants. Geotechnical services include all phases of soil mechanics and foundation engineering, including foundation and lateral load analysis, slope stability analysis, site preparation recommendations, see page analysis, pavement design, and settlement analysis.

O'Donnell & Associates materials testing laboratory is certified by AASHTO Accreditation Program for the testing of Soils, Aggregate, Hot Mix Asphalt and Portland Cement Concrete. A copy of our laboratory certification is included with this proposal. In addition to in-house training, field and laboratory technicians participate in a variety of certification programs, including those sponsored by the American Concrete Institute (ACI) and Illinois Department of Transportation (IDOT).

Describing *certifications* (approvals by recognized industry associations or government agencies) helps build the company's credibility.

Costs

On the basis of our understanding of the scope of the work, we estimate the total cost of the two projects to be $100,260.00, as follows:

(continued)

Figure 15.3 **External Solicited Proposal (*continued*)**

For digital distribution, unless your audience specifically requests a word processor file, provide documents as portable document format (PDF) files. Using Adobe Acrobat or similar products, you can quickly convert reports and proposals to PDF files that are easy to share digitally. PDFs are generally considered safer than word processor files, but keep in mind that they can also be used to transmit computer viruses.[8]

Many businesses use the Adobe portable document format (PDF) to distribute reports electronically.

If your company or client expects you to distribute your reports via a web-based content management system, a shared workspace, or some other online location, double-check that you've uploaded the correct file(s) to the correct location. Verify the on-screen display of your reports after you've posted them, making sure graphics, charts, links, and other elements are in place and operational.

For a reminder of the tasks involved in producing formal reports and proposals, see "Checklist: Producing Formal Reports and Proposals."

Cost Estimates

Cost Estimate: Mass Grading	Units	Rate ($)	Total Cost ($)
Field Inspection			
Labor	1,320 hours	$38.50	$ 50,820.00
Nuclear Moisture Density Meter	132 days	35.00	4,620.00
Vehicle Expense	132 days	45.00	5,940.00
Laboratory Testing			
Proctor Density Tests (ASTM D-1557)	4 tests	130.00	520.00
Engineering/Project Management			
Principal Engineer	16 hours	110.00	1,760.00
Project Manager	20 hours	80.00	1,600.00
Administrative Assistant	12 hours	50.00	600.00
Subtotal			**$ 65,860.00**

Cost Estimate: Utility Work	Units	Rate ($)	Total Cost ($)
Field Inspection			
Labor	660 hours	$ 38.50	$ 25,410.00
Nuclear Moisture Density Meter	66 days	5.00	2,310.00
Vehicle Expense	66 days	45.00	2,970.00
Laboratory Testing			
Proctor Density Tests (ASTM D-1557)	2 tests	130.00	260.00
Engineering/Project Management			
Principal Engineer	10 hours	110.00	1,100.00
Project Manager	20 hours	80.00	1,600.00
Administrative Assistant	15 hours	50.00	750.00
Subtotal			**$ 34,400.00**
Total Project Costs			**$100,260.00**

> A clear and complete itemization of estimated costs builds confidence in the dependability of the project's financial projections.

This estimate assumes full-time inspection services. However, our services may also be performed on an as-requested basis, and actual charges will reflect time associated with the project. We have attached our standard fee schedule for your review. Overtime rates are for hours in excess of 8.0 hours per day, before 7:00 a.m., after 5:00 p.m., and on holidays and weekends.

> To give the client some budgetary flexibility, the proposal offers an alternative to the fixed-fee approach—which may lower any resistance to accepting the bid.

Figure 15.3   External Solicited Proposal (*continued*)

(continued)

CHECKLIST ✓   Producing Formal Reports and Proposals

A. Prefatory parts
- Use your company's standard report covers, if available.
- Include a concise, descriptive title on the cover.
- Include a title fly only if you want an extra-formal touch.
- On the title page, list (1) the report title; (2) the name, title, and address of the group or person who authorized the report; (3) the name, title, and address of the group or person who prepared the report; and (4) the date of submission.
- Include a copy of the letter of authorization, if appropriate.
- If responding to an RFP, follow its instructions for including a copy or referring to the RFP by name or tracking number.
- Include a letter of transmittal that introduces the report.
- Provide a table of contents in outline form, with headings worded exactly as they appear in the body of the report.
- Include a list of illustrations if the report contains a large number of them.
- Include a synopsis (brief summary of the report) or an executive summary (a condensed, "mini" version of the report) for longer reports.

B. Body of the report
- Draft an introduction that prepares the reader for the content that follows.
- Provide information that supports your conclusions, recommendations, or proposals in the body of the report.
- Don't overload the body with unnecessary detail.
- Close with a summary of your main idea.

C. Supplementary parts
- Use appendixes to provide supplementary information or supporting evidence.
- List in a bibliography any secondary sources you used.
- Provide an index if your report contains a large number of terms or ideas and is likely to be consulted over time.

Ms. Joyce Colton, AGI Builders   Page 4   July 31, 2017

Authorization

With a staff of over 30 personnel, including registered professional engineers, resident engineers, geologists, construction inspectors, laboratory technicians, and drillers, we are confident that O'Donnell & Associates is capable of providing the services required for a project of this magnitude.

The brief close emphasizes the bidder's qualifications and asks for a decision.

If you would like our firm to provide the services as outlined in this proposal, please sign this letter and return it to us along with a certified check in the amount of $10,000 (our retainer) by August 14, 2017. Please call me if you have any questions regarding the terms of this proposal or our approach.

Sincerely,

Dixon O'Donnell

Dixon O'Donnell
Vice President

Enclosures

The call to action clarifies the steps needed to put the project in motion.

Accepted for AGI BUILDERS, INC.

By_____   Date _____

The customer's signature will make the proposal a binding contract.

Figure 15.3   External Solicited Proposal (*continued*)

Writing Requests for Proposals

At some point in your career, you might be in a position to solicit proposals, and learning how to request effective proposals will simplify the process considerably. When writing an RFP, remember that it is more than just a request; it's an informational report that provides potential bidders with the information they need in order to craft effective proposals. Writing an RFP demands careful consideration because it starts a process that leads to a proposal, a contract, and eventually the delivery of a product or the performance of a service. In other words, mistakes at the RFP stage can ripple throughout the process and create costly headaches for everyone involved.

An RFP's specific content will vary widely from industry to industry, but all RFPs should include some combination of the following elements:[9]

- **Company background.** Give potential bidders some background information on your organization, your business priorities, and other information they might need in order to respond in an informed manner.

5 LEARNING OBJECTIVE
Identify the elements to include in a request for proposals (RFP).

- **Project description.** Put your requirements in context; are you seeking bids for routine supplies or services, or do you need a major computer system?
- **Requirements.** The requirements section should spell out everything you expect from potential vendors; don't leave anything to unstated assumptions. Will potential vendors provide key equipment or will you? Will you expect vendors to work under confidentiality restrictions, such as a nondisclosure agreement? Who will pay if costs run higher than expected? Will you require ongoing service or support? Providing this information can be a lot of work, but again, overlooking anything at this point is likely to create considerable problems once the project gets rolling.
- **Decision criteria.** Let bidders know how you'll be making the decision. Is quality more important than cost? Will you consider only certain types of vendors or only those that use certain processes or technologies? Will you entertain bids from companies that have never worked in your particular industry? The answers to such questions not only help bidders determine whether they're right for your project but also help them craft proposals that meet your needs.
- **Proposal requirements.** Explain exactly what you expect to see in the proposal itself—which sections, what media, how many copies, and so on.
- **Submission and contact information.** A well-written RFP answers most potential questions, and it also tells people when, where, and how to respond. In addition, effective RFPs always give bidders the name of a contact within the organization who can answer detailed questions.

A smart approach to managing RFPs can minimize the work involved for everyone and maximize the effectiveness of the RFP. First, identify your decision criteria and then brainstorm the information you need to measure against those criteria. Don't ask bidders to submit information about every aspect of their operations if such details aren't relevant to your decision. Making such unreasonable demands is unfair to bidders, will unnecessarily complicate your review process, and will discourage some potentially attractive bidders from responding.

Second, to get quality responses that match your unique business needs, give bidders plenty of time to respond. Successful companies are usually busy responding to other RFPs and working on other projects; you can't expect them to drop everything to focus solely on your RFP.

Third, if your company generates numerous RFPs, tracking proposals can become a full-time job. Consider establishing an online system for tracking responses automatically.[10]

Analyzing a Formal Report

The report presented in the following pages was prepared by Linda Moreno, the cost accounting manager at Electrovision. Electrovision's main product is optical character recognition equipment, which is used by the U.S. Postal Service for sorting mail. Moreno's job is to help analyze the company's costs, and she has this to say about the background of the report:

> For the past three or four years, Electrovision has been on a roll. Our A-12 optical character reader was a real breakthrough, and the post office grabbed up as many as we could make. Our sales and profits kept climbing, and morale was fantastic. Everybody seemed to think that the good times would last forever. Unfortunately, everybody was wrong. When the Postal Service announced that it was postponing all new equipment purchases because of cuts in its budget, we woke up to the fact that we are essentially a one-product company with one customer. At that point, management started scrambling around looking for ways to cut costs until we could diversify our business a bit.
>
> The vice president of operations, Dennis McWilliams, asked me to help identify cost-cutting opportunities in travel and entertainment. On the basis of his personal observations, he felt that Electrovision was overly generous in its travel policies and that we might be able to save a significant amount by controlling these costs more carefully. My investigation confirmed his suspicion.
>
> I was reasonably confident that my report would be well received. I've worked with Dennis for several years and know what he likes: plenty of facts, clearly stated conclusions, and specific recommendations for what should be done next. I also knew that my report would be passed on to other Electrovision executives, so I wanted to create a good impression. I wanted the report to be accurate and thorough, visually appealing, readable, and appropriate in tone.

When writing the analytical report that follows, Moreno based the organization on conclusions and recommendations presented in direct order. The first two sections of the report correspond to Moreno's two main conclusions: that Electrovision's travel and entertainment costs are too high and that cuts are essential. The third section presents recommendations for achieving better control over travel and entertainment expenses. As you review the report, analyze both the mechanical aspects and the way Moreno presents her ideas. Be prepared to discuss the way the various components convey and reinforce the main message.

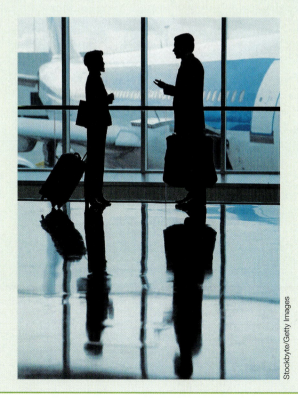

Stockbyte/Getty Images

**Reducing Electrovision's
Travel and Entertainment Costs**

Prepared for

Dennis McWilliams,

Vice President of Operations

Electrovision, Inc.

Prepared by

Linda Moreno, Manager

Cost Accounting Services

Electrovision, Inc.

February 16, 2018

← Large, bold type distinguishes the title from the other elements on the cover.

← The name of the recipient, if applicable, typically comes after the title.

← Generous use of white space between elements gives the cover an open feel.

Dating the report gives it a feeling of currency when it is submitted and, conversely, as time passes, signals to future readers that the material might be out of date at that point.

The "how-to" tone of Moreno's title is appropriate for an action-oriented report that emphasizes recommendations. A more neutral title, such as "An Analysis of Electrovision's Travel and Entertainment Costs," would be more suitable for an informational report.

The memo format is appropriate for this internal report; the letter format would be used for transmitting an external report.

The tone is conversational yet still businesslike and respectful.

Acknowledging help given by others is good etiquette and a way to foster positive working relationships.

MEMORANDUM

TO: Dennis McWilliams, Vice President of Operations
FROM: Linda Moreno, Manager of Cost Accounting Services *LM*
DATE: February 16, 2018
SUBJECT: Reducing Electrovision's Travel and Entertainment Costs

Here is the report you requested January 28 on Electrovision's travel and entertainment costs.

Your suspicions were right. We are spending far too much on business travel. Our unwritten policy has been "anything goes," leaving us with no real control over T&E expenses. Although this hands-off approach may have been understandable when Electrovision's profits were high, we can no longer afford the luxury of going first class.

The solutions to the problem seem rather clear. We need to have someone with centralized responsibility for travel and entertainment costs, a clear statement of policy, an effective control system, and a business-oriented travel service that can optimize our travel arrangements. We should also investigate alternatives to travel, such as videoconferencing.

Getting people to economize is not going to be easy. In the course of researching this issue, I've found that our employees are deeply attached to their generous travel privileges. I think some would almost prefer a cut in pay to a loss in travel status. We'll need a lot of top management involvement to sell people on the need for moderation.

I'm grateful to Mary Lehman and Connie McIllvain for their considerable help in rounding up and sorting through five years' worth of expense reports.

Thanks for giving me the opportunity to work on this assignment. It's been a real education. If you have any questions about the report, please give me a call.

Moreno expects a positive response, so she presents her main conclusion right away.

She closes graciously, with thanks and an offer to discuss the results.

In this report, Moreno decided to write a brief memo of transmittal and include a separate executive summary. Short reports (fewer than 10 pages) often combine the synopsis or executive summary with the memo or letter of transmittal.

The table of contents doesn't include any elements that appear before the "Contents" page.

The headings are worded exactly as they appear in the text.

Moreno lists the figures because they are all significant, and the list is fairly short.

This and other prefatory pages are numbered with Roman numerals.

CONTENTS

The table lists only the page number on which a section begins, not the entire range of numbers.

LIST OF ILLUSTRATIONS

Moreno included only first- and second-level headings in her table of contents, even though the report contains third-level headings. She prefers a shorter table of contents that focuses attention on the main divisions of thought. She used informative titles, which are appropriate for a report to a receptive audience.

The executive summary begins by stating the purpose of the report.

Moreno presents the points in the executive summary in the same order as they appear in the report, using subheadings that summarize the content of the main sections of the report.

EXECUTIVE SUMMARY

This report analyzes Electrovision's travel and entertainment (T&E) costs and presents recommendations for reducing those costs.

Travel and Entertainment Costs Are Too High

Travel and entertainment is a large and growing expense category for Electrovision. The company spends over $16 million per year on business travel, and these costs have been increasing by 12 percent annually. Company employees make roughly 3,390 trips each year at an average cost per trip of $4,720. Airfares are the biggest expense, followed by hotels, meals, and rental cars.

The nature of Electrovision's business does require extensive travel, but the company's costs are excessive: Our employees spend more than twice the national average on travel and entertainment. Although the location of the company's facilities may partly explain this discrepancy, the main reason for our high costs is a management style that gives employees little incentive to economize.

Cuts Are Essential

Electrovision management now recognizes the need to gain more control over this element of costs. The company is currently entering a period of declining profits, prompting management to look for every opportunity to reduce spending. At the same time, rising airfares and hotel rates are making T&E expenses more significant.

Electrovision Can Save $6 Million per Year

Fortunately, Electrovision has a number of excellent opportunities for reducing T&E costs. Savings of up to $6 million per year should be achievable, judging by the experience of other companies. A sensible travel-management program can save companies as much as 35 percent a year (Gilligan 39–40), and we should be able to save even more, since we purchase many more business-class tickets than the average. Four steps will help us cut costs:

1. Hire a director of travel and entertainment to assume overall responsibility for T&E spending, policies, and technologies, including the hiring and management of a national travel agency.
2. Educate employees on the need for cost containment, both in avoiding unnecessary travel and reducing costs when travel is necessary.
3. Negotiate preferential rates with travel providers.
4. Implement technological alternatives to travel, such as virtual meetings.

As necessary as these changes are, they will likely hurt morale, at least in the short term. Management will need to make a determined effort to explain the rationale for reduced spending. By exercising moderation in their own travel arrangements, Electrovision executives can set a good example and help other employees accept the changes. On the plus side, using travel alternatives such as web conferencing will reduce the travel burden on many employees and help them balance their business and personal lives.

Her audience is receptive, so the tone in the executive summary is forceful; a more neutral approach would be better for hostile or skeptical readers.

The executive summary uses the same font and paragraph treatment as the text of the report.

The page numbering in the executive summary continues with Roman numerals.

Moreno decided to include an executive summary because her report is aimed at a mixed audience, some of whom are interested in the details of her report and others who just want the "big picture." The executive summary is aimed at the second group, giving them enough information to make a decision without burdening them with the task of reading the entire report.

Her writing style matches the serious nature of the content without sounding distant or stiff. Moreno chose the formal approach because several members of her audience are considerably higher up in the organization, and she did not want to sound too familiar. In addition, her company prefers the impersonal style for formal reports.

A color bar highlights the report title and the first-level headings; a variety of other design treatments are possible as well.

REDUCING ELECTROVISION'S TRAVEL AND ENTERTAINMENT COSTS

INTRODUCTION

Electrovision has always encouraged a significant amount of business travel. To compensate employees for the stress and inconvenience of frequent trips, management has authorized generous travel and entertainment (T&E) allowances. This philosophy has been good for morale, but last year Electrovision spent $16 million on travel and entertainment—$7 million more than it spent on research and development.

The introduction opens by establishing the need for action.

This year's T&E costs will affect profits even more because of increases in airline fares and hotel rates. Also, the company anticipates that profits will be relatively weak for a variety of other reasons. Therefore, Dennis McWilliams, Vice President of Operations, has asked the accounting department to explore ways to reduce the T&E budget.

The purpose of this report is to analyze T&E expenses, evaluate the effect of recent hotel and airfare increases, and suggest ways to tighten control over T&E costs. The report outlines several steps that could reduce Electrovision's expenses, but the precise financial impact of these measures is difficult to project. The estimates presented here provide a "best guess" of what Electrovision can expect to save.

In preparing this report, the accounting department analyzed internal expense reports for the past five years to determine how much Electrovision spends on travel and entertainment. These figures were then compared with average statistics compiled by Dow Jones (publisher of the *Wall Street Journal*) and presented as the Dow Jones Travel Index. We also analyzed trends and suggestions published in a variety of business journal articles to see how other companies are coping with the high cost of business travel.

Moreno mentions her sources and methods to increase credibility and to give readers a complete picture of the study's background.

THE HIGH COST OF TRAVEL AND ENTERTAINMENT

Although many companies view travel and entertainment as an incidental cost of doing business, the dollars add up. At Electrovision the bill for airfares, hotels, rental cars, meals, and entertainment totaled $16 million last year. Our T&E budget has increased by 12 percent per year for the past five years. Compared with the average U.S. business traveler, Electrovision's expenditures are high, largely because of management's generous policy on travel benefits.

A *running footer* that contains the report title and the page number appears on every page.

In her brief introduction, Moreno counts on topic sentences and transitions to indicate that she is discussing the purpose, scope, and limitations of the study.

$16 Million per Year Spent on Travel and Entertainment

Electrovision's annual budget for T&E is only 8 percent of sales. Because this is a relatively small expense category compared with such things as salaries and commissions, it is tempting to dismiss T&E costs as insignificant. However, T&E is Electrovision's third-largest controllable expense, directly behind salaries and information systems.

Last year Electrovision personnel made about 3,390 trips at an average cost per trip of $4,720. The typical trip involved a round-trip flight of 3,000 miles, meals, hotel accommodations for two or three days, and a rental car. Roughly 80 percent of trips were made by 20 percent of the staff—top management and sales personnel traveled most, averaging 18 trips per year.

Figure 1 illustrates how the T&E budget is spent. The largest categories are airfares and lodging, which together account for $7 of every $10 that employees spend on T&E. This spending breakdown has been relatively steady for the past five years and is consistent with the distribution of expenses experienced by other companies.

Figure 1
Airfares and Lodging Account for Over
Two-Thirds of Electrovision's T&E Budget

Although the composition of the T&E budget has been consistent, its size has not. As mentioned earlier, these expenditures have increased by about 12 percent per year for the past five years, roughly twice the rate of the company's sales growth (see Figure 2). This rate of growth makes T&E Electrovision's fastest-growing expense item.

Figure 2
T&E Expenses Continue to Increase as a
Percentage of Sales

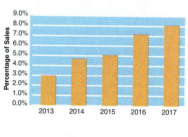

The visual is placed as close as possible to the point it illustrates.

Each visual has a title that clearly indicates what it's about; titles are consistently placed to the left of each visual.

Moreno opens the first main section of the body with a topic sentence that introduces an important fact about the subject of the section. Then she orients the reader to the three major points developed in the section.

Electrovision's Travel Expenses Exceed National Averages

Much of our travel budget is justified. Two major factors contribute to Electrovision's high T&E budget:

- With our headquarters on the West Coast and our major customer on the East Coast, we naturally spend a lot of money on cross-country flights.

- A great deal of travel takes place between our headquarters here on the West Coast and the manufacturing operations in Detroit, Boston, and Dallas. Corporate managers and division personnel make frequent trips to coordinate these disparate operations.

However, even though a good portion of Electrovision's travel budget is justifiable, the company spends considerably more on T&E than the average business traveler (see Figure 3).

Figure 3
Electrovision Employees Spend Over Twice as Much as the Average Business Traveler

Source: *Wall Street Journal* and company records

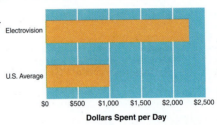

Dollars Spent per Day

The Dow Jones Travel Index calculates the average cost per day of business travel in the United States, based on average airfare, hotel rates, and rental car rates. The average fluctuates weekly as travel companies change their rates, but it has been running at about $1,000 per day for the last year or so. In contrast, Electrovision's average daily expense over the past year has been $2,250—a hefty 125 percent higher than average. This figure is based on the average trip cost of $4,720 listed earlier and an average trip length of 2.1 days.

Spending Has Been Encouraged

Although a variety of factors may contribute to this differential, Electrovision's relatively high T&E costs are at least partially attributable to the company's philosophy and management style. Since many employees do not enjoy business travel, management has tried to make the trips more pleasant by authorizing business-class airfare, luxury hotel accommodations, and full-size rental cars. The sales staff is encouraged to entertain clients at top restaurants and to invite them to cultural and sporting events.

The visuals are numbered consecutively and referred to by their numbers in the text.

Moreno introduces visuals before they appear and indicates what readers should notice about the data.

The chart in Figure 3 is simple but effective; Moreno includes just enough data to make her point. Notice how she is as careful about the appearance of her report as she is about the quality of its content.

The cost of these privileges is easy to overlook, given the weakness of Electrovision's system for tracking T&E expenses:

A bulleted list makes it easy for readers to identify and distinguish related points.

- The monthly financial records do not contain a separate category for travel and entertainment; the information is buried under Cost of Goods Sold and under Selling, General, and Administrative Expenses.

- Each department head is given authority to approve any expense report, regardless of how large it may be.

- Receipts are not required for expenditures less than $100.

- Individuals are allowed to make their own travel arrangements.

- No one is charged with the responsibility for controlling the company's total spending on travel and entertainment.

GROWING IMPACT ON THE BOTTOM LINE

During the past three years, the company's healthy profits have resulted in relatively little pressure to push for tighter controls over all aspects of the business. However, as we all know, the situation is changing. We're projecting flat to declining profits for the next two years, a situation that has prompted all of us to search for ways to cut costs. At the same time, rising airfares and hotel rates have increased the impact of T&E expenses on the company's financial results.

Lower Profits Underscore the Need for Change

The next two years promise to be difficult for Electrovision. After several years of steady increases in spending, the Postal Service is tightening procurement policies for automated mail-handling equipment. Funding for the A-12 optical character reader has been canceled. As a consequence, the marketing department expects sales to drop by 15 percent. Although Electrovision is negotiating several other promising R&D contracts, the marketing department does not foresee any major procurements for the next two to three years.

At the same time, Electrovision is facing cost increases on several fronts. As we have known for several months, the new production facility now under construction in Salt Lake City, Utah, is behind schedule and over budget. Labor contracts in Boston and Dallas will expire within the next six months, and plant managers there anticipate that significant salary and benefits concessions may be necessary to avoid strikes.

Moreover, marketing and advertising costs are expected to increase as we attempt to strengthen these activities to better cope with competitive pressures. Given the expected decline in revenues and increase in costs, the Executive Committee's prediction that profits will fall by 12 percent in the coming fiscal year does not seem overly pessimistic.

Informative headings focus reader attention on the main points. Such headings are appropriate when a report uses the direct approach and is intended for a receptive audience. However, descriptive headings are more effective when a report uses the indirect approach and readers are less receptive.

Moreno designed her report to include plenty of white space so even those pages that lack visuals are still attractive and easy to read.

Moreno supports her argument with objective facts and sound reasoning.

The recommendations are realistic, noting both the benefits and the risks of taking action.

Airfares and Hotel Rates Are Rising

Business travelers have grown accustomed to frequent fare wars and discounting in the travel industry in recent years. Excess capacity and aggressive price competition, particularly in the airline business, made travel a relative bargain.

However, that situation has changed as weaker competitors have been forced out and the remaining players have grown stronger and smarter. Airlines and hotels are better at managing inventory and keeping occupancy rates high, which translates into higher costs for Electrovision. Last year saw some of the steepest rate hikes in years. Business airfares (tickets most likely to be purchased by business travelers) jumped more than 40 percent in many markets. The trend is expected to continue, with rates increasing another 5 to 10 percent overall (Phillips 331; "Travel Costs Under Pressure" 30; Dahl B6).

Given the fact that air and hotel costs account for almost 70 percent of our T&E budget, the trend toward higher prices in these two categories will have serious consequences, unless management takes action to control these costs.

METHODS FOR REDUCING T&E COSTS

By implementing a number of reforms, management can expect to reduce Electrovision's T&E budget by as much as 40 percent. This estimate is based on the general assessment made by American Express (Gilligan 39) and on the fact that we have an opportunity to significantly reduce air travel costs by eliminating business-class travel. However, these measures are likely to be unpopular with employees. To gain acceptance for such changes, management will need to sell employees on the need for moderation in T&E allowances.

Four Ways to Trim Expenses

By researching what other companies are doing to curb T&E expenses, the accounting department has identified four prominent opportunities that should enable Electrovision to save about $6 million annually in travel-related costs.

Institute Tighter Spending Controls

A single individual should be appointed director of travel and entertainment to spearhead the effort to gain control of the T&E budget. More than a third of all U.S. companies now employ travel managers ("Businesses Use Savvy Managers" 4). The director should be familiar with the travel industry and should be well versed in both accounting and information technology. The director should also report to the vice president of operations. The director's first priorities should be to establish a written T&E policy and a cost-control system.

Electrovision currently has no written policy on T&E, a step that is widely recommended by air travel experts (Smith D4). Creating a policy would clarify management's position and serve as a vehicle for communicating the need for moderation.

Moreno creates a forceful tone by using action verbs in the third-level subheadings of this section. This approach is appropriate to the nature of the study and the attitude of the audience. However, in a status-conscious organization, the imperative verbs might sound a bit too presumptuous coming from a junior member of the staff.

At a minimum, the policy should include the following:

- All T&E should be strictly related to business and should be approved in advance.

- Except under special circumstances to be approved on a case-by-case basis, employees should travel by coach and stay in mid-range business hotels.

- The T&E policy should apply equally to employees at all levels.

To implement the new policy, Electrovision will need to create a system for controlling T&E expenses. Each department should prepare an annual T&E budget as part of its operating plan. These budgets should be presented in detail so that management can evaluate how T&E dollars will be spent and can recommend appropriate cuts. To help management monitor performance relative to these budgets, the director of travel should prepare monthly financial statements showing actual T&E expenditures by department.

The director of travel should also be responsible for retaining a business-oriented travel service that will schedule all employee business trips and look for the best travel deals, particularly in airfares. In addition to centralizing Electrovision's reservation and ticketing activities, the agency will negotiate reduced group rates with hotels and rental car firms. The agency selected should have offices nationwide so that all Electrovision facilities can channel their reservations through the same company. This is particularly important in light of the dizzying array of often wildly different airfares available between some cities. It's not uncommon to find dozens of fares along commonly traveled routes (Rowe 30). In addition, the director can help coordinate travel across the company to secure group discounts whenever possible (Barker 31; Miller B6).

Reduce Unnecessary Travel and Entertainment

One of the easiest ways to reduce expenses is to reduce the amount of traveling and entertaining that occurs. An analysis of last year's expenditures suggests that as much as 30 percent of Electrovision's T&E is discretionary. The professional staff spent $2.8 million attending seminars and conferences last year. Although these gatherings are undoubtedly beneficial, the company could save money by sending fewer representives to each function and perhaps by eliminating some of the less valuable seminars.

Similarly, Electrovision could economize on trips between headquarters and divisions by reducing the frequency of such visits and by sending fewer people on each trip. Although there is often no substitute for face-to-face meetings, management could try to resolve more internal issues through telephone, electronic, and written communication.

Electrovision can also reduce spending by urging employees to economize. Instead of flying business class, employees can fly coach class or take advantage of discount fares. Rather than ordering a $50 bottle of wine, employees can select a less expensive bottle or dispense with alcohol entirely. People can book rooms at moderately priced hotels and drive smaller rental cars.

In addition to making key points easy to find, bulleted lists help break up the text to relieve the reader's eye.

Moreno lists the steps needed to implement her recommendations.

Moreno takes care not to overstep the boundaries of her analysis. For instance, she doesn't analyze the value of the seminars that employees attend every year, so she avoids any absolute statements about reducing travel to seminars.

Obtain Lowest Rates from Travel Providers

Apart from urging employees to economize, Electrovision can also save money by searching for the lowest available airfares, hotel rates, and rental car fees. Currently, few employees have the time or knowledge to seek out travel bargains. When they need to travel, they make the most convenient and comfortable arrangements. A professional travel service will be able to obtain lower rates from travel providers.

Judging by the experience of other companies, Electrovision may be able to trim as much as 30 to 40 percent from the travel budget simply by looking for bargains in airfares and negotiating group rates with hotels and rental car companies. Electrovision should be able to achieve these economies by analyzing its travel patterns, identifying frequently visited locations, and selecting a few hotels that are willing to reduce rates in exchange for guaranteed business. At the same time, the company should be able to save up to 40 percent on rental car charges by negotiating a corporate rate.

The possibilities for economizing are promising; however, making the best travel arrangements often requires trade-offs such as the following:

- The best fares might not always be the lowest. Indirect flights are usually cheaper, but they take longer and may end up costing more in lost work time.

- The cheapest tickets often require booking 14 or even 30 days in advance, which is often impossible for us.

- Discount tickets are usually nonrefundable, which is a serious drawback when a trip needs to be canceled at the last minute.

Replace Travel with Technological Alternatives

Online meeting systems such as WebEx and GoTo Meeting offer a compelling alternative to many instances of business travel. With webcam video, application/ screen sharing, and collaboration tools such as virtual whiteboards, they have made great strides toward replicating the in-person meeting experience.

As effective as they can be, though, they shouldn't automatically replace every in-person meeting. When establishing a business relationship, for example, meeting face to face is an important part of building trust and getting past the uncertainties of working with a new partner. Part of the new travel director's job would be to draft guidelines for choosing travel or online meeting options.

By pointing out possible difficulties and showing that she has considered all angles, Moreno builds reader confidence in her judgment.

Note how Moreno makes the transition from section to section. The first sentence under the second heading on this page refers to the subject of the previous paragraph and signals a shift in thought.

An informative title in the table is consistent with the way headings are handled throughout this report, and it is appropriate for a report to a receptive audience.

The Impact of Reforms

By implementing tighter controls, reducing unnecessary expenses, negotiating more favorable rates, and exploring alternatives to travel, Electrovision should be able to reduce its T&E budget significantly. As Table 1 illustrates, the combined savings should be in the neighborhood of $6 million, although the precise figures are somewhat difficult to project.

Table 1
Electrovision Can Trim Travel and Entertainment Costs by an Estimated $6 Million per Year

SOURCE OF SAVINGS	ESTIMATED SAVINGS
Switching from business-class to coach airfare	$2,300,000
Negotiating preferred hotel rates	940,000
Negotiating preferred rental car rates	460,000
Systematically searching for lower airfares	375,000
Reducing interdivisional travel	675,000
Reducing seminar and conference attendance	1,250,000
TOTAL POTENTIAL SAVINGS	**$6,000,000**

To achieve the economies outlined in the table, Electrovision will incur expenses for hiring a director of travel and for implementing a T&E cost-control system. These costs are projected at $115,000: $105,000 per year in salary and benefits for the new employee and a one-time expense of $10,000 for the cost-control system. The cost of retaining a full-service travel agency is negligible, even with the service fees that many are now passing along from airlines and other service providers.

The measures required to achieve these savings are likely to be unpopular with employees. Electrovision personnel are accustomed to generous T&E allowances, and they are likely to resent having these privileges curtailed. To alleviate their disappointment

- Management should make a determined effort to explain why the changes are necessary.

- The director of corporate communication should be asked to develop a multi-faceted campaign that will communicate the importance of curtailing T&E costs.

- Management should set a positive example by adhering strictly to the new policies.

- The limitations should apply equally to employees at all levels in the organization.

The in-text reference to the table highlights the key point the reader should get from the table.

Including financial estimates helps management envision the impact of the suggestions, even though the estimated savings are difficult to project accurately.

Note how Moreno calls attention in the first paragraph to items in the following table, without repeating the information in the table.

She uses a descriptive heading for the last section of the text. In informational reports, this section is often called "Summary"; in analytical reports, it is called "Conclusions" or "Conclusions and Recommendations."

Presenting the recommendations in a list gives each one emphasis.

Moreno summarizes her conclusions in the first two paragraphs—a good approach because she organized her report around conclusions and recommendations, so readers have already been introduced to them.

CONCLUSIONS AND RECOMMENDATIONS

Electrovision is currently spending $16 million per year on T&E. Although much of this spending is justified, the company's costs are high relative to competitors' costs, mainly because Electrovision has been generous with its travel benefits.

Electrovision's liberal approach to T&E was understandable during years of high profitability; however, the company is facing the prospect of declining profits for the next several years. Management is therefore motivated to cut costs in all areas of the business. Reducing T&E spending is particularly important because the bottom-line impact of these costs will increase as airline fares increase.

Electrovision should be able to reduce T&E costs by as much as 40 percent by taking four important steps:

1. *Institute tighter spending controls.* Management should hire a director of travel and entertainment who will assume overall responsibility for T&E activities. Within the next six months, this director should develop a written travel policy, institute a T&E budget and a cost-control system, and retain a professional, business-oriented travel agency that will optimize arrangements with travel providers.

2. *Reduce unnecessary travel and entertainment.* Electrovision should encourage employees to economize on T&E spending. Management can accomplish this by authorizing fewer trips and by urging employees to be more conservative in their spending.

3. *Obtain lowest rates from travel providers.* Electrovision should also focus on obtaining the best rates on airline tickets, hotel rooms, and rental cars. By channeling all arrangements through a professional travel agency, the company can optimize its choices and gain clout in negotiating preferred rates.

4. *Replace some travel with technological alternatives.* Online meeting system should be adequate for most of our tactical meetings with established clients and for most internal communication as well.

Because these measures may be unpopular with employees, management should make a concerted effort to explain the importance of reducing travel costs. The director of corporate communication should be given responsibility for developing a plan to communicate the need for employee cooperation.

Moreno doesn't introduce any new facts in this section. In a longer report she might have divided this section into subsections, labeled "Conclusions" and "Recommendations," to distinguish between the two.

WORKS CITED

Barker, Julie. "How to Rein in Group Travel Costs." *Successful Meetings* Feb. 2017: 31. Print.

"Businesses Use Savvy Managers to Keep Travel Costs Down." *Christian Science Monitor* 17 July 2016: 4. Print.

Dahl, Jonathan. "2000: The Year Travel Costs Took Off." *Wall Street Journal* 29 Dec. 2016: B6. Print.

Gilligan, Edward P. "Trimming Your T&E Is Easier Than You Think." *Managing Office Technology* Nov. 2015: 39–40. Print.

Miller, Lisa. "Attention, Airline Ticket Shoppers." *Wall Street Journal* 7 July 2015: B6. Print.

Phillips, Edward H. "Airlines Post Record Traffic." *Aviation Week & Space Technology* 8 Jan. 2016: 331. Print.

"Product Overview: Cisco WebEx Meeting Center," *Webex.com.* Web Ex, n.d. 2 Feb. 2016. Web.

Rowe, Irene Vlitos. "Global Solution for Cutting Travel Costs." *European Business* 12 Oct. 2016: 30. Print.

Smith, Carol. "Rising, Erratic Airfares Make Company Policy Vital." *Los Angeles Times* 2 Nov. 2017: D4. Print.

Solheim, Shelley. "Web Conferencing Made Easy." *eWeek* 22 Aug. 2017: 26. Web.

"Travel Costs Under Pressure." *Purchasing* 15 Feb. 2016: 30. Print.

MLA style lists references alphabetically by the author's last name, and when the author is unknown, by the title of the reference. (See Appendix B for additional details on preparing reference lists.)

Moreno's list of references follows the style recommended in the *MLA Style Manual*. The box below shows how these sources would be cited following American Psychological Association (APA) style.

REFERENCES

Barker, J. (2017, February). How to rein in group travel costs. *Successful Meetings*, p. 31.

Businesses use savvy managers to keep travel costs down. (2016, July 17). *Christian Science Monitor*, p. 4.

Dahl, J. (2016, December 29). 2000: The year travel costs took off. *Wall Street Journal*, p. B6.

Gilligan, E. (2015, November). Trimming your T&E is easier than you think. *Managing Office Technology*, pp. 39–40.

Miller, L. (2015, July 7). Attention, airline ticket shoppers. *Wall Street Journal*, p. B6.

Phillips, E. (2016, January 8). *Aviation Week & Space Technology*, p. 331.

Rowe, I. (2016, October 12). Global solution for cutting travel costs. *European*, p. 30.

Smith, C. (2017, November 2). Rising, erratic airfares make company policy vital. *Los Angeles Times*, D4.

Solheim, S. (2017, August 22). Web conferencing made easy. *eWeek*, p. 26.

Travel costs under pressure. (2016, February 15). *Purchasing*, p. 30.

WebEx.com. (2017). Cisco WebEx Meeting Center. Retrieved from http://www.webex.com/product-overview/index.html

COMMUNICATION CHALLENGES AT **WPP**

You've joined the corporate communications department at WPP's headquarters in London, where you get to work on a variety of major projects. Address these challenges.

INDIVIDUAL CHALLENGE: Visit the Reading Room on WPP's website at wpp.com (look for the tab along the top of the screen). Browse the topic categories down the left side (Advertising, Branding, Consumer Insights, and so on). Find any article that interests you and prepare a brief summary (no more than 250 words) that would be easy to read on a small mobile device.

TEAM CHALLENGE: Find WPP's latest Sustainability Report on the company's website (you should see a "Sustainability" link at the top of the page). Select the report and find the "Client case studies," a series of short multimedia reports on communication campaigns the company has done for various nonprofits and nongovernmental organizations (NGOs). Find three cases that you feel highlight creative approaches to solving community challenges. Prepare a one-page summary report that could be offered on the WPP website as a downloadable PDF (create a PDF if your instructor directs you to). Be sure to brainstorm a compelling title for your report, and as you summarize the three cases, point out how communication techniques were used to solve pressing, significant problems.

Quick Learning Guide

KEY TERMS

abstract Name usually given to a synopsis that accompanies long technical, professional, or academic reports

appendix Supplementary section that contains materials related to the report but not included in the text because they are too long or perhaps not relevant to everyone in the audience

bibliography List of the secondary sources consulted in the preparation of a report

executive summary A brief but complete version of the report; may contain headings, well-developed transitions, and even visual elements

index An alphabetical list of names and subjects mentioned in a report, along with the pages on which they occur

letter of authorization Written authorization to prepare a report

letter of transmittal A specialized form of cover letter that introduces a report to the audience

synopsis A brief overview (one page or less) of a report's most important points, designed to give readers a quick preview of the contents

title fly A single sheet of paper with only the title of the report on it

title page Page that includes the report title; the name, title, and address of the person or organization that authorized the report (if anyone); the name, title, and address of the person or organization that prepared the report; and the date on which the report was submitted

SUMMARY OF LEARNING OBJECTIVES

1 Explain how to adapt to your audiences when writing reports and proposals. Adapt to your audience by demonstrating sensitivity to their needs (adopting the "you" attitude, maintaining a strong sense of etiquette, emphasizing the positive, and using bias-free language), building a strong relationship with your audience (making sure your writing reflects the desired image of your organization and building your credibility), and controlling your style and tone to achieve the appropriate degree of formality for the situation.

Effective reports help readers navigate the document by using three elements: (1) headings (and links for online reports), which set off important ideas and provide the reader with clues as to the report's framework and shifts in discussion; (2) transitions, which tie together ideas and keep readers moving along; and (3) previews and reviews, which prepare readers for new information and summarize previously discussed information.

2 Name five characteristics of effective report content, and list the topics commonly covered in the introduction, body, and close of formal reports. Effective report content is accurate if it is factually correct and error free. It is complete if it includes all necessary information and supports all key assertions. It is balanced if it presents all sides of an argument. It is clear and logical if it is well written and organized logically. It is properly documented if credit is given to all primary and secondary sources of information used.

The introduction highlights the person(s) who authorized the report, the purpose and scope of the report, necessary background material, the sources or methods used to gather information, important definitions, any limitations, and the order in which the various topics are covered. The body can discuss such details as problems, opportunities, facts, evidence, trends, results of studies or investigations, analysis of potential courses of action and their advantages and disadvantages, process procedures and steps, methods and approaches, evaluation criteria for options, conclusions, recommendations, and supporting reasons. The close summarizes key points, restates conclusions and recommendations, if appropriate, and lists action items.

3 List six strategies to strengthen a proposal argument, and list the topics commonly covered in the introduction, body, and close of formal reports. To strengthen your argument, you should demonstrate your knowledge, provide concrete examples, research the competition, prove that your proposal is workable, adopt a "you" attitude, and make your proposal attractive and error free.

The most common elements in the introduction of a proposal are background information or a statement of the problem or opportunity, an overview of the proposed solution, a delineation of the scope of the proposal, and a description of how the proposal is organized. The body can contain a full description of the proposed solution, a work plan with schedules and other key implementation information, a statement of the firm's qualifications, and a breakdown of project costs. The close usually contains a summary of key points, a brief reminder of the benefits readers will realize from the solution and the merits of the proposed approach, a quick summary of qualifications, and a call to action in terms of a request for a decision.

4 Summarize the four tasks involved in completing business reports and proposals. The four completion tasks of revising, producing, proofreading, and distributing all need to be accomplished with care, given the size and complexity of many reports. The production stage for a formal report or proposal can involve creating a number of elements not found in most other business documents. Possible prefatory parts (those coming before the main text of the report or proposal) include a cover, a title fly, a title page, a letter of authorization, a letter of transmittal, a table of contents, a list of illustrations, and a synopsis (a brief overview of the report) or an executive summary (a miniature version of the report). Possible supplemental parts (those coming after the main text of the report or proposal) include one or more appendixes, a bibliography, and an index.

5 Identify the elements to include in a request for proposals (RFP). The content of RFPs varies widely from industry to industry and project to project, but most include background on the company, a description of the project, solution requirements, the criteria that will be used to make selection decisions, expectations for submitted proposals, and any relevant submission and contact information.

MyBCommLab
Go to **mybcommlab.com** to complete the problems marked with this icon .

Test Your Knowledge

To review chapter content related to each question, refer to the indicated Learning Objective.

15-1. What writing choices can you make to adjust the formality of your reports? [LO-1]

15-2. What navigational elements can you use to help readers follow the structure and flow of information in a long report? [LO-1]

15-3. What are three supplementary parts often included in formal reports? [LO-2]

15-4. Why must the introduction of an unsolicited proposal include a statement of the problem or opportunity that the proposal addresses? [LO-3]

15-5. Why is the work plan a key component of a proposal? [LO-3]

15-6. How should you refer to the RFP in a solicited proposal? [LO-3]

15-7. What is the equivalent of a letter of authorization for a proposal? [LO-4]

15-8. How does a synopsis differ from an executive summary? [LO-4]

15-9. Why does writing an RFP require such careful thought? [LO-5]

Apply Your Knowledge

To review chapter content related to each question, refer to the indicated Learning Objective.

15-10. How would you report on a confidential survey in which employees rated their managers' capabilities? Both employees and managers expect to see the results. Would you give the same report to employees and managers? What components would you include or exclude for each audience? Explain your choices. [LO-1]

15-11. What are the risks of not explaining the purpose of a proposal within the introduction? [LO-3]

15-12. If a company receives a solicited formal proposal outlining the solution to a particular problem, is it ethical for the company to adopt the proposal's recommendations without hiring the firm that submitted the proposal? Why or why not? [LO-3]

15-13. Is an executive summary a persuasive message? Explain your answer. [LO-4]

Practice Your Skills

15-14. Message 15.A: Executive Summaries [LO-2] To access the document for this exercise, go to **real-timeupdates.com/bct14**, select Student Assignments, and select Chapter 15, Message 15.A. Download the PDF file, which is the executive summary of *Dietary Guidelines for Americans*, a publication from the U.S. Center for Nutrition Policy and Promotion. Using the information in this chapter, analyze the executive summary and offer specific suggestions for revising it.

Exercises

Each activity is labeled according to the primary skill or skills you will need to use. To review relevant chapter content, you can refer to the indicated Learning Objective. In some instances, supporting information will be found in another chapter, as indicated.

15-15. Message Strategies: Informational Reports [LO-1] Imagine that you and a classmate are helping Linda Moreno prepare her report on Electrovision's travel and entertainment costs (see the Report Writer's Notebook on pages 431–445). This time, however, the report is to be informational rather than analytical, so it will not include recommendations. Review the existing report and determine what changes would be needed to make it an informational report. Be as specific as possible. For example, if your team decides the report needs a new title, what title would you use? Draft a transmittal memo for Moreno to use in conveying this informational report to Dennis McWilliams.

15-16. Message Strategies: Informational Reports [LO-1] Review a long article in a business magazine (print or online). Highlight examples of how the article uses headings, links (if online), transitions, previews, and reviews to help readers navigate through the content.

15-17. Message Strategies: Analytical Reports; Communication Ethics: Resolving Ethical Dilemmas [LO-1], Chapter 1 Your boss has asked you to prepare a feasibility report to determine whether the company should advertise its custom-crafted cabinetry in the weekly neighborhood newspaper. Based on your primary research, you think it should. As you draft the introduction to your report, however, you discover that the survey administered to the neighborhood newspaper subscribers was flawed. Several of the questions were poorly written and misleading. You used the survey results, among other findings, to justify your recommendation. The report is due in three days. What actions might you want to take, if any, before you complete your report?

15-18. Completing: Producing Formal Reports [LO-4] You are president of the Friends of the Library, a not-for-profit group that raises funds and provides volunteers to support your local library. Every February you send a report of the previous year's activities and accomplishments to the County Arts Council, which provides an annual grant of $1,000 toward your group's summer reading festival. Now it's February 6, and you've completed your formal report. Here are the highlights:

- Back-to-school book sale raised $2,000
- Holiday craft fair raised $1,100

- Promotion and prizes for summer reading festival cost $1,450
- Materials for children's program featuring a local author cost $125
- New reference databases for library's career center cost $850
- Bookmarks promoting library's website cost $200

Write a letter of transmittal to Erica Maki, the council's director. Because she is expecting this report, you can use the direct approach. Be sure to express gratitude for the council's ongoing financial support.

15-19. Distributing Reports; Communication Ethics: Resolving Ethical Dilemmas [LO-4], Chapter 1 You submitted what you thought was a masterful report to your boss more than three weeks ago. The report analyzes current department productivity and recommends several steps you think will improve employee output without increasing individual workloads. Brilliant, you thought. But you haven't heard a word from your boss. Did you overstep your boundaries by making recommendations that might imply that she has not been doing a good job? Did you overwhelm her with your ideas? You'd like some feedback. In your last email to her, you asked whether she had read your report. So far you've received no reply.

Then yesterday, you overheard the company vice president talk about some productivity changes in your department—the same changes you recommended in your report. Now you're worried that your boss submitted your report to senior management and will take full credit for your terrific ideas. What, if anything, should you do? Should you confront your boss about this? Should you ask to meet with the company vice president? Discuss this situation with your teammates and develop a solution to this sticky situation. Present your solution to the class, explaining the rationale behind your decision.

15-20. Revising for Clarity and Conciseness [LO-4] The following sentence appears in your first draft of a report that analyzes perceived shortcomings in your company's employee health benefits:

> Among the many criticisms and concerns expressed by the workforce, at least among the 376 who responded to our online survey (out of 655 active employees), the issues of elder care, health insurance during retirement, and the increased amount that employees are being forced to pay every month as the company's contribution to health insurance coverage has declined over the past two years were identified as the most important.

Revise this 69-word sentence to make it shorter, more direct, and more powerful.

15-21. Producing Formal Reports [LO-4] Government reports vary in purpose and structure. Read through the Department of Education's report "Helping Your Child Become a Reader," available at **www.ed.gov**. What is the purpose of this document? Does the title communicate this purpose? What type of report is this, and what is the report's structure? Which prefatory and supplementary parts are included? Now analyze the visuals. What types of visuals are included in this report? Are they all necessary? Are the titles and legends sufficiently informative? How does this report take advantage of the online medium to enhance readability?

Expand Your Skills

Critique the Professionals

Download the latest issue of the *International Trade Update* from **trade.gov**. What techniques does the report use to help readers find their way through the document or direct readers to other sources of information? What techniques are used to highlight key points in the document? Are these techniques effective? Using whatever medium your instructor requests, write a brief summary of your analysis.

Sharpen Your Career Skills Online

Bovée and Thill's Business Communication Web Search, at **websearch.businesscommunicationnetwork.com**, is a unique research tool designed specifically for business communication research. Use the Web Search function to find a website, video, article, podcast, or presentation that offers advice on creating effective business reports. Write a brief email message to your instructor or a post for your class blog, describing the item that you found and summarizing the career skills information you learned from it.

Cases

For all cases, feel free to use your creativity to make up any details you need in order to craft effective messages.

Short Reports

15-22. Message Strategies: Informational Reports [LO-1]
Concern is growing in many youth sports about the negative consequences of existing approaches to player development and competition. The long-term athlete development (LTAD) approach aims to instill methods and mindsets that will make athlete development more successful in the long run while making sports more enjoyable for kids. The American Development Model (ADM) used by USA Hockey is one example of the LTAD approach in a specific sport.

Your task: Visit USA Hockey's ADM website at **www.admkids .com**. Read the material on the Athlete Development page, then write a brief informational report (one to two pages) on the ADM concept, including the rationale behind it and the benefits it offers youth athletes.

PORTFOLIO BUILDER

15-23. Message Strategies: Analytical Reports [LO-1]
Redecorating and remodeling to meet your specific needs and tastes are among the great joys of owning a home. Many people are content with superficial changes, such as new paint or new accessories, but some are more ambitious. These homeowners want to move walls, add rooms, redesign kitchens, convert garages to home theaters—the big stuff.

With many consumer trends, publishers try to create magazines that appeal to carefully identified groups of potential readers and the advertisers who'd like to reach them. The do-it-yourself (DIY) market is already served by numerous magazines, but you see an opportunity in those homeowners who tackle the heavy-duty projects. **Case Tables 15.1** through **15.3** summarize

CASE TABLE 15.1 Rooms Most Frequently Remodeled by DIYers

Room	Homeowners Surveyed Who Have Tackled or Plan to Tackle at Least a Partial Remodel (%)
Kitchen	60
Bathroom	48
Home office/study	44
Bedroom	38
Media room/home theater	31
Den/recreation room	28
Living room	27
Dining room	12
Sun room/solarium	8

CASE TABLE 15.2 Average Amount Spent on Remodeling Projects

Estimated Amount	Surveyed Homeowners (%)
Under $5K	5
$5–10K	21
$10–20K	39
$20–50K	22
More than $50K	13

CASE TABLE 15.3 Tasks Performed by Homeowner on a Typical Remodeling Project

Task	Surveyed Homeowners Who Perform or Plan to Perform Most or All of This Task Themselves (%)
Conceptual design	90
Technical design/architecture	34
Demolition	98
Foundation work	62
Framing	88
Plumbing	91
Electrical	55
Heating/cooling	22
Finish carpentry	85
Tile work	90
Painting	100
Interior design	52

the results of some preliminary research you asked your company's research staff to conduct.

Your task: You think the data show a real opportunity for a "big projects" DIY magazine, although you'll need more extensive research to confirm the size of the market and refine the editorial direction of the magazine. Prepare a brief analytical report that presents the data you have, identifies the opportunity or opportunities you've found (suggest your own ideas based on the tables), and requests funding from the editorial board to pursue further research.

15-24. Message Strategies: Informational Reports [LO-1]
Anyone contemplating stock market investing is likely to shudder at least a little bit at the market's penchant for taking a tumble now and again.

Your task: Write a brief informational report that contains a chart of one of the major stock market indexes (such as the Dow Jones Industrial Average or the S&P 500) over the past 20 years.

Choose four significant drops in the index during this time period and investigate economic or political events that occurred immediately before or during these declines. Briefly describe the events and their likely effect on the stock market.

15-25. Message Strategies: Informational Reports [LO-1], [LO-2] As you may know, the procedural requirements involved in getting a degree or certificate can be nearly as challenging as any course you could take.

Your task: Prepare an interim progress report that details the steps you've taken toward completing your graduation or certification requirements. After examining the requirements listed in your college catalog, indicate a realistic schedule for completing those that remain. In addition to course requirements, include steps such as completing the residency requirement, filing necessary papers, and paying necessary fees. Use a memo format for your report and address it to anyone who is helping or encouraging you through school.

15-26. Message Strategies: Informational Reports [LO-1], [LO-2] Success in any endeavor doesn't happen all at once. For example, success in college is built one quarter or semester at a time, and the way to succeed in the long term is to make sure you succeed in the short term. After all, even a single quarter or semester of college involves a significant investment of time, money, and energy.

Your task: Imagine you work for a company that has agreed to send you to college full-time, paying all your educational expenses. You are given complete freedom in choosing your courses, as long as you graduate by an agreed-upon date. All your employer asks in return is that you develop your business skills and insights as much as possible so that you can make a significant contribution to the company when you return to full-time work after graduation. To make sure that you are using your time—and your company's money—wisely, the company requires a brief personal activity report at the end of every quarter or semester (whichever your school uses). Write a brief informational report summarizing how you spent your quarter or semester. Itemize the classes you took, how much time you spent studying and working on class projects, whether you got involved in campus activities and organizations that help you develop

CASE TABLE 15.4 Selected Employment Data for Engineers and Marketing Staff

Employment Statistic	Engineering Department	Marketing Department
Average number of years of work experience	18.2	16.3
Average number of years of experience in current profession	17.8	8.6
Average number of years with company	12.4	7.9
Average number of years of college education	6.9	4.8
Average number of years between promotions	6.7	4.3
Salary range	$58–165k	$45–85k
Median salary	$77k	$62k

leadership or communication skills, and what you learned that you can apply in a business career. (For the purposes of this assignment, your time estimates don't have to be precise.) Email the final report to your instructor.

15-27. Message Strategies: Informational Reports [LO-1], [LO-4] You've been in your new job as human resources director for only a week, and already you have a major personnel crisis on your hands. Some employees in the marketing department got their hands on a confidential salary report and learned that, on average, marketing employees earn less than engineering employees. In addition, several top performers in the engineering group make significantly more than anybody in marketing. The report was instantly passed around the company by email, and now everyone is discussing the situation. You'll deal with the data security issue later; for now, you need to address the dissatisfaction in the marketing group.

Case Table 15.4 lists the salary and employment data you were able to pull from the employee database. You also had the opportunity to interview the engineering and marketing directors to get their opinions on the pay situation; their answers are listed in **Case Table 15.5.**

CASE TABLE 15.5 Summary Statements from Department Director Interviews

Question	Engineering Director	Marketing Director
1. Should engineering and marketing professionals receive roughly similar pay?	In general, yes, but we need to make allowances for the special nature of the engineering profession. In some cases, it's entirely appropriate for an engineer to earn more than a marketing person.	Yes.
2. Why or why not?	Several reasons: (1) Top engineers are extremely hard to find, and we need to offer competitive salaries; (2) the structure of the engineering department doesn't provide as many promotional opportunities, so we can't use promotions as a motivator the way marketing can; (3) many of our engineers have advanced degrees, and nearly all pursue continuing education to stay on top of the technology.	Without marketing, the products the engineers create wouldn't reach customers, and the company wouldn't have any revenue. The two teams make equal contributions to the company's success.
3. If we decide to balance pay between the two departments, how should we do it?	If we do anything to cap or reduce engineering salaries, we'll lose key people to the competition.	If we can't immediately increase payroll to raise marketing salaries, the only fair thing to do is freeze raises in engineering and gradually raise marketing salaries over the next few years.

Your task: The CEO has asked for a short report summarizing whatever data and information you have on engineering and marketing salaries. Feel free to offer your own interpretation of the situation as well (make up any information you need), but keep in mind that because you are a new manager with almost no experience in the company, your opinion might not have a lot of influence.

15-28. Message Strategies: Analytical Reports [LO-1], [LO-2] Your company develops a mobile phone app that helps people get detailed technical information about products while they are shopping. The original plan was to incorporate Quick Response (QR) codes into the app so that people could scan QR stickers placed on product displays in retail stores. After decoding the QR code, the app would then pull up information about the product on display. However, you've recently learned about *near-field communication* (NFC), a short-range radio technology that might able to accomplish the same thing in a way that is simpler for consumers to use.

Your task: Research the prospects for QR codes and NFC technology, and write a short comparative report. Draw a conclusion about which technology you think will dominate in the coming years.

15-29. Message Strategies: Analytical Reports [LO-2] Assume you will have time for only one course next term.

Your task: List the pros and cons of four or five courses that interest you and use the yardstick method to settle on the course that is best for you to take at this time. Write your report in memo format, addressing it to your academic adviser.

15-30. Message Strategies: Analytical Reports [LO-1], [LO-5] Anyone looking at the fragmented 21st-century landscape of media and entertainment options might be surprised to learn that poetry was once a dominant medium for not only creative literary expression but also philosophical, political, and even scientific discourse. Alas, such is no longer the case.

Your task: With a team of fellow students, your challenge is to identify opportunities to increase sales of poetry—any kind of poetry, in any medium. The following suggestions may help you get started:

- Research recent bestsellers in the poetry field and try to identify why they have been popular.
- Interview literature professors, professional poets, librarians, publishers, and bookstore personnel.
- Consider art forms and venues in which verse plays an essential role, including popular music and poetry slams.
- Conduct surveys and interviews to find out why consumers don't buy more poetry.
- Review professional journals that cover the field of poetry, including *Publishers Weekly* and *Poets & Writers*, from both business and creative standpoints.

Summarize your findings in a brief formal report; assume that your target readers are executives in the publishing industry.

15-31. Message Strategies: Informational Reports [LO-1] Health-care costs are a pressing concern at every level in the economy, from individual households to companies of all sizes to state and federal governments. Many companies are responding with *wellness programs* and other efforts to encourage employees to live healthier lifestyles and thereby reduce their need for expensive health care.

Your task: Research the wellness efforts at any U.S. company and draft a brief report (one to two pages) that describes the company's strategy, the details of the wellness program, and any measured outcomes that reflect its success or failure.

Long Reports

15-32. Message Strategies: Analytical Reports [LO-1] Like any other endeavor that combines factual analysis and creative free thinking, the task of writing business plans generates a range of opinions.

Your task: Find at least six sources of advice on writing successful business plans (focus on start-up businesses that are likely to seek outside investors). Use at least two books, two magazine or journal articles, and two websites or blogs. Analyze the advice you find and identify points where most or all the experts agree and points where they don't agree. Wherever you find points of significant disagreement, identify which opinion you find most convincing and explain why. Summarize your findings in a formal report.

15-33. Message Strategies: Informational Reports [LO-1], [LO-4] Your company is the largest private employer in your metropolitan area, and the 43,500 employees in your workforce have a tremendous impact on local traffic. A group of city and county transportation officials recently approached your CEO with a request to explore ways to reduce this impact. The CEO has assigned you the task of analyzing the workforce's transportation habits and attitudes as a first step toward identifying potential solutions. He's willing to consider anything from subsidized bus passes to company-owned shuttle buses to telecommuting, but the decision requires a thorough understanding of employee transportation needs. Case Tables 15.6 through 15.10 summarize data you collected in an employee survey.

Your task: Present the results of your survey in an informational report, using the data provided in the tables.

CASE TABLE 15.6 Employee Carpool Habits

Frequency of Use: Carpooling	Portion of Workforce
Every day, every week	10,138 (23%)
Certain days, every week	4,361 (10%)
Randomly	983 (2%)
Never	28,018 (64%)

CASE TABLE 15.7   Use of Public Transportation

Frequency of Use: Public Transportation	Portion of Workforce
Every day, every week	23,556 (54%)
Certain days, every week	2,029 (5%)
Randomly	5,862 (13%)
Never	12,053 (28%)

CASE TABLE 15.8   Effect of Potential Improvements to Public Transportation

Which of the Following Would Encourage You to Use Public Transportation More Frequently? (check all that apply)	Portion of Respondents
Increased perception of safety	4,932 (28%)
Improved cleanliness	852 (5%)
Reduced commute times	7,285 (41%)
Greater convenience: fewer transfers	3,278 (18%)
Greater convenience: more stops	1,155 (6%)
Lower (or subsidized) fares	5,634 (31%)
Nothing could encourage me to take public transportation	8,294 (46%)

Note: This question was asked of respondents who use public transportation randomly or never, a subgroup that represents 17,915 employees, or 41 percent of the workforce.

CASE TABLE 15.9   Distance Traveled to/from Work

Distance You Travel to Work (One Way)	Portion of Workforce
Less than 1 mile	531 (1%)
1–3 miles	6,874 (16%)
4–10 miles	22,951 (53%)
11–20 miles	10,605 (24%)
More than 20 miles	2,539 (6%)

CASE TABLE 15.10   Is Telecommuting an Option?

Does the Nature of Your Work Make Telecommuting a Realistic Option?	Portion of Workforce
Yes, every day	3,460 (8%)
Yes, several days a week	8,521 (20%)
Yes, random days	12,918 (30%)
No	18,601 (43%)

PORTFOLIO BUILDER

15-34. Message Strategies: Analytical Reports [LO-1], [LO-5]
As a college student and an active consumer, you may have considered one or more of the following questions at some point in the past few years:

- What criteria distinguish the top-rated MBA programs in the country? How well do these criteria correspond to the needs and expectations of business? Are the criteria fair for students, employers, and business schools?
- Which of three companies you might like to work for has the strongest corporate ethics policies?
- What will the music industry look like in the future? What's next after online stores such as Apple's iTunes and digital players such as the iPod?
- Which industries and job categories are forecast to experience the greatest growth—and therefore the greatest demand for workers—in the next 10 years?
- What has been the impact of Starbucks's aggressive growth on small, independent coffee shops? On midsized chains or franchises? In the United States or in another country?
- How large is the "industry" of major college sports? How much do the major football or basketball programs contribute—directly or indirectly—to other parts of a typical university?
- How much have minor-league sports—baseball, hockey, arena football—grown in small- and medium-market cities? What is the local economic impact when these municipalities build stadiums and arenas?

Your task: Answer one of the preceding questions using information from secondary research sources. Be sure to document your sources using the format your instructor indicates. Give conclusions and offer recommendations where appropriate.

PORTFOLIO BUILDER

15-35. Message Strategies: Analytical Reports [LO-1]   An observer surveying the current consumer electronics landscape and seeing Apple products everywhere might be surprised to learn that during part of the company's history, it was regarded by some as a fairly minor player in the computer industry—and at times a few pundits even wondered whether the company would survive.

Your task: In a two- to three-page report, identify the reasons Apple has been successful and explain how other companies can apply Apple's strategies and tactics to improve their business results.

PORTFOLIO BUILDER/TEAM SKILLS

15-36. Message Strategies: Informational Reports [LO-1]
The partners in your accounting firm have agreed to invest some of the company's profits in the stock market. They plan to diversify the portfolio by spreading the investment across several industries. In the web services/social networking arena, they've narrowed their choices down to Facebook and LinkedIn. Now

they've assigned you and another first-year colleague the task of comparing these two companies in the following areas:

- Internal strengths and weaknesses
- External threats (can be anything from emerging competitors and shift in the economy to potential changes in consumer habits or new government regulations)
- Growth opportunities
- Management styles and strategies
- Examples of how the company has succeeded in the face of challenges
- Brief company background information
- Brief comparative statistics, such as annual sales, market share, number of employees, number of customers, sources of revenue, and any other numbers you think might help the partners choose between the two

Your task: Write a formal informational report comparing the two companies according to these parameters.

15-37. Message Strategies: Analytical Reports [LO-1]
After 15 years in the corporate world, you're ready to strike out on your own. Rather than building a business from the ground up, however, you think that buying a franchise is a better idea. Unfortunately, some of the most lucrative franchise opportunities, such as the major fast-food chains, require significant start-up costs—some more than a half-million dollars. Fortunately, you've met several potential investors who seem willing to help you get started in exchange for a share of ownership. Between your own savings and money from these investors, you estimate that you can raise from $350,000 to $600,000, depending on how much ownership share you want to cede to the investors.

You've already worked in several functional areas, including sales and manufacturing, so you have a fairly well-rounded business résumé. You're open to just about any type of business, too, as long as it provides the opportunity to grow; you don't want to be so tied down to the first operation that you can't turn it over to a hired manager and expand into another market.

Your task: To convene a formal meeting with the investor group, you first need to draft a report that outlines the types of franchise opportunities you'd like to pursue. Write a brief report identifying five franchises that you would like to explore further. (Choose five based on your own personal interests and the criteria already identified.) For each possibility, identify the nature of the business, the financial requirements, the level of support the company provides, and a brief statement of why you could run such a business successfully (make up any details you need). Be sure to carefully review the information you find about each franchise company to make sure you can qualify for it. For instance, McDonald's doesn't allow investment partnerships to buy franchises, so you won't be able to start up a McDonald's outlet until you have enough money to do it on your own. For a quick introduction to franchising, see How Stuff Works (**www .howstuffworks.com**) and search for "Franchising." You can learn more about the business of franchising at Franchising.com (**www.franchising.com**) and search for specific franchise opportunities at Francorp Connect. In addition, many companies that sell franchises, such as Subway, offer additional information on their websites.

Proposals

15-38. Message Strategies: Proposals [LO-1] Select a product you are familiar with and imagine that you are the manufacturer trying to get a local retail outlet to carry it.

Your task: Research the product online and in person if possible to learn as much as you can about it, then write an unsolicited sales proposal in letter format to the owner (or manager) of the store, proposing that the item be stocked. Use the information you gathered on the product's features and benefits to make a compelling case for why the product would be a strong seller for the store. Then make up some reasonable figures, highlighting what the item costs, what it can be sold for, and what services your company provides (return of unsold items, free replacement of unsatisfactory items, necessary repairs, and so on).

PORTFOLIO BUILDER

15-39. Message Strategies: Proposals [LO-3] Your boss, the national sales manager, insists that all company sales reps continue to carry full-size laptop computers for making presentations to clients and to manage files and communications tasks. In addition to your laptops, you and you colleagues have to carry a bulky printed catalog and a variety product samples—up and down stairs, on and off airplanes, and in and out of your cars. You are desperate to lighten the load, and you think switching from laptops to tablets would help.

Your task: Write an informal proposal suggesting that the company equip its traveling salespeople with tablets instead of laptops. Making up any information you need, address three questions you know your boss will have. First, can sales reps type at an adequate speed on tablets, without a conventional keyboard? Second, can sales reps make informal "table top" presentations on tablets, the way they can on their laptops? (Currently, sales reps can sit at a conference room table and give a PowerPoint or Prezi presentation to two or three people, without the need for a projector screen.) Third, do tablets have a sufficient selection of business software, from word processing to database management software?

15-40. Message Strategies: Proposals [LO-3] One of the banes of apartment living is those residents who don't care about the condition of their shared surroundings. They might leave trash all over the place, dent walls when they move furniture, spill food and beverages in common areas, destroy window screens, and otherwise degrade living conditions for everyone. Landlords obviously aren't thrilled about this behavior, either, because it raises the costs of cleaning and maintaining the facility.

Your task: Assume that you live in a fairly large apartment building some distance from campus. Write an email proposal that you could send to your landlord, suggesting that fostering a sense of stronger community among residents in your building might help reduce incidents of vandalism and neglect. Propose that the little-used storage area in the basement of the building be converted to a community room, complete with a simple kitchen and a large-screen television. By attending Super Bowl parties and other events there, residents could get to know one another and perhaps forge bonds that would raise the level of shared concern for their living environment. You can't offer any proof of this in advance, of course, but share your belief that a modest investment in this room could pay off long term in lower repair and maintenance costs. Moreover, it would be an attractive feature to entice new residents.

15-41. Message Strategies: Proposals [LO-1], [LO-3]

Presentations can make—or break—both careers and businesses. A good presentation can bring in millions of dollars in new sales or fresh investment capital. A bad presentation might cause any number of troubles, from turning away potential customers to upsetting fellow employees to derailing key projects. To help business professionals plan, create, and deliver more effective presentations, you offer a three-day workshop that covers the essentials of good presentations:

- Understanding your audience's needs and expectations
- Formulating your presentation objectives
- Choosing an organizational approach
- Writing openings that catch your audience's attention
- Creating effective graphics and slides
- Practicing and delivering your presentation
- Leaving a positive impression on your audience
- Avoiding common mistakes with presentation slides
- Making presentations online using webcasting tools
- Handling questions and arguments from the audience
- Overcoming the top 10 worries of public speaking (including *How can I overcome stage fright?* and *I'm not the performing type; can I still give an effective presentation?*)

Workshop benefits: Students will learn how to prepare better presentations in less time and deliver them more effectively.

Who should attend: Top executives, project managers, employment recruiters, sales professionals, and anyone else who gives important presentations to internal or external audiences.

Your qualifications: Eighteen years of business experience, including 14 years in sales and 12 years of public speaking. Experience speaking to audiences as large as 5,000 people. More than a dozen speech-related articles published in professional journals. Have conducted successful workshops for nearly 100 companies.

Workshop details: Three-day workshop (9 A.M. to 3:30 P.M.) that combines lectures, practice presentations, and both individual and group feedback. Minimum number of students per workshop: 6. Maximum number of students: 12.

Pricing: The cost is $3,500, plus $100 per student; 10 percent discount for additional workshops.

Other information: Each attendee will have the opportunity to give three practice presentations that will last from three to five minutes. Everyone is encouraged to bring Power-Point files containing slides from actual business presentations. Each attendee will also receive a workbook and a digital video recording of his or her final class presentation on DVD. You'll also be available for phone or email coaching for six months after the workshop.

Your task: Identify a company in your local area that might be a good candidate for your services. Learn more about the company by visiting its website so you can personalize your proposal. Using the information listed above, prepare a sales proposal that explains the benefits of your training and what students can expect during the workshop.

PORTFOLIO BUILDER

15-42. Message Strategies: Proposals [LO-1], [LO-3] For years, a controversy has been brewing over the amount of junk food and soft drinks being sold through vending machines in local schools. Schools benefit from revenue-sharing arrangements, but many parents and health experts are concerned about the negative effects of these snacks and beverages. You and your brother have almost a decade of experience running espresso and juice stands in malls and on street corners, and you'd love to find some way to expand your business into schools. After a quick brainstorming session, the two of you craft a plan that makes good business sense while meeting the financial concerns of school administrators and the nutritional concerns of parents and dietitians. Here are the notes from your brainstorming session:

- Set up portable juice bars on school campuses, offering healthy fruit and vegetable drinks along with simple, healthy snacks
- Offer schools 30 percent of profits in exchange for free space and long-term contracts
- Provide job-training opportunities for students (during athletic events, for example)
- Provide a detailed dietary analysis of all products sold
- Establish a nutritional advisory board comprising parents, students, and at least one certified health professional
- Assure schools and parents that all products are safe (for example, no stimulant drinks, no dietary supplements)
- Support local farmers and specialty food preparers by buying locally and giving these vendors the opportunity to test-market new products at your stands

Your task: Based on the ideas listed, draft a formal proposal to the local school board outlining your plan to offer healthier alternatives to soft drinks and prepackaged snack foods. Invent any details you need to complete your proposal.

PORTFOLIO BUILDER/TEAM SKILLS

15-43. Message Strategies: Proposals [LO-1], [LO-3] It seems like everybody in your firm is frustrated. On the one hand, top executives complain about the number of lower-level employees who want promotions but just don't seem to "get it" when it comes to dealing with customers and the public, recognizing when to speak out and when to be quiet, knowing how to push new ideas through the appropriate channels, and performing other essential but difficult-to-teach tasks. On the other hand, ambitious employees who'd like to learn more feel that they have nowhere to turn for career advice from people who've been there. In between, a variety of managers and midlevel executives are overwhelmed by the growing number of mentoring requests they're getting, sometimes from employees they don't even know.

You've been assigned the challenge of proposing a formal mentoring program—and a considerable challenge it is:

- The number of employees who want mentoring relationships far exceeds the number of managers and executives willing and able to be mentors. How will you select people for the program?
- The people most in demand for mentoring also tend to be some of the busiest people in the organization.
- After several years of belt tightening and staff reductions, the entire company feels overworked; few people can imagine adding another recurring task to their seemingly endless to-do lists.
- What's in it for the mentors? Why would they be motivated to help lower-level employees?
- How will you measure the success or failure of the mentoring effort?

Your task: With a team assigned by your instructor, identify potential solutions to the issues (make up any information you need) and draft a proposal to the executive committee for a formal, companywide mentoring program that would match selected employees with successful managers and executives.

PORTFOLIO BUILDER/TEAM SKILLS

15-44. Message Strategies: Proposals [LO-1] Either to create opportunities in a slow job market or to avoid traditional employment altogether, some college graduates create their own jobs as independent freelancers or as entrepreneurs launching new companies.

Your task: Assemble a team of classmates as your instructor directs, then brainstorm all the services you could perform for local businesses. Identify as many services as you can that are related to you and your teammates' college majors and career interests, but also include anything you are willing to do to generate revenue. Next, identify a specific company that might have some opportunities for you. Outline and draft a short proposal that describes what your team can do for this company, how the company would benefit from your services, why you're the right people for the job, and how much you propose to charge for your services. Remember that this is an unsolicited proposal, so be sure introduce it accordingly.

MyBCommLab

Go to **mybcommlab.com** for Auto-graded writing questions as well as the following Assisted-graded writing questions:

15-45. How do previews and reviews work in tandem to help readers? [LO-1]

15-46. Why is the close of a report or proposal so important? [LO-2]

Endnotes

1. *WPP 2014 Annual Report*, wpp.com; Norman Pearlstine, *Fortune CEO Daily* (email newsletter), 3 August 2015.
2. A. S. C. Ehrenberg, "Report Writing—Six Simple Rules for Better Business Documents," *Admap*, June 1992, 39–42.
3. Michael Netzley and Craig Snow, *Guide to Report Writing* (Upper Saddle River, N.J.: Prentice Hall, 2001), 15.
4. David A. Hayes, "Helping Students Grasp the Knack of Writing Summaries," *Journal of Reading* (November 1989): 96–101.
5. Philip C. Kolin, *Successful Writing at Work*, 6th ed. (Boston: Houghton Mifflin, 2001), 552–555.
6. Qvidian website, accessed 26 June 2012, www.qvidian.com.
7. John Morkes and Jakob Nielsen, "Concise, Scannable, and Objective: How to Write for the Web," UseIt.com, accessed 13 November 2006, www.useit.com.
8. Martin James, "PDF Virus Spreads Without Exploiting Any Flaw," *IT Pro*, 8 April 2010, www.itpro.co.uk.
9. Andrea Obana, "How to Write a Request for Proposal (RFP)," Fine Brand Media website, accessed 22 January 2004, www.finebrand.com; Toby B. Gooley, "Ocean Shipping: RFPs That Get Results," *Logistics Management*, July 2003, 47–52.
10. Obana, "How to Write a Request for Proposal (RFP)"; Gooley, "Ocean Shipping," 47–52; "Writing a Good RFP," Infrastructure Issues, Mead & Hunt website, accessed 23 January 2004, www.meadhunt.com.

Developing and Delivering Business Presentations

Presentations give you the opportunity to put all your communication skills on display, from audience analysis and research to the design of presentation materials to public speaking. Learn how to plan effective presentations, overcome the anxieties that every speaker feels, respond to questions from the audience, and embrace the Twitter-enabled backchannel. Discover some tips and techniques for succeeding with online presentations, an increasingly common mode of communication in today's environment. Complement your talk with compelling visual materials, and learn how to create presentation slides that engage and excite your audience.

Rawpixel.com/ShutterStock

LEARNING OBJECTIVES

After studying this chapter, you will be able to

1 Describe the tasks involved in analyzing the situation for a presentation and organizing a presentation.

2 Explain how to adapt to your audience and develop an effective opening, body, and close for a presentation.

3 Discuss five steps for delivering a successful presentation.

4 Explain the growing importance of the backchannel in presentations, and list six steps for giving effective presentations online.

MyBCommLab®

⭐ **Improve Your Grade!** More than 10 million students improved their results using Pearson MyLabs. Visit **mybcommlab.com** for simulations, tutorials, and end-of-chapter problems.

COMMUNICATION CLOSE-UP AT
Barnett International

barnettinternationalconsulting.com

Presentations have much in common with other business communication efforts, from analyzing the situation and defining your purpose to gathering information and crafting audience-focused messages. They have one major difference, of course: Presentations are *performances*, and a good message isn't enough. How you perform in front of an audience has a major influence on how they respond to your message.

Max Gordon/Barnett International Inc.

Communication coach Gina Barnett advises speakers to learn how to read and use their body's signals to become more relaxed, open, and engaging.

From her years of experience in the theater, communication coach Gina Barnett knows that the performance makes or breaks the presentation. A strong performance makes any message more compelling, whereas a weak performance can undermine even the best messages.

While performance is vital, it's a mistake to think that only actors or extroverts have some special performance gift. All business professionals can learn to use their bodies to perform more effectively while giving speeches and making presentations. Being mindful of your physical habits and mannerisms, from how you hold your head to the way you use your feet, can make you a more effective speaker. And there's a bonus: You'll enjoy it more, too. A body-mindful approach to speaking can help you control the anxiety that every presenter feels and harness that energy for a more natural and engaging experience.

In her performance-coaching work with corporate executives, Barnett helps presenters explore the key centers in the human body that regulate how speakers feel and how they come across to others, both visually and vocally. For example, it's easy to think a smile is merely a *reaction* to a pleasant thought or experience, but smiles can also instigate positive thoughts. The physical act of smiling can trigger improvements in your own mood and in the moods of people watching you. A warm smile helps the audience connect with you and conveys your confidence in yourself and in your message. Smiling also forces you to relax your jaw and facial muscles, which helps to release pent-up stress and improve your vocal clarity and projection. With so many benefits to offer, the simple act of smiling as you step onto the stage can launch your presentation on a strong note.

Barnett tells speakers to think of their bodies as communication instruments and to use them to their full potential, in much the same way musicians use their instruments. Like a musical instrument, your body can be treated well or poorly and played with varying degrees of success.

Using your physical self to full advantage starts with understanding the signals your body is sending to you and the people in your audience. Tune in to your body and listen to its signals. If you are anxious leading up to a presentation, you may feel this signal in your shoulders, your jaw, or wherever you tend to "collect" stress. Explore that emotion and try to identify why you feel that way. You may identify some reasons that are real and relevant to the situation and some that are noise or distractions, at least as far as the immediate situation is concerned.

A real and extremely relevant reason might be that you haven't prepared thoroughly and therefore lack confidence in your ability to present your message or respond to audience questions. Assuming you've given yourself enough time, you can address this source of anxiety by finishing your preparation. A less relevant source of stress might be a buried memory of being embarrassed in front of your class as a child. This emotional mishap might still be stuck in your memory at some deep level, but it doesn't need to be part of who you are as a professional adult.

Barnett emphasizes that by dismissing irrelevant sources of stress and proactively dismantling relevant sources of stress, your mind can then tell your body that you're ready to go. This confidence will change the way you carry and present yourself on stage, it will give your voice fresh energy, and it will spread to your audience—your confidence in yourself will make them more confident in you, too. Rather than rushing through your presentation with your mind a nervous whirl, hoping only to make it through in one piece and get off the stage, you'll enjoy being in the moment and sharing your ideas and inspiration.[1]

Planning a Presentation

1 LEARNING OBJECTIVE
Describe the tasks involved in analyzing the situation for a presentation and organizing a presentation.

Business presentations involve all of your communication skills, from research through nonverbal communication, and they let you demonstrate your business acumen as well.

Feeling nervous is perfectly normal when you're faced with a presentation; the good news is there are positive steps you can take to reduce your anxiety.

Gina Barnett (profiled in the chapter-opening Communication Close-Up) recognizes the importance of being your best and most authentic self when you're giving presentations. Presentations offer important opportunities to put all your communication skills on display, including research, planning, writing, visual design, and interpersonal and nonverbal communication. Presentations also let you demonstrate your ability to think on your feet, grasp complex business issues, and handle challenging situations—all attributes that executives look for when searching for talented employees to promote.

If the thought of giving a speech or presentation makes you nervous, keep three points in mind. First, everybody gets nervous when speaking in front of groups. Second, being nervous is actually a good thing; it means you care about the topic, your audience, and your career success. Third, with practice, you can convert those nervous feelings into positive energy that helps you give more compelling presentations. You can take control of the situation by using the three-step writing process to prepare for successful presentations (see Figure 16.1).

Planning presentations is much like planning any other business message: You analyze the situation, gather information, select the right medium, and organize the information.

Gathering information for presentations is essentially the same as for written communication projects. The other three planning tasks have some special applications when it comes to presentations; they are covered in the following sections.

On the subject of planning, be aware that preparing a professional-quality business presentation takes time. Nancy Duarte, a presentation design expert profiled in Chapter 17, offers this rule of thumb: For a 1-hour presentation that uses 30 slides, allow 36 to 90 hours to research, conceive, create, and practice.[2] Not every one-hour presentation justifies a week or two of preparation, of course, but the important presentations that can make your career or your company certainly can.

ANALYZING THE SITUATION

As with written communications, analyzing the situation for a presentation involves defining your purpose and developing an audience profile. The purpose of most of your presentations will be to inform or to persuade, although you may occasionally need to make a collaborative presentation, such as when you're leading a problem-solving or brainstorming session. Given the time limitations of most presentations and the live nature of the event, make sure your purpose is crystal clear so that you make the most of the opportunity and show respect for your listeners' time and attention.

Creating a high-quality presentation for an important event can take many days, so be sure to allow enough time.

The purpose of most business presentations is to inform or persuade; you may also give presentations designed primarily to collaborate with others.

1 Plan →	**2** Write →	**3** Complete
Analyze the Situation Define your purpose and develop a profile of your audience, including their likely emotional states and language preferences.	**Adapt to Your Audience** Adapt your content, presentation style, and room setup to the audience and the specific situation. Be sensitive to audience needs and expectations with a "you" attitude, politeness, positive emphasis, and bias-free language. Plan to establish your credibility as required.	**Revise the Message** Evaluate your content and speaking notes.
Gather Information Determine audience needs and obtain the information necessary to satisfy those needs.		**Master Your Delivery** Choose your delivery mode and practice your presentation.
Choose Medium and Channel Identify the best combination for the situation, message, and audience, including handouts and other support materials.	**Compose Your Presentation** Outline an attention-getting introduction, body, and close. Prepare supporting visuals and speaking notes.	**Prepare to Speak** Verify facilities and equipment, including online connections and software setups. Hire an interpreter if necessary.
Organize the Information Define your main idea, limit your scope and verify timing, select the direct or indirect approach, and outline your content.		**Overcome Anxiety** Take steps to feel more confident and appear more confident on stage.

Figure 16.1 The Three-Step Process for Developing Presentations
Although you rarely "write" a presentation or speech in the sense of composing every word ahead of time, the tasks in the three-step writing process adapt quite well to the challenge of planning, creating, and delivering presentations.

Knowing your audience's state of mind will help you adjust both your message and your delivery.

When you develop your audience profile, try to anticipate the likely emotional state of your audience members. Figure 16.2 offers tips for dealing with a variety of audience mindsets.

You also need to determine whether your audience is comfortable listening to the language you speak. Listening to an unfamiliar language is much more difficult than reading that language, so an audience that might be able to read a written report might not be able to understand a presentation covering the same material (see "Communicating Across Cultures: Making Sure Your Message Doesn't Get Lost in Translation").

Learn as much as you can about the setting and circumstances of your presentation, from the size of the audience to seating arrangements to potential interruptions.

Also consider the circumstances in which you'll be making your presentation. Will you speak to five people in a conference room where you can control everything from light to sound to temperature? Or will you be demonstrating a product on the floor of a trade show, where you might have from 1 to 100 listeners and little control over the environment? Will everyone be in the same room, or will some or all of your audience participate from remote locations via the Internet? What equipment will you have at your disposal?

For in-person presentations, pay close attention to seating arrangements. The four basic formats have distinct advantages and disadvantages:

- **Classroom or theater seating,** in which all chairs or desks face forward, helps keep attention focused on the speaker and is usually the best method for accommodating large audiences. However, this arrangement inhibits interaction among audience members, so it is not desirable for brainstorming or other collaborative activities.
- **Conference table seating,** in which people sit along both sides of a long table and the speaker stands at one end, is a common arrangement for smaller meetings. It promotes interaction among attendees, but it tends to isolate the speaker at one end of the room.
- **Horseshoe, or *U*-shaped, seating,** in which tables are arranged in the shape of a *U*, improves on conference table seating by allowing the speaker to walk between the tables to interact with individual audience members.

Supportive: Reward their goodwill with a presentation that is clear, concise, and upbeat; speak in a relaxed, confident manner.

Interested but neutral: Build your credibility as you present compelling reasons to accept your message; address potential objections as you move forward; show confidence in your message but a willingness to answer questions and concerns.

Uninterested: Use the techniques described in this chapter to get their attention and work hard to hold it throughout; find ways to connect your message with their personal or professional interests; be well organized and concise.

Worried: Don't dismiss their fears or tell them they are mistaken for feeling that way; if your message will calm their fears, use the direct approach; if your message will confirm their fears, consider the indirect approach to build acceptance.

Hostile: Recognize that angry audiences care deeply but might not be open to listening; consider the indirect approach to find common ground and to diffuse anger before sharing your message; work to keep your own emotions under control.

Figure 16.2 **Planning for Various Audience Mindsets**
Try to assess the emotional state of your audience ahead of time so you can plan your presentation approach accordingly.

Making Sure Your Message Doesn't Get Lost in Translation

When speaking to an international audience, keep in mind that audience members' language fluency might vary widely. So take special care to ensure clear communication:

- **Speak slowly and distinctly.** The most common complaint of international audiences is that English speakers talk too fast. Articulate each word carefully, emphasize consonants for clarity, and pause frequently.
- **Repeat key words and phrases.** When audiences are not very familiar with your language, they need to hear important information more than once. Also, they may not be familiar with synonyms, so word key points in the same way throughout your presentation.
- **Aim for clarity.** Keep your message simple. Avoid complex sentence structures, abbreviations, acronyms, and metaphors. Replace two-word verbs with one-word alternatives (such as *review* instead of *look over*). Such verbs are confusing because the definition of each separate word differs from the meaning of the two words combined. Similarly, avoid slang and cultural idioms, such as *once in a blue moon*, which may be unfamiliar to an international audience. If you use words or phrases from the audience's native language, make sure you understand them fully.
- **Communicate with body language.** Emphasize and clarify verbal information with gestures and facial expressions. For instance, smile to emphasize positive points and use gestures to illustrate the meaning of words such as *up*, *down*, or *under*.

- **Support your spoken message with visuals.** Simple, clear visuals can help you describe your key points and keep the audience engaged. If possible, prepare captions in both English and your audience's native language.

CAREER APPLICATIONS

1. One of the most important changes speakers need to make when addressing audiences in other cultures is to avoid colloquial figures of speech. Listen carefully to the next three course lectures you attend and identify phrases that could cause confusion (such as "hit one out of the park," "go for broke," or "get your ducks in a row"). Review your list and replace the problematic phrases with wording that is more likely to be understood by nonnative English speakers or audiences in other countries.

2. Make a list of 10 two-word verbs. How does the meaning of each separate word differ from the definition of the combined words? Replace each two-word verb with a single, specific word that will be clearer to an international audience.

Sources: Adapted from Ramez Naguib, "International Audiences," Toastmasters International, accessed 8 February 2013, www.toastmasters.org; Patricia L. Kurtz, *The Global Speaker* (New York: AMACOM, 1995), 35–47, 56–68, 75–82, 87–100; David A. Victor, *International Business Communication* (New York: Harper-Collins Publishers, 1992), 39–45; Lalita Khosla, "You Say Tomato," *Forbes*, 21 May 2001, 36; Stephen Dolainski, "Are Expats Getting Lost in the Translation?" *Workforce*, February 1997, 32–39.

- **Café seating**, in which people sit in groups at individual tables, is best for breakout sessions and other small-group activities. However, this arrangement is less than ideal for anything more than short presentations because it places some in the audience with their backs to the speaker, making it awkward for both them and the presenter.

If you can't control the seating arrangement, at least be aware of what it is so you can adjust your plans if necessary.

All these variables can influence not only the style of your presentation but the content. For instance, in a public environment full of distractions and uncertainties, you're probably better off keeping your content simple and short because chances are you won't be able to keep everyone's attention for the duration of your presentation.

Table 16.1 on the next page offers a summary of the key steps in analyzing an audience for presentations. For even more insight into audience evaluation (including emotional and cultural issues), consult a good public-speaking textbook.

SELECTING THE BEST COMBINATION OF MEDIA AND CHANNELS

For some presentations, you'll be expected to use whatever media and channels your audience, your boss, or the circumstances require. For example, you might be required to use specific presentation software and a conference room's built-in display system or your company's online meeting software.

For other presentations, though, you might have an array of choices, from live, in-person presentations to **webcasts** (online presentations that people either view live or download later from the web), **screencasts** (recordings of activity on computer displays

TABLE 16.1 Analyzing Audiences for Business Presentations

Task	Actions
To determine audience size and composition	• Estimate how many people will attend (in person and online). • Identify what they have in common and how they differ. • Analyze the mix of organizational position, professions, language fluencies, and other demographic factors that could influence your content and delivery choices.
To predict the audience's probable reaction	• Analyze why audience members are attending the presentation. • Determine the audience's general attitude toward the topic: interested, moderately interested, unconcerned, open-minded, or hostile. • Analyze your audience's likely mood when you speak to them. • Find out what kind of supporting information will help the audience accept and respond to your message: technical data, historical information, financial data, demonstrations, samples, and so on. • Consider whether the audience has any biases that might work against you. • Anticipate possible objections or questions.
To gauge the audience's experience	• Analyze whether everybody has the same background and level of understanding. • Determine what the audience already knows about the subject. • Consider whether the audience is familiar with the vocabulary you intend to use. • Analyze what the audience expects from you. • Think about the mix of general concepts and specific details you will need to present.

with audio voiceover), or **twebinars** (the use of Twitter as a *backchannel* —see page 477— for real-time conversation during a web-based seminar[3]).

ORGANIZING A PRESENTATION

Linear presentations generally follow a fixed path from start to finish.

The possibilities for organizing a business presentation fall into two basic categories: *linear* or *nonlinear*. Linear presentations are like printed documents in the sense that they are outlined like conventional messages and follow a predefined flow from start to finish. The linear model is appropriate for speeches, technical and financial presentations, and other presentations in which you want to convey your message point by point or build up to a conclusion following logical steps.

Nonlinear presentations can move back and forth between topics and up and down in levels of detail.

In contrast, a nonlinear presentation doesn't flow in any particular direction but rather gives the presenter the option to move back and forth between topics and up and down in terms of level of detail. Nonlinear presentations can be useful when you want to be able to show complicated relationships between multiple ideas or elements, to zoom in and out between the "big picture" and specific details, to explore complex visuals, or to have the flexibility to move from topic to topic in any order.

The difference between the two styles can be seen in the type of software typically used to create and deliver a presentation. Microsoft PowerPoint, Apple Keynote, Google Slides, and similar packages use sequences of individual slides, often referred to as a *slide deck*. They don't necessarily need to be presented in a strict linear order, because the presenter does have the option of jumping out of the predefined order, but in most presentations using slides, the speaker moves from start to finish in that order.

Prezi is the best-known nonlinear presentation software and doesn't use the concept of individual slides. Instead, you start from a main screen, or canvas, which often presents the big picture overview of your topic (see Figure 16.3). From there, you add individual objects (including blocks of text, photos, or videos) that convey specific information points. When you present, you can zoom in and out, discussing the individual objects and their relationship to the big picture and each other. You can also define a narrative flow by creating a path from one object to the next, which also lets people view the presentation on their own[4] (and effectively turns a Prezi presentation into a linear presentation).

Remember that presentations— using any software or system— are not about flash and dazzle; they are about sharing ideas, information, and emotions with your audience.

Prezi is sometimes viewed as a more dynamic and engaging way to present, and it certainly has that potential. However, keep several points in mind if you have a choice of which approach to take and which software to use. First, match the tool to the task, not the other way around. A detailed technical discussion might need a linear presentation, whereas a free-form brainstorming session might benefit from a nonlinear approach, for

Figure 16.3 Nonlinear Presentations
Nonlinear presentations, particularly those using the cloud-based Prezi system, give the presenter more freedom to zoom in and out between the big picture to the details and to cover topics in any order.

example. Second, if they are used well, software features can help you tell your story, but your story is what matters—not the software. If they are used poorly, software features only get in the way. (Overuse of zooming in Prezi is a good example of this.[5]) Third, in spite of their reputation, PowerPoint and other conventional slide programs aren't limited to creating boring, linear flows of bullet points (see "Choosing Structured or Free-Form Slides" on page 489 in Chapter 17).

Defining Your Main Idea

Regardless of which overall approach you take, a successful presentation starts with a clear picture of the main idea you want to share with your audience. Start by composing a one-sentence summary that links your subject and purpose to your audience's frame of reference. Here are some examples:

> Convince management that reorganizing the technical support department will improve customer service and reduce employee turnover.

> Convince the board of directors that we should build a new plant in Texas to eliminate manufacturing bottlenecks and improve production quality.

> Address employee concerns regarding a new health-care plan by showing how the plan will reduce costs and improve the quality of their care.

Each of these statements puts a particular slant on the subject, one that directly relates to the audience's interests. Make sure your purpose is based on a clear understanding of audience needs so that you can deliver information your audience truly cares about.[6] For example, a group of new employees will be much more responsive to your discussion of plant safety procedures if you focus on how the procedures can save lives and prevent injuries rather than on how they will save the company money or conform to government regulations.

Limiting Your Scope

Limiting your scope is important with any message, but it's particularly vital with presentations, for two reasons. First, for most presentations, you must work within strict time limits. Second, the longer you speak, the more difficult it is to hold the audience's attention and the more difficult it is for your listeners to retain your key points.[7]

The only sure way to know how much material you can cover in a given time is to practice your presentation after you complete it. As an alternative, if you're using

Limiting your scope is important for two reasons: to ensure that your presentation fits the allotted time and to make sure you respect your audience members' time and attention.

The only sure way to measure the length of your presentation is to complete a practice run.

conventional structured slides (see page 489), you can figure on three or four minutes per slide as a rough guide.[8] Of course, be sure to factor in time for introductions, coffee breaks, demonstrations, question-and-answer sessions, and anything else that takes away from your speaking time.

Approaching time constraints as a creative challenge can actually help you develop more effective presentations. Limitations can force you to focus on the most essential message points that are important to your audience.[9]

If you're having trouble meeting a time limit or just want to keep your presentation as short as possible, consider a hybrid approach in which you present your key points in summary form and give people printed handouts with additional detail.[10]

Choosing Your Approach

Organize a short presentation the same way you would a brief written message; organize a longer presentation as you would a report.

With a well-defined main idea to guide you and a clearly defined scope for your presentation, you can begin to arrange your message. If you have 10 minutes or less to deliver your message, organize your presentation much as you would a brief written message: Use the direct approach if the subject involves routine information or good news; use the indirect approach if the subject involves negative news or persuasion. Plan to spend a minute or two during your introduction to arouse interest and to give a preview of what's to come. For the body of the presentation, be prepared to explain the who, what, when, where, why, and how of your subject. In the final few moments, review the points you've made and close with a statement that will help your audience remember the subject of your speech (see Figure 16.4).

Longer presentations are organized like reports. If the purpose is to inform, use the direct approach and a structure imposed naturally by the subject: importance, sequence, chronology, spatial orientation, geography, or category. If your purpose is to analyze,

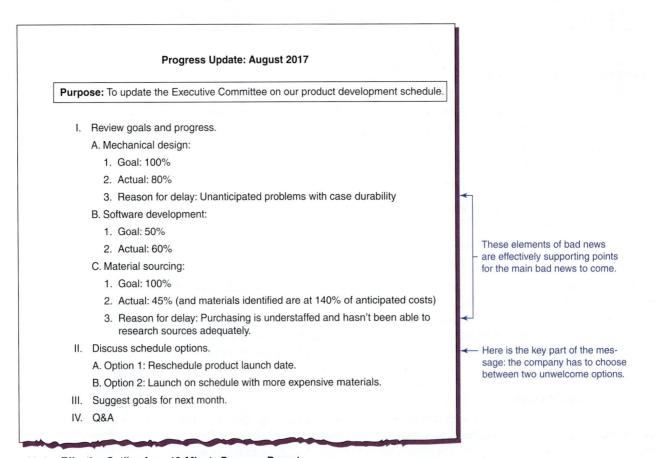

Figure 16.4 **Effective Outline for a 10-Minute Progress Report**
Here is an outline of a short presentation that updates management on the status of a key project. The presenter has some bad news to deliver (either the product launch will have to be delayed or the materials costs will be higher than anticipated), so she opted for an indirect approach to lay out the reasons for the delay before sharing the news.

persuade, or collaborate, organize your material around conclusions and recommendations or around a logical argument. Use the direct approach if the audience is receptive and the indirect approach if you expect resistance.

As you develop your presentation, keep in mind that presentations have one important advantage over written reports: You can adjust your outline on the fly if you need to. Identify the critical points in your presentation and ask yourself some "what if" questions to address possible audience reactions. For instance, if you're worried the audience might not agree with the financial assumptions you've made, you might prepare a detailed analysis that you can include in case you sense that a negative reaction is building or if someone openly questions you about it. Most presentation software makes it easy to adjust your presentation as you move along, allowing you to skip over any parts you decide not to use or to insert backup material at the last minute.

Regardless of the length of your presentation, remember to keep your organization clear and simple. If listeners lose the thread of your presentation, they'll have a hard time catching up and following your message in the remainder of your speech. Explain at the beginning how you've organized your material and try to limit the number of main points to three or four.

> Simplicity is critical in the organization of presentations.

With every presentation, look for opportunities to integrate storytelling (see page 117) into the structure of your presentation. The dramatic tension (not knowing what will happen to the "hero") at the heart of effective storytelling is a great way to capture and keep the audience's attention.

Preparing Your Outline

A presentation outline helps you organize your message, and it serves as the foundation for delivering your speech. Prepare your outline in several stages:[11]

> In addition to planning your speech, a presentation outline helps you plan your speaking notes as well.

- State your purpose and main idea and then use these to guide the rest of your planning.
- Organize your major points and subpoints in logical order, expressing each major point as a single, complete sentence.
- Identify major points in the body first and then outline the introduction and close.
- Identify transitions between major points or sections and then write these transitions in full-sentence form.
- Prepare your bibliography or source notes; highlight those sources you want to identify by name during your talk.
- Choose a compelling title. Make it brief, action oriented, and focused on what you can do for the audience.[12]

Many speakers like to prepare both a detailed *planning outline* (see Figure 16.5 on the next page) and a simpler *speaking outline* that provides all the cues and reminders they need to present their material. Follow these steps to prepare an effective speaking outline:[13]

> You may find it helpful to create a simpler speaking outline from your planning outline.

- Start with the planning outline and then strip away anything you don't plan to say directly to your audience.
- Condense points and transitions to key words or phrases.
- Add delivery cues, such as places where you plan to pause for emphasis or use visuals.
- Arrange your notes on numbered cards or use the notes capability in your presentation software.

Crafting Presentation Content

Although you usually don't write out a presentation word for word, you still engage in the writing process—developing your ideas, structuring support points, phrasing your transitions, and so on. Depending on the situation and your personal style, the eventual presentation might follow your initial words closely, or you might express your thoughts in fresh, spontaneous language. This section covers the tasks of adapting to your audience and developing your presentation; Chapter 17 covers the task of creating slides to accompany your talk.

> **2 LEARNING OBJECTIVE**
> Explain how to adapt to your audience and develop an effective opening, body, and close for a presentation.

A clear statement of purpose helps the presenter stay focused on her message while she develops her outline.

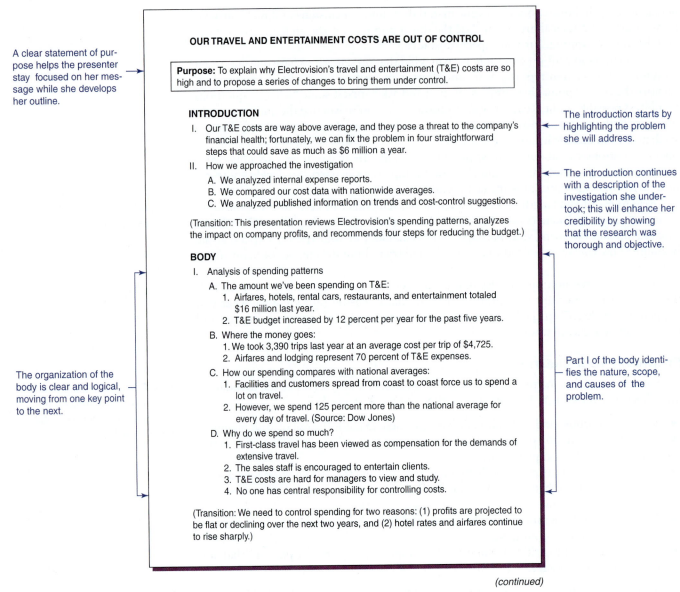

OUR TRAVEL AND ENTERTAINMENT COSTS ARE OUT OF CONTROL

Purpose: To explain why Electrovision's travel and entertainment (T&E) costs are so high and to propose a series of changes to bring them under control.

INTRODUCTION

I. Our T&E costs are way above average, and they pose a threat to the company's financial health; fortunately, we can fix the problem in four straightforward steps that could save as much as $6 million a year.

II. How we approached the investigation
   A. We analyzed internal expense reports.
   B. We compared our cost data with nationwide averages.
   C. We analyzed published information on trends and cost-control suggestions.

(Transition: This presentation reviews Electrovision's spending patterns, analyzes the impact on company profits, and recommends four steps for reducing the budget.)

BODY

I. Analysis of spending patterns
   A. The amount we've been spending on T&E:
      1. Airfares, hotels, rental cars, restaurants, and entertainment totaled $16 million last year.
      2. T&E budget increased by 12 percent per year for the past five years.
   B. Where the money goes:
      1. We took 3,390 trips last year at an average cost per trip of $4,725.
      2. Airfares and lodging represent 70 percent of T&E expenses.
   C. How our spending compares with national averages:
      1. Facilities and customers spread from coast to coast force us to spend a lot on travel.
      2. However, we spend 125 percent more than the national average for every day of travel. (Source: Dow Jones)
   D. Why do we spend so much?
      1. First-class travel has been viewed as compensation for the demands of extensive travel.
      2. The sales staff is encouraged to entertain clients.
      3. T&E costs are hard for managers to view and study.
      4. No one has central responsibility for controlling costs.

(Transition: We need to control spending for two reasons: (1) profits are projected to be flat or declining over the next two years, and (2) hotel rates and airfares continue to rise sharply.)

The introduction starts by highlighting the problem she will address.

The introduction continues with a description of the investigation she undertook; this will enhance her credibility by showing that the research was thorough and objective.

Part I of the body identifies the nature, scope, and causes of the problem.

The organization of the body is clear and logical, moving from one key point to the next.

(continued)

Figure 16.5 **Effective Outline for a 30-Minute Presentation**
This outline (based on Linda Moreno's report in Chapter 15) clearly identifies the purpose and the distinct points to be made in the introduction, body, and close. Notice also how the presenter wrote her major transitions in full-sentence form to be sure she can clearly phrase these critical passages when it's time to speak.

ADAPTING TO YOUR AUDIENCE

Adapting to your audience addresses a number of issues, from speaking style to technology choices.

Your audience's size, the venue (in person or online), your subject, your purpose, your budget, the time available for preparation, and the time allotted for your talk all influence the style of your presentation. If you're speaking to a small group, particularly people you already know, you can use a casual style that encourages audience participation. Use simple visuals and invite your audience to interject comments. Deliver your remarks in a conversational tone, using notes to jog your memory if necessary.

If you're addressing a large audience or if the event is important, establish a more formal atmosphere. During formal presentations, speakers are often on a stage or platform, standing behind a lectern and using a microphone so that their remarks can be heard throughout the room or captured for broadcasting or webcasting.

When you deliver a presentation to people from other cultures, you may need to adapt the content of your presentation. It is also important to take into account any cultural

REAL-TIME UPDATES
LEARN MORE BY WATCHING THIS VIDEO

How to establish an emotional connection with any audience

Entertainment executive Peter Guber talks about the art of purposeful storytelling. Go to **real-timeupdates.com/bct14** and select Learn More in the Students section.

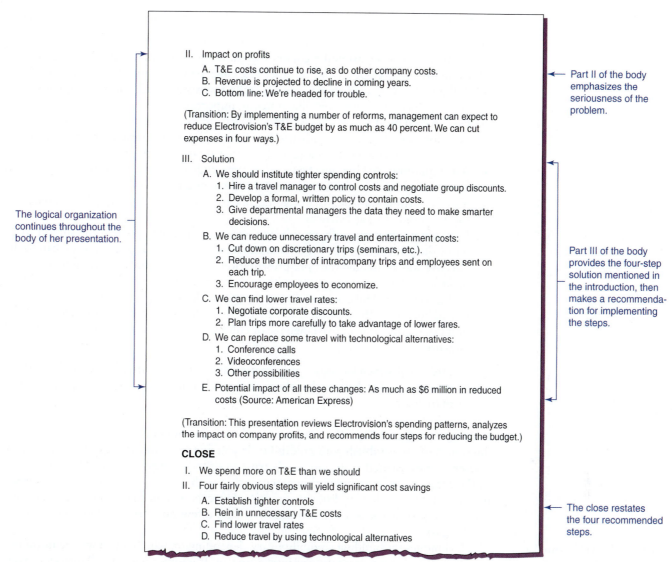

The logical organization continues throughout the body of her presentation.

II. Impact on profits
   A. T&E costs continue to rise, as do other company costs.
   B. Revenue is projected to decline in coming years.
   C. Bottom line: We're headed for trouble.

(Transition: By implementing a number of reforms, management can expect to reduce Electrovision's T&E budget by as much as 40 percent. We can cut expenses in four ways.)

III. Solution
   A. We should institute tighter spending controls:
      1. Hire a travel manager to control costs and negotiate group discounts.
      2. Develop a formal, written policy to contain costs.
      3. Give departmental managers the data they need to make smarter decisions.
   B. We can reduce unnecessary travel and entertainment costs:
      1. Cut down on discretionary trips (seminars, etc.).
      2. Reduce the number of intracompany trips and employees sent on each trip.
      3. Encourage employees to economize.
   C. We can find lower travel rates:
      1. Negotiate corporate discounts.
      2. Plan trips more carefully to take advantage of lower fares.
   D. We can replace some travel with technological alternatives:
      1. Conference calls
      2. Videoconferences
      3. Other possibilities
   E. Potential impact of all these changes: As much as $6 million in reduced costs (Source: American Express)

(Transition: This presentation reviews Electrovision's spending patterns, analyzes the impact on company profits, and recommends four steps for reducing the budget.)

CLOSE

I. We spend more on T&E than we should
II. Four fairly obvious steps will yield significant cost savings
   A. Establish tighter controls
   B. Rein in unnecessary T&E costs
   C. Find lower travel rates
   D. Reduce travel by using technological alternatives

Part II of the body emphasizes the seriousness of the problem.

Part III of the body provides the four-step solution mentioned in the introduction, then makes a recommendation for implementing the steps.

The close restates the four recommended steps.

Figure 16.5 **Effective Outline for a 30-Minute Presentation (*continued*)**

preferences for appearance, mannerisms, and other customs. An interpreter or event host can suggest appropriate changes for a specific audience or particular occasion.

DEVELOPING YOUR PRESENTATION

Like written documents, presentations comprise distinct elements: the introduction, the body, and the close.

Presentation Introduction

A good introduction arouses the audience's interest in your topic, establishes your credibility, and prepares the audience for what will follow. That's a lot to pack into the first few minutes of your presentation, so give yourself plenty of time to prepare the words and visuals you'll use to get your presentation off to a great start.

Arousing Audience Interest Some subjects are naturally more interesting to some audiences than others. If you will be discussing a matter of profound significance that will personally affect the members of your audience, chances are they'll listen, regardless of how you begin. All you really have to do is announce your topic, and you'll have their

If your audience isn't likely to be naturally interested in your topic, your introduction will need to build interest by relating the subject to their personal concerns.

attention. Other subjects call for more imagination. Here are six ways to arouse audience interest:[14]

- **Unite the audience around a common goal.** Invite listeners to help solve a problem, capitalize on an opportunity, or otherwise engage in the topic of your presentation.
- **Tell a story.** Well-told stories are naturally interesting and can be compelling. Of course, make sure your story illustrates an important and relevant point.
- **Pass around product samples or other objects.** If your company is in the textile business, for example, let the audience handle some of your fabrics. The more of their senses you can engage, the more likely people are to remember your message.
- **Ask a question.** Asking questions will get the audience actively involved in your presentation and give you information about them and their needs.
- **Share a startling statistic.** An intriguing, unexpected, or shocking detail can often grab the attention of your listeners.
- **Use humor.** Opening with an amusing observation about yourself, the subject matter of the presentation, or the circumstances surrounding the presentation can be an effective way to lighten the "pre-presentation jitters" for you and the audience or to make an emotional connection with your listeners. However, humor must be used with great care. Make sure any comments are relevant, appropriate, and not offensive to anyone in the audience. In general, avoid humor when you and the audience don't share the same native language or culture; it's too easy for humor to fall flat or backfire.

Regardless of which technique you choose, make sure you can give audience members a reason to care and to believe that the time they're about to spend listening to you will be worth their while.[15]

Building Your Credibility   In addition to grabbing the audience's attention, your introduction needs to establish your credibility. If you're a well-known expert in the subject matter or have earned your audience's trust in other situations, you're already ahead of the game. If you have no working relationship with your audience or if you're speaking in an area outside your known expertise, however, you need to establish credibility and do so quickly; people tend to decide within a few minutes whether you're worth listening to.[16]

> If someone else will be introducing you to the audience, you can ask this person to present your credentials.

Techniques for building credibility vary, depending on whether you will be introducing yourself or having someone else introduce you. If another person will introduce you, he or she can present your credentials so that you don't appear boastful. If you will be introducing yourself, keep your comments simple, but don't be afraid to mention your relevant experience and accomplishments. Your listeners will be curious about your qualifications, so tell them briefly who you are and why you're the right person to be giving this presentation. Here's an example:

I'm Karen Whitney, a market research analyst with Information Resources Corporation. For the past five years, I've specialized in studying high-technology markets. Your director of engineering, John LaBarre, has asked me to talk to you about recent trends in computer-aided design so that you'll have a better idea of how to direct your research efforts.

This speaker establishes credibility by tying her credentials to the purpose of her presentation, without boasting. By mentioning her company's name, her specialization and position, and the name of the audience's boss, she lets her listeners know immediately that she is qualified to tell them something they need to know. She connects her background to their concerns.

Previewing Your Message   In addition to arousing audience interest and establishing your credibility, a good introduction gives your audience members a preview of what's ahead, helping them understand the structure and content of your message. A report reader can learn these things by looking at the table of contents and scanning the headings, but in a presentation you need to provide that framework with a preview.

Your preview should summarize the main idea of your presentation, identify major supporting points, and indicate the order in which you'll develop those points. Tell your listeners in so many words, "This is the subject, and these are the points I will cover." Once you've established the framework, you can be confident that the audience will understand how the individual facts and figures are related to your main idea as you move into the body of your presentation. If you are using an indirect approach, your preview can discuss the nature of your main idea without disclosing it.

> Use the preview to help your audience understand the importance, the structure, and the content of your message.

Presentation Body

The bulk of your speech or presentation is devoted to a discussion of the main supporting points from your outline. Whether you're using the direct or indirect approach, make sure the organization of your presentation is clear and your presentation holds the audience's attention.

Connecting Your Ideas Help your listeners move from one key point to the next with generous use of transitions. Between sentences and paragraphs, use transitional words and phrases such as *therefore, because, in addition, in contrast, moreover, for example, consequently, nevertheless,* and *finally.* To link major sections of a presentation, use complete sentences or paragraphs, such as "Now that we've reviewed the problem, let's take a look at some solutions." Every time you shift topics, be sure to stress the connection between ideas. Summarize what's been said and then preview what's to come. You might also want to call attention to the transitions by using gestures, changing your tone of voice, or introducing a new slide or other visual.

> Use transitions to repeat key ideas and help the audience follow along, particularly in longer presentations.

Holding Your Audience's Attention After you've successfully captured your audience's attention in your introduction, you need to work to keep it throughout the body of your presentation. Here are a few helpful tips for keeping the audience tuned in to your message:

- **Relate your subject to your audience's needs.** People are naturally most interested in things that affect them personally.
- **Anticipate your audience's questions.** Try to anticipate as many questions as you can and address these questions in the body of your presentation. You'll also want to prepare and reserve additional material to use during the question-and-answer period, in case the audience asks for greater detail.
- **Use clear, vivid language.** If your presentation involves abstract ideas, show how those abstractions connect with everyday life. Use familiar words, short sentences, and concrete examples. Be sure to use some variety as well; repeating the same words and phrases puts people to sleep.
- **Explain the relationship between your subject and familiar ideas.** Show how your subject is related to ideas that audience members already understand and give people a way to categorize and remember your points.[17]
- **Ask for opinions or pause occasionally for questions or comments.** Audience feedback helps you determine whether your listeners understand a key point before you launch into another section. Asking questions or providing comments also gives your audience members a chance to switch for a time from listening to participating, which helps them engage with your message and develop a sense of shared ownership.
- **Illustrate your ideas with visuals.** As Chapter 17 discusses, visuals enliven your message, help you connect with audience members, and help people more effectively remember your message.

> The most important way to hold an audience's attention is to show how your message relates to their individual needs and concerns.

REAL-TIME UPDATES

LEARN MORE BY VISITING THIS WEBSITE

Quick tips for a variety of speaking situations

Use these ideas for some of the most common public speaking scenarios. Go to **real-timeupdates.com/bct14** and select Learn More in the Students section.

Presentation Close

The close of a speech or presentation has two critical jobs to accomplish: making sure your listeners leave with the key points from your talk clear in their minds and putting

> Plan your close carefully so that your audience leaves with your main idea clear in their minds.

your audience in the appropriate emotional state. For example, if the purpose of your presentation is to warn managers that their out-of-control spending threatens the company's survival, you want them to leave with that message ringing in their ears—and with enough concern for the problem to stimulate changes in their behavior.

Restating Your Main Points   Use the close to succinctly restate your main points, emphasizing what you want your listeners to do or to think. For example, to close a presentation on your company's executive compensation program, you could repeat your specific recommendations and then conclude with a memorable statement to motivate your audience to take action:

> We can all be proud of the way our company has grown. However, if we want to continue that growth, we need to take four steps to ensure that our best people don't start looking for opportunities elsewhere:
>
> - First, increase the overall level of compensation
>
> - Second, establish a cash bonus program
>
> - Third, offer a variety of stock-based incentives
>
> - Fourth, improve our health insurance and pension benefits
>
> By taking these steps, we can ensure that our company retains the management talent it needs to face our industry's largest competitors.

By summarizing the key ideas, you improve the chance that your audience will leave with your message clearly in mind.

Ending with Clarity and Confidence   If you've been successful with the introduction and body of your presentation, your listeners have the information they need and are in the right frame of mind to put that information to good use. Now you're ready to end on a strong note that confirms expectations about any actions or decisions that will follow the presentation—and to bolster the audience's confidence in you and your message one final time.

Some presentations require the audience to reach a decision or agree to take specific action, in which case the close provides a clear wrap-up. If the audience agrees on an issue covered in the presentation, briefly review the consensus. If they don't agree, make the lack of consensus clear by saying something like, "We seem to have some fundamental disagreement on this question." Then be ready to suggest a method of resolving the differences.

If you expect any action to occur as a result of your speech, be sure to explain who is responsible for doing what. List the action items and, if possible within the time available, establish due dates and assign responsibility for each task.

Make sure your final remarks are memorable and expressed in a tone that is appropriate to the situation. If your presentation is a persuasive request for project funding, you might emphasize the importance of this project and your team's ability to complete it on schedule and within budget. Expressing confident optimism sends the message that you believe in your ability to perform. Conversely, if your purpose is to alert the audience to a problem or risk, false optimism undermines your message.

Whatever final message is appropriate, think through your closing remarks carefully before stepping in front of the audience. You don't want to wind up on stage with nothing to say but "Well, I guess that's it."

Plan your final statement carefully so you can end on a strong, positive note.

If you need to have the audience make a decision or agree to take action, make sure the responsibilities for doing so are clear.

Make sure your final remarks are memorable and have the right emotional tone.

Delivering a Presentation

3 LEARNING OBJECTIVE Discuss five steps for delivering a successful presentation.

With an outline, speaking notes, and any visual aids you plan to use, you're almost ready to deliver your presentation. This section covers five essential topics that will help you prepare for and deliver engaging and effective presentations, starting with choosing your method.

CHOOSING YOUR PRESENTATION METHOD

Depending on the circumstance of your presentation, you can choose from a variety of delivery methods:

- **Memorizing.** Except for extremely short speeches, trying to memorize an entire presentation is not a good idea. In the best of circumstances, you'll probably sound stilted; in the worst, you might forget your lines. Besides, you'll often need to address audience questions during your speech, so you need to be flexible enough to adjust your speech as you go. However, memorizing a quotation, an opening paragraph, and some strong finishing remarks can bolster your confidence and strengthen your delivery.

- **Reading.** In a few rare instances you may need to read a speech from a prepared script. For instance, policy statements and legal documents are sometimes read in full because the wording can be critical. However, unless you're required or expected to read your presentation verbatim, reading is not a good choice. You won't talk as naturally as you would otherwise, and the result will be a monotonous, uninspiring presentation.[18] If you must read your speech for some reason, practice enough so that you can still make periodic eye contact with your audience and make sure the printout of your speech is easy to read.

- **Speaking from an outline or notes.** Speaking with the help of an outline or note cards is nearly always the easiest and most effective delivery mode. The outline or notes guide you through the flow of the speech while giving you the freedom to speak naturally and spontaneously, to maintain eye contact with your listeners, and to respond and improvise as circumstances warrant. If you print note cards, use heavy note cards instead of regular paper. They're quieter and easier to flip through as you talk.

- **Impromptu speaking.** From time to time, you may be called upon unexpectedly to give an *impromptu* or *extemporaneous* speech on the spot, without the benefit of any planning or practice. Take a few seconds to identify the one key idea you want to share with the audience. That idea alone may be enough to meet the audience's expectations, or it might be enough to get you started and allow you to piece together additional ideas on the fly. Then think about a structure that would help convey that idea. Telling a brief story can be particularly effective in these situations because the structure helps you organize what you want to say, even as you're speaking. If you are asked to speak on a topic and simply don't have the information at hand, don't try to fake it. Instead, offer to get the information to the audience after the meeting or ask whether anyone else in the room can respond. Finally, before you even enter the meeting or other setting, if there is a chance you might be called on to say a few words, you can "prepare for the surprise" by thinking through what you might say in response to potential questions.[19]

Whichever delivery mode you use, be sure that you're thoroughly familiar with your subject. Knowing what you're talking about is the best way to build your self-confidence. If you stumble, get interrupted, or suffer equipment failures, your expertise will help you get back on track.

PRACTICING YOUR DELIVERY

Practicing your presentation is essential. Practice boosts your confidence, gives you a more professional demeanor, and lets you verify the operation of your visuals and equipment. A test audience can tell you if your slides are understandable and whether your delivery is effective. A day or two before you're ready to step on stage for an important talk, make sure you and your presentation are ready:

- Can you present your material naturally, without reading your slides?
- Is the equipment working, and do you know how to use it?
- Could you still make a compelling and complete presentation if you experience an equipment failure and have to proceed without using your slides at all?

MOBILE APP
authorSTREAM lets you replay webcasts and other recorded presentations on your mobile device.

Speaking from carefully prepared notes is the best delivery mode for nearly all presentations.

The more you practice, the more confidence you'll have in yourself and your material.

Make sure you're comfortable with the equipment you'll be expected to use; you don't want to be fumbling with controls while the audience is watching and waiting.

- Is your timing on track?
- Can you easily pronounce all the words you plan to use?
- Have you anticipated likely questions and objections?

With experience, you'll get a feel for how much practice is enough in any given situation. Practicing helps keep you on track, helps you maintain a conversational tone with your audience, and boosts your confidence and composure.

> You'll know you've practiced enough when you can present the material at a comfortable pace and in a natural, conversational tone.

PREPARING TO SPEAK

In addition to knowing your material thoroughly and practicing your delivery, make sure your location is ready, you have everything you'll need, and you're prepared to address audiences from other cultures, if that applies.

Whenever you can, scout the location for your presentation in advance. Check the seating arrangement to confirm it's appropriate for your needs and the audience's. Verify the availability and operation of all the equipment and supplies you're counting on, from the projection system to simple but vital necessities such as flip charts and marking pens. If you're using slides, make sure you know how to get the file from your computer or other device to the projection system.

> If possible, visit the speaking venue ahead of time to familiarize yourself with the facilities and the equipment.

If you're addressing audience members who speak a different native language, consider using an interpreter. Working with an interpreter does constrain your presentation somewhat. For instance, you must speak slowly enough for the interpreter to keep up with you. Send your interpreter a copy of your speaking notes and your visuals as far in advance as possible. If your audience is likely to include persons with hearing impairments, team up with a sign-language interpreter as well.

When you deliver a presentation to people from other cultures, take into account cultural differences in appearances, mannerisms, and other customs. Your interpreter or host will be able to suggest appropriate changes for a specific audience or occasion.

OVERCOMING ANXIETY

Recognize that nervousness is an indication that you care about your audience, your topic, and the occasion. These techniques will help you convert anxiety into positive energy:[20]

> Preparation is the best antidote for anxiety; it gives you confidence that you know your material and that you can recover from any glitches you might encounter.

- **Put yourself into a positive frame of mind before you start.** Remind yourself of how well you know the material and how much you enjoy sharing useful or inspirational information. If appropriate for the setting, smile as you take the stage.
- **Stop worrying about being perfect.** Successful speakers focus on making an authentic connection with their listeners, rather than on trying to deliver a note-perfect presentation.
- **Know your subject.** The more familiar you are with your material, the less panic you'll feel.
- **Practice, practice, practice.** The more you rehearse, the more confident you will be.
- **Visualize success.** Visualize mental images of yourself in front of the audience feeling confident, prepared, and able to handle any situation that might arise.[21] Remember that your audience wants you to succeed, too.
- **Remember to breathe.** Tension can lead people to breathe in a rapid and shallow fashion, which can create a lightheaded feeling. Breathe slowly and deeply to maintain a sense of calm and confidence.
- **Be ready with your opening line.** Have your first sentence memorized and on the tip of your tongue.
- **Be comfortable.** Dress appropriately but as comfortably as possible. Drink plenty of water ahead of time to hydrate your voice (bring water with you, too).
- **Take a three-second break.** If you sense that you're starting to race or ramble, pause and arrange your notes or perform some other small task while taking several deep breaths. Then start again at your normal pace.

- **Concentrate on your message and your audience, not on yourself.** When you're busy thinking about your subject and observing your audience's response, you tend to forget your fears.
- **Maintain eye contact with friendly audience members.** Eye contact not only makes you appear sincere, confident, and trustworthy but can give you positive feedback as well.
- **Keep going.** Things usually get better as you move along, with each successful minute giving you more and more confidence.

No one enjoys mistakes, equipment failures, and other troubles, but they are survivable. To learn how several experienced presenters have overcome some serious glitches, see "The Art of Professionalism: Recovering from Disasters."

Confident delivery starts as soon as you become the focus of attention, before you even begin to speak, so don't rush. As you approach the front of the room, walk with confidence, breathe deeply, and stand up straight. Face your audience, adjust the microphone and other equipment as needed, count to three slowly, and then scan the audience. When you find a friendly face, make eye contact and smile. Look away, count to three again, and then begin your presentation.[22] If you are nervous, this slow, controlled beginning will help you establish rapport and appear more confident. Make sure your nonverbal signals send a message of confidence.

As Gina Barnett advises, your posture helps you project confidence. Stand tall, with your weight on both feet and your shoulders back. Avoid gripping the lectern

> **REAL-TIME UPDATES**
> LEARN MORE BY READING THIS ARTICLE
> ### Two secrets to presenting like a pro
> Read how to build your confidence and stay in the moment. Go to **real-timeupdates.com/bct14** and select Learn More in the Students section.

Nonverbal signals tell the audience how you're feeling, so pay attention to the signals you send.

Recovering from Disasters

You've researched your topic, analyzed your audience, prepared a compelling message, crafted eye-catching visuals, and practiced until you're running like a smooth machine. You're ready to go.

Then you wake up with a sore throat and half a voice. You grab a few lozenges, hope for the best, and drive to the conference facility in plenty of time to set up your equipment. Oops, somebody forgot to tell you that your presentation has been moved up by an hour, and your audience is already in the room waiting for you. You scramble to turn on your laptop and get it connected to the projector, only to discover that you forgot the power cord and your battery is low. But that won't be a problem: Your laptop is dead anyway. Feeling smart, you pull out a CD-ROM with a backup copy of your PowerPoint slides and ask to use one of the several laptops you see scattered around the room. Nice idea, but they're equipped only with USB flash drives, so your CD is useless. The audience is getting restless; a few people get up to leave. You keep hoping you'll wake up from this bad dream so that your great day can really start. Sorry. This *is* your day.

Ask any business speaker with a few years of experience, and you'll hear all these horror stories and a few more: people who have driven to the wrong conference center, hit themselves in the head with a microphone, tripped over wires, started with a sure-fire joke that generated nothing but cold stares, or been rendered speechless by tough questions. Hoping you'll be spared isn't an effective response. You must be prepared for when—not if—something goes wrong.

If you assume that something *will* go wrong at some point, you can make peace with the possibility and focus on backup planning. Experts suggest that you make a list of every major problem you might encounter and imagine how you'll respond when these calamities strike you on the day of a big presentation. As much as possible, create a backup plan, such as calling ahead to reserve a second projector in the event that yours gets lost in transit. You won't be able to put backup resources in place for every possible glitch, but by at least thinking through the possibilities, you can decide how you'll respond. When disaster does strike, you'll look like a polished pro instead of a befuddled novice.

CAREER APPLICATIONS

1. If you spy trouble ahead in your presentation, such as noticing that your laptop battery is about to go dead or that you somehow have an old copy of the presentation file, should you tell your audience what's wrong? Or should you try to "wing it"? Explain your answer.
2. What steps can you take to make absolutely sure you have a usable backup copy of your presentation slides outside your office? Why is this important?

Sources: Based in part on C. Peter Guiliano and Frank J. Currilo, "Going Blank in the Boardroom," Public Relations Quarterly, Winter 2003, 35+; Jennifer Rotondo and Mike Rotondo Jr., Presentation Skills for Managers (New York: McGraw-Hill, 2002), 160–162; Mark Merritt, "No More Nightmares," Presentations, April 2001, 44+.

or other physical structure. Use your hands to emphasize your remarks with appropriate gestures. Meanwhile, vary your facial expressions to make the message more dynamic.

Finally, think about the sound of your voice. Studies indicate that people who speak with lower pitches at a slightly faster-than-average rate are perceived as being more credible.[23] Try to sound poised and confident, varying your pitch and speaking rate to add emphasis. For instance, slow down slightly when you're making an important point.[24] Speak clearly and crisply, articulating all the syllables, and sound enthusiastic about what you're saying. Use silence instead of meaningless filler words such as *um*, *you know*, *okay*, and *like*. Silence adds dramatic punch and gives the audience time to think about your message.

HANDLING QUESTIONS RESPONSIVELY

Don't leave the question-and-answer period to chance: anticipate likely questions and think through your answers.

Whether you take questions during a formal question-and-answer (Q&A) period or as they come up during your presentation, audience queries are often one of the most important parts of a presentation. They give you a chance to obtain important information, to emphasize your main idea and supporting points, and to build enthusiasm for your point of view. When you're speaking to high-ranking executives in your company, the Q&A period will often consume most of the time allotted for your presentation.[25]

Note that you may not always have the option of establishing ground rules for Q&A. If you're presenting to a small group of upper managers or potential investors, for example, you will probably have no say in the matter: Audience members will likely ask as many questions as they want, whenever they want, to get the information they need. On the other hand, if you are presenting to your peers or a large public audience, establish some guidelines, such as the number of questions allowed per person and the overall time limit for questions.

Don't assume you can handle whatever comes up without some preparation.[26] Learn enough about your audience members to get an idea of their concerns and think through answers to potential questions.

When people ask questions, pay attention to nonverbal signals to help determine what each person really means. Repeat the question to confirm your understanding and to ensure that the entire audience has heard it. If the question is vague or confusing, ask for clarification; then give a simple, direct answer.

If you don't have the complete answer to an important question, offer to provide it after the presentation.

If you are asked a difficult or complex question, avoid the temptation to sidestep it. Offer to meet with the questioner afterward if the issue isn't relevant to the rest of the audience or if giving an adequate answer would take too long. If you don't know the answer, don't pretend you do. Instead, offer to get a complete answer as soon as possible or ask if someone else can offer information on the topic.

Be on guard for audience members who use questions to make impromptu speeches or to take control of your presentation. Without offending anyone, find a way to stay in control. You might admit that you and the questioner have differing opinions and, before calling on someone else, offer to get back to the questioner after you've done more research.[27]

If you ever face hostile questions, respond honestly and directly while keeping your cool.

If a question ever puts you on the hot seat, respond honestly but keep your cool. Look the person in the eye, answer the question as well as you can, and keep your emotions under control. Defuse hostility by paraphrasing the question and asking the questioner to confirm that you've understood it correctly. Maintain a businesslike tone of voice and a pleasant expression.[28]

No matter how the presentation has gone, conclude in a strong, confident manner.

When the time allotted for your presentation is almost up, prepare the audience for the end by saying something like, "We have time for one more question." After you reply to that last question, summarize the main idea of the presentation and thank people for their attention. Conclude with the same confident demeanor you've had from the beginning.

Incorporating Technology in Your Presentation

Like much of the rest of business communication, presentations can be high-tech affairs in many companies. Two aspects you will most likely encounter on the job are the backchannel and online presentations.

EMBRACING THE BACKCHANNEL

Many business presentations these days involve more than just the spoken conversation between the speaker and his or her audience. Using Twitter and other digital media, audience members often carry on their own parallel communication during a presentation via the **backchannel**, which the presentation expert Cliff Atkinson defines as "a line of communication created by people in an audience to connect with others inside or outside the room, with or without the knowledge of the speaker."[29] Chances are you've participated in an informal backchannel already, such as when texting with your classmates or live-blogging during a lecture.

The backchannel presents both risks and rewards for business presenters. On the negative side, for example, listeners can research your claims the instant you make them and spread the word quickly if they think your information is shaky. The backchannel also gives contrary audience members more leverage, which can cause presentations to spin out of control. On the plus side, listeners who are excited about your message can build support for it, expand on it, and spread it to a much larger audience in a matter of seconds. You can also get valuable feedback during and after presentations.[30]

By embracing the backchannel, rather than trying to fight it or ignore it, presenters can use this powerful force to their advantage. Follow these tips to make the backchannel work for you:[31]

- **Integrate social media into the presentation process.** For example, you can create a website for the presentation so that people can access relevant resources during or after the presentation, create a Twitter hashtag that everyone can use when sending tweets, or display the Twitterstream during Q&A so that everyone can see the questions and comments on the backchannel.
- **Monitor and ask for feedback.** Using a free service such as TweetDeck to organize tweets by hashtag and other variables, you can monitor comments from the audience. To avoid trying to monitor the backchannel while speaking, you can schedule "Twitter breaks," during which you review comments and respond as needed.
- **Review comments to improve your presentation.** After a presentation is over, review comments on audience members' Twitter accounts and blogs to see which parts confused them, which parts excited them, and which parts seemed to have little effect (based on few or no comments).
- **Automatically tweet key points from your presentation while you speak.** Add-ons for presentation software can send out prewritten tweets as you show specific slides during a presentation. By making your key points readily available, you make it easy for listeners to retweet and comment on your presentation.
- **Establish expectations with the audience.** Explain that you welcome audience participation but that to ensure a positive experience for everyone, comments should be civil, relevant, and productive.

GIVING PRESENTATIONS ONLINE

Online presentations offer many benefits, including the opportunity to communicate with a geographically dispersed audience at a fraction of the cost of travel and the ability for a project team or an entire organization to meet at a moment's notice. However, this format also presents some challenges for the presenter, thanks to that

4 LEARNING OBJECTIVE
Explain the growing importance of the backchannel in presentations, and list six steps for giving effective presentations online.

Twitter and other social media are dramatically changing business presentations by making it easy for all audience members to participate in the *backchannel*.

Resist the urge to ignore or fight the backchannel; instead, learn how to use it to your advantage.

MOBILE APP
SlideShark lets you present and share PowerPoint slides with mobile and PC users.

Online presentations give you a way to reach more people in less time, but they require special preparation and skills.

layer of technology between you and your audience. Many of those "human moments" that guide and encourage you through an in-person presentation won't travel across the digital divide. For instance, it's sometimes difficult to tell whether audience members are bored or confused if your view of them is confined to small video images (and sometimes not even that). To ensure successful online presentations, keep the following advice in mind:

- **Consider sending preview study materials ahead of time.** Doing so allows audience members to familiarize themselves with any important background information. Also, by using a free service such as SlideShare, you can distribute your presentation slides to either public or private audiences, and you can record audio narrative to make your presentations function on their own.[32] Some presenters advise against giving out your slides ahead of time, however, because doing so gives away the ending of your presentation. If time allows, you can prepare preview materials that don't include your entire slide set.

- **Rehearse using the system live, if at all possible.** Presenting online has all the challenges of other presentations, with the additional burden of operating the presentation system while you are talking. Practice with at least one test viewer so you're comfortable using the system.[33]

- **Keep your presentation as simple as possible.** Break complicated slides down into multiple slides if necessary and keep the direction of your discussion clear so that no one gets lost.

With online presentations, you often can't rely on nonverbal signals to sense audience confusion or disagreement, so check in with your listeners frequently to see if they have questions.

- **Ask for feedback frequently.** Except on the most advanced telepresence systems, you won't have as much of the visual feedback that alerts you when audience members are confused, and many online viewers will be reluctant to call attention to themselves by interrupting you to ask for clarification. Setting up a backchannel via Twitter or as part of your online meeting system will help in this regard.

- **Consider the viewing experience from the audience members' point of view.** Will they be able to see what you think they can see? For instance, webcast video is sometimes displayed in a small window on screen, so viewers may miss important details. People logging in on mobile devices (smartphones in particular) may not get the same visual experience as people sitting in front of full-size computer screens.

- **Allow plenty of time for everyone to get connected and familiar with the screen they're viewing.** Build extra time into your schedule to ensure that everyone is connected and ready to start. If the meeting will require them to download and install meeting software, make sure to let them know well in advance.

Last but not least, don't get lost in the technology. Use these tools whenever they'll help, but remember that the most important aspect of any presentation is getting the audience to receive, understand, and embrace your message.

For a reminder of the steps to take in developing a presentation, refer to "Checklist: Developing Presentations." For the latest advice on planning presentations, visit **real-timeupdates.com/bct14** and select Chapter 16.

CHECKLIST ✔ Developing Presentations

A. Planning your presentation
- Analyze the situation by defining your purpose and developing an audience profile.
- Select the best medium.
- Organize your presentation by defining the main idea, limiting the scope, choosing your approach, and preparing your outline.

B. Developing your presentation
- Adapt to your audience by tailoring your style and language.
- Compose your presentation by preparing an introduction, a body, and a close.
- Use your introduction to arouse audience interest, build your credibility, and preview your message.
- Use the body to connect your ideas and hold your audience's attention.
- Close with confidence and clarity, restating your main points and describing the next steps.

C. Delivering your presentation
- Choose a presentation method, which should be speaking from an outline or notes in nearly all situations.
- Practice until you can deliver your material naturally, without reading your slides.

- Prepare to speak by verifying the operation of all the equipment you'll need to use.
- Determine whether you should use an interpreter.
- Overcome anxiety by preparing thoroughly.
- Handle questions responsively.

D. Embracing the backchannel
- Integrate social media into the presentation process.
- Monitor and ask for feedback.
- Review comments to improve your presentation.
- Automatically tweet key points from your presentation while you speak.
- Establish expectations with the audience.

E. Giving presentations online
- Consider sending preview study materials ahead of time.
- Rehearse using the system live, if at all possible.
- Keep your presentation as simple as possible.
- Ask for feedback frequently.
- Consider the viewing experience from the audience members' point of view.
- Allow plenty of time for everyone to get connected and familiar with the screen they're viewing.

COMMUNICATION CHALLENGES AT Barnett International

You are a communication coach at Barnett International, helping corporate clients improve their presentations using Gina Barnett's insights and strategies. In addition to presentation skills and stage presence, you also counsel clients on the content of important presentations.

INDIVIDUAL CHALLENGE: One of your clients wants to give an inspirational speech about how his grandparents founded a company during the Great Depression, built it up over four decades, and passed it on to their children, who then passed it on to him. He now serves as the CEO and wants to give his employees a sense of the company's history and values. After several attempts, however, he has given up and declared that he is simply not a storyteller. You believe he could benefit from a good example to study.

Revisit the story of Sarah Calhoun and Red Ants Pants on page 329 in Chapter 12. Construct a brief outline that would convey Calhoun's founding story in roughly 10 minutes. You can also visit **redantpants.com** and search for some of the articles published about her for more on the company's history.

TEAM CHALLENGE: Merge the outlines you and your teammates created in the individual exercise and then develop the content for this presentation. Brainstorm your way through the introduction, the body, and the close, identifying key message points and ideas for supporting visuals (anything from Red Ants Pants products to photographs to presentation slides). You don't have to create the visuals, but identify and describe them. Prepare a speaking outline with notes that convey all the key message points you've identified.

Quick Learning Guide

KEY TERMS

backchannel A social media conversation that takes place during a presentation, in parallel with the speaker's presentation

screencasts Recordings of activity on computer displays with audio voiceover

twebinars The use of Twitter as a backchannel to facilitate organized discussions

webcasts Online presentations that people either view live or download later from the web

SUMMARY OF LEARNING OBJECTIVES

1 Describe the tasks involved in analyzing the situation for a presentation and organizing a presentation. Although you rarely want to write out a presentation word for word, the three-step writing process is easy to adapt to presentations. The steps you take in planning presentations are generally the same as with any other business message: analyze the situation, gather information, select the right medium, and organize the information. The purpose of most business presentations is to inform or to persuade, although you may occasionally need to make a collaborative presentation. When you develop your audience profile, anticipate the likely emotional state of your audience members and plan to diffuse emotional situations if necessary.

Organizing a presentation requires the same general tasks as organizing a written message (define your main idea, limit your scope, select the direct or indirect approach, and outline your content), but pay special attention to the demands a presentation puts on listeners. They are largely captive to your timing and sequence, so make doubly sure you have a clear purpose, and limit your scope to convey your main idea and necessary supporting points within your allotted time frame. At the same time, take advantage of the flexibility you have with speeches and presentations to adjust the flow and level of detail on the fly if you sense that the audience wants different information than you originally planned. After you complete your *planning outline*, consider simplifying it to create a *speaking outline* to guide you during your presentation.

2 Explain how to adapt to your audience and develop an effective opening, body, and close for a presentation. To adapt to your audience, assess the size of your audience and the venue (in person or online); your subject, purpose, and budget; and the time available for preparation and allotted for your presentation. Determine whether you need to adjust your presentation or engage an interpreter when addressing audiences from other cultures, and assess the specific circumstances in which you'll be making your presentation.

You rarely write out a presentation in full, but plan your word and phrase choices so you can speak in a way that delivers planned messages in a spontaneous way. This step also includes creating whatever visual support materials you plan to use.

An effective introduction arouses audience interest in your topic, builds your credibility, and gives your audience a preview of your message. If your topic doesn't naturally interest the audience, you need to work extra hard in your introduction (and throughout the presentation) to relate the material to the audience in as personal a manner as possible. If you can't demonstrate credibility in your subject area, you can "borrow" credibility from recognized experts by incorporating their insights and opinions into your presentation (giving proper credit, of course). Previewing your message in the introduction helps the audience members recognize the importance of your material and gives them a chance to prepare for it by understanding how you plan to present it.

The bulk of your speech or presentation is devoted to a discussion of the main supporting points from your outline. Throughout the body of your talk, take care to connect your supporting points so that listeners can follow your thinking. Also work to hold your audience's attention by relating your subject to their needs, anticipating their questions, using clear and vivid language, relating your subject to familiar ideas, asking for questions or comments, and illustrating your ideas with visuals.

The close of a speech or presentation has two critical jobs to accomplish: making sure your listeners leave with the key points from your talk clear in their minds and putting your audience in the appropriate emotional state.

3 Discuss five steps for delivering a successful presentation. First, choose the best delivery method, which is speaking naturally and spontaneously from notes or a speaking outline in nearly all instances. Second, practice until you can deliver your material naturally, without reading your slides. Third, prepare to speak by making sure that your location is ready, you have everything you'll need, and you're prepared to address audiences from other cultures, if that applies. Fourth, work to overcome anxiety before and during your presentation by letting go of worrying about being perfect, preparing more material than necessary, visualizing your success, remembering to breathe, being ready with your opening line, making yourself comfortable, taking a three-second break if you sense that you're starting to race, concentrating on your message and your audience rather than on yourself, maintaining eye contact with friendly audience members, and going on even if you stumble. Fifth, handle questions responsively by determining whether you can set boundaries for the Q&A period, prepare answers to potential questions, pay attention to nonverbal signals, be sure to respond to all questions, don't let questioners take control of the presentation, face hostile questions head-on without getting defensive, and alert the audience when the Q&A period is almost over.

4 Explain the growing importance of the backchannel in presentations, and list six steps for giving effective presentations online. The backchannel is a parallel conversation taking place among audience members and other interested parties using Twitter and other media. To take advantage of the backchannel, you can integrate social media into your presentation, monitor and ask for feedback, review comments point by point to improve your presentation, automatically tweet key points from your presentation while you speak, and establish expectations with the audience.

To ensure a successful online presentation, consider sending preview materials ahead of time, keep your content and presentation as simple as possible, ask for feedback frequently, consider the viewing experience from the audience's side, and give participants time to get connected.

MyBCommLab

Go to **mybcommlab.com** to complete the problems marked with this icon .

Test Your Knowledge

To review chapter content related to each question, refer to the indicated Learning Objective.

16-1. What skills do business presentations give you the opportunity to practice and demonstrate? [LO-1]

16-2. What are the two most common purposes for giving presentations? [LO-1]

16-3. How do linear and nonlinear presentations differ? [LO-1]

16-4. How can outlines help you write and deliver a presentation? [LO-1]

16-5. How can you get and keep the audience's attention? [LO-2]

16-6. How does the delivery method of impromptu speaking differ from the delivery method of speaking from notes? [LO-3]

16-7. As a speaker, what nonverbal signals can you send to appear more confident? [LO-3]

16-8. What can speakers do to maintain control during the question-and-answer period of a presentation? [LO-3]

16-9. What is the backchannel? [LO-4]

Apply Your Knowledge

To review chapter content related to each question, refer to the indicated Learning Objective.

16-10. You just gave an in-depth presentation on the company's new marketing programs, intended for the specialists in the marketing department. The marketing manager then asked you to give a shorter version of the presentation to the company's top executives. In general, how should you modify the scope of your presentation for this new audience? [LO-1], [LO-2]

16-11. What role can entertainment play in an effective presentation? [LO-2]

16-12. If you're worried about forgetting your key message points, should you write them out and read them during your presentation? Why or why not? [LO-3]

16-13. Letting go of the idea that you have to be perfect can reduce your anxiety before a presentation. However, is it possible to create ethical problems by being too relaxed about your message and your performance? Explain your answer. [LO-3]

16-14. What are the possible consequences of ignoring the backchannel during a presentation to a public audience (such as at a convention)? [LO-4]

Practice Your Skills

Messages for Analysis

16-15. Message 16.A: Analyzing the Structure of a Presentation [LO-1] Find the transcript of a business-oriented speech or presentation by searching online for "speech transcription" or "presentation transcription." You can also browse **www.americanrhetoric.com**, which has thousands of transcriptions from speeches on a variety of subjects. Examine both the introduction and the close and analyze how these two sections work together to emphasize the main idea. Does the speaker want the audience to take any specific actions? To change any particular beliefs or feelings?

Next, identify the transitional sentences or phrases that clarify the speech's structure for the listener, especially those that help the speaker shift between supporting points. Using these transitions as clues, list the main message and supporting points, then indicate how each transitional phrase links the current supporting point to the succeeding one. Finally, prepare a brief (two- to three-minute) presentation summarizing your analysis for your class.

16-16. Message 16.B: Did the Introduction Get Your Attention? [LO-2] To access this message, visit **real-timeupdates .com/bct14**, select Student Assignments, then select Chapter 16, Message 16.B. Download and listen to this podcast, which is the introduction of a presentation to college seniors. Identify at least two techniques the speaker uses to try to grab your attention.

Exercises

Each activity is labeled according to the primary skill or skills you will need to use. To review relevant chapter content, you can refer to the indicated Learning Objective. In some instances, supporting information will be found in another chapter, as indicated.

16-17. Presentations: Planning and Developing [LO-1], [LO-2] With a team of three other students, prepare a detailed outline (including descriptions of any visuals you would plan to use) for a 10-minute presentation on the advantages of attending your college or university. The presentation would be delivered by someone from the admissions office, and the audience would be visiting high school students and their family members. After completing the outline together, each team member should individually develop a 60-second introduction to the presentation. Meet again, have each team member present his or her introduction, and then discuss which was most effective and why. Be prepared to discuss your conclusion with the class.

Presentations: Planning and Developing [LO-1], [LO-2] Choose a topic from this list and prepare a brief speech or presentation (5–10 minutes), with or without visuals, as your instructor indicates.

16-18. What I expected to learn in this course—and what I have learned

16-19. Past public speaking experiences: the good, the bad, and the ugly

16-20. I would be good at teaching _____.

16-21. I am afraid of _____.

16-22. It's easy for me to _____.

16-23. I get angry when _____.

16-24. I am happiest when I _____.

16-25. People would be surprised if they knew that I _____.

16-26. My favorite older person

16-27. My favorite charity

16-28. My favorite place

16-29. My favorite sport

16-30. My favorite store

16-31. My favorite television show

16-32. The town you live in suffers from a great deal of juvenile vandalism. Explain to a group of community members why juvenile recreational facilities should be built instead of a juvenile detention complex.

16-33. You are speaking to the Humane Society. Support or oppose the use of animals for medical research purposes.

16-34. You are talking to civic leaders of your community. Try to convince them to build an art gallery.

16-35. You are speaking to a first-grade class at an elementary school. Explain why they should brush their teeth after meals.

16-36. You are speaking to a group of first-time drivers. Convince them of the dangers of texting while driving.

16-37. You are speaking to a group of elderly people. Convince them to adopt an exercise program.

16-38. Energy issues (supply, conservation, alternative sources, national security, global warming, pollution, etc.)

16-39. Financial issues (banking, investing, family finances, etc.)

16-40. Government (domestic policy, foreign policy, Social Security taxes, welfare, etc.)

16-41. Interesting new technologies (virtual reality, geographic information systems, nanotechnology, bioengineering, etc.)

16-42. Politics (political parties, elections, legislative bodies and legislation, the presidency, etc.)

16-43. Sports (amateur and professional, baseball, football, golf, hang gliding, hockey, rock climbing, tennis, etc.)

16-44. **Presentations: Planning, Developing, and Delivering [LO-1], [LO-2], [LO-3]** Identify a company whose prospects look bright over the next few years because of highly competitive products, strong leadership, fundamental changes in the market, or any other significant reason. Prepare a five-minute speech, without visuals, explaining why you think this company is going to do well in the near future.

16-45. **Presentations: Mastering Delivery [LO-3]** Watch any talk that interests you at the TED website, **www.ted.com/talks,** and compare the speaker's delivery with this chapter's "Checklist: Developing Presentations." Write a brief

report (one to two pages) analyzing the speaker's performance and suggesting improvements.

16-46. **Presentations: Mastering Delivery; Communication Ethics: Making Ethical Choices [LO-3], Chapter 1** Think again about the presentation you observed and analyzed in the previous exercise. How could the speaker have used nonverbal signals to unethically manipulate the audience's attitudes or actions?

16-47. **Presentations: Using the Backchannel; Collaboration: Team Projects [LO-4], Chapter 2** In teams assigned by your instructor, develop a 15-minute slide presentation on any topic that interests you. Nominate one person to give the presentation; the others will participate via a Twitter backchannel. Set up private Twitter accounts if your class doesn't already use them, and create a hashtag that everyone on the team can follow using TweetDeck or a similar tool. During the presentation, the audience members should tweet comments and questions, and the presenter can take a Twitter break partway through to respond to backchannel messages. Be ready to discuss your experience with the entire class.

Expand Your Skills

Critique the Professionals

Find a product demonstration video on YouTube for any product that is appropriate to discuss in class. (Find a video that is at least two minutes long and was uploaded by the company that makes the product, not by a customer or other outside party.) Study the effectiveness of the demonstration, including the use of visuals and the presenter's speech and mannerisms. Did you find the demonstration compelling? Why or why not? If not, what would've made it more compelling? Using whatever medium your instructor requests, write a brief summary of your analysis. Be sure to include a link to the video.

Sharpening Your Career Skills Online

Bovée and Thill's Business Communication Web Search, at **websearch.businesscommunicationnetwork.com,** is a unique research tool designed specifically for business communication research. Use the Web Search function to find a website, video, article, podcast, or presentation that offers advice on public speaking or presentations in business. Write a brief email message to your instructor, describing the item that you found and summarizing the career skills information you learned from it.

MyBCommLab

Go to **mybcommlab.com** for Auto-graded writing questions as well as the following Assisted-graded writing questions:

16-48. What three goals should you accomplish during the introduction of a presentation? [LO-2]

16-49. Can you prepare for an impromptu speech? Explain your answer. [LO-3]

Endnotes

1. Kate Torgovnick May and Emily Ludolph, "A TED Speaker Coach Shares 11 Tips for Right Before You Go on Stage," TED blog, 14 February 2016, blog.ted.com; Laura Montini, "Steal This TED Coach's Top 3 Public Speaking Tricks," *Inc.*, 4 June 2015, www.inc.com; Barnett International website, accessed 5 May 2016, barnettinternationalconsulting.com; Gina Barnett, "Play the Part: Master Body Signals to Connect and Communicate for Business Success," Talks at Google, video, 24 June 2015, www.youtube.com/watch?v=q3nxsdQt7Rg; "TED Conference Coach Gina Barnett Offers Public Speaking Tips," CBC News, 19 March 2015, www.cbc.ca; Gina Barnett, "Like, Totally Don't Talk Like This to Get Ahead in Business?" *Fortune*, 6 July 2015, www.fortune.com; Gina Barnett, *Play the Part: Master Body Signals to Connect and Communicate for Business Success* (New York: McGraw-Hill, 2015).

2. Nancy Duarte, *slide:ology: The Art and Science of Creating Great Presentations* (Sebastopol, Calif.: O'Reilly Media, 2008), 13.

3. Amber Naslund, "Twebinar: GE's Tweetsquad," 4 August 2009, www.radian6.com/blog.

4. "Get Started with Prezi," Prezi website, accessed 2 May 2014, prezi.com.

5. Adam Noar, "PowerPoint vs. Prezi: What's the Difference?" Presentation Panda blog, 21 February 2012, presentationpanda.com.

6. Irwin Pollack, "Don't Just Give Presentations, Impact Your Audience," *Fort Worth Business Press*, 1 May 2006, 10.

7. Carmine Gallo, "How to Deliver a Presentation Under Pressure," *BusinessWeek* online, 18 September 2008, www.businessweek.com.

8. Sarah Lary and Karen Pruente, "Powerless Point: Common PowerPoint Mistakes to Avoid," *Public Relations Tactics*, February 2004, 28.

9. Garr Reynolds, *Presentation Zen: Simple Ideas on Presentation Design and Delivery* (Berkeley, Calif.: New Riders, 2008), 39–42.

10. Reynolds, *Presentation Zen*, 66.

11. Sherwyn P. Morreale and Courtland L. Bovée, *Excellence in Public Speaking* (Fort Worth, Tex.: Harcourt Brace College Publishers, 1998), 234–237.

12. John Windsor, "Presenting Smart: Keeping the Goal in Sight," *Presentations*, 6 March 2008, www.presentations.com.

13. Morreale and Bovée, *Excellence in Public Speaking*, 241–243.

14. Adapted from Eric J. Adams, "Management Focus: User-Friendly Presentation Software," *World Trade*, March 1995, 92.

15. Carmine Gallo, "Grab Your Audience Fast," *BusinessWeek*, 13 September 2006, 19.

16. Walter Kiechel III, "How to Give a Speech," *Fortune*, 8 June 1987, 180.

17. *Communication and Leadership Program* (Santa Ana, Calif.: Toastmasters International, 1980), 44, 45.

18. Steve Adubato, "Throw Away That Script, Use an Outline Instead," *NJBiz*, 23 October 2006, 17.

19. Cheryl Wiles, "Impromptu Speaking," *Harvard Management Communication Letter*, December 2001, 7–8.

20. Richard Zeoli, "The Seven Things You Must Know About Public Speaking," *Forbes*, 3 June 2009, www.forbes.com; Morreale and Bovée, *Excellence in Public Speaking*, 24–25.

21. Jennifer Rotondo and Mike Rotondo Jr., *Presentation Skills for Managers* (New York: McGraw-Hill, 2002), 9.

22. Judy Linscott, "Getting On and Off the Podium," *Savvy*, October 1985, 44.

23. Iris R. Johnson, "Before You Approach the Podium," *MW*, January–February 1989, 7.

24. "Advice from a Voice Coach: Say It and Sell It," *Presentations*, 6 November 2006, www.presentations.com.

25. Rick Gilbert, "Presentation Advice for Boardroom Success," *Financial Executive*, September 2005, 12.

26. Rotondo and Rotondo, *Presentation Skills for Managers*, 151.

27. Teresa Brady, "Fielding Abrasive Questions During Presentations," *Supervisory Management*, February 1993, 6.

28. Robert L. Montgomery, "Listening on Your Feet," *Toastmaster*, July 1987, 14–15.

29. Cliff Atkinson, *The Backchannel* (Berkeley, Calif.: New Riders, 2010), 17.

30. Atkinson, *The Backchannel*, 51, 68–73.

31. Olivia Mitchell, "10 Tools for Presenting with Twitter," Speaking About Presenting blog, 3 November 2009, www.speakingaboutpresenting.com; Atkinson, *The Backchannel*, 51, 68–73, 99.

32. SlideShare website, accessed 3 August 2010, www.slideshare.net.

33. Geoffrey James, "How to Give an Online Presentation," BNET, 23 February 2011, www.bnet.com.

LEARNING OBJECTIVES

After studying this chapter, you will be able to

1 Explain the role of visuals in business presentations, and list the types of visuals commonly used.

2 Explain the difference between structured and free-form slides, and suggest when each design strategy is more appropriate.

3 Outline the decisions involved in using a key visual and selecting color, artwork, and typefaces to create effective slide designs.

4 Explain how to create effective slide content.

5 Explain the role of navigation slides, support slides, and handouts.

MyBCommLab®

⭐ **Improve Your Grade!** More than 10 million students improved their results using Pearson MyLabs. Visit **mybcommlab.com** for simulations, tutorials, and end-of-Chapter problems.

COMMUNICATION CLOSE-UP AT

Duarte

www.duarte.com

When managers of top consumer brands, global experts in a wide variety of topics, and campaigners for major social causes need help getting their messages across, many of them turn to the services of Duarte, a Silicon Valley firm that specializes in presentation design. You don't have to be a major corporation or well-known speaker to benefit from Duarte's expertise, however. In her books and in various presentations, CEO and founder Nancy Duarte offers advice that all business communicators can use to create more compelling presentation slides.

Duarte suggests five principles of effective slide design that echo the audience-centered approach you've been practicing throughout this course. The first and most important is to make your presentation about your audience and their needs. If you are pitching a new business idea to potential investors, for example, do it in a way that addresses their interests in finding profitable investment opportunities. In other words, don't make it all about you and how clever you are. Use slides and other visuals to show audience members how they can make money by climbing on board with you.

Second, don't try to transfer truckloads of data and information to your audience. Instead, focus on sharing meaning and connecting with audiences at an emotional level. If you're training your sales force on a new product, give them the technical details and market information, but also fire them up with stories about how people can use this product to improve their lives or do amazing things in their businesses. Use images and video to

Follow Nancy Duarte's slide design principles to create compelling, audience-focused visuals for your presentations.

convey the human side of whatever business proposition you're discussing. And with every slide or visual, strive for simplicity. Overloaded slides exhaust and confuse audiences.

Third, use your visual medium to full effect. This might sound obvious, since presentation slides are a visual medium to begin with, but too many presenters rely too heavily on verbal content. Showing your audience one slide after another with nothing but words on them is not very far removed from handing them a written report. In addition, when it comes to learning and under-standing, many people respond better to visual content and rep-resentations of ideas. For each major point in your presentation, see if you can find a way to present the key information visually—through a flowchart, a diagram, a photo, a mindmap, or any other visual tool. PowerPoint and other slide programs offer a host of easy-to-use drawings that help you present ideas and information.

Fourth, think *design*, not *decoration*, when it comes to creating your slides. When choosing fonts, colors, artwork, animation, and other visual elements, consider how each piece can support the meaning you want your audience to receive. Don't add things to your slides to "liven them up" or because you stumbled on a cool-looking special effect in your slide software—some of these add little or no value while distracting the audience from your message.

Fifth, remember that slides and other visuals are simply part of the channel between you and your audience. Because slides are so visible, it's easy for presenters to fall into the trap of treat-ing their slides as the centerpiece of a presentation. But slides are just a conduit for moving ideas, meaning, and inspiration from your mind to your audience's minds. By following some time-tested principles of good design, you can create slides that help you make those important connections with every audience.[1]

Planning Your Presentation Visuals

1 **LEARNING OBJECTIVE**
Explain the role of visuals in business presentations and list the types of visuals commonly used.

The three-step development process in Chapter 16 helps ensure that you have a well-crafted, audience-focused message. The techniques in this chapter, which reflect the advice offered by experts such as Nancy Duarte (profiled in the chapter-opening Communication Close-Up), will help you enhance the delivery of that message with creative and effective visuals.

Visuals can improve the quality and impact of any presentation by creating interest, illustrating points that are difficult to explain with words alone, adding variety, and increasing the audience's ability to absorb and remember information. Behavioral research has shown that visuals can improve learning by up to 400 percent because humans can process visuals 60,000 times faster than text.[2]

Remember that the purpose of visuals is to support your spoken message, not replace it.

For all the communication power of visuals, however, don't make the mistake of think-ing that your visuals *are* your presentation. Particularly when using software such as Prezi or Microsoft PowerPoint, communicators sometimes fall into the trap of letting the visuals take center stage. Remember that your message is the presentation, not your visuals; your visuals are there to help support and clarify what you have to say.[3]

SELECTING THE TYPE OF VISUALS TO USE

You can select from a variety of visuals to enhance presentations, each with unique advan-tages and disadvantages:

Presentation slides and Prezis are the most common visual supports for presentations, but don't limit yourself to these.

- **Prezis.** Chapter 16 discusses the differences between linear and nonlinear presenta-tions, with Prezis as the dominant example of nonlinear presentations. The biggest advantages of Prezis are flexibility (both in how you structure your visuals and in how you access them during your presentation), the ability to incorporate video and other media elements, and a more dynamic look and feel than conventional slide shows. The potential disadvantages of Prezis include fewer design options, the chance of viewers "losing the plot" as the presenter jumps from topic to topic, and the possibil-ity of viewers feeling dizzy or even getting motion sickness if zooming is overused.[4]

- **Slides.** Slides created with PowerPoint or similar pro-grams have a number of advantages: They are easy to create and edit (at least for simple slides), designs are easy to customize, and slides are easy to incorporate into online meetings and webcasts. The biggest potential dis-advantage of slides is the linear nature of the presenta-tion. Changing the flow of the presentation or jumping to specific slides is more difficult in presentation software than it is with a Prezi. Note that for both Prezi and slide software, the disadvantages people sometimes mention are usually a result of how the tools are used, rather than limitations in the software itself.

- **Overhead transparencies.** Overhead transparencies are the very definition of old school, but they do have advantages. They can be created with nothing more than a marking pen, they don't require the latest computer or projection equipment, you can write on them during a presentation, and they never malfunction. On the downside, they're limited to static displays, they're virtually impossible to edit once you've printed them, you need to have the right equipment, and you or a partner must stand next to the projector throughout the entire presentation.

- **Chalkboards and whiteboards.** Chalkboards and whiteboards are effective tools for recording points made during small-group sessions. With digital whiteboards, you can print, save, and share copies of whatever is written, too.

- **Flip charts.** Flip charts are another dependable low-tech tool for meetings and presentations. They are great for recording comments and questions during a presentation or for creating a "group memory" during brainstorming sessions, keeping track of all the ideas the team generates.

- **Other visuals.** Be creative when choosing visuals to support your presentation. A video of a focus group talking about your company can have much more impact than a series of text slides that summarize what the group said. In technical or scientific presentations, a sample of a product or material lets your audience experience your subject directly. Designers and architects use mock-ups and models to help people envision what a final creation will look like. You might also want to incorporate other software into your presentation, such as a live spreadsheet to show financial data or a computer-aided design program to show a new product's design. If you're demonstrating the use of a software program, you can create a screencast that shows the software in action. Screencasting software also lets you add on-screen annotations and record an audio track to explain what is happening on screen.

This chapter focuses on slide presentations, although most of these design tips apply to other visuals as well.

THE FUTURE OF COMMUNICATION

Holograms

If you've ever wanted to be in two places at once, your wish could be coming true soon. At a recent executive meeting of the global management and technology consulting firm Accenture, the attendees included CEO Pierre Nanterme and human resources chief Ellyn Shook. During the meeting, which took place near Chicago, they chatted with other managers, pitched and listened to ideas, and even shared a few ceremonial fist bumps. Nothing remarkable there, except that Nanterme was in Paris and Shook was in New York City. Their three-dimensional selves were beamed in as holograms over the company's hyper-advanced information network.

Accenture has long been on the leading edge of communication technology, including the use of advanced telepresence facilities that help its huge workforce stay connected from outposts all over the world. As much as Nanterme would like to meet frequently with employees in person, the fact that there are 375,000 of them spread over 120 counties makes that impossible.

Vastly oversimplified, in this context holograms are created by scanning a person or an object with a laser, transmitting the resulting data to a second location, then re-creating the person or object as a three-dimensional "figure." The figure is made entirely of light, but today's systems can make that figure look extremely lifelike. And researchers at the University of Tokyo have invented a system that combines holograms with ultrasonic haptic technology that simulates the sensation of touch, making it possible to "touch" a hologram.

Few companies have the resources to pull off what Accenture can do with holograms, and as a technology consulting firm, it has other business reasons to keep pushing the limits of technology. If this use of holograms moves into the mainstream, however, it could change the way far-flung companies communicate. And holograms are already being used in such areas as research and product design, letting people interact with objects that aren't really there.

WHAT'S YOUR PREDICTION?

Research the current state of holograms to identify one way in which the technology has the potential to change business communication practices. Do you agree with the predictions the experts make? Why or why not?

Sources: Jena McGregor, "Star Wars Meets the C-Suite: This CEO's Hologram Is Beaming into Meetings," *Washington Post*, 13 April 2016, www.washingtonpost .com; Alan Murray, "The CEO as Hologram," *Fortune*, 16 December 2015, fortune.com; Jason Hahn, "Japanese Researchers Have Created Holograms You Can Touch, Poke, and Push," *Digital Trends*, 26 December 2015, www.digitaltrends .com; Microsoft HoloLens website, accessed 7 May 2016, www.microsoft.com /microsoft-hololens.

VERIFYING YOUR DESIGN PLANS

Think through your presentation outline carefully before designing your visuals.

After you have chosen the medium or media for your visuals, think through your presentation plan carefully before you start creating anything. Discerning audience members—the sort of people who can influence the direction of your career—are not easily fooled by visual razzle-dazzle. If your analysis is shaky or your conclusions are suspect, an over-the-top visual production won't help your presentation succeed. Review the plan for each visual and ask yourself how it will help your audience understand and appreciate your message.

Next, make sure your presentation style is appropriate for the subject matter, the audience, and the setting (see Figure 17.1). Take the time to double-check any cultural assumptions that might be inappropriate. Are you highlighting with a color that has negative emotional connotations in your audience's culture? Would your materials be too playful for a serious audience? Too serious for an audience that values creativity?

When it comes time to make design choices, from selecting fonts to deciding whether to include a photo, remember the advice from Chapter 16 and designers such as Garr Reynolds: Let simplicity be your guide. Doing so has several advantages. First, creating simple materials often takes less time. Second, simple visuals reduce the chances of distraction and misinterpretation. Third, the more complex your presentation, the more likely something might go wrong.

Finally, use your time wisely. Presentation software seems to encourage experimentation and fiddling around with details and special effects, which can eat up hours of time you probably don't have. Based on your audience and the situation, decide up front how much visual design is sufficient for your purpose and then stop when you get there. Use the time you'll save to rehearse your presentation—practice is far more important than minor design issues on your slides.

Figure 17.1 **Presentation Style**
Presentation software lets you create a variety of visual styles, from quiet and plain to bold and busy. These four slides contain the same text but send different nonverbal messages. Make sure you choose a style that is appropriate for your audience and your message.

Choosing Structured or Free-Form Slides

The most important design choice you face when creating slides is whether to use conventional **structured slides** or the looser, **free-form slides** that many presentation specialists now advocate. Compare the two rows of slides in Figure 17.2. The structured slides in the top row follow the same basic format throughout the presentation; in fact, they're based directly on the templates built into PowerPoint, which tend to feature lots of bullet points.

The free-form slides in the bottom row don't follow a rigid structure. However, choosing a free-form design strategy does not mean you should just randomly change the design from one slide to the next. Effectively designed slides should still be unified by design elements such as color and typeface selections, as Figures 17.2c and 17.2d show. Also, note how Figure 17.2d combines visual and textual messages to convey the point about listening without criticizing. This complementary approach of pictures and words is a highlight of free-form design.

2 LEARNING OBJECTIVE
Explain the difference between structured and free-form slides, and suggest when each design strategy is more appropriate.

Structured slides are usually based on templates that give all the slides in a presentation the same general look.

Free-form slides typically don't follow any set design plan but are unified by color and other elements.

ADVANTAGES AND DISADVANTAGES OF STRUCTURED SLIDES

Structured slides have the advantage of being easy to create; you simply choose an overall design scheme for the presentation, select a template for a new slide, and start typing. If you're in a schedule crunch, going the structured route might save the day because at least

Figure 17.2a

Figure 17.2b

Figure 17.2c

Figure 17.2d

Figure 17.2 **Structured Versus Free-Form Slide Design**
Compare the rigid, predictable design of the two slides in the top row with the free-form designs in the bottom row. Although the two free-form slides don't follow the same design structure, they are visually linked by color and font choices. As you compare these two styles, you can imagine how free-form designs require more slides to cover the same subject and require the speaker to convey more of the message. (Note that Figure 17.2d is a light-hearted but effective way of conveying the first bullet point in Figure 17.2b.)

Structured slides are usually the best choice for project updates and other routine information presentations, particularly if the slides are intended to be used only once.

Structured slide designs, which can lead to screen after screen of identical-looking bullet points, can be boring and overwhelming.

Well-designed free-form slides help viewers understand, process, and remember the speaker's message while keeping the focus on what the speaker is saying.

A key disadvantage of free-form slide designs is the time and effort that can be required to create them.

you'll have *something* ready to show. Given the speed and ease of creating them, structured slides can be a more practical choice for routine presentations such as project status updates.

Also, because more information can usually be packed onto each slide, carefully designed structured slides can be more effective at conveying complex ideas or sets of interrelated data to the right audiences. For example, if you are talking to a group of executives who must decide where to make budget cuts across the company's eight divisions, at some point in the presentation they will probably want to see summary data for all eight divisions on a single slide for easy comparison. Such a slide would be overcrowded by the usual definition, but this might be the only practical way to get a "big picture" view of the situation. (The best solution is probably some high-level, summary slides supported by a detailed handout, as "Creating Effective Handouts" on page 502 explains.)

The primary disadvantage of structured design is the mind-numbing effect of text-heavy slides that all look alike. Slide after slide of dense, highly structured bullet points with no visual relief can put an audience to sleep.

ADVANTAGES AND DISADVANTAGES OF FREE-FORM SLIDES

Free-form slide designs can overcome the drawbacks of text-heavy structured design. Such slides can fulfill three criteria researchers have identified as important for successful presentations: (1) providing complementary information through both textual and visual means, (2) limiting the amount of information delivered at any one time to prevent cognitive overload, and (3) helping viewers process information by identifying priorities and connections, such as by highlighting the most important data points in a graph.[5] (Of course, well-designed structured slides can also meet these criteria, but the constraints of prebuilt templates make doing so more of a challenge.)

With appropriate imagery and thoughtful design, free-form designs can also create a more dynamic and engaging experience for the audience. Given their ability to excite and engage, free-form designs are particularly good for motivational, educational, and persuasive presentations—particularly when the slides will be used multiple times and therefore compensate for the extra time and effort required to create them. By taking advantage of the animation capabilities in PowerPoint or Keynote, it is also possible to create some of the dynamic, flowing feel of a Prezi.

Free-form slides have several potential disadvantages, however. First, effectively designing slides with both visual and textual elements is more creatively demanding and more time consuming than simply typing text into preformatted templates. The emphasis on visual content also requires more images, which take time to find.

Second, because far less textual information tends to be displayed on screen, the speaker is responsible for conveying more of the content. Ideally, of course, this is how a presentation *should* work, but presenters sometimes find themselves in less-than-ideal circumstances, such as being asked to fill in for a colleague on short notice.

Third, if not handled carefully, the division of information into smaller chunks can make it difficult to present complex subjects in a cohesive, integrated manner. For instance, if you're discussing a business problem that has five interrelated causes, it might be helpful to insert a conventional bullet-point slide as a summary and reminder after discussing each problem on its own.

Designing Effective Slides

Businesspeople have had to sit through so many poorly conceived presentations that you may hear the phrase "death by PowerPoint" to describe the agony of sitting through dull, slide-heavy presentations. However, the problem is not with PowerPoint itself (or with Apple Keynote or any other presentation program). The software is just a tool and, like other tools, can be used well or poorly. Unfortunately, lack of design awareness, inadequate training, schedule pressures, and the instinctive response of doing things the way they've always been done can lead to ineffective slides and lost opportunities to really connect with audiences.

Another reason for ineffective slides is the practice of treating slide sets as standalone documents that can be read on their own, without a presenter. These "slideument" hybrids that try to function as both presentation visuals and printed documents often don't work well as either: They usually have too much information to be effective visuals and too little to be effective reports (in addition to being clumsy to read).

As the section "Creating Effective Handouts" on page 502 explains, the ideal solution is to create an effective slide set and a separate handout document that provides additional details and supporting information. This way, you can optimize each piece to do the job it is really meant to do. An alternative is to use the notes field in your presentation software to include your speaking notes for each slide. Anyone who gets a copy of your slides can at least follow along by reading your notes, although you will probably need to edit and expand them to make them understandable by others.

However, if creating slideuments is truly your only option, be sure to emphasize clarity and simplicity. If you have to add more slides to avoid packing individual slides with too much text, by all means do so. Having a larger number of simpler slides is a better compromise all around than having a smaller number of jam-packed slides. Remember that the primary purpose of the slides is to support your presentation, so make sure your slides work well for that purpose.

> "Slideuments" are hybrids that try to function as both presentation slides and printed documents—and often fail at both tasks.

> The ideal solution for many presentations is an effective set of slides and a complementary handout.

> If you must create a slideument, make the slides as simple and clear as possible.

DESIGNING SLIDES AROUND A KEY VISUAL

With both structured and free-form design strategies, it is often helpful to structure specific slides around a key visual that helps organize and explain the points you are trying to make. For example, a pyramid suggests a hierarchical relationship, and a circular flow diagram emphasizes that the final stage in a process loops back to the beginning of the process. Figure 17.3 on the next page shows six of the many types of visual designs you can use to organize information on a slide.

> Organizing a slide around a key visual can help the audience quickly grasp how ideas are related.

SELECTING DESIGN ELEMENTS

As you design and create slides, always keep the audience's experience in mind: What will it be like to view this slide while listening to a speaker? Chapter 9 highlights six principles of effective design: consistency, contrast, balance, emphasis, convention, and simplicity. Pay close attention to these principles as you select the design elements for your slides (covered in this section) and create content for each slide (covered in the following section).

> To design effective slides, remember the six principles of effective design: consistency, contrast, balance, emphasis, convention, and simplicity (review Chapter 9 for a refresher).

Color

Color is a critical design element, far more than mere decoration. It grabs the viewer's attention, emphasizes important ideas, creates contrast, and isolates slide elements. Color sends a powerful nonverbal message, too, whether it's elegance, technical sophistication, fiscal prudence, or hipster trendiness. You can study this effect as you view various websites or advertisements, for instance. A palette of cool grays and blues "says" something different from a palette of warm oranges and browns, which says something different from a palette of hot pink and lime green.

Color can also play a key role in the overall acceptance of your message. Research shows that color visuals can account for 60 percent of an audience's acceptance or rejection of an idea. Color can increase willingness to read by up to 80 percent, and it can enhance learning and improve retention by more than 75 percent.[6]

Your color choices can also stimulate various emotions, as Table 17.1 on the next page suggests. For instance, if you want to excite your audience, add warm colors, such as red and orange, to your slides. If you want to achieve a more relaxed and receptive environment, blue is a better choice.[7]

> Color is much more than mere decoration: It provides emphasis, isolation, and contrast; it increases readability and retention; it sends powerful nonverbal signals; and it can stimulate desired emotional responses.

REAL-TIME UPDATES
LEARN MORE BY VISITING THIS WEBSITE
Advice and free templates for more effective slideuments

The free e-book and a pair of PowerPoint templates will help you make more effective slide-document hybrids. Go to **real-timeup-dates.com/bct14** and select Learn More in the Students section.

Figure 17.3a

Figure 17.3b

Figure 17.3c

Figure 17.3d

Figure 17.3e

Figure 17.3f

Figure 17.3 **Using a Key Visual to Organize Points on a Slide**
Simple graphical elements such as these "SmartArt" images in Microsoft PowerPoint make it easy to organize slide content using a key visual. Whether you're trying to convey the relationship of ideas in a hierarchy, a linear process, a circular process, or just about any other configuration, a key visual can work in tandem with your written and spoken messages to help audiences get your message.

TABLE 17.1 Color and Emotion

Color	Emotional Associations (for U.S. audiences)	Best Uses
Blue	Peaceful, soothing, tranquil, cool, trusting	Background for business presentations (usually dark blue); safe and conservative
White	Neutral, innocent, pure, wise	Font color of choice for most business presentations with a dark background
Yellow	Warm, bright, cheerful, enthusiastic	Text bullets and subheadings with a dark background
Red	Passionate, dangerous, active, painful	For promoting action or stimulating the audience; seldom used as a background ("in the red" specifically refers to financial losses)
Green	Assertive, prosperous, envious, relaxed	Highlight and accent color (green symbolizes money in the United States but not in other countries)

Source: Claudyne Wilder and David Fine, *Point, Click & Wow!!: A Quick Guide to Brilliant Laptop Presentations* (San Francisco: Jossey-Bass Pfeiffer, 1996), 63, 527.

Remember, color may have a different meaning in certain cultures, so if you are creating slides for international audiences, research those cultural differences.

When selecting color, limit your choices to a few compatible ones and keep in mind that some colors work better together than others. Contrasting colors, for example, increase readability, so when selecting colors for backgrounds, titles, and text, avoid choosing those that are close in hue, such as brown on green or blue on purple.[8] If you'll be presenting in a dark room, use dark colors such as blue for the background, a midrange of brightness for illustrations, and light colors for text. If you are presenting in well-lit rooms, reverse the colors: Use light colors for the background and dark colors for text. If you have some reason to change colors between slides, don't switch back and forth from very dark to very bright; the effect is jarring to the audience's eyes.[9]

Artwork

Every slide has two layers or levels of visual elements: the background and foreground. The *background* is the equivalent of paper in a printed report and often stays the same from slide to slide, particularly with structured designs. The *foreground* contains the unique text and graphic elements that make up each individual slide.

In general, the less the background does, the better. As Nancy Duarte explains, the background "should be open, spacious, and simple."[10] Cluttered or flashy backgrounds tend to distract from your message. The background needs to stay in the background; it shouldn't compete with the foreground elements. Be careful when using the design templates that come with your software. Many have backgrounds that are too busy, and some are too playful for business use. Bear in mind that you don't *need* to use a background at all, other than perhaps a solid color to set type and images against.

> The background should stay in the background, not compete with the foreground.

In the background, all artwork is essentially decorative. In the foreground, artwork can be either functional or decorative. *Functional artwork* includes photos, technical drawings, charts, and other visual elements containing information that is part of your message. In contrast, *decorative artwork* doesn't deliver textual or numerical information, and it may or may not be helpful. Decorative artwork can be helpful if it establishes an appropriate emotional tone or amplifies the message of a slide, in part because simple, high-impact images are easier to remember than text.[11] However, decorative artwork is unhelpful if it doesn't add value, is off topic, conveys an unprofessional image, or pulls viewer attention away from the essential elements on a slide (see Figure 17.4). Decorative artwork is usually the least important element of any slide, but it often causes the most trouble. *Clip art*, collections of drawings you can insert in slides and other documents, is probably the biggest troublemaker of them all. You can find thousands of pieces of free

> Artwork can be either decorative or functional; use decorative artwork only if it supports the message of the slide in question.

Figure 17.4a

Figure 17.4b

Figure 17.4   Effective and Ineffective Artwork

Slide artwork can carry your message, support your message, or totally get in the way. Figure 17.4a could be an effective way to introduce a talk about teamwork, with one ant helping its "teammate" out of a tough spot. If this image were created using clip art, it would probably be too cartoony for a professional presentation. However, this image has a sophisticated, almost elegant, look in spite of the fact that it features ants. The slide in Figure 17.4b is a disaster. The visual confusion created by the clutter and mixed styles of artwork will distract the audience and obscure the message.

clip art in presentation software or online, but few of them have any information value, and many give your slides an unprofessional, cartoony appearance.

Typefaces and Type Styles

When selecting typefaces and type styles for slides, follow these guidelines:

Many of the typefaces available on your computer are difficult to read when projected, so they aren't good choices for presentation slides.

- Avoid script or decorative typefaces, except for limited, special uses.
- Use serif typefaces with care and only with larger text.
- Limit the number of typefaces to one or two per slide.
- When using thinner typefaces, use boldface so that letters don't disappear on screen.
- Avoid most italicized type; it is usually difficult to read when projected.
- Avoid all-capitalized words and phrases.
- Allow extra white space between lines of text.
- Be consistent with typefaces, type styles, colors, and sizes.

When selecting type sizes, consider the room(s) in which you'll be presenting. The farther the audience is from the screen, the larger your type must be in order to be readable from everywhere in the room. The investor and author Guy Kawasaki, who has sat through hundreds and hundreds of presentations, suggests using no type smaller than 30 points. Doing so not only ensures readable slides but forces you to distill every idea down to its essential core, simply because you won't have space to be wordy.[12]

After you have selected your fonts and type styles, test them for readability by viewing sample slides from your audience's viewing location. If you don't have access to the meeting room, a clever way to test readability at your computer is to stand back as many feet from the screen as your screen size in inches (17 feet for a 17-inch screen, for example). If the slides are readable at this distance, you're probably in good shape.[13]

MAINTAINING DESIGN CONSISTENCY

Design inconsistencies confuse and annoy audiences; don't change colors and other design elements randomly throughout your presentation.

Audiences start to assign meaning to visual elements beginning with your first slide. For instance, if the first slide presents the most important information in dark red, 36-point, Arial typeface, your audience will expect the same type treatment for the most important information on the remaining slides as well. Don't force viewers to repeatedly figure out the meaning of design elements by making arbitrary changes from slide to slide.

Fortunately, presentation software makes consistency easy to achieve, particularly for structured slide designs. You simply adjust the *slide master* using the colors, fonts, and other design elements you've chosen; these choices will then automatically show up on every slide in the presentation. In addition, you can maintain consistency by choosing a predefined layout from those available in your software—which helps ensure that bulleted lists, charts, graphics, and other elements show up in predictable places on each slide. Something as simple as switching from a single column of bullet points to two columns can cause problems for readers as they try to figure out the meaning of the new arrangement. The less work readers have to do to interpret your slide designs, the more attention they can give to your message.

REAL-TIME UPDATES

LEARN MORE BY VISITING THIS WEBSITE

The latest tools and trends in presentations

From design trends to new software tools, this blog covers the newest ideas in presentations. Go to real-timeupdates.com/bct14 and select Learn More in the Students section.

Creating Effective Slide Content

4 LEARNING OBJECTIVE
Explain how to create effective slide content.

No matter which design strategy you use, limit the amount of information on each slide to avoid overloading your viewers.

With some design fundamentals in mind, you're ready to create the textual and visual content for your slides. For every slide, remember to watch out for information overload. When slides have too much content—textual, visual, or both—particularly for several slides in a row, viewers can't process the incoming information fast enough to make sense of it and eventually tune out. Keep your slides clear and easy to grasp, and pace the flow of information at a speed that lets people connect your ideas from one slide to the next.[14]

WRITING READABLE CONTENT

One of the most common mistakes beginners make—and one of the chief criticisms leveled at structured slide designs in general—is stuffing slides with too much text. Doing so overloads the audience with too much information too fast, takes attention away from the speaker by forcing people to read more, and requires the presenter to use smaller type.

Effective text slides supplement your words and help the audience follow the flow of ideas. In a sense, slide text serves as the headings and subheadings for your presentation. Accordingly, choose words and short phrases that help your audience follow the flow of ideas, without forcing them to read in depth. You want your audience to *listen*, not to *read*. Use your slides to highlight key points, summarize and preview your message, signal major shifts in thought, illustrate concepts, or help create interest in your spoken message. If the audience can benefit from additional written information, provide those details in handouts .

When writing content for text slides, keep your message short and simple (see Figure 17.5):

- Limit each slide to one thought, concept, or idea (without dividing things so far that the audience has trouble seeing the big picture).
- Limit text content to four or five lines with four or five words per line. For selected slides, it might make sense to exceed these limits, but do so infrequently.
- Don't show a large number of text-heavy slides in a row; give the audience some visual relief.

> Use slide text sparingly and only to emphasize key points, not to convey your entire message.

Figure 17.5a

Figure 17.5b

Figure 17.5c

Figure 17.5d

Figure 17.5   **Writing Text for Slides**
Effective text slides are clear, simple guides that help the audience understand and remember the speaker's message. Notice the progression toward simplicity in these slides: Figure 17.5a is a paragraph that would distract the audience for an extended period of time. Figure 17.5b offers concise, readable bullets, although too many slides in a row in this structured design would become tedious. Figure 17.5c distills the message down to a single thought that is complete on its own but doesn't convey all the information from the original and would need embellishment from the speaker. Figure 17.5d pushes this to the extreme, with only the core piece of the message to serve as an "exclamation point" for the spoken message. Figure 17.5c and especially Figure 17.5d could be more even more powerful with a well-chosen visual that illustrates the idea of following the flow.

- Write short, bulleted phrases rather than long sentences.
- Use sentences only when you need to share a quotation or some other text item verbatim.[15]
- Phrase list items in parallel grammatical form to facilitate quick reading.
- Use the active voice.
- Include short, informative titles.
- When combining visuals with text, the more information the visual can convey, the less work your text needs to do.

CREATING CHARTS AND TABLES FOR SLIDES

Many graphics that work well in printed form need to be simplified for use in presentations because they are too dense and too complicated to be easily viewed on screen.

Charts and tables for presentations need to be simpler than visuals for printed documents. Detailed images that look fine on the printed page can be too dense and too complicated for presentations. Remember that your audience will view your slides from across the room—not from a foot or two away, as you do while you create them. Don't force the audience to study your charts and graphs in order to get the message. Follow these guidelines:

- **Reduce the detail.** Eliminate anything that is not absolutely essential to the message. If necessary, break information into more than one slide. If a deeper level of detail is helpful or necessary, hand out printed visuals that people can review during or after the presentation.
- **Simplify.** For example, if a bar chart is segmented by week, don't write "Week of 12/01," "Week of 12/08," and so on. Use the "Week of" label once and then just include the dates. Similarly, you might be able to remove the vertical scale from the left side of the chart and just show individual values above each bar.[16]
- **Shorten numbers.** If doing so doesn't hide essential details, you can round off numbers such as $12,500.72 to $12 or $12.5 and then label the axis to indicate thousands.
- **Limit the amount of data shown.** Line charts look busy when they have more than two or three lines, bar charts look crowded with more than five or six bars, and tables are difficult to read if they have too many rows or columns.

- **Highlight key points.** Use arrows, boldface type, and color to direct your audience's eyes to the main point of a visual. Summarize the intent of the graphic in one clear title, such as "Earnings up by 15%."
- **Adjust the size and design.** Modify the size of a graphic to accommodate the size of a slide. Leave plenty of white space so that audience members can view and interpret content from a distance. Use colors that stand out from the slide's background and choose a typeface for labels that is clear and easy to read.

ADDING ANIMATION AND MULTIMEDIA

MOBILE APP

Haiku Deck is a mobile-first presentation app that lets you create and present from your iOS phone or tablet.

Today's presentation software offers a wide array of options for livening up your slides, including sound, animation, video clips, transition effects from one slide to the next, and hyperlinks to websites and other resources. As with every other visual element, the key is to make sure any effects you use support your message. Always consider the impact that all these effects will have on your audience members and their desire to understand your message.[17]

Animation and special effects can be grouped into four categories: functional animation, transitions and builds, hyperlinks, and multimedia. These capabilities are briefly discussed in the following sections; to learn more about using them, consult the Help menu in your software.

Although you can animate just about everything in a presentation, resist the temptation to do so. Make sure each animation has a purpose.

Functional Animation

PowerPoint and other presentation packages offer a mind-boggling set of tools for moving and changing things on screen. You can have a block of text cartwheel in from outer space, change colors, change font and font size, spin around in circles, blink on and off, wave back and forth, crawl around the screen following a predefined path, and then disappear one letter at a time, like some sort of erasing typewriter. You *can* do all this, but *should* you?

Just as static graphic elements can be either functional or decorative, so too can animated elements. For instance, having each bullet point fly in from the left side of the screen doesn't add any functional value to your communication effort. In contrast, a highlight arrow or color bar that moves around the screen to emphasize specific points in a technical diagram can be an effective use of animation and a welcome alternative to a laser pointer. You can control every aspect of the animation, so it's easy to coordinate the movement with the points you're making in your presentation.

Using carefully controlled functional animation is also a great way to demonstrate sequences and procedures. For a training session on machinery repair, for example, you can show a schematic diagram of the machinery and walk your audience through each step of the troubleshooting process, highlighting each step on screen as you address it verbally. Again, use animation in support of your message, not simply for animation's sake.

Transitions and Builds

In addition to animating specific elements on your slides, you can choose from various options for adding motion between slides. These **slide transitions** control how one slide replaces another on screen. Subtle transitions can ease your viewers' gaze from one slide to the next—such as having the current slide gently fade out before the next one fades in. However, many of the transitions currently available (such as checkerboards, pinwheels, and spinning "newsflashes") are like miniature animated shows themselves and are therefore distracting. These pointless transition effects not only disrupt the flow of your presentation, they can make the whole thing seem amateurish. If you use a transition effect, use the same one throughout the presentation (so that audiences won't wonder whether there is some significance to a new transition at some point during the presentation), and choose the effect carefully. Aim for a smooth, subtle effect that is easy on the eye. And unless a sound effect is somehow integral to the message, there is no reason to add audio to a transition.

> Use subtle transition animations between slides to ease the viewer from one slide to the next; most transitions available in presentation software are too distracting.

Builds are much more useful than transitions, at least when used with care and thought. These effects control the release of text, graphics, and other elements on individual slides. For instance, with builds you can make a list of bullet points appear one at a time rather than having all of them appear at once, which makes it difficult to focus on a single point. This controlled release of information helps draw audience members' attention to the point being discussed and keeps them from reading ahead.

> Using carefully designed builds can be a great way to reveal information in easy-to-process pieces.

As with transitions, stick with the subtle, basic options for builds. The point of a build is to release information in a controlled fashion, not to distract or entertain the audience. Another useful option is to change the color of bullet points as you discuss each one. For instance, if your primary text color is a strong blue, you might have the text in each bullet point change to a light gray after you've finished talking about it. This subtle approach keeps the audience's attention focused on the bullet point you are currently discussing.

After you've assigned builds to your slides, you can control the build activity with a mouse or a remote control device. Experiment with the options in your software to find the most effective build scheme. In addition to building up text, you can build up graphical elements. For instance, to discuss monthly sales of three products over the past year, you can have a line graph of the first product appear by itself while you discuss it, and then you can click the mouse to display the second product's sales line, then the third.

Hyperlinks

Hyperlinks and action buttons can be quite handy when you need flexibility in your presentations or want to share different kinds of files with the audience. A **hyperlink** instructs your computer to jump to another slide in your presentation, to a website, or to another program entirely. Depending on your presentation software, hyperlinks can be underlined text, invisible *hotspots* in graphical elements, or clearly labeled *action buttons*.

THE ART OF PROFESSIONALISM

Being a Team Player

Professionals know that they are contributors to a larger cause, that it's not all about them. Just as in athletics and other team efforts, being a team player in business is something of a balancing act. On the one hand, you need to pay enough attention to your own efforts and skills to make sure you're pulling your own weight. On the other hand, you need to pay attention to the overall team effort to make sure the team succeeds. Remember that if the team fails, you fail, too.

Great team players know how to make those around them more effective, whether it's by lending a hand during crunch time, sharing resources, removing obstacles, making introductions, or offering expertise. In fact, the ability to help others improve their performance is one of the key attributes executives look for when they want to promote people into management.

Being a team player also means showing loyalty to your organization and protecting your employer's reputation—one of the most important assets any company has. Pros don't trash their employers in front of customers or in their personal blogs. When they have a problem, they solve it; they don't share it.

CAREER APPLICATIONS

1. If you prefer to work by yourself, should you take a job in a company that uses a team-based organization structure? Why or why not?

2. You can see plenty of examples of unprofessional business behavior in the news media and in your own experiences as a consumer and an employee. Why should you bother being professional yourself?

You can increase the flexibility of your presentation slides with hyperlinks that let you jump to different slides, websites, or other software screens with the click of a mouse.

Using hyperlinks is also a great way to customize your presentations, giving a linear presentation some of the flexibility of a nonlinear presentation. For instance, if you work in sales and call on a variety of customers, you can't be sure what sort of situation you'll encounter at each customer's site. You might be prepared to give an in-depth technical presentation to a group of engineers, only to have the company president walk in and request a brief financial overview instead. Or you might prepare a set of detailed technical slides but not show them unless the audience asks detailed questions.

Another challenging situation is finding out at the last minute that you have less time than you thought to make your presentation. If you've built in some flexibility, you won't need to rush through your entire presentation or scramble on the spot to find the most important slides. Instead, you can simply click an action button labeled "Five-minute overview" and jump right to the two or three most important slides in your presentation. With hyperlinks, you can even switch from the indirect approach to the direct approach or vice versa, based on the response you're getting from your audience. By building in links that accommodate these various scenarios, you can adjust your presentation at a moment's notice—and look polished and professional while you do it.

Multimedia Elements

Video clips can add memorable, engaging content to your presentations—as long as they are relevant, interesting, and brief.

Multimedia elements offer the ultimate in active presentations. Using audio and video clips can be an effective way to complement your live message, such as including a recorded message from a company executive or scenes from a customer focus group. Just be sure to keep these elements brief and relevant—as supporting points for your presentation, not as replacements for it.

INTEGRATING MOBILE DEVICES IN PRESENTATIONS

Smartphones and tablets offer a variety of ways to enhance presentations for presenters as well as audience members (see Figure 17.6). For example, you can get around the problem of everyone in the audience not having a clear view of the screen by using systems that broadcast your slides to tablets and smartphones. In fact, these systems can eliminate a conventional projection system entirely; everyone in the audience can view your slides on their mobile devices. You can also broadcast a live presentation to mobile users anywhere in the world. Each time you advance to a new slide, it is sent to the phone or tablet of everyone who is subscribed to your presentation.[18]

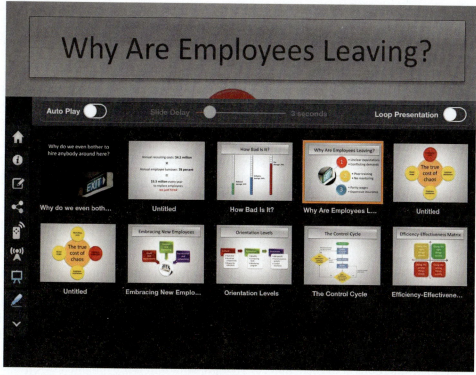

Figure 17.6 Using Mobile Devices in Presentations
A variety of mobile apps and cloud-based systems can free presenters and audiences from the constraints of a conventional conference room.

Completing Slides and Support Materials

Just as you would review any message for content, style, tone, readability, clarity, and conciseness, you should apply the same quality control to your slides and other visuals. As you look over your presentation for the final time, make sure that all visuals are

- **Readable.** Can text be read from the back of the room? Does the text stand out from the background?
- **Consistent.** Are colors and design elements used consistently?
- **Simple.** Is each slide and the entire presentation as simple as possible? Can you eliminate any slides?
- **Audience centered.** Are the message and the design focused on the audience?
- **Clear.** Is the main point of a slide obvious? Easy to understand? Can the audience grasp the main point in just a few seconds?[19]
- **Concise and grammatical.** Is text written in concise phrases? Are bulleted phrases grammatically parallel?
- **Focused.** Does each slide cover only one thought, concept, or idea (or summarize a group of related ideas)? Does the slide grab the viewer's attention in the right place and support the key points of the message? Are arrows, symbols, or other techniques used to draw the audience's attention to the key sections of a chart or diagram?
- **Fully operational.** Have you verified every slide in your presentation? Do all the animations and other special effects work as you intended?

The *slide sorter* view (different programs have different names for this feature) lets you see some or all of the slides in your presentation on a single screen. Use this view to add and delete slides, reposition slides, check slides for design consistency, and verify the operation of any effects. Moreover, the slide sorter is a great way to review the flow of your story.[20]

With your slides working properly and in clear, logical order, you're just a few steps away from being ready. Now is a good time to think about a backup plan. What will you do if your laptop won't turn on or the projector dies? Can you get by without your slides? For important presentations, consider having backup equipment on standby, loaded with

5 LEARNING OBJECTIVE
Explain the role of navigation slides, support slides, and handouts.

Review each slide carefully to make sure it is clear and readable.

Use the slide sorter view to verify and modify the organization of your slides.

your presentation and ready to go. At the very least, have enough printed handouts ready to give the audience so that, as a last resort, you can give your presentation "on paper."

CREATING NAVIGATION AND SUPPORT SLIDES

Now that the content slides are ready, enhance your presentation with several slides that add "finish" to your presentation and provide additional information to benefit your audience:

- **Title slide(s).** Make a good first impression on your audience with one or two title slides, the equivalent of a report's cover and title page. A title slide should contain the title of your presentation (and subtitle, if appropriate), your name, your department affiliation (for internal audiences), and your company affiliation (for external audiences). You may also include the presentation date and an appropriate graphic element. Depending on the amount of information you need to convey at this point, two title slides might be appropriate: one focusing on the topic of the presentation and a second with your affiliation and other information. This second slide can also be used to introduce the speaker and list his or her credentials.
- **Agenda and program details.** You can use these slides to communicate the agenda for your presentation and any additional information your audience might need. Because presentations pull your audience members away from their daily routines and work responsibilities, they can have questions about anything from break times or lunch plans to the password needed to log onto the facility's wireless network. By answering these questions at the beginning of your presentation, you'll minimize disruptions later and help the audience stay focused on your message.
- **Navigation slides.** To tell your audience where you're going and where you've been, you can use a series of **navigation slides** based on your outline or agenda. This technique is most useful in longer presentations with several major sections. As you complete each section, repeat the slide but indicate which material has been covered and which section you are about to begin (see Figure 17.7). This sort of slide is sometimes referred to as a *moving blueprint*. You can then use the original slide again in the close of your presentation to review the points you've covered. As an alternative to the repeating agenda slide, you can insert a simple *bumper slide* at each major section break, announcing the title of the section you're about to begin.[21]

Figure 17.8 illustrates some of the many options you have for presenting various types of information. Note that although these slides don't follow a rigid structure of text-heavy bullet points, they are unified by the color scheme (a silver background and bold color accents) and typeface selections.

Navigation slides help your audience keep track of what you've covered already and what you plan to cover next.

Figure 17.7a "Muting" topics already covered

Figure 17.7b Highlighting the next topic

Figure 17.7 **Blueprint Slides**
Here are two of the ways you can use a *blueprint slide* as a navigational aid to help your audience stay on track with the presentation. Figure 17.7a visually "mutes" and checks off the sections of the presentation that have already been covered. In contrast, Figure 17.7b uses a sliding highlight box to indicate the next section to be covered.

Left: This introductory slide is a blunt attention-getter, something that would have to be used with caution and only in special circumstances.

Right: This simple math equation gets the point across about how expensive high employee turnover is.

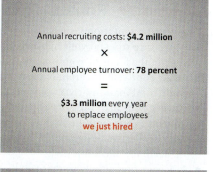

Left: This stylized bar graph sends a stark visual message about how bad the company's turnover really is.

Right: This slide is essentially a bullet list, with three groups of two bullets each. Repeating the photo element from the introductory slide emphasizes the message about employee turnover.

These two *navigation slides* show one way to introduce each of the four subtopics in this particular section. As the highlight moves around the central circle, the audience is reminded of which subtopics have been covered and which subtopic is going to be covered next. And each time it is shown, the message is repeated that all these problems are the "true cost of chaos" in the company's employment practices.

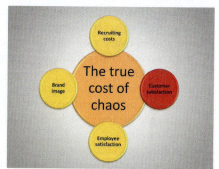

Left: This slide introduces three key points the speaker wants to emphasize in this particular section.

Right: This slide shows a linear flow of ideas, each with bulleted subpoints. This slide could be revealed one section at a time to help the speaker keep the audience's attention focused on a single topic.

Left: This flowchart packs a lot of information onto one slide, but seeing the sequence of events in one place is essential.

Right: This simple visual highlights the presenter's spoken message about being careful to choose the right tasks to focus on and then completing them quickly.

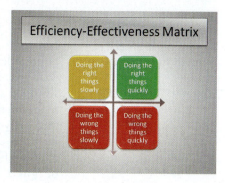

Figure 17.8 **Designing Effective Visuals: Selected Slides**
These slides, from a presentation that addresses a company's high employee turnover rate, illustrate the wide variety of design options you have for creating effective, appealing slides. (All the slides were created using features in PowerPoint.)

CHECKLIST ✔ Enhancing Presentations with Visuals

A. Plan your presentation visuals.
- Make sure you and your message, not your visuals, remain the focus of your presentation.
- Select your visuals carefully to support your message; use a combination of visuals if needed.
- Review your plan for each visual to make sure it truly supports your message.
- Follow effective design principles, with an emphasis on accuracy and simplicity.
- Use your time wisely so that you have plenty of time to practice your presentation.

B. Choose structured or free-form slides.
- Structured slides using bullet-point templates are easy to create, require little time or skill to design, and can be completed in a hurry. Best uses: routine, internal presentations.
- Primary disadvantages of structured slides are mind-numbing repetition of bullet-point format and the common tendency of stuffing too much information on them.
- Free-form slides make it easier to combine textual and visual information, to create a more dynamic and engaging experience, and to maintain a conversational connection with the audience. Best uses: motivational, educational, and persuasive presentations.
- Primary disadvantages of structured slides are the time, skill, and imagery required; added responsibilities for the speaker; and the possibility of fragmenting complex topics.

C. Design effective slides.
- If you can, avoid creating "slideuments," slides that are so packed with information that they can be read as standalone documents.
- Use color to emphasize important ideas, create contrast, isolate visual elements, and convey intended nonverbal signals.
- Limit color to a few compatible choices and use them consistently.
- Make sure your slide background doesn't compete with the foreground.

- Use decorative artwork sparingly and only to support your message.
- Emphasize functional artwork—photos, technical drawings, charts, and other visual elements containing information that is part of your message.
- Choose typefaces that are easy to read on screen; limit the number of typefaces and use them consistently.
- Use slide masters to maintain consistency throughout your presentation.

D. Create effective slide content.
- Write content that will be readable from everywhere in the room.
- Write short, active, parallel phrases that support, not replace, your spoken message.
- Avoid complete sentences unless you need to quote verbatim.
- Limit the amount of text so that your audience can focus on listening, not reading.
- Simplify print graphics for use on slides but don't oversimplify.
- Use functional animation when it can support your message.
- Make sure slide transitions are subtle, if used at all.
- Use builds carefully to control the release of information.
- Use hyperlinks and action buttons to add flexibility to your presentation.
- Incorporate multimedia elements that can help engage your audience and deliver your message.

E. Complete slides and support materials.
- Review every slide carefully to ensure accuracy, consistency, and clarity.
- Make sure that all slides are fully operational.
- Use the slide sorter to verify and adjust the sequence of slides, if needed.
- Have a backup plan in case your slide plan fails.
- Create navigation and support slides.
- Create handouts to give the audience additional information and to minimize the amount of information you need to put on your slides.

CREATING EFFECTIVE HANDOUTS

View handouts as an integral part of your presentation strategy so that they work in harmony with your slides and spoken message.

Handouts, any printed materials you give the audience to supplement your talk, should be considered an integral part of your presentation strategy. Plan them in tandem with your presentation slides so that you use each medium as effectively as possible. Your presentation should paint the big picture, convey and connect major ideas, set the emotional tone, and rouse the audience to action (if that is relevant to your talk). Your handouts can then carry the rest of the information load, providing the supporting details that audience members can consume at their own speed, on their own time. You won't need to worry about stuffing every detail into your slides because you have the more appropriate medium of printed documents to do that.[22]

Possibilities for good handout materials include the following:[23]

- **Complex charts and diagrams.** Charts and tables that are too unwieldy for the screen or that demand thorough analysis make good handouts.
- **Articles and technical papers.** Magazine articles that supplement the information in your presentation make good handout materials, as do technical papers that provide in-depth coverage of the material you've highlighted in your presentation.
- **Case studies.** Summaries of business case studies can make good supplemental reading material.
- **Recommended resources.** Lists of websites, blogs, and other online resources related to your topic can be useful. For each source, provide a URL and a one- or two-sentence summary of its content.
- **Copies of presentation slides.** Audiences often like to have print versions of the slides used by a speaker, containing the speaker's comments about each slide and blank lines for note taking. Use the page and print setup options in your software to choose the more useful arrangement.

Timing the distribution of handouts depends on their content, the nature of your presentation, and your personal preference. Some speakers like to distribute handout copies of their slides before the presentation begins so that the audience can take notes on them. Doing so can be risky, however, particularly if you've organized your talk with the indirect approach, because the audience can read ahead and reach the conclusion and recommendations before you're able to build up to them yourself. Other speakers simply advise the audience of the types of information covered in handouts but delay distributing anything until they have finished speaking.

For a quick review of the key steps in creating effective visuals, see "Checklist: Enhancing Presentations with Visuals." For the latest information on presentation design, visit **real-timeupdates.com/bct14** and select Chapter 17.

Use handout materials to support the points made in your presentation and to offer the audience additional information on your topic.

COMMUNICATION CHALLENGES AT **Duarte**

You've joined the dozens of designers, trainers, and information specialists at Duarte. Use what you've learned in this chapter to address these two challenges.

INDIVIDUAL CHALLENGE: You've just been given the assignment to create presentation slides for a new client. The client, House-You, is a start-up that aims to compete with Airbnb in the private room- and house-rental business. The purpose of the presentation is to pitch the business idea to investors.

Your first task is to choose a color palette for the slides, which will also be used in the company's other promotional materials. Using any program or app you're comfortable with, choose five standard colors or mix your own. You'll need one dark color to use for slide backgrounds, one contrasting color for type on this dark background, and three compatible accent colors to use for various purposes. Study Airbnb's logo and make sure you don't choose any colors that are too similar. Using PowerPoint, Keynote, or Google Slides, create a few slides that show how your color palette could be used in a presentation. (Don't worry about the content of the presentation; use any text and visual material that lets you show your five colors.)

TEAM CHALLENGE: With a team of classmates, search the Creative Commons website for attractive photos that could be used on slides to help illustrate or emphasize the following message points in a presentation:

- Trends in health-care costs
- Competition
- High levels of employee engagement (the energy, enthusiasm, and effort employees put into their work)
- Consumer hyperchoice (situations in which shoppers have such an overwhelming array of choices in a given product category that purchase decisions become difficult and stressful)
- Scalability (the ease with which a business process or an entire company can be expanded to handle a greater number of transactions)

For each message point, find three good images and then decide as a team which one conveys the point most effectively and in the most appropriate style for a fairly formal business presentation. Create a slide show in which you show the photos, describe how each one conveys the concept in question, and explain why you chose the one you think is most effective. Make sure you follow the usage and attribution guidelines for any photos you find online.

Quick Learning Guide

KEY TERMS

builds Effects that control the release of text, graphics, and other elements on individual slides

free-form slides Presentation slides that are not based on a template, often with each slide having a unique look but unified by typeface, color, and other design choices; tend to be much more visually oriented than structured slides

hyperlink Link embedded in a presentation that instructs your computer to jump to another slide in your presentation, to a website, or to another program

navigation slides Noncontent slides that tell your audience where you're going and where you've been

slide transitions Software effects that control how one slide replaces another on screen

structured slides Presentation slides that follow the same design templates throughout and give all the slides in a presentation the same general look; they emphasize textual information in bullet-point form

SUMMARY OF LEARNING OBJECTIVES

1 **Explain the role of visuals in business presentations and list the types of visuals commonly used.** Visuals create interest, illustrate and clarify important points, add variety, and help the listener absorb the information you're presenting. In most businesses today, Prezi-style and conventional slide presentations are the most common tools, but you might also use overhead transparencies, chalkboards and whiteboards (including digital whiteboards), flip charts, product samples, models, video, and various software programs.

2 **Explain the difference between structured and free-form slides, and suggest when each design strategy is more appropriate.** Structured slides follow the same design plan for most or all of the slides in a presentation. They are often created by using the templates provided with PowerPoint and other presentation programs. Structured slides tend to convey most of their information through bullet points. In contrast, free-form slides do not follow any set design scheme from slide to slide, although they can and should use color, font selection, and other design choices to create a unified feel across a presentation. Free-form slides often have just a single statement on each slide, requiring many more slides to cover the same amount of material as the typical structured design.

The ease and speed with which structured slides can be created make them most useful for routine presentations such as project update meetings, particularly for internal audiences and in situations in which the slide deck will be used only once. They can also be useful when the audience needs to see a number of information points on screen simultaneously in order to make comparisons. Given their ability to excite and engage, free-form designs are particularly good for motivational, educational, and persuasive presentations—particularly when the slides will be used multiple times and therefore compensate for the extra time and effort often required to create them.

3 **Outline the decisions involved in using a key visual and selecting color, artwork, and typefaces to create effective slide designs.** Using a key visual involves selecting a single, simple visual element as a structure for the elements on a slide. For example, a circle can be used to identify the points in a repeating process, and a triangle can establish the interrelationship of three entities.

Color is a critical design element because it can grab the viewer's attention, emphasize important ideas, create contrast, isolate particular slide elements, stimulate emotions, and send powerful nonverbal messages such as elegance or technical sophistication. Color also affects the acceptance and retention of messages. When selecting color, limit your choices to a few compatible ones and use them consistently.

Slides have two layers of visual elements, the *background* (which should be as unobtrusive as possible) and the *foreground*, which carries the information content of the slide. Artwork on the background and foreground can be divided into *functional*, which conveys information directly, and *decorative*, which does not. Well-designed functional artwork is always useful and a great way to convey message points quickly. Decorative artwork can be useful if it supports the message point on a slide, but it can be distracting otherwise.

Typefaces and type styles need careful consideration to ensure that they are easily readable from every point in the presentation room. Clean, sans serif typefaces are usually the best choice, although serif typefaces can be useful when used in large sizes. In general, avoid decorative typefaces except for limited, special purposes.

4 **Explain how to create effective slide content.** Slide content can be divided into three groups: text, tables and graphics, and animation and multimedia. To choose effective words and phrases, think of the text on your slides as a guide to the content, not the content itself. For all-text slides, try to limit the content to four or five lines, with four or five words per line, and use short phrases rather than full sentences.

To create effective tables and graphics, keep in mind that visuals for projection need to be simpler than those used for print documents. If necessary, create simplified versions for your slides and provide the full-detail versions in a printed handout.

Like artwork, animation can be functional or decorative. Functional animation can be a powerful way to demonstrate processes and procedures. Decorative animation is nearly always a distraction and should be avoided. Slide transitions, which control how one slide replaces another on screen, are a form of animation. Except for subtle transitions such as a gentle fade to black, avoid using most of the transitions that come with your software. Builds, on the other hand, can be extremely helpful by letting you control the release of individual text points or graphical elements on a slide.

Hyperlinks instruct your computer to jump to another slide in your presentation, to a website, or to another program entirely. They can be handy for designing flexibility into your presentations and for sharing other types of files with the audience.

Audio, video, and other multimedia files can complement your live message, but make sure they support your message rather than replace it.

5 **Explain the role of navigation slides, support slides, and handouts.** In addition to the slides that convey your content, you can create one or more *title slides* to introduce your presentation (and yourself, if necessary), *agenda and program detail slides* that tell viewers what to expect during the presentation and provide information to help them plan their time, and *navigation slides* that help you and your audience keep track of where you are in the presentation. Particularly for longer presentations, a *moving blueprint* slide is a great way to show the audience what has been covered so far and what is still to come.

Handouts should be considered an integral part of your presentation, working in conjunction with your slides and spoken message to provide audience members with additional details, supporting documents, and other material too detailed to include in the presentation itself.

MyBCommLab

Go to **mybcommlab.com** to complete the problems marked with this icon .

Test Your Knowledge

To review chapter content related to each question, refer to the indicated Learning Objective.

17-1. What are your options for supporting a presentation with visuals? [LO-1]

17-2. What are the potential disadvantages of Prezi-style presentations? [LO-1]

17-3. How do structured and free-form slide designs differ? [LO-2]

17-4. What should the role of the background be in a slide? [LO-3]

17-5. How does Guy Kawasaki's "30-point rule" for fonts (see page 494) help ensure readable and memorable slide content? [LO-3]

17-6. Why is it important to avoid arbitrarily changing colors throughout a presentation? [LO-3]

17-7. What is the recommended number of fonts to use per slide? [LO-4]

17-8. How do slide transitions differ from builds? [LO-4]

17-9. How is a moving blueprint slide used in a presentation? [LO-5]

17-10. How does the slide sorter view facilitate the editing process for a presentation? [LO-5]

Apply Your Knowledge

To review chapter content related to each question, refer to the indicated Learning Objective.

17-11. Would you choose a structured or free-form design plan for a presentation about upcoming changes in international accounting regulations? Why? [LO-2]

17-12. What is the fundamental problem with "slideuments"? [LO-2]

17-13. How can you use slide masters to enhance the effectiveness of your slides? [LO-3]

17-14. Is it ethical to use design elements and special effects to persuade an audience? Why or why not? [LO-3]

17-15. If you are giving a presentation to company management using the indirect approach to recommend that the company consolidate its manufacturing operations (a traumatic change that would result in the loss of hundreds of jobs, including a dozen management positions), would it be wise to hand out copies of your slides at the beginning of the presentation? Why or why not? [LO-5]

Practice Your Skills

Messages for Analysis

17-16. **Message 17.A: Improving a Slide** Examine the slide in Figure 17.9 and point out any problems you notice. How would you correct these problems?

17-17. **Message 17.B: Modifying for Presentation** Examine the graph in Figure 17.10 and explain how to modify it for a presentation, using the guidelines discussed in this chapter.

17-18. **Message 17.C: Analyzing the Animation** To access this PowerPoint presentation, visit **real-timeupdates.com/ bct14**, select Student Assignments, and select Chapter 17, Message 17.C. Download and watch the presentation in slideshow mode. After you've watched the presentation, identify at least three ways in which various animations, builds, and transitions either enhanced or impeded your understanding of the subject matter.

Figure 17.9 **Piece of Cake Bakery Customer Survey**

Figure 17.10   **CommuniCo Employee Training Costs**

Exercises

Each activity is labeled according to the primary skill or skills you will need to use. To review relevant chapter content, you can refer to the indicated Learning Objective.

17-19. **Designing Effective Slides [LO-2]** Find a business-related slide presentation on SlideShare (**www.slideshare.net**) and analyze the design. Do you consider it structured or free form? Does the design help the audience understand and remember the message? Why or why not? What improvements to the design would you suggest? Is the slide set understandable on its own?

17-20. **Designing Effective Slides [LO-3]** Think about a company you might like to start after graduation and imagine that you are giving a 20-minute presentation to potential investors. Review the design templates or themes available in whatever presentation software you have available, such as Microsoft PowerPoint, Apple Keynote, or Google Slides. Choose a template and color palette that best support the message you want to convey to these financiers. Write a one-page report or brief blog post that includes a sample slide using this theme and color palette and an explanation of how this design supports your message.

17-21. **Creating Effective Slide Content [LO-4]** Look through recent issues of several business periodicals for an article that discusses issues a specific company or industry is facing. Based on the information in the article and the guidelines discussed in this chapter, create three to five presentation slides summarizing these issues.

17-22. **Creating Effective Slide Content [LO-4]** Locate one of the tables elsewhere in the book and convert it to presentation slides so that the content is easily readable in a large conference room. (Be sure to select one of the shorter tables.) Choose whether to use free-form or structured slides, and

decide how much content will be on the slides and how much will be spoken by the presenter. Provide speaker's notes along with your slides.

17-23. **Creating Effective Slide Content; Mobile Skills [LO-4]** Find a business-oriented presentation on SlideShare or another online source. Re-create four of the slides so they will be more effective on small mobile screens, then assemble a before-and-after presentation that highlights the changes you made.

Expand Your Skills

Critique the Professionals

Dave Paradi, the author of *The Visual Slide Revolution*, specializes in helping presenters transform text-heavy slides into more readable and more effective visuals. Visit his YouTube channel at **www.youtube.com/thinkoutsidetheslide**, watch several of his "PowerPoint Slide Makeover" videos, and select the one that you find most helpful or enlightening. Using whatever medium your instructor requests, summarize the changes Paradi made to the slide in question and explain in your own words why these changes made the slide more effective.

Sharpening Your Career Skills Online

Bovée and Thill's Business Communication Web Search, at **websearch.businesscommunicationnetwork.com**, is a unique research tool designed specifically for business communication research. Use the Web Search function to find a website, video, article, podcast, or presentation that offers advice on creating slides and other presentation visuals. Write a brief email message to your instructor, describing the item that you found and summarizing the career skills information you learned from it.

Cases

For all cases, feel free to use your creativity to make up any details you need in order to craft effective messages.

PRESENTATION SKILLS

17-24. Planning, Designing, and Creating Presentation Slides [LO-1], [LO-2], [LO-3], [LO-4] Select the Communication Close-Up from the beginning of any chapter in the book and decide whether free-form or structured slides would be the most effective way to present this story to an audience of business professionals.

Your task: Using whichever design approach you think is better, create a brief presentation (slides and speaking notes) to tell the story.

PRESENTATION SKILLS

17-25. Planning, Designing, and Creating Presentation Slides [LO-1], [LO-2], [LO-3], [LO-4] Not long ago, snowboarding seemed to be on pace to pass skiing as the country's favorite way to zoom down snowy mountains, but the sport's growth has cooled off in recent years.[24]

Your task: Research and prepare a 10-minute presentation on participation trends in snowboarding and skiing, including explanations for the relative popularity of both sports. Include at least three quotations to emphasize key points in your presentation. Use either structured or free-form slides.

PRESENTATION SKILLS

17-26. Planning, Designing, and Creating Presentation Slides [LO-1], [LO-2], [LO-3], [LO-4] Many companies publish stories of their founding and early years as a way to convey the company's strengths and values.

Your task:? Choose a company that has been in business for at least two decades and prepare a 10-minute presentation on its history.

PRESENTATION SKILLS/TEAM SKILLS

17-27. Planning, Designing, and Creating Presentation Slides [LO-1], [LO-2], [LO-3], [LO-4] Changing a nation's eating habits is a Herculean task, but the physical and financial health of the United States depends on it. You work for the USDA Center for Nutrition Policy and Promotion (**www.cnpp .usda.gov**), and it's your job to educate people on the dangers of unhealthy eating and the changes they can make to eat more balanced and healthful diets.

Your task: Visit **real-timeupdates.com/bct14,** select Student Assignments, and download Chapter 17, *Dietary Guidelines for Americans*. With your team, develop a presentation no longer than 15 minutes, using a Prezi or free-form slides, that conveys

the key points from Chapter 3 of the *Guidelines*, "Food and Food Components to Reduce." The objectives of your presentation are to alert people to the dangers of excessive consumption of the five components discussed in the chapter and to let them know what healthy levels of consumptions are. This chapter has a lot of information, but you don't need to pack it all into your slides; you can assume that the chapter will be available as a handout to anyone who attends your presentation. Along with your presentation, draft speaking notes that someone outside your team could use to give the presentation. You can use images from the *Guidelines* PDF, the websites of the U.S. Department of Agriculture and the U.S. Department of Health and Human Services, or a nongovernment source such as Creative Commons (**creativecommons.org**). Make sure you follow the usage and attribution guidelines for any photos you find on nongovernment sites.

PRESENTATION SKILLS

17-28. Planning, Designing, and Creating Presentation Slides [LO-1], [LO-2], [LO-3], [LO-4] *PechaKucha* is a style of presentation that might be the ultimate in creative constraint: The speaker is limited to 20 slides, each of which is displayed for exactly 20 seconds before automatically advancing. PechaKucha Nights, which are open to the public, are now put on in cities all over the world. Visit **www.pechakucha.org** for more information on these events or to view some archived presentations.

Your task: Chose any topic that interests you and develop a PechaKucha-style presentation with 20 slides, each designed to be displayed for 20 seconds. Use the slide timing capabilities in your presentation software to control the pace. Make sure you practice before presenting to your class so that you can hit the precise timing requirements.[25]

PRESENTATION SKILLS

17-29. Planning, Designing, and Creating Presentation Slides [LO-1], [LO-2], [LO-3], [LO-4] Learning to play a musical instrument offers children multiple benefits, beyond the joys of creating and appreciating music.

Your task: Research the benefits of learning and playing an instrument, then prepare a brief presentation that conveys these benefits in a way that most parents would find compelling.

PRESENTATION SKILLS/PORTFOLIO BUILDER

17-30. Planning, Designing, and Creating Presentation Slides [LO-1], [LO-2], [LO-3], [LO-4] Small farmers looking for more predictable revenue and consumers who want to eat fresh local produce have found a match in *community-supported agriculture (CSA)*. CSA is essentially a subscription service in which consumers sign up for regular allotments of fruits and vegetables from a local farm. At regular intervals during the growing season, each subscriber gets a box of whatever produce is ripe and ready at that time.

Your task: Research CSA options in your area and prepare a brief presentation on how these programs work and how they benefit farmers and consumers. If you can't find any local programs, choose any location in the United States where CSA is available.

PRESENTATION SKILLS/PORTFOLIO BUILDER

17-31. Planning, Designing, and Creating Presentation Slides [LO-1], [LO-2], [LO-3], [LO-4]   One could argue that sleep is the single most important element of healthy living. Not only is adequate sleep essential for the body on its own, but getting enough sleep enables other activities that are essential for health, including getting exercise and taking the time to eat a healthy diet. Unfortunately, millions of people who recognize the value of sleep and want nothing more than to get enough sleep every night are often unable to do so.

Your task: Research the types and causes of insomnia and the cures most often recommended by sleep specialists. Using Prezi or slide software, prepare a 10- to 15-minute presentation on why insomnia affects so many people and the steps people can take to reduce or eliminate it.

PRESENTATION SKILLS/TEAM SKILLS/ PORTFOLIO BUILDER

17-32. Planning, Designing, and Creating Presentation Slides [LO-1], [LO-2], [LO-3], [LO-4]   In your job as a business development researcher for a major corporation, you're asked to gather and process information on a wide variety of subjects. Management has gained confidence in your research and analysis skills and would now like you to begin making regular presentations at management retreats and other functions. Topics are likely to include the following:

- Offshoring of U.S. jobs
- Foreign ownership of U.S. firms
- Employment issues involving workers from other countries
- Tax breaks offered by local and state governments to attract new businesses
- Economic impact of environmental regulations

Your task: With a team assigned by your instructor, choose one of the topics from the list and conduct enough research to familiarize yourself with it. Identify at least three important issues that anyone involved with this topic should know about. Prepare a 10-minute presentation that introduces the topic, comments on its importance to the U.S. economy, and discusses the issues you've identified. Assume that your audience is a cross section of business managers who don't have any particular experience in the topic you've chosen.

PRESENTATION SKILLS/PORTFOLIO BUILDER

17-33. Planning, Designing, and Creating Presentation Slides [LO-1], [LO-2], [LO-3], [LO-4]   Depending on the sequence your instructor chose for this course, you've probably covered at least a dozen chapters at this point and learned or improved many valuable skills. Think through your progress and identify five business communication skills that you've either learned for the first time or developed during this course.

Your task: Create a 10-minute Prezi or slide presentation that describes each of the five skills you've identified. Be sure to explain how each skill could help you in your career. Use any visual style that you feel is appropriate for the assignment.

PRESENTATION SKILLS/TEAM SKILLS/ PORTFOLIO BUILDER

17-34. Planning, Designing, and Creating Presentation Slides [LO-1], [LO-3], [LO-4]   In its competitive battles with AT&T and other phone and Internet service providers, Verizon seeks to attract and keep not just customers but top employees. Engineers and technicians obviously play a vital role in a technology company such as Verizon, but the firm also needs specialists in everything from accounting to public relations to real estate.

Your task: Prepare a brief presentation (Prezi or slides) that Verizon recruiters could use at job fairs and other venues to entice both new graduates and experienced professionals to consider joining the company. Create an appropriate amount of visual material for a presentation that is at least 10 minutes but no longer than 15 (not including a question-and-answer period). Assume the audience members have heard of Verizon but don't have any in-depth knowledge about the company. Visit the company's website to learn more about the benefits of working there.

MyBCommLab

Go to **mybcommlab.com** for Auto-graded writing questions as well as the following Assisted-graded writing questions:

17-35.   Why is it important to use your time carefully when creating presentation materials? [LO-1]

17-36.   How do structured and free-form slide designs differ from one another? [LO-2]

Endnotes

1. Duarte website, accessed 9 May 2016, www.duarte.com; Nancy Duarte, *slide:ology: The Art and Science of Creating Great Presentations* (Sebastopol, Calif.: O'Reilly Media, 2008), 251–261; Marta Kagan, "Nancy Duarte's Five Rules for Creating Great Presentations," HubSpot, 22 July 2011, blog.hubspot.com.

2. "Polishing Your Presentation," 3M Meeting Network, accessed 8 June 2001, www.mmm.com/meetingnetwork/readingroom/meetingguide_pres.html.

3. Michael Hyatt, "Five Rules to Better PowerPoint Presentations," 21 June 2005, Working Smart blog, www.michaelhyatt.com.

4. Jeff Herb, "Prezi—Advantages and Disadvantages," Instructional Tech Talk blog, 29 December 2012, instructionaltechtalk.com.

5. Cliff Atkinson, "The Cognitive Load of PowerPoint: Q&A with Richard E. Mayer," *Sociable Media*, accessed 15 August 2009, www.sociablemedia.com/articles_mayer.htm.

6. Margo Halverson, "Choosing the Right Colors for Your Next Presentation," 3M Meeting Network, accessed 8 June 2001, www.mmm.com/meetingnetwork/readingroom/meetingguide_right_color.html.

7. Carol Klinger and Joel G. Siegel, "Computer Multimedia Presentations," *CPA Journal*, June 1996, 46.

8. Jon Hanke, "Five Tips for Better Visuals," 3M Meeting Network, accessed 25 May 2007, www.3m.com/meetingnetwork/presentations/pmag_better_visuals.html.

9. Hanke, "Five Tips for Better Visuals."

10. Duarte, *slide:ology*, 118.

11. Garr Reynolds, *Presentation Zen: Simple Ideas on Presentation Design and Delivery* (Berkeley, Calif.: New Riders, 2008), 132.

12. Guy Kawasaki, "Rule of Thumb," *Entrepreneur*, May 2008, 44.

13. Duarte, *slide:ology*, 152.

14. Eric Markowitz, "How to Create a Great PowerPoint Presentation," *Inc.*, 7 February 2011, www.inc.com.

15. Jerry Weissman, *Presenting to Win: The Art of Telling Your Story* (Upper Saddle River, N.J.: Pearson Prentice Hall, 2006), 124.

16. Weissman, *Presenting to Win*, 144–147.

17. Sarah Lary and Karen Pruente, "Powerless Point: Common PowerPoint Mistakes to Avoid," *Public Relations Tactics*, February 2004, 28.

18. Greg Anderson, "Presefy Syncs and Controls Presentations over Your Phone," Arctic Startup, 14 March 2013, www.arcticstartup.com; Kanda Software website, accessed 2 May 2014, www.kandasoft.com; Heather Clancy, "Broadcast Your Mobile Presentations to Remote Attendees," ZDNet, 27 March 2013, www.zdnet.com.

19. Nancy Duarte, "Avoiding the Road to PowerPoint Hell," *Wall Street Journal*, 22 January 2011, online.wsj.com.

20. Reynolds, *Presentation Zen*, 85.

21. Weissman, *Presenting to Win*, 162.

22. Reynolds, *Presentation Zen*, 66.

23. Ted Simons, "Handouts That Won't Get Trashed," *Presentations*, February 1999, 47–50.

24. Hugo Martin, "Snowboarding Craze Fades, Skiing Becomes Cool Again," *Seattle Times*, 7 February 2013, seattletimes.com.

25. PechaKucha20×20 website, accessed 4 August 2010, www.pechakucha.org; Reynolds, *Presentation Zen*, 41.

The same techniques you use to succeed in your career can also help you launch and manage that career. Understand the employer's perspective on the hiring process so that you can adapt your approach and find the best job in the shortest possible time. Learn the best ways to craft a résumé and the other elements in your job-search portfolio. Understand the interviewing process to make sure you're prepared for every stage and every type of interview.

Laflor/Getty Images

18

Building Careers and Writing Résumés

LEARNING OBJECTIVES

After studying this chapter, you will be able to

1 List eight key steps to finding the ideal opportunity in today's job market.

2 Explain the process of planning your résumé, including how to choose the best résumé organization.

3 Describe the tasks involved in writing your résumé, and list the major sections of a traditional résumé.

4 Characterize the completing step for résumés, including the six most common formats in which you can produce a résumé.

MyBCommLab®
⭐ **Improve Your Grade!** More than 10 million students improved their results using Pearson MyLabs. Visit **mybcommlab.com** for simulations, tutorials, and end-of-chapter problems.

COMMUNICATION CLOSE-UP AT
Burning Glass

burning-glass.com

Finding a job opening that matches your interests and qualifications—and then convincing employers you are the best person for the job—can be one of the most complicated, aggravating, and downright mystifying tasks you ever undertake.

If you eventually move into management or take the entrepreneurial plunge and build your own company, you'll encounter this matchmaking challenge from the other side of the table. When a single job opening can attract dozens or hundreds of applicants, how can you sort through all the possibilities to identify the most promising candidates who warrant the time and expense of interviewing?

The challenge of matching the right people with the right jobs isn't limited to employees and employers, either. It's a vital

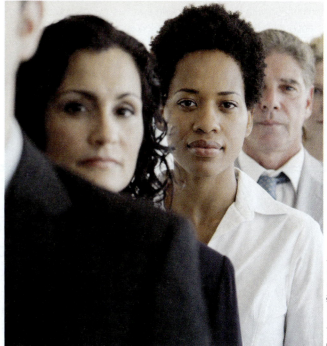

Burning Glass applies artificial intelligence to the challenges of matching employer needs with employee skill sets.

Tetra Images/Shutterstock

issue for governments and educational institutions as well. Government bodies from the local up to the national level need to make workforce policy and investment decisions that reflect the real-world problems employees and employers encounter. And in the career-related facets of their broader educational missions, high schools, colleges, and universities need to understand what employers are looking for in order to provide the training and education that best prepare students for the job market.

In other words, matching people and job opportunities is one of society's most important challenges, and doing it well or poorly has a tremendous impact on everyone's financial well-being.

To a large degree, at every level this challenge is all about getting one's hands on the right data and using them to make smart decisions. With more than 150 million employees in the Unites States alone, though, the total collection of this workforce data is massive.

To extract usable insights from this ocean of data, the Boston-based firm Burning Glass applies the power of artificial intelligence in a specialty known as *job market analytics.* In particular, it studies millions of job postings and career transitions to figure out what employers are looking for, what employees have to offer, and where gaps exist between the two sides. (Incidentally, when it studied the most important "baseline skills" across all professions, the company identified overall communication abilities as the most important skill and writing as the third-most important skill.)

Burning Glass integrates these job market insights into a variety of software tools that are used by employers, job seekers, colleges, and other parties involved in meeting the job-match challenge. In the human resources area, this software works in conjunction with *applicant tracking systems*, which you are sure to encounter at some point in your job search. Before a human being reads your résumé, it will likely be "read" by such a system, designed to help company recruiters find the most promising candidates and manage communication and data collection all the way through the recruiting, hiring, and orientation stages.

It's difficult to fault the basic concept of an applicant tracking system. Software helps business professionals make all kinds of decisions, and most medium-sized and large companies get swamped with so many résumés that they have to rely on software to help recruiters manage the flow. However, the technology has developed a negative reputation in some quarters. Applicants express frustration that they can't get past a "robot" and explain their qualifications to an actual human being. Employers get frustrated when people clog their systems by applying for jobs for which they are clearly not qualified or when applicants try to game the system by loading up their résumés with stacks of *keywords* they think the system is looking for. And employers sometimes complain they can't find enough good applicants, even as good applicants are banging on the door but can't get in. Overly aggressive filtering can be a problem with poorly configured systems or for employers who dial up the qualification requirements to the point that only a superhero could make it over the barrier.

Companies such as Burning Glass aim to make this process work better for everybody by moving beyond simple keyword searches and résumé cataloging. For example, Burning Glass's technology analyzes how keywords are used in a résumé in order to separate candidates who describe themselves legitimately and naturally from those who are simply stuffing their résumés with keywords. The software is learning to read résumés the way human recruiters do, evaluating keywords in context to make informed judgments about the quality and currency of the skills someone has included. If the system is searching for candidates with database design experience, for instance, it can tell whether somebody took a class in the subject ten years or ago or is currently applying those skills in a professional capacity.

From an applicant's perspective, the best way to "beat the robots" is to stop trying to beat them. Don't try to trick the system by including every keyword you can find or try to improve your odds by blasting your application to hundreds of openings. Instead, take the time to read job descriptions carefully so you can concentrate on the ones where you fit best and so you can understand employers' needs well enough that you can explain how your skills and experience align with those needs. Even though you may have to go through a machine to get to an actual human, using the same audience-focused skills and techniques you've been practicing throughout this course is the best way to get there.[1]

Finding the Ideal Opportunity in Today's Job Market

1 LEARNING OBJECTIVE
List eight key steps to finding the ideal opportunity in today's job market.

Software developers such as Burning Glass (profiled in the chapter-opening Communication Close-Up) play an important role in today's job market, particularly with **applicant tracking systems,** computer systems that help companies manage job applications and identify promising candidates.

Identifying and landing a job can be a long and challenging process. Fortunately, the skills you're developing in this course will give you a competitive advantage. This section offers a general job-search strategy with advice that applies to just about any career path you might want to pursue. As you craft your personal strategy, keep these three guidelines in mind:

If you haven't already, read the Prologue, "Building a Career with Your Communication Skills," before studying this chapter.

- **Get organized.** Your job search could last many months and involve multiple contacts with dozens of companies. You need to keep all the details straight to ensure that you don't miss opportunities or make mistakes such as losing someone's email address or forgetting an appointment.

- **Start now and stick to it.** Even if you are a year or more away from graduation, now is not too early to get started with some of the essential research and planning tasks. If you wait until the last minute, you might miss opportunities and you won't be as prepared as other candidates.

- **Look for stepping-stone opportunities.** Particularly in today's tough job market, you might not find the opportunity you're looking for right away. You might need to take a job that doesn't meet your expectations while you keep looking to get on the right track. But view every job as an opportunity to learn workplace skills, observe effective and ineffective business practices, and fine-tune your sense of how you'd like to spend your career.

WRITING THE STORY OF YOU

Writing or updating your résumé is a great opportunity to step back and think about where you've been and where you'd like to go. Do you like the path you're on, or is it time for a change? Are you focused on a particular field, or do you need some time to explore?

What's your story? Thinking about where you've been and where you want to go will help focus your job search.

You might find it helpful to think about the "story of you"—the things you are passionate about, your skills, your ability to help an organization reach its goals, the path you've been on so far, and the path you want to follow in the future (see Figure 18.1 on the next page). Think in terms of an image or a theme you'd like to project. Are you academically gifted? An effective leader? A well-rounded professional with wide-ranging talents? A creative problem solver? A technical wizard? Writing your story is a valuable planning exercise that helps you think about where you want to go and how to present yourself to target employers.

LEARNING TO THINK LIKE AN EMPLOYER

When you know your side of the hiring equation a little better, switch sides and look at it from an employer's perspective. Recognize that companies take risks with every hiring decision—the risk that the person hired won't meet expectations and the risk that a better candidate has slipped through their fingers. Many companies judge the success of their recruiting efforts by *quality of hire*, a measure of how closely new employees meet the company's needs.[2] Given this perspective, what steps can you take to present yourself as the low-risk, high-reward choice?

Employers judge their recruiting success by *quality of hire*, and you can take steps to be—and look like—a high-quality hire.

Of course, your perceived ability to perform the job is an essential part of your potential quality as a new hire. However, hiring managers consider more than just your ability to handle the job. They want to know if you'll be reliable and motivated—if you're somebody who "gets it" when it comes to being a professional in today's workplace. A great way to get inside the heads of corporate recruiters is to "listen in" on their professional conversations by reading periodicals such as *Workforce Management* and blogs such as Fistful of Talent and The HR Capitalist.

Follow the online conversations of professional recruiters to learn what their hot-button issues are.

RESEARCHING INDUSTRIES AND COMPANIES OF INTEREST

Learning more about professions, industries, and individual companies is a vital step in your job search. It also impresses employers, particularly when you go beyond the easily available sources such as a company's own website. "Detailed research, including talking to our customers, is so rare it will almost guarantee you get hired," explains the recruiting manager at Alcon Laboratories.[3]

Table 18.1 on page 517 lists some of the many websites where you can learn more about companies and find job openings. Start with The Riley Guide, which offers advice for online job searches as well as links to hundreds of specialized websites that post openings in specific industries and professions. Your college's career center placement office probably maintains an up-to-date list as well.

My Story

Where I Have Been

- Honor student and all around big shot in high school (but discovered that college is full of big shots!)
- Have worked several part-time jobs; only thing that really appealed to me in any of them was making improvements, making things work better

Where I Am Now

- Junior; on track to graduate in 2018
- Enjoy designing creative solutions to challenging problems
- Not a high-end techie in an engineering sense, but I figure most things out eventually
- Not afraid to work hard, whatever it takes to get the job done
- I can tolerate some routine, as long as I have the opportunity to make improvements if needed
- Tend to lead quietly by example, rather than by visibly and vocally taking charge
- Knowing that I do good work is more important than getting approval from others
- I tend not to follow fads and crowds; sometimes I'm ahead of the curve, sometimes I'm behind the curve

Where I Want to Be

- Get an advanced degree; not sure what subject area yet, though
- Haven't really settled on one industry or profession yet; working with systems of any kind is more appealing than any particular profession that I've learned about so far
- Develop my leadership and communication skills to become a more "obvious" leader
- Collaborate with others while still having the freedom to work independently (may be become an independent contractor or consultant at some point?)
- Have the opportunity to work internationally, at least for a few years
- I like the big bucks that corporate executives earn, but I don't want to live in the public eye like that or have to "play the game" to get ahead
- Believe I would be good manager, but not sure I want to spend all my time just managing people
- What to be known as an independent thinker and creative problem solver, as somebody who can analyze tough situations and figure out solutions that others might not consider
- Are there jobs where I could focus on troubleshooting, improving processes, or designing new systems?

← What experiences from your past give you insight into where you would like to go in the future?

← Where do you stand now in terms of your education and career, and what do you know about yourself?

← What would you like your future to be? What do you like and dislike? What would you like to explore? If you haven't figured everything out yet, that's fine—as long as you've started to think about the future.

Figure 18.1   Writing the Story of You
Writing the "story of you" is a helpful way to think through where you've been in your life and career so far, where you are now, and where you would like to go from here. Remember that this is a private document designed to help you clarify your thoughts and plans, although you probably will find ways to adapt some of what you've written to various job-search documents, including your résumé.

Employers expect you to be familiar with important developments in their industries, so stay on top of business news.

MOBILE APP
The **Indeed.com** mobile app lets you search for jobs and apply for them from your phone.

To learn more about contemporary business topics, peruse leading business periodicals and newspapers with significant business sections (in some cases you may need to go through your library's online databases to access back issues).

Thousands of bloggers, microbloggers, and podcasters offer news and commentary on the business world. AllTop is another good resource for finding people who write about topics that interest you. In addition to learning more about professions and opportunities, this research will help you get comfortable with the jargon and buzzwords currently in use in a particular field, including essential keywords to use in your résumé.

Take advantage of job-search apps as well, including those offered by job-posting websites and major employers. You can use them to learn more about the company as well as specific jobs. See "Job-Search Strategies: Maximize Your Mobile" for more tips on using a smartphone in your job search.

TABLE 18.1   Selected Job-Search Websites

Website*	URL	Highlights
Riley Guide	www.rileyguide.com	Vast collection of links to both general and specialized job sites for every career imaginable; don't miss this one—it could save you hours of searching
CollegeRecruiter.com	www.collegerecruiter.com	Focused on opportunities for graduates with fewer than three years of work experience
Monster	www.monster.com	One of the most popular job sites, with hundreds of thousands of openings, many from hard-to-find small companies; extensive collection of advice on the job-search process
MonsterCollege	college.monster.com	Focused on job searches for new college grads; your school's career center site probably links here
CareerBuilder	www.careerbuilder.com	One of the largest job boards; affiliated with more than 150 newspapers around the country
Jobster	www.jobster.com	Uses social networking to link employers with job seekers
USAJOBS	www.usajobs.gov	Official job-search site for the U.S. government, featuring everything from jobs for economists to astronauts to border patrol agents
IMDiversity	imdiversity.com	Good resource on diversity in the workplace, with job postings from companies that have made a special commitment to promoting diversity in their workforces
Dice.com	www.dice.com	One of the best sites for high-technology jobs
TopTechJobs	toptechjobs.com	Concentrates on jobs for IT specialists and engineers; also incorporates NetTemps.com for contractors and freelancers looking for short-term assignments
Internship Programs	internshipprograms.com	Posts listings from companies looking for interns in a wide variety of professions
SimplyHired Indeed	www.simplyhired.com www.indeed.com	Two specialized search engines that look for job postings on hundreds of websites world-wide; they find many postings that aren't listed on job board sites such as Monster

Note: This list represents only a small fraction of the hundreds of job-posting sites and other resources available online; be sure to check with your college's career center for the latest information.

Sources: Individual websites, all accessed 10 May 2016.

TRANSLATING YOUR GENERAL POTENTIAL INTO A SPECIFIC SOLUTION FOR EACH EMPLOYER

An important aspect of the employer's quality-of-hire challenge is trying to determine how well a candidate's attributes and experience will translate into the demands of a specific position. Customizing your résumé to each job opening is an important step in showing employers that you will be a good fit. As you can see from the sample résumés in Figures 18.4 through 18.6 on pages 529–531, customizing your résumé is not difficult if you have done your research. In fact, from your initial contact all the way through the interviewing process you will have opportunities to impress recruiters by explaining how your general potential translates to the specific needs of the position.

> An essential task in your job search is presenting your skills and accomplishments in a way that is relevant to the employer's business challenges.

TAKING THE INITIATIVE TO FIND OPPORTUNITIES

When it comes to finding the right opportunities for you, the easiest ways are not always the most productive ways. The major job boards such as Monster and classified services such as Craigslist might have thousands of openings, but thousands of job seekers are looking at and applying for these same openings. Moreover, posting job openings on these sites is often a company's last resort, after it has exhausted other possibilities.

To maximize your chances, take the initiative and seek opportunities. Identify the companies you want to work for and focus your efforts on them. Get in touch with their human resources departments (or individual managers, if possible), describe what you can offer the company, and ask to be considered if any opportunities come up.[4] Reach out to company representatives on social networks. Your message might appear right when a company is busy looking for someone but hasn't yet advertised the opening to the outside world. And be sure to take advantage of the growing number of career-related mobile apps (see Figure 18.2 on page 519).

> Don't hesitate to contact interesting companies even if they haven't advertised job openings to the public yet; they might be looking for somebody just like you.

DIGITAL + SOCIAL + MOBILE: TODAY'S COMMUNICATION ENVIRONMENT

Job-Search Strategies: Maximize Your Mobile

The mobile business communication revolution is changing the way employers recruit new talent and the way job candidates look for opportunities. Many companies have optimized their careers websites for mobile access, and some have even developed mobile apps that offer everything from background information on what it's like to work there to application forms that you can fill out right on your phone.

However, don't be too quick to abandon a job application or an investigation into an employer just because the firm doesn't have a careers app or a mobile-friendly job site. Creating apps and mobile-friendly websites takes time and money, and many employers are still in the process of optimizing their online career materials for mobile devices. In a recent survey, 40 percent of mobile users said they would abandon a non-mobile job application—a distressingly high number in a slow job market. Don't miss a great opportunity just because an employer hasn't caught up to your mobile habits.

In addition to researching companies and applying for openings, integrating a mobile device into your job-search strategy can help with networking and staying on top of your active job applications. For instance, some companies don't wait long after extending an offer; if they don't hear from the top candidate in a short amount of time, they'll move on their next choice. By staying plugged in via your mobile device, you won't let any opportunities pass you by.

Think of ways to use your mobile device to enhance your personal brand and your online portfolio. If you want to work in retail, for example, you could take photos of particularly good or particularly bad merchandizing displays and post them with commentary on your social media accounts. Employers doing background research on you on will see these posts and recognize you as a candidate who is invested in his or her career and the industry as a whole. Many of the tools you can use to build your personal brand are available as mobile apps, including blogging platforms, Twitter, Facebook, and LinkedIn.

Dozens of apps are available to help with various aspects of your job search. Résumé creation apps let you quickly modify your résumé if you come across a good opportunity. Business card scanning apps make it easy to keep digital copies of business cards, so you'll never lose important contact information. Note-taking apps are a great way to plan for interviews and record your postinterview notes. Use your phone's scheduling capability to make sure you never miss an interviewing or a filing deadline. Polish your interviewing skills with your phone's audio- and video-recording features or a practice-interview app. If an employer wants to interview you via Cisco WebEx or another online meeting system, those apps are available for your phone or tablet as well.

You've been paying a lot for your mobile service—now make that mobile work for you by helping you land a great job.

CAREER APPLICATIONS

1. Would it be a good idea to present your online portfolio on your smartphone during a job interview? Why or why not?

2. Is it wise for applicants to shun a company that doesn't have a mobile-friendly careers website or a career app? Why or why not?

Sources: David Cohen, "Social Recruiting Goes Mobile," AllFacebook blog, 23 December 2013, allfacebook.com; Ryan Rancatore, "The 33 Best iPhone Apps for Personal Branding," Personal Branding 101 blog, 27 December 2009, personalbranding101.com; Jule Gamache, "The Rise of Mobile Job Search," Come Recommended blog, 12 June 2013, comerecommended.com.

BUILDING YOUR NETWORK

Start thinking like a networker now; your classmates could turn out to be some of your most important business contacts.

Networking is the process of making informal connections with mutually beneficial business contacts. Networking takes place wherever and whenever people talk: at industry functions, at social gatherings, at alumni reunions—and all over the Internet, from LinkedIn and Twitter to Facebook and Google+. In addition to making connections through social media tools, you might get yourself noticed by company recruiters.

Networking is more essential than ever because the vast majority of job openings are never advertised to the general public. To avoid the time and expense of sifting through thousands of applications and the risk of hiring complete strangers, most companies prefer to ask their employees for recommendations first.[5] The more people who know you, the better chance you have of being recommended for one of these hidden job openings.

Put your network in place before you need it.

Start building your network now, before you need it. Your classmates could end up being some of your most valuable contacts, if not right away, then possibly later in your career. Then branch out by identifying people with similar interests in your target professions, industries, and companies. Read news sites, blogs, and other online sources. Follow industry leaders on Twitter. You can also follow individual executives at your target companies to learn about their interests and concerns.[6] Be on the lookout for career-oriented *Tweetups*, in which people who've connected on Twitter get together for in-person networking events. Connect with people on LinkedIn and Facebook, particularly in groups

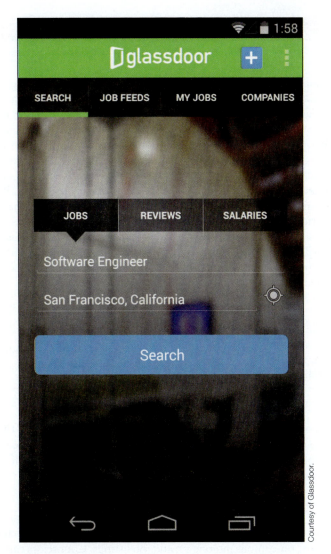

Courtesy of Glassdoor.

Figure 18.2   Mobile Job-Search Tools
Put your mobile phone or tablet to work in your job search, using some of the many employment apps now available.

dedicated to particular career interests. Depending on the system and the settings on individual users' accounts, you may be able to introduce yourself via public or private messages. Just make sure you are respectful of people, and don't take up much of their time.[7]

Participate in student business organizations, especially those with ties to professional organizations. Visit *trade shows* to learn about various industries and rub shoulders with people who work in those industries.[8] Don't overlook volunteering; you not only meet people but also demonstrate your ability to solve problems, manage projects, and lead others. You can do some good while creating a network for yourself.

Remember that networking is about people helping each other, not just about other people helping you. Pay close attention to networking etiquette: Try to learn something about the people you want to connect with, don't overwhelm others with too many messages or requests, be succinct in all your communication efforts, don't give out other people's names and contact information without their permission to do so, never email your résumé to complete strangers, and remember to say thank you every time someone helps you.[9]

To become a valued network member, you need to be able to help others in some way. You may not have any influential contacts yet, but because you're researching industries and trends as part of your own job search, you probably have valuable information you can share via your online and offline networks. Or you might simply be able to connect one person with another who can help. The more you network, the more valuable you become in your network—and the more valuable your network becomes to you.

MOBILE APP
Stay in touch with your professional network with the **LinkedIn** mobile app.

Networking is a mutually beneficial activity, so look for opportunities to help others in some way.

THE ART OF PROFESSIONALISM

Striving to Excel

Pros are good at what they do, and they never stop improving. No matter what your job might be at any given time—even if it is far from where you aspire to be—strive to perform at the highest possible level. Not only do you have an ethical obligation to give your employer and your customers your best effort, but excelling at each level in your career is also the best way to keep climbing up to new positions of responsibility. Plus, being good at what you do delivers a sense of satisfaction that is hard to beat.

In many jobs and in many industries, performing at a high level requires a commitment to continuous learning and improvement. The nature of the work often changes as markets and technologies evolve, and expectations of quality tend to increase over time as well. View this constant change as a positive thing, as a way to avoid stagnation and boredom.

Striving to excel can be a challenge when there is a mismatch between the job's requirements and your skills and knowledge. If you are underqualified for a job, you need to identify your weaknesses quickly and come up with a plan to address them. A supportive manager will help you identify these areas and encourage improvement through training or mentoring. Don't wait for a boss to tell you your work is sub-par, however. If you know you're floundering, ask for help.

If you are overqualified for a job, it's easy to slip into a rut and eventually underperform simply because you aren't being challenged. However, current and future bosses aren't going to judge you on how well you performed relative to your needs and expectations; they're going to judge you on how well you performed relative to the job's requirements. Work with your boss to find ways to make your job more challenging if possible, or start looking for a better job if necessary, but be sure to maintain your level of performance until you can bring your responsibilities and talents into closer alignment.

CAREER APPLICATIONS

1. Should you ever try to sell yourself into a job for which you are not yet 100 percent qualified? Explain your answer.
2. Do you agree that you have an ethical obligation to excel at your job? Why or why not?

Finally, be aware that your online network reflects on who you are in the eyes of potential employers, so exercise some judgment in making connections. Also, many employers now contact people in a candidate's public network for background information, even if the candidate doesn't list those people as references.[10]

SEEKING CAREER COUNSELING

Don't overlook the many resources available through your college's career center.

Your college's career center probably offers a wide variety of services, including individual counseling, job fairs, on-campus interviews, and job listings. Counselors can advise on career planning and provide workshops on job-search techniques, résumé preparation, job readiness training, interview techniques, self-marketing, and more.[11] You can also find career-planning advice online. Many of the websites listed in Table 18.1 offer articles and online tests to help you choose a career path, identify essential skills, and prepare to enter the job market.

AVOIDING MISTAKES

Don't let a silly mistake knock you out of contention for a great job.

While you're making all these positive moves to show employers you will be a quality hire, take care to avoid the simple blunders that can torpedo a job search, such as not catching mistakes in your résumé, misspelling the name of a manager you're writing to, showing up late for an interview, tweeting something unprofessional, failing to complete application forms correctly, asking for information that you can easily find yourself on a company's website, or making any other error that could flag you as someone who is careless or disrespectful. Assume that every employer will conduct an online search on you. Busy recruiters will seize on these errors as a way to narrow the list of candidates they need to spend time on, so don't give them a reason to reject your résumé.

Planning Your Résumé

2 LEARNING OBJECTIVE
Explain the process of planning your résumé, including how to choose the best résumé organization.

Although you will create many messages during your career search, your **résumé**—a structured, written summary of your education, employment background, and job qualifications—will be the most important document in this process. You will be able to use it directly in many instances, adapt it to a variety of uses such an e-portfolio or a social media résumé, and reuse pieces of it in social networking profiles and online application forms.

Even if you apply to a company that doesn't want to see résumés from applicants, the process of developing your résumé will prepare you for interviewing and preemployment testing.

Developing a résumé is one of those projects that benefits from multiple planning, writing, and completing sessions spread out over several days or weeks. You are trying to summarize a complex subject (yourself!) and present a compelling story to strangers in a brief document. Follow the three-step writing process (see Figure 18.3) and give yourself plenty of time.

Before you dive in to your résumé, be aware that you will find a wide range of opinions about résumés, regarding everything from appropriate length, content, design, distribution methods, and acceptable degrees of creativity to whether it even makes sense to write a traditional résumé in this age of online applications. For example, you may encounter a prospective employer that wants you to tweet your résumé or submit all the links that make up your online presence, rather than submit a conventional résumé.[12] You may run across examples of effective résumés that were produced as infographics, interactive videos, simulated search engine results, puzzles, games, graphic novels—you name it, somebody has probably tried it.

When you hear conflicting advice or see trendy concepts that you might be tempted to try, remember the most important question in business communication: What is the most effective way to adapt your message to the individual needs of each member of your audience? An approach that is wildly successful with one company or in one industry could be a complete disaster in another industry. To forge your own successful path through this maze of information, get inside the heads of the people you are trying to reach—try to think the way they think—and then apply the principles of effective communication you are learning in this course.

> You will see lots of ideas and even some conflicting advice about résumés; use what you know about effective business communication to decide what is right for your résumés.

1 Plan →	**2** Write →	**3** Complete
Analyze the Situation Recognize that the purpose of your résumé is to get an interview, not to get a job.	**Adapt to Your Audience** Plan your wording carefully so that you can catch a recruiter's eye within seconds; translate your education and experience into attributes that target employers find valuable.	**Revise the Message** Evaluate content and review readability and then edit and rewrite for conciseness and clarity.
Gather Information Research target industries and companies so that you know what they're looking for in new hires; learn about various jobs and what to expect; learn about the hiring manager, if possible.	**Compose the Message** Write clearly and succinctly, using active, powerful language that is appropriate to the industries and companies you're targeting; use a professional tone in all communications.	**Produce the Message** Use effective design elements and suitable layout for a clean, professional appearance; seamlessly combine text and graphical elements. When printing, use quality paper and a good printer.
Choose Media and Channels Start with a traditional paper résumé and develop scannable, plain text, PDF, and social/online versions, as needed. Consider other formats as supplements.		**Proofread the Message** Review for errors in layout, spelling, and mechanics; mistakes can cost you interview opportunities.
Organize the Information Choose an organizational model that highlights your strengths and downplays your shortcomings; use the chronological approach unless you have a strong reason not to.		**Distribute the Message** Deliver your résumé, carefully following the specific instructions of each employer or job board website.

Figure 18.3 Three-Step Writing Process for Résumés
Following the three-step writing process will help you create a successful résumé in a short time. Remember to pay particular attention to the "you" attitude and presentation quality.

ANALYZING YOUR PURPOSE AND AUDIENCE

Once you view your résumé as a persuasive business message, it's easier to decide what should and shouldn't be in it.

Planning an effective résumé starts with understanding its true function—as a brief, persuasive business message intended to stimulate an employer's interest in meeting you and learning more about you (see Table 18.2). In other words, the purpose of a résumé is not to get you a job but rather to get you an interview.[13]

As you conduct your research on various professions, industries, companies, and individual managers, you will have a better perspective on your target readers and their information needs. Learn as much as you can about the individuals who may be reading your résumé. Many professionals and managers are bloggers, Twitter users, and LinkedIn members, for example, so you can learn more about them online even if you've never met them. Any bit of information can help you craft a more effective message.

Thanks to Twitter, LinkedIn, and other social media, you can often learn valuable details about individual managers at your target employers.

By the way, if employers ask to see your "CV," they're referring to your *curriculum vitae*, the term used instead of *résumé* in academic professions and in many countries outside the United States. Résumés and CVs are essentially the same, although CVs can be much more detailed and include personal information that is not included in a résumé.

REAL-TIME UPDATES

LEARN MORE BY VISITING THIS WEBSITE

Converting your résumé to a CV

If you need to convert your U.S.-style résumé to the curriculum vitae format used in many other countries (and in many academic positions in the United States), this website will tell you everything you need to know. Go to **real-timeupdates.com/bct14** and select Learn More in the Students section.

GATHERING PERTINENT INFORMATION

If you haven't been building an employment portfolio thus far, you may need to do some research on yourself at this point. Gather all the pertinent personal history you can think of, including all the specific dates, duties, and accomplishments from any previous jobs you've held. Compile all your educational accomplishments, including formal degrees, training certificates, professional and technical certifications, academic awards, and scholarships. Also, gather information about school or volunteer activities that might be relevant to your job search, including offices you have held in any club or professional organization, presentations given, and online or print publications. You probably won't use every piece of information you come up with, but you'll want to have it at your fingertips.

SELECTING THE BEST MEDIA AND CHANNELS

You should expect to produce your résumé in several media and formats. "Producing Your Résumé" on page 532 discusses your options.

ORGANIZING YOUR RÉSUMÉ AROUND YOUR STRENGTHS

Although there are a number of ways to organize a résumé, most are some variation of chronological, functional, or a combination of the two. The right choice depends on your background and your goals.

TABLE 18.2   Fallacies and Facts About Résumés

Fallacy	Fact
The purpose of a résumé is to list all your skills and abilities.	The purpose of a résumé is to kindle employer interest and generate an interview.
A good résumé will get you the job you want.	All a résumé can do is get you in the door.
Your résumé will always be read carefully and thoroughly.	In most cases, your résumé needs to make a positive impression within a few seconds; only then will someone read it in detail. Moreover, it will likely be screened by a computer looking for keywords first—and if it doesn't contain the right keywords, a human being may never see it.
The more good information you present about yourself in your résumé, the better, so stuff your résumé with every positive detail.	Recruiters don't need that much information about you at the initial screening stage, and they probably won't read it.

The Chronological Résumé

In a **chronological résumé**, the work experience section dominates and is placed immediately after your contact information and introductory statement (see Figure 18.6 on page 531 for an example). The chronological approach is the most common way to organize a résumé, and many employers prefer this format because it presents your professional history in a clear, easy-to-follow arrangement.[14] If you're just graduating from college and have limited professional experience, you can vary this chronological approach by putting your educational qualifications before your experience.

Develop your work experience section by listing your jobs in reverse chronological order, beginning with the most recent one and giving more space to the most recent positions you've held. For each job, start by listing the employer's name and location, your official job title, and the dates you held the position (write "to present" if you are still in your most recent job). Next, in a short block of text, highlight your accomplishments in a way that is relevant and understandable to your readers. If the general responsibilities of the position are not obvious from the job title, provide a little background to help readers understand what you did.

The chronological résumé is the most common approach, but it might not be right for you at this stage in your career.

The Functional Résumé

A **functional résumé**, sometimes called a *skills résumé*, emphasizes your skills and capabilities, identifying employers and academic experience in subordinate sections. This arrangement stresses individual areas of competence rather than job history. The functional approach has three benefits: (1) Without having to read through job descriptions, employers can get an idea of what you can do for them; (2) you can emphasize previous job experience through the skills you gained in those positions; and (3) you can deemphasize any lengthy unemployment or lack of career progress. However, you should be aware that because the functional résumé can obscure your work history, many employment professionals are suspicious of it.[15] Moreover, it lacks the evidence of job experience that supports your skills claims. If you don't believe the chronological format will work for you, consider the combination résumé instead.

The functional résumé is often considered by people with limited or spotty employment history, but many employers are suspicious of this format.

The Combination Résumé

A **combination résumé** meshes the skills focus of the functional format with the job history focus of the chronological format. Figures 18.4 (page 529) and 18.5 (page 530) show examples of combination résumés. The chief advantage of this format is that it allows you to highlight your capabilities and education when you don't have a long or steady employment history, without raising concerns that you might be hiding something about your past.

As you look at a number of sample résumés, you'll probably notice many variations on the three basic formats presented here. Study these other options in light of the effective communication principles you've learned in this course and the unique circumstances of your job search. If you find one that seems like the best fit for your unique situation, by all means use it.

If you don't have a lot of work history to show, consider a combination résumé to highlight your skills while still providing a chronological history of your employment.

ADDRESSING AREAS OF CONCERN

Many people have gaps in their careers or other issues that could be a concern for employers. Here are some common issues and suggestions for handling them in a résumé:[16]

- **Frequent job changes.** If you've had a number of short-term jobs of a similar type, such as independent contracting and temporary assignments, you can group them under a single heading. Also, if past job positions were eliminated as a result of layoffs or mergers, find a subtle way to convey that information (if not in your résumé, then in your cover letter). Reasonable employers understand that many professionals have been forced to job hop by circumstances beyond their control.
- **Gaps in work history.** Mention relevant experience and education you gained during employment gaps, such as volunteer or community work.
- **Inexperience.** Mention related volunteer work and membership in professional groups. List relevant course work and internships.

- **Overqualification.** Tone down your résumé, focusing exclusively on the experience and skills that relate to the position.
- **Long-term employment with one company.** Itemize each position held at the firm to show growth within the organization and increasing responsibilities along the way.
- **Job termination for cause.** Be honest with interviewers and address their concerns with proof, such as recommendations and examples of completed projects.
- **Criminal record.** You don't necessarily need to disclose a criminal record or time spent incarcerated on your résumé, but you may be asked about it on job application forms. Laws regarding what employers may ask (and whether they can conduct a criminal background check) vary by state and profession, but if you are asked and the question applies to you, you are legally bound to answer truthfully. Use the interview process to explain any mitigating circumstances and to emphasize your rehabilitation and commitment to being a law-abiding, trustworthy employee.[17]

REAL-TIME UPDATES
LEARN MORE BY READING THIS ARTICLE
Smart strategies to explain gaps in your work history

Get three key pieces of advice if you have been or were out of work for a period of time. Go to **real-timeupdates.com/bct14** and select Learn More in the Students section.

Writing Your Résumé

3 **LEARNING OBJECTIVE**
Describe the tasks involved in writing your résumé, and list the major sections of a traditional résumé.

If you're uncomfortable writing your own résumé, you might try to trade with a classmate and write each other's résumé.

With the necessary information and a good plan in hand, you're ready to begin writing. If you feel uncomfortable writing about yourself, you're not alone. Many people, even accomplished writers, can find it difficult to write their own résumés. If you get stuck, imagine you are somebody else, writing a résumé for this person called you. By "being your own client" in this sense, you might find the words and ideas flow more easily. You can also find a classmate or friend who is writing a résumé and swap projects for a while. Working on each other's résumés might speed up the process for both of you.

KEEPING YOUR RÉSUMÉ HONEST

Résumé fraud has reached epidemic proportions, but employers are fighting back with more rigorous screening techniques.

Estimates vary, but one comprehensive study uncovered lies about work history in more than 40 percent of the résumés tested.[18] And dishonest applicants are getting bolder all the time—going so far as to buy fake diplomas online, pay a computer hacker to insert their names into prestigious universities' graduation records, and sign up for services that offer phony employment verification or phony references.[19] "It's becoming common to cheat," observes Professor George Gollin of the University of Illinois, Urbana, mentioning the 200,000 fake college degrees sold every year as one example.[20]

Applicants with integrity know they don't need to stoop to lying. If you are tempted to stretch the truth, bear in mind that professional recruiters have seen all sorts of fraud by job applicants, and frustrated employers are working aggressively to uncover the truth. Nearly all employers do some form of background checking, from contacting references and verifying employment to checking criminal records and sending résumés through verification services.[21] Employers are also beginning to craft certain interview questions specifically to uncover dishonest résumé entries.[22]

Most companies that find lies on résumés refuse to hire the offending applicants, even if that means withdrawing formal job offers.[23] And if you do sneak past these filters and get hired, you'll probably be exposed on the job when you can't live up to your own résumé. Given the networked nature of today's job market, lying on a résumé could haunt you for years—and you could be forced to keep lying throughout your career to hide the misrepresentations on your original résumé.[24]

REAL-TIME UPDATES
LEARN MORE BY READING THIS ARTICLE
Tempted to twist the truth on your resume?

Lying on a résumé can have legal ramifications. Go to **real-timeup dates.com/bct14** and select Learn More in the Students section.

ADAPTING YOUR RÉSUMÉ TO YOUR AUDIENCE

Translate your past accomplishments into a compelling picture of what you can do for employers in the future.

The importance of adapting your résumé to your target readers' needs and interests cannot be overstated. In a competitive job market, the more you seem like a good fit—a quality hire—the better your chances of securing interviews. Address your readers' business concerns by showing how your capabilities meet the demands and expectations of the position and the organization as a whole.

For example, an in-house public relations (PR) department and an independent PR agency perform many of the same tasks, but the outside agency must also sell its services to multiple clients. Consequently, it needs employees who are skilled at attracting and keeping paying customers in addition to being skilled at PR. If you are applying for both in-house and agency PR jobs, you need to adapt your résumé for each of these audiences.

An essential step in adapting your résumé is using the same terminology as the employer uses to describe job responsibilities and professional accomplishments. In Figures 18.4 through 18.6 starting on page 529, you can see how the sample résumés do this, incorporating key terms and phrases from the job postings.

If you are applying for business positions after military service or moving from one industry to another, you may need to "translate" your experience into the language of your target employers. For instance, military experience can help you develop many skills that are valuable in business, but military terminology can sound like a foreign language to people who aren't familiar with it. Isolate the important general concepts and present them in the business language your target employers use.

REAL-TIME UPDATES
LEARN MORE BY EXPLORING THIS INTERACTIVE WEBSITE
See how well your résumé matches a target job description

Increase your chances of getting past a company's résumé filters by comparing your résumé with the wording of a target job description. Go to **real-timeupdates.com/bct14** and select Learn More in the Students section.

Military service and other specialized experiences may need to be "translated" into terms more readily understandable by your target readers.

COMPOSING YOUR RÉSUMÉ

Write your résumé using a simple and direct style. Use short, crisp phrases instead of whole sentences and focus on what your reader needs to know. Avoid using the word *I*, which can sound both self-involved and repetitive by the time you outline all your skills and accomplishments. Instead, start your phrases with strong action verbs such as these:[25]

Draft your résumé using short, crisp phrases built around strong verbs and nouns.

accomplished	coordinated	initiated	participated	set up
achieved	created	installed	performed	simplified
administered	demonstrated	introduced	planned	sparked
approved	developed	investigated	presented	streamlined
arranged	directed	launched	proposed	strengthened
assisted	established	maintained	raised	succeeded
assumed	explored	managed	recommended	supervised
budgeted	forecasted	motivated	reduced	systematized
chaired	generated	negotiated	reorganized	targeted
changed	identified	operated	resolved	trained
compiled	implemented	organized	saved	transformed
completed	improved	oversaw	served	upgraded

For example, you might say, "Created a campus organization for students interested in entrepreneurship" or "Managed a fast-food restaurant and four employees." Whenever you can, quantify the results so that your claims don't come across as empty puffery. Don't just say that you're a team player or detail oriented—show that you are by offering concrete proof.[26] Here are some examples of phrasing accomplishments using active statements that show results:

Instead of This	Write Active Statements That Show Results
Responsible for developing a new filing system	Developed a new filing system that reduced paperwork by 50 percent
I was in charge of customer complaints and all ordering problems	Handled all customer complaints and resolved all product order discrepancies
I won a trip to Europe for opening the most new customer accounts in my department	Generated the highest number of new customer accounts in my department
Member of special campus task force to resolve student problems with existing cafeteria assignments	Assisted in implementing new campus dining program that balances student wishes with cafeteria capacity

Providing specific supporting evidence is vital, but make sure you don't go overboard with details.[27] Carefully select the most compelling evidence so that your message is clear and immediate.

In addition to clear writing with specific examples, the particular words and phrases used throughout your résumé are critically important. The majority of résumés are now subjected to *keyword searches* in an applicant tracking system or other database, in which a recruiter searches for résumés most likely to match the requirements of a particular job. Résumés that don't closely match the requirements may never be seen by a human reader, so it is essential to use the words and phrases that a recruiter is most likely to search on. (Although most experts used to advise including a separate *keyword summary* as a stand-alone list, the trend nowadays is to incorporate your keywords into your introductory statement and other sections of your résumé.)[28]

> Include relevant *keywords* in your introductory statement, work history, and education sections.

Identifying these keywords requires some research, but you can uncover many of them while you are looking into various industries and companies. In particular, study job descriptions carefully. In contrast to the action verbs that catch a human reader's attention, keywords that catch a computer's attention are usually nouns that describe the specific skills, attributes, and experiences an employer is looking for in a candidate. Keywords can include the business and technical terms associated with a specific profession, industry-specific jargon, names or types of products or systems used in a profession, job titles, and college degrees.[29]

REAL-TIME UPDATES
LEARN MORE BY VISITING THIS WEBSITE
Find the keywords that will light up your résumé
This list of tips and tools will help you find the right keywords to customize your résumé for every opportunity. Go to **real-timeupdates .com/bct14** and select Learn More in the Students section.

Name and Contact Information

> Be sure to provide complete and accurate contact information; mistakes in this section of the résumé are surprisingly common.

Your name and contact information constitute the heading of your résumé; include the following:

- Name
- Address (both permanent and temporary, if you're likely to move during the job-search process)
- Email address
- Phone number(s)
- The URL of your personal webpage, e-portfolio, or social media résumé (if you have one)

> Use a professional-sounding email address for business correspondence, such as firstname .lastname@something.com.

If the only email address you have is through your current employer, get a free personal email address from one of the many services that offer them. It's not fair to your current employer to use company resources for a job search, and doing so sends a bad signal to potential employers. Also, if your personal email address is anything like precious .princess@something.com or PsychoDawg@something.com, get a new email address for your business correspondence.

Introductory Statement

You have three options for a brief introductory statement that follows your name and contact information:[30]

> You can choose to open with a career objective, a qualifications summary, or a career summary.

- **Career objective.** A career objective identifies either a specific job you want to land or general career track you would like to pursue. Some experts advise against including a career objective because it can categorize you so narrowly that you miss out on interesting opportunities, and it is essentially about fulfilling your desires, not about meeting the employer's needs. In the past, most résumés included a career objective, but in recent years more job seekers are using a qualifications summary or a career summary. However, if you have little or no work experience in your target profession, a career objective might be your best option. If you do opt for an objective, word it in a way that relates your qualifications to employer needs.

> If you have a reasonably focused skill set but don't yet have a long career history, a qualifications summary is probably the best type of introductory statement for you.

- **Qualifications summary.** A qualifications summary offers a brief view of your key qualifications. The goal is to let a reader know within a few seconds what you can deliver. You can title this section generically as "Qualifications Summary" or "Summary of Qualifications," or, if you have one dominant qualification, you can use that as the title. Consider using a qualifications summary if you have one or more important qualifications but don't yet have a long career history. Also, if you haven't been working long but your college education has given you a dominant professional "theme," such as multimedia design or statistical analysis, you can craft a qualifications summary that highlights your educational preparedness.

- **Career summary.** A career summary offers a brief recap of your career with the goal of presenting increasing levels of responsibility and performance (see Figure 18.6 on page 531 for an example). A career summary can be particularly useful for managers who have demonstrated the ability to manage increasingly larger and more complicated business operations—a key consideration when companies look to hire upper-level executives.

Whichever option you choose, make sure it includes many of the essential keywords you identified in your research—and adapt these words and phrases to each job opportunity as needed.

MOBILE APP
Need a simple résumé in a hurry? **Resume App Pro** and **Resume Builder Pro** let you build one right on your phone.

Education

If you're still in college or have recently graduated, education is probably your strongest selling point. Present your educational background in depth, choosing facts that support your professional theme. Give this section a heading such as "Education," "Technical Training," or "Academic Preparation," as appropriate. Then, starting with the most recent, list the name and location of each school you have attended, the month and year of your graduation (say "anticipated graduation: _____" if you haven't graduated yet), your major and minor fields of study, significant skills and abilities you've developed in your course work, and the degrees or certificates you've earned. Fine-tune your message by listing courses that are most relevant to each job opening, and indicate any scholarships, awards, or academic honors you've received.

If you are early in your career, your education is probably your strongest selling point.

The education section should also include relevant training sponsored by business or government organizations. Mention high school or military training only if the associated achievements are pertinent to your career goals.

Whether you list your grade point average depends on the job you want and the quality of your grades. If you don't show your GPA on your résumé—and there's no rule saying you have to—be prepared to answer questions about it during the interview process because many employers will assume that your GPA is not spectacular if you didn't list it on your résumé. If you choose to show a grade point average, be sure to mention the scale, especially if it isn't a four-point scale. If your grades are better within your major than in other courses, you can also list your GPA as "Major GPA" and include only those courses within your major.

Work Experience, Skills, and Accomplishments

This section can be called "Work Experience," "Professional Experience," or "Work and Volunteer Experience," if you have limited work experience and want to bolster that with volunteer experience. Like the education section, the work experience section should focus on your overall theme in a way that shows how your past can contribute to an employer's future. Use keywords to call attention to the skills you've developed on the job and to your ability to handle responsibility. Emphasize what you accomplished in each position, not just the generic responsibilities of the job.

When you describe past job responsibilities, identify the skills and knowledge that you can apply to a future job.

List your jobs in reverse chronological order, starting with the most recent. Include military service and any internships and part-time or temporary jobs related to your career objective. Include the name and location of the employer, and if readers are unlikely to recognize the organization, briefly describe what it does. When you want to keep the name of your current employer confidential, you can identify the firm by industry only ("a large video game developer"). If an organization's name or location has changed since you worked there, state the current name and location and include the old information preceded by "formerly . . ." Before or after each job listing, state your job title and give the years you worked in the job; use the phrase "to present" to denote current employment. Indicate whether a job was part time.

Devote the most space to jobs that are related to your target position.

Devote the most space to the jobs that are most recent or most closely related to your target position. If you were personally responsible for something significant, be sure to mention it. Facts about your skills and accomplishments are the most important information you can give a prospective employer, so quantify them whenever possible.

One helpful exercise is to write a 30-second "commercial" for each major skill you want to highlight. The commercial should offer proof that you really do possess the skill. For your résumé, distill the commercials down to brief phrases; you can use the more detailed proof statements in cover letters and as answers to interview questions.[31]

If you have a number of part-time, temporary, or entry-level jobs that don't relate to your career objective, you have to use your best judgment when it comes to including or excluding them. Too many minor and irrelevant work details can clutter your résumé, particularly if you've been in the professional workforce for a few years. However, if you don't have a long employment history, including these jobs shows your ability and willingness to keep working.

Activities and Achievements

Include personal accomplishments only if they suggest special skills or qualities that are relevant to the jobs you're seeking.

This optional section can be used to highlight activities and achievements outside of a work or educational context—but only if they make you a more attractive job candidate. For example, traveling, studying, or working abroad and fluency in multiple languages could weigh heavily in your favor with employers who do business internationally.

Because many employers are involved in their local communities, they tend to look positively on applicants who are active and concerned members of their communities as well. Consider including community service activities that suggest leadership, teamwork, communication skills, technical aptitude, or other valuable attributes.

You should generally avoid indicating membership or significant activity in religious or political organizations (unless, of course, you're applying to such an organization) because doing so might raise concerns for people with differing beliefs or affiliations. However, if you want to highlight skills you developed while involved with such a group, you can refer to it generically as a "not-for-profit organization."

Finally, if you have little or no job experience and not much to discuss outside of your education, indicating involvement in athletics or other organized student activities lets employers know that you don't spend all your free time hanging around your apartment playing video games. Also consider mentioning publications, projects, and other accomplishments that required relevant business skills.

Personal Data and References

When applying to U.S. companies, your résumé should not include any personal data such as age, marital status, physical description, or Social Security number.

In nearly all instances your résumé should not include any personal data beyond the information described in the previous sections. When applying to U.S. companies, never include any of the following: physical characteristics, age, gender, marital status, sexual orientation, religious or political affiliations, race, national origin, salary history, reasons for leaving jobs, names of previous supervisors, names of references, Social Security number, or student ID number.

However, be aware that standards can vary in other countries. For example, some international employers might require you to include your citizenship, nationality, or marital status.[32]

Prepare a list of references but don't include them on your résumé.

The availability of references is assumed, so you don't need to put "References available upon request" at the end of your résumé. However, be sure to have a list of several references ready when you begin applying for jobs. Prepare your reference sheet with your name and contact information at the top. For a finished look, use the same design and layout you use for your résumé. Then list three or four people who have agreed to serve as references. Include each person's name, job title, organization, address, telephone number, email address (if the reference prefers to be contacted by email), and the nature of your relationship.

Figures 18.4 through 18.6 show how a job applicant can put these guidelines to work in three job-search scenarios:

- **Scenario 1: Positioning yourself for an ideal opportunity** (when you've found a job opening that aligns closely with your career goals and your academic and professional credentials)

The Scenario

You are about to graduate and have found a job opening that is in your chosen field. You don't have any experience in this field, but the courses you've taken in pursuit of your degree have given you a solid academic foundation for this position.

The Opportunity

The job opening is for an associate market analyst with Living Social, the rapidly growing advertising and social commerce service that describes itself as "the online source for discovering valuable local experiences." (A market analyst researches markets to find potentially profitable business opportunities.)

The Communication Challenge

You don't have directly relevant experience as a market analyst, and you might be competing against people who do. Your education is your strongest selling point, so you need to show how your coursework relates to the position.

Don't let your lack of experience hold you back; the job posting makes it clear that this is an entry-level position. For example, the first bullet point in the job description says "Become an expert in market data . . .," and the required skills and experience section says that "Up to 2 years of experience with similar research and analysis is preferred." The important clues here are *become* (the company doesn't expect you to be an expert already) and *preferred* (experience would be great if you have it, but it's not required).

Keywords and Key Phrases

You study the job posting and highlight the following elements:

1. Working in a team environment
2. Research, including identifying trendy new businesses
3. Analyzing data using Microsoft Excel
4. Managing projects
5. Collaborating with technical experts and sales staff
6. Creating new tools to help maximize revenue and minimize risks
7. Bachelor's degree is required
   Natural curiosity and desire to
8. learn
9. Detail oriented
10. Hands-on experience with social media

Emma Gomes
(847) 555–2153
emma.gomes@mailsystem.net
emmawrites.blogspot.com

Address:
860 North 8th Street, Terre Haute, IN 47809

Permanent Address:
993 Church Street, Barrington, IL 60010

Summary of Qualifications

- In-depth academic preparation in marketing analysis techniques
- Intermediate skills with a variety of analytical tools, including Microsoft Excel and Google Analytics
- Front-line experience with consumers and business owners
- Multiple research and communication projects involving the business applications of social media

Education

B.S. in Marketing (Marketing Management Track), Indiana State University, Terre Haute, IN, anticipated graduation: May 2016

Program coursework

- 45 credits of core business courses, including Business Information Tools, Business Statistics, Principles of Accounting, and Business Finance
- 27 credits of marketing and marketing management courses, including Buyer Behavior, Marketing Research, Product and Pricing Strategy, and seminars in e-commerce and social media

Special projects

- "Handcrafting a Global Marketplace: The Etsy Phenomenon," in-depth analysis of how Etsy transformed the market for handmade craft items by bringing e-commerce capabilities to individual craftspeople
- "Hybrid Communication Platforms for Small Businesses," team service project for five small businesses in Terre Haute, recommending best practices for combining traditional and social-media methods of customer engagement and providing a customized measurement spreadsheet for each company

Work and Volunteer Experience

Independent math tutor, 2011-present. Assist students with a variety of math courses at the elementary, junior high, and high school level; all clients have achieved combined test and homework score improvements of at least one full letter grade, with an average improvement of 38 percent

LeafSpring Food Bank, Terre Haute, IN, 2014-present (weekends during college terms), Volunteer. Stock food and supply pantries; prepare emergency baskets for new clients; assist director with public relations activities, including website updates and social media news releases.

Owings Ford, Barrington, IL, 2013–2015 (summers), Customer care agent. Assisted the service and sales managers of this locally owned car dealership with a variety of customer-service tasks; scheduled service appointments; designed and implemented improvements to service-center waiting room to increase guest comfort; convinced dealership owners to begin using Twitter and Facebook to interact with current and potential customers.

Professional Engagement

- Collegiate member, American Marketing Association; helped establish the AMA Collegiate Chapter at Indiana State
- Participated in AMA International Collegiate Case Competition, 2013-2014

Awards

- Dean's List: 2014, 2015
- Forward Youth award, Barrington Chamber of Commerce, 2012

Notice how Gomes adapts her résumé to "mirror" the keywords and phrases from the job posting:

1. Offers concrete evidence of teamwork (rather than just calling herself a "team player," for example)
2. Emphasizes research skills and experience in multiple instances
3. Calls out Microsoft Excel, as well as Google Analytics, a key online tool for measuring activity on websites
4. Indicates the ability to plan and carry out projects, even if she doesn't have formal project management experience
5. Indicates some experience working in a supportive or collaborative role with technical experts and sales specialists (the content of the work doesn't translate to the new job, but the concept does)
6. Suggests the ability to work with new analytical tools
7. Displays her B.S. degree prominently
8. Demonstrates a desire to learn and to expand her skills
9. Tracking the progress of her tutoring clients is strong evidence of a detail-oriented worker—not to mention someone who cares about results and the quality of her work
10. Lists business-oriented experience with Facebook, Twitter, and other social media

---

Gomes includes phone and email contacts, along with a blog that features academic-oriented writing.

Using a *summary of qualifications* for her opening statement lets her target the résumé and highlight her most compelling attributes.

Her education is a much stronger selling point than her work experience, so she goes into some detail—carefully selecting course names and project descriptions to echo the language of the job description.

She adjusts the descriptions and accomplishments of each role to highlight the aspects of her work and volunteer experience that are relevant to the position.

The final sections highlight activities and awards that reflect her interest in marketing and her desire to improve her skills.

Figure 18.4 Crafting Your Résumé, Scenario 1: Positioning Yourself for an Ideal Opportunity
Even for an ideal job-search scenario, where your academic and professional experiences and interests closely match the parameters of the job opening, you still need to adapt your résumé content carefully to "echo" the specific language of the job description.[43]

- **Scenario 2: Positioning yourself for an available opportunity** (when you can't find a job in your chosen field and need to adapt to whatever opportunities are available)
- **Scenario 3: Positioning yourself for more responsibility** (after you have some experience in your field and want to apply for positions of greater responsibility)

Emma Gomes
(847) 555–2153
emma.gomes@mailsystem.net
emmawrites.blogspot.com

Address:
860 North 8th Street, Terre Haute, IN 47809

Permanent Address:
993 Church Street, Barrington, IL 60010

Summary of Qualifications

- (8) • Front-line customer service experience with consumers and business owners
- • Strong business sense based on work experience and academic preparation
- (6) • Intermediate skills with a variety of software tools, including Microsoft Excel and Google Analytics
- (10) • Record of quality work in both business and academic settings

Education

B.S. in Marketing (Marketing Management Track), Indiana State University, Terre Haute, IN, expected graduation May 2016

Program coursework

- (6) • 45 credits of core business courses, including Business Information Tools, Business Statistics, Principles of Accounting, and Business Finance
- (1) • 27 credits of marketing and marketing management courses, including Marketing Fundamentals, Buyer Behavior, Marketing Research, Retail Strategies and seminars in e–commerce and social media

Special projects

- (1)(2) • "Handcrafting a Global Marketplace: The Etsy Phenomenon," in-depth analysis of how the Etsy e-commerce platform helps craftspeople and artisans become more successful merchants
- (1)(2)(9) • "Hybrid Communication Platforms for Small Businesses," team service project for five small businesses in Terre Haute, recommending best practices for combining traditional and social–media methods of customer engagement and providing a customized measurement spreadsheet for each company

Work and Volunteer Experience

- (3)(4)(10) **Independent math tutor, 2011-present.** Assist students with a variety of math courses at the elementary, junior high, and high school level; all clients have achieved combined test and homework score improvements of at least one full letter grade, with an average improvement of 38 percent
- (2) **LeafSpring Food Bank, Terre Haute, IN, 2014-present (weekends during college terms), Volunteer.** Stock food and supply pantries; prepare emergency baskets for new clients; assist director with public relations activities, including website updates and social media news releases.
- (8)(5) **Owings Ford, Barrington, IL, 2013–2015 (summers), Customer care agent.** Assisted the service and sales managers of this locally owned car dealership with a variety of customer-service tasks; scheduled service appointments; designed and implemented improvements to service-center waiting room to increase guest comfort; convinced dealership owners to begin using Twitter and Facebook to interact with current and potential customers.

Professional Engagement

- (7) • Collegiate member, American Marketing Association; helped establish the AMA Collegiate Chapter at Indiana State
- • Participated in AMA International Collegiate Case Competition, 2013–2014

Awards

- (3)(4)(10) • Dean's List: 2014, 2015
- (1) • Forward Youth award, Barrington Chamber of Commerce, 2012

Notice how Gomes adapts her résumé to "mirror" the keywords and phrases from the job posting:

1. Suggests strong awareness of the needs of various businesses
2. Examples of experience with written business communication; she can demonstrate oral communication skills during phone, video, or in-person interviews
3. Results-oriented approach to tutoring business suggests high degree of professionalism, as do the two awards
4. The ability to work successfully as an independent tutor while attending high school and college is strong evidence of self-motivation and good time management
5. Indicates ability to understand problems and design solutions
6. Suggests the ability to work with a variety of software tools
7. Demonstrates a desire to learn and to expand her skills
8. Highlights customer service experience
9. Offers concrete evidence of teamwork (rather than just calling herself a "team player," for example)
10. Tracking the progress of her tutoring clients is strong evidence of someone who cares about results and the quality of her work; Dean's List awards also suggest quality of work; record of working while attending high school and college suggests strong productivity

Figure 18.5   Crafting Your Résumé, Scenario 2: Repositioning Yourself for Available Opportunities
If you can't find an ideal job opening, you'll need to adjust your plans and adapt your résumé to the openings that are available. Look for opportunities that meet your near-term financial needs while giving you the chance to expand your skill set so that you'll be even more prepared when an ideal opportunity does come along.[44]

Emma Gomes
(847) 555–2153
emma.gomes@mailsystem.net
Twitter: www.twitter.com/emmagomes
1605 Queen Anne Avenue North, Seattle, WA 98109

Market and Strategy Analyst

- Five years of experience in local and online retailing, with three years of focus on market opportunity analysis
- Strong business sense developed through more than 60 marketing programs across a range of retail sectors, including hospitality, entertainment, and fashion
- Recognized by senior management for ability to make sound judgment calls in situations with incomplete or conflicting data
- Adept at coordinating research projects and marketing initiatives across organizational boundaries and balancing the interests of multiple stakeholders
- Advanced skills with leading analysis and communication tools, including Excel, PowerPoint, and Google Analytics

Professional Experience

LivingSocial, Seattle, WA (July 2013–present), Associate market analyst. Analyzed assigned markets for such factors as consumer demand, merchandising opportunities, and seller performance; designed, launched, and managed marketing initiatives in 27 retailing categories, including fashions and accessories; met or exceeded profit targets on 90 percent of all marketing initiatives; appointed team lead/trainer in recognition of strong quantitative and qualitative analysis skills; utilized both established and emerging social media tools and helped business partners use these communication platforms to increase consumer engagement in local markets.

Amazon, Seattle WA (July 2011–June 2013), Seller support associate. Worked with more than 300 product vendors, including many in the fashion and accessories sectors, to assure profitable retailing activities on the Amazon e-commerce platform; resolved vendor issues related to e-commerce operations, pricing, and consumer communication; anticipated potential vendor challenges and assisted in the development of more than a dozen new selling tools that improved vendor profitability while reducing Amazon's vendor support costs by nearly 15 percent.

Education

Evening MBA program, University of Washington, Seattle, WA; anticipated graduation: May 2017. Broad-based program combining financial reporting, marketing strategy, competitive strategy, and supply chain management with individual emphasis on quantitative methods, financial analysis, and marketing decision models.

B.S. in Marketing (Marketing Management Track), Indiana State University, Terre Haute, IN, May 2011. Comprehensive coursework in business fundamentals, accounting and finance, marketing fundamentals, retailing, and consumer communications.

Professional Engagement

- Member, American Marketing Association
- Member, International Social Media Association
- Active in National Retail Federation and Retail Advertising & Marketing Association

Awards

- Living Social Top Ten Deals (monthly employee achievement award for designing the most profitable couponing deals); awarded seven times, 2013–2015
- Social Commerce Network's Social Commerce Innovators: 30 Under 30; 2014

Notice how Gomes adapts her résumé to "mirror" the keywords and phrases from the job posting:

1. Highlights her experience in market and business analysis and her continuing education in this area
2. Mentions skill at coordinating cross-functional projects
3. Lists experiences that relate to the collection and analysis of retail data
4. Emphasizes the work she has done with fashion-related retailing and retailing in general
5. Identifies experience and education that relates to quantitative and qualitative analysis (this point overlaps #1 and #3 to a degree)
6. Mentions project management experience
7. Lists areas that suggest effective communication skills
8. Lists education, with emphasis on coursework that relates most directly to the job posting
9. Mentions work experience and educational background related to these topics
10. Includes these programs in the list of software tools she uses

Figure 18.6   Crafting Your Résumé, Scenario 3: Positioning Yourself for More Responsibility
When you have a few years of experience under your belt, your résumé strategy should shift to emphasize work history and accomplishments. Here is how Emma Gomes might reshape her résumé if she had held the two jobs described in Figures 18.4 and 18.5 and is now ready for a bigger challenge.[45] (For an application message that could accompany this résumé, see Figure 19.3 on page 549.)

Completing Your Résumé

4 **LEARNING OBJECTIVE** Characterize the completing step for résumés, including the six most common formats in which you can produce a résumé.

Completing your résumé involves revising it for optimum quality, producing it in the various forms and media you'll need, and proofreading it for any errors before distributing it or publishing it online.

REVISING YOUR RÉSUMÉ

Revise your résumé until it is as short and clear as possible.

Revising your résumé for clarity and conciseness is essential. Recruiters and hiring managers want to find key pieces of information about you, including your top skills, your current job, and your education, in a matter of seconds. Many are overwhelmed with résumés, and if they have to work to find or decode this information, chances are they'll toss yours aside and move on to the next one in the pile. Remember the fundamental purpose of the résumé—to get you an interview, not to get you a job. Weed out details and irrelevant information until your résumé is tight, clear, and focused.

If your employment history is brief, keep your résumé to one page.

The ideal length of your résumé depends on the depth of your experience and the level of the positions for which you are applying. As a general guideline, if you have fewer than five years of professional experience, keep your conventional résumé to one page. For online résumé formats, you can always provide links to additional information. If you have more experience and are applying for a higher-level position, you may need to prepare a somewhat longer résumé.[33] For highly technical positions, longer résumés are often the norm as well because the qualifications for such jobs can require more description.

PRODUCING YOUR RÉSUMÉ

Effective résumé designs are clear, clean, and professional.

No matter how many media and formats you eventually choose for producing your résumé, a clean, professional-looking design is a must. Recruiters and hiring managers typically skim your essential information in a matter of seconds, and anything that distracts or delays them will work against you.

Choosing a Design Strategy for Your Résumé

Don't pick a résumé style just because it's trendy or different; make sure it works for your specific needs.

You'll find a wide range of résumé designs in use today, from text-only documents that follow a conventional layout to full-color infographics with unique designs. As with every type of business message, keep your audience, your goals, and your resources in mind. Don't choose a style just because it seems trendy or flashy or different. For example, you can find many eye-catching infographic résumés online, but many of those are created by graphic designers applying for visual jobs in advertising, fashion, web design, and other areas in which graphic design skills are a must. In other words, the intended audience expects an applicant to have design skills, and the résumé is a good opportunity to demonstrate those. In contrast, a colorful, graphically intense résumé might just look odd to recruiters in finance, engineering, or other professions.

The sample résumés in Figures 18.4 through 18.6 use a classic, conservative design that will serve you well for most business opportunities. Notice how they feature simplicity, an easy-to-read layout, effective use of white space, and clear typefaces. Recruiters can pick out the key pieces of information in a matter of seconds.

You can certainly enhance your résumé beyond this style, but do so carefully and always with an eye on what will help the reader and avoid confusing an applicant tracking system. Make subheadings easy to find and easy to read. Avoid big

With any résumé design, make sure that readers can find essential information in a matter of seconds.

blocks of text, and use lists to itemize your most important qualifications. Above all, don't make the reader work to find the key points of story. Your résumé should be a high-efficiency information delivery system, not a treasure hunt. Simple formatting and clean design are essential for dealing with an applicant tracking system because complicated formats can confuse the system. If you want a more "designed" résumé to hand out during networking events or for other uses, you can always create a second version.[34]

Depending on the companies you apply to, you might want to produce your résumé in as many as six formats (all are explained in the following sections):

- Printed traditional résumé
- Printed scannable résumé
- Digital plain-text file
- Microsoft Word file
- Online résumé
- PDF file

Unfortunately, no single format or medium will work for all situations, and employer expectations continue to change as technology evolves. Find out what each employer or job-posting website expects, and provide your résumé in that specific format.

Be prepared to produce versions of your résumé in multiple formats.

Considering Photos, Videos, Presentations, and Infographics

As you produce your résumé in various formats, you will encounter the question of whether to include a photograph of yourself on or with your résumé. For print or digital documents that you will be submitting to employers or job websites, the safest advice is to avoid photos. The reason is that seeing visual cues of the age, ethnicity, and gender of candidates early in the selection process exposes employers to complaints of discriminatory hiring practices. In fact, some employers won't even look at résumés that include photos, and some applicant tracking systems automatically discard résumés with any extra files.[35] However, photographs are acceptable and expected for social media résumés and other online formats where you are not actively submitting a résumé to an employer.

Do not include or enclose a photo in résumés that you send to employers or post on job websites.

> **REAL-TIME UPDATES**
> LEARN MORE BY READING THIS ARTICLE
> ### Make friends with the résumé robots
> Follow these tips to make sure your résumé doesn't get snagged in an applicant tracking system. Go to **real-timeupdates .com/bct14** and select Learn More in the Students section.

In addition to the six main résumé formats, some applicants create PowerPoint or Prezi presentations, videos, or infographics to supplement a conventional résumé. Two key advantages of a presentation supplement are flexibility and multimedia capabilities. For instance, you can present a menu of choices on the opening screen and allow viewers to click through to sections of interest. (Note that most of the things you can accomplish with a presentation can be done with an online résumé, which is probably more convenient for most readers.)

A video résumé can be a compelling supplement as well, but be aware that some employment law experts advise employers not to view videos, at least not until after candidates have been evaluated solely on their credentials. The reason for this caution is the same as with photographs. In addition, videos are more cumbersome to evaluate than paper or digital résumés, and many recruiters refuse to watch them.[36] However, not all companies share this concern over videos, so you'll have to research their individual preferences. In fact, the online retailer Zappos encourages applicant videos and provides a way to upload videos on its job application webpage.[37] Research the preferences of the companies on your target list before you decide to invest time and money in a video résumé or supplement.

An infographic résumé attempts to convey a person's career development and skill set graphically through a visual metaphor such as a timeline or subway map or as a poster with an array of individual elements. A well-designed infographic could be an intriguing element of the job-search package for candidates in certain situations and professions because it can definitely stand out from traditional résumés and can show a high level of skill in visual communication. However, infographics are likely to be incompatible with most applicant tracking systems and with the screening habits of most recruiters, so while you might stand out with an infographic, you might also get tossed out if you try to use an infographic in place of a conventional résumé. In virtually every situation, an infographic should complement a conventional résumé, not replace it. In addition, successful infographics require graphical design skills that many job seekers don't have.

Producing a Traditional Printed Résumé

Even though most of your application activity will take place online, having a copy of a conventional printed résumé is important for taking to job fairs, interviews, and other events. Many interviewers expect you to bring a printed résumé to the interview, even if

Use high-quality paper when printing your résumé.

you applied online. The résumé can serve as a note-taking form or discussion guide, and it is tangible evidence of your attention to professionalism and detail.[38] When printing a résumé, choose a heavier, higher-quality paper designed specifically for résumés and other important documents. White or slightly off-white is the best color choice. Avoid papers with borders or backgrounds.

Printing a Scannable Résumé

Some employers still prefer résumés in scannable format, but most now want online submissions.

You might encounter a company that prefers *scannable résumés*, a type of printed résumé that is specially formatted to be compatible with optical scanning systems that convert printed documents to digital text. These systems were once quite common, but their use has been declining rapidly as more employers prefer email submissions or website application forms.[39] If you need to produce a scannable résumé, search online for "formatting a scannable résumé" to get detailed instructions.

Creating a Plain-Text File of Your Résumé

A plain-text version of your résumé is simply a computer file without any of the formatting that you typically apply using word-processing software.

A *plain-text file* (sometimes known as an ASCII text file) is a digital version of your résumé that has no font formatting, no bullet symbols, no colors, no lines or boxes, and no other special formatting. The plain-text version can be used in two ways. First, you can include it in the body of an email message, for employers who want email delivery but don't want file attachments. Second, you can copy and paste the sections into the application forms on an employer's website.

Make sure you verify the plain-text file that you create with your word processor; it might need a few manual adjustments using a text editor such as NotePad.

A plain-text version is easy to create with your word processor. Start with the file you used to create your résumé, use the "Save As" choice to save it as "plain text" or whichever similarly labeled option your software has, and verify the result using a basic text editor (such as Microsoft Notepad). If necessary, reformat the page manually, moving text and inserting space as needed. For simplicity's sake, align headings with the left margin, rather than trying to center them manually.

Creating a Word File of Your Résumé

Some employers and websites want your résumé in Microsoft Word format; make sure your computer is thoroughly scanned for viruses first, however.

In some cases an employer or job-posting website will want you to upload a Microsoft Word file or attach it to an email message. (Although there are certainly other word-processing software programs available, Microsoft Word is the de facto standard in business these days.) This method of transferring information preserves the design and layout of your résumé and saves you the trouble of creating a plain-text version. However, before you submit a Word file to anyone, make sure your computer is free of viruses. Infecting a potential employer's computer will not make a good first impression.

Creating a PDF Version of Your Résumé

Creating a PDF file is a simple procedure, depending on the software you have. In newer versions of Microsoft Word, you can save a document directly as a PDF file. The advantages of creating PDFs are that you preserve the formatting of your résumé (unlike pasting plain text into an email message), and you create a file type that is less vulnerable to viruses than word-processer files.

Creating an Online or Social Media Résumé

You have many options for creating an online résumé, from college-hosted e-portfolios to multimedia résumés on commercials websites.

A variety of online résumé formats, variously referred to as *e-portfolios*, *interactive résumés*, or *social media résumés*, provide the opportunity to create a dynamic, multimedia presentation of your qualifications. You can expand on the information contained in your basic résumé with links to projects, publications, screencasts, online videos, course lists, blogs, social networking profiles, and other elements that give employers a more complete picture of who you are and what you can offer.

You have a number of options for hosting an online résumé. Start with your college's career center; many such centers offer hosting for e-portfolios, for example, where you can showcase your academic achievements. You can also chose one of the commercial résumé hosting services, such as LinkedIn. In addition to being free (for basic services, at least), these sites provide easy-to-use tools for creating your online profile. You can also use them to peruse examples of various résumés, from students just about to enter the workforce full time all the way up to corporate CEOs.

Regardless of the approach you take to creating an online résumé, keep these helpful tips in mind:

- **Remember that your online presence is a career management tool.** The way you are portrayed online can work for you or against you, and it's up to you to create a positive impression.
- **Take advantage of social networking.** Use whatever tools are available to direct people to your online résumé, such as including your URL in your Twitter profile.
- **During the application process, don't expect or ask employers to retrieve a résumé from a website.** Submit your résumé using whatever method and medium each employer prefers. If employers then want to know more about you, they will likely do a web search on you and find your site, or you can refer them to your site in your résumé or application materials.

PROOFREADING YOUR RÉSUMÉ

Employers view your résumé as a concrete example of your attention to quality and detail. Your résumé doesn't need to be good or pretty good—it needs to be *perfect*. Although it may not seem fair, just one or two errors in a job application package are enough to doom a candidate's chances. A human reader will likely view errors as signs of carelessness, and an applicant tracking system can be programmed to automatically reject résumés with spelling errors.[40]

Your résumé is one of the most important documents you'll ever write, so don't rush or cut corners when it comes to proofreading. Check all headings and lists for clarity and parallelism, and be sure your grammar, spelling, and punctuation are correct. Double-check all dates, phone numbers, email addresses, and other essential data. Ask at least three other people to read it, too. As the creator of the material, you could stare at a mistake for weeks and not see it.

> Your résumé can't be "pretty good" or "almost perfect"—it needs to be *perfect*, so proofread it thoroughly and ask several other people to verify it, too.

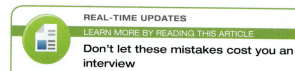

REAL-TIME UPDATES
LEARN MORE BY READING THIS ARTICLE
Don't let these mistakes cost you an interview
Make sure you don't commit these nine costly blunders. Go to real-timeupdates.com/bct14 and select Learn More in the Students section.

DISTRIBUTING YOUR RÉSUMÉ

How you distribute your résumé depends on the number of employers you target and their preferences for receiving résumés. Employers usually list their requirements on their websites, so verify this information and follow it carefully. Beyond that, here are some general distribution tips:

- **Mailing printed résumés.** Take some care with the packaging. Spend a few extra cents to mail these documents in a flat 9 × 12 envelope, or better yet, use a Priority Mail flat-rate envelope, which gives you a sturdy cardboard mailer and faster delivery for just a few more dollars.
- **Emailing your résumé.** Some employers want applicants to include the text of their résumés in the body of an email message; others prefer an attached Microsoft Word or PDF file. If you have a reference number or a job ad number, include it in the subject line of your email message.
- **Submitting your résumé to an employer's website.** Many employers, including most large companies, now prefer or require applicants to submit their résumés online. In some instances you will be asked to upload a complete file. In others you will need to copy and paste sections of your résumé into individual boxes in an online application form.
- **Posting your résumé on job websites.** You can post your résumé on general-purpose job websites such as Monster and CareerBuilder, on more specialized job boards that address specific professions, or with staffing services such as Volt. Roughly 100,000 job boards are now online, so you'll need to spend some time looking for sites that specialize in your target industries, regions, or professions.[41] Before you upload your

> When distributing your résumé, pay close attention to the specific instructions provided by every employer, job website, or other recipient.

> Don't post a résumé on any public website unless you understand its privacy and security policies.

résumé to any site, however, learn about its privacy protection. Some sites allow you to specify levels of confidentiality, such as letting employers search your qualifications without seeing your personal contact information or preventing your current employer from seeing your résumé. Don't post your résumé to any website that doesn't give you the option of restricting the display of your contact information. Only employers that are registered clients of the service should be able to see your contact information.[42]

For a quick summary of the steps to take when planning, writing, and completing your résumé, refer to "Checklist: Writing an Effective Résumé." For the latest information on résumé writing and distribution, visit **real-timeupdates.com/bct14** and select Chapter 18.

CHECKLIST ✔ Writing an Effective Résumé

A. Plan your résumé.
- Analyze your purpose and audience carefully to make sure your message meets employers' needs.
- Gather pertinent information about your target companies.
- Select the required media types by researching the preferences of each employer.
- Organize your résumé around your strengths, choosing the chronological, functional, or combination structure. (Be careful about using the functional structure.)

B. Write your résumé.
- Keep your résumé honest.
- Adapt your résumé to your audience to highlight the qualifications each employer is looking for.
- Choose a career objective, qualifications summary, or career summary as your introductory statement—and make it concise, concrete, and reader-focused.
- Use powerful language to convey your name and contact information, introductory statement, education, work experience, skills, work or school accomplishments, and activities and achievements.

C. Complete your résumé.
- Revise your résumé until it is clear, concise, compelling—and perfect.
- Produce your résumé in all the formats you might need: traditional printed résumé, scannable, plain-text file, Microsoft Word file, PDF, or online.
- Proofread your résumé to make sure it is absolutely perfect.
- Distribute your résumé using the means that each employer prefers.

COMMUNICATION CHALLENGES AT **Burning Glass**

You work as a recruiter in the human resources department at Burning Glass's Boston headquarters, where part of your responsibility involves using the applicant tracking system to identify promising job candidates. Solve these challenges by using what you've learned about presenting oneself effectively on a résumé.

INDIVIDUAL CHALLENGE: One of today's tasks is selecting candidates to be interviewed for a management trainee position. This position involves significant interaction with other departments, so communication skills are vital. The applicant tracking system has turned up two candidates with almost identical qualifications. You have time to interview only one of them, however. Based on the way the two candidates described their education, which one would you invite in for an interview—and why?

1. **Morehouse College, Atlanta, GA, 2011–2015.** Received BA degree with a major in Business Administration and a minor in Finance. Graduated with a 3.65 grade point average. Played varsity football and basketball. Worked 15 hours per week in the library. Coordinated the local student chapter of the American Management Association. Member of Alpha Phi Alpha social fraternity.

2. I attended Wayne State University in Detroit, Michigan, for two years and then transferred to the University of Michigan at Ann Arbor, where I completed my studies. My major was economics, but I also took many business management courses, including employee motivation, small-business administration, history of business start-ups, and organizational behavior. I selected courses based on the professors' reputations for excellence, and I received mostly As and Bs. Unlike many other college students, I viewed the acquisition of knowledge—rather than career preparation—as my primary goal. I believe I have received a well-rounded education that has prepared me to approach management situations as problem-solving exercises.

TEAM CHALLENGE: To find candidates for an accounting associate position (a job typically filled by college graduates rather than more experienced professionals), you searched the applicant tracking system and found the following rather unconventional résumé. With one or two other students, decide whether you

should (1) invite this candidate for an interview; (2) reject the application without further analysis; (3) review the candidate's web-based e-portfolio, then make a decision about inviting him in for an interview; or (4) compare the candidate's qualifications relative to those of other applicants and invite him in for an interview only if you cannot find several qualified applicants. Explain your choice.

Darius Jaidee
809 N. Perkins Rd, Stillwater, OK 74075
Phone: (405) 369-0098
Email: dariusj@okstate.edu

Career Objective: To build a successful career in financial management

Summary of Qualifications: As a student at the University of Oklahoma, Stillwater, completed a wide variety of assignments that demonstrate skills related to accounting and management. For example:

Planning Skills: As president of the university's foreign affairs forum, organized six lectures and workshops featuring 36 speakers from 16 foreign countries within a nine-month period. Identified and recruited the speakers, handled their travel arrangements, and scheduled the facilities.

Communication Skills: Wrote more than 25 essays and term papers on various academic topics, including at least 10 dealing with business and finance. As a senior, wrote a 20-page analysis of financial trends in the petroleum industry, interviewing five high-ranking executives in accounting and finance positions at ConocoPhillip's refinery in Ponca City, Oklahoma, and company headquarters in Houston, Texas.

Accounting and Computer Skills: Competent in all areas of Microsoft Office, including Excel spreadsheets and Access databases. Assisted with bookkeeping activities in parents' small business, including the conversion from paper-based to computer-based accounting (Peachtree software). Have taken courses in accounting, financial planning, database design, web design, and computer networking.

For more information, including employment history, please access my e-portfolio at **http://dariusjaidee.com**.

Quick Learning Guide

KEY TERMS

applicant tracking systems Computer systems that capture and store incoming résumés and help recruiters find good prospects for current openings

chronological résumé Format that emphasizes work experience, with past jobs shown in reverse chronological order; the most common résumé format

combination résumé Format that includes the best features of the chronological and functional approaches

functional résumé Format that emphasizes skills and capabilities while identifying employers and academic experience in subordinate sections; many recruiters view this format with suspicion

networking The process of making connections with mutually beneficial business contacts

résumé A structured, written summary of a person's education, employment background, and job qualifications

SUMMARY OF LEARNING OBJECTIVES

1 List eight key steps to finding the ideal opportunity in today's job market. The eight steps discussed in this chapter are (1) writing the story of you, which involves describing where you have been in your career so far and where you would like to go in the future; (2) learning to think like an employer so you can present yourself as a quality hire; (3) researching industries and companies of interest to identify promising opportunities and to learn the language of hiring managers; (4) translating your general potential into a specific solution for each employer so that you look like a good fit for each opening; (5) taking the initiative to approach interesting companies even if they haven't yet posted any job openings; (6) building your network so you and your connections can help each other in the job-search process; (7) seeking career counseling if appropriate; and (8) avoiding the easily avoidable mistakes that can ruin your chances of getting a job.

2 Explain the process of planning your résumé, including how to choose the best résumé organization. Planning a résumé starts with recognizing what it is: a persuasive message designed to get you job interviews. Gathering the necessary information involves learning about target industries, professions, companies, and specific positions, as well as gathering information about yourself. Choosing the best résumé organization depends on your background and your goals. A chronological résumé helps employers easily locate necessary information, highlights your professional growth and career progress, and emphasizes continuity and stability. If you can use the chronological format, you should because it is the approach employers tend to prefer. A functional résumé helps employers easily see what you can do for them, allows you to emphasize earlier job experience, and lets you downplay any lengthy periods of unemployment or a lack of career progress. However, many employers are suspicious of functional résumés for this very reason. The combination approach uses the best features of the other two and is often the best choice for recent graduates.

3 Describe the tasks involved in writing your résumé, and list the major sections of a traditional résumé. Adapting to the audience is crucial because readers are looking to see how well you understand their businesses and can present a solution to their talent needs. The major sections to consider including in your résumé are (1) your name and contact information; (2) an introductory statement, which can be a career objective, a qualifications summary, or a career summary; (3) your education; (4) your work experience; and (5) activities and achievements that are professionally relevant. Most résumés do not need to include any personal data.

4 Characterize the completing step for résumés, including the six most common formats in which you can produce a résumé. Quality is paramount with résumés, so the tasks of revising and proofing are particularly important. The six common résumé formats are traditional printed résumé, scannable résumé, electronic plain-text file, Microsoft Word file, PDF, and online résumé (which might be called a personal webpage, an e-portfolio, or a social media résumé).

MyBCommLab

Go to **mybcommlab.com** to complete the problems marked with this icon .

Test Your Knowledge

To review chapter content related to each question, refer to the indicated Learning Objective.

18-1. What does *quality of hire* mean? [LO-1]

18-2. Why is it important to have an organized approach to finding a new job? [LO-1]

18-3. Why is it important to contribute to any networks you belong to, in addition to looking for assistance for your own career? [LO-1]

18-4. What is the purpose of a résumé? [LO-2]

18-5. Why are some employers suspicious of the functional résumé? [LO-2]

18-6. What are keywords? [LO-3]

18-7. Should you include personal data on a résumé? Explain your answer. [LO-3]

18-8. What is a plain-text résumé? [LO-4]

Apply Your Knowledge

To review chapter content related to each question, refer to the indicated Learning Objective.

18-9. How can you "think like an employer" if you have no professional business experience? [LO-1]

18-10. If you were a team leader at a summer camp for children with special needs, should you include this in your employment history if you are applying for work that is unrelated? Explain your answer. [LO-3]

18-11. Can you use a qualifications summary if you don't yet have extensive professional experience in your desired career? Why or why not? [LO-3]

18-12. Some people don't have a clear career path when they enter the job market. If you're in this situation, how would your uncertainty affect the way you write your résumé? [LO-3]

18-13. Between your sophomore and junior years, you quit school for a year to earn the money to finish college. You worked as a loan-processing assistant in a finance company, checking references on loan applications, typing, and filing. Your manager made a lot of the fact that he had never attended college. He seemed to resent you for pursuing your education, but he never criticized your work, so you thought you were doing okay. After you'd been working there for six months, he fired you, saying that you'd failed to be thorough enough in your credit checks. You were actually glad to leave, and you found another job right away at a bank, doing similar duties. Now that you've graduated from college, you're writing your résumé. Will you include the finance company job in your work history? Explain. [LO-3]

Practice Your Skills

Message For Analysis

Read the following résumé information and then (1) analyze the strengths or weaknesses of the information and (2) revise the résumé so that it follows the guidelines presented in this chapter.

18-14. Message 18.A: Writing a Résumé [LO-3]

Sylvia Manchester
765 Belle Fleur Blvd.
New Orleans, LA 70113
(504) 312-9504
smanchester@rcnmail.com

PERSONAL: Single, excellent health, 5'7", 136 lbs.; hobbies include cooking, dancing, and reading.

JOB OBJECTIVE: To obtain a responsible position in marketing or sales with a good company.

EDUCATION: BA degree in biology, University of Louisiana, 1998. Graduated with a 3.0 average. Member of the varsity cheerleading squad. President of Panhellenic League. Homecoming queen.

WORK EXPERIENCE

Fisher Scientific Instruments, 2015 to now, field sales representative. Responsible for calling on customers and explaining the features of Fisher's line of laboratory instruments. Also responsible for writing sales letters, attending trade shows, and preparing weekly sales reports.

Fisher Scientific Instruments, 2011–2014, customer service representative. Was responsible for handling incoming phone calls from customers who had questions about delivery, quality, or operation of Fisher's line of laboratory instruments. Also handled miscellaneous correspondence with customers.

Medical Electronics, Inc., 2008–2011, administrative assistant to the vice president of marketing. In addition to handling typical secretarial chores for the vice president of marketing, I was in charge of compiling the monthly sales reports, using figures provided by members of the field sales force. I also was given responsibility for doing various market research activities.

New Orleans Convention and Visitors Bureau, 2005–2008, summers, tour guide. During the summers of my college years, I led tours of New Orleans for tourists visiting the city. My duties included greeting conventioneers and their spouses at hotels, explaining the history and features of the city during an all-day sightseeing tour, and answering questions about New Orleans and its attractions. During my fourth summer with the bureau, I was asked to help train the new tour guides. I prepared a handbook that provided interesting facts about the various tourist attractions, as well as answers to the most commonly asked tourist questions. The Bureau was so impressed with the handbook they had it printed up so that it could be given as a gift to visitors.

University of Louisiana, 2005–2008, part-time clerk in admissions office. While I was a student in college, I worked 15 hours a week in the admissions office. My duties included filing, processing applications, and handling correspondence with high school students and administrators.

Exercises

Each activity is labeled according to the primary skill or skills you will need to use. To review relevant chapter content, you can refer to the indicated Learning Objective. In some instances, supporting information will be found in another chapter, as indicated.

18-15. **Career Management: Researching Career Opportunities [LO-1]** Based on the preferences you identified in your career self-assessment (see page xl in the Prologue) and the academic, professional, and personal qualities you have to offer, perform an online search for a career that matches your interests (starting with the websites listed in Table 18.1). Draft a brief report for your instructor, indicating how the career you select and the job openings you find match your strengths and preferences.

18-16. **Message Strategies: Writing a Résumé [LO-3]** Change the following statements to make them more effective for a résumé by using action verbs.

a. Have some experience with database design.

b. Assigned to a project to analyze the cost accounting methods for a large manufacturer.

c. I was part of a team that developed a new inventory control system.

d. Am responsible for preparing the quarterly department budget.

e. Was a manager of a department with seven employees working for me.

f. Was responsible for developing a spreadsheet to analyze monthly sales by department.

g. Put in place a new program for ordering supplies.

18-17. **Completing a Résumé [LO-4]** Using your revised version of the résumé in Message for Analysis 18.A, create a plain-text file that Sylvia Manchester could use to include in email messages.

18-18. **Completing a Résumé [LO-4]** Imagine you are applying for work in a field that involves speaking in front of an audience, such as sales, consulting, management, or training. Using material you created for any of the exercises or cases in Chapter 17, record a two- to three-minute video demonstration of your speaking and presentation skills. Record yourself speaking to an audience, if one can be arranged.

Expand Your Skills

Critique the Professionals

Locate an example of an online résumé (a sample or an actual résumé). Analyze the résumé following the guidelines presented in this chapter. Using whatever medium your instructor requests, write a brief analysis (no more than one page) of the résumé's strengths and weaknesses, citing specific elements from the résumé and support from the chapter. If you are analyzing a real résumé, do not include any personally identifiable data, such as the person's name, email address, or phone number, in your report.

Sharpen Your Career Skills Online

Bovée and Thill's Business Communication Web Search, at **websearch.businesscommunicationnetwork.com**, is a unique research tool designed specifically for business communication research. Use the Web Search function to find a website, video, article, podcast, or presentation that offers advice on creating effective online résumés. Write a brief email message to your instructor or a post for your class blog, describing the item that you found and summarizing the career skills information you learned from it.

Cases

For all cases, feel free to use your creativity to make up any details you need in order to craft effective messages.

CAREER SKILLS/EMAIL SKILLS

18-19. Career Planning: Researching Career Opportunities [LO-1]   Knowing the jargon and "hot-button" issues in a particular profession or industry can give you a big advantage when it comes to writing your résumé and participating in job interviews. You can fine-tune your résumé for both human readers and applicant tracking systems, sound more confident and informed in interviews, and present yourself as a professional individual with an inquiring mind.

Your task: Imagine a specific job category in a company that has an informative, comprehensive website (to facilitate the research you'll need to do). This doesn't have to be a current job opening, but a position you know exists or is likely to exist in this company, such as a business systems analyst at Apple or a brand manager at Unilever.

Explore the company's website and other online sources to find the following: (1) a brief description of what this job entails, with enough detail that you could describe it to a fellow student; (2) some of the terminology used in the profession or industry, both formal terms that might serve as keywords on your résumé and informal terms and phrases that insiders are likely to use in publications and conversations; (3) an ongoing online conversation among people in this profession, such as a LinkedIn Group, a popular industry or professional blog that seems to get quite a few comments, or an industry or professional publication that attracts a lot of comments; and (4) at least one significant issue that will affect people in this profession or companies in this industry over the next few years. For example, if your chosen profession involves accounting in a publicly traded corporation, upcoming changes in international financial reporting standards would be a significant issue. Similarly, for a company in the consumer electronics industry, the recycling and disposal of e-waste is an issue. Write a brief email message summarizing your findings and explaining how you could use this information on your résumé and during job interviews.

CAREER SKILLS/EMAIL SKILLS

18-20. Career Management: Researching Career Opportunities [LO-1]   Perhaps you won't be able to land your ultimate dream job right out of college, but that doesn't mean you shouldn't start planning right now to make that dream come true.

Your task: Using online job-search tools, find a job that sounds just about perfect for you, even if you're not yet qualified for it. It might even be something that would take 10 or 20 years to reach. Don't settle for something that's not quite right—find a job that is so "you" and so exciting that you would jump out of bed every morning, eager to go to work (such jobs really do exist!). Start with the job description you found online and then supplement it with additional research so that you get a good picture of what this job and career path are all about. Compile a list of all the qualifications you would need to have a reasonable chance of landing such a job. Now compare this list with your current résumé. Write a brief email message to your instructor that identifies all the areas in which you would need to improve your skills, work experience, education, and other qualifications in order to land your dream job.

CAREER SKILLS/TEAM SKILLS

18-21. Planning a Résumé [LO-2]   If you haven't begun your professional career yet or you are pursuing a career change, the employment history section on your résumé can sometimes be a challenge to write. A brainstorming session with your wise and creative classmates could help.

Your task: In a team assigned by your instructor, help each other evaluate your employment histories and figure out the best way to present your work backgrounds on a résumé. First, each member of the team should compile his or her work history, including freelance projects and volunteer work if relevant, and share this information with the team. After allowing some time for everyone to review each other's information, meet as a team (in person if you can, or online otherwise). Discuss each person's history, pointing out strong spots and weak spots, and then brainstorm the best way to present each person's employment history.

Note: If there are aspects of your employment history you would rather not share with your teammates, substitute a reasonably similar experience of the same duration.

CAREER SKILLS/TEAM SKILLS

18-22. Writing a Résumé [LO-3]   The introductory statement of a résumé requires some careful thought, both in deciding which of the three types of introductory statement (see page 526) to use and what information to include in it. Getting another person's perspective on this communication challenge can be helpful. In this activity, in fact, someone else is going to write your introductory statement for you, and you will return the favor.

Your task: Pair off with a classmate. Provide each other with the basic facts about your qualifications, work history, education, and career objectives. Then meet in person or online for an informal interview, in which you ask each other questions to flesh out the information you have on each other. Assume that each of you has chosen to use a qualifications summary for your résumé. Now, write each other's qualifications summary, then trade them for review. As you read what your partner wrote about you, ask yourself whether this feels true to what you believe about yourself and your career aspirations. Do you think it introduces you effectively to potential employers? What might you change about it?

PRESENTATION SKILLS/PORTFOLIO BUILDER

18-23. Message Strategies: Completing a Résumé [LO-4]

Creating presentations and other multimedia supplements can be a great way to expand on the brief overview that a résumé provides.

Your task: Starting with any version of a résumé you've created for yourself, create a PowerPoint presentation that expands on your résumé information to give potential employers a more complete picture of what you can contribute. Include samples of your work, testimonials from current or past employers and colleagues, videos of speeches you've made, and anything else that tells the story of the professional "you." If you have a specific job or type of job in mind, focus your presentation on that. Otherwise, present a more general picture that shows why you would be a great employee for any company to consider. Be sure to review the information from Chapters 16 and 17 about creating professional-quality presentations.

CAREER SKILLS/VIDEO SKILLS

18-24. Message Strategies: Completing a Résumé [LO-4]

In the right circumstances, brief videos can be an effective complement to a traditional job-search communication package.

Your task: Find a job opening that interests you (something you are at least partially qualified for at this stage of your career) and produce a two-minute video profile of yourself, highlighting the skills mentioned in the job description. For tips on producing effective video, visit **www.indie-film-making.com**.

MyBCommLab

Go to **mybcommlab.com** for Auto-graded writing questions as well as the following Assisted-graded writing questions:

18-25. How does writing "the story of you" help you prepare a résumé and other communication pieces during your job search? [LO-1]

18-26. Explain the difference between a qualifications summary and a career summary. [LO-3]

Endnotes

1. Scott Bittle, "Graphic: What's the Most Important Baseline Skill? It Depends," Burning Glass, 19 November 2015, burning-glass.com; "About Us," Burning Glass, accessed 17 May 2016, burning-glass .com; James Hu, "8 Things You Need To Know About Applicant Tracking Systems," Jobscan blog, 19 July 2014, www.jobscan.co; Rob Nightingale, "How to Get Your Resume Past the Applicant Tracking System," *MakeUseOf*, 12 November 2015, www.makeuseof.com; Lisa Vaas, "Resume, Meet Technology: Making Your Resume Format Machine-Friendly," Ladders, accessed 17 May 2016, www.theladders.com; Russ Banham, "2016 Trends In Applicant Tracking Systems," *HR Today*, 2 February 2016, www .hrtoday.com; Hannah Morgan, "5 Things You Need to Know About Applicant Tracking Systems," *Career Sherpa*, 10 February 2016, careersherpa.net.
2. Courtland L. Bovée and John V. Thill, *Business in Action*, 8th ed. (Boston: Pearson Prentice Hall, 2017), 256.
3. Anne Fisher, "How to Get Hired by a 'Best' Company," *Fortune*, 4 February 2008, 96.
4. Eve Tahmincioglu, "Revamping Your Job-Search Strategy," MSNBC.com, 28 February 2010, www.msnbc.com.
5. Jessica Dickler, "The Hidden Job Market," CNNMoney.com, 10 June 2009, money.cnn.com.
6. Tara Weiss, "Twitter to Find a Job," *Forbes*, 7 April 2009, www.forbes.com.
7. Miriam Saltpeter, "Using Facebook Groups for Job Hunting," Keppie Careers blog, 13 November 2008, www.keppiecareers.com.
8. Anne Fisher, "Greener Pastures in a New Field," *Fortune*, 26 January 2004, 48.
9. Liz Ryan, "Etiquette for Online Outreach," Yahoo! Hotjobs website, accessed 26 March 2008, hotjobs.yahoo.com.
10. Eve Tahmincioglu, "Employers Digging Deep on Prospective Workers," MSNBC.com, 26 October 2009, www.msnbc.com.
11. Career and Employment Services, Danville Area Community College website, accessed 9 June 2016, www.dacc.edu/career; Career Services Programs for Students, Sarah Lawrence College website, accessed 9 June 2016, www.sarahlawrence.edu; Cheryl L. Noll, "Collaborating with the Career Planning and Placement Center in the Job-Search Project," *Business Communication Quarterly* 58, no. 3 (1995): 53–55.
12. Rachel Emma Silverman, "No More Résumés, Say Some Firms," *Wall Street Journal*, 24 January 2012, online.wsj.com.
13. Randall S. Hansen and Katharine Hansen, "What Résumé Format Is Best for You?" QuintCareers.com, accessed 7 August 2010, www.quintcareers.com.
14. Hansen and Hansen, "What Résumé Format Is Best for You?"
15. Katharine Hansen, "Should You Consider a Functional Format for Your Resume?" QuintCareers.com, accessed 7 August 2010, www.quintcareers.com.
16. Kim Isaacs, "Resume Dilemma: Criminal Record," Monster .com, accessed 23 May 2006, www.monster.com; Kim Isaacs, "Resume Dilemma: Employment Gaps and Job-Hopping," Monster.com, accessed 23 May 2006, www.monster.com; Susan Vaughn, "Answer the Hard Questions Before Asked," *Los Angeles Times*, 29 July 2001, W1–W2.
17. John Steven Niznik, "Landing a Job with a Criminal Record," About.com, accessed 12 December 2006, jobsearchtech.about.com.
18. "How to Ferret Out Instances of Résumé Padding and Fraud," *Compensation & Benefits for Law Offices*, June 2006, 1.

19. "Resume Fraud Gets Slicker and Easier," CNN.com, accessed 11 March 2004, www.cnn.com.

20. "Resume Fraud Still Major Problem HR Needs to Address," *HR Focus*, July 2012, 13–15.

21. Cari Tuna and Keith J. Winstein, "Economy Promises to Fuel Résumé Fraud," *Wall Street Journal*, 17 November 2008, online.wsj.com; Lisa Takeuchi Cullen, "Getting Wise to Lies," *Time*, 1 May 2006, 59; "Resume Fraud Gets Slicker and Easier"; Employment Research Services website, accessed 18 March 2004, www.erscheck.com.

22. "How to Ferret Out Instances of Résumé Padding and Fraud."

23. Jacqueline Durett, "Redoing Your Résumé? Leave Off the Lies," *Training*, December 2006, 9; "Employers Turn Their Fire on Untruthful CVs," *Supply Management*, 23 June 2005, 13.

24. Cynthia E. Conn, "Integrating Writing Skills and Ethics Training in Business Communication Pedagogy: A Résumé Case Study Exemplar," *Business Communication Quarterly*, June 2008, 138–151; Marilyn Moats Kennedy, "Don't Get Burned by Résumé Inflation," *Marketing News*, 15 April 2007, 37–38.

25. Rockport Institute, "How to Write a Masterpiece of a Résumé," accessed 9 August 2010, www.rockportinstitute.com.

26. Lora Morsch, "25 Words That Hurt Your Resume," CNN.com, 20 January 2006, www.cnn.com.

27. Liz Ryan, "The Reengineered Résumé," *BusinessWeek*, 3 December 2007, SC12.

28. Katharine Hansen, "Tapping the Power of Keywords to Enhance Your Resume's Effectiveness," QuintCareers.com, accessed 7 August 2010, www.quintcareers.com.

29. Hansen, "Tapping the Power of Keywords to Enhance Your Resume's Effectiveness."

30. Anthony Balderrama, "Resume Blunders That Will Keep You from Getting Hired," CNN.com, 19 March 2008, www.cnn.com; Michelle Dumas, "5 Resume Writing Myths," Distinctive Documents blog, 17 July 2007, blog.distinctiveweb.com; Kim Isaacs, "Resume Dilemma: Recent Graduate," Monster.com, accessed 26 March 2008, career-advice.monster.com.

31. Karl L. Smart, "Articulating Skills in the Job Search," *Business Communication Quarterly* 67, no. 2 (June 2004): 198–205.

32. "When to Include Personal Data," ResumeEdge.com, accessed 25 March 2008, www.resumeedge.com.

33. "Résumé Length: What It Should Be and Why It Matters to Recruiters," *HR Focus*, June 2007, 9.

34. Lisa Rangel, "The Easy How-To Guide to Formatting Resumes for Applicant Tracking Systems," LinkedIn, accessed 9 June 2016, www.linked.com.

35. Lisa Vaas, "13 Ways Your Resume Can Say 'I'm Unprofessional,'" Ladders, accessed 10 May 2016, www.theladders.com; John Hazard, "Resume Tips: No Pictures, Please and No PDFs," Career-Line.com, 26 May 2009, www.career-line.com; "25 Things You Should Never Include on a Resume," HR World website, 18 December 2007, www.hrworld.com.

36. Caroline M. L. Potter, "Video Resumes: Let the Applicant Beware," Monster, accessed 10 May 2016, www.monster.com; John Sullivan, "Résumés: Paper, Please," *Workforce Management*, 22 October 2007, 50; "Video Résumés Offer Both Pros and Cons During Recruiting," *HR Focus*, July 2007, 8.

37. Jobs page, Zappos website, accessed 24 March 2011, about.zappos.com/jobs.

38. Rachel Louise Ensign, "Is the Paper Résumé Dead?" *Wall Street Journal*, 24 January 2012, online.wsj.com.

39. Nancy M. Schullery, Linda Ickes, and Stephen E. Schullery, "Employer Preferences for Résumés and Cover Letters," *Business Communication Quarterly*, June 2009, 163–176.

40. Nightingale, "How to Get Your Resume Past the Applicant Tracking System"; "10 Reasons Why You Are Not Getting Any Interviews," *Miami Times*, 7–13 November 2007, 6D.

41. Deborah Silver, "Niche Sites Gain Monster-Sized Following," *Workforce Management*, March 2011, 10–11.

42. "Protect Yourself from Identity Theft When Hunting for a Job Online," *Office Pro*, May 2007, 6.

43. Job description keywords and key phrases quoted or adapted in part from "Associate Market Analyst" job opening posted on the LivingSocial website, accessed 9 July 2012, corporate.livingsocial.com.

44. Job description keywords and key phrases quoted or adapted in part from "Seller Support Associate" job opening posted on the Amazon website, accessed 12 July 2012, us-amazon.icims.com/jobs.

45. Job description keywords and key phrases quoted or adapted in part from "Senior Strategy Analyst" job opening posted on the Nordstrom website, accessed 17 July 2012, careers.nordstrom.com.

19

Applying and Interviewing for Employment

LEARNING OBJECTIVES

After studying this chapter, you will be able to

1 Explain the purposes of application letters, and describe how to apply the AIDA organizational approach to them.

2 Describe the typical sequence of job interviews, the major types of interviews, and the attributes employers look for during an interview.

3 List six tasks you need to complete to prepare for a successful job interview.

4 Explain how to succeed in all three stages of an interview.

5 Identify the most common employment messages that follow an interview and explain when you would use each one.

MyBCommLab®

⭐ **Improve Your Grade!** More than 10 million students improved their results using Pearson MyLabs. Visit **mybcommlab.com** for simulations, tutorials, and end-of-chapter problems.

COMMUNICATION CLOSE-UP AT

VMWare

www.vmware.com

Innovative businesspeople are always on the lookout for better ways to work and for any developments in the business environment that can give their companies a competitive edge. Back in 2009, James Malloy, a recruiting manager at VMWare, picked up on the early buzz surrounding *social recruiting* and wanted to know whether his company might benefit from the growth of LinkedIn, Facebook, and other social platforms.

Social networking wasn't a new technology at that point, but most companies were still feeling their way through this new world and trying to figure out whether or how to use all these new tools. In addition, corporate recruiters already had well-established systems for finding, evaluating, and recruiting new talent, and few companies knew whether social media could add value to such a vital business process.

Moreover, even though social media were taking off with consumers and many consumer-oriented companies, VMWare is about as far from the front lines of consumer activity as a company can get. Its specialty is *virtualization*, a software technique that lets a single computer act like multiple independent machines. Virtualization is a critical technology behind cloud computing and much of today's information technology (IT) infrastructure, but it's not exactly the sort of trendy topic that blows up on Twitter or prompts a million "you have to see this" shares on Facebook.

Kristoffer Tripplaar/Alamy Stock Photo

James Malloy's hunch that social media might benefit VMWare's employee recruiting set off a revolution in how the company finds, evaluates, and recruits top talent.

However, Malloy was intrigued by social recruiting and decided to conduct a low-risk experiment on Facebook to test its potential. He set up a page and began posting job openings to it—and the effort caught on quickly as interested candidates found the openings. Importantly, the Facebook presence brought VMWare in touch with talented people it hadn't been in contact with before.

Technology companies compete fiercely with one another to attract the best software designers and other specialists, so anything that gives recruiters an advantage is going to get attention. Malloy's simple Facebook experiment was so successful that VMWare's top management decided to realign its entire recruiting strategy around social networking.

Recruiting isn't the only aspect of company operations that adopted social media with gusto. The company is social through and through, with hundreds of official social media accounts and groups focused on specific technical or business issues,

including nearly a hundred Twitter accounts. Four of those accounts are dedicated to careers and recruiting, including @VMWareU, the account for the VMWare University Recruiting Team. Through this account, the company announces job openings targeted at recent graduates, internship opportunities, and news of interest to potential employees.

The company's social recruiting strategy goes far beyond simple announcements, however. Molloy and his colleagues use these channels to build relationships with potential hires, to share videos and other media that showcase the VMWare corporate culture, and to brand VMWare as an exciting, supportive place to work. The social recruiting effort has been so successful that the company continues to expand it. Moving forward, it is focusing on expanding its use of mobile recruiting apps and in helping employees become effective "brand advocates" for the company in their own social networks.[1]

Submitting Your Résumé

1 **LEARNING OBJECTIVE**
Explain the purposes of application letters, and describe how to apply the AIDA organizational approach to them.

VMWare's experience with social recruiting (profiled in the chapter-opening Communication Close-Up) gives you an idea of the investment that leading companies put into the recruiting process in order to find and land the best employees. To find and land the best job, you need to approach the process with a similar level of preparation. Your résumé (see Chapter 18) is the centerpiece of your job-search package, but it usually requires support from several other employment messages, including application letters, job-inquiry letters, application forms, and follow-up notes.

WRITING APPLICATION LETTERS

Adapt your application letter to each job opening and situation.

Whenever you mail, email, hand-deliver, or upload your résumé, you should include an **application letter**, also known as a *cover letter*, to let readers know what you're sending, why you're sending it, and how they can benefit from reading it. (Even though this message is often not a printed letter anymore, many professionals still refer to it as a letter.) Take the same care with your application letter that you took with your résumé. A poorly written application letter can prompt employers to skip over your résumé, even if you are a good fit for a job.[2] Staffing specialist Abby Kohut calls the application letter "a writing-skills evaluation in disguise" and emphasizes that even a single error can get you bounced from contention.[3]

As with proposals, the best approach for an application letter depends on whether your application is solicited or unsolicited.

The best approach for an application letter depends on whether you are applying for an identified job opening or are *prospecting*—taking the initiative to write to companies even though they haven't announced a job opening that is right for you.[4] In many ways, the difference between the two is like the difference between solicited and unsolicited proposals (see page 404).

Figure 19.1 shows an application message written in response to a posted job opening. The writer knows exactly what qualifications the organization is seeking and can "echo" those attributes back in his letter.

Writing a prospecting letter is more challenging because you don't have the clear target you have with a solicited letter, and the message is unexpected. You will need to do more research to identify the qualities that a company would probably seek for the position you hope to occupy (see Figure 19.2 on page 548). Also, search for news items that involve the company, its customers, the profession, or the individual manager to whom you are writing. Using this information in your application letter helps you establish common ground with your reader—and it shows that you are tuned in to what is going on in the industry.

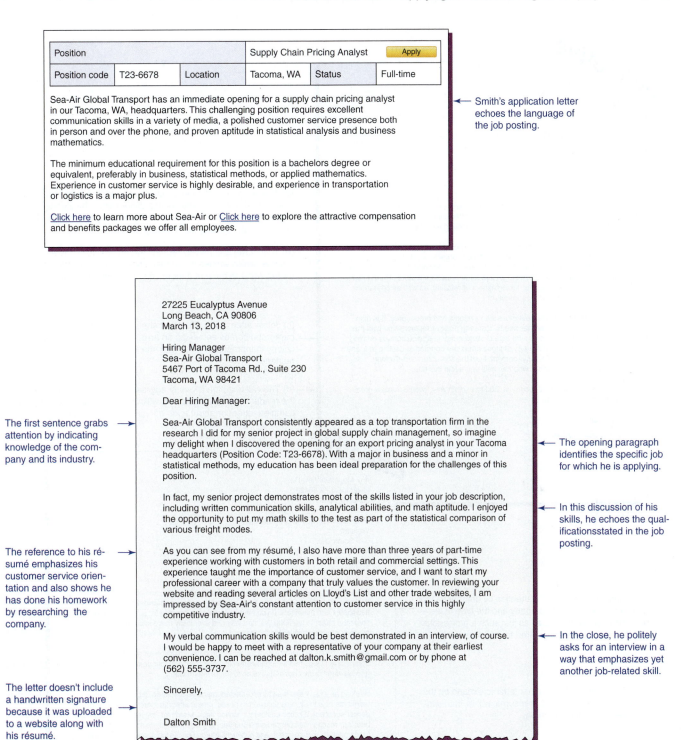

Position			Supply Chain Pricing Analyst		Apply
Position code	T23-6678	Location	Tacoma, WA	Status	Full-time

Sea-Air Global Transport has an immediate opening for a supply chain pricing analyst in our Tacoma, WA, headquarters. This challenging position requires excellent communication skills in a variety of media, a polished customer service presence both in person and over the phone, and proven aptitude in statistical analysis and business mathematics.

The minimum educational requirement for this position is a bachelors degree or equivalent, preferably in business, statistical methods, or applied mathematics. Experience in customer service is highly desirable, and experience in transportation or logistics is a major plus.

Click here to learn more about Sea-Air or Click here to explore the attractive compensation and benefits packages we offer all employees.

Smith's application letter echoes the language of the job posting.

27225 Eucalyptus Avenue
Long Beach, CA 90806
March 13, 2018

Hiring Manager
Sea-Air Global Transport
5467 Port of Tacoma Rd., Suite 230
Tacoma, WA 98421

Dear Hiring Manager:

Sea-Air Global Transport consistently appeared as a top transportation firm in the research I did for my senior project in global supply chain management, so imagine my delight when I discovered the opening for an export pricing analyst in your Tacoma headquarters (Position Code: T23-6678). With a major in business and a minor in statistical methods, my education has been ideal preparation for the challenges of this position.

In fact, my senior project demonstrates most of the skills listed in your job description, including written communication skills, analytical abilities, and math aptitude. I enjoyed the opportunity to put my math skills to the test as part of the statistical comparison of various freight modes.

As you can see from my résumé, I also have more than three years of part-time experience working with customers in both retail and commercial settings. This experience taught me the importance of customer service, and I want to start my professional career with a company that truly values the customer. In reviewing your website and reading several articles on Lloyd's List and other trade websites, I am impressed by Sea-Air's constant attention to customer service in this highly competitive industry.

My verbal communication skills would be best demonstrated in an interview, of course. I would be happy to meet with a representative of your company at their earliest convenience. I can be reached at dalton.k.smith@gmail.com or by phone at (562) 555-3737.

Sincerely,

Dalton Smith

The first sentence grabs attention by indicating knowledge of the company and its industry.

The reference to his résumé emphasizes his customer service orientation and also shows he has done his homework by researching the company.

The letter doesn't include a handwritten signature because it was uploaded to a website along with his résumé.

The opening paragraph identifies the specific job for which he is applying.

In this discussion of his skills, he echoes the qualificationsstated in the job posting.

In the close, he politely asks for an interview in a way that emphasizes yet another job-related skill.

Figure 19.1   Solicited Application Message
In this response to an online job posting, Dalton Smith highlights his qualifications while mirroring the requirements specified in the posting. Following the AIDA model (see page 334), he grabs attention immediately by letting the reader know he is familiar with the company and the global transportation business.

For either type of letter, follow these tips to be more effective:[5]

- Resist the temptation to stand out with gimmicky application letters; impress with knowledge and professionalism instead.
- If the name of an individual manager is findable, address your letter to that person. (And if it is findable, make sure you find it, because other applicants will.) Search

Ineffective

457 Mountain View Rd.
Clear Lake, IA 50428
June 16, 2018

Ms. Patricia Downing, Store Manager
Walmart
840 South Oak
Iowa Falls, IA 50126

Dear Ms. Downing:

Do you have any openings for people who want to move into store manage-ment? I am really looking for an opportunity to get a job like yours, even if it takes starting at a low level and working my way up.

Allow me to list some highlights from my enclosed résumé. First, I have a BA degree in retailing, which included such key courses as retailing, marketing, management, and business information systems. Second, I have worked as a clerk and as an assistant manager in a large department store. Third, I have experience in the customer-facing aspect of retailing, as well as operations, marketing, and personnel supervision.

Successful retailing is about more than systems and procedures. It is also about anticipating customer needs, fostering positive relationships with the community, and delivering the type of service that keeps customers coming back. Retailers that fail in any of these areas are doomed to decline in today's hypercompetitive sales environment. I am the sort of forward-thinking, customer-focused leader who can help you avoid this fate.

I will call you next Wednesday at 2:00 to explain why I would make a great addition to your team.

Sincerely,

Glenda Johns

Glenda Johns
Enclosure

(a) The writer commits three major mistakes in the first paragraph: asking a question that she could answer herself by visiting the company's website, failing to demonstrate any knowledge of the company, and making the message all about her.

(b) This paragraph merely repeats information from the enclosed résumé, which wastes the reader's time and wastes the opportunity for the writer to present a more complete picture of herself.

(c) Johns attempts to show that she understands retailing, but this paragraph comes across as an arrogant lecture. The tone is particularly inappropriate, given that she is writing to the store's top manager.

(d) The call to action is overly aggressive, and it presumes that the reader will be available and willing to take a phone call from a complete stranger about a job opening that might not even exist.

Effective

(a) Johns gets the reader's attention by demonstrating good awareness of the company and the type of people it hires, presents herself as just such a professional, and then asks to be considered for any relevant job openings.

(b) Johns uses the body of her letter to expand on the information presented in her résumé, rather than simply repeating that information.

(c) The close builds the reader's interest by demonstrating knowledge of the company's policy regarding promotion.

(d) The call to action is respectful, and it makes a response easy for the reader by providing both phone and email contact information.

457 Mountain View Rd.
Clear Lake, IA 50428
June 16, 2018

Ms. Patricia Downing, Store Manager
Walmart
840 South Oak
Iowa Falls, IA 50126

Dear Ms. Downing:

Even with its world-class supply chain, admired brand name, and competitive prices, Walmart obviously would not be the success it is without enthusiastic, service-driven associates and managers. If you have or foresee an opening for such a professional, someone eager to learn the Walmart way and eventually move into a management position, please consider me for the opportunity.

As an associate or management trainee, I can bring a passion for retailing and the perspective I've gained through academic preparation and four years of experience. (Please refer to my enclosed résumé for more information.)

Working as a clerk and then as an assistant manager in a large department store taught me how to anticipate customer needs, create effective merchandising, and deliver service that keeps customers coming back. Moreover, my recent BA degree in retailing, which encompassed such courses as retailing concepts, marketing fundamentals, management, and business information systems, prepared me with in-depth awareness of contemporary retailing issues and strategies.

I understand Walmart prefers to promote its managers from within, and I would be pleased to start out with an entry-level position until I gain the necessary experience. Could we have a brief conversation about the possibilities of joining your team? I am available by phone at 641-747-2222 or email at glendajohns@mailnet.com.

Sincerely,

Glenda Johns

Glenda Johns
Enclosure

Figure 19.2 **Unsolicited Application Letter**
Demonstrating knowledge of the employer's needs and presenting your qualifications accordingly are essential steps in an unsolicited application letter.

LinkedIn, the company's website, industry directories, Twitter, and anything else you can think of to locate an appropriate name. Ask the people in your network if they know a name. If you can't find a name, addressing your letter to "Dear Hiring Manager" is perfectly acceptable.

- Clearly identify the opportunity you are applying for or expressing interest in.
- Show that you understand the company and its marketplace.
- Never volunteer salary history or requirements unless an employer has asked for this information.
- Keep it short—no more than three or four brief paragraphs. Remember that all you are trying to do at this point is move the conversation forward one step.
- Show some personality while maintaining a business-appropriate tone. The letter gives you the opportunity to balance the facts-only tone of your résumé.
- Project confidence without being arrogant.
- Don't just repeat information from your résumé; use the conversational tone of the letter to convey additional professional and personal qualities and the reasons that you're a good candidate for this particular job (see Figure 19.3).

Because application letters are persuasive messages, the AIDA approach you learned in Chapter 12 is ideal, as the following sections explain.

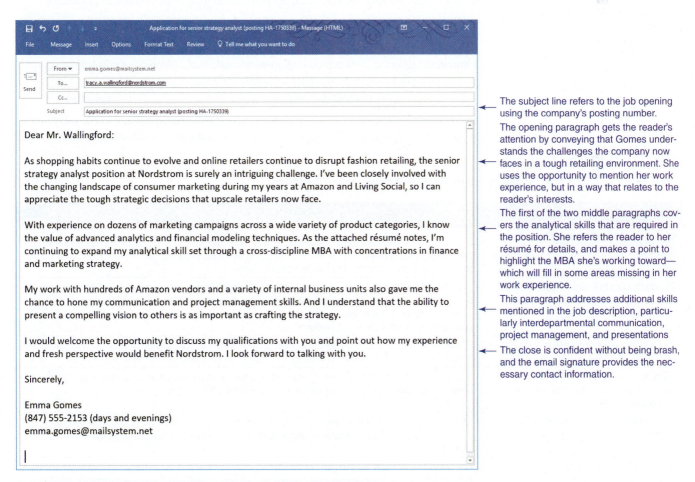

Figure 19.3 Complementing Your Résumé With an Application Message
When writing a letter or email message to accompany your résumé, use the opportunity to complement the information already contained in your résumé. Highlight how your qualifications match the needs of the position, without repeating the information from your résumé. Here is a message that could accompany the résumé in Figure 18.6 on page 531.

Getting Attention

The opening paragraph of your application letter needs to clearly convey the reason you're writing and give the recipient a compelling reason to keep reading.

The opening paragraph of your application letter must accomplish two essential tasks: (1) explain why you are writing and (2) give the recipient a reason to keep reading by demonstrating that you have some immediate potential for meeting the company's needs. Consider this opening:

> With the recent slowdown in corporate purchasing, I can certainly appreciate the challenge of new fleet sales in this business environment. With my high energy level and 16 months of new-car sales experience, I believe I can produce the results you listed as vital in the job posting on your website.

This applicant does a smooth job of echoing the company's stated needs while highlighting his personal qualifications and providing evidence that he understands the broader market. He balances his relative lack of experience with enthusiasm and knowledge of the industry. Table 19.1 suggests some other ways you can spark interest and grab attention in your opening paragraph.

Building Interest and Increasing Desire

Use the middle section of your application letter to expand on your opening and present a more complete picture of your strengths.

The middle section of your letter presents your strongest selling points in terms of their potential benefit to the organization, thereby building interest in you and creating a desire to interview you. Be specific and back up your assertions with convincing evidence:

> **Poor:** I completed three college courses in business communication, earning an A in each course, and have worked for the past year at Imperial Construction.

> **Improved:** Using the skills gained from three semesters of college training in business communication, I developed a collection system for Imperial Construction that reduced annual bad-debt losses by 25 percent.

In a solicited letter, be sure to discuss each major requirement listed in the job posting. If you are deficient in any of these requirements, stress other solid selling points to help

TABLE 19.1   Tips for Getting Attention in Application Letters

Tip	Example
Unsolicited Application Letters	
Show how your strongest skills will benefit the organization.	If you need a regional sales specialist who consistently meets sales targets while fostering strong customer relationships, please consider my qualifications.
Describe your understanding of the job's requirements and show how well your qualifications fit them.	Your annual report stated that improving manufacturing efficiency is one of the company's top priorities for next year. Through my postgraduate research in systems engineering and consulting work for several companies in the industry, I've developed reliable methods for quickly identifying ways to cut production time while reducing resource use.
Mention the name of a person known to and highly regarded by the reader.	When Janice McHugh of your franchise sales division spoke to our business communication class last week, she said you often need promising new marketing graduates at this time of year.
Refer to publicized company activities, achievements, changes, or new procedures.	Today's issue of the *Detroit News* reports that you may need the expertise of computer programmers versed in robotics when your Lansing tire plant automates this spring.
Use a question to demonstrate your understanding of the organization's needs.	Can your fast-growing market research division use an interviewer with two years of field survey experience, a B.A. in public relations, and a real desire to succeed? If so, please consider me for the position.
Use a catchphrase opening if the job requires ingenuity and imagination.	*Haut monde*—whether referring to French, Italian, or Arab clients, it still means "high society." As an interior designer for your Beverly Hills showroom, not only could I serve and sell to your distinguished clientele, but I could also do it in all these languages. I speak, read, and write them fluently.
Solicited Application Letters	
Identify where you discovered the job opening; describe what you have to offer.	Your job posting on Monster.com for a cruise-line social director caught my eye. My eight years of experience as a social director in the travel industry would equip me to serve your new Caribbean cruise division well.

strengthen your overall presentation. Don't restrict your message to just core job duties, either. Also highlight personal characteristics that apply to the targeted position, such as your ability to work hard or handle responsibility:

> While attending college full-time, I worked part-time during the school year and up to 60 hours a week each summer in order to be totally self-supporting while in college. I can offer your organization the same level of effort and perseverance.

Mention your salary requirements only if the organization has asked you to state them. If you don't know the salary appropriate for the position and someone with your qualifications, you can find typical salary ranges at the U.S. Bureau of Labor Statistics website, **www.bls.gov**, or a number of commercial websites. If you do state a target salary, tie it to the value you would offer:

Don't bring up salary in your application letter unless the recipient has asked you to include your salary requirements.

> For the past two years, I have been helping a company similar to yours organize its database marketing efforts. I would therefore like to receive a salary in the same range (the mid-60s) for helping your company set up a more efficient customer database.

Toward the end of this section, refer the reader to your résumé by citing a specific fact or general point covered there:

> As you can see in the attached résumé, I've been working part-time with a local publisher since my sophomore year. During that time, I've used client interactions as an opportunity to build strong customer service skills.

REAL-TIME UPDATES
LEARN MORE BY EXPLORING THIS INTERACTIVE WEBSITE
How much are you worth?
Find real-life salary ranges for a wide range of jobs. Go to **real-timeupdates.com/bct14** and select Learn More in the Students section.

Motivating Action

The final paragraph of your application letter has two important functions: to ask the reader for a specific action (usually an interview) and to facilitate a reply. Offer to come to the employer's office at a convenient time or, if the firm is some distance away, to meet with its nearest representative or arrange a telephone or Skype interview. Include your email address and phone number, as well as the best times to reach you:

In the final paragraph of your application letter, respectfully ask for specific action and make it easy for the reader to respond.

> After you have reviewed my qualifications, could we discuss the possibility of putting my marketing skills to work for your company? I am available at (360) 555-7845 from 2 p.m. to 10 p.m. Monday to Friday or by email at john.wagner462@gmail.com.

After editing and proofreading your application letter, give it a final quality check by referring to "Checklist: Writing Application Letters." Then send it along with your résumé promptly, especially if you are responding to an advertisement or online job posting.

CHECKLIST ✔ **Writing Application Letters**

- Take the same care with your application letter that you took with your résumé.
- If you are *prospecting* using an unsolicited message, do deep research to identify the qualities the company likely wants.
- For solicited messages in response to a posted job opening, word your message in a way that echoes the qualifications listed in the posting.
- Open the letter by capturing the reader's attention in a businesslike way.
- Use specific language to clearly state your interests and objectives.

- Build interest and desire in your potential contribution by presenting your key qualifications for the job.
- Link your education, experience, and personal qualities to the job requirements.
- Outline salary requirements only if the organization has requested that you provide them.
- Request an interview at a time and place that is convenient for the reader.
- Make it easy to comply with your request by providing your complete contact information and good times to reach you.
- Adapt your style for cultural variations, if required.

Think creatively about a follow-up message; show that you've continued to add to your skills or that you've learned more about the company or the industry.

FOLLOWING UP AFTER SUBMITTING A RÉSUMÉ

Deciding if, when, and how to follow up after submitting your résumé and application letter is one of the trickiest parts of a job search. First and foremost, keep in mind that employers continue to evaluate your communication efforts and professionalism during this phase, so don't say or do anything to leave a negative impression. Second, adhere to whatever instructions the employer has provided. If a job posting says "no calls," for example, don't call. Third, if the job posting lists a *close date*, don't call or write before then because the company is still collecting applications and will not have made a decision about inviting people for interviews. Wait a week or so after the close date. If no close date is given and you have no other information to suggest a timeline, you can generally contact the company starting a week or two after submitting your résumé.[6]

When you follow up by email or telephone, you can share an additional piece of information that links your qualifications to the position (keep an eye out for late-breaking news about the company, too) and ask a question about the hiring process as a way to gather some information about your status. Good questions to ask include:[7]

- Has a hiring decision been made yet?
- Can you tell me what to expect next in terms of the hiring process?
- What is the company's time frame for filling this position?
- Could I follow up in another week if you haven't had the chance to contact me yet?
- Can I provide any additional information regarding my qualifications for the position?

Whatever the circumstances, a follow-up message can demonstrate that you're sincerely interested in working for the organization, persistent in pursuing your goals, and committed to upgrading your skills.

If you don't land a job at your dream company on the first attempt, don't give up. You can apply again if a new opening appears, or you can send an updated résumé with a new unsolicited application letter that describes how you have gained additional experience, taken a relevant course, or otherwise improved your skill set. Many leading employers take note of applicants who came close but didn't quite make it and may extend offers when positions open up in the future.[8]

Understanding the Interviewing Process

2 LEARNING OBJECTIVE
Describe the typical sequence of job interviews, the major types of interviews, and the attributes employers look for during an interview.

Start preparing early for your interviews—and be sure to consider a wide range of options.

An **employment interview** is a meeting during which both you and the prospective employer ask questions and exchange information. The employer's objective is to find the best talent to fill available job openings, and your objective is to find the right match for your goals and capabilities.

As you get ready to begin interviewing, keep two vital points in mind. First, recognize that the process takes time. Start your preparation and research early; the best job offers usually go to the best-prepared candidates. Second, don't limit your options by looking at only a few companies. By exploring a wide range of firms and positions, you might uncover great opportunities that you would not have found otherwise. You'll increase the odds of getting more job offers, too.

THE TYPICAL SEQUENCE OF INTERVIEWS

During the screening stage of interviews, use the limited time available to confirm your fit for the position.

Most employers interview an applicant multiple times before deciding to make a job offer. At the most selective companies, you might have a dozen or more individual interviews across several stages.[9] Depending on the company and the position, the process may stretch out over many weeks, or it may be completed in a matter of days.[10]

Employers start with the *screening stage*, in which they filter out applicants who are unqualified or otherwise not a good fit for the position. Screening can take place on your school's campus, at company offices, via telephone (including Skype or another Internet-based phone service), or through a computer-based screening system. Time is limited in screening interviews, so keep your answers short while providing a few key points that confirm your fit for the position. If your screening interview will take place by phone, try to schedule it for a time when you can be focused and free from interruptions.[11]

The next stage of interviews, the *selection stage*, helps the organization identify the top candidates from all those who qualify. During these interviews, show keen interest in the job, relate your skills and experience to the organization's needs, listen attentively, and ask questions that show you've done your research.

If the interviewers agree that you're a good candidate, you may receive a job offer, either on the spot or a few days later by phone, mail, or email. In other instances you may be invited back for a final evaluation, often by a higher-ranking executive. The objective of the *final stage* is often to sell you on the advantages of joining the organization.

COMMON TYPES OF INTERVIEWS

Be prepared to encounter a variety of interviewing approaches. These can be distinguished by the way they are structured, the number of people involved, and the purpose of the interview.

Structured Versus Unstructured Interviews

In a **structured interview**, the interviewer (or a computer program) asks a series of questions in a predetermined order. Structured interviews help employers identify candidates who don't meet basic job criteria, and they allow the interview team to compare answers from multiple candidates.[12]

In contrast, in an **open-ended interview**, the interviewer adapts his or her line of questioning based on the answers you give and any questions you ask. Even though it may feel like a conversation, remember that it's still an interview, so keep your answers focused and professional.

Panel and Group Interviews

Although one-on-one interviews are the most common format, some employers use panel or group interviews as well. In a **panel interview**, you meet with several interviewers at once.[13] Try to make a connection with each person on the panel, and keep in mind that each person has a different perspective, so tailor your responses accordingly.[14] For example, an upper-level manager is likely to be interested in your overall business sense and strategic perspective, whereas a potential colleague might be more interested in your technical skills and ability to work in a team. In a **group interview**, one or more interviewers meet with several candidates simultaneously. A key purpose of a group interview is to observe how the candidates interact.[15] Group interviews can be tricky because you want to stand out while coming across as a supportive team player. Be sure to treat your fellow candidates with respect, while looking for opportunities to demonstrate the depth of knowledge you have about the company and its needs.

Behavioral, Situational, Working, and Stress Interviews

Interviewing techniques also vary based on the types of questions you are asked. Perhaps the most common type of interview these days is the **behavioral interview**, in which you are asked to relate specific incidents and experiences from your past.[16] In contrast to generic questions that can often be answered with "canned" responses, behavioral questions require candidates to use their own experiences and attributes to craft answers. Studies show that behavioral interviewing is a much better predictor of success on the job than traditional interview questions.[17] To prepare for a behavioral interview, review your work or college experiences to recall several instances in which you demonstrated an important job-related attribute or dealt with a challenge such as uncooperative team members or heavy workloads. Get ready with responses that quickly summarize the situation, the actions you took, and the outcome of those actions.[18]

MOBILE APP

Add the **Skype** mobile app to your phone to be ready for video interviews.

During the selection stage, continue to show how your skills and attributes can help the company.

During the final stage, the interviewer may try to sell you on working for the firm.

A structured interview follows a set sequence of questions, allowing the interview team to compare answers from all candidates.

In an open-ended interview, the interviewer adapts the line of questioning based on your responses and questions.

In a panel interview, you meet with several interviewers at once; in a group interview, you and several other candidates meet with one or more interviewers at once.

In a behavioral interview, you are asked to describe how you handled situations from your past.

A **situational interview** is similar to a behavioral interview except that the questions focus on how you would handle various hypothetical situations on the job. The situations will likely relate closely to the job you're applying for, so the more you know about the position, the better prepared you'll be.

A **working interview** is the most realistic type of interview: You actually perform a job-related activity during the interview. You may be asked to lead a brainstorming session, solve a business problem, engage in role playing, or even make a presentation.[19]

The most unnerving type of interview is the **stress interview**, during which you might be asked questions designed to unsettle you or might be subjected to long periods of silence, criticism, interruptions, and or even hostile reactions by the interviewer. The theory behind this approach is that you'll reveal how well you handle stressful situations, although some experts find the technique of dubious value.[20] If you find yourself in a stress interview, recognize what is happening and collect your thoughts for a few seconds before you respond.

You might encounter two or more types of interview questions within a single interview, so stay alert and try to understand the type of question you're facing before you answer each one.

INTERVIEW MEDIA

Expect to be interviewed through a variety of media. Employers trying to cut travel costs and the demands on staff time now interview candidates via telephone, email, instant messaging, virtual online systems, and videoconferencing, in addition to traditional face-to-face meetings.

To succeed at a telephone interview, make sure you treat it as seriously as an in-person interview. Be prepared with a copy of all the materials you have sent to the employer, including your résumé and any correspondence. In addition, prepare some note cards with key message points you'd like to make and questions you'd like to ask. And remember that you won't be able to use a pleasant smile, a firm handshake, and other nonverbal signals to create a good impression. A positive, alert tone of voice is therefore vital.[21]

Email and IM are also sometimes used in the screening stage. Although you have almost no opportunity to send and receive nonverbal signals with these formats, you do have the major advantage of being able to review and edit each response before you send it. Maintain a professional style in your responses, and be sure to ask questions that demonstrate your knowledge of the company and the position.[22]

Many employers use video technology for both live and recorded interviews. For instance, the online clothing retailer Zappos uses video interviews on Skype to select the top two or three finalists for each position and then invites those candidates for in-person interviews.[23] Recruiters can also use mobile apps for interviews. With recorded video interviews, an online system asks a set of questions and records the respondent's answers. Recruiters then watch the videos as part of the screening process.[24] Prepare for a video interview as you would for an in-person interview—including dressing and grooming—and take the extra steps needed to become familiar with the equipment and the process. If you're interviewing from home, arrange your space so that the webcam doesn't pick up anything distracting or embarrassing in the background. During any video interview, remember to sit up straight and focus on the camera.

Online interviews can range from simple structured questionnaires and tests to sophisticated job simulations that are similar to working interviews (see Figure 19.4). These simulations help identify good candidates, give applicants an idea of what the job is like, and reduce the risk of employment discrimination lawsuits because they closely mimic actual job skills.[25]

REAL-TIME UPDATES

LEARN MORE BY WATCHING THESE VIDEOS

Five TED talks that will help you prepare for interviews

MIT career advisor Lily Zhang hand-picked these talks for the insights they can give all job hunters. Go to **real-timeupdates.com/bct14** and select Learn More in the Students section.

Figure 19.4   Job Task Simulations
Computer-based job simulations are an increasingly popular approach to testing job-related skills.

WHAT EMPLOYERS LOOK FOR IN AN INTERVIEW

Interviews give employers the chance to go beyond the basic data of your résumé to get to know you and to answer two essential questions. The first is whether you can handle the responsibilities of the position. Naturally, the more you know about the demands of the position, and the more you've thought about how your skills match those demands, the better you'll be able to respond.

The second essential question is whether you will be a good fit with the organization and the target position. All good employers want people who are confident, dedicated, positive, curious, courteous, ethical, and willing to commit to something larger than their own individual goals. Companies also look for fit with their individual cultures. Just like people, companies have different "personalities." Some are intense; others are more laid back. Some emphasize teamwork; others expect employees to forge their own way and even to compete with one another. Expectations also vary from job to job within a company and from industry to industry. An outgoing personality is essential for sales but less so for research, for instance.

Suitability for a specific job is judged on the basis of such factors as
- Academic preparation
- Work experience
- Job-related personality traits

Compatibility with an organizational culture and a position is judged on such factors as personal background, attitudes, and communication style.

PREEMPLOYMENT TESTING AND BACKGROUND CHECKS

In an effort to improve the predictability of the selection process, many employers now conduct a variety of preemployment evaluations and investigations. Here are types of assessments you are likely to encounter during your job search:[26]

- **Integrity tests.** Integrity tests attempt to measure how truthful and trustworthy a candidate is likely to be.
- **Personality tests.** Personality tests are designed to gauge such aspects as attitudes toward work, interests, managerial potential, dependability, commitment, and motivation.
- **Cognitive tests.** Cognitive tests measure a variety of attributes involved in acquiring, processing, analyzing, using, and remembering information. Typical tests involve reading comprehension, mathematics, problem solving, and decision making.
- **Language proficiency.** You may be asked to take a reading or writing test.
- **Job knowledge and job-skills tests.** These assessments measure the knowledge and skills required to succeed in a particular position. An accounting candidate, for

Preemployment tests attempt to provide objective, quantitative information about a candidate's skills, attitudes, and habits.

example, might be tested on accounting principles and legal matters (knowledge) and asked to create a simple balance sheet or income statement (skills).

- **Substance tests.** A majority of companies perform some level of drug and alcohol testing. Many employers believe such testing is necessary to maintain workplace safety, ensure productivity, and protect companies from lawsuits, but others view it as an invasion of employee privacy.

- **Background checks.** In addition to testing, most companies conduct some sort of background check, including reviewing your credit record, checking to see whether you have a criminal history, and verifying your education. Moreover, you should assume that every employer will conduct a general online search on you. To help prevent a background check from tripping you up, verify that your college transcripts are current, look for any mistakes or outdated information in your credit record, plug your name into multiple search engines to see whether anything embarrassing shows up, and scour your social network profiles and connections for potential problems.

Preemployment assessments are a complex and controversial aspect of workforce recruiting. For instance, even though personality testing is widely used, some research suggests that commonly used tests are not a reliable predictor of job success.[27] However, expect to see more innovation in this area and greater use of testing in general in the future as companies try to reduce the risks and costs of poor hiring decisions.

If you're concerned about any preemployment test, ask the employer for more information or ask your college career center for advice. You can also get more information from the Equal Employment Opportunity Commission at **www .eeoc.gov**.

Preparing for a Job Interview

Now that you're armed with insights into the interviewing and assessment process, you're ready to begin preparing for your interviews. Preparation will help you feel more confident and perform better under pressure, and preparation starts with learning about the organization.

LEARNING ABOUT THE ORGANIZATION AND YOUR INTERVIEWERS

Interviewers expect you to know some basic information about the company and its industry.

Employers expect serious candidates to demonstrate an understanding of the company's operations, its markets, and its strategic and tactical challenges.[28] You've already done some initial research to identify companies of interest, but when you're invited to an interview, it's time to dig a little deeper (see Table 19.2). Making this effort demonstrates your interest in the company, and it identifies you as a business professional who knows the importance of investigation and analysis.

In addition to learning about the company and the job opening, try to find out as much as you can about the managers who will be interviewing you, if you can get their names. Search LinkedIn in particular. It's also perfectly acceptable to ask your contact at the company for the names and titles of the people who will be interviewing you.[29] Whatever information you can find, think about ways to use it during your interview. For example, if an interviewer lists membership in a particular professional organization, you might ask whether the organization is a good forum for people to learn about vital issues in the profession or industry. This question gives the interviewer an opportunity to talk about his or her own interests and experiences for a moment, which builds rapport and might reveal vital insights into the career path you are considering. Just make sure your questions are sincere and not uncomfortably personal.

TABLE 19.2 Investigating an Organization and a Job Opportunity

Where to Look and What You Can Learn

- *Company website, blogs, and social media accounts:* Overall information about the company, including key executives, products and services, locations and divisions, employee benefits, job descriptions
- *Competitors' websites, blogs, and social media accounts:* Similar information from competitors, including the strengths these companies claim to have
- *Industry-related websites and blogs:* Objective analysis and criticism of the company, its products, its reputation, and its management
- *Marketing materials (print and online):* The company's marketing strategy and customer communication style
- *Company publications (print and online):* Key events, stories about employees, new products
- *Your social network contacts:* Names and job titles of potential contacts within a company
- *Periodicals (newspapers and trade journals, both print and online):* In-depth stories about the company and its strategies, products, successes, and failures; you may find profiles of top executives
- *Career center at your college:* Often provides a wide array of information about companies that hire graduates
- *Current and former employees:* Insights into the work environment

Points to Learn About the Organization

- Full name
- Location (headquarters and divisions, branches, subsidiaries, or other units)
- Ownership (public or private; whether it is owned by another company)
- Brief history
- Products and services
- Industry position (whether the company is a leader or a minor player; whether it is an innovator or more of a follower)
- Key financial points (such as stock price and trends, if a public company)
- Growth prospects (whether the company is investing in its future through research and development; whether it is in a thriving industry)

Points to Learn About the Position

- Title
- Functions and responsibilities
- Qualifications and expectations
- Possible career paths
- Salary range
- Travel expectations and opportunities
- Relocation expectations and opportunities

THINKING AHEAD ABOUT QUESTIONS

Planning ahead for the interviewer's questions will help you handle them more confidently and successfully. In addition, you will want to prepare insightful questions of your own.

Planning for the Employer's Questions

Many general interview questions are "stock" queries you can expect to hear again and again during your interviews. Get ready to face these six at the very least:

- **What is the hardest decision you've ever had to make?** Be prepared with a good example (that isn't too personal), explaining why the decision was difficult, how you made the choice you made, and what you learned from the experience.

- **What is your greatest weakness?** This question seems to be a favorite of some interviewers, although it probably rarely yields useful information. One good strategy is to mention a skill or attribute you haven't had the opportunity to develop yet but would like to in your next position.[30] Another option is to discuss a past shortcoming you took steps to correct.

- **Where do you want to be five years from now?** This question tests (1) whether you're merely using this job as a stopover until something better comes along and (2) whether you've given thought to your long-term goals. Your answer should reflect your desire to contribute to the employer's long-term goals, not just your own goals. Whether this question often yields useful information is also a matter of debate, but be prepared to answer it.[31]

You can expect to face a number of common questions in your interviews, so be sure to prepare for them.

- **What didn't you like about previous jobs you've held?** Answer this one carefully: The interviewer is trying to predict whether you'll be an unhappy or difficult employee.[32] Describe something that you didn't like in a way that puts you in a positive light, such as having limited opportunities to apply your skills or education. Avoid making negative comments about former employers or colleagues.
- **Tell me something about yourself.** One good strategy is to briefly share the "story of you" (see page 515)—quickly summarizing where you have been and where you would like to go—in a way that aligns your interests with the company's. Alternatively, you can focus on a specific skill you know is valuable to the company, share something business-relevant that you are passionate about, or offer a short summary of what colleagues or customers think about you.[33] Whatever tactic you choose, this is not the time to be shy or indecisive, so be ready with a confident, memorable answer.
- **How do you spend your free time?** This question can pop up late in an interview, after the interviewer has covered the major work-related questions and wants to get a better idea of what sort of person you are.[34] Prepare an answer that is honest and that puts you in a positive light, without revealing more than you are comfortable revealing or suggesting that you might not fit in the corporate culture. Sports, hobbies, reading, spending time with family, and volunteer work are all "safe" answers.

Continue your preparation by planning a brief answer to each question in Table 19.3.

REAL-TIME UPDATES

LEARN MORE BY READING THIS ARTICLE

Prepare your answers to these tough interview questions

Use this advice to get ready for five questions you're likely to encounter. Go to **real-timeupdates.com/bct14** and select Learn More in the Students section.

TABLE 19.3   Twenty-Five Common Interview Questions

Questions About College

1. What courses in college did you like most? Least? Why?
2. Do you think your extracurricular activities in college were worth the time you spent on them? Why or why not?
3. When did you choose your college major? Did you ever change your major? If so, why?
4. Do you feel you did the best scholastic work you are capable of?
5. How has your college education prepared you for this position?

Questions About Employers and Jobs

6. Why did you leave your last job?
7. Why did you apply for this job opening?
8. Why did you choose your particular field of work?
9. What are the disadvantages of your chosen field?
10. What do you know about our company?
11. What do you think about how this industry operates today?
12. Why do you think you would like this particular type of job?

Questions About Work Experiences and Expectations

13. What was your biggest failure?
14. What is your biggest weakness?
15. Describe an experience in which you learned from one of your mistakes.
16. What motivates you? Why?
17. What do you think determines a person's progress in a good organization?
18. What have you done that shows initiative and willingness to work?
19. Why should we hire you?

Questions About Work Habits

20. Do you prefer working with others or by yourself?
21. What type of boss do you prefer?
22. Have you ever had any difficulty getting along with colleagues or supervisors? With instructors? With other students?
23. What would you do if you were given an unrealistic deadline for a task or project?
24. How do you feel about overtime work?
25. How do you handle stress or pressure on the job?

Sources: "50 Most Common Interview Questions," Glassdoor blog, 25 March 2016, www.glassdoor.com; Alison Green, "The 10 Most Common Job Interview Questions," *U.S. News & World Report*, 27 April 2015, money.usnews.com; Carole Martin, "10 Most Common Interview Questions," Monster, accessed 14 May 2016, www.monster.com.

As you prepare answers, look for ways to frame your responses as brief stories (30 to 90 seconds) rather than simple declarative answers.[35] Cohesive stories tend to stick in the listener's mind more effectively than disconnected facts and statements.

Look for ways to frame your responses as brief stories rather than as dry facts or statements.

Planning Questions of Your Own

Remember that an interview is a two-way conversation: The questions you ask are just as important as the answers you provide. By asking insightful questions, you can demonstrate your understanding of the organization, steer the discussion into areas that allow you to present your qualifications to best advantage, and verify for yourself whether this is a good opportunity. Plus, interviewers expect you to ask questions, and they look negatively on candidates who don't have any questions to ask. For good questions that you might use as a starting point, see Table 19.4.

Preparing questions of your own helps you understand the company and the position, and it sends an important signal that you are truly interested.

BOOSTING YOUR CONFIDENCE

Interviewing is stressful for everyone, so some nervousness is natural. However, you can take steps to feel more confident. Start by reminding yourself that you have value to offer the employer and that the employer already thinks highly enough of you to invite you to an interview.

The best way to build your confidence is to prepare thoroughly and address shortcomings as best you can. In other words, take action.

If some aspect of your appearance or background makes you uneasy, correct it if possible or offset it by emphasizing positive traits such as warmth, wit, intelligence, or charm. Instead of dwelling on your weaknesses, focus on your strengths. Instead of worrying about how you will perform in the interview, focus on how you can help the organization succeed. As with public speaking, the more prepared you are, the more confident you'll be.

POLISHING YOUR INTERVIEW STYLE

Competence and confidence are the foundation of your interviewing style, and you can enhance them by giving the interviewer an impression of poise, good manners, and good judgment. You can develop a smooth style by staging mock interviews with a friend or

Staging mock interviews with a friend is one good way to hone your style.

TABLE 19.4 Ten Questions to Consider Asking an Interviewer

Question	Reason for Asking
1. What are the job's major responsibilities?	A vague answer could mean that the responsibilities have not been clearly defined, which is almost guaranteed to cause frustration if you take the job.
2. What qualities do you want in the person who fills this position?	This will help you go beyond the job description to understand what the company really wants.
3. How do you measure success for someone in this position?	A vague or incomplete answer could mean that the expectations you will face are unrealistic or ill defined.
4. What is the first problem that needs the attention of the person you hire?	Not only will this help you prepare, but it can also signal whether you're about to jump into a problematic situation.
5. How well do my qualifications align with the current and future needs of this position?	This gives you the opportunity to address any unspoken concerns the interviewer might have.
6. Why is this job now vacant?	If the previous employee got promoted, that's a good sign. If the person quit, that might not be such a good sign.
7. What makes your organization different from others in the industry?	The answer will help you assess whether the company has a clear strategy to succeed in its industry and whether top managers communicate this to lower-level employees.
8. How would you define your organization's managerial philosophy?	You want to know whether the managerial philosophy is consistent with your own working values.
9. What is a typical workday like for you?	The interviewer's response can give you clues about daily life at the company.
10. What are the next steps in the selection process? What's the best way to follow up with you?	Knowing where the company is in the hiring process will give you clues about following up after the interview and possibly give you hints about where you stand.

Sources: Jacquelyn Smith and Natalie Walters, "The 29 Smartest Questions to Ask at the End of Every Job Interview," *Business Insider*, 28 January 2016, www.businessinsider.com; Heather Huhman, "5 Must-Ask Questions at Job Interviews," Glassdoor blog, 7 February 2012, www.glassdoor.com.

Figure 19.5 **Interview Simulators**
A number of mobile apps are available to help you practice and polish your interviewing skills.

using an interview simulator on your phone or tablet (see Figure 19.5). Record these mock interviews so you can evaluate yourself. Your college's career center may have computer-based systems for practicing interviews as well.

After each practice session, look for opportunities to improve. Have your mock interview partner critique your performance, or critique yourself if you're able to record your practice interviews, using the list of warning signs shown in Table 19.5. Pay close attention to the length of your planned answers as well. Interviewers want you to give complete answers, but they don't want you to take up valuable time or test their patience by chatting about minor or irrelevant details.[36]

Evaluate the length and clarity of your answers, your nonverbal behavior, and the quality of your voice.

In addition to reviewing your answers, evaluate your nonverbal behavior, including your posture, eye contact, facial expressions, and hand gestures and movements. Do you come across as alert and upbeat or passive and withdrawn? Pay close attention to your speaking voice as well. If you tend to speak in a monotone, for instance, practice speaking in a livelier style, with more inflection and emphasis. And watch out for "filler words" such as *uh* and *um*. Many people start sentences with a filler without being conscious of doing so. Train yourself to pause silently for a moment instead as you gather your thoughts and plan what to say.

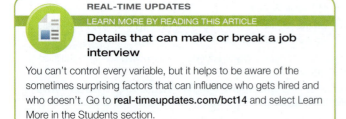

REAL-TIME UPDATES
LEARN MORE BY READING THIS ARTICLE

Details that can make or break a job interview

You can't control every variable, but it helps to be aware of the sometimes surprising factors that can influence who gets hired and who doesn't. Go to **real-timeupdates.com/bct14** and select Learn More in the Students section.

PRESENTING A PROFESSIONAL IMAGE

Dress conservatively and be well groomed for every interview.

Clothing and grooming are important elements of preparation because they reveal something about a candidate's personality, professionalism, and ability to sense the unspoken "rules" of a situation. Your research into various industries and professions should give you insight into expectations for business attire. If you're not sure what to wear, ask someone who works in the same industry or even visit the company at the end of the day and see what employees are wearing as they leave the office. You don't need to spend a

TABLE 19.5 Warning Signs: 25 Attributes Interviewers Don't Like to See

1. Poor personal appearance	13. Poor scholastic record
2. Overbearing, overaggressive, or conceited demeanor; a "superiority complex"; a know-it-all attitude	14. Unwillingness to start at the bottom; expecting too much too soon
3. Inability to express ideas clearly; poor voice, diction, or grammar	15. Tendency to make excuses
4. Lack of knowledge or experience	16. Evasive answers; hedging on unfavorable factors in record
5. Poor preparation for the interview	17. Lack of tact
6. Lack of interest in the job	18. Lack of maturity
7. Lack of planning for career; lack of purpose or goals	19. Lack of courtesy and common sense, including answering mobile phones, texting, or chewing gum during the interview
8. Lack of enthusiasm; passive and indifferent demeanor	20. Being critical of past or present employers
9. Lack of confidence and poise; appearance of being nervous and ill at ease	21. Lack of social skills
10. Insufficient evidence of achievement	22. Marked dislike for schoolwork
11. Failure to participate in extracurricular activities	23. Lack of vitality
12. Overemphasis on money; interest only in the best offer	24. Failure to look interviewer in the eye
	25. Limp, weak handshake

Sources: Donna Fuscaldo, "Seven Deadly Interview Sins," Glassdoor blog, 4 April 2012, www.glassdoor.com; "Employers Reveal Outrageous and Common Mistakes Candidates Made in Job Interviews, According to New CareerBuilder Survey," CareerBuilder, 12 January 2011, www.careerbuilder.com; *The Northwestern Endicott Report* (Evanston, Ill.: Northwestern University Placement Center).

fortune on interview clothes, but your clothes must be clean, pressed, and appropriate. The following look will serve you well in most interview situations:[37]

- Neat, "adult" hairstyle
- For more formal environments, a conservative business suit (for women, that means no exposed midriffs, short skirts, or plunging necklines) in a dark solid color or a subtle pattern such as pinstripes; white shirt and understated tie for men; coordinated blouse for women
- For less formal environments, smart-looking "business casual," including a pressed shirt or blouse and nice slacks or a skirt

COMMUNICATING ACROSS CULTURES

Successfully Interviewing Across Borders

Interviewing for a job in another country can be one of the most exciting steps in your career. To succeed, you need to pay close attention to the important elements of the interviewing process, including personal appearance, an awareness of what interviewers are really trying to learn about you, and things you should learn about the organization you're hoping to join.

Some countries and cultures place a much higher importance on dress and personal grooming than many employees in the United States are accustomed to; moreover, expectations of personal appearance can vary dramatically from country to country. Ask people who've been to the country before and observe local businesspeople when you arrive. Many people interpret inappropriate dress as more than a simple fashion mistake; they view it as an inability or unwillingness to understand another culture. Even if you are interviewing via Skype, as is often the case in the early rounds, make sure your on-screen appearance is appropriate.

For instance, the business image consultant Ashley Rothschild points out that you could get away with wearing a boldly colored suit in Italy but probably not in Japan. Business professionals tend to dress formally in Italy, but as a worldwide fashion leader, the country has a broad definition of what is appropriate business attire.

Smart recruiters always analyze both nonverbal signals and verbal messages to judge whether an applicant truly has the qualities necessary for a job. In international employment situations, you'll probably be under even closer scrutiny. Recruiters abroad will want to know if you really have what it takes to succeed in unfamiliar social settings, how your family will handle the transition, and whether you can adapt your personal work style and habits enough to blend in with the hiring organization.

Remember to ask plenty of questions and do your research, both before and after the interview. Some employees view overseas postings as grand adventures, only to collide headfirst with the reality of what it's like to live and work in a completely different culture. For instance, if you've grown accustomed to the independent work style you enjoy in your current job or in school, could you handle a more structured work environment with a hierarchical chain of command? Make sure to get a sense of the culture both within the company and within its social community before you commit to a job in another country.

CAREER APPLICATIONS

1. Explain how you could find out what is appropriate dress for a job interview in South Africa.
2. Would it be appropriate to ask an interviewer to describe the culture in his or her country? Explain your answer.

Sources: Sharon Ann Holgate, "Gaining an Edge in Overseas Interviews," *Science Careers,* 4 August 2014; sciencecareers.sciencemag.org; Jean-Marc Hachey, "Interviewing for an International Job," excerpt from *The Canadian Guide to Working and Living Overseas,* 3rd ed., accessed 23 February 2004, www.workingoverseas.com; Rebecca Falkoff, "Dress to Impress the World: International Business Fashion," Monster, accessed 23 February 2004, www.monster.com; Mary Ellen Slater, "Navigating the Details of Landing an Overseas Job," *Washington Post,* 11 November 2002, E4.

- Limited jewelry (men, especially, should wear very little jewelry)
- No visible piercings other than one or two earrings (for women only)
- No visible tattoos, although this expectation is changing in some industries
- Stylish but professional-looking shoes (no extreme high heels or casual shoes)
- Clean hands and nicely trimmed fingernails
- Little or no perfume or cologne (some people are allergic and many people are put off by strong smells)
- Subtle makeup (for women)
- Exemplary personal hygiene

If you want to be taken seriously, dress and act seriously.

An interview is not the place to express your individuality or to let your inner rebel run wild. Send a clear signal that you understand the business world and know how to adapt to it. You won't be taken seriously otherwise.

BEING READY WHEN YOU ARRIVE

Be ready to go the minute you arrive at the interviewing site; don't fumble around for your résumé or your list of questions.

When you go to your interview, take a small notebook, a pen, a list of the questions you want to ask, several copies of your résumé (protected in a folder), an outline of what you have learned about the organization, and any past correspondence about the position. You may also want to take a small calendar, a transcript of your college grades, a list of references, and a portfolio containing samples of your work, performance reviews, and certificates of achievement.[38] Think carefully if you plan to use a tablet computer or any other device for note taking or reference during an interview. You don't want to waste any of the interviewer's time fumbling with it. Also, turn off your mobile phone; in a recent survey of hiring professionals, answering calls or texting while in an interview was identified as the most common mistake job candidates make during their interviews.[39]

Be sure you know when and where the interview will be held. The worst way to start any interview is to be late. Verify the route and time required to get there, even if that means traveling there ahead of time. Plan to arrive early, but don't approach the reception desk until 5 minutes or so before your appointed time.[40] Chances are the interviewer won't be ready to receive you until the scheduled time.

If you have to wait for the interviewer, use this time to review the key messages about yourself you want to get across in the interview. Conduct yourself professionally while waiting. Show respect for everyone you encounter, and avoid chewing gum, eating, or drinking. Anything you do or say at this stage may get back to the interviewer, so make sure your best qualities show from the moment you enter the premises. To review the steps for planning a successful interview, see "Checklist: Planning for a Successful Job Interview."

CHECKLIST ✔ Planning for a Successful Job Interview

- Learn about the organization, including its operations, markets, and challenges.
- Learn as much as you can about the people who will be interviewing you, if you can find their names.
- Plan for the employer's questions, including questions about tough decisions you've made, your perceived shortcomings, what you didn't like about previous jobs, and your career plans.
- Plan questions of your own to find out whether this is really the job and the organization for you and to show that you've done your research.
- Bolster your confidence by removing as many sources of apprehension as you can.

- Polish your interview style by staging mock interviews.
- Present a professional appearance with appropriate dress and grooming.
- Be ready when you arrive and bring along a pen, paper, a list of questions, copies of your résumé, an outline of your research on the company, and any correspondence you've had regarding the position.
- Double-check the location and time of the interview and map out the route beforehand.
- Relax and be flexible; the schedule and interview arrangements may change when you arrive.

Interviewing for Success

At this point, you have a good sense of the overall process and know how to prepare for your interviews. The next step is to get familiar with the three stages of every interview: the warm-up, the question-and-answer session, and the close.

4 LEARNING OBJECTIVE
Explain how to succeed in all three stages of an interview.

THE WARM-UP

Of the three stages, the warm-up is the most important, even though it may account for only a small fraction of the time you spend in the interview. Studies suggest that many interviewers make up their minds within the first 20 seconds of contact with a candidate.[41] Don't let your guard down if the interviewer engages in what feels like small talk; these exchanges are every bit as important as structured questions.

The first minute of the interview is crucial, so stay alert and be on your best business behavior.

Body language is crucial at this point. Stand or sit up straight, maintain regular but natural eye contact, and don't fidget. When the interviewer extends a hand, respond with a firm but not overpowering handshake. Repeat the interviewer's name when you're introduced ("It's a pleasure to meet you, Ms. Litton"). Wait until you're asked to be seated or the interviewer has taken a seat. Let the interviewer start the discussion, and be ready to answer one or two substantial questions right away. The following are some common openers:[42]

- Why do you want to work here?
- What do you know about us?
- Tell me a little about yourself.

Recognize that you could face substantial questions as soon as your interview starts, so make sure you are prepared and ready to go.

THE QUESTION-AND-ANSWER STAGE

Questions and answers usually consume the greatest part of the interview. Depending on the type of interview, the interviewer will likely ask about your qualifications, discuss some of the points mentioned in your résumé, and ask about how you have handled particular situations in the past or would handle them in the future. You'll also be asking questions of your own.

MOBILE APP
The **Monster** mobile app offers helpful tips to help you prepare for your next job interviews.

Answering and Asking Questions

Let the interviewer lead the conversation and never answer a question before he or she has finished asking it. Not only is this type of interruption rude, but the last few words of the question might alter how you respond. As much as possible, avoid one-word yes or no answers. Use the opportunity to expand on a positive response or explain a negative response. If you're asked a difficult question or the offbeat questions that companies such as Zappos and Google are known to use, pause before responding. Think through the implications of the question. For instance, the recruiter may know that you can't answer a question and only wants to know how you'll respond under pressure or whether you can construct a logical approach to solving a problem.

Listen carefully to questions before you answer.

Whenever you're asked if you have any questions, or whenever doing so naturally fits the flow of the conversation, ask a question from the list you've prepared. Probe for what the company is looking for in its new employees so that you can show how you meet the firm's needs. Also try to zero in on any reservations the interviewer might have about you so that you can dispel them.

REAL-TIME UPDATES
LEARN MORE BY LISTENING TO THIS PODCAST
Expert tips for successful phone interviews
Recruiting experts offer invaluable advice on nailing a phone interview. Go to **real-timeupdates.com/bct14** and select Learn More in the Students section.

Listening to the Interviewer

Paying attention when the interviewer speaks can be as important as giving good answers or asking good questions. Review the tips on listening offered in Chapter 2. The interviewer's facial expressions, eye movements, gestures, and posture may tell you the real meaning of what is being said. Be especially aware of how your answers are received. Does the interviewer nod in agreement or smile to show approval? If so, you're making progress. If not, you might want to introduce another topic or modify your approach.

Paying attention to both verbal and nonverbal messages can help you turn the question-and-answer stage to your advantage.

Handling Potentially Discriminatory Questions

Federal, state, and local laws prohibit employment discrimination based on a variety of factors, and well-trained interviewers know to avoid questions that could be used to discriminate in the hiring process.

A variety of federal, state, and local laws prohibit employment discrimination on the basis of race, ethnicity, gender, age (at least if you're between 40 and 70), marital status, religion, national origin, or disability. Interview questions designed to elicit information on these topics are potentially illegal.[43] Table 19.6 compares some specific questions that employers are and are not allowed to ask during an employment interview.

Think about how you might respond if you were asked a potentially unlawful question.

If an interviewer asks a potentially unlawful question, consider your options carefully before you respond. You can answer the question as it was asked, you can ask tactfully whether the question might be prohibited, you can simply refuse to answer it, or you can try to answer "the question behind the question."[44] For example, if an interviewer inappropriately asks whether you are married or have strong family ties in the area, he or she might be trying to figure out if you're willing to travel or relocate—both of which are acceptable questions. Only you can decide which is the right choice based on the situation.

Even if you do answer the question as it was asked, think hard before accepting a job offer from this company if you have alternatives. Was the off-limits question possibly accidental (it happens) and therefore not really a major concern? If you think it was intentional, would you want to work for an organization that condones illegal or discriminatory questions or that doesn't train its employees to avoid them?

If you believe an interviewer's questions to be unreasonable, unrelated to the job, or an attempt to discriminate, you have the option of filing a complaint with the U.S. Equal Employment Opportunity Commission or with the agency in your state that regulates fair employment practices.

THE CLOSE

Like the warm-up, the end of the interview is more important than its brief duration would indicate. These last few minutes are your final opportunity to emphasize your value to the organization and to correct any misconceptions the interviewer might have. Be aware that many interviewers will ask whether you have any more questions at this point, so save one or two from your list.

Concluding Gracefully

Conclude an interview with courtesy and enthusiasm.

You can usually tell when the interviewer is trying to conclude the session. He or she may ask whether you have any more questions, check the time, summarize the discussion, or simply tell you that the allotted time for the interview is up. When you get the signal, be sure to thank the interviewer for the opportunity and express your interest in the

TABLE 19.6 Acceptable Versus Potentially Discriminatory Interview Questions

Interviewers May Ask This . . .	But Not This
What is your name?	What was your maiden name?
Are you over 18?	When were you born?
Did you graduate from high school?	When did you graduate from high school?
[Questions about race are not allowed.]	What is your race?
Can you perform [specific tasks]?	Do you have physical or mental disabilities?
[Questions about alcohol use are not allowed.]	Do you drink alcoholic beverages?
Are you currently using illegal drugs?	Have you ever been addicted to drugs in the past?
Would you be able to meet the job's requirement to frequently work weekends?	Would working on weekends conflict with your religion?
Do you have the legal right to work in the United States?	What country are you a citizen of?
Have you ever been convicted of a felony?	Have you ever been arrested?
This job requires that you speak Spanish. Do you?	What language did you speak in your home when you were growing up?

Sources: Dave Johnson, "Illegal Job Interview Questions," *CBS Money Watch*, 27 February 2012, www.cbsnews.com; "5 Illegal Interview Questions and How to Dodge Them," *Forbes*, 20 April 2012, www.forbes.com; Vivian Giang, "11 Common Interview Questions That Are Actually Illegal," *Business Insider*, 5 July 2013, www .businessinsider.com.

organization. If you can do so comfortably, try to pin down what will happen next, but don't press for an immediate decision.

If this is your second or third visit to the organization, the interview may end with an offer of employment. If you have other offers or need time to think about this offer, it's perfectly acceptable to thank the interviewer for the offer and ask for some time to consider it. If no job offer is made, the interview team may not have reached a decision yet, but you may tactfully ask when you can expect to know the decision.

Discussing Salary

If you receive an offer during the interview, you'll naturally want to discuss salary. However, let the interviewer raise the subject. If asked your salary requirements during the interview or on a job application, you can say that your requirements are open or negotiable or that you would expect a competitive compensation package.[45]

How far you can negotiate depends on several factors, including market demand for your skills, the strength of the job market, the company's compensation policies, the company's financial health, and any other job offers you may be considering. Remember that you're negotiating a business deal, not asking for personal favors, so focus on the unique value you can bring to the job. The more information you have, the stronger your position will be.

If salary isn't negotiable, look at the overall compensation and benefits package. You may find flexibility in a signing bonus, profit sharing, retirement benefits, health coverage, vacation time, and other valuable elements.[46]

To review the important tips for successful interviews, see "Checklist: Making a Positive Impression in Job Interviews."

Research salary ranges in your job, industry, and geographic region before you try to negotiate salary.

Negotiating benefits may be one way to get more value from an employment package.

INTERVIEW NOTES

Maintain a notebook or simple database with information about each company, interviewers' answers to your questions, contact information for each interviewer, the status of follow-up communication, and upcoming interview appointments. Carefully organized notes will help you decide which company is the right fit for you when it comes time to choose from among the job offers you receive.

For the latest information on interviewing strategies, visit **real-timeupdates.com/bct14** and select Chapter 19.

Keeping a careful record of your job interviews is essential.

CHECKLIST ✔ Making a Positive Impression in Job Interviews

A. **Be ready to make a positive impression in the warm-up stage.**
- Be alert from the moment you arrive; even initial small talk is part of the interviewing process.
- Greet the interviewer by name, with a smile and direct eye contact.
- Offer a firm (not crushing) handshake if the interviewer extends a hand.
- Take a seat only after the interviewer invites you to sit or has taken his or her own seat.
- Listen for clues about what the interviewer is trying to get you to reveal about yourself and your qualifications.
- Exhibit positive body language, including standing up straight, walking with purpose, and sitting up straight.

B. **Convey your value to the organization during the question-and-answer stage.**
- Let the interviewer lead the conversation.
- Never answer a question before the interviewer finishes asking it.
- Listen carefully to the interviewer and watch for nonverbal signals.
- Don't limit yourself to simple yes or no answers; expand on the answer to show your knowledge of the company (but don't ramble on).
- If you encounter a potentially discriminatory question, decide how you want to respond before you say anything.
- When you have the opportunity, ask questions from the list you've prepared; remember that interviewers expect you to ask questions.

C. **Close on a strong note.**
- Watch and listen for signs that the interview is about to end.
- Quickly evaluate how well you've done and correct any misperceptions the interviewer might have.
- If you receive an offer and aren't ready to decide, it's entirely appropriate to ask for time to think about it.
- Don't bring up salary but be prepared to discuss it if the interviewer raises the subject.
- End with a warm smile and a handshake and thank the interviewer for meeting with you.

Following Up After the Interview

5 **LEARNING OBJECTIVE** Identify the most common employment messages that follow an interview and explain when you would use each one.

Staying in contact with a prospective employer after an interview shows that you really want the job and are determined to get it. Doing so also gives you another chance to demonstrate your communication skills and sense of business etiquette. Following up brings your name to the interviewer's attention once again and reminds him or her that you're actively looking and waiting for the decision.

Any time you hear from a company during the application or interview process, be sure to respond quickly. Companies flooded with résumés may move on to another candidate if they don't hear back from you within 24 hours.[47]

FOLLOW-UP MESSAGE

A follow-up message after an interview is more than a professional courtesy; it's another chance to promote yourself to an employer.

Send a follow-up message within two days of the interview, even if you feel you have little chance of getting the job. These messages are often referred to as "thank-you notes," but they give you an important opportunity to go beyond merely expressing your appreciation. You can use the message to reinforce the reasons you are a good choice for the position, modify any answers you gave during the interview if you realize you made a mistake or have changed your mind, and respond to any negatives that might have arisen in the interview (see Figure 19.6).[48] Email is usually acceptable for follow-up messages, unless the interviewer has asked you to use other media.

MESSAGE OF INQUIRY

Use the model for a direct request when you write an inquiry about a hiring decision.

If you're not advised of the interviewer's decision by the promised date or within two weeks, you might make an inquiry. A message of inquiry (which can be handled by email if the interviewer has given you his or her email address) is particularly appropriate if you've received a job offer from a second firm and don't want to accept it before you have an answer from the first. The following message illustrates the general model for a direct request:

> When we talked on April 7 about the fashion coordinator position in your Park Avenue showroom, you indicated that a decision would be made by May 1. I am still enthusiastic about the position and eager to know what conclusion you've reached.

◄— Identifies the position and introduces the main idea

> To complicate matters, another firm has now offered me a position and has asked that I reply within the next two weeks.

◄— Places the reason for the request second

> Because your company seems to offer a greater challenge, I would appreciate knowing about your decision by Thursday, May 12. If you need more information before then, please let me know.

◄— Makes a courteous request for specific action last, while clearly stating a preference for this organization

REQUEST FOR A TIME EXTENSION

If you receive a job offer while other interviews are still pending, you can ask the employer for a time extension. Open with a strong statement of your continued interest in the job, ask for more time to consider the offer, provide specific reasons for the request, and assure the reader that you will respond by a specific date (see Figure 19.7 on page 568).

LETTER OF ACCEPTANCE

Use the model for positive messages when you write a letter of acceptance.

When you receive a job offer you want to accept, reply within five days. Begin by accepting the position and expressing thanks. Identify the job you're accepting. In the next paragraph, cover any necessary details. Conclude by saying that you look forward to reporting for work. As always, a positive letter should convey your enthusiasm and eagerness to cooperate:

> I'm delighted to accept the graphic design position in your advertising department at the salary of $3,875 per month.

◄— Confirms the specific terms of the offer with a good-news statement at the beginning

Ineffective

Thanks! - Message (HTML)

MESSAGE   INSERT   OPTIONS   FORMAT TEXT   REVIEW

To... serena.reynolds@westcoasttv.com

Cc...

Subject   Thanks!

Dear Ms. Reynolds:

The talk, the tour, watching commercials being filmed—I had a great time interviewing with you yesterday! That was nice of you to take so much time to show me around.

You guys are doing so many cool things there, and your tour convinced me that I would really enjoy working on the various film and TV productions you do there.

Again, thank you for the chat. I really believe you and I hit it off and would make a great team. Please let me know your decision as soon as possible.

Sincerely,

Michael Espinosa
585 Montoya Road
Las Cruces, NM 88005
(505) 555-6208
espinosam@newm.com

(a) The subject line is too generic and doesn't give the reader any clues about the content of the message.

(b) The message oozes with enthusiasm but beyond that it doesn't really say anything to further the candidate's cause.

(c) The writer fails to use this opportunity to confirm his ability to perform the job.

(d) The tone here is too personal, and the closing line is too demanding.

Effective

thank you for yesterday's interview and tour - Message (HTML)

INSERT   OPTIONS   FORMAT TEXT   REVIEW

To... serena.reynolds@westcoasttv.com

Cc...

Subject   Thank you for yesterday's interview and tour

Dear Ms. Reynolds:

After talking with you yesterday, touring your sets, and watching commercials being filmed, I remain enthusiastic about the possibility of joining your staff as a production assistant. Thanks for taking so much time to show me around.

During our meeting, I said I would prefer not to relocate, but I've reconsidered the matter. I would be pleased to relocate wherever you might need my skills in set decoration and prop design.

Now that you've explained the details of your operation, I feel quite strongly that I can make a contribution to the sorts of productions you are lining up. You can also count on me to be an energetic employee and a positive addition to your crew. I look forward to hearing your decision.

Sincerely,

Michael Espinosa
585 Montoya Road
Las Cruces, NM 88005
(505) 555-6208

serena.reynolds@westcoasttv.com No Items

(a) The subject line lets the reader know what the message is about, which increases the chances she'll read it.

(b) The opening expresses appreciation and enthusiasm without overdoing it.

(c) Espinosa takes the opportunity to provide additional information—in this instance, reversing something he said in the interview.

(d) He uses the close to confirm his ability to do the job and to emphasize some positive personal characteristics.

Figure 19.6   Follow-Up Message
Use the follow-up message after an interview to express continued interest in the opportunity, to correct or expand on any information you provided in the interview, and to thank the interviewer for his or her time.

Enclosed are the health insurance forms you asked me to complete and sign. I've already given notice to my current employer and will be able to start work on Monday, January 18.

← Covers miscellaneous details in the body

The prospect of joining your firm is exciting. Thank you for giving me this opportunity, and I look forward to making a positive contribution.

← Closes with another reference to the good news and a look toward the future

Be aware that a job offer and a written acceptance of that offer can constitute a legally binding contract, for both you and the employer. Before you send an acceptance letter, be sure you want the job.

Written acceptance of a job offer can be considered a legally binding contract.

Ineffective

Request for extension - Message (HTML)

MESSAGE   INSERT   OPTIONS   FORMAT TEXT   REVIEW   DEVELOPER

To... frank.lapuzo@lonestarfoods.com
Cc...
Subject Request for extension

Dear Mr. Lapuzo:

I need more time to give you a decision about your offer of the e-commerce director position at Lone Star Foods. I am thrilled to get the offer, don't get me wrong, but I have another iron the fire, as they say.

To make a long story short, I had a follow-up interview with another company on my schedule before my interview with you. Although I am truly interested in your organization because of its commitment to quality and team-based management style, this other job bears looking into.

I am so sorry to hold you up, but you certainly understand my need to verify and compare this other opportunity. I'll let you know by January 25, possibly earlier if I can.

Sincerely,

(a) "I need" is a blunt and fairly offensive way to start any message, and particularly so when one is asking the reader to make an accommodation.

(b) "To make a long story short" only makes the story longer, and saying "this other job bears looking into" sounds self-centered.

(c) Apologizing isn't necessary under the circumstances, but the writer then commits a serious blunder by failing to ask for the extension to January 25.

Effective

Request for extension - Message (HTML)

MESSAGE   INSERT   OPTIONS   FORMAT TEXT   REVIEW   DEVELOPER

To... frank.lapuzo@lonestarfoods.com
Cc...
Subject Request for extension

Dear Mr. Lapuzo:

The e-commerce director position at Lone Star Foods is an exciting challenge, and I am thrilled that you offered me the position.

Because of another commitment, I would appreciate your giving me until January 25 to make a decision. Before our interview, I scheduled a follow-up interview with another company. I'm interested in your organization because of its commitment to quality and team-based management style, but I do feel obligated to keep my appointment.

If you need my decision immediately, I certainly understand. However, if you can allow me the added time to fulfill this earlier commitment, I would be grateful. Please let me know at your earliest convenience.

Sincerely,

Chang Li
1448 Solsbury Avenue
Thunderhawk, SD 57655
(605) 555-6897

(a) This positive opener confirms the writer's interest in the job and serves as buffer before the upcoming request.

(b) Phrasing this as the need to meet a prior commitment is a graceful way to communicate the idea of wanting to explore the other opportunity, without coming right out and saying so.

(c) The respectful close acknowledges that it might not be possible for the reader to accommodate the request for an extension. The conditional phrasing ("if you can") is a good way to make the request without coming across as demanding.

Figure 19.7   Request for a Time Extension
Needing more time to decide on a job offer is not uncommon, particularly for candidates with desirable credentials. However, make the request in a respectful and subtle way. The reader understands you are comparing opportunities and looking for the best offer, so you don't need to belabor this point.

LETTER DECLINING A JOB OFFER

If you decide to decline a job offer, do so tactfully, using the model for negative messages.

After all your interviews, you may find that you need to write a letter declining a job offer. Use the techniques for negative messages (see Chapter 11): Open warmly, state the reasons for refusing the offer, decline the offer explicitly, and close on a pleasant note that expresses gratitude. By taking the time to write a sincere, tactful letter, you leave the door open for future contact:

Thank you for your hospitality during my interview at your Durham facility last month. I'm flattered that you would offer me the computer analyst position that we talked about.

← Uses a buffer in the opening paragraph

I was fortunate to receive two job offers during my search. Because my desire to work abroad can more readily be satisfied by another company, I have accepted that job offer. ←— Precedes the bad news with tactfully phrased reasons for the applicant's unfavorable decision

I deeply appreciate the time you spent talking with me. Thank you again for your consideration and kindness. ←— Lets the reader down gently with a sincere and cordial ending

LETTER OF RESIGNATION

If you get a job offer while employed, you can maintain good relations with your current employer by writing a thoughtful letter of resignation to your immediate supervisor. Follow the advice for negative messages and make the letter sound positive, regardless of how you feel. Say something favorable about the organization, the people you work with, or what you've learned on the job. Then state your intention to leave and give the date of your last day on the job. Be sure you give your current employer at least two weeks' notice.

Letters of resignation should always be written in a gracious and professional style that avoids criticism of your employer or your colleagues.

My sincere thanks to you and to all the other Emblem Corporation employees for helping me learn so much about serving the public these past two years. You have given me untold help and encouragement. ←— Uses an appreciative opening to serve as a buffer

You may recall that when you first interviewed me, my goal was to become a customer relations supervisor. Because that opportunity has been offered to me by another organization, I am submitting my resignation. I will miss my friends and colleagues at Emblem, but I want to take advantage of this opportunity. ←— States reasons before the bad news itself, using tactful phrasing to help keep the relationship friendly, should the writer later want letters of recommendation

I would like to terminate my work here two weeks from today (June 13) but can arrange to work an additional week if you want me to train a replacement. ←— Discusses necessary details in an extra paragraph

My sincere thanks and best wishes to all of you. ←— Tempers any disappointment with a cordial close

To verify the content and style of your follow-up messages, consult the tips in "Checklist: Writing Follow-Up Messages."

CHECKLIST ✔ Writing Follow-Up Messages

A. Thank-you messages
- Write a brief thank-you letter within two days of the interview.
- Acknowledge the interviewer's time and courtesy.
- Restate the specific job you're applying for.
- Express your enthusiasm about the organization and the job.
- Add any new facts that may help your chances.
- Politely ask for a decision.

B. Messages of inquiry
- If you haven't heard from the interviewer by the promised date, write a brief message of inquiry.
- Use the direct approach: main idea, necessary details, specific request.

C. Requests for a time extension
- Request an extension if you have pending interviews and need time to decide about an offer.
- Open on a friendly note.
- Explain why you need more time and express continued interest in the company.
- In the close, promise a quick decision if your request is denied and ask for a confirmation if your request is granted.

D. Letters of acceptance
- Send this message within five days of receiving the offer.
- State clearly that you accept the offer, identify the job you're accepting, and confirm vital details such as salary and start date.
- Make sure you want the job; an acceptance letter can be treated as a legally binding contract.

E. Letters declining a job offer
- Use the indirect approach for negative messages.
- Open on a warm and appreciative note and then explain why you are refusing the offer.
- End on a sincere, positive note.

F. Letters of resignation
- Send a letter of resignation to your current employer as soon as possible.
- Begin with an appreciative buffer.
- In the middle section, state your reasons for leaving and actually state that you are resigning.
- Close cordially.

COMMUNICATION CHALLENGES AT **VMWare**

You work as a recruiter in the human resources department at VMWare, and the company is currently expanding its roster of customer support professionals. Use what you've learned about interviewing to address these challenges.

INDIVIDUAL CHALLENGE: Customer support employees can get hit with some off-the-wall questions and requests from time to time, and you want to make sure the people you hire can handle these questions with grace and tact. Come up with three fairly outlandish questions you could use during interviews to see how candidates react. You're not particularly interested in precise answers; you want to see how they handle the situation and how they go about solving odd challenges. For example, you might ask them to estimate how many mobile phone batteries will be thrown away in the next 10 years or to explain the concept of a human family to an alien from another planet.

TEAM CHALLENGE: Although VMWare operates in a highly technical industry, its customer support specialists need the same "soft" skills that every company must have to keep customers productive and happy. With your team, brainstorm the soft-skill attributes of an ideal customer service specialist, such as active listening and communicating with people who have different native languages. (Review Chapters 2 and 3 for ideas.) Next, write five interview questions that could help you judge how well candidates match this profile.

Quick Learning Guide

KEY TERMS

application letter Message that accompanies a résumé to let readers know what you're sending, why you're sending it, and how they can benefit from reading it

behavioral interview Interview in which you are asked to relate specific incidents and experiences from your past

employment interview Formal meeting during which a candidate and an employer ask questions and exchange information

group interview Interview in which one or more interviewers meet with several candidates simultaneously

open-ended interview Interview in which the interviewer adapts his or her line of questioning based on the answers given or questions asked by the interviewee

panel interview Interview in which the candidate meets with several interviewers at once

situational interview Similar to a behavioral interview, except the questions focus on how the candidate would handle various hypothetical situations on the job

stress interview Interview in which the candidate might be asked questions designed to unsettle him/her or is subjected to long periods of silence, criticism, interruptions, and/or hostile reactions by the interviewer

structured interview Interview in which the interviewer (or a computer) asks a series of prepared questions in a set order

working interview Interview in which the candidate performs a job-related activity

SUMMARY OF LEARNING OBJECTIVES

1 Explain the purposes of application letters, and describe how to apply the AIDA organizational approach to them. The purposes of an application letter are to introduce your résumé, persuade an employer to read it, and request an interview. With the AIDA model, get attention in the opening paragraph by showing how your work skills could benefit the organization, by explaining how your qualifications fit the job, or by demonstrating an understanding of the organization's needs. Build interest and desire by showing how you can meet the job requirements and, near the end of this section, be sure to refer your reader to your résumé. Finally, motivate action by making your request easy to fulfill and by including all necessary contact information.

2 Describe the typical sequence of job interviews, the major types of interviews, and the attributes employers look for during an interview. The typical sequence of interviews involves three stages. During the screening stage, employers filter out unqualified applicants and identify promising candidates. During the selection stage, the pool of applicants is narrowed through a variety of structured and unstructured interviewing methods. In the final stage, employers select the candidates who will receive offers and, if necessary, promote the benefits of joining the company.

Interviews can be distinguished by the way they are structured (structured or unstructured interviews), the number of people involved (one-on-one, panel, or group interviews), and the purpose of the interview (behavioral, situational, working, or stress interviews). The behavioral interview, probably the most common in terms of purpose, requires candidates to use their own experiences and attributes to craft answers. The situational interview is similar, but instead of using incidents from the candidate's past, it explores how the candidate would respond to hypothetical situations in the future. In a working interview, you are asked to perform job-related tasks. Stress interviews are designed to see how well you perform under stress.

Employers look for two things during an employment interview. First, they seek evidence that an applicant is qualified for the position. Second, they seek reassurance that an applicant will be a good fit with the "personality" of the organization and the position.

3 List six tasks you need to complete to prepare for a successful job interview. To prepare for a successful job interview, (1) complete the research you started when planning your résumé, (2) think ahead about questions you'll need to answer and questions you'll want to ask, (3) boost your confidence by focusing on your strengths and preparing thoroughly, (4) polish your interviewing style, (5) present a professional image with businesslike clothing and good grooming, and (6) arrive on time and ready to begin.

4 Explain how to succeed in all three stages of an interview. All employment interviews have three stages. The warm-up stage is the most important because first impressions greatly influence an interviewer's decision. Pay close attention to your body language and etiquette with everyone you encounter, and be ready to answer common openers such as "Tell me about yourself." The question-and-answer stage, during which you will answer and ask questions, is the longest. Be prepared to answer the common interview questions, and find ways to work in questions of your own that you have prepared. Listen carefully to every question, view each question as an opportunity to expand on the information presented in your résumé, and be prepared to handle difficult or potentially discriminatory questions. The close is your final opportunity to promote your value to the organization and counter any misconceptions the interviewer may have. End with a warm smile and a firm handshake to leave the interviewer with a positive impression.

5 Identify the most common employment messages that follow an interview and explain when you would use each one. Following an interview, send a thank-you message to show appreciation, emphasize your strengths, and politely ask for a decision. Send an inquiry if you haven't received the interviewer's decision by the date promised or within one or two weeks of the interview—especially if you've received a job offer from another firm. You can request a time extension if you need more time to consider an offer. Send a letter of acceptance after receiving a job offer you want to take. Send a letter declining a job offer when you want to refuse an offer tactfully. Finally, if you are currently employed, send a letter of resignation after you have accepted the offer of another job.

Test Your Knowledge

To review chapter content related to each question, refer to the indicated Learning Objective.

19-1. What two message elements can you use when writing a follow-up message after submitting a résumé? [LO-1]

19-2. How can you apply the AIDA model to an application letter? [LO-1]

19-3. What information or questions can you use when writing a follow-up message after submitting a résumé? [LO-1]

19-4. What should your objective be for an interview during the selection stage? [LO-2]

19-5. Why do many employers now use situational or behavioral interviews? [LO-2]

19-6. How does a structured interview differ from an open-ended interview? [LO-2]

19-7. What are the three stages of every interview, and which is the most important? [LO-4]

19-8. How should you respond if an interviewer at a company where you want to work asks you a question that seems too personal or unethical? [LO-4]

Apply Your Knowledge

To review chapter content related to each question, refer to the indicated Learning Objective.

19-9. If you lack one important qualification for a job but have made it past the initial screening stage, how should you prepare to handle this issue during the next round of interviews? Explain your answer. [LO-3]

19-10. What is an interviewer likely to conclude about you if you don't have any questions to ask during the interview? [LO-3]

19-11. Why is it important to distinguish unethical or illegal interview questions from acceptable questions? Explain. [LO-4]

19-12. What should you do if your mind goes blank after an interviewer asks you a question? [LO-4]

Practice Your Skills

Messages for Analysis

Read the following messages and then (1) analyze the strengths or weaknesses of each document and (2) revise each document so that it follows this chapter's guidelines.

19-13. **Message 19.A: Writing an Application Letter [LO-1]**

I'm writing to let you know about my availability for the brand manager job you advertised. As you can see from my enclosed résumé, my background is perfect for the position. Even though I don't have any real job experience, my grades have been outstanding, considering that I went to a top-ranked business school.

I did many things during my undergraduate years to prepare me for this job:

- Earned a 3.4 out of a 4.0, with a 3.8 in my business courses
- Elected representative to the student governing association
- Selected to receive the Lamar Franklin Award
- Worked to earn a portion of my tuition

I am sending my résumé to all the top firms, but I like yours better than any of the rest. Your reputation is tops in the industry, and I want to be associated with a business that can pridefully say it's the best.

If you wish for me to come in for an interview, I can come on a Friday afternoon or anytime on weekends when I don't have classes. Again, thanks for considering me for your brand manager position.

19-14. **Message 19.B: Writing Application Follow-Up Messages [LO-1]**

Did you receive my résumé? I sent it to you at least two months ago and haven't heard anything. I know you keep résumés on file, but I just want to be sure that you keep me in mind. I heard you are hiring health-care managers and certainly would like to be considered for one of those positions.

Since I last wrote you, I've worked in a variety of positions that have helped prepare me for management. To wit, I've become lunch manager at the restaurant where I work, which involved a raise in pay. I now manage a waitstaff of 12 girls and take the lunch receipts to the bank every day.

Of course, I'd much rather be working at a real job, and that's why I'm writing again. Is there anything else you would like to know about me or my background? I would really like to know more about your company. Is there any literature you could send me? If so, I would really appreciate it.

I think one reason I haven't been hired yet is that I don't want to leave Atlanta. So I hope when you think of me, it's for a position that wouldn't require moving. Thanks again for considering my application.

19-15. **Message 19.C: Thank-You Message [LO-5]**

Thank you for the really marvelous opportunity to meet you and your colleagues at Starret Engine Company. I really enjoyed touring your facilities and talking with all the people there. You have quite a crew! Some of the other companies I have visited have been so rigid and uptight that I can't imagine how I would fit in. It's a relief to run into a group of people who seem to enjoy their work as much as all of you do.

I know that you must be looking at many other candidates for this job, and I know that some of them will probably be more experienced than I am. But I do want to emphasize that my two-year hitch in the Navy involved a good deal of engineering work. I don't think I mentioned all my shipboard responsibilities during the interview.

Please give me a call within the next week to let me know your decision. You can usually find me at my dormitory in the evening after dinner (phone: 877-9080).

19-16. Message 19.D: Letter of Inquiry [LO-5]

I have recently received a very attractive job offer from the Warrington Company. But before I let them know one way or another, I would like to consider any offer that your firm may extend. I was quite impressed with your company during my recent interview, and I am still very interested in a career there.

I don't mean to pressure you, but Warrington has asked for my decision within 10 days. Could you let me know by Tuesday whether you plan to offer me a position? That would give me enough time to compare the two offers.

19-17. Message 19.E: Letter Declining a Job Offer [LO-5]

I'm writing to say that I must decline your job offer. Another company has made me a more generous offer, and I have decided to accept. However, if things don't work out for me there, I will let you know. I sincerely appreciate your interest in me.

Exercises

Each activity is labeled according to the primary skill or skills you will need to use. To review relevant chapter content, you can refer to the indicated Learning Objective. In some instances, supporting information will be found in another chapter, as indicated.

19-18. Career Management: Preparing for Interviews [LO-3] Google yourself, Bing yourself, scour your social networking profiles, review your Twitter messages, and explore every other possible online source you can think of that might have something about you. If you find anything potentially embarrassing, remove it if possible. Write a summary of your search-and-destroy mission (you can skip any embarrassing details in your report to your instructor!).

Career Management: Researching Target Employers [LO-3] Select a medium-sized or large company (one that you can easily find information on) where you might like to work. Use online sources to gather some preliminary research on the company; don't limit your search to the company's own website.

19-19. What did you learn about this organization that would help you during an interview there?

19-20. What online sources did you use to obtain this information?

19-21. Armed with this information, what aspects of your background do you think might appeal to this company's recruiters?

19-22. Based on what you've learned about this company's culture, what aspects of your personality should you try to highlight during an interview?

19-23. Career Management: Interviewing; Collaboration: Team Projects [LO-4], Chapter 2 Divide the class into two groups. Half the class will be recruiters for a large chain of national department stores, looking to fill manager trainee positions (there are 16 openings). The other half of the class will be candidates for the jobs. The company is specifically looking for candidates who demonstrate these three qualities: initiative, dependability, and willingness to assume responsibility.

- Have each recruiter select and interview an applicant for 10 minutes.
- Have all the recruiters discuss how they assessed the applicant in each of the three desired qualities. What questions did they ask or what did they use as an indicator to determine whether the candidate possessed the quality?
- Have all the applicants discuss what they said to convince the recruiters that they possessed each of these qualities.

19-24. Career Management: Interviewing [LO-3] Write a short email to your instructor, discussing what you believe are your greatest strengths and weaknesses from an employment perspective. Next, explain how these strengths and weaknesses would be viewed by interviewers evaluating your qualifications.

19-25. Career Management: Interviewing [LO-3] Prepare written answers to 10 of the questions listed in Table 19.3.

Message Strategies: Employment Messages, Communication Ethics: Resolving Ethical Dilemmas [LO-5], Chapter 1 You have decided to accept a new position with a competitor of your company. Write a letter of resignation to your supervisor, announcing your decision.

19-26. Will you notify your employer that you are joining a competing firm? Explain.

19-27. Will you use the direct or the indirect approach? Explain.

19-28. Will you send your letter by email, send it by regular mail, or place it on your supervisor's desk?

Expand Your Skills

Critique the Professionals

Find an online video of a business professional being interviewed by a journalist. Using whatever medium your instructor requests, write a brief assessment (no more than one page) of the professional's performance and any tips that you picked up that could you use in job interviews.

Sharpen Your Career Skills Online

Bovée and Thill's Business Communication Web Search, at **websearch.businesscommunicationnetwork.com**, is a unique research tool designed specifically for business communication research. Use the Web Search function to find a website, video, article, podcast, or presentation that offers advice on successful interviewing techniques. Write a brief email message to your instructor or a post for your class blog describing the item that you found and summarizing the career skills information you learned from it.

Cases

For all cases, feel free to use your creativity to make up any details you need in order to craft effective messages.

Application Messages

VIDEO SKILLS

19-29. Media Skills: Video; Message Strategies: Employment Messages [LO-1], Chapter 9 With its encouragement of video applications and abandonment of traditional job postings, Zappos might be starting a mini-trend toward a new style of employment application.

Your task: Identify a company where you would like to work and assume that it encourages candidates to submit video introductions. Plan, record, and produce a short video (no longer than three minutes) that you might submit to this employer. Don't worry too much about fancy production quality, but make sure your content and presentation match the company's style and brand image.

EMAIL SKILLS

19-30. Message Strategies: Employment Messages [LO-1] Use one of the websites listed in Table 18.1 on page 517 to find a job opening in your target profession. If you haven't narrowed down to one career field yet, choose a business job for which you will have at least some qualifications at the time of your graduation.

Your task: Write an email message that would serve as your application letter if you were to apply for this job. Base your message on your actual qualifications for the position, and be sure to "echo" the requirements listed in the job description. Include the job description in your email message when you submit it to your instructor.

MICROBLOGGING SKILLS

19-31. Message Strategies: Employment Messages [LO-1] If you want to know whether job candidates can express themselves clearly on Twitter, why not test them as part of the application process? That's exactly what the Minneapolis advertising agency Campbell Mithun does. Rather than having them using conventional application methods, the company asks intern candidates to tweet their applications in 13 messages.[49]

Your task: Find a job opening on Twitter by searching on any of the following hashtags: #hiring, #joblisting, or #nowhiring.[50] Next, write an "application letter" composed of 13 individual tweets. If your class is set up with private Twitter accounts, go ahead and send the tweets. Otherwise, email them to your instructor or post them on your class blog, as your instructor indicates.

EMAIL SKILLS

19-32. Message Strategies: Employment Messages [LO-1] Finding job openings that align perfectly with your professional interests is wonderful, but it doesn't always happen. Sometimes you have to widen your search and go after whatever opportunities happen to be available. Even when the opportunity is not ideal, however, you still need to approach the employer with enthusiasm and a focused, audience-centric message.

Your task: Find a job opening for which you will be qualified when you graduate (or close to being qualified, for the purposes of this activity), but make it one that is outside your primary field of interest. Write an email application letter for this opening, making a compelling case that you are the right candidate for this job.

Interviewing

BLOGGING SKILLS/TEAM SKILLS

19-33. Career Management: Researching Target Employers [LO-3] Research is a critical element of the job-search process. With information in hand, you increase the chance of finding the right opportunity (and avoiding bad choices), and you impress interviewers in multiple ways by demonstrating initiative, curiosity, research and analysis skills, an appreciation for the complex challenges of running a business, and willingness to work to achieve results.

Your task: With a small team of classmates, use online job listings to identify an intriguing job opening that at least one member of the team would seriously consider pursuing as graduation approaches. (You'll find it helpful if the career is related to at least one team member's college major or on-the-job experience so that the team can benefit from some knowledge of the profession in question.) Next, research the company, its competitors, its markets, and this specific position to identify five questions that would (1) help the team member decide whether this is a good opportunity and (2) show an interviewer that you've really done your homework. Go beyond the basic and obvious questions to identify current, specific, and complex issues that only deep research can uncover. For example, is the company facing significant technical, financial, legal, or regulatory challenges that threaten its ability to grow or perhaps even survive in the long term? Or is the market evolving in a way that positions this particular company for dramatic growth? In a post for your class blog, list your five questions, identify how you uncovered the issue, and explain why each is significant.

TEAM SKILLS

19-34. Career Management: Interviewing [LO-4] Interviewing is a skill that can be improved through observation and practice.

Your task: You and all other members of your class are to write letters of application for an entry-level or management-trainee position that requires an engaging personality and intelligence but a minimum of specialized education or experience. Sign your letter with a fictitious name that conceals your identity. Next, polish (or create) a résumé that accurately identifies you and your educational and professional accomplishments.

Now, three members of the class who volunteer as interviewers divide up all the anonymously written application letters. Then each interviewer selects a candidate who seems the most convincing in his or her letter. At this time, the selected candidates identify themselves and give the interviewers their résumés.

Each interviewer then interviews his or her chosen candidate in front of the class, seeking to understand how the items on the résumé qualify the candidate for the job. At the end of the interviews, the class decides who gets the job and discusses why this candidate was successful. Afterward, retrieve your letter, sign it with the right name, and submit it to the instructor for credit.

TEAM SKILLS

19-35. Career Management: Interviewing [LO-4] Select a company in an industry in which you might like to work and then identify an interesting position within the company. Study the company and prepare for an interview with that company.

Your task: Working with a classmate, take turns interviewing each other for your chosen positions. Interviewers should take notes during the interview. When the interview is complete, critique each other's performance. (Interviewers should critique how well candidates prepared for the interview and answered the questions; interviewees should critique the quality of the questions asked.) Write a follow-up letter thanking your interviewer and submit the letter to your instructor.

Following up After an Interview

LETTER-WRITING SKILLS

19-36. Message Strategies: Employment Messages [LO-5] Because of a mix-up in your job application scheduling, you accidentally applied for your third-choice job before going after the one you really wanted. What you want to do is work in retail marketing with the upscale department store Neiman Marcus in Dallas; what you have been offered is a job with Longhorn Leather and Lumber, 65 miles away in the small town of Commerce, Texas.

You review your notes. Your Longhorn interview was three weeks ago with the human resources manager, R. P. Bronson, who has just written to offer you the position. The store's address is 27 Sam Rayburn Drive, Commerce, TX 75428. Mr. Bronson notes that he can hold the position open for 10 days. You have an interview scheduled with Neiman Marcus next week, but it is unlikely that you will know the store's decision within this 10-day period.

Your task: Write to Mr. Bronson, requesting a reasonable delay in your consideration of his job offer.

LETTER-WRITING SKILLS/EMAIL SKILLS

19-37. Message Strategies: Employment Messages [LO-5] Fortunately for you, your interview with Neiman Marcus (see the previous case) went well, and you've just received a job offer from the company.

Your task: Write a letter to R. P. Bronson at Longhorn Leather and Lumber declining his job offer, and write an email message to Clarissa Bartle at Neiman Marcus accepting her job offer. Make up any information you need when accepting the Neiman Marcus offer.

LETTER-WRITING SKILLS

19-38. Message Strategies: Employment Messages (Letters of Resignation) [LO-5] Leaving a job is rarely stress free, but it's particularly difficult when you are parting ways with a mentor who played an important role in advancing your career. A half-dozen years into your career, you have benefited greatly from the advice, encouragement, and professional connections offered by your mentor, who also happens to be your current boss. She seemed to believe in your potential from the beginning and went out of her way on numerous occasions to help you. You returned the favor by becoming a stellar employee who has made important contributions to the success of the department your boss leads.

Unfortunately, you find yourself at a career impasse. You believe you are ready to move into a management position, but your company is not growing enough to create many opportunities. Worse yet, you joined the firm during a period of rapid expansion, so there are many eager and qualified internal candidates at your career level interested in the few managerial jobs that do become available. You fear it may be years before you get the chance to move up in the company. Through your online networking activities, you found an opportunity with a firm in another industry and have decided to pursue it.

Your task: You have a close relationship with your boss, so you will announce your intention to leave the company in a private, one-on-one conversation. However, you also recognize the need to write a formal letter of resignation, which you will hand to your boss during this meeting. This letter is addressed to your boss, but as formal business correspondence that will become part of your personnel file, it should not be a "personal" letter. Making up whatever details you need, write a brief letter of resignation.

MyBCommLab

Go to **mybcommlab.com** for Auto-graded writing questions as well as the following Assisted-graded writing questions:

19-39.   How should your application letter work in conjunction with your résumé? [LO-1]

19-40.   How can you prepare for a situational or behavioral interview if you have no experience with the job for which you are interviewing? [LO-2]

Endnotes

1. Ladan Nikravan, "Socially Exceptional Recruiting," *Talent Management*, 6 March 2015, www.talentmgt.com; VMWare website, accessed 9 May 2016, www.vmware.com; VMWare Careers profile on LinkedIn, accessed 9 May 2016, www.linkedin.com/company/vmware/careers; VMWare University Twitter account, accessed 9 May 2016, twitter.com/vmwareu; VMWare Community portal, accessed 9 May 2016, communities.vmware.com; James Molloy profile on LinkedIn, accessed 9 May 2016, www.linkedin.com/in/jmolloy.

2. Matthew Rothenberg, "Manuscript vs. Machine," Ladders, 15 December 2009, www.theladders.com; Joann Lublin, "Cover Letters Get You in the Door, So Be Sure Not to Dash Them Off," *Wall Street Journal*, 6 April 2004, B1.

3. Lisa Vaas, "How to Write a Great Cover Letter," Ladders, 20 November 2009, www.theladders.com.

4. Allison Doyle, "Introduction to Cover Letters," About.com, accessed 13 August 2010, jobsearch.about.com.

5. Alison Green, "Are You Making These 8 Mistakes on Your Cover Letter?" *U.S. News & World Report*, 18 July 2012, money.usnews.com; Doyle, "Introduction to Cover Letters"; Vaas, "How to Write a Great Cover Letter"; Toni Logan, "The Perfect Cover Story," *Kinko's Impress* 2 (2000): 32, 34.

6. Lisa Vaas, "How to Follow Up a Résumé Submission," Ladders, 9 August 2010, www.theladders.com.

7. Alison Doyle, "How to Follow Up After Submitting a Resume," About.com, accessed 13 August 2010, jobsearch.about.com; Vaas, "How to Follow Up a Résumé Submission."

8. Anne Fisher, "How to Get Hired by a 'Best' Company," *Fortune*, 4 February 2008, 96.

9. Fisher, "How to Get Hired by a 'Best' Company."

10. Sarah E. Needleman, "Speed Interviewing Grows as Skills Shortage Looms; Strategy May Help Lock in Top Picks; Some Drawbacks," *Wall Street Journal*, 6 November 2007, B15.

11. Scott Beagrie, "How to Handle a Telephone Job Interview," *Personnel Today*, 26 June 2007, 29.

12. John Olmstead, "Predict Future Success with Structured Interviews," *Nursing Management*, March 2007, 52–53.

13. Fisher, "How to Get Hired by a 'Best' Company," 96.

14. Erinn R. Johnson, "Pressure Sessions," *Black Enterprise*, October 2007, 72.

15. "What's a Group Interview?" About.com Tech Careers, accessed 5 April 2008, jobsearchtech.about.com.

16. Fisher, "How to Get Hired by a 'Best' Company."

17. Katherine Hansen, "Behavioral Job Interviewing Strategies for Job-Seekers," QuintCareers.com, accessed 13 August 2010, www.quintcareers.com.

18. Hansen, "Behavioral Job Interviewing Strategies for Job-Seekers."

19. Chris Pentilla, "Testing the Waters," *Entrepreneur*, January 2004, www.entrepreneur.com; Terry McKenna, "Behavior-Based Interviewing," *National Petroleum News*, January 2004, 16; Nancy K. Austin, "Goodbye Gimmicks," *Incentive*, May 1996, 241.

20. William Poundstone, "Beware the Interview Inquisition," *Harvard Business Review*, May 2003, 18.

21. Peter Vogt, "Mastering the Phone Interview," Monster.com, accessed 13 December 2006, www.monster.com; Nina Segal, "The Global Interview: Tips for Successful, Unconventional Interview Techniques," Monster.com, accessed 13 December 2006, www.monster.com.

22. Segal, "The Global Interview."

23. Barbara Kiviat, "How Skype Is Changing the Job Interview," *Time*, 20 October 2009, accessed 13 August 2010, www.time.com.

24. HireVue website, accessed 4 April 2008, www.hirevue.com; in2View website, accessed 4 April 2008, www.in2view.biz; Victoria Reitz, "Interview Without Leaving Home," *Machine Design*, 1 April 2004, 66.

25. Gina Ruiz, "Job Candidate Assessment Tests Go Virtual," *Workforce Management*, January 2008, www.workforce.com; Connie Winkler, "Job Tryouts Go Virtual," *HR Magazine*, September 2006, 131–134.

26. U.S. Equal Employment Opportunity Commission, "Employment Test and Selection Procedures," EEOC website, accessed 24 July 2012, www.eeoc.gov; Jonathan Katz, "Rethinking Drug Testing," *Industry Week*, March 2010, 16–18; Ashley Shadday, "Assessments 101: An Introduction to Candidate Testing," *Workforce Management*, January 2010, www.workforce.com; Dino di Mattia, "Testing Methods and Effectiveness of Tests," *Supervision*, August 2005, 4–5; David W. Arnold and John W. Jones, "Who the Devil's Applying Now?" *Security Management*, March 2002, 85–88; Matthew J. Heller, "Digging Deeper," *Workforce Management*, 3 March 2008, 35–39.

27. Frederick P. Morgeson, Michael A. Campion, Robert L. Dipboye, John R. Hollenbeck, Kevin Murphy, and Neil Schmitt, "Are We Getting Fooled Again? Coming to Terms with Limitations in the Use of Personality Tests in Personnel Selection," *Personnel Psychology* 60, no. 4 (Winter 2007): 1029–1049.

28. Austin, "Goodbye Gimmicks."

29. Hannah Morgan, "The Ultimate Interview Prep Checklist," *U.S. News & World Report*, 23 April 2014, money.usnews.com.

30. Rachel Zupek, "How to Answer 10 Tough Interview Questions," CNN.com, 4 March 2009, www.cnn.com; Barbara Safani, "How to Answer Tough Interview Questions Authentically," Ladders, 5 December 2009, www.theladders.com.

31. Nick Corcodilos, "How to Answer a Misguided Interview Question," *Seattle Times*, 30 March 2008, www.seattletimes.com.

32. Katherine Spencer Lee, "Tackling Tough Interview Questions," *Certification Magazine*, May 2005, 35.

33. Scott Ginsberg, "10 Good Ways to 'Tell Me About Yourself,'" Ladders, 26 June 2010, www.theladders.com.

34. Richard A. Moran, "The Number One Interview Trap Question," *Business Insider*, 23 April 2014, www.businessinsider.com.

35. Joe Turner, "An Interview Strategy: Telling Stories," Yahoo! HotJobs website, accessed 5 April 2008, hotjobs.yahoo.com.

36. "A Word of Caution for Chatty Job Candidates," *Public Relations Tactics*, January 2008, 4.

37. Randall S. Hansen, "When Job-Hunting: Dress for Success," QuintCareers.com, accessed 5 April 2008, www.quintcareers.com; Alison Doyle, "Dressing for Success," About.com, accessed 5 April 2008, jobsearch.about.com.

38. William S. Frank, "Job Interview: Pre-Flight Checklist," *Career Advisor*, accessed 28 September 2005, careerplanning.about.com.

39. "Employers Reveal Outrageous and Common Mistakes Candidates Made in Job Interviews, According to New CareerBuilder Survey," CareerBuilder.com, accessed 24 March 2011, www.careerbuilder.com.

40. Alison Green, "10 Surefire Ways to Annoy a Hiring Manager," *U.S. News & World Report*, accessed 24 July 2012, money.usnews.com.

41. T. Shawn Taylor, "Most Managers Have No Idea How to Hire the Right Person for the Job," *Chicago Tribune*, 23 July 2002, www.ebsco.com.

42. "10 Minutes to Impress," *Journal of Accountancy*, July 2007, 13.

43. Steven Mitchell Sack, "The Working Woman's Legal Survival Guide: Testing," FindLaw.com, accessed 22 February 2004, www.findlaw.com.

44. Todd Anten, "How to Handle Illegal Interview Questions," Yahoo! HotJobs website, accessed 7 August 2009, hotjobs .yahoo.com.

45. "Negotiating Salary: An Introduction," *InformationWeek*, accessed 22 February 2004, www.informationweek.com.

46. "Negotiating Salary."

47. Lisa Vaas, "Resume, Meet Technology: Making Your Resume Format Machine-Friendly," Ladders, accessed 13 August 2010, www.theladders.com.

48. Alison Green, "How a Thank-You Note Can Boost Your Job Chances," *U.S. News & World Report*, 27 June 2012, money.usnews .com; Joan S. Lublin, "Notes to Interviewers Should Go Beyond a Simple Thank You," *Wall Street Journal*, 5 February 2008, B1.

49. Tiffany Hsu, "Extreme Interviewing: Odd Quizzes, Weird Mixers, Improve Pitches. Can You Get Past the Hiring Gatekeepers?" *Los Angeles Times*, 19 February 2012, B1.

50. From Ritika Trikha, "The Best Tips for Tweeting Your Way to a Job," *U.S. News & World Report*, 24 July 2012, money.usnews.com.

The format and layout of business documents vary from country to country. In addition, many organizations develop their own variations of standard styles, adapting documents to the types of messages they send and the kinds of audiences they communicate with. The formats described here are the most common approaches used in U.S. business correspondence, but be sure to follow whatever practices are expected at your company.

First Impressions

Your documents tell readers a lot about you and about your company's professionalism. So all your documents must look neat, present a professional image, and be easy to read. Your audience's first impression of a document comes from the quality of its paper, the way it is customized, and its general appearance.

PAPER

To give a quality impression, businesspeople consider carefully the paper they use. Several aspects of paper contribute to the overall impression:

- **Weight.** Paper quality is judged by the weight of four reams (each a 500-sheet package) of letter-size paper. The weight most commonly used by U.S. business organizations is 20-pound paper, but 16- and 24-pound versions are also used.
- **Cotton content.** Paper quality is also judged by the percentage of cotton in the paper. Cotton doesn't yellow over time the way wood pulp does, plus it's both strong and soft. For letters and outside reports, use paper with a 25 percent cotton content. For memos and other internal documents, you can use a lighter-weight paper with lower cotton content. Airmail-weight paper may save money for international correspondence, but make sure it isn't too flimsy.[1]
- **Size.** In the United States, the standard paper size for business documents is 8½ by 11 inches. Standard legal documents are 8½ by 14 inches. Executives sometimes have heavier 7-by-10-inch paper on hand (with matching envelopes) for personal messages such as congratulations.[2] They may also have a box of note cards imprinted with their initials and a box of plain folded notes for condolences or for acknowledging formal invitations.

- **Color.** White is the standard color for business purposes, although neutral colors such as gray and ivory are sometimes used. Memos can be produced on pastel-colored paper to distinguish them from external correspondence. In addition, memos are sometimes produced on various colors of paper for routing to separate departments. Light-colored papers are appropriate, but bright or dark colors make reading difficult and may seem too frivolous.

CUSTOMIZATION

For letters to outsiders, U.S. businesses commonly use letterhead stationery, which may be either professionally printed or designed in-house using word-processing templates and graphics. Letterhead typically contains the company name, logo, address, telephone and fax numbers, general email address, website URL, and possibly one or more social media URLs.

In the United States, businesses always use letterhead for the first page of a letter. Successive pages are usually plain sheets of paper that match the letterhead in color and quality. Some companies use a specially printed second-page letterhead that bears only the company's name.

APPEARANCE

Nearly all business documents are produced using an inkjet or laser printer; make sure to use a clean, high-quality printer. Certain documents, however, should be handwritten (such as a short informal memo or a note of condolence). Be sure to handwrite, print, or type the envelope to match the document. However, even a letter on the best-quality paper with the best-designed letterhead may look unprofessional if it's poorly produced. So pay close attention to all the factors affecting appearance, including the following:

- **Margins.** Business letters typically use 1-inch margins at the top, bottom, and sides of the page, although these parameters are sometimes adjusted to accommodate letterhead elements.
- **Justification.** For all routine business documents, all lines (body text and headings) should be left-justified.
- **Character spacing.** Use proper spacing between characters and after punctuation. For example, U.S. conventions include leaving one space after commas, semicolons, colons, and sentence-ending periods. Each letter in a person's initials is followed by a period and a

single space. However, abbreviations such as U.S.A. or MBA may or may not have periods, but they never have internal spaces.

- **Special symbols.** Take advantage of the many special symbols available with your computer's selection of fonts. In addition, see whether your company has a style guide for documents, which may include particular symbols you are expected to use.
- **Corrections.** Messy corrections are unacceptable in business documents. If you notice an error after printing a document with your word processor, correct the mistake and reprint. (With informal memos to members of your own team or department, the occasional small correction in pen or pencil is acceptable, but never in formal documents.)

Letters

All business letters have certain elements in common. Several of these elements appear in every letter; others appear only when desirable or appropriate. In addition, these letter parts are usually arranged in one of three basic formats.

STANDARD LETTER PARTS

The letter in Figure A.1 shows the placement of standard letter parts. The writer of this business letter had no letterhead available but correctly included a heading. All business letters typically include these seven elements.

Heading

The elements of the letterhead make up the heading of a letter in most cases. If letterhead stationery is not available, the heading includes a return address (but no name) and starts 13 lines from the top of the page, which leaves a 2-inch top margin.

Date

If you're using letterhead, place the date at least one blank line beneath the lowest part of the letterhead. Without letterhead, place the date immediately below the return address. The standard method of writing the date in the United States uses the full name of the month (no abbreviations), followed by the day (in numerals, without *st*, *nd*, *rd*, or *th*), a comma, and then the year: July 31, 2018 (7/31/2018). Many

Figure A.1 **Standard Letter Parts**

TABLE A.1   Common Date Forms

Convention	Order	Examples
U.S. standard	Month day year	July 31, 2018
		7/31/2018
		7-31-2018
Japan	Year month day	18/07/31
Europe (most countries)	Day month year	31 July 2018
		31/07/18
		31.07.18
International (ISO) format	Year month day	2018-07-31

other countries use other formats (see Table A.1), which can create confusion in international correspondence. To avoid misinterpretation in such cases, spell out the month.[3]

Inside Address

The inside address identifies the recipient of the letter. For U.S. correspondence, begin the inside address at least one line below the date. Precede the addressee's name with a courtesy title, such as *Dr., Mr.,* or *Ms.* The accepted courtesy title for women in business is *Ms.,* although a woman known to prefer the title *Miss* or *Mrs.* is always accommodated. If you don't know whether a person is a man or a woman (and you have no way of finding out), omit the courtesy title. For example, *Terry Smith* could be either a man or a woman. The first line of the inside address would be just *Terry Smith,* and the salutation would be *Dear Terry Smith.* The same is true if you know only a person's initials, as in *S. J. Adams.*

Spell out and capitalize titles that precede a person's name, such as *Professor* or *General* (see Table A.2 on the next page for the proper forms of address). The person's organizational title, such as *Director,* may be included on this first line (if it is short) or on the line below; the name of a department may follow. In addresses and signature lines, don't forget to capitalize any professional title that follows a person's name:

Mr. Ray Johnson, Dean

Ms. Patricia T. Higgins
Assistant Vice President

However, professional titles not appearing in an address or signature line are capitalized only when they directly precede the name:

President Kenneth Johanson will deliver the speech.

Maria Morales, president of ABC Enterprises, will deliver the speech.

The Honorable Helen Masters, senator from Arizona, will deliver the speech.

If the name of a specific person is unavailable, you may address the letter to the department or to a specific position within the department. Also, be sure to spell out company names in full, unless the company itself uses abbreviations in its official name.

Other address information includes the treatment of buildings, house numbers, and compass directions (see Table A.3 on the next page). The following example shows all the information that may be included in the inside address and its proper order for U.S. correspondence:

Ms. Linda Coolidge, Vice President
Corporate Planning Department
Midwest Airlines
Kowalski Building, Suite 21-A
7279 Bristol Ave.
Toledo, OH 43617

Canadian addresses are similar, except that the name of the province is usually spelled out:

Dr. H. C. Armstrong
Research and Development
Commonwealth Mining Consortium
The Chelton Building, Suite 301
585 Second St. SW
Calgary, Alberta T2P 2P5

The order and layout of address information vary from country to country. So when addressing correspondence for other countries, carefully follow the format and information that appear in the company's letterhead. However, when you're sending mail from the United States, be sure that the name of the destination country appears on the last line of the address in capital letters. Use the English version of the country name so that your mail is routed from the United States to the right country. Then, to be sure your mail is routed correctly within the destination country, use the foreign spelling of the city name (using the characters and diacritical marks that would be commonly used in the region). For example, the following address uses *Köln* instead of *Cologne:*

H. R. Veith, Director	Addressee
Eisfieren Glaswerk	Company name
Blaubachstrasse 13	Street address
Postfach 10 80 07	Post office
D-5000 Köln I	District, city
GERMANY	Country

TABLE A.2   Forms of Address

Person	In Address	In Salutation
Personal Titles		
Man	Mr. [first & last name]	Dear Mr. [last name]:
Woman*	Ms. [first & last name]	Dear Ms. [last name]:
Two men (or more)	Mr. [first & last name] and Mr. [first & last name]	Dear Mr. [last name] and Mr. [last name] *or* Messrs. [last name] and [last name]:
Two women (or more)	Ms. [first & last name] and Ms. [first & last name]	Dear Ms. [last name] and Ms. [last name] *or* Mses. [last name] and [last name]:
One woman and one man	Ms. [first & last name] and Mr. [first & last name]	Dear Ms. [last name] and Mr. [last name]:
Couple (married with same last name)	Mr. [husband's first name] and Mrs. [wife's first name] [couple's last name]	Dear Mr. and Mrs. [last name]:
Couple (married with different last names)	Mr. [first & last name of husband] Ms. [first & last name of wife]	Dear Mr. [husband's last name] and Ms. [wife's last name]:
Couple (married professionals with same title and same last name)	[title in plural form] [husband's first name] and [wife's first name] [couple's last name]	Dear [title in plural form] [last name]:
Couple (married professionals with different titles and same last name)	[title] [first & last name of husband] and [title] [first & last name of wife]	Dear [title] and [title] [last name]:
Professional Titles		
President of a college or university	[title] [first & last name], President	Dear President [last name]:
Dean of a school or college	Dean [first & last name] *or* Dr., Mr., or Ms. [first & last name], Dean of [title]	Dear Dean [last name]: *or* Dear Dr., Mr., *or* Ms. [last name]:
Professor	Professor *or* Dr. [first & last name]	Dear Professor *or* Dr. [last name]:
Physician	[first & last name], M.D.	Dear Dr. [last name]:
Lawyer	Mr. *or* Ms. [first & last name], Attorney at Law	Dear Mr. *or* Ms. [last name]:
Military personnel	[full rank, first & last name, abbreviation of service designation] (add *Retired* if applicable)	Dear [rank] [last name]:
Company or corporation	[name of organization]	Ladies and Gentlemen: *or* Gentlemen and Ladies:
Governmental Titles		
President of the United States	The President	Dear Mr. *or* Madam President:
Senator of the United States	The Honorable [first & last name]	Dear Senator [last name]:
Cabinet member	The Honorable [first & last name]	Dear Mr. *or* Madam Secretary:
Attorney General	The Honorable [first & last name]	Dear Mr. *or* Madam Attorney General:
Mayor	The Honorable [first & last name], Mayor of [name of city]	Dear Mayor [last name]:
Judge	The Honorable [first & last name]	Dear Judge [last name]:

*Use *Mrs.* or *Miss* only if the recipient has specifically requested that you use one of these titles; otherwise *always* use *Ms.* in business correspondence. Also, never refer to a married woman by her husband's name (for example, Mrs. Robert Washington) unless she specifically requests that you do so.

TABLE A.3   Inside Address Information

Description	Example
Capitalize building names.	Empire State Building
Capitalize locations within buildings (apartments, suites, rooms).	Suite 1073
Use numerals for all house or building numbers, except the number one.	One Trinity Lane; 637 Adams Ave., Apt. 7
Spell out compass directions that fall within a street address.	1074 West Connover St.
Abbreviate compass directions that follow the street address.	783 Main St., N.E., Apt. 27

Be sure to use organizational titles correctly when addressing international correspondence. Job designations vary around the world. In England, for example, a managing director is often what a U.S. company would call its chief executive officer or president, and a British deputy is the equivalent of a vice president. In France, responsibilities are assigned to individuals without regard to title or organizational structure, and in China the title *project manager* has meaning, but the title *sales manager* may not.

In addition, be aware that businesspeople in some countries sign correspondence without their names typed below.

In Germany, for example, the belief is that employees represent the company, so it's inappropriate to emphasize personal names.[4]

REAL-TIME UPDATES
LEARN MORE BY VISITING THIS WEBSITE
Addressing international correspondence
The Universal Postal Union offers examples for most countries around the world. Go to **real-timeupdates.com/bct14**. and select Learn More in the Students section.

Salutation

In the salutation of your letter, follow the style of the first line of the inside address. If the first line is a person's name, the salutation is *Dear Mr.* or *Ms. Name*. The formality of the salutation depends on your relationship with the addressee. If in conversation you would say "Mary," your letter's salutation should be *Dear Mary*, followed by a colon. Otherwise, include the courtesy title and last name, followed by a colon. Presuming to write *Dear Lewis* instead of *Dear Professor Chang* demonstrates a disrespectful familiarity that the recipient will probably resent.

If the first line of the inside address is a position title such as *Director of Personnel*, then use *Dear Director*. If the addressee is unknown, use a polite description, such as *Dear Alumnus, Dear SPCA Supporter,* or *Dear Voter*. If the first line is plural (a department or company), then use *Ladies and Gentlemen* (look again at Table A.2). When you do not know whether you're writing to an individual or a group (for example, when writing a reference or a letter of recommendation), use *To whom it may concern*.

In the United States some letter writers use a "salutopening" on the salutation line. A salutopening omits *Dear* but includes the first few words of the opening paragraph along with the recipient's name. After this line, the sentence continues a double space below as part of the body of the letter, as in these examples:

Thank you, Mr. Brown, for your prompt payment of your bill.   Salutopening

Your payment of $88.13 was received on January 24, 2018.   Body

Whether your salutation is informal or formal, be especially careful that names are spelled correctly. A misspelled name is glaring evidence of carelessness, and it belies the personal interest you're trying to express.

Body

The body of the letter is your message. Almost all letters are single-spaced, with one blank line before and after the salutation or salutopening, between paragraphs, and before the complimentary close. The body may include indented lists, entire paragraphs indented for emphasis, and even subheadings. If it does, all similar elements should be treated in the same way. Your department or company may select a format to use for all letters.

Complimentary Close

The complimentary close begins on the second line below the body of the letter. Alternatives for wording are available, but the current trend seems to be toward one-word closes, such as *Sincerely* and *Cordially*. In any case, the complimentary close reflects the relationship between you and the person you're writing to. Avoid cute closes, such as *Yours for bigger profits*. If your audience doesn't know you well, your sense of humor may be misunderstood.

Signature Block

Leave three blank lines for a written signature below the complimentary close, and then include the sender's name (unless it appears in the letterhead). The person's title may appear on the same line as the name or on the line below:

Cordially,

Raymond Dunnigan
Director of Personnel

Your letterhead indicates that you're representing your company. However, if your letter is on plain paper or runs to a second page, you may want to emphasize that you're speaking legally for the company. The accepted way of doing that is to place the company's name in capital letters, a double space below the complimentary close, and then include the sender's name and title four lines below that:

Sincerely,
WENTWORTH INDUSTRIES

Helen B. Taylor
President

If your name could be taken for either a man's or a woman's, a courtesy title indicating gender should be included, with or without parentheses. Also, women who prefer a particular courtesy title should include it:

Mrs. Nancy Winters
(Ms.) Juana Flores
Ms. Pat Li
(Mr.) Jamie Saunders

ADDITIONAL LETTER PARTS

Letters vary greatly in subject matter and thus in the identifying information they need and the format they adopt. The letter in Figure A.2 shows how these additional parts should be arranged. The following elements may be used in any combination, depending on the requirements of the particular letter:

- **Addressee notation.** Letters that have a restricted readership or that must be handled in a special way should include such addressee notations as *PERSONAL, CONFIDENTIAL,* or *PLEASE FORWARD.* This sort of notation appears a double space above the inside address, in all-capital letters.

- **Attention line.** Although not commonly used today, an attention line can be used if you know only the last name of the person you're writing to. It can also direct a letter to a position title or department. Place the attention line on the first line of the inside address and put the company name on the second.[5] Match the address

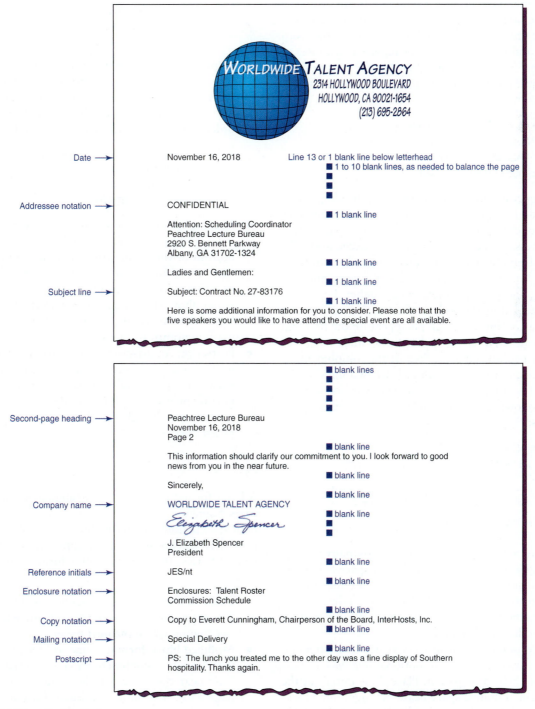

Figure A.2   Additional Letter Parts

on the envelope with the style of the inside address. An attention line may take any of the following forms or variants of them:

> Attention Dr. McHenry
> Attention Director of Marketing
> Attention Marketing Department

- **Subject line.** The subject line tells recipients at a glance what the letter is about (and indicates where to file the letter for future reference). It usually appears below the salutation, either against the left margin, indented (as a paragraph in the body), or centered. It can be placed above the salutation or at the very top of the page, and it can be underscored. Some businesses omit the word *Subject*, and some organizations replace it with *Re:* or *In re:* (meaning "concerning" or "in the matter of"). The subject line may take a variety of forms, including the following:

> Subject: RainMaster Sprinklers
> Re: About your February 2, 2018, order
> In re: FALL 2018 SALES MEETING
> Reference Order No. 27920

- **Second-page heading.** Use a second-page heading whenever an additional page is required. Some companies have second-page letterhead (with the company name and address on one line and in a smaller typeface). The heading bears the name (person or organization) from the first line of the inside address, the page number, the date, and perhaps a reference number. Leave two blank lines before the body. Make sure that at least two lines of a continued paragraph appear on the first and second pages. Never allow the closing lines to appear alone on a continued page. Precede the complimentary close or signature lines with at least two lines of the body. Also, don't hyphenate the last word on a page. All the following are acceptable forms for second-page headings:

> Ms. Melissa Baker
> May 10, 2018
> Page 2
>
> Ms. Melissa Baker, May 10, 2018, Page 2
>
> Ms. Melissa Baker-2-May 10, 2018

- **Company name.** If you include the company's name in the signature block, put it a double space below the complimentary close. You usually include the company's name in the signature block only when the writer is serving as the company's official spokesperson or when letterhead has not been used.
- **Reference initials.** When one person dictates a letter and another person produces it, optional *reference initials* show who helped prepare it. Place these initials at the left margin, a double space below the signature block, using one of the following forms: *RSR/sm*, *RSR:sm*, or

RSR:SM (writer/preparer). See "JES/nt" in Figure A.2 for an example. When the signature block includes the writer's name, some companies use only the preparer's initials. When the writer and the signer are different people, you can include both their initials as well as the typist's: *JFS/RSR/sm* (signer/writer/preparer).

- **Enclosure notation.** Enclosure notations appear at the bottom of a letter, one or two lines below the reference initials. Some common forms include the following:

> Enclosure
> Enclosures (2)
> Enclosures: Résumé
>   Photograph
>   Brochure

- **Copy notation.** Copy notations may follow reference initials or enclosure notations. They indicate who's receiving a *courtesy copy* (*cc*). Recipients are listed in order of rank or (rank being equal) in alphabetical order. Among the forms used are the following:

> cc: David Wentworth, Vice President
> Copy to Hans Vogel
> 748 Chesterton Road
> Snohomish, WA 98290

- **Mailing notation.** You may place a mailing notation (such as *Special Delivery* or *Registered Mail*) at the bottom of the letter, after reference initials or enclosure notations (whichever is last) and before copy notations. Or you may place it at the top of the letter, either above the inside address on the left side or just below the date on the right side. For greater visibility, mailing notations may appear in capital letters.
- **Postscript.** A postscript is presented as an afterthought to the letter, a message that requires emphasis, or a personal note. It is usually the last thing on any letter and may be preceded by *P.S., PS., PS:,* or nothing at all. A second afterthought would be designated *P.P.S.* (post postscript).

LETTER FORMATS

A letter format is the way of arranging all the basic letter parts. Sometimes a company adopts a certain format as its policy; sometimes the individual letter writer or preparer is allowed to choose the most appropriate format. In the United States, three major letter formats are commonly used:

- **Block format.** Each letter part begins at the left margin. The main advantage is quick and efficient preparation (see Figure A.3 on the next page).
- **Modified block format.** Same as block format, except that the date, complimentary close, and signature block start near the center of the page (see Figure A.4 on page 586). The modified block format does permit indentions as an option. This format mixes preparation

Delauny Music
56 Commerce Circle • Davenport, IA 52806
(563) 555-400▸ delaunymusic.net

June 21, 2018   Line 13 or one line below letterhead
■ 1 to 10 blank lines, as needed to balance the page
■

Ms. Claudia Banks
122 River Heights Drive
Bettendorf, IA 52722

■ 1 blank line

Dear Ms. Banks:

■ 1 blank line

Thank you for your recent purchase. We wish you many years of satisfaction with your new Yamaha CG1 grand piano. The CG1 carries more than a century of Yamaha's heritage in design and production of world-class musical instruments and will give you many years of playing and listening pleasure.

■ 1 blank line

Our commitment to your satisfaction doesn't stop with your purchase, however. As a vital first step, please remember to call us sometime within three to eight months after your piano was delivered to take advantage of the Yamaha Servicebond ℠ Assurance Program. This free service program includes a thorough evaluation and adjustment of the instrument after you've had some time to play your piano and your piano has had time to adapt to its environment.

■ 1 blank line

In addition to this important service appointment, a regular program of tuning is essential to ensure your piano's impeccable performance. Our piano specialists recommend four tunings during the first year and two tunings every year thereafter. As your local Yamaha dealer, we are ideally positioned to provide you with optimum service for both regular tuning and any maintenance or repair needs you may have.

■ 1 blank line

Sincerely,

■ 3 blank lines
■
■

Madeline Delauny
Owner

Figure A.3   **Block Letter Format**

speed with traditional placement of some letter parts. It also looks more balanced on the page than the block format does. (Note: The address and contact information in the left margin of this letter is part of this company's particular stationery design; other designs put this information at the top or bottom of the page.)

- **Simplified format.** Instead of using a salutation, this format often weaves the reader's name into the first line or two of the body and often includes a subject line in capital letters (see Figure A.5 on page 587). This format does not include a complimentary close, so your signature appears immediately below the body text. Because certain letter parts are eliminated, some line spacing is changed.

These three formats differ in the way paragraphs are indented, in the way letter parts are placed, and in some punctuation. However, the elements are always separated by at least one blank line, and the printed name is always separated from the line above by at least three blank lines to allow space for a signature. If paragraphs are indented, the indention is normally five spaces. The most common formats for intercultural business letters are the block style and the modified block style.

In addition to these three letter formats, letters may also be classified according to their style of punctuation. *Standard*, or *mixed, punctuation* uses a colon after the salutation (a comma if the letter is social or personal) and a comma after the complimentary close. *Open punctuation* uses no colon or comma after the salutation or the complimentary close. Although the most popular style in business communication is mixed punctuation, either style of punctuation may be used with block or modified block letter formats. Because the simplified letter format has no salutation or complimentary close, the style of punctuation is irrelevant.

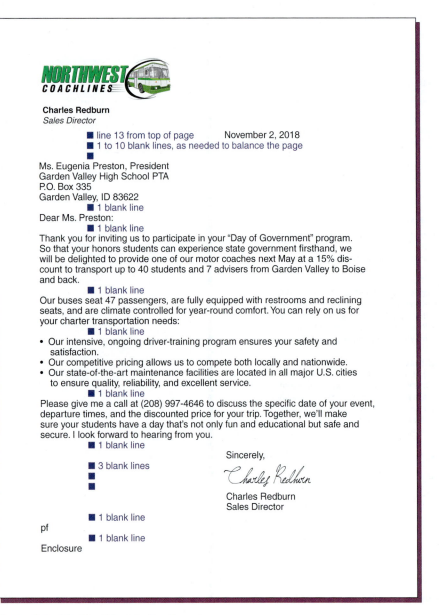

Figure A.4   **Modified Block Letter Format**

Envelopes

For a first impression, the quality of the envelope is just as important as the quality of the stationery. Letterhead and envelopes should be of the same paper stock, have the same color ink, and be imprinted with the same address and logo. Most envelopes used by U.S. businesses are No. 10 envelopes 9½ which are sized for an 8½-by-11-inch piece of paper folded in thirds. Some occasions call for a smaller, No. 6¾ envelope or for envelopes proportioned to fit special stationery. Figure A.6 shows the two most common sizes.

ADDRESSING THE ENVELOPE

No matter what size the envelope, the address is always single-spaced with all lines aligned on the left. The address on the envelope is in the same style as the inside address and presents the same information. The order to follow is from the smallest division to the largest:

1. Name and title of recipient
2. Name of department or subgroup
3. Name of organization
4. Name of building
5. Street address and suite number, or post office box number
6. City, state, or province, and zip code or postal code
7. Name of country (if the letter is being sent abroad)

Because the U.S. Postal Service uses optical scanners to sort mail, envelopes for quantity mailings, in particular, should be addressed in the prescribed format. Everything is in capital letters, no punctuation is included, and

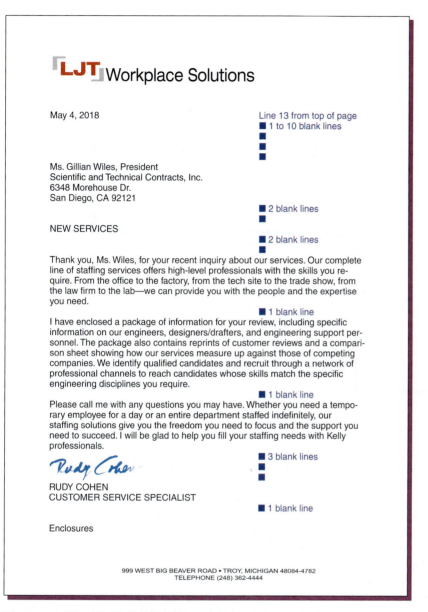

Figure A.5   Simplified Letter Format

all mailing instructions of interest to the post office are placed above the address area (see Figure A.6). Canada Post requires a similar format, except that only the city is all in capitals, and the postal code is placed on the line below the name of the city. The post office scanners read addresses from the bottom up, so if a letter is to be sent to a post office box rather than to a street address, the street address should appear on the line above the box number. Figure A.6 also shows the proper spacing for addresses and return addresses.

The U.S. Postal Service and the Canada Post Corporation have published lists of two-letter mailing abbreviations for states, provinces, and territories (see Table A.4 on page 589). Postal authorities prefer no punctuation with these abbreviations. Quantity mailings should always follow post office requirements. For other letters, a reasonable compromise is to use traditional punctuation, uppercase and lowercase letters for names and street addresses, but two-letter state or province abbreviations, as shown here:

Mr. Kevin Kennedy
2107 E. Packer Dr.
Amarillo, TX 79108

Canadian postal codes are alphanumeric, with a three-character "area code" and a three-character "local code" separated by a single space (K2P 5A5). Zip and postal codes should be separated from state and province names by one space. Canadian postal codes may be treated the same or may be positioned alone on the bottom line of the address all by itself.

FOLDING TO FIT

The way a letter is folded also contributes to the recipient's overall impression of your organization's professionalism.

Small envelope, No. 6³/₄, is 6¹/₂ by 3⁵/₈ inches.

Figure A.6 **Prescribed Envelope Format**

When sending a standard-size piece of paper in a No. 10 envelope, fold it in thirds, with the bottom folded up first and the top folded down over it (see Figure A.7 on the next page); the open end should be at the top of the envelope and facing out. Fit smaller stationery neatly into the appropriate envelope simply by folding it in half or in thirds. When sending a standard-size letterhead in a No. 6¾ envelope, fold it in half from top to bottom and then in thirds from side to side.

INTERNATIONAL MAIL

Postal service differs from country to country, so it's always a good idea to investigate the quality and availability of various services before sending messages and packages internationally. Also, compare the services offered by delivery companies such as UPS and FedEx to find the best rates and options for each destination and type of shipment. No matter which service you choose, be aware that international mail requires more planning than domestic mail. For example, for anything beyond simple letters, you generally need to prepare *customs forms* and possibly other documents, depending on the country of destination and the type of shipment. You are responsible for following the laws of the United States and any countries to which you send mail and packages.

The U.S. Postal Service currently offers four classes of international delivery, listed here from the fastest (and most expensive) to the slowest (and least expensive):

- **Global Express Guaranteed** is the fastest option. This service, offered in conjunction with FedEx, provides delivery in one to three business days to more than 190 countries and territories.
- **Express Mail International** guarantees delivery in three to five business days to a limited number of countries, including Australia, China, Hong Kong, Japan, and South Korea.
- **Priority Mail International** offers delivery guarantees of 6 to 10 business days to more than 190 countries and territories.
- **First Class Mail International** is an economical way to send correspondence and packages weighing up to four pounds to virtually any destination worldwide.

To prepare your mail for international delivery, follow the instructions provided at the U.S. Postal Service website (**www.usps.com**). There you'll find complete information on the international services available through the USPS, along with advice on addressing and packaging mail, completing customs forms, and calculating postage rates and fees. The *International Mail Manual*, also available on this website, offers the latest information and regulations for both outbound and inbound international mail. For instance, you can select individual country names to see current information about restricted or prohibited items and materials, required customs forms, and rates for various classes of service.[6] Various countries have specific and often extensive lists of items that may not be sent by mail at all or that must be sent using particular postal service options.

TABLE A.4   Two-Letter Mailing Abbreviations for the United States and Canada

State/Territory/Province	Abbreviation	State/Territory/Province	Abbreviation	State/Territory/Province	Abbreviation
United States		Maryland	MD	Tennessee	TN
Alabama	AL	Massachusetts	MA	Texas	TX
Alaska	AK	Michigan	MI	Utah	UT
American Samoa	AS	Minnesota	MN	Vermont	VT
Arizona	AZ	Mississippi	MS	Virginia	VA
Arkansas	AR	Missouri	MO	Virgin Islands	VI
California	CA	Montana	MT	Washington	WA
Canal Zone	CZ	Nebraska	NE	West Virginia	WV
Colorado	CO	Nevada	NV	Wisconsin	WI
Connecticut	CT	New Hampshire	NH	Wyoming	WY
Delaware	DE	New Jersey	NJ	**Canada**	
District of Columbia	DC	New Mexico	NM	Alberta	AB
Florida	FL	New York	NY	British Columbia	BC
Georgia	GA	North Carolina	NC	Manitoba	MB
Guam	GU	North Dakota	ND	New Brunswick	NB
Hawaii	HI	Northern Mariana	MP	Newfoundland and Labrador	NL
Idaho	ID	Ohio	OH	Northwest Territories	NT
Illinois	IL	Oklahoma	OK	Nova Scotia	NS
Indiana	IN	Oregon	OR	Nunavut	NU
Iowa	IA	Pennsylvania	PA	Ontario	ON
Kansas	KS	Puerto Rico	PR	Prince Edward Island	PE
Kentucky	KY	Rhode Island	RI	Quebec	QC
Louisiana	LA	South Carolina	SC	Saskatchewan	SK
Maine	ME	South Dakota	SD	Yukon Territory	YT

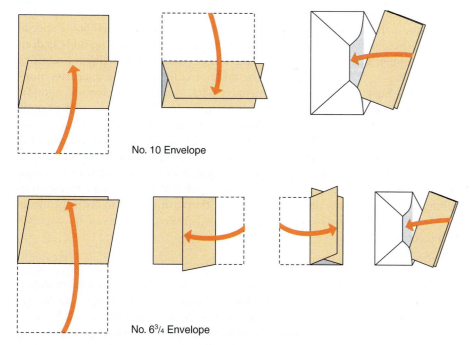

No. 10 Envelope

No. 6¾ Envelope

Figure A.7   **Folding Standard-Size Letterhead**

Memos

Digital media have replaced most internal printed memos in many companies, but you may have occasion to send printed memos from time to time. These can be simple announcements or messages, or they can be short reports using the memo format.

On your document, include a title such as MEMO or INTEROFFICE CORRESPONDENCE (all in capitals) centered at the top of the page or aligned with the left margin. Also at the top, include the words *To*, *From*, *Date*, and *Subject*—followed by the appropriate information—with a blank line between as shown here:

MEMO

TO:
FROM:
DATE:
SUBJECT:

Sometimes the heading is organized like this:

MEMO

TO:	FROM:
DATE:	SUBJECT:

The following guidelines will help you effectively format specific memo elements:

- **Addressees.** When sending a memo to a long list of people, include the notation *See distribution list* or *See below* in the *To* position at the top; then list the names at the end of the memo. Arrange this list alphabetically, except when high-ranking officials deserve more prominent placement. You can also address memos to groups of people—*All Sales Representatives, Production Group, New Product Team.*
- **Courtesy titles.** You need not use courtesy titles anywhere in a memo; first initials and last names, first names, or even initials alone are often sufficient. However, use a courtesy title if you would use one in a face-to-face encounter with the person.
- **Subject line.** The subject line of a memo helps busy colleagues quickly find out what your memo is about, so take care to make it concise and compelling.
- **Body.** Start the body of the memo on the second or third line below the heading. Like the body of a letter, it's usually single-spaced with blank lines between paragraphs. Indenting paragraphs is optional. Handle lists, important passages, and subheadings as you do in letters.
- **Second page.** If the memo carries over to a second page, head the second page just as you head the second page of a letter.
- **Writer's initials.** Unlike a letter, a memo doesn't require a complimentary close or a signature because your name is already prominent at the top. However, you may initial the memo—either beside the name appearing at the top of the memo or at the bottom of the memo.

- **Other elements.** Treat elements such as reference initials and copy notations just as you would in a letter. One difference between letters and memos is that while letters use the term *enclosure* to refer to other pieces included with the letter, memos usually use the word *attachment*.

Memos may be delivered by hand, by the post office (when the recipient works at a different location), or through interoffice mail. Interoffice mail may require the use of special reusable envelopes that have spaces for the recipient's name and department or room number; the name of the previous recipient is simply crossed out. If a regular envelope is used, the words *Interoffice Mail* appear where the stamp normally goes, so that it won't accidentally be stamped and mailed with the rest of the office correspondence.

Informal, routine, or brief reports for distribution within a company are often presented in memo form. Don't include report parts such as a table of contents and appendixes, but write the body of the memo report just as carefully as you'd write a formal report.

Reports

Enhance the effectiveness of your reports by paying careful attention to their appearance and layout. Follow whatever guidelines your organization prefers, always being neat and consistent throughout. If it's up to you to decide formatting questions, the following conventions may help you decide how to handle margins, headings, and page numbers.

MARGINS

All margins on a report page should be at least 1 inch wide. The top, left, and right margins are usually the same, but the bottom margins can be 1½ times deeper. Some special pages also have deeper top margins. Set top margins as deep as 2 inches for pages that contain major titles: prefatory parts (such as the table of contents or the executive summary), supplementary parts (such as the reference notes or bibliography), and textual parts (such as the first page of the text or the first page of each chapter).

If you're going to bind your report at the left or at the top, add half an inch to the margin on the bound edge (see Figure A.8): The space taken by the binding on left-bound reports makes the center point of the text a quarter inch to the right of the center of the paper. Be sure to center headings between the margins, not between the edges of the paper.

HEADINGS

If you don't have a template supplied by your employer, choose a design for headings and subheadings that clearly distinguishes the various levels in the hierarchy. The first-level headings should be the most prominent, on down to the lowest-level subheading.

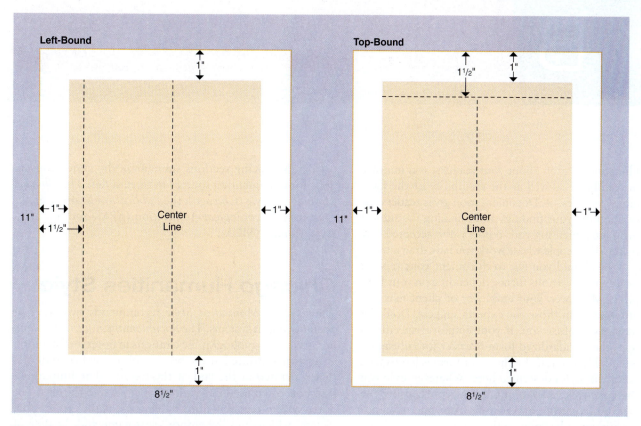

Figure A.8 **Margins for Formal Reports**

PAGE NUMBERS

Every page in a report is counted; however, not all pages show numbers. The first page of the report, normally the title page, is unnumbered. All other pages in the prefatory section are numbered with a lowercase roman numeral, beginning with *ii* and continuing with *iii*, *iv*, *v*, and so on. Start numbering again with arabic numerals (1, 2, and so on) starting at the first page of the body.

You have many options for placing and formatting the page numbers, although these choices are usually made for you in a template. If you're not using a standard company template, position the page number where it is easy to see as the reader flips through the report. If the report will be stapled or otherwise bound along the left side, for instance, the best place for the page number is the upper right or lower right corner.

Endnotes

1. Mary A. De Vries, *Internationally Yours* (Boston: Houghton Mifflin, 1994), 9.
2. Patricia A. Dreyfus, "Paper That's Letter Perfect," *Money*, May 1985, 184.
3. Linda Driskill, *Business and Managerial Communication: New Perspectives* (Orlando, Fla.: Harcourt Brace Jovanovich, 1992), 470.

4. Lennie Copeland and Lewis Griggs, *Going International: How to Make Friends and Deal Effectively in the Global Marketplace*, 2nd ed. (New York: Random House, 1985), 24–27.
5. De Vries, *Internationally Yours*, 8.
6. U.S. Postal Service, *International Mail Manual*, Issue 34, 14 May 2007, www.usps.gov.

By providing information about your sources, you improve your own credibility as well as the credibility of the facts and opinions you present. Documentation gives readers the means for checking your findings and pursuing the subject further. Also, documenting your report is the accepted way to give credit to the people whose work you have drawn from.

What style should you use to document your report? Experts recommend various forms, depending on your field or discipline. Moreover, your employer or client may use a form different from those the experts suggest. Don't let this discrepancy confuse you. If your employer specifies a form, use it; the standardized form is easier for colleagues to understand. However, if the choice of form is left to you, adopt one of the styles described here. Whatever style you choose, be consistent within any given report, using the same order, punctuation, and format from one reference citation or bibliography entry to the next.

A wide variety of style manuals provide detailed information on documentation. These publications explain the three most commonly used styles:

- American Psychological Association, *Publication Manual of the American Psychological Association*, 6th ed. (Washington, D.C.: American Psychological Association, 2013). Details the author-date system, which is preferred in the social sciences and often in the natural sciences as well.
- *The Chicago Manual of Style,* 16th ed. (Chicago: University of Chicago Press, 2010). Often referred to only as *"Chicago"* and widely used in the publishing industry; provides detailed treatment of source documentation and many other aspects of document preparation.
1. Joseph Gibaldi, *MLA Style Manual and Guide to Scholarly Publishing,* 3rd ed. (New York: Modern Language Association, 2008). Serves as the basis for the note and bibliography style used in much academic writing and is recommended in many college textbooks on writing term papers; provides many examples in the humanities.

For more information on these three guides, visit **realtimeupdates.com/bct14** and select Appendix B. Although many schemes have been proposed for organizing the information in source notes, all of them break the information into parts: (1) information about the author (name), (2) information about the work (title, edition, volume number), (3) information about the publication (place, publisher), (4) information about the date, and (5) information on relevant page ranges.

The following sections summarize the major conventions for documenting sources in three styles: *The Chicago Manual of Style (Chicago)*, the *Publication Manual of the American Psychological Association* (APA), and the *MLA Style Manual* (MLA).

Chicago Humanities Style

The Chicago Manual of Style recommends two types of documentation systems. The *documentary-note,* or *humanities,* style gives bibliographic citations in notes—either footnotes (when printed at the bottom of a page) or endnotes (when printed at the end of the report). The humanities system is often used in literature, history, and the arts. The other system recommended by *Chicago* is the *author-date* system, which cites the author's last name and the date of publication in the text, usually in parentheses, reserving full documentation for the reference list (or bibliography). For the purpose of comparing styles, this section concentrates on the humanities system, which is described in detail in *Chicago*.

IN-TEXT CITATION—CHICAGO HUMANITIES STYLE

To document report sources in text, the humanities system relies on superscripts—arabic numerals placed just above the line of type at the end of the reference:

> Toward the end of his speech, Myers sounded a note of caution, saying that even though the economy is expected to grow, it could easily slow a bit.[10]

The superscript lets the reader know how to look for source information in either a footnote or an endnote (see Figure B.1 on the next page). Some readers prefer footnotes so that they can simply glance at the bottom of the page for information. Others prefer endnotes so that they can read the text without a clutter of notes on the page. Also, endnotes relieve the writer from worrying about how long each note will be and how much space it will take away from the page. Both footnotes and endnotes can be handled automatically by today's word-processing software.

For the reader's convenience, you can use footnotes for *content notes* (which may supplement your main text with asides about a particular issue or event, provide a crossreference to another section of your report, or direct the

Notes

Journal article with volume and issue numbers
1. Jonathan Clifton, "Beyond Taxonomies of Influence," *Journal of Business Communication* 46, no. 1 (2009): 57–79.

Brochure
2. BestTemp Staffing Services, *An Employer's Guide to Staffing Services*, 2d ed. (Denver: BestTemp Information Center, 2016), 31.

Newspaper article, no author
3. "Might Be Harder Than It Looks," *Los Angeles Times*, 30 January 2015, sec. A, 22.

Annual report
4. The Walt Disney Company, *2015 Annual Report* (Burbank, Calif.: The Walt Disney Company, 2016), 48.

Magazine article
5. Kerry A. Dolan, "A Whole New Crop" *Forbes*, 2 June 2013, 72–75.

Television broadcast
6. Daniel Han, "Trade Wars Heating Up Around the Globe," *CNN Headline News* (Atlanta: CNN, 5 March 2013).

Internet, World Wide Web
7. "Intel—Company Capsule," Hoover's Online, accessed June 19, 2011, www.hoovers.com/intel/-ID_13787-/free-co-factsheet.xhtml.

Book, component parts
8. Sonja Kuntz, "Moving Beyond Benefits," in *Our Changing Workforce*, ed. Randolf Jacobson (New York: Citadel Press, 2001), 213–27.

Unpublished dissertation or thesis
9. George H. Morales, "The Economic Pressures on Industrialized Nations in a Global Economy" (PhD diss., University of San Diego, 2001), 32–47.

Paper presented at a meeting
10. Charles Myers, "HMOs in Today's Environment" (paper presented at the Conference on Medical Insurance Solutions, Chicago, Ill., August 2001), 16–17.

Online magazine article
11. Leo Babauta, "17 Tips to Be Productive with Instant Messaging," *Web Worker Daily* updated November 14, 2012; accessed February 14, 2016, http://webworkerdaily.com.

Interview
12. Georgia Stainer, general manager, Day Cable and Communications, interview by author, Topeka, Kan., 2 March 2011.

Newspaper article, one author
13. Evelyn Standish, "Global Market Crushes OPEC's Delicate Balance of Interests," *Wall Street Journal*, 19 January 2016, sec. A, 1.

Book, two authors
14. Miriam Toller and Jay Fielding, *Global Business for Smaller Companies* (Rocklin, CA: Prima Publishing, 2001), 102–3.

Government publication
15. U.S. Department of Defense, *Stretching Research Dollars: Survival Advice for Universities and Government Labs* (Washington, D.C.: GPO, 2002), 126.

Online video
16. Adam Grant, "The Surprising Habits of Original Thinkers," TED video, filmed February 2016; available from www.ted.com/talks/adam_grant_the_surprising _habits_of_original_thinkers.

Figure B.1   Sample Endnotes—*Chicago* Humanities Style
(Note: This is a collection of sample entries, not a page from an actual report.)

reader to a related source). Then you can use endnotes for *source notes* (which document direct quotations, paraphrased passages, and visual aids). Consider which type of note is most common in your report, and then choose whether to present these notes all as endnotes or all as footnotes. Regardless of the method you choose for referencing textual information in your report, notes for visual aids (both content notes and source notes) are placed on the same page as the visual.

BIBLIOGRAPHY—*CHICAGO* HUMANITIES STYLE

The humanities system may or may not be accompanied by a bibliography (because the notes give all the necessary bibliographic information). However, endnotes are arranged in order of appearance in the text, so an alphabetical bibliography can be valuable to your readers. The bibliography may be titled *Bibliography*, *Reference List*, *Sources*, *Works Cited* (if you include only those sources you actually cited in your report), or *Works Consulted* (if you include uncited sources as well). This list of sources may also serve as a reading list for those who want to pursue the subject of your report further, so you may want to annotate each entry—that is, comment on the subject matter and viewpoint of the source, as well as on its usefulness to readers. Annotations may be written in either complete or incomplete sentences. A bibliography may also be more manageable if you subdivide it into categories (a classified bibliography), either by

Bibliography

Online magazine article	Babauta, Leo. "17 Tips to Be Productive with Instant Messaging," In *Web Worker Daily* [online], San Francisco, 2011. Updated November 14, 2012, accessed February 14, 2016. http://webworkerdaily.com.
Brochure	BestTemp Staffing Services. *An Employer's Guide to Staffing Services.* 2d ed. Denver: BestTemp Information Center, 2016.
Journal article with volume and issue numbers	Clifton, Jonathan. "Beyond Taxonomies of Influence." *Journal of Business Communication* 46, no. 1 (2009): 57–79.
Magazine article	Dolan, Kerry A. "A Whole New Crop," *Forbes,* 2 June 2013, 72–75.
Online video	Grant, Adam. "The Surprising Habits of Original Thinkers." Filmed February 2016. TED video, 15:25. Posted April 2016. www.ted.com/talks/adam_grant_the_surprising_habits_of_original_thinkers
Television broadcast	Han, Daniel. "Trade Wars Heating Up Around the Globe." *CNN Headline News.* Atlanta: CNN, March 5, 2013.
Internet, World Wide Web	"Intel—Company Capsule." *Hoover's Online,* 3 screens. Accessed June 19, 2015. www.hoovers.com/intel/-ID_13787-/free-co-factsheet.xhtml.
Book, component parts	Kuntz, Sonja. "Moving Beyond Benefits." In *Our Changing Workforce,* edited by Randolf Jacobson, 104–114. New York: Citadel Press, 2001.
Newspaper article, no author	"Might Be Harder Than It Looks." *Los Angeles Times,* 30 January 2015, sec. A, 22.
Unpublished dissertation or thesis	Morales, George H. "The Economic Pressures on Industrialized Nations in a Global Economy." PhD diss., University of San Diego, 2001.
Paper presented at a meeting	Myers, Charles. "HMOs in Today's Environment." Paper presented at the Conference on Medical Insurance Solutions, Chicago, IL, August 2001.
Interview	Stainer, Georgia, general manager, Day Cable and Communications. Interview by author. Topeka, KS, March 2, 2011.
Newspaper article, one author	Standish, Evelyn. "Global Market Crushes OPEC's Delicate Balance of Interests." *Wall Street Journal,* 19 January 2016, sec. A, 1.
Book, two authors	Toller, Miriam, and Jay Fielding. *Global Business for Smaller Companies.* Rocklin, CA: Prima Publishing, 2001.
Government publication	U.S. Department of Defense. *Stretching Research Dollars: Survival Advice for Universities and Government Labs.* Washington, DC: GPO, 2002.
Annual report	The Walt Disney Company, *2015 Annual Report.* Burbank, CA: The Walt Disney Company, 2016.

Figure B.2   **Sample Bibliography—*Chicago* Humanities Style**
(Note: This is a collection of sample entries, not a page from an actual report.)

type of reference (such as books, articles, and unpublished material) or by subject matter (such as government regulation, market forces, and so on). Following are the major conventions for developing a bibliography according to *Chicago* style (see Figure B.2):

- Exclude any page numbers that may be cited in source notes, except for journals, periodicals, newspapers, and book chapter page ranges.
- Alphabetize entries by the last name of the lead author (listing last name first). The names of second and succeeding authors are listed in normal order. Entries without an author name are alphabetized by the first important word in the title.
- Format entries as hanging indents (indent the second and succeeding lines three to five spaces).

- Arrange entries in the following general order: (1) author name, (2) title information, (3) publication information, (4) date, (5) periodical page range.
- Use quotation marks around the titles of articles from magazines, newspapers, and journals. Capitalize the first and last words, as well as all other important words (except prepositions, articles, and coordinating conjunctions).
- Use italics to set off the names of books, newspapers, journals, and other complete publications. Capitalize the first and last words, as well as all other important words.
- For journal articles, include the volume number and the issue number (if necessary). Include the year of publication inside parentheses and follow with a colon and the page range of the article: *Journal of Business Communication*

46, no. 1 (2009): 57–79. (In this source, the volume is 46, the number is 1, and the page range is 57–79.)

- Use brackets to identify all electronic references: [Online database] or [CD-ROM].
- Explain how electronic references can be reached if it's not obvious from the URL.
- Give the access date for online references: Accessed August 23, 2018.

APA Style

The American Psychological Association (APA) recommends the author-date system of documentation, which is popular in the physical, natural, and social sciences. When using this system, you simply insert the author's last name and the year of publication within parentheses following the text discussion of the material cited. Include a page number if you use a direct quotation. This approach briefly identifies the source so that readers can locate complete information in the alphabetical reference list at the end of the report. The author-date system is both brief and clear, saving readers time and effort.

IN-TEXT CITATION—APA STYLE

To document report sources in text using APA style, insert the author's surname and the date of publication at the end of a statement. Enclose this information in parentheses. If the author's name is referred to in the text itself, then the name can be omitted from parenthetical material.

> Some experts recommend both translation and back-translation when dealing with any non-English-speaking culture (Clifton, 2013).
> Toller and Fielding (2015) make a strong case for small companies succeeding in global business.

Personal communications and interviews conducted by the author would not be listed in the reference list. Such citations appear in the text only.

> Increasing the role of cable companies is high on the list of Georgia Stainer, general manager at Day Cable and Communications (personal communication, March 2, 2015).

LIST OF REFERENCES—APA STYLE

For APA style, list only those works actually cited in the text (so you would not include works for background or for further reading). Following are the major conventions for developing a reference list according to APA style (see Figure B.3):

- Format entries as hanging indents.
- List all author names in reversed order (last name first), and use only initials for the first and middle names.
- Arrange entries in the following general order: (1) author name, (2) date, (3) title information, (4) publication information, (5) periodical page range.

- Follow the author name with the date of publication in parentheses.
- List titles of articles from magazines, newspapers, and journals without underlines or quotation marks. Capitalize only the first word of the title, any proper nouns, and the first word to follow an internal colon.
- Italicize titles of books, capitalizing only the first word, any proper nouns, and the first word to follow a colon.
- Italicize titles of magazines, newspapers, journals, and other complete publications. Capitalize all the important words in the title.
- For journal articles, include the volume number (in italics) and, if necessary, the issue number (in parentheses). Finally, include the page range of the article: *Journal of Business Communication, 46*(1), 57–79. (In this example, the volume is 46, the number is 1, and the page range is 57–79.)
- Include personal communications (such as letters, memos, emails, and conversations) only in text, not in reference lists.
- Electronic references include author, date of publication, title of article, name of publication (if one), volume, and the URL.
- For electronic references, indicate the actual year of publication.
- For web pages with extremely long URLs, use your best judgment to determine which URL from the site to use. For example, rather than giving the URL of a specific news release with a long URL, you can provide the URL of the "Media relations" webpage.
- APA citation guidelines for social media are still evolving. For the latest information, visit the APA Style Blog (**blog.apastyle.org**).
- For online journals or periodicals that assign a digital object identifier (DOI), include that instead of a conventional URL. If no DOI is available, include the URL of the publication's home page.

MLA Style

The style recommended by the Modern Language Association of America is used widely in the humanities, especially in the study of language and literature. Like APA style, MLA style uses brief parenthetical citations in the text. However, instead of including author name and year, MLA citations include author name and page reference.

IN-TEXT CITATION—MLA STYLE

To document report sources in text using MLA style, insert the author's last name and a page reference inside parentheses following the cited material: (Matthews 63). If the author's name is mentioned in the text reference, the name can be omitted from the parenthetical citation: (63). The citation indicates that the reference came from page 63 of

References

Online magazine article	Babauta, L. (2007, November 14). 17 tips to be productive with instant messaging. *Web Worker Daily*. Retrieved from http://webworkerdaily.com
Brochure	BestTemp Staffing Services. (2016). *An employer's guide to staffing services* (2nd ed.) [Brochure]. Denver, CO: BestTemp Information Center.
Journal article with volume and issue numbers	Clifton, J. (2009). Beyond taxonomies of influence. *Journal of Business Communication, 46*(1), 57.
Magazine article	Dolan, K. A. (2013, June 2). A whole new crop. *Forbes*, 72–75.
Online video	Grant, A. (2016, April 26). *The surprising habits of original thinkers* [Video file]. Retrieved from www.ted.com/talks/adam_grant_the_surprising_habits_of_original_thinkers
Television broadcast	Han, D. (2013, March 5). Trade wars heating up around the globe. *CNN Headline News* [Television broadcast]. Atlanta, GA: CNN.
Internet, World Wide Web	Hoover's Online. (2011). *Intel—company capsule*. Retrieved from http://www.hoovers.com/intel/-ID_13787-/free-co-factsheet.xhtml
Book, component parts	Kuntz, S. (2001). Moving beyond benefits. In R. Jacobson (Ed.), *Our changing workforce* (pp. 213–227). New York, NY: Citadel Press.
Newspaper article, no author	Might be harder than it looks. (2015, January 30). *Los Angeles Times*, p. A22.
Unpublished dissertation or thesis	Morales, G. H. (2001). *The economic pressures on industrialized nations in a global economy* (Unpublished doctoral dissertation) University of San Diego.
Paper presented at a meeting	Myers, C. (2001, August). *HMOs in today's environment*. Paper presented at the Conference on Medical Insurance Solutions, Chicago, IL.
Interview	*Cited in text only, not in the list of references.*
Newspaper article, one author	Standish, E. (2016, January 19). Global market crushes OPEC's delicate balance of interests. *Wall Street Journal*, p. A1.
Book, two authors	Toller, M., & Fielding, J. (2001). *Global business for smaller companies*. Rocklin, CA: Prima Publishing.
Government publication	U.S. Department of Defense. (2002). *Stretching research dollars: Survival advice for universities and government labs*. Washington, DC: U.S. Government Printing Office.
Annual report	The Walt Disney Company. (2016). *2015 Annual report*. Burbank, CA: The Walt Disney Company.

Figure B.3   Sample References—APA Style
(Note: This is a collection of sample references, not a page from an actual report. Also, it is single-spaced as is the norm for business reports; APA references are double-spaced in academic reports.)

a work by Matthews. With the author's name, readers can find complete publication information in the alphabetically arranged list of works cited that comes at the end of the report.

> Some experts recommend both translation and back-translation when dealing with any non-English-speaking culture (Clifton 57).
> Toller and Fielding make a strong case for small companies succeeding in global business (102–03).

LIST OF WORKS CITED—MLA STYLE

The *MLA Style Manual* recommends preparing the list of works cited first so that you will know what information to give in the parenthetical citation (for example, whether to add a short title if you're citing more than one work by the same author, or whether to give an initial or first name if you're citing two authors who have the same last name). The list of works cited appears at the end of your report, contains all the works that you cite in your text, and lists them in alphabetical order. Following are the major conventions for developing a reference list according to MLA style (see Figure B.4 on the next page):

- Format entries as hanging indents.
- Arrange entries in the following general order: (1) author name, (2) title information, (3) publication information, (4) date, (5) periodical page range.
- List the lead author's name in reverse order (last name first), using either full first names or initials. List second and succeeding author names in normal order.

Works Cited

Online magazine article	Babauta, Leo. "17 Tips to Be Productive with Instant Messaging," *Web Worker Daily* 14 Nov. 2012. 14 Feb. 2016. http://webworkerdaily.com
Brochure	BestTemp Staffing Services. *An Employer's Guide to Staffing Services.* 2d ed. Denver: BestTemp Information Center, 2016.
Journal article with volume and issue numbers	Clifton, Jonathan. "Beyond Taxonomies of Influence." *Journal of Business Communication* 46, 1 (2009): 57–79.
Magazine article	Dolan, Kerry A. "A Whole New Crop" *Forbes*, 2 June 2013: 72–75.
Online video	Grant, Adam. "The surprising habits of original thinkers." TED. April 2016. Lecture.
Television broadcast	Han, Daniel. "Trade Wars Heating Up Around the Globe." *CNN Headline News.* CNN, Atlanta. 5 Mar. 2013.
Internet, World Wide Web	"Intel—Company Capsule." *Hoover's Online.* 2011. Hoover's Company Information. 19 June 2011 http://www.hoovers.com/intel/-ID_13787/free-co-factsheet.xhtml
Book, component parts	Kuntz, Sonja. "Moving Beyond Benefits." *Our Changing Workforce.* Ed. Randolf Jacobson. New York: Citadel Press, 2001. 213–27.
Newspaper article, no author	"Might Be Harder Than It Looks." *Los Angeles Times,* 30 Jan. 2013: A22.
Unpublished dissertation or thesis	Morales, George H. "The Economic Pressures on Industrialized Nations in a Global Economy." Diss. U of San Diego, 2001.
Paper presented at a meeting	Myers, Charles. "HMOs in Today's Environment." Conference on Medical Insurance Solutions. Chicago. 13 Aug. 2001.
Interview	Stainer, Georgia, general manager, Day Cable and Communications. Telephone interview. 2 Mar. 2011.
Newspaper article, one author	Standish, Evelyn. "Global Market Crushes OPEC's Delicate Balance of Interests." *Wall Street Journal,* 19 Jan. 2016: A1.
Book, two authors	Toller, Miriam, and Jay Fielding. *Global Business for Smaller Companies.* Rocklin, CA: Prima Publishing, 2001.
Government publication	United States. Department of Defense. *Stretching Research Dollars: Survival Advice for Universities and Government Labs.* Washington: GPO, 2002.
Annual report	The Walt Disney Company, *2015 Annual Report.* Burbank, Calif.: The Walt Disney Company, 2016.

Figure B.4   Sample Works Cited—MLA Style

(Note: This is a collection of sample references, not a page from an actual report. Also, it is single-spaced as is the norm for business reports; MLA works cited are double-spaced in academic reports.)

- Use quotation marks around the titles of articles from magazines, newspapers, and journals. Capitalize all important words.
- Italicize the names of books, newspapers, journals, and other complete publications, capitalizing all main words in the title.
- For journal articles, include the volume number and the issue number (if necessary). Include the year of publication inside parentheses and follow with a colon and the page range of the article: *Journal of Business Communication* 46.1 (2009): 57. (In this source, the volume is 46, the number is 1, and the page is 57.)
- Electronic sources are less fixed than print sources, and they may not be readily accessible to readers. So citations for electronic sources must provide more information. Always try to be as comprehensive as possible, citing whatever information is available (however, see the note about extremely long URLs).

- The date for electronic sources should contain both the date assigned in the source (if no date is shown, write "n.d." instead) and the date accessed by the researcher.
- The URL for electronic sources must be as accurate and complete as possible, from access-mode identifier (such as http or ftp) to all relevant directory and file names. If the URL is extremely long, however, use the URL of the website's home page or the URL of the site's search page if you used the site's search function to find the article. The *MLA Style Manual* no longer requires writers to include URLs for materials retrieved online. However, follow whatever guidelines your instructor gives you in this regard.
- MLA style requires you to indicate the medium of publication. For most sources, this will be "Web" or "Print," but you may also cite "CD-ROM" and other media, as appropriate.

C Correction Symbols

Instructors often use these short, easy-to-remember correction symbols and abbreviations when evaluating students' writing. You can use them as well to understand your instructor's suggestions and to revise and proofread your own letters, memos, and reports. Refer to the Handbook of Grammar, Mechanics, and Usage (page 601) for further information.

Content and Style

Acc	Accuracy. Check to be sure information is correct.
ACE	Avoid copying examples.
ACP	Avoid copying problems.
Adp	Adapt. Tailor message to reader.
App	Follow proper organization approach. (Refer to Chapter 4.)
Assign	Assignment. Review instructions for assignment.
AV	Active verb. Substitute active for passive.
Awk	Awkward phrasing. Rewrite.
BC	Be consistent.
BMS	Be more sincere.
Chop	Choppy sentences. Use longer sentences and more transitional phrases.
Con	Condense. Use fewer words.
CT	Conversational tone. Avoid using overly formal language.
Depers	Depersonalize. Avoid attributing credit or blame to any individual or group.
Dev	Develop. Provide greater detail.
Dir	Direct. Use direct approach; get to the point.
Emph	Emphasize. Develop this point more fully.
EW	Explanation weak. Check logic; provide more proof.
Fl	Flattery. Avoid compliments that are insincere.
FS	Figure of speech. Find a more accurate expression.

GNF	Good news first. Use direct order.
GRF	Give reasons first. Use indirect order.
GW	Goodwill. Put more emphasis on expressions of goodwill.
H/E	Honesty/ethics. Revise statement to reflect good business practices.
Imp	Imply. Avoid being direct.
Inc	Incomplete. Develop further.
Jar	Jargon. Use less specialized language.
Log	Logic. Check development of argument.
Neg	Negative. Use more positive approach or expression.
Obv	Obvious. Do not state point in such detail.
OC	Overconfident. Adopt humbler language.
OM	Omission.
Org	Organization. Strengthen outline.
OS	Off the subject. Close with point on main subject.
Par	Parallel. Use same structure.
Pom	Pompous. Rephrase in down-to-earth terms.
PV	Point of view. Make statement from reader's perspective rather than your own.
RB	Reader benefit. Explain what reader stands to gain.
Red	Redundant. Reduce number of times this point is made.
Ref	Reference. Cite source of information.
Rep	Repetitive. Provide different expression.
RS	Resale. Reassure reader that he or she has made a good choice.
SA	Service attitude. Put more emphasis on helping reader.
Sin	Sincerity. Avoid sounding glib or uncaring.
SL	Stereotyped language. Focus on individual's characteristics instead of on false generalizations.
Spec	Specific. Provide more specific statement.

SPM	Sales promotion material. Tell reader about related goods or services.
Stet	Let stand in original form.
Sub	Subordinate. Make this point less important.
SX	Sexist. Avoid language that contributes to gender stereotypes.
Tone	Tone needs improvement.
Trans	Transition. Show connection between points.
UAE	Use action ending. Close by stating what reader should do next.
UAS	Use appropriate salutation.

UAV	Use active voice.
Unc	Unclear. Rewrite to clarify meaning.
UPV	Use passive voice.
USS	Use shorter sentences.
V	Variety. Use different expression or sentence pattern.
W	Wordy. Eliminate unnecessary words.
WC	Word choice. Find a more appropriate word.
YA	"You" attitude. Rewrite to emphasize reader's needs.

Grammar, Mechanics, and Usage

Ab	Abbreviation. Avoid abbreviations in most cases; use correct abbreviation.
Adj	Adjective. Use adjective instead.
Adv	Adverb. Use adverb instead.
Agr	Agreement. Make subject and verb or noun and pronoun agree.
Ap	Appearance. Improve appearance.
Apos	Apostrophe. Check use of apostrophe.
Art	Article. Use correct article.
BC	Be consistent.
Cap	Capitalize.
Case	Use cases correctly.
CoAdj	Coordinate adjective. Insert comma between coordinate adjectives; delete comma between adjective and compound noun.
CS	Comma splice. Use period or semicolon to separate clauses.
DM	Dangling modifier. Rewrite so that modifier clearly relates to subject of sentence.
Exp	Expletive. Avoid expletive beginnings, such as it is, there are, there is, this is, and these are.
F	Format. Improve layout of document.
Frag	Fragment. Rewrite as complete sentence.
Gram	Grammar. Correct grammatical error.
HCA	Hyphenate compound adjective.

lc	Lowercase. Do not use capital letter.
M	Margins. Improve frame around document.
MM	Misplaced modifier. Place modifier close to word it modifies.
NRC	Nonrestrictive clause (or phrase). Separate from rest of sentence with commas.
P	Punctuation. Use correct punctuation.
Par	Parallel. Use same structure.
PH	Place higher. Move up on page.
PL	Place lower. Move down on page.
Prep	Preposition. Use correct preposition.
RC	Restrictive clause (or phrase). Remove commas that separate clause from rest of sentence.
RO	Run-on sentence. Separate two sentences with comma and coordinating conjunction or with semicolon.
SC	Serial comma. Add comma before *and* or *or*.
Sp	Spelling error. Consult dictionary.
S-V	Subject-verb pair. Do not separate with comma.
Syl	Syllabification. Divide word between syllables.
WD	Word division. Check dictionary for proper end-of-line hyphenation.
WW	Wrong word. Replace with another word.

Proofreading Marks

Symbol	Meaning	Symbol Used in Context	Corrected Copy
═	Align horizontally	meaningful result	meaningful result
‖	Align vertically	1. Power cable 2. Keyboard	1. Power cable 2. Keyboard
bf	Boldface	Recommendations bf	**Recommendations**
≡	Capitalize	Pepsico, Inc.	PepsiCo, Inc.
⊐⊏	Center	Awards Banquet	Awards Banquet
⌣	Close up space	self- confidence	self-confidence
ℓ	Delete	harrassment and abuse	harrassment
ds	Double-space	text in first line text in second line ds	text in first line text in second line
∧	Insert	tirquoise shirts (u / and white)	turquoise and white shirts
∨	Insert apostrophe	our teams goals	our team's goals
⋏	Insert comma	a, b and c	a, b, and c
=	Insert hyphen	third quarter sales	third-quarter sales
⊙	Insert period	Harrigan et al	Harrigan et al.
∀ ∀	Insert quotation marks	This team isn't cooperating.	This "team" isn't cooperating.
#	Insert space	real estate testcase	real estate test case
ital	Italics	Quarterly Report ital	*Quarterly Report*
/	Lowercase	TULSA, South of here	Tulsa, south of here
⌐⌐	Move down	Sincerely,	Sincerely,
⌐	Move left	Attention: Security	Attention: Security
⌐	Move right	February 2, 2018	February 2, 2018
⌐⌐	Move up	THIRD-QUARTER SALES	THIRD-QUARTER SALES
STET	Restore	staff talked openly and frankly STET	staff talked openly
⌒	Run lines together	Manager, Distribution	Manager, Distribution
ss	Single space	text in first line text in second line ss	text in first line text in second line
⬭	Spell out	COD	cash on delivery
sp	Spell out	Assn. of Biochem. Engrs.	Association of Biochemical Engineers
⌐	Start new line	Marla Fenton, Manager, Distri- bution	Marla Fenton, Manager, Distribution
¶	Start new paragraph	The solution is easy to determine but difficult to implement in a competitive environment like the one we now face.	The solution is easy to determine but difficult to implement in a competitive environment like the one we now face.
∼	Transpose	airy, light, casual tone	light, airy, casual tone

The rules of grammar, mechanics, and usage provide the guidance every professional needs in order to communicate successfully with colleagues, customers, and other audiences. These rules help you in two important ways. First, they determine how meaning is encoded and decoded in the communication process. If you don't encode your messages using the same rules your readers or listeners use to decode them, chances are your audiences will not extract your intended meaning from your messages. Without a firm grasp of the basics of grammar, mechanics, and usage, you risk being misunderstood, damaging your company's image, losing money for your company, and possibly even losing your job. In other words, if you want to get your point across, you need to follow the rules of grammar, mechanics, and usage. Second, apart from successfully transferring meaning, following the rules tells your audience that you respect the conventions and expectations of the business community.

You can think of *grammar* as the agreed-on structure of a language, the way that individual words are formed and the manner in which those words are then combined to form meaningful sentences. *Mechanics* are style and formatting issues such as capitalization, spelling, and the use of numbers and symbols. *Usage* involves the accepted and expected way in which specific words are used by a particular community of people—in this case, the community of businesspeople who use English. This handbook can help you improve your knowledge and awareness in all three areas. It is divided into the following sections:

- **Diagnostic Test of English Skills.** Testing your current knowledge of grammar, mechanics, and usage helps you find out where your strengths and weaknesses lie. This test offers 50 items taken from the topics included in this handbook.
- **Assessment of English Skills.** After completing the diagnostic test, use the assessment form to highlight the areas you most need to review.
- **Essentials of Grammar, Mechanics, and Usage.** This section helps you quickly review the basics. You can study the things you've probably already learned but may have forgotten about grammar, punctuation, mechanics (including capitalization, abbreviation, number style, and word division), and vocabulary (including frequently confused words, frequently misused words, frequently misspelled words, and transitional words and phrases). Use this essential review not only to study and improve your English skills but also as a reference for any questions you may have during this course.

Diagnostic Test of English Skills

Use this test to determine whether you need more practice with grammar, punctuation, mechanics, or vocabulary. When you've answered all the questions, ask your instructor for an answer sheet so that you can score the test. On the Assessment of English Skills form (page 603), record the number of questions you answered incorrectly in each section.

The following choices apply to items 1–5. Write in each blank the letter of the choice that best describes the part of speech that is underlined.

A. noun
B. pronoun
C. verb
D. adjective
E. adverb
F. preposition
G. conjunction
H. article

_____ 1. The new branch location will be decided <u>by</u> next week.
_____ 2. We must hire only <u>qualified</u>, ambitious graduates.
_____ 3. After their <u>presentation</u>, I was still undecided.
_____ 4. See <u>me</u> after the meeting.
_____ 5. Margaret, pressed for time, turned in <u>unusually</u> sloppy work.

In the blanks for items 6–15, write the letter of the word or phrase that best completes each sentence.

_____ 6. (A. Russ's, B. Russ') laptop was stolen last week.
_____ 7. Speaking only for (A. me, B. myself), I think the new policy is discriminatory.
_____ 8. Of the five candidates we interviewed yesterday, (A. who, B. whom) do you believe is the best choice?
_____ 9. India has increased (A. it's, B. its) imports of corn and rice.
_____10. Either the New York head office or the regional offices will need to reduce (A. their, B. its) staffing costs.
_____11. If the IT department can't (A. lie, B. lay) the fiber-optic cable by March 1, the plant will not open on schedule.
_____12. Starbucks (A. is, B. are) opening five new stores in San Diego in the next year.

_____13. The number of women-owned small businesses (A. has, B. have) increased sharply in the past two decades.

_____14. Greg and Bernyce worked (A. good, B. well) together.

_____15. They distributed the supplies (A. among, B. between) the six staff members.

The following choices apply to items 16–20. Identify the issue that best describes the problem with each sentence's structure.

A. sentence fragment
B. comma splice
C. misplaced modifier
D. fused sentence
E. lack of parallelism
F. unclear antecedent

_____16. The number of employees who took the buyout offer was much higher than expected, now the entire company is understaffed.

_____17. The leader in Internet-only banking.

_____18. Diamond doesn't actually sell financial products rather it acts as an intermediary.

_____19. Helen's proposal is for not only the present but also for the future.

_____20. When purchasing luxury products, quality is more important than price for consumers.

For items 21–30, circle the letter of the preferred choice in each of the following groups of sentences.

21. A. What do you think of the ad slogan "Have it your way?"
    B. What do you think of the ad slogan "Have it your way"?

22. A. Send copies to Jackie Cross, Uniline, Brad Nardi, Peale & Associates, and Tom Griesbaum, MatchMakers.
    B. Send copies to Jackie Cross, Uniline; Brad Nardi, Peale & Associates; and Tom Griesbaum, MatchMakers.

23. A. They've recorded 22 complaints since yesterday, all of them from long-time employees.
    B. They've recorded 22 complaints since yesterday; all of them from long-time employees.

24. A. We are looking for two qualities in applicants: experience with computers and an interest in people.
    B. We are looking for two qualities in applicants; experience with computers and an interest in people.

25. A. At the Center for the Blind the clients we serve have lost vision, due to a wide variety of causes.
    B. At the Center for the Blind, the clients we serve have lost vision due to a wide variety of causes.

26. A. Replace your standard light bulbs with new, compact fluorescent bulbs.
    B. Replace your standard light bulbs with new, compact, fluorescent bulbs.

C. Replace your standard light bulbs with new compact fluorescent bulbs.

27. A. Blue Cross of California may have changed its name to Anthem Blue Cross but the company still has the same commitment to California.
    B. Blue Cross of California may have changed its name to Anthem Blue Cross, but the company still has the same commitment to California.

28. A. Only eight banks in this country—maybe nine can handle transactions of this magnitude.
    B. Only eight banks in this country—maybe nine— can handle transactions of this magnitude.

29. A. Instead of focusing on high-growth companies, we targeted mature businesses with only one or two people handling the decision making.
    B. Instead of focusing on high growth companies, we targeted mature businesses with only one or two people handling the decision-making.

30. A. According to board president Damian Cabaza "having a crisis communication plan is a high priority."
    B. According to board president Damian Cabaza, "Having a crisis communication plan is a high priority."

For items 31–40, select the best choice from among those provided.

31. A. At her previous employer, Mary-Anne worked in Marketing Communications and Human Resources.
    B. At her previous employer, Mary-Anne worked in marketing communications and human resources.

32. A. By fall, we'll have a dozen locations between the Mississippi and Missouri rivers.
    B. By Fall, we'll have a dozen locations between the Mississippi and Missouri Rivers.

33. A. The Board applauded President Donlan upon her reelection for a fifth term.
    B. The board applauded president Donlan upon her reelection for a fifth term.
    C. The board applauded President Donlan upon her reelection for a fifth term.

34. A. If you want to travel to France, you need to be au courant with the business practices.
    B. If you want to travel to France, you need to be "au courant" with the business practices.

35. A. As the company's CEO, Thomas Spurgeon handles all dealings with the FDA.
    B. As the company's C.E.O., Thomas Spurgeon handles all dealings with the F.D.A.

36. A. The maximum speed limit in most states is 65 mph.
    B. The maximum speed limit in most states is 65 m.p.h.

37. A. Sales of graphic novels increased nine percent between 2008 and 2009.
    B. Sales of graphic novels increased 9 percent between 2008 and 2009.

38. A. Our store is open daily from nine a.m. to seven p.m.
    B. Our store is open daily from 9:00 a.m. to 7:00 p.m.

39. A. The organizing meeting is scheduled for July 27, and the event will be held in January 2018.
   B. The organizing meeting is scheduled for July 27th, and the event will be held in January, 2018.
40. A. We need six desks, eight file cabinets, and 12 trashcans.
   B. We need 6 desks, 8 file cabinets, and 12 trashcans.

For items 41–50, write in each blank the letter of the word that best completes each sentence.

_____ 41. Will having a degree (A. affect, B. effect) my chances for promotion?
_____ 42. Try not to (A. loose, B. lose) this key; we will charge you a fee to replace it.
_____ 43. I don't want to discuss my (A. personal, B. personnel) problems in front of anyone.
_____ 44. Let us help you choose the right tie to (A. complement, B. compliment) your look.
_____ 45. The repairman's whistling (A. aggravated, B. irritated) all of us in accounting.
_____ 46. The bank agreed to (A. loan, B. lend) the Smiths $20,000 for their start-up.
_____ 47. The credit card company is (A. liable, B. likely) to increase your interest rate if you miss a payment.
_____ 48. The airline tries to (A. accommodate, B. accomodate) disabled passengers.
_____ 49. Every company needs a policy regarding sexual (A. harrassment, B. harassment).
_____ 50. Use your best (A. judgment, B. judgement) in selecting a service provider.

Assessment of English Skills

In the space provided, record the number of questions you answered incorrectly.

Questions	Skills Area	Number of Incorrect Answers
1–5	Parts of speech	_____
6–15	Usage	_____
16–20	Sentence structure	_____
21–30	Punctuation	_____
31–40	Mechanics	_____
41–50	Vocabulary	_____

If you had more than two incorrect answers in any of the skills areas, focus on those areas in the appropriate sections of this handbook.

Essentials of Grammar, Mechanics, and Usage

The following sentence looks innocent, but is it really?

We sell tuxedos as well as rent.

You sell tuxedos, but it's highly unlikely that you sell rent—which is what this sentence says. Whatever you're selling, some people will ignore your message because of a blunder like this. The following sentence has a similar problem:

Vice President Eldon Neale told his chief engineer that he would no longer be with Avix, Inc., as of June 30.

Is Eldon or the engineer leaving? No matter which side the facts are on, the sentence can be read the other way. Now look at this sentence:

The year before we budgeted more for advertising sales were up.

Confused? Perhaps this is what the writer meant:

The year before, we budgeted more for advertising.
Sales were up.

Or maybe the writer meant this:

The year before we budgeted more for advertising, sales were up.

These examples show that even short, simple sentences can be misunderstood because of errors on the part of the writer. As you've learned in numerous courses over your schooling, an English sentence consists of the parts of speech being combined with punctuation, mechanics, and vocabulary to convey meaning. Making a point of brushing up on your grammar, punctuation, mechanics, and vocabulary skills will help ensure that you create clear, effective business messages.

1.0 Grammar

Grammar is the study of how words come together to form sentences. Categorized by meaning, form, and function, English words fall into various parts of speech: nouns, pronouns, verbs, adjectives, adverbs, prepositions, conjunctions, articles, and interjections. You will communicate more clearly if you understand how each of these parts of speech operates in a sentence.

1.1 NOUNS

A **noun** names a person, a place, a thing, or an idea. Anything you can see or detect with one of your senses has a noun to name it. Some things you can't see or sense are also nouns—ions, for example, or space. So are things that exist as ideas, such as accuracy and height. (You can see that something is accurate or that a building is tall, but you can't see the idea of accuracy or the idea of height.) These names for ideas are known as **abstract nouns**. The simplest nouns are the names of things you can see or touch: *car, building, cloud, brick*; these are termed **concrete nouns**. A few nouns, such as *algorithm, software*, and *code*, are difficult to categorize as either abstract or concrete but can reasonably be considered concrete even though they don't have a physical presence.

1.1.1 Proper Nouns and Common Nouns

So far, all the examples of nouns have been **common nouns**, referring to general classes of things. The word *building* refers to a whole class of structures. Common nouns such as *building* are not capitalized.

If you want to talk about one particular building, however, you might refer to the Glazier Building. The name is capitalized, indicating that *Glazier Building* is a **proper noun**.

Here are three sets of common and proper nouns for comparison:

Common	Proper
city	Kansas City
company	Blaisden Company
store	Books Galore

1.1.2 Nouns as Subject and Object

Nouns may be used in sentences as subjects or objects. That is, the person, place, thing, or idea that is being or doing (subject) is represented by a noun. So is the person, place, idea, or thing that is being acted on (object). In the following sentence, the nouns are underlined:

The <u>web designer</u> created the <u>homepage</u>.

The web designer (subject) is acting in a way that affects the homepage (object). The following sentence is more complicated:

The <u>installer</u> delivered the <u>carpet</u> to the <u>customer</u>.

Installer is the subject. *Carpet* is the object of the main part of the sentence (acted on by the installer), and *customer* is the object of the phrase *to the customer*. Nevertheless, both *carpet* and *customer* are objects.

1.1.3 Plural Nouns

Nouns can be either singular or plural. The usual way to make a plural noun is to add *s* or *es* to the singular form of the word:

Singular	Plural
file	files
tax	taxes
cargo	cargoes

Many nouns have other ways of forming the plural. Some plurals involve a change in a vowel (*mouse/mice, goose/geese, woman/women*), the addition of *en* or *ren* (*ox/oxen, child/children*), the change from *y* to *ies* (*city/cities, specialty/specialties*), or the change from *f* to *v* (*knife/knives, half/halves*; some exceptions: *fifes, roofs*). Some words of Latin origin offer a choice of plurals (*phenomena/phenomenons, indexes/indices, appendixes/appendices*). It's always a good idea to consult a dictionary if you are unsure of the correct or preferred plural spelling of a word.

The plurals of compound nouns are usually formed by adding *s* or *es* to the main word of the compound (*fathers-in-law, editors-in-chief, attorneys-at-law*).

Some nouns are the same whether singular or plural (*sleep, deer, moose*). Some nouns are plural in form but singular in use (*ethics, measles*). Some nouns are used in the plural only (*scissors, trousers*).

Letters, numbers, and words used as words are sometimes made plural by adding an apostrophe and an *s* (*A's, Ph.D.'s, I's*). However, if no confusion would be created by leaving off the apostrophe, it is common practice to just add the *s* (*1990s, RFPs, DVDs*).

1.1.4 Possessive Nouns

A noun becomes possessive when it's used to show the ownership of something. Then you add *'s* to the word:

the man's car	the woman's apartment

However, ownership does not need to be legal:

the secretary's desk	the company's assets

Also, ownership may be nothing more than an automatic association:

a day's work	the job's prestige

An exception to the rule about adding *'s* to make a noun possessive occurs when the word is singular and already has two "s" sounds at the end. In cases like the following, an apostrophe is all that's needed:

crisis' dimensions	Mr. Moses' application

When the noun has only one "s" sound at the end, however, retain the *'s*:

Chris's book	Carolyn Nuss's office

With compound (hyphenated) nouns, add *'s* to the last word:

Compound Noun	Possessive Noun
mother-in-law	mother-in-law's
mayor-elect	mayor-elect's

To form the possessive of plural nouns, just begin by following the same rule as with singular nouns: add *'s*. However, if the plural noun already ends in an *s* (as most do), drop the one you've added, leaving only the apostrophe:

the clients' complaints	employees' benefits

To denote joint possession by two or more proper nouns, add the *'s* to the last name only (*Moody, Nation,* and *Smith's* ad agency). To denote individual possession by two or more persons, add an *'s* to each proper noun (*Moody's, Nation's,* and *Smith's* ad agencies).

1.1.5 Collective Nouns

Collective nouns encompass a group of people or objects: *crowd, jury, committee, team, audience, family, couple, herd, class.* They are often treated as singular nouns. (For more on collective nouns, see Section 1.3.4, Subject–Verb Agreement.)

1.2 PRONOUNS

A **pronoun** is a word that stands for a noun; it saves repeating the noun:

> Employees have some choice of weeks for vacation, but *they* must notify the HR office of *their* preference by March 1.

The pronouns *they* and *their* stand in for the noun *employees.* The noun that a pronoun stands for is called the **antecedent** of the pronoun; *employees* is the antecedent of *they* and *their.*

When the antecedent is plural, the pronoun that stands in for it has to be plural; *they* and *their* are plural pronouns because *employees* is plural. Likewise, when the antecedent is singular, the pronoun has to be singular:

> We thought the contract had expired, but we soon learned that *it* had not.

However, you should be aware that expectations are changing regarding the use of *they* (and its variants *their, them,* and *themselves*) as singular pronouns, and these evolving expectations will be a source of uncertainty for some time to come. The problem stems from the fact that English does not have a gender-neutral singular pronoun to refer to people. In the past, many writers defaulted to *he* and its variants in order to be grammatically correct, even though doing so created situations in which the language was sexist. The solutions of using *he or she* or switching back and forth between *he* and *she* in a document can be awkward, particularly in paragraphs that require multiple pronouns based on the same antecedent.

In response to this need for a gender-neutral pronoun, many linguists and some style guides now consider it grammatically acceptable to use *they* and *their* to refer to a singular noun, as in this sentence:

> Any employee seeking a promotional opportunity must check with *their* supervisor first to make sure all performance reviews are up to date.

Using *their* in this case neatly avoids the problems of sexist and awkward language and will probably become even more widely accepted in the coming years. However, some readers still continue to view it as a grammatical error and an instance of careless writing, which creates a dilemma for business communicators.

The simplest solution is often to rewrite sentences in order to make all the affected nouns and pronouns plural:

> *All employees* seeking *promotional opportunities* must check with *their supervisors* first to make sure all performance reviews are up to date.

If rewriting the sentence isn't feasible, you have to decide whether using *they* or one of its variants will diminish your credibility in the eyes of your readers. Using *he or she* is still perfectly acceptable, although it can feel overly formal in some contexts.

(Note that even as the usage of *they* evolves, the rule of matching singular pronouns with singular nouns and plural pronouns with plural nouns stays intact. The change taking place is that *they* is gradually becoming both a singular and plural term, depending on context, just as *you* can be singular or plural).

1.2.1 Multiple Antecedents

Sometimes a pronoun has a double (or even a triple) antecedent:

Kathryn Boettcher and Luis Gutierrez went beyond *their* sales quotas for January.

If taken alone, *Kathryn Boettcher* is a singular antecedent. So is *Luis Gutierrez*. However, when together they are the plural antecedent of a pronoun, so the pronoun has to be plural. Thus the pronoun is *their* instead of *her* or *his*.

1.2.2 Unclear Antecedents

In some sentences the pronoun's antecedent is unclear:

Sandy Wright sent Jane Brougham *her* production figures for the previous year. *She* thought they were too low.

To which person does the pronoun *her* refer? Someone who knew Sandy and Jane and knew their business relationship might be able to figure out the antecedent for *her*. Even with such an advantage, however, a reader might receive the wrong meaning. Also, it would be nearly impossible for any reader to know which name is the antecedent of *she*.

The best way to clarify an ambiguous pronoun is usually to rewrite the sentence, repeating nouns when needed for clarity:

Sandy Wright sent her production figures for the previous year to Jane Brougham. Jane thought they were too low.

The noun needs to be repeated only when the antecedent is unclear.

1.2.3 Pronoun Classes

Personal pronouns consist of *I, you, we/us, he/him, she/her, it,* and *they/them.*

Compound personal pronouns are created by adding *self* or *selves* to simple personal pronouns: *myself, ourselves, yourself, yourselves, himself, herself, itself, themselves*. Compound personal pronouns are used either *intensively*, to emphasize the identity of the noun or pronoun (I *myself* have seen the demonstration), or *reflexively*, to indicate that the subject is the receiver of his or her own action (I promised *myself* I'd finish by noon). Compound personal pronouns are used incorrectly if they appear in a sentence without their antecedent:

Walter, Virginia, and *I* (not *myself*) are the top salespeople.

You need to tell *her* (not *herself*) about the mixup.

Relative pronouns refer to nouns (or groups of words used as nouns) in the main clause and are used to introduce clauses:

Purina is the brand *that* most dog owners purchase.

The relative pronouns are *which, who, whom, whose,* and *what*. Other words used as relative pronouns include *that, whoever, whomever, whatever,* and *whichever*.

Interrogative pronouns are those used for asking questions: *who, whom, whose, which,* and *what*.

Demonstrative pronouns point out particular persons, places, or things:

That is my desk.   *This* can't be correct.

The demonstrative pronouns are *this, these, that,* and *those*.

Indefinite pronouns refer to persons or things not specifically identified. They include *anyone, someone, everyone, everybody, somebody, either, neither, one, none, all, both, each, another, any, many,* and similar words.

1.2.4 Case of Pronouns

The case of a pronoun tells whether it's acting or acted upon:

She sells an average of five packages each week.

In this sentence, *she* is doing the selling. Because *she* is acting, *she* is said to be in the **nominative case**. Now consider what happens when the pronoun is acted upon:

After six months, Ms. Browning promoted *her*.

In this sentence, the pronoun *her* is acted upon and is thus said to be in the **objective case**.

Contrast the nominative and objective pronouns in this list:

Nominative	Objective
I	me
we	us
he	him
she	her
they	them
who	whom
whoever	whomever

Objective pronouns may be used as either the object of a verb (such as *promoted*) or the object of a preposition (such as *with*):

Rob worked with *them* until the order was filled.

In this example, *them* is the object of the preposition *with* because Rob acted upon—worked with—them. Here's a sentence with three pronouns, the first one nominative, the second the object of a verb, and the third the object of a preposition:

> *He* paid *us* as soon as the check came from *them*.

He is nominative; *us* is objective because it's the object of the verb *paid*; *them* is objective because it's the object of the preposition *from*.

Every writer sometimes wonders whether to use *who* or *whom*:

> (*Who, Whom*) will you hire?

Because this sentence is a question, it's difficult to see that *whom* is the object of the verb *hire*. You can figure out which pronoun to use if you rearrange the question and temporarily try *she* and *her* in place of *who* and *whom*: "Will you hire *she?*" or "Will you hire *her?*" *Her* and *whom* are both objective, so the correct choice is "Whom will you hire?" Here's a different example:

> (*Who, Whom*) logged so much travel time?

Turning the question into a statement, you get:

> He logged so much travel time.

Therefore, the correct statement is:

> Who logged so much travel time?

1.2.5 Possessive Pronouns

Possessive pronouns work like possessive nouns—they show ownership or automatic association:

her job	their preferences
his account	its equipment

However, possessive pronouns are different from possessive nouns in the way they are written. Possessive pronouns never have an apostrophe:

Possessive Noun	Possessive Pronoun
the woman's estate	her estate
Roger Franklin's plans	his plans
the shareholders' feelings	their feelings
the vacuum cleaner's attachments	its attachments

The word *its* is the possessive of *it*. Like all other possessive pronouns, *its* has no apostrophe. Some people confuse *its* with *it's*, the contraction of *it is*. (Contractions are discussed in Section 2.9, Apostrophes.)

1.2.6 Pronoun-Antecedent Agreement

Like nouns, pronouns can be singular or plural. Pronouns must agree in number with their antecedents—a singular antecedent requires a singular pronoun:

> The president of the board tendered *his* resignation.

Multiple antecedents require a plural pronoun:

> The members of the board tendered *their* resignations.

A pronoun referring to singular antecedents connected by *or* or *nor* should be singular:

> Neither Sean nor Terry made his quota.

But a pronoun referring to a plural and a singular antecedent connected by *or* or *nor* should be plural:

> Neither Sean nor the twins made *their* quotas.

Formal English prefers the nominative case after the linking verb *to be*:

> It is *I*.   That is *he*.

However, for general usage it's perfectly acceptable to use the more natural "It's me" and "That's him."

1.3 VERBS

A **verb** describes an action or acts as a link between a subject and words that define or describe that subject:

> They all *quit* in disgust.
>
> Working conditions *were* substandard.

The English language is full of **action verbs**. Here are a few you'll often run across in the business world:

verify	perform	fulfill
hire	succeed	send
leave	improve	receive
accept	develop	pay

You could undoubtedly list many more.

The most common **linking verbs** are all the forms of *to be*: I *am*, *was*, or *will be*; you *are*, *were*, or *will be*. Other words that can serve as linking verbs include *seem*, *become*, *appear*, *prove*, *look*, *remain*, *feel*, *taste*, *smell*, *sound*, *resemble*, *turn*, and *grow*:

> It *seemed* a good plan at the time.
>
> She *sounds* impressive at a meeting.
>
> The time *grows* near for us to make a decision.

These verbs link what comes before them in the sentence with what comes after; no action is involved. (See Section 1.7.5 for a fuller discussion of linking verbs.)

An **auxiliary verb** is one that helps another verb and is used for showing tense, voice, and so on. A verb with its helpers is called a **verb phrase**. Verbs used as auxiliaries include *do*, *did*, *have*, *may*, *can*, *must*, *shall*, *might*, *could*, *would*, and *should*.

1.3.1 Verb Tenses

English has three simple verb tenses: present, past, and future.

> | | |
> |---|---|
> | **Present:** | Our branches in Hawaii *stock* other items. |
> | **Past:** | We *stocked* Purquil pens for a short time. |
> | **Future:** | Rotex Tire Stores *will stock* your line of tires when you begin a program of effective national advertising. |

With most verbs (the regular ones), the past tense ends in *ed*, and the future tense always has *will* or *shall* in front of it. But the present tense is more complex, depending on the subject:

> | | First Person | Second Person | Third Person |
> |---|---|---|---|
> | **Singular** | I stock | you stock | he/she/it stocks |
> | Plural | we stock | you stock | they stock |

The basic form, *stock*, takes an additional *s* when *he*, *she*, or *it* precedes it. (See Section 1.3.4 for more on subject–verb agreement.)

In addition to the three simple tenses, the three **perfect tenses** are created by adding forms of the auxiliary verb *have*. The present perfect tense uses the past participle (regularly the past tense) of the main verb, *stocked*, and adds the present-tense *have* or *has* to the front of it:

> (I, we, you, they) *have stocked*.
>
> (He, she, it) *has stocked*.

The past perfect tense uses the past participle of the main verb, *stocked*, and adds the past-tense *had* to the front of it:

> (I, you, he, she, it, we, they) *had stocked*.

The future perfect tense also uses the past participle of the main verb, *stocked*, but adds the future-tense *will have*:

> (I, you, he, she, it, we, they) *will have stocked*.

Verbs should be kept in the same tense when the actions occur at the same time:

> When the payroll checks *came in*, everyone *showed up* for work.
>
> We *have found* that everyone *has pitched* in to help.

When the actions occur at different times, you may change tense accordingly:

> The shipment *came* last Wednesday, so if another one *comes* in today, please return it.
>
> The new employee *had been* ill at ease, but now she *has become* a full-fledged member of the team.

1.3.2 Irregular Verbs

Many verbs don't follow some of the standard patterns for verb tenses. The most irregular of these verbs is *to be*:

> | Tense | Singular | Plural |
> |---|---|---|
> | **Present:** | I *am* | we *are* |
> | | you *are* | you *are* |
> | | he, she, it *is* | they *are* |
> | **Past:** | I *was* | we *were* |
> | | you *were* | you *were* |
> | | he, she, it *was* | they *were* |

The future tense of *to be* is formed in the same way that the future tense of a regular verb is formed.

The perfect tenses of *to be* are also formed as they would be for a regular verb, except that the past participle is a special form, *been*, instead of just the past tense:

> | | |
> |---|---|
> | **Present perfect:** | you have been |
> | **Past perfect:** | you had been |
> | **Future perfect:** | you will have been |

Here's a sampling of other irregular verbs:

Present	Past	Past Participle
begin	began	begun
shrink	shrank	shrunk
know	knew	known
rise	rose	risen
become	became	become
go	went	gone
do	did	done

Dictionaries list the various forms of other irregular verbs.

1.3.3 Transitive and Intransitive Verbs

Many people are confused by three particular sets of verbs:

lie/lay	sit/set	rise/raise

Using these verbs correctly is much easier when you learn the difference between transitive and intransitive verbs.

Transitive verbs require a receiver; they "transfer" their action to an object. **Intransitive verbs** do not have a receiver for their action. Some intransitive verbs are complete in themselves and need no help from other words (prices *dropped*; we *won*). Other intransitive words must be "completed" by a noun or adjective called a **complement**. Complements occur with linking verbs.

Here are some sample uses of transitive and intransitive verbs:

Intransitive	Transitive
We should include in our new offices a place to *lie* down for a nap.	The workers will be here on Monday to *lay* new carpeting.
Even the way an interviewee *sits* is important.	That crate is full of stemware, so *set* it down carefully.
Salaries at Compu-Link, Inc., *rise* swiftly.	They *raise* their level of production every year.

The workers *lay* carpeting, you *set down* the crate, they *raise* production; each action is transferred to something. In the intransitive sentences, a person *lies down*, an interviewee *sits*, and salaries *rise* without affecting anything else. Intransitive sentences are complete with only a subject and a verb; transitive sentences are not complete unless they also include an object; or something to transfer the action to.

Tenses are a confusing element of the *lie/lay* problem:

Present	Past	Past Participle
I *lie*	I *lay*	I *have lain*
I *lay* (something down)	I *laid* (something down)	I *have laid* (something down)

The past tense of *lie* and the present tense of *lay* look and sound alike, even though they're different verbs.

1.3.4 Subject-Verb Agreement

Whether regular or irregular, every verb must agree with its subject, both in person (first, second, or third) and in number (single or plural).

	First Person	Second Person	Third Person
Singular	I *am*	you *are*	he/she/it *is*
	I *write*	you *write*	he/she/it *writes*
Plural	we *are*	you *are*	they *are*
	we *write*	you *write*	they *write*

In a simple sentence, making a verb agree with its subject is a straightforward task:

Hector Ruiz *is* a strong competitor. (third-person singular)

We *write* to you every month. (first-person plural)

Confusion sometimes arises when sentences are a bit more complicated. For example, be sure to avoid agreement problems when words come between the subject and verb. In the following examples, the verb appears in italics, and its subject is underlined:

The <u>analysis</u> of existing documents *takes* a full week.

Even though *documents* is a plural, the verb is in the singular form. That's because the subject of the sentence is *analysis*, a singular noun. The phrase *of existing documents* can be disregarded. Here is another example:

The <u>answers</u> for this exercise *are* in the study guide.

Take away the phrase *for this exercise* and you are left with the plural subject *answers*. Therefore, the verb takes the plural form.

Verb agreement is also complicated when the subject is a collective noun or pronoun or when the subject may be considered either singular or plural. In such cases, you often have to analyze the surrounding sentence to determine which verb form to use:

The <u>staff</u> *is* quartered in the warehouse.

The <u>staff</u> *are* at their desks in the warehouse.

The <u>computers</u> and the <u>staff</u> *are* in the warehouse.

Neither the staff nor the <u>computers</u> *are* in the warehouse.

<u>Every</u> computer *is* in the warehouse.

Many a <u>computer</u> *is* in the warehouse.

Did you notice that words such as *every* use the singular verb form? In addition, when an *either/or* or a *neither/nor* phrase combines singular and plural nouns, the verb takes the form that matches the noun closest to it.

In the business world, some subjects require extra attention. Company names, for example, are considered singular and therefore take a singular verb in most cases—even if they contain plural words:

> Stater Brothers *offers* convenient grocery shopping.

In addition, quantities are sometimes considered singular and sometimes plural. If a quantity refers to a total amount, it takes a singular verb; if a quantity refers to individual, countable units, it takes a plural verb:

> Three hours *is* a long time.
>
> The eight dollars we collected for the fund *are* tacked on the bulletin board.

Fractions may also be singular or plural, depending on the noun that accompanies them:

> One-third of the warehouse *is* devoted to this product line.
>
> One-third of the products *are* defective.

To decide whether to use a singular or plural verb with subjects such as *number* and *variety*, follow this simple rule: If the subject is preceded by *a*, use a plural verb:

> *A* number of products *are* being displayed at the trade show.

If the subject is preceded by *the*, use a singular verb:

> *The* variety of products on display *is* mind-boggling.

For a related discussion, see Section 1.7.1, Longer Sentences.

1.3.5 Voice of Verbs

Verbs have two voices, active and passive. When the subject comes first, the verb is in **active voice**; when the object comes first, the verb is in **passive voice**:

> **Active:**   The buyer *paid* a large amount.
>
> **Passive:**   A large amount *was paid* by the buyer.

The passive voice uses a form of the verb *to be*, which adds words to a sentence. In the example, the passive-voice sentence uses eight words, whereas the active-voice sentence uses only six to say the same thing. The words *was* and *by* are unnecessary to convey the meaning of the sentence. In fact, extra words usually clog meaning. So be sure to opt for the active voice when you have a choice.

At times, however, you have no choice:

> Several items *have been taken*, but so far we don't know who took them.

The passive voice becomes necessary when you don't know (or don't want to say) who performed the action; the active voice is bolder and more direct.

1.3.6 Mood of Verbs

Verbs can express one of three moods: indicative, imperative, or subjunctive. The **indicative mood** is used to make a statement or to ask a question:

> The secretary mailed a letter to each supplier.
>
> Did the secretary mail a letter to each supplier?

Use the **imperative mood** when you wish to command or request:

> Please mail a letter to each supplier.

With the imperative mood, the subject is the understood *you*.

The **subjunctive mood** is used to express doubt or a wish or a condition contrary to fact:

> If I *were* you, I wouldn't send that email.

The subjunctive is also used to express a suggestion or a request:

> I asked that Rosario *be* [not *is*] present at the meeting.

1.3.7 Verbals

Verbals are verbs that are modified to function as other parts of speech. They include infinitives, gerunds, and participles.

Infinitives are formed by placing a *to* in front of the verb (*to go, to purchase, to work*). They function as nouns. Although many of us were taught that it is incorrect to split an infinitive—that is, to place an adverb between the *to* and the verb—this "rule" never had much logical linguistic basis and is no longer rigidly advocated by many contemporary language experts. In some cases, the adverb is best placed in the middle of the infinitive to avoid awkward constructions or ambiguous meaning:

> Production of steel is expected to *moderately exceed* domestic use.

Gerunds are verbals formed by adding *ing* to a verb (*going, having, working*). Like infinitives, they function as nouns. Gerunds and gerund phrases take a singular verb:

> *Borrowing* from banks *is* preferable to getting venture capital.

Participles are verb forms used as adjectives. The present participle ends in *ing* and generally describes action going on at the same time as other action:

> *Checking* the schedule, the contractor was pleased with progress on the project.

The **past participle** is usually the same form as the past tense and generally indicates completed action:

> When *completed*, the project will occupy six city blocks.

The **perfect participle** is formed by adding *having* to the past participle:

> *Having completed* the project, the contractor submitted his last invoice.

1.4 ADJECTIVES

An **adjective** modifies (tells something about) a noun or pronoun. Each of the following phrases says more about the noun or pronoun than the noun or pronoun would say alone:

> an *efficient* staff   a *heavy* price
>
> *brisk* trade   *light* web traffic

Adjectives modify nouns more often than they modify pronouns. When adjectives do modify pronouns, however, the sentence usually has a linking verb:

> They were *attentive*.   It looked *appropriate*.
>
> He seems *interested*.   You are *skillful*.

1.4.1 Types of Adjectives

Adjectives serve a variety of purposes. **Descriptive adjectives** express some quality belonging to the modified item (*tall, successful, green*). **Limiting** or **definitive adjectives**, on the other hand, point out the modified item or limit its meaning without expressing a quality. Types include:

- Numeral adjectives (*one, fifty, second*)
- Articles (*a, an, the*)
- Pronominal adjectives: pronouns used as adjectives (*his* desk, *each* employee)
- Demonstrative adjectives: *this, these, that, those* (*these* tires, *that* invoice)

Proper adjectives are derived from proper nouns:

> *Chinese* customs   *Orwellian* overtones

Predicate adjectives complete the meaning of the predicate and are introduced by linking verbs:

> The location is *perfect*.   Prices are *high*.

1.4.2 Comparative Degree

Most adjectives can take three forms: simple, comparative, and superlative. The simple form modifies a single noun or pronoun. Use the comparative form when comparing two items. When comparing three or more items, use the superlative form:

Simple	Comparative	Superlative
hard	harder	hardest
safe	safer	safest
dry	drier	driest

The comparative form adds *er* to the simple form, and the superlative form adds *est*. (The *y* at the end of a word changes to *i* before the *er* or *est* is added.)

A small number of adjectives are irregular, including these:

Simple	Comparative	Superlative
good	better	best
bad	worse	worst
little	less	least

When the simple form of an adjective has two or more syllables, you usually add *more* to form the comparative and *most* to form the superlative:

Simple	Comparative	Superlative
useful	more useful	most useful
exhausting	more exhausting	most exhausting
expensive	more expensive	most expensive

The most common exceptions are two-syllable adjectives that end in *y*:

Simple	Comparative	Superlative
happy	happier	happiest
costly	costlier	costliest

If you choose this option, change the *y* to *i* and tack *er* or *est* onto the end. (Note that when *more, most*, or any other adjective is used to modify another adjective, it becomes an adverb. See 1.5.2, Adverb-Adjective Confusion.)

Some adjectives cannot be used to make comparisons because they themselves indicate the extreme. For example, if something is perfect, nothing can be more perfect. If something is unique or ultimate, nothing can be more unique or more ultimate.

1.4.3 Hyphenated Adjectives

Many adjectives used in the business world are actually combinations of words: *up-to-date* report, *last-minute* effort, *fifth-floor* suite, *well-built* engine. As you can see, they are hyphenated when they come before the noun they modify. However, when such word combinations come after the noun they modify, they are not hyphenated. In the following example, the adjectives appear in italics and the nouns they modify are underlined:

> The <u>report</u> is *up to date* because of our team's *last-minute* <u>efforts</u>.

Hyphens are not used when part of the combination is a word ending in *ly* (because that word is usually not an adjective). Hyphens are also omitted from word combinations that are used so frequently that readers are used to seeing the words together and are therefore unlikely to misread them without hyphens:

> We live in a *rapidly shrinking* world.
>
> Our *highly motivated* employees will be well paid.
>
> Please consider renewing your *credit card* account.
>
> Send those figures to our *data processing* department.
>
> Our new intern is a *high school* student.

1.5 ADVERBS

An **adverb** modifies a verb, an adjective, or another adverb:

Modifying a verb:	Our marketing department works *efficiently*.
Modifying an adjective:	She was not dependable, although she was *highly* intelligent.
Modifying another adverb:	When signing new clients, he moved *extremely* cautiously.

An adverb can be a single word (*clearly*), a phrase (*very clearly*), or a clause (*because it was clear*).

1.5.1 Types of Adverbs

Simple adverbs are simple modifiers:

> The door opened *automatically*.
>
> The order arrived *yesterday*.
>
> Top companies were *there*.

Interrogative adverbs ask a question:

> *Where* have you been?

Conjunctive adverbs connect clauses:

> The boardroom isn't available for the meeting; *however*, the conference room should be clear.
>
> We met all our sales goals for April; *therefore*, all sales reps will get a bonus.

Words frequently used as conjunctive adverbs include *however*, *nevertheless*, *therefore*, *similarly*, *thus*, and *meanwhile*.

Negative adverbs include *not*, *never*, *seldom*, *rarely*, *scarcely*, *hardly*, and similar words. Negative adverbs are powerful words and therefore do not need any help in conveying a negative thought. Avoid using double negatives like these:

> I don't want no mistakes.
>
> (Correct: "I don't want any mistakes," or "I want no mistakes.")
>
> They couldn't hardly read the report.
>
> (Correct: "They could hardly read the report," or "They couldn't read the report.")
>
> They scarcely noticed neither one.
>
> (Correct: "They scarcely noticed either one," or "They noticed neither one.")

1.5.2 Adverb-Adjective Confusion

Many adverbs are adjectives turned into adverbs by adding *ly*: *highly*, *extremely*, *officially*, *closely*, *really*. In addition, many words can be adjectives or adverbs with no change in spelling, depending on their usage in a particular sentence:

The *early* bird gets the worm. [adjective]	We arrived *early*. [adverb]
It was a *hard* decision. [adjective]	He hit the wall *hard*. [adverb]
I enjoy *most* forms of jazz. [adjective]	My finances are my *most* important problem. [adverb]

Because of this situation, some adverbs are difficult to distinguish from adjectives. For example, in the following sentences, is the underlined word an adverb or an adjective?

> They worked <u>well</u>.
>
> The baby is <u>well</u>.

In the first sentence, *well* is an adverb modifying the verb *worked*. In the second sentence, *well* is an adjective modifying the noun *baby*. You may find it helpful to remember that a *linking verb* (such as *is* in "The baby is well") connects an adjective to the noun it modifies. In contrast, an *action verb* is modified by an adverb:

Adjective	Adverb
He is a *good* worker.	He works *well*.
(What kind of worker is he?)	(How does he work?)
It is a *real* computer.	It *really* is a computer.
(What kind of computer is it?)	(To what extent is it a computer?)
The traffic is *slow*.	The traffic moves *slowly*.
(What quality does the traffic have?)	(How does the traffic move?)
This food tastes *bad* without salt.	This food *badly* needs salt.
(What quality does the food have?)	(How much is it needed?)

1.5.3 Comparative Degree

Like adjectives, adverbs can be used to compare items. Generally, the basic adverb is combined with *more* or *most*, just as long adjectives are. However, some adverbs have one-word comparative forms:

One Item	Two Items	Three Items
quickly	more quickly	most quickly
sincerely	less sincerely	least sincerely
fast	faster	fastest
well	better	best

1.6 OTHER PARTS OF SPEECH

Nouns, pronouns, verbs, adjectives, and adverbs carry most of the meaning in a sentence. Four other parts of speech link them together in sentences: prepositions, conjunctions, articles, and interjections.

1.6.1 Prepositions

A **preposition** is a word or group of words that describes a relationship between other words in a sentence. A simple preposition is made up of one word: *of, in, by, above, below*. A *compound preposition* is made up of two prepositions: *out of, from among, except for, because of*.

A **prepositional phrase** is a group of words introduced by a preposition that functions as an adjective (an adjectival phrase) or as an adverb (adverbial phrase) by telling more about a pronoun, noun, or verb:

The shipment will be here *by next Friday*.

Put the mail *in the out-bin*.

Prepositional phrases should be placed as close as possible to the element they are modifying:

Shopping *on the Internet* can be confusing for the uninitiated. (*not* Shopping can be confusing for the uninitiated *on the Internet*.)

Some prepositions are closely linked with a verb. When using phrases such as *look up* and *wipe out*, keep them intact and do not insert anything between the verb and the preposition.

You may have been told that it is unacceptable to put a preposition at the end of a sentence. However, that is not a hard-and-fast rule, and trying to follow it can sometimes be a challenge. You can end a sentence with a preposition as along as the sentence sounds natural and as long as rewording the sentence would create awkward wording:

I couldn't tell what they were interested in.

What did she attribute it to?

What are you looking for?

Avoid using unnecessary prepositions. In the following examples, the prepositions in parentheses should be omitted:

All (of) the staff members were present.

I almost fell off (of) my chair with surprise.

Where was Mr. Steuben going (to)?

They couldn't help (from) wondering.

The opposite problem is failing to include a preposition when you should. Consider these two sentences:

Sales were over $100,000 for Linda and Bill.

Sales were over $100,000 for Linda and for Bill.

The first sentence indicates that Linda and Bill had combined sales over $100,000; the second, that Linda and Bill each had sales over $100,000, for a combined total in excess of $200,000. The preposition *for* is critical here.

When the same preposition can be used for two or more words in a sentence without affecting the meaning, only the last preposition is required:

We are familiar (with) and satisfied with your company's products.

But when different prepositions are normally used with the words, all the prepositions must be included:

We are familiar with and interested in your company's products.

Some prepositions have come to be used in a particular way with certain other parts of speech. Here is a partial list of some prepositions that have come to be used with certain words:

according to	independent of
agree to (a proposal)	inferior to
agree with (a person)	plan to
buy from	prefer to
capable of	prior to
comply with	reason with
conform to	responsible for
differ from (things)	similar to
differ with (person)	talk to (without interaction)
different from	talk with (with interaction)
get from (receive)	wait for (person or thing)
get off (dismount)	wait on (like a waiter)

If you are unsure of the correct idiomatic expression, check a dictionary.

Some verb-preposition idioms vary depending on the situation: You agree *to* a proposal but *with* a person, *on* a price, or *in* principle. You argue *about* something, *with* a person, and *for* or *against* a proposition. You compare one item *to* another to show their similarities; you compare one item *with* another to show differences.

Here are some other examples of preposition usage that have given writers trouble:

among/between: *Among* is used to refer to three or more (Circulate the memo *among* the staff); *between* is used to refer to two (Put the copy machine *between* Judy and Dan).

as if/like: *As if* is used before a clause (It seems *as if* we should be doing something); *like* is used before a noun or pronoun (He seems *like* a nice guy).

have/of: *Have* is a verb used in verb phrases (They should *have* checked first); *of* is a preposition and is never used in such cases.

in/into: *In* is used to refer to a static position (The file is *in* the cabinet); *into* is used to refer to movement toward a position (Put the file *into* the cabinet).

1.6.2 Conjunctions

Conjunctions connect the parts of a sentence: words, phrases, and clauses. A **coordinating conjunction** connects two words, phrases, or clauses of equal rank. The simple coordinating conjunctions include *and, but, or, nor, for, yet,* and *so.* **Correlative conjunctions** are coordinating conjunctions used in pairs: *both/and, either/or, neither/nor, not only/but also.* Constructions with correlative conjunctions should be parallel, with the same part of speech following each element of the conjunction:

The purchase was *not only* expensive *but also* unnecessary.

The purchase *not only was* expensive *but also was* unnecessary.

Conjunctive adverbs are adverbs used to connect or show relationships between clauses. They include *however, nevertheless, consequently, moreover,* and *as a result.*

A **subordinate conjunction** connects two clauses of unequal rank; it joins a dependent (subordinate) clause to the independent clause on which it depends (for more on dependent and independent clauses, see Section 1.7.1). Subordinate conjunctions include *as, if, because, although, while, before, since, that, until, unless, when, where,* and *whether.*

1.6.3 Articles and Interjections

Only three **articles** exist in English: *the, a,* and *an.* These words are used, like adjectives, to specify which item you are talking about. *The* is called the *definite article* because it indicates a specific noun; *a* and *an* are called the *indefinite articles* because they are less specific about what they are referring to.

If a word begins with a vowel (soft) sound, use *an;* otherwise, use *a.* It's *a history,* not *an history, a hypothesis,* not *an hypothesis.* Use *an* with an "h" word only if it is a soft "h," as in *honor* and *hour.* Use *an* with words that are pronounced with a soft vowel sound even if they are spelled beginning with a consonant (usually in the case of abbreviations): *an SEC application, an MP3 file.* Use *a* with words that begin with vowels if they are pronounced with a hard sound: *a university, a Usenet account.*

Repeat an article if adjectives modify different nouns: *The red house and the white house are mine.* Do not repeat an article if all adjectives modify the same noun: *The red and white house is mine.*

Interjections are words that express no solid information, only emotion:

Wow!	Well, well!
Oh, no!	Good!

Such purely emotional language has its place in private life and advertising copy, but it only weakens the effect of most business writing.

1.7 SENTENCES

Sentences are constructed with the major building blocks, the parts of speech. Take, for example, this simple two-word sentence:

Money talks.

It consists of a noun (*money*) and a verb (*talks*). When used in this way, the noun works as the first requirement for a sentence, the **subject**, and the verb works as the second requirement, the **predicate**. Without a subject (who or what does something) and a predicate (the doing of it), you have merely a collection of words, not a sentence.

1.7.1 Longer Sentences

More complicated sentences have more complicated subjects and predicates, but they still have a simple subject and a predicate verb. In the following examples, the subject is underlined once, the predicate verb twice:

Marex and Contron enjoy higher earnings each quarter.

Marex [and] *Contron* do something; *enjoy* is what they do.

My interview, coming minutes after my freeway accident, did not impress or move anyone.

Interview is what did something. What did it do? It *did* [not] *impress* [or] *move*.

In terms of usable space, a steel warehouse, with its extremely long span of roof unsupported by pillars, makes more sense.

Warehouse is what *makes*.

These three sentences demonstrate several things. First, in all three sentences, the simple subject and predicate verb are the "bare bones" of the sentence, the parts that carry the core idea of the sentence. When trying to find the subject and predicate verb, disregard all prepositional phrases, modifiers, conjunctions, and articles.

Second, in the third sentence, the verb is singular (*makes*) because the subject is singular (*warehouse*). Even though the plural noun *pillars* is closer to the verb, *warehouse* is the subject. So *warehouse* determines whether the verb is singular or plural. Subject and predicate must agree.

Third, the subject in the first sentence is compound (*Marex* [and] *Contron*). A compound subject, when connected by *and*, requires a plural verb (*enjoy*). Also, the second sentence shows how compound predicates can occur (*did* [not] *impress* [or] *move*).

Fourth, the second sentence incorporates a group of words—*coming minutes after my freeway accident*—containing a form of a verb (*coming*) and a noun (*accident*). Yet, this group of words is not a complete sentence for two reasons:

- **Not all nouns are subjects:** *Accident* is not the subject of *coming*.
- **Not all verbs are predicates:** A verb that ends in *ing* can never be the predicate of a sentence (unless preceded by a form of *to be*, as in *was coming*).

Because they don't contain a subject and a predicate, the words *coming minutes after my freeway accident* (called a **phrase**) can't be written as a sentence. That is, the phrase cannot stand alone; it cannot begin with a capital letter and end with a period. So a phrase must always be just one part of a sentence.

Sometimes a sentence incorporates two or more groups of words that do contain a subject and a predicate; these word groups are called **clauses**:

My interview, because it came minutes after my freeway accident, did not impress or move anyone.

The **independent clause** is the portion of the sentence that could stand alone without revision:

My *interview* did not impress or move anyone.

The other part of the sentence could stand alone only by removing *because*:

(because) It came minutes after my freeway accident.

This part of the sentence is known as a **dependent clause**; although it has a subject and a predicate (just as an independent clause does), it's linked to the main part of the sentence by a word (*because*) showing its dependence.

In summary, the two types of clauses—dependent and independent—both have a subject and a predicate. Dependent clauses, however, do not bear the main meaning of the sentence and are therefore linked to an independent clause. Nor can phrases stand alone, because they lack both a subject and a predicate. Only independent clauses can be written as sentences without revision.

1.7.2 Types of Sentences

Sentences come in four main types, depending on the extent to which they contain clauses. A **simple sentence** has one subject and one predicate; in short, it has one main independent clause:

Boeing is the world's largest aerospace company.

A **compound sentence** consists of two independent clauses connected by a coordinating conjunction (*and*, *or*, *but*, etc.) or a semicolon:

Airbus outsold Boeing for several years, but Boeing has recently regained the lead.

A **complex sentence** consists of an independent clause and one or more dependent clauses:

Boeing is betting [independent clause] that airlines will begin using moderately smaller planes to fly passengers between smaller cities [dependent clause introduced by *that*].

A **compound-complex sentence** has two main clauses, at least one of which contains a subordinate (dependent clause):

> Boeing is betting [independent clause] that airlines will begin using moderately smaller planes to fly passengers between smaller cities [dependent clause], and it anticipates that new airports will be developed to meet passenger needs [independent clause].

1.7.3 Sentence Fragments

An incomplete sentence (a phrase or a dependent clause) that is written as though it were a complete sentence is called a **fragment**. Consider the following sentence fragments:

> Marilyn Sanders, having had pilferage problems in her store for the past year. Refuses to accept the results of our investigation.

This serious error can easily be corrected by putting the two fragments together:

> Marilyn Sanders, having had pilferage problems in her store for the past year, refuses to accept the results of our investigation.

The actual details of a situation will determine the best way for you to remedy a fragment problem.

The ban on fragments has one exception. Some advertising copy contains sentence fragments, written knowingly to convey a certain rhythm. However, advertising is the only area of business in which fragments are acceptable.

1.7.4 Fused Sentences and Comma Splices

Just as there can be too little in a group of words to make it a sentence, there can also be too much:

> All our mail is run through a postage meter every afternoon someone picks it up.

This example contains two sentences, not one, but the two have been blended so that it's hard to tell where one ends and the next begins. Is the mail run through a meter every afternoon? If so, the sentences should read:

> All our mail is run through a postage meter every afternoon. Someone picks it up.

Perhaps the mail is run through a meter at some other time (morning, for example) and is picked up every afternoon:

> All our mail is run through a postage meter. Every afternoon someone picks it up.

The order of words is the same in all three cases; sentence division makes all the difference. Either of the last two cases is grammatically correct. The choice depends on the facts of the situation.

Sometimes these so-called **fused sentences** have a more obvious point of separation:

> Several large orders arrived within a few days of one another, too many came in for us to process by the end of the month.

Here, the comma has been put between two independent clauses in an attempt to link them. When a lowly comma separates two complete sentences, the result is called a **comma splice**. A comma splice can be remedied in one of three ways:

- **Replace the comma with a period and capitalize the next word:** " . . . one another. Too many . . . "
- **Replace the comma with a semicolon and do not capitalize the next word:** " . . . one another; too many . . . " This remedy works only when the two sentences have closely related meanings.
- **Change one of the sentences so that it becomes a phrase or a dependent clause.** This remedy often produces the best writing, but it takes more work.

The third alternative can be carried out in several ways. One is to begin the sentence with a subordinating conjunction:

> Whenever several large orders arrived within a few days of one another, too many came in for us to process by the end of the month.

Another way is to remove part of the subject or the predicate verb from one of the independent clauses, thereby creating a phrase:

> Several large orders arrived within a few days of one another, too many for us to process by the end of the month.

Finally, you can change one of the predicate verbs to its *ing* form:

> Several large orders arrived within a few days of one another, too many coming in for us to process by the end of the month.

In many cases, simply adding a coordinating conjunction can separate fused sentences or remedy a comma splice:

> You can fire them, or you can make better use of their abilities.

> Margaret drew up the designs, and Matt carried them out. We will have three strong months, but after that sales will taper off.

Be careful with coordinating conjunctions: Use them only to join simple sentences that express similar ideas.

Also, because they say relatively little about the relationship between the two clauses they join, avoid using coordinating conjunctions too often: *and* is merely an addition sign; *but* is just a turn signal; *or* only points to an alternative. Subordinating conjunctions such as *because* and *whenever* tell the reader a lot more.

1.7.5 Sentences with Linking Verbs

Linking verbs were discussed briefly in the section on verbs (Section 1.3). Here, you can see more fully the way they function in a sentence. The following is a model of any sentence with a linking verb:

A (*verb*) B.

Although words such as *seems* and *feels* can also be linking verbs, let's assume that the verb is a form of *to be*:

A *is* B.

In such a sentence, A and B are always nouns, pronouns, or adjectives. When one is a noun and the other is a pronoun, or when both are nouns, the sentence says that one is the same as the other:

She is president.

Rachel is president.

She is forceful.

Recall from Section 1.3.3 that the noun or adjective that follows the linking verb is called a *complement*. When it is a noun or noun phrase, the complement is called a *predicate nominative*, when the complement is an adjective, it is referred to as a *predicate adjective*.

1.7.6 Misplaced Modifiers

The position of a modifier in a sentence is important. The movement of *only* changes the meaning in the following sentences:

Only we are obliged to supply those items specified in your contract.

We are obliged only to supply those items specified in your contract.

We are obliged to supply only those items specified in your contract.

We are obliged to supply those items specified only in your contract.

In any particular set of circumstances, only one of those sentences would be accurate. The others would very likely cause problems. To prevent misunderstanding, place such modifiers as close as possible to the noun or verb they modify.

For similar reasons, whole phrases that are modifiers must be placed near the right noun or verb. Mistakes in placement create ludicrous meanings:

Antia Information Systems bought programmers the new computer chairs with more comfortable seats.

The anatomy of programmers is not normally a concern of business writers. Obviously, the comfort of the chairs was the issue:

Antia Information Systems bought new computer chairs for the programmers with more comfortable seats.

Here is another example:

I asked him to file all the letters in the cabinet that had been answered.

In this ridiculous sentence, the cabinet has been answered, even though no cabinet in history is known to have asked a question. *That had been answered* is too far from *letters* and too close to *cabinet*. Here's an improvement:

I asked him to file in the cabinet all the letters that had been answered.

The term **dangling modifier** is often used to refer to a clause or phrase that because of its position in the sentence seems to modify a word that it is not meant to modify. For instance:

Lying motionless, co-workers rushed to Barry's aid.

Readers expect an introductory phrase to modify the subject of the main clause. But in this case it wasn't the *co-workers* who were lying motionless but rather *Barry* who was in this situation. Like this example, most instances of dangling modifiers occur at the beginning of sentences. The source of some danglers is a passive construction:

To find the needed information, the whole book had to be read.

In such cases, switching to the active voice can usually remedy the problem:

To find the needed information, you will need to read the whole book.

1.7.7 Parallelism

Two or more sentence elements that have the same relation to another element should be in the same form. Otherwise, the reader is forced to work harder to understand the meaning of the sentence. When a series consists of phrases or clauses, the same part of speech (preposition, gerund, etc.) should introduce them. Do not mix infinitives with participles or adjectives with nouns. Here are some examples of nonparallel elements:

> Andersen is hiring managers, programmers, and people who work in accounting. [nouns not parallel]
>
> Andersen earns income by auditing, consulting, and by bookkeeping. [prepositional phrases not parallel]
>
> Andersen's goals are to win new clients, keeping old clients happy, and finding new enterprises. [infinitive mixed with gerunds]

2.0 Punctuation

On the highway, signs tell you when to slow down or stop, where to turn, and when to merge. In similar fashion, punctuation helps readers negotiate your prose. The proper use of punctuation keeps readers from losing track of your meaning.

2.1 PERIODS

Use a period (1) to end any sentence that is not a question, (2) with certain abbreviations, and (3) as a decimal with numbers (for example, between dollars and cents in an amount of money).

2.2 QUESTION MARKS

Use a question mark after any direct question that requests an answer:

> Are you planning to enclose a check, or shall we bill you?

Don't use a question mark with commands phrased as questions for the sake of politeness:

> Will you send us a check today.

A question mark should precede quotation marks, parentheses, and brackets if it is part of the quoted or parenthetical material; otherwise, it should follow:

> This issue of *Inc.* has an article titled "What's Your Entrepreneurial IQ?"
>
> Have you read the article "Five Principles of Guerrilla Marketing"?

Do not use the question mark with indirect questions or with requests:

> Mr. Antonelli asked whether anyone had seen Nathalia lately.

Do not use a comma or a period with a question mark; the question mark takes the place of these punctuation marks.

2.3 EXCLAMATION POINTS

Use exclamation points after highly emotional language. Because business writing almost never calls for emotional language, you will seldom use exclamation points.

2.4 SEMICOLONS

Semicolons have three main uses. One is to separate two closely related independent clauses:

> The outline for the report is due within a week; the report itself is due at the end of the month.

A semicolon should also be used instead of a comma when the items in a series have commas within them:

> Our previous meetings were on November 11, 2016; February 20, 2017; and April 27, 2018.

Finally, a semicolon should be used to separate independent clauses when the second one begins with a conjunctive adverb such as *however*, *therefore*, or *nevertheless* or a phrase such as *for example* or *in that case*:

> Our supplier has been out of part D712 for 10 weeks; however, we have found another source that can ship the part right away.
>
> His test scores were quite low; on the other hand, he has a lot of relevant experience.

Section 4.4 provides more information on using transitional words and phrases.

Semicolons should always be placed outside parentheses:

> Events Northwest has the contract for this year's convention (August 23–28); we haven't awarded the contract for next year yet.

2.5 COLONS

Use a colon after the salutation in a business letter. You should also use a colon at the end of a sentence or phrase introducing a list or (sometimes) a quotation:

> Our study included the three most critical problems: insufficient capital, incompetent management, and inappropriate location.

A colon should not be used when the list, quotation, or idea is a direct object of the verb or preposition. This rule applies whether the list is set off or run in:

> We are able to supply
>
> > staples
> >
> > wood screws
> >
> > nails
> >
> > toggle bolts
>
> This shipment includes 9 DVDs, 12 CDs, and 4 USB flash drives.

Another way you can use a colon is to separate the main clause and another sentence element when the second explains, illustrates, or amplifies the first:

> Management was unprepared for the union representatives' demands: this fact alone accounts for their arguing well into the night.

However, in contemporary usage, such clauses are frequently separated by a semicolon.

Like semicolons, colons should always be placed outside parentheses:

> He has an expensive list of new demands (none of which is covered in the purchase agreement): new carpeting, network cabling, and a new security system.

2.6 COMMAS

Commas have many uses; the most common is to separate items in a series:

> He took the job, learned it well, worked hard, and succeeded.
>
> Put paper, pencils, and paper clips on the requisition list.

Company style may dictate omitting the final comma in a series. However, if you have a choice, use the final comma; it's often necessary to prevent misunderstanding.

A second place to use a comma is between independent clauses that are joined by a coordinating conjunction (*and*, *but*, or *or*):

> She spoke to the sales staff, and he spoke to the production staff.
>
> I was advised to proceed, and I did.

A third use for the comma is to separate a dependent clause at the beginning of a sentence from an independent clause:

> Because of our lead in the market, we may be able to risk introducing a new product.

However, a dependent clause at the end of a sentence is separated from the independent clause by a comma only when the dependent clause is unnecessary to the main meaning of the sentence:

> We may be able to introduce a new product, although it may involve some risk.

A fourth use for the comma is after an introductory phrase or word:

> Starting with this amount of capital, we can survive in the red for one year.
>
> Through more careful planning, we may be able to serve more people.
>
> Yes, you may proceed as originally planned.

However, with short introductory prepositional phrases and some one-syllable words (such as *hence* and *thus*), the comma is often omitted:

> Before January 1 we must complete the inventory.
>
> Thus we may not need to hire anyone.
>
> In July we will complete the move to Tulsa.

Fifth, paired commas are used to set off nonrestrictive clauses and phrases. A **restrictive clause** is one that cannot be omitted without altering the meaning of the main clause, whereas a **nonrestrictive clause** can be:

> The *Time* magazine website, which is produced by Steve Conley, has won several design awards. [nonrestrictive: the material set off by commas could be omitted]
>
> The website that is produced by Steve Conley has won several design awards. [restrictive: no commas are used before and after *that is produced by Steve Conley* because this information is necessary to the meaning of the sentence—it specifies which website]

A sixth use for commas is to set off appositive words and phrases. (An **appositive** has the same meaning as the word it is in apposition to.) Like nonrestrictive clauses, appositives can be dropped without changing or obscuring the meaning of the sentence:

> Conley, a freelance designer, also produces the websites for several nonprofit corporations.

Seventh, commas are used between adjectives modifying the same noun (coordinate adjectives):

> She left Monday for a long, difficult recruiting trip.

To test the appropriateness of such a comma, try reversing the order of the adjectives: *a difficult, long recruiting trip*. If the order cannot be reversed, leave out the comma (a *good old friend* isn't the same as an *old good friend*). A comma should not be used when one of the adjectives is part of the noun. Compare these two phrases:

> a distinguished, well-known figure
>
> a distinguished public figure

The adjective-noun combination of *public* and *figure* has been used together so often that it has come to be considered a single thing: *public figure*. So no comma is required.

Eighth, commas are used both before and after the year in sentences that include month, day, and year:

> It will be sent by December 14, 2018, from our Cincinnati plant.

Some companies use the European style: 15 December 2018. No commas should be used in that case. Nor is a comma needed when only the month and year are present (December 2018).

Ninth, commas are used to set off a variety of parenthetical words and phrases within sentences, including state names, dates, abbreviations, transitional expressions, and contrasted elements:

> They were, in fact, prepared to submit a bid.
>
> Habermacher, Inc., went public in 1999.
>
> Our goal was increased profits, not increased market share.
>
> Service, then, is our main concern.
>
> The factory was completed in Chattanooga, Tennessee, just three weeks ago.
>
> Joanne Dubiik, M.D., has applied for a loan from First Savings.
>
> I started work here on March 1, 2003, and soon received my first promotion.

Tenth, a comma is used to separate a quotation from the rest of the sentence:

> Your warranty reads, "These conditions remain in effect for one year from date of purchase."

However, the comma is left out when the quotation as a whole is built into the structure of the sentence:

> He hurried off with an angry "Look where you're going."

Finally, a comma should be used whenever it's needed to avoid confusion or an unintended meaning. Compare the following:

> Ever since they have planned new ventures more carefully.
>
> Ever since, they have planned new ventures more carefully.

2.7 DASHES

Use dashes to surround a comment that is a sudden turn in thought:

> Membership in the IBSA—it's expensive but worth it—may be obtained by applying to our New York office.

A dash can also be used to emphasize a parenthetical word or phrase:

> Third-quarter profits—in excess of $2 million—are up sharply.

Finally, use dashes to set off a phrase that contains commas:

> All our offices—Milwaukee, New Orleans, and Phoenix—have sent representatives.

Don't confuse a dash with a hyphen. A dash separates and emphasizes words, phrases, and clauses more strongly than commas or parentheses can; a hyphen ties two words so tightly that they almost become one word.

When using a computer, use the em dash symbol. When typing a dash in email, type two hyphens with no space before, between, or after.

A second type of dash, the en dash, can be produced with computer word processing and page-layout programs. This kind of dash is shorter than the regular dash and longer than a hyphen. It is reserved almost exclusively for indicating "to" or "through" with numbers such as dates and pages: *2017–2018, pages 30–44.*

2.8 HYPHENS

Hyphens are mainly used in three ways. The first is to separate the parts of compound words beginning with such prefixes as *self-, ex-, quasi-,* and *all-*:

> self-assured   quasi-official
>
> ex-wife   all-important

However, do not use hyphens in words that have prefixes such as *pro, anti, non, re, pre, un, inter,* and *extra*:

> prolabor   nonunion
>
> antifascist   interdepartmental

Exceptions occur when (1) the prefix occurs before a proper noun or (2) the vowel at the end of the prefix is the same as the first letter of the root word:

pro-Republican	anti-American
anti-inflammatory	extra-atmospheric

When in doubt, consult your dictionary.

Hyphens are used in some types of spelled-out numbers. For instance, they are used to separate the parts of a spelled-out number from *twenty-one* to *ninety-nine* and for spelled-out fractions: *two-thirds, one-sixth* (although some style guides say not to hyphenate fractions used as nouns).

Certain compound nouns are formed by using hyphens: *secretary-treasurer, city-state*. Check your dictionary for compounds you're unsure about.

Hyphens are also used in some compound adjectives, which are adjectives made up of two or more words. Specifically, you should use hyphens in compound adjectives that come before the noun:

an interest-bearing account	well-informed executives

However, you need not hyphenate when the adjective follows a linking verb:

This account is interest bearing.

Their executives are well informed.

You can shorten sentences that list similar hyphenated words by dropping the common part from all but the last word:

Check the costs of first-, second-, and third-class postage.

Finally, hyphens may be used to divide words at the end of a typed line. Such hyphenation is best avoided, but when you have to divide words at the end of a line, do so correctly (see Section 3.5). Dictionaries show how words are divided into syllables.

2.9 APOSTROPHES

Use an apostrophe in the possessive form of noun (but not in a pronoun):

On his desk was a reply to Bette *Ainsley's* application for the *manager's* position.

Apostrophes are also used in place of the missing letter(s) of a contraction:

Whole Words	Contraction
we will	we'll
do not	don't
they are	they're

2.10 QUOTATION MARKS

Use quotation marks to surround words that are repeated exactly as they were said or written:

The collection letter ended by saying, "This is your third and final notice."

Remember: (1) When the quoted material is a complete sentence, the first word is capitalized. (2) The final comma or period goes inside the closing quotation marks.

Quotation marks are also used to set off the title of a newspaper story, magazine article, or book chapter:

You should read "Legal Aspects of the Collection Letter" in *Today's Credit*.

Quotation marks may also be used to indicate special treatment for words or phrases, such as terms that you're using in an unusual or ironic way:

Our management "team" spends more time squabbling than working to solve company problems.

When you are defining a word, put the definition in quotation marks:

The abbreviation *etc.* means "and so forth."

When using quotation marks, take care to insert the closing marks as well as the opening ones.

Although periods and commas go inside any quotation marks, colons and semicolons generally go outside them. A question mark goes inside the quotation marks only if the quotation is a question:

All that day we wondered, "Is he with us?"

If the quotation is not a question but the entire sentence is, the question mark goes outside:

What did she mean by "You will hear from me"?

For quotes within quotes, use single quotation marks within double:

Bonnie Schulman fired up the project team by saying, "We've all heard the doubts that this team can meet the goals outlined in '2015: The Strategic Imperative,' but I have total confidence in your ability and commitment."

Otherwise, do not use single quotation marks for anything, including titles of works—that's British style.

2.11 PARENTHESES AND BRACKETS

Use parentheses to surround comments that are entirely incidental or to supply additional information:

> Our figures do not match yours, although (if my calculations are correct) they are closer than we thought.

> Sally Wagner (no relation to our own John Wagner) was just promoted to general manager of the Detroit office.

Parentheses are used in legal documents to surround figures in arabic numerals that follow the same amount in words:

> Remittance will be one thousand two hundred dollars ($1,200).

Be careful to put punctuation marks (period, comma, and so on) outside the parentheses unless they are part of the statement in parentheses. And keep in mind that parentheses have both an opening and a closing mark; both should always be used, even when setting off listed items within text: (*1*), not *1*.

Brackets are used for notation, comment, explanation, or correction within quoted material:

> When asked for a reason, Jackson said, "The dismissal was a carefully considered decision, with input from every member [of the board of directors]."

Brackets are also used for parenthetical material that falls within parentheses:

> Drucker's magnum opus (*Management: Tasks, Responsibilities, Practices* [Harper & Row, 1979]) has influenced generations of entrepreneurs.

2.12 ELLIPSES

Use ellipsis points, or three evenly spaced periods, to indicate that material has been left out of a direct quotation. Use them only in direct quotations and only at the point where material was left out. In the following example, the first sentence is quoted in the second:

> The Dow Jones Industrial Average fell 276.39 points, or 2.6%, during the week to 10292.31.

> According to the *Wall Street Journal*, "The Dow Jones Industrial Average fell 276.39 points . . . to 10,292.31."

The number of dots in ellipses is not optional; always use three. Occasionally, the points of an ellipsis come at the end of a sentence, where they seem to grow a fourth dot. Don't be fooled: One of the dots is a period. Ellipsis points should always be preceded and followed by a space.

Avoid using ellipses to represent a pause in your writing; use a dash for that purpose:

> At first we had planned to leave for the conference on Wednesday—but then we changed our minds. [not *on Wednesday . . . but then*]

3.0 Mechanics

The most obvious and least tolerable mistakes that a business writer makes are probably those related to grammar and punctuation. However, a number of small details, known as writing mechanics, demonstrate the writer's polish and reflect on the company's professionalism.

When it comes to mechanics, also called *style*, many of the "rules" are not hard and fast. Publications and organizations vary in their preferred styles for capitalization, abbreviations, numbers, italics, and so on. Here, we'll try to differentiate between practices that are generally accepted and those that can vary. When you are writing materials for a specific company or organization, find out the preferred style (such as *The Chicago Manual of Style* or *Webster's Style Manual*). Otherwise, choose a respected style guide. The key to style is consistency: If you spell out the word *percent* in one part of a document, don't use the percent sign in a similar context elsewhere in the same document.

3.1 CAPITALIZATION

With capitalization, you can follow either an "up" style (when in doubt, capitalize: *Federal Government, Board of Directors*) or a "down" style (when in doubt, use lowercase: *federal government, board of directors*). The trend over the last few decades has been toward the down style. Your best bet is to get a good style manual and consult it when you have a capitalization question. Following are some rules that most style guides agree on.

Capital letters are used at the beginning of certain word groups:

- Complete sentence: Before hanging up, he said, "We'll meet here on Wednesday at noon."
- Formal statement following a colon: She has a favorite motto: Where there's a will, there's a way.
- Phrase used as sentence: Absolutely not!
- Quoted sentence embedded in another sentence: Scott said, "Nobody was here during lunch hour except me."
- List of items set off from text:

> Three preliminary steps are involved:
> Design review
> Budgeting
> Scheduling

Capitalize proper adjectives and proper nouns (the names of particular persons, places, and things):

> Darrell Greene lived in a Victorian mansion.

> We sent Ms. Larson an application form, informing her that not all applicants are interviewed.

Let's consider opening a branch in the West, perhaps at the west end of Tucson, Arizona.

As office buildings go, the Kinney Building is a pleasant setting for TDG Office Equipment.

We are going to have to cancel our plans for hiring French and German sales reps.

Larson's name is capitalized because she is a particular applicant, whereas the general term *applicant* is left uncapitalized. Likewise, *West* is capitalized when it refers to a particular place but not when it means a direction. In the same way, *office* and *building* are not capitalized when they are general terms (common nouns), but they are capitalized when they are part of the title of a particular office or building (proper nouns). Some proper adjectives are lowercased when they are part of terms that have come into common use, such as *french fries* and *roman numerals*.

Titles within families or companies as well as professional titles may also be capitalized:

I turned down Uncle David when he offered me a job.

I wouldn't be comfortable working for one of my relatives.

We've never had a president quite like President Sweeney.

People's titles are capitalized when they are used in addressing a person, especially in a formal context. They are not usually capitalized, however, when they are used merely to identify the person:

Address the letter to Chairperson Anna Palmer.

I wish to thank Chairperson Anna Palmer for her assistance.

Anna Palmer, chairperson of the board, took the podium.

Also capitalize titles if they are used by themselves in addressing a person:

Thank you, Doctor, for your donation.

Always capitalize the first word of the salutation and complimentary close of a letter:

Dear Mr. Andrews: *Yours* very truly,

The names of organizations are capitalized, of course; so are the official names of their departments and divisions. However, do not use capitals when referring in general terms to a department or division, especially one in another organization:

Route this memo to Personnel.

Larry Tien was transferred to the Microchip Division.

Will you be enrolled in the Psychology Department?

Someone from the personnel department at EnerTech stopped by the booth.

Capitalization is unnecessary when using a word like *company*, *corporation*, or *university* alone:

The corporation plans to issue 50,000 shares of common stock.

Likewise, the names of specific products are capitalized, although the names of general product types are not:

Apple Inc.   Xerox machine
Tide laundry detergent

When it comes to government terminology, here are some guides to capitalization: (1) Lowercase *federal* unless it is part of an agency name; (2) capitalize names of courts, departments, bureaus, offices, and agencies but lowercase such references as *the bureau* and *the department* when the full name is not used; (3) lowercase the titles of government officers unless they precede a specific person's name: *the secretary of state, the senator, the ambassador, the governor, and the mayor* but *Mayor Gonzalez* (Note: style guides vary on whether to capitalize *president* when referring to the president of the United States without including the person's name); (4) capitalize the names of laws and acts: *the Sherman Antitrust Act, the Civil Rights Act*; (5) capitalize the names of political parties but lowercase the word *party: Democratic party, Libertarian party*.

When writing about two or more geographic features of the same type, it is now accepted practice to capitalize the common noun in addition to the proper nouns, regardless of word order:

Lakes Ontario and Huron

Allegheny and Monongahela Rivers

Corson and Ravenna Avenues

The names of languages, races, and ethnic groups are capitalized: Japanese, Caucasian, Hispanic. But racial terms that denote only skin color are not capitalized: black, white.

When referring to the titles of books, articles, magazines, newspapers, reports, movies, and so on, you should capitalize the first and last words and all nouns, pronouns, adjectives, verbs, and adverbs, and capitalize prepositions and conjunctions with five letters or more. Except for the first and last words, do not capitalize articles:

Economics During the Great War

"An Investigation into the Market for Long-Distance Services"

"What Successes Are Made Of"

When *the* is part of the official name of a newspaper or magazine, it should be treated this way too:

The Wall Street Journal

Style guides vary in their recommendations regarding capitalization of hyphenated words in titles. A general guide is to capitalize the second word in a temporary compound (a compound that is hyphenated for grammatical reasons and not spelling reasons), such as *Law-Abiding Citizen*, but to lowercase the word if the term is always hyphenated, such as *Son-in-law*).

References to specific pages, paragraphs, lines, and the like are not capitalized: *page 73, line 3*. However, in most other numbered or lettered references, the identifying term is capitalized:

> Chapter 4   Serial No. 382-2203   Item B-11

Finally, the names of academic degrees are capitalized when they follow a person's name but are not capitalized when used in a general sense:

> I received a bachelor of science degree.
>
> Thomas Whitelaw, Doctor of Philosophy, will attend.

Similarly, general courses of study are not capitalized, but the names of specific classes are:

> She studied accounting as an undergraduate.
>
> She is enrolled in Accounting 201.

3.2 UNDERSCORES AND ITALICS

Usually a line typed underneath a word or phrase either provides emphasis or indicates the title of a book, magazine, or newspaper. If possible, use italics instead of an underscore. Italics (or underlining) should also be used for defining terms and for discussing words as words:

> In this report, *net sales* refers to after-tax sales dollars.

Also use italics to set off foreign words, unless the words have become a common part of English:

> Top Shelf is considered the *sine qua non* of comic book publishers.
>
> Chris uses a laissez-faire [no italic] management style.

3.3 ABBREVIATIONS

Abbreviations are used heavily in tables, charts, lists, and forms. They're used sparingly in prose. Here are some abbreviation situations to watch for:

- In most cases do not use periods with acronyms (words formed from the initial letter or letters of parts of a term): *CEO, CD-ROM, DOS, YWCA, FDA*; but *Ph.D., M.A., M. D.*

- Use periods with abbreviations such as *Mr., Ms., Sr., Jr., a.m., p.m., B.C.,* and *A.D.*
- The trend is away from using periods with such units of measure as *mph, mm,* and *lb.*
- Use periods with such Latin abbreviations as *e.g., i.e., et al.,* and *etc.* However, style guides recommend that you avoid using these Latin forms and instead use their English equivalents (*for example, that is, and others,* and *and so on,* respectively). If you must use these abbreviations, such as in parenthetical expressions or footnotes, do not put them in italics.
- Some companies have abbreviations as part of their names (*&, Co., Inc., Ltd.*). When you refer to such firms by name, be sure to double-check the preferred spelling, including spacing: *AT&T; Barnes & Noble; Carson Pirie Scott & Company; PepsiCo; Kate Spade, Inc.; National Data Corporation; Siemens Corp.; Glaxo Wellcome PLC; US Airways; U.S. Business Reporter.*
- Most style guides recommend that you spell out *United States* as a noun and reserve *U.S.* as an adjective preceding the noun modified.

One way to handle an abbreviation that you want to use throughout a document is to spell it out the first time you use it, follow it with the abbreviation in parentheses, and then use the abbreviation in the remainder of the document.

3.4 NUMBERS

Numbers may be correctly handled many ways in business writing, so follow company style. In the absence of a set style, however, generally spell out all numbers from one to nine and use arabic numerals for the rest.

There are some exceptions to this general rule. For example, never begin a sentence with a numeral:

> Twenty of us produced 641 units per week in the first 12 weeks of the year.

Use numerals for the numbers one through nine if they're in the same list as larger numbers:

> Our weekly quota rose from 9 to 15 to 27.

Use numerals for percentages, time of day (except with o'clock), dates, and (in general) dollar amounts:

> Our division is responsible for 7 percent of total sales.
>
> The meeting is scheduled for 8:30 a.m. on August 2. Add $3 for postage and handling.

When using numerals for time, be consistent: It should be *between 10:00 a.m. and 4:30 p.m.*, not *between 10 a.m. and 4:30 p.m.* Expressions such as *4:00 o'clock* and *7 a.m. in the morning* are redundant.

Use a comma in numbers expressing thousands (1,257), unless your company specifies another style. When dealing with numbers in the millions and billions, combine words and figures: 7.3 million, 2 billion.

When writing dollar amounts, use a decimal point only if cents are included. In lists of two or more dollar amounts, use the decimal point either for all or for none:

> He sent two checks, one for $67.92 and one for $90.00.

When two numbers fall next to each other in a sentence, use figures for the number that is largest, most difficult to spell, or part of a physical measurement; use words for the other:

> I have learned to manage a classroom of 30 twelve-year-olds.
>
> She won a bonus for selling 24 thirty-volume sets.
>
> You'll need twenty 3-inch bolts.

In addresses, all street numbers except One are in numerals. So are suite and room numbers and zip codes. For street names that are numbered, practice varies so widely that you should use the form specified on an organization's letterhead or in a reliable directory. All the following examples are correct:

> One Fifth Avenue   297 Ninth Street
> 1839 44th Street   11026 West 78 Place

Telephone numbers are always expressed in numerals. Parentheses may separate the area code from the rest of the number, but a slash or a hyphen may be used instead, especially if the entire phone number is enclosed in parentheses:

> 382-8329   (602/382-8329)   602-382-8329

Percentages are always expressed in numerals. The word *percent* is used in most cases, but % may be used in tables, forms, and statistical writing.

Ages are usually expressed in words—except when a parenthetical reference to age follows someone's name:

> Mrs. Margaret Sanderson is seventy-two.
>
> Mrs. Margaret Sanderson, 72, swims daily.

Also, ages expressed in years and months are treated like physical measurements that combine two units of measure: *5 years, 6 months.*

Physical measurements such as distance, weight, and volume are also often expressed in numerals: *9 kilometers, 5 feet 3 inches, 7 pounds 10 ounces.*

Decimal numbers are always written in numerals. In most cases, add a zero to the left of the decimal point if the number is less than one and does not already start with a zero:

> 1.38   .07   0.2

In a series of related decimal numbers with at least one number greater than one, make sure that all numbers smaller than one have a zero to the left of the decimal point: 1.20, 0.21, 0.09.

Simple fractions are written in words, but more complicated fractions are expressed in figures or, if easier to read, in figures and words:

> two-thirds   9/32   2 hundredths

When typing ordinal numbers, such as *3rd edition* or *21st century,* your word processing program may automatically make the letters *rd* (or *st, th,* or *nd*) into a superscript. Do yourself a favor and turn that formatting function off in your "Preferences," as superscripts should not be used in regular prose or even in bibliographies.

3.5 WORD DIVISION

In general, avoid dividing words at the end of lines. When you must do so, follow these rules:

- Don't divide one-syllable words (such as *since, walked,* and *thought*), abbreviations (*mgr.*), contractions (*isn't*), or numbers expressed in numerals (*117,500*).
- Divide words between syllables, as specified in a dictionary or word-division manual.
- Make sure that at least three letters of the divided words are moved to the second line: *sin-cerely* instead of *sincere-ly.*
- Do not end a page or more than three consecutive lines with hyphens.
- Leave syllables consisting of a single vowel at the end of the first line (*impedi-ment* instead of *imped-iment*), except when the single vowel is part of a suffix such as *-able, -ible, -ical,* or *-ity* (*re-spons-ible* instead of *re-sponsi-ble*).
- Divide between double letters (*tomor-row*), except when the root word ends in double letters (*call-ing* instead of *cal-ling*).
- Wherever possible, divide hyphenated words at the hyphen only: instead of *anti-inde-pendence,* use *anti-independence.*
- Whenever possible, do not break URLs or email addresses. If you have to break a long URL or email address, do not insert a hyphen at the end of the first line. If the break happens at an interior period (e.g., after "blogs" in http://blogs.company.com), place the period at the beginning of the second line so that it isn't misinterpreted as a sentence-ending period at the end of the first line.

4.0 Vocabulary

Using the right word in the right place is a crucial skill in business communication. However, many pitfalls await the unwary.

4.1 FREQUENTLY CONFUSED WORDS

Because the following sets of words sound similar, be careful not to use one when you mean to use the other:

Word	Meaning
accede	to comply with
exceed	to go beyond
accept	to take
except	to exclude
access	admittance
excess	too much
advice	suggestion
advise	to suggest
affect	to influence
effect	a result
allot	to distribute
a lot	much or many
all ready	completely prepared
already	completed earlier
born	given birth to
borne	carried
capital	money; chief city
capitol	a government building
cite	to quote
sight	a view
site	a location
complement	complete amount; to go well with
compliment	expression of esteem; to flatter
corespondent	party in a divorce suit
correspondent	letter writer
council	a panel of people
counsel	advice; a lawyer
defer	to put off until later
differ	to be different
device	a mechanism
devise	to plan
die	to stop living; a tool
dye	to color
discreet	careful
discrete	separate
envelop	to surround
envelope	a covering for a letter

Word	Meaning
forth	forward
fourth	number four
holey	full of holes
holy	sacred
wholly	completely
human	of people
humane	kindly
incidence	frequency
incidents	events
instance	example
instants	moments
interstate	between states
intrastate	within a state
its	indicates possession
it's	contracted form of "it is"
later	afterward
latter	the second of two
lead	a metal; to guide
led	guided
lean	to rest at an angle
lien	a claim
levee	embankment
levy	tax
loath	reluctant
loathe	to hate
loose	free; not tight
lose	to mislay
material	substance
materiel	equipment
miner	mineworker
minor	underage person
moral	virtuous; a lesson
morale	sense of well-being
ordinance	law
ordnance	weapons
overdo	to do in excess
overdue	past due
peace	lack of conflict
piece	a fragment
pedal	a foot lever
peddle	to sell
persecute	to torment
prosecute	to sue
personal	private
personnel	employees

Word	Meaning
precedence	priority
precedents	previous events
principal	sum of money; chief; main
principle	general rule
rap	to knock
wrap	to cover
residence	home
residents	inhabitants
right	correct
rite	ceremony
write	to form words on a surface
role	a part to play
roll	to tumble; a list
root	part of a plant
rout	to defeat
route	a traveler's way
shear	to cut
sheer	thin, steep
stationary	immovable
stationery	paper
than	as compared with
then	at that time
their	belonging to them
there	in that place
they're	they are
to	a preposition
too	excessively; also
two	the number
waive	to set aside
wave	a swell of water; a gesture
weather	atmospheric conditions
whether	if
who's	contraction of "who is" or "who has"
whose	possessive form of "who"

In the preceding list, only enough of each word's meaning is given to help you distinguish between the words in each group. Several meanings are left out entirely. For more complete definitions, consult a dictionary.

4.2 FREQUENTLY MISUSED WORDS

The following words tend to be misused for reasons other than their sound. Reference books (including the *Random House College Dictionary*, revised edition; Follett's *Modern American Usage*; and Fowler's *Modern English Usage*) can help you with similar questions of usage:

a lot: When the writer means "many," *a lot* is always two separate words, never one.

aggravate/irritate: *Aggravate* means "to make things worse." Sitting in the smoke-filled room *aggravated* his sinus condition. *Irritate* means "to annoy." Her constant questions *irritated* [not *aggravated*] me.

anticipate/expect: *Anticipate* means "to prepare for": Macy's *anticipated* increased demand for athletic shoes in spring by ordering in November. In formal usage, it is incorrect to use *anticipate* for *expect*: I *expected* (not *anticipated*) a better response to our presentation than we actually got.

> The company's distribution division *comprises* four departments.

compose/comprise: The whole comprises the parts:

> The company's distribution division *is comprised of* four departments.

The following usage is incorrect:

In that construction, *is composed of* or *consists of* would be preferable. It might be helpful to think of *comprise* as meaning "encompasses" or "contains."

continual/continuous: *Continual* refers to ongoing actions that have breaks:

> Her *continual* complaining will accomplish little in the long run.

Continuous refers to ongoing actions without interruptions or breaks:

> A *continuous* stream of paper came out of the malfunctioning printing press.

convince/persuade: One is *convinced* of a fact or that something is true; one is *persuaded* by someone else to do something. The use of *to* with *convince* is unidiomatic—you don't convince someone to do something, you persuade them to do it.

correspond with: Use this phrase when you are talking about exchanging letters. Use *correspond to* when you mean "similar to." Use either *correspond with* or *correspond to* when you mean "relate to."

dilemma/problem: Technically, a *dilemma* is a situation in which one must choose between two undesirable alternatives. It shouldn't be used when no choice is actually involved.

disinterested: This word means "fair, unbiased, having no favorites, impartial." If you mean "bored" or "not interested," use *uninterested*.

etc.: This abbreviated form of the Latin phrase *et cetera* means "and so on" or "and so forth," so it is never correct to write *and etc*. The current tendency among business writers is to use English rather than Latin.

flaunt/flout: To *flaunt* is to be ostentatious or boastful; to *flout* is to mock or scoff at.

impact: Avoid using *impact* as a verb when *influence* or *affect* is meant.

imply/infer: Both refer to hints. Their great difference lies in who is acting. The writer *implies*, the reader *infers*, sees between the lines.

its/their: Use *its* to indicate possession by a singular entity such as a company, not *their*. "HP released its quarterly results" is correct; "HP released their quarterly results" is not.

lay: This word is a transitive verb. Never use it for the intransitive *lie*. (See Section 1.3.3.)

lend/loan: *Lend* is a verb; *loan* is a noun. Usage such as "Can you loan me $5?" is therefore incorrect.

less/fewer: Use *less* for uncountable quantities (such as amounts of water, air, sugar, and oil). Use *fewer* for countable quantities (such as numbers of jars, saws, words, pages, and humans). The same distinction applies to *much* and *little* (uncountable) versus *many* and *few* (countable).

liable/likely: *Liable* means "responsible for": I will hold you *liable* if this deal doesn't go through. It is incorrect to use *liable* for "possible": Anything is *likely* (not *liable*) to happen.

literally: *Literally* means "actually" or "precisely"; it is often misused to mean "almost" or "virtually." It is usually best left out entirely or replaced with *figuratively*.

many/much: See *less/fewer*.

regardless: The *less* suffix is the negative part. No word needs two negative parts, so don't add *ir* (a negative prefix) to the beginning. There is no such word as *irregardless*.

try: Always follow with *to*, never *and*.

verbal: People in the business community who are careful with language frown on those who use *verbal* to mean "spoken" or "oral." Many others do say "verbal agreement." Strictly speaking, *verbal* means "of words" and therefore includes both spoken and written words. Follow company usage in this matter.

4.3 FREQUENTLY MISSPELLED WORDS

All of us, even the world's best spellers, sometimes have to check a dictionary for the spelling of some words. People who have never memorized the spelling of commonly used words must look up so many that they grow exasperated and give up on spelling words correctly.

Don't expect perfection and don't surrender. If you can memorize the spelling of just the words listed here, you'll need the dictionary far less often and you'll write with more confidence:

absence	disappoint
absorption	disbursement
accessible	discrepancy
accommodate	dissatisfied
accumulate	dissipate
achieve	
advantageous	eligible
affiliated	embarrassing
analyze	endorsement
apparent	exaggerate
appropriate	exceed
argument	exhaust
asphalt	existence
assistant	extraordinary
asterisk	
auditor	fallacy
	familiar
bankruptcy	flexible
believable	fluctuation
brilliant	forty
bulletin	
	gesture
calendar	grievous
campaign	
category	haphazard
ceiling	harassment
changeable	holiday
clientele	
collateral	illegible
committee	immigrant
comparative	incidentally
competitor	indelible
concede	independent
congratulations	indispensable
connoisseur	insistent
consensus	intermediary
convenient	irresistible
convertible	
corroborate	jewelry
criticism	judgment
	judicial
definitely	labeling
description	legitimate
desirable	leisure
dilemma	license
disappear	litigation

maintenance

mathematics

mediocre

minimum

necessary

negligence

negotiable

newsstand

noticeable

occurrence

omission

parallel

pastime

peaceable

permanent

perseverance

persistent

personnel

persuade

possesses

precede

predictable

preferred

privilege

procedure

proceed

pronunciation

psychology

pursue

questionnaire

receive

recommend

repetition

rescind

rhythmical

ridiculous

salable

secretary

seize

separate

sincerely

succeed

suddenness

superintendent

supersede

surprise

tangible

tariff

technique

tenant

truly

unanimous

until

vacillate

vacuum

vicious

> Production delays are inevitable; _____, our current lag time in filling orders is one month.

Now read the sentence with *nevertheless* in the blank space. Then try *therefore, incidentally, in fact,* and *at any rate* in the blank. Each substitution changes the meaning of the sentence.

Here are some transitional words (conjunctive adverbs) that will help you write more clearly:

accordingly	furthermore	moreover
anyway	however	otherwise
consequently	incidentally	still
finally	likewise	therefore
	meanwhile	

The following transitional phrases are used in the same way:

as a result	in other words
for example	in the second place
in fact	on the other hand
	to the contrary

When one of these words or phrases joins two independent clauses, it should be preceded by a semicolon and followed by a comma:

> The consultant recommended a complete reorganization; moreover, she suggested that we drop several products.

4.4 TRANSITIONAL WORDS AND PHRASES

The following sentences don't communicate as well as they could because they lack a transitional word or phrase:

> Production delays are inevitable. Our current lag time in filling orders is one month.

A semicolon between the two sentences would signal a close relationship between their meanings, but it wouldn't even hint at what that relationship is. Here are the sentences again, now linked by means of a semicolon, with a space for a transitional word or phrase:

Brand, Organization, Name, and Website Index

*Indicates a fictitious company used in examples or student activities.

*Indicates a fictitious company used in examples or student activities.

Subject Index